California

Brett Atkinson, Amy C Balfour, Andrew Bender, Alison Bing, Cristian Bonetto, Celeste Brash, Jade Bremner, Bailey Freeman, Michael Grosberg, Ashley Harrell, Anita Isalska, Mark Johanson, Andrea Schulte-Peevers, Wendy Yanagihara

PLAN YOUR TRIP

PAUL ROJAS /GETTY IMAGES ©

YOSEMITE NATIONAL PARK P680

JOSEPH SOHM / SHUTTERSTOCK ©

SANTA MONICA P399

ON THE ROAD

Contents

ON THE ROAD

SEAN PAVONE / SHUTTERSTOCK ©

SAN DIEGO P460

Contents

UNDERSTAND

SURVIVAL GUIDE

SPECIAL FEATURES

COVID-19

We have re-checked every business in this book before publication to ensure that it is still open after 2020's COVID-19 outbreak. However, the economic and social impacts of COVID-19 will continue to be felt long after the outbreak has been contained, and many businesses, services and events referenced in this guide may experience ongoing restrictions. Some businesses may be temporarily closed, have changed their opening hours and services, or require bookings; some unfortunately could have closed permanently. We suggest you check with venues before visiting for the latest information.

Right: Zabriskie Point (p530), Death Valley National Park

WELCOME TO

California

After my first visit to California many moons ago, I was instantly so smitten that I ended up moving to LA from Germany. There were the predictable lures: the sunshine, the beaches, the celebrities. But it was the unexpected gems that intrigued me more, be they hot springs in the mountains, an artist colony in the desert or a magic club in a Victorian mansion. Every exploration opened up new perspectives on humanity in this cauldron of cultures, with all its vexing complexities and hope for a grand future.

By Andrea Schulte-Peevers, Writer

@aschultepeevers @aschultepeevers

For more about our writers, see p800

California

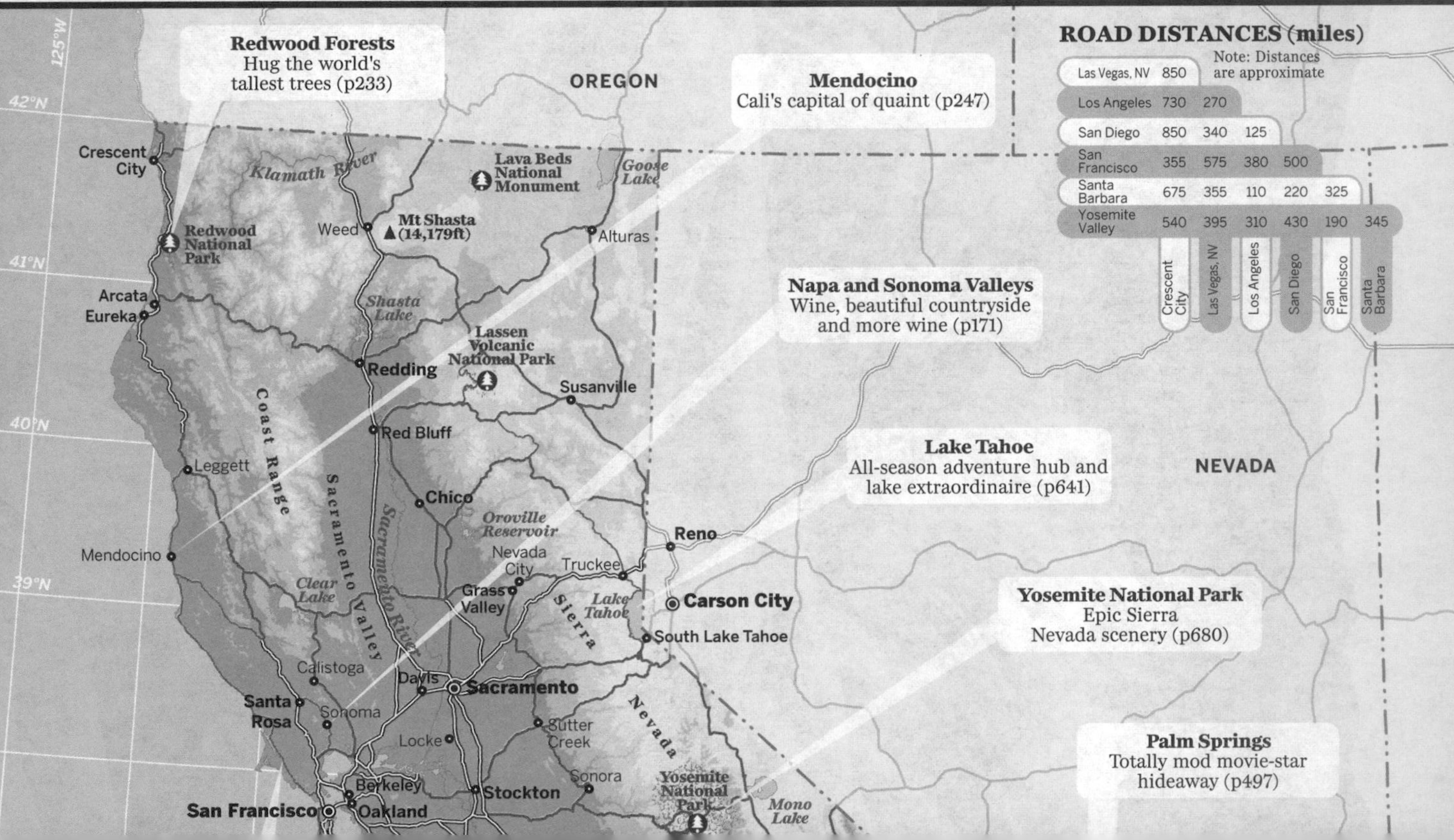

	Crescent City	Las Vegas, NV	Los Angeles	San Diego	San Francisco	Santa Barbara
Las Vegas, NV	850					
Los Angeles	730	270				
San Diego	850	340	125			
San Francisco	355	575	380	500		
Santa Barbara	675	355	110	220	325	
Yosemite Valley	540	395	310	430	190	345

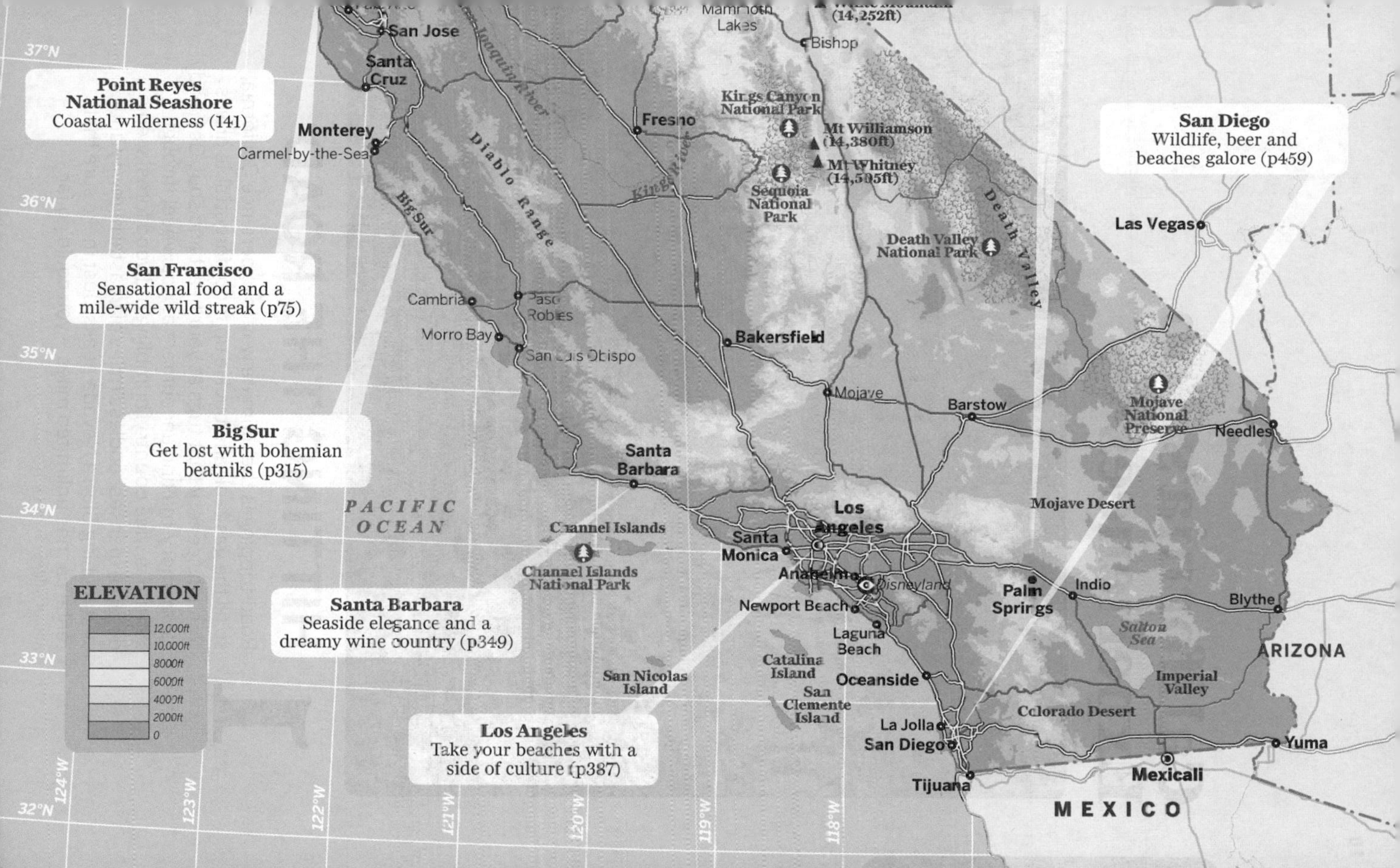

Point Reyes National Seashore
Coastal wilderness (141)
San Francisco
Sensational food and a mile-wide wild streak (p75)
Big Sur
Get lost with bohemian beatniks (p315)
Santa Barbara
Seaside elegance and a dreamy wine country (p349)
Los Angeles
Take your beaches with a side of culture (p387)
San Diego
Wildlife, beer and beaches galore (p459)
ELEVATION
12,000ft
10,000ft
8000ft
6000ft
4000ft
2000ft
0
San Jose
Santa Cruz
Monterey
Carmel-by-the-Sea
Big Sur
Diablo Range
Cambria
Paso Robles
Morro Bay
San Luis Obispo
Fresno
Kings River
Kings Canyon National Park
Mt Williamson (14,380ft)
Mt Whitney (14,505ft)
Sequoia National Park
Mammoth Lakes
Bishop
(14,252ft)
Death Valley National Park
Death Valley
Las Vegas
Bakersfield
Mojave
Barstow
Mojave National Preserve
Needles
Santa Barbara
PACIFIC OCEAN
Channel Islands
Channel Islands National Park
Los Angeles
Santa Monica
Anaheim
Disneyland
Newport Beach
Laguna Beach
Catalina Island
San Nicolas Island
San Clemente Island
Oceanside
La Jolla
San Diego
Tijuana
Mojave Desert
Palm Springs
Indio
Blythe
Salton Sea
ARIZONA
Imperial Valley
Colorado Desert
Yuma
Mexicali
MEXICO
37°N
36°N
35°N
34°N
33°N
32°N
124°W
123°W
122°W
121°W
120°W
119°W
118°W

California's Top Experiences

ALISA_CH / SHUTTERSTOCK©

1 HITTING THE ROAD

Road-tripping is the ultimate way to experience California, so fill the gas tank and buckle up for unforgettable drives through scenery that tugs at your heart and soul. Get ready for memory-making encounters as you wheel through sensuous wine country, humbling redwood forests, epic desert expanses, endless miles of coastal highway and skytouching Sierra Nevada peaks. Just make sure that rental car has unlimited miles – you could go far.

Above: Whitney Portal Rd (p732)

Route 66

Get your kicks on America's 'Mother Road', which brought Dust Bowl refugees, Hollywood starlets and hippies to California. Cruise from the desert to the Pacific Ocean, pulling up alongside retro relics, sleeping in a tipi hotel and fueling up in neon-lit diners.

➡ **Route 66** p502

SKY NOIR PHOTOGRAPHY BY BILL DICKINSON / GETTY IMAGES ©

MARK SCHWETTMANN / SHUTTERSTOCK ©

MICHAEL OVERSTREET / SHUTTERSTOCK ©

Pacific Coast Highway

No matter if you follow the entire 656 miles or just a short stretch of coast-hugging Hwy 1, you'll hit the Insta jackpot. Posing options include dramatic sea cliffs, sun-soaked surfing towns, playful harbor seals and the Golden Gate Bridge.

➡ **Pacific Coast Highway** p235

Avenue of the Giants

This incredible 32-mile road is canopied by the world's tallest trees, some of which were seedlings during the Roman Empire. The best time is in the morning when sunlight glints off dew-drenched ferns.

➡ **Humboldt Redwoods State Park** p269

2 URBAN IMMERSION

California's cities have more flavors than a jar of jelly beans. They will seduce you with a cultural kaleidoscope that spans the arc from art museums, architectural showpieces and vibrant theater to tantalizing food scenes and high-octane nightlife. LA and San Francisco may hog the spotlight, but you'll also find ample charm and diversions in smaller towns like San Luis Obispo, Palm Springs and Chico.

San Francisco

This scene-stealing city keeps pushing boundaries with trendsetting food, social movements, art and technology. Once you cling to the side of a cable car, you know that it you're in for one heck of a ride, from the Marina's chic waterfront to the edgy Mission District.

➡ **San Francisco** p75

JAYLAND MASUDA / GETTY IMAGES ©

JON BILOUS / SHUTTERSTOCK ©

NAN728 / SHUTTERSTOCK ©

Above: Venice Boardwalk (p401), Los Angeles; La Jolla (p483), San Diego

Left: San Francisco (p75)

Los Angeles

LA runs deeper than its beaches, bottle-blonde celebutantes and reality-TV entourages might have you believe. Ultimately, it's LA's cultural diversity and vibrant immigrant cultures that make the biggest impression. Bewildering as it is exciting, LA will leave an indelible impression.

➡ **Los Angeles** p387

San Diego

San Diego's breezy confidence and sunny countenance are irresistible. It's tough to decide where to start your exploration. Do as locals do: Grab a fish taco and hit the beach or Balboa Park's art, cultural and science museums.

➡ **San Diego** p459

Below: camping, Joshua Tree National Park (p516); Truckee River (p660)

Left: Travertine Hot Spring (p712)

3 OUTDOOR ADVENTURE

An irresistible combo of forests, mountains, ocean and desert, California's outdoors is nothing short of extraordinary and the menu of options is seemingly inexhaustible. So get out of the car and get your blood pumping. Make memories while hiking in a fairy-tale forest, plunging into a gem-colored mountain lake, clambering around massive dunes or schussing down epic slopes. Adventure, after all, is about embracing the elements as much as embracing unique experiences.

Pitch a tent in Joshua Tree

Bed down under a heavenly blanket of stars, surrounded by evocatively eroded boulders, fan-palm oases and vestiges of old homesteads in this dreamy

➡ **SoCal desert park** p516

ROBCOCQUYT / SHUTTERSTOCK ©

VERNONWILEY / GETTY IMAGES ©

Hot Springs & Swimming Holes

Calistoga's volcanic mud baths may just be exactly be what the doctor ordered after a day of wine tasting. Alternatively, dip into natural hot-springs pools scattered throughout the state.

➡ **Calistoga** p190

Rafting the American River

California's premier white-water destination is ready-made for families and thrill-seekers. Embark on a short expedition or a full-on, multiday adventure at rivers throughout the state.

➡ **Truckee River** p660

Below: Hearst Castle (p323)

4 QUIRKY SURPRISES

ALIZADA STUDIOS / SHUTTERSTOCK ©

California is full of bizarre roadside attractions and hidden surprises. SoCal's deserts and the North Coast, both traditional magnets for free spirits, deliver a disproportionate share of kooky gems, but loopy LA and bohemian SF are just as jam-packed with memorable oddities. Outdoor sculpture gardens, houses built of bottles, a museum dedicated to crocheted animals, dinosaurs by the freeway – it's all part of California's quirky DNA.

Slab City

Mingle with artists and misfits in this off-grid community that sprawls across the sun-scorched desert floor at the foot of Salvation Mountain, a colorful showpiece of American folk art.

➡ **Slab City** p528

Hearst Castle

Take a tour of William Randolph Hearst's hilltop estate with its sparkling outdoor Neptune Pool, interiors lavishly decorated in European antiquities and jewels, and stunning sunsets from the balcony.

➡ **Hearst Castle** p323

Integratron

Built with the help of aliens (of course!), this giant 'rejuvenation and time machine' awaits near Joshua Tree. Book way ahead to channel the vibes in a mind-altering sound bath.

➡ **Integratron** p522

Below: Russian River Valley grapes

Left: Napa vineyard; Santa Ynez vineyard party

5 GRAPE DELIGHTS

No matter where you go in California, you'll rarely be far from a vineyard. World-class vintages are grown and bottled here, just waiting to be tasted and drained. Raise a toast to California's wine-producing regions that are pioneering sustainable practices and brimming with natural wonders: blooming biodynamic orchards, sun-dappled organic olive groves, lazy bicycle rides to LEED-certified tasting rooms, and restaurants pairing cult wines with seasonally inspired dishes.

YINYANG / GETTY IMAGES ©

GERI LAVROV / GETTY IMAGES ©

GIBSON OUTDOOR PHOTO / SHUTTERSTOCK ©

Napa Valley

Sample America's best wines in famous Napa, a region that has emerged from devastating wildfires and economic setbacks with newfound commitments to creativity and sustainability.

➡ **Napa Valley** p174

Santa Ynez Valley

Watch the 2004 Oscar-winning *Sideways*, then sip soft pinot noir *in situ* on a tour of these sylvan hillsides quilted with oaks, olive trees and endless rows of vineyards.

➡ **Santa Ynez Valley** p351

Russian River Valley

One of California's best-kept secrets, this is Napa's rebel cousin, with sparkling wines offered in tasting rooms and cult biodynamic vintages you won't find anywhere else.

➡ **Russian River Valley** p218

Below: tacos; Ferry Building (p81), San Francisco

6 EPIC EPICUREAN

REGGIE BARROGA / SHUTTERSTOCK ©

MICHAEL LEE / GETTY IMAGES ©

California is the epicenter of good eating in the United States, if not the world. Where else is the natural bounty fresher or more varied, the kitchen creativity more boundary-pushing or the flavors and textures more international? New cravings have been invented at California's cultural crossroads for over 200 years, so don't hold back! Get adventurous with the latest food trends, from hip food halls to Cal-Japanese tasting menus to indigenous cooking.

Tacomania

Tacos are a staple of the SoCal food scene, especially in San Diego where the humble Baja-style fish taco is a local obsession. Savor it in such places as Pacific Beach Fish Shop.

➡ **Pacifc Beach Fish Shop** p477

Ferry Building

Duck inside this 19th-century ferry terminal in San Francisco that's been rebooted as a delectable showcase of top bounty from regional, sustainable and artesanal food producers.

➡ **Ferry Building** p81

Grand Central Market

Mingle with hipsters, office jockeys and visitors at this neon-festooned beaux art gourmet market hall in Downtown LA's that kept the hungry fed since 1917.

➡ **Grand Central Market** p410

Below: Yosemite Village (p682); Lassen Volcanic National Park (p556)

Left: Zabriskie Point (p530), Death Valley National Park

7 BIG NATURE

In California, Mother Nature has been as prolific as Picasso in his prime. Blissful beaches, unspoiled wilderness, big-shouldered mountains, trees as tall as the Statue of LIberty, lakes as blue as Paul Newman's eyes – this land is an intoxicating mosaic that has inspired visionaries, artists and wanderers for centuries. Plunge in to create memories sure to last a lifetime.

Yosemite National Park

Feeling so small has never felt grander than in Yosemite. To achieve maximum wonder, stop at Glacier Point under a full moon or drive the high country's Tioga Rd.

➡ **Yosemite National Park** p682

ARMIN ADAMS / GETTY IMAGES ©

PATRICK LEITZ / GETTY IMAGES ©

Death Valley National Park

Twist your way through canyons, zoom across crackled salt flats, descend into volcanic craters and stop at the lowest point in North America in larger-than-life Death Vallley.

➡ **Death Valley NP** p529

Lassen Volcanic National Park

Explore this otherworldly natural mosaic of lava fields, azure crater lakes and sulfuric mud pots, all lorded over by a snow-capped dormant volcano.

➡ **Lassen Volcanic National Park** p556

Below: TCL Chinese Theatre (p392)

8 MOVIE MAGIC

FJPHOTO / SHUTTERSTOCK ©

To Shakespeare all the world may have been a stage, but in California, it's actually more of a film set. And although movies were born in France, they certainly came of age in Hollywood. Even without any celebrities to snare your stare, you can still stand in their footprints, look behind the scenes on a studio tour or hop on a bus to see where the stars live.

Hollywood

Snap a selfie outside TCL Chinese Theatre, then duck into Hollywood & Highland for a photo op with the iconic Hollywood sign and revel in your 15 minutes of social media fame.

➡ **Hollywood** p392

Disneyland Resort

Waltz down Main Street arm in arm with beloved cartoon characters and watch fireworks explode over Sleeping Beauty Castle in the Magic Kingdom, aka the 'Happiest Place on Earth'.

➡ **Disneyland Resort** p429

Universal Studios Hollywood

An action-packed day at this legendary movie studio and cinematic theme park is filled with a backlot tram tour, movie-themed rides, live-action shows and slick special effects.

➡ **Universal Studios Hollywood** p395

Below: greater white-fronted geese

Left: tule elk, Point Reyes National Seashore (p141); sea lions, Channel Islands National Park (p382)

9 ANIMAL ENCOUNTERS

People love California, and so do animals! This may explain the state's mind-blowing biodiversity. No matter where you go, wildlife encounters are pretty much guaranteed. Sea otters and seals frolic around harbor piers, while whales serenely cruise offshore. From black bears in the forests to monarch butterflies in eucalyptus groves, tortoises in the desert and skies filled with millions of migrating birds, this state is a critter's paradise.

JULIE VADER / SHUTTERSTOCK ©

DOUGLAS KLUG / GETTY IMAGES ©

TOM REICHNER / SHUTTERSTOCK ©

Point Reyes National Seashore

Come to this peninsula for windswept beaches with migrating whales offshore, a colony of elephant seals, free-roaming tule elk and birds galore.

➡ **Point Reyes National Seashore** p141

Channel Islands National Park

Commune with coral-reef creatures and giant colonies of pinnipeds while hiking, snorkeling or kayaking around the uninhabited Channel Islands.

➡ **Channel Islands National Park** p382

Klamath Basin National Wildlife Refuges

Whip out your binoculars for close-ups of hundreds of thousands of winged creatures passing through on the Pacific Flyway.

➡ **Klamath Basin National Wildlife Refuges** p575

Below: Bodie State Historic Park (p713); Pioneertown (p523)

10 WILD WEST ADVENTURES

JEFF HUNTER / GETTY IMAGES ©

DAVID HRUBARL / SHUTTERSTOCK ©

'Go west, young man!' was the rallying cry of tens of thousands of pioneers who arrived in California during the state's infamous gold rush, starting in 1848. Heed the call as you plunge back into the past for a glimpse of how the west was won, in a fascinating but anything-but-romantic era. Tap into stories of gun-slinging outlaws, out-of-control barroom brawls, frenzied gold strikes and broken hearts (after the mines ran dry).

Gold Country

Follow Hwy 49 through the rough-and-tumble Sierra Nevada foothills that are a stronghold of gold-rush history, with thrilling, mostly true tales of banditry, bordellos and bloodlust.

➡ **Gold Country** p617

Bodie State Historic Park

Barrel along a bumpy road to Bodie, one of the West's most authentic and best-preserved mining ghost towns, renowned in its heyday for its opium dens and 60 saloons.

➡ **Bodie State Historic Park** p713

Pioneertown

Just outside Joshua Tree National Park, Pioneertown was built as a Wild West movie set in 1946 and is now famous for its mock gun fights and rocking honky-tonk.

➡ **Pioneertown** p523

Below: Huntington Beach (p439); Big Sur (p315)

Left: Santa Monica Pier (p399)

11 COASTAL PLEASURES

Life's a beach in California, and so much more. When the coastal fog lifts, the state's 840 miles of shoreline truly give its 'golden' moniker justice. Find family fun in La Jolla, watch world-class surfers in Huntington Beach, mingle with eccentrics on Venice Beach, cuddle at sunset in a Big Sur cove or find yourself on the stunning Lost Coast Trail.

Santa Monica Beach

Santa Monica's endless summers are fueled by a solar-powered Ferris wheel, carnival games on the old-fashioned pier, tidal touch pools in the aquarium and soul-stirring sunsets.

➡ **Santa Monica** p399

Surf City USA

Even if you never set foot on a board – you should, like, *totally* check out Huntington Beach. Surfing defines California pop culture, from street slang to movies and fashion.

➡ **Huntington Beach** p439

Big Sur

Cradled by mossy redwood forests, the rocky Big Sur coast is a mystical place. Search out hidden waterfalls and hot springs and watch for endangered California condors while scrambling along sea cliffs.

➡ **Big Sur** p315

Below:Alcatraz (p85)

12 HIGH ON HISTORY

F11PHOTO / SHUTTERSTOCK ©

It's been quite a wild ride for California, from the days of mammoths and saber-toothed tigers to the world's fifth-largest economy. Follow in the footsteps of countless generations that have shaped the state in ways both dark and golden. Hike to sacred Native American waterfalls, confront the moral complexities of the mission system, reflect upon the frenzied rush for gold and finish up with a martini in Humphrey Bogart's favorite watering hole.

Sonoma State Historic Park

Dive deep in California's history as far back as the 1820s, with stops at an adobe mission, 19th-century military barracks and a gorgeously restored hotel.

➡ **Sonoma State Historic Park** p198

Mission San Juan Capistrano

Roam around this 1776 'Jewel of the Missions', world-famous for the swallows that nest in its walls on their return from South America in spring.

➡ **Mission San Juan Capistrano** p454

Alcatraz

Watch Clint Eastwood in *Escape from Alcatraz* in preparation for visiting 'The Rock' – America's first military prison – on a tiny island rising offshore from San Francisco.

➡ **Alcatraz** p82

Below: Palm Springs (p497)

Left: Pfeiffer Beach (p318), Big Sur; Mendocino (p247)

13 ROMANTIC ESCAPES

Whether you're on your honeymoon, celebrating an anniversary or wishing to escape the daily grind with your loved one, California is tailor-made for romance. Bed down in a Victorian B&B or in a tent under a canopy of stars. Clink glasses in a winery bistro or over a mountaintop picnic. Surrender to slothdom in a chic spa or hike out to an isolated forest cabin. The only limit is your own imagination.

CHINTLA / SHUTTERSTOCK ©

N. F. PHOTOGRAPHY / SHUTTERSTOCK ©

CREB DESIGN / SHUTTERSTOCK ©

Big Sur

Following your bliss inevitably leads to Big Sur. Waterfalls splash down in rainbow mists, and coastal cliffs cradle purple-sand beaches, while you cuddle in a blufftop yurt or a luxe retreat.

➡ **Big Sur** p315

Mendocino

Heed the call of romance in this former whaling village with an artistic pedigree, century-old rose-covered cottages and quiet country inns made for serenely drifting off to dreamland.

➡ **Mendocino** p247

Palm Springs

Let this classy desert town sweep you off your feet: dine under the stars, sipping potent cocktails in chic bars and lounge poolside at your mid-century yet modern hotel.

➡ **Palm Springs** p495

Below: Lake Tahoe (p641); Mono Lake (p715)

14 LIVING IT UP LAKESIDE

TOPSELLER / SHUTTERSTOCK ©

GEORGE LAMSON / SHUTTERSTOCK ©

Lake Tahoe

High in the Sierra Nevada Mountains, this all-seasons adventure base camp invites splashing, kayaking and even scuba diving in its gem-colored waters. In winter, it's California's prime ski resort.

➡ **Lake Tahoe** p641

Mono Lake

Canoe or kayak on North America's second-oldest lake, famous for its salty tufa castles rising from subterranean springs, and observe migrating birds feasting on clouds of lake flies.

➡ **Mono Lake** p716

Shasta Lake

Party with your friends on a houseboat, or find tranquility hiking along the shoreline of California's largest reservoir. Bald eagles pilot the skies while the waters teem with 20 species of fish.

➡ **Shasta Lake** p555

California is clearly defined by the Pacific Ocean, but there are plenty of bodies of water in the mountains and inland areas where just as much aquatic fun can be had. Kayaking, swimming and boating are major activities, but fishing is also popular (license required). From vast reservoirs to calm pools cradled by mighty peaks, lakes are an integral part of the state's stunning natural beauty.

Need to Know

For more information, see Survival Guide (p765)

Currency
US dollars ($)

Language
English

Visas
Generally not required for stays of 90 days or less for citizens of Visa Waiver Program (VWP) countries with ESTA approval (https://esta.cbp.dhs.gov) – apply online at least 72 hours in advance.

Money
ATMs are widely available. Credit cards are usually required for reservations. Traveler's checks (US dollars) are rarely accepted. Tipping is not optional.

Cell Phones
Foreign phones that may work in the USA include LTE, GSM and UMTS multiband models. Buy prepaid SIM cards locally. Coverage can be spotty in remote areas.

Time
Pacific Standard Time (GMT/UTC minus eight hours)

When to Go

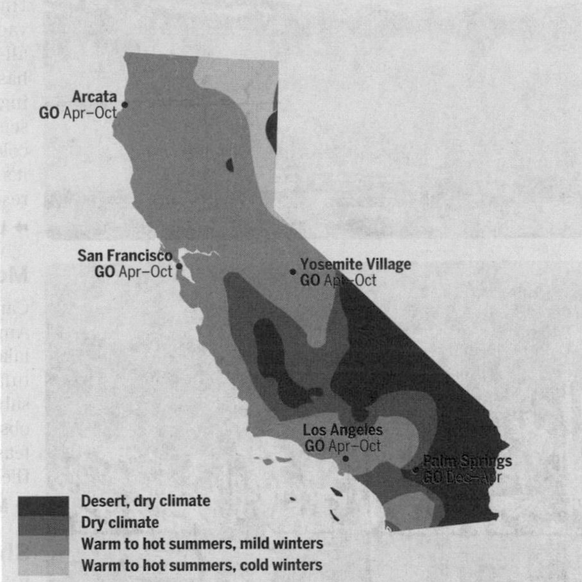

High Season
(Jun–Aug)

➡ Accommodations prices up 50% to 100% on average.

➡ Major holidays are even busier and more expensive.

➡ Summer is low season in the desert, where temperatures exceed 100°F (38°C).

Shoulder
(Apr–May & Sep–Oct)

➡ Crowds and prices drop, especially on the coast and in the mountains.

➡ Mild temperatures and sunny, cloudless days.

➡ Typically wetter in spring, drier in autumn.

Low Season
(Nov–Mar)

➡ Accommodations rates lowest along the coast.

➡ Chilly temperatures, frequent rainstorms and heavy snow in the mountains.

➡ Winter is peak season in SoCal's desert regions.

Useful Websites

Visit California (www.visitcalifornia.com) Multilingual trip-planning guides.

Lonely Planet (www.lonelyplanet.com/usa/california) Destination information, hotel bookings, traveler forum and more.

LA Times Travel (www.latimes.com/travel) Travel news, deals and blogs.

California State Parks (www.parks.ca.gov) Outdoor activities and camping.

CalTrans (www.dot.ca.gov) Current highway conditions.

Important Numbers

All phone numbers have a three-digit area code followed by a seven-digit local number. For long-distance and toll-free calls, dial 1 plus all 10 digits.

Country code	☎1
International dialing code	☎011
Operator	☎0
Emergency (ambulance, fire & police)	☎911
Directory assistance (local)	☎411

Exchange Rates

Australia	A$1	$0.73
Canada	C$1	$0.76
China	Y10	$1.52
Euro zone	€1	$1.18
Japan	¥100	$0.96
Mexico	MXN10	$0.50
New Zealand	NZ$1	$0.69
UK	£1	$1.33

For current exchange rates see www.xe.com.

Daily Costs

Budget: Less than $100

- Hostel dorm beds: $30–70
- Takeout meal: $7–12

Midrange: $100–300

- Motel or hotel double room: $100–250
- Sit-down restaurant meal: $20–40

Top End: More than $300

- Upscale hotel or beach resort room: from $250
- Three-course meal in top restaurant excluding drinks: $80–120

Opening Hours

Businesses, restaurants and shops may close earlier and on additional days during the winter off-season (November to March). Otherwise, standard opening hours are as follows:

Banks 9:30am–4pm (some later) Monday to Friday, some 9am–noon or later Saturday

Bars 4pm–2am daily

Business hours (general) 9am–5pm Monday to Friday

Nightclubs 10pm–4am Thursday to Saturday

Post offices 8:30am–5pm Monday to Friday, some 8:30am–noon or later Saturday

Restaurants 11am–3pm and 5:30pm–10pm daily, some open later Friday and Saturday

Shops 10am–7pm Monday to Saturday, 11am–6pm Sunday (malls open later)

Supermarkets 8am–9pm or 10pm daily, some 24 hours

Arriving in California

Los Angeles International Airport (p779) Taxis to most destinations ($30 to $50) take 30 minutes to one hour; fares for ride-hailing companies are cheaper. Door-to-door shuttles ($15 to $20) operate 24 hours. FlyAway bus ($9.75) runs to Downtown LA. Free shuttles connect with LAX City Bus Center and Metro Rail station.

San Francisco International Airport (p779) Taxis into the city ($45 to $65) take 25 to 50 minutes; fares for ride-hailing companies are cheaper. Door-to-door shuttles (from $19) operate 24 hours. BART trains ($9.65, 30 minutes) serve the airport, running from 5:30am (later on weekends) to midnight daily.

Getting Around

Most people self-drive around California. You can also fly (it's expensive) or take cheaper long-distance buses or scenic trains. In cities, when distances are too far to walk, hop aboard buses, trains, streetcars, cable cars or trolleys, or grab a taxi or a rideshare.

Car Metro-area traffic can be nightmarish, especially during weekday commuter rush hours (roughly 6am to 10am and 3pm to 7pm). City parking is often an expensive hassle.

Train The fastest way to get around the San Francisco Bay Area and LA, but lines don't go everywhere. Pricier regional and long-distance Amtrak trains scenically connect some destinations.

Bus Usually the cheapest and slowest option, but with extensive metro-area networks. Intercity, regional and long-distance Greyhound routes are limited and more expensive.

For much more on **getting around**, see p32

What's New

California dreamin' has of late been hit with an unwelcome dose of unpleasant reality, from wildfires to a pandemic and an economic downturn. But don't worry: the Golden State has shed almost none of its natural glitter and boundary-pushing coolness that's forever fueled its intoxicating lure.

Pot's Hot

Since 2018 it has been legal for those over 21 to buy pot in California, no ostensible medical problems required. New dispensaries have continued to pop up all over the state with a stunning array of plants, edibles, oils, infusions and tinctures on the menu. Up in Humboldt County, in California's 'Emerald Triangle,' tourists can take educational tours of pot farms and stay in government-permitted 'bud-and-breakfasts.'

A Museum's Premier

After going massively over budget, LA's Academy Museum of Motion Pictures (p396) was due to be unveiled in April 2021. With a daring design by celebrated architect Renzo Piano, the new 300,000-sq-ft museum pays homage to the magic of the cinema with everything from props, memorabilia and costumes to screenings and events.

Lake Tahoe's Latest

These days, California's adventure capital is offering new routes to walk, cycle, climb and even scuba dive. The East Shore Trail (p671) is a 3-mile paved pedestrian and bicycle path that linked Incline Village with Sand Harbor State Park in 2019. Squaw Valley's new via ferrata route up Tram Face has opened, along with Tram Car Bar (p664), a 1970s ski tram car converted into a bar. Finally, the Emerald Bay Maritime Heritage Underwater Trail, a

LOCAL KNOWLEDGE

WHAT'S HAPPENING IN CALIFORNIA

By Andrea Schulte-Peevers, Lonely Planet writer

Since Gavin Newsom took the helm as California's governor in 2019, the Golden State has literally been under fire as record-breaking wildfires torched more than 4 million acres, including wide swaths of some of the state's most beloved parks. Climate scientists say the situation will only get worse, although a growing number of countermeasures being implemented throughout the state, including solar parks and water-saving initiatives, may help mitigate the situation.

Of course, these events left first-degree burns in comparison with 2020's Covid-19 pandemic, which shuttered the state for months, decimating its economy (the world's fifth-largest) and wreaking havoc on its ever-increasing homeless population. The silver linings? Less traffic and more affordable housing. Meanwhile, California has also taken the lead on such global issues as environmental standards, online privacy, LGBT+ advocacy and immigrant rights.

And there were also signs in 2020 that California is still 'golden' when the LA Lakers became NBA champions, the LA Dodgers won the World Series and former California attorney general and US Senator Kamala Harris was elected the country's first women and biracial vice president.

scuba-diving route past sunken boats and barges, opened in Emerald Bay in 2018.

Table to Farm

Visitors to the Point Reyes National Seashore can now investigate the origins of the region's finest cheeses, oysters and meat products on food and farm tours (p139).

Recently Uncorked

California's wine industry is sprawling and highly innovative, with frequent newcomers to the scene. On Berkeley's 'wine block' a half-dozen tasting rooms (p158) specializing in natural wine have become popular stops in the city's Gilman District. Underdog wine region Amador County offers family-owned wineries and gold-rush history, along with a lovely new boutique hotel, Rest (p631).

More Beer (and Liquor)

California boasts by far the most craft breweries of any US state, and the intoxicating options are ever-expanding. New notables include Humble Sea Brewing Company (p298), a nautically themed taproom in Santa Cruz that's also a top spot to try some of the best hazy IPAs in the region. Over in the East Bay, Alameda's Spirits Alley has been making a splash with its liquor distilleries (p146).

Palm Springs, Rejuvenated

With the opening of Kimpton's Rowan Palm Springs (p513) high-rise hotel and an array of snazzy boutiques and restaurants, the city has injected a much-needed dose of contemporary cool into its once-sleepy downtown. In addition, work on a new downtown park and cultural complex (p497) by the local Agua Caliente band of Cahuilla people also kicked off in 2020.

Magical Mitchell Caverns

After a seven-year closure, and $1 million of repairs to the Providence Mountains State Recreation Area, the dramatic Mitchell Caverns are back in business. Book ahead for close-ups of the LED-illuminated stalagmite and stalactite formations on a guided tour.

LISTEN, WATCH AND FOLLOW

For inspiration and up-to-date news, visit www.lonelyplanet.com/usa/california/articles.

The California Report (www.kqed.org/californiareport) KQED's California news and culture podcast.

Eater (www.eater.com/california) Website covering food and restaurants in California.

LAist; SFist (www.laist.com; www.sfist.com) Websites covering news, events, food and culture in their respective cities.

California Through My Lens (www.californiathroughmylens.com) A blog focused on California travel.

California Sunday Magazine (www.californiasunday.com) The state's weekend magazine.

FAST FACTS

Food trend Indigenous cuisine

Acres of redwood forest 110,000

Miles of coastline 840

Population 39.9 million

population per sq mile

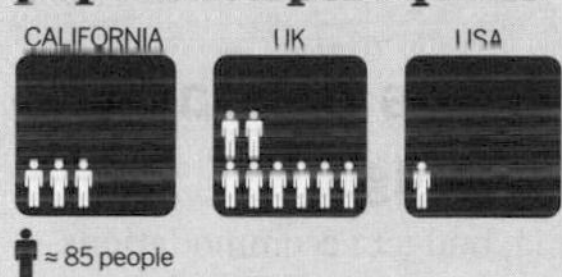

Airport Takes Off

Once no longer closed due to COVID-19, the Eastern Sierra Regional Airport (aka Bishop Airport) is expected to begin serving commercial airlines. The move would allow direct flights to and from Los Angeles and possibly a few other destinations. The airport is picking up the slack of nearby Mammoth Yosemite Airport, which often had to cancel flights due to weather and access issues.

Accommodations

Find more accommodations reviews throughout the On the Road chapters (from p75)

Accommodations Types

Campgrounds Not just a cheap sleep, but the best way to experience California's great outdoors by the beach, under the redwoods or nestled in desert dunes.

Hostels Budget-friendly dorm stays in key locations, including coastal parks and city centers.

B&Bs Home-style inns range from romantic vineyard cottages to historic Victorian mansions.

Motels Handy for road-trippers and less expensive than hotels; some have swimming pools.

Hotels & Resorts Upscale options come with prime locations, views and deluxe amenities.

Best Places to Stay

Best on a Budget

In California, budget accommodations include campgrounds and hostels, both of which are in large supply. National and state parks almost always offer scenic campgrounds, while independent hostels are scattered throughout the state but are particularly common in coastal cities like San Francisco and Los Angeles.

Best budget accommodations:

➡ Trinidad Inn (p280), Trinidad

➡ Yosemite Bug Rustic Mountain Resort (p696), Merced River Canyon

➡ Mellow Mountain Hostel (p650), South Lake Tahoe

➡ HI Pigeon Point Lighthouse (p169), Pescadero

➡ Newport Dunes Waterfront Resort (p444), Newport Beach

➡ HI San Francisco Fisherman's Wharf (p102), San Francisco

Best for Families

Family-friendly accommodations can be found in all destinations across the state. And although there is often a surcharge for the third and fourth person, children under a certain age (this varies) may stay free. Cribs or rollaway cots usually incur an additional fee.

Best family-travel accommodations:

➡ Paradise Pier Hotel (p432), Disneyland Resort

➡ Legoland Hotel (p490), San Diego

➡ Featherbed Railroad Co (p259), Clear Lake

➡ Evergreen Lodge (p690), Yosemite National Park

➡ Lake Siskiyou Beach & Camp (p569), Mt Shasta City

PRICE RANGES

Accommodation prices can vary according to demand, or there may be different rates for online, phone or walk-in bookings. The following price ranges refer to a double room with bath during high season, unless otherwise specified. Taxes, breakfast and resort fees are not normally included in the price.

$ less than $150 (less than $200 for San Francisco)

$$ $150–$250 ($200–$350 for San Francisco)

$$$ more than $250 (more than $350 for San Francisco)

Best for Solo Travelers

Unfortunately for solo travelers, rooms are often priced by the size and number of beds, rather than the number of occupants. A room with one double or queen-size bed usually costs the same for one or two people, while a room with a king-size bed or two double beds costs more.

Best solo-traveler accommodations:

➡ Silver Lake Pool & Inn (p407), Silver Lake & Echo Park

➡ Cosmopolitan Hotel (p470), San Diego

➡ Caravan Outpost (p379), Ojai

➡ Harbin Hot Springs (p260), Clear Lake

➡ Basecamp South Hotel (p652), South Lake Tahoe

➡ Eastside Guesthouse & Bivy (p725), Bishop

Best for Ecofriendliness

Some of California's hotels and motels are making environmental progress, with LEED-certified green buildings and state-mandated air-and water-saving initiatives. For lodgings that make extra sustainability efforts, look for our leaf icon. Also check out the California Green Lodging Program (www.calrecycle.ca.gov/epp/greenlodging), a state-run certification scheme.

Best ecofriendly travel accommodations:

➡ Samesun (p410), Venice

➡ Stanford Inn & Resort (p250) Mendocino

➡ Pacific Blue Inn (p296), Santa Cruz

➡ Cedar House Sport Hotel (p667), Truckee

➡ Rush Creek Lodge (p690), Yosemite National Park

➡ LOGE Mt Shasta (p569), Mt Shasta City

Booking

High season stretches from June to August everywhere, except the deserts and mountain ski areas, where December through April are the busiest months. Reservations are recommended for weekend and holiday travel year-round, and every day of the week during high season. Generally midweek rates are lower, except at urban hotels geared toward business travelers.

Cosmopolitan Hotel (p470), San Diego.

Lonely Planet (www.lonelyplanet.com/hotels) Find independent reviews, as well as recommendations on the best places to stay – and book them online.

Cabbi (www.cabbi.com) Lists a small, high-quality selection of B&Bs in California.

Hipcamp (www.hipcamp.com) A selection of campsites on farms, vineyards, nature preserves and parks across California, with an option to book.

Hostelling International USA (www.hiusa.com) A network of the state's best hostels; you can book through the site as well.

HotelTonight (www.hoteltonight.com) Hotel-search app offering last-minute discounted bookings.

Recreation.gov (www.recreation.gov) Book lodgings in California's national parks.

ReserveCalifornia (www.reservecalifornia.com) Book campsites and lodgings within state parks.

Vrbo (www.bedandbreakfast.com) Listings include local B&Bs and neighborhood inns.

Getting Around

For more information, see Transport (p778)

Traveling by Car

California's love affair with cars runs deep for at least one practical reason: the state is so big, public transportation can't cover it. For flexibility and convenience, you'll probably want a car, but rental rates and gas prices can eat up a good chunk of your trip budget. Also note that metro-area traffic can be nightmarish, especially during weekday commuter rush hours (roughly 6am to 10am and 3pm to 7pm). City parking is often an expensive hassle.

Car Hire

To rent your own wheels, you'll typically need to be at least 25 years old, hold a valid driver's license and have a major credit card, not a check or debit card. A few companies may rent to drivers under 25 but over 21 for a hefty surcharge. If you don't have a credit card, large cash deposits are infrequently accepted.

With advance reservations, you can often get an economy-size vehicle with unlimited mileage from around $30 per day, plus insurance, taxes and fees. Weekend and weekly rates are usually the most economical. Airport locations may have cheaper rates but higher add-on fees; if you get a fly-drive package, local taxes may be extra when you pick up the car. City-center branches sometimes offer free pickups and drop-offs.

Driving Conditions

In places where winter driving is an issue, mountain passes may periodically close, or snow tires and tire chains may

RESOURCES

California Department of Transportation (www.dot.ca.gov) Up-to-date highway conditions, including road closures and construction updates for California.

American Automobile Association (AAA; www.aaa.com) Walk-in offices throughout California, add-on coverage for RVs and motorcycles, and reciprocal agreements with some international auto clubs (eg CAA in Canada, AA in the UK).

Better World Club (www.betterworldclub.com) Ecofriendly auto club offering add-on or stand-alone emergency roadside assistance for cyclists.

be required. Carry your own chains and know how to use them. Otherwise, chains can usually be bought or rented (but not cheaply) on the highway, at gas stations or in the nearest town. Most car-rental companies don't permit the use of chains and also prohibit driving off-road or on dirt roads.

In rural areas, livestock sometimes graze next to unfenced roads. These areas are typically signed as 'Open Range,' with the silhouette of a steer. Where deer and other wild animals frequently appear roadside, you'll see signs with the silhouette of a leaping deer. Take these signs seriously, particularly at night.

In coastal areas thick fog may impede driving – slow down and if it's too soupy, get off the road. Along coastal cliffs and in the mountains, watch out for falling rocks, mudslides and avalanches that could damage or disable your car if struck.

No Car?

Bus

California buses are a cheap but slow option, with extensive metro-area networks. Intercity and regional buses are limited and more expensive, while Greyhound (www.greyhound.com) and FlixBus (https://global.flixbus.com/bus/united-states) buses are an economical way to travel between major cities and points along the coast. Still, they won't get you off the beaten path or to national parks. Frequency varies; main routes have service several times daily.

Train

Trains are the fastest way to get around the San Francisco Bay Area and LA, but the lines offer limited reach. Pricier regional and long-distance Amtrak (www.amtrak.com) trains comfortably connect some major cities and limited towns, but are occasionally tardy. At some stations Thruway buses provide onward connections or replace trains.

Bicycle

Although cycling around California is a 'green' way to travel, the distances involved demand a high level of fitness and make it hard to cover much ground.

DRIVING FAST FACTS

- ➡ Drive on the right.
- ➡ All passengers must use seat belts in a private vehicle. In a taxi, backseat passengers aren't required to buckle up.
- ➡ Speed limits: 65mph on freeways, 55mph on two-lane highways, 35mph on major city streets, 25mph in residential districts.
- ➡ Driving under the influence of alcohol or drugs is illegal.

ROAD DISTANCES (miles)
NOTE: Distances are approximate

	Los Angeles	Sacramento	San Diego	San Francisco
Sacramento	385			
San Diego	120	510		
San Francisco	380	90	500	
Truckee/Lake Tahoe	480	100	605	190

Month by Month

TOP EVENTS

Pride Month, June

Coachella Valley Music & Arts Festival, April

California State Fair, July

Comic-Con International, July

Tournament of Roses Parade, January

January

January is the wettest month in California, and a slow time for coastal travel – but this is when mountain ski resorts and Southern California deserts hit their stride.

☆ Tournament of Roses Parade

The famous New Year's parade (https://tournamentofroses.com) held before the Tournament of Roses college football game draws over 700,000 spectators to the LA suburb of Pasadena. Expect marching bands, prancing equestrians and flower-festooned floats displayed for days after the event concludes.

February

As California sunshine breaks through the drizzle, skiers hit the slopes in T-shirts, wildflowers burst into bloom, and romantics scramble for Valentine's Day reservations at restaurants and hotels.

Lunar New Year

Firecrackers, parades, lion dances and Chinatown night markets usher in the Lunar New Year, falling on February 1, 2022, and January 22, 2023. California's biggest parade happens in San Francisco, where tiny-tot martial artists chase a 200ft dragon. (p96)

☆ Academy Awards

Hollywood rolls out the red carpet for movie-star entrances on Oscars night (www.oscars.org) in late February or early March. Fans wait patiently in bleachers and jostle paparazzi for a glimpse of the action when stretch limos arrive.

March

As ski season winds down the beaches warm up, just in time for spring break (exact dates vary with school schedules and the Easter holiday).

Mendocino Coast Whale Festivals

Mendocino, Fort Bragg and nearby towns toast the whale migration with wining and dining, art shows and naturalist-guided walks and talks over three weekends in March. (p249)

April

As wildflower season peaks in the high desert, the southern desert bursts into song and San Francisco twinkles with international film stars. Shoulder season in the mountains and along the coast brings lower hotel prices.

☆ Coachella Valley Music & Arts Festival

Headliners, indie rockers, rappers and cult DJs converge outside Palm Springs for a three-day musical extravaganza usually held over two weekends in mid-April. Book well ahead – this festival is huge. (p510)

☆ San Francisco International Film Festival

The nation's oldest film festival lights up San Francisco

nights with star-studded US premieres of hundreds of films from around the globe, usually held over two weeks in April. (p96)

May

Weather starts to heat up statewide, although some coastal areas are blanketed by 'May gray' fog. Memorial Day holiday weekend marks the official start of summer, and one of the year's busiest travel times.

Cinco de Mayo

¡Viva México! California celebrates its Mexican heritage and the victory of Mexican forces over the French army on May 5, 1862. LA and San Diego have the biggest celebrations, but you'll find margaritas, music and dancing across the state.

Bay to Breakers

On the third Sunday in May, costumed joggers, inebriated idlers and renegade streakers make the annual dash from San Francisco's Embarcadero to Ocean Beach. Watch out for participants dressed as salmon, who run upstream from the finish line. (p96)

Kinetic Grand Championship

Artists spend months preparing for this 'triathlon of the art world,' inventing outlandish human-powered and self-propelled sculptural contraptions to cover 42 miles from Arcata to Ferndale over three days. (p276)

June

Once school lets out for the summer, everyone heads to California beaches – only to shiver through San Francisco as 'June gloom' coastal fog descends. Mountain resorts offer cool escapes, but the deserts are just too darn hot.

Pride Month

California celebrates LGBT+ pride not just for a day but for the entire month of June, with costumed parades, film fests, marches and streets parties. SF Pride sets the global parade standard, with more than a million people, tons of glitter and ounces of bikinis. San Diego celebrates in mid-July, Palm Springs in November. (p96)

Summer Solstice Celebration

Since 1974, Santa Barbara's summer throw-down reminds residents of what the place was like before it got fancy. Expect floats, dance troupes and inventive miscellany sashaying down State St. (p358)

July

California's campgrounds, beaches and theme parks hit peak popularity, especially on the July 4 holiday – summer's biggest travel weekend.

California State Fair

A million people come to this fair to ride the giant Ferris wheel, cheer on pie-eating contests and horseback jockeys, browse the blue-ribbon agricultural and arts-and-crafts exhibits, taste California wines and craft beers, and listen to live bands. It's held in Sacramento over two weeks in late July.

Festival of Arts & Pageant of the Masters

Laguna Beach is so prolifically creative, the local Festival of Arts stretches over July and August, featuring art shows and demos by 140 artists in media ranging from scrimshaw to furniture. The festival culminates with a reenactment of famous paintings by costumed actors, accompanied by an orchestra. (p453)

Comic-Con International

Affectionately known as 'Nerd Prom,' the nation's biggest annual convention of comic-book fans, hardcore pop-culture collectors, and sci-fi and anime devotees brings out-of-this-world costumed madness to San Diego in late July. (p469)

August

School summer vacations may technically be over, but you'd never guess in California – beaches and parks are still packed. Travel slows only slightly before the Labor Day holiday weekend.

Outside Lands

Three days of debauchery in Golden Gate Park: Outside Lands is out to reinvent the Summer of

Love every August with headliner music and comedy acts plus gourmet food, beer and wine. (p98)

Eureka Street Art Festival

Eureka's weeklong extravaganza of mural painting and street artistry takes place across Old Town. (p273)

Old Spanish Days Fiesta

Santa Barbara shows off its early Spanish, Mexican and American *rancho* roots with parades, rodeo events, arts-and-crafts exhibits, and live music and dance shows in early August.

September

Summer's last hurrah is Labor Day holiday weekend, which is busy almost everywhere in California (except hot SoCal deserts). After Labor Day, prices drop and availability goes up statewide.

Tall Ships Festival

In early September, the West Coast's biggest gathering of historical tall ships happens at Dana Point in Orange County, with knot-tying and scrimshaw-carving demonstrations and other kid-friendly maritime activities. (p456)

Monterrey Jazz Festival

Old-school jazz cats, cross-cultural sensations and fusion rebels all line up to play the West Coast's legendary jazz festival, held on the Central Coast over a long weekend in mid-September. (p307)

October

Summer arrives at last in Northern California, and Southern Californians take a breather after a long summer of nonstop beach-going. The mellow fall shoulder season is a prime time for sweet travel deals along the coast and in cities.

Hardly Strictly Bluegrass

Over half a million people converge for free outdoor concerts in Golden Gate Park during the first weekend in October. Headliners like Emmylou Harris, Elvis Costello and Gillian Welch share seven stages with 100-plus folk, blues and jazz musicians. (p98)

Vineyard Festivals

All month long under sunny skies, California's wine countries celebrate bringing in the vineyard harvest with food-and-wine events, harvest fairs, barrel tastings and grape-stomping 'crush' parties.

Halloween

Hauntings and fright-fests take place all month at theme parks, and on the 31st, hundreds of thousands of revelers descend on West Hollywood for all-day partying and live entertainment. Over-the-top scary and not safe for work costumes must be seen to be believed.

November

Temperatures drop statewide, the first raindrops fall along the coast, and with any luck, ski season begins in the mountains. Consider this your opportunity to explore without crowds or traffic, except around the Thanksgiving holiday.

Dia de los Muertos

Mexican communities honor deceased relatives on November 2 with costumed parades, sugar skulls, graveyard picnics, candlelight processions and fabulous altars, including in San Francisco, LA and San Diego.

December

As winter rains reach coastal areas, SoCal's sunny, dry deserts become magnets for travelers. Christmas and New Year's Eve are extremely crowded travel times, but worth it for California's palm-tree light displays and holiday cheer.

Parades of Lights

Deck the decks with boughs of holly: boats bedecked with holiday cheer and twinkling lights float through coastal California harbors, including Orange County's Newport Beach and San Diego.

Itineraries

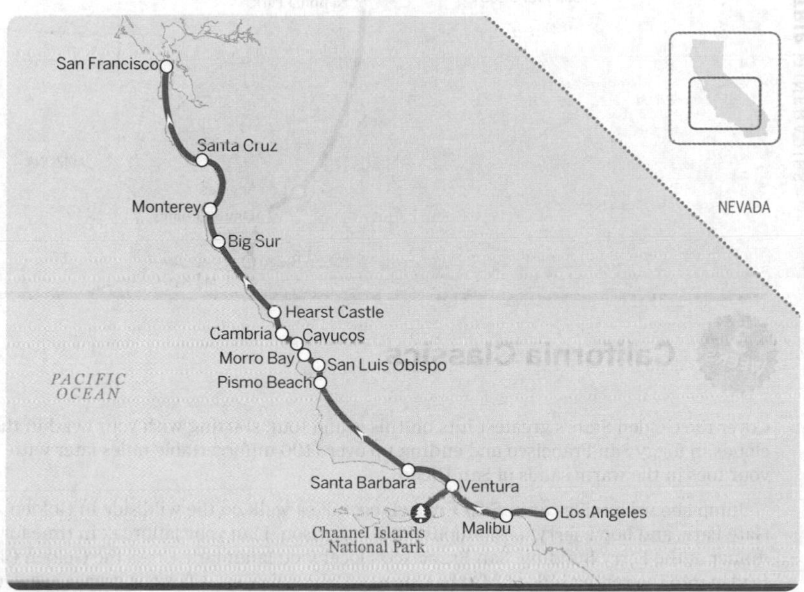

Los Angeles to San Francisco

You've got one whole week to settle California's longest-running debate: which is California's better half, North or South?

Start in **Los Angeles** for Hollywood star-spotting, world-class museums and live music on Sunset Strip. Cruise north to the beaches of **Malibu**, and hop a boat from **Ventura** to explore **Channel Islands National Park**. Arrive for happy hour in seaside **Santa Barbara**, at the edge of SoCal wine country. Follow the monarch-butterfly trail to retro-1950s **Pismo Beach**, and arrive in **San Luis Obispo** hungry for local BBQ. Take coastal Hwy 1 past offbeat beach towns like **Morro Bay**, **Cayucos** and **Cambria** before a stop at the eccentric **Hearst Castle**. Wind north along cliff edges through soul-stirring **Big Sur**, where redwood forests rise and waterfalls crash onto the beach. Dive into California's best aquarium in maritime **Monterey**, and take a bone-rattling roller-coaster ride over **Santa Cruz**' beach boardwalk. Hwy 1 leads you past lighthouses and strawberry farms, staggering bluffs and fishing harbors to the countercultural capital of **San Francisco**. You may not have settled the great North/South debate – but now you can see both sides.

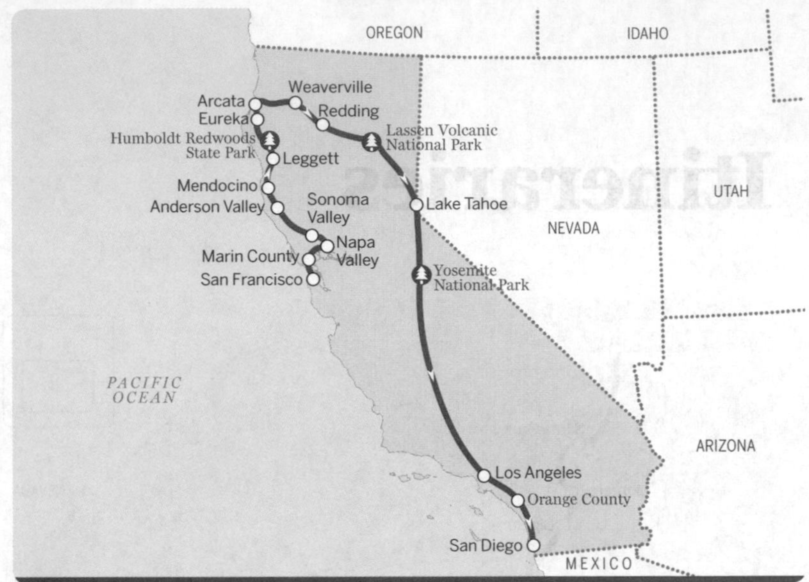

California Classics

Cover the Golden State's greatest hits on this grand tour, starting with your head in the clouds in foggy San Francisco and ending up over 1400 unforgettable miles later with your toes in the warm sands of San Diego.

Jump aboard a cable car in **San Francisco**, take a walk on the wild side in Golden Gate Park, and hop a ferry to infamous Alcatraz prison. Plan your jailbreak in time for dinner at the Ferry Building, San Francisco's local food landmark. Cross the Golden Gate Bridge into the rolling hills of **Marin County**. California's most famous grapes grow just east in down-home **Sonoma Valley** and chichi **Napa Valley**. Detour west through more vineyards and apple orchards in rural **Anderson Valley**, and head through redwood forests to emerge in **Mendocino**, a postcard-perfect Victorian seaside town. Swing onto Hwy 101 at **Leggett**, where your magical mystery tour of the Redwood Empire really begins. In **Humboldt Redwoods State Park**, you'll stand in the shadows of the tallest trees on earth. Kick back in the candy-colored Victorian harbor town of **Eureka**, or head north to hang out with artists and environmentalists in the outlandish outpost of **Arcata**. Turn east on Hwy 299 for a long, scenic trip to hidden **Weaverville**, skirting the lake-laced Trinity Alps. Keep trucking east, then south on I-5 to **Redding**, where families throng Turtle Bay Exploration Park. Climb east on Hwy 44 to the otherworldly moonscapes of **Lassen Volcanic National Park**, at the southern tip of the Cascades Range. Go southeast on Hwy 89 to **Lake Tahoe**, the Sierra Nevada's scenic outdoor playground. Roll down the Eastern Sierra's Hwy 395, taking the back-door route via Tioga Rd (open seasonally) into **Yosemite National Park**. Gawk at waterfalls tumbling over granite cliffs, and enjoy moments of silence in groves of giant sequoias, the world's biggest trees. Zoom south to **Los Angeles** to find as-seen-on-TV beaches, fleets of food trucks and colorful neighborhood characters. Walk in stars' footsteps through Hollywood, then sprawl on the sand in hip Santa Monica or quirky Venice Beach. Cruise south past swanky **Orange County**'s beaches to hang-loose **San Diego** for epic surf and serious fish tacos. Dude, you've totally got the hang of California.

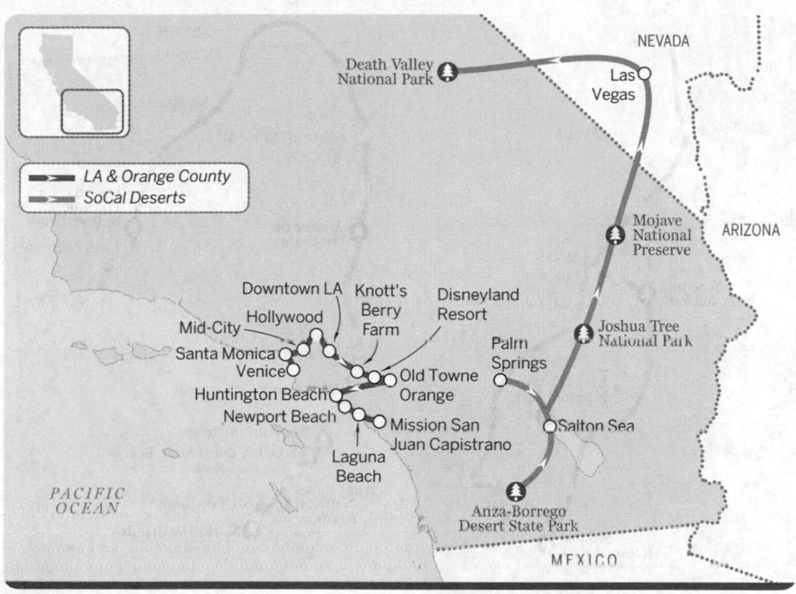

5 DAYS LA & Orange County

All-star attractions, bodacious beaches and fresh seafood are yours on this Southern California sojourn, covering 100 miles of sun, sand and surf.

Kick things off in Los Angeles. Skate north from oddball **Venice** to oceanfront **Santa Monica** for sunset carnival rides on the pier. Cram your social feeds with selfies on the star-studded sidewalks of **Hollywood**, then go highbrow with art museums in **Mid-City**, and Walt Disney Concert Hall and Grammy Museum in **downtown LA**. Do lunch at Grand Central Market, then over in Anaheim you've got a hot date with Mickey at Disneyland and wild rides at Disney California Adventure. If **Disneyland Resort** isn't enough adrenaline, hit the thrill rides over at **Knott's Berry Farm**, and recuperate in nostalgic **Old Towne Orange**. Cruise west to 'Surf City USA', **Huntington Beach**, to rent a board, play beach volleyball and make s'mores over a beach bonfire. Swing by **Newport Beach** for sunset strolls by the piers, then roll south to the upscale artists' colony of **Laguna Beach**. Slingshot back toward the I-5, and make for the historic **Mission San Juan Capistrano**.

10 DAYS SoCal Deserts

You might think you've arrived on another planet, with giant sand dunes, palm-tree oases and volcanic craters – but you're just a few hours from LA. Get lost – and find yourself – on this 800-mile desert drive.

Start in glam **Palm Springs**, where stars from Elvis to DiCaprio hole up in sleek mid-century-modern hideaways. Sip mojitos poolside, hike to palm-studded canyons and ride a tram into cool pine-scented mountains. Drive past the Coachella Valley's date farms and along the shores of the mirage like **Salton Sea**, turning west into wild **Anza-Borrego Desert State Park** to see bighorn sheep and wind-sculpted caves. Boomerang north to **Joshua Tree National Park**, with its precariously balanced boulders and iconic namesake trees. Keep motoring north into the **Mojave National Preserve**, where sand dunes sing with the wind and wander the world's largest Joshua-tree forest. Ready for a change of pace? **Las Vegas**, baby. Quit while you're ahead at the Strip's casinos, and head for **Death Valley National Park**. These crackled salt flats and marbled canyons make Mars seem overrated.

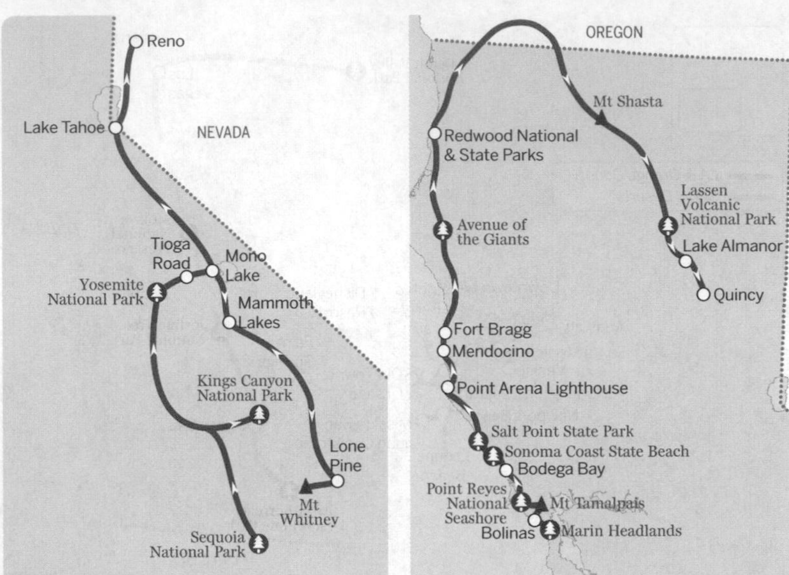

Sierra Nevada Ramble

Nothing can prepare you for the monumental mountain scenery of the Sierra Nevada, with acres of wildflower meadows, gleaming alpine lakes and sun-catching peaks. Take this 850-mile trip in summer, when all roads are open.

To gaze up at the world's biggest trees and down at a gorge deeper than the Grand Canyon, start in **Sequoia and Kings Canyon National Parks**. Go west, then north to **Yosemite National Park**, where thunderous waterfalls and eroded granite monoliths overhang a verdant valley. Soar over the Sierra Nevada's snowy rooftop on Yosemite's high-elevation **Tioga Road** (open seasonally). It's a quick trip south on Hwy 395 to **Mammoth Lakes**, an all-seasons adventure base camp, and 100 more miles to **Lone Pine**, in the shadow of mighty **Mt Whitney**. Backtracking north, gaze out over **Mono Lake** and its odd-looking tufa formations, which you can paddle past in a kayak. Head to **Lake Tahoe**, a deep-blue jewel framed by jutting peaks with hiking trails and ski-resort slopes. Roll to Nevada for casino nightlife in **Reno**, and return to Tahoe for restorative hot springs.

North Coast & Mountains

Follow the coastline north of SF, where Hwy 1 skirts rocky shores, secluded coves and wind-sculpted beaches, before joining Hwy 101. Loop back via the majestic Northern Mountains for an 800-mile journey.

Across the Golden Gate Bridge, hike over the **Marin Headlands** or around **Mt Tamalpais**. Locals keep hiding the road signs to **Bolinas**, but you'll find this eccentric cove north of Stinson Beach. Head up to blustery **Point Reyes National Seashore**, and, passing **Bodega Bay**, picnic at stunning **Sonoma Coast State Beach** or **Salt Point State Park**. Next, scale **Point Arena Lighthouse**, step through pot-scented mists into enchanted **Mendocino** and ride the Skunk Train at **Fort Bragg**. Hwy 1 curves inland to Hwy 101, running north into hippie Humboldt County. Hug ancient redwoods on the **Avenue of the Giants** or wander through misty **Redwood National and State Parks**. Cutting east through Oregon to the I-5 southbound, you'll hit the stunning **Mt Shasta**. Snap photos and head southeast to **Lassen Volcanic National Park**, a geological wonderland. Take a dip in **Lake Almanor**, near the laid-back mountain town of **Quincy**.

Top: Mt Whitney (p734)

Bottom: Point Arena Lighthouse (p245)

ANDREW ZARIVNY / SHUTTERSTOCK ©

Off the Beaten Track

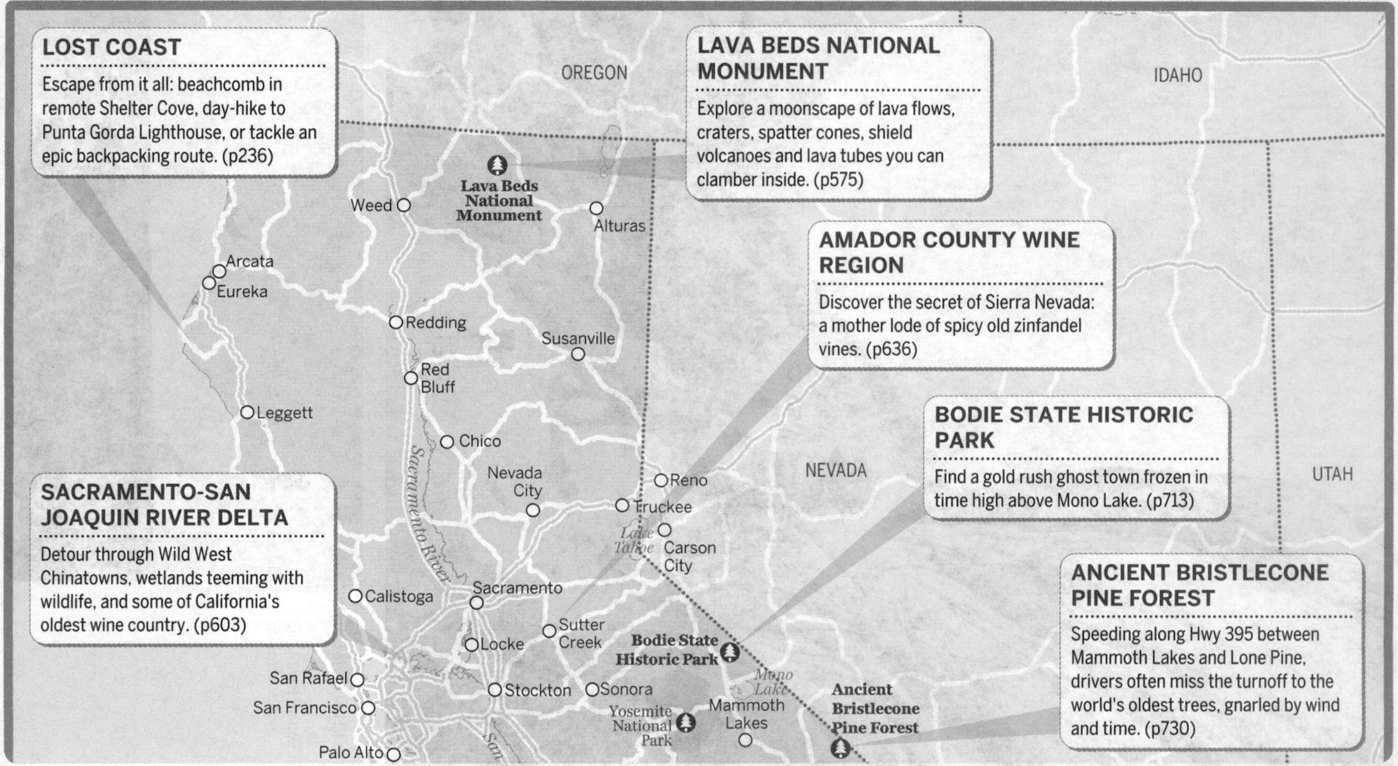

LOST COAST

Escape from it all: beachcomb in remote Shelter Cove, day-hike to Punta Gorda Lighthouse, or tackle an epic backpacking route. (p236)

LAVA BEDS NATIONAL MONUMENT

Explore a moonscape of lava flows, craters, spatter cones, shield volcanoes and lava tubes you can clamber inside. (p575)

AMADOR COUNTY WINE REGION

Discover the secret of Sierra Nevada: a mother lode of spicy old zinfandel vines. (p636)

BODIE STATE HISTORIC PARK

Find a gold rush ghost town frozen in time high above Mono Lake. (p713)

SACRAMENTO-SAN JOAQUIN RIVER DELTA

Detour through Wild West Chinatowns, wetlands teeming with wildlife, and some of California's oldest wine country. (p603)

ANCIENT BRISTLECONE PINE FOREST

Speeding along Hwy 395 between Mammoth Lakes and Lone Pine, drivers often miss the turnoff to the world's oldest trees, gnarled by wind and time. (p730)

0 200 km
0 100 miles
OREGON
IDAHO
NEVADA
UTAH
Lava Beds National Monument
Weed
Alturas
Arcata
Eureka
Redding
Susanville
Red Bluff
Leggett
Chico
Sacramento River
Nevada City
Reno
Truckee
Lake Tahoe
Carson City
Calistoga
Sacramento
Sutter Creek
Locke
Bodie State Historic Park
San Rafael
Stockton
Sonora
Mono Lake
San Francisco
Yosemite National Park
Mammoth Lakes
Ancient Bristlecone Pine Forest
Palo Alto
San

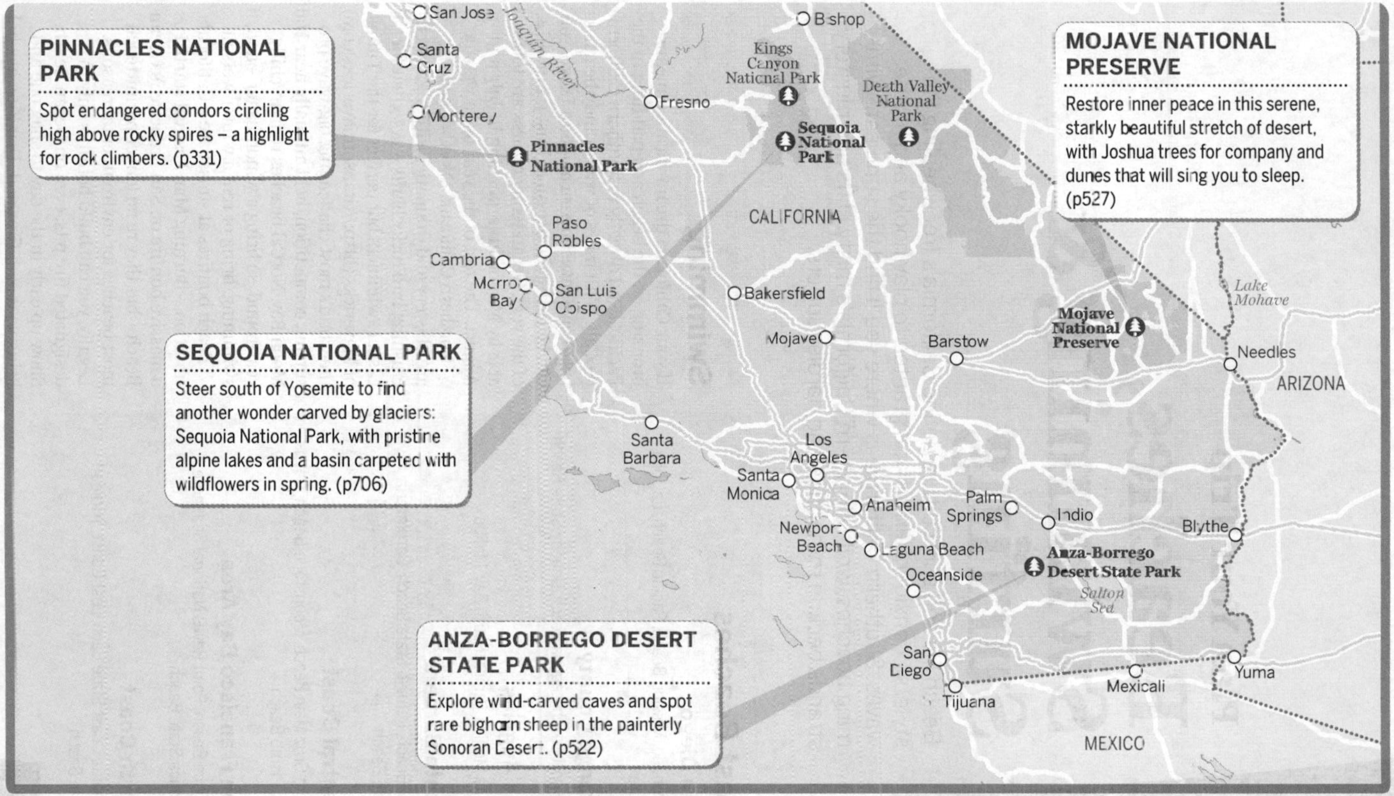

PINNACLES NATIONAL PARK

Spot endangered condors circling high above rocky spires – a highlight for rock climbers. (p331)

SEQUOIA NATIONAL PARK

Steer south of Yosemite to find another wonder carved by glaciers: Sequoia National Park, with pristine alpine lakes and a basin carpeted with wildflowers in spring. (p706)

MOJAVE NATIONAL PRESERVE

Restore inner peace in this serene, starkly beautiful stretch of desert, with Joshua trees for company and dunes that will sing you to sleep. (p527)

ANZA-BORREGO DESERT STATE PARK

Explore wind-carved caves and spot rare bighorn sheep in the painterly Sonoran Desert. (p522)

San Jose
Santa Cruz
Monterey
Joaquin River
Fresno
Bishop
Kings Canyon National Park
Death Valley National Park
Sequoia National Park
Pinnacles National Park
CALIFORNIA
Paso Robles
Cambria
Morro Bay
San Luis Obispo
Bakersfield
Mojave
Barstow
Mojave National Preserve
Lake Mohave
Needles
ARIZONA
Santa Barbara
Los Angeles
Santa Monica
Anaheim
Palm Springs
Indio
Blythe
Newport Beach
Laguna Beach
Oceanside
Anza-Borrego Desert State Park
Salton Sea
San Diego
Tijuana
Mexicali
Yuma
MEXICO

Plan Your Trip

Beaches, Swimming & Surfing

Beach life and surf culture define California's freewheeling lifestyle, so consider permission granted to play hooky and hit the waves. Southern California is where you'll find the sunniest swimming beaches, while Northern California's misty cliffs and blustery strands beckon romantics and hardier surfers.

Best Beaches

San Diego

Coronado, Mission Beach, Pacific Beach, La Jolla Shores

Orange County

Newport Beach, Laguna Beach, Doheny State Beach

Los Angeles

Santa Monica, Venice, South Bay, Malibu

Santa Barbara

East Beach, Refugio State Beach, Carpinteria State Beach

Central Coast

Santa Cruz Main Beach, Moonstone Beach, Cayucos, Pismo Beach

San Francisco Bay Area

Stinson Beach, Point Reyes National Seashore, Pacifica State Beach

North Coast

Sonoma Coast State Bach, Lost Coast, Trinidad State Beach

Swimming

If your California dream vacation means bronzing on the beach and paddling in the Pacific, head directly to Southern California (SoCal). With miles of wide, sandy beaches between Santa Barbara and San Diego, you can be living the dream at least six months of the year. Ocean temperatures are tolerable by May or June, peaking in July and August. The rest of the year use a wetsuit.

Northern California (NorCal) beaches are blustery and dramatic, with high swells crashing into rocky bluffs – not great for casual swimmers but perfect for the Titans of Mavericks (http://titansofmavericks.com), the world's most challenging big-wave pro surfing competition, held annually near Half Moon Bay. NorCal beaches remain chilly year-round, so bring a windbreaker – and, if swimming, bring or rent a winter wetsuit.

Beach bonfires at sunset are a California tradition – Burning Man Festival started as a massive bonfire on San Francisco's Ocean Beach – but they're no longer permitted at most beaches for environmental reasons. Legally, you can build bonfires only in designated fire pits, even on Ocean Beach. Show up early in the day to snag one and bring your own firewood. Drinking alcohol

Top: La Jolla Shores (p483)

Bottom: Santa Monica beach (p399)

HOLBOX / SHUTTERSTOCK ©

WARNING! RIPTIDES

If you find yourself being carried offshore by a dangerous ocean current called a riptide, the important thing is to just keep afloat. Don't panic or try to swim against the current, as this will quickly exhaust you. Instead, swim parallel to the shoreline and once the current stops pulling you out, swim back to shore.

is usually prohibited on beaches, except at campgrounds.

During the hottest dog days of summer, families skip the beach and head inland for a dip at theme parks like Legoland (p490) in San Diego's North County and Knott's Soak City (p434) near Disneyland.

Safety Tips

➡ Most California beaches have flags to distinguish between surfer-only sections and sections for swimmers. Flags also alert beachgoers to dangerous water conditions – and even seasoned California surfers know these warnings need to be taken seriously. The most important is red – don't swim.

➡ Popular beaches in Southern California have lifeguards, but can still be dangerous places to swim. Obey all posted warning signs and ask about local conditions before venturing out.

➡ Stay out of the ocean for at least three days after a major rainstorm, when dangerously high levels of pollutants flush out through storm drains, washing road debris with them.

➡ Water quality varies from beach to beach and day to day. For current water-safety conditions and beach closures, check the Beach Report Card issued by the nonprofit organization Heal the Bay (http://brc.healthebay.org).

Best Family-Friendly Beaches

La Jolla Shores (p483) San Diego

Santa Monica State Beach (p399) Los Angeles

Leo Carrillo State Park (☎310-457-8143; www.parks.ca.gov; 35000 W Pacific Coast Hwy, Malibu; per car $12; ⌚8am-10pm; 🅿👪) Malibu

Balboa Peninsula (p443) Newport Beach

Carpinteria State Beach (p376) Santa Barbara County

Arroyo Burro Beach County Park (p356) Santa Barbara

Avila Beach (p340) San Luis Obispo County

Natural Bridges State Beach (p294) Santa Cruz

Stinson Beach (p137) Marin County

Trinidad State Beach (p279) North Coast

Best Places for Beach Volleyball

Manhattan Beach (www.citymb.info; 🚌MTA 126, 439) LA's South Bay

Hermosa Beach LA's South Bay

Huntington City Beach (p440) Orange County

Mission Bay (p467) San Diego

East Beach (p356) Santa Barbara

Surfing

Surf's up! Even if you've never set foot on a board, now's the time. There's no denying the influence of surfing on every aspect of California life. Surfing is an obsession up and down the coast, particularly in Santa Cruz, San Diego and Orange County.

The most powerful ocean swells arrive along California's coast during late fall and winter. May and June are generally the flattest months, although they do bring warmer water. Without a wetsuit, you'll likely freeze your butt off except at the height of summer – especially north of Santa Barbara.

Crowds can be a problem at many surf spots, as are territorial surfers. Befriend a local surfer for an introduction before hitting Cali's most famous waves, such as notoriously agro Windansea Beach, Trestles and sometimes Malibu Surfrider Beach.

Sharks do inhabit California waters, but attacks are rare. Most take place in the so-called 'Red Triangle' between Monterey on the Central Coast, Tomales Bay north of San Francisco and the offshore Farallon Islands.

Rentals & Lessons

You'll find board rentals on just about every patch of beach where surfing is possible. Expect to pay about $25 per half-day fo; with wetsuit rental add another $10 or so.

Huntington Beach Pier (p439)

Two-hour group lessons for beginners start at around $100 per person, while private, two-hour instruction easily costs more than $125. If you've got bigger ambitions, surf schools offer longer surf clinics and weeklong 'surfari' camps.

Stand-up paddleboarding (SUP) on flat water is more relaxing and easier than learning to surf on waves. You'll find board-and-paddle rentals and lessons popping up all along the coast, from San Diego to north of San Francisco Bay. Kiteboarding is also big along NorCal's windy coast, and you can get started with rentals in Santa Cruz and San Francisco.

Best Surf Breaks for Beginners

The best spots to learn to surf are the long bays, where waves are small and rolling. Surf schools dot the California coast from San Diego to Santa Cruz, and popular places for beginners include:

San Diego

Mission Beach (Map p474; ☎858-483-8837; www.missionsurf.com; 4320 Mission Blvd, Pacific Beach; surfboard rentals soft-top/hardboard from $10/20; ⏲10am-7pm)

Pacific Beach (p468),

La Jolla (Map p462; ☎858-454-8273; www.surfdiva.com; 2160 Avenida de la Playa; group surf lessons from $75, surfboard rental per hour from $9; ⏲store 8:30am-5pm, lesson hours vary)

Orange County

Seal Beach (p438)

Huntington Beach (p440)

Newport Beach (p442)

Los Angeles

Malibu (☎310-456-8508; www.malibusurf-shack.com; 22935 Pacific Coast Hwy, Malibu; kayaks per hour/day $25/40, surfboards per day $30-40, SUP per 2hr/overnight $45/75, wetsuits per day $10-15, surf/SUP lessons per person $125/115; ⏲10am-6pm)

Santa Barbara County

Leadbetter Beach (p356)

Carpinteria (p376)

Central Coast

Santa Cruz (p295)

Cayucos (p326)

Bodyboarding & Bodysurfing

There are other ways to catch your dream wave – bodysurfing and bodyboarding let you ride rolling waves for 50ft or more. To increase your speed and control, use some fins. It's pretty easy, and you'll be beaming with glee once you catch that first wave.

Online Resources

➡ Browse live beach webcams and surf reports at Huntington Beach–based Surfline (www.surfline.com), and get the lowdown on the best swells from San Diego to Humboldt County.

➡ Orange County–based *Surfer* magazine's website (www.surfermag.com) has travel reports, gear reviews, blogs, forums and totally gnarly videos.

➡ Surfers have led California's coastal conservation efforts for more than 40 years. Join their ongoing efforts through the nonprofit Surfrider Foundation (www.surfrider.org).

Plan Your Trip
California Camping & Outdoors

California is an all-seasons destination for outdoor fun. Hike among desert wildflowers in spring, dive into the Pacific in summer, mountain bike through fall foliage and ski down wintry mountain slopes. Once California gets your adrenaline pumping, you'll also be ready to hang glide off ocean bluffs, scuba past coastal shipwrecks, scale sheer granite cliffs or white-water raft the rapids.

When & Where

Best Times to Go

Cycling & mountain biking Apr–Oct

Hiking Apr–Oct

Kayaking, snorkeling & scuba diving Jul–Oct

Rock climbing Apr–Oct

Skiing & snowboarding Dec–Mar

Whale-watching Jan–Mar

White-water rafting Apr–Oct

Windsurfing Apr–Oct

Top Experiences

Backpacking John Muir Trail

Cycling Pacific Coast Hwy

Hiking Redwood National & State Parks

Mountain biking Lake Tahoe

Rock climbing Yosemite National Park

Sea kayaking Channel Islands

Snorkeling & scuba diving La Jolla

White-water rafting Sierra Nevada

Camping

In California, camping is much more than just a cheap way to spend the night. Pitch a tent beside alpine lakes and streams beneath snaggletoothed Sierra Nevada peaks, nestle into shimmering SoCal sand dunes beneath the full moon, and drift off on NorCal redwood forest floors beneath the tallest trees on earth. No five-star-hotel views can compare to this kind of scenery. If you didn't bring your own tent, you can buy (and occasionally rent) camping gear at outdoor outfitters and sporting-goods shops in most cities and some towns, especially near national parks.

Campground Types & Amenities

Primitive campsites Usually have fire pits, picnic tables and access to drinking water and vault toilets; most common in United States Forest Service (USFS) forests and on Bureau of Land Management (BLM) land.

Developed campgrounds Typically found in state and national parks, these offer more amenities,

California's Best Places to Camp

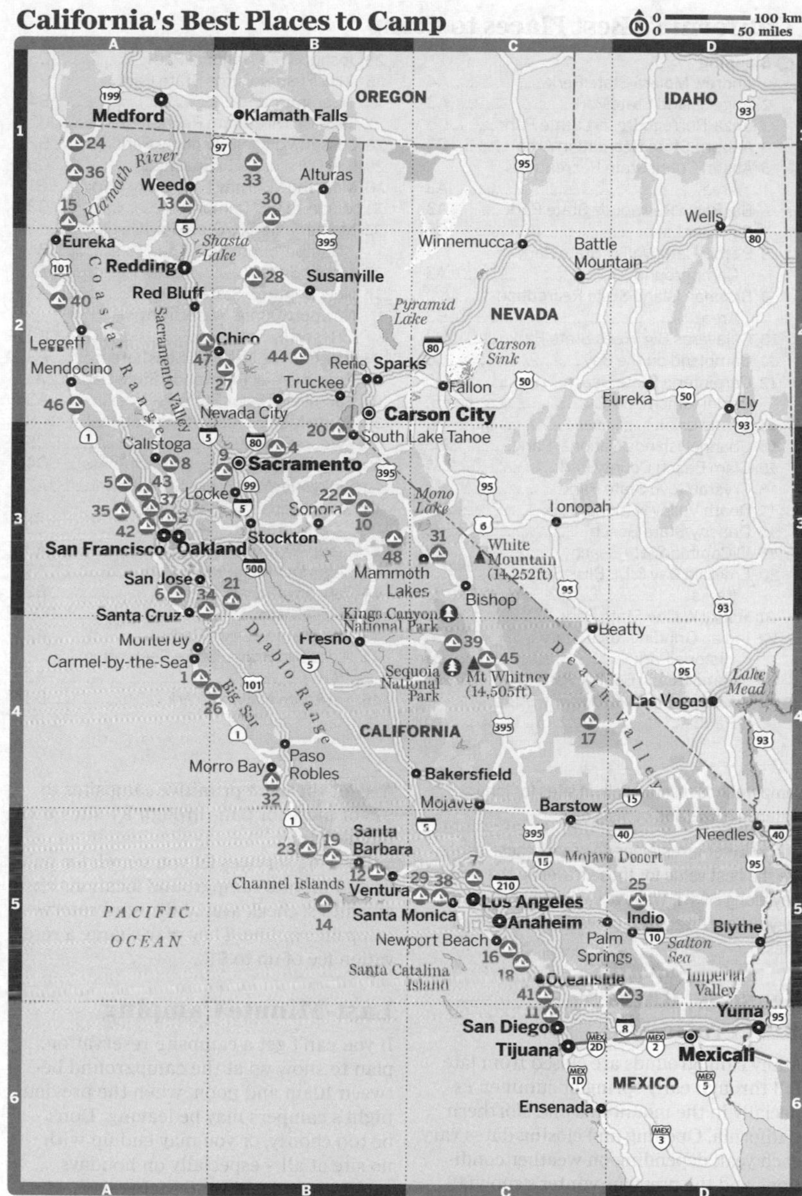

including flush toilets, barbecue grills and occasionally hot showers.

Private campgrounds Often cater to RVs (recreational vehicles), with full electricity and water hookups and dump stations; tent sites may be sparse and uninviting. Hot showers and a coin-operated laundry are usually available, plus possibly a swimming pool, wi-fi and camping cabins.

Walk-in (environmental) sites Provide more peace and privacy, and may be significantly cheaper than drive-in sites. A few state-park

California's Best Places to Camp

Sleeping

1 Andrew Molera State Park A4
2 Angel Island State Park A3
3 Anza-Borrego Desert State Park D5
4 Auburn State Recreation Area B3
5 Austin Creek State Recreation Area A3
6 Big Basin Redwoods State Park A3
7 Big Bear Lake C5
8 Bothe-Napa Valley State Park Campground A3
9 Brannan Island State Recreation Area B3
10 Calaveras Big Trees State Park B3
11 Campland on the Bay C6
12 Carpinteria State Beach B5
Casini Ranch .... (see 5)
13 Castle Lake A1
14 Channel Islands National Park B5
15 Clam Beach County Park A1
16 Crystal Cove State Park C5
17 Death Valley National Park C4
18 Doheny State Beach C5
19 El Capitán State Beach B5
20 Emerald Bay & DL Bliss State Parks B3
21 Henry W Coe State Park B3
22 Indian Grinding Rock State Historic Park B3
23 Jalama Beach County Park B5
24 Jedediah Smith Redwoods State Park A1
25 Joshua Tree National Park D5
26 Julia Pfeiffer Burns State Park Campground B4
27 Lake Oroville State Recreation Area B2
28 Lassen Volcanic National Park B2
29 Leo Carrillo State Beach C5
30 McArthur-Burney Falls State Park B1
31 Minaret Falls Campground C3
32 Montaña de Oro State Park Campground B4
33 Mount Shasta B1
34 New Brighton State Beach A3
Newport Dunes Waterfront Resort .... (see 16)
35 Point Reyes National Seashore A3
36 Prairie Creek Redwoods State Park A1
37 Samuel P Taylor State Park A3
38 Santa Monica Mountains National Recreation Area C5
39 Sequoia-Kings Canyon Wilderness C4
40 Sinkyone Wilderness State Park A2
41 South Carlsbad State Park Campground C5
42 Steep Ravine A3
43 Sugarloaf Ridge State Park A3
44 Tahoe National Forest B2
45 Tuttle Creek C4
46 Van Damme State Park A2
47 Woodson Bridge State Recreation Area A2
48 Yosemite National Park B3

campgrounds reserve walk-in sites for long-distance hikers and cyclists only.

Hiker/biker sites Along the coast these spots are the best value for those traveling the slow way along Hwy 1. While occasionally crowded, they reward hikers and cyclists with excellent sites.

Seasons, Rates & Reservations

Many campgrounds are closed from late fall through early spring or summer, especially in the mountains and Northern California. Opening and closing dates vary each year, depending on weather conditions and the previous winter's snowfall. Private campgrounds are often open year-round, especially those closest to cities, beaches and major highways.

Many public and private campgrounds accept reservations for all or some of their sites, while a few are strictly first-come, first-served. Overnight rates range from free for the most primitive campsites to $75 or more for pull-through RV sites with full hookups.

Booking services let you search for public and private campground locations and amenities, check availability and reserve campsites online. They may charge a reservation fee of up to $10.

Last-Minute Camping

If you can't get a campsite reservation, plan to show up at the campground between 10am and noon, when the previous night's campers may be leaving. Don't be too choosy, or you may end up with no site at all – especially on holidays, summer weekends and spring days when wildflowers are in bloom. Park rangers, visitor centers and campground hosts can often tell you where spaces may still be available, if there are any. Otherwise, ask about overflow and dispersed camping nearby.

BUT WAIT, THERE'S MORE

ACTIVITY	LOCATION	REGION
Bird-watching	Klamath Basin National Wildlife Refuges (p576)	Northern Mountains
	Mono Lake (p714)	Sierra Nevada
	Arcata Marsh & Wildlife Sanctuary (p276)	North Coast
	Humboldt Bay National Wildlife Refuge (p272)	North Coast
Caving	Lava Beds National Monument (p575)	Northern Mountains
	Crystal Cave (Map p51; www.recreation.gov; Crystal Cave Rd, off Generals Hwy; tours adult/child/youth from $16/5/8; ⏰late May-late Sep; p700)	Sierra Nevada
	Pinnacles National Park (p331)	Central Coast
Fishing	Dana Point (p455)	Orange County
	San Diego (p468)	San Diego
	Bodega Bay (p235)	North Coast
	Trinity Alps (p577)	Northern Mountains
Golf	**Palm Springs & Coachella Valley** (☎760-321-2665; www.standbygolf.com; ⏰7am-7pm)	The Deserts
	Pebble Beach (p312)	Central Coast
	Torrey Pines (p483)	San Diego
Hang gliding & paragliding	Torrey Pines (p483)	San Diego
	Santa Barbara (p349)	Santa Barbara County
Horseback riding	Yosemite National Park (p686)	Sierra Nevada
	Wild Horse Sanctuary (p562)	Northern Mountains
	South Lake Tahoe (p649)	Lake Tahoe
Hot-air ballooning	Temecula (p<OT>)	San Diego
	Napa Valley (p174)	Napa & Sonoma Wine Country
Kayaking & canoeing	Channel Islands National Park (p382)	Santa Barbara County
	Elkhorn Slough (p301)	Central Coast
	Mendocino (p249)	North Coast
	Tomales Bay (p139)	Marin County
	Russian River (p226)	Napa & Sonoma Wine Country
	San Diego (p468)	San Diego
	Sacramento Delta (p603)	Sacramento County
Kiteboarding & windsurfing	Crissy Field (p88)	San Francisco
	Mission Bay (p467)	San Diego
	Donner Lake (p664)	Lake Tahoe
	Belmont Shore (Long Beach; 🚌Red Passport, 🚌Long Beach Transit routes 121,131)	Los Angeles
Rock climbing	Yosemite National Park (p685)	Sierra Nevada
	Joshua Tree National Park (p517)	The Deserts
	Pinnacles National Park (p331)	Central Coast
	Bishop (p725)	Eastern Sierra
	Mission Bay (p467)	San Diego

Cycling & Mountain Biking

California has outstanding cycling terrain offering varying experiences: leisurely spins along the beach, adrenaline-fueled mountain rides or multiday road-cycling tours down the coast. The cycling season runs year-round in most coastal areas, although coastal fog may rob you of views in winter and during 'May gray' and 'June gloom.' Avoid the North Coast and the mountains during winter (too much rain and snow at higher elevations) and SoCal's deserts in summer (too dang hot).

Road Rules

➡ In national parks, bicycles are usually limited to paved and dirt roads, and are not allowed on trails or in designated wilderness areas.

➡ Most national forests and BLM lands are open to mountain bikers. Stay on already established tracks and always yield to hikers and horseback riders.

➡ At California's state parks, trails are off-limits to bikes unless otherwise posted, while paved and dirt roads are usually open to cyclists and mountain bikers.

Best Places to Cycle

➡ Even heavily trafficked urban areas may have good cycling routes, especially in SoCal. Take the scenic route along LA's beachside South Bay Bicycle Trail (p400) and down shoreline bike paths in Santa Barbara, Newport Beach and other beach towns.

➡ In the Bay Area, cruise through San Francisco's Golden Gate Park (p91) and over the Golden Gate Bridge (p85), then hop on the ferry back across the bay from Sausalito. Angel Island is another great bike-and-ferry combo.

➡ On the Central Coast, ocean-view Monterey Peninsula Recreational Trail (p305) and scenic 17-Mile Drive (p312) attract cyclists of all skill levels.

➡ California's wine countries offer beautiful DIY and guided bike tours, especially in Napa (p174) and Sonoma's Dry Creek Valley (p224).

➡ For road cyclists, nothing surpasses winding, coastal Hwy 1, especially the dizzying stretch through Big Sur (p315).

➡ Up north in Humboldt Redwoods State Park (p269), take a gentle ride past the world's tallest trees on the Avenue of the Giants.

➡ In Sierra Nevada, Yosemite Valley (p680) has paved recreational paths that pass meadows, waterfalls and granite spires.

➡ The new East Shore Trail (p671) in Incline Village Trails is one of several paved bikes trails along or near the shores of Lake Tahoe.

Best Mountain-Biking Areas

➡ Just north of San Francisco, the Marin Headlands offer a bonanza of trails for fat-tire fliers. Mt Tamalpais State Park (p134) is where the sport of mountain biking began, and the adrenaline-pumping trails here have inspired video games. Another option for mountain biking in Marin is China Camp State Park (p132).

➡ Top-rated single-track rides near Lake Tahoe include Mr Toad's Wild Ride and the Flume Trail (p672). In the neighboring Gold Country, Downieville offers an enormous downhill rush (p625).

➡ Speed freaks can't get enough of Eastern Sierra's Mammoth Mountain (p718), where the summer bike park offers more than 80 miles of single-track challenges. Other ski areas also open trails and chairlifts to mountain bikers in summer, including Big Bear Mountain Resort (p425) outside LA and Northstar (p664) at Lake Tahoe.

➡ Joshua Tree (p516) and Death Valley (p529) National Parks offer miles of backcountry roads for desert mountain biking. For more desert terrain, hit Anza-Borrego Desert State Park (p523) outside San Diego and the Santa Monica Mountains (www.nps.gov/samo/index.htm) north of LA.

➡ State parks especially popular with mountain bikers include NorCal's Prairie Creek Redwoods (p282), Montaña de Oro (p328) on the Central Coast and Orange County's Crystal Cove (p447).

➡ A hidden gem inland from Monterey, Fort Ord National Monument (p305) has more than 80 miles of dirt single tracks and fire roads for mountain bikers.

Maps & Online Resources

Local bike shops and some tourist offices can supply you with more cycling route ideas, maps and advice. For online forums and reviews of mountain-biking trails in California, search www.mtbr.com and www.socaltrailriders.org.

TAKE A HIKE

An invitation to get lost may sound like an insult elsewhere, but in California, it's a fantastic dare. Legendary long-distance trails cut right through the state, including the 2650-mile **Pacific Crest National Scenic Trail** (PCT; www.pcta.org), which takes hikers from Mexico to Canada. Running mostly along the PCT, the 211-mile **John Muir Trail** (JMT; www.pcta.org/discover-the-trail/john-muir-trail) links Yosemite Valley and Mt Whitney via Sierra Nevada's high country. Trace the footsteps of pioneers and Native Americans along the 165-mile **Tahoe Rim Trail** (www.tahoerimtrail.org), and you'll swear you've never seen a bluer lake or brighter sky. But there are still more trails to blaze here: the **California Coastal Trail Association** (www.coastwalk.org) is already more than halfway through building a 1200-mile trail along California's shoreline.

California Bicycle Coalition (http://calbike.org) Links to free online cycling maps, bike-sharing programs and community bike shops.

Adventure Cycling Association (www.adventurecycling.org) Sells long-distance cycling route guides and touring maps covering the entire Pacific Coast.

League of American Bicyclists (www.bikeleague.org) Can help you find bicycle specialty shops and local cycling clubs.

Hiking

With epic scenery, California is the perfect place to explore on foot. If you stay in the car, you'll miss experiencing the state's iconic highlights: strolling the beach at sunset, trekking past Joshua trees in desert oases, summitting 14,000ft craggy peaks, admiring alpine lakes and walking under the world's tallest, largest and oldest trees. In spring and early summer, the Golden State is touched with a painter's palette as wildflowers bloom down coastal hillsides, across mountain meadows and along desert sands.

Best Places to Hike

No matter where you find yourself in California, you're never far from a trail, even in metropolitan areas. National and state parks offer a wide variety of trails, from easy nature walks negotiable by wheelchairs and strollers to multiday backpacking routes through rugged wilderness.

Sierra Nevada In Yosemite (p680), Sequoia & Kings Canyon National Parks (p698) and around Lake Tahoe (p641), clamber toward waterfalls, wildflower meadows and alpine lakes, tackle mighty granite domes and peaks, and wander through pine-scented forests.

SoCal's Deserts Best hiked in spring and fall, Death Valley (p529) and Joshua Tree (p516) National Parks, Mojave National Preserve (p527) and Anza-Borrego Desert State Park (p523) lead you to palm-canyon oases and mining ghost towns, up volcanic cinder cones and across sand dunes and salt flats.

San Francisco Bay Area Marin Headlands (p123), Muir Woods National Monument (p136), Mt Tamalpais State Park (p134) and Point Reyes National Seashore (p141) are crisscrossed by dozens of superb hiking trails – and they're all within a 90-minute drive of San Francisco.

North Coast Redwood National and State Parks (p281) and the Avenue of the Giants (p269) offer misty walks through groves of old-growth redwoods, or you can scout out wilder beaches along the challenging Lost Coast Trail.

Northern Mountains Summiting Mt Shasta (p565) is a spiritually uplifting experience, while Lassen Volcanic National Park (p556) is a bizarre landscape of smoking fumaroles, cinder cones and craters.

Los Angeles Ditch your car in the Santa Monica Mountains National Recreation Area, where many movies and TV shows are filmed – or get away from the LA scene in the cool mountain climate of Big Bear Lake (p425).

Fees & Wilderness Permits

➡ Most California state parks charge a daily parking fee of $5 to $15. There's often no charge for pedestrians or cyclists. Californians give serious side-eye to people who park their cars just outside the gate then walk in – California's

OCEAN IMAGE PHOTOGRAPHY / SHUTTERSTOCK ©

Catalina Island (p423)

state parks are chronically underfunded and need the support.

➡ National park entry runs $25 to $35 per vehicle for seven consecutive days. Some national parks offer free admission, including the Channel Islands and Redwood National Parks.

➡ For unlimited admission to national parks, national forests and other federal recreation lands, buy an 'America the Beautiful' annual pass (12-month pass $80). It's sold at national park visitor centers and entry stations, online (https://store.usgs.gov/pass) and at most USFS ranger stations.

➡ If you don't have an 'America the Beautiful' annual pass, you'll need a National Forest Adventure Pass (per day $5; annual pass $30) to park in some recreational areas of SoCal's national forests. Buy passes from USFS ranger stations and local vendors, such as sporting-goods stores.

➡ Often required for overnight backpacking trips and a few extended day hikes, wilderness permits are issued at ranger stations and park visitor centers. Costs vary from free to $15, plus possible reservation fees if booked online. Daily quotas may be in effect during peak periods, usually late spring through early fall. Some wilderness permits can be reserved, and the most popular trails (such as Half Dome and Mt Whitney) may sell out several months in advance.

Maps & Online Resources

➡ There are bulletin boards showing basic trail maps and safety information at most major trailheads, some of which also have trail-guide brochure dispensers.

➡ For short, established hikes in national and state parks, free maps handed out at visitor centers or ranger stations are usually sufficient. A more detailed topographical map may be necessary for longer backcountry hikes.

➡ Topo maps are sold at park bookstores, visitor centers, ranger stations and outdoor-gear shops. The USGS Store (https://store.usgs.gov) offers its (sometimes outdated) topographic maps as free downloadable PDFs, or you can order print copies online.

➡ Learn how to minimize your impact on the environment while traipsing through the wilderness at the Leave No Trace Center for Outdoor Ethics online (http://lnt.org).

Scuba Diving & Snorkeling

All along California's coast, rocky reefs, shipwrecks and kelp beds teem with sea creatures ready for their close-up. Ocean waters are warmest in SoCal, but wetsuits are recommended for divers year-round.

Local dive shops are your best resource for equipment, guides, instructors and boat trips. With Professional Association of Diving Instructors (PADI) certification, you can book one-tank boat dives for $70 to $130, while two-tank dives start at about $100; reserve at least a day in advance.

Snorkelers can rent a mask, snorkel and fins from most dive shops or beach concessionaires for about $20 to $45 per day. If you're going to take the plunge more than once or twice, it's probably worth buying your own mask and fins. Remember not to touch anything while you're out snorkeling, and never snorkel alone. Sunblock can hurt reefs; choose a 'reef-safe' brand, or better yet, wear a UV-protection suit.

Best Scuba Diving & Snorkeling Spots

➡ San Diego–La Jolla Underwater Park Ecological Reserve (p483) is a great place for beginning divers, while La Jolla Cove attracts snorkelers.

➡ More experienced divers and snorkelers head for Orange County's Crystal Cove State Park (p447), Divers Cove (p450) in Laguna Beach or explore shipwrecks off San Diego's Mission Beach (p467).

➡ Offshore from LA and Ventura, Catalina Island (p423) and Channel Islands National Park (p382) are major diving and snorkeling destinations.

➡ With its national marine sanctuary, Monterey Bay (p302) offers world-renowned diving and snorkeling – although in these chilly waters, you'll need a thick wetsuit.

➡ Just south of Monterey, Point Lobos State Natural Reserve (p313) is another gem for scuba divers and snorkelers (permit reservations required).

➡ See sunken barges and boats on the underwater Emerald Bay Maritime Heritage Trail in Emerald Bay State Park (p656) at Lake Tahoe.

White-Water Rafting

California has dozens of white-water rivers, and hurtling down their surging rapids beats any roller-coaster ride. Swelled by snowmelt and ripping through sheer canyons, these river rapids collapse your entire vocabulary into just two words: 'dude!' and 'go!' You'll find river challenges here to suit any skill level, from beginning paddlers to hardcore river rats. The premier river runs are in the Sierra Nevada and Gold Country, but the Northern Mountains also offer some rollicking rides.

You don't get thrills without some spills – in rough conditions, it's not unusual for participants to fall out of the raft. But serious injuries are rare, and most trips are without incident. No prior experience is needed for guided river trips up to Class III, but Class IV is recommended for excellent swimmers in good shape, with paddling experience under your life-jacket belt.

Seasons, Rates & Online Resources

The main river-running season is from April to October, although exact months depend on which river you're rafting and the spring snowmelt runoff from the mountains. During drought years, the season can end midsummer. You'll be hurtling along either in large rafts holding a dozen or more people, or in smaller ones seating half a dozen. Smaller rafts tend to be more exhilarating because everyone paddles and they can tackle rougher rapids. Be sure

BEST WHITE-WATER RAFTING RIVERS

RIVER	CLASS	SEASON	DESCRIPTION
American	II-V	Apr-Oct	The South Fork is best for rafting newbies, while the more challenging Middle and North Forks carve through deep gorges.
Kaweah	II-IV+	Apr-Jul	Expect steep drops past Sequoia National Park, then mellow out past Three Rivers.
Kern	II-V	Apr-Sep	The Upper and Lower Forks offer some of the southern Sierra's best white water.
Kings	III-V	Apr-Jul	One of California's most powerful rivers, with put-ins (starting points) outside Kings Canyon National Park.
Merced	III-IV	Apr-Jul	Starting near Yosemite National Park, this canyon run is the Sierra Nevada's best one-day intermediate trip.
Stanislaus	II-IV	Apr-Oct	The North Fork provides rafting trips for all, from novices to the more adventure-minded.
Truckee	II-IV	Apr-Aug	Near Lake Tahoe, this gentle river is a great beginners' run, especially for families.
Tuolumne	IV-V	Apr-Sep	Experienced paddlers prefer ferocious runs on 'the T'; in summer, experts-only Cherry Creek is a legendary Sierra Nevada run.

to inquire whether or not you will be expected to paddle.

Commercial rafting outfitters run a variety of trips, from morning or afternoon floats to overnight and multiday expeditions. Book ahead and expect to pay $115 and up for a one-day trip.

Whale-Watching

During their annual migration, gray whales can be spotted off the California coast from December to April, while blue, humpback and sperm whales pass by in summer and fall. You can try your luck whale-watching from lighthouses and other coastal perches along the shore – but you're less likely to see whales and you'll be removed from all the action.

Just about every port town along the coast worth its sea salt offers whale-watching boat excursions, especially during winter. Bring binoculars and dress in warm, waterproof layers. Fair warning: choppy seas can be nauseating. To avoid seasickness, sit outside on the boat's second level – but not too close to the diesel fumes in the back.

Half-day whale-watching cruises cost from $50 per adult (up to $20 less for children). Make reservations at least a day ahead. Better tour boats limit the number of passengers and have a trained naturalist on board. Some tour companies let you go again for free if you don't spot any whales on your first trip.

Snow Sports

California winter vacations have it all: alpine scenery, luxury mountain cabins, killer après-ski happy hours, high-speed modern ski lifts, slopes dusted with fresh powder, and trails ranging from easy-peasy 'Sesame Street' to black-diamond 'Death Wish.' All that, and you're still just a short drive from a beach. Now you get why people move here.

Ski season runs from late November or early December until late March or early April, although this depends on weather conditions and elevation. The Sierra Nevada Mountains offer the best slopes and trails for skiers and snowboarders, although snow conditions have been unreliable in recent years due to unusually low winter snowfall. All resorts have ski schools, rent equipment and offer a variety of lift tickets, including cheaper half-day and multiday versions. Prices vary tremendously, from about $65 to $169 per day for adults; discounts for children, teens and seniors are typically available. Many of the large ski conglomerates now offer expensive season passes (a good value if used frequently), covering their various resorts. For example, the Epic Pass includes Heavenly, Northstar and Kirkwood, among others. 'Ski & stay' lodging packages may offer big savings.

Best Places for Snow Sports

Around Lake Tahoe For sheer variety, the dozen-plus downhill skiing and snowboarding resorts ringing Lake Tahoe are unbeatable. Alongside world-famous ski resorts like Squaw Valley (p663), site of the 1960 Winter Olympic Games, you'll find scores of smaller operations, many of them with lower lift-ticket prices, smaller crowds and great runs for beginners and families. Royal Gorge (p664), near Truckee, is North America's largest cross-country ski resort. Family-friendly 'sno-parks' offer sledding hills and snow play.

Mammoth & June Mountains Mammoth Mountain (p717) is a favorite of downhill devotees, because it usually has the longest ski and snowboarding season. Beginning and intermediate skiers and snowboarders hit the less crowded slopes of nearby June Mountain (p715).

Yosemite National Park In the glacier-carved winter wonderland of Yosemite National Park, Badger Pass (p686) welcomes families and beginning skiers and snowboarders. This is California's oldest ski resort and a launchpad for cross-country skiing and snowshoe treks – and kids will love the snow-tubing hill. You can snowshoe or cross-country ski among giant sequoias elsewhere in Yosemite.

Sequoia & Kings Canyon National Parks Lots of wonderful snowshoe and cross-country skiing trails, such as at Panoramic Point (p701) in Kings Canyon.

Northern Mountains Mt Shasta Ski Park (p567) is popular with families, offering a range of challenges for all skill levels.

Near Los Angeles Sunny Southern California gets in on the snow action at Big Bear Mountain Resort (p425).

Top: Skiing in Squaw Valley (p662)

Bottom: Humpback whale, Monterey Bay (p305)

Dungeness crab

Plan Your Trip

Eat & Drink Like a Local

As you graze the Golden State, you'll often want to compliment the chef – and that chef will pass it on to the staff, local farmers, fishers, ranchers, winemakers and artisan food producers that make their menu possible. California cuisine is a team effort that changes with every season – and it's changed the way the world eats.

SALTY VIEW / SHUTTERSTOCK ©

The Year in Food

Most of America's fruit and specialty vegetables are grown in California and you get the pick of the crop year-round.

Fall

Experience your first crush at harvest in wine country, get lost in corn mazes and pumpkin patches, and give thanks for California's bounty of fresh-fruit pies.

Winter

Make the most of long winter nights with seafood feasts of Dungeness crab, oysters and sand dabs. Celebrate Lunar New Year with lucky mandarins, and let citrus-spiked craft cocktails with locally distilled spirits warm you from the inside out.

Spring

When the sun comes out, farmers markets fill city streets with salad makings, fish-taco trucks flock to California beaches, and lines bend around the block for organic artisanal ice cream studded with just-picked berries.

Summer

Beach barbecues are better with wild coho salmon, Brentwood corn on the cob, fresh salsa made with heirloom tomatoes, and grilled peaches topped with edible lavender flowers.

California Cuisine: Then & Now

'Let the ingredients speak for themselves!' is the rallying cry of California cuisine. With fruit, vegetables, meats and seafood this fresh, heavy sauces and fussy tweezered garnishes aren't required to make meals memorable. So when New York chefs David Chang and Anthony Bourdain mocked chef Alice Waters' California cuisine as merely putting an organic fig on a plate, Californian chefs retorted that New Yorkers shouldn't knock it until they tried a real Mission fig. This flavor-bursting fruit is one of hundreds of rare California heirloom produce varietals cultivated here since the late 18th century for their unique flavor, not their refrigerator shelf life. In California, even fast food gets the California-fresh treatment: one grass-fed burger with heirloom-tomato ketchup, coming right up!

California's Food Revolution

Seasonal, locavore eating has become mainstream, but California started the movement more than 40 years ago. As the turbulent 1960s wound down, many disillusioned idealists concluded that the revolution was not about to be delivered on a platter – but California's pioneering organic farmers weren't about to give up.

In 1971 Alice Waters opened her now-legendary restaurant Chez Panisse (p157) in a converted house in Berkeley with the then-radical notion of making the most of California's organically farmed, sustainably sourced bounty. Waters combined rustic French finesse with California's seasonal flavors, and diners tasted the difference.

Waters' call for 'good, clean, fair food' was heard around the world, inspiring Italy's Carlo Petrini to cofound the worldwide Slow Food movement in the 1980s. Meanwhile in California, crowds flock year-round to 800 certified farmers markets across the state, stocking up on farm-fresh ingredients direct from 2500 local producers.

Global Soul Food

Beyond its exceptionally fertile farmland, California has another culinary advantage: an experimental attitude toward food that dates from its Wild West days. Most gold-rush miners were men not accustomed to cooking for themselves, which resulted in such doomed mining-camp experiments as jelly omelets. But the era also introduced California to the Hangtown fry, a strike-it-rich scramble of eggs, bacon and deep-fried cornbread-battered oysters – a combination of ingredients that cost around $300 in today's terms. Miners ate adventurously and cross-culturally, pairing whiskey and wine with tamales and Chinese noodles, and becoming regulars at America's first Italian restaurant, which opened in San Francisco in 1886.

Some 150 years later, fusion is not a fad but second nature in California, where chefs can hardly resist adding international twists to local flavors. Menus often infuse ingredients and kitchen craft borrowed from California's deep Latin American heritage, from shipping-route neighbors around the Pacific Rim and across Asia, and from the distant shores of the Mediterranean, where the climate and soil are similar to California's.

Keep in mind that California belonged to Mexico before it became a US state in 1850, and almost 40% of the state's population today is Latinx. It's no surprise that Californian versions of Mexican classics remain go-to comfort foods, and upscale restaurants are constantly adding new twists to staple tamales and tacos. Culinary cross-pollination has yielded such New American standards as the California burrito – a mega-meal bursting out of a giant flour tortilla – and the Korean taco, with grilled marinated beef and spicy pickled kimchi.

California's Regional Specialties

San Francisco Bay Area

For miners converging here for the gold rush, San Francisco offered an unrivaled variety of novelties and cuisines, from Chinese street food to French fine dining. Today, San Francisco's adventurous eaters support the most restaurants per capita of any US city – five times more than New York – and year-round farmers markets.

Some of San Francisco's novelty dishes have extraordinary staying power, including chocolate bars (invented by the Ghirardelli family as power bars for miners), ever-popular cioppino (seafood stew), and sourdough bread, with original gold-rush era mother dough still yielding local loaves with a distinctive tang. To sample SF classics and the latest local inventions, stop by San Francisco's monument to food: the Ferry Building (p81).

Today no Bay Area star chef's menu would be complete without a few foraged ingredients – including wild chanterelles found beneath California oaks, miner's lettuce from Berkeley hillsides, and edible nasturtium flowers from SF backyards. But some pioneering Bay Area chefs have taken local a step further, growing herbs and hosting beehives on neighborhood rooftops and urban gardens. When COVID-19 hit, San Francisco restaurants doubled down on community-minded cooking, launching nonprofits to cook and deliver 4000-plus free meals a week to neighbors in need under quarantine. The Bay Area isn't only committed to locavore cooking – this is a new movement in local community cuisine.

Napa & Sonoma Wine Country

With international acclaim for Napa and Sonoma wines in the 1970s came woozy Wine Country visitors in need of food, and local cheese-makers and restaurateurs graciously obliged. Chef Sally Schmitt transformed a 1900s Yountville saloon into an international foodie landmark called French Laundry (p184), where current chef/owner Thomas Keller dazzles diners with garden-grown organic produce in casually elegant, multicourse feasts. Other chefs eager to make their names and fortunes among free-spending wine tasters descended on this 30-mile valley – and now the night skies over Napa Valley are crowded with 11 Michelin stars, and local food offerings fill Napa's Oxbow Public Market (p180).

As the price of launching food businesses rose up in Napa, many innovators moved over to Sonoma County to launch their businesses. With farmers as neighbors and seafood and foraged ingredients fresh from Sonoma's beaches and redwood forests, cooks are bringing Sonoma's immigrant roots and sustainable farm-to-table practices to the plate – and reinventing Wine Country cooking. El Molino (p200) uses local, sustainable ingredients in sensational dishes inspired by the Yucatán, and triple-Michelin-starred SingleThread (p228) serves dozens of Pacific-inspired, Sonoma-grown dishes on a driftwood log.

When firestorms swept through Sonoma and Napa in 2017, 2019 and 2020, the losses were devastating to farmers, workers, restaurants and the hospitality industry. But even before the smoke cleared, the community rallied, launching initiatives like Sonoma Family Meal and UndocuFund to ensure everyone affected by the fires could feed themselves and their families. When COVID-19 struck, systems were already in place to provide meals to neighbors in need – and restaurants including El Molino and SingleThread rapidly pivoted to cooking

Oxbow Public Market (p180), Napa

meals for frontline workers, seniors and other at-risk neighbors. Wine Country cooking has always benefitted from cream-of-the-crop ingredients – but this food ecosystem has also shown its powerful roots, setting global standards for resilience.

North Coast

After millennia of habitation, native foodways run deep on the North Coast, where you'll taste the influence of Ohlone, Pomo and Miwok traditions. Nature has been kind to this landscape, yielding bonanzas of wildflower honey, berries, wild grains and nuts. Along this rugged coastline, you'll find traditional shellfish collection and Native Californian–run fishing operations, alongside sustainable oyster farms and fish hatcheries. Fearless foragers have identified every edible plant from wood sorrel to Mendocino sea vegetables here – though key spots for wild morel mushrooms remain closely guarded local secrets.

Hippies headed back to the land here in the 1960s to find a more self-sufficient lifestyle, adopting Native Californian foodways and reviving Wild West traditions of making bread, cheese and beer from scratch in small batches. Early adopters of pesticide-free, zero-chemical-fertilizer farming, these hippie homesteaders innovated hearty, organic cuisine that was health-minded – yet still satisfied the munchies of the region's many pot growers. Today, legal dispensaries across Mendocino and Humboldt keep local farmers and food artisans busy, feeding the now-legal cravings of adults (aged 21-plus, with ID) for gourmet edibles (including baked goods, sweet treats and beer) that incorporate cannabis with psychoactive THC and/or relaxing (but non-intoxicating) CBD. Up north, a new category of California food is emerging: farm-to-dispensary cuisine.

Central Valley & Central Coast

Most of California's produce is grown in the hot, irrigated Central Valley, south of Sacramento – but road-tripping foodies tend to bolt through the sunny farmlands, if only to make it past stinky cattle feedlots without losing their appetites. Much of the region remains dedicated to large-scale agribusiness, but valley farms that have converted to organic methods have helped

RICK POON / GETTY IMAGES ©

Oysters

make California the top US producer of organic foods.

Over on the Central Coast, some of California's freshest seafood is harvested from Monterey Bay. For help choosing the most sustainable catch on restaurant menus, check out the handy report card of the Monterey Bay Aquarium (p302) at www.seafoodwatch.org. Excellent wine tasting awaits in the fog-kissed Santa Cruz Mountains, the sun-drenched hills around Paso Robles and the lush valleys north of Santa Barbara. Look for farm-stand produce pit stops all along the coast, offering everything from Watsonville strawberries to Carpinteria avocados. In San Luis Obispo, the weekly farmers market celebrates local farms with smoky, soulful Santa Maria–style barbecue.

Southern California

In the movies, SoCal scenery is a stand-in for many geographic locations around the world – and it brings that same versatility to the plate. Follow authenticity-seeking Angelenos to Koreatown for flavor-bursting *kalbi* (marinated, grilled beef short ribs), East LA for tacos *al pastor* (marinated, fried pork), Torrance for ramen noodles made fresh daily, and the San Gabriel Valley for Chinese dim sum. Further south, San Diego and Orange County surfers cruise from Ocean Beach to Huntington Beach in search of epic waves, but also for the ultimate Cal-Mex fish taco.

Ever since Austrian-born chef Wolfgang Puck launched the celebrity-chef trend with his Sunset Strip restaurant Spago in 1982, reservations at dining hot spots are as sought-after as VIP party invites. As with Hollywood blockbusters, trendy LA restaurants don't always live up to the hype – for honest opinions, read reviews in the *Los Angeles Times*.

True Californian foodies insist that immortality isn't achieved with a star in a Michelin guide or on the Hollywood Walk of Fame, but by having a dish named in your honor. Bob Cobb was the celebrity owner of Hollywood's Brown Derby Restaurant, and his legend lives on with his namesake salad: lettuce, tomato, avocado, egg, chicken and blue cheese. First concocted in the 1930s, it's been the regular order of Hollywood hopefuls ever since.

When salads fail to satisfy, make late-night raids on local food trucks – fleets are standing by in LA and San Diego. For mouthwatering reviews of legendary Cal-Mex street food, check out LA Taco (www.lataco.com). In Hollywood, barflies hit diners that have survived since the '50s with only minor remodeling – more than you can say for some celebrities around here.

Wine, Beer & Beyond

Powerful drink explains a lot about California. Mission vineyards first planted in the 18th century gave California a taste for wine, and the mid-19th-century gold rush brought a rush on the bar. By 1850, San Francisco had 500 saloons selling hooch to gold-rush prospectors who struck it rich – or didn't. Today California's traditions of wine, beer and cocktails are being reinvented by cult winemakers, craft brewers and microdistillers – and, for the morning after, specialty coffee roasters come in mighty handy.

Wine

During the gold rush, when imported French wine was slow to arrive in California via Australia, three brothers from Bohemia named Korbel started making their own bubbly in 1882. Today, the Russian River winery they founded has become the biggest US maker of sparkling wines – and the misty, redwood-lined Russian River Valley has earned acclaim as America's foremost producer of complex, cool-climate pinot noir.

Many California vines survived federal scrutiny during Prohibition (1920–33) with a flimsy alibi: the grapes were needed for sacramental wines back east. The authorities bought this story, or at least the bribes that came with it. The ensuing bootlegging bonanza kept West Coast speakeasies well supplied, and saved old vinestock from being torn out by the authorities.

By 1976, California had an established reputation for mass-market plonk and bottled wine spritzers, when upstart Napa Valley and Santa Cruz Mountains wineries suddenly gained international status. At a landmark blind tasting by international critics, their cabernet sauvignon and chardonnay beat venerable French wines to take top honors. This event became known as the Judgment of Paris, as amusingly retold in the movie *Bottle Shock* (2008).

During the internet bubble of the late 1990s, owning a vineyard became the ultimate Silicon Valley status symbol. It seemed like a comparatively solid investment – until a phylloxera blight made a catastrophic comeback, and acres of infected vines across the state had to be dug out from the roots. But disaster brought breakthroughs: winemakers rethought their approach, using organic and biodynamic methods to keep the soil healthy and pests at bay. So whether you order a red, white or pink small-production California vintage, chances are your wine is green.

Beer

At least 400 craft breweries are based in California – more than any other US state. Even the most laid-back surfer here geeks out over Belgian tripels, and will passionately debate optimum hoppiness levels. You won't get attitude for ordering beer with fancy food here, and many sommeliers are happy to suggest beer pairings with your five-star meal.

Any self-respecting California city has at least one brewery or brewpub of note, serving quality small-batch brews you won't find elsewhere. The well-established craft beer scenes in San Diego and along the North Coast will spoil you for choice – but you'll also find memorable microbrews around the San Francisco Bay Area, Sonoma, and along the Central Coast,

WINE-TASTING TIPS

Swirl Before tasting a just-opened bottle of wine, swirl your glass to oxygenate the wine and release the flavors.

Sniff Dip your nose (without getting it wet) into the glass for a good whiff. This sniff prompts your senses and your salivary glands to fully appreciate the wine.

Swish Take a swig, and roll it over the front of your gums and sides of your tongue to get the full effect of complex flavors and textures on all your tastebuds. After you swallow, breathe out through your nose to appreciate the finish.

If you're driving or cycling, don't swallow Sips are hard to keep track of at tastings, so perfect your graceful arc into the spit bucket.

You don't have to buy anything No one expects you to buy, especially if you're paying to taste or take a tour – but it's customary to buy a bottle before winery picnics, and tasting fees are sometimes refunded with purchases.

Take it slow and easy There's no need for speed. Plan to visit three wineries a day maximum.

Don't smoke Not in the gardens either. Wait until you're off-property so you don't kill that mellow buzz your fellow wine-tasters have worked so diligently to achieve.

especially around Santa Cruz and Santa Barbara.

Some of the best beer you'll try in California might actually come in a can. California's craft breweries are increasingly canning craft beer (and wine) to make it cheaper, more ecofriendly and easier to distribute across California. There's nothing as satisfying as popping the tab of a cold one after a hot California day on hiking trails or at the beach – especially if it's a California craft microbrew.

Cocktails

Cocktails have been shaken and stirring up trouble in Northern California since San Francisco's Barbary Coast days, when they were used to sedate unsuspecting guests - who were then delivered unconscious onto outbound ships in need of crews. Today the kidnapping rings are gone, but bartenders still pour a mean drink. California's drink historians are researching old recipes and inventing new cocktail traditions, aided and abetted by local distillers. Don't be surprised to see NorCal's own St George absinthe poured into cordial glasses of Sazerac, or holiday eggnog spiked with Sonoma Spirit Works rye and organic orange peel. And in the COVID-19 era, with many bars closed, California's indie distillers are producing a new specialty: hand sanitizer.

Legend has it that the martini was invented when a boozehound walked into an SF bar and demanded something to tide him over until he reached Martinez across the bay – a likely story, but one you'll probably hear at a California bar. The original Martinez was made with vermouth, gin, bitters, lemon, maraschino cherry and ice – though by the days of Sinatra's Rat Pack, the martini was reduced to gin with vermouth vapors and a briny California olive or two.

Beach weather calls for tropical drinks made with shipping-route ingredients, and for over 100 years, California has obliged at legendary tiki bars such as Bootlegger Tiki (p514) in Palm Springs and **Trader Sam's Enchanted Tiki Lounge** (p430) in Disneyland. The mai tai (with rum, orgeat, curaçao and lime juice) is another cocktail allegedly invented in the Bay Area, at Trader Vic's tiki bar in Oakland in the 1940s. For those who like their cocktails less sweet and turbo-charged, margaritas (made with tequila, lime, Cointreau, ice and salt) have been SoCal's poolside drink of choice since the 1940s.

STEAM BREWING

Blowing off steam took on new meaning during the gold rush, when entrepreneurs trying to keep up with the demand for drink started brewing beer at higher temperatures. The result was an amber color, malted flavor and such powerful effervescence that when a keg was tapped a mist would rise like steam. San Francisco's Anchor Brewing Company has made its signature Anchor Steam amber ale this way since 1896, using copper distilling equipment. Today, brewpubs across California offer steam-brewed beer with lunch and brunch, so you don't have to wait until until the end of a workday to let off some steam.

Coffee

California is the home of 'third-wave' coffee. LA's Pulitzer Prize–winning critic Jonathan Gold defined this movement as coffee directly sourced from small farms instead of plantations, and roasted to maximize the bean's unique characteristics. The university towns of Berkeley and Santa Cruz were early adopters, and Santa Cruz still sets coffee standards at Verve Coffee Roasters (p297). LA's third-wave coffee shops tend not to roast their own, but cherry-pick the best beans from microroasters along the West Coast and Chicago.

Oakland's Blue Bottle Coffee Company (p148) added a 'fourth-wave' element of showmanship to coffee geekery, introducing a $20,000 Japanese coffee siphon to filter its brews. SF's **Sightglass Coffee** (Map p78; ☎415-861-1313; www.sightglasscoffee.com; 270 7th St; ⏲7am-7pm; 🚌12, 14, 19, Ⓑ Civic Center, Ⓜ Civic Center) and **Ritual Coffee Roasters** (Map p94; ☎415-641-1011; www.ritualroasters.com; 1026 Valencia St; ⏲6am-8pm Mon-Fri, from 7am Sat & Sun; 🚌14, 49, Ⓑ 24th St Mission) roast beans in-house in small batches and leaded guided tastings at cupping bars. It may sound precious, but there's no denying the laid-back California appeal of their popular 'pour-over': water poured slowly over custom-ground specialty coffees.

Wine tasting, Napa Valley (p174)

Food Trucks & Pop-Up Restaurants

Weekday lunches may last only 30 minutes for Californians, and every minute counts. California's legendary food trucks deliver gourmet options on the go, from Indian curry-and-naan wraps to Chinese buns packed with roast duck and fresh mango. One way to find trucks coming soon to a curb near you is by searching for 'food truck' and your location on Twitter. Come prepared with cash and sunblock: most trucks don't accept plastic cards, and lines can be long.

With restaurants closing in the wake of COVID-19, many California food businesses are pivoting, and finding new ways to cook and deliver excellent food. Chef-made meals have been popping up in unexpected urban spaces, including parks, warehouses, storefronts and farmers markets. Foodies seek out these overnight taste sensations via Twitter, food-critic picks on local news websites, and dedicated food websites such as www.eater.com. Bring cash and arrive early, as popular dishes run out fast.

Vegans & Vegetarians Welcome

To all you beleaguered vegetarians accustomed to making do with reheated vegetarian lasagna: relax, you're in California now. Your needs are not an afterthought in California cuisine, which revolves around seasonal produce instead of the standard American meat and potatoes. Decades before actress Alicia Silverstone (of *Clueless* fame) championed a vegan diet in her cookbook *The Kind Diet* and website (www.thekindlife.com), LA, SF and North Coast restaurants were already catering to vegans. You don't have to go out of your way to find vegetarian and vegan options: bakeries, bistros and even mom-and-pop joints in the remote Sierras are ready for meat-free, dairy-free, eggless requests. To locate vegetarian and vegan restaurants and health-food stores near you in California, consult the free online directory at Happy Cow (www.happycow.net).

Plan Your Trip

Family Travel

California is a tailor-made destination for family travel. The kids will be begging to go to theme parks, and teens to celebrity hot spots. Then take 'em into the great outdoors – from sunny beaches shaded by palm trees to misty redwood forests and four-seasons mountain playgrounds.

Keeping Costs Down

Hotels vs Motels

Look for 'kids stay free' and/or 'free family breakfast' promotions at hotels. Motels are cheaper on average, most have two queen-sized beds and some have kitchenettes.

Avoid Theme-Park Meals

If you're visiting theme parks, carry a cooler in the car and have a picnic in the parking lot (although be sure to get everyone's hand stamped for park re-entry before you do) to avoid expensive and often sugar-laden options inside.

Fabulous & Free

From endless beaches and mountains for frolicking on to top museums like California Science Center and the La Brea Tar Pits to explore, some of the most family-friendly activities in California are free.

Transportation

If you stay in areas with large concentrations of family-friendly activities, you may be able to avoid the inevitable -- renting a car -- at least for a day or two. Explore on foot, by bicycle, roller skates or short taxi rides.

Children Will Love . . .

Theme Parks

Disneyland Park (p429) and Disney California Adventure (p431) Kids of all ages, even teens, and the young-at-heart adore the 'Magic Kingdom'.

Knott's Berry Farm (p434) NearDisneyland, SoCal's original theme park offers thrills-a-minute, especially on spooky, haunted Halloween nights.

Universal Studios Hollywood, LA (p395) Movie-themed action rides, the Wizarding World of Harry Potter and a working studio tour entertain tweens and teens.

Legoland California Resort, Carlsbad (p490) This fantasyland of building blocks in San Diego's North County is made for tots and youngsters.

Aquariums & Zoos

Monterey Bay Aquarium (p302) Meet aquatic denizens of the deep at a national marine sanctuary.

San Diego Zoo (p461) and Safari Park (p491) Journey around the world with exotic wildlife at California's best and biggest zoo, then go on safari.

Aquarium of the Pacific, LA (p402) Long Beach's aquarium houses critters from Baja California to the north Pacific, including a shark lagoon.

Los Angeles Zoo & Botanical Gardens (☎323-644-4200; www.lazoo.org; 5333 Zoo Dr, Griffith Park; adult/senior/child $22/19/17; ⏱10am-5pm;

Monterey Bay Aquarium (p302)

P 🅿; Metro Line 96) What was once the home of retired circus animals is today a center for endangered-species conservation.

Beaches

Los Angeles (p387) Carnival fun and an aquarium await on Santa Monica Pier, or hit perfect beaches in Malibu.

Orange County (p433) Pick from beautiful pier-side strands in Newport Beach, miles of million-dollar sands in Laguna Beach, Huntington Beach (aka 'Surf City, USA') or old-fashioned Seal Beach.

San Diego (p459) Head over to Coronado's idyllic Silver Strand, play in Mission Bay by SeaWorld, lap up La Jolla or unwind in a half dozen surf-style beach towns in North County.

Santa Barbara County (p347) and Central Coast (p289) Laze on unmatched beaches in Santa Barbara then roll all the way north to the famous beach boardwalk in Santa Cruz.

Lake Tahoe (p641) In summer it's California's favorite high-altitude escape: a sparkling diamond tucked in the craggy Sierra Nevada Mountains.

Parks

Yosemite National Park (p680) Get an epic slice of Sierra Nevada scenery, with gushing waterfalls, alpine lakes, glacier-carved valleys and peaks.

Redwood National & State Parks (p281) A string of nature preserves on the North Coast protect magnificent wildlife and the planet's tallest trees.

Griffith Park, LA (p68) Bigger than NYC's Central Park, this greenspace has tons of fun for younger kids, from miniature train rides and a merry-go-round to planetarium shows.

Channel Islands National Park (p382) Sail across to California's version of the Galapagos for wildlife-watching, sea kayaking, hiking and camping adventures – best for teens.

Museums

San Francisco (p77) The city is a mind-bending classroom for kids, especially at the interactive Exploratorium, multimedia Children's Creativity Museum and ecofriendly California Academy of Sciences in Golden Gate Park.

Los Angeles (p390) See the real stars at the Griffith Observatory, movie stars at the Academy

Museum of Motion Pictures, or dinosaur bones at the La Brea Tar Pits & Museum.

San Diego (p461) Balboa Park is jam-packed with museums and a world-famous zoo; take younger kids to the engaging New Children's Museum downtown and let teens and tweens clamber aboard the USS Midway Museum.

Orange County (p434) Bring budding lab geeks to the Discovery Cube and get a pint-sized dose of arts and culture in the Kidseum at the Bowers Museum, all near Disneyland Resort.

Region by Region

Los Angeles

See stars in Hollywood and get behind the movie magic at Universal Studios (p395), then hit the beaches and Griffith Park (p394) for fun in the sun.

Disneyland & Orange County

Theme parks like Disneyland (p429), excellent kid-friendly museums including the Discovery Cube (p434), sandy beaches – this is kid wonderland.

San Diego & Around

San Diego Zoo (p461) is paws-down the best zoo in California, plus there's the zoo's safari park (p491) in Escondido, and colorful Legoland (p490) in Carlsbad.

Palm Springs & the Deserts

Learn about the region at the Living Desert Zoo & Gardens (p509), then see it from the Palm Springs Aerial Tramway (p507). Stop at the World's Biggest Dinosaurs roadside attraction.

Santa Barbara County

Enjoy sandy stretches like Arroyo Burro Beach (p356) and learn about native flora at the Santa Barbara Botanic Garden (p353). Take an adventurous trip to the magical Channel Islands (p382).

Central Coast

Don't miss the Monterey Bay Aquarium (p302) but there's plenty more to excite, from the Santa Cruz Beach Boardwalk (p291) to tide pooling.

San Francisco

Explore hands-on museums, hear barking sea lions at **Pier 39** (Map p88; ☎415-623-4734; www.pier39.com; Pier 39, cnr Beach St & the Embarcadero; 24hr; ; 47, Powell-Mason, E, F), traipse through Golden Gate Park (p91) and ride SF's cable cars.

Marin County & the Bay Area

Wander the redwood forests of Muir Woods (p136), the wild coastline of Point Reyes (p141), or head to Silicon Valley to visit tech giants and the Computer History Museum (p158).

Yosemite & the Sierra Nevada

Gawk at Yosemite's waterfalls (p682) and granite domes, then go hiking among groves of giant sequoias.

Lake Tahoe

Ski and snowboard at world-class resorts such as Squaw Valley (p663) or smaller spots like Homewood (p658). In summer, play in the lake, mountain bike and hike to glorious vistas.

Gold Country

Tall tales of forty-niners, gun-slinging bandits and treasure-hunters are brought to life in historic towns such as Columbia State Historic Park (p637) and Nevada City (p624).

North Coast & Redwoods

Hike through forests of Redwood National and State Parks (p281), drive through a big tree in Leggit, frolic on the beaches, climb lighthouses or get a visceral history lesson at Fort Ross Historic State Park (p241).

Napa & Sonoma Wine Country

It's not all wine, there's also Old Faithful Geyser (p191) in Calistoga and the Russian River to play in. Snoopy fans won't want to miss the Charles M Schulz Museum (p207) in Santa Rosa.

Sacramento & Central Valley

Hit up the California Museum (p588) that sums up the state's history. The surrounding areas are home to acres of farmland.

Northern Mountains

Escape the crowds at lake campsites, marvel at the geothermal displays in Lassen Volcanic National Park (p556) and explore caves in Lava Beds National Monument (p575).

Good to Know

Look out for the icon for family-friendly suggestions throughout this guide.

Children's discounts Available for everything from museum admission and movie tickets to bus fares. The definition of a 'child' varies from 'under 18' to age six. A limited number of venues offer student discounts for older children and university students.

Amusement parks Some rides may have minimum-height requirements, so let younger kids know about this in advance, to avoid disappointment – and tears.

Dining out Casual eateries in well-trafficked neighborhoods typically have high chairs and children's menus available. Generally, dining earlier (say, before 6pm) is better for families with young ones.

Public toilets Many restrooms have a baby-changing table. Bigger, private 'family' bathrooms may be available at airports, museums etc.

Car travel Any child under the age of six or weighing less than 60lb must be buckled up in the car's back seat in a child or infant safety seat – book ahead when renting a car. Bring in-car distractions for inevitable traffic delays.

Prams & strollers Urban areas are great for strollers but if you plan on enjoying the great outdoors, child carriers are definitely a better option.

Stuff for babies Basics are available in supermarkets and drug stores 24/7, while organics and fancier specialty items can be found at natural-food stores and smaller boutiques.

Carousel at Pier 39, San Francisco

Useful Resources

Lonely Planet Kids (www.lonelyplanetkids.com) Loads of activities and family-travel blog content.

Visit California (www.visitcalifornia.com) The state's official tourism website lists family-friendly attractions, activities and more – just search for 'Family Fun' and 'Events'.

My Family Travel Map: North America (shop.lonelyplanet.com) Unfolds into a colorful poster for kids to personalize with stickers marking their family's travels.

Travel for Kids (www.travelforkids.com) Listings of kid-friendly sights, activities, hotels and recommended children's books for every region of California.

Regions at a Glance

California's cities have more flavors than a jar of jellybeans. Start from San Francisco, where earth mother meets geek chic, and head toward Los Angeles, where even juice-cleansing starlets can't resist Koreatown BBQ. On sunny days when the coastal fog lifts, over 1100 miles of ocean beaches await. Drift down the coast past palm-lined avenues to surfer-dude-central San Diego – and when you're tanned enough and ready for a change of scenery, escape to the craggy Sierra Nevada mountains, soul-search in SoCal's desert moonscapes, and find your better nature in northern redwood forests. And no matter where you go, California's vineyards never seem far away.

San Francisco

Food
Culture
Arts

California's 'Left Coast' reputation is made in SF, where DIY self-expression, sustainability and spontaneity are the highest virtues, and freethinkers, techies and chefs reinvent San Francisco anew each day.

p75

Marin County & the Bay Area

Hiking & Cycling
Food
Cities

Outdoorsy people love Marin County for its beaches, ranches, wildlife and hiking and cycling trails – but indoorsy people will appreciate the counterculture hubs of 'Bezerkely' and 'Oaktown' along with Silicon Valley.

p121

Napa & Sonoma Wine Country

Wineries
Food
Cycling & Canoeing

Sun-washed valleys and cool coastal fog have turned Napa and Sonoma into California's most iconic wine-growing regions. Local ranches and specialty produce also thrive, yielding bountiful farm-to-table meals.

p171

North Coast & the Redwoods

Wildlife
Hiking
Scenic Drives

Lumber barons wised up and conserved primeval redwood forests along the misty, rugged and wild North Coast. Let your hippie flag fly in Humboldt County, and swap seafaring stories at fishing villages.

p233

Central Coast

Beaches
Wildlife
Scenic Drives

Surf south from hippy-dippy Santa Cruz to studious San Luis Obispo, stopping to whale-watch at Monterey Bay, hike past Big Sur's coastal waterfalls and gawk at Hearst Castle.

p289

Santa Barbara County

Beaches
Wineries
Outdoor Sports

Santa Barbara keeps a low, Spanish Colonial profile behind white-sand beaches, with world-class vineyards right next door. Sparkling waters invite snorkeling, diving or kayaking in the nearby national park.

p347

Los Angeles

Nightlife
Food
Culture

There's more to life in La La Land than just sunny beaches and air-kissing celebrities. Explore its bounty of art and architecture, feast on eclectic cuisines and visit sharply contrasting and vibrant neighborhoods.

p347

Disneyland & Orange County

Theme Parks
Beaches
Surfing

The OC's beaches are packed with rugged surfers, volleyball champions and retouched reality stars. And if you think this scenery is surreal, check out the hyper-reality of the Disneyland Resort.

p387

San Diego & Around

Beaches
Mexican Food
Museums

California's southernmost city is on permanent vacation, with a near-perfect year-round climate and booming craft-brewery scene. Explore Balboa Park's quirky museums or wander laid-back beach towns.

p459

Palm Springs & the Deserts

Resorts & Spas
Wildflowers
Hiking & Climbing

Palm Springs is making a comeback with its Coachella festival, LGBT+ scene, speakeasies and restored mid-century-modern motels. Go hiking or climbing in Joshua Tree, then test your 4WD mettle in Death Valley.

p495

Northern Mountains

Mountains
Lakes
Scenic Drives

Mt Shasta is a magnet for shamans, new-age poets and ice-axe-wielding alpinists. There's more wilderness as you head north along backcountry byways, passing pristine lakes to Lassen's volcanic Bumpass Hell.

p549

Sacramento & the Central Valley

History
Farms & Fairs
Beer

Arrive in the capital in summer for epic farmers markets, then visit the Sacramento River Delta, where riverside towns resemble their 1930s heyday, or cool off in Chico's swimming holes.

p583

Gold Country

History
Caving & Rafting
Wineries

Head for the Sierra Nevada foothills to find the Wild West alive and well in historic gold-mining country. Get thrills on river-rafting trips, chills on underground cave tours and swills at rustic winery tasting rooms.

p617

Lake Tahoe

Winter Sports
Water Sports
Cabins & Camping

North America's largest alpine lake is a year-round playground. Come for Olympic-worthy skiing in winter, or cool off by the beaches in summer. Flashy casinos are a bonus nearby attraction.

p641

Yosemite & the Sierra Nevada

Wildlife
Hiking & Climbing
Scenic Drives

This iconic mountain range is a wonder, with granite peaks, natural hot springs, deep canyons, groves of sequoias, and alpine meadows and lakes. Summer is for outdoor adventures in America's wildest backyard.

p679

On the Road

North Coast & Redwoods
p233
Northern Mountains
p549
Gold Country
p617
Lake Tahoe
p641
Napa & Sonoma Wine Country
p171
Yosemite & the Sierra Nevada
p677
San Francisco
p75
Marin County & the Bay Area
p121
Sacramento & Central Valley
p583
Central Coast
p289
Palm Springs & the Deserts
p495
Santa Barbara County
p347
Los Angeles
p387
Disneyland & Orange County
p427
San Diego & Around
p459

AT A GLANCE

POPULATION
891,590

AREA
47.9 sq miles

BEST MARKET
Ferry Plaza Farmers Market (p106)

BEST DIM SUM
Good Mong Kok (p104)

BEST VICTORIAN B&B
Parsonage (p103)

WHEN TO GO

Jan–Mar
Low-season rates, brisk but rarely cold days, and Lunar New Year parade fireworks.

May–Aug
Farmers markets and festivals make up for high-season rates and chilly afternoon fog.

Sep–Nov
Blue skies, free concerts, bargain hotel rates and some flavor-bursting harvest cuisine.

Coit Tower (p81) and downtown San Francisco
MATT MOLDENHAUER / SHUTTERSTOCK ©
ARCHITECT: ARTHUR BROWN JR

San Francisco

Get to know the capital of weird from the inside out, from mural-lined alleyways named after poets to clothing-optional beaches on a former military base. But don't be too quick to dismiss San Francisco's wild ideas. Biotech, gay rights, the internet, cable cars and organic fine dining were once considered outlandish, before San Francisco introduced these ideas into the mainstream decades ago. San Francisco's morning fog erases the boundaries between land and ocean, reality and possibility.

Rules are never strictly followed here. Golden Gate Bridge and Alcatraz are entirely optional. Instead of sightseeing, just follow your bliss through Golden Gate Park, past flamboyantly painted Victorian homes, and through mural-lined Mission streets. Just don't be late for your sensational, sustainable dinner: in San Francisco, you can find happiness and eat it too.

INCLUDES

San Francisco Highlights

❶ **Golden Gate Park** (p91) Following your bliss through San Francisco's mile-wide wild streak.

❷ **Exploratorium** (p85) Discovering how real life is even weirder than science fiction.

❸ **Golden Gate Bridge** (p85) Watching fog dance atop the art-deco towers.

❹ **San Francisco Museum of Modern Art** (p77) Seeing where San Francisco gets its most outlandish ideas.

❺ **Alcatraz** (p85) Plotting your escape from San Francisco's notorious island prison.

❻ **Chinatown** (p81) Wandering through 150 years of turbulent California history.

❼ **The Castro** (p92) Celebrating LGBT+ history at the center of the gay universe.

❽ **Coit Tower** (p81) Seeing censored murals below and all of SF from above.

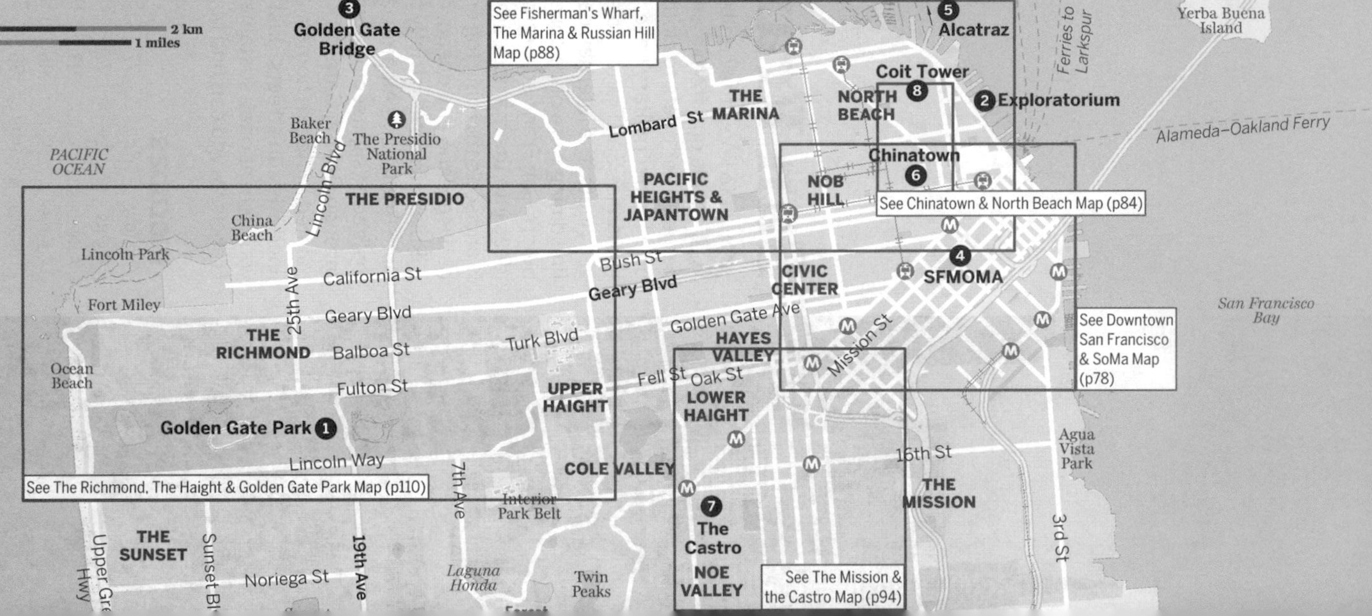

DON'T MISS...

Green everything Reports rank San Francisco as the greenest city in North America, with its pioneering parklets, LEED-certified sustainable hotels, citywide composting and the USA's biggest stretch of urban greenery: Golden Gate Park (p91).

Queer culture From America's first GLBT History Museum (p92) in the Castro to the Tenderloin's (Map p78) **Transgender Cultural District**, SF welcomes all to come out and celebrate LGBTQ pioneers somewhere over the rainbow.

Creative California cuisine Year-round farmers markets, award-winning chefs and daring diners have kept SF's polyglot Pacific Rim cuisine fresh over 170 years.

Saloons The Barbary Coast is roaring back to life with historically researched whiskey cocktails and staggering gin concoctions in San Francisco's great Western-saloon revival.

History

Oysters and acorn bread were prime dinner options in the Mexico-run Ohlone settlement of San Francisco circa 1848 – but a year and some gold nuggets later, Champagne and chow mein were served by the bucket. Gold found in nearby Sierra Nevada foothills turned a sleepy 800-person village into a port city of 100,000 prospectors, con artists, inventors, entertainers and dockworkers – all thronging the city's 300 saloons.

Panic struck when Australia glutted the gold market in 1854. Rioters burned waterfront 'Sydney-Town' before turning on SF's Chinese community, who were subjected to anti-Chinese exclusion laws that effectively restricted them to Chinatown for 73 years. Chinese laborers were left with few outside employment options besides dangerous work building railroads for San Francisco's robber barons, who dynamited, mined and clear-cut their way across the Golden West, and built Nob Hill mansions above Chinatown.

But the city's grand ambitions came crashing down in 1906, when earthquake and fire reduced the city to rubble. Theater troupes and opera divas performed for free amid smoldering ruins, and reconstruction hummed along at an astounding rate of 15 buildings per day.

During WWII, soldiers accused of insubordination and homosexuality were dismissed in San Francisco, as though that would teach them a lesson. Instead San Francisco's counterculture thrived, with North Beach jazz and Beat poetry. When the Central Intelligence Agency (CIA) tested LSD on willing volunteer and *One Flew Over the Cuckoo's Nest* author Ken Kesey, he slipped some into Kool-Aid at 1966 Trips Festival in North Beach's Longshoremen's Hall – and the scene turned psychedelic. As the Grateful Dead jammed and dancers flailed, organizer and Whole Earth Catalog founder Steward Brand hallucinated a computer shrunk to fit his hand. Forty years later, Steve Jobs thanked him for the inspiration.

Across town, the 1967 Summer of Love brought free food, love and music to the Haight. In the Castro, pioneering gay activists helped elect Harvey Milk as San Francisco supervisor – America's first out gay official. When San Francisco witnessed devastating losses from HIV/AIDS in the 1980s, the city rallied to establish a global model for epidemic treatment and prevention. In 2020, that model was put to the test with Covid-19 – and again, the city rallied.

San Francisco's unconventional thinking launched the web in the 1990s tech boom, ending with the 2000 dot-com crash. But risk-taking SF continued to float outlandish new ideas – social media, mobile apps, biotech. Congratulations: you're just in time for San Francisco's next wild ride.

Sights

Downtown, Civic Center & SoMa

★San Francisco Museum of Modern Art MUSEUM

(SFMOMA; Map p78; ☎415-357-4000; www.sfmoma.org; 151 3rd St; adult/ages 19-24yr/under 18yr $25/19/free; ⏲10am-5pm Fri-Tue, to 9pm Thu, atrium from 8am Mon-Fri; 👪; 🚌5, 6, 7, 14, 19, 21, 31, 38, Ⓜ Montgomery, Ⓑ Montgomery) The mind boggles at SFMOMA, where boundary-pushing modern and contemporary masterworks sprawl over seven floors of galleries. Start with the world-class 3rd-floor photography collection, meditate in Agnes Martin's secluded shrine behind 4th-floor

Downtown San Francisco & SoMa

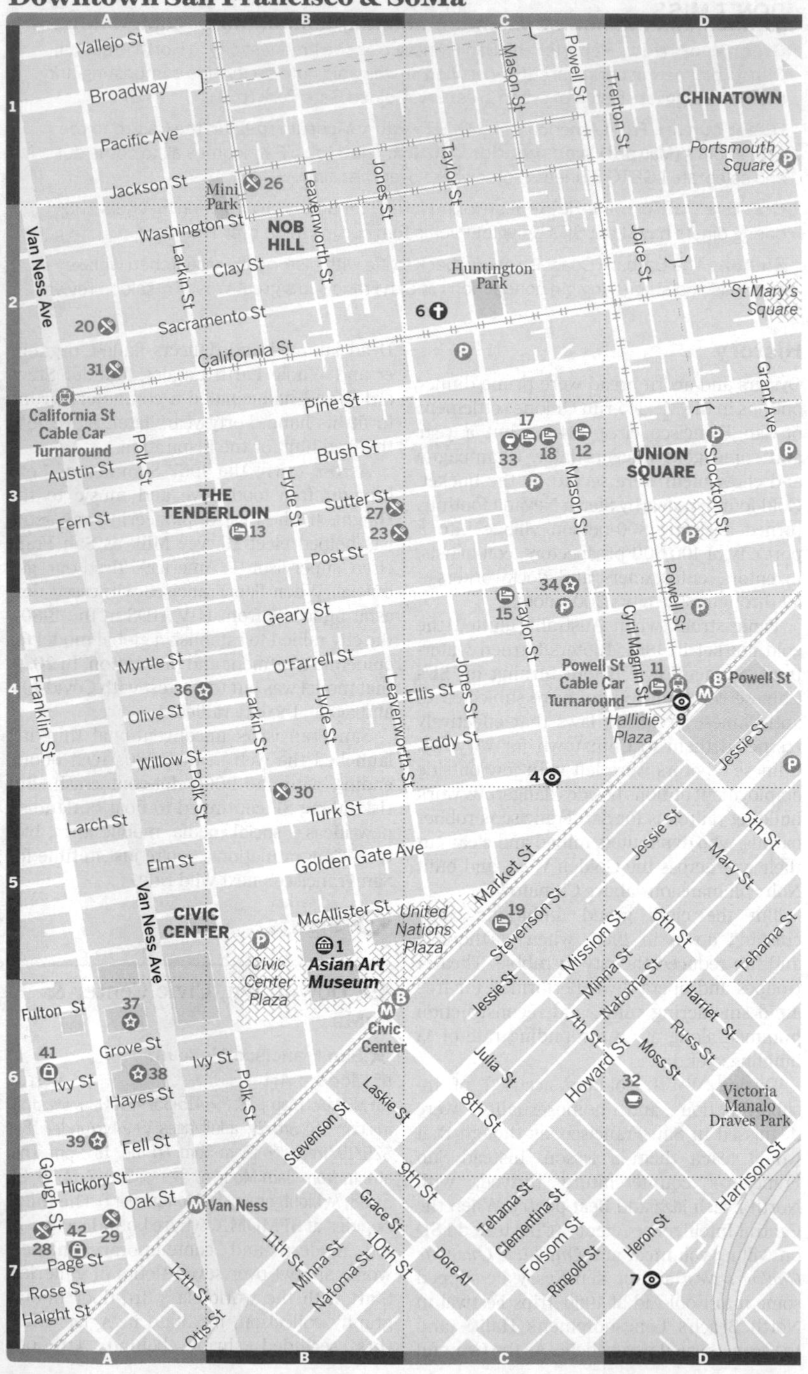

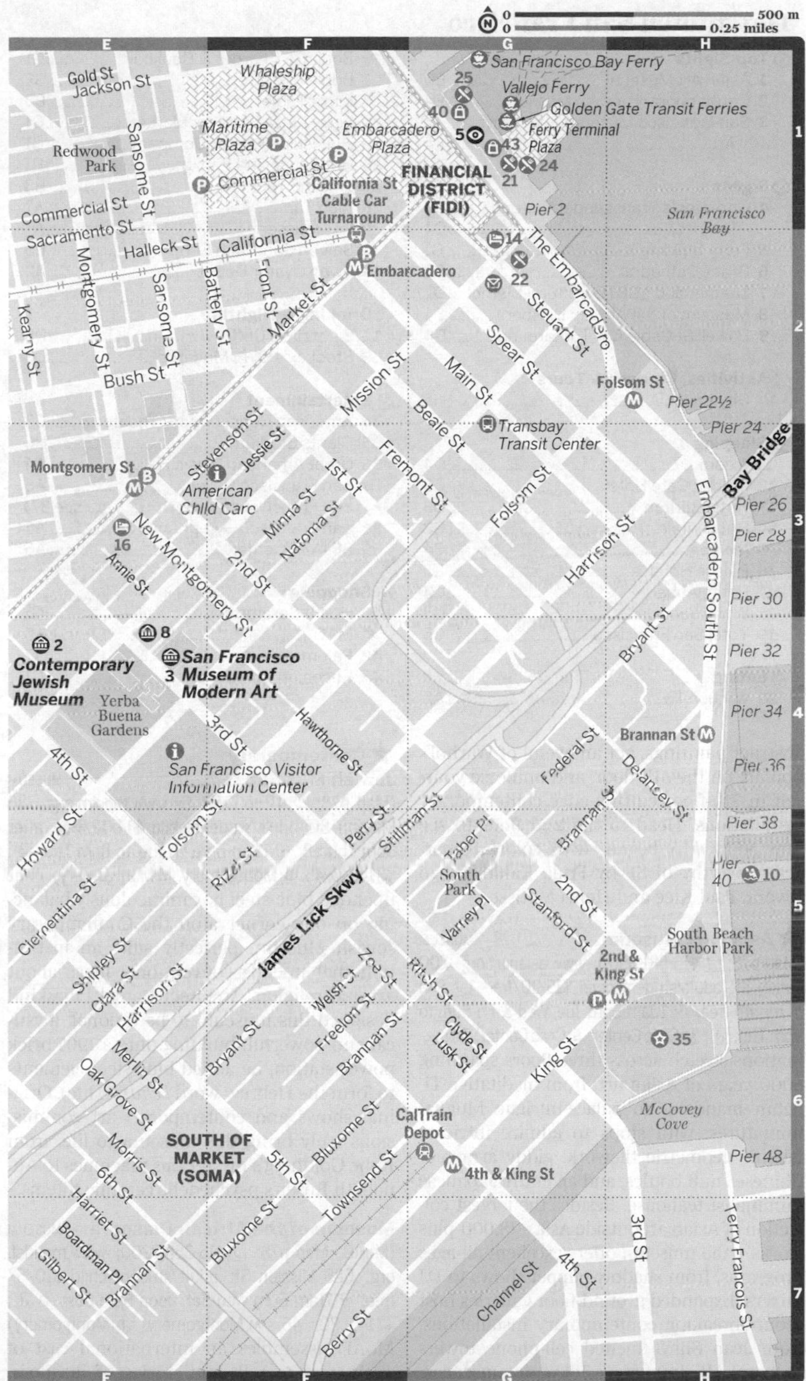

San Francisco Bay Ferry
Vallejo Ferry
Golden Gate Transit Ferries
Ferry Terminal Plaza
Whaleship Plaza
Maritime Plaza
Embarcadero Plaza
Redwood Park
FINANCIAL DISTRICT (FIDI)
California St Cable Car Turnaround
Embarcadero
Pier 2
San Francisco Bay
Folsom St
Pier 22½
Pier 24
Bay Bridge
Transbay Transit Center
Montgomery St
American Child Care
Pier 26
Pier 28
Pier 30
Pier 32
Pier 34
Pier 36
Pier 38
Pier 40
Contemporary Jewish Museum
San Francisco Museum of Modern Art
Yerba Buena Gardens
San Francisco Visitor Information Center
Brannan St
South Park
South Beach Harbor Park
2nd & King St
James Lick Skwy
McCovey Cove
Pier 48
CalTrain Depot
4th & King St
SOUTH OF MARKET (SOMA)

Downtown San Francisco

Top Sights
1 Asian Art Museum B5
2 Contemporary Jewish Museum E4
3 San Francisco Museum of Modern Art E4

Sights
4 Compton's Transgender Cultural District C4
5 Ferry Building G1
6 Grace Cathedral C2
7 Leather and LGBTQ Cultural District ... D7
8 Museum of the African Diaspora E4
9 Powell St Cable Car Turnaround D4

Activities, Courses & Tours
10 City Kayak H5

Sleeping
11 Axiom D4
12 Golden Gate Hotel C3
13 Hotel Carlton B3
14 Hotel Vitale G2
15 Marker C4
16 Palace Hotel E3
17 Petite Auberge C3
18 White Swan Inn C3
19 Yotel San Francisco C5

Eating
20 Acquerello A2
21 Boulette's Larder & Boulibar G1
22 Boulevard G2
23 Farm:Table B3
24 Ferry Plaza Farmers Market G1
25 Hog Island Oyster Company G1
26 Hot Sauce and Panko B1
27 Liholiho Yacht Club B3
28 Rich Table A7
29 RT Rotisserie A7
30 Saigon Sandwich Shop B5
31 Swan Oyster Depot A2

Drinking & Nightlife
32 Sightglass Coffee D6
33 Stookey's Club Moderne C3

Entertainment
34 American Conservatory Theater C3
35 Giants Stadium H6
36 Great American Music Hall A4
37 San Francisco Ballet A6
San Francisco Opera .... (see 37)
38 San Francisco Symphony A6
39 SFJAZZ Center A6

Shopping
40 Heath Ceramics G1
41 MAC A6
42 Paloma A7
43 Recchiuti Confections G1

abstract paintings, get an eyeful of Warhol's pop art on the 5th floor, and immerse yourself in 7th-floor cutting-edge contemporary installations. Head to the 2nd floor to see how SFMOMA began, with colorful characters worthy of SF by Frida Kahlo, Diego Rivera, Paul Klee and Henri Matisse.

★Asian Art Museum — MUSEUM

(Map p78; ☎415-581-3500; www.asianart.org; 200 Larkin St; adult/student/child $15/10/free, 1st Sun of month free; ⊙10am-5pm Tue, Wed & Fri-Sun, to 9pm Thu; ; M Civic Center, B Civic Center) Imaginations stretch across three floors spanning 6000 years of Asian art, from meditative Tibetan mandalas to palace-intrigue Mughal miniatures, with stops to admire intricate Islamic geometric tilework, giddy arrays of Chinese snuff bottles, and an entire Japanese minimalist teahouse. Besides the largest collection of Asian art outside Asia – 18,000-plus works – the museum offers excellent all-ages programs, from shadow-puppet shows to DJ mixers. Expanded ground-floor galleries host groundbreaking contemporary installations, from Jean Shin's melted cell-phone towers to teamLAB's immersive Tokyo dreamscapes.

★Contemporary Jewish Museum — MUSEUM

(Map p78; ☎415-655-7856; www.thecjm.org; 736 Mission St; adult/student/child $14/12/free, after 5pm Thu $8; ⊙11am-5pm Fri-Tue, to 8pm Thu; ; 14, 30, 45, B Montgomery, M Montgomery) That upended blue-steel box miraculously balancing on one corner atop the Contemporary Jewish Museum perfectly suits an institution that upends conventional ideas about art and religion. Architect Daniel Libeskind designed this museum to be rational, mystical and powerful: building onto a 1907 brick power station, he added blue-steel elements to form the Hebrew word *l'chaim* (life). Original shows and contemporary-art commissions truly bring this museum to life, from Rube Goldberg's mysterious machines to Annabeth Rosen's psychedelic ceramic totems.

Museum of the African Diaspora — MUSEUM

(MoAD; Map p78; ☎415-358-7200; www.moadsf.org; 685 Mission St; adult/student/child $10/5/free; ⊙11am-6pm Wed-Sat, noon-5pm Sun; P ; 14, 30, 45, M Montgomery, B Montgomery) MoAD assembles an international cast of characters to tell epic stories of diaspora, starting with a moving video of slave narratives featuring Maya Angelou. Standouts among quarterly changing exhibits have included homages to Harlem's queer ballroom scene, Kwame Brathwaite's uplifting 1960s Black Is Beautiful photography, and Angela Hennessey's altarpieces made entirely of woven hair. Public events include poetry slams, artist talks, film screenings, concerts with SFJAZZ, and Third Thursday nights, when the museum is free and open until 8pm.

Ferry Building LANDMARK
(Map p78; ☎415-983-8000; www.ferrybuildingmarketplace.com; cnr Market St & the Embarcadero; ⌚10am-7pm Mon-Fri, 8am-6pm Sat, 11am-5pm Sun; ♿; 🚌2, 6, 9, 14, 21, 31, Ⓜ Embarcadero, Ⓑ Embarcadero) Hedonism interrupts commutes at this historic transit hub that's become a local sustainable-food destination, where crowds happily miss their ferries over Sonoma oysters and bubbly, SF craft beer and Marin-raised beef burgers, locally roasted coffee and just-baked cupcakes. Star chefs are spotted year-round at the Saturday waterfront farmers market (p106), while farm-to-table kiosks line the curb Tuesdays and Thursdays.

North Beach & Chinatown

★Chinatown Alleyways AREA
(Map p84; btwn Grant Ave, Stockton St, California St & Broadway; 🚌1, 30, 45, 🚋Powell-Hyde, Powell-Mason, California) The 41 historic alleyways packed into Chinatown's 22 blocks have seen it all since 1849: gold rushes and revolution, incense and opium, fire and icy receptions. Brick temple balconies jut out over bakeries, laundries and barbers just as they have since 1870, when Chinese exclusion laws restricted Chinese immigration, employment and housing. These racist laws remained in force for 73 years. With nowhere to go after the 1906 earthquake, the community ingeniously rebuilt using burned clinker bricks.

★City Lights Books CULTURAL CENTER
(Map p84; ☎415-362-8193; www.citylights.com; 261 Columbus Ave; ⌚10am-midnight; ♿; 🚌8, 10, 12, 30, 41, 45, 🚋Powell-Mason, Powell-Hyde, Ⓜ T) FREE Free speech and free spirits have rejoiced here since 1957, when City Lights founder and poet Lawrence Ferlinghetti and manager Shigeyoshi Murao won a landmark ruling defending their right to publish Allen Ginsberg's magnificent epic poem *Howl*. Celebrate your freedom to read freely in the designated Poet's Chair upstairs overlooking Jack Kerouac Alley, load up on zines on the mezzanine and entertain radical ideas downstairs in the new Pedagogies of Resistance section.

★Coit Tower PUBLIC ART
(Map p84; ☎415-249-0995; www.sfrecpark.org; Telegraph Hill Blvd; nonresident elevator fee adult/child $9/6, mural tour full/2nd fl only $8/5; ⌚10am-6pm Apr-Oct, to 5pm Nov-Mar; 🚌39) The exclamation mark atop Telegraph Hill is Coit Tower, dedicated to SF first responders by firefighting millionaire Lillie Hitchcock Coit. The lobby is lined with 1930s murals celebrating SF workers – initially denounced as communist, but now landmarked. For a parrot's-eye panoramic view of San Francisco 210ft above the city, take the elevator to the tower's open-air platform. Book docent-led, 30- to 40-minute mural tours online – tour all murals or just the seven recently restored hidden stairwell murals.

★Waverly Place STREET
(Map p84; 🚌1, 30, 🚋California, Powell-Mason, Ⓜ T) Grant Ave is Chinatown's economic heart, but its soul is Waverly Place, lined with historic clinker-brick buildings and flag-festooned temple balconies. Nineteenth-century race-based planning restrictions left Chinatown nowhere to go but up – so family associations and temples were built atop barber shops, laundries and restaurants lining Waverly Place. Through world wars and Prohibition gunfights, Waverly Place calmly stood its ground. Temple services have been held here since 1852 – even after San Francisco's 1906 earthquake and fire, when altars were still smoldering.

Chinese Historical Society of America MUSEUM
(CHSA; Map p84; ☎415-391-1188; www.chsa.org; 965 Clay St; ⌚11am-4pm Wed-Sun; ♿; 🚌1, 8, 30, 45, 🚋California, Powell-Mason, Powell-Hyde, Ⓜ T) FREE Picture what it was like to be Chinese in America during the gold rush, Beat era, and women's rights movements in this 1932 landmark, built as Chinatown's YWCA. CHSA historians unearth fascinating artifacts: 1920s silk *qipao* dresses, WWII Chinatown nightclub posters, and Frank Wong's Chinatown miniatures. Exhibits share personal insights and historical perspectives on Chinese American historical milestones – including the Civil Rights movement, Transcontinental Railroad construction, and the 1882 Chinese Exclusion Act, denying Chinese immigrants US citizenship and civil rights.

Alcatraz

A HALF-DAY TOUR

Book a ferry from Pier 33 and ride 1.5 miles across the bay to explore America's most notorious former prison. The trip itself is worth the money, providing stunning views of the city skyline. Once you've landed at the ❶ **Ferry Dock & Pier**, you begin the 580yd walk to the top of the island and prison; if you need assistance to reach the top, there's a twice-hourly tram.

As you climb toward the ❷ **Guardhouse**, notice the island's steep slope; before it was a prison, Alcatraz was a fort. In the 1850s, the military quarried the rocky shores into near-vertical cliffs. Ships could then only dock at a single port, separated from the main buildings by a sally port (a drawbridge and moat in what became the guardhouse). Inside, peer through floor grates to see Alcatraz' original prison.

Volunteers tend the brilliant ❸ **Officers' Row Gardens**, an orderly counterpoint to the overgrown rose bushes surrounding the burned-out shell of the ❹ **Warden's House**. At the top of the hill, by the front door of the ❺ **Main Cellhouse**, beautiful shots unfurl all around, including a view of the ❻ **Golden Gate Bridge**. Above the main door of the administration building, notice the ❼ **historic signs & graffiti**, before you step inside the dank, cold prison to find the ❽ **Frank Morris cell**, former home to Alcatraz' most notorious jail-breaker.

TOP TIPS

➡ Book at least one month prior for self-guided daytime visits, longer for ranger-led night tours. For info on garden tours, see www.alcatraz gardens.org.

➡ Be prepared to hike; a steep path ascends from the ferry landing to the cell block. Most people spend two to three hours on the island. You need only reserve for the outbound ferry; take any ferry back.

➡ There's no food (just water) but you can bring your own; picnicking is allowed at the ferry dock only. Dress in layers as weather changes fast and it's usually windy.

ADRIEN_G/SHUTTERSTOCK ©

Historic Signs & Graffiti
During their 1969–71 occupation, Native Americans graffitied the water tower: 'Home of the Free Indian Land.' Above the cellhouse door, examine the eagle-and-flag crest to see how the red-and-white stripes were changed to spell 'Free.'

DOPTIS/SHUTTERSTOCK ©

Warden's House
Fires destroyed the warden's house and other structures during the Native American occupation. The government blamed the Native Americans; the Native Americans blamed agents provocateurs acting on behalf of the Nixon administration to undermine public sympathy.

Parade Grounds

Officers' Row Gardens
In the 19th century soldiers imported topsoil to beautify the island with gardens. Well-trusted prisoners later gardened – Elliott Michener said it kept him sane. Historians, ornithologists and archaeologists choose today's plants.

FRANK VAN DEN BERGH / GETTY IMAGES ©

Main Cellhouse

During the mid-20th century, the maximum-security prison housed the day's most notorious troublemakers, including Al Capone and Robert Stroud, the 'Birdman of Alcatraz' (who actually conducted his ornithology studies at Leavenworth).

FRANCKREPORTER/GETTY IMAGES ©

View of the Golden Gate Bridge

The Golden Gate Bridge stretches wide on the horizon. Best views are from atop the island at Eagle Plaza, near the cellhouse entrance, and at water level along the Agave Trail (September to January only).

Power House

Recreation Yard

Water Tower

Officers' Club

Lighthouse

Guard Tower

Guardhouse

Alcatraz' oldest building dates to 1857 and retains remnants of the original drawbridge and moat. During the Civil War the basement was transformed into a military dungeon – the genesis of Alcatraz as a prison.

Frank Morris Cell

Peer into cell 138 on B-Block to see a recreation of the dummy's head that Frank Morris left in his bed as a decoy to aid his notorious – and successful – 1962 escape from Alcatraz.

OSCITY/SHUTTERSTOCK ©

STEVE ROSSET/SHUTTERSTOCK ©

Ferry Dock & Pier

A giant wall map helps you get your bearings. Inside nearby Building 64, short films and exhibits provide historical perspective on the prison and details about the Native American Occupation.

North Beach & Chinatown

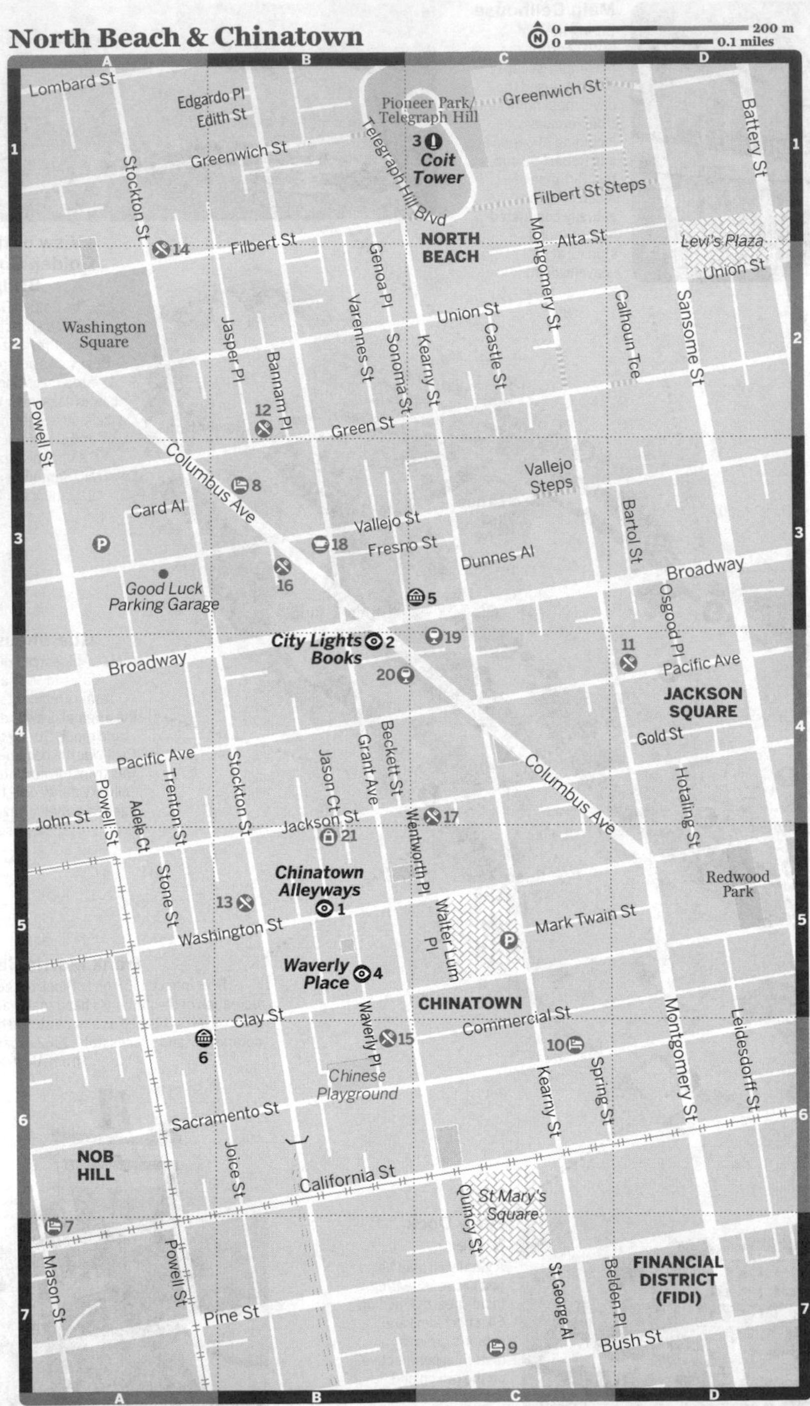

North Beach & Chinatown

Top Sights
1 Chinatown Alleyways B5
2 City Lights Books B4
3 Coit Tower C1
4 Waverly Place B5

Sights
5 Beat Museum C3
6 Chinese Historical Society of America A6

Sleeping
7 Fairmont San Francisco A7
8 Hotel Boheme B3
9 Orchard Garden Hotel C7
10 Pacific Tradewinds Hostel C6

Eating
11 Cotogna D4
12 Golden Boy B2
13 Good Mong Kok B5
14 Liguria Bakery A2
15 Mister Jiu's B6
16 Molinari B3
17 Z & Y C4

Drinking & Nightlife
18 Caffe Trieste B3
19 Specs C4
20 Vesuvio B4

Shopping
21 Golden Gate Fortune Cookies B5

Beat Museum MUSEUM

(Map p84; 800-537-6822; www.kerouac.com; 540 Broadway; adult/student $8/5; museum 10am-7pm, walking tours 2-4pm Sat; 8, 10, 12, 30, 41, 45, Powell-Mason, T) The closest you can get to the complete Beat experience without breaking a law. The 1000-plus artifacts in this museum's collection of literary ephemera include the sublime (the banned edition of Ginsberg's *Howl*, with the author's own annotations) and the ridiculous (those Kerouac bobblehead dolls are definite head-shakers). Downstairs, watch Beat-era films in ramshackle theater seats redolent with odors of literary giants, pets and pot. Upstairs, pay your respects at shrines to individual Beat writers. Bookstore entry and poetry readings are free.

★**Exploratorium** MUSEUM

(Map p88; 415-528-4444; www.exploratorium.edu; Pier 15/17; adult/child $29.95/19.95, 6-10pm Thu $19.95, Tactile Dome 30/60min $8/15; 10am-5pm Tue-Sun, over 18yr only 6-10pm Thu; ; E, F) Can you stop time, sculpt fog, or make sand sing? At San Francisco's hands-on, living laboratory of science and human perception, you'll discover superhuman abilities you never knew you had. But the Exploratorium's not just for kids: After Dark Thursdays offer mad-scientist cocktails, technology-assisted sing-alongs and themed exhibits for 18-plus crowds. Book ahead to slide, climb and feel your way in total darkness through the labyrinthine Tactile Dome, and emerge with a renewed sense of wonder (reservations required).

The Marina, Fisherman's Wharf & the Piers

★**Alcatraz** HISTORIC SITE

(Alcatraz Cruises 415-981-7625; www.alcatrazcruises.com; tours adult/child 5-11yr day $39.90/24.40, night $47.30/28, behind the scenes $92.30 (over 12yr only); call center 8am-7pm, ferries depart Pier 33 half-hourly 8:45am-3:50pm, night tours 5:55pm & 6:30pm;) Alcatraz: for over 150 years, the name has given the innocent chills and the guilty cold sweats. Over the decades, it's been a military prison, a forbidding maximum-security penitentiary and disputed territory between Native American activists and the FBI. Today, first-person accounts of daily life in the Alcatraz lockup are included on the award-winning audio tour. But take your headphones off to hear carefree city life across the bay: this torment made perilous prison escapes into riptides worth the risk.

DON'T MISS

GOLDEN GATE BRIDGE

Hard to believe the Navy almost nixed SF's signature art-deco **landmark** (toll information 877-229-8655; www.goldengatebridge.org/visitors; Hwy 101; northbound free, southbound $5-8; 28, all Golden Gate Transit buses) by architects Gertrude and Irving Murrow and engineer Joseph B Strauss. Photographers, take your cue from Hitchcock: seen from Fort Point (p90), the 1937 bridge induces a thrilling case of vertigo. Fog aficionados prefer Marin's Vista Point, watching gusts billow through bridge cables like dry ice at a Kiss concert. For the full effect, hike or bike the 1.7-mile span.

POWELL & MA
13
OUR
TOURIS
SAN FRA
TWO STANDEES
ONLY

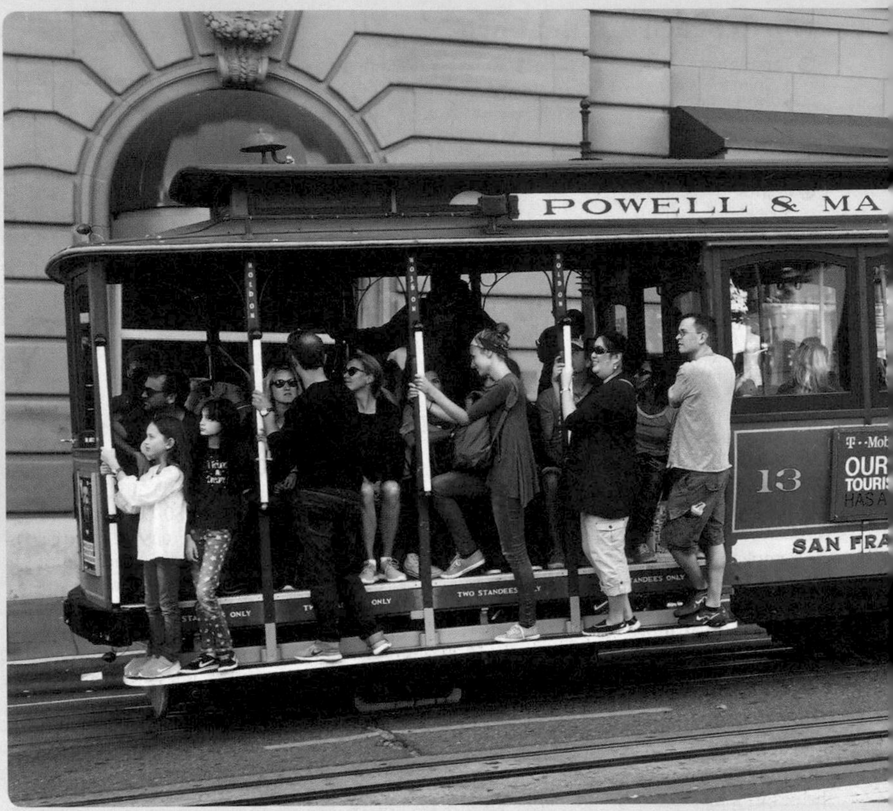

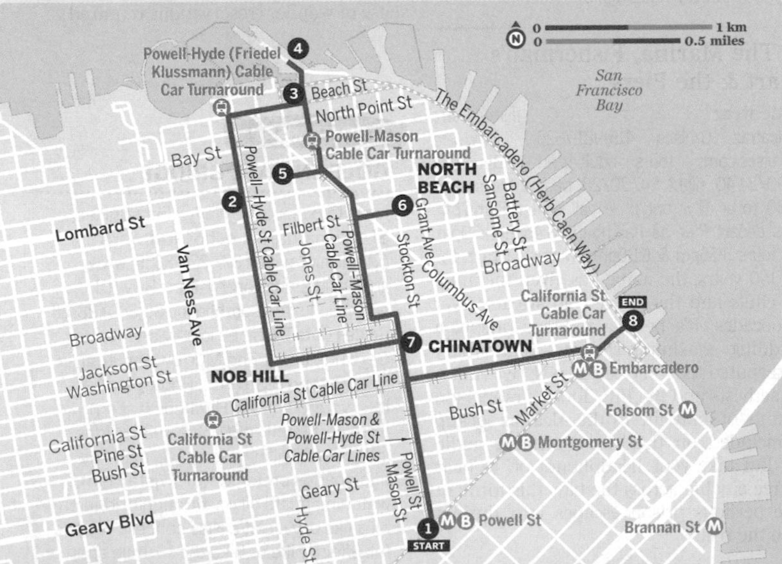

0 1 km
0 0.5 miles
N
San Francisco Bay
Powell-Hyde (Friedel Klussmann) Cable Car Turnaround
4
3
Beach St
North Point St
The Embarcadero (Herb Caen Way)
Powell-Mason Cable Car Turnaround
Bay St
Powell–Hyde St Cable Car Line
5
NORTH BEACH
2
6
Lombard St
Filbert St
Jones St
Powell–Mason Cable Car Line
Stockton St
Grant Ave
Columbus Ave
Sansome St
Battery St
Broadway
Van Ness Ave
California St Cable Car Turnaround
END
8
Broadway
7
CHINATOWN
Jackson St
Washington St
NOB HILL
M B Embarcadero
California St Cable Car Line
Market St
Bush St
Folsom St M
California St Cable Car Turnaround
Powell-Mason & Powell-Hyde St Cable Car Lines
M B Montgomery St
California St
Pine St
Bush St
Geary St
Powell St
Mason St
Geary Blvd
Hyde St
1
START
M B Powell St
Brannan St M

PACK-SHOT / SHUTTERSTOCK ©

HOLEOX / SHUTTERSTOCK ©

Top: City center cable car
Bottom: Powell-Hyde line cable car

San Francisco by Cable Car

Carnival rides can't compare to cable cars, San Francisco's vintage public transit. Novices slide into strangers' laps – cable cars were invented in 1873, long before seat belts – but regular commuters just grip the leather hand straps, lean back and enjoy the ride. On this trip, you'll master the San Francisco stance, and conquer SF hills without breaking a sweat.

At the 1**Powell St Cable Car Turnaround** (Map p78; www.sfmta.com; cnr Powell & Market Sts; Powell-Mason, Mason-Hyde, M Powell, B Powell), operators turn the car atop a revolving wooden platform and there's a vintage kiosk where you can buy an all-day Muni Clipper card for $16, instead of paying $8 per ride. Board the red-signed Powell Hyde cable car, and begin your 338ft ascent up Nob Hill.

Nineteenth century city planners were skeptical of inventor Andrew Hallidie's 'wire-rope railway' – but after more than a century of near-continuous operation, his wire-and-hemp cables have seldom broken.

On the 2**Powell-Hyde car**, you'll enjoy Bay views as you careen past zig-zagging Lombard Street (p90) toward 3**Fisherman's Wharf**. At the wharf you can see SF as sailors did, then enter underwater mode inside the submarine 4**USS Pampanito** (Map p88; 415-775-1943; www.maritime.org/pamphome.htm; Pier 45; adult/child/family $20/10/45; 9am-6pm Sun-Thu, to 8pm Fri & Sat; can vary seasonally; ; 19, 30, 47, Powell-Hyde, M E, F) before hitching the Powell-Mason cable car to North Beach.

Hop off to see Diego Rivera's 1931 cityscape in the 5**Diego Rivera Gallery** (Map p88; 415-771-7020; www.sfai.edu; 800 Chestnut St; 9am-7pm; 30, Powell-Mason) FREE at the San Francisco Art Institute, or follow your rumbling stomach directly to 6**Liguria Bakery** (p104). Stroll through North Beach and Chinatown alleyways, or take the Powell-Mason line to time-travel through the 7**Chinese Historical Society of America** (p81). Nearby, catch a ride on the city's oldest line: the California St cable car. The terminus is near the 8**Ferry Building** (p81), where champagne-and-oyster happy hour awaits.

Fisherman's Wharf, The Marina & Russian Hill

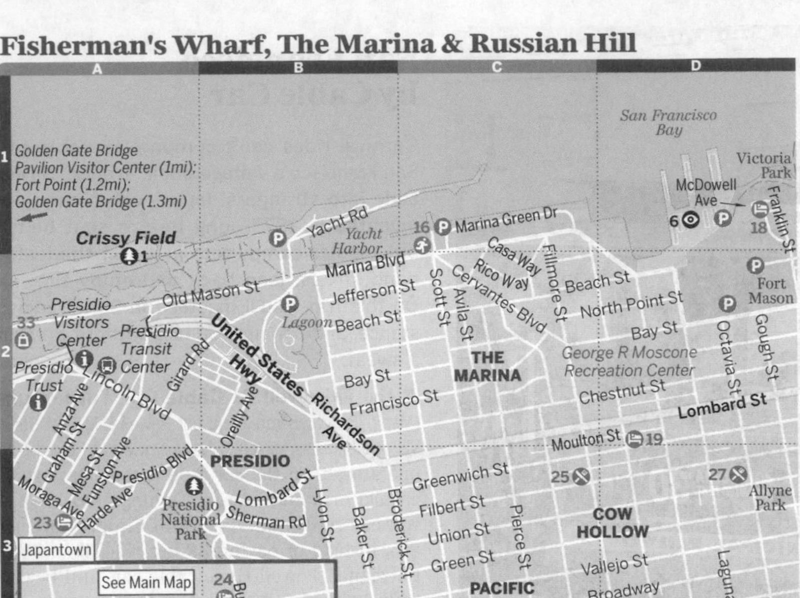

★Crissy Field PARK

(Map p88; ☎415-561-4700; www.nps.gov; 1199 East Beach; P 🐾; 🚌30, PresidiGo Shuttle) War is for the birds at Crissy Field, a military airstrip turned waterfront nature preserve with knockout Golden Gate views. Where military planes once zoomed in for landings, bird-watchers now huddle in the quiet rushes of a reclaimed tidal marsh. No more secret Army missions here – just puppies chasing kite fliers, joggers pounding beachfront trails, and kitesurfers skimming bay waters. On foggy days, stop by the certified-green cafe Warming Hut to browse California field guides and warm up with fair-trade coffee.

Maritime National Historical Park HISTORIC SITE

(Map p88; ☎415-447-5000; www.nps.gov/safr; 499 Jefferson St, Hyde St Pier; 7-day ticket adult/child under 16 $15/free; ⏰9:30am-5pm Oct-May, to 5:30pm Jun-Sep; 👪; 🚌19, 30, 47, 🚋Powell-Hyde, Ⓜ F) Five historic ships are floating museums at Fisherman's Wharf's most enduring attraction. Moored along Hyde St Pier, the three-star attractions are the 1891 schooner *Alma,* which hosts guided sailing trips in summer; 1890 steamboat *Eureka;* and iron-hulled 1886 *Balclutha,* which brought coal to San Francisco. It's free to walk the pier; pay only to board ships. The park includes the 1939 **Aquatic Park Bathhouse** (10am to 4pm), featuring Maritime Museum exhibits and fabulous art-deco friezes by African American sculptor Sargent Johnson.

Baker Beach BEACH

(Map p110; ☎10am-5pm 415-561-4323; www.nps.gov/prsf; ⏰sunrise-sunset; P; 🚌29, PresidiGo Shuttle) Picnic amid wind-sculpted pines, fish from craggy rocks or frolic nude at mile-long Baker Beach, with spectacular views of the Golden Gate. Crowds come weekends, especially on fog-free days; arrive early. For nude sunbathing among straight women and gay men, head to the north. Families in

clothing stick to the south, nearer parking. Mind the currents and the c-c-cold water.

Cartoon Art Museum MUSEUM

(Map p88; ☎415-227-8666; http://cartoonart.org; 781 Beach St; adult/child $10/4; ⊙11am-5pm Thu-Tue; 🚌19, 30, 47, 🚋Powell-Hyde) Founded on a grant from Bay Area cartoon legend Charles M Schultz of *Peanuts* fame, this museum showcases cartoon classics from Batman blockbusters to *Calvin & Hobbes* strips. But these curators aren't afraid of the dark or serious subjects, either, showcasing R Crumb's underground comics, Gemma Correll's *Worrier Girl*, and George Takei's graphic-novel memoir of Japanese American internment camps. Lectures and openings are rare opportunities to mingle with comic legends, local Pixar Studios animators and obsessive comic collectors.

Fort Mason Center AREA

(Map p88; ☎415-345-7500; www.fortmason.org; cnr Marina Blvd & Laguna St; P; 🚌22, 28, 30, 43, 47, 49) San Francisco takes subversive glee in turning military installations into civilian playgrounds. Fort Mason was an embarkation point for WWII troops, but today its warehouses contain cultural centers, galleries, cutting-edge **Magic Theater** (Map p88; ☎415-441-8822; www.magictheatre.org; Fort Mason Center, Bldg D, 3rd fl, cnr Marina Blvd & Laguna St; tickets $30-85; 🚌22, 28, 30, 43, 47, 49) and **BATS Improv** (Map p88; ☎415-474-6776; www.improv.org; Fort Mason Center, Bldg B, 3rd fl, cnr Marina Blvd & Laguna St; tickets $17-20; ⊙shows 8pm Fri & Sat; 🚌22, 28, 30, 43) comedy workshops. Waterfront Herbst Pavilion includes arts and craft fairs among its arsenal of events, ex-shipyards host **farmers markets** (9:30am to 1:30pm Sunday and Wednesday) and **Off the Grid** (Map p88; ☎415-339-5888; www.offthegridsf.com; 2 Marina Blvd, Fort Mason Center; items $6-15; ⊙5-10pm Fri Mar-Oct; 👪; 🚌22, 28) food trucks, and army mess halls are replaced by leisurely Interval Bar & Cafe (p112)

Fisherman's Wharf, The Marina & Russian Hill

and Zen-community-run Greens (p105) vegetarian restaurant.

Fort Point HISTORIC SITE

(☎415-504-2334; www.nps.gov/fopo; Marine Dr; ⏰10am-5pm Fri-Sun; P; 🚌28) FREE This triple-decker, brick-walled US military fortress was completed in 1861, with 126 cannons, to protect the bay against certain invasion during the Civil War...or not, as it turned out. Without a single shot fired, Fort Point was quietly abandoned in 1900. Alfred Hitchcock made it famous in his 1956 film *Vertigo* – this is where Kim Novak jumped into the bay. Now the fort showcases Civil War displays and knockout panoramic viewing decks of the bridge's underside.

Nob Hill, Russian Hill & Fillmore

Grace Cathedral CHURCH

(Map p78; ☎415-749-6300; www.gracecathedral.org; 1100 California St; suggested donation adult/child $3/2; ⏰8am-6pm Mon-Sat, to 7pm Sun, services 8:30am, 11am & 6pm Sun; 🚌1, 🚋California) San Francisco's reinforced-concrete Gothic hilltop cathedral took 40 years to complete, with spectacular 'Human Endeavor' stained-glass windows celebrating science – look for Albert Einstein amid swirling nuclear particles. Murals commemorate the 1906 earthquake and 1945 UN charter signing, and Grace's Interfaith AIDS Memorial Chapel features a bronze angel altarpiece by artist-activist Keith Haring – his final work before his 1990 death from AIDS. Locals light candles here and at the feet of Beniamino Bufano's smiling statue of the city's patron saint.

Lombard Street STREET

(Map p88; 🚋Powell-Hyde) You've seen its eight switchbacks in movies, but Lombard St doesn't deserve its nickname as 'San Francisco's crookedest street' – Vermont St in Potrero Hill deserves that honor. Lombard is more scenic, with flowerbeds lining its brick-paved 900 block. It wasn't always so bent: it plunged straight downhill until too many joyriders crashed in the 1920s. Today traffic is slow and skating is banned – so Lombard St thrills featured in Tony Hawk's Pro Skater video game are strictly virtual.

Vallejo Street Steps ARCHITECTURE

(Map p88; Vallejo St, btwn Mason & Jones Sts; 🚋Powell-Mason, Powell-Hyde) Reach staggering heights with spectacular views along this staircase connecting North Beach with Russian Hill. Ascend Vallejo toward Mason St, where stairs rise toward Jones St,

DON'T MISS

GOLDEN GATE PARK

When San Franciscans refer to 'the park,' there's only one that gets the definite article. Everything they hold dear is in **Golden Gate Park** (Map p110; https://goldengatepark.com; btwn Stanyan St & Great Hwy; P 🚻; 🚌5, 7, 18, 21, 28, 29, 33, 44, MN) 🍃, including free spirits, free music, Frisbee and bison.

At the east end you can join year-round drum circles at Hippie Hill, sweater-clad dandies at the historic **Lawn Bowling Club**, toddlers clinging for dear life onto the 100-year-old **carousel**, and meditators in the contemplative **AIDS Memorial Grove**. To the west, turtles paddle past model yachts at **Spreckels Lake**, offerings are made at pagan altars behind the baseball diamond, and free concerts are held in the **Polo Fields**, site of 1967's hippie Human Be-In.

When New York's Central Park architect Frederick Law Olmsted balked at transforming 1013 acres of dunes into the world's largest developed park, San Francisco's green scheme fell to tenacious young civil engineer William Hammond Hall. He insisted that park features should include **botanical gardens** (Strybing Arboretum; Map p110; ☎415-661-1316; www.sfbg.org; 1199 9th Ave; adult/child $9/2, before 9am daily & 2nd Tue of month free; ⏰7:30am-5pm, extended hours in summer & spring, last entry 1hr before closing, bookstore 10am-4pm; 🚌6, 7, 44, MN) 🍃, a dedicated **Buffalo Paddock** (Map p110; www.golden-gate-park.com/buffalo-paddock.html; ⏰sunrise-sunset; 🚌5, 21), and waterfalls at **Stow Lake**. Today the park offers 7.5 miles of bicycle trails, 12 miles of equestrian trails, an archery range, fly-casting pools, four soccer fields, and 21 tennis courts. Sundays, when John F Kennedy Dr closes to traffic around 9th Ave, join roller disco and Lindy Hop in the park. Don't miss these park highlights:

de Young Museum (Map p110; ☎415-750-3600; http://deyoung.famsf.org; 50 Hagiwara Tea Garden Dr; adult/child $15/free, 1st Tue of month free ; ⏰9:30am-5:15pm Tue-Sun; 🚌5, 7, 44, MN) Follow sculptor Andy Goldsworthy's artificial fault line in the sidewalk into Herzog & de Meuron's sleek, copper-clad building that's oxidizing green to blend into the park. Don't be fooled by the camouflaged exterior: shows here boldly broaden artistic horizons, from Oceanic ceremonial mask displays to Frida Kahlo retrospectives, and Black Power movement posters to AI-assisted artwork. Don't miss James Turrell's domed *Skyspace* installation built under the sculpture garden. Avail of a $2 discount with a Bay Area public transit ticket. Ticket includes free same-day entry to the **Legion of Honor** (Map p110; ☎415-750-3600; http://legionofhonor.famsf.org; 100 34th Ave; adult/child $15/free, discount with Muni ticket $2, 1st Tue of month free; ⏰9:30am-5:15pm Tue-Sun; 🚌1, 2, 18, 38).

California Academy of Sciences (Map p110; ☎415-379-8000; www.calacademy.org; 55 Music Concourse Dr; adult/student/child $36.50/31.25/28; ⏰9:30am-5pm Mon-Sat, from 11am Sun; P 🚻; 🚌5, 6, 7, 21, 31, 33, 44, MN) Architect Renzo Piano's landmark LEED-certified green building houses 40,000 animals in a four-story rainforest, split-level aquarium and planetarium, all under a 'living roof' of wildflowers. Inside, butterflies flit around the Osher Rainforest Dome, giant pink Pacific octopuses roam Steinhart Aquarium, penguins waddle in the African Hall, and Claude the albino alligator stalks the mezzanine swamp. Explore California in the Giants of Land and Sea exhibit – brave an earthquake simulation, virtually climb a redwood and get lost in a fog room. See website for weekday and sustainable transit discounts.

Japanese Tea Garden (Map p110; ☎415-752-1171; www.japaneseteagardensf.com; 75 Hagiwara Tea Garden Dr; adult/child $10/3, Mar-Sep $12/3, before 10am Mon, Wed & Fri free; ⏰9am-5:45pm Mar-Sep, to 4:45pm Oct-Feb; P; 🚌5, 7, 44, MN) Since 1894, this 5-acre garden has blushed pink with cherry blossoms in spring and turned flaming red with maple leaves in fall. The century-old bonsai grove was cultivated by generations of Hagiwara family gardeners, until they were forced to leave for WWII Japanese American interment camps. After the war, the Hagiwaras discovered their prized evergreens had been sold by profiteers, and they spent decades rebuilding the tiny forest. Don't miss the meditative Zen Garden and Tea House fortune cookies (introduced right here).

passing poetic **Ina Coolbrith Park** (Map p88; www.sfparksalliance.org/our-parks/parks/ina-coolbrith-park; cnr Vallejo & Taylor Sts; 🚌41, 45, 🚋Powell-Mason). Pause at the top for nighttime views of the shimmering Bay Bridge lights, then continue west to Polk St for nightlife.

The Haight & Hayes Valley

★Haight Street Art Center ARTS CENTER

(Map p94; ☎415-363-6150; https://haightstreetart.org; 215 Haight St; ⏱noon-6pm Wed-Sun; 🚌6, 7, 22, Ⓜ F) FREE Jeremy Fish's bronze bunny-skull sculpture guides you into a wonderland of screen-printed posters, San Francisco's signature art form. Glimpse rock-concert posters in progress at the on-site screen-printing studio, plus jaw-dropping gallery shows featuring Stanley Mouse's psychedelic Grateful Dead posters and Ralph Steadman's original illustrations for Hunter S Thompson's *Fear and Loathing in Las Vegas*. Gracing the stairwell is a hidden SF treasure: Ruben Kaddish's 1937 WPA fresco *Dissertation on Alchemy,* surely the trippiest mural ever commissioned by the US government.

★Alamo Square Park PARK

(Map p94; www.sfparksalliance.org/our-parks/parks/alamo-square; cnr Hayes & Steiner Sts; ⏱sunrise-sunset; 👪🐾; 🚌5, 21, 22, 24) Hippie communes and Victorian bordellos, czarist bootleggers and jazz legends: these genteel 'Painted Lady' Victorian mansions have hosted them all since 1857, and survived elegantly intact. Pastel 'Postcard Row' mansions (aka the *Full House* sitcom backdrop) along the southeastern edge of this hilltop park pale in comparison with the colorful, turreted, outrageously ornamented Victorians along the northwestern end – especially the 1889 Italianate Westerfield mansion, where Church of Satan rituals were filmed in the tower by Kenneth Anger.

The Castro & Noe Valley

★Rainbow Honor Walk LANDMARK

(Map p94; http://rainbowhonorwalk.org; Castro St & Market St; Ⓜ Castro St) You're always in excellent company in the Castro, where sidewalk plaques honor LGBTQ heroes. The walk runs along Market St from Noe St to Casto St and down Castro St from Market St to 20th St. Portraits are etched into the bronze plaques, and many are familiar faces: civil-rights activist James Baldwin, artist Keith Haring, author Virginia Woolf, disco diva Sylvester. Honorees are suitably bathed in glory every night, when they're illuminated by rainbow LEDs.

GLBT History Museum MUSEUM

(Map p94; ☎415-621-1107; www.glbthistory.org/museum; 4127 18th St; adult/child $10/free, 1st Wed of month free; ⏱11am-6pm Mon-Sat, noon-5pm Sun, closed Tue fall-spring; Ⓜ Castro St) America's first gay-history museum showcases a century of San Francisco LGBTQ ephemera – Harvey Milk's campaign literature, matchbooks from long-gone bathhouses, photographs of early marches – alongside insightful installations highlighting queer culture milestones and struggles for acceptance throughout history. Multimedia stories put civil-rights efforts into personal perspective, and provide community introductions for queer folk and allies alike. The shop sells reproductions of '80s pink triangle tees,'70s pride pins, and Harvey Milk fridge magnets citing his words: 'You gotta give 'em hope.' Indeed.

Human Rights Campaign Action Center HISTORIC SITE

(Harvey Milk's Camera Store; Map p94; ☎415-431-2200; http://shop.hrc.org/san-francisco-hrc-store; 575 Castro St; ⏱10am-8pm Mon-Sat, to 7pm Sun; Ⓜ Castro St) FREE From the Oscar-winning movie *Milk*, you might recognize this as the storefront where Harvey Milk launched his campaign to become America's first out gay city official. Today it houses the civil-rights nonprofit championing marriage equality and transgender identity rights, with a rainbow mural quoting Milk: 'If a bullet should enter my brain, let that bullet destroy every closet door.' Activists scan bulletin boards and sign petitions, while shoppers score stylish HRC tees, with proceeds supporting LGBTQ civil-rights initiatives.

The Mission, Dogpatch & Potrero Hill

★826 Valencia CULTURAL CENTER

(Map p94; ☎415-642-5905; www.826valencia.org; 826 Valencia St; ⏱noon-6pm; 👪; 🚌14, 33, 49, Ⓑ16th St Mission, Ⓜ J) FREE Avast, ye scurvy scallywags! If ye be shipwrecked without yer eye patch or McSweeney's literary anthology, lay down ye doubloons and claim yer booty at this here nonprofit pirate store. Below decks, kids be writing tall tales for dark nights a'sea, and ye can study writing movies, science fiction and suchlike, if that be yer dastardly inclination.

★**Dolores Park** PARK

(Map p94; http://sfrecpark.org; Dolores St, btwn 18th & 20th Sts; ⏲6am-10pm; 🚸🐾; 🚌14, 33, 49, Ⓑ16th St Mission, ⓂJ) Welcome to San Francisco's sunny side, the land of street ball and Mayan-pyramid playgrounds, semiprofessional tanning and glorious taco picnics. Grassy slopes are dedicated to the fine art of lolling, while lowlands host soccer, Frisbee, political protests and other local sports. Good weather brings cultural events, including Easter's Hunky Jesus drag contest, free summer movie nights, and fall SF Mime Troupe performances. Fair warning: secondhand highs copped near the refurbished bathroom may have you chasing the *helados* (ice-cream) cart.

★**Women's Building** NOTABLE BUILDING

(Map p94; ☎415-431-1180; www.womensbuilding.org; 3543 18th St; 🚌14, 22, 33, 49, Ⓑ16th St Mission, ⓂJ) A renowned and beloved Mission landmark since 1979, the nation's first women-owned-and-operated community center has housed 150 women's organizations – but it's recognized around the world for its awe-inspiring wraparound murals. Painted in 1994 by dozens of SF women muralists, *Maestrapeace* murals depict feminist icons from around the world, including Nobel Prize–winner Rigoberta Menchú, poet Audre Lorde, artist Georgia O'Keeffe and former US Surgeon General Dr Joycelyn Elders.

★**Balmy Alley** PUBLIC ART

(Map p94; ☎415-285-2287; www.precitaeyes.org; btwn 24th & 25th Sts; 🚌10, 12, 14, 27, 48, Ⓑ24th St Mission) When Mission *muralistas* objected to US policy in Latin America in the 1970s, they took to the streets with paintbrushes. Inspired by Diego Rivera's 1930s San Francisco murals, Mujeres Muralistas ('Women Muralists') and Placa ('Mark-making') covered Balmy Alley garage doors and back fences with murals of pride and protest. Today Balmy Alley artworks span three decades, from memorials honoring Salvadoran activist Archbishop Romero to a homage to Frida Kahlo. Nonprofit Precita Eyes commissions and upkeeps these murals, plus dozens more throughout the Mission.

★**Clarion Alley** PUBLIC ART

(Map p94; https://clarionalleymuralproject.org; btwn 17th & 18th Sts; 🚌14, 22, 33, Ⓑ16th St Mission, Ⓜ16th St Mission) Spot street artists touching up pieces and making new ones in this open-air gallery, maintained by neighbors and Clarion Alley Collective's curators. Only a few pieces survive for years, such as Megan Wilson's daisy-covered *Tax the Rich* or Jet Martinez' glimpse of Clarion Alley inside a forest spirit. Incontinent art critics often take over the alley's eastern end – pee-eew! – so topical murals usually go up on the western end.

★**Anglim Gilbert Gallery** GALLERY

(☎415-433-2710; http://anglimgilbertgallery.com; 1275 Minnesota St, 2nd fl; ⏲11am-6pm Tue-Sat; 🚌48, 🚋T) FREE For 30-plus years this has been where Bay Area art movements hit the big time, from Beat assemblage to Bay Area conceptualists. Major gallery artists range from political provocateur Enrique Chagoya to sublime bronze sculptor Deborah Butterfield – yet shows here maintain the element of surprise, from Lynn Hershman's sugary dystopias to Ala Ebtekar's blocked doors to the cosmos.

Mission Dolores CHURCH

(Misión San Francisco de Asís; Map p94; ☎415-621-8203; www.missiondolores.org; 3321 16th St; adult/child $7/5; ⏲9am-4:30pm May-Oct, to 4pm Nov-Apr; 🚌22, 33, Ⓑ16th St Mission, ⓂJ) The city's oldest building and its namesake, whitewashed adobe Misión San Francisco de Asís is better known as Mission Dolores (Mission of the Sorrows) – tragically apt for Native conscripts who built it in 1776–82. Subjected to harsh living conditions and introduced diseases, some 5000 Ohlone and Miwok laborers were buried on Mission lands. Today you can pay respects at a graveyard memorial, and glimpse recently restored Native American handiwork: a Native basket-patterned ceiling, and an original Ohlone sacred heart mural.

Activities

Cycling & Skating

Basically Free Bike Rentals CYCLING

(Map p88; ☎415-934-2922; www.basicallyfree.com; 1196 Columbus Ave; half-/full-day bike rentals regular $24/32, electric $42/$65, child $15/20, tandem $50/60; ⏲8am-6pm; 🚸; 🚌F, 30, 47, 🚋Powell-Mason, Powell-Hyde) This quality bike-rental shop cleverly gives you the choice of paying for your rental or taking the cost as credit for purchases (valid for 72 hours) at sporting-goods store **Sports Basement** (Map p88; ☎415-934-2900; www.sportsbasement.com; 610 Old Mason St; ⏲9am-9pm Mon-Fri, 8am-8pm Sat & Sun; 🚌30, 43, PresidiGo Shuttle), in the Presidio en route to the Golden Gate Bridge. Guided 2.5-hour bike tours of the Golden Gate Bridge include

The Mission & The Castro

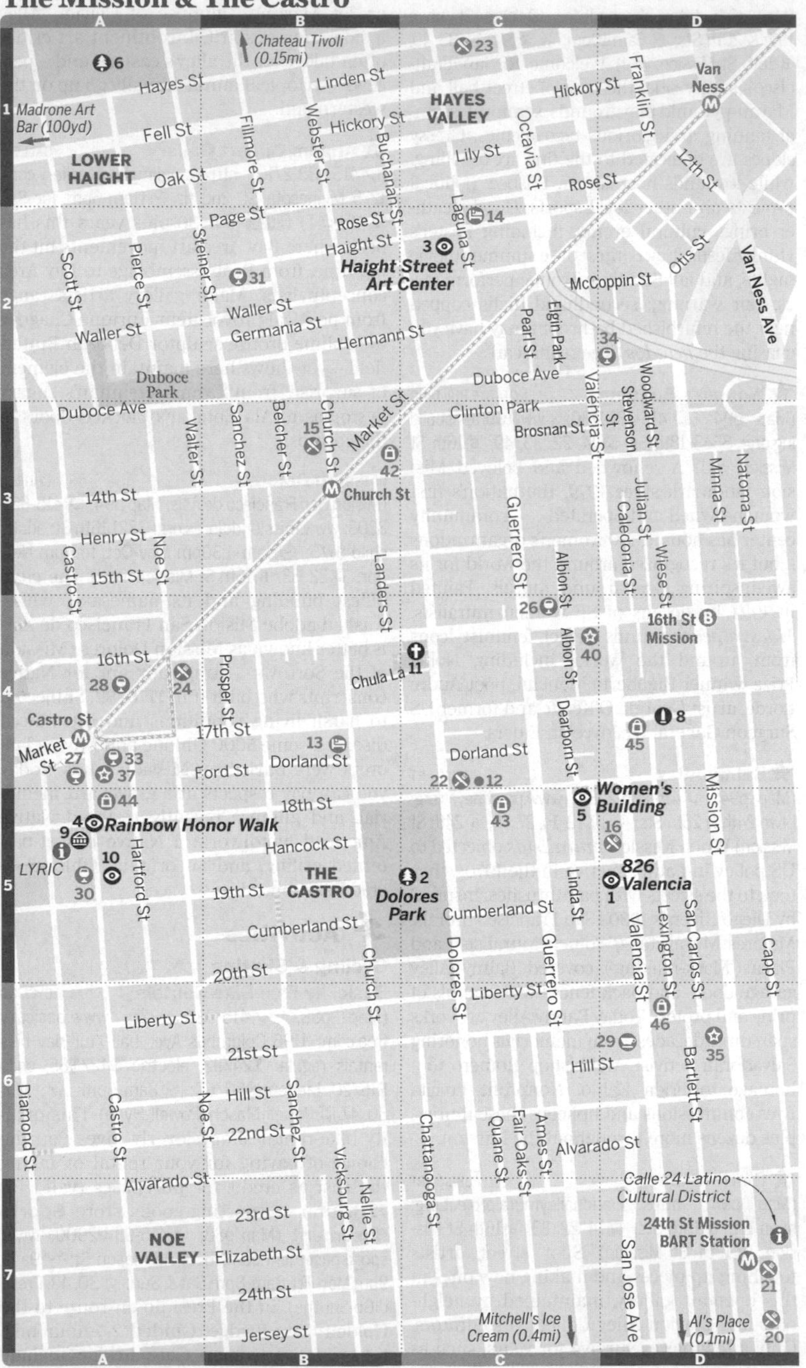

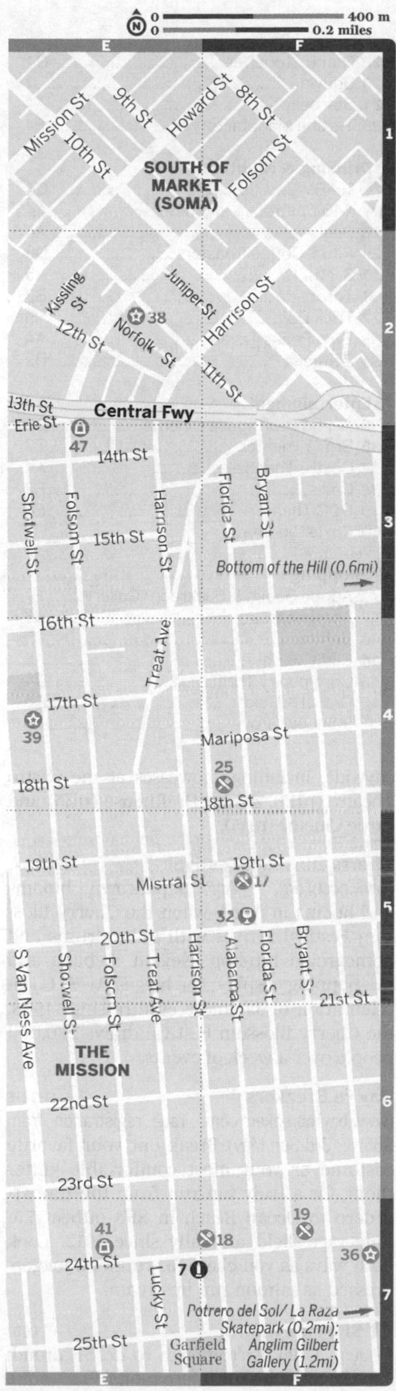

all-day bike rentals ($23 to $30 extra per person).

Kayaking & Whale-Watching

★Oceanic Society Expeditions CRUISE

(Map p88; ☎415-256-9604; www.oceanicsociety.org; 3950 Scott St; whale-watching trips per person $150; ⊙office 9am-5pm Mon-Fri; 🚌30) The Oceanic Society runs top-notch, naturalist-led, oceangoing weekend boat trips to the Farallon Islands and/or Half Moon Bay during whale-migration seasons. Cruises depart from the yacht harbor and last all day. Reservations required; group pricing and private charters are also available. Kids must be 10 years or older.

City Kayak KAYAKING

(Map p78; ☎415-294-1050, 888-966-0953; www.citykayak.com; Pier 40, South Beach Harbor; kayak rentals per hour $35-128, lesson & rental $54, tours $54-89; ⊙rentals noon-3pm, return by 5pm Thu-Mon; 🚌30, 45, Ⓜ N, T) You haven't seen San Francisco until you've seen it from the water. Newbies to kayaking can take lessons and paddle calm waters near the Bay Bridge; experienced paddlers can rent kayaks to brave currents near the Golden Gate (conditions permitting; get advice first). Sporty romantics: twilight tours past the Bay Bridge lights are ideal for proposals. Check website for details.

Spas

★Kabuki Springs & Spa BATHHOUSE

(Map p88; ☎415-922-6000; www.kabukisprings.com; 1750 Geary Blvd; adult $30; ⊙10am-10pm, all-gender Tue, women-identified Wed, Fri & Sun, men-identified Mon, Thu & Sat; 🚌22, 38) Gooong! That's a subtle hint to chatty spa-goers to shush, restoring meditative silence to Japantown's communal, clothing-optional bathhouse. Salt-scrub in the steam room, soak in the hot pool, take a cold plunge, reheat in the sauna, rinse and repeat. Men/transmen and women/transwomen alternate days except all-gender Tuesdays, when bathing suits are required. Bath access is $15 with spa treatments, including shiatsu massage.

Courses

★18 Reasons COOKING

(Map p94; ☎415-568-2710; https://18reasons.org; 3674 18th St; classes & dining events $15-125; 👪; 🚌22, 33, Ⓜ J) 🌿 Go gourmet at this Bi-Rite-affiliated (p117) community food nonprofit, offering deliciously educational events and chef-led classes, including cheesemaking

The Mission & The Castro

Top Sights

1 826 Valencia ... D5
2 Dolores Park ... C5
3 Haight Street Art Center ... C2
4 Rainbow Honor Walk ... A5
5 Women's Building ... C5

Sights

6 Alamo Square Park ... A1
7 Balmy Alley ... E7
8 Clarion Alley ... D4
9 GLBT History Museum ... A5
10 Human Rights Campaign Action Center ... A5
11 Mission Dolores ... C4

Activities, Courses & Tours

12 18 Reasons ... C4

Sleeping

13 Parker Guest House ... B4
14 Parsonage ... C2

Eating

15 Beit Rima ... B3
16 Craftsman & Wolves ... D5
17 Farmhouse Kitchen Thai Cuisine ... F5
Foreign Cinema ... (see 35)
18 Humphry Slocombe ... F7
19 La Palma Mexicatessen ... F7
20 La Taqueria ... D7
21 Mr Pollo ... D7
22 Namu Stonepot ... C4
23 Souvla ... C1
24 Starbelly ... A4
25 Tartine Manufactory ... F4

Drinking & Nightlife

26 %ABV ... C4
27 440 Castro ... A4
28 Beaux ... A4
29 Ritual Coffee Roasters ... D6
30 Swirl ... A5
31 Toronado ... B2
32 Trick Dog ... F5
33 Twin Peaks Tavern ... A4
34 Zeitgeist ... D2

Entertainment

35 Alamo Drafthouse Cinema ... D6
36 Brava Theater ... F7
37 Castro Theatre ... A4
38 Oasis ... E2
39 ODC Theater ... E4
40 Roxie Cinema ... C4

Shopping

41 Adobe Books & Backroom Gallery ... E7
42 Apothecarium ... B3
43 Bi-Rite ... C5
44 Cliff's Variety ... A5
45 Community Thrift ... D4
46 Gravel & Gold ... D6
47 Rainbow Grocery ... E3

courses, knife-skills workshops and culinary boot camps. Mingle with fellow foodies at family-friendly $15 community suppers and multicourse winemaker dinners ($95 to $125). The website lists bargain guest-chef pop-ups and low-cost classes with cookbook authors. Spots fill quickly – book early.

Festivals & Events

★Lunar New Year CULTURAL

(www.chineseparade.com; Feb) Chase the 200ft dragon, legions of lion dancers and local politicians on floats tossing lucky *lai see* (red envelopes with chocolate coins) during Chinatown's Lunar New Year celebrations. Firecrackers and fierce troops of tiny-tot martial artists make this parade the highlight of San Francisco winters.

San Francisco International Film Festival FILM

(https://sffilm.org; Apr) The nation's oldest film festival has kept audiences riveted for 60 years with hundreds of films, including star-studded premieres and directors' cuts from around the world. Plan ahead for two weeks of screenings citywide, including showcases at the Castro Theatre (p115), Alamo Drafthouse (p115) and Roxie Cinema (p115).

Cherry Blossom Festival CULTURAL

(www.nccbf.org; Apr) Japantown blooms and booms in April, when the Cherry Blossom Festival arrives with taiko drums and homegrown hip-hop, elegant ikebana and eye-popping cosplay. The biggest West Coast celebration of Japanese culture since 1968, the Cherry Blossom Festival draws 220,000 people over a week of events.

Bay to Breakers SPORTS

(www.baytobreakers.com; race registration from $65; 3rd Sun May) Break out your favorite costume or your most comfortable glitter thong for a truly fun run from the Embarcadero to Ocean Beach in SF's offbeat 7.5-mile race, held annually since 1912. Look both ways as you cheer for runners: joggers dressed as salmon run upstream.

★SF Pride Month LGBT

(Jun) A day isn't enough to do SF proud: June begins with the international **Frameline**

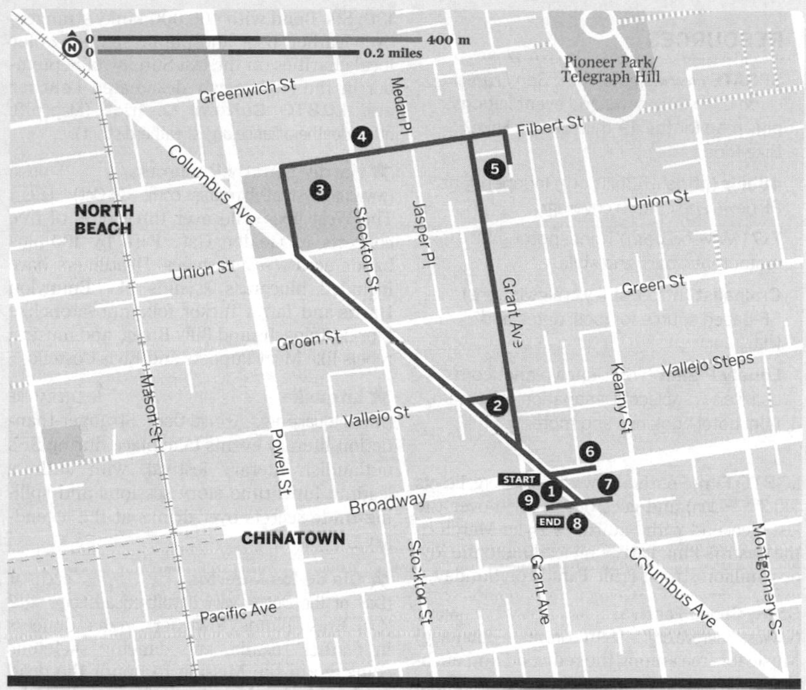

City Walk
North Beach Beat

START CITY LIGHTS BOOKS
END VESUVIO
LENGTH 1.5 MILES; TWO HOURS

At **1 City Lights Books** (p81), home of Beat poetry and free speech, pick up something to inspire your journey into literary North Beach – Ferlinghetti's *San Francisco Poems* and Ginsberg's *Howl* make excellent company.

Head to **2 Caffe Trieste** (p111) for opera on the jukebox and potent espresso in the back booth, where Francis Ford Coppola drafted *The Godfather* screenplay.

At **3 Washington Square**, you'll spot parrots in the treetops and octogenarians in tai chi tiger stances on the lawn – pure poetry in motion. At the corner, **4 Liguria Bakery** (p104) will give you something to write home about: focaccia hot from a century-old oven.

Peaceful **5 Bob Kaufman Alley** was named for the legendary street-corner poet who kept a 12-year vow of silence that lasted until the Vietnam War ended – when he finally walked into a North Beach cafe and recited his poem 'All Those Ships That Never Sailed.'

Dylan jam sessions erupt in the bookshop, Allen Ginsberg spouts poetry nude in backroom documentary screenings, and stoned visitors grin beatifically at it all. Welcome to the **6 Beat Museum** (p85), spiritual home to all 'angelheaded hipsters burning for the ancient heavenly connection' (to quote Ginsberg's *Howl*).

The obligatory literary bar crawl begins at **7 Specs** (p111) amid merchant-marine memorabilia, tall tales from old-timers, and pitchers of Anchor Steam. *On the Road* author Jack Kerouac once blew off Henry Miller to go on a bender across the street at **8 Vesuvio** (p112), until bartenders ejected him into the street now named for him: **9 Jack Kerouac Alley**. Note the words of Chinese poet Li Po embedded in the alley: 'In the company of friends, there is never enough wine.'

Follow the lead of Kerouac and Ginsberg and end your night at Vesuvio – there may not be enough wine here, but there's plenty of beer.

RESOURCES

SFGATE (www.sfgate.com) *San Francisco Chronicle* news and event listings, plus map for the 49-mile Scenic Hike/Bike Ride.

48hills (https://48hills.org) Independent SF news and culture coverage.

7x7 (www.7x7.com) Trendspotting SF restaurants, bars and style.

Craigslist (http://sfbay.craigslist.org) SF-based source for jobs, dates and free junk.

Lonely Planet (www.lonelyplanet.com/usa/san-francisco) Destination information, hotel bookings and more.

LGBTQ Film Festival (www.frameline.org; tickets $10-35; ⌚Jun) and goes out in style over the last weekend with Saturday's Dyke March to the Castro's Pink Party – all leading to the joyous, million-strong Pride Parade on Sunday.

Stern Grove Festival MUSIC
(www.sterngrove.org; Stern Grove; ⌚Jun-Aug) Music for free among the redwood and eucalyptus trees every summer since 1938. Stern Grove's 2pm Sunday concerts include hip-hop, world music and jazz, but the biggest events are usually performances by the SF Ballet, SF Symphony and SF Opera.

AIDS Walk San Francisco SPORTS
(http://sf.aidswalk.net; ⌚3rd Sun Jul) Until AIDS takes a hike, you can: this 10km fundraiser walk through Golden Gate Park directly benefits numerous HIV/AIDS organizations. Over three decades, this walk has raised more than $90 million to fight the pandemic and support those living with HIV.

Outside Lands MUSIC
(www.sfoutsidelands.com; 3-day pass standard/VIP $375/795; ⌚Aug) Score tickets the minute they go on sale mid-May to attend the music festival *Billboard* named America's best, featuring marquee acts that range from artsy (Childish Gambino, Lorde) to legendary (Tribe Called Quest, Paul Simon). Golden Gate Park is the site for three days of gleeful debauchery assisted by Wine Lands, Beer Lands and star-chef food trucks.

Folsom Street Fair STREET CARNIVAL
(www.folsomstreetfair.com; ⌚last Sun Sep) Bondage enthusiasts emerge from dungeons worldwide for the world's biggest leather street party, on Folsom St between 8th and 13th Sts. Bond with 400,000 kinky strangers over leather, beer and public spankings for local charities on the last Sunday of September in the city's newly designated **Leather and LGBTQ Cultural District** (Map p78; http://leatheralliance.org/sfleatherdistrict).

★ **Hardly Strictly Bluegrass** MUSIC
(www.hardlystrictlybluegrass.com; ⌚Oct) FREE The West goes wild over three days of free concerts in Golden Gate Park by 100-plus bands across seven stages. Headliners have included bluegrass legends like Emmylou Harris and Tanya Tucker, folk innovators like Flor de Toloache and Billy Bragg, and musical rebels like Meat Puppets and Elvis Costello.

★ **Litquake** LITERATURE
(www.litquake.org; ⌚mid-Oct) Stranger-than-fiction literary events take place during SF's outlandish literary festival, with authors leading lunchtime story sessions and spilling trade secrets over drinks at the legendary Lit Crawl.

★ **Día de los Muertos** CULTURAL
(Day of the Dead; www.dayofthedeadsf.org; ⌚2 Nov) Brass bands, lowriders, Aztec dancers in feather regalia, and dancing skeletons converge in the Mission to honor the dead on Día de los Muertos. Offerings line the processional route along 24th St, culminating in moving outdoor community altars at **Potrero del Sol/La Raza Skate Park** (cnr 25th & Utah Sts; ⌚8am-9pm; 🚌9, 10, 27, 33, 48, Ⓑ24th St Mission). This is a true community gathering – grassroots and family-friendly, with zero corporate sponsorship.

Sleeping

Downtown, Civic Center & SoMa

Yotel San Francisco HOTEL $
(Map p78; ☎415-829-0000; www.yotel.com/en/hotels/yotel-san-francisco; 1095 Market St; d $179-209; ❄📶; 🚌6, 7, 9, 21, Ⓑ Civic Center, Ⓜ Civic Center) Surprise: inside the yellow-brick Grant building are hip, compact, high-tech 'sky cabins' (studio lofts) in a convenient (if gritty) location. Smart design choices save time with self-check-in kiosks and space with adjustable 'smartbeds' with extra-long mattresses that morph into couches. Mingle at the panoramic rooftop bar or chill out with Netflix on the in-room TV – or work with high-speed wi-fi and a 24-hour gym.

★Hotel Vitale BOUTIQUE HOTEL $$

(Map p78; ☎415-278-3700; www.hotelvitale.com; 8 Mission St; d $249-509; ❄@📶🐾; Ⓜ Embarcadero, Ⓑ Embarcadero) When your love interest or executive recruiter books you into the waterfront Vitale, you know it's serious. The office-tower exterior disguises a snazzy, SF-certified green hotel with sleek, up-to-the-minute luxuries. Beds are dressed with silky-soft 450-thread-count sheets, and the on-site spa features rooftop hot tubs. Rooms facing the bay offer spectacular Bay Bridge views, and Ferry Building dining awaits across the street.

Marker BOUTIQUE HOTEL $$

(Map p78; ☎415-292-0100, 844-736-2753; http://themarkersanfrancisco.com; 501 Geary St; d from $209; ❄@📶🐾; 🚌38, 🚋Powell-Hyde, Powell-Mason) Snazzy Marker gets details right, with guest-room decor in bold colors – lipstick-red lacquer, navy-blue velvet and shiny purple silk – and thoughtful amenities like high-thread count sheets, ergonomic workspaces, digital-library access, multiple electrical outlets and ample space in drawers, closets and bathroom vanities. Extras include a small gym, an evening wine reception and bragging rights to stylish downtown digs.

Axiom BOUTIQUE HOTEL $$

(Map p78; ☎415-392-9466; www.axiomhotel.com; 28 Cyril Magnin St; d $238-374; @📶🐾; 🚋Powell-Mason, Powell-Hyde, Ⓑ Powell, Ⓜ Powell) Of all the downtown SF hotels aiming for high-tech appeal, this one gets it right. The lobby is razzle-dazzle LED, marble and riveted steel, but the games room looks like a start-up HQ, with arcade games and foosball tables. Guest rooms have low-slung, gray-flannel couches, king platform beds, dedicated routers for high-speed wireless streaming to Apple/Google/Samsung devices, and Bluetooth-enabled everything.

Hotel Carlton DESIGN HOTEL $$

(Map p78; ☎800-922-7586, 415-673-0242; www.hotelcarltonsf.com; 1075 Sutter St; d from $269; @📶🐾; 🚌2, 3, 19, 38, 47, 49) World travelers feel right at home at the Carlton amid Moroccan tea tables, Indian bedspreads, West African wax-print throw pillows and carbon-offsetting LEED-certified initiatives (note the rooftop solar panels). It's not the most convenient location – 10 minutes from Union Sq – but offers good value for colorful, spotlessly clean rooms. The quietest rooms are those with the suffix -08 to -19.

Palace Hotel HOTEL $$

(Map p78; ☎415-512-1111; www.marriott.com; 2 New Montgomery St; d from $179-499; ❄@📶🏊🐾; Ⓜ Montgomery, Ⓑ Montgomery) The 1906 landmark Palace remains a monument to turn-of-the-century grandeur, with 100-year-old Austrian-crystal chandeliers and Maxfield Parrish paintings. Cushy but corporate Marriott accommodations cater to business travelers, but prices drop at weekends. Even if you're not staying here, visit the opulent Garden Court to sip tea beneath a translucent glass ceiling. There's also a spa; kids love the big pool.

North Beach & Chinatown

Pacific Tradewinds Hostel HOSTEL $

(Map p84; ☎415-433-7970; www.san-francisco-hostel.com; 680 Sacramento St; dm $39-43, refundable security deposit $20; ⏲front desk 8am-midnight; 🚭@📶; 🚌1, Ⓑ Montgomery, 🚋California) San Francisco's smartest all-dorm hostel has a nautical theme, fully equipped kitchen (free coffee, tea, and peanut-butter-and-jelly sandwiches), spotless showers, laundry (free sock wash), luggage storage and no lockout time. Bunks are bolted to the wall, ending bed-shaking when bunkmates roll. No elevator means hauling bags up three flights – but it's worth it. Great service; fun staff.

★Hotel Bohème BOUTIQUE HOTEL $$

(Map p84; ☎415-433-9111; www.hotelboheme.com; 444 Columbus Ave; d $185-295; 🚭@📶; 🚌10, 12, 30, 41, 45, Ⓜ T) Eclectic, historic and unabashedly romantic, this quintessential North Beach boutique hotel has jazz-era color schemes, wrought-iron beds, paper-umbrella lamps, Beat poetry and original artwork. The vintage rooms are smallish with teensy bathrooms, some face noisy Columbus Ave (quieter rooms are in the back) and there's no elevator – but novels practically write themselves here, with City Lights and legendary bars as handy inspiration.

★Orchard Garden Hotel BOUTIQUE HOTEL $$

(Map p84; ☎415-393-9917; www.theorchardgardenhotel.com; 466 Bush St; d $278-389; Ⓟ🚭❄@📶; 🚌2, 3, 30, 45, Ⓑ Montgomery) San Francisco's original LEED-certified, all-green-practices hotel uses sustainably grown wood, chemical-free cleaning products and recycled fabrics in its soothingly quiet rooms. Don't think you'll be trading comfort for conscience: rooms have unexpectedly luxe touches, like high-end down

Where to Stay in San Francisco

Nob Hill & Russian Hill
Stately hilltop hotels and romantic hideaway B&Bs surrounded by historic bars and cable cars.

Best For Honeymooners and high rollers

Transport Cable cars up steep hills

Price Mostly top end

Japantown, Fillmore & Pacific Heights
Mid-century modern and Victorian splendor, with Japanese restaurants and spas, boutiques galore and legendary concert venues.

Best For Style, SF history and local scene

Transport Muni bus 20 minutes from downtown

Price Midrange to top end

The Haight & Hayes Valley
Flower power lives on between Golden Gate Park and City Hall, with '60s landmarks and boho hotels.

Best For Dreamers and diners

Transport Muni bus and N Judah streetcar

Price Mostly midrange

Golden Gate Park & the Avenues
Parkside motels and oceanfront surfer hangouts with cafes, breweries and fog.

Best For Outdoor enthusiasts

Transport Muni bus and N Judah streetcar

Price Budget to midrange

The Castro
LGBT+ magnet, with Victorian B&Bs tucked away amid community landmarks and bars.

Best For Well-heeled travelers, star spotters

Transport Muni streetcar

Price Mostly midrange

Alcatraz

North Beach & Chinatown
Historic cultural hot spot, with literary landmarks, crossroads restaurants, actual saloons and boho boardinghouses.

Best For Cultural immersion in SF's artistic hub

Transport Cable cars from downtown

Price Mostly top end

The Marina, Fisherman's Wharf & the Piers
Waterfront views, scenic hikes and kid-friendly motels and attractions, if a bit of a tourist trap.

Best For Families and sporty types

Transport Cable cars and F streetcars; buses for the Marina

Price Midrange to top end

The Marina, Fisherman's Wharf & the Piers

Coit Tower

Nob Hill & Russian Hill

North Beach & Chinatown

Grace Cathedral

Japantown, Filmore & Pacific Heights

San Francisco Museum of Modern Art (SFMOMA)

Downtown, Center & SoMa

Downtown, Civic Center & SoMa
Wide selection of hotels surrounded by sights, restaurants and nightlife; street smarts required.

Best For Business travel and budget stays

Transport Cable cars, CalTrain and BART

Price Budget to top end

Alamo Square Park

The Haight & Hayes Valley

The Mission, Dogpatch & Potrero Hills
Mural-lined center for Latinx culture, SF arts and biotech, with limited short-term stays.

Best For Community, creative inspiration, political imagination

Transport BART, bus and bikes

Price Mostly midrange

Rainbow Honor Walk

Women's Building

The Castro

The Mission, Dogpatch & Potrero Hills

pillows, Egyptian-cotton sheets and organic bath products. Toast sunsets with a cocktail on the rooftop terrace. Book directly for deals, free breakfast and parking.

The Marina, Fisherman's Wharf & the Piers

★HI San Francisco Fisherman's Wharf HOSTEL $

(Map p88; ☎415-771-7277; www.hiusa.org; Fort Mason, Bldg 240; dm $41-51, d $125-160; P@; 28, 30, 47, 49) Trading downtown convenience for a glorious parklike setting with million-dollar waterfront views, this hostel occupies a former army-hospital building, with bargain-priced private rooms and dorms (some coed) with four to 22 beds (avoid bunks one and two – they're by the doorways). All bathrooms are shared. There's a huge kitchen offering free breakfasts and a cafe overlooking the bay. Limited free parking.

★Hotel del Sol MOTEL $

(Map p88; ☎415-921-5520; www.jdvhotels.com; 3100 Webster St; d $99-210; P@; 22, 28, 30, 43) Cartoons come to life in this 1950s motor lodge redone in eye-popping beach-ball colors, with a palm-lined courtyard and heated outdoor pool – a rare treat in San Francisco. Kids aren't an afterthought but are honored guests treated to afternoon cookies, board games, a movie library and hammocks. The quiet Marina District location is near restaurants, parks and Fort Mason; parking costs $30 per night.

Hotel Zephyr DESIGN HOTEL $$

(Map p88; ☎415-617-6565, 844-617-6555; www.hotelzephyrsf.com; 250 Beach St; d $250-500; P@; 8, 39, 47, Powell-Mason, M E, F) Completely revamped in 2015, this vintage 1960s hotel surrounds a vast courtyard with fire pits and lounge chairs, nautical flotsam repurposed as modern art, and games like table tennis in a tube – reminders you're here to play, not work. Rooms are fresh and spiffy, with up-to-date amenities, including smart TV that links with your devices. Book waterfront rooms; parking costs $60.

★Inn at the Presidio HOTEL $$$

(Map p88; ☎415-800-7356; www.presidiolodging.com; 42 Moraga Ave; d $310-495; P@; 43, PresidiGo Shuttle) Built in 1903 as bachelor quarters for army officers, this three-story, redbrick building in the Presidio was transformed in 2012 into a smart national-park lodge, styled with leather, linen and wood. Oversized rooms are plush, including feather beds with Egyptian-cotton sheets, and suites have gas fireplaces. Downtown seems a world away – here nature surrounds you, with hiking trailheads out back.

Argonaut Hotel BOUTIQUE HOTEL $$$

(Map p88; ☎415-345-5519, 415-563-0800; www.argonauthotel.com; 495 Jefferson St; d $269-474; P; 19, 47, 49, Powell-Hyde) Originally built as a cannery in 1908, Fisherman's Wharf's top hotel remains a waterfront character, with exposed-brick walls, century-old beams, and nautical decor. Guest rooms are fit for a first mate, with shiplap walls, plush navy-blue furnishings and ultracomfy beds with compass bedheads. All rooms are shipshape, but some are so tiny and dark, you might feel like a stowaway. Parking runs $65.

Nob Hill, Russian Hill, Japantown & Pacific Heights

★Hotel Kabuki HOTEL $$

(Map p88; ☎415-922-3200; www.jdvhotels.com; 1625 Post St; d $160-570; P@; 2, 3, 38) Welcome to the Steve Jobs of SF hotels – austerely minimalist outside, but sneaky psychedelic touches inside make you wonder who's been microdosing magic mushrooms. Japanese mid-century modern meets '60s SF in cleverly updated decor: Noguchi tables flank *shibori* tie-dyed bedheads, and trippy Jonathan Adler prints adorn slate-gray walls. Book directly for free Kabuki Springs & Spa (p95) passes; reserve dinner on-site at Nari (p106).

★White Swan Inn BOUTIQUE HOTEL $$

(Map p78; ☎415-775-1755; www.whiteswaninnsf.com; 845 Bush St; d $237-305; P@; 2, 3, 27) If a Nob Hill socialite had a fling with a rebellious royal, they'd hide out at White Swan. Each room has its own eccentric English character – cabbage-rose wallpaper, terrier portraits, mod lamps, fireplaces – without sacrificing Californian creature comforts: soaking tubs, pillow-top beds, gourmet pizza delivery. Don't miss high tea in Christian Lacroix wingback lounge chairs, or fireside yoga in the library (yes, really).

The Kimpton Buchanan BOUTIQUE HOTEL $$

(Map p88; ☎415-921-4000; www.thebuchananhotel.com; 1800 Sutter St; d $218-294; P) Roll out of bed and find shopping, spas and shabu-shabu dining at your doorstep. Mid-century modern luxe city-view rooms offer views of Japantown's Peace Pagoda from the considerable comfort of your king bed, and spa king corner rooms have Japanese soaking tubs. Cheeky style – like the whiskey-crate-paneled lounge – and thoughtful amenities, including bicycles at your disposal.

Golden Gate Hotel HOTEL $$
(Map p78; ☎415-392-3702; www.goldengatehotel.com; 775 Bush St; d $240-260, with shared bath $160-180; @ 📶; 🚌2, 3, 🚋Powell-Hyde, Powell-Mason) Like an old-fashioned *pension*, the Golden Gate has kindly owners and simple rooms with cheerful cottage furnishings, in a 1913 Edwardian hotel perched above the downtown fray. Rooms are snug, clean and comfortable, and most have private bathrooms – some with antique claw-foot bathtubs. Enormous croissants, homemade cookies, and a resident cat provide TLC after long days of sightseeing.

Petite Auberge BOUTIQUE HOTEL $$
(Map p78; ☎415-928-6000; www.petiteaubergesf.com; 863 Bush St; d $229-299; P 📶; 🚌2, 3, 27) No one expects a French country inn on Nob Hill, but voilà! The Auberge is a sunshine-yellow charmer, with vintage books flanking cozy gas fireplaces. Rooms are snug, floral and eccentrically posh, though some overlook a gloomy, echoing alley (request a quiet room). Breakfast, freshly baked cookies and afternoon wine are served fireside in the salon. Valet parking available.

Fairmont San Francisco HOTEL $$$
(Map p84; ☎415 772 5000; www.fairmont.com; 950 Mason St; d from $359; P ❄ @ 📶 🐾; 🚋California, Powell-Mason, Powell-Hyde) Heads of state choose the Fairmont for its grand hotel swagger – magnificent marble lobby, opulent mosaic penthouse suite, bacchanalian brunches – plus San Francisco eccentricity, including tiki Tonga Room and deco circus-mural Cirque bar. Guest rooms offer business-class comfort, but comparatively less character and luxury than public spaces. For historic appeal, reserve in the original 1906 building; for jaw-dropping views, go for the tower.

Hotel Drisco BOUTIQUE HOTEL $$$
(Map p88; ☎415-346-2880; www.hoteldrisco.com; 2901 Pacific Ave; d $378-540; @ 📶; 🚌3, 24, 45) Towering atop Pacific Heights, this stately 1903 apartment hotel has a privileged perch tucked between mansions. Revamped rooms are pure relaxation in foggy grey tones and luxurious natural fabrics, with thoughtful details like the pillow menu and heated bathroom floors. It's a bus, taxi or workout to get anywhere, so relax and enjoy the hilltop views and attentive service.

The Castro

★Parker Guest House B&B $$
(Map p94; ☎415-621-3222; www.parkerguesthouse.com; 520 Church St; d $249-289, with shared bath $209-249; P @ 📶; 🚌33, M J) 🍃 Make your gay getaway in grand style at this Edwardian estate, covering two sunny yellow mansions linked by secret gardens. Dashingly handsome guest rooms feature stately beds piled with down duvets, gleaming retro-tiled bathrooms and generous closets for coming out of. Unwind over wine in the sunroom, linger over continental breakfasts, or get cozy with sherry by the library fireplace.

The Haight & Hayes Valley

★Parsonage B&B $$
(Map p94; ☎415-863-3699; www.theparsonage.com; 198 Haight St; d $260-290; @ 📶; 🚌6, 71, M F) Social graces come naturally at this 1883 Italianate Victorian, with original Carrara-marble fireplaces, rose-brass chandeliers and period furnishings. Six spacious, antique-adorned guest rooms are named after San Francisco's grand dames – millionaire Alma Spreckles has a claw-foot tub and four-poster bed, but architect Julia Morgan gets the best views. Take breakfast in the formal dining room, and brandy and chocolates before bed. Two-night minimum.

Chateau Tivoli B&B $$
(☎415-776-5462; www.chateautivoli.com; 1057 Steiner St; d $205-215, with shared bath $160-185, q $220-325; 📶; 🚌5, 22) The source of neighborhood gossip since 1892, this gilded, turreted mansion graciously hosted Isadora Duncan, Mark Twain and (rumor has it) the ghost of a Victorian opera diva – now you too can be Chateau Tivoli's guest. Nine antique-filled rooms named after San Francisco artistes set the scene for romance; some have four-poster beds and claw-foot bathtubs, two share a bathroom. No elevator or TVs.

Eating

Downtown, Civic Center & SoMa

Farm:Table AMERICAN $
(Map p78; ☎415-300-5652; www.farmtablesf.com; 754 Post St; dishes $6-14; ⏰7:15am-1pm Tue-Fri, 8am-2pm Sat & Sun; 🌶; 🚌2, 3, 27, 38) 🍃 A ray of sunshine in the concrete heart of the city, this plucky little storefront showcases seasonal California organics in just-baked

breakfasts and farmstead-fresh lunches. Daily specials include a rotation of homemade cereals, zesty tuna melts and game-changing toast – mmmm, ginger peach and fresh mascarpone on whole-wheat sourdough! Tiny space, but immaculate kitchen and locally roasted espresso drinks.

Saigon Sandwich Shop VIETNAMESE **$**
(Map p78; ☎415-474-5698; 560 Larkin St; sandwiches $4-5; ⏲7am-5:30pm; 🚌19, 31) Don't get distracted by Tenderloin street scenes while you wait – be ready to order your banh mi (Vietnamese sandwiches) when the Saigon boss ladies call 'Next!' or you'll get skipped. Act fast and be rewarded with a baguette piled high with your choice of roast pork, chicken, pâté, meatballs or tofu, plus pickled carrots, cilantro, jalapeño and thinly sliced onion.

★**Liholiho Yacht Club** HAWAIIAN, CALIFORNIAN **$$**
(Map p78; ☎415-440-5446; http://lycsf.com; 871 Sutter St; dishes $11-37; ⏲5-10:30pm Mon-Thu, to 11pm Fri & Sat; 🚌2, 3, 27, 38, 🚋California) Who needs yachts to be happy? Aloha comes naturally with Liholiho's pucker-up-tart cocktails and gleefully creative dishes – surefire mood enhancers include spicy beef-tongue *bao,* duck-liver mousse with pickled pineapple on brioche, and Vietnamese slaw with tender squid and crispy tripe. Reservations are tough; arrive early/late for bar dining, or head downstairs to Louie's Gen-Gen Room speakeasy for blissfully indulgent bone-marrow-butter waffles.

Cotogna ITALIAN **$$**
(Map p84; ☎415-775-8508; www.cotognasf.com; 490 Pacific Ave; mains $19-38; ⏲11:30am-10:30pm Mon-Thu, to 11pm Fri & Sat, 5-9:30pm Sun; 🌶; 🚌10, 12) Chef-owner Michael Tusk racks up James Beard Awards for gracefully performing a tricky Italian balancing act: he strikes ideal proportions among a few pristine flavors in rustic pastas, wood-fired pizzas and salt-crusted branzino. Reserve, especially for bargain $69 multicourse Sunday suppers with $35 wine pairings – or plan a walk-in late lunch/early dinner. Top-value Italian wine list (bottles from $50).

★**Boulevard** CALIFORNIAN **$$$**
(Map p78; ☎415-543-6084; www.boulevardrestaurant.com; 1 Mission St; mains lunch $16-30, dinner $29-54; ⏲11:30am-2pm & 5:30-9:30pm Mon-Thu, to 10pm Fri, 5:30-10pm Sat, 5:30-9:30pm Sun; Ⓜ Embarcadero, Ⓑ Embarcadero) The 1889 belle-epoque Audiffred Building once housed the Coast Seamen's Union, but James Beard Award–winning chef Nancy Oakes made it a culinary landmark. Dates and deals are made over reliably tasty, effortlessly elegant dishes, like juicy wood-oven-roasted Berkshire pork chops, crisp California quail, and wild halibut with scallop-prawn dumplings – plus decadent, nostalgia-inducing cakes and SF's best service.

North Beach & Chinatown

★**Golden Boy** PIZZA **$**
(Map p84; ☎415-982-9738; www.goldenboypizza.com; 542 Green St; slices $3.25-4.25; ⏲11:30am-midnight Sun-Thu, to 2am Fri & Sat; 🚌8, 30, 39, 41, 45, 🚋Powell-Mason) 'If you don't see it don't ask 4 it' reads the menu – Golden Boy has kept punks in line since 1978, serving Genovese focaccia-crust pizza that's chewy, crunchy and hot from the oven. You'll have whatever second-generation Sodini family *pizzaioli* (pizza-makers) are making and like it – especially pesto and clam-and-garlic. Grab square slices and draft beer at the bomb-shelter counter and boom: you're golden.

★**Good Mong Kok** DIM SUM **$**
(Map p84; ☎415-397-2688; 1039 Stockton St; dumpling orders $2-5; ⏲7am-6pm; 🚌30, 45, 🚋Powell-Mason, California, ⓂT) Ask Chinatown neighbors about their go-to dim sum and the answer is either grandma's or Good Mong Kok. Join the line outside this counter bakery for dumplings whisked from vast steamers into takeout containers to enjoy in Portsmouth Sq. The menu changes by the minute/hour, but expect classic pork *siu mai,* shrimp *har gow* and BBQ pork buns; BYO chili sauce and black vinegar.

★**Liguria Bakery** BAKERY **$**
(Map p84; ☎415-421-3786; 1700 Stockton St; focaccia $4-6; ⏲8am-2pm Tue-Fri, from 7am Sat, 7am-noon Sun; 🌶👪; 🚌8, 30, 39, 41, 45, 🚋Powell-Mason, ⓂT) Bleary-eyed art students and Italian grandmothers line up by 8am for cinnamon-raisin focaccia hot out of the 100-year-old oven, leaving 9am dawdlers a choice of tomato or classic rosemary and garlic. Latecomers, beware: when they run out, they close. Get yours in waxed paper or boxed for picnics – just don't kid yourself that you'll save some for later. Cash only.

Molinari DELI **$**
(Map p84; ☎415-421-2337; www.molinarisalame.com; 373 Columbus Ave; sandwiches $11-14.50; ⏲9am-6pm Mon-Fri, to 5:30pm Sat; 🚌8, 10, 12, 30,

39, 41, 45, Powell-Mason, T) Observe this quasi-religious North Beach noon ritual: enter Molinari and grab a number. When your number's called, let wisecracking staff pile a crusty roll or focaccia with heavenly fixings: milky buffalo mozzarella, tangy sun-dried tomatoes, translucent sheets of prosciutto di Parma, slabs of legendary house-cured salami, drizzles of olive oil and balsamic. Enjoy hot from the panini press at sidewalk tables.

Z & Y SICHUAN **$**

(Map p84; 415-981-8988; www.zandyrestaurant.com; 655 Jackson St; mains $9-20; 11am-9:30pm Sun-Thu, to 10:30pm Fri & Sat; 8, 10, 12, 30, 45, Powell-Mason, Powell-Hyde, T) Graduate from ho-hum sweet-and-sour and middling *mu shu* to sensational Sichuan dishes that go down in a blaze of glory. Warm up with spicy pork dumplings and heat-blistered string beans, take on the housemade *tantan* noodles with peanut-chili sauce, and leave lips buzzing with fish poached in flaming chili oil and buried under red Szechuan chili peppers. Go early; worth the inevitable wait.

Mister Jiu's CHINESE, CALIFORNIAN **$$**

(Map p84; 415-857-9688; http://misterjius.com; 28 Waverly Pl; mains $14-45; 5:30-10:30pm Tue-Sat; 30, California, T) Success has been celebrated in this historic Chinatown banquet hall since the 1880s – but today, scoring a table is reason enough for celebration. Build memorable banquets from chef Brandon Jew's ingenious Chinese–Californian signatures: quail and Mission-fig sticky rice, hot and sour Dungeness crab soup, Wagyu sirloin and tuna-heart fried rice. Don't skip dessert – pastry chef Melissa Chou's salted plum sesame balls are flavor bombs.

The Marina, Fisherman's Wharf & the Piers

★Kaiyo JAPANESE, PERUVIAN **$$**

(Map p88; 415-525-4804; https://kaiyosf.com; 1838 Union St; small plates $12-28, share plates $19-28; 5-10pm Tue, Wed & Sun, to 11pm Thu & Sat, 10:30am-3pm Sat & Sun; 41, 45) Fusion is more fun at this Nikkei (Japanese-Peruvian) bistro, where Pisco and whiskey cocktails are named for anime characters and neon-green moss streaks like lightning across the dining-room wall. But the real adventure here is the menu, featuring such daring feats of Pacific Rim fusion as smoked duck-breast sashimi, Hokkaido scallop *tiradito*, and *cusquena*-brined, organic Sonoma chicken.

Greens VEGETARIAN, CALIFORNIAN **$$**

(Map p88; 415-771-6222; www.facebook.com/greensrestaurant; 2 Marina Blvd, Bldg A, Fort Mason Center; mains $18-28; 5:30-9pm Mon, 11:30am-2:30pm & 5:30-9pm Tue-Thu, 11:30am-2:30pm & 5-9pm Fri, 10:30am-2:30pm & 5-9pm Sat & Sun; 22, 28, 30, 43, 47, 49) Career carnivores won't realize there's zero meat in the hearty black-bean chili or the other flavor-packed vegetarian dishes – all made using ingredients from a Zen farm in Marin. The on-site cafe serves to-go lunches, and light bites are served on reclaimed-redwood-stump tables – but book ahead for stellar weekend brunches with breathtaking Golden Gate Bridge views in the window-lined dining room.

★Atelier Crenn FRENCH **$$$**

(Map p88; 415-440-0460; www.ateliercrenn.com; 3127 Fillmore St; tasting menu $335; 5-9pm Tue-Sat; 22, 28, 30, 43) The menu arrives in the form of a poem, with white chocolate spheres containing a burst of apple cider – followed by geoduck rice tart in a liquid nitrogen-frosted glass dome, and a dozen more daydream-worthy dishes inspired by the Brittany childhood of James Beard Award–winning, triple Michelin-starred chef Dominique Crenn. Book two months ahead; see website for reservation details.

Nob Hill, Russian Hill & Japantown

★Benkyodo JAPANESE **$**

(Map p88; 415-922-1244; www.benkyodocompany.com; 1747 Buchanan St; mochi $1.50; 8am-5pm Tue-Fri, to 4pm Sat; 2, 3, 22, 38) Since 1906, family-owned Benkyodo has survived earthquakes, world wars, even Japanese American internment – and still the Okamura family keeps making life sweeter each day with handmade mochi and *manju* (rice-based confections). Every morning, rice is pounded into pillowy, chewy wrappers that envelop seasonal fillings – fragrant mango, crowd-pleasing peanut butter and best of all, velvety red bean. Cash only.

Hot Sauce and Panko CHICKEN **$**

(Map p78; 415-359-1908; http://hotsauceandpanko.com; 1468 Hyde St; wings $7-11; 11:30am-7pm Wed-Sat, to 5pm Sun; Powell-Hyde) What's for lunch? Just wing it at Hot Sauce and Panko, an obsessive hilltop corner store stocking hundreds of versions of two namesake items, plus 30 (!) variations on chicken wings.

THE FERRY BUILDING

San Francisco's monument to food, the Ferry Building (p81) still doubles as a trans-bay transit hub – but with dining options like these, you may never leave.

Ferry Plaza Farmers Market (Map p78; 415-291-3276; www.cuesa.org; cnr Market St & the Embarcadero; street food $3-12; 10am-2pm Tue & Thu, from 8am Sat; ; 2, 6, 9, 14, 21, 31, M Embarcadero, B Embarcadero) The pride and joy of SF foodies, the Ferry Building market showcases more than 100 prime purveyors of California-grown organic produce, pasture-raised meats and gourmet prepared foods at accessible prices. On Saturdays, join top chefs early for prime browsing, and stay for eclectic bayside picnics of Namu Korean tacos, Dirty Girl tomatoes, Nicasio cheese samples and Frog Hollow fruit turnovers.

Boulette's Larder & Boulibar (Map p78; 415-399-1155; www.boulettesIarder.com; 1 Ferry Bldg, cnr Market St & the Embarcadero; mains $18-24; Larder 8-10:30am & 11:30am-3pm Tue-Sat, 10am-2:30pm Sun, Boulibar 11:30am-3pm & 6-9:30pm Tue-Fri, 11:30am-3pm & 4:30-8pm Sat; M Embarcadero, B Embarcadero) Dinner theater can't beat brunch at Boulette's communal table, strategically placed inside a working kitchen amid a swirl of chefs with views of the Bay Bridge. At adjoining Boulibar, get tangy Middle Eastern mezze platters, beautifully blistered wood-fired pizzas and flatbreads at indoor picnic-style tables – perfect for people-watching, despite sometimes rushed service. Get inspiration to go with Larder spice mixes.

Hog Island Oyster Company (Map p78; 415-391-7117; www.hogislandoysters.com; 1 Ferry Bldg, cnr Market St & the Embarcadero; 6 oysters $19-21; 11am-9pm; 2, 6, 9, 14, 21, 31, M Embarcadero, B Embarcadero) Slurp the bounty of the North Bay with East Bay views at this local, sustainable oyster bar. Get them raw, grilled with chipotle-bourbon butter, or Rockefeller (cooked with spinach, Pernod and cream). Not the cheapest oysters in town, but consistently the best, with excellent local wines – hence the waits for seating. Stop by Hog Island's farmers-market stall 8am to 2pm Saturday.

House hot sauce gives a sensational slow burn and lime-chili fish sauce is a flavor bomb – but housemade *gochujang* (fermented-chili sauce) will have you licking your lips for hours afterwards.

Marufuku Ramen RAMEN $

(Map p88; 415-872-9786; www.marufukuramen.com; 1581 Webster St, Suite 235, Japan Center, West Wing, 2nd fl; ramen $13-17; 11:30am-2:30pm & 5:30-10pm Mon-Fri, 11:30am-10pm Sat-Sun; 22,38) No Silicon Valley technology excites as much local geekery as a bowl of Marufuku ramen. Its advantages are much discussed: *tonkotsu* broth cooked for 20 hours to achieve milky density, noodles handcut ultrathin to avoid clumping, topped with egg that's soft-cooked, never hard-boiled. Here's all you need to know: rich, slurp-worthy noodles. Save some broth and get extra noodles for $2.50.

★Swan Oyster Depot SEAFOOD $$

(Map p78; 415-673-1101; https://swanoysterdepot.us; 1517 Polk St; dishes $10-28; 10:30am-5:30pm Mon-Sat; 1, 19, 47, 49, California) Seafood fresh enough to impress sailors since 1912. First-timers get oysters mignonette and Dungeness salads with crab-fat vinaigrette, regulars order secret-menu specials – try 'dozen eggs' (scallop sashimi in ponzu puddles) or 'crabsanthemum' (leg-only crab Louie). Arrive before 11am or strike up conversations over hour-long waits for counter stools. Introverts, get your 'salad-sandwich combo' (hollowed-out sourdough crab salad) to go. Cash only.

★Nari THAI $$

(415-868-6274; www.narisf.com; 1625 Post St; mains $14-47; 5:30-10pm) 'Breathe through it,' the server recommends – which might not seem like a promising dinner omen. But it's excellent advice for enjoying *kapi plah,* challengingly pungent fermented shrimp paste with just enough Meyer-lemon sass to achieve acquired-taste status. Crowd-pleasing regional Thai curries delight between intriguingly sweet oysters with water-beetle mignonette and unabashedly charred fish-sauce cabbage. Nari is SF's best dare.

Sasa JAPANESE $$

(Map p88; 415-683-9674; www.sasasf.com; 22 Peace Plaza, Japan Center, East Wing, 2nd fl; 6-10 small plates $25-60, individual plates $5-18;

⌚noon-2:30pm & 5:30-9:30pm Tue-Sun; 🚌22,38) Settle into driftwood-strewn decor for a *kaiseki* (seasonally inspired tasting menu) as exciting as any San Francisco parade. Delight arrives in unexpected details: katsu made with *kurobuta* pork, silken organic *chawanmushi* (egg custard) studded with Dungeness crab, and thoughtfully sourced Santa Barbara sea urchin and Hokkaido scallop *nigiri*. Never has the 2nd floor of a mall seemed this close to heaven.

State Bird Provisions CALIFORNIAN $$

(Map p88; ☎415-795-1272; http://statebirdsf.com; 1529 Fillmore St; dishes $8-30; ⌚5:30-10pm Sun-Thu, to 11pm Fri & Sat; 🚌22, 38) 🌿 Even before winning multiple James Beard Awards, State Bird attracted lines not seen since the Dead played neighboring Fillmore Auditorium (p113). Carts arrive tableside laden with California-inspired, dim-sum-sized 'provisions' like jerk octopus and pastrami pancakes. Progress to larger but equally esoteric seasonal signatures, from kimchi spiced Dungeness crab with bottarga to parmesan-feathered quail atop slow-cooked onions. Book ahead or line up before 5pm for walk-ins.

★Acquerello CALIFORNIAN, ITALIAN $$$

(Map p78; ☎415-567-5432; www.acquerello.com; 1722 Sacramento St; 3-/4-/5-course menu $105/130/150; ⌚5:30-9:30pm Tue-Thu, to 10pm Fri & Sat; 🚌1, 19, 47, 49, 🚋California) A converted chapel is a fitting location for feasts that turn Italian culinary purists into true believers in Cal-Italian cuisine. Chef Suzette Gresham's ingenious handmade pastas and seasonal signatures include heavenly abalone risotto, devilish lamb with sweetbreads, and truffled squab cannelloni. An anteroom where brides once steadied their nerves is lined with limited production Italian vintages seldom seen outside Tuscan castles.

The Haight & Hayes Valley

★RT Rotisserie CALIFORNIAN $

(Map p78; www.rtrotisserie.com; 101 Oak St; dishes $9-14; ⌚11am-9pm; 🥗👶; 🚌5, 6, 7, 21, 47, 49, Ⓜ Van Ness) 🌿 An all-star menu makes ordering mains easy – you'll find bliss with entire chickens hot off the spit, succulent lamb and pickled onions, or surprisingly decadent roast cauliflower with earthy beet tahini sauce – but do you choose porcini-powdered fries or signature salad with that? A counter staffer calls it: 'Look, I don't normally go for salads, but this one's next-level.' So true. No reservations.

Brenda's Meat & Three SOUTHERN US $

(☎415-926-8657; http://brendasmeatandthree.com; 919 Divisadero St; mains $9-20; ⌚8am-10pm Wed-Mon; 🚌5, 21, 24, 38) Southerners know the name promises one meaty main course plus three sides – though only superheroes finish ham steak with Creole red-eye gravy and exemplary grits, let alone cream biscuits and eggs. Chef Brenda Buenviaje's portions are defiantly Southern, which explains brunch lines of marathoners and partiers who forgot to eat last night. Arrive early, share sweet-potato pancakes, and pray for crawfish specials.

Souvla GREEK $

(Map p94; ☎415-400-5458; www.souvlasf.com; 517 Hayes St; sandwiches & salads $12-15; ⌚11am-10pm; 🚌5, 21, 47, 49, Ⓜ Van Ness) Ancient Greek philosophers didn't think too hard about lunch, and neither should you at Souvla. Step in line for no-fail choices: signature spit-fired lamb atop kale with yogurt dressing, or organic chicken with pickled onion, *mizithra* cheese and sweet potatoes. Go early/late for skylit communal seating, or head to Patricia's Green park with takeout. Additional locations citywide, including 531 Divisadero; see website.

★Rich Table CALIFORNIAN $$

(Map p78; ☎415-355-9085; http://richtablesf.com; 199 Gough St; mains $17-37; ⌚5:30-10pm Sun-Thu, to 10:30pm Fri & Sat; 🚌5, 6, 7, 21, 47, 49, Ⓜ Van Ness) 🌿 Impossible cravings begin with mind-blowing inventions like porcini doughnuts, sardine chips, and burrata funnel cake. Join married co-chefs/owners Sarah and Evan Rich for the world's friendliest culinary competition – Sarah's Southern roots shine in biscuits with chicken-liver mousse and fried chicken skin, while Evan jet-sets from Tokyo to Rome with *cacio e pepe* pasta. For maximum surprise, get the chef's menu ($99).

The Castro

Beit Rima MIDDLE EASTERN $

(Map p94; ☎415-710-2397; www.beitrimasf.com; 138 Church St; small plates $8-12; ⌚11am-8:30pm; 🥗👶; 🚌22, Ⓜ J, K, L, M, N) Bond over meze inspired by chef-owner Samir Mogannam's mom, plus stints at the bay's top Mediterranean restaurants. Hummus traditionalists and root-vegetable radicals kiss and make up over Samir's classic version, with just enough

SAN FRANCISCO TREATS

Life is sweet in San Francisco, where chocolate bars were invented in the Gold Rush and velvet ropes keep ice-cream lines from getting ugly. Before you dismiss dessert, consider these Mission District temptations.

Craftsman & Wolves (Map p94; ☎415-913-7713; http://craftsman-wolves.com; 746 Valencia St; pastries $3-16; ⏰6am-5pm Mon-Fri, from 8am Sat & Sun; 🚌14, 22, 33, 49, Ⓑ16th St Mission, ⓂJ) Breakfast rules are made to be broken by the Rebel Within: a sausage-spiked Asiago-cheese muffin with a silken soft-boiled egg baked inside. SF's surest pick-me-up is a Bellwether latte with matcha (green tea) cookies, but gorgeous pastries are their own occasion – yuzu coconut cakes are ideal for non-birthdays, while imaginary holidays require hazelnut mousse and passion fruit atop sesame praline.

Humphry Slocombe (Map p94; ☎415-550-6971; www.humphryslocombe.com; 2790 Harrison St; ice creams $4-7; ⏰1-11pm Mon-Fri, from noon Sat & Sun; 🚌12, 14, 49, Ⓑ24th St Mission) Indie-rock organic ice cream may permanently spoil you for Top 40 flavors. Once 'Elvis: The Fat Years' (banana and peanut butter) and 'Hibiscus Beet Sorbet' have rocked your taste buds, cookie dough seems basic. Ordinary sundaes can't compare to 'Secret Breakfast' (bourbon and cornflakes) and 'Blue Bottle Vietnamese Coffee' drizzled with hot fudge, California olive oil and sea salt.

Mitchell's Ice Cream (☎415-648-2300; www.mitchellsicecream.com; 688 San Jose Ave; ice creams $4-9; ⏰11am-11pm; 🚌14, 49, Ⓑ24th St Mission, ⓂJ) When you see happy dances break out on Mission sidewalks, you must be getting close to Mitchell's. One glance at the menu induces gleeful gluttony: classic Kahlua mocha cream, exotic tropical *macapuno* (young coconut)…or both?! Avocado and *ube* (purple yam) are acquired tastes, but they've been local favorites for generations – Mitchell's has kept fans coming back for seconds since 1953.

lemon to make you pucker up – kibbe-style spiced beef optional. Palestinian lager pairs with garlicky *ful* (fava dip), juicy, smokey *shish taouk* (grilled chicken) and nutty, tangy *muhamarra* (almond/pepper spread).

Starbelly CALIFORNIAN, PIZZA **$$**
(Map p94; ☎415-252-7500; https://starbellysf.com; 3583 16th St; dishes $8-25; ⏰11:30am-3:30pm & 5-11pm Mon-Thu, to midnight Fri, 10am-3:30pm & 5pm-midnight Sat, to 11pm Sun; 🍷👶; ⓂCastro St) 🌿 All the sun-drenched flavors you'd expect from California, at totally chill prices. The Castro farmers market is across the street, and you can taste it in Starbelly's sustainably sourced, market-fresh salads, seasonal dumplings, and thin-crust pizzas with cave-aged Gruyère and wild local mushrooms. Salami is house-cured and Prather Ranch burgers are the Castro's best. For quiet conversation, request patio seating.

The Mission

★Reem's BAKERY, MIDDLE EASTERN **$**
(www.reemscalifornia.com; 2901 Mission St; pastries $3.50-6, mains $12-18; ⏰11am-3pm & 4-7pm Tue-Fri) The best meal of your SF trip may be a meze (appetizer spread) at Reem's. Acclaimed Syrian-Palestinian chef Reem Assil opened her sustainable, Beirut-meets-SF bakery amid the coronavirus epidemic, and her to-go *sabanikh* (spinach and onion turnover), *musakhan* (baked sumac chicken) and *baba ghanouj* (eggplant dip) with just-baked *khobz* (pita) sustained the neighborhood. Save room for urban-legendary *knafeh* (cheese pastry with rosewater syrup).

★La Palma Mexicatessen MEXICAN **$**
(Map p94; ☎415-647-1500; www.lapalmasf.com; 2884 24th St; tamales, tacos & huaraches $3-10; ⏰8am-6pm Mon-Sat, to 5pm Sun; 🍷; 🚌12, 14, 27, 48, Ⓑ24th St Mission) 🌿 Follow the applause: that's the clapping sound of organic tortilla-making in progress. You've found the Mission mother lode of handmade tamales, *huaraches* (stuffed masa), and *pupusas* (tortilla pockets) with potato and *chicharones* (pork crackling), *carnitas* (slow-roasted pork), *cotija* (Oaxacan cheese) and La Palma's own tangy tomatillo sauce. Get takeout or bring a small army to finish feasts at sunny sidewalk tables.

La Taqueria MEXICAN **$**
(Map p94; ☎415-285-7117; www.facebook.com/LaTaqSF; 2889 Mission St; burritos $3-11; ⏰11am-

8:45pm Mon-Sat, to 7:45pm Sun; ; 12, 14, 48, 49, B 24th St Mission) SF's definitive burrito has no saffron rice, spinach tortilla or mango salsa – just perfectly grilled meats, slow-cooked beans and tomatillo or mesquite salsa in a flour tortilla. You'll pay extra to skip the beans at James Beard Award–winning La Taqueria, because they add more meat. For total burrito bliss, add spicy pickles and *crema* (sour cream). Worth the wait, always.

★Al's Place CALIFORNIAN **$$**
(415-416-6136; www.alsplacesf.com; 1499 Valencia St; share plates $15-21; 5:30-10pm Wed-Sun; ; 12, 14, 49, M J, B 24th St Mission) The Golden State dazzles on Al's plates, featuring heirloom ingredients, pristine Pacific seafood, and meadow-fed meat. Painstaking preparation yields sun-drenched flavors and exquisite textures: goat's-milk curd grits with chanterelles, crispy-skin cod with preserved-lime froth. Dishes are half the size but thrice the flavor of mains elsewhere – get three or the family-style menu (five courses $73), and you'll be California dreaming.

Tartine Manufactory CALIFORNIAN **$$**
(Map p94; 415-757-0007; www.tartinemanufactory.com; 595 Alabama St; mains $16-38; 8am-10pm; ; 12, 22, 27, 33) What began as a bakehouse has become a powerhouse of artisan foods, in a converted factory so awash in sunshine and good vibes, it seems Instagram-filtered. Join the line for specialty coffee drinks and grab-and-go pastry at indoor picnic tables – or reserve ahead for sit-down smørrebrød brunches, roasted-lamb flatbread lunches, and five-spiced duck dinners, plus wine pairings or craft cocktails.

Farmhouse Kitchen Thai Cuisine THAI **$$**
(Map p94; 415-814-2920; www.farmhousethai.com; 710 Florida St; share plates $10-24; 11am-2pm & 5-10pm Mon-Thu, to 10:30pm Fri, noon-10:30pm Sat, to 10pm Sun; ; 22, 27) California farm-to-table gets Thai street smarts in this warehouse restaurant showcasing organic local ingredients and regional Thai street-food inspirations. Skewered Sonoma BBQ chicken marinated in fresh turmeric packs a savory punch, but spicy eggplant with blue rice teaches your taste buds Thai kickboxing. Pricey for lunch, but worth it – embrace the decadence with local wines and croissant-bread pudding.

Namu Stonepot KOREAN **$$**
(Map p94; 415-431-6268; www.namusf.com; 499 Dolores St; share plates $10-21; 5:30-10pm Tue, 11:30am-3pm & 5:30-10pm Wed-Fri, 10:30am-4pm & 5-10pm Sat & Sun; 14, 22, 33, 49, M J, B 16th St Mission) SF's unfair culinary advantages – organic local ingredients, Pacific Rim roots and street-skater, try-anything attitude – are showcased in Namu's Korean-inspired soul food. Bold flavors abound in ultrasavory shiitake-mushroom dumplings, meltingly tender lamb meatballs and Namu's version of bibimbap: Wagyu beef, organic vegetables, kimchi, spicy *gochujang* (fermented chili sauce) and farm egg atop *koshihikari* rice, served sizzling in a stone pot.

★Mr Pollo INTERNATIONAL **$$$**
(Map p94; 2823 Mission St; 4-course tasting menu $35; 6-10pm Mon-Sat; 12, 14, 48, 49, B 24th St Mission) Travel the world taste buds first at one of six tables squeezed into this hole-in-the-wall restaurant. Mr Pollo dishes up four-course seasonal meals inspired by the chef's travels, including meat dishes and arepas (honoring the namesake Colombian restaurant that was once here). No substitutions or vegetarian alternatives, but excellent wine and beer pairings. Make reservations through Yelp a month in advance.

Foreign Cinema CALIFORNIAN **$$$**
(Map p94; 415-648-7600; www.foreigncinema.com; 2534 Mission St; mains $28-36; 5:30-10pm Sun-Wed, to 11pm Thu-Sat, brunch 11am-2:30pm Sat & Sun; 12, 14, 33, 48, 49, B 24th St Mission) Chef Gayle Pirie's acclaimed California classics are the star attractions here, including grilled Monterey calamari and crisp sesame fried chicken – but subtitled films by Luis Buñuel and François Truffaut screening in the courtyard are mighty handy when conversation lags with first dates or business colleagues. Get the red-carpet treatment with valet parking ($15) and a well-stocked oyster bar.

Golden Gate Park & the Avenues

★Dragon Beaux DIM SUM **$**
(Map p110; 415-333-8899; www.dragonbeaux.com; 5700 Geary Blvd; dumplings $5-9; 11am-2:30pm & 5:30-9:45pm Mon-Fri, 10am-3pm & 5:30-9:45pm Sat & Sun; 2, 38) Hong Kong meets Vegas at SF's most glamorous, decadent Cantonese restaurant. Say yes to cartloads of succulent roast meats – hello, duck and pork belly – and creative dumplings, especially XO dumplings with plump, brandy-laced shrimp in spinach wrappers. Expect premium teas, sharp service and impeccable Cantonese

The Richmond, The Haight & Golden Gate Park

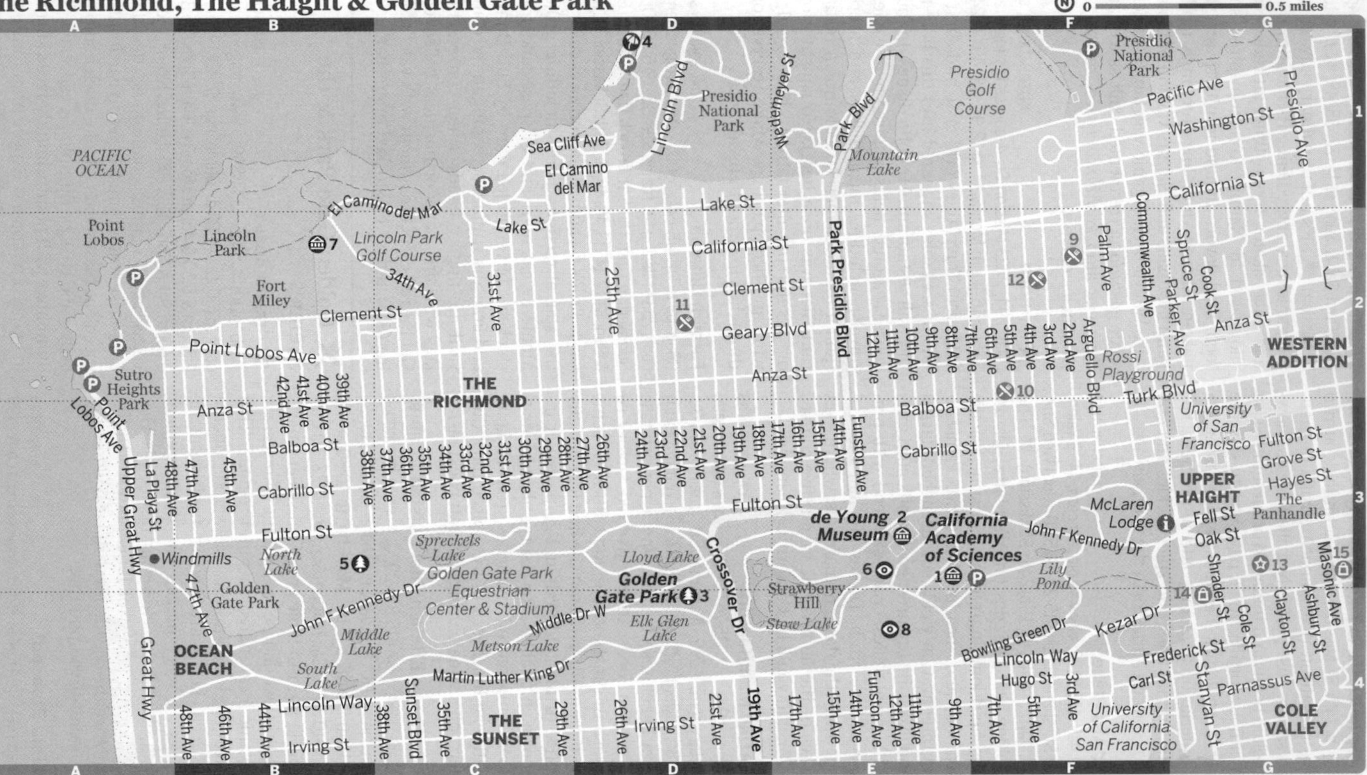

The Richmond, The Haight & Golden Gate Park

standards, including Chinese doughnuts, *har gow* (shrimp dumplings) and Chinese broccoli in housemade oyster sauce.

Arsicault Bakery BAKERY $
(Map p110; 415-750-9460; https://arsicault-bakery.com; 397 Arguello Blvd; pastries $3-7; 7am-2:30pm Mon-Fri, to 3:30pm Sat & Sun; 1, 2, 33, 38, 44) Armando Lacayo left his job in finance because – like his Parisian grandparents before him – he was obsessed with croissants. After perfecting his technique, Lacayo opened a modest bakery in the Inner Richmond. Within a year, *Bon Appétit* magazine declared it the best new bakery in America. Go early: his golden, flaky, buttery croissants regularly sell out.

Cinderella Russian Bakery RUSSIAN $
(Map p110; 415-751-6723; www.cinderellabakery.com; 436 Balboa St; pastries $1.50-3.50, mains $7-14; 7am-7pm; 5, 21, 31, 33) Fog banks and cold wars are no match for the heartwarming powers of the Cinderella, serving traditional Russian treats since 1953. Join SF's Russian community in Cinderella's parklet near Golden Gate Park for scrumptious, just-baked egg-and-green-onion piroshki, hearty borscht and decadent dumplings – all at neighborly prices.

★ **Wako** JAPANESE $$$
(Map p110; 415-682-4875; www.sushiwakosf.com; 211 Clement St; 9-course menu $135; 5:30-10pm Tue-Sat; 1, 2, 33, 38, 44) Chef-owner Tomoharu Nakamura's driftwood-paneled bistro is as quintessentially San Franciscan as the landmark bonsai grove at nearby Japanese Tea Garden (p91). Each *omakase* (chef's choice) dish is a miniature marvel of Japanese seafood with a California accent – Santa Cruz abalone *nigiri,* seared tuna belly with California caviar, steamed crab *mushimono* with yuzu grown by a neighbor. *Domo arigato,* dude.

Drinking & Nightlife

No matter what you're having, SF bars, cafes and clubs are here to oblige, serving up California wines, Bay spirits and local roasts. Adventurous drinking is abetted by local bartenders, who continue gold-rush saloon traditions with potent drinks in deceptively delicate vintage glasses. Craft is a given: bartenders brew their own bitters, SF baristas take their micro-roasts seriously, and local DJs invent their own software.

North Beach & Chinatown

★ **Specs** BAR
(Specs Twelve Adler Museum Cafe; Map p84; 415-421-4112; www.facebook.com/specsbarsf; 12 William Saroyan Pl; 5pm-2am Mon-Fri; 8, 10, 12, 30, 41, 45, Powell-Mason, M T) The walls here are plastered with merchant-marine memorabilia, and you'll be plastered too if you try to keep up with the salty characters holding court in the back. Surrounded by seafaring mementos – including a massive walrus organ over the bar – your order seems obvious: pitcher of Anchor Steam, coming right up. Cash only.

★ **Caffe Trieste** CAFE
(Map p84; 415-392-6739; www.caffetrieste.com; 601 Vallejo St; 6:30am-10pm Sun-Thu, to 11pm Fri & Sat; ; 8, 10, 12, 30, 41, 45, M T) Opera on the jukebox, live accordion jams and Beat poetry on bathroom walls: Caffe Trieste remains North Beach at its best, since the 1950s. Linger over espresso drinks and scribble your screenplay under the Sardinian fishing mural just as young Francis Ford Coppola did. Perhaps you've heard of the movie: *The Godfather*. Cash only.

Vesuvio BAR

(Map p84; ☎415-362-3370; www.vesuvio.com; 255 Columbus Ave; ⏰8am-2am; 🚌8, 10, 12, 30, 41, 45, 🚋Powell-Mason) Guy walks into a bar, roars and leaves. Without missing a beat, the bartender says to the next customer, 'Welcome to Vesuvio, honey – what can I get you?' Jack Kerouac blew off Henry Miller to go on a bender here and, after you've joined neighborhood characters on the stained-glass mezzanine for 8pm microbrews or 8am Kerouacs (rum, tequila and OJ), you'll see why.

The Marina, Fisherman's Wharf & the Piers

★**Interval Bar & Cafe** BAR

(Map p88; www.theinterval.org; 2 Marina Blvd, Fort Mason Center, Bldg A; ⏰10am-midnight; 🚌10, 22, 28, 30, 47, 49) Lose track of time over aged Tom Collins or freshly roasted coffee at the Interval, specifically designed to stimulate philosophical discussion. The bar-cafe doubles as HQ for nonprofit Long Now Foundation, dedicated to long-term thinking – hence Brian Eno's fourth-dimensional digital artwork over the bar, the interdisciplinary library overhead, and the sculptural prototype of a 10,000-year clock.

Buena Vista Cafe BAR

(Map p88; ☎415-474-5044; www.thebuenavista.com; 2765 Hyde St; ⏰9am-2am Mon-Fri, from 8am Sat & Sun; 📶; 🚌30, 45, 47, 🚋Powell-Hyde) Warm your cockles with a prim little goblet of bitter-creamy Irish coffee, introduced to America at this destination bar that once served sailors and cannery workers. That old Victorian floor creaks under carousers and families alike, served community-style at round tables overlooking the cable-car turnaround at Victoria Park.

Nob Hill, Russian Hill & Japantown

★**Stookey's Club Moderne** LOUNGE

(Map p78; www.stookeysclubmoderne.com; 895 Bush St; ⏰4:30pm-2am; 🚌1, 🚋Powell-Hyde, Powell-Mason, California) Dangerous dames lure unsuspecting sailors into late-night schemes over potent hooch at this art-deco bar straight out of a Dashiell Hammett thriller. Chrome-lined 1930s Streamline Moderne decor sets the scene for intrigue, and wisecracking white-jacketed bartenders shake the stiffest Corpse Reviver cocktails in town. Arrive early to find room on the hat rack for your fedora, especially on live jazz nights.

The Haight & Hayes Valley

★**Toronado** PUB

(Map p94; ☎415-863-2276; www.toronado.com; 547 Haight St; ⏰11:30am-2am; 🚌6, 7, 22, Ⓜ N) Glory hallelujah, beer-lovers: your prayers are answered. Genuflect before the chalkboard altar that lists 40-plus beers on tap and hundreds more bottled, including sensational seasonal microbrews. Bring cash and score sausages from the next-door grill to accompany ale made by Trappist monks. Sometimes it gets too loud in here to hear your date talk, but you'll hear angels sing.

Madrone Art Bar BAR

(☎415-241-0202; www.madroneartbar.com; 500 Divisadero St; cover free-$5; ⏰4pm-2am Tue-Sat, 3pm-1:30am Sun; 🚌5, 6, 7, 21, 24) Drinking becomes an art form at this Victorian parlor crammed with graffiti installations and absinthe fountains. Daily 4pm-to-7pm happy hours bring $1 off well drinks, including mules – but nothing beats monthly Prince/Michael Jackson throwdown dance parties fueled by Madronis (gin, Campari, Carpano). Performers redefine genres: punk-grass (bluegrass/punk), blunt-funk (reggae/soul) and church, no chaser (Sunday-morning jazz organ). Cash only.

The Castro

★**Twin Peaks Tavern** GAY

(Map p94; ☎415-864-9470; www.twinpeakstavern.com; 401 Castro St; ⏰noon-2am Mon-Fri, from 8am Sat & Sun; Ⓜ Castro St) The vintage rainbow neon sign points the way to a local landmark – Twin Peaks was the world's first gay bar with windows open to the street. If you're not here for the Castro's best people-watching, cozy up to the Victorian carved-wood bar for cocktails and conviviality, or grab a back booth to discuss movies at the Castro (p115) over wine by the glass.

440 Castro GAY

(Map p94; ☎415-621-8732; www.the440.com; 440 Castro St; ⏰noon-2am; 🚌24, 33, Ⓜ F, K, L, M) The most happening bar on the street, 440 draws bearded, gym-fit 30- and 40-something dudes – especially on scruffy Sundays and weekend nights, when go-go boys twirl – and an odd mix of Peter Pans for Monday's underwear night. If you think the monthly Battle of the Bulges contest has something to do with WWII, this is not your bar, honey.

Beaux GAY & LESBIAN
(Map p94; www.beauxsf.com; 2344 Market St; cover free-$5; 4pm-2am Mon-Fri, from noon Sat & Sun; 24, 33, M F, K, L, M) The candy store of Castro clubs, Beaux serves every gay flavor. Highlights include Club Papi Wednesdays, '90s–'00s Throwback Thursdays, go-go Manimal Fridays, and Nitty Gritty dirty disco Saturdays (find the mezzanine for best views over the floor). On Big Top Sundays, *Rupaul's Drag Race* stars emcee. Weekends are rainbow-spectrum and straight-but-questioning; arrive before 10pm to beat lines and cover.

Swirl WINE BAR
(Map p94; 415-864-2262; www.swirloncastro.com; 572 Castro St; 1:30-8pm Mon-Thu, to 9pm Fri, noon-9pm Sat, to 8pm Sun; 24, 33, F, M K, L, M) Come as you are – pinstripes or leather, gay, straight or whatever – to toast equality with sublime bubbly after GLBT History Museum (p92) visits, or find liquid courage for sing-alongs at the Castro Theatre (p115) in flights of bold reds. This wine shop with a bar in the back has universal appeal, with reliably delicious wine at fair prices in neighborly company.

The Mission

★Trick Dog BAR
(Map p94; 415-471-2999; www.trickdogbar.com; 3010 20th St; 3pm-2am; 12, 14, 49) Drink in SF inspiration with clever cocktails inspired by local obsessions like the Whole Earth Catalog, Mission muralists or Chinese horoscopes. Every six months, Trick Dog adopts a new theme and the menu changes – proof you can teach an old dog new tricks and improve on classics like the Manhattan. Arrive early for bar stools or hit the mood-lit loft for high-concept bar bites.

★Zeitgeist BAR
(Map p94; 415-255-7505; www.zeitgeistsf.com; 199 Valencia St; 11:30am-2am Mon-Fri, from 10:30am Sat & Sun; 14, 22, 49, B 16th St Mission) You've got two seconds flat to order from tough-gal barkeeps used to putting macho bikers in their place – but with 48 beers on draft, you're spoiled for choice. Epic afternoons unfold in the beer garden, with folks hanging out and smoking at long tables. SF's longest happy hour lasts 11:30am to 6pm weekdays. Cash only; no photos.

%ABV COCKTAIL BAR
(Map p94; 415-400-4748; www.abvsf.com; 3174 16th St; 2pm-2am; 14, 22, B 16th St Mission, M J) As kindred spirits deduce from the name (the abbreviation for 'percent alcohol by volume'), these cocktail crafters know their Rittenhouse rye from their Japanese malt whiskey. Top-notch hooch is served with zero pretension, including excellent Cali wine and beer, and original historically inspired cocktails like the Sutro Swizzle (Armagnac, grapefruit shrub, maraschino liqueur). Order tasty bar bites early, before the place packs.

☆ Entertainment

Live Music

★SFJAZZ Center JAZZ
(Map p78; 866-920-5299; www.sfjazz.org; 201 Franklin St; tickets $25-120; ; 5, 6, 7, 21, 47, 49, M Van Ness) Jazz legends and singular talents from Argentina to Yemen are showcased at America's largest jazz center. Hear fresh takes on classic jazz albums and poets riffing with jazz combos in downstairs Joe Henderson Lab, and witness main-stage collaborations by Kid Koala and Del the Funky Homosapien, raucous all-women mariachis Flor de Toluache, and tap virtuoso Savion Glover improvising with a jazz trio.

★Fillmore Auditorium LIVE MUSIC
(Map p88; 415-346-6000; http://thefillmore.com; 1805 Geary Blvd; tickets from $20; box office 10am-3pm Sun, plus 30min before doors open to 10pm show nights; 22, 38) Jimi Hendrix, Janis Joplin, the Grateful Dead – they all played the Fillmore, and the upstairs bar is lined with vintage psychedelic posters to prove it. Bands that sell out stadiums keep rocking this historic, 1250-capacity dance hall, and for major shows, free posters are still handed out. To squeeze up to the stage, be polite and lead with the hip.

Bottom of the Hill LIVE MUSIC
(415-621-4455; www.bottomofthehill.com; 1233 17th St; tickets $5-20; shows generally 9pm Tue-Sat; 10, 19, 22) The bottom of Potrero Hill tops the list for rocking with punk legends the Avengers, Pansy Division and The Dills, and newcomers worth checking out for their names alone (Playboy Manbaby, Try the Pie, The Freak Accident). The patio is covered in handbills and ruled by a cat that prefers music to people – totally punk rock. Anchor Steam on tap; cash-only bar.

Great American Music Hall LIVE MUSIC
(Map p78; 415-885-0750; www.gamh.com; 859 O'Farrell St; tickets $20-45; box office noon-6pm Mon-Fri, 5pm-close on show nights; ; 19, 38, 47,

DON'T MISS

TICKETS TO SAN FRANCISCO'S NEXT BIG GAME

Sports fans, you're in luck: you've got 81 chances each year to see the San Francisco Giants play baseball on their home turf at the **Giants Stadium** (AT&T Park; Map p78; 415-972-2000, tours 415-972-2400; http://sanfrancisco.giants.mlb.com; 24 Willie Mays Plaza; tickets $14-349, stadium tour adult/senior/child $22/17/12; tour times vary; ; N, T) on their way to their next World Series win. Better yet: you might be able to catch some Giants action for free behind the park, on the Embarcadero waterfront boardwalk.

But wait, there's more: the Golden State Warriors play NBA basketball to win, and they've moved back to SF to hold court in their brand new stadium, Chase Center (www.chasecenter.com).

Football fans aren't quite so lucky. To see the **49ers** (415-656-4900; www.sf49ers.com; Levi's Stadium, Santa Clara; tickets $48-570; Caltrain Santa Clara Station) in action, you'd need to drive an hour south of SF to Santa Clara, where they now play in Levi's Stadium.

Tickets can be booked through team websites or Ticketmaster (www.ticketmaster.com). If games are sold out, search the 'Tickets' category on www.craigslist.org. The *San Francisco Chronicle* (www.sfgate.com) offers complete sports coverage, but *The Examiner* (www.sfexaminer.com) also has sports stats and predictions.

49) Everyone busts out their best sets at this opulent 1907 bordello turned all-ages venue – global sensations like Latin Grammy–winner Monsieur Periné fly in just for the night, Grateful Dead tribute acts pack the house with patchouli, and John Waters hosts Christmas extravaganzas. Pay $25 extra for dinner with prime balcony seating, or rock out with the standing-room scrum downstairs.

Classical Music & Dance

★San Francisco Symphony CLASSICAL MUSIC
(Map p78; box office 415-864-6000, rush-ticket hotline 415-503-5577; www.sfsymphony.org; Grove St, btwn Franklin St & Van Ness Ave; tickets $20-150; 21, 45, 47, M Van Ness, B Civic Center) From the moment cutting-edge conductor and composer Esa-Pekka Salonen raises his baton, the audience is on the edge of their seats for another world-class performance by the Grammy-winning SF Symphony. Don't miss signature Bach and Stravinsky, world premieres of Symphony-commissioned contemporary works, live performances with such films as *Star Trek*, and collaborations with artists from Wynton Marsalis to Renée Fleming.

★San Francisco Opera OPERA
(Map p78; 415-864-3330; www.sfopera.com; 301 Van Ness Ave, War Memorial Opera House; tickets from $10; 21, 45, 47, 49, B Civic Center, M Van Ness) Opera was SF's gold-rush soundtrack – and today crowds rush to SF Opera premieres of original works, from Margaret Atwood's gripping *The Handmaid's Tale* to Grammy-winning *The (R)Evolution of Steve Jobs*. Painter David Hockney's radical sets and haute-couture costumes complement Eun Sung Kim's bold musical direction – and you can score $10 same-day standing-room tickets at 10am. Check the website for Opera Lab pop-ups.

San Francisco Ballet DANCE
(Map p78; 415-865-2000; www.sfballet.org; 301 Van Ness Ave, War Memorial Opera House; tickets $22-150; ticket sales over the phone 10am-4pm Mon-Fri; 5, 21, 47, 49, M Van Ness, B Civic Center) The USA's oldest ballet company is looking sharp in more than 100 shows annually, from *The Nutcracker* (the US premiere was here) to modern originals. Performances are at the War Memorial Opera House from January to May, and you can score $15 to $20 same-day standing-room tickets at the box office (open four hours before curtain on performance days only).

Theater & Performing Arts

★Oasis CABARET
(Map p94; 415-795-3180; www.sfoasis.com; 298 11th St; tickets $15-35; 9, 12, 14, 47, M Van Ness) Forget what you've learned about drag on TV – at this dedicated dragstravaganza venue in a former gay bathhouse, the shows are so fearless, freaky-deaky and funny you'll laugh until it stops hurting. Drag icon and owner D'Arcy Drollinger hosts drag-comedians like Ben de la Creme and mounts original shows – sometimes literally – including drag spoofs of *Star Trek*, *Buffy the Vampire Slayer* and *Sex and the City*.

★ODC Theater DANCE
(Oberlin Dance Collective; Map p94; box office 415-863-9834, classes 415-549-8519; www.odctheater.org; 3153 17th St; drop-in classes from

$15, shows $20-50; 12, 14, 22, 33, 49, 16th St Mission) For 45 years ODC has been redefining dance with risky, raw performances and the sheer joy of movement. ODC's season runs from September to December, but its stage presents year-round shows featuring local and international artists. Down the block at 351 Shotwell St, ODC Dance Commons offers 200-plus classes a week from flamenco to vogue for all dance levels.

★ **Booksmith** LIVE PERFORMANCE

(Map p110; 415-863-8688; www.booksmith.com; 1644 Haight St; events free-$25; 10am-10pm Mon-Sat, to 8pm Sun; ; 6, 7, 43, N) Throw a stone in SF and you'll probably hit a writer (ouch) or reader (ouch again) headed to/from Booksmith. Literary figures organize Booksmith book signings, raucous poetry readings, extra-short fiction improv, and politician-postcard-writing marathons. Head to sister shop-salon-bar **Bindery** (1727 Haight St) for boozy book swaps, comedy nights, and silent reading parties hosted by Daniel Handler (aka Lemony Snicket).

San Francisco Mime Troupe PERFORMING ARTS

(www.sfmt.org) Uproarious, Tony-winning original political satire since 1961, combining musical theater, Japanese kabuki, slapstick and Italian *commedia dell'arte*. Performances are free in Dolores Park every summer.

Brava Theater THEATER

(Map p94; 415-641-7657; www.brava.org; 2781 24th St; 12, 27, 33, 48) Brava's been producing women-run theater for 30-plus years, hosting acts from comedian Sandra Bernhard to V-day monologist Eve Ensler, and it's the nation's first company with a commitment to producing original works by women of color and LGBTQ playwrights. Brava honors the Mission's Mexican roots with community fiestas, holiday shows and hand-painted posters modeled after Mexican cinema billboards.

American Conservatory Theater THEATER

(ACT; Map p78; 415-749-2228; www.act-sf.org; 405 Geary St; box office 10am-6pm Mon, to curtain Tue-Sun; 8, 30, 38, 45, Powell-Mason, Powell-Hyde, Powell, Powell) Breakthrough shows launch at this turn-of-the-century landmark, which has hosted ACT's productions of Tony Kushner's *Angels in America* and Robert Wilson's *Black Rider*, with William S Burroughs' libretto and music by Tom Waits. Major playwrights like Tom Stoppard, Dustin Lance Black and Eve Ensler premiere work here, while the ACT's newer **Strand Theater** stages more experimental works.

Cinema

★ **Castro Theatre** CINEMA

(Map p94; 415-621-6120; www.castrotheatre.com; 429 Castro St; adult/child, senior & matinee $13/10; 22, 33, F, K, L, M) Every night at the Castro, crowds roar as the mighty organ rises – and no, that's not a euphemism. Showtime at this 1922 art-deco movie palace is heralded with Wurlitzer organ show tunes, culminating in sing-alongs to the Judy Garland anthem 'San Francisco.' Don't miss uproarious drag reenactments of cult flicks – from *Valley of the Dolls* to *Mean Girls* – and signature *Wizard of Oz* sing-alongs.

★ **Alamo Drafthouse Cinema** CINEMA

(Map p94; 415-549-5959; https://drafthouse.com/sf; 2550 Mission St; tickets $6-20; 14, 24th St Mission) The landmark 1932 New Mission cinema is restored to its original Timothy Pfleuger–designed art-deco glory, and it's on a mission to upgrade dinner-and-a-movie dates. Staff deliver cocktails, beer and pizza to your plush banquette seats while you enjoy premieres, cult revivals (especially Music Mondays) or SF favorites, from *Mrs Doubtfire* to *Dirty Harry* – sometimes followed by filmmaker Q&As.

Roxie Cinema CINEMA

(Map p94; 415-863-1087; www.roxie.com; 3117 16th St; regular screening $12-13, matinee $10; 14, 22, 33, 49, 16th St Mission) This vintage 1909 cinema is a neighborhood nonprofit with an international reputation for distributing documentaries and showing controversial films banned elsewhere. Tickets to film-festival premieres, rare revivals and raucous Oscars telecasts sell out – buy them online – but if the main show's packed, discover riveting documentaries in teensy next-door Little Roxy instead. No ads, plus personal introductions to every film.

Shopping

For indie boutiques, local designers and vintage scores, skip downtown and head directly to the Mission, Hayes Valley, the Haight or North Beach. Union Square is the city's main commercial shopping district, with big-brand flagship stores, department stores and international chains. Downtown shopping-district borders are (roughly) Powell St (west), Sutter St (north), Kearny St (east) and Market St (south). The epicenter of the Union Square shopping area is around Post St, near Grant Ave.

★Adobe Books & Backroom Gallery BOOKS

(Map p94; ☎415-864-3936; www.adobebooks.com; 3130 24th St; ⊙noon-8pm Mon-Fri, from 11am Sat & Sun; 🚌12, 14, 48, 49, Ⓑ24th St Mission) Wall-to-wall inspiration – just-released fiction, limited-edition art books, rare cookbooks, well-thumbed poetry – plus zine-launch parties, comedy nights and art openings. Mingle with Mission characters debating all-time-greatest pulp-fiction covers and SF history (founder Andrew is a whiz) and see SF artists at the Backroom Gallery before they hit Whitney Biennials. Adobe is a member-supported cooperative; purchases underwrite community events and prison library programs.

★Gravel & Gold HOMEWARES

(Map p94; ☎415-552-0112; www.gravelandgold.com; 3266 21st St; ⊙noon-7pm Mon-Sat, to 5pm Sun; 🚌12, 14, 49, Ⓑ24th St Mission) Get back to the land and in touch with California's roots without leaving sight of a Mission sidewalk. Gravel & Gold celebrates California's hippie homesteader movement with hand-printed smock-dresses, signature boob-print totes and wiggly stoner-striped throw pillows. Find your own style with hand-thrown stoneware mugs, Risograph posters and rare books on '70s beach-shack architecture – plus frequent maker workshops (see the website).

★Apothecarium DISPENSARY

(Map p94; ☎415-500-2620; https://apothecarium.com; 2029 Market St; ⊙9am-9pm; 🚌22, 37, ⓂF, J, K, L, M) What's that alluring frosted-glass emporium – the lovechild of an Apple Store and Victorian lingerie boutique? It's America's best-designed marijuana dispensary, according to *Architectural Digest*. For the full effect, consult expert staff about edibles for your desired state, from mellow to giddy – and then you can *really* appreciate the local art on thoughtfully provided designer couches. It's 18-plus only; ID required.

★MAC FASHION & ACCESSORIES

(Map p78; ☎415-863-3011; http://macmodernappealingclothing.com; 387 Grove St; ⊙11am-7pm Mon-Sat, noon-6pm Sun; 🚌5, 21, 47, 49) 'Modern Appealing Clothing' is what this store promises – and it delivers for men and women alike, with streamlined chic from Engineered Garments, Junya Watanabe's sculptural shifts, and pop-art tops made exclusively for MAC by SF designer Dema. Fashion-forward-thinking staff are on your side, finding perfect fits and scores from the 40%- to 75%-off sales rack – including that luxe Dries Van Noten suit Jay-Z rocked.

★Golden Gate Fortune Cookies FOOD & DRINKS

(Map p84; ☎415-781-3956; www.goldengatefortunecookies.com; 56 Ross Alley; ⊙9am-6pm; 🚌8, 30, 45, 🚋Powell-Mason, Powell-Hyde, ⓂT) Find your fortune at this bakery, where cookies are stamped from vintage presses – just as they were in 1909, when fortune cookies were invented for SF's Japanese Tea Garden (p91). Write your own fortunes for custom cookies (50¢ each), or get cookies with regular or risqué fortunes (or just add 'in bed' to regular ones). Cash only; $1 tip per photo.

Amoeba Music MUSIC

(Map p110; ☎415-831-1200; www.amoeba.com; 1855 Haight St; ⊙11am-8pm; 🚌6, 7, 33, 43, ⓂN) Enticements are hardly necessary to lure fans to the West Coast's most eclectic collection of new and used music and video, but Amoeba offers listening stations, free zines with uncannily accurate staff reviews, and a free concert series that recently starred Billy Bragg, Karl Denson's Tiny Universe, Violent Femmes, and Mike Doughty – plus a foundation that's saved one million acres of rainforest.

Bound Together Anarchist Book Collective BOOKS

(Map p110; ☎415-431-8355; http://boundtogetherbooks.wordpress.com; 1369 Haight St; ⊙11:30am-7:30pm; 🚌6, 7, 33, 37, 43) Since 1976 this volunteer-run, nonprofit anarchist bookstore has kept free thinkers supplied with organic-permaculture manuals, prison literature and radical comics, all while coordinating the annual spring **Anarchist Book Fair** (http://bayareaanarchistbookfair.com) and retouching Emma Goldman's portrait in the *Anarchists of the Americas* storefront mural – makes us tools of the state look like slackers. Hours are impressively regular, but call ahead to check.

Community Thrift CLOTHING

(Map p94; ☎415-861-4910; www.communitythriftsf.org; 623 Valencia St; ⊙10am-6:30pm; 🚌14, 22, 33, 49, Ⓑ16th St Mission) When local collectors and retailers have too much of a good thing, they donate it to nonprofit Community Thrift, where proceeds go to 200-plus local charities – all the more reason to gloat over your $3 porcelain teacup, $9 vintage suede platform heels and $14 aloha-print romper. Donate your cast-offs (until 5pm daily) and show some love to the community.

Cliff's Variety HOMEWARES
(Map p94; www.cliffsvariety.com; 479 Castro St; ⏲10am-8pm Mon-Sat, to 6pm Sun; Ⓜ Castro St) None of the hardware maestros at Cliff's will raise an eyebrow if you express a dire need for a jar of rubber nuns, some silver body paint, and a case of cocktail toothpicks – though they might angle for an invitation. A community institution since 1936, Cliff's stocks drag supplies galore in the annex and celebrates the seasons with gay-gasp-worthy window displays.

Heath Ceramics HOMEWARES
(Map p78; ☎415-399-9284; www.heathceramics.com; 1 Ferry Bldg, cnr Market St & the Embarcadero; ⏲10am-7pm Mon-Fri, 8am-6pm Sat, 10am-5pm Sun; Ⓜ Embarcadero, Ⓑ Embarcadero) Odds are your favorite SF meal was served on Heath Ceramics, Bay Area chefs' tableware of choice ever since Alice Waters started using Heath's modern, hand-thrown dishes at Chez Panisse. Heath's muted colors and streamlined, mid-century designs stay true to Edith Heath's originals c 1948. Plates are priced for fine dining, but affordable bud vases make fantastic host gifts (hint, hint).

Bi-Rite FOOD & DRINKS
(Map p94; ☎415-241-9760; www.biritemarket.com; 3639 18th St; ⏲8am-9pm; 🚻; 🚌14, 22, 33, 49, Ⓑ 16th St Mission, Ⓜ J) 🍃 Diamond counters can't compare to the dazzle of Bi-Rite's sublime wall of local artisan chocolates, treasure boxes of organic fruit and California wine and cheese selections expertly curated by upbeat, knowledgeable staff. Step up to the altar-like deli counter to provision five-star Dolores Park picnics. An institution since 1940, Bi-Rite champions good food for all through its nonprofit 18 Reasons (p95).

Recchiuti Confections CHOCOLATE
(Map p78; ☎415-834-9494; www.recchiuticonfections.com; 1 Ferry Bldg, cnr Market St & the Embarcadero; ⏲10am-7pm Mon-Fri, 8am-6pm Sat, 10am-5pm Sun; Ⓜ Embarcadero, Ⓑ Embarcadero) 🍃 No San Franciscan can resist award-winning Recchiuti: Pacific Heights parts with old money for its *fleur de sel* caramels; foodie Marina kids prefer S'more Bites to the campground variety; North Beach toasts to the red-wine-pairing chocolate box; and the Mission approves SF-landmark chocolates designed by Creativity Explored – proceeds benefit the Mission arts-education nonprofit.

Paloma FASHION & ACCESSORIES
(Map p78; ☎415-342-2625; https://palomahayes.com; 112 Gough St; ⏲noon-7pm Tue-Sat; 🚌5, 6, 7, 21, 47, 49, Ⓜ Van Ness) Like ransacking a poet's attic, this SF maker collective yields evocative, imaginative handmade finds. You might discover hand-patched indigo scarves, caps made from camp blankets, wallets made from footballs, and real buffalo nickels adorning handbags made on-site by artisan Laureano Faedi. His love of history shows in SF motorcycle-gang coasters and tees advertising long-lost amusement park Playland at the Beach.

Rainbow Grocery FOOD & DRINKS
(Map p94; ☎415-863-0620; www.rainbow.coop; 1745 Folsom St; ⏲9am-9pm; 🚌9, 12, 33, 47) 🍃 This legendary cooperative attracts crowds to buy eco/organic/fair-trade products in bulk, sample the bounty of local cheeses, and flirt in the artisan-chocolate aisle. To answer your questions about where to find what in the Byzantine bulk section, ask a fellow shopper – staff can be elusive. Small but well-priced wine and craft-beer selections; no meat products.

ℹ Information

DANGERS & ANNOYANCES

Keep your city smarts and wits about you, especially at night in the Tenderloin, South of Market (SoMa) and the Mission. If you're alone in these areas at night, consider rideshare or a taxi instead of waiting for a bus.

➡ Homelessness remains a troubling fact of life in San Francisco, as in urban centers worldwide – though SF crime rates are comparatively low. SF's pioneering navigation centers provide transitional housing support, but you'll probably see some people camped out Downtown, in SoMa and the Mission.

➡ The Bayview–Hunters Point neighborhood (south of Dogpatch) isn't for wandering tourists, due to ongoing issues with policing, petty crime and gentrification.

➡ After dark, Mission Dolores Park, Buena Vista Park, and the entry to Golden Gate Park at Haight and Stanyan Sts are used for drug deals and casual sex hookups. If you're there at night, you may get propositioned.

➡ Avoid using your smartphone unnecessarily on the street, or laptops near cafe doors – snatch-and-grab theft can happen.

EMERGENCY & MEDICAL SERVICES

Before traveling, contact your health-insurance provider to learn what medical care they will cover outside your hometown (or home country). Overseas visitors should acquire travel insurance that covers medical situations in the US, where nonemergency care for uninsured patients can be very expensive.

For nonemergency appointments at hospitals, you'll need proof of insurance, a credit card or cash. Even with insurance, you'll most likely have to pay up-front for nonemergency care and then wrangle afterward with your insurance company to get reimbursed. San Francisco has excellent medical facilities, plus alternative medical practices and herbal apothecaries.

San Francisco General Hospital (Zuckerberg San Franciso General Hospital and Trauma Center; ☎ emergency 415-206-8111, main hospital 415-206-8000; https://zuckerberg-sanfranciscogeneral.org; 1001 Potrero Ave; ⌚24hr; 🚌9, 10, 33, 48) Best for serious trauma. Provides care to uninsured patients, including psychiatric care; no documentation required beyond ID.

University of California San Francisco Medical Center (☎415-476-1000; www.ucsfhealth.org; 505 Parnassus Ave; ⌚24hr; 🚌6, 7, 43, Ⓜ N) ER at leading university hospital.

Strut (☎415-437-3400; www.strutsf.org; 470 Castro St; ⌚10am-6pm Mon & Sat, to 8pm Tue-Thu; 🚌24, 33, Ⓜ F, K, L, M) Nonprofit LGBTQ community health and wellness, including free/low-cost Pre-Exposure Prophylaxis (PrEP), walk-in counseling, support groups and health screenings.

San Francisco City Clinic (☎415-487-5500; www.sfcityclinic.org; 356 7th St; ⌚8am-3pm Mon, Wed & Fri, 1-5pm Tue) Low-cost treatment for sexually transmitted diseases (STDs), including emergency contraception and post-exposure prevention (PEP) for HIV.

American College of Traditional Chinese Medicine (☎415-282-9603; www.actcm.edu; 450 Connecticut St; ⌚8:30am-9pm Mon-Thu, 9am-5:30pm Fri & Sat; 🚌10, 19, 22) Affordable community acupuncture, herbal remedies and other traditional Chinese medical treatments.

INTERNET ACCESS

See **San Francisco WiFi** (http://sfgov.org/sfc/sanfranciscowifi) for free wi-fi hot spots.

POST

Rincon Center Post Office (Map p78; ☎800-275-8777; www.usps.com; 180 Steuart St; ⌚7:30am-5pm Mon-Fri, 9am-2pm Sat; Ⓜ Embarcadero, Ⓑ Embarcadero) Postal services plus historic murals; check the website for other post-office locations throughout San Francisco.

TOURIST INFORMATION

California Welcome Center (Map p88; ☎415-981-1280; www.visitcwc.com; Pier 39, 2nd fl; ⌚9am-7pm; 🚌47, 🚋Powell-Mason, Ⓜ E, F) Handy resource for stroller and wheelchair rental, plus luggage storage, phone charging, and ideas for broader California travel.

San Francisco Visitor Information Center (Map p78; ☎415-391-2000; www.sftravel.com/visitor-information-center; 749 Howard St, Moscone Center; ⌚9am-5pm Mon-Fri, to 3pm Sat & Sun; 🚌14, Ⓜ Powell, Ⓑ Powell) Inside Moscone Center, this helpful tourist information center offers practical multilingual information, sells transportation passes, and publishes maps and booklets.

ℹ Getting There & Away

If you've got unlimited time, consider taking the train, instead of driving or flying, to minimize traffic hassles and carbon emissions.

AIR

The Bay Area has three international airports: San Francisco (SFO) (p779), Oakland (OAK) (p779) and San Jose (SJC) (p165). Direct flights from Los Angeles take 60 minutes; Chicago, four hours; Atlanta, five hours; New York, six hours. Factor in additional transit time – and cost – to reach San Francisco proper from Oakland or San Jose, and note that what you save in airfare you may wind up spending on ground transportation.

BUS

San Francisco's intercity hub is the Transbay Transit Center. From here you can catch the following buses:

AC Transit (p150) Buses to the East Bay.

Greyhound (☎800-231-2222; www.greyhound.com) Buses leave daily for Los Angeles ($39 to $90, eight to 12 hours), Truckee near Lake Tahoe ($35 to $46, 5½ hours) and other major destinations.

Megabus (p166) Low-cost bus service to San Francisco from Los Angeles, Sacramento and Reno.

SamTrans (p119) Southbound buses to Palo Alto and the Pacific Coast.

CAR & MOTORCYCLE

Major car-rental operators have offices at airports and downtown. Driving downtown isn't recommended, and hills make parking tricky.

TRAIN

Easy on the eyes and light on carbon emissions, train travel is a good way to visit the Bay Area and beyond.

Amtrak (☎800-872-7245; www.amtrak.com) Serves San Francisco via stations in Oakland and Emeryville (near Oakland), with free shuttle-bus connections to San Francisco's Ferry Building and Caltrain station, and Oakland's Jack London Sq. Amtrak offers rail passes good for 15 days of travel in California within a 330-day period (from $459).

Caltrain (www.caltrain.com; cnr 4th & King Sts) Connects San Francisco with Silicon Valley hubs and San Jose.

Getting Around

When San Franciscans aren't pressed for time, most walk, bike or ride Muni instead of taking a car, cab or SF-invented rideshare services Uber and Lyft. Traffic is notoriously bad at rush hour, and parking is next to impossible in downtown neighborhoods. Avoid driving until it's time to leave town – or drive during off-peak hours.

For Bay Area transit options, departures and arrivals, call 511 or check www.511.org. A detailed *Muni Street & Transit Map* is available free online.

BART High-speed transit to East Bay, Mission St, SF airport and Millbrae, where it connects with Caltrain. Within SF, one-way fares start at $2.50.

Cable cars Frequent, slow and scenic, from 6am to 12:30am daily. Single rides cost $7; for frequent use, get a Muni Passport ($23 per day).

Muni streetcar and bus Reasonably fast, but schedules vary wildly by line; infrequent after 9pm. Fares are $2.75 cash, or $2.50 with a reloadable Clipper card (also good for BART and ferries).

Taxi Fares are about $3 per mile, plus 15%; meters start at $3.50. **Green Cab** (415-626-4733; www.greencabsf.com) is a worker-owned collective offering fuel-efficient hybrids. **Homobiles** (415-574-5023; www.homobiles.org; donations appreciated) offer secure, reliable, donation-based transport for the LGBTQ community 24/7 – text for fastest service.

TO/FROM THE AIRPORT

Rideshare services Lyft and Uber serve SFO. Fares range from $35 to $60 off-peak for a direct-to-destination ride and take between 30 to 45 minutes, depending on traffic and SF destination. Rideshares meet curbside at the upstairs Departures level in the International Terminal. In domestic terminals, rideshares meet at level 5 of the domestic parking garage.

SamTrans (800-660-4287; www.samtrans.com; $2.50) Express bus 398 takes about 30 to 45 minutes to run from San Francisco International Airport to SF's **Transbay Transit Center** (Map p78; cnr Howard & Main Sts; 5, 38, 41, 71).

Airport Express (800-327-2024; www.airportexpressinc.com) Runs a scheduled shuttle every hour from 5:30am to 12:30am between San Francisco International Airport and Sonoma ($38) and Marin ($30) counties.

BART

The fastest link between downtown and the Mission District (30 minutes) also offers transit to San Francisco International Airport ($9.65), Oakland ($4) and Berkeley ($4.60). Four of the system's five lines pass through SF before terminating at Daly City or SFO.

BICYCLE

Bike-sharing is available citywide through **Bay Wheels** (855-480-2453; www.lyft.com/bikes/bay-wheels; single ride/day pass $2/10) – bring your own helmet. Contact the San Francisco Bicycle Coalition (p128) for maps, information and laws regarding cyclists.

Bicycles can be taken on BART, but not aboard crowded trains, and never in the first car, nor in the first three cars during weekday rush hours; folded bikes are allowed in all cars at all times. On Amtrak, bikes can be checked as baggage for $10.

BOAT

With the reinvention of the Ferry Building (p81) as a gourmet dining destination, commuters and tourists alike are dining before taking the scenic ferry across the bay.

Alcatraz Cruises (Map p88; 415-981-7625; www.alcatrazcruises.com; Pier 33; tours day adult/child/family $38.35/23.50/115.70, night adult/child $45.50/27.05; M E, F) Has ferries departing Pier 33 for Alcatraz every half-hour from 8:45am to 3:50pm and at 5:55pm and 6:30pm for night tours. Reservations essential.

San Francisco Bay Ferry (p150) Operates from both Pier 41 and the Ferry Building to Oakland/Alameda. During baseball season, a Giants ferry service runs directly from the landing at AT&T Park's Seals Plaza entrance to Oakland and Alameda. Fares cost $7.20.

Blue & Gold Fleet (Map p88; 415-705-8200; www.blueandgoldfleet.com; Pier 41; adult/child 60min ferry tour $33/22, 30min high-speed boat ride $30/21; 9am-6:30pm, varies seasonally; ; 47, M E, F) operates ferries to Tiburon or Sausalito (one way $12.50) from Pier 41.

Golden Gate Transit Ferries (Map p78; 415-455-2000; www.goldengateferry.org; 6am-9:30pm Mon-Fri, 10am-6pm Sat & Sun) runs regular ferry services from the Ferry Building to Larkspur and Sausalito (one way $12.50), plus game-day ferries to Warriors and Giants games ($14 one way). Transfers to Muni bus services are available and bicycles are permitted.

Vallejo Ferry (Map p78; 877-643-3779, 707-643-3779; http://sanfranciscobayferry.com; one way $15.10) Get to Napa car-free (weekdays only) with departures from the Ferry Building docks about every hour from 6:35am to 7pm; bikes are permitted. The Route 10 VINE bus connects the Vallejo Ferry Terminal to downtown Napa, where you can catch bus 10 to Yountville, St Helena or Calistoga; fares are $1.60.

AT A GLANCE

POPULATION
5.8 million

AREA
4500 sq miles

BEST HIKE
Dipsea Trail (p133)

BEST TACOS
Taqueria El Paisa@.com (p148)

BEST TOUR
Food and Farm Tours (p139)

WHEN TO GO

Dec–Mar
Elephant seal pupping season and gray whale migration along the coast.

Mar–Apr
Wildflowers hit their peak on trails throughout the region.

Aug–Sep
Sunny days at the beaches, and farmers markets overflow with seasonal goodness.

Giant Redwoods at Muir Woods National Monument (p136)
ZACK FRANK / SHUTTERSTOCK ©

Marin County & the Bay Area

The San Francisco Bay Area encompasses a bonanza of natural vistas and wildlife. Cross the Golden Gate Bridge into Marin County to visit wizened ancient redwoods, and herds of elegant tule elk on the bluffs of Tomales Bay. Gray whales show some fluke off the Point Reyes peninsula, while hawks surf the skies over the Marin Headlands.

Stanford University draws academics and students from around the world while the city of Berkeley sparked the state's locavore food movement and, together with its university, continues to be at the forefront of environmental and left-leaning political causes. South of San Francisco, Hwy 1 traces miles of undeveloped coastline and sandy pocket beaches as it winds seductively south to Santa Cruz.

INCLUDES

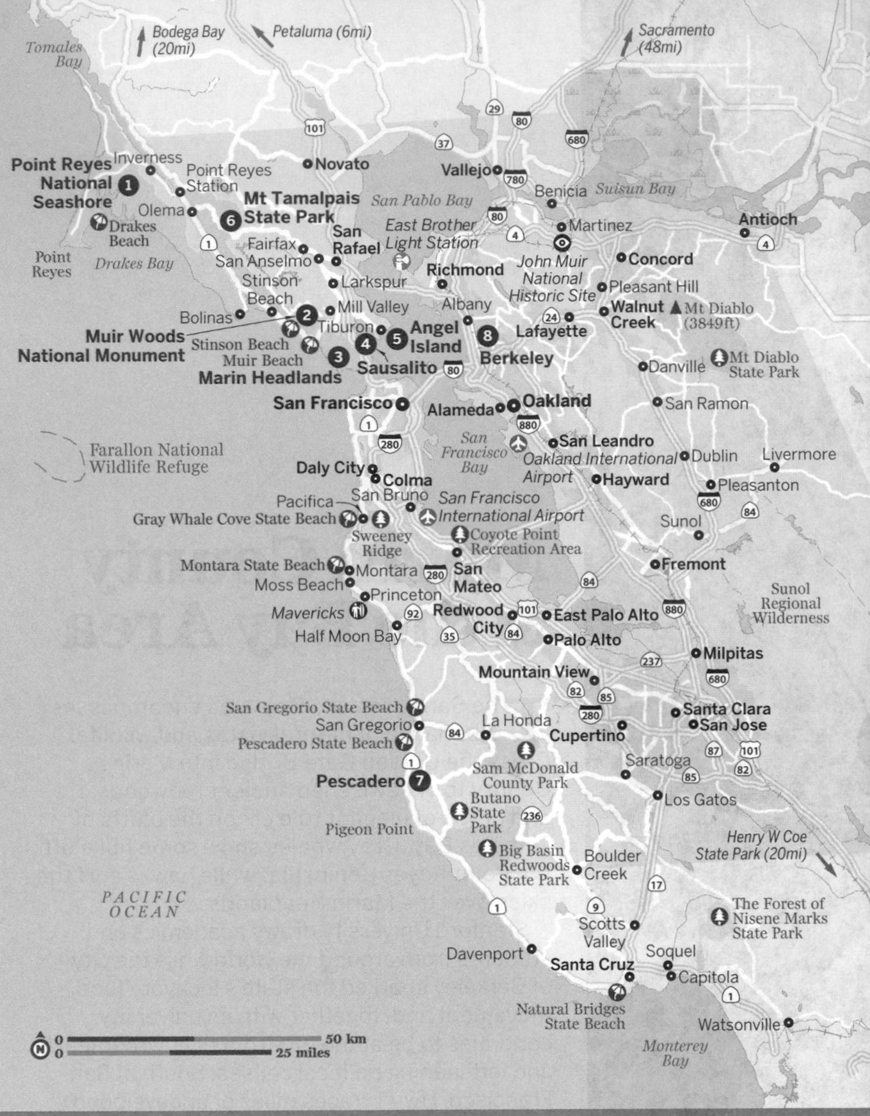

Marin County & the Bay Area Highlights

❶ **Point Reyes National Seashore** (p141) Cavorting with tule elk and spotting gray whales from the lighthouse.

❷ **Muir Woods National Monument** (p136) Gazing at majestic redwood canopies.

❸ **Marin Headlands** (p123) Catching the best views of the Golden Gate Bridge from stunning trails and beaches.

❹ **Sausalito** (p127) Ferrying from San Francisco to bohemian, bobbing houseboats.

❺ **Angel Island** (p131) Hiking and cycling amidst bay views and immigration history.

❻ **Mt Tamalpais** (p134) Exploring forest trails, lakes and panoramas by foot or bike.

❼ **Pescadero** (p168) Cove-hopping along Hwy 1 and tasting farm-fresh bounty.

❽ **Berkeley** (p151) Hanging with radicals, hippies, students and foodies.

MARIN COUNTY

Just across the Golden Gate Bridge from San Francisco, Marin County is a collection of wealthy, wooded hamlets that hang tenuously by haute hippie roots as a more conservative tech-era population moves in. The 'common' folk here eat organic, vote far left and drive Teslas. Tons of old rockers, from members of the Grateful Dead to Metallica, have owned properties in these hills and are testament to the county's wilder days of yore.

Geographically, Marin County is a near mirror image of San Francisco. Its southern peninsula nearly touches the north-pointing tip of the city, and is surrounded by ocean and bay. But Marin is wilder and more mountainous. Redwoods grow on the coastside hills, surf crashes against cliffs, and hiking and cycling trails crisscross scenic Point Reyes, Muir Woods and Mt Tamalpais. These glorious natural surrounds make Marin County an excellent day trip or weekend escape from San Francisco.

Marin Headlands

The headlands rise majestically out of the water at the north end of the Golden Gate Bridge, their rugged beauty all the more striking given the fact that they're only a few miles from San Francisco's urban core. A few forts and bunkers are left over from a century of US military occupation – which is, ironically, the reason the headlands are today protected parklands, free of development.

Sights

★Golden Gate National Recreation Area PARK

(Map p124; ☎415-561-4700; www.nps.gov/goga; 🅿) It's no mystery why this is one of the Bay Area's most popular hiking and cycling destinations. As the trails wind beside the Pacific Ocean and San Francisco Bay and through the Marin Headlands, they afford stunning views of the sea, the Golden Gate Bridge and the city of San Francisco.

★Point Bonita Lighthouse LIGHTHOUSE

(Map p124; ☎415-331-1540; www.nps.gov/goga/pobo.htm; ⏲12:30-3:30pm Sun & Mon, hours may vary; 🅿) FREE This historical lighthouse is a breathtaking half-mile walk from Field Rd parking area. From the tip of Point Bonita, you can see the Golden Gate Bridge and the San Francisco skyline. Harbor seals haul out seasonally on nearby rocks. It's worth coming out here even when the lighthouse is closed. Call ahead to reserve a spot on one of the free monthly sunset tours of the promontory.

Nike Missile Site SF-88 HISTORIC SITE

(Map p124; ☎415-331-1540; www.nps.gov/goga/nike-missile-site.htm; Field Rd; ⏲12:30-3:30pm Sat, & Fri in summer); 🅿) FREE File past guard shacks with uniformed mannequins to witness the area's not-too-distant military history at this fascinating Cold War museum staffed by veterans. Watch them place a now-warhead-free missile into position, then explore the cavernous underground silo to see the multikeyed launch controls that thankfully were never set in motion.

Rodeo Beach BEACH

(Map p124; www.parksconservancy.org/visit/park-sites/rodeo-beach.html; off Bunker Rd; 🅿) At the western end of Bunker Rd sits Rodeo Beach, partly protected from wind by high cliffs. It's known to locals as 'Fort Cronkhite' for the old military post that sits behind it. Kids will love the colorful pebbles on the beach. It's also a popular surf spot.

Activities

Hiking

All along the coastline you'll find cool old battery sites – abandoned concrete bunkers dug into the ground with fabulous views. **Battery Townsley**, a half-mile walk or bike ride up from the **Fort Cronkite** parking lot, opens for free subterranean tours from noon to 4pm on the first Sunday of the month.

Tennessee Valley Trail HIKING

(Map p124; www.nps.gov/goga/planyourvisit/tennessee_valley.htm) This trail offers beautiful views of the rugged coastline and is one of the most popular hikes in Marin (expect crowds on weekends), especially for families. It has easy, level access to the cove beach and ocean, and is a short 3.5-mile round-trip. The parking lot and trailhead are at the end of Tennessee Valley Rd.

Coastal Trail HIKING

(Map p124; www.nps.gov/goga/planyourvisit/coastal-trail.htm) From nearby Rodeo Beach, the Coastal Trail meanders 3.5 miles inland, past abandoned military bunkers, to intersect the Tennessee Valley Trail. It then continues almost 3 miles along the blustery headlands all the way to Muir Beach (p137).

Marin County

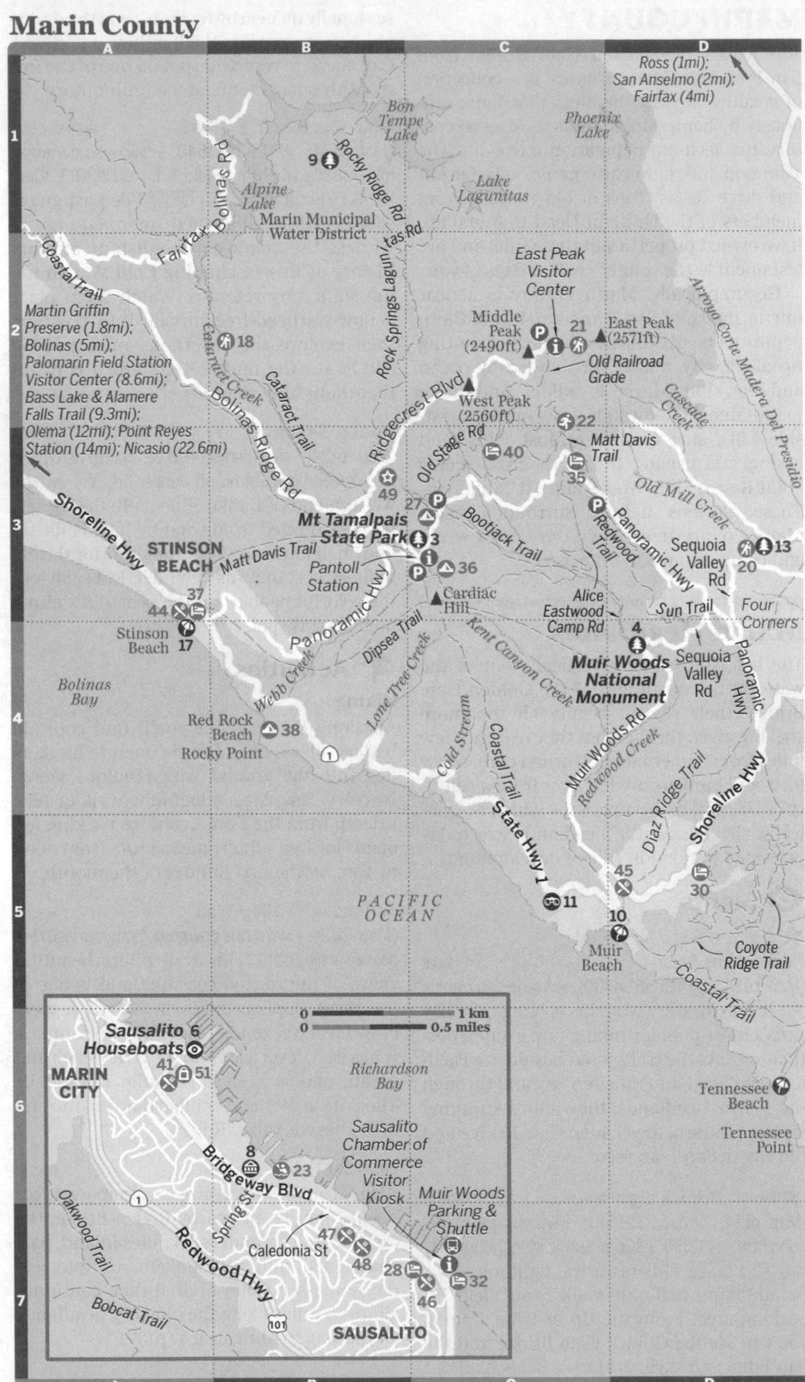

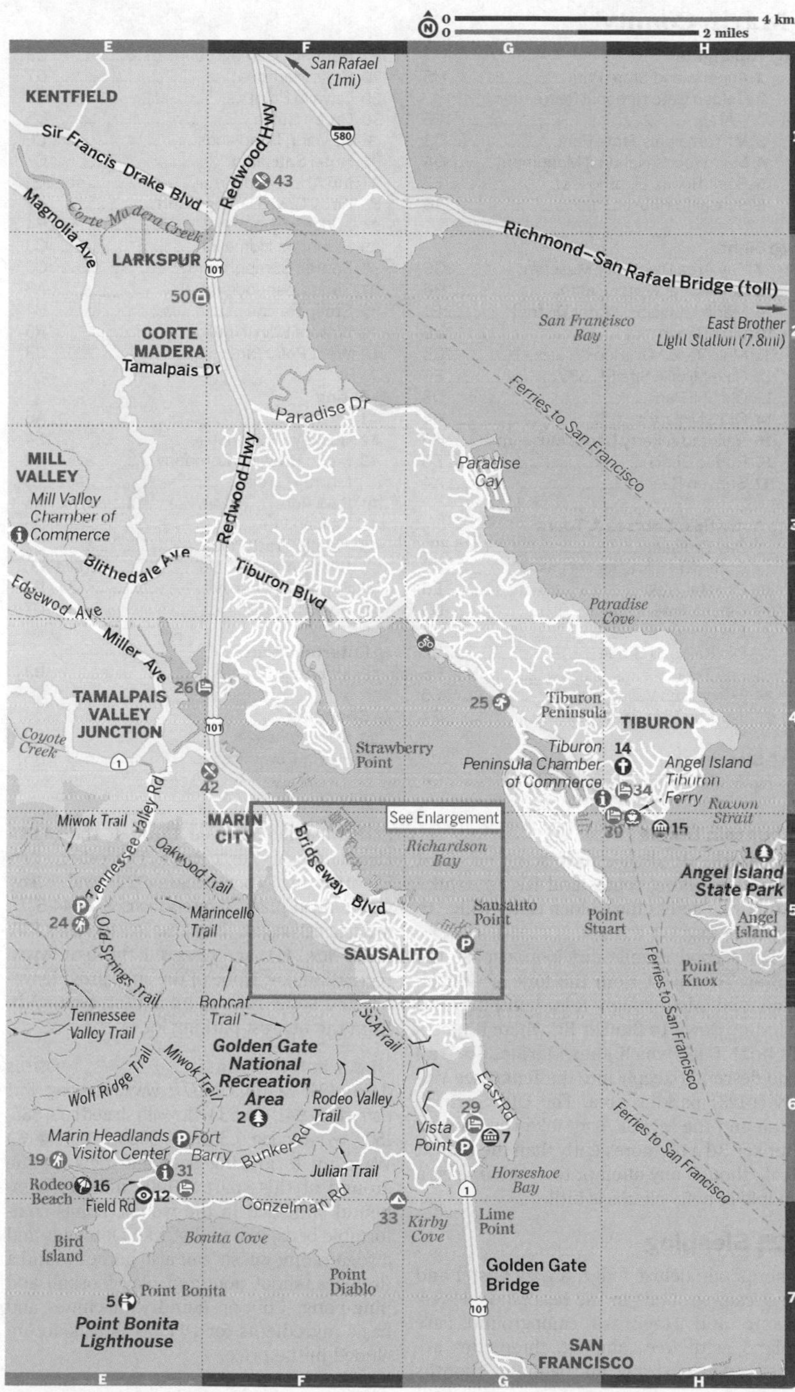

KENTFIELD
San Rafael (1mi)
Sir Francis Drake Blvd
Redwood Hwy
43
Magnolia Ave
Corte Madera Creek
Richmond–San Rafael Bridge (toll)
LARKSPUR
50
CORTE MADERA
Tamalpais Dr
San Francisco Bay
East Brother Light Station (7.8mi)
Ferries to San Francisco
Paradise Dr
MILL VALLEY
Mill Valley Chamber of Commerce
Paradise Cay
Blithedale Ave
Tiburon Blvd
Edgewood Ave
Miller Ave
Paradise Cove
26
TAMALPAIS VALLEY JUNCTION
25
Tiburon Peninsula
TIBURON
Coyote Creek
Strawberry Point
Tiburon Peninsula Chamber of Commerce
14
Angel Island Tiburon Ferry
34
Racoon Strait
42
MARIN CITY
See Enlargement
30
15
Miwok Trail
Tennessee Valley Rd
Richardson Bay
1
Angel Island State Park
Oakwood Trail
Bridgeway Blvd
24
Marincello Trail
Sausalito Point
Point Stuart
Angel Island
Old Springs Trail
SAUSALITO
Point Knox
Bobcat Trail
Tennessee Valley Trail
SCA Trail
Golden Gate National Recreation Area
Wolf Ridge Trail
Miwok Trail
East Rd
Rodeo Valley Trail
29
2
Marin Headlands Visitor Center
Fort Barry
Vista Point
7
Bunker Rd
19
Julian Trail
31
Horseshoe Bay
Rodeo Beach
16
Field Rd
12
Conzelman Rd
33
Kirby Cove
Lime Point
Bird Island
Bonita Cove
Point Diablo
Golden Gate Bridge
5
Point Bonita
Point Bonita Lighthouse
SAN FRANCISCO
4 km
2 miles

Marin County

Top Sights
1 Angel Island State Park H5
2 Golden Gate National Recreation Area F6
3 Mt Tamalpais State Park C3
4 Muir Woods National Monument D4
5 Point Bonita Lighthouse E7
6 Sausalito Houseboats A6

Sights
7 Bay Area Discovery Museum G6
8 Bay Model Visitor Center B6
9 Marin Municipal Water District B1
10 Muir Beach D5
11 Muir Beach Overlook C5
12 Nike Missile Site SF-88 ..... E6
13 Old Mill Park D3
14 Old St Hilary's H4
15 Railroad & Ferry Depot Museum H5
16 Rodeo Beach E6
17 Stinson Beach A4

Activities, Courses & Tours
Bay Cruises ..... (see 39)
18 Cataract Falls & Alpine Lake B2
19 Coastal Trail E6
20 Dipsea Trail D3
21 East Peak C2
22 Old Railroad Grade C2
23 Sea Trek B6
24 Tennessee Valley Trail E5
25 Tiburon Bike Path G4

Sleeping
26 Acqua Hotel E4
27 Bootjack Campground C3
28 Casa Madrona C7
29 Cavallo Point G6
30 Green Gulch D5
31 HI Marin Headlands E6
32 Hotel Sausalito C7
Inn Above Tide ..... (see 32)
33 Kirby Cove Campground F7
34 Lodge at Tiburon H4
35 Mountain Home Inn C3
36 Pantoll Campground C3
37 Sandpiper Lodging A3
38 Steep Ravine B4
39 Waters Edge Hotel H5
40 West Point Inn C3

Eating
41 Avatar's A6
42 Buckeye Roadhouse F4
43 Marin Brewing Company F1
Murray Circle ..... (see 29)
44 Parkside A3
45 Pelican Inn D5
46 Poggio Trattoria C7
Sam's Anchor Cafe ..... (see 39)
47 Sausalito Gourmet B7
48 Sushi Ran B7

Entertainment
49 Mountain Theater B3

Shopping
50 Book Passage E2
51 Heath Ceramics A6

Mountain Biking

The Marin Headlands have some excellent mountain biking routes and it's an exhilarating ride across the Golden Gate Bridge to reach them.

For a good 12-mile dirt loop, choose the **Julian Trail** west from the fork of Conzelman and McCullough Rds, bumping and winding down to Bunker Rd where it meets **Bobcat Trail**, which joins **Marincello Trail** and descends steeply into the Tennessee Valley (p123) parking area. The **Old Springs Trail** and the **Miwok Trail** take you back to Bunker Rd a bit more gently than the Bobcat Trail, though any attempt to avoid at least a couple of hefty climbs is futile.

Sleeping

There's one deluxe lodge, a cozy hostel and four campgrounds in the headlands. **Hawk Camp** and **Haypress** campgrounds are inland, with free camping; these sites are open only in spring and summer months and must be reserved through the Marin Headlands Visitor Center. The other sites, **Bicentennial** (per person $20) and **Kirby Cove** (Map p124; reservations 877-444-6777; www.recreation.gov; Kirby Cove Rd; tent sites $30; Apr-Nov; P), are reserved through www.recreation.gov. None of the sites provide water, and some require hiking (or cycling) in from the nearest parking lot.

HI Marin Headlands HOSTEL **$**
(Map p124; 415-331-2777; www.hiusa.org; Fort Barry, Bldg 941; dm $33-41, r with shared bath $85-150; reception 7:30am-10:30pm; P @) Wake up to grazing deer and dew on the ground at this spartan 1907 military compound snuggled in the woods. It has comfortable beds, two well-stocked kitchens and a yoga room; guests can also gather round a fireplace, shoot pool and play foosball and ping-pong. Coin-op laundry machines and basic ingredients for DIY breakfasts are included in the price.

Cavallo Point LODGE $$$
(Map p124; ☎415-339-4700; www.cavallopoint.com; 601 Murray Circle; r from $400; P ⊜ @ 📶 🐾) Spread over 45 acres of the Bay Area's most scenic parkland, Cavallo Point lodge flaunts an eco-conscious focus with a full-service spa, restaurant and bar, and easy access to outdoor activities. Choose from richly renovated rooms in the landmark Fort Baker officers' quarters or contemporary, stylish 'green' accommodations with exquisite bay views (including a turret of the Golden Gate Bridge).

Eating

It's easiest to bring a picnic lunch, trail snacks and plenty of water from somewhere such as Sausalito Gourmet (p129). But you can also do a sit-down lunch at the Cavallo Point lodge or the children's museum (p128) near Sausalito. On Saturday through Monday, the YMCA operates a small eatery called Point Bonita Café near the lighthouse parking lot.

Murray Circle AMERICAN $$$
(Map p124; ☎415-339-4750; www.cavallopoint.com; 601 Murray Circle; dinner mains $25-36; ⏰7-11am Mon-Fri, 11:30am-2pm Mon, 11:30am-9pm Tue-Thu, 11:30am-10:30pm Fri, 7am-10:30pm Sat, 7-9am Sun; 🍷) At Cavallo Point lodge, dine on locally sourced meats, seafood and produce – perhaps grass-fed organic beef burgers or Dungeness crab BLT sandwiches – in a club-by dining room topped by a pressed tin ceiling. Reservations recommended for dinner and weekend brunch.

Information

Information is available from the Golden Gate National Recreation Area (p123) and the **Marin Headlands Visitors Center** (Map p124; ☎415-331-1540; www.nps.gov/goga/marin-headlands.htm; Bunker Rd, Fort Barry; ⏰9:30am-4:30pm Wed-Mon), in an old chapel off Bunker Rd near Fort Barry.

Getting There & Away

By car, take the Alexander Ave exit just after crossing north over the Golden Gate Bridge. Take a left on Bunker Rd, which leads to the headlands through a one-way tunnel (when the light is red, the wait is five minutes). Arrive before 2pm on weekends to avoid traffic and parking congestion, or cycle over the bridge instead.

On Saturdays, Sundays and holidays, **Muni** (☎415-701-2311, 511; www.sfmta.com; fare $3) bus 76X runs every 60 to 90 minutes from San Francisco's Financial District to the Marin Headlands Visitor Center, Rodeo Beach (p123) and several other stops. Buses are equipped with bicycle racks. Note that cellphone service is spotty; you can arrive via ridesharing services but may have a tough time summoning a ride out.

Sausalito

Perfectly arranged on a secure little harbor on the bay, Sausalito is undeniably lovely. Named for the tiny willows that once populated the banks of its creeks, it's famous for its colorful houseboats bobbing in the bay. Much of the well-heeled downtown has uninterrupted views of San Francisco and Angel Island, and due to the ridgeline at its back, fog generally skips it.

Sausalito is (understandably) a major tourist trap, jam-packed with souvenir shops and costly boutiques. It's the first town you encounter after crossing the Golden Gate Bridge from San Francisco, so daytime

WHY IS IT SO FOGGY?

When the summer sun's rays warm the air over the chilly Pacific, fog forms and hovers offshore. To grasp how it moves inland requires an understanding of California's geography. The vast agricultural region in the state's interior, the Central Valley, is ringed by mountains like a giant bathtub. The only substantial sea-level break in these mountains occurs at the Golden Gate to the west, which happens to be the direction from which prevailing winds blow. As the inland valley heats up and the warm air rises, it creates a deficit of air at surface level, generating wind that gets sucked through the only opening it can find: the Golden Gate. It happens fast and it's unpredictable. Gusty wind is the only indication that the fog is about to roll in. But even this is inconsistent: there can be fog at the beaches south of the Golden Gate and sun a mile to the north. Hills block fog – especially at times of high atmospheric pressure, as often happens in summer. Because of this, weather forecasters speak of the Bay Area's 'microclimates.' In July it's not uncommon for inland areas to top 100°F (38°C), while the mercury at the coast barely reaches 70°F (21°C).

DON'T MISS

HIKING & CYCLING THE GOLDEN GATE BRIDGE

Walking or cycling across the Golden Gate Bridge to Sausalito is a fun way to avoid traffic and get some great ocean views and fresh air. Getting to Sausalito is a relatively easy journey, mostly flat or downhill when heading north from San Francisco. Cycling back isn't nearly as fun; the return trip involves a big climb out of Sausalito. Unless you want a workout, simply hop on a ferry back to SF.

The trip is about 4 miles from the south end of the bridge and takes less than an hour. Pedestrians have access to the bridge's east walkway between 5am and 9pm daily (until 6:30pm in winter). Cyclists generally use the west side, except on weekdays between 5am and 3:30pm, when they share the east side with pedestrians (who have the right-of-way). After 9pm, cyclists can still cross the bridge on the east side through a security gate. Check the bridge website for changes (www.goldengate.org).

For more ambitious cyclists, the Cal Park Hill Tunnel is a safe subterranean passage from Larkspur (another ferry terminus) to San Rafael.

More information and resources are available at the websites of the **San Francisco Bicycle Coalition** (415-431-2453; www.sfbike.org) and the **Marin County Bicycle Coalition** (MCBC; 415-456-3469; www.marinbike.org).

crowds turn up in droves and make parking difficult. Ferrying over from San Francisco makes for a more relaxing excursion.

The town sits on Richardson Bay, a smaller bay within San Francisco Bay. The commercial district is mainly one street, Bridgeway Blvd, which runs alongside the waterfront.

Sights

★Sausalito Houseboats ARCHITECTURE

(Map p124; Richardson Bay) Bohemia still thrives along the shoreline of Richardson Bay, where free spirits inhabit quirky homes that bob in the waves among the seabirds and seals. Structures range from psychedelic mural-splashed castles to dilapidated salt-sprayed shacks and immaculate three-story floating mansions. You can poke around the houseboat docks located off Bridgeway Blvd between Gate 5 and Gate 6½ Rds.

Bay Model Visitor Center MUSEUM

(Map p124; 415-289-3007; www.spn.usace.army.mil/missions/recreation/baymodelvisitorcenter.aspx; 2100 Bridgeway Blvd; 9am-4pm Tue-Fri, 10am-5pm Sat summer, 9am-4pm Tue-Sat rest of year; P) FREE One of the coolest things in town, fascinating to both kids and adults, is the Army Corps of Engineers' primarily solar-powered visitor center. Housed in one of the old (and cold!) Marinship warehouses, it's a 1.5-acre hydraulic model of San Francisco Bay and the delta region. Self-guided audio tours ($5) take you over and around it as the water flows.

Bay Area Discovery Museum MUSEUM

(Map p124; 415-339-3900; https://bayareadiscoverymuseum.org; 557 McReynolds Rd; $16, first Wed of every other month free; 9am-4pm Tue-Fri, to 5pm Sat & Sun; P) Below the north tower of the Golden Gate Bridge, at Fort Baker, this excellent hands-on activity museum is designed for children. Multilingual exhibits include an oversized kitchen sink called Wobbleland, an interactive outdoors exhibit emphasizing Bay Area features, and a large playground area with a shipwreck to romp around. The museum's **Bean Sprouts Café** has healthy nibbles.

Activities

Sea Trek KAYAKING

(Map p124; 415-332-8494; www.seatrek.com; 2100 Bridgeway Blvd; kayak or SUP rental per hour from $25, tours from $75; 9am-5pm Mon-Fri, 8:30am-5pm Sat & Sun Apr-Oct, 9am-4pm daily Nov-Mar) On a sunny day, Richardson Bay is irresistible. Kayaks and stand-up paddleboard (SUP) sets can be rented here. No experience is necessary; lessons and group outings are also available. Guided kayaking excursions include full-moon and starlight tours and an adventurous crossing to Angel Island. May through October is the best time to paddle.

Sausalito Bike Rentals BICYCLE RENTAL

(415-331-2453; www.sausalitobikerentals.com; 34a Princess St; bicycle rental per hour/day from $15/40; 9:30am-7pm) Rents road, mountain, hybrid, tandem and electric bicycles by the hour or the day.

Sleeping

Most of the lodgings in town charge a pretty penny, with a two-night minimum on weekends. On the outskirts of town, midrange chain motels and hotels line Hwy 101.

Hotel Sausalito HISTORIC HOTEL **$$**
(Map p124; ☎415-332-0700; www.hotelsausalito.com; 16 El Portal St; r $175-375; P ⊖ ❄ ≋) Steps away from the ferry in the middle of downtown, this grand 1915 hotel has loads of period charm, paired with modern touches such as satellite TV and DVD players. Each guest room is decorated in Mediterranean hues and some enjoy partial bay views. Parking is $20.

★**Casa Madrona** BOUTIQUE HOTEL **$$$**
(Map p124; ☎415-332-0502; www.casamadrona.com; 801 Bridgeway Blvd; d from $325; P ⊖ ≋) A multimillion-dollar revamp has catapulted this classic Sausalito hotel into the 21st century. Canopy beds now offer smart mattresses that track guests' sleep on tablets, meditation headbands send feedback to an app and Alexa assists with room service. The property remains divided into a 12-room, 'hillside' mansion and a collection of 'harborside' cottages, all with gorgeous bay views.

Inn Above Tide BOUTIQUE HOTEL **$$$**
(Map p124; ☎415-332-9535; www.innabovetide.com; 30 El Portal; r $425-1755; P ⊖ ❄ @ ≋) Ensconce yourself in one of 33 modern and spacious rooms and suites – most with private deck and fireplace – that practically levitate over the water. There are envy-inducing bay views from your window; scan the horizon with the in-room binoculars. Parking is $24 per day; bicycles are complimentary. Located next to the ferry terminal.

Eating

Bridgeway Blvd is packed with moderately priced cafes and many more expensive bay-view seafood restaurants. Budget-friendly options are limited to local delis; our favorite is **Sausalito Gourmet** (Map p124; ☎415-332-4880; www.sausalitogourmet.com; 209 Caledonia St; sandwiches $9-12; ⏲11am-6:30pm Mon-Sat).

★**Avatar's** INDIAN **$$**
(Map p124; ☎415-332-8083; www.facebook.com/avatarsrestaurant; 2656 Bridgeway Blvd; mains $13-19; ⏲11am-3pm & 5-9:30pm Mon-Sat; ✎) Boasting a cuisine of 'ethnic confusions,' the Indian-fusion dishes here incorporate Mexican, Italian and Caribbean ingredients and will bowl you over with flavor and creativity. Think Punjabi enchiladas with curried sweet potato, or spinach fettuccine with mild-curry tomato sauce. All diets (vegan, gluten-free etc) are graciously accommodated. It sounds weird, but it's all amazing.

Poggio Trattoria ITALIAN **$$**
(Map p124; ☎415-332-7771; www.poggiotrattoria.com; 777 Bridgeway Blvd; mains $16-38; ⏲6:30am-9pm Sun-Thu, to 10pm Fri & Sat) A classic Northern Italian restaurant specializing in handmade pastas, wood-fired pizzas and tasty salad grown in the owner's spring-fed garden. It's all served up in a swanky, old-world dining room or on the lively outdoor patio. Service is flawless. *Bollito misto* (a rich, meaty Northern Italian stew) graces the menu each winter.

Sushi Ran JAPANESE **$$$**
(Map p124; ☎415 332 3620; www.sushiran.com; 107 Caledonia St; shared dishes $18-38; ⏲11:45am-2:30pm Mon-Fri, 5-10pm Sun-Thu, 5-11pm Fri & Sat) Many Marin residents claim this place is the best sushi spot around and it's hard to argue. If you didn't reserve ahead, the wine and sake bar eases the pain of the long wait for a table.

Shopping

Heath Ceramics HOMEWARES
(Map p124; ☎415-332-3732; www.heathceramics.com; 400 Gate 5 Rd; ⏲10am-6pm Mon-Sat, from 11am Sun) Near Sausalito's houseboat docks, this factory has been baking and glazing iconic dinnerware and homewares made of clay since 1959. Even chef Alice Waters adores the earth-toned place settings, which show arts-and-crafts styling. The showroom discounts overstock and seconds. Reserve ahead for free factory tours on Fridays, Saturdays and Sundays.

Information

Sausalito Chamber of Commerce (Map p124; ☎415-331-1093; www.sausalito.org; foot of El Portal St; ⏲11am-4pm) Offers local information at a visitor kiosk by the ferry terminal.

Getting There & Away

Driving to Sausalito from San Francisco, take the Alexander Ave exit (the first exit after the Golden Gate Bridge) and follow the signs into downtown. There are five municipal parking lots in town, each charging varying rates; you can get three hours of free parking in the lot at the foot of Locust St, off Bridgeway Blvd. Street parking (metered or free, but time-limited) is difficult to find.

The ferry is a fun and easy way to travel to Sausalito. **Golden Gate Ferry** (☎511, 415-455-2000; www.goldengateferry.org) operates to and from San Francisco's Ferry Building ($13, 25 to 30 minutes) several times daily. **Blue & Gold Fleet** (☎415-705-8200; www.blueandgoldfleet.com) sails to Sausalito several times daily from the Fisherman's Wharf area in San Francisco ($13, 30 to 55 minutes). Both ferries operate year-round and transport bicycles for no additional charge.

Golden Gate Transit (p173) bus 30 runs hourly to Sausalito from downtown San Francisco ($7, 40 to 55 minutes). **West Marin Stagecoach** (☎415-526-3239; www.marintransit.org/stage.html) route 61 ($2) connects Bolinas to Sausalito, with stops in Mt Tamalpais State Park and Stinson Beach. The seasonal **Muir Woods Shuttle** (Map p124; ☎800-410-2419; www.gomuirwoods.com; parking $8, round-trip shuttle adult/child under 16 $3.25/free) connects with San Francisco ferries arriving in Sausalito before 3pm.

Tiburon

At the end of a small peninsula pointing out into the center of the bay, Tiburon is blessed with gorgeous views. The name comes from its original Spanish title, Punta de Tiburon (Shark Point). Take the ferry from San Francisco, browse the shops on Main St, grab a bite to eat and you've seen downtown Tiburon. For further exploration, hike up to **Old St Hilary's** (Map p124; ☎415-435-1853; http://landmarkssociety.com/landmarks/st-hilarys; 201 Esperanza St; ⏲1-4pm Sun Apr-Oct) and its surrounding trails, or rent a bicycle to enjoy the gorgeous waterfront **bike path** (Map p124). The town is also a jumping-off point for nearby Angel Island.

Upper Main St, also known as Ark Row, is where old houseboats have taken root on dry land and metamorphosed into classy shops and boutiques.

Sights & Activities

Railroad & Ferry Depot Museum MUSEUM
(Map p124; ☎415-435-1853; http://landmarkssociety.com/landmarks/railroad-ferry-museum; 1920 Paradise Dr; suggested donation $5; ⏲1-4pm Wed-Sun Apr-Oct) Formerly the terminus for a 3000-person ferry to San Francisco and a railroad that once reached north to Ukiah, this late 19th-century building showcases a scale model of Tiburon's commercial hub, circa 1900. The restored stationmaster's quarters can be visited upstairs.

Bay Cruises CRUISE
(Map p124; ☎415-435-2131; http://angelislandferry.com; 21 Main St; 90min cruise adult/child $30/15; ⏲usually 6:30-8pm Fri & Sat mid-May–mid-Oct) The Angel Island Tiburon Ferry (runs San Francisco Bay sunset cruises on weekend evenings in summer and fall. Reserve ahead and bring your own picnic dinner to enjoy outside on the deck.

Sleeping

Tiburon has only two places to stay downtown. Midrange motels and chain hotels line Hwy 101.

Lodge at Tiburon HOTEL $$
(Map p124; ☎415-435-3133; www.lodgeattiburon.com; 1651 Tiburon Blvd; r $135-309; P ⊖ ❄ @ ᯤ ≋ 🐾) A stylish and comfortable contemporary hotel, although concrete hallways and staircases testify to the more basic motel it once was. The best value in town, it's a short stroll to anywhere – including the ferry – and there's a pool, DVD library, tavern, rental bikes, free parking and a rooftop deck with a fireplace and heady Mt Tamalpais views.

Waters Edge Hotel BOUTIQUE HOTEL $$$
(Map p124; ☎415-789-5999; www.marinhotels.com; 25 Main St; r from $289; P ⊖ ❄ @ ᯤ) At this hotel, with its deck extending over the bay, tasteful rooms have an elegant minimalism that combines comfort and style. Rooms with rustic high wood ceilings are quite romantic and all afford bay views. Complimentary bicycles and evening wine-and-cheese included. Parking is $15.

Eating

Downtown, Tiburon Blvd and Main St feature several pricey cafes and restaurants, some with excellent waterfront locations.

★ **Sam's Anchor Cafe** SEAFOOD $$
(Map p124; ☎415-435-4527; www.samscafe.com; 27 Main St; mains $13-34; ⏲11:30am-10pm Mon-Wed, to midnight Thu & Fri, 10am-midnight Sat, 10am-8pm Sun) Since 1920 Sam's has been slinging seafood and burgers on the waterfront, where a weekend cocktail brunch remains a quintessential Bay Area experience. In 2018 a new owner and a $2 million revamp brought a chic new design, expanded indoor/outdoor space and a new menu with significantly tastier food.

Grab a table under a snazzy new patio umbrella and try a prickly-pear margarita with crab and avo toast or a yummy burger. Have a few more drinks and stay till late – the patio banquettes offer heated seating.

WORTH A TRIP

ANGEL ISLAND

Angel Island (Map p124; ☎415-435-5390; www.parks.ca.gov/AngelIsland) FREE, in San Francisco Bay, has a mild climate with fresh bay breezes, which makes it pleasant for hiking and cycling. For a unique treat, picnic in a protected cove overlooking the surrounding cities. The island's history is apparent in its buildings – it was a hunting and fishing ground for the Miwok people, served as a military base, an immigration station, a WWII Japanese internment camp and a Nike missile site. There are 13 miles of roads and trails around the island, including a hike to the summit of 788ft **Mt Livermore** (no bicycles) and a 5-mile perimeter trail.

The **Immigration Station** (USIS; ☎415-435-5537; www.aiisf.org/visit; adult/child $5/3, incl tour $7/5, cash only; ⊙11am-3pm Wed-Sun), which operated from 1910 to 1940, was the Ellis Island of the West Coast. But this facility was primarily a screening and detention center for Chinese immigrants, who were at that time restricted from entering the US under the **Chinese Exclusion Act**. Many detainees were cruelly held for long periods before ultimately being sent home. The mournful Chinese poetry etched into the barrack walls is a heartbreaking testament to their trials. The site is now a museum with excellent interpretive exhibits; tours include admission fees and can be purchased on-site. Large groups may reserve ahead.

Sea Trek (p128) runs kayaking excursions around the island. You can rent bicycles (per hour/day $15/60) and e-bikes (per hour/day $25/90) at **Ayala Cove**, and there are **tram tours** ($16.50) and **Segway tours** ($80) around the island. Tour schedules vary seasonally; go to http://angelisland.com for information.

You can camp on the island, and when the last ferry sails for the night, the place is your own – except for the very persistent raccoons. The dozen hike-, bicycle- or kayak-in **campsites** (☎reservations 800-444-7275; www.reservecalifornia.com; tent sites from $30, one-time service fee $7) are usually reserved months in advance. Near the ferry dock, there's a cafe serving sandwiches and snacks.

Getting There & Away

All ferry tickets are sold on a first-come, first-served basis. From San Francisco's Pier 41, take a Blue & Gold Fleet (p129) ferry (one-way adult/child $9.75/5.50). There are three or four daily sailings year-round. Check the online schedule for details. From Tiburon, take the Angel Island Tiburon Ferry, which runs daily from April to August (weekends only September to March). As you board, pay fares (one-way adult/child $15/13) by cash or check only.

Information

Tiburon Peninsula Chamber of Commerce (Map p124; ☎415-435-5633; www.tiburonchamber.org; 96b Main St; ⊙hours vary) Provides area information.

Getting There & Away

On Hwy 101, look for the off-ramp for Tiburon Blvd/E Blithedale Ave/Hwy 131. Drive about 4 miles east to downtown, where Tiburon Blvd intersects Main St.

Golden Gate Transit (p173) commuter bus 8 runs direct between San Francisco and Tiburon ($7, 60 to 80 minutes) once or twice on weekdays.

Blue & Gold Fleet (p129) sails several times daily from San Francisco's Pier 41 to Tiburon ($13, 30 to 50 minutes). Golden Gate Ferry (p129) connects San Francisco's Ferry Building with Tiburon ($13, 30 minutes) during weekday commuter hours only. You can transport bicycles for free on both ferry services.

In downtown Tiburon, the smaller **Angel Island Tiburon Ferry** (Map p124; ☎415-435-2131; http://angelislandferry.com; 21 Main St; round-trip adult/child/bicycle $15/13/1) departs from a nearby dock. It operates daily between April and October, and on weekends from November through March (no reservations, payment by cash or check only).

Sir Francis Drake Boulevard & Around

The towns along and nearby the Sir Francis Drake Blvd corridor – including Larkspur, Corte Madera, Ross, San Anselmo and Fairfax – evoke charmed small-town life, even though things get busy around Hwy 101.

Starting from the eastern section in **Larkspur**, window-shop along Magnolia Ave or explore the redwoods in nearby **Baltimore Canyon**. On the east side of the freeway is the hulking mass of **San Quentin State Penitentiary**, California's oldest and most notorious prison, founded in 1852.

Take the bicycle and pedestrian bridge from the ferry terminal across the road to the **Marin Country Mart**, a shopping center with a excellent eateries and outdoor seating. One favorite is the **Marin Brewing Company** (Map p124; ☎415-461-4677; www.marinbrewing.com; 1809 Larkspur Landing Circle, Larkspur; mains $12-19; ⏰11:30am-11pm Sun-Thu & Sat, to midnight Fri; 📶) brewpub, where you can see the glassed-in kettles behind the bar. The head brewer, Arne Johnson, has won many awards, and the Mt Tam Pale Ale complements the menu of pizza, burgers and hearty sandwiches.

Just south, **Corte Madera** is home to one of the Bay Area's best bookstores, **Book Passage** (Map p124; ☎415-927-0960; www.bookpassage.com; 51 Tamal Vista Blvd, Corte Madera; ⏰9am-9pm; 📶), in the Marketplace shopping center. It has a strong travel section and frequently hosts big-name author appearances and workshops. West along Sir Francis Drake, **San Anselmo** is a cute downtown area along San Anselmo Ave. The attractive center of neighboring **Fairfax** has ample dining and shopping options, along with a bohemian aesthetic best experienced via the cozy floor cushions, psychedelic tapestries and medicinal elixirs at **Wu Wei Tea Temple** (☎415-516-2578; www.wuweiteatemple.com; 1820 Sir Francis Drake Blvd, Fairfax; ⏰11am-10pm).

Six miles east of Olema on Sir Francis Drake Blvd, **Samuel P Taylor State Park** (☎415-488-9897; www.parks.ca.gov/samuelptaylor; 8889 Sir Francis Drake Blvd, Lagunitas; per car $8; ⏰8am-sunset; P🐾) has beautiful, secluded campsites in redwood groves and a coveted handful of new five-person cabins with electricity and wood stoves. The park's also located on the paved **Cross Marin Trail**, with miles of creekside landscape to explore along a former railroad grade.

San Rafael

The oldest and largest town in Marin, San Rafael is slightly less upscale than most of its neighbors but doesn't lack atmosphere. It's a common stop for travelers on their way to Point Reyes. Two blocks south of the 19th-century Spanish **Catholic mission** (☎415-454-4455; www.saintraphael.com; 1104 5th Ave; by donation; ⏰11am-4pm Wed-Fri, 10am-3pm some Sun) that gives the town its name, San Rafael's main drag, 4th St, is lined with cafes and shops. If you follow it west out of downtown San Rafael, it meets Sir Francis Drake Blvd and continues west to the coast. Just north of San Rafael, Lucas Valley Rd heads west toward Nicasio, passing George Lucas' Skywalker Ranch.

Sights

Marin County Civic Center ARCHITECTURE
(☎415-473-3762; www.marincounty.org/depts/cu/tours; 3501 Civic Center Dr; tour adult/child $10/5; ⏰8:30am-4:30pm; guided tour 10:30am Wed & Fri; P) Although he didn't live to see it built, this was architect Frank Lloyd Wright's final commission. He designed the horizontal hilltop buildings to flow with the natural beauty of the county's landscape, with sky-blue roofs and sand-colored walls. Come Wednesday or Friday morning for a 90-minute guided tour, or access the prerecorded audioguide and self-guiding tour brochure online anytime.

China Camp State Park STATE PARK
(☎415-456-0766; www.friendsofchinacamp.org; 100 China Camp Village Rd; per car $5, trail fee $3; ⏰8am-sunset; P) About 6 miles northeast of San Rafael, this is Marin's top spot for mountain biking, with 15 miles of lovely trails. It's also a decent stop for picnics and hikes. A Chinese shrimp-fishing village once stood here and a small museum exhibits interesting artifacts from the 19th-century settlement. From Hwy 101, take the N San Pedro Rd exit and continue east.

Sleeping & Eating

China Camp State Park Campground CAMPGROUND $
(☎reservations 800-444-7275; www.reservecalifornia.com; 730 N San Pedro Rd; tent sites $35; P) Pretty waterfront park with 31 walk-in tent sites. It has pleasant shade, and coin-op hot showers.

Panama Hotel B&B $$
(☎415-457-3993; www.panamahotel.com; 4 Bayview St; r $145-235, with shared bath from $128; ⏰reception 8am-6pm; ❄📶🐾) Basic rooms at this B&B, in a building dating from 1910, each have their own unique style and artsy decor such as crazy quilts and vibrant accent walls. The hotel restaurant offers a

homemade continental breakfast and particularly good fish tacos. Weekends require a two-night minimum stay.

★ Sunday Marin Farmers Market MARKET $
(☎ 415-472-6100; www.agriculturalinstitute.org; 3501 Civic Center Dr; ⊙ 8am-1pm Sun; P ♿) Nowhere else in Marin County do as many farmers, ranchers, fishers and gourmet-food makers gather than at this Sunday-morning farmers market, happening rain or shine at the Marin County Civic Center off Hwy 101. Browse the season's most luscious fruit, freshest vegetables, richest honey and cheeses, aromatic breads, colorful flowers and even handmade art, jewelry and crafts.

Sol Food PUERTO RICAN $$
(☎ 415-451-4765; www.solfoodrestaurant.com; 903 Lincoln Ave; mains $8-17; ⊙ 8am-10pm Sun-Thu, to 1am Fri & Sat) Lazy ceiling fans, tropical plants and the pulse of Latin rhythms create a soothing atmosphere for delicious dishes such as a *jíbaro* sandwich (made with fried plantain patties instead of bread) with thinly sliced steak, and other island-inspired meals concocted with plantains, organic veggies and free-range meats. This place is wildly popular. A sister restaurant has opened in Mill Valley.

☆ Entertainment

★ Terrapin Crossroads LIVE MUSIC
(☎ 415-524-2773; www.terrapincrossroads.net; 100 Yacht Club Dr; Cover charge free-$99; ⊙ 4-9:30pm Mon-Fri, from 11am Sat & Sun) Do you or did you miss the Marin of yesteryear? Terrapin Crossroads is your portal. Owner and Grateful Dead bassist – Phil Lesh regularly plays here with people he likes to jam with. All the archetypes come out of the woodwork – from bra-burners who never went back to guys in tie-dyes who personify the dancing bear.

Smith Rafael Film Center CINEMA
(☎ 415-454-1222; www.rafaelfilm.cafilm.org; 1118 4th St; tickets $9-11.75; ⊙ hours vary) Restored downtown cinema offering innovative art-house programming on three screens in state-of-the-art surrounds.

ℹ Information

Marin Convention & Visitors Bureau (☎ 415-925-2060; www.visitmarin.org; 1 Mitchell Blvd; ⊙ 9am-5pm Mon-Fri, hours can vary) Provides tourist information for the entire county.

ℹ Getting There & Away

Several Golden Gate Transit (p173) buses operate between San Francisco and the San Rafael Transit Center at 3rd and Hetherton Sts ($7.50, one hour). From the transit center, local buses ($2) run by Golden Gate Transit and **Marin Transit** (☎ 415-455-2000, 511; www.marintransit.org) fan out across the county.

For ambitious cyclists, the Cal Park Hill Tunnel is a safe subterranean passage from Larkspur – a terminus for Golden Gate Ferry (p129) services from San Francisco – to San Rafael.

Mill Valley

It's still hanging on to its bohemian roots, but beautiful Mill Valley, nestled under the redwoods at the base of Mt Tamalpais, is nowadays home to expensive houses, luxury cars and pricey boutiques. It's one of the Bay Area's most picturesque hamlets and is a great place to stay, visit or use as a base for forays to the mountain and the county's beaches.

Mill Valley was originally a logging town, its name stemming from an 1830s sawmill – the first in the Bay Area to provide lumber. Though the 1892 Mill Valley Lumber Company still greets motorists on Miller Ave, the town is a vastly different place today. Mill Valley also once served as the starting point for the scenic railway that carried visitors up Mt Tamalpais. The tracks were removed in 1940; today the Depot Bookstore & Cafe occupies the former rail station.

Activities

★ Dipsea Trail HIKING
(Map p124) A beloved though demanding hike, the 7-mile Dipsea Trail climbs over the coastal range and down to Stinson Beach (p137), cutting through a corner of Muir Woods (p136). This classic trail starts at **Old Mill Park** (Map p124; ☎ 415-383-1370; www.cityofmillvalley.org; Throckmorton Ave & Cascade Dr; ⊙ dawn-dusk; 👪) with a climb up 676 steps in three separate flights, and includes a few more ups and downs before reaching the ocean.

Festivals & Events

Mill Valley Film Festival FILM
(☎ 415-383-5256; www.mvff.com; adult/child per film $16.50/8; ⊙ Oct) An innovative, internationally regarded program of independent films screened in Mill Valley and San Rafael.

Sleeping & Eating

Lackluster midrange motels stand beside Hwy 101. Boutique hotels and inns shelter by the waterfront and on the forested hillsides around Mt Tamalpais.

Acqua Hotel BOUTIQUE HOTEL **$$**
(Map p124; ☎415-380-0400; www.acquahotel.com; 555 Redwood Hwy; r from $229; P ⊖ ❄ @ 📶 🐾) With views of the bay and Mt Tamalpais, plus a lobby with a welcoming fireplace, this boutique hotel doesn't lack for eye candy. Contemporary rooms are sleekly designed, featuring beautiful fabrics and aromatherapy bath products. Perks include free loaner bikes for guests, a morning espresso bar, and – in the evening – a wine service and freshly baked cookies.

★**Mountain Home Inn** INN **$$$**
(Map p124; ☎415-381-9000; www.mtnhomeinn.com; 810 Panoramic Hwy; r $215-400; ⊖ 📶) Set amid redwood, spruce and pine trees on a ridge of Mt Tamalpais with trails spreading in all directions, this retreat is both modern and rustic. The larger (more expensive) rooms are rugged beauties, with unfinished timbers forming floor-to-ceiling columns, as though the forest is shooting up through the floor. Smaller rooms are cozy dens for two.

Buckeye Roadhouse AMERICAN **$$**
(Map p124; ☎415-331-2600; www.buckeyeroadhouse.com; 15 Shoreline Hwy; dinner mains $22-37; ⏲11:30am-10:30pm Mon-Thu, to 11pm Fri & Sat, 10:30am-10pm Sun) Originally opened as a roadside stop in the 1930s, the Buckeye is a Marin County classic, and it always feels festive here. Stop off for upscale American favorites including barbecued baby back ribs, oysters Bingo and a devilish wedge of s'mores pie before getting back on Hwy 101.

Information

Mill Valley Chamber of Commerce (Map p124; ☎415-388-9700; www.enjoymillvalley.com; 85 Throckmorton Ave; ⏲10am-4pm Tue-Sat) Offers tourist information and maps.

Getting There & Away

From San Francisco or Sausalito, take Hwy 101 north to the Mill Valley/Stinson Beach/Hwy 1 exit. Follow Hwy 1/Shoreline Hwy to Almonte Blvd (which becomes Miller Ave), then follow Miller Ave into downtown Mill Valley.

From the north, take the E Blithedale Ave exit from Hwy 101, then head west into downtown Mill Valley.

Golden Gate Transit (p173) bus 4 runs directly from San Francisco to Mill Valley ($7, one hour, every 20 to 60 minutes) on weekdays. Marin Transit (p133) route 17 ($2, 30 minutes, every 30 to 60 minutes) connects Mill Valley with the Sausalito ferry terminal daily.

Mt Tamalpais State Park

Standing guard over Marin County, majestic Mt Tamalpais (Mt Tam) holds more than 60 miles of hiking and biking trails, lakes, streams, waterfalls and an impressive array of wildlife – from plentiful newts and hawks to rare foxes and mountain lions. Wind your way through meadows, oaks and madrone trees to breathtaking vistas over the San Francisco Bay, Pacific Ocean, towns, cities and forested hills rolling into the distance.

It's hard to believe that this serene 2572ft mountain (comprising **Mt Tamalpais State Park** (Map p124; ☎415-388-2070; www.parks.ca.gov/mttamalpais; per car $8; ⏲7am-sunset; P) 🍃, the **Marin Municipal Water District** (Map p124; ☎415-945-1455; www.marinwater.org), Muir Woods National Monument (p136), several Marin County open space areas and part of the Golden Gate Recreation Area) lies within an hour's drive of one of the state's largest metropolitan areas. It's still a bit of a secret and is the pride, love and *raison d'etre* for many Marin County residents.

Mt Tam was a sacred place to the Coast Miwok people for thousands of years before the arrival of Europeans and Americans. By the late 19th century, San Franciscans were escaping the bustle of the city with all-day outings on the mountain, and in 1896 the 'world's crookedest railroad' (281 turns) was completed from Mill Valley to the summit. Though the railroad was closed in 1930, Old Railroad Grade is today one of Mt Tam's most popular and scenic hiking and cycling paths.

Activities

Panoramic Hwy climbs from Mill Valley through the park to Stinson Beach. From Pantoll Station, it's 4.2 miles by car to **East Peak Summit**; take Pantoll Rd and then panoramic Ridgecrest Blvd to the top. A 10-minute hike leads to a fire lookout at the very top and awesome sea-to-bay views.

Mountain Biking

Cyclists must stay on the fire roads (and off the single-track trails) and keep to speeds under 15mph. Rangers are prickly about these rules and a ticket can result in a steep fine.

The most popular ride is the Old Railroad Grade from Mill Valley to Mt Tam's East Peak. Alternatively, from just west of Pantoll Station, cyclists can take either the **Deer Park Fire Road** – which runs close to the Dipsea Trail (p133) through giant redwoods to the main entrance of Muir Woods (p136) – or the aptly named **Coast View Trail**, which joins Hwy 1 north of Muir Beach Overlook (p136). Both options require a return to Mill Valley via Frank Valley/Muir Woods Rd, which climbs steadily (800ft) to Panoramic Hwy, then becomes Sequoia Valley Rd as it drops toward Mill Valley.

For more information on bicycle routes and rules, contact the Marin County Bicycle Coalition (p128); its *Marin Bicycle Map* ($12) is the gold standard for local cycling.

Old Railroad Grade MOUNTAIN BIKING
(Map p124) For a sweaty, 6-mile, 2500ft climb, start in Mill Valley at the end of W Blithedale Ave and cycle up to East Peak. For a head start, begin partway up at the Mountain Home Inn and follow Gravity Car Rd to the Old Railroad Grade, an easy half-hour ride to the summit.

Hiking

Mt Tamalpais is a hiking paradise. You can download a map of the mountain's trails and get lots of hiking ideas at OneTam (www.onetam.org), an excellent website combining all of the parts that make up the Mt Tamalpais recreation area into 'One Tam.'

One of the best hikes on the mountain is the **Steep Ravine Trail**. From Pantoll Station, it follows a wooded creek on to the coast (about 2.1 miles each way). For a longer hike, veer right (northwest) after 1.5 miles onto the Dipsea Trail (p133), which meanders through trees for 1 mile before ending at Stinson Beach (p137). Grab some lunch, then walk north through town and follow signs for the **Matt Davis Trail**, which leads 2.7 miles back to Pantoll Station.

Other top picks include the woodsy and watery 6-mile round-trip Cataract Falls & Alpine Lake hike and a 2.5 mile ramble with the best views of the Bay Area at the **East Peak** (Map p124).

Cataract Falls & Alpine Lake HIKING
(Map p124) A worthy hiking option on Mt Tam is the **Cataract Trail**, which runs along Cataract Creek. From the trailhead along Pantoll Rd, it's less than 3 miles to Alpine Lake. The last mile or so is a spectacular rooty staircase that descends alongside Cataract Falls, at its prettiest immediately after winter or spring rainfall.

Sleeping

Book ahead for a coveted cabin or tent site at Steep Ravine, try your luck finding a last-minute site at **Bootjack** (Map p124; info 415-388-2070; www.parks.ca.gov; Panoramic Hwy; tent sites $25; P 🐾) or **Pantoll** (Map p124; info 415-388-2070; www.parks.ca.gov; Panoramic Hwy; tent sites $25; P 🐾) campgrounds, or hike in to rustic West Point Inn.

★ **Steep Ravine** CAMPGROUND $
(Map p49; reservations 800-444-7275; www.reservecalifornia.com; tent sites $25, cabins $100, reservation fee $8; P) Just off Hwy 1, about 1 mile south of Stinson Beach, this jewel has seven primitive beachfront tent sites and nine rustic five-person cabins with woodstoves overlooking the ocean. Both options book up solid, very far in advance; reservations can be made up to seven months ahead.

West Point Inn LODGE $
(Map p124; info 415-388-9955; www.westpointinn.com; 100 Old Railroad Grade, Mill Valley; r with shared bath per adult/child $50/25, linen rental $20; 🚭) Load up your sleeping bag and hike 2 miles from Pantoll Station to this rustic 1904 hilltop hideaway built as a stopover for the Mill Valley and Mt Tamalpais Scenic Railway. It hosts pancake breakfasts (adult/child $10/5) every second Sunday of the month during summer.

Entertainment

Mountain Theater THEATER
(Cushing Memorial Amphitheater; Map p124; 415-383-1100; www.mountainplay.org; off Pantoll Rd; adult/child $40/25; late May–mid-Jun; 👪) Built by the Civilian Conservation Corps in the 1930s, the park's natural-stone, 3750-seat theater hosts the annual family-friendly 'Mountain Play' series on weekend afternoons in late spring and early summer. Shuttles run from Mill Valley (adult/child $10/5); otherwise, parking is $25 to $30.

Information

Pantoll Station (Map p124; 415-388-2070; www.parks.ca.gov; 801 Panoramic Hwy; hours vary; 📶) The park headquarters. Detailed park maps are sold here.

East Peak Visitor Center (Map p124; www.friendsofmttam.org; off Ridgecrest Blvd; 11am-4pm Sat & Sun) Small center with nature and historical exhibits and a gift shop.

Getting There & Away

To reach Pantoll Station (p135) by car, take Hwy 1 to the Panoramic Hwy and look for the signs. Panoramic Hwy climbs from Mill Valley through the park, then winds downhill to Stinson Beach.

From Fairfax, Bolinas Rd winds up over the mountain past many trailheads including Cataract Falls & Alpine Lake (p135). It ends, like the name says, in the tiny coastal town of Bolinas.

West Marin Stagecoach (p130) route 61 runs a few times per day on weekdays from Marin City via Mill Valley (more frequent weekend and holiday service from the Sausalito ferry terminal) to Pantoll Station ($2, 55 minutes).

Muir Woods National Monument

Walking through an awe-inspiring stand of some of the world's tallest trees is an experience to be had only in Northern California and a small part of southern Oregon. The old-growth redwoods at **Muir Woods** (Map p124; ☎415-561-2850; www.nps.gov/muwo; 1 Muir Woods Rd, Mill Valley; adult/child $15/free; ⏲8am-8pm mid-Mar–mid-Sep, to 7pm mid-Sep–early Oct, to 6pm Feb–mid-Mar & early Oct-early Nov, to 5pm early Nov-Jan; P) , just 12 miles north of the Golden Gate Bridge, make up the closest redwood stand to San Francisco; more grandiose redwood forests are found further north in Mendocino and Humboldt counties. The trees were initially eyed by loggers, and Redwood Creek, as the area was known, seemed ideal for a dam. Those plans were halted when power couple William Kent (a congressman and naturalist) and Elizabeth Thatcher Kent (a women's rights activist) bought a section of Redwood Creek and, in 1907, donated 295 acres to the federal government. President Theodore Roosevelt made the site a national monument in 1908, the name honoring John Muir, naturalist and founder of environmental organization the Sierra Club.

From 2020 to 2023, Muir Woods will be undergoing various renewal projects to protect and restore park resources. The monument will remain open, but you may encounter construction in some areas. You'll also notice large crowds, especially on weekends. Try to come midweek, early in the morning or late in the afternoon, when tour buses are less of a problem. Even at busy times, a short hike will get you out of the densest crowds and onto trails with huge trees and stunning vistas. A lovely cafe serves local and organic goodies and hot drinks that hit the spot on foggy days.

Activities

The 1-mile Main Trail Loop is a gentle walk alongside Redwood Creek to the 1000-year-old trees at **Cathedral Grove**; it returns via **Bohemian Grove**, where the tallest tree in the park stands more than 258ft high. The **Dipsea Trail** is a good 2-mile hike up to the top of aptly named Cardiac Hill.

You can also walk down into Muir Woods by taking trails from the Panoramic Hwy, such as the **Bootjack Trail** from the Bootjack picnic area, or from Mt Tamalpais' Pantoll Station campground, along the **Ben Johnson Trail**.

The flat trails of Muir Woods are particularly friendly to guests with disabilities.

Getting There & Away

Online reservations must be made in advance for Muir Woods parking, and during busy periods (most weekends and during summer), you'll be required to take a shuttle to/from Sausalito. The Muir Woods Shuttle (p130) leaves from Sausalito, where the ferries from San Francisco arrive.

To get there by car, drive north on Hwy 101, exit at Hwy 1 and continue north along Hwy 1/ Shoreline Hwy to the Panoramic Hwy (a right-hand fork). Follow that for about 1 mile to Four Corners, where you turn left onto Muir Woods Rd (there are plenty of signs).

Note that you may arrive by rideshare but there is no cell service, making it impossible to depart this way. Same goes for any vehicle requiring cell service to start the ignition.

Muir Beach

Muir Beach is a quiet hamlet with a pretty gray-sand beach. With a short, view-filled hike directly from the beach and a low-key, dog-friendly vibe (off-leash is allowed) it's a great place to spend an hour or two before grabbing lunch or a beer at the very British Pelican Inn.

Sights

Muir Beach Overlook VIEWPOINT

(Map p124; www.nps.gov/goga/planyourvisit/muirbeach.htm; Shoreline Hwy; P) Just over a mile northwest of Pelican Inn along Hwy 1, this overlook offers superb coastal views. During WWII scouts kept watch from the surrounding concrete lookouts for invading Japanese ships.

Muir Beach BEACH
(Map p124; www.nps.gov/goga/planyourvisit/muirbeach.htm; off Pacific Way; P) The turnoff from Hwy 1 is next to the coast's longest row of mailboxes at Mile 5.7, just before Pelican Inn. Aside from the beach, there are wetlands, creeks, lagoons and sand dunes providing a habitat for birds, California red-legged frogs and coho salmon. In winter you might spot monarch butterflies roosting in Monterey pines, and migratory whales swimming offshore.

Sleeping & Eating

Most people visit Muir Beach on a day trip from San Francisco.

Green Gulch LODGE $$
(Map p124; 415-383-3134; www.sfzc.org/greengulch; 1601 Shoreline Hwy; incl all meals s $100-175, d $175-250; P) In the hills above Muir Beach, this Zen Buddhist retreat center's contemporary accommodations are for personal retreats or those attending the center's workshops (see the website for a calendar of options). Delicious buffet-style vegetarian meals are included. Many vegetables come from the center's gorgeous organic gardens.

Pelican Inn PUB FOOD $$$
(Map p124; 415-383-6000; www.pelicaninn.com; 10 Pacific Way; dinner mains $15-38; 8-11am Sat & Sun, 11.30am-3pm & 5:30-9pm Sun-Fri, to 9.30pm Sat) The oh-so-English Pelican Inn lures in visitors almost as much as the beach itself. Hikers, cyclists and families come for pub lunches inside its dark, timbered restaurant and cozy bar, perfect for a pint, bangers-and-mash and a game of darts. Enjoy the lawn in sunshine or warm up beside the open fire when it's colder.

Upstairs are seven cozy rooms (from $224) with half-canopy beds.

Stinson Beach

Just 5 miles north of Muir Beach, wide, blond Stinson Beach is positively buzzing on warm weekends. The town flanks Hwy 1 for about three blocks and is speckled with a few shops, a small handful of eateries and lots of vacation rentals. The beach is often blanketed with fog, but when the sun's shining it's filled with surfers, families and gawkers. There are views of Point Reyes and San Francisco on clear days, and the beach is long enough for an invigorating stroll.

Sights

Stinson Beach BEACH
(Map p124; lifeguard tower 415-868-0942; www.nps.gov/goga/stbe.htm; off Hwy 1; from 9am daily, closing time varies seasonally; P) Stinson Beach (3 miles long) is a popular surf spot, with swimming advised from late May to mid-September only. For updated weather and surf conditions call 415-868-1922. The beach is one block west of Hwy 1. There's free parking but the lot often fills up before noon on sunny days.

Martin Griffin Preserve WILDLIFE RESERVE
(415-868-9244; www.egret.org/preserves_martin_griffin; 4900 Shoreline Hwy; suggested donation $20; hours vary; P) One of four regional Audubon Canyon Ranch preserves, this place hides in the hills above Bolinas Lagoon. It's a major nesting ground for great blue herons and great egrets; viewing scopes are set up behind blinds where you can watch these magnificent birds congregate to nest and hatch their chicks in tall redwoods. At low tide, harbor seals often doze on sandbars in the lagoon.

Sleeping & Eating

Sandpiper Lodging CABIN $$
(Map p124; 415-868-1632; www.sandpiperstinsonbeach.com; 1 Marine Way; r $145-180, cabins $220-250, cottage $350; P) Just off Hwy 1 and a quick stroll to the beach, Sandpiper's rooms, cabins and cottage are all comfortable and truly adorable. All have a gas fireplace and kitchenette, and are ensconced in a lush garden and picnic area. Two-night minimum stay on weekends and holidays between April and October. Bright and friendly management.

Parkside CAFE $$
(Map p124; 415-868-1272; www.parksidecafe.com; 43 Arenal Ave; restaurant mains $16-30, snack bar $4-9; 7:30am-9pm, coffee bar from 6am;) Famous for its hearty breakfasts and lunches, this cozy eatery next to the beach serves wood-fired pizzas and an array of fresh seasonal seafood at dinner, when reservations are recommended. The bakery cranks out decadent and delicious Gruyère levain bread and pastries, luring families, beachgoers, hikers and cyclists.

Parkside's outdoor snack bar serves burgers, sandwiches, fruit smoothies, baked goods and ice cream. Expect a queue.

Getting There & Away

Stinson Beach is nearly an hour's drive by car from San Francisco, though on weekends you should plan for toe-tapping traffic delays. Note that the closest gas station is in Bolinas.

West Marin Stagecoach (p130) route 61 runs a few daily minibuses ($2) from Marin City (one hour), with more frequent weekend and holiday services connecting with Sausalito ferries (75 minutes).

Bolinas

Here's a town where the farm stand is on the honor system, there's a giant 'free' box next to the central organic market, and most of the population wear a gray ponytail, carry a surfboard or both. The community became famous for taking down the 'Bolinas' signs on the highway so nonlocals wouldn't know how to get here. Be polite and discrete if you do find it, and you won't be run out of town.

Known as Jugville during the gold-rush days, the sleepy beachside hamlet later became home to writers, musicians and fisherfolk who cherish their bohemian culture and Bolinas' Victorian architecture, chilled-out beach and surrounding agricultural fields.

Sights & Activities

Palomarin Field Station Visitor Center NATURE CENTER
(☎415-868-0655; www.pointblue.org; 999 Mesa Rd; ⊙dawn-dusk; P) FREE Formerly Point Reyes Bird Observatory, Point Blue's Palomarin Field Station has bird-banding and netting demonstrations, an unstaffed visitor center and a nature trail. Banding demonstrations are held Tuesday to Sunday mornings from May through late November, and on Wednesday, Saturday and Sunday the rest of the year. Show up between 8am and 11am for the best bird-watching.

★**Bass Lake & Alamere Falls Trail** HIKING
(www.nps.gov/pore/planyourvisit/alamere_falls.htm) At the end of Mesa Rd, the Palomarin parking lot accesses various hiking trails in the southern part of Point Reyes National Seashore (p141), including the easy (and very popular) 3-mile trail to lovely **Bass Lake**. Continuing another 1.5 miles northwest, you'll reach an unmaintained trail to **Alamere Falls**, a fantastic flume plunging 30ft off a cliff and onto the beach.

A sweet inland spot buffered by tall trees, small Bass Lake is perfect for a swim on a toasty day. You can dive in wearing your birthday suit (or not), bring an inner tube to float about, or do a long lap all the way across.

Approaching Alamere Falls, sketchy beach access may make it more enjoyable to hike another 1.5 miles along the trail to Wildcat Beach, then backtrack a mile south on sand. Note that this trail has become so popular that on weekends parking becomes nearly impossible.

2 Mile Surf Shop SURFING
(☎415-868-0264, surf report 415-868-2412; www.2milesurf.com; 22 Brighton Ave; surfboard rental 3hr/full day $30/40; ⊙9am-6pm May-Oct, 10am-5pm Nov-Apr) Surfing's popular in these parts, and this shop behind the post office rents boards and wetsuits and also gives lessons.

Sleeping & Eating

Bolinas has one historical **inn** (☎415-868-1311; http://smileyssaloon.com; 41 Wharf Rd; r $135-225;) to stay in, though during research it was being renovated. There's also a B&B above the pizza place, or you could stay in Stinson Beach 6 miles south.

Eleven Wharf PIZZA $$
(☎415-868-1133; www.11wharfroad.com; 11 Wharf Rd; pizzas $14-17; ⊙5-9pm Thu-Mon;) This chic, sister-owned 'backyard-to-table' restaurant offers freshly shucked oysters, delicious Neapolitan-style pizza (topped with fresh local produce) and a mostly natural wine list. Save space for the *fior di latte gelato* made with local water-buffalo milk.

You can also stay in one of the two small, elegant rooms (from $180) with cozy bathrooms and splashes of bohemia, including Mexican throw-blankets and Balinese hardwood accents.

Coast Cafe AMERICAN $$
(☎415-868-2298; www.coastcafebolinas.com; 46 Wharf Rd; dinner mains $16-29; ⊙11:30am-3pm & 5-8pm Tue-Thu, to 9pm Fri, 8am-3pm & 5-9pm Sat, to 8pm Sun) Everyone in town jockeys for outdoor seats among the flower boxes for fish and chips, barbecued oysters, or buttermilk pancakes with damn good coffee. Live music on Thursday and Sunday nights.

Getting There & Away

By car, follow Hwy 1 north from Stinson Beach and turn west for Bolinas at the first road north of the lagoon. At the first stop sign, take a left onto Olema–Bolinas Rd and follow it 2 miles to town.

West Marin Stagecoach (p130) route 61 travels four times daily from the Marin City transit hub to downtown Bolinas ($2); a more frequent weekend and holiday service connects with the Sausalito ferry.

Olema & Nicasio

These two tiny towns – Olema in a shady grove near the junction of Hwy 1 and Sir Francis Drake Blvd, and Nicasio, in the midst of horse ranches and grassy open hillsides – are about 10 miles apart.

Olema was the main settlement in West Marin in the 1860s. Back then, there was stagecoach service to San Rafael and six saloons. In 1875, when the railroad was built through Point Reyes Station instead of Olema, the town's importance began to fade.

Nicasio's claim to fame is that it's the geographic center of Marin County.

The **Bolinas Ridge Trail** (www.nps.gov/goga/planyourvisit/bolinas.htm), a 10.5-mile series of ups and downs for hikers or cyclists, starts about 1 mile east of Olema, off Sir Francis Drake Blvd. It has great views.

In the former Olema Inn, a creaky 1876 building, hyper local **Sir & Star** (☎415-663-1034; www.sirandstar.com; 10000 Sir Francis Drake Blvd, Olema; mains $15-34, Sat prix-fixe menu $85; ⏲5-9pm Thu-Sun; 📶) restaurant delights with seasonal bounty such as Tomales Bay oysters, seafood bouillabaisse and duck 'faux' gras. Reservations recommended.

A few minutes away in Nicasio, get free tastings at the **Nicasio Valley Cheese Company** (☎415-662-6200; http://nicasiocheese.com; 5300 Nicasio Valley Rd, Nicasio; ⏲10am-5pm), one of Marin County's most renowned cheesemaking shops. Crafted on a ranch started by a Swiss immigrant family, these soft cheeses – such as the award-winning Foggy Morning *fromage blanc* – appear on chef's menus and at farmers markets around the Bay Area.

You can get a dose of local flavor at the tiny town's music venue, **Rancho Nicasio** (☎415-662-2219; www.ranchonicasio.com; 1 Old Rancheria Rd, Nicasio; tickets free-$45; ⏲11:30am-9pm Mon-Thu, to midnight Fri, 11am-midnight Sat & Sun), a rustic saloon that regularly attracts local and national blues, rock and country performers.

Getting There & Away

Olema is about 13 miles northwest of Stinson Beach via Hwy 1. Nicasio is at the west end of Lucas Valley Rd, 10 miles from Hwy 101.

West Marin Stagecoach (p130) route 68 runs several times daily to Olema from the San Rafael Transit Center, stopping at Samuel P Taylor State Park (p132).

Point Reyes Station

Though the railroad stopped coming through in 1933 and the town is small, Point Reyes Station is nevertheless the hub of western Marin County. Dominated by dairies and ranches, the region was invaded by artists in the 1960s. Today Main St is a diverting blend of art galleries, tourist shops, restaurants and cafes. The town has a rowdy **saloon** (☎415-663-1661; 11201 Hwy 1; ⏲10am-2am Mon-Sat, to midnight Sun) and the occasional smell of cattle on the afternoon breeze.

Activities & Tours

Blue Waters Kayaking KAYAKING
(☎415-669-2600; www.bluewaterskayaking.com; 11401 Shoreline Hwy; rentals/tours from $70/78; ⏲usually 9am-5pm, last rental 3pm) This long-running outfit offers guided tours of Tomales Bay; otherwise, you can get a kayak delivered to your lodgings and paddle to secluded beaches on your own. No experience necessary. Book ahead for full-moon and bioluminescence excursions.

★**Food and Farm Tours** FOOD & DRINK
(☎415-599-9222; https://foodandfarmtours.com; tours $195 per person; ⏲tour times vary) These intimate tours highlight the agricultural bounty of West Marin through behind-the-scenes farm visits, sustainability discussions and oodles of delicious samples. The most popular and comprehensive tour, 'Flavors of Point Reyes,' features a creamery, an oyster farm, a bakery, a **meadery** (☎415-663-9122; www.heidrunmeadery.com; 11925 Hwy 1; tasting $15, incl tour $35; ⏲11am-4pm Mon & Wed-Fri, to 5pm Sat & Sun) and an organic veggie farm. More specialized tours focus on oyster (p140) and **cheese** (The Fork; ☎800-591-6878; www.pointreyescheese.com/fork; 14700 Shoreline Hwy; tours from $25; ⏲tours by appointment only) operations.

Sleeping

Cute little cottages, cabins and B&Bs are plentiful in and around Point Reyes. The **West Marin Chamber of Commerce** (☎415-663-9232; www.pointreyes.org; 60 4th St; ⏲11am-3pm Fri-Sun) and the Point Reyes Lodging Association (www.ptreyes.com) have additional listings.

Windsong Cottage Guest Yurt YURT $$
(☎415-663-9695; www.windsongcottage.com; 25 McDonald Lane; d $195-230; P ⊖ 📶) A wood-burning stove, private outdoor hot tub, California king bed and kitchen stocked with breakfast supplies make this round skylighted abode a slice of rural heaven. Book at least six weeks in advance.

Nick's Cove COTTAGE $$$
(☎415-663-1033; www.nickscove.com; 23240 Hwy 1, Marshall; cottages $315-850; P ⊖ 📶 🐾) Fronting a peaceful cove at Tomales Bay, these water-view and waterfront vacation cottages are expensive, but oh-so romantic. Some have a wood-burning fireplace, deep soaking tub, private deck and TV. Two-night minimum stay on weekends and holidays. It's about a 20-minute drive north of Point Reyes Station.

Eating

★Hog Island Oyster Company SEAFOOD $
(☎415-663-9218; www.hogislandoysters.com; 20215 Hwy 1, Marshall; dozen oysters $14-36, picnic per person $5; ⏲shop 9am-5pm daily, picnic area from 10:30am, cafe & bar 11am-5pm Fri-Mon) Ten miles north of Point Reyes Station you'll find the salty turnout for Hog Island Oyster Company. There's not much to see: just some picnic tables and BBQ grills, an outdoor cafe and a window selling the famously silky oysters and a few other provisions. A picnic at the farm makes an unforgettable lunch; it's popular, and reservations are required.

If you don't feel like shucking your own, order (at the bar) oysters on the half shell or grilled, along with beer, wine and dishes made from local ingredients.

★Cowgirl Creamery & Cantina DELI $
(☎415-663-9335; www.cowgirlcreamery.com; 80 4th St; deli items $3-12; ⏲10am-5pm Wed-Sun; ✎) Perhaps the best cheeses made in Northern California, Marin, and probably beyond. The milk is local and organic, with vegetarian rennet in soft cheeses.The cheesemaking facility is in an indoor deli and marketplace in an old barn that also sells farm-fresh picnic items, organic produce and local clothing and crafts.

Bovine Bakery BAKERY $
(☎415-663-9420; www.bovinebakeryptreyes.com; 11315 Hwy 1; most items $2-6; ⏲6:30am-5pm Mon-Fri, 7am-5pm Sat, 7am-4pm Sun; ✎) Don't leave town without sampling something buttery from this tiny, beloved country bakery. Indulging in a sweet bear-claw pastry and an organic coffee is a good way to kick off your morning.

Marshall Store SEAFOOD $$
(☎415-663-1339; www.themarshallstore.com; 19225 Hwy 1, Marshall; mains $11-25; ⏲10am-4pm Wed-Fri & Mon, to 5pm Sat & Sun) This former country store is now a relaxed waterfront eatery, perfect for slurping down BBQ or raw Tomales Bay oysters (the oyster farm is owned by the same people). Smoked-seafood plates and sandwiches aren't half bad either. It's a 15-minute drive north of Point Reyes Station.

Getting There & Away

From Hwy 101 and San Rafael, it's about a 45-minute drive to Point Reyes Station. Driving the coast, it's less than 30 minutes from Bolinas. Hwy 1 becomes Main St in town, running right through the center.

West Marin Stagecoach (p130) route 68 runs to Point Reyes Station several times daily from the San Rafael Transit Center ($2, 75 minutes) via Bear Valley Visitor Center at Point Reyes National Seashore .

Inverness

The last outposts on the journey westward toward the tip of Point Reyes, the two tiny adjacent towns of Inverness Park and Inverness stretch out along the west side of Tomales Bay. Several great beaches are but a short drive away.

Sleeping

Cottages at Point Reyes Seashore COTTAGE $$
(☎415-669-7250; www.cottagespointreyes.com; 13275 Sir Francis Drake Blvd; r $159-249; P ⊖ 📶 ≋ 🐾) Tucked into the woods, this family-friendly place offers contemporary kitchenette rooms in A-frame structures, plus a tennis court, hot tub, croquet, horseshoe pitches, barbecue grills and a saltwater pool. There's also a garden and private nature trail.

★Dancing Coyote Beach Cottages COTTAGE $$$
(☎415-669-7200; www.dancingcoyotebeach.com; 12794 Sir Francis Drake Blvd; cottages $200-325; P ⊖ 📶 🐾) Serene and comfortable, these four modern cottages back right onto Tomales Bay, with skylights and decks extending the views in all directions. Full kitchens

contain locally sourced breakfast foods, and fireplaces are stocked with firewood for foggy nights.

Getting There & Away

From Hwy 1, Sir Francis Drake Blvd heads northwest straight into Inverness. West Marin Stagecoach (p130) route 68 from San Rafael ($2) makes several daily runs here via Olema and Point Reyes Station.

Point Reyes National Seashore

Windswept Point Reyes peninsula is a rough-hewn beauty that has always lured marine mammals and migratory birds; it's also home to scores of shipwrecks. In 1579, Sir Francis Drake landed here to repair his ship, the *Golden Hind*. During his five-week stay he mounted a brass plaque near the shore claiming this land for England. In 1595 the first of many ships lost in these waters went down. The *San Augustine* was a Spanish treasure ship out of Manila, laden with luxury goods; to this day bits of its cargo still wash up on shore. Despite modern navigation, the dangerous waters here continue to claim the occasional boat.

Point Reyes National Seashore (Map p49; ☎415-654-5100; www.nps.gov/pore; P) FREE protects 100 sq miles of pristine ocean beaches and coastal wilderness and has excellent hiking and camping opportunities. Be sure to bring warm clothing, as even the sunniest days can quickly turn cold and foggy.

Sights & Activities

Point Reyes Lighthouse LIGHTHOUSE
(☎415-669-1534; www.nps.gov/pore/planyourvisit/lighthouse.htm; end of Sir Francis Drake Blvd; ⊙10am-4:30pm Fri-Mon, first gallery 2:30-4pm Fri-Mon (weather permitting); P) FREE With wild terrain and ferocious winds, this spot feels like the end of the earth and offers the best whale-watching along the coast. The lighthouse, which reopened in late 2019 after a multimillion-dollar renovation, sits below the headlands; to reach it you need to descend more than 300 stairs.

Five Brooks Ranch HORSEBACK RIDING
(☎415-663-1570; www.fivebrooks.com; 8001 Shoreline Hwy, Olema; trail rides $50-280; ⊙9am-5pm; 👪) Explore the Point Reyes landscape on horseback with a trail ride. Take a slow amble through a pasture or ascend Inverness Ridge for views of the Olema Valley. If you can stay in the saddle for six hours, ride along the coastline to Alamere Falls (p138) via Wildcat Beach.

Chimney Rock HIKING
(www.nps.gov/pore/planyourvisit/chimney_rock.htm; off Sir Francis Drake Blvd) Not far from the lighthouse, Chimney Rock is a fine short hike, especially in spring when wildflowers are blossoming. During winter, a viewing area allows you to spy on an elephant seal colony hauled out below the cliffs. The large seals are males; keep a safe distance.

Sleeping

Wake up to deer nibbling under a blanket of fog at one of Point Reyes' very popular **backcountry campgrounds** (☎reservations 877-444-6777; www.nps.gov/pore/planyourvisit/campgrounds.htm; tent sites $20), or stay at the pastoral hostel. More inns, motels and B&Bs are found in nearby Inverness, off Sir Francis Drake Blvd.

HI Point Reyes HOSTEL $
(☎415-663-8811; www.hiusa.org/pointreyes; 1390 Limantour Spit Rd; dm $35-39, r with shared bath $105-130; ⊙reception 7:30-10:30am & 4:30-10pm; P 🚭 @) 🌿 Just off Limantour Rd, this rustic hostel has bunkhouses with warm and cozy front rooms, big-view windows and outdoor areas with hill vistas. A newer ecofriendly building has four private rooms (two-night minimum stay on weekends) and a modern kitchen. It's in a beautiful secluded valley 2 miles from the ocean and surrounded by lovely hiking trails.

Information

At park headquarters, a mile west of Olema, **Bear Valley Visitor Center** (☎415-464-5100; www.nps.gov/pore; 1 Bear Valley Rd, Point Reyes Station; ⊙10am-5pm Mon-Fri, 9am-5pm Sat & Sun) has information and maps. Stop here if you have questions or need advice planning your adventure. You can also get information at the Point Reyes Lighthouse and the **Kenneth Patrick Center** (☎415-669-1250; www.nps.gov/pore; 1 Drakes Beach Rd; ⊙9:30am-4:30pm Sat, Sun & holidays late Dec-late Mar or early Apr) (seasonal) at Drakes Beach.

Getting There & Away

By car you can get to Point Reyes a few different ways. The curviest is along Hwy 1, through Stinson Beach and Olema. More direct is to exit

Hwy 101 in San Rafael and follow Sir Francis Drake Blvd all the way to the tip of Point Reyes. By either route, it's less than 1½ hours to Olema from San Francisco barring weekend and rush-hour traffic jams.

Just north of Olema, where Hwy 1 and Sir Francis Drake Blvd come together, is Bear Valley Rd; turn left to reach Bear Valley Visitor Center (p141). If you're heading to the outermost reaches of Point Reyes, follow Sir Francis Drake Blvd north toward Point Reyes Station, turning left and heading out onto the peninsula (at least a 45-minute drive).

West Marin Stagecoach (p130) route 68 from San Rafael stops several times daily at the Bear Valley Visitor Center ($2, 70 minutes) before continuing to the town of Point Reyes Station.

Getting Around

On weekends and holidays from late December through mid-April, visitors may be required to ride a shuttle bus from **Drakes Beach** (www.nps.gov/pore/planyourvisit/beaches.htm) to the lighthouse (p141) and Chimney Rock (p141) areas. Purchase shuttle bus tickets ($7) at Kenneth Patrick Center (p141). First tickets are sold at 9:30am and last tickets at 3pm; the bus comes every 15 to 20 minutes.

EAST BAY

Berkeley and Oakland are what most San Franciscans think of as the East Bay, though the area includes numerous other suburbs that swoop up from the bayside flats into exclusive enclaves in the hills. Many residents of the 'West Bay' would like to think they needn't ever cross the Bay Bridge or take a Bay Area Rapid Transit (BART) train through an underwater tunnel. But a wealth of museums and historical sites, a world-famous university, excellent restaurants and bars, a creative arts scene, offbeat shopping, woodsy parks and better weather are just some of the attractions that lure travelers from San Francisco over to the sunny side of the bay.

Oakland

Oakland is where San Francisco's diverse, artsy and radical folks have fled to escape an astronomical cost of living. Oaklanders are fiercely proud their home retains the mixed ethnic tableau and unapologetic left-wing politics San Francisco once enshrined, and they know this backdrop is threatened by million-dollar residential homes, already present even in middle-class neighborhoods.

Is this the last of what the Bay Area was? We're not sure, but between the food, nightlife and fabulous outdoors scene, Oakland is a great example of what the Bay Area can be.

Sights & Activities

Oakland is full of historical buildings and a growing number of colorful businesses. With such easy access from San Francisco via BART or ferry, it's worth spending part of a day exploring here on foot or by bicycle.

Downtown, Chinatown & Waterfront

Pedestrianized **City Center**, between Broadway and Clay St, 12th and 14th Sts, forms the heart of downtown Oakland. There's also a newly car-free corridor along 13th St between Broadway and Franklin. Nearby **City Hall** (Map p144; www.oaklandca.gov; 1 Frank H Ogawa Plaza; 9am-5pm Mon-Fri; 12th St Oakland City Center) is a beautifully refurbished 1914 beaux-arts building.

Old Oakland, west of Broadway between 8th and 10th Sts, is lined with restored historical buildings dating from the late 19th century. The area has a lively restaurant and after-work scene, and a farmers market every Friday from 8am until 2pm.

East of Broadway and bustling with commerce, Oakland's Chinatown centers on Franklin and Webster Sts, as it has since the 1850s. Jack London Sq is on the waterfront further south.

Oakland Museum of California MUSEUM

(OMCA; Map p144; 510-318-8427, 510-318-8400; www.museumca.org; 1000 Oak St; adult/child $16/7, 1st Sun each month free; 11am-5pm Wed, Thu, Sat & Sun, to 9pm Fri; P; Lake Merritt) Every museum has an educational mission, and this one is dedicated to California. You'll find rotating exhibitions on artistic and scientific themes, and permanent galleries dedicated to the state's diverse ecology and history, as well as California art, from traditional landscapes to reimagined cartography. Start your weekend here on a Friday night (after 5pm), when DJs, food trucks and free art workshops for kids make it a fun hangout.

Uptown & Lake Merritt

North of downtown Oakland, the Uptown district has many of the city's art deco beauties, such as the Fox Theater (p149) and Paramount Theatre (p149), and a proliferating arts, restaurant and nightlife scene. The area stretches between Telegraph and Broadway, bounded by Grand Ave to the north.

Follow Grand Ave east of Broadway and you'll run into the shores of Lake Merritt. Grand Ave (north of the lake) and Lakeshore Ave (east of the lake) are pedestrian-friendly streets for local shops, restaurants, cafes and bars.

Lake Merritt LAKE

(Map p144; 510-238-3187; www.lakemerritt.org; sunrise-sunset; P; B Lake Merritt) FREE An urban respite, Lake Merritt is a popular place to stroll or go running (a 3.2-mile paved path circles the lake), with bonsai and botanical gardens, a children's amusement park, bird sanctuary, green spaces, a **boathouse** (Map p144; 510 238 2196; www.oaklandca.gov/topics/boating-at-lake-merritt-boating-center; 568 Bellevue Ave; boat rentals per hour $15-25; daily Mar-Oct, Sat & Sun Nov-Feb; AC Transit 12) and **gondola rides** (Map p144; 510-663-6603; www.gondolaservizio.com; 1520 Lakeside Dr; 30/50min cruise from $60/85; B Lake Merritt). The two main commercial streets skirting Lake Merritt are Grand Ave, running along the north shore, and Lakeshore Ave on the eastern edge of the lake.

Children's Fairyland AMUSEMENT PARK

(Map p144; 510-452-2259; www.fairyland.org; 699 Bellevue Ave; $12, child under 1yr free; 10am-4pm Mon-Fri, to 5pm Sat & Sun Jun-Aug, off-season hours vary; P; AC Transit 12) This 10-acre kiddie attraction dates from 1950, and hasn't changed a whole lot since. We mean that as a compliment! Children's Fairyland, with its little Aesop theater and Peter Rabbit's garden, has all of the nostalgia feels. In a stark contrast to most hyper-frenetic contemporary kids' play parks, there's a raw authenticity to the faded attractions. That said, the park's oldest ride – an *Alice in Wonderland*-themed carousel dubbed the Wonder-Go-Round – was beautifully restored in 2019.

Jack London Square

Jack London Square SQUARE

(Map p144; 510-645-9292; www.jacklondonsquare.com; Broadway & Embarcadero; 24hr, shop, restaurant & bar hours vary; P; Broadway Shuttle) The area where writer and adventurer Jack London once raised hell now bears his name. It offers grand opportunities for kayaking around the harbor or strolling the waterfront, especially when the Sunday **farmers market** (415-291-3276; www.cuesa.org;; 10am-3pm Sun;) takes over. At the time of writing, a 40,000-sq-ft, two-level food hall was being constructed at 55 Harrison St. Contemporary redevelopment has previously added a cinema complex, condo development and popular restaurants and bars.

A replica of Jack London's Yukon **cabin** (Map p144; 1-199 Webster St Tube; Broadway Shuttle) stands at the eastern end of the square. Oddly, people throw coins inside as if it's a fountain. Another interesting historical stop, adjacent to the tiny cabin, is Heinold's First & Last Chance Saloon (p148). Catch a ferry from San Francisco – a worthwhile excursion in itself – and you'll land just paces away.

USS Potomac SHIP

(Map p144; 510 627 1215; www.usspotomac.org; 540 Water St; adult/child $10/free; tours 11am-2pm Wed, Fri & Sun; Broadway Shuttle) Franklin D Roosevelt's 'floating White House,' the 165ft USS *Potomac*, is moored at Clay and Water Sts by the ferry dock, and is open for dockside tours. Two- and three-hour cruises (adult/child two hour $55/35, three hour including lunch $75/55) are scheduled several times a month from March through November (book far in advance).

Piedmont Ave, Temescal & Rockridge

North of downtown Oakland, Broadway becomes a lengthy strip of car dealerships called Auto Row. Detour a couple of blocks east to Piedmont Ave, wall-to-wall with vintage-clothing stores, coffeehouses, restaurants and an art-house cinema.

A half-dozen or so long blocks west of Broadway, Temescal has a reputation for artiness and hipness. Find unique shops, creative restaurants and happening bars on Telegraph Ave north of 40th St.

Rockridge, a leafy, upscale neighborhood, is further north between Broadway and Telegraph Ave. College Ave is lined with upmarket boutiques, a bookstore, pubs and cafes and a few fancy restaurants.

Mountain View Cemetery CEMETERY

(Map p155; 510-658-2588; www.mountainviewcemetery.org; 5000 Piedmont Ave; 6:30am-

Central Oakland

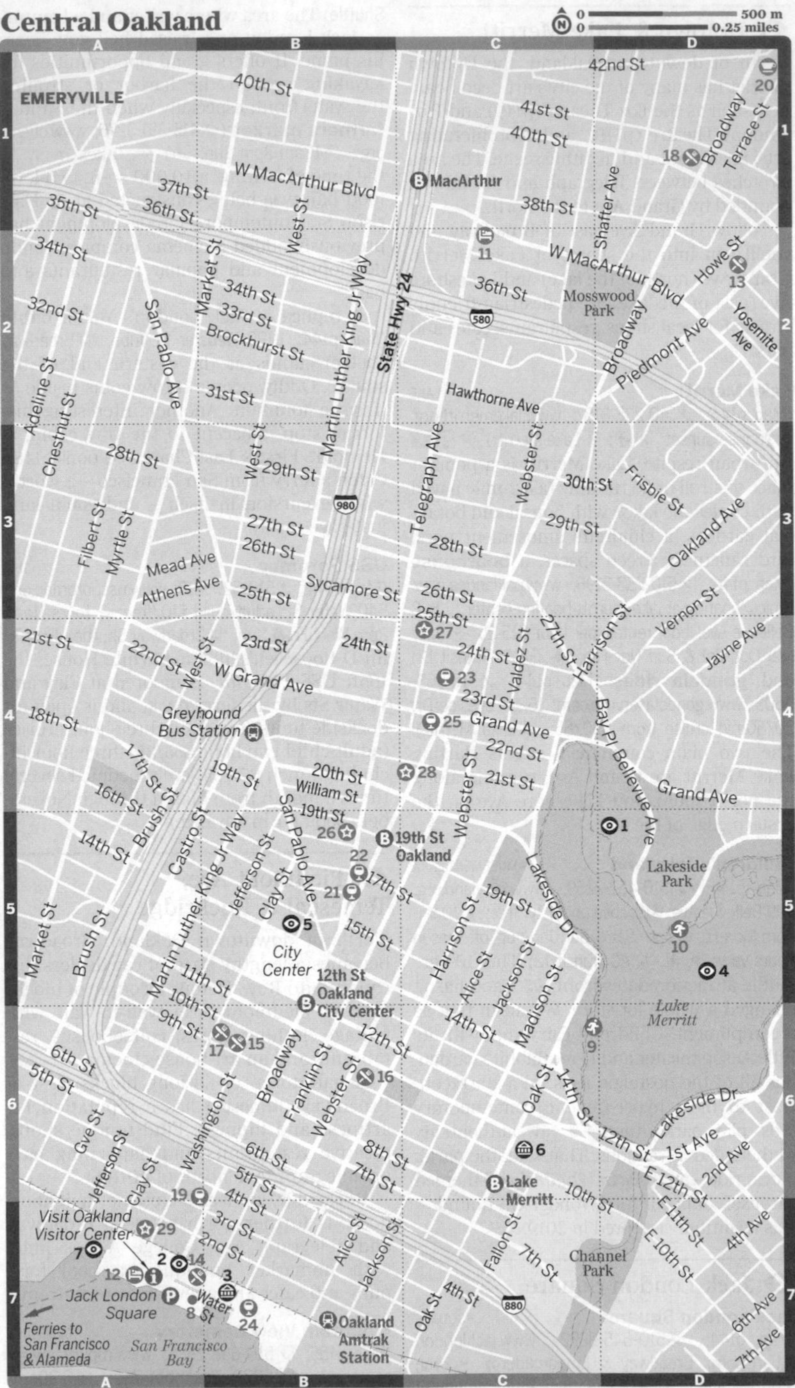

Central Oakland

6:30pm; P; AC Transit 12) At the northern end of Piedmont Ave, this is perhaps the most serene and lovely artificial landscape in the East Bay. Designed by Frederick Law Olmsted (the landscape architect of New York City's Central Park), its 226 acres are great for walking and the views are stupendous.

Oakland Hills

The large parks of the Oakland Hills are ideal for day hiking and challenging cycling. The **East Bay Regional Parks** (888-327-2757; www.ebparks.org; per car free-$6; hours vary;) manages more than 1200 miles of trails in 65 regional parks, preserves and recreation areas in the Alameda and Contra Costa Counties.

Off Hwy 24, **Robert Sibley Volcanic Regional Preserve** is the northernmost of the Oakland Hills parks. It has great views of the Bay Area from its **Round Top Peak** (1761ft). From Sibley, Skyline Blvd runs south past **Redwood Regional Park** (Map p155; 888-327-2757; www.ebparks.org/parks/redwood; 7867 Redwood Rd; per vehicle $5; 5am-10pm;) and adjacent **Joaquin Miller Park** to **Anthony Chabot Regional Park**. A hike or mountain-bike ride through the groves and along the hilltops of any of these sizable parks will make you forget you're in an urban area. At the southern end of Chabot Park is the enormous **Lake Chabot**, with an easy trail along its shore, and canoes, kayaks and other boats for rent from the **Lake Chabot Marina** (510-247-2526; www.lakechabotrecreation.com; 17936 Lake Chabot Rd, Castro Valley; rentals from $27; 6:30am-6pm Mon-Thu, to 7:30pm Fri-Sun May-early Sep, off-season hours vary;).

★Chabot Space & Science Center MUSEUM
(Map p155; 510-336-7300; www.chabotspace.org; 10000 Skyline Blvd; adult/child $18/14; 10am-5pm Wed-Sun; P; AC Transit 339) Stargazers will go gaga over this kid-oriented science and technology center in the Oakland Hills with loads of exhibits on subjects such as space travel and eclipses, as well as cool planetarium shows. When the weather's good, check out the free Friday and Saturday evening viewings using a 20in refractor telescope.

Admission is just $5 on the first Friday evening of each month (6pm to 10pm), when the museum organizes hands-on activities, science demonstrations, movies and night hikes.

Festivals & Events

Oakland First Fridays STREET CARNIVAL
(510-361-0615; www.oaklandfirstfridays.org; Telegraph Ave; entry by donation; 5-9pm 1st Fri each month; ; B 19th St Oakland) A kinetic street festival takes place on the first Friday of the month, when a five-block stretch of Telegraph Ave closes to car traffic. Thousands of people turn out for food vendors, live music and performances.

WORTH A TRIP

SPIRITS ALLEY

Ever fancied a boozy stroll through a former Naval Air Station? The western tip of Alameda Island has been transformed for this purpose and dubbed Spirits Alley, with artisan distilleries, wine-tasting rooms and breweries springing up in historical buildings and long-deserted airplane hangars.

Perched along Monarch Street, top draws include distillery tours at Hangar 1 Vodka, wine tasting in Rock Wall's geodesic dome and learning some (drunken) history at **St George Spirits** (Map p155; ☎510-769-1601; www.stgeorgespirits.com; 2601 Monarch St, Alameda; tour & tasting $20; ⊙tastings & tours Thu-Sun), the alley's anchor. St George established its distillery here in 1982, and the tours of the 65,000-sq-ft facility are as informative as they are intoxicating.

Before you start seeing double, be sure to check out the striking panoramic views of the San Francisco skyline across the bay, and ward off those hangovers with food truck goodness. The experience is all the more delightful for those who arrive and depart by San Francisco Bay Ferry (p150); it's a quick and scenic trip from San Francisco's Ferry Building or Pier 41 (one-way $7.20, 15-25 minutes).

Sleeping

Oakland has surprisingly few places to stay, apart from chain motels and hotels off the freeways, downtown and near the airport.

Anthony Chabot Regional Park CAMPGROUND $
(☎reservations888-327-2757;www.reserveamerica.com; end of Marciel Rd, Castro Valley; tent sites $25, RV sites with hookups $30-40; P 🐾) In the East Bay's forested hills, this 3304-acre park has 75 campsites and hot showers. Open year-round.

Inn at Temescal MOTEL $$
(Map p144; ☎510-652-9800; www.innattemescal.com; 3720 Telegraph Ave; r $119-189; P 📶; B MacArthur) There's a fair bit of mid-century, swinging Cali charm at this motel, located a short walk from the BART and Temescal's main strip. Walk through exterior doors painted in avocado green and sunset orange to find clean-lined rooms with pillow-top mattresses, wall-sized historical photos and retro accents. Expect some street noise

★**Claremont Resort & Spa** RESORT $$$
(Map p155; ☎510-843-3000; www.fairmont.com/claremont-berkeley; 41 Tunnel Rd; d from $300; P @ 📶 🏊 🐾) The East Bay's classy crème de la crème, this Fairmont-owned historical hotel is a glamorous white 1915 building with elegant restaurants, a fitness center, swimming pools, tennis courts and a full-service spa. The bay-view rooms are superb. It's located at the foot of the Berkeley Hills, off Hwy 13 (Tunnel Rd), but is technically located in Oakland. Parking is $30.

Waterfront Hotel BOUTIQUE HOTEL $$$
(Map p144; ☎510-836-3800; www.hyatt.com; 10 Washington St; r $127-489, ste $509-599; P @ 📶 🏊 🐾) Paddle-printed wallpaper and lamps fashioned from faux lanterns round out the playful nautical theme of this cheerful harborside hotel. A huge brass-topped fireplace warms the foyer, and comfy rooms include iPad docking stations and coffeemakers. Unless you're an avid train-spotter, water-view rooms are preferred, as trains rattle by on the city side. Complimentary wine-and-cheese reception on weekdays. Parking is $32.

Eating

Oakland's eateries nearly rival those of foodie neighbor San Francisco, largely because immigrant and young chefs can more readily afford to start a business here. Downtown, Old Oakland, Chinatown, West Oakland and East Oakland abound with budget-friendly local favorites. Uptown, Temescal and Rockridge attract culinary trend-spotters. Ethnic enclave neighborhoods are the obvious best place for the cuisine of their respective demographics.

Uptown, Downtown & Jack London Square

Shandong Restaurant CHINESE $
(Map p144; ☎510-839-2299; www.shandongoakland.com; 328 10th St; mains $10-15; ⊙11am-3pm & 4-9pm Sun-Thu, to 9:30pm Fri & Sat; B 12th St Oakland City Center) This restaurant makes a claim to serving the best pork dumplings around, and the Chinese fare is solid (though not necessarily the best around). Local families still pack the place, so it's worth a visit

partly for a glimpse into the old-school Oakland Chinatown vibe.

Miss Ollie's CARIBBEAN $$
(Map p144; ☎510-285-6188; www.realmissolliesoakland.com; 901 Washington St; $10-24; ⏰11:30am-3pm & 5:30-9pm Tue-Thu, to 10pm Fri, noon-3pm & 5:30-10pm Sat; ; B 12th St Oakland City Center) Get back to the islands by way of **Swan's Market** (Map p144; ☎510-287-5353; www.swansmarket.com; 510 9th St; most mains $8-20; ⏰9am-10pm Mon-Sat; B 12th St Oakland City Center), Oakland's own food bazaar. Its standout restaurant Miss Ollie's lets you go cheap and vegan with a seasonal curry, and also serves up wildly popular skillet-fried chicken. Throw in some cornmeal fritters or plantains to finish a meal inspired by the African diaspora.

Piedmont Ave, Temescal & Rockridge

★Fentons ICE CREAM $
(Map p155; ☎510-658-7000; www.fentonscreamery.com; 4226 Piedmont Ave; ice cream from $5, mains $8-15; ⏰11am-11pm Mon-Thu, 9am-midnight Fri & Sat, 9am-11pm Sun; ; AC Transit 12, C) If you have children, or love ice cream, you owe it to yourself to stop by this institution. The range of ice cream flavors is encyclopedic in range, stretching from mocha royale to pistachio raspberry swirl, and the scoops are more than generous. Plenty of sundae options, plus burgers and grilled sandwiches for those not indulging their sweet tooth.

Boichik Bagels BAGELS $
(Map p155; ☎510-858-5189; https://boichikbagels.com; 3170 College Ave; bagel from $3; ⏰6:30am-2pm Wed-Fri, from 7:30am Sat & Sun; B Rockridge) Upon Boichik's 2019 arrival on the border of Oakland and Berkeley, a long-standing debate about whether good bagels could exist in the Bay Area was settled: yes. A line regularly snarls around the block for these vegan, kosher, New York-style delights, which derive their authentic barley-malt sweetness from fermentation, kettle-boiling and then baking atop a gas-fired revolving stone deck oven.

Millennium VEGAN $$
(Map p155; ☎510-735-9459; www.millenniumrestaurant.com; 5912 College Ave; mains $21-25; ⏰5:30-9:30pm Sun-Thu, to 10:30pm Fri & Sat, 10:30am-2pm Sun; ; B Rockridge) Oaklanders rejoiced when San Francisco's classiest vegan restaurant hopped across the bay in 2015, bringing the beloved pumpkin tamales and parsnip *okonomikaki* (Japanese savory pancakes) along with it. The newer space is cozy but chic, with dark-wood finishes and a lively back patio. The creative plant and grain-based dishes are made with mostly organic, locally grown foods.

Teni East BURMESE $$
(Map p144; ☎510-597-1860; http://tenieastkitchen.com; 4015 Broadway; mains $16-23; ⏰11:30am-2:30pm daily, 5-9:30pm Sun-Thu, to 10pm Fri & Sat; ; AC Transit 51A, 57, C) With Teni East, Cal-Burmese cuisine has arrived. And why shouldn't a tableside tea-leaf salad involve baby kale? Thai, Indian and even Ethiopian cooking styles also influence these playful dishes thanks to the diverse background of the owner. The curries are excellent, particularly the beef, and so are the *balachaung-* (a Burmese chili oil) and tamarind-tossed wings.

★Commis CALIFORNIAN $$$
(Map p144; ☎510-653-3902; www.commisrestaurant.com; 3859 Piedmont Ave; 8-course dinner $185, wine & beer pairings $100; ⏰5:30-9:15pm Wed-Sat, 5-8:45pm Sun; AC Transit 51A) At the East Bay's only Michelin-starred restaurant, the discreet dining room counts a minimalist decór and some coveted counter real estate where patrons can watch the two-Michelin-star award-winning team piece together creative and innovative dishes. Don't miss the raw sea scallops, the slow-poached egg yolk with smoked dates, or the warm levain bread with chicken skin butter. Reservations essential.

Lake Merritt

★Oakland–Grand Lake Farmers Market MARKET $
(Map p155; ☎415-472-6100; www.agriculturalinstitute.org; Lake Park Ave, at Grand Ave; ⏰9am-2pm Sat; ; AC Transit 12) A rival to San Francisco's Ferry Plaza Farmers Market, this bountiful weekly market hauls in bushels of fresh fruit, vegetables, seafood, ranched meats, artisanal cheese and baked goods from as far away as Marin County and the Central Valley. The northern side of the market is cheek-by-jowl with food trucks and hot-food vendors – don't skip the dim-sum tent.

Arizmendi Bakery BAKERY $
(Map p155; ☎510-268-8849; www.arizmendilakeshore.com; 3265 Lakeshore Ave; pizza slices $3.25; ⏰7am-8pm Tue-Sun; ; AC Transit 12)

DON'T MISS

OAKLAND'S TOP TACO SHOP

Taqueria El Paisa@.com (510-610-6398; www.facebook.com/pg/elpaisa77; 4610 International Blvd; tacos from $3; 9am-9pm; AC Transit 1) is the name of the place, and no, we don't know how to say it out loud (a lot of locals just call it 'El Paisa'). Honestly, we would call this taco joint whatever it wants to be called, because the tacos are good beyond all superlatives: simple, fresh and garnished with cilantro, onions and *nopales* (cactus). Hands down delicious.

Look for a low-slung little restaurant with a green awning, popular with lots of families and Oakland's Mexican population, and strap in: this is one of the best meals going in the East Bay. Bonus: it's not just excellent, it's dirt cheap.

Great for breakfast or lunch but beware: this bakery co-op is not for the weak-willed. Gourmet vegetarian pizza, chewy breads and gigantic scones: all baked fresh, all addictive. The menu offerings shift depending on the day and what's been harvested.

Sister PIZZA $$
(Map p155; 510-763-2668; www.sisteroakland.com; 3308 Grand Ave; pizzas from $20; 8am-2pm Tue-Sun, 5:30-10pm Tue-Thu, to 10:30pm Fri & Sat, to 9:30pm Sun; ; AC Transit 12) Patrons pack this cozy brick-walled space for its wood-fired pizzas, original cocktails and creative antipasti made from sustainably sourced fresh ingredients. From November to July, the Tuesday menu includes a Dungeness crab special with garlic noodles. On Wednesdays, wine bottles are half price.

Drinking & Nightlife

Oakland's busiest and hippest bars are in the Uptown district, often a short stumble from BART. You'll find watering holes near Jack London Sq and in Old Oakland. Students and grown-ups pretending to be students hang out in Rockridge, while a mix of locals gravitate to bars around Lake Merritt, along Piedmont Ave and on Temescal's main drag.

★**Blue Bottle Coffee Company** CAFE
(Map p144; www.bluebottlecoffee.com; 4270 Broadway; coffee from $3.50; 6am-6pm Mon-Fri, from 6:30am Sat & Sun; AC Transit 51A) This Blue Bottle cafe is inside the beautiful WC Morse Building, a 1920s truck showroom. Communal tables, lofty ceilings and minimalist white decor invite the sipping of a Gibraltar – similar to a cortado (espresso with a dash of milk), but made with more milk – or a cold-brew iced coffee.

★**Cafe Van Kleef** BAR
(Map p144; 510-763-7711; www.facebook.com/cafevankleef; 1621 Telegraph Ave; 4pm-2am Mon, from noon Tue-Fri, from 6pm Sat & Sun; 19th St Oakland) Order a Greyhound (with freshly squeezed grapefruit juice) and take a gander at the profusion of antique musical instruments, fake taxidermy heads, sprawling formal chandeliers and bizarro ephemera clinging to every surface possible. Quirky even *before* you get lit, it features live blues, jazz, soul, funk and the occasional rock band on weekends.

Drake's Dealership BEER GARDEN
(Map p144; 510-568-2739; www.drinkdrakes.com/dealership; 2325 Broadway; 11:30am-11pm Sun-Wed, to 1am Thu-Sat; ; 19th St Oakland) East Bay craft brewer Drake's Brewing Company has transformed a humdrum Dodge dealership into a lively restaurant, bar and outdoor beer garden with fire pits that crackle on foggy nights. Order a pint of Flyway Pils or Best Coast IPA with a wood-oven-fired pizza.

Dogwood COCKTAIL BAR
(Map p144; www.facebook.com/bardogwood; 1644 Telegraph Ave; 4pm-2am; 19th St Oakland) A hip, tattooed young crowd hobnobs inside this red-brick-walled bar on a busy corner of Uptown. Order a creative house cocktail or classic concoction such as the Brooklyn from mixologists behind the bar. Simple sandwiches and meat-and-cheese plates keep stomachs from growling.

Heinold's First & Last Chance Saloon BAR
(Map p144; 510-839-6761; www.heinoldsfirstandlastchance.com; 48 Webster St; 3-11pm Mon, noon-11pm Tue & Wed, to 11:30pm Thu-Sat, 11am-9:30pm Sun; Broadway Shuttle) At this 1883 bar constructed from wood scavenged from an old whaling ship, you really have to hold on to your beer. Keeled to a severe slant during the 1906 earthquake, the building's tilt might make you feel self-conscious about stumbling before you even order. Its big claim to fame is that adventure writer Jack London was a regular patron.

Luka's Taproom & Lounge LOUNGE
(Map p144; ☎510-451-4677; www.lukasoakland.com; 2221 Broadway; ⊙11:30am-midnight Sun-Wed, to 1am Thu, to 2am Fri & Sat; Ⓑ19th St Oakland) Go Uptown to get down. At this long-running restaurant and lounge, DJs spin a soulful mix of hip-hop, R&B and Latin grooves Thursday to Sunday nights (cover charge $5 to $10).

Beer Revolution BAR
(Map p144; ☎510-452-2337; http://beer-revolution.com; 464 3rd St; ⊙noon-11pm Sun-Thu, to midnight Fri & Sat; 🚇Broadway Shuttle) With 50 beers on tap and hundreds more in bottles, there's a lifetime of discovery ahead, so kick back on the sunny deck or park yourself at that barrel table embedded with bottle caps. Bonuses include a punk-rock soundtrack played at conversation-friendly levels.

☆ Entertainment

Most of Oakland's smaller live-music and performing-arts venues are Uptown, but you can find gigs in Temescal and along College Ave.

Two pro sports venues, the outdoors Oakland-Alameda County Coliseum and Oakland Arena off I-880, have lost or are losing their respective teams. A new professional indoor football team, the Oakland Panthers, started playing at Oakland Arena in 2020, while the Oakland A's were planning to build a new stadium, Howard Terminal Ballpark, near Jack London Sq.

★ **Fox Theater** THEATER
(Map p144; ☎510-302-2250; www.thefoxoakland.com; 1807 Telegraph Ave; tickets from $35; ⊙hours vary; Ⓑ19th St Oakland) A phoenix arisen from the urban ashes, this restored 1928 art deco stunner adds dazzle and neon lights to Telegraph Ave, where it's a cornerstone of the happening Uptown theater and nightlife district. Once a movie house, it's now a popular concert venue for edgy and independent Californian, national and international music acts. Buy tickets early; many shows sell out.

Paramount Theatre CINEMA
(Map p144; ☎510-465-6400; www.paramounttheatre.com; 2025 Broadway; ⊙hours vary; 🚇19th St Oakland) This massive 1931 art deco masterpiece shows classic films a few times each month and is also home to the Oakland Symphony and Oakland Ballet. It periodically books big-name concerts and screens classic flicks. Guided tours ($5) are given at 10am on the first and third Saturdays of the month (no reservations).

Yoshi's JAZZ
(Map p144; ☎510-238-9200; www.yoshis.com; 510 Embarcadero W; ⊙hours vary; 🚇Broadway Shuttle) Yoshi's has a solid jazz calendar, with talent from around the world passing through on a near-nightly basis. It's also a Japanese restaurant, so if you enjoy a sushi dinner before the show, you'll be rewarded with reserved cabaret-style seating. Otherwise, resign yourself to limited high-top tables squeezed along the back walls of this intimate club.

Grand Lake Theatre CINEMA
(Map p155; ☎510-452-3556; www.renaissancerialto.com; 3200 Grand Ave; regular/3D features $12/13.50, matinee $6.50; ⊙hours vary; 🚇AC Transit 12) Once a vaudeville theater and silent-movie house, this 1926 beauty near Lake Merritt lures you in with its huge corner marquee (which sometimes displays left-leaning political messages) and keeps you coming with a fun balcony and a Wurlitzer organ playing on weekends.

New Parkway Theater CINEMA
(Map p144; ☎510-338-3228; www.thenewparkway.com; 474 24th St; tickets $10; ⊙films at 6pm Mon-Wed, 3:30pm Thu & Fri, noon Sat & Sun; 🚇AC Transit 6) This laid-back movie house, pub and community-events space shows second-run and throwback indie films. Reasonably priced beer, wine, sandwiches and pizza are delivered to your couch seat.

Oakland A's BASEBALL
(☎510-638-4900; www.mlb.com/athletics; 7000 Coliseum Way; tickets from $17; ⊙Mar-Sep; ⒷColiseum) When the San Francisco Giants are away, the Oakland A's are usually home, which expands the possibilities for those desperate for a summer baseball fix. The team has plans to build a new stadium, Howard Terminal Ballpark, near Jack London Sq.

ℹ Information

MEDIA

Oakland's daily newspaper is the *East Bay Times* (www.eastbaytimes.com). The free weekly *East Bay Express* (www.eastbayexpress.com) has good Oakland and Berkeley listings.

TOURIST INFORMATION

Visit Oakland Visitor Center (Map p144; ☎510-839-9000; www.visitoakland.com; 481 Water St; ⊙9am-5pm Mon-Fri, 10am-5pm

Sat & Sun) At Jack London Sq, offering maps, brochures, itineraries, clothing, snacks, ferry tickets, tours and more.

Getting There & Away

AIR

Oakland International Airport (OAK) is less crowded and sometimes cheaper to fly into than San Francisco International Airport (SFO) across the bay. OAK airport is connected to Oakland, Berkeley and San Francisco by frequent BART trains.

BART

Within the Bay Area, the most convenient way to get to Oakland and back is by **BART** (Bay Area Rapid Transit; www.bart.gov). Trains run on a set schedule approximately every 10 minutes or so from around 5am to 12:30am on weekdays, 6am to midnight on Saturday and 8am to midnight on Sunday.

Downtown BART stations are on Broadway at 12th and 19th Sts; other Oakland stations are on the south side of Lake Merritt, close to Chinatown; near Temescal (MacArthur station) and in Rockridge.

To get to downtown Oakland, catch a Richmond or Antioch–SFO/Millbrae train. The fare to Oakland's 12th or 19th St stations from any BART station in downtown San Francisco is $3.70 to $4.20. Rockridge is on the Antioch–SFO/Millbrae line, while all Berkeley stops are on the Richmond line. To Lake Merritt or the Coliseum (for connections to Oakland's airport), catch a BART train heading toward Warm Springs/South Fremont or Dublin/Pleasanton.

BUS

AC Transit (510-891-4777; www.actransit.org; single ride East Bay/trans-Bay $2.50/6) runs convenient buses from San Francisco's Salesforce Transit Center to downtown Oakland (single ride $6). Local (East Bay) buses run along numbered lines, while transbay buses are lettered.

After BART trains stop, late-night transportation between downtown San Francisco and downtown Oakland is with the AC Transit bus 800 line, which runs hourly on weekdays and every 30 minutes on weekends.

Between downtown Berkeley and downtown Oakland, take fast and frequent AC Transit bus 6 along Telegraph Ave. Alternatively, take AC Transit bus 18 via Martin Luther King Jr Way and Shattuck Ave.

Greyhound (p779) operates direct buses from Oakland, including to Vallejo (from $5, 30 minutes), San Jose (from $11, one hour), Sacramento (from $11, two hours) and Los Angeles (from $20, seven to 12 hours), among other destinations. Its **bus station** (Map p144; 510-832-4730; www.greyhound.com; 2103 San Pablo Ave; B 19th St Oakland) is pretty seedy. Discount carrier **Megabus** (Map p155; 877-462-6342; http://us.megabus.com) has daily service to LA (from $20, seven to eight hours) departing from outside the West Oakland BART station.

CAR & MOTORCYCLE

From San Francisco by car, cross the Bay Bridge and enter Oakland via one of two ways: I-580, which leads to I-980 heading to downtown Oakland; or I-880, which curves through West Oakland and lets you off near the south end of Broadway. I-880 then continues to the Coliseum, Oakland International Airport and, eventually, San Jose. Driving back westbound from the East Bay to San Francisco, the bridge toll is $5 or $7 on weekdays, depending on the time of day, and $6 on weekends.

FERRY

From San Francisco's Ferry Building and Pier 41, **San Francisco Bay Ferry** (415-705-8291; http://sanfranciscobayferry.com) sails to Jack London Sq (one way $7.20, 30 to 45 minutes) and Alameda (one way $7.20, 30 to 45 minutes) more frequently on weekdays than on weekends. Mobile ticketing is available with the Hopthru mobile app, and Clipper cards provide a discount on ferry tickets and transfers on MUNI and AC Transit buses.

TRAIN

Oakland is a regular stop for Amtrak (p779) trains operating up and down the coast. From Oakland's **Amtrak station** (reservations 800-872-7245; www.amtrak.com; 245 2nd St; Broadway Shuttle) at Jack London Sq, catch AC Transit bus 12 or the free Broadway Shuttle to downtown Oakland, or take a ferry across the bay to San Francisco.

Amtrak passengers with reservations on to San Francisco disembark at the **Emeryville Amtrak station** (www.amtrak.com; 5885 Horton St), one stop north of Oakland. From there, an Amtrak bus can shuttle you to San Francisco's Ferry Building stop, Pier 39, the Financial District bus stop, or the San Francisco Shopping Center bus stop.

Emeryville is also the terminus for Amtrak's daily California Zephyr train service to/from Chicago. The free **Emery Go Round** (510-451-3862; www.emerygoround.com; 6am-10pm Mon-Fri, 8am-10pm Sat, 9am-7pm Sun) shuttle runs a circuit including the Emeryville Amtrak and MacArthur BART stations.

Getting Around

The best ways to get around much of central Oakland are walking, cycling, scootering, ridesharing or taking public buses.

TO/FROM THE AIRPORT

Flying into **Oakland International Airport** (OAK; ☎510-563-3300; www.oaklandairport.com; 1 Airport Dr; 📶; Ⓑ Oakland International Airport), car rentals are available from all the major agencies. Outside the terminal, free shuttle buses depart every 10 minutes for the airport's rental-car center.

BART is the easiest public transportation option. Opposite the terminal, catch a BART shuttle train to Coliseum Station, where you'll pay the fare to your final destination when changing trains. BART trains run on weekdays between 5am and 12:30am (from 6am on Saturday, 8am on Sunday).

There are several door-to-door shuttle services operating out of Oakland International Airport. One-way service to San Francisco/Oakland destinations starts at around $75/55 for up to four people.

A taxi from Oakland International Airport to downtown Oakland costs about $40; to downtown San Francisco about $70. Ridesharing services are often significantly cheaper.

BUS

AC Transit has a comprehensive bus network within Oakland. Local bus fares are single ride/day pass $2.50/6; pay with cash (bring exact change) or a Clipper card.

The free **Broadway Shuttle** (☎510-891-4777; www.oaklandca.gov/topics/free-broadway-shuttle; ⏰7am-10pm Mon-Fri) runs along Broadway between Jack London Sq and 27th St, stopping at Old Oakland/Chinatown, downtown BART stations, Lake Merritt and the Uptown district. Buses arrive every 12 to 15 minutes.

Berkeley

Berkeley is synonymous with protest, activism and left wing politics. Beyond those tropes is a busy, attractive city, a blend of yuppie and hippie and student, all existing side by side with great Asia-Pacific regional restaurants, twee toy stores, Latin American groceries, high-end organic food halls and the misty green campus of the University of California, Berkeley. It's easy to stereotype 'Beserkeley' for some of its recycle-or-else PC crankiness and occasional overbearing self-righteousness. But some of that attitude is justified: at the end of the day Berkeley has, more often than not, been on the right side of environmental and political issues that have defined the rest of the nation.

Berkeley is also home to a large South Asian community, as evidenced by an abundance of sari shops on University Ave and an unusually large number of Indian, Pakistani and Nepalese restaurants.

Sights & Activities

University of California, Berkeley

The Berkeley campus of the University of California (UCB, called 'Cal' by both students and locals) is the oldest university in the state. The decision to found the college was made in 1866, and the first students arrived in 1873. Today UCB has more than 40,000 students, more than 1500 professors and more Nobel laureates than you could point a particle accelerator at.

From Telegraph Ave, enter the campus via Sproul Plaza and Sather Gate, a center for people-watching, soapbox oration and pseudotribal drumming. Or you can enter from Center St and Oxford Lane, near the downtown BART station.

Campanile LANDMARK

(Sather Tower; Map p152; ☎510-642-6000; http://campanile.berkeley.edu; adult/child $4/3; ⏰10am-3:45pm Mon-Fri, to 4:45pm Sat, 10am-1:30pm & 3-4:45pm Sun; Ⓑ Downtown Berkeley) Officially called Sather Tower, the Campanile was modeled on St Mark's Basilica in Venice. The 307ft spire offers fine views of the Bay Area, and at the top you can stare up into the carillon of 61 bells, ranging from the size of a cereal bowl to that of a Volkswagen. Carillon concerts are held at 2pm on Sundays

Phoebe A Hearst Museum of Anthropology MUSEUM

(Map p152; ☎510-642-3682; www.hearstmuseum.berkeley.edu; Bancroft Way, at College Ave; adult/child $6/free; ⏰11am-5pm Sun-Wed & Fri, to 8pm Thu, 10am-6pm Sat; 🚌AC Transit 6, 51B) South of the Campanile in Kroeber Hall, this small museum includes exhibits from indigenous cultures around the world, including ancient Peruvian, Egyptian and African items. There's also a large collection highlighting Native Californian cultures.

BAMPFA MUSEUM

(UC Berkeley Art Museum and Pacific Film Archive; Map p152; ☎510-642-0808; www.bampfa.org; 2155 Center St; adult/child $14/free; ⏰11am-7pm Wed-Sun; Ⓑ Downtown Berkeley) With a stainless-steel exterior wrapping around a 1930s printing plant, this museum holds multiple galleries showcasing a limited number of artworks, from ancient Chinese

Central Berkeley

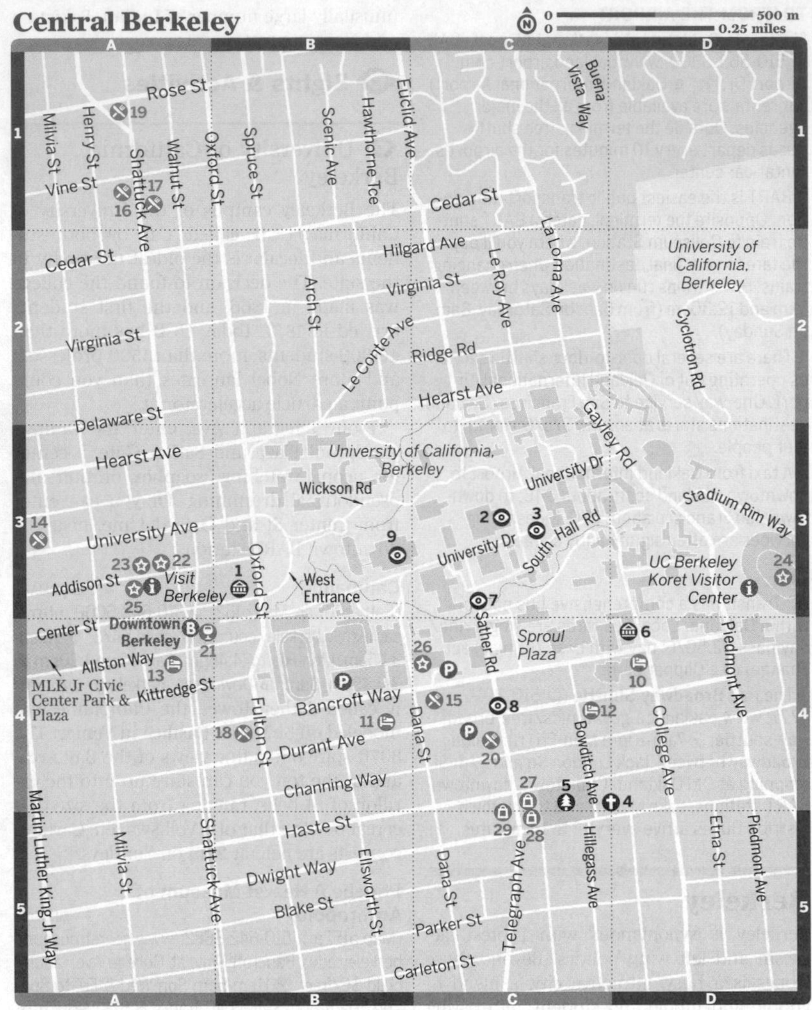

to cutting-edge contemporary. The complex also houses a bookstore, cafe and the much-loved Pacific Film Archive (p159).

Bancroft Library LIBRARY

(Map p152; www.lib.berkeley.edu/libraries/bancroft-library; University Dr; ⏲archives 10am-4:45pm Mon-Fri; Ⓑ Downtown Berkeley) FREE The Bancroft houses, among other gems, the papers of Mark Twain, a copy of Shakespeare's folios and a diary from the Donner Party. Its small public exhibits of historical Californiana include the surprisingly small gold nugget that sparked the 1849 gold rush. Rotating temporary exhibits spotlight history and art, with pieces from the library's own collections.

Sather Gate GATE

(Map p152; www.berkeley.edu; Sather Rd; 🚌AC Transit 6, 51B) The frenetic energy buzzing from the university's Sather Gate on any given day is a mixture of youthful posthippies reminiscing about days before their time and fashion-conscious hipsters and punk rockers who sneer at tie-dyed nostalgia. Political activists still hand out leaflets here at the south entrance to campus.

UC Museum of Paleontology RESEARCH CENTER

(Map p152; ☎510-642-1821; www.ucmp.berkeley.edu; Campanile Way; Ⓑ Downtown Berkeley) FREE Despite the title, this is actually a research

Central Berkeley

facility that's closed to the public. That said, the location within the Valley Life Sciences Building is fronted by an accessible atrium area that includes some cool fossil exhibits, including a life-size cast of a Tyrannosaurus rex skeleton. The Life Sciences building is usually open to the public from 9am to 10pm, but may be closed during holidays, weekends and parts of summer.

South of Campus

South of campus along College Ave is the **Elmwood District**, a charming nook of shops and restaurants that offers a calming alternative to the frenetic buzz around Telegraph Ave. Continue further south and you'll be in Rockridge, in the neighboring city of Oakland.

Telegraph Avenue STREET

(Map p152; shop & restaurant hours vary; P; AC Transit 6) Telegraph Ave has traditionally been the throbbing heart of studentville in Berkeley, the sidewalks crowded with undergrads, postdocs and youthful shoppers squeezing their way past throngs of vendors, buskers and panhandlers. Street stalls hawk everything from crystals to bumper stickers to self-published tracts. Several cafes and budget eateries cater to students.

First Church of Christ, Scientist CHURCH

(Map p152; 510-845-7199; www.friendsoffirstchurch.org; 2619 Dwight Way; tour 12:15pm 1st Sun each month; P; AC Transit 6) FREE Bernard Maybeck's impressive 1910 church uses concrete and wood in its blend of arts-and-crafts, Asian and Gothic influences. Maybeck was a professor of architecture at UC Berkeley and designed San Francisco's Palace of Fine Arts, plus many landmark homes in the Berkeley Hills.

People's Park PARK

(Map p152; 2556 Haste St; AC Transit 6) This park, just east of Telegraph Ave, is a marker in local history as a political battleground between residents and the city and state government in the late 1960s. Occasional festivals do still happen here, but it's a bit run-down and serves mostly as a gathering spot for Berkeley's homeless.

Downtown

Berkeley's downtown, centered on Shattuck Ave between University Ave and Dwight Way, has few traces of the city's tie-dyed reputation. Today it abounds with shops, restaurants and restored public buildings.

The nearby **arts district** revolves around the acclaimed thespian stomping grounds of the Berkeley Repertory Theatre (p159) and Aurora Theatre Company (p159), and live music at the historical Freight & Salvage Coffeehouse (p159), all on Addison St.

North Berkeley & Albany

Not too far north of the university campus, North Berkeley is a neighborhood filled with lovely garden-front homes and parks. The popular **Gourmet Ghetto** stretches along Shattuck Ave north of University Ave for several blocks, anchored by acclaimed restaurant Chez Panisse (p157). Further northwest, **Solano Avenue**, which crosses from Berkeley into Albany, is lined with offbeat shops and family-friendly restaurants.

Berkeley Rose Garden GARDENS
(Map p155; 510-981-6700; www.cityofberkeley.info; 1200 Euclid Ave; dawn-dusk; AC Transit 65) FREE In North Berkeley, the Berkeley Rose Garden features a terraced amphitheater of colorful explosions. Relax on a quiet bench and admire 1500 rose bushes in near perpetual bloom, arranged by hue. Across the street, **Cordornices Park** has a children's playground with a 40ft concrete slide.

The Berkeley Hills

★Tilden Regional Park PARK
(Map p155; 510-544-2747; www.ebparks.org/parks/tilden; 5am-10pm; AC Transit 67) FREE This 2079-acre park, up in the hills east of town, is Berkeley's best. It has nearly 40 miles of hiking and multiuse trails of varying difficulty, from paved paths to hilly scrambles, including part of the magnificent Bay Area Ridge Trail. There's also a miniature steam train ($3), a children's farm and environmental education center, a wild-looking botanical garden and an 18-hole golf course. Lake Anza is good for picnics and from spring through fall you can swim ($3.50).

UC Botanical Garden at Berkeley GARDENS
(Map p155; 510-643-2755; http://botanicalgarden.berkeley.edu; 200 Centennial Dr; adult/child $15/7; 9am-5pm, last entry 4:30pm, closed 1st & 3rd Tue each month; Bear Transit H) With 34 acres and more than 10,000 types of plants, this garden in the hills above campus has one of the most varied collections in the country. Flora from every continent except Antarctica are lovingly tended here, with special emphasis on Mediterranean species that grow in California, the Americas, the Mediterranean and southern Africa.

Lawrence Hall of Science MUSEUM
(Map p155; 510-642-5132; www.lawrencehallofscience.org; 1 Centennial Dr; adult/child $16/12; 10am-5pm Tue-Sun, daily mid-Jun–early Sep; AC Transit 65) Near Grizzly Peak Blvd, this science hall is named after Ernest Lawrence, who won the Nobel Prize for his invention of the cyclotron particle accelerator. He was a key member of the WWII Manhattan Project, and he's also the name behind the Lawrence Berkeley and Lawrence Livermore national laboratories. The museum has interactive (if kinda dated) exhibits geared mainly toward young children.

West Berkeley

Adventure Playground PARK
(Map p155; 510-981-6720; www.cityofberkeley.info/adventureplayground; 160 University Ave; 11am-5pm mid-Jun–mid-Aug, 11am-4pm Sat & Sun only rest of year; AC Transit 51B) FREE At the Berkeley Marina, this is one of the coolest play spaces in the Bay Area – a free outdoor park encouraging creativity and cooperation where supervised kids of any age can help build and paint their own structures. There's an awesome zipline too. Dress the tykes in play clothes, because they *will* get dirty.

Takara Sake USA Tasting Room MUSEUM
(Map p155; 510-540-8250; www.takarasake.com; 708 Addison St; tasting fee $10-20; noon-6pm Wed-Mon, to 5pm Tue, last tastings one hour before close; AC Transit 51B, 80) Stop in to see the traditional wooden tools used for making sake and a short video of the brewing process. Tours of the factory aren't offered, but you can view elements of modern production and bottling through a window. Sake flights are poured in a spacious tasting room constructed with reclaimed wood and floor tiles fashioned from recycled glass, all set beneath 'Song of the Sky,' a kinetic sculpture by Susumu Shingu.

Berkeley Marina MARINA
(Map p155; 510-981-6740; www.berkeley-marina.com; 201 University Ave; office 8am-4pm; AC Transit 51B) At the west end of University Ave is the marina, frequented by seagulls and on windy weekends, families flying colorful kites. It offers sweeping waterfront views from paved walking, cycling and running paths. A commuter ferry operated by Tideline runs four times daily from the marina to San Francisco piers 1.5 and 52.

Sleeping

Lodging rates spike during special university events such as graduation (mid-May) and home football games. A number of older, less expensive motels along University Ave can be handy during peak demand, as can chain motels and hotels off I-80 in Emeryville or Vallejo.

Around Berkeley & Oakland

Around Berkeley & Oakland

Top Sights
1 Chabot Space & Science Center D3
2 Tilden Regional Park C1

Sights
Adventure Playground .... (see 3)
3 Berkeley Marina A2
4 Berkeley Rose Garden B1
5 Lawrence Hall of Science C1
6 Mountain View Cemetery C3
7 Redwood Regional Park D3
8 Takara Sake USA Tasting Room A2
9 UC Botanical Garden at Berkeley C1

Activities, Courses & Tours
Cal Adventures .... (see 3)
Cal Sailing Club .... (see 3)

Sleeping
10 Claremont Resort & Spa C2

Eating
11 Arizmendi Bakery C4
12 Berkeley Bowl West A2
13 Boichik Bagels B2
14 Fentons C3
15 Millennium B2
16 Oakland–Grand Lake Farmers Market C4
17 Sister C3
18 Vik's Chaat Corner A2

Drinking & Nightlife
19 Albatross A2
20 Broc Cellars A1
21 Fieldwork Brewing Company A1
22 St George Spirits A4

Entertainment
23 924 Gilman A1
24 Ashkenaz A1
25 California Shakespeare Theater A2
26 Grand Lake Theatre C4
27 La Peña Cultural Center B2
28 Shotgun Players B2

WATERSPORTS ON THE BAY

As well as making for a lovely postcard or iconic snapshot, San Francisco Bay offers plenty of options for getting out on the water.

California Canoe & Kayak (Map p144; ☎510-893-7833; www.calkayak.com; 409 Water St; kayak & SUP rentals per hour $25-50, tours from $79; ⏰10am-5pm; 🚌Broadway Shuttle) Rents kayaks and stand-up paddleboard (SUP) sets at Oakland's Jack London Sq. Book ahead for moonlight paddles along the waterfront.

Cal Adventures (Map p155; ☎510-642-4000; https://recsports.berkeley.edu/cal-adventures; 124 University Ave; rentals/classes from $20/45; ⏰hours vary; 🚌AC Transit 51B) Run by the UC Aquatic Center at Berkeley Marina, it organizes sailing, windsurfing, SUP and sea-kayaking classes and rentals.

Cal Sailing Club (Map p155; www.cal-sailing.org; 124 University Ave; 3-month membership $120; ⏰lesson hours vary; 🚌AC Transit 51B) Membership-based, volunteer-run nonprofit offering sailing and windsurfing programs at Berkeley Marina.

Boardsports California (☎415-385-1224; www.boardsportscalifornia.com; rentals/lessons from $45/65; ⏰hours vary) Offers lessons and rentals for kiteboarding, windsurfing, SUP and kayaking, with locations at Alameda in the East Bay, and Coyote Point Recreation Area in San Mateo.

Sea Trek (p128) This long-running Sausalito outfit has kayaks and SUP sets for rent, plus a fabulous array of tours, including bay crossings to Angel Island.

Graduate Berkeley BOUTIQUE HOTEL **$$**
(Map p152; ☎510-845-8981; www.graduatehotels.com/berkeley; 2600 Durant Ave; d $180-1000; P ⊖ @ ☜ 🐾; 🚌AC Transit 51B, 7, 9) Located a block from campus, this classic 1928 hotel has been cheekily renovated to highlight the connection to the university. The lobby is decorated in collegiate plaids and velvet sofas, room keys are pseudo student IDs, and smallish rooms have bongs repurposed into bedside lamps. Overnight parking is $35.

Berkeley City Club HISTORIC HOTEL **$$**
(Map p152; ☎510-848-7800; www.berkeleycityclub.com; 2315 Durant Ave; d $235-265; P ⊖ @ ☜ ≋; 🚌AC Transit 51B, 79) Designed by Julia Morgan (the architect of Hearst Castle), the 38 rooms and dazzling common areas of this refurbished 1929 historical landmark building (which is also a private club) feel like a glorious time warp into a more refined era. The hotel contains lush and serene Italianate courtyards, with a bocci court and a stunning indoor pool. Parking is $29.

Hotel Shattuck Plaza HOTEL **$$**
(Map p152; ☎510-845-7300; www.hotelshattuckplaza.com; 2086 Allston Way; d $210-449; P ⊖ @ ☜; Ⓑ Downtown Berkeley) This 100-year-old downtown jewel features a foyer of red Italian glass lighting, flocked Victorian-style wallpaper – and yes, a peace sign tiled into the floor. Colorful, vintage-chic hallways lead guests to fairly plain if comfortable rooms with down comforters. The attached Mediterranean restaurant Zino offers a classy bar and killer weekend brunch.

Bancroft Hotel HISTORIC HOTEL **$$**
(Map p152; ☎510-549-1000; www.bancrofthotel.com; 2680 Bancroft Way; d $134-202; P ⊖ @ ☜; 🚌AC Transit 51B, 52) A gorgeous 1928 arts-and-crafts building that was originally a women's club, the Bancroft is just across the street from campus and two blocks from Telegraph Ave (p153). It has small, simply furnished rooms (some with lovely balconies) and a spectacular bay-view rooftop, though no elevator. Limited parking.

Eating

Telegraph Ave is packed with cafes, pizza counters and cheap restaurants. Berkeley's Little India runs along the University Ave corridor. Many more restaurants can be found along Shattuck Ave near the Downtown Berkeley BART station. The section of Shattuck Ave north of University Ave, nicknamed the 'Gourmet Ghetto,' is home to excellent restaurants and cafes for all budgets.

Downtown & Around Campus

Tacos Sinaloa TACOS **$**
(Map p152; ☎510-665-7895; www.facebook.com/TacosSinaloaBerkeley; 2384 Telegraph Ave; tacos from $2, mains $6-14; ⏰11am-11pm; 🚌AC Transit 51B) After this authentic, casual taco joint

graduated from food truck to restaurant in 2015, Berkeley students wondered if they should postpone their own graduations; the shrimp, carnitas and asado tacos are *that* tasty. More adventurous eaters can sample the *lengua* (beef tongue), *tripitas* (pork intestines) and *buche* (pork stomach).

Butcher's Son VEGAN $

(Map p152; ☎510-984-0818; www.thebutchersveganson.com; 1954 University Ave; mains $13-16; ⏰11am-8pm Mon, Thu & Fri, to 3pm Tue & Wed, 10am-5pm Sat & Sun; ; Ⓑ Downtown Berkeley) What could be more in tune with Berkeley's granola-crunchy, latter-day-hippie vibe than a vegan deli? Gorge on imitation deli meats and cheeses, scratch that itch for a smoked jackfruit sandwich, or go to town on hot pesto 'chicken' on sourdough. All are made without any animal products.

North Berkeley Farmers Market MARKET $

(Map p152; ☎510-548-3333; www.ecologycenter.org; Shattuck Ave, at Rose St; ⏰3-7pm Thu; ; AC Transit 79) Pick up some organic produce or tasty prepared food at North Berkeley's weekly farmers market, operating year-round. Also operates a market downtown (Martin Luther King Jr Way and Center St, 10am to 3pm Saturday) and in South Berkeley (Adeline and 63rd St, 2pm to 6:30pm Tuesday).

Great China Restaurant CHINESE $$

(Map p152; ☎510-843-7996; www.greatchinaberkeley.com; 2190 Bancroft Way; mains $14-25; ⏰11:30am-2:30pm Wed-Mon, 5:30-9pm Mon, Wed & Thu, to 9:30pm Fri, 5-9:30pm Sat & Sun; Ⓑ Downtown Berkeley) Berkeley does not lack for good Chinese food, but this enormous upscale restaurant elevates the genre with Northern Chinese specialties such as duck-bone soup, cumin-braised lamb, ginger scallion prawns and thrice-cooked pork belly. Come with friends and order as much as you can – your taste buds will not forget this.

★ **Cafe Ohlone** NATIVE AMERICAN $$$

(Map p152; www.makamham.com/cafeohlone; 2430 Bancroft Way, University Press Books; prix/fixe lunch/dinner from $30/150; ⏰hours vary; AC Transit 51B) Berkeley's most delightful new pop-up restaurant resurrects the cuisine of California's native Ohlone people, with a contemporary spin. The prix-fixe lunches, dinners and tea ceremonies take place on a cozy outdoor patio behind University Press Books (p160), where guests learn about Ohlone history and culture as they feast on delicacies including dandelion soup, sweet acorn pancakes, sorrel salad and wood-smoked venison.

The organizers are passionate members of modern-day Ohlone communities, and the events are as enlightening as they are delicious.

North Berkeley

Cheese Board Collective PIZZA $

(Map p152; ☎510-549-3183; www.cheeseboardcollective.coop; 1504 & 1512 Shattuck Ave; slices/half-pizzas/whole pizzas $2.75/11/22; ⏰7am-1pm Mon, to 6pm Tue-Fri, 8am-5pm Sat; ; AC Transit 7) Worker-owned since 1971, this co-op boasts (surprise) a great collection of cheese, a bakery with a changing selection of fresh bread, and a new vegetarian pizza and salad every day; options may include asparagus and onion or crushed tomato and goat cheese. Live music is often playing at this delicious Berkeley institution. Expect lines!

★ **Chez Panisse** CALIFORNIAN $$$

(Map p152; ☎cafe 510-548-5049, restaurant 510-548-5525; www.chezpanisse.com; 1517 Shattuck Ave; cafe dinner mains $23-35, restaurant prix fixe dinner $75-125; ⏰cafe 11:30am-2:45pm & 5-10:30pm Mon-Thu, 11:30am-3pm & 5-11pm Fri & Sat, restaurant seatings 5:30pm & 8pm Mon-Sat; ; AC Transit 7) Foodies come to worship here at the church of Alice Waters, inventor of California cuisine. Panisse is located in a lovely arts-and-crafts house in Berkeley's 'Gourmet Ghetto.' Pull out all the stops with a prix-fixe meal downstairs or go less expensive and a tad less formal in the upstairs café. Reservations accepted one month ahead.

The restaurant is as good and popular as it ever was, and despite its fame, the place has retained a welcoming atmosphere. The ever-changing menu showcases the bounty of California in ways both creative and delicious, from sea scallops with watermelon radishes to wild nettle soup and trout rillettes.

West Berkeley

Berkeley Bowl West MARKET $

(Map p155; ☎510-898-9555; www.berkeleybowl.com; 920 Heinz Ave; ⏰9am-8pm Mon-Sat, 10am-7pm Sun; Ⓟ; AC Transit 36) The go-to East Bay market is a veritable smorgasbord of fresh produce, cheese, seafood, natural products, baked goods, ethnic foods, meat and everything else a person might dream of eating or drinking. Has a parking area

NERD'S NIRVANA

Touted as the largest computer-history exhibition in the world, the **Computer History Museum** (☎650-810-1010; www.computerhistory.org; 1401 N Shoreline Blvd, Mountain View; adult $17.50, student & senior $13.50; ⏰10am-5pm Wed-Sun; 🅿) has rotating exhibits drawn from its 100,000-item collection. Artifacts range from the abacus to the iPod, including Cray-1 supercomputers, a Babbage Difference Engine (a Victorian-era automatic computing engine), the first Google server and a Waymo self-driving car.

Though there are no tours of the **Googleplex** (☎650-214-3308; www.google.com/about/company/facts/locations; 1600 Amphitheatre Pkwy, Mountain View; ⏰store 10am-6:30pm Thu & Fri; 🅿), visitors can stroll the campus and gawk at the public art on the leafy grounds, where scads of Googlers zoom about on primary-colored bicycles. Don't miss the 'dessert yard' outside Building 44, with lawn sculptures of Android operating systems (a cupcake! a doughnut! a robot!), and across the street, a toothy Tyrannosaurus rex festooned in pink flamingos next to the volleyball court. During research, Google was readying to build a second headquarters, which will include a transit center, a corporate hotel and oodles of green space, in San Jose.

At the Intel headquarters, the **Intel Museum** (☎408-765-5050; www.intel.com/museum; 2200 Mission College Blvd, Santa Clara; ⏰9am-6pm Mon-Fri, 10am-5pm Sat; 🅿) FREE has displays on the birth and growth of the computer industry with special emphasis, not surprisingly, on microchips and Intel's involvement. Reserve ahead if you want to schedule a tour.

and a coffee-and-juice bar serving breakfast, sandwiches, salads and other deliciousness.

Vik's Chaat Corner INDIAN $

(Map p155; ☎510-644-4412; https://vikschaat.com; 2390 4th St; mains $6-12; ⏰11am-6pm Mon-Thu, to 8pm Fri-Sun; 🌶; 🚌AC Transit 80) In West Berkeley, this long-standing popular *chaat* house gets mobbed at lunchtime by regulars that include equal numbers of hungry office workers, students and Indian families. Order samosas or a puffy *bhature* (flatbread) with *chole* (chickpea curry), an *uttapam* (savory pancake) or one of many filling *dosas* (savory crepes). Colorful Indian sweets, sold by the piece or pound, are irresistible.

Drinking & Nightlife

You'll never come up short of places to imbibe in Berkeley. Join students at bars and pubs scattered around downtown, on side streets near the university campus or along College Ave in Elmwood. Detour to industrial areas of West Berkeley to visit craft breweries, natural wineries and a sake distillery (p154).

Fieldwork Brewing Company BREWERY

(Map p155; ☎510-898-1203; www.fieldworkbrewing.com; 1160 6th St; ⏰11am-10pm Sun-Thu, to 11pm Fri & Sat; 🐾; 🚌AC Transit 12) At this industrial brewery taproom you can sit down on the outdoor patio with a tasting flight of IPAs or a glass of rich Mexican hot-chocolate stout. It's dog-friendly, and there are racks for hanging up your bicycle inside the front door. There's also a short menu of Mexican-Californian food.

Broc Cellars WINERY

(Map p155; ☎510-542-9463; www.broccellars.com; 1300 5th St; tastings $25; ⏰3-7pm Fri, 1-5pm Sat & Sun) 🍃 One of the first tasting rooms on Berkeley's 'wine block' in the Gilman district. Like the other half-dozen wineries in the vicinity, Broc Cellars specializes in natural wine made with biodynamically grown grapes and minimal intervention during fermenting. The owner also delights in using lesser-known grapes from obscure regions when creating his earthy, low-alcohol wines.

Albatross PUB

(Map p155; ☎510-843-2473; www.albatrosspub.com; 1822 San Pablo Ave; ⏰6pm-2am Sun-Tue, from 4:30pm Wed-Sat; 🚌AC Transit 51B) Berkeley's oldest pub is one of the most inviting and friendly in the city. Some serious darts are played here and board games get a workout on many of the worn-out tables. Sunday is trivia quiz night.

Jupiter PUB

(Map p152; ☎510-843-8277; www.jupiterbeer.com; 2181 Shattuck Ave; ⏰11:30am-12:30am Mon-Thu, to 1:30am Fri, noon-1:30am Sat, noon-11:30pm Sun; Ⓑ Downtown Berkeley) This downtown pub has loads of regional microbrews, a beer garden and firepit, decent pizza and live bands most nights. Sit upstairs for a bird's-eye view of bustling Shattuck Ave.

Caffe Strada CAFE
(Map p152; ☎510-843-5282; 2300 College Ave; ⏰6am-11pm; 📶; 🚌AC Transit 51B) Try the strong espressos or a sweet white-chocolate mocha at this popular hangout with an inviting shaded patio. With a clientele of almost all Cal students, this is a spot to sample (or relive) university days.

☆ Entertainment

Berkeley's arts district, centered on Addison St between Milvia St and Shattuck Ave, anchors downtown's extremely energetic performing-arts scene.

Berkeley also has plenty of intimate live-music venues. Cover charges usually range from $5 to $20, and several venues are all-ages or 18-and-over.

Freight & Salvage Coffeehouse LIVE MUSIC
(Map p152; ☎510-644-2020; www.thefreight.org; 2020 Addison St; tickets $5-65; ⏰shows daily; Ⓑ Downtown Berkeley) This legendary club has almost 50 years of history and is conveniently located in the downtown arts district. It features great traditional folk, country and bluegrass, and welcomes all ages, with half-price tickets for patrons under 21. A newly upgraded concessions area serves pizza and sandwiches, and music classes are offered on nights and weekends.

924 Gilman LIVE MUSIC
(Map p155; ☎510-524-8180; www.924gilman.org; 924 Gilman St; tickets from $10; ⏰Fri, Sat & Sun; 🚌AC Transit 12) This volunteer-run and booze-free all-ages space is a West Coast punk-rock institution. Its claim to fame is launching Green Day (then banning the group and all others on major labels in an effort to keep the scene independent). Check the online calendar for upcoming shows.

Ashkenaz DANCE
(Map p155; ☎510-525-5054; www.ashkenaz.com; 1317 San Pablo Ave; free-$20; ⏰office 2-7pm Mon-Fri; 🚌AC Transit 52) Ashkenaz is a 'music and dance community center' attracting activists, hippies and fans of folk, swing, world music and more who love to dance (lessons offered).

La Peña Cultural Center WORLD MUSIC
(Map p155; ☎510-849-2568; www.lapena.org; 3105 Shattuck Ave; ⏰hours vary; Ⓑ Ashby) This warmhearted community center presents dynamic dance classes and musical and visual arts events with a social justice bent. Look for a vibrant mural outside and the on-site Mexican cafe Los Cilantros, perfect for grabbing drinks and a preshow bite.

Berkeley Repertory Theatre THEATER
(Map p152; ☎510-647-2949; www.berkeleyrep.org; 2025 Addison St; tickets $15-105; ⏰box office noon-7pm Tue-Sun; Ⓑ Downtown Berkeley) This highly respected company has produced bold versions of classical and modern plays since 1968. Most shows have half-price tickets for patrons under 35.

California Shakespeare Theater THEATER
(Map p155; ☎510-548-9666; www.calshakes.org; 701 Heinz Ave; tickets $39-63; ⏰late May-early Oct; 🚌AC Transit 36, 80) Headquartered in Berkeley, with the fantastic outdoor Bruns Amphitheater east of the Berkeley Hills in Orinda as a venue, 'Cal Shakes' carries on a a warm-weather tradition of alfresco Shakespeare and other classic productions.

Zellerbach Hall PERFORMING ARTS
(Map p152; ☎510-642-9988; www.calperformances.org; off Bancroft Way; tickets from $10; ⏰ticket office usually noon-5:30pm Tue-Fri, 1-5pm Sat & Sun; 🚌AC Transit 51B) At the south end of the University of California, Berkeley campus near Bancroft Way and Dana St, Zellerbach Hall features dance events, musical concerts and performances of all types by national and international touring artists. The on-site Cal Performances Ticket Office sells tickets.

Shotgun Players THEATER
(Map p155; ☎510-841-6500; www.shotgunplayers.org; 1901 Ashby Ave; varies; ⏰hours vary; Ⓑ Downtown Berkeley) 🍃 Berkeley's solar-powered theater company stages exciting and provocative works in an intimate space. Offers pay-what-you-can tickets for preview shows, and $7 admission for under-25s if you show up an hour before a show (space permitting).

Aurora Theatre Company THEATER
(Map p152; ☎510-843-4822; www.auroratheatre.org; 2081 Addison St; tickets from $25; ⏰box office usually 1-5pm Tue-Fri; Ⓑ Downtown Berkeley) Intimate downtown theater performing contemporary, thought-provoking plays staged with subtle aesthetics.

Pacific Film Archive CINEMA
(PFA; Map p152; ☎510-642-0808; www.bampfa.org; 2155 Center St; adult/child from $14/10; ⏰hours vary; Ⓑ Downtown Berkeley) A world-renowned film center with an ever-changing

WORTH A TRIP

EAST BROTHER LIGHT STATION

Most Bay Area residents have never heard of this speck of an island off the East Bay city of Richmond, and even fewer know that the **East Brother Light Station** (☎510-233-2385; www.ebls.org; 1900 Stenmark Dr, Richmond; d incl breakfast & dinner $347-457; ⊙Thu-Sun) is a five-room, adults-only Victorian B&B. Guests stay in the romantic lighthouse or fog-signal building (the foghorn blares from October 1 to April 1), and resident innkeepers serve afternoon hors d'oeuvres and champagne. After the four-course dinner (which includes wine pairings), you can stroll around the breezy 0.75-acre islet and rummage through historical photos and artifacts.Access is by boat, and guests must be capable of climbing a ladder. Showers are only available to guests staying two or more nights. Reserve ahead.

schedule of international and classic films – cineastes should seek out this place. The spacious theater has seats comfy enough for hours-long movie marathons.

Shopping

Heading south of the university campus, Telegraph Ave caters mostly to students, hawking a steady dose of urban hippie gear, handmade sidewalk-vendor jewelry and head-shop paraphernalia. Audiophiles will swoon over the music stores.

Berkeley's other shopping corridors include College Ave in the Elmwood District (on the Oakland border), 4th St (north of University Ave) and Solano Ave (heading into Albany).

Amoeba Music MUSIC
(Map p152; ☎510-549-1125; www.amoeba.com; 2455 Telegraph Ave; ⊙11am-8pm Sun-Thu, to 10pm Fri & Sat; 🚌6) If you're a music junkie, you might plan on spending a few hours at the original Berkeley branch of Amoeba Music, packed with massive quantities of new and used CDs, DVDs, tapes and records (yes, lots of vinyl).

Hi-Fidelity DISPENSARY
(Map p152; ☎510-838-2400; www.hifigreen.com; 2465 Telegraph Ave; eighth from $25; ⊙10am-9pm) 🍃 From the owners of the neighboring Amoeba Music comes Berkeley's top cannabis dispensary. The array of pot products is sourced from small farmers, independent collectives and boutique purveyors who minimize their carbon footprints and produce superior strains.

University Press Books BOOKS
(Map p152; ☎510-548-0585; www.universitypressbooks.com; 2430 Bancroft Way; ⊙11am-7pm Mon-Fri, noon-5pm Sat & Sun; 🚌AC Transit 51B) Across the street from campus, this academic and scholarly bookstore stocks works by UC Berkeley professors and other academic and museum publishers, with frequent author appearances.

Moe's Books BOOKS
(Map p152; ☎510-849-2087; www.moesbooks.com; 2476 Telegraph Ave; ⊙10am-10pm; 🚌6) A long-standing local favorite, Moe's offers four floors of new, used and remaindered books for hours of browsing.

Information

MEDICAL SERVICES

Alta Bates Summit Medical Center, Ashby Campus (☎510-204-4444; www.sutterhealth.org; 2450 Ashby Ave; ⊙24hr; 🚌AC Transit 6) Emergency services.

TOURIST INFORMATION

UC Berkeley Koret Visitor Center (Map p152; ☎510-642-5215; http://visit.berkeley.edu; 2227 Piedmont Ave; ⊙8:30am-4:30pm Mon-Fri, 9am-1pm Sat & Sun; 🚌AC Transit 36) Campus maps and information are available at this visitor center on Goldman Plaza at **California Memorial Stadium** (Map p152; ☎510-642-2730; https://calbears.com/sports/2020/6/18/california-memorial-stadium.aspx; 2227 Piedmont Ave; ⊙hours vary; 👪; 🚌AC Transit 52). Free 90-minute campus walking tours usually start at 10am daily (online reservations required in advance).

Visit Berkeley (Map p152; ☎510-549-7040; www.visitberkeley.com; 2030 Addison St; ⊙9am-1pm & 2-5pm Mon-Fri; Ⓑ Downtown Berkeley) The helpful Berkeley Convention & Visitors Bureau prints a free visitors guide (also available online) and provides complimentary maps, trail guides, brochures, performing arts information and more.

Getting There & Away

BART

To get to Berkeley, catch a Richmond-bound train to one of three BART (p150) stations: Ashby, Downtown Berkeley or North Berkeley. After

9pm Monday through Thursday, 11pm on Friday, 7pm on Saturday and all day Sunday, there is no direct train service operating from San Francisco to Berkeley; instead, catch an Antioch train, then transfer at 19th St station in Oakland.

BUS

On AC Transit (p150), the F line leaves from the Salesforce Transit Center in San Francisco for downtown Berkeley and the university campus approximately every half-hour ($6, 40 minutes).

Between downtown Berkeley and downtown Oakland, take fast and frequent AC Transit bus 6 along Telegraph Ave. Alternatively, take bus 18 via Martin Luther King Jr Way and Shattuck Ave. Bus 51B travels along University Ave past Downtown Berkeley BART station to the Berkeley Marina. One-way local bus fares on AC Transit are $2.50 (though Clipper cards offer a slight discount).

CAR & MOTORCYCLE

From San Francisco, drive over the Bay Bridge and then follow either I-80 (for University Ave, Berkeley Marina, downtown Berkeley and the university campus) or Hwy 24 (for College Ave and the Berkeley Hills).

TRAIN

Amtrak does stop in Berkeley, but the platform is not staffed and direct connections are few. More convenient is Emeryville Amtrak station (p150), about 2 miles south.

To reach the Emeryville station from downtown Berkeley, take AC Transit bus F or ride BART to the MacArthur station and then catch the free Emery Go Round (p150) shuttle bus.

Getting Around

Local buses, ridesharing, cycling, scootering and walking are the best ways to get around Berkeley.

BICYCLE

By Downtown Berkeley BART station, **Bike Station** (510-548-7433; www.bikehub.com/rentals; 2023 Center St; per day/week/month $35/95/200; 7am-8pm Mon-Fri) rents bicycles with a helmet and U-lock.

BUS

AC Transit (p150) operates local public buses in and around Berkeley. The one-way fare is $2.50; pay with cash (exact change required) or a Clipper card.

The university's **Bear Transit** (510-643-7701; http://pt.berkeley.edu) runs a shuttle from Downtown Berkeley BART station to various points on campus. From Bear Transit's on-campus stop at Hearst Mining Circle, the H Line runs along Centennial Dr to the upper parts of the campus. For visitors, each ride costs $1 (bring cash).

CAR & MOTORCYCLE

Drivers should note that numerous barriers have been set up to prevent car traffic from traversing residential streets at high speeds, so zigzagging is necessary in some neighborhoods.

Downtown and near the university campus, pay-parking lots are well signed. Metered street-parking spots are rarely empty.

John Muir National Historic Site

Naturalist John Muir's **former residence** (925-228-8860; www.nps.gov/jomu; 4202 Alhambra Ave, Martinez; Muir Home 10am-4:45pm, Mt Wanda sunrise-sunset; P) FREE sits in a pastoral patch of farmland in bustling, modern Martinez. Though Muir wrote of sauntering the Sierra Nevada with a sack of tea and bread, it may be a shock for those familiar with the iconic Sierra Club founder's ascetic weather-beaten appearance that this house (built by his father-in-law) is a model of Victorian Italianate refinement, with a tower cupola, a daintily upholstered parlor and splashes of white lace.

Muir's 'scribble den' has been left as it was during his life, with crumbled papers overflowing from wire wastebaskets and dried-bread balls – his preferred snack – resting on the mantelpiece.

Acres of the family's fruit orchards still stand, and visitors can enjoy seasonal samples. The grounds include the 1849 Martinez Adobe, part of the ranch on which the house was built, and oak-speckled hiking trails on nearby Mt Wanda, named for one of Muir's daughters. Check the website for special campfire programs, wildflower walks and full-moon hikes.

The park is just north of Hwy 4. **County Connection** (925-676-7500; www.countyconnection.com; one way $2-2.50) buses 16 and 98X from nearby Amtrak and BART stations stop here.

THE PENINSULA

South of San Francisco, squeezed tightly between the bay and the coastal foothills, a vast swath of suburbia continues toward San Jose. Dotted inside this area are Palo Alto – home of Stanford University – and Silicon

Valley, the epicenter of the Bay Area's tech industry.

You won't find Silicon Valley on any map: it's a nickname. As silicon chips form the basis of modern microcomputers, and the Santa Clara Valley – stretching from Palo Alto through Mountain View, Sunnyvale and Cupertino to San Jose – is thought of as the birthplace of the microcomputer, the region is dubbed 'Silicon Valley.' It's hard to imagine that even after WWII this was still a wide expanse of orchards and farms.

Further west, the 70-mile stretch of coastal Hwy 1 from San Francisco to Santa Cruz is one of California's most bewitching oceanside drives. For the most part, it's winding, two-lane blacktop, passing beach after beach.

San Francisco to San Jose

South of the San Francisco peninsula, I-280 is the divide between the densely populated South Bay area and the rugged, lightly populated Pacific Coast. With sweeping views of hills and reservoirs, it's a more scenic choice than Hwy 101. Unfortunately, both these parallel north–south arteries are often clogged with traffic.

A historical site where European explorers first set eyes on San Francisco Bay, **Sweeney Ridge** (www.nps.gov/goga/sweeney.htm; end of Sneath Lane, San Bruno) straddles a prime spot between Pacifica and San Bruno, offering hikers awe-inspiring ocean and bay views. From I-280, exit at Sneath Lane and follow it 2 miles southwest until it dead-ends at the trailhead.

On the bay at the northern edge of San Mateo, 4 miles south of San Francisco International Airport, is **Coyote Point Recreation Area** (650-573-2592; https://parks.smcgov.org/coyote-point-recreation-area; 1701 Coyote Point Dr, San Mateo; per car $6; 8am-8pm Apr-Aug, to 5pm, 6pm or 7pm Sep-Mar; P), a popular park and windsurfing destination. The main attraction is **CuriOdyssey** (650-342-7755; www.curiodyssey.org; 1651 Coyote Point Dr, Coyote Point Recreation Area; adult/child $15.95/12.95; 10am-5pm Tue-Sun; P), an innovative museum with conservation-minded wildlife exhibits. Exit Hwy 101 at Coyote Point Dr.

Stanford University

Sprawled over 8180 leafy acres in Palo Alto, Stanford University (www.stanford.edu) was founded by Leland Stanford, one of the Central Pacific Railroad's 'Big Four' founders and a former governor of California. When the Stanfords' only child died of typhoid during a European tour in 1884, they decided to build a university in his memory. The campus was built on the site of the Stanfords' horse-breeding farm and, as a result, Stanford is still known as 'The Farm.'

Sights

Main Quad PLAZA

(650-723-2560; off Palm Dr) Auguste Rodin's *Burghers of Calais* bronze sculpture marks the entrance to Stanford University's Main Quad, an open plaza where the original 12 campus buildings – a mix of Romanesque and Mission Revival styles – were joined by Memorial Church in 1903. The church is noted for its beautiful mosaic-tiled frontage, stained-glass windows and five organs with more than 8000 pipes.

Free guided tours of 'MemChu' are offered at 1pm every Friday and 11:30am on the first Sunday of the month.

Hoover Tower TOWER

(650-723-2053; adult/child $4/3; 10am-4pm, last entry 3:30pm) A campus landmark at the east of the Main Quad, the 285ft-high Hoover Tower is part of the conservative Hoover Institution on War, Revolution and Peace, a Stanford-affiliated public policy research center. An observation platform on the 14th floor offers superb views, and the building also houses a university library, offices and a couple of free exhibition rooms, one of which contains a 900lb piece of the Berlin Wall.

The tower was struck by lightning in August 2020; at the time of writing, the full extent of the damage was still unknown.

Cantor Arts Center MUSEUM

(650-723-4177; https://museum.stanford.edu; 328 Lomita Dr; 11am-5pm Wed & Fri-Mon, to 8pm Thu; P) FREE The Cantor Center for Visual Arts is a beautiful large museum originally dating from 1894. Its collection spans works from ancient civilizations to contemporary art, sculpture (including a Rodin garden) and photography. Rotating exhibits are eclectic in scope, and the new *OY/YO* letter sculpture out front has drawn considerable attention.

Information

Stanford Visitor Center (650-723-2560; http://visit.stanford.edu; 295 Galvez St; 8:30am-5pm Mon-Fri, 11am-5pm Sat & Sun) Offers free 70-minute walking tours of the campus at 11:30am and 3:30pm daily, except

WORTH A TRIP

MT DIABLO STATE PARK

Collecting a light dusting of snowflakes on the coldest days of winter, Mt Diablo (3849ft) is more than 1200ft higher than Mt Tamalpais in Marin County. On a clear day (early on a winter morning is a good bet) the views from Diablo's summit are vast and sweeping. To the west you can see over the bay and out to the Farallon Islands; to the east you can look out over the Central Valley to the Sierra Nevada. Additional draws include rock climbing, stargazing, wildflowers in springtime and the tarantula mating season in the fall.

Most easily accessed from Danville or Walnut Creek, the **park** (☎925-837-2525; www.mdia.org; off Summit Rd, Walnut Creek; per vehicle $10; ⌚8am-sunset) is threaded by more than 170 miles of hiking trails. You can also drive to the summit, where there's a **visitor center** (☎925-837-6119; www.parks.ca.gov; ⌚10am-4pm), and spend the night in the park's **campgrounds** (☎reservations 800-444-7275; www.reservecalifornia.com; tent & RV sites $30).

during academic breaks and some holidays. Special-interest tours also available.

Getting There & Away

Stanford University's free public shuttle, **Marguerite** (☎650-724-4309; http://transportation.stanford.edu/marguerite), provides service from Caltrain's Palo Alto and California Ave stations to the campus. All shuttles are wheelchair-accessible and most are equipped with bicycle racks. Parking on campus is difficult and expensive.

San Jose

Though culturally diverse and historical, San Jose – awash in Silicon Valley's suburbia – has always been in San Francisco's shadow. Founded in 1777 as El Pueblo de San José de Guadalupe, San Jose is California's oldest Spanish civilian settlement. Its downtown is relatively small and quiet for a city of its size, though it does bustle with twentysomething clubgoers on weekends. Industrial parks, high-tech computer firms and look-alike housing developments are sprawled across the city's landscape, taking over from where farms, ranches and open spaces once spread between the bay and the surrounding hills.

Sights

History Park MUSEUM

(☎408-287-2290; http://historysanjose.org; 635 Phelan Ave; ⌚12:30-5pm Mon-Fri, from 8am Sat & Sun; P) FREE Historical buildings from all over San Jose have been brought together in this open-air history museum. The centerpiece is a scaled-down replica of the 1881 **Electric Light Tower**. Other buildings include the 1880 **Pacific Hotel**, which houses an old-timey ice cream parlor and rotating art exhibits. The **Trolley Barn** restores trolley cars to operate on San Jose's light-rail line.

On weekends you can ride a streetcar along the park's own short line at no charge.

Tech Interactive MUSEUM

(The Tech; ☎408-294-8324; www.thetech.org; 201 S Market St; adult/child $25/20, incl IMAX movie $31/24; ⌚10am-5pm; 👪) Opposite **Plaza de Cesar Chavez**, San Jose's excellent technology museum examines subjects from robotics to biofeedback, genetics to virtual reality. The museum also includes an IMAX dome theater, which screens newly released films throughout the day.

MACLA GALLERY

(Movimiento de Arte y Cultura Latino Americana; ☎408-998-2783; www.maclaarte.org; 510 S 1st St; ⌚noon-7pm Wed & Thu, to 5pm Fri & Sat) FREE A cutting-edge gallery highlighting themes by both established and emerging Latino artists, MACLA is one of the Bay Area's best community arts spaces, with open-mike performances, live music shows, experimental theater and well-curated, thought-provoking visual-arts exhibits.

Rosicrucian Egyptian Museum MUSEUM

(☎408-947-3635; www.egyptianmuseum.org; 1660 Park Ave; adult/child $9/5; ⌚9am-5pm Wed-Fri, 10am-6pm Sat & Sun; P) West of downtown, this educational Egyptian museum is one of San Jose's more unusual attractions. Its extensive collection includes statues, household items and mummies (both human and animal); there's even a two-room walk-through reproduction of an ancient subterranean tomb.

Sleeping

Conventions and trade shows keep downtown hotels busy year-round, with midweek rates often higher than those on weekends. Midrange motels and hotels hug freeways on the outskirts of the city and by the airport.

Hotel De Anza HISTORIC HOTEL $$$
(408-286-1000; www.hoteldeanza.com; 233 W Santa Clara St; r from $299;) Opened during the Jazz Age, this downtown hotel is a restored art deco beauty that pays homage to the property's history. Guest rooms offer plush comforts (those facing south are a tad larger) and there's full concierge service. Complimentary late-night snack boxes, in-room espresso makers and a 24-hour fitness center seal the deal.

Hotel Valencia BOUTIQUE HOTEL $$$
(408-551-0010; www.hotelvalencia-santanarow.com; 355 Santana Row; r from $299;) A tranquil and conveniently located 215-room boutique hotel in the **Santana Row** (408-551-4611; www.santanarow.com; 377 Santana Row; 10am-9pm Mon-Sat, 11am-7pm Sun) shopping complex. In-room minibars and bathrobes plus an outdoor pool and hot tub create a stylish oasis of contemporary design. Valet overnight parking is $26.

Westin San Jose HISTORIC HOTEL $$$
(408-295-2000; www.marriott.com; 302 S Market St; r from $369;) Formerly the Sainte Claire, this atmospheric 1926 landmark hotel overlooking Plaza de Cesar Chavez (p163) has a drop-dead gorgeous lobby with stretched-leather ceilings. Guest rooms are smallish, but have been remodeled. Overnight valet parking is $45.

Eating

San Jose rarely comes to mind as a culinary hub. But in 2016 one of its restaurants, Adega, won a Michelin star – a first in the city's history.

Thanks to large populations of Mexican, Vietnamese, Indian and Portuguese immigrants, restaurants specializing in those cuisines have tended to thrive here. Downtown and Japantown offer lively dining scenes, and you'll find plenty of budget-friendly cafes in the city's eastern stretches near the SJSU campus.

San Pedro Square Market FOOD HALL $
(www.sanpedrosquaremarket.com; 87 N San Pedro St; most mains $6-20; 11am-10pm Sun-Thu, to midnight Fri & Sat;) Always busy, this indoor/outdoor marketplace downtown showcases a few shining local food stars such as Pizza Bocca Lupo, Konjoe Burger Bar and Treatbot ice cream. All seating is first-come, first-served. There's live music almost every night, and on Sunday afternoons.

Falafel's Drive-in MIDDLE EASTERN $
(408-294-7886; www.falafelsdrivein.com; 2301 Stevens Creek Blvd; falafel pita & banana shake $10; 10am-8pm;) At this San José institution of more than 50 years, the pitas brim with crunchy, herby falafel, creamy tahini, veggies, pepper sauce and ketchup. Defying explanation, a banana shake is the pita's perfect complement.

Back A Yard CARIBBEAN $
(408-294-8626; https://backayard.net; 80 N Market St; mains $9-17; 11am-8:30pm Mon-Thu, to 9pm Fri, from noon Sat) Jamaican jerk chicken, pork, salmon and tofu are the house specialties of this beloved Caribbean-barbecue kitchen, which also serves the occasional plate of beef oxtails or curried goat. The at-

WINCHESTER MYSTERY HOUSE

A bizarre, sprawling structure commissioned by the heir to the Winchester-rifle fortune, this ridiculous Victorian **mansion** (408-247-2101; www.winchestermysteryhouse.com; 525 S Winchester Blvd; mansion tours adult/child $39/20; incl Explore More tour adult/child $54/25; 9am-7pm, to 5pm early Sep-late May;) features 160 rooms of various sizes and little utility, with dead-end hallways, pointless staircases and doors to nowhere that seem designed by a toddler playing architect. The standard hour-long guided mansion tour covers most of the (apparently haunted) home, while the newer 'Explore More' tour involves a romp through the stables and gardens plus entry to unfinished areas of the the house that were off-limits for decades. A shooting gallery and axe-throwing game round out offerings.

One theory holds that Sarah Winchester spent 38 years constructing this oddity because the spirits of the people killed by Winchester rifles told her to. Regardless, no expense was spared in the construction, the extreme results of which sprawl over 4 acres.

The house is west of central San Jose and just north of I-280, perched incongruously across the street from Santana Row shopping center.

mosphere is festive, with tropically colored murals adorning the red-brick walls.

Tofoo Com Chay VIETNAMESE $
(☎408-286-6335; www.tofoocomchaydeli.com; 388 E Santa Clara St; mains $7-15; ⏰9am-9pm Mon-Fri, 10am-6pm Sat; 🌱) Students and vegetarians queue for Vietnamese dishes such as the faux-meat pho and the heaped combo plates. Conveniently located on the border of the San Jose State University campus.

★ **Adega** PORTUGUESE $$$
(☎408-926-9075; www.adegarest.com; 1614 Alum Rock Ave; set tasting menu $89; ⏰5-9:30pm Wed-Sun) In San José's Little Portugal neighborhood, this family-owned Portuguese restaurant holds the city's first and only Michelin star. The setting is rustic-cozy, with wood floors and and beamed ceilings, and the tasting menu is as exotic as it is satisfying: salted codfish, rich duck rice, rabbit casserole, egg-topped steak. The colossal Portuguese wine list includes more than 500 bottles.

Drinking & Nightlife

Original Gravity Public House CRAFT BEER
(☎408-915-2337; www.originalgravitypub.com; 66 S 1st St; ⏰noon-10pm Sun-Wed, to midnight Thu, to 1am Fri & Sat) With nearly three dozen rotating taps of brews, including ciders and meads, as well as scores of bottles, this crowded yet friendly pub will confound you with choices. Consider the options while you nosh on housemade gourmet sausages, a grilled cheese sandwich or duck-fat poutine.

Paper Plane COCKTAIL BAR
(☎408-713-2625; www.paperplanesj.com; 72 S 1st St; ⏰4:30pm-midnight Sun-Tue, to 2am Wed-Sat) Downtown at this industrial-chic watering hole with wall-sized, backlit shelves of liquor, tattooed bartenders willingly customize your drink if nothing on the menu of old-school classics and imaginative modern mixology tempts. Share a pitcher and appetizers with friends.

Haberdasher COCKTAIL BAR
(☎408-792-7356; www.haberdashersj.com; 43 W San Salvador St; ⏰5pm-midnight Sun, Tue & Wed, to 1am Thu-Sat) A cool basement lounge where sharply dressed bartenders artfully mix cocktails, with some recipes dating to before Prohibition. It's a justifiably popular place; you can (and should) book ahead for a table Friday and Saturday nights to guarantee your spot.

Entertainment

Earthquakes Stadium SPECTATOR SPORT
(1123 Coleman Rd) Located near San Jose's airport, this is the home of the **San Jose Earthquakes** (☎408-556-7700; www.sjearthquakes.com), the city's professional soccer team (season runs from February through October).

SAP Center STADIUM
(☎408-287-9200; www.sapcenteratsanjose.com; 525 W Santa Clara St) The **San Jose Sharks** (☎800-559-2333; www.nhl.com/sharks) – the city's tremendously popular professional hockey team – play at this massive glass-and-metal stadium (formerly the HP Pavilion) from September through April. Megaconcerts by touring acts go on stage year-round.

California Theatre THEATER
(☎408-792-4111; http://sanjosetheaters.org/theaters/california-theatre; 345 S 1st St) The absolutely stunning Spanish Colonial interior of this landmark entertainment venue could be mistaken for that of a cathedral. The theater is home to Opera San Jose and Symphony Silicon Valley.

Information

San Jose Convention & Visitors Bureau (☎408-792-4511; www.sanjose.org; 408 Almaden Blvd; ⏰8am-5pm Mon-Fri) Free visitor information, guides and maps. Good website too.

Santa Clara Valley Medical Center (☎408-885-5000; www.scvmc.org; 751 S Bascom Ave; ⏰24hr) 24-hour emergency services.

Getting There & Away

AIR

Four miles northwest of downtown between Hwy 101 and I-880, **Norman Y. Mineta San Jose International Airport** (SJC; ☎408-392-3600; www.flysanjose.com; 1701 Airport Blvd) has free wi-fi and mostly domestic US flights from two terminals.

BART

To access the BART (p150) system, VTA (p166) bus 181 runs between downtown San Jose and the Fremont BART station ($7.60, 35 to 45 minutes). Construction is underway for a downtown San Jose station but it's not expected to be completed until 2026.

BUS

Greyhound (p779) buses to Los Angeles ($20 to $37, 6½ to 10½ hours) leave from **San Jose**

Diridon Station (65 Cahill St). Discount carrier **Megabus** (☎877-462-6342; https://us.megabus.com) offers daily service between San Jose and Burbank, Los Angeles or Anaheim ($10 to $40, six to seven hours), with departures outside Diridon Station.

The **VTA** (Valley Transport Authority; ☎408-321-2300; www.vta.org) Hwy 17 Express bus plies a handy route between Diridon Station and Santa Cruz ($7, 55 minutes, every 30 minutes).

CAR & MOTORCYCLE

San Jose is at the southern end of the San Francisco Bay, about 40 miles from Oakland (via I-880) or 50 miles from San Francisco (via Hwy 101 or I-280). Expect lots of traffic at all times of day on Hwy 101 from San Francisco; although I-280 is slightly longer, it's much prettier and usually less congested. Heading south, Hwy 17 leads over the mountains to Santa Cruz.

TRAIN

A double-decker commuter rail service operating up and down the Peninsula, **Caltrain** (☎800-660-4287; www.caltrain.com) runs between San Jose and San Francisco ($10.50, 65 to 85 minutes). Trains run hourly on weekends and more frequently on weekdays. Bicycles may be brought on designated cars only. San Jose's terminal, Diridon Station (p165), is just south of the Alameda.

Diridon Station is also the terminal for Amtrak (p779) trains serving Seattle, Los Angeles and Sacramento, and also for **Altamont Commuter Express** (ACE; ☎800-411-7245; www.acerail.com; Diridon Station) trains, which run to **Great America** (☎408-988-1776; www.cagreatamerica.com; 4701 Great America Pkwy, Santa Clara; ticket $40, ticket incl parking & a meal $50; ⏰Apr-Nov, hours vary; 👪), Livermore and Stockton (among other places).

VTA runs a free weekday shuttle (known as the Downtown Area Shuttle or DASH) from Diridon Station to downtown San Jose.

ℹ Getting Around

VTA buses run all over Silicon Valley. Fares for VTA buses (except express lines) and light-rail trains are $2.50 for a single ride (day pass $7.50).

From the airport (p165), free VTA Airport Flyer shuttles (route 60) run every 15 to 20 minutes to the Metro/Airport Light Rail station, where you can catch the light rail to downtown San Jose; shuttles also go to the Santa Clara Caltrain station.

The main San Jose light-rail line runs north–south from the city center. Heading south gets you as far as Santa Teresa. The northern route runs to Japantown, the airport and Tasman, where it connects with another line that heads west past Great America to downtown Mountain View.

In San Jose, many downtown retailers offer two-hour parking validation. Otherwise, city-owned lots and garages downtown charge a $5 flat rate after 6pm on weekdays and all day on weekends.Rideshare is another simple way to get around.

Pacifica & Devil's Slide

The lazy beach town of Pacifica, just 15 miles from downtown San Francisco, signals the end of the city's urban sprawl and the start of wild Pacific coastline. Once a fairly down-trodden, cluttered town – its claim to fame is having the world's most scenic Taco Bell (which now serves booze) – Pacifica is gentrifying thanks to its easy-to-reach location and beautiful white beaches that get pounded regularly by surfable waves.

Immediately south of Pacifica is the Devil's Slide, a gorgeous coastal cliff area now bypassed by a car tunnel.

Pacifica State Beach BEACH
(Linda Mar Beach; ☎650-738-7381; www.parks.ca.gov; 5000 Pacific Coast Hwy; per car $7-9; ⏰5am-dusk; P) Getting a suntan or catching a wave are the main attractions at popular Pacifica State Beach, as well as at Rockaway Beach just north.

Nor-Cal Surf Shop SURFING
(☎650-738-9283; 5440 Coast Hwy, Pedro Point Shopping Center; ⏰9am-6pm Sun-Fri, from 8am Sat, open to 7pm in summer) Rents surfboards (half/full day $15/20), wetsuits (half-full day $12.50/16.50) and SUP sets (half-full day $28/45) next to Pacifica State Beach. Book ahead for surf lessons (from $98).

Devil's Slide Trail HIKING
(☎650-355-8289; http://parks.smcgov.org/devils-slide-trail; Hwy 1; ⏰8am-8pm Apr-Aug, closes earlier Sep-Mar) Hikers and cyclists cruise along the Devil's Slide Coastal Trail, a paved 1.3-mile section of the old highway. Heading south or north on Hwy 1, turn off into the trailhead parking lots before entering the tunnels.

Pacifica to Half Moon Bay

These tiny hamlets front a stretch of coast dotted by white-sand beaches and surf-pounded cliffs. If you're driving it's fun to drop in to the towns and admire the humble Victorian-era beach houses with

THE CULINARY COAST

Pescadero is renowned for Duarte's Tavern (p169), but loads of other tidbits are close by. **Arcangeli Grocery Company** (Norm's Market; ☎650-879-0147; www.normsmarket.com; 287 Stage Rd; sandwiches $8-10; ⏰10am-6pm;) supplies made-to-order deli sandwiches, chilled bottles of California wine, and a famous artichoke garlic herb bread, baked fresh almost hourly. **Harley Farms Goat Dairy** (☎650-879-0480; www.harleyfarms.com; 250 North St; ⏰11am-4pm Fri-Sun; P) is a local food treasure and baby-goat haven, with a split-level farm shop hawking creamy artisanal goat cheeses festooned with fruit, nuts and edible flowers. Definitely hit the brakes for **Pie Ranch** (☎650-879-9281; www.pieranch.org; 2080 Cabrillo Hwy; ⏰noon-5pm Mon & Wed-Fri, 10am-5pm Sat & Sun), a roadside farm stand known for its fresh produce, eggs, coffee and amazing fruit pies (they sell out fast). And down at the **Swanton Berry Farm Stand** (☎650-469-8804; www.swantonberryfarm.com; 25 Swanton Rd, Davenport; ⏰8am-8pm late May-early Sep, closes 5pm rest of year; P), you'll roll up those shirtsleeves and pick your own fruit. There's also indoor and outdoor seating, bluegrass music on the stereo and hot drinks including strawberry cider.

gingerbread trim and colorful paint. There are plenty of larger beaches and preserves to stop at as well.

Montara State Beach STATE PARK
(☎650-726-8819; www.parks.ca.gov; Hwy 1; ⏰8am-sunset; P) FREE About 5 miles south of the town of Pacifica, this wide-open crescent is a local favorite for its pristine sand. Inland the park encompasses **McNee Ranch**, which has hiking and cycling trails aplenty, including a strenuous ascent to a panoramic viewpoint atop **Montara Mountain** (1898ft); it's a 7.6-mile round-trip from Hwy 1.

Fitzgerald Marine Reserve NATURE RESERVE
(☎650-728-3584; www.fitzgeraldreserve.org; 200 Nevada Ave, Moss Beach; ⏰8am-8pm Apr-Aug, closes earlier Sep-Mar; P) FREE At Moss Beach, this marine reserve protects tide pools teeming with sea life. Walk out among the pools at low tide – wearing shoes that you can get wet – and observe countless crabs, sea stars, mollusks and rainbow-colored sea anemone. Note that it's illegal to remove any creatures, shells or even rocks from the marine reserve.

★**HI Point Montara Lighthouse** HOSTEL $
(☎650-728-7177; www.norcalhostels.org/montara; cnr Hwy 1 & 16th St, Montara; dm $35-40, r with shared bath $100-140; ⏰reception 7:30am-10:30pm; P) Starting life as a fog station in 1875, this hostel is adjacent to the current lighthouse and has ramshackle yet beautiful Victorian architecture plus sea views to die for. There's a living room, decent kitchen and outdoor fire pit plus a few private rooms for couples or families. Make reservations two weeks in advance, especially for weekends and summer.

Moss Beach Distillery BAR
(☎650-728-5595; www.mossbeachdistillery.com; 140 Beach Way, Moss Beach; ⏰from noon Mon-Sat, from 11am Sun (closing time varies);) Overlooking the cove where bootleggers used to unload Prohibition-era liquor, the restaurant's heated ocean-view deck is perfectly positioned to catch sunset. In fair weather it's the best place for miles to have a leisurely cocktail and snack, but head elsewhere for a meal if you're hungry.

Half Moon Bay

Home to a long coastline, mild weather and Mavericks – one of the biggest and scariest surf breaks on the planet – Half Moon Bay is prime real estate. The Ohlone people lived here for thousands of years before Spanish missionaries set up shop in the late 1700s; it was developed as a beach resort in the early 1900s. Today, it's the main coastal town between San Francisco (29 miles north) and Santa Cruz (49 miles south).

Its long stretches of sandy beach and coastal bluffs attract surfers, hikers and other rambling weekenders, while a 1919 jail house (now a **museum** (☎650-479-1935; http://halfmoonbayhistory.org; 505 Johnston St; ⏰10am-4pm Sat & Sun) FREE – beckons history enthusiasts. While its services spread out along Hwy 1/Cabrillo Hwy, Half Moon Bay itself is still relatively small.

Half Moon Bay Kayak Co WATER SPORTS
(☎650-773-6101; www.hmbkayak.com; 2 Johnson Pier; kayak or SUP set rental per hour/day $25/75, bicycle rental $20/50; ⏰9am-5pm Jun-Sep, rest of the year Wed-Mon, winter hours 10am-4pm) When the bay is calm, get out and cruise around

on the water for a few hours with Half Moon Bay Kayak Co, which rents kayaks and SUP sets. It also rents bicycles. Book ahead for harbor, sunset or full-moon tours.

Mavericks SURFING

Mavericks is an intense surf break that once attracted pro big-wave riders to battle its huge, steep and very dangerous waves. The invitational Mavericks Challenge, called on a few days' notice when the swells get huge, was held annually between November and March. It hasn't taken place since 2016, though, and was cancelled indefinitely in 2019.

Sea Horse Ranch HORSEBACK RIDING

(650-726-9903; www.seahorseranch.org; 1828 Cabrillo Hwy; trail ride $80-100; 8am-4pm;) Just over a mile north of the Hwy 92 junction, Sea Horse Ranch offers daily horseback rides along the beach. Minimum age for riders is seven years; weight limits and clothing restrictions apply. Book ahead.

Half Moon Bay Brewing Company PUB FOOD $$

(650-728-2739; www.hmbbrewingco.com; 390 Capistrano Rd; mains $15-27; 11am-9pm Mon-Fri, 10am-10pm Sat, 10am-8pm Sun;) Chomp on seafood and burgers while you swill pints from a respectable menu of local brews and gaze out at the bay from a sheltered, heated outdoor patio. Live music every weekend.

Getting There & Away

SamTrans bus 294 operates hourly between the Caltrain (p166) Hillsdale station in San Mateo and Half Moon Bay ($2.25, 45 minutes). From Half Moon Bay, SamTrans bus 17 heads up the coast to Moss Beach, Montara and Pacifica ($2.25, one hour) every hour or two daily, with limited weekday service south to Pescadero ($2.25, 25 minutes).

Pescadero

A foggy speck of coastal crossroads between Half Moon Bay and Santa Cruz, 167-year-old Pescadero is a close-knit rural town of sugar-lending neighbors and community pancake breakfasts. But on weekends the tiny downtown strains its seams with long-distance cyclists panting for carbohydrates and day-trippers dive-bombing in from the oceanfront highway. They're all drawn to the winter vistas of emerald-green hills parched to burlap-brown in summer, the wild Pacific beaches populated by seals and pelicans, and the unbelievably fresh food from local farms and ranches. With its cornucopia of tide-pool coves and parks of sky-blotting redwood canopies, city dwellers come here to slow down and smell the sea breeze wafting over fields of bushy artichokes.

Sights

Pigeon Point Light Station State Historic Park LIGHTHOUSE

(650-879-2120; www.parks.ca.gov; 210 Pigeon Point Rd; 8am-sunset, visitor center 10am-4pm Thu-Mon; P) A half-dozen miles south of Pescadero along the coast, this 115ft-high light station is one of the tallest lighthouses on the West Coast. The 1872 landmark had to close access to the upper tower when chunks of its cornice began to rain from the sky (future restorations are planned), but the automated LED beacon still flashes brightly and the bluff is a prime – though blustery – spot to scan for breaching gray whales in winter.

Bean Hollow State Beach BEACH

(650-726-8819; www.parks.ca.gov; off Hwy 1; 8am-sunset; P) FREE Pretty sand beaches speckle the coast, though one of the most interesting places to stop is Pebble Beach, a jewel less than 2 miles south of Pescadero Creek Rd (and part of Bean Hollow State Beach). The shore is awash with bite-sized eye candy of agate, jade and carnelian, and sandstone troughs are pockmarked by groovy honeycombed formations called tafoni.

Butano State Park STATE PARK

(650-879-2040; www.parks.ca.gov; 1500 Cloverdale Rd; per car $10; sunrise-sunset; P) Five miles south of Pescadero, bobcats and coyotes reside discreetly in this pretty park's 4600 acres of dense redwood canyon and uplands laced with hiking and mountain-biking trails and shady **campsites** (reservations 800-444-7275; www.reserveamerica.com; 1500 Cloverdale Rd; tent & RV sites from $35; P). From Pescadero Creek Rd in downtown Pescadero, follow Cloverdale Rd south for 4 miles to the turnoff.

Pescadero State Beach & Marsh Natural Preserve STATE PARK

(650-726-8819; www.parks.ca.gov; off Hwy 1; per car $8; 8am-sunset; P) Fifteen miles south of Half Moon Bay, this beach and marshland preserve attract beachcombers and birders. Pull over and get out of the car to explore the marine-life-rich coastal tide pools on rocky outcroppings.

Sleeping & Eating

★HI Pigeon Point Lighthouse HOSTEL $
(☎650-879-0633; www.norcalhostels.org/pigeon; 210 Pigeon Point Rd; dm $38, r with shared bath $96-134, r with private bath $228; ⊙reception 7:30am-10:30pm; P ⊜ @ ☎) Not your workaday hostel, this highly coveted coastside lodging is all about its absolutely stunning location. Book ahead and check in early to snag a spot in the outdoor hot tub ($8 per person per 30 minutes) and contemplate roaring waves as the lighthouse beacon races through a starburst sky.

It's about 6 miles south of Pescadero.

Costanoa LODGE $$
(☎650-879-1100; www.costanoa.com; 2001 Rossi Rd; tent bungalows/cabin from $145/175, lodge r from $175; P ⊜ ☎) Although this coastal resort, about 10 miles south of Pescadero, includes a **campground** (☎650-879-7302; http://koa.com/campgrounds/santa-cruz-north; 2001 Rossi Rd; tent/RV sites with hookups from $42/82; P ☎ 🐾), nobody can pull a straight face and declare they're actually roughing it here. Down bedding swaddles guests in canvas-sided tent bungalows with shared bathrooms, and in hard-sided Douglas-fir cabins with private ones.

Pescadero Creek Inn INN $$
(☎650-879-1898; www.pescaderocreekinn.com; 393 Stage Rd; d $175-255; P ⊜ ☎) Unwind in the private two-room cottage or one of the spotless Victorian rooms in a restored 100-year-old farmhouse with a tranquil creekside garden.

Duarte's Tavern AMERICAN $$
(☎650-879-0464; www.duartestavern.com; 202 Stage Rd; mains $9-42; ⊙7am-8pm Wed-Mon) You'll rub shoulders with fancy-pants foodies, spandex-swathed cyclists and dusty cowboys at this casual, surprisingly unpretentious fourth-generation family restaurant. Duarte's is this town's culinary magnet, though some critics say it's resting on its laurels. Feast on crab cioppino and a half-and-half split of cream of artichoke and green-chili soups, then bring it home with a wedge of olallieberry pie.

Getting There & Away

By car, the town is 3 miles east of Hwy 1 on Pescadero Creek Rd, leading inland from Pescadero State Beach. On weekdays, **SamTrans** (☎511, 800-660-4287; www.samtrans.com) bus 17 runs twice a day to and from Half Moon Bay ($2.25, 25 minutes).

Año Nuevo State Park

Just over a dozen miles southeast of Pescadero State Beach, **Año Nuevo State Park** (☎park office 650-879-2025, recorded info 650-879-0227, tour reservations 800-444-4445; www.parks.ca.gov/anonuevo; 1 New Years Creek Rd; per car $10, 2½hr tour per person $7 (plus a $4 reservation fee); ⊙8:30am-sunset Apr-Nov, guided tours only 8.30am-3.30pm Dec 15-Mar 31; P) is home to the world's largest mainland breeding colonies of northern elephant seals. More raucous than a full-moon beach rave, up to 10,000 boisterous animals party year-round on the dunes of Año Nuevo Point, their squeals and barks reaching fever pitch during the winter pupping season.

Northern elephant seals were just as fearless two centuries ago as they are today. Unfortunately, seal trappers were not as friendly as today's tourists; during the 19th century, northern elephant seals were driven to the edge of extinction. Only a handful survived around the Guadalupe Islands off the Mexican state of Baja California. With the availability of substitutes for seal oil and the conservationist attitudes of more recent times, northern elephant seals have come back, reappearing on the southern California coast during the 1920s. They returned to Año Nuevo Beach in 1955.

In peak season, during the mating and birthing time from mid-December to the end of March, visitors are only permitted access to the reserve on guided tours. For the busiest period, from mid-January to mid-February, it's recommended you book two months ahead. Although the park office can answer general questions, tours must be arranged through ReserveCalifornia (www.reservecalifornia.com).

The rest of the year, advance reservations aren't necessary, but visitor permits from the entrance station are required; arrive before 3:30pm April to November. From the ranger station it's a 3- to 4-mile round-trip hike on sand; allow two to three hours. Dogs are not allowed on-site and no visitors are permitted during the first two weeks of December.

The park is less than 7 miles southeast of Pigeon Point or more than 20 miles northwest of Santa Cruz.

AT A GLANCE

POPULATION
630,800

WINERIES IN NAPA
475

BEST MUD BATH
Indian Springs Spa (p191)

BEST GOURMET MARKET
Oxbow Public Market (p180)

BEST WINERY
Tres Sabores (p185)

WHEN TO GO

Jan–Feb Bright yellow flowers carpet the valleys; enjoy bargain stays and spa getaways.

Apr–May Bask in sunshine on vineyard tours before it gets busy.

Sep–Oct 'Crush' time is crunch time at wineries and fun times at harvest fairs.

Napa Valley vineyard
INGENIEURIN / SHUTTERSTOCK ©

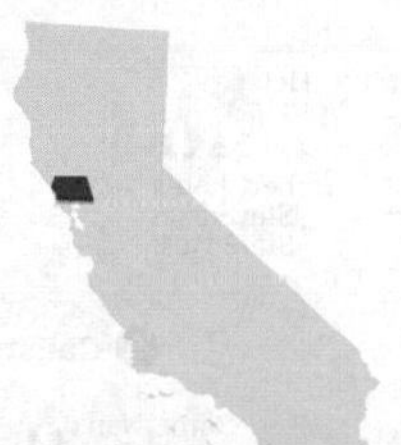

Napa & Sonoma Wine Country

In a single day in Napa, you can wallow in volcanic mud, throw axes like a lumberjack, and spend a wild night among giraffes on a Wine Country safari. Or head to Sonoma to wander thousand-year-old redwoods, pop open a bottle of bubbly, eat the meal of your life off a driftwood log, and meet the budding talent behind farm-to-spliff dispensaries.

The two valleys are California's most climate-resilient tourist destination, with nonprofit-managed parklands, pioneering regenerative agriculture, and close-knit networks of first responders, star chefs and hospitality workers. So raise a toast to Napa and Sonoma: living proof that with exceptional dedication and a splash of liquid courage, California dreams really do come true.

INCLUDES

Getting There & Away

From San Francisco or Oakland, public transportation and/or rideshares can get you to Napa Valley or Sonoma County. For public-transit information, dial 511, or check www.transit.511.org.

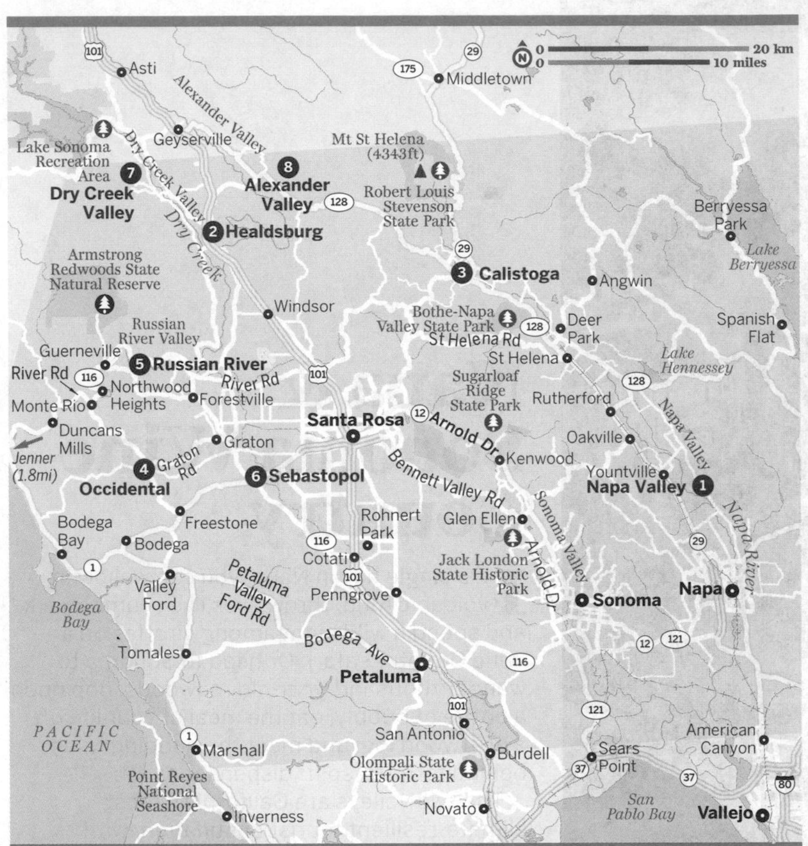

Napa & Sonoma Wine Country Highlights

1 Napa Valley (p174) Wining and dining like a rock star, with California's most prized reds, world-acclaimed chefs' tasting menus and restorative brunches at five-star resorts.

2 Healdsburg (p224) Wine tasting and boutique-browsing your way around the plaza before dinner of a lifetime at California's best new restaurant.

3 Calistoga (p190) Slipping into a volcanic-ash mud bath at a historic hot-springs resort, then curling up in your Victorian cottage B&B.

4 Occidental (p216) Wandering and ziplining through mighty redwoods and hanging with resident artists and ecologists at the heart of the Bohemian Hwy.

5 Russian River (p218) Floating in a canoe, kayak or inner tube down NorCal's laziest river, docking in Guerneville to toast progress.

6 Sebastopol (p209) Getting to know local winemakers, bakers, distillers, musicians, gardeners and budtenders in California's most prolifically creative farm town.

7 Dry Creek Valley (p224) Picnicking and pedaling between wineries along sunny, vineyard-lined West Dry Creek Rd.

8 Alexander Valley (p229) Raising a toast to resilience with spectacular reds in barns that are scorched by firestorms but still standing.

If you want to go vineyard-hopping, a car or bicycle will be useful. Both Napa and Sonoma Valleys are a 90-minute drive from San Francisco and Oakland, and both valleys offer scenic, relatively flat bike riding.

The names here are confusing: Napa and Sonoma counties each have an eponymous city and valley. Downtown Sonoma is at the southern end of Sonoma Valley, in Sonoma County. Likewise, downtown Napa is in southern Napa Valley, in Napa County.

AIR

Visitors fly into San Francisco International Airport (p779), Oakland International Airport (p779), **Sonoma County Airport** (Charles M Schulz; Map p220; ☎707-565-7240; www.sonomacountyairport.org; 2200 Airport Blvd, Santa Rosa) or Sacramento International Airport (p779). The drive from any of these airports to Napa Valley takes about 1½ to two hours.

Some visitors fly directly into Sonoma County Airport in Santa Rosa, at the north end of Sonoma Valley; otherwise, Sonoma County is easiest to reach from OAK (one to two hours) or SFO (two to 2½ hours).

BOAT

To reach Napa from SF via public transit, take the **San Francisco Bay Ferry** (☎877-643-3779; www.sanfranciscobayferry.com) from the Ferry Building to the Vallejo Ferry Terminal (adult/child $15.30/7.50, 60 minutes); connect with Napa Valley Vine bus 29 (weekdays) or bus 11 (daily). With some coordination, you can catch the Bay Ferry to Marin's Larkspur Landing, and take the SMART train shuttle to reach Santa Rosa.

BUS

Evans Transportation (☎707-255-1559; www.evanstransportation.com; ⏲sales & customer service 7:30am-9pm) Shuttles ($40) to Napa from San Francisco and Oakland airports.

Golden Gate Transit (☎415-455-2000, 511; www.goldengatetransit.org) Bus from San Francisco to Petaluma (adult/child $13/6.50) and Santa Rosa (adult/child $13/6.50); board at 1st and Mission Sts. Connects with **Sonoma County Transit** (☎707-576-7433; www.sctransit.com) buses.

Greyhound (☎800-231-2222; www.greyhound.com; 📶) Buses run from San Francisco to Santa Rosa ($16 to $38).

Napa Valley Vine (☎707-251-2800; www.ridethevine.com; Napa) Operates local bus 10 daily from downtown Napa to Calistoga ($1.60); express bus 29 Monday to Friday from the Vallejo Ferry Terminal ($3.25) and El Cerrito del Norte BART station via Napa to Calistoga ($5.50); and local bus 11 daily from the Vallejo Ferry Terminal to downtown Napa ($1.60).

Sonoma County Airport Express (☎707-837-8700; www.airportexpressinc.com; 📶) Shuttles ($38) between Sonoma County Airport (Santa Rosa) and San Francisco and Oakland airports.

CAR & MOTORCYCLE

Sonoma County has more than 425 wineries, including around 40 in Sonoma Valley. To reach Sonoma from San Francisco, take Hwy 101 north over the Golden Gate Bridge. For Sonoma Valley, turn off 101 to take Hwy 37 east to Hwy 121 north; expect 60 to 90 minutes, depending on traffic. Otherwise, stay on 101 to reach Santa Rosa (one to two hours) and Healdsburg (1½ to 2½ hours).

Napa is further inland, with about 475 wineries and more visitors – factor in heavy traffic on summer weekends. To get to Napa Valley from SF, take Hwy 101 to 12/121 east, then head northbound on Hwy 29. Plan for 70 minutes in light traffic, two hours during the weekday 3pm-to-7pm commute.

From the East Bay (or downtown SF), take I-80 east to Hwy 37 west (north of Vallejo). To reach Napa, head northbound on Hwy 29. For Sonoma Valley, continue on Hwy 37 west to Hwy 121 north.

Tolls are automated on the Golden Gate Bridge and Bay Bridge, so you'll need to sign up for a toll pass with your rental-car company.

TRAIN

Amtrak (☎800-872-7245; www.amtrak.com) trains travel to Martinez (south of Vallejo), with connecting buses to Napa (45 minutes), Santa Rosa (1¼ hours) and Healdsburg (1¾ hours). From San Francisco, take **BART** (☎415-989-2278; www.bart.gov) Richmond-line train to reach the Amtrak station.

BART also runs from San Francisco to El Cerrito del Norte ($4.30, 30 minutes). Napa Valley Vine bus 29 runs weekdays from that same BART stop to Calistoga, via Napa ($5.50); on Saturdays take **SolTrans** (☎707-648-4666; www.soltransride.com) from BART to Vallejo ($5, 30 minutes), then connect with Napa Valley Vine bus 11 to Napa and Calistoga ($1.60). On Sundays, there's no connecting bus service from BART.

From the Bay Ferry Larkspur Landing dock in Marin, you can catch a shuttle to the commuter **SMART** (Sonoma-Marin Area Rail Transit; www.sonomamarintrain.org; $3.50-11.50, depending on zones) train to downtown Santa Rosa.

ℹ Getting Around

You may want a car or bicycle to vineyard-hop, or you can leave the navigation to the pros and join a guided tour – perhaps in a hot-air balloon or auto-rickshaw. If you'd rather stroll, the towns with the best selection of tasting rooms are Healdsburg, downtown Napa and downtown Sonoma.

You can get around Sonoma and Napa with buses and shuttles, but it's slow going.

Rideshares and taxis are also options, but spotty cell-phone coverage means you might not always be able to get a ride when you need one.

BICYCLE

Wine Country is a dream for cyclists. For many, the highlight of a California trip is the sun-dappled, winery-lined stretch of West Dry Creek Rd, northwest of Healdsburg. But don't stop there – roads and trails linking valley wineries are scenic, mostly flat, and easy enough for beginners.

From downtown Santa Rosa transit centers, trails fan out to West Sonoma County back roads. The West County Regional Trail covers 5.5 miles of scenic farmland on old railway lines linking Sebastopol, Graton and Forestville; free maps are available at https://parks.sonomacounty.ca.gov/Visit/West-County-Regional-Trail.

Crossing between the Sonoma Valley and Napa is challenging via steep Oakville Grade and Trinity Rd (between Glen Ellen and Oakville). To avoid the mountains, take the long way around, via southern Carneros lowlands. Through Sonoma Valley, take scenic, winding Arnold Dr instead of Hwy 12.

In Napa Valley, the new Napa Valley Vine Trail connects downtown Napa and Yountville along old stagecoach and rail lines. Tree-lined trails are being extended from Vallejo Ferry Terminal to Calistoga; see current routes at https://www.vinetrail.org/pub/htdocs/route.html. To bike onward to Calistoga, take tree-lined Silverado Trail instead of hot, traffic-heavy Hwy 29.

Bicycles are allowed on the San Francisco Bay Ferry (p173) to Vallejo and Larkspur Landing and on the SMART (p173) train to Santa Rosa – first come, first served.

Bicycles in boxes can be checked on Greyhound (p173) buses for $30 to $40; bike boxes cost $10 (call ahead). You can also transport bicycles on Golden Gate Transit (p173) buses, which usually have free racks available (first come, first served).

BUS

Sonoma County Transit (p173) buses travel around Santa Rosa, Healdsburg, Sebastopol, Petaluma, Kenwood, Glen Ellen, Russian River towns, Sonoma Valley and Geyserville. Prices range from $1.50 to $4.80, depending on how many zones you pass through on your journey. Child prices range from $1.25 to $4.55.

Napa Valley Vine (p173) local bus 10 runs daily from downtown Napa to Calistoga (adult/child $1.60/1.10).

CAR & MOTORCYCLE

Don't drive buzzed. Alcohol and cannabis are legal in California for adults (aged 21-plus with ID), but driving under the influence isn't – and police watch like hawks for traffic violators.

Fair warning: the American Automobile Association ranks Napa Valley among America's most congested rural vacation destinations. Plan accordingly, especially on late summer afternoons.

There are a number of shortcuts between the Napa and Sonoma Valleys: from Oakville, take Oakville Grade to Trinity Rd; from St Helena, take Spring Mountain Rd into Calistoga Rd; from Calistoga, take Petrified Forest Rd to Calistoga Rd.

Rideshare

Ridesharing services Uber and Lyft operate in Napa Valley, but attempts to get a ride can go awry in some areas due to spotty cell-phone reception. Sonoma's cell service is even more variable.

NAPA VALLEY

Wining and dining is a glorious way of life in Napa today – but decades ago, this 5-by-35-mile strip of farmland seemed forgotten by time. Grapes have been grown here since the gold rush, when speculators built Victorian greenhouses and hot-springs resorts in Calistoga. But earthquakes and juice-sucking phylloxera bugs struck the valley, and grand plans were abandoned. Then came the one-two punch of Prohibition and the Great Depression. Napa had 140 wineries in the 1890s, but by the 1960s only around 25 were left.

Speculators returned to Napa, spotting potential for postwar suburban development. But local farmers rallied in 1968, declaring the 'Napa Valley Agricultural Preserve' to block future valley development for non-ag purposes. The law prohibited the subdivision of valley-floor land under 40 acres, which helped preserve the valley's natural beauty.

Then renegade local winemakers entered a few bottles into a 1976 blind tasting competition in Paris – and to the world's surprise, Napa wines took top honors. As Napa's reputation grew, global wine conglomerates moved into the valley. With land priced at up to $1 million an acre, independent, family-owned wineries had to work extra hard just to stand their ground against stiff competition.

But as they say in Napa: adversity makes wine taste even better. Traveling through this resilient valley, you'll notice that Napa has emerged from recent droughts and fires with even stronger commitments to sustainability and local character. Right off Hwy 29, organic family wineries are daring to make wines besides classic cabernets, and indie

TOURING NAPA & SONOMA WINE COUNTRY

Bicycle Tours & Rentals

Guided tours start at around $90 per day including bikes, tastings and lunch. Daily rentals cost $25 to $85; make reservations.

Getaway Adventures (☎800-499-2453; www.getawayadventures.com; tours 1-day $139-250, multiday $899-2500) Explore Dry Creek's natural side, from all-ages bike and wine tours to challenging Velo and Vino tours, with three tasting and picnic pit stops (guides collect your purchases). Take it easy on Sonoma brewery tours by e-bike, become a bi-athlete with Russian River kayak/bike rides, or explore Sonoma's coastline and/or redwood groves on customized hiking tours. Napa trips also available.

Napa Valley Bike Tours (Map p181; ☎707-944-2953; www.napavalleybiketours.com; 6500 Washington St, Yountville; bicycle rental per day $45-85, tours $124-189; ⊙8:30am-5pm) Hit the Napa Valley Vine Trail on a rental from this bike shop, which also offers tours ranging from easy to moderately difficult – when in doubt, reserve an e-bike. The second location's at the end of the Vine Trail in downtown Napa at 3259 California Blvd; rent in one location and drop off in the other for $10 extra.

Calistoga Bike Shop (Map p188; ☎707-942-9687; www.calistogabikeshop.com; 1318 Lincoln Ave, Calistoga; bicycle rental per day from $28, tours from $149; ⊙10am-6pm) Rents full-suspension mountain bikes, hybrids, road bikes and tandem models and provides reliable trail information. DIY touring packages ($110 per day) include two or three free tastings and wine pickup; electric-assist hybrid bikes are available. If you brought your own bike but it needs repairs, shop technicians can patch you up and get you back on the road.

Spoke Folk Cyclery (Map p220; ☎707-433-7171; www.spokefolk.com; 201 Center St, Healdsburg; bike rental per hour $20-25, per day $40-100) Since 1976, Healdsburg's Spoke Folk have been getting visitors to vineyards on rental bikes. Choose from cruisers, tandems, and top-end road bikes; rentals include helmet, lock and pack. Since cell-phone signal is spotty in Sonoma, go to Spoke Folk's website to download free Sonoma ride maps, ranging from the scenic 12-mile Dry Creek loop to the challenging 30-mile Old Redwood Highway excursion.

Other Tours

Active Wine Adventures (☎707-927-1058; www.activewineadventures.com; per person $125) This innovative tour company covering Napa and Sonoma works up your appetite for gourmet food, wine and craft beer with your choice of adventures – including forest strolls, local art walks, and hikes to mountaintop vistas. Prices range from $110 for downtown Napa walking tours to $79 per hour for customized tours for up to six people. Transportation is provided in SUVs.

Laces and Limos (Map p177; ☎707-501-8089; www.lacesandlimos.com; 2480a Oak St, Napa; tuk-tuk tour per person $119) Take the slow, scenic route around Napa Valley in a chauffered *tuk-tuk* (auto-rickshaw). The adventure begins in downtown Napa at 11:30am, when you're picked up to start tasting at your choice of partner wineries – ask what's available when you book, and note that tasting fees aren't included in the tour fee. Tours accommodate up to six people.

Platypus Wine Tours (☎707-253-2723; www.platypustours.com; join-in tour per person $110) Billed as the anti-wine-snob tour, Platypus specializes in back-road vineyards, historic wineries and family-owned operations. There's a daily 'join-in' tour that shuttles guests to four wineries and provides a picnic lunch, and private tours with a dedicated driver and vehicle. The Napa tours are the most popular, but Platypus also takes people to Sonoma, Russian River and Dry Creek Valleys.

Beau Wine Tours (Map p177; ☎707-938-8001; www.beauwinetours.com; 1754 2nd St, Suite B, Napa; per person from $125) For an affordable day trip from San Francisco, Beau's 'dynamic wine tours' pick up from the Vallejo ferry stop and shuttle you around Napa wineries – including a picnic lunch from Sonoma's tasty Girl & the Fig (p201). Winery tours in sedans and stretch limos charge a base rate of $65 to $205 per hour (four- to six-hour minimum), plus gas, tax and tip.

winemakers have opened up shop on Napa's revitalized 1st St. Bicyclists commuting between former valley stagecoach stops wave hello to sous-chefs, weeding organic kitchen gardens to seed farm-to-table menus. The signs are clear: you're right on time for Napa's renaissance.

Getting There & Away

Napa Valley is about a 90-minute drive from San Francisco and an hour's drive from Oakland.

Public transportation can get you to Napa, but coordinating ferry and bus schedules can get tricky on weekends. For public-transit information, dial 511, or check www.transit.511.org.

From outside the Vallejo Ferry Terminal, you can hop Napa Valley Vine (p173) express bus 11x (weekdays, 40 minutes, $3) or 11 (daily, 90 minutes, $1.60), which takes you to the downtown Napa bus terminal. From there, take bus 10 to St Helena or Calistoga (daily, 40 minutes, $1.60).

Weekdays from the East Bay, Vine bus 29 picks up at El Cerrito del Norte BART station and drops off at the downtown Napa bus terminal and Calistoga (50 minutes, $5.50).

Getting Around

BICYCLE

Napa Valley Vine Trail (707-252-3547; www.vinetrail.org) aims to connect the entire valley via tree-lined bike trails – complete maps are available at https://www.vinetrail.org/pub/htdocs/route.html.

BUS

Vine (p173) bus 10 takes you from downtown Napa to St Helena and Calistoga.

CAR

Summer and fall weekend traffic crawls, especially on Hwy 29 between downtown Napa and St Helena around 5pm, when wineries close.

Downtown Napa & Around

Your first stop in Napa may be the only one you need for a dream Wine Country getaway. With laid-back downtown tasting rooms, historic music halls, and Oxbow Public Market (p180) offering affordable gourmet fare, downtown Napa is where locals come to relax.

Join the 'golden hour' stroll past brave Western storefront facades and lovingly restored Victorians, and take a breather along grassy riverbanks. Look around: you'd never know this was the site of a major earthquake in 2014, Napa River floods, and the 2017, 2019 and 2020 wildfires. Today, Napa's revitalized 1st St is lined with indie wine-tasting rooms and casual bistros with California-grown, globe-trotting menus.

Nature is making a comeback too, as you can see on Napa's lush hillsides and riverbank parks – part of the town's sustainable 'living river' design to manage seasonal floods. The new Napa Valley Vine Trail connecting downtown Napa to Yountville provides a welcome respite from Hwy 29 traffic. Downtown Napa has been raising its profile with film and music festivals – but between events, Napa remains the sweet spot where wine flows and conversation meanders.

Sights

★Hess Collection GALLERY, WINERY

(707-255-1144; www.hesscollection.com; 4411 Redwood Rd; gallery free, tastings from $25; 10am-5pm, last tasting 5pm) Welcome to California's finest private contemporary-art collection. Head upstairs to galleries brimming with thought-provoking installation art, starting with Leopoldo Maler's 1974 burning typewriter – an homage to his uncle, a newspaper editor killed by Argentina's junta. Highlights include Anselm Kiefer's lead-lined bunker made of shingles from collapsed Cologne Cathedral, and Andy Goldsworthy's curtain of thorns loosely held together by gravity.

★CIA at Copia MUSEUM

(Culinary Institute of America; Map p177; 707-967-2500; www.ciaatcopia.com; 500 1st St; 10:30am-9pm) FREE You don't have to be a chef to find inspiration at the Culinary Institute of America's public food and wine showplace. Turn left at the Winemaker Wall of Fame (salute Merry Edwards, the sole woman!) for gourmet-themed art, including vintage portraits of Julia Child taken before she was famous. Upstairs is fabulous, free **Chuck Williams Culinary Arts Museum**, with its dazzling wall of copper baking molds (10:30am to 5pm daily). Check online for cooking classes, demos, documentaries and too-spicy-for-TV star-chef panels.

★Brown Downtown TASTING ROOM

(Map p177; 707-963-2435; www.brownestate.com; 1005 Coombs St; flights from $40; 11am-7pm) Find liquid courage with Duppy Conqueror, Jamaican folklore hero of Bob Marley songs and namesake of the epic white wine from Brown Estate, Napa's first (and only)

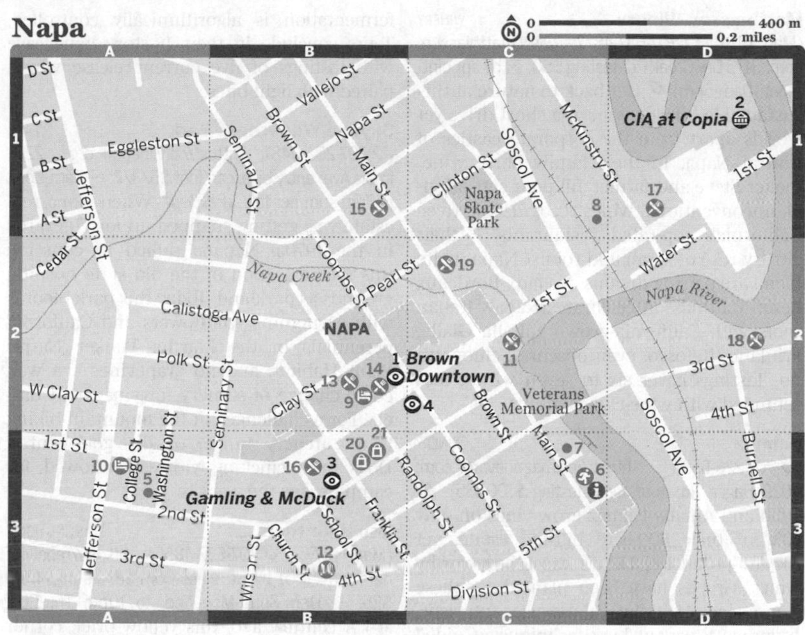

Napa

Top Sights
1 Brown Downtown B2
2 CIA at Copia D1
3 Gamling & McDuck B3

Sights
4 Rebel Vinters C2

Activities, Courses & Tours
5 Beau Wine Tours A3
6 Laces and Limos C3
7 Napa Valley Gondola C3
8 Napa Valley Wine Train C1

Sleeping
9 Archer B2
10 Blackbird Inn A3

Eating
11 Bounty Hunter Wine Bar & Smokin' BBQ C2
12 Clemente's at Val's Liquors B3
13 Compline B2
14 Eiko's B2
15 La Gran Eléctrica B1
16 Oenotri B3
17 Oxbow Public Market D1
18 Taquería María D2
19 Torc C2

Shopping
20 Antiques on Second B3
21 Betty's Girl B3

black-owned winery. Taste Napa turf on the Zinapalooza flight, where subtle differences of soil, sun and altitude yield four distinctive California zinfandels. Cheese boards ($20 to $40) offer further excuses to lounge on velvet couches with classic R&B.

★Gamling & McDuck TASTING ROOM
(Map p177; ☎707-819-2835; www.gamlingandmcduck.com; 1420 2nd St; tastings from $25; ⊙by reservation 10am & 11:30am, 1-7pm Thu-Mon) Get to know your friendly neighborhood winemaker/cartoonist Adam McClary and his cat Theodosia in Napa's most punk-rock tasting room. No neckties or snooty cabs here – 'Do Not Sneak This Wine into Movie Theaters' cab franc comes in a handy split, which you should definitely not stash in pockets to pair with Snickers. Elegant, silky chenin blancs knock the sweaty socks off Napa chards, and Adam's adorable cat label on cab franc rosé cleverly disguises a minerally, hardcore pink. Reserve ahead.

Matthiasson Winery WINERY
(Map p181; ☎707-637-4877; www.matthiasson.com; 3175 Dry Creek Rd; tasting $50; ⏲by appointment 10am-5pm) Get back to nature at this sustainable hillside winery, a short drive yet worlds apart from the corporate castles of central Napa. In their family barn, winemaker Steve and farmer Jill pour sensational, unconventional wines recognizable from California's top-rated restaurants – their citrusy rosé of syrah and robust Napa white blend are pairing dreams. No faux-Bordeaux here: Matthiasson celebrates Napa's Italian roots with California-grown Ribolla Gialla, Friulano, Refosco, even obscure Schioppettino. Tastings cover six to seven wines; fees refunded with wine-club sign-ups.

Palmaz WINERY
(☎707-226-5587; https://palmazvineyards.com; 4029 Hagen Rd; tours with tasting $100-135) Julio and Amalia Palmaz grow vines on only 10% of their 600-acre hillside estate, yet they're producing Napa's most buzzworthy wines. Grapes have been planted on these slopes since 1881, but Palmaz uses futuristic, proprietary winemaking techniques. Guided two-hour tours in English and/or Spanish ($135) cover their high-tech gravity flow facility, including the underground dome where fermentation is algorithmically controlled. Tours conclude in their 18-story wine cave with tastings of five current-release wines, paired with light bites.

Skyline Wilderness Park PARK
(☎707-252-0481; https://skylinepark.org; 2201 Imola Ave; entry bike/car/foot $5/3/2; ⏲7am-5pm, to 7pm summer-fall;) When Napa real estate was getting snapped up for vineyards in the 1970s, Napans rallied to conserve this scenic section of the old state hospital grounds as parkland. Today this park blooms with springtime wildflowers and California perennials in the Martha Walker Native Plant Habitat, and no grapevines – a welcome change of scenery for vineyard workers. For a challenge, hit the mountain-biking trails, archery range, or disc-golf course. Dogs and picnicking with wine allowed; for camping, see the website.

Rebel Vintners TASTING ROOM
(Map p177; ☎707-637-4855; https://rebelvintners.com; 1201 1st St; glass from $8, tastings from $25; ⏲11am-8pm Mon-Wed, to 10pm Thu-Sun;) A century ago, this yellow-brick corner housed the Sons of the Golden West clubhouse – but Rebel Vintners have thrown open the doors to everyone, with board games on tables, graffiti art on the walls, and California indie wines lining the bar. Enjoy generous pours of non-cabernets by glass or flight from three family-owned wineries: Uncharted, Leaf & Vine, and Cadle Family. Wine menus change daily; look for Uncharted picpoul, Leaf & Vine cool-climate merlot, and Cadle sangiovese.

BEST NAPA WINERIES TO SUIT YOUR STYLE

Classic and historic Schramsberg (p190), Grgich Hills Estate (p185)

Chill California vibes Brown Downtown (p176), Vincent Arroyo (p190), Gamling & McDuck (p177)

Natural and sustainable Tres Sabores (p185), Matthiasson Winery, Frog's Leap (p184)

World-class art and architecture Hess Collection (p176), Quixote (p182), Hall (p186)

Proposal-worthy views Artesa, (p194), Pride Mountain (p186)

Drinking your way to genius Joseph Phelps (p186), Palmaz

Inspired food and wine pairings Robert Sinskey Vineyards (p182), **Long Meadow Ranch** (Map p188; ☎707-963-4555; www.longmeadowranch.com; 738 Main St; tasting $30, with food pairing $45-60; ⏲11am-6pm;)

Tours

Napa Valley Wine Train RAIL
(Map p177; ☎707-253-2111; www.winetrain.com; 1275 McKinstry St; ticket incl dining from $160) Chug through Napa Valley in plush vintage Pullman dining cars, covering tracks laid in 1864 from downtown Napa to St Helena. The *Gourmet Express* (2½ hours, seat/Vista Dome from $160/245, lunch included) is more easygoing fun than the *Quattro Vino* (four-course meal plus three mega-winery tours, six hours, from $385) – but there's no better location for a costumed *Murder Mystery* (from $290).

Napa Valley Gondola BOATING
(Map p177; ☎707-373-2100; https://napavalleygondola.com; 700 Main St; boat trips 40/60min $90/125) Glide downstream on your private gondola, watching the sun set over

the city. Your gondolier can serenade you in Italian, but the scenery and wine on offer are totally California, dude. On this single-oared boat, you and up to five friends can hang out with ducks, spot heron and otters, and see how ecologists are restoring Napa River.

Festivals & Events

★BottleRock Music Festival MUSIC
(www.bottlerocknapavalley.com; 575 3rd St, Napa Valley Expo; ⌚end May) This three-day music, food and wine festival attracts marquee names with intergenerational appeal, including Janelle Monáe, Red Hot Chili Peppers, Miley Cyrus and Blondie. General admission starts around $164 for a one-day pass, with prices shooting up to $599 for VIP options such as viewing decks with bar service; three-day passes start around $300.

★Napa Valley Film Festival FILM
(www.napavalleyfilmfest.org; passes from $125; ⌚Nov) Movies about food and wine are obvious crowd-pleasers, but there's also plenty of food for thought at Napa's five-day mid-November celebration of documentary and narrative storytelling. Flex passes ($125) include five films plus afternoon wine tastings, while unlimited festival passes (from $225) include films, wine and culinary demonstrations. Recent star sightings include Damian Lewis, Geena Davis and Laurence Fishburne.

Sleeping

Hennessey House B&B $$
(Map p181; ☎707-226-3774; https://hennesseyhouse.com; 1727 Main St; d $159-389;) Star in your own romantic costume drama at this lovely lavender Victorian mansion, recently renovated to accommodate guests with modern comforts (some have jetted tubs) and impressive antiques. Main-house rooms have more period charm; carriage-house rooms have more space. Innkeepers Lorri and Ken Walsh treat guests to lavish breakfasts and wine-and-cheese hour in the sunny courtyard.

Blackbird Inn B&B $$
(Map p177; ☎707-226-2450; www.blackbirdinnnapa.com; 1755 1st St; d $229-350;) Spend the weekend with a ruggedly handsome California Craftsman – an authentic 1902 cottage with eight plush rooms lined with original woodwork, tapestries and mood lighting, some with fireplaces. Gather around the living-room fireplace for afternoon wine, cheese and just-baked cookies, and enjoy communal brunches in a sunny breakfast nook. Four rooms in next-door Finch House offer Victorian drama.

★White House BOUTIQUE HOTEL $$$
(Map p181; ☎707-254-9301; www.whitehouseinnnapa.com; 443 Brown St; d from $329;) International affairs improve in just one weekend at Napa's glam 17-bedroom mansion. Guest-room decor is chic and cheeky, with money-green velvet chairs, polka-dot carpets, original art, cozy fireplaces and vast beds. New alliances form over wine in the chandeliered salon, and proposals are accepted in the rose garden. Perks include pool lounging and fresh breakfasts, plus on-site spa treatments and yoga.

Archer HOTEL $$$
(Map p177; ☎707-690-9800; www.archerhotel.com; 1230 1st St; d from $330;) Live like a vintner who's just won double gold at the Archer, downtown Napa's most happening hotel. The vibe is barrel-room chic, all sleek wood paneling and chiseled stone – and guest-room balconies overlook city lights and vineyards beyond. Head to the rooftop to lounge poolside or fireside with a glass of Napa's finest. Spa upstairs, Charlie Palmer steakhouse downstairs: win-win.

Milliken Creek Inn INN $$$
(Map p181; ☎707-255-1197; www.millikencreekinn.com; 1815 Silverado Trail; d $299-580;) Understatedly elegant Milliken Creek combines small-inn charm, boutique-hotel service and Napa indulgence. With four-poster beds draped in high-thread-count linens and breakfasts delivered to your private balcony, you might want to rethink early wine-tasting appointments. Book a breezy river-view rooms and if you don't want to leave your spot by the fireplace, in-room spa treatments are available.

Cottages of Napa Valley BUNGALOW $$$
(Map p181; ☎707-252-7810; www.napacottages.com; 1012 Darms Lane; cottages $400-600;) Next to a vineyard and under towering pines hide eight snug cottages made for romantic hideaways, with extra-long soaking tubs, indoor gas fireplaces, and outdoor campfire pits. Low-key for a luxury stay, but with sweet perks, from heated floors to Bouchon bakery breakfasts – plus in-room massages are available. Cottages 4 and 8 have private porches and swinging chairs.

Eating

★Oxbow Public Market MARKET $

(Map p177; ☎707-226-6529; www.oxbowpublicmarket.com; 610 & 644 1st St; items from $3; ⊙7:30am-9:30pm;) Why commit to just one dining establishment when you could graze a dozen of Napa's finest? Assemble the meal of your California dreams with all-star dishes – perhaps Hog Island Oyster Co oysters mignonette, C Casa duck-confit tacos and Eiko's *hamachi* sushi bonbons with Fieldwork Brewing Company farmhouse ale, followed by Ritual Coffee espresso.

Clemente's at Val's Liquors ITALIAN $

(Map p177; ☎707-224-2237; 1531 3rd St; dishes $5.75-11.99; ⊙10am-8pm Tue-Sat, to 7pm Sun;) Joanne Cittoni Gonzalez and her papa Clemente hand-roll *malfatti* ('badly made') for a family recipe dating from 1925, when a Napa restaurant out of pasta rolled ravioli filling in flour, then served it in meaty sauce. You'll spot Clemente in his paper hat at Val's back counter, dishing Napa's original comfort-food takeout – grab a local red and *buon appetito*.

Taqueria Maria MEXICAN $

(Map p177; ☎707-257-6925; 640 3rd St; mains $8-20; ⊙9am-9pm;) Satisfy taco cravings on Taqueria Maria's sunny wraparound deck, and graduate to a whole new obsession with *camarones al mojo de ajo* (garlicky shrimp). David Reynoso was Taqueria Maria's chef before he bought the place, and expanded it – all while keeping a sharp eye on quality.

Eiko's JAPANESE $

(Map p177; ☎707-501-4444; http://eikosnapa.com; 1300 1st St; rolls $7-16; ⊙11:30am-9pm Mon-Thu, to 11pm Fri & Sat;) Napa's been sushi-obsessed since 1986, when Eiko Nakamura opened her first restaurant here. Now apprentices honor her legacy with signature *makimono* (rolls): *unagi*-topped Super California, jalapeño-laced Hot Mama, and kelp-wrapped Eiko. For quick bites, hit Eiko's Oxbow kiosk or pick up bargain *bentō* boxes – sesame chicken, rice, miso soup, California roll and *gyoza* (dumplings) runs $14.

★Oenotri ITALIAN $$

(Map p177; ☎707-252-1022; www.oenotri.com; 1425 1st St; brunch $13-18, dinner mains $19-34; ⊙5:30-9pm Sun-Thu, to 10pm Fri & Sat, brunch 10am-3pm Sat & Sun;) Celebrate Napa's Italian farming roots with rustic feasts sourced from chef Tyler Rodde's organic garden. Handmade pasta dishes are generous enough to share – theoretically speaking – and pizzas made with Napa Valley olive oil are wood-fired, for blistered crusts that would make Napa papas proud. Come back for brunch: eggs Benedict on focaccia and skillet pancakes with caramelized peaches. Bravo.

La Gran Eléctrica MEXICAN, CALIFORNIAN $$

(Map p177; ☎707-258-1313; www.granelectrica.com; 1313 Main St; dishes $7-24; ⊙4-8pm Tue-Sun;) This Brooklyn-born restaurant became a Napa crossover hit with the ingenuity of local chef Ignacio Beltran, who reinvents Mexican staples daily with NorCal ingredients. Sunny days demand beet margaritas and duck-mole tacos on the patio, under the DJ Agana mural; cold weather calls for fireside mezcal and *menudo* (stew) indoors.

Bounty Hunter Wine Bar & Smokin' BBQ BARBECUE $$

(Map p177; ☎707-226-3976; www.bountyhunterwinebar.com; 975 1st St; mains $14-38; ⊙11am-10pm Sun-Thu, to midnight Fri & Sat;) When your stagecoach passengers need victuals, hit this 1888 gastro-saloon. Tear into beer-can chicken – whole chicken roasted over a can of Tecate – or get cowboy combos of house-smoked pulled pork with Napa-grown Rancho Gordo baked beans and Yankee cornbread. Libations include 40 local beers, 40 whiskeys and 400 wines (40 by the glass).

Torc CALIFORNIAN $$$

(Map p177; ☎707-252-3292; www.torcnapa.com; 1140 Main St; mains $26-45; ⊙5-9:30pm Wed-Mon;) Chef Sean O'Toole's seasonal dishes capture California moments in time with a photographer's rapt attention. Silky Pacific halibut crudo zooms into sharp focus with hibiscus *kosho* (fermented yuzu-chili paste), while cannelloni envelop an entire Napa spring landscape of wild herbs. Original stone walls, flattering lighting and simple pinewood tables keep the focus on food, company and, oh yes, wine.

Compline CALIFORNIAN $$$

(Map p177; ☎707-492-8150; https://complinewine.com; 1300 1st St No 312; mains $25-34; ⊙10am-midnight Wed-Mon) Hidden in the heart of Napa, this cozy, unpretentious bistro/wine bar offers a short, seasonal menu of hearty dishes designed to complement wine: burger with duck-fat fries, jerk chicken with red beans and rice, steak smothered in trumpet mushrooms. Compline's corkage policy is generous ($15, four-bottle maximum), but

Napa Valley South

Top Sights
1 French Laundry Gardens B6
2 Frog's Leap B1
3 Quixote B3
4 Robert Sinskey Vineyards B3
5 Tres Sabores A1

Sights
6 Grgich Hills Estate A1
7 Matthiasson Winery A5

Activities, Courses & Tours
8 Aloft B7
9 Balloons Above the Valley A7
10 Napa Valley Balloons A5
11 Napa Valley Bike Tours B7

Sleeping
12 Auberge du Soleil B1
13 Bardessono B7
14 Cottages of Napa Valley A4
15 Hennessey House A6
16 Lavender Inn B6
17 Milliken Creek Inn B6
18 Napa Valley Railway Inn B7
19 Petit Logis B7
20 Poetry Inn B3
21 Rancho Caymus A1
22 White House A7

Eating
23 Ad Hoc + Addendum B3
24 Bouchon Bakery B7
25 Ciccio B6
26 French Laundry B6
27 La Luna Taqueria & Market A1
28 Oakville Grocery A2
29 Southside Cafe B6
30 Tacos Garcia B6

Shopping
31 Kelly's Filling Station B6
32 Kollar Chocolates B7

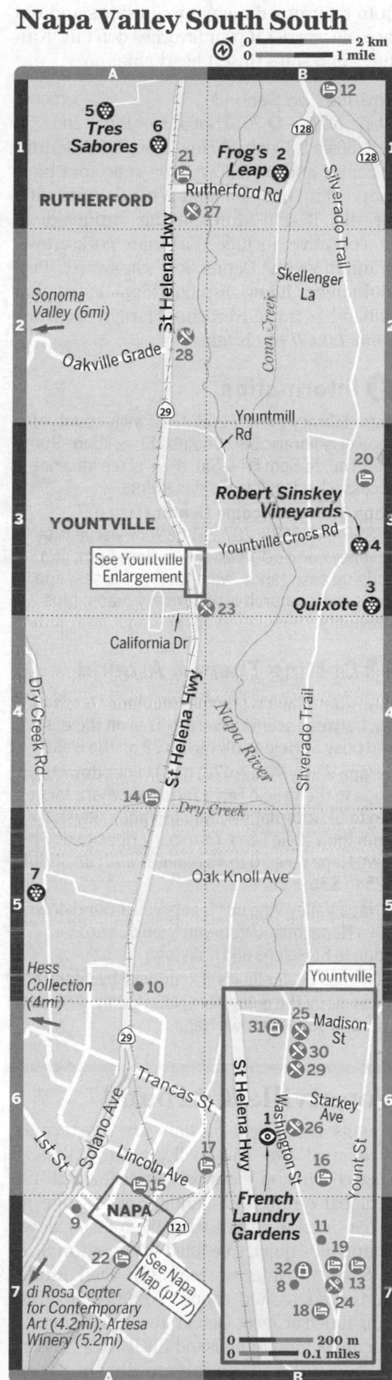

the extensive selection of top-notch wines under $40 is Napa's best-value list.

Shopping

★ **Betty's Girl** VINTAGE, FASHION & ACCESSORIES

(Map p177; ☎707-254-7560; www.bettysgirlnapa.com; 1320 2nd St; ⏲10am-5:30pm Mon & Thu-Sat, 11am-5pm Sun) When your Instagram following demands more than 'Wine Not?' tees, Kim Northrup will get you BottleRocking Napa's signature boho style: vintage cowboy boots, 1970s denim, hand-tooled leather belts, and flowy white dresses Kim custom-makes from repurposed men's tuxedo shirts and old lace. No worries if your favorites don't fit: Kim alters and ships (insert heart emoji).

Antiques on Second ANTIQUES
(Map p177; 707-252-6353; 1370 2nd St; 10:30am-5:30pm) How thoughtful: Jennifer Smith and 25 fellow Napa collectors have rounded up one-of-a-kind Wine Country gifts for you. Recent scores at this antique-dealer collective include Victorian corkscrews, uranium-green Depression glassware, Prohibition-era home distilling kits – sorry, that Italian bar tray advertising Marilyn Monroe's *Some Like It Hot* is taken.

Information

Napa Library (707-253-4241; www.countyofnapa.org/library; 580 Coombs St; 10am-9pm Mon-Thu, to 6pm Fri & Sat;) Free internet access; check online for kids events.

Napa Valley Welcome Center (Map p177; 855-847-6272, 707-251-5895; www.visitnapavalley.com; 600 Main St; 9am-5pm;) Lodging assistance, wine-tasting passes, spa deals and comprehensive winery maps, plus souvenirs.

Getting There & Around

Downtown Napa is centrally located in Napa Valley, between scenic Silverado Trail on the east and busy St Helena Hwy/Hwy 29 on the west.

Napa Valley Vine (p173) bus 11 links downtown Napa to the Vallejo Ferry Terminal, where ferries run to SF. Alternatively, you can get a rideshare from the Vallejo Ferry Terminal – rides to downtown Napa take 30 to 45 minutes and run about $25 to $35.

Napa Valley Vine bus C gets you around downtown Napa; bus 10 gets you from downtown Napa to St Helena and Calistoga.

Get hungry for lunch in Yountville by biking 6 miles along the completed Napa Valley Vine Trail (p176) from downtown Napa.

Yountville & Around

Planets and Michelin stars are mysteriously aligned over Yountville, a tiny Western stagecoach stop that's been transformed into a global dining destination. Sounds like an urban legend – until you take a stroll down Yountville's quiet, tree-lined Washington St.

Say hey to interns weeding French Laundry herb gardens and trainee sommeliers grabbing lunch at Tacos Garcia. You've just met the talents behind a thousand meals of a lifetime each week – and you can probably buy them a beer later. Once you've been to Yountville, you'll know firsthand how legends are made.

Sights

★**Robert Sinskey Vineyards** WINERY
(Map p181; 707-944-9090; www.robertsinskey.com; 6320 Silverado Trail; bar tasting $40, seated food & wine pairings $70-175; 10am-4:30pm; P) Angel choirs seem to echo through this redwood-cathedral tasting room, where organic, biodynamic wines and gourmet bites hit high notes together. Even skeptics of lighter reds will sing the praises of Sinskey's silky pinot noir and merlot, specifically crafted to harmonize with food – and you may find heaven in the vin gris or pinot noir. Reserve ahead. Bottles run $22 to $100.

★**Quixote** WINERY
(Map p181; 707-944-2659; https://quixotewinery.com; 6126 Silverado Trail; tasting $45, with tour $65, tour & barrel tasting with food pairings $125; 10am-5pm) When you spot a gold-leafed onion dome sprouting from a grassy knoll, you've found Napa's most quixotic attraction. No, you're not drunk (yet) and yes, there is a winery beneath the olive trees on that living roof. This is the only US building by visionary Austrian eco-architect Friedensreich Hundertwasser, whose signature crayon-colored ceramic pillars frame broken-tile mosaic walls. Enter a wonderland of original, organically farmed, acclaimed Stag's Leap estate cabs and petit syrah ($50 to $140).

★**French Laundry Gardens** GARDENS
(Map p181; www.thomaskeller.com/tfl; 6639 Washington St; morning-sunset) FREE The secret to French Laundry feasts is hiding in plain sight right across the street: a lush organic culinary garden. Walk among these neatly boxed plots, and see if you can guess the obscure heirloom varietals destined for dinner – if you can't tell your Mokum carrots from your Hakurei turnips, check the framed cheat-sheet at the front. Tables and seats are thoughtfully provided near the flowerbeds for lazy summer afternoons.

Sleeping

Napa Valley Railway Inn INN $$
(Map p181; 707-944-2000; www.napavalleyrailwayinn.com; 6523 Washington St; d $205-280; P) Rest your tired caboose in a converted railroad car. Two trains are parked alongside a covered platform, where guests read and mingle on rocking chairs.

Eight snug rail-car guest rooms are comfortable, though not soundproofed – bring earplugs, or you might be awakened by morning hot-air-balloon flights. Book the skylit caboose, and enjoy breakfast at on-site Model Bakery.

Petit Logis INN $$
(Map p181; ☎707-944-2332; www.petitlogis.com; 6527 Yount St; d $169-$295;) Live the Yountville dream in this cedar-shingled bungalow, where you wake to the aroma of croissants from Bouchon Bakery and the sound of birds chirping smugly in the garden. Each of the five country-cottage-style rooms has a gas fireplace and jetted tub.

★**Lavender Inn** INN $$$
(Map p181; ☎707-944-1388; www.lavendernapa.com; 2020 Webber Ave; d $349-449;) This stately Yountville farmhouse has been entertaining visitors since the 1860s, and today Lavender innkeepers extend gracious welcomes with afternoon wine, abundant treats and gourmet breakfasts. All six artistic, contemporary rooms have fireplaces and tubs; courtyard cottage rooms are more secluded, while the historic main house offers sunny rooms overlooking a park. Call for deals.

Bardessono LUXURY HOTEL $$$
(Map p181; ☎707-204-6000; www.bardessono.com; 6524 Yount St; d $500-1400;) Retreat to secret pavilions in the heart of Yountville, surrounded by olive trees, sleek sculpture and meandering waterways. California's first LEED-platinum-certified green hotel celebrates the outdoors indoors, with cloud-like organic duvets, tubs overlooking private courtyards, and windows cleverly framing vineyard views. The on-site spa and rooftop pool are ideal for mornings after French Laundry (p184), right up the block.

Poetry Inn INN $$$
(Map p181; ☎707-944-0646; www.poetryinn.com; 6380 Silverado Trail; d $760-1500;) Spend an epic night at this contemporary inn with staggering views over Stag's Leap vineyards. Recite sonnets on your balcony, compose haikus by your fireplace, and commune with nature in indoor/outdoor showers. Five vast guest rooms are named after poets – Robert Frost overlooks roads less traveled from a garden hammock, while Emily Dickinson offers unexpected perspectives from the bathroom.

Eating

Tacos Garcia TACOS $
(Map p181; ☎707-980-4896; 6764 Washington St; tacos $4.50-10; ⏲11am-8pm) Most day-trippers without reservations wait in vain for bar seating at Yountville bistros, but taco aficionados know the deal: follow your nose to Pancha's parking lot, and line up at Napa Valley's best taco truck. Go with juice-dripping *carne asada* (steak), smoky *al pastor* (spice-rubbed pork) or tender *lengua* (tongue) – or during Napa Valley marathons or harvests, double-meat burritos. Cash only.

Southside Cafe CALIFORNIAN $
(Map p181; ☎707-947-7120; www.southsidenapa.com; 6752 Washington St; items $7-16; ⏲8am-3pm;) It's worth interrupting your busy day of wine tasting for these brunches: mascarpone-topped grilled strawberry toast made with Model Bakery bread, *tortas* (sandwiches) packed with ancho-chili-braised beef and charred onions, and California's obligatory avocado toast with smoked salmon and pepitas. The Southside welcomes your entire crew with excellent artisan coffee, an affordable kids menu, and a sunny courtyard for dogs and their humans.

Bouchon Bakery BAKERY $
(Map p181; ☎707-944-2253; www.bouchonbakery.com; 6528 Washington St; items from $3; ⏲7am-7pm Mon-Fri, from 6:30am Sat & Sun;) Make the Yountville morning pilgrimage to Thomas Keller's bakery for buttered-heaven croissants and perfectly Parisian ham baguette sandwiches, and you'll do a double take when you see what's in the glowing altar-like pastry case: sly artisan takes on convenience-store snacks, including the aptly named 'oh-oh' chocolate rolls and 'better-nutter' sandwich cookies.

Ad Hoc + Addendum CALIFORNIAN $$
(Map p181; ☎707-944-2487; www.thomaskeller.com/adhoc; 6476 Washington St; prix-fixe meals $20-55; ⏲5-9pm Fri-Mon) You'll have whatever the chef's making at Thomas Keller's family-style restaurant. Ad Hoc offers four courses of comfort food inspired by Napa grandmas and farmers. Check out what's cooking online; pray for buttermilk fried chicken. Reserve three-course Sunday brunches or score pulled-pork sandwiches to go.

★**Ciccio** ITALIAN $$$
(Map p181; ☎707-945-1000; www.ciccionapavalley.com; 6770 Washington St; pizzas & mains $24-

A LOVELY SPOT FOR A PICNIC

Strict zoning laws make it tricky to find places to picnic legally in Napa. If you're heading to a winery, call ahead to see if picnicking is allowed – never hurts to ask. If the winery allows it, bear in mind that it's customary to buy a bottle of your host's wine. If you don't finish your bottle, stash it in the trunk – California law forbids driving with an uncorked bottle in the car.

Here's a short list of prime picnic spots, in south–north order.

- Skyline Wilderness Park (p178)
- French Laundry Gardens (p182)
- Pride Mountain (p186)
- Old Faithful Geyser (p191)

32; 5-9pm Wed-Sun) The pick of the day at the family farm determines today's menu at Ciccio, where the Altamura family of farmers-restaurateurs showcase Napa-fresh flavors. Take your pick of wood-fired pizzas topped with just-picked herbs, ranch-raised meat or Pacific seafood mains, and a rainbow of sun-ripened vegetables in salads or atop homemade pasta. Don't miss the negroni cocktail bar.

French Laundry CALIFORNIAN **$$$**
(Map p181; 707-944-2380; www.thomaskeller.com/tfl; 6640 Washington St; prix-fixe dinner from $350; seatings 5-9pm daily, 11am-12:30pm Fri-Sun) Whether you've won a Nobel or survived a quarantine, Thomas Keller's world-renowned restaurant is here to celebrate life. Strut through the hidden door of this historic Western saloon, and the star treatment begins with bubbly and amuse-bouches – and it won't quit through nine opulent, original courses, from signature 'oysters and pearls' (oyster-caviar custard) to 'doughnuts and coffee' (cappuccino semifreddo) grand finales.

Shopping

★**Kollar Chocolates** CHOCOLATE
(Map p181; www.kollarchocolates.com; 6525 Washington St, Marketplace at the Yountville Estate; 10am-5:30pm;) Um, did someone abandon toothpaste and a toothbrush inside Yountville's upscale shopping center? Nope, it's sculpted from single-origin chocolate – and yes, it's delicious. Chef Chris Kollar is a confectionary artist with a sneaky sense of humor and impeccable taste – his zinfandel truffles are vintner-acclaimed.

Kelly's Filling Station WINE
(Map p181; 707-944-8165; 6795 Washington St; 7am-8pm) Only in Yountville can you fill your tank while you browse vintage Champagne. Your checkout clerk does double duty as sommelier, and can school you on blending philosophies of Napa Meritages versus Super Tuscans. Snack racks feature artisan salumi and single-origin chocolate – and instead of gag gifts at checkout, they sell hip flasks. Possibly the world's fanciest gas station.

Getting There & Away

Yountville is about a 90-minute drive from San Francisco. For scenic drives from Yountville, follow Silverado Trail north, or take Mt Veeder Rd through pristine countryside west of Yountville.

Note that Napa Valley Vine (p173) doesn't stop in Yountville proper, but across Hwy 29 at the Veteran's Home.

The new Napa Valley Vine Trail (p176) connects downtown Napa and Yountville along old stagecoach and rail lines. To bike onward to Calistoga, take tree-lined Silverado Trail instead of hot, traffic-heavy Hwy 29.

Oakville & Rutherford Area

Today when wine aficionados look at this green valley, they see red – thanks in no small part to Robert Mondavi, the visionary vintner who knew back in the 1960s that Napa was capable of more than jug wine. His marketing savvy launched Napa's premium reds to cult status, including his own Opus One 'Meritage'. Meanwhile up the road, trailblazing winemaker Mike Grgich made history in 1976 with the first Napa chardonnay to win over French judges in international wine competitions.

Yet beyond the historic 1881 Oakville Grocery, the hamlets of Oakville and Rutherford seem practically invisible. Sprawling winery complexes along Hwy 29 dominate the landscape with gilded signs and gated entrances – including Mondavi and Grgich Hills – while modest farmhouses hang back from the road. Turn off Hwy 29 onto cross-valley roads, and you'll find a 50-year-old taqueria, offbeat organic wineries, and low-key, high-end hotels hidden in the heart of Napa Valley.

Sights

★**Frog's Leap** WINERY
(Map p181; 707-963-4704; www.frogsleap.com; 8815 Conn Creek Rd, Rutherford; tasting & tour $35-55; by appointment 10am-4pm; P)

Follow vineyard cats through enchanted gardens, and drink in the views from the loft of an 1884 barn. Your human hosts supply witty barnyard banter, plus insights you can taste in organically farmed wines. Sauvignon blanc is the critical darling, but merlot has all the texture and drama of a black-velvet Elvis painting, and rebel zinfandel will make you want to boogie barefoot (bottles $26 to $76).

Grgich Hills Estate WINERY
(Map p181; ☎707-963-2784; www.grgich.com; 1829 St Helena Hwy, Rutherford; tasting $40; ⏲9:30am-4:30pm; P) 'Do something better every day' was the motto that led maverick winemaker Mike Grgich from Croatia to Napa to Paris, where his Napa Valley chardonnay won top honors in the legendary 1976 Judgment of Paris. Wineries worldwide recruited him – but Mike became a farmer instead. He championed sustainable methods, growing grapes biodynamically without artificial pesticides, using wild yeast for fermentation, and solar powering his operations. Toast 'something better' with effortlessly elegant fumé blanc and 'cabernet-lover's merlot' (bottles $31 to $149); walk-ins welcome.

Sleeping & Eating

★Auberge du Soleil LUXURY HOTEL $$$
(Map p181; ☎707-963-1211; www.aubergedusoleil.com; 180 Rutherford Hill Rd, Rutherford; d $1325-4025;) With such romantic views, Michelin-starred three-course brunches ($75) are almost upstaged. To play the lead in your own version of Napa Valley's best recurring rom-com, book a valley-view room with panoramic balconies. Auberge's hillside cottages supply every modern comfort, including soaking tubs and cozy fireplaces, so there's no need to leave your room. Honeymooners may prefer private garden-view rooms with outdoor tubs in secret courtyards.

Rancho Caymus HOTEL $$$
(Map p181; ☎707-200-9300, 800-845-1777; www.ranchocaymusinn.com; 1140 Rutherford Rd, Rutherford; d $276-596; P@) Kick off your boots and stay awhile in this Western-style spa-ranch built by pioneering vintner Mary Tilden Morton. Handsome, sprawling rooms accommodate discerning Napa cowboys with leather couches, gas fireplaces and secluded patios. Handcrafted details surround you: barnwood ceilings, terra-cotta tiles, stained-glass windows. Enjoy complimentary breakfasts and wine poolside, plus exclusive tastings arranged by your concierge.

★La Luna Taqueria & Market TACOS $
(Map p181; ☎707-963-3211; www.lalunamarket.com; 1153 Rutherford Rd, Rutherford; tacos from $2.75; ⏲7am-7pm Mon-Fri, 8am-6pm Sat, to 5pm Sun; P) 'Tacos y vinos' says the wine-fridge sign – an excellent pairing suggestion made possible by La Luna for 50 years. Complement generous super-tacos ($4.25) with top-value Napa wines: unoaked Maldonado Farm Worker chardonnay ($20) with crispy fish tacos, and Elouan rosé ($18) with soulful *pollo adobado* (adobo-marinated chicken). One-stop-shop for picnics, camping supplies, and fiestas complete with piñatas.

Oakville Grocery DELI $
(Map p181; ☎707-944-8802; www.oakvillegrocery.com; 7856 Hwy 29, Oakville; sandwiches $10-14, pizzas $15-16; ⏲7am-5pm Sun-Thu, to 6pm Fri & Sat;) Since 1881 the definitive Napa Valley deli has supplied wine-worthy picnics – gooey local cheeses, artisan charcuterie, Dungeness crab-cake sandwiches – and now they serve made-to-order pizzas hot from the patio's wood-fired oven. Consult staff to find a new favorite Napa wine, and they'll open it and hand you wineglasses to toast the good life on picnic benches. Great gourmet gifts, too.

St Helena & Around

Even people with places to go and wine to drink can't resist downtown St Helena, which looks like a Western movie set. Three blocks of Main St are a designated national historic site, including one of the oldest cinemas in America still in operation.

This area was native Wappo land until it was claimed by Spain, then Mexico – more specifically, the property of Doña Maria Ygnacia Soberanes. She gave her daughter Isadora Bale Grist Mill (still grinding flour today) and prime vineyards to her daughter Caroline, who married a German winemaker named Charles Krug. Together they founded the first commercial winery in Napa in 1858.

Today if you're thirsty, you're in luck: there's more than an acre of wine grapes per resident in St Helena. Raise a toast to the women who put that wine in your glass, and their hearts into building this charming town.

Sights

★Tres Sabores WINERY
(Map p181; ☎707-967-8027; www.tressabores.com; 1620 Sth Whitehall Lane; tour & tasting $40; ⏲by appointment 10:30am-3pm;) Julie Johnson

and her vineyard dogs had just harvested her organically grown zinfandel in 2005 when disaster struck: fire hit her off-site fermentation facility. Rather than risk smoke-taint, owner/winemaker/farmer/chef Julie ingeniously repurposed the juice for barbecue sauce, and her winery rebounded. Today Tres Sabores' soulful zin is the toast of Napa Valley, the sauvignon blanc was named a *New York Times* top-10 pick, and rare rosé is a collectors' favorite – you might even score legendary Por Que No? (Why Not?) BBQ sauce.

★ Joseph Phelps WINERY
(☎800-707-5789; www.josephphelps.com; 200 Taplin Rd; ⏲by appointment 10am-4pm) Here's the secret to Phelps' iconic red blend Insignia, made with each season's best grapes since 1974: there are no rules. In fact, Phelps invites you to make your own version of Insignia, blending the same six components winemaker Ashley Hepworth used for the current release – and then taste them side by side ($125, 90 minutes, 11am and 2pm). Or you can just lounge under California oaks with a panoramic terrace tasting, and raise a toast to rule-breaking ($85, 75 minutes).

Pride Mountain WINERY
(☎707-963-4949; www.pridewines.com; 4026 Spring Mountain Rd; tasting & tour $30-45, summit experience $90; ⏲by appointment only; P) High atop Spring Mountain and smack on the county boundary, this family-owned winery is the pride of both Napa and Sonoma. Winemaker Sally Johnson and David Orozco's sustainable-farming vineyard team share credit for cult-status cabernet and merlot, and they also collaborate on wines only available onsite –) aromatic viognier and spicy cab franc reward trips up the mountain (bottles $45 to $145). After your tasting, head to Viewpoint for top-of-the-world vistas, or Ghost Winery for a shaded picnic amid historic ruins.

Hall WINERY
(Map p188; ☎707-967-2626; www.hallwines.com; 401 St Helena Hwy; tasting & tour from $50; ⏲10am-5:30pm; P) When you see a giant chrome rabbit leaping over the vines, you've come to the right place for cabernet with an unexpected kick. The wines at Hall are as big and bold as the installation art – party-ready sauvignon blancs reflect Nick Cave's collage of disco costumes, and stormy merlots mirror Graham Caldwell's rain of red glass droplets. Hourly tours cover the grounds, artwork, and noteworthy wine tastings under Nenna Okore's newspaper-and-rope tapestry (bottles $26 to $185).

Sleeping

★ El Bonita MOTEL $
(Map p188; ☎707-963-3216; www.elbonita.com; 195 Main St; d $145-215; P) Free up funds for vintage wines by staying at this affordable vintage motel. Instagrammers pose by original neon signs, wine-tasters nap poolside under California oaks, and cyclists recover from Sugarloaf Ridge rides in the hot tub and sauna. Rooms are spacious, cheerful and remodeled, with headboards hand-painted with California scenes. Request a quieter room in the back; two-night minimum on weekends.

Harvest Inn RESORT $$$
(Map p188; ☎707-963-9463; www.harvestinn.com; 1 Main St; d $269-494;) Get in touch with nature at this wooded wine estate, with Tudor-timbered lodges, stone-pillared bungalows, and cedar-shingled cabins dotted around old-growth trees and vineyards. All 78 rooms are contemporary and spacious, many with bonuses: brick fireplaces, vineyard views and private hot tubs. Relax after complimentary wine-tastings with pool dips, organic spa treatments, Harvest Bar's flaming cocktails, and Harvest Table's farm-to-fork cuisine.

Wydown Hotel BOUTIQUE HOTEL $$$
(Map p188; ☎707-963-5100; www.wydownhotel.com; 1424 Main St; d $359-495; P) Live the dream promised by Wine Country magazines in a historic St Helena inn redone by a contemporary art collector. Twelve guest rooms are smart and easygoing, with sprawling beds and gleaming subway-tiled bathrooms. Complimentary breakfasts are served in the tea room. Ask savvy staff for hot tips on dinner and wine tasting, or just wander down charming, sycamore-lined Main St.

Eating

★ Model Bakery BAKERY $
(Map p188; ☎707-963-8192; www.themodelbakery.com; 1357 Main St; pastries $3-10; ⏲6:30am-5pm Mon-Sat, from 7am Sun;) Baked goods are even better at Model Bakery, where Napa babies instinctively reach for fluffy cornmeal-dusted English muffins, and tiny birds hop around the threshold for crumbs of crusty spelt boules. For lunch, go with the savory galette of the day – but leave room

for salted-caramel tarts or accurately named 'chocolate rad' cookies with top-notch coffee.

Napa Valley Olive Oil Company MARKET $
(Map p188; 707-963-4173; www.nvoliveoilmfg.com; 835 Charter Oak Ave; 8am-5:30pm) Salami swings from the rafters as you enter the screen door of the country market that's supplied Napa with Italian delicacies for almost a century. Wooden crates brim with picnic possibilities – crusty bread, nutty cheeses, meaty olives – plus Napa's freshest olive oil. Ask nicely for a knife and a board to picnic at rickety tables outside. Cash only.

WF Giugni & Son DELI $
(Map p188; 707-963-3421; 1227 Main St; sandwiches from $9; 9am-5pm;) Vintages vary, but Giugni's has remained a Napa classic for 50 years. Pile meats (mortadella, peppered salami, hot coppa, roast chicken or beef) onto deli bread (ideally rosemary, rye or Dutch crunch) until your sandwich looks like it belongs in a comic strip, then drizzle with 'Giugni juice' (red-wine-vinegar). Cash only.

Gott's Roadside AMERICAN $
(Map p188; 707-963-3486; www.gotts.com; 933 Main St; mains $8-16; 10am-10pm May-Sep, to 9pm Oct-Apr;) Welcome to the retro roadside burger joint you were fantasizing about mid-cab-tasting. Sprawl on the grassy lawn and feast on Niman Ranch grass-fed beef burgers oozing with Point Reyes blue cheese – or enjoy Mary's free-range fried-chicken sandwiches or massive Greenleaf Farms Cobb salads. Call ahead, order online or try Oxbow Public Market (p180); Gott's is often busy supporting community-wide recovery efforts.

★Charter Oak CALIFORNIAN $$
(Map p188; 707-302-6996; www.thecharteroak.com; 1050 Charter Oak Ave; mains $20-30; 5-8:30pm Mon-Thu, from 11:30am Fri-Sun; P) The dining-room fireplace isn't just for looks at Charter Oak: sensational dishes emerge from the blazing hearth and arrive tableside still bubbling in enamel cookware. Each dish showcases a signature seasonal ingredient or two, often from Charter Oak's farm – black cod sizzles like gossip atop vineyard-cover-crop mustard greens, and slow-smoked short ribs slide drunkenly off the bone into cabernet-grape saba.

Cook St Helena ITALIAN $$
(Map p188; 707-963-7088; www.cooksthelena.com; 1310 Main St; mains $19-35; 11:30am-9pm Tue-Thu, to 10pm Fri & Sat) Small space, small menu and big flavors are signatures of this storefront bistro, where earthy Cal-Italian cooking keeps crowds coming all day. Browse today's dream menu – recently, foraged mushroom risotto, eggplant parmesan with a proper béchamel, braised short ribs and pillowy parmesan polenta – or go straight for homemade pasta slathered with homemade ricotta. Expect waits, even with reservations.

Shopping

★Woodhouse Chocolates CHOCOLATE
(Map p188; 800 966 3468; www.woodhousechocolate.com; 1367 Main St; 10am-6pm) The best light-blue-boxed gifts in Napa aren't jewelry, but a gift you can't possibly refuse: chocolates handmade by CIA-trained mother-daughter team Tracy and Christina Anderson. Chocolate this good needs no adornment, but it's delightful to devour a dark-chocolate Tyrannosaurus Rex, or milk-chocolate Easter bunnies on a scooter. For folks back home, they'll send Home Sweet Home care packages.

★New West KnifeWorks HOMEWARES
(Map p188; 707-244-5188; www.newwestknifeworks.com; 1380 Main St; 10am-6pm Mon-Fri, from 9:30am Sat & Sun) Thwack! Was that a flying axe? Yes...but don't worry, it wasn't aimed at you. The target's that wooden stump on the wall – try it! Just don't get distracted by walls of gleaming, high-performance artisan knives

BOOKING APPOINTMENTS AT WINERIES

To make sure the winery of your choice can accommodate you for a tasting, book online or call ahead. Due to strict county zoning laws, some Napa wineries can't legally receive drop-in visitors – and many small wineries just don't have spare staff to handle impromptu guests.

Most Napa wineries ask that you allow 60 to 90 minutes for a tasting. Fair enough – it took farmers and winemakers a long time to pack all that flavor into a bottle, and wine this special deserves its moment to breathe and shine. Besides, look around you: you're in Wine Country, where's the rush? Plan for one or two tastings a day, plus a lunch or dinner reservation, maybe a stroll, bike ride, spa or nap – and that's it, you've done Wine Country right.

Napa Valley North

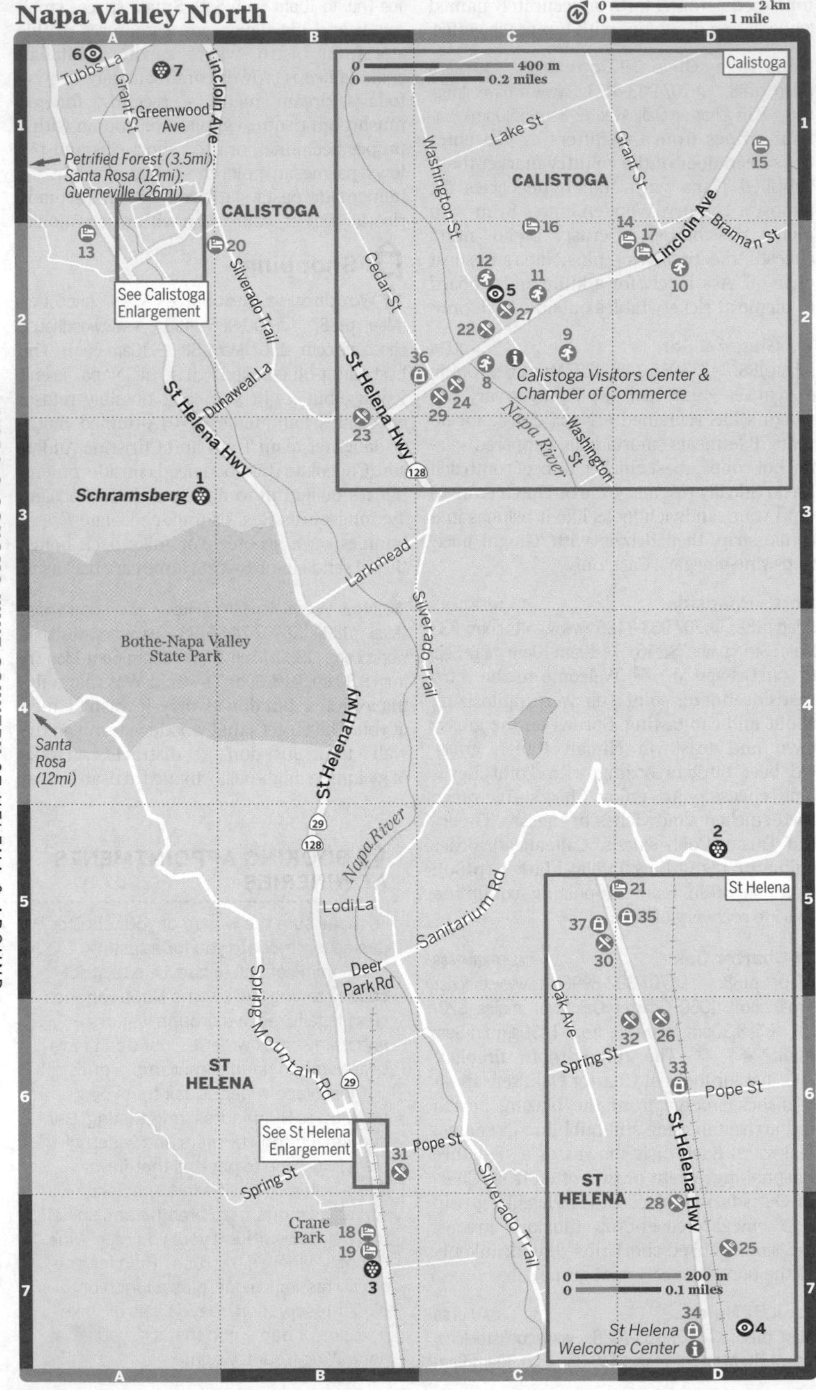

Napa Valley North

Top Sights
1 Schramsberg ... A3

Sights
2 Cade ... D5
3 Hall ... B7
4 Long Meadow Ranch ... D7
5 Olabisi Wines ... C2
6 Old Faithful Geyser ... A1
7 Vincent Arroyo ... A1

Activities, Courses & Tours
8 Calistoga Bike Shop ... C2
9 Calistoga Spa Hot Springs ... C2
10 Indian Springs Spa ... D2
11 Mount View Spa ... C2
12 Roman Spa Hot Springs Resort ... C2

Sleeping
13 Aurora Park Cottages ... A2
14 Brannan Cottage Inn ... D2
15 Calistoga Motor Lodge & Spa ... D1
Calistoga Spa Hot Springs ... (see 9)
16 Chelsea Garden Inn ... C2
17 Cottage Grove Inn ... D2
18 El Bonita ... B7
19 Harvest Inn ... B7
Indian Springs Resort ... (see 10)
Mount View Hotel & Spa ... (see 11)
20 Solage ... B2
21 Wydown Hotel ... D5

Eating
22 Bella Bakery ... C2
23 Buster's Southern BBQ ... B3
24 Calistoga Inn & Brewery ... C2
25 Charter Oak ... D7
26 Cook St Helena ... D6
27 Evangeline ... C2
28 Gott's Roadside ... D7
29 Lovina ... C2
30 Model Bakery ... C5
31 Napa Valley Olive Oil Company ... B6
Solbar ... (see 20)
32 WF Giugni & Son ... D6

Shopping
33 Lolo's Consignment ... D6
34 Napa Soap Company ... D7
35 New West KnifeWorks ... D5
36 Rags to Riches ... C2
37 Woodhouse Chocolates ... C5

with ergonomic handles, hand-carved cutting boards, and colorful blown glass olive-oil decanters – ideal gifts for your personal chef.

Napa Soap Company COSMETICS
(Map p188; 707-963-5010; www.napasoap.com; 655 Main St; 10am-5:30pm) Cabernet Soapignon, Shea-R-donnay, Gard-iongnier...the names of these ecofriendly soaps are meant to make you laugh, remind you of Napa, and make handwashing less of a chore. Napa Soap Company bath products, candles and balms are made locally, with a commitment to sustainable sourcing – and without sodium lauryl sulfate, parabens or phthalates.

Lolo's Consignment VINTAGE
(Map p188; 707-963-7972; www.lolosconsignment.com; 1120 Main St; 10am-4pm Mon, to 5:30pm Tue-Sat, 11am-4pm Sun) Whether you forgot to bring a sweater for wine-cellar tastings or packed heels that are slowing your roll through vineyards, Kristine and her Lolo's crew are here for you. Score cast-off cashmere and sleek sandals, and sell those stilettos on consignment. Lolo's vintage housewares like grapevine tea towels and cow-shaped creamers make affordable gourmet souvenirs.

Information

St Helena Welcome Center (Map p188; 707-963-4456; www.sthelena.com; 657 Main St, Suite A; 9am-5pm Mon-Fri, 10am-4pm Sat, 11am-5pm Sun) The visitor center has information and lodging assistance.

Getting There & Around

St Helena is an 80-minute drive from San Francisco. Napa Valley Vine (p173) connects St Helena to downtown Napa and Calistoga on bus 10, and also provides transit around town on the St Helena Shuttle. The shuttle provides door-to-door service for just $1; to schedule a pickup, call 707-963-3007 during operating hours (7:45am to 6pm Monday to Thursday, to 11pm Friday, 10am to 11pm Saturday, and noon to 7pm Sunday).

Parking downtown is next to impossible on summer weekends. Tip: look behind the visitor center.

The Napa Valley Wine Train (p178) takes you from downtown Napa to St Helena and back in a plush vintage dining car, with meal service included and optional winery stops – if you choose one, make it historic Grgich Hills (p185).

Calistoga & Around

With soothing natural hot springs, bubbling volcanic mud pools and a dramatically spurting geyser, the settlement of Nilektsonoma was renowned across Talahalusi (Napa Valley) by the indigenous Wappo people for some 8000 years. Then in 1859, legendary speculator Sam Brannan talked some bankers into backing his scheme to transform Nilektsonoma into Calistoga, California's signature spa resort. But California cowboys preferred dirt, and by 1873 Sam cut his losses in Calistoga and left town. Only a few Brannan cottages remain from his original resort, including Brannan Cottage Inn (p192).

Some 150 years later, Brannan's dream seems to have come true. Local hills dotted with defunct silver and mercury mines are reclaimed as parkland, and Calistoga spring water still appears on store shelves today. For a century, Calistoga's extraordinary geology has been a featured attraction at the Petrified Forest and Old Faithful Geyser. Meanwhile at Calistoga's hot-springs spas, brochures still extoll the curative powers of mineral springs and bubbling mud baths.

Sights

★Schramsberg WINERY

(Map p188; 707-942-4558; www.schramsberg.com; 1400 Schramsberg Rd; tour & tasting $70, tour & sparkling-wine tasting $95, reserve wine & cheese pairing $125; by appointment at 9:30am, 10am, 11:30am, noon, 1:30pm & 2:30pm) This enchanted winery has survived miraculously intact since 1862, and it's hit a 50-year winning streak producing California's most distinctive brut sparkling wines. Explore the historic caves to glimpse the traditional riddling and racking process firsthand, then emerge to the Napa Green–certified wine estate to sample the *tête de cuvées* (best of the vintage). Go with the giddy all-sparkling experience to concentrate on signature *blanc de blancs* (bottles $29 to $110).

Vincent Arroyo WINERY

(Map p188; 707-942-6995; www.vincentarroyo.com; 2361 Greenwood Ave; tasting $20; by appointment 10am-4pm) Signature wines are named after vineyard dogs and the tasting room is a garage – welcome to Napa's most winsome winery, keeping it low-key while winning high praise since 1984. The Arroyo family's all-estate-grown petite syrah, cab and syrah blends are so consistently memorable that 75% of production is sold before it's bottled (bottles $16 to $68). The Arroyos sell directly to people, not corporations, so you won't find these wines anywhere but right here – and you can pet the dogs, too.

Cade WINERY

(Map p188; 707-965-2746; www.cadewinery.com; 360 Howell Mountain Rd S, Angwin; tasting & tour $80; by appointment only; P) Ascend Howell Mountain for hawk-eye views 1800ft above the valley at Napa's pioneering LEED Gold–certified sustainable winery. Before he became Governor of California, Gavin Newsom was the founder/owner of Cade – and this place showcases Californian ingenuity, from the WWII submarine-hull table in the wine cave to the manzanita-branch chandelier in the hilltop tasting room. Organically farmed, complex cabernet and bright sauvignon blanc balance French and Californian styles – French-Californian winemaker Danielle Cyrot's effortlessly elegant wines are bottled diplomacy (bottles $34 to $110).

Petrified Forest FOREST

(707-942-6667; www.petrifiedforest.org; 4100 Petrified Forest Rd; adult/child 6-11yr/youth 12-18yr $12/6/8; 10am-7pm late May-early Sep, to 6pm Apr-late May & early Sep-Oct, to 5pm Nov-Mar; P) Three million years ago, a volcanic eruption at Mt St Helena blew down a stand of redwoods. Their trunks gradually turned to stone, and in 1914, enterprising environmentalist Ollie Bockee preserved this land as an educational roadside attraction – and her vision remains remarkably intact today. Wildfires struck in 2017, but the petrified redwoods were spared – and the redwoods are recovering beautifully. Two half-mile trails are open to explore independently or on one-hour educational tours (11am, 1pm and 3pm Wednesday to Saturday).

Olabisi Wines TASTING ROOM

(Map p188; 707-942-4472; www.olabisiwines.com; 1226 Washington St; tasting $25; 11am-6pm) Wild yeast and wild notions make these unconventional wines perfectly suited to the Wild West scenery of downtown Calistoga. Ted and Kim make extremely small-production wines from highly specific vineyards, producing less than 1000 cases a year – boot-stomping cabs, zesty sauvignon blancs, floral pinots, old-vine zins and celebration-worthy Time Machine blends sell out quickly (bottles $40 to $75).

Old Faithful Geyser GEYSER

(Map p188; ☎707-942-6463; www.oldfaithfulgeyser.com; 1299 Tubbs Lane, between Hwys 128 & 29; adult/child/child under 4yr $15/9/free; ⏲8:30am-7pm, shorter hours Oct-Feb; P 👪) 'Many notable people have come to see, hear and learn the mysteries of this "Wonder of Nature" that captivates the imagination – it's amazing!' brags a vintage sign at this geothermal roadside attraction. Scientists do gush about this geyser, which shoots boiling water 30ft to 80ft into the air every 20 to 40 minutes – though brief spurts can be anticlimactic. Make the most of admission with picnics, bocce, geology displays, and a barnyard petting zoo.

Activities

Spas

Calistoga is bubbling with mineral hot springs, but it's most famous as the best place in the West to wallow in the mud. Calistoga mud is a blend of volcanic ash, peat and hot mineral spring water. Baths with higher volcanic ash content are silkier and more decadent.

Mud-bath packages take 60 to 90 minutes and cost $95 to $110. You start semi-submerged in hot mud, then soak in hot mineral water – a steam bath and blanket-wrap typically follow. Most spas offer multi-treatment packages, and some offer discounted spa-lodging packages. A massage increases the cost (around $140 and up).

Baths are typically taken solo, though some offer couples options. Variations include thin, painted-on clay-mud wraps (called 'fango' baths, good for those uncomfortable sitting in mud), herbal wraps and seaweed baths. Discount coupons are sometimes available from the visitors center (p194). Reservations are essential.

★ **Indian Springs Spa** SPA

(Map p188; ☎844-378-3635; www.indianspringscalistoga.com; 1712 Lincoln Ave; mud bath $110; ⏲by appointment 8:15am-7pm) Smart updates to California's longest-running spa make this retro resort a winner. Modern concrete tubs are filled with volcanic mud, and mineral hot springs feed the massive pool (access with treatment weekday/weekend $25/50). Add a massage (from $150 per 50 minutes), and you may have to roll home. Inn guests gain free pool access, and shuffle into Sam's Social Club (p193) for bathrobed happy hours.

Mount View Spa SPA

(Map p188; ☎707-942-1500; www.mountviewhotel.com; 1457 Lincoln Ave; mud bath per person 25/45min single $75/95, couple $50/65; ⏲by appointment 8:30am-7pm) Ease into mud bathing with a lighter, shorter, sweeter version. This historic spa hotel uses lighter, mineral-rich mud as warming as thicker mud, but easier to wash off. Soothe sore knees after mountain biking and tired elbows post-wine-toasting with CBD bath bombs in seasonal scents ($5 extra) and/or CBD-oil massage ($145 per 50 minutes) for THC-free relaxation. Check lodging/spa packages online.

Roman Spa Hot Springs Resort HOT SPRINGS

(Map p188; ☎707-942-2122; www.romanspahotsprings.com; 1300 Washington St; ⏲9am-7pm) Other Roman spas are famous, but this Italian-themed spa motel just off Calistoga's main street remains a favorite local secret. Besides mud baths, Roman Spa is known for

FLYING & BALLOONING

If you think Wine Country scenery is breathtaking, wait until you see it from 3000ft up in the air. Biplanes and balloons have limited capacity, so be sure to book ahead and prepare yourself for this once-in-a-lifetime, adrenaline-rush experience.

The Vintage Aircraft Company (p199) flies over Sonoma in a vintage biplane with an expert pilot who'll do loop-the-loops on request (add $50).

Napa Valley's signature hot-air balloon flights leave early, around 6am or 7am, when the air is coolest and the mists are rising from the vineyard. Many offer a Champagne toast or brunch on landing – definitely helps offset the adrenaline! Adults pay around $200 to $250, and kids $150 to $175. Call **Balloons Above the Valley** (Map p181; ☎800-464-6824, 707-253-2222; www.balloonrides.com; 603 California Blvd, Napa; balloon rides & tours $189-344; ⏲8am-5pm), **Napa Valley Balloons** (Map p181; ☎800-253-2224, 707-944-0228; www.napavalleyballoons.com; 4086 Byway E, Napa; per person $219, 2-person private flight $2200) or **Aloft** (Map p181; ☎855-944-4408; https://nvaloft.com; 6525 Washington St, Yountville; balloon rides from $200; 👪), Napa's most established ballooning outfit.

affordable massages with THC-free, hemp CBD for harvest-time muscle-pain relief (50/80 minutes $165/125), weekday morning early-bird deals on massage and spa treatments, and two-for-one specials Tuesday and Friday. Lodging/spa specials available online.

Calistoga Spa Hot Springs SPA
(Map p188; ☎707-942-6269; www.calistogaspa.com; 1006 Washington St; mud bath $105; ⏲by appointment 9am-4pm Mon-Thu, to 7pm Fri-Sun;) Mud the whole family can enjoy. This motel complex offers volcanic mud baths followed by mineral baths with colored light (try purple!), eucalyptus-scented steam baths, and blanket wraps. Mud bathers get free access to four outdoor, geothermal swimming pools; pass for one non-mud bather available for $25. Kids are welcome, as long as an adult stays with them. Lodging/spa deals online.

Sleeping

★Indian Springs Resort RESORT $$
(Map p188; ☎707-942-4913; www.indianspringscalistoga.com; 1712 Lincoln Ave; d/cottages from $229/559;) The definitive old-school Calistoga resort, Indian Springs has vintage bungalows beneath swaying palm trees strung with hammocks. A grand drive leads to the historic spa, new Sam's Social Club bar/grill, and massive mineral-hot-springs pool. Bungalows can accommodate families, but the mellow, upscale 1930s lodge is exclusively for adults.

★Mount View Hotel & Spa HISTORIC HOTEL $$
(Map p188; ☎707-942-6877; www.mountviewhotel.com; 1457 Lincoln Ave; d $239-259;) Welcoming Calistoga visitors for a century, this family-owned Mission Revival hotel is a charming character with art deco flair – enjoy welcome wine and complimentary breakfast in the 1930s speakeasy – and a big heart: 50% of profits are donated to charity. Guest rooms are cushy, stylish and surprisingly quiet, with gleaming bathrooms. Unwind in the mineral-water Jacuzzi, heated pool and spa.

Calistoga Motor Lodge & Spa MOTEL $$
(Map p188; ☎707-942-0991; www.calistogamotorlodge.com; 1880 Lincoln Ave; d & ste from $186;) A 1947 American classic, reinvented. Each cleverly updated motel room is unique, with mid-century-modern details: swiveling lights, bucket chairs, geometric carpets. Suites have a fold-down dining table that converts into an extra bed. You'll keep busy with free, family-friendly activities, including Pilates, yoga and bocce – plus three hot-springs pools and on-site spa.

Aurora Park Cottages COTTAGE $$
(Map p188; ☎877-942-7700, 707-942-6733; www.aurorapark.com; 1807 Foothill Blvd; cottages from $179;) Sitting back from Calistoga's main road amid trees and flower gardens is this quiet row of sunny yellow cottages. All six are immaculately kept, with shining polished-wood floors, fluffy feather beds and private sundecks. There's also a two-bedroom rental home equipped with a full kitchen ($395 per night). The innkeeper offers wine-tasting discounts plus complimentary breakfasts with direct bookings.

Calistoga Spa Hot Springs MOTEL $$
(Map p188; ☎707-942-6269; www.calistogaspa.com; 1006 Washington St; d $197-267;) Pool parties and snack-bar treats for kids, spa treatments and wine for parents – what more does anyone want from a family vacation? This motel resort has recently remodeled, colorful rooms with kitchenettes, surrounded by fantastic pools: two full-size outdoor geothermal pools, a kiddie pool with mini-waterfall, and a huge Jacuzzi for adults.

Chelsea Garden Inn B&B $$
(Map p188; ☎707-942-0948; www.chelseagardeninn.com; 1443 2nd St; d $165-400;) Palms, flowers and grapevines frame the entrance of this trellis-covered inn on a quiet Calistoga side street. The five country-style rooms have floral-print armchairs, gas fireplaces, fridges and cable TV. Each has its own private entrance that opens onto blooming courtyard gardens. Laze around the pool (open May to October), or sip the house Chelsea cabernet ($20) in the library-lounge.

★Brannan Cottage Inn BOUTIQUE HOTEL $$$
(Map p188; ☎707-942-4200; www.brannancottageinn.com; 109 Wappo Ave; d from $309;) Stay in the iconic 1862 gingerbread cottage of Samuel Brannan, the hustler/entrepreneur who imagined Calistoga as the best resort in the West – and after staying here, you'll be inclined to agree. Six updated guest rooms offer historic charm plus pillow-top beds, flat screens and espresso machines. Access to a neighboring spa resort is included, and so is breakfast if you book directly.

Solage RESORT $$$
(Map p188; ☎707-226-0800; www.aubergeresorts.com/solage; 755 Silverado Trail; d $530-675, ste $835-1275;) Modern luxury

sets Solage apart from Calistoga's spa-hotel crowd. Ranch meets loft in guest studios with platform beds and sliding doors opening onto outdoor patios – some have fireplaces and tubs and/or pebble-floor showers. At the heart of the resort, palm trees surround a glam pool and spa. Cruiser bikes are provided to work up Solbar appetites.

Cottage Grove Inn BUNGALOW **$$$**
(Map p188; ☎707-942-8400; www.cottagegrove.com; 1711 Lincoln Ave; cottages from $269; P ⊖ ❄ 📶 🐾) Get cozy in sweet little white-washed cottages with wood-burning fireplaces, two-person Jacuzzis, and rocking chair front porches. They're just big enough to accommodate an additional guest ($75, ages 12-plus only) and/or a small dog. Bicycles are provided, though it's a short stroll to anywhere in downtown Calistoga. Breakfast is complimentary. Checkout is 11am.

Eating & Drinking

★Bella Bakery BAKERY **$**
(Map p188; ☎707-942-1443; 1353 Lincoln Ave; pastries $2-7; ⊙6am-1pm Mon-Sat, from 7am Sun) Your friendly neighborhood world-class bakery and coffee bar. At their hometown bakery, Jen and Paul Crudo perfect the classics – their quiche crust is wafer-thin yet crispy, and the chocolate layer cake defies gravity, with airy frosting lifting dense cake. Pick up snacks for the ride home at your own risk – those oatmeal cookies will make you turn your car around.

Buster's Southern BBQ BARBECUE **$**
(Map p188; ☎707-942-5605; www.bustersouthernbbq.com; 1207 Foothill Blvd; meals $11-22; ⊙10am-7pm; 🍷 👪) Make small talk with the sheriff while you wait for your tri-tip – Buster's is where all of Napa Valley bonds over barbecue, since 1965. Smoky ribs are served with beer or wine at outdoor tables, with a side of live jazz and blues from 2pm to 5pm Sunday.

★Lovina CALIFORNIAN **$$**
(Map p188; ☎707-942-6500; www.lovinacalistoga.com; 1107 Cedar St; lunch/brunch dishes $10-29, dinner $20-36; ⊙5:30pm-late Thu, 11:30am-3pm & 5:30pm-late Fri & Sat, 9:30am-3pm Sun; 🌶 👪) Lunch in the garden here is a dream – and nonstop inspiration for chef Leticia Martinez, who composes produce from restaurateur Jennifer Bennet's garden into California sensations like Napa wild-mushroom risotto, herb-spiked green-goddess salads, and rich *cioppino* (tomato seafood stew). For brunch, her Jalisco-style chilaquiles will 'soak up the tannins' (read: fix wine-tasting hangovers).

Evangeline CREOLE **$$**
(Map p188; ☎707-341-3131; www.evangelinenapa.com; 1226 Washington St; mains $15-34; ⊙11:30am-2pm & 5:30-9pm Mon-Fri, from 10am Sat & Sun) The MVPs of California's gold rush were New Orleans chefs and bartenders, who kept gold miners going through triumphs and trials – and Evangeline's works that same magic for Napa winemakers, who swap harvest tales here over bracing Sazeracs, mood-boosting gumbo, and soulful shrimp and grits. Call ahead to nab a table, or dine at the marble bar among new friends.

Calistoga Inn & Brewery AMERICAN **$$**
(Map p188; ☎707-942-4101; www.calistogainn.com; 1250 Lincoln Ave; dinner mains $15-45; ⊙11:30am-9:30pm Mon-Fri, from 11am Sat & Sun) Bicycle right up to the bar for a drink or brunch in Napa Valley's most happening beer garden, with a microbrewery at the back of the patio and live music on summer weekends. For classic American country dinners – hot wings, thick pork chops, buttermilk mashed potatoes, iceberg-wedge salads – take a seat at oakwood tables.

Solbar CALIFORNIAN **$$$**
(Map p188; ☎707-226-0860; www.aubergeresorts.com/solage/dine; 755 Silverado Trail N; lunch/brunch dishes $16-36, dinner mains $26-55; ⊙7am-9pm Sun-Thu, to 9:30pm Fri & Sat) 🌿 Farm meets resort at this bar/restaurant strong on creative cocktails and small plates. Mains are more Hamptons club than NorCal spa, featuring blue-chip comfort food like truffle pasta, Maine diver scallops, and lobster mac and cheese – but those 48-hour ribs are worth every hour.

Shopping

★Rags to Riches ANTIQUES
(Map p188; ☎707-616-3750; 1125 Lincoln Ave; ⊙11am-6pm Thu-Mon) 🌿 Hopscotch from the sidewalk into this arts-and-crafts cottage, transformed into a spellbinding art installation by Napa artist duo the Baker Sisters. The front parlor is Alice's Wonderland: deco teapots pour out fountain pens, and brass bands play on wax-cylinder recordings. The den is a DJ's dream, lined with Fillmore posters and crates of deep cuts, from owner/collector Gary Himelfarb's reggae-music-producing days.

Information

Calistoga Visitors Center & Chamber of Commerce (Map p188; ☎707-942-6333; www.visitcalistoga.com; 1133 Washington St; ⏰9am-5pm) Lodging info, maps, tasting passes and spa-deal coupons.

Getting There & Away

Calistoga is about a 100-minute drive from San Francisco.

Napa Valley Vine (p173) bus 10 connects Calistoga to St Helena and downtown Napa, where you can catch bus 11 to the Vallejo Ferry Terminal.

Getting Around

Downtown Calistoga is flat, easy and charming to walk or bike. If you're planning to visit restaurants, wineries or resorts further afield, you may want to drive. Hwys 128 and 29 split in Calistoga, where Hwy 29 turns east and becomes Lincoln Ave, continuing across Silverado Trail, toward Clear Lake. Hwy 128 continues north as Foothill Blvd.

Napa Valley Vine (p173) operates a Calistoga Shuttle, providing door-to-door service within city limits. To schedule a pickup, call 707-963-4229 during operating hours (7am to 9pm Monday to Thursday, to 11pm Friday and Saturday, 11am to 9pm Sunday). The service is free to guests staying at Calistoga motels and resorts, and just $1 for day visitors.

CARNEROS

Uncommon wine comes from this extraordinary stretch of common land. Historically, Carneros was shared by Patwin people on the east and Coastal Miwok to the west. When the US made California a state, Carneros became shared pastureland, spanning the boundaries of Napa and Sonoma counties. Mexican shepherds named these lowlands Los Carneros ('The Rams') back in the 1830s – and until recently, sheep had the run of the place.

In the 20th century, local ecologists saw land getting snapped up for development across California, so they formed the Sonoma Land Trust in 1976, conserving rare wetlands. Carneros conservation efforts helped preserve the cool coastal microclimates that make this land perfect for wooly sheep – and sun-sensitive, thin-skinned pinot noir grapes. Carneros began to bubble with excitement, producing some of California's most distinctive sparkling wines. Environmentally-minded Carneros grape-farmers also set aside private land for conservation, celebrating the local scenery with outdoor sculpture – including Donum Estate and di Rosa Center for Contemporary Art, where you'll notice steel sheep on the grassy hillside.

The losses from 2017 and 2019 wildfires were devastating, and Carneros faced an uncertain future. But flocks of sheep have come to the rescue: as they graze Carneros farms, vineyards and common land, they clear weeds that could become fire hazards and fertilize dry patches. So when you raise a toast in Carneros, don't forget to thank the sheep.

Sights

★di Rosa Center for Contemporary Art — ARTS CENTER

(☎707-226-5991; www.dirosaart.org; 5200 Hwy 121; adult/child under 17yr $18/free; ⏰10am-4pm Thu-Mon May-Dec; Ⓟ) Scrap-metal sheep dotting the hillside hint that something unusual is afoot on these 217 acres of Carneros countryside: contemporary art has taken over this farmstead. This groundbreaking collection was the passion of free-spirited reporter-turned-grape-farmer Rene di Rosa, who hung hyperrealist Robert Bechtle paintings on the ceiling and installed spooky Tony Oursler videos in his cellar. Today the gatehouse gallery showcases Viola Frey's monumental 1970s ceramic sculpture, David Best's art cars, and works by visiting California artists.

★Donum Estate — WINERY

(☎707-732-2200; www.thedonumestate.com; 24500 Ramal Rd; tours with tasting & food pairing from $95; ⏰10am-4pm, tours by appointment) Craving some Ai Weiwei with your chardonnay? You're in the right place: Donum Estate's jaw-dropping contemporary-art collection is literally put out to pasture, surrounded by lavender fields, vineyards and an organic farm. Take the 90-minute tour with a glass of chardonnay, wandering among Ai Weiwei's Chinese Zodiac bronzes, around Yayoi Kusama's polka-dotted pumpkin, through Gao Weigang's brass-tube maze, to Keith Haring's embracing figures – and discuss art over pairings of current-release wines and farm-to-fork bites ($95).

Artesa — WINERY

(☎707-254-2126; www.artesawinery.com; 1345 Henry Rd; tastings from $35, tour/glass $45/15; ⏰10am-5pm, last pour 4:30pm) 🍃 Enter the mysterious pyramid built into the Carneros hillside to discover a stunning all-white lounge with a tiled bar, pairing San Pablo Bay views with winemaker Ana Diogo-Draper's inspired lineup of albariño, rosé of pinot noir, and Galatea red blends (bottles $30 to $80). You may recognize this place from your dreams and/or the Maya Rudolph/Amy Poehler/Tina Fey buddy comedy *Wine Country* – and if you want to stage your own buddy comedy, they'll ship you a tasting kit of new-release wines.

Domaine Carneros WINERY
(☎707-257-0101; www.domainecarneros.com; 1240 Duhig Rd; tastings from $40; ⊙10am-5:30pm; P) 'In victory you deserve it, in defeat you need it,' Napoleon famously said. He meant Champagne, of course – who would expect a proper cuvée from California swampland? But that was before French Champagne house Taittinger opened Domaine Carneros, turning brut absolutists into California dreamers. Taste creamy cuvées on the Sparkling Flight ($40) or Bubbles and Bites pairing ($85), which easily passes as lunch. The cuvée-and-caviar tasting for two makes a fine occasion to pop the question while popping fish eggs ($350).

Patz & Hall WINERY
(☎707-265-7700; www.patzhall.com; 21200 8th St E; tastings $45-75; ⊙10am-4pm) Old friendships produce exceptional old wines at Patz & Hall, maker of prized California chardonnays. Cofounders/friends James Hall, Anne Moses, Donald and Heather Patz figured they could make wines to showcase exceptional grapes Sonoma friends were growing, and you can taste the results in tastings of four single-vineyard wines ($45) or six sparkling and still wines ($50). To explore the difference age can make for wine and friendships, take an old friend to taste library wines ($75, 90 minutes).

Robledo WINERY
(☎707-939-6903; www.robledofamilywinery.com; 21901 Bonness Rd; tasting $35; ⊙10am-5pm Mon-Sat, 11am-4pm Sun) Taste the American Dream at the Carneros winery built from the ground up by Reynoldo Robledo, who started in the industry as a farm worker in 1968 and became Sonoma's go-to vineyard expert. Reynoldo's kids run the family winery. Highlights include non-oaked sauvignon blancs, aged cabernets that haven't lost their edge, and heartwarming Los Braceros red blend – dedicated to the Mexican farm workers who kept America fed during WWII (bottles $20 to $110).

Scribe WINERY
(☎707-939-1858; www.scribewinery.com; 2100 Denmark St; tasting $35, food pairing $65; ⊙by appointment 11:30am-4pm Thu-Mon) In 1858 this hacienda was already growing grapes – but it's never been this hip. Brothers Andrew and Adam Mariani are the fourth-generation farmers who gave it new life, adding Nordic sofas, preserving fireplaces, and installing lighting that gives visitors angelic halos. At outdoor tables made from fallen redwoods, regulars dig into food pairings with terroir-driven pinot noir rosé and sparkling chardonnay. Traditionalists mock Scribe's millennial target-marketing, but subScribers helped sustain this estate through wildfires – so raise a toast to millennials, already.

Cornerstone Sonoma GARDENS
(☎707-933-3010; www.cornerstonesonoma.com; 23570 Arnold Dr; ⊙10am-5pm, gardens to 4pm; P) FREE This Wine Country garden and design showplace features 10 landscape-artist-designed gardens, five kid-friendly experiential-education gardens, local design boutiques, wine-tasting parlors, and on-site Sonoma Valley Visitors Bureau (p197) that's generous with trip advice and tasting-room passes. Stop by for farm-fresh local fare at family-friendly, indoor-outdoor **Palooza Beer Gardens**.

Activities

Sonoma Raceway RACING
(☎800-870-7223; www.sonomaraceway.com; 29355 Arnold Dr; tickets from $15; ⊙drag & drift races 4-10pm Wed) Maybe you're here to watch the pros at Nascar events, or to witness the summer spectacle of vintage cars hitting the track – but why not try it yourself? For $50, you can race your own car in Wednesday-night drag-and-drift races, where racers converge to compete for bragging rights.

Sleeping & Eating

Carneros Resort & Spa RESORT $$$
(☎707-299-4900; www.carnerosresort.com; 4048 Sonoma Hwy; d from $600; P) Guest cottages are chic sheds, with simple board-and-batten walls and corrugated-metal roofs – but inside they're low-key luxury, with cherry-wood floors, wood-burning fireplaces, heated-tile bathroom floors, giant tubs and indoor-outdoor showers. Mellow out in the hilltop infinity pool (for adults), make a splash in the family-friendly fitness pool, and indulge in the guest-only spa.

Angelo's Wine Country Deli DELI $
(☎707-938-3688; www.angelossmokehouse.com; 23400 Arnold Dr; sandwiches $7; ⊙9am-5pm) Look for the cow on the roof of this roadside deli south of town for fat sandwiches Angelo Ibleto makes with smoked meats and *un pizzico*

d'amore (a pinch of love). Try free samples of his famous homemade turkey and beef jerky, and score a jar of the must-have martini ingredient for any self-respecting Sonoma bartender: Angelo's jalapeño-stuffed olives.

Getting There & Away

Carneros is an AVA (American Viticulture Area) that spans Napa and Sonoma counties. If you're driving, Carneros is about 15 minutes from downtown Napa, 10 minutes from downtown Sonoma, and an hour from San Francisco.

Rideshares can get you to Carneros, but cellphone coverage is spotty.

Carneros' rolling hills pose a moderate challenge for cyclists.

SONOMA COUNTY

Sonoma is a vast county with an independent streak just as wide. Miwok, Pomo, Wintun and Wappo people thrived in this fertile land for about 10,000 years before they began trading with Russian trappers and Spanish ranchers, some 300 years ago. In the 1830s when Spain lost California to Mexico, the government decreed that Spanish mission territory should revert to native control – but that memo was somehow mislaid. Settlers snapped up extensive mission lands across Sonoma, including ranches and vineyards.

Then one drunken night in 1846, a motley group of partiers took over the Sonoma barracks, staggered over to Mexican General Vallejo's home to confiscate his brandy, and proclaimed a breakaway republic. The next morning, Sonoma awoke to a hangover for the ages and the realization that they were now living in the 'Bear Flag Republc' [sic], with a flag emblazoned with what looked like a wombat. After a month, the US military took over Sonoma, Vallejo became a US citizen and Sonoma's first state senator, and the barracks were converted into (what else?) a winery.

Sonoma County has remained a magnet for free spirits. In the 1880s, freed slave, self-made millionaire and civil rights pioneer Mary Ellen Pleasant opened her Sonoma Valley getaway Beltane Ranch, entertaining California's freewheeling elite with horse races and barnstorming dances. Adventure author Jack London built his dream ranch in Glen Ellen, attracting like-minded bohemians to Sonoma Valley. Romantics and rebels headed to Russian River Valley to frolic in the redwoods, establishing Guerneville as a pioneering LGBT+ resort in the early 1900s.

Sonoma's historic terraced vineyards and pristine forest parklands survived earthquakes, wildfires, even Prohibition amazingly intact – thanks to cleverly repackaged 'communion wine' sold by the trainload. Pioneering conservation initiatives have protected West Sonoma's ancient redwoods, and forward-thinking fire prevention directives help keep everyone safe. Across Sonoma, a new bear flag was raised in 2020: this time, the bear wears a fire helmet and hospital mask, and the slogan reads: 'Thank you first responders.' This calls for a toast: to resilient, life-loving, singular Sonoma.

Sonoma Valley

Sonoma Valley is an easy groove to fall into. Hwy 12 follows the footsteps of Miwok, Pomo and Wintun people, who called this enchanted place 'Valley of the Moon' – and its charms are undeniable. Century-old vines and community farms thrive in this uniquely rich soil, downhill from extinct volcano Mt St Helena to the east, and watered by underground mineral springs in the western Sonoma mountain range. Even a novelist can farm land this fertile, as you can see at Jack London State Park, where the adventure author preserved land from slash-and-burn agriculture and pioneered sustainable methods. Through the efforts of London and other pioneering Sonoma ecologists, some 13,000 acres are set aside as parkland.

The Valley of the Moon is a quick escape back to nature from San Francisco. But take a closer look at those hills: purple-brown burn scars reveal where wildfires swept through the valley in 2017, 2019 and 2020. While volunteer firefighters contained blazes, neighbors opened homes to evacuees, restaurants opened as service kitchens to keep everyone fed, and volunteers painstakingly cleared miles of debris on Sugarloaf Ridge. Consider this your chance to be a hero among heroes, and be mindful of fire advisories.

Now the valley has resumed its role as delightful host – fun-loving and down to earth, with a distinct gourmet flair. Most journeys here start in historic downtown Sonoma, with its lively town square, farm-proud restaurants, indie boutiques and dozens of tasting rooms. Heading up the valley, the tiny, quaint 19th-century resort town of Glen Ellen is full of surprises: acclaimed restaurants, recycled art masterpieces, rare Japanese maples, and luxury cottage hideaways. Further north, the collection of vineyards known as Kenwood lures you with wine, lavish picnics, and Sugarloaf hikes to appreciate where you've been – and how far this valley has come, while staying true to its roots.

Information

Sonoma Valley Visitors Bureau (Map p202; 866-966-1090; www.sonomavalley.com; 453 1st St E; 9am-5pm Mon-Sat, from 10am Sun) Offers guides, maps, pamphlets, wine-tasting passes and information on deals and events. There's another branch at **Cornerstone Sonoma** (707-996-1090; www.sonomavalley.com; 23570 Hwy 121; 10am-4pm).

Getting There & Away

Public transport is not convenient, but it can be done in a pinch. Call 511 or check online at www.transit.511.org.

Sonoma Valley is a 90-minute drive from San Francisco and about 45 minutes from Santa Rosa. You can get a rideshare to downtown Sonoma, but cell-phone coverage is spotty, so it might be tricky to get one when and where you need it.

To reach Sonoma Valley from San Francisco, take Hwy 101 north over the Golden Gate Bridge. Turn off 101 to take Hwy 37 east to Hwy 121 north; expect 60 to 90 minutes, depending on traffic.

From the East Bay (or downtown San Francisco), take I-80 east to Hwy 37 west (north of Vallejo). In Carneros, take Hwy 121 north to reach Sonoma Valley.

Getting Around

Sonoma County has more than 425 wineries, including around 40 in Sonoma Valley. If you want to go vineyard-hopping, you may want a car or bicycle.

Sonoma Hwy/Hwy 12 is lined with wineries and runs from Sonoma to Santa Rosa, then to western Sonoma County. Arnold Dr has less traffic (but few wineries) and runs parallel up the valley's western side to Glen Ellen.

Plan for at least five hours to visit the valley from bottom to top.

Downtown Sonoma & Around

Enchanted downtown Sonoma seems a world apart from mundane everyday life, and that's the way it's been for centuries. Native Americans once converged here at the village of Huichi to trade goods and songs, but many died in outbreaks of measles and smallpox that arrived with the Spanish priests of Mission Solano. Sonoma's mission vineyards were claimed by settlers, who proclaimed the short-lived Bear Flag Republic in 1846.

Sonoma remains staunchly independent-minded and proud of its singular vision, as you can see at community-run urban farm the Patch (p202) and the Huihuicha music festival at historic Gundlach-Bundschu Winery (p198). The town's pride and joy is the plaza – the largest town square in all of California, surrounded by local history, food and oh, yes: drink. Local wineries damaged by fires in 2017 and 2019 have mostly recovered, and the inspired vintages they're producing are proudly splashed across Sonoma menus.

Stroll downtown Sonoma blocks lined with trees and Victorians, and you'll find heritage inns, acclaimed bistros, indie boutiques and some 30 tasting rooms. A bicycle ride away are more parks, historic sites and (how did you guess?) more wineries. If you can ever tear yourself away, downtown Sonoma can be your launching pad to Carneros and Sonoma Valley. Just don't try launching your own republic, or the whole town might join you.

Sights

★Hanzell Vineyards — WINERY

(707-996-3860; https://hanzell.com; 18596 Lomita Ave; tasting $45, with farm tour $65; 11am-3pm Tue & Wed, to 4pm Thu & Sun, to 4:30pm Fri, Sat & Mon; P) Chickens perch on pigs snoring in the vineyards, as sheep graze all around: it's all in a day's work at Hanzell, Sonoma's most idyllic winery. First planted by philanthropist James Zellerbach in 1953, these vineyards are farmed holistically and organically to produce exceptional cool-climate chardonnays and pinot noirs. Take your seat in the historic stone barn alongside the resident cats, and you'll taste mists and sunshine swirling around your wineglass as you overlook Sonoma all the way to the bay.

★Sonoma Plaza — SQUARE

(Map p202; www.sonomaplaza.com; btwn Napa, Spain & 1st Sts) The largest plaza in California showcases everything Sonoma holds dear – food, community, art, history – flanked by indie restaurants, galleries and wine-tasting rooms. The Mission Revival–style city hall was inaugurated in 1908 with four identical facades, reportedly because plaza businesses all demanded City Hall face their direction. At the plaza's northeast corner, the **Bear Flag Monument** (Map p202; Sonoma Plaza) commemorates Sonoma's drunken independ-

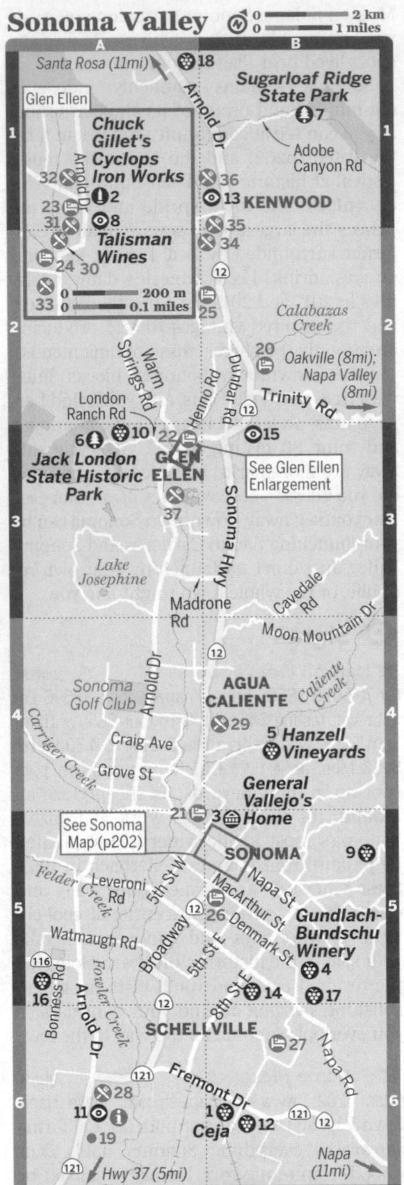

ence movement. The weekly farmers market (5:30pm to 8pm Tuesdays, April to October) showcases Sonoma's incredible produce.

★**General Vallejo's Home** HISTORIC BUILDING
(☎707-938-9559; www.sonomaparks.org; 363 3rd St W; adult/child $3/2; ⏲10am-5pm) When Mexico lost California to the US, General Vallejo lost his official position as Comandante of California Norte – but master strategist Vallejo quickly became a US citizen, a California senator, and spring-water supplier to the city of Sonoma. His estate was called Lachryma Montis (Latin for 'Tears of the Mountain' and a translation of its original Native name, Chiucuyem), after its natural spring. The Carpenter's Gothic-Victorian home he built next to the spring remained in the family until 1933, when the state bought it as a museum.

★**Gundlach-Bundschu Winery** WINERY
(☎707-938-5277; www.gunbun.com; 2000 Denmark St; tasting $25-35, incl tour $55-60; ⏲11am-5:30pm Sun-Fri, to 7pm Sat Apr-Oct, to 4:30pm Nov-Mar; Ⓟ) California's oldest family-run winery looks like a castle, but everyone gets a royal welcome at the bar. Six generations of Bundschus have kept the delightful dry Gewürztraminer flowing since 1858, while innovating winery practices – 'Gun-Bun' was the first American winery to introduce phylloxera-resistant vines, produce 100% merlot and install water-recycling ponds. Bike down a country lane past farmstead donkeys for wine tasting, tours of the 1800-barrel cave ($55) and picnics by the pond (bottles $20 to $50).

★**Sonoma State Historic Park** HISTORIC SITE
(Map p202; ☎707-938-9560; www.parks.ca.gov; 363 3rd St W; adult/child $3/2; ⏲10am-5pm; Ⓟ) Time-travel across 200 years of California history, with multiple sites in action-packed downtown Sonoma blocks – one ticket covers them all. Start your time-travel adventure in 1823 in **Mission San Francisco Solano** (Map p202; ☎707-938-1519; www.sonomaparks.org; 114 E Spain St; adult/child $3/2; ⏲10am-5pm), the adobe structure that anchors the plaza where the Native American village of Huichi once stood. Sonoma Barracks captures 19th-century life, and describes how Sonoma's Bear Flag Republic started. The 1886 **Toscano Hotel** (Map p202; ☎707-938-9560; www.sonomaparks.org; 20 E Spain St; adult/child $3/2; ⏲10am-5pm) lobby is beautifully preserved – peek inside – and Vallejo's stately 1852 home is a half-mile northwest.

Bartholomew Estate Winery WINERY
(☎707-509-0450; www.bartholomewestate.com; 1000 Vineyard Lane; tasting $25, with vineyard tour $45; ⏲11am-4:30pm; Ⓟ) This estate has seen it all: the 1857 start of California's wine industry under Hungarian count Agoston Haraszthy, devastation by phylloxera and

Sonoma Valley

Top Sights
1 Ceja ... B6
2 Chuck Gillet's Cyclops Iron Works ... A1
3 General Vallejo's Home ... B5
4 Gundlach-Bundschu Winery ... B5
5 Hanzell Vineyards ... B4
6 Jack London State Historic Park ... A3
7 Sugarloaf Ridge State Park ... B1
8 Talisman Wines ... A1

Sights
9 Bartholomew Estate Winery ... B5
10 Benziger ... A3
11 Cornerstone Sonoma ... A6
12 Homewood ... B6
13 Muscardini Cellars ... B1
14 Patz & Hall ... B5
15 Quarryhill Botanical Garden ... B3
16 Robledo ... A5
17 Scribe ... B5
18 St Francis Winery & Vineyards ... A1

Activities, Courses & Tours
Triple Creek Horse Outfit ... (see 6)
19 Vintage Aircraft Company ... A6

Sleeping
20 Beltane Ranch ... B2
21 El Pueblo Inn ... A5
22 Gaige House Inn ... A3
23 Glen Ellen Cottages ... A1
24 Jack London Lodge ... A2
25 Kenwood Inn & Spa ... B2
26 MacArthur Place ... B5
Sugarloaf Ridge State Park Camping ... (see 7)
27 Windhaven Cottage ... B6

Eating
28 Angelo's Wine Country Deli ... A6
29 El Molino Central ... B4
30 Fig Cafe & Winebar ... A2
31 Glen Ellen Inn & Martini Bar ... A1
32 Glen Ellen Star ... A1
33 Les Pascals Patisserie ... A2
34 Mayo Family Winery Reserve Room ... B2
35 Salt & Stone ... B1
36 Wine Truffle Boutique ... B1
37 Yeti ... A3

bankruptcy, the 1885 castle construction for millionaire philanthropist Kate Johnson and her 42 cats, and its 1919 conversion into a home for 'delinquent women' (read: sex workers and addicts) before fires destroyed it. A winery arose from the ashes, and despite fires in 2017 and 2019, these certified-organic vineyards are again producing sauvignon blanc, cabernet sauvignon and zinfandel.

Bedrock Wine TASTING ROOM
(Map p202; ☎707-343-1478; www.bedrockwine co.com; 414 1st St E; tasting $30; ⊙10am-3:30pm Wed-Sun) Every vintage is a taste of history, but at Bedrock Wines those flavors go back 150 years. Maverick winemaker Morgan Twain-Petersen is reviving California's old vine-field blends with grapes sourced from tiny NorCal blocs, including classic zinfandels, untrendy varietals like riesling, and obscure ones like alicante bouschet. In a historic saltbox cottage you can taste wines visitors may have sipped here 150 years ago.

Hawkes TASTING ROOM
(Map p202; ☎707-938-7620; www.hawkeswine.com; 383 1st St W; tasting $45-60; ⊙11am-6pm Thu-Mon) Step into a low-key downtown Sonoma bungalow to discover big-hearted cabernet sauvignons from Hawkes family-owned vineyards in Alexander Valley, where they've produced landmark single-varietal cabernets since 1972. Cab fans, reserve ahead for the 90-minute tasting of six estate cabs accompanied by a platter of cheese and charcuterie ($60). On sunny days, take that bottle of Hawkes' rosé or chardonnay to a sunny spot outside on the patio (bottles $30 to $70).

Activities

Wine Country Cyclery CYCLING
(Map p202; ☎707-966-6800; www.winecountry cyclery.com; 262 W Napa St; bicycle rental per day $30-80; ⊙11am-4pm Mon, Tue, Thu & Fri, 10am-5pm Sat & Sun) Downtown Sonoma is small, relatively flat and perfect for biking, and this reliable bike shop rents road bikes, electric bikes, hybrids, kids bikes and even tandem sport bikes (aka 'divorce-makers') to get you where you want to go for an hour or all day. Rentals include helmets, handlebar bag, and – crucially – a winery map. Book ahead.

Vintage Aircraft Company SCENIC FLIGHTS
(☎707-938-2444; www.vintageaircraft.com; 23982 Arnold Dr; 20min flight 1/2 people $175/270; ⊙Thu & Fri Apr-Oct by appointment, 10:30am-4pm Sat & Sun year-round;) See Sonoma vineyards from above in biplanes, with an option to add aerobatic maneuvers ($50 extra). Daredevils can do loops in open-cockpit biplanes, while gearheads geek out over 1942 navy fighter planes. Weekends are for walk-ins, so you can hop in that cockpit before you change your

mind. Flights run 20 minutes, and only take off when weather permits; ages 10-plus.

Sleeping

An Inn 2 Remember INN $$
(Map p202; ☎707-938-2909; www.aninn2remember.com; 171 W Spain St; d/ste from $185/245; ⊙closed Jan 1-15; P ⊖ ❄ 📶) Steps from Sonoma Plaza, this vintage 1910 charmer offers warm welcomes and private, comfortable lodgings with soothing modern farmhouse decor. Delightful Italian owners Paolo and Alice have thought of everything you need for a dream getaway, including in-room continental breakfasts, free bikes, picnic baskets and wine-tasting passes. The suites in the back have private entrances, candlelit fireplaces and secret garden patios.

Windhaven Cottage COTTAGE $$
(☎707-543-1621; www.windhavencottage.com; 21700 Pearson Ave; cottages $165-175; ⊖ ❄ 📶) Live the Sonoma life in a wooden cottage surrounded by edible gardens and vineyard views, with barbecues and bikes at the ready. Choose from two private hideaways with hot tubs and kitchenette: a romantic cottage with vaulted wooden ceilings and fireplace, or the handsome 800-sq-ft studio.

Hidden Oak Inn B&B $$
(Map p202; ☎707-996-9863; www.hiddenoakinn.com; 214 E Napa St; d $225-315; ⊖ ❄ 📶 🏊) Step under the wisteria bower into a 1914 California arts-and-crafts cottage, where three guest rooms have antique beds piled with fluffy down comforters. Guests are treated to personal attention from hosts and two cute dogs, with homemade breakfasts, afternoon wine and cheese, and the use of a couple of bicycles. Two-night minimum.

El Pueblo Inn MOTEL $$
(☎707-996-3651; www.elpuebloinn.com; 896 W Napa St; d $119-384; ⊖ ❄ @ 📶 🏊) One mile west of downtown, family-owned El Pueblo inn has sleek, lodge-style rooms with cushy beds. The spacious lawns and heated pool are perfect for kids; parents appreciate the 24-hour hot tub. Larger Sonoma rooms can accommodate families with extra beds, while smart-value California rooms have fireplaces, king beds and private patios. Check the website for deals.

MacArthur Place INN $$$
(☎707-938-2929; www.macarthurplace.com; 29 E MacArthur St; d/ste from $399/555; ⊖ ❄ @ 📶 🏊) A historic homestead nestled in 7-acre gardens is a freshly remodeled inn, full of easy graces. Luxury guest rooms along garden paths provide secluded hideaways, even though you're only a few blocks from the plaza. Best value are 1860s Burris House rooms, lavished with light and natural materials. Lounge away days at MacArthur's legit cocktail bar, porch cafe, on-site spa and organic Mediterranean bistro.

El Dorado Hotel BOUTIQUE HOTEL $$$
(Map p202; ☎707-996-3030; www.eldoradosonoma.com; 405 1st St W; d Sun-Thu $225-330, Fri & Sat $385-500; P ⊖ ❄ 📶 🏊) 🌿 Stylish stays in a local landmark right on Sonoma Plaza. The original 1843 adobe building has been thoughtfully remodeled with smart guest rooms that are eco-conscious, compact and comfortable, with high-end linens and private balconies overlooking the plaza or the fig-shaded courtyard. Enjoy the solar-heated saltwater pool, free bikes, tasty farm-to-table restaurant, and famous ice cream drizzled with Sonoma olive oil.

Eating

★**El Molino Central** MEXICAN $
(☎707-939-1010; www.elmolinocentral.com; 11 Central Ave; mains $12-16; ⊙9am-9pm; P 🍸 👪 🐾) 🌿 Unforgettable Wine Country meals combine sustainably homegrown ingredients and Sonoma's deeply rooted Mexican culinary traditions at this 1930s roadside diner. Zoraida's mother's red mole is as profound and tangy as the finest California zinfandel – get it slathered on banana-leaf-wrapped tamales or poblano-chicken enchiladas. *Tatemada birria* (slow-cooked goat) tacos with slapped-to-order organic stone-ground tortillas earn California-wide cult followings.

Taste of the Himalayas TIBETAN, NEPALI $
(Map p202; ☎707-996-1161; 464 1st St E; mains $10-20; ⊙11am-2:30pm Tue-Sun, 5-9pm daily; P 🍸 👪) Anyone can pair cabernet with burgers – raise the bar and try your newest Sonoma wine finds with *momos* (Tibetan dumplings), luscious lentil soup, and sizzling platters of tandoori lamb and plump chicken. With your day's haul of aromatic Carneros whites and Sonoma Valley old-vine zins (corkage $15), this casual Himalayan joint delivers peak Wine Country dining, Sonoma-style.

★**Tasca Tasca** TAPAS $$
(Map p202; ☎707-996-8272; www.tascatasca.com; 122 W Napa St; meals $16-26; ⊙11:30am-10pm Sun-Thu, to 11pm Fri & Sat; ❄) Sea, garden, land: choose where your next culinary adventure

begins, and this inspired tapas bar menu takes you there. Select three to seven small plates for a whirlwind tour that leads from Portuguese goat stew with potatoes to NorCal Dungeness crab empanadas, ending with sea-salt chocolate tarts and Sonoma olive-oil ice cream with 40-year-old madeira. Bravo.

Red Grape ITALIAN $$
(Map p202; ☎707-996-4103; http://theredgrape.com; 529 1st St W; pizzas & pastas $17-20; ⏲11:30am-9pm;) Choose red or white pizzas to go with red or white wines: you can't go wrong with downtown Sonoma's crowd-pleasing thin-crust pizzas. Prosciutto-arugula-goat cheese is a sauceless sensation, and the good-value wine list runs 300 deep. Local crowds pack the cavernous space on weekends.

Della Santina's ITALIAN $$
(Map p202; ☎707-935-0576; www.dellasantinas.com; 133 E Napa St; mains $19-28; ⏲11:30am-3pm & 5-9:30pm) The waiters have been here forever and specials rarely change, because Della Santina's classic Italian-American cooking is timeless: lasagna Bolognese oozing with béchamel, roast Sonoma duck with risotto, organic rotisserie chicken hot off the spit, and gnocchi *della nonna* (grandma's style). Reserve seats in the brick courtyard in summer, or bide your time with Sonoma-grown, Italian-varietal wines at the next-door enoteca.

Hopmonk Tavern Sonoma PUB FOOD $$
(Map p202; ☎707-935-9100; www.hopmonk.com; 691 Broadway; mains $16-19; ⏲11:30am-11pm Sun-Wed, to midnight Thu-Sat) An 1880 farmhouse comes roaring back to life as a booming tavern and year-round beer garden, serving a dozen Hopmonk microbrews plus guest beers on tap in type-specific glassware to gratify craft-beer sticklers. Stick around for live music Friday through Sunday, and brace for the Wednesday open mikes starting at 8pm.

★**Cafe La Haye** CALIFORNIAN $$$
(Map p202; ☎707-935-5994; www.cafelahaye.com; 140 E Napa St; mains $26-42; ⏲5:30-9pm Tue-Sat) Warm feelings are mutual between farmers and chefs, regulars and visitors at cozy La Haye, which champions produce sourced within 60 miles. Neighboring farmers earn co-star credits on seasonal favorites, including sherry-basted Wolfe Ranch quail with sourdough stuffing and hearty chopped salads with George's farm eggs and Humboldt Fog goat cheese. Save room for simple, sensational desserts such as yuzu-citrus cheesecake.

Girl & the Fig FRENCH $$$
(Map p202; ☎707-938-3634; www.thegirlandthefig.com; 110 W Spain St; mains $22-36; ⏲11:30am-10pm Mon-Thu, from 11am Fri & Sat, from 3pm Sun) French accents aren't required to order up hearty feasts of rustic fare here – Sondra Bernstein and her garden keep these bistro tables loaded with house-cured salami, velvety duck cassoulet, and aptly named roast-cauliflower steaks. The all-day and late-night menus accommodate busy wine-tasting schedules, including the three-course prix-fixe menu ($42) and obligatory Fig Royale (sparkling wine and house-made fig liqueur).

La Salette PORTUGUESE $$$
(Map p202; ☎707-938-1927; www.lasalette-restaurant.com; 452 1st St E; mains lunch $24-27, dinner $24-36; ⏲11:30am-2:30pm & 5:30-9pm Mon-Fri, 11:30am-9pm Sat & Sun) Turn up the romance at chef/owner Manuel Azevedo's contemporary Portuguese bistro, hidden behind the plaza. After grazing bar snacks at wine tastings, this is a dream retreat for elegant sit-down, white-tablecloth dinners of reinvented, locally sourced Portuguese classics like *caldeirada* (fisherman's stew) or *bacalhau no forno* (baked salt cod), followed by dessert platters paired with port or madeira.

☆ Entertainment

★**Sebastiani Theatre** CINEMA
(Map p202; ☎707-996-2020; www.sebastianitheatre.com; 476 1st St E; adult/child $11/9, 3D $14/11;) Offbeat is what Sonoma does best, and the plaza's community-run, 1934 Mission Revival cinema encourages that independent streak with global indie art-house films, director-led screenings of award contenders, locally produced documentaries on mushrooms and other Sonoma obsessions, and outrageously fun events like the Cat Video Festival – it's no competition, because every video is purr-fect.

Shopping

★**Vella Cheese Co** FOOD
(Map p202; ☎707-938-3232; www.vellacheese.com; 315 2nd St E; ⏲9:30am-6pm Mon-Fri, to 5pm Sat;) Move over, parmesan: Vella's two-year-aged dry jack is meant for shaving atop rustic dishes, and it has been making spaghetti Western for almost 100 years. The Mezzo Secco is another aged umami bomb, ideal for pairing with Sonoma's hearty reds.

Sonoma

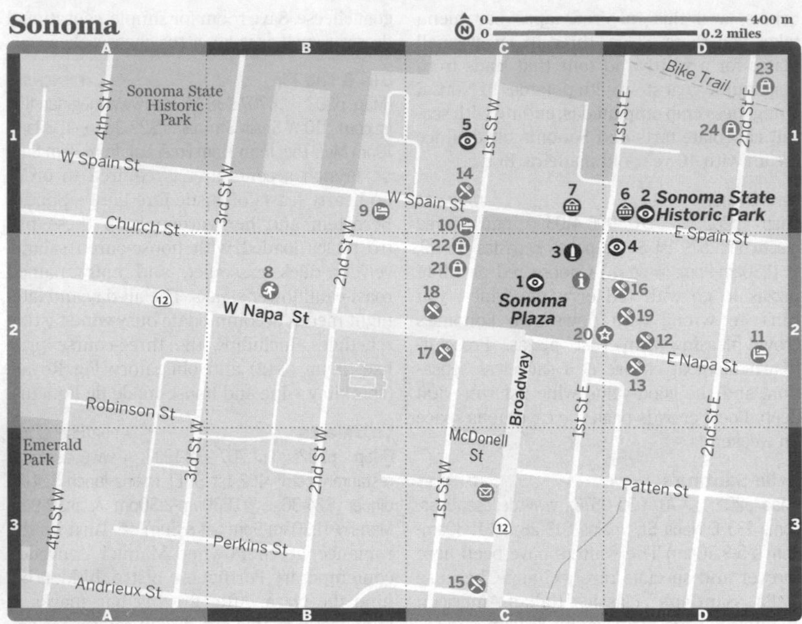

Sonoma

Top Sights
1 Sonoma Plaza C2
2 Sonoma State Historic Park D1

Sights
3 Bear Flag Monument C2
4 Bedrock Wine D2
5 Hawkes C1
6 Mission San Francisco Solano D1
7 Toscano Hotel C1

Activities, Courses & Tours
8 Wine Country Cyclery B2

Sleeping
9 An Inn 2 Remember B1
10 El Dorado Hotel C1
11 Hidden Oak Inn D2

Eating
12 Cafe La Haye D2
13 Della Santina's D2
14 Girl & the Fig C1
15 Hopmonk Tavern Sonoma C3
16 La Salette D2
17 Red Grape C2
18 Tasca Tasca C2
19 Taste of the Himalayas D2

Entertainment
20 Sebastiani Theatre D2

Shopping
21 Chateau Sonoma C2
22 Global Heart Fair Trade C2
23 Patch D1
Tiddle E Winks .... (see 13)
24 Vella Cheese Co D1

Staff graciously provide samples before purchase, and will vacuum-pack for shipping.

★ Patch FOOD
(Map p202; 260 2nd St E; ⏲9am-2pm Mon-Sat May-Nov; 👪) Right in downtown Sonoma, this historic patch is California's oldest community-run urban farm, beloved by neighbors and protected from developers for at least 150 years. Their pesticide-free, peak picnic produce is yours to select, weigh and pay for on the honor system – if no one's here, just leave your cash on the box.

Chateau Sonoma HOMEWARES
(Map p202; ☎707-309-1993; www.chateausonoma.com; 453 1st St W; ⏲10am-5pm) France whimsy meets California quirk at Sarah Anderson's curiosity cabinet of a shop, brimming with unique finds from scouring the countryside across continents. Here home decor doubles as Wine Country installation

art – scented soaps spill out of birds' nests, tarnished medicine cabinets hold sleek barware, vineyard cuttings become centerpieces in vintage enamel pitchers.

Global Heart Fair Trade GIFTS & SOUVENIRS

(Map p202; 707-939-2847; http://globalheartfairtrade.com; 423 1st Street W; 10am-6pm;) Everything you need to celebrate an occasion – unique handmade gifts, festive clothing and jewelry, cheerful recyclable decorations, artisan chocolates – plus a cause worth celebrating: all sales ensure living wages for talented makers worldwide. Global Heart is not only pro worker, it's worker-owned. Sonoman Sofie Wastell worked here for a decade before taking over the business.

Tiddle E Winks TOYS

(Map p202; 707-939-6933; www.tiddleewinks.com; 115 E Napa St; 10:30am-5:30pm Mon-Sat, 11am-5pm Sun;) Step back in time at this retro 1950s five-and-dime store, packed with nostalgic fun for all ages: wind-up toys, classic board games, lunch boxes for retro picnics, striped peppermint sticks and other penny candy – prices are adjusted for inflation, but totally worth it. They'll put together custom care packages for your favorite people – family, friends, teachers and first responders.

Getting There & Away

Downtown Sonoma is an hour's drive north from San Francisco. You can get a rideshare to downtown Sonoma, where many wine-tasting rooms, restaurants and attractions are within walking or cycling distance. Public transport is not convenient, but it can be done.

Glen Ellen & Around

A contender for the quaintest village in Sonoma, and quite possibly Northern California, tiny Glen Ellen (population 800) is a jumble of little cottages behind white picket fences along a poplar-lined creek.

Back in 1905, Glen Ellen was a swinging resort town with natural hot springs that lured California's rich and famous – including the world's most famous author at the time, Jack London, who built Beauty Ranch here as his writing retreat and pioneering organic farm. His widow, editor and fellow writer Charmian Kittredge London donated their estate to form Jack London State Historic Park, so that others could find inspiration in this retreat. The town has remained a magnet for trailblazing writers and artists, including gonzo journalist Hunter S Thompson, food writer MFK Fisher, Pixar animator John Lasseter (who now owns Glen Ellen railroad) and junk-art maestro Chuck Gillet.

Glen Ellen was badly scorched in the 2017 and 2019 fires, but nature is staging another glorious comeback here. Minus the distractions of bright city lights or star attractions, the nighttime sky above leafy Glen Ellen blazes with stars.

Sights & Activities

★ Jack London State Historic Park PARK

(707-938-5216; www.jacklondonpark.com; 2400 London Ranch Rd; per car $10, cottage admission $3; 9:30am-5pm;) He wrote the world's longest-running bestseller, *Call of the Wild*, and traveled the world over – but Jack London (1876–1916) claimed his greatest work was rescuing this 1400-acre preserve from early settlers' slash-and-burn farming methods. Beauty Ranch remains as Jack left it: Yokohama sailor shirts overflowing steamer trunks, cowboy hat hanging by his desk. A short but rugged hiking trail leads past Jack's gravesite to ruined Wolf House and House of Happy Walls (10am to 5pm), featuring Jack's rejection letters in the bookshop.

★ Chuck Gillet's Cyclops Iron Works PUBLIC ART

(Brazen Estates; 13623 Arnold Dr) Maestro of mess, recycling genius, folk-art legend: neighbors call Chuck Gillet, Esquire by many names, but people tend to forget he's a lawyer once they see the work of art he's made of his Glen Ellen home-studio. Over decades, he's reassembled rusted farm tools and auto parts into post-apocalyptic gargoyles that completely cover the 7ft-high fence. 'Private but peek freely,' says the sign next to a garden-sheared bat, peering shyly from the ivy. Message received: invitation accepted, artist respected.

★ Talisman Wines TASTING ROOM

(707-721-1628; www.talismanwine.com; 13651 Arnold Dr; tasting $30-40; noon-5pm) Talisman founder/winemaker team Scott and Marta Rich worked in major Napa wineries before they jumped the county line, collaborating with legendary pinot growers from Carneros to the Sonoma Coast. Join knowledgeable pourers and wine-collector regulars for a flight to remember, including sought-after library wines. Tasting fee waived with three-bottle purchase (bottles $30 to $70); call ahead.

Quarryhill Botanical Garden GARDENS
(707-996-3166; www.quarryhillbg.org; 12841 Hwy 12; adult/child 13-17yr $12/8; 9am-4pm) Just when you thought the vineyards would never end along Hwy 12, along comes this world-renowned 25-acre botanical garden specializing in the flora of Asia. Vines wouldn't grow on this abandoned quarry site, but over 30 years, founder Jane Davenport Jansen and a team of dedicated conservationists cultivated an artful woodland of Asian magnolias, dogwood, lilies and maples – including some that are now endangered in their native lands.

Benziger WINERY
(707-935-3000; www.benziger.com; 1883 London Ranch Rd; tastings $25-50, tours incl tasting for adults $30-55, kids $10; 11am-5pm Mon-Fri, from 10am Sat & Sun;) If you're new to wine, head to Benziger for Sonoma Valley's best crash course in winemaking. The worthwhile tour (45 or 90 minutes; reserve online) includes an open-air tram ride (weather permitting) through biodynamic vineyards, wine-cave visit and five-wine tasting. Picnics come with panoramic views of green hills badly scorched by 2017 and 2019 fires, but already rebounding wonderfully. Benziger's large-production wine is OK (head for the estate reserves); the tour's the thing. Bottles run $20 to $80.

Sleeping

Jack London Lodge MOTEL $
(707-938-8510; www.jacklondonlodge.com; 13740 Arnold Dr; d Mon-Fri $119-249, Sat & Sun $219-349;) Sprawl in a spacious, well-kept room with big comfy beds at this recently refurbished motel. Outside there's a pool and hot tub; continental breakfast buffets are included and held creekside, next door to the historic saloon. Walls are thin, so bring earplugs and request a room in the back. Check for online deals; two-night minimum during high-season weekends.

★**Beltane Ranch** INN $$
(707-833-4233; www.beltaneranch.com; 11775 Hwy 12; d $185-375;) African American millionaire venture capitalist and civil-rights pioneer Mary Ellen Pleasant built this ranch in 1892 as a country getaway to entertain influential friends, with a horse-racing track out front and dances in the barn. Beltane remains enchanted – the sunny yellow gingerbread-trimmed ranch house has wraparound porches where guests laze away days amid vineyards, parklands and horses grazing in pastures. Each suite has a discreet private entrance, and no phone or TV means zero distraction from pastoral bliss.

Glen Ellen Cottages BUNGALOW $$
(707-996-1174; www.glenelleninn.com; 13670 Arnold Dr; cottages Sun-Thu $159-189, Fri & Sat $239-329;) Hidden behind Glen Ellen Inn, these five creekside cottages are designed for romance, with oversized jetted soaking tubs, steam showers and gas fireplaces. After oysters and a nightcap at the inn's Martini Bar, you can drift off to the murmur of Calabazas Creek at your doorstep – and rest assured that coffee's in your room for tomorrow morning.

★**Gaige House Inn** INN $$$
(707-935-0237; www.thegaigehouse.com; 13540 Arnold Dr; d/ste from $279/699;) Down to earth meets fabulous at Gaige House. In the 1890s house, sleek, modern guest rooms are refurbished with elemental luxury: platform beds, cushy duvets, leather chairs. For rock-star-worthy hideaways, book a Japanese-inspired 'Ryokan Zen suite' that faces Calabazas Creek, complete with atrium rock garden, stone fireplace, and freestanding tub made from a hollowed-out boulder. Pricey but classy; breakfast and aperitifs included.

Eating

★**Les Pascals Patisserie** BAKERY, FRENCH $
(707-934-8378; www.lespascalspatisserie.com; 13798 Arnold Dr; pastries $3-8; 6am-6pm Mon, Tue, Thu & Fri, 7am-4pm Sat & Sun;) Everyone in Glen Ellen seems to have picked up a French accent since Les Pascals owner Pascale Merle and her husband, pâtissier Pascal Merle, moved to town. Once you try these flaky, butter-glossed croissants, impeccable baguettes and savory quiches, you too will be saying *ooh lala* – and there's an entire case of tarts, macarons and mille-feuille for dessert.

Fig Cafe & Winebar FRENCH, CALIFORNIAN $$
(707-938-2130; www.thefigcafe.com; 13690 Arnold Dr; mains $21-27, 3-course meal $39; dinner from 5pm;) Sondra Bernstein's earthy California comfort food is as satisfying as dinner gets. On the seasonal menu, look for succulent Sonoma duck, fig and arugula salad, and decadent steak frites with blue-cheese butter. Service is downright neighborly – through wildfires and COVID-19, these folks kept neighbors and staff fed. No reservations; complimentary corkage.

Yeti NEPALI $$
(707-996-9930; www.yetirestaurant.com; 14301 Arnold Dr; mains $14-26; 11:30am-3pm &

5-9:30pm; P ❄ ✐ 🚸) An old watermill that belongs on a Western movie set seems an unlikely destination for Nepali home cooking, but what a find. Tandoori lamb and chicken platters and naan are made to order in the wood-fired oven, while the well-annotated wine list proves you're in Sonoma. Reserve ahead to score a spot on the creekside patio.

Glen Ellen Inn & Martini Bar AMERICAN **$$**
(☎707-996-6409; www.glenelleninn.com; 13670 Arnold Dr; mains $16-25; ⏲3-9pm) Start with oysters with Bloody Mary sauce and pre-dinner drinks in the creekside garden, and you may never get around to dinner. Choose from creative vodka martinis (get the cucumber), classic Western gin martinis (dirty, extra olives),or signature Sonoma lavender lemon drop – but get all three and you might fall asleep in your tasty chicken pot pie.

Glen Ellen Star CALIFORNIAN, ITALIAN **$$$**
(☎707-343-1384; www.glenellenstar.com; 13648 Arnold Dr; pizzas $17-20, mains $24-50; ⏲5:30-9pm Sun-Thu, to 9:30pm Fri & Sat; ✐) The Wine Country star power here is formidable – co-owners are *Food & Wine* star chef Ari Weiswasser and Erinn Benziger-Weiswasser, from Benziger Winery – yet the vibes are relaxed, with easy banter in the open kitchen and buzzy crowds awaiting wood-fired-oven pizza, roasted fish, and pasta with spring-lamb ragù. Organic produce comes from Benziger gardens; definitely get those bacon-marmalade brussels sprouts.

Getting There & Away

Glen Ellen is an hour's drive north from San Francisco. It's also a nice bike ride from Sonoma – just 7 miles on quiet country roads. If you go over to Arnold Dr, Kenwood is another 5 miles north.

Kenwood & Around

If you think you must have missed downtown Kenwood, not to worry: there isn't one. This was Wappo country for roughly 10,000 years before Spanish and Mexican settlers claimed it and renamed it Rancho Los Guilicos. Later Anglophone arrivals found the name tricky to pronounce, and called it Kenwood instead. Today you can just call it vineyards, which stretch almost as far as the eye can see.

A few Kenwood-area landmarks have stood the test of time – including the 1860s little red schoolhouse, now Muscardini Cellars tasting room, and Sugarloaf Ridge, which narrowly survived 2017 and 2019 fires only through the heroic efforts of firefighters and local volunteers. Take a hike, raise a toast and enjoy a picnic, and you can say you did justice to vineyards – erm, Kenwood.

WHAT'S CRUSH?

Crush is autumn harvest, the time of year Wine Country lives for, when vine leaves turn brilliant colors and you can smell fermenting fruit on the breeze. Farmers throw big parties with vineyard workers to celebrate everyone's work. No one wants to miss the good times, and room rates skyrocket – reserve ahead and budget accordingly. To score party invitations, join your favorite winery's wine club.

Sights & Activities

★Sugarloaf Ridge State Park PARK
(☎707-833-5712; www.sugarloafpark.org; 2605 Adobe Canyon Rd; per car $8; P 🚸) Detour for beauty at this scenic park with 25 miles of fantastic hiking and biking. On clear days, Bald Mountain views stretch to the Pacific, while Brushy Peaks Trail overlooks Napa Valley. Both trails are moderately strenuous; plan on three hours round trip. For mellower nature experiences, check online for ecologist-guided forest-bathing walks and weekend stargazing at on-site Robert Ferguson Observatory. Temperatures can be blazingly hot in summer and fall, when wildfires are a concern – check conditions at the volunteer-run visitors center.

VJB Cellars WINERY
(☎707-833-2300; http://vjbcellars.com; 60 Shaw Ave; tasting $15; ⏲10am-4pm; P 🚸) Immigrants everywhere can relate: when the flavors you grew up with are half a world away, those cravings become insatiable. So the Belmonte family made a plan: start a restaurant, plant a vineyard, then join the two with a sunny piazza and call it VJB Cellars. You can taste the triumph in prized Italian wines grown in Sonoma that aren't often imported to the US, including robust white Friulano, summer-stormy aleatico rosé, plush red negroamaro, and cherry-chocolate barbera port. Bravi!

St Francis Winery & Vineyards WINERY
(☎707-538-9463; www.stfranciswinery.com; 100 Pythian Rd at Hwy 12; tasting $20, wine & food pairing $85; ⏲10am-5pm; P) St Francis' lovely vineyards look even better through the bottom

of your wineglass – but with food pairings, you might glimpse heaven. Friendly wine guides introduce five elegant, seasonal courses paired with sustainably Sonoma-grown St Francis wines – recent highlights include sunny rosé with earthy roasted beet ravioli, zesty zinfandel with juicy duck, and rich port with chocolate *budino*.

Sleeping

Sugarloaf Ridge State Park Camping CAMPGROUND **$**
(707-833-6084; www.reservecalifornia.com/CaliforniaWebHome; 2605 Adobe Canyon Rd; tent & RV sites $35, online reservation fee $7.99;) Camp out at this lovely hilltop park near Kenwood, with 48 drive-in sites, clean coin-operated showers and great hiking. The community pitches in to clear debris and maintain the self-guided nature trail. Show your support by buying dry firewood on-site to minimize sparks, practicing fire safety, and packing out what you bring in.

Kenwood Inn & Spa INN **$$$**
(707-833-1293; www.kenwoodinn.com; 10400 Sonoma Hwy; d $230-825;) Pass through lush gardens to reach secluded courtyards, where you can hear the fountain burbling and feel your blood pressure instinctively drop. For complete stress relief, the 30-room inn is equipped with two hot tubs, swanky on-site spa and private poolside cabanas ($209 per day). No kids; book an upstairs balcony room.

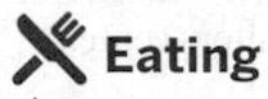

Eating

★La Cucina at VJB ITALIAN **$**
(707-833-2300; http://vjbcellars.com/la-cucina; 60 Shaw Ave; meals $8.50-20; 10am-4pm;) For Sonoma Valley's most authentic Italian fare, order at the counter of VJB's Italian-varietal winery. Chef/VJB co-founder Maria Belmonte makes her *sugo* (sauce), pesto and mozzarella from scratch, for impeccable caprese panini and sauce-dunked meatballs – but you may discover new favorites in her *porchetta* (slow-roasted pork) with grilled eggplant, and arugula salads lavished with ricotta, pistachios and lemon vinaigrette.

★Wine Truffle Boutique CHOCOLATE, ICE CREAM **$**
(707-238-2042; www.winetruffleboutique.com; 60 Shaw Ave, at VJB Winery Marketplace; gelato $4-6, chocolates from $4; noon-4pm;) Trust your chocolate cravings to Sonoma chocolatiers Libby Miller and Regina Taormina Rolland, who customize boxes of truffles infused with California wines. That glowing cold-case features their artisan gelato, including dark chocolate made with 65% Dutch-process cocoa and fresh cream, seasonal Sonoma flavors like Meyer lemon, and lactose-free wonders like peach *bellini sorbetto* with freshly pureed peaches and prosecco.

Salt & Stone CALIFORNIAN, FRENCH **$$**
(707-833-6362; www.saltstonekenwood.com; 9900 Hwy 12; mains $15-25; 11am-9pm Thu-Mon, 2:30-9pm Tue & Wed) Stop here for a fortifying lunch of French, Sonoma-grown bistro fare. Find a patio spot by the fountain to begin with an oyster flight, or proceed directly to duck confit Cobb salad, crab Louie, or a fresh take on a *croque madame*: prosciutto and Gruyère with roasted tomato, leeks and broccolini.

Mayo Family Winery Reserve Room CALIFORNIAN **$$$**
(707-833-5504; www.mayofamilywinery.com; 9200 Sonoma Hwy; 7-course menu incl wine pairing $70; by appointment 10:30am-6:30pm Thu-Mon) Wining and dining are better together at Mayo Family Winery, where seven-course menus of seasonal small plates are designed to showcase its reserve wines. On recent menus, silky grenache blanc brought out the sweetness in Dungeness crab *temaki* (hand rolls), old-vine zinfandel added spice to Tunisian chicken couscous, and reserve alicante bouschet brightened earthy Korean short ribs.

Getting There & Away

Kenwood is about 75 minutes by car from San Francisco. It's 12 miles north of downtown Sonoma and 5 miles north of Glen Ellen – a nice bike ride through scenic vineyards. Santa Rosa is another 20 minutes north of Kenwood by car.

Santa Rosa

The Sonoma County seat is a city of flowering, pleasant neighborhoods and startlingly bold initiatives, starting with its 1841 founding by *ranchera* María Ygnacia Lopez de Carrillo. Her son Julio Carrillo become a forward-thinking urban planner, laying out a neat city grid with a public square at the center. Cheerful retro storefronts still beckon visitors into mom-and-pop shops around Old Courthouse Sq, and historic Railroad Sq greets commuters arriving on tracks first laid by local Chinese laborers in the 1870s.

Wine Country's biggest town is timeless Americana, with neighbors waving hello from cottage rose gardens at bicyclists peddling rails-to-trails greenway Joe Rodota Trail. Seems like a vintage comic-strip backdrop, because it is: *Peanuts* creator Charles Schulz lived, dreamed and doodled here, as you'll see in his cartoon museum.

Walk around the tree-shaded, mural-lined streets of **SofA**, the South of A St Art District, and you can't help but stop and smell the flowers – many are fragrant heirloom varietals developed for delight, usefulness and sustainability just up the street at Luther Burbank Home & Gardens. Santa Rosa is so leafy and laid-back, it's hard to believe it survived two earthquakes and wildfires – but the city named for the patron saint of first responders was always destined to be a survivor.

Sights & Activities

Charles M Schulz Museum MUSEUM
(707-579-4452; www.schulzmuseum.org; 2301 Hardies Lane; adult/child $12/5; 11am-5pm Mon & Wed-Fri, from 10am Sat & Sun; P) Beloved in 75 countries, *Peanuts* comic strip was drawn in Santa Rosa by cartoonist Charles Schulz – and this museum follows the journey of Snoopy, Charlie Brown, Lucy and the gang from their 1950 introduction to last laughs in 2000. Downstairs are original Schulz drawings; upstairs are artists' tributes to *Peanuts*, plus an exacting recreation of Schulz' art studio.

Luther Burbank Home & Gardens GARDENS
(707-524-5445; www.lutherburbank.org; 204 Santa Rosa Ave; grounds free, tour adult/child $10/5; gardens 8am-7pm Apr-Dec, to 5pm Nov-Mar, museum 10am-4pm Tue-Sat, 11am-3pm Sun) Pioneering horticulturist Luther Burbank (1849–1926) cultivated 800 hybrid plant species over 50 years, aiming for delight, usefulness and sustainability. He used his own backyard as a testing ground, and you can see his experiments with flowers, cacti and medicinal plants in these well-annotated gardens. Burbank's Greek-revival home and the adjoining **Carriage Museum** showcase his life and work, but you can also take a free self-guided cell-phone tour of the grounds.

Farmers Market MARKET
(www.wednesdaynightmarket.org; Old Courthouse Sq; 5-8:30pm Wed mid-May–Aug;) A street party disguised as a farmers market fills Old Courthouse Sq on Wednesday summer nights. Join barnstorming good times starring Sonoma's organic farmers, live music, craft beer gardens and mom-and-pop food vendors. If you're really just after produce, a second smaller farmers market meets year-round, rain or shine, on Wednesdays and Saturdays 9am to 1pm at Santa Rosa Veterans Building.

Festivals & Events

Sonoma Harvest Fair WINE
(http://harvestfair.org; 1350 Bennett Valley Rd, Sonoma County Fairgrounds; Oct) All that wine tasting prepared you for this: a grand tasting of Sonoma's best, from 100 wineries. This is America's biggest and arguably toughest wine competition – 1000 wines judged blind, by winemakers, sommeliers and critics – but try and see if you agree with Double Gold winners. Feast on award-winning food, and witness the spectacularly splashy World Championship Grape Stomp.

Sleeping

Sandman MOTEL $$
(707-293-2100; www.sandmansantarosa.com; 3421 Cleveland Ave; d $120-300; P) Chill out California-style at this retro-hip motel brimming with cheeky art, shaggy macramé, and laid-back Sonoma swagger. Rooms are spacious, relaxed and good value, with

BEST SONOMA WINERIES FOR EVERY INTEREST

Vineyard walks Sutro Wine (p230), Hanzell Vineyards (p197), Donum Estate (p194)

Natural and sustainable wines Preston (p225), Porter Creek (p222), Pax Wines (p210)

Drinking for a cause Equality Vines (p222)

Inspiring views Iron Horse (p214), Bella (p225), Soda Rock Winery (p230)

Rebels and trailblazers Merry Edwards (p210), Gundlach-Bundschu Winery (p198), **Ceja** (707-255-3954; www.cejavineyards.com; 22989 Burndale Rd; tastings from $20; 10am-5pm; P)

Hidden gems Porter-Bass (p221), Carpenter Wine (p230), Emmit-Scorsone Wine (p225)

Food and wine pairings House of Flowers (p222), Idlewild (p225)

Collector favorites Bohème Wines (p216), Talisman Wines (p203)

complimentary breakfast bar, gym and morning yoga classes. Kick back outside in the heated pool, hot tub, pool house bar, bocce court, fire-pit patio, and backyard where local musicians play sets on summer weekends.

Hotel E BOUTIQUE HOTEL $$
(☎707-481-3750; www.hotelesantarosa.com; 37 Old Courthouse Sq; d $199-217) Towering grandly over Old Courthouse Sq, this beaux arts beauty with its signature clock tower is Santa Rosa's newest boutique hotel. Once a Bank of Italy outpost, the 1908 Empire Building now offers stylish stays in cozy rooms with cushy beds and tall windows, with imperial views over the Santa Rosa skyline.

Hotel La Rose HISTORIC HOTEL $$
(☎707-579-3200; www.hotellarose.com; 308 Wilson St; d Mon-Fri $149-199, Sat & Sun $209-269;) Step off the train and back in time at this historic Railroad Sq inn. Built by Italian stonemasons after the 1906 earthquake leveled Santa Rosa, it's a symbol of Sonoma's resilience. Request characterful inn rooms featuring sloping eaves, floral patterns galore and four-poster beds piled with duvets, rather than boxy condo rooms at the 1985 'carriage house' across the street.

Eating

Criminal Baking Co BAKERY $
(☎707-888-3546; www.criminalbaking.com; 808 Donahue St; baked goods $2-6; 7:30am-2pm Mon-Fri, from 8am Sat & Sun;) Slip through a warehouse side door, and join the line of regulars about to do something Criminal. Approach the counter for triple-cheese knishes, deep-dish quiches, quinoa salad bowls and toasted-rye chocolate-chip cookies. There's sometimes room in the back, with live music on weekends – or make a clean getaway to the park across the street for a picnic.

Taqueria Las Palmas MEXICAN $
(☎707-546-3091; 415 Santa Rosa Ave; dishes $3-11; 9am-9pm;) Tucked away in the corner of a parking lot, Las Palmas invites passersby indoors with a cacophony of color on the walls and the unmistakable aroma of *carnitas* (barbecued pork) on the grill. Load up tacos or forearm-size burritos with homemade salsas, and head to the park up the block for an urban Wine Country picnic.

Cascabel MEXICAN $$
(☎707-521-9444; 909 Village Ct; mains $10-22; 4-9pm;) Welcome to California, where suburban strip-mall Mexican may just rock your world. Tangy-spicy ancho-guajillo tortilla soup warms the toes, *cochinita pibil* (slow-braised pork) melting into plump charro beans stirs the soul, and *aguachile* (shrimp, cucumber, and serrano chili pickled in lime juice) sends taste buds surfing. Sonoma winemakers throng tequila-fueled 3pm to 6pm happy hours.

Rosso Pizzeria & Wine Bar PIZZA $$
(☎707-544-3221; www.rossopizzeria.com; 53 Montgomery Dr; pizzas $16-19; 11:30am-9pm Sun-Thu, to 10pm Fri & Sat;) No opera aria compares to the sound of Sonoma-grown ingredients sizzling atop crisp Neapolitan pizzas, fresh from Rosso's wood-fired oven. Get the margherita with housemade mozzarella – local mushrooms or prosciutto optional – plus a pile of oven-roasted, caramelized beets or brussels sprouts on the side. Trust your sommelier-trained server to pair Sonoma wines from the 100-strong wine list.

Bird & Bottle AMERICAN $$$
(☎707-568-4000; www.birdandthebottle.com; 1055 4th St; small plates $10-23; 11:30am-9:30pm Sun-Thu, to 10pm Fri & Sat;) When you're not sure what you're craving, try a little bit of everything at Bird & Bottle: Dungeness crab hush puppies, Nashville spicy fried chicken, pork-belly Cobb salad, pastrami street tacos. Share three to five small plates of rich dishes to feel decadent, but not overly full – plus inspired craft cocktails like blood-orange Macho pisco sours in solo and shareable sizes.

Drinking & Entertainment

★**Russian River Brewing Co** BREWERY
(☎707-545-2337; www.russianriverbrewing.com; 729 4th St; 11am-midnight;) Santa Rosa is the craft-beer capital of Wine Country, and this always-busy brewery is one major reason why – releases of its notoriously bitter double IPA Pliny the Elder prompt campouts at the door. Watch bearded brew fanatics take their first timid sips of brain-rattling, triple-IPA Pliny the Younger, and get pizza to go with that wine-barrel-aged sour beer.

Willi's Wine Bar WINE BAR
(☎707-526-3096; https://starkrestaurants.com/stark-restaurant/willis-wine-bar; 1415 Town & Country Dr; 11:30am-9:30pm Tue-Sat, 5-9pm Sun & Mon) Choose your own wine-tasting adventure with a vast menu of wines available as 2oz pours, plus flights comparing Sonoma and international wines. Grab a spot on the heated patio or sociable bar, and pair with

Sonoma cheese platters or chef Mark Stark's Mediterranean tapas – including Moroccan lamb chops, skillet-roasted shrimp and craving-inducing roasted carrots.

A'Roma Roasters CAFE
(☎707-576-7765; www.aromaroasters.com; 95 5th St, Railroad Sq; ⏲6am-11pm Mon-Thu, to midnight Fri, 7am-midnight Sat, to 11pm Sun; 📶) Even the aroma of coffee roasted on-site at A'Roma is powerful enough to propel Railroad Sq commuters onto their trains, while cyclists stop by to power up on Babe's Rocket Fuel blend before hitting the Joe Rodota Trail. Join regulars for live acoustic music on Saturday evenings and anything-goes Monday open-mike nights.

Moonlight Brewery BREWERY
(☎707-528-2537; https://moonlightbrewing.com; 3350 Coffey Lane, Suites A & D; ⏲4-9pm Wed-Fri, from 1pm Sat & Sun) Beer fans don't trek out to this industrial-park brewery for the atmosphere, the pub grub or cornhole – all nonexistent. They're lured here by Death and Taxes, Moonlight's memorable black lager. But this taproom also pours five other styles with original twists, including Misspent Youth pale ale and Reality Czech pilsner.

Shopping

★Flora Terra DISPENSARY
(☎707-978-5978; https://floraterraca.com; 1825 Empire Industrial Ct, Suite A; ⏲10am-9pm) Cannabis farmers across Northern California converge in Santa Rosa's warehouse district to process cannabis into THC edibles, CBD-enriched products and other adult treats – but here at Sonoma's farm-to-spliff destination dispensary, you can actually say hi(gh) to the plants growing on-site. Flora Terra offers organic, local, indie products for 'cannascurs,' from High Gorgeous CBD facials to Garden Society THC-chocolates. ID required.

★Miracle Plum FOOD & DRINKS, ARTS & CRAFTS
(☎707-708-7986; www.miracleplum.com; 208 Davis St; ⏲10am-7pm Tue-Sat, to 4pm Sun) Cross a Sonoma farmers market with an art gallery, and hello, Miracle Plum. The front gallery showcases trippy drawings, deconstructed stoneware pitchers and Kesslyr Dean block-print napkins. The adjoining Wild West–style general store is lined with finds from curators-owners Sallie Miller and Gwen Gunheim: Meyer lemon paste, solstice candles, Sonoma olive oil, stellar natural wines, and playing cards featuring women culinary legends.

★Made Local GIFTS & SOUVENIRS
(☎707-583-7667; www.madelocalmarketplace.com; 529 4th St; ⏲10am-6pm) One-stop shopping for one-of-a-kind, made-in-the-North-Bay finds: Sonoma cabernet ice tea, obligatory tie-dyed baby onesies for Sonoma farmers market outings, Sonoma wool cat toys filled with organic catnip, and striking candle holders carved from a storm-felled Sonoma redwood. Prices vary by individual maker, but are typically lower than you'll find elsewhere – proceeds go to the makers in this collective market.

Batcave Comics & Toys COMICS, TOYS
(☎707-755-3432; https://batcavecomicsandtoys.com; 100 4th St; ⏲10am-8pm Wed-Sun) Of course the hometown of *Peanuts* creator Charles Schulz has a dream basement vintage comic-book and toy store. Owner Mike Holbrook knows that one toy that got away still haunts you – that's why he's tracked down original 1980s Donkey Kong video games, 1970s radio-controlled R2-D2s, and *Spider-Man* issues all the way back to the 1960s.

Information

California Welcome Center & Santa Rosa Visitors Bureau (☎800-404-7673, 707-577-8674; www.visitsantarosa.com; 9 4th St; ⏲9am-5pm) Same-day lodging assistance. At Railroad Sq, west of Hwy 101; take downtown exit from Hwy 12 or 101.

Santa Rosa Memorial Hospital (☎707-525-5300; www.stjoesonoma.org; 1165 Montgomery Dr; ⏲24hr) Wide range of health services; houses the region's trauma center.

Getting There & Away

Sonoma County Airport Express (p173) runs shuttles ($38) between Sonoma County Airport (p173) (Santa Rosa) and San Francisco and Oakland airports.

Golden Gate Transit (p173) buses run between San Francisco and Santa Rosa (adult/youth $13/6.50); board at 1st and Mission Sts in SF.

Greyhound (p173) buses run from San Francisco to Santa Rosa ($21 to $38).

SMART (p173) offers train service from the Sonoma County Airport station (1 mile from the airport via Sonoma County Transit bus 55) and Santa Rosa's Railroad Sq to Marin's Larkspur ferry terminal, where you can catch the Bay Ferry (p173) to San Francisco.

Sebastopol

No amount of fermented grapes can explain free-spirited Sebastopol. In the 19th century, independent Pomo villagers and immigrant apple farmers formed a US township in the Pomo homeland of Bitakomtara. According to legend, an epic local bar brawl was jokingly compared to the famous Crimean War battlefront, and the nickname Sebastopol stuck.

While the rest of Wine Country started growing grapes, Sebastopol kept growing heirloom apples and wildflowers developed by local horticulture hero Luther Burbank. Back-to-the-land hippies brought fresh ideas to western Sonoma, including organic farming, home beekeeping and marijuana cultivation. You can visit many trailblazing local farms using the **Sonoma County Farm Trails Guide** (www.farmtrails.org), and admire the fruits of local labor at Sebastopol's organic market. At Solful (p213) farm-to-spliff cannabis dispensary you might meet Robert Jacob, the first cannabis dispensary owner to be elected mayor of a US town at age 36.

Anywhere you go in Sebastopol, you can't miss the local characters. Tom Waits lives on the outskirts of town, and Grateful Dead drummer Mickey Hart occasionally joins jam sessions at People's Music (p213). Or take a walk down Florence Ave, lined with recycled-art creatures Patrick Amiot made for his neighbors. Even after 160 years, Sebastopol keeps bringing legends to life.

Sights

★Merry Edwards — WINERY

(Map p220; ☎888-388-9050; www.merryedwards.com; 2959 Gravenstein Hwy N; ⏰walk-ins 9:30am-4pm, in-depth tastings by appointment 9:30am, 11am, 1pm, 2:30pm & 4pm; P) While chef Alice Waters established California cuisine, Merry Edwards was championing California wine – becoming the first woman in Napa's Winemakers' Hall of Fame, and earning her James Beard Award. But in 1973, as one of the first women to earn her master's from UC Davis' esteemed oenology program, she couldn't get hired in Napa. So Merry came to Sonoma, and discovered that a virus attacking pinot noir was susceptible to heat – saving vines and putting California pinots on the map.

★Pax Wines — TASTING ROOM

(Map p220; ☎707-331-1393; https://paxwine.com; 6780 McKinley St No 170; tastings $16-20; ⏰11am-6pm Sun-Thu, to 8pm Fri & Sat; P) Sunlight streams through the garage door, the vinyl's spinning, and over on the scuffed leather couch, your flight is taking off with Pax Trousseau Gris. Like every natural wine Pax and Pam Mahle make, it's been massaged into existence – raised with zero chemicals, crushed by hand, fermented with natural yeast, and left alone to absorb the mysteries of the universe before bottling. Your flight reaches giddy granite peaks with gamay noir, before mellowing into signature cool-climate syrahs: bliss.

★Patrick Amiot Junk Art — GALLERY

(Map p220; ☎707-824-9388; www.patrickamiot.com; 382 Florence Ave; P) FREE A cow rides a tractor, a rocket blasts off the lawn, and a dinosaur grabs a red convertible for lunch: it's all happening on Florence Ave, in sculptures Patrick Amiot made for neighbors' yards from recycled junk. You'll spot more around Sebastopol, but Amiot's block hosts three of the best: tin-can firefighters in a bathtub-sized fire truck, a sprinting waitress made of cutlery and – in a driveway with a powder-blue VW Beetle – a tiny driver in a recycled-fuel-can Beetle.

★Sebastopol Farmers Market — MARKET

(Map p220; ☎707-522-9305; www.sebastopolfarmmarket.org; 6932 Sebastopol Ave; ⏰10am-1:30pm Sun;) Vats of organic kombucha, small-batch elderberry syrup, dried maitake-mushroom jerky: this isn't your standard farmers market fare, and Sebastopol is proud of it. Kids instinctively skip toward this market, where local musicians perform and free samples and good vibes abound. Artists and activists converge here too – for a donation, you can pick up artist Michael Bridge's hand-drawn greeting card of a toilet saying, 'Raise Your Consciousness: Lower the Lid.' Park where you can; arrive hungry and open-minded.

★Spirit Works Distillery — DISTILLERY

(Map p220; ☎707-634-4793; www.spiritworksdistillery.com; 6790 McKinley St No 100; tasting 4/6/cocktails $12/18/16; ⏰11am-5pm Wed-Sun) Take it slow and easy at Spirit Works, where dangerously smooth-drinking small-batch spirits like sloe gin, rye whiskey, barrel gin and vodka come from organic California red-winter wheat. Taste current releases straight (1.5oz total) to savor the 'grain-to-glass' process – all milling, mashing, fermenting and distilling happens on-site. Sample inspired mini-cocktails, from refreshing Bees Knees (barrel gin, lemon, Sonoma honey) to the Bessie Williamson (sloe gin, basil, apricot shrub, bitters, lime), named for the first woman to run a Scottish whiskey distillery.

★ Barlow MARKET
(Map p220; ☎707-824-5600; www.thebarlow.net; cnr Sebastopol Ave & Morris St; ⏲hours vary; P 👪) Sebastopol's old apple-cannery sheds have been creatively repurposed by upstart makers into a hip, 12-acre village of indie food producers, artists, winemakers, coffee roasters, gardeners, distillers and restaurateurs. Wander shed to shed, meet artisans in their workshops, and accept generous offers to taste everything – especially Pax Mahle's natural wines, Two Dog Night's Sonoma-cream gelato, and Spirit Works' craft cocktails. Drift over to Fern Bar for dinner and live music, and toast to Sebastopol's uncanny creativity.

Luther Burbank's Gold Ridge Experiment Farm GARDENS
(Map p220; ☎707-829-2361; https://wschs.org/farm; 7777 Bodega Ave; ⏲sunrise-sunset) Radical ideas have quietly taken root in this Sebastopol garden over 140 years. This sunny hillock is where pioneering horticulturalist Luther Burbank cultivated 800 heirloom varietals for sustainability and utility, but also sheer delight – the stately, blight-resistant 1885 walnut tree here was one of his earliest successes, but the popular favorites remain Shasta daisies, the hybrid of daisies from three continents introduced here in 1901. Plants are thoughtfully labeled and picnic tables provided for all to enjoy.

Littorai WINERY
(Map p220; ☎707-823-9586; www.littorai.com; 788 Gold Ridge Rd; tasting $40, tour & tasting $60; ⏲by appointment 10am-4pm Mon-Sat; P) Climbing the hillside to Littorai, you may wonder: where are the grapes? Vineyards are a minority crop on Littorai's 30-acre biodynamic estate: 8 acres are woodlands, 14 are cow pastures, and the rest are vineyards and companion gardens that attract bees, birds and beneficial insects for an integrated ecosystem. Take the tour, or head directly into the winery for private single-vineyard tastings (six people maximum), and taste the difference a year or plot can make in sustainable Sonoma chardonnays and pinot noirs.

Horse & Plow TASTING ROOM
(Map p220; ☎707-827-3486; 1272 Gravenstein Hwy N; flights cider/wine/with cheese pairing $15/20/22; ⏲11am-5pm; P 👪) Chickens pose on one leg and fluff their feathers importantly – they're used to admirers flocking to their barnyard for long, sunny afternoons of hard cider and easy living. Heirloom apples from the backyard orchard and Sebastopol's pioneering organic farmers come shining through thanks to minimal-intervention cider-making methods – and the Gravenstein's a tart standout. Biodynamically farmed grapes are handled just as gently, yielding natural wines that open with a fizz and settle into plush, offbeat charmers.

Festivals & Events

Gravenstein Apple Fair FOOD & DRINK
(www.gravensteinapplefair.com; 500 Ragle Rd, Ragle Ranch Park; ⏲Aug; 👪) Celebrate Sebastopol's heirloom Gravenstein apple harvest with a weekend of live entertainment, local arts and crafts, Sonoma-grown food, cider, microbrews and wine, kids activities and the wildest apple-pie baking contest in the West.

Sleeping

Fairfield Inn & Suites HOTEL $$
(☎707-829-6677; www.marriott.com; 1101 Gravenstein Hwy S; d $149-354;) Modern farmhouse styling makes this Marriott a bit more relatable than other chain hotels in Sonoma, and extras like in-room refrigerators, flat-screens with cable, and slick bathrooms sweeten the deal. Downstairs there's a gym, convenience store, and cafe for complimentary breakfast buffets; outdoors, there's a pool plus hot tub. From here, it's a mile to downtown Sebastopol.

Eating

★ Sebastopol Cookie Co BAKERY $
(☎707-824-4040; 168A N Main St; pastries $2-5; ⏲6:30am-5pm Wed-Sun; 👪) When spirits and blood sugar dip, follow tantalizing aromas into this indie bakery for restorative triple-chocolate cookies, snickerdoodles, and signature backpacker cookies – with oats, raisins, chips and love, it's everything you need to conquer mountains. They open early to serve farmers coffee and hot pastries, and help hikers power up with homemade trail mix and white-chocolate lavender lattes.

★ Mom's Apple Pie DESSERTS $
(Map p220; ☎707-823-8330; www.momsapplepieusa.com; 4550 Gravenstein Hwy N; pies $7-17; ⏲10am-6pm; 👪) 'Mom' Betty Carr began her search for the ultimate all-American pie in the 1960s, leading from her native Japan to Sonoma, where she fell in love with an apple farmer – and the rest is edible history. Enjoy her signature cinnamon-sprinkled

Gravenstein pie or seasonal-favorite olallieberry still warm, piled with vanilla ice cream.

Bohemian Creamery CHEESE $

(Map p220; www.bohemiancreamery.com; 7380 Occidental Rd; cheese from $4; ⌚10am-6pm Fri-Sun; P 👪) Break free from boring cheese molds at Bohemian, where you'll witness cheese being hand-formed from local, organic milk – including Surf and Turf, aged goat's cheese with toasted Sonoma *nori* (seaweed), and Flower Power, organic cow's-milk cheese sprinkled with bee pollen. Taste a dozen ($15 to $20) or reserve a fun cheese-making tour plus tasting (60 minutes, $20; kids free).

Screamin' Mimi ICE CREAM $

(☎707-823-5902; www.screaminmimisicecream.com; 6902 Sebastopol Ave; ice cream $3-8; ⌚11am-10pm Sun-Thu, to 11pm Fri & Sat; 👪) Create your dream dessert with homemade ice cream served by the ounce ($0.73), so you never have to make impossible choices between classic peppermint stick, chocolate sin (dark chocolate with fudge) and birthday cake (vanilla with chocolate cake and rainbow sprinkles). Lactose-challenged friends, rejoice: vegan salted caramel is made with coconut milk, and dairy-free passion-fruit and grapefruit Campari sorbets are decadent treats.

★ La Bodega Kitchen MEDITERRANEAN $$

(☎707-827-1832; www.sonomawineshop.com; 2295 Gravenstein Hwy S; shared plates $17-27; ⌚4-9pm Tue-Fri, from noon Sat & Sun; P 🖉) Shhhhh, don't call it a restaurant – cook/owner/dynamo Meekk cooks Sonoma's most inspired Mediterranean 'food pairings' to accompany wine from the adjoining wine store. Bright local, organic flavors turbo-charge Mediterranean standards: Meyer lemon–zested greens bring zing to *bourekkas* (feta turnovers), wild morels add umami power to Normandy chicken, and Sonoma's best lamb, eggs and flour explain your meatball-fettuccini dreams tonight.

★ Fork Roadhouse CALIFORNIAN $$

(☎707-634-7575; www.forkcatering.com; 9890 Bodega Hwy; mains $15-25; ⌚9am-2pm & 5:30-8:30pm Wed-Sat, to 2pm Sun; P 🖉 👪 🐾) Get cozy by the fireplace at this rural ranch house, and warm up to farm-to-table fare with a wild streak. Chef/owner Sarah Piccolo sources Sonoma's most intriguing organic ingredients for mod-Mediterranean dishes: wild-nettle pesto lasagna makes basil seem bland, house-fermented sauerkraut wakes breakfast tacos with a slap, and caramelized onions and Sonoma cheese oozing into trumpet-mushroom melts totally outclass tuna.

★ Fern Bar CALIFORNIAN $$

(☎707-861-9603; https://fernbar.square.site; 6780 Depot St No 120; shared plates $9-27; ⌚5-11pm Tue-Sun; P ❄ 🖉) Come for '70s fern-bar atmosphere, with stained glass and amber lighting – stay for the food. Choose your Sonoma-proud shared plates: seasonal standouts include local trout with green garlic and 'umami bomb' mushroom-cream broccolini on yeast-dusted sticky rice. 'Yes, this is my dinner,' says the winemaker the next stool over, dunking churros into spiced chocolate sauce. She's possibly a genius.

Ramen Gaijin RAMEN $$

(☎707-827-3609; www.ramengaijin.com; 6948 Sebastopol Ave; ramen $18; ⌚noon-2:30pm & 3:30-10pm Tue-Sat) That street party is actually the back patio of Sonoma's best ramen shop. The upbeat mood is fueled by (so spicy!) pork-belly ramen and (so tasty!) short ribs slumping sideways into noodles. Add Sonoma farm eggs and pickles, pair with legendary Pliny the Elder on tap or milky Jozen Nigori sake, and finish with black sesame-miso gelato – the party's in your mouth now.

Handline CALIFORNIAN $$

(☎707-827-3744; www.handline.com; 935 Gravenstein Ave; mains $14-23; ⌚11am-10pm; P 👪) Seafood served the way Sonoma likes it: fresh, tasty, sustainable, easygoing. Inside this converted Foster's Freeze drive-in, wait at the counter to order grilled oysters (get yours with uni-chive butter or bacon and wilted greens), creative tostadas loaded with poached calamari, avocado and grapefruit, or classic fish tacos: beer-battered and fried rockfish, with pickled onion and avocado on fresh tortillas.

Drinking & Nightlife

Hardcore Espresso CAFE

(☎707-823-7588; 81 Bloomfield Rd; ⌚5am-7pm Mon-Fri, from 6am Sat & Sun; 📶) Organic coffee, smoothies, tea and turmeric lattes make fine excuses to hang out with Sebastopol's resident artists and hippies in an indoor-outdoor found-art installation that doubles as a cafe. It's off-the-grid and south of downtown – look for the roadside giant chair, order at the corrugated-metal-roofed shack, and find your niche: bathtub bench, fortune-teller booth, hand-painted lounge chair.

Woodfour Brewing Co BREWERY

(☎707-823-3144; www.woodfourbrewing.com; 6780 Depot St; ⊙noon-7pm Mon-Thu, to 8pm Fri & Sat, 11am-6pm Sun) Not your grandpa's brewery, this solar-powered establishment produces original craft brews light on alcohol and hops – including coffee-infused black lager, whiskey-barrel-aged Belgian ale, and spontaneously fermented sour ales. Bar snacks go above and beyond – corn dogs are housemade, and tortillas are made to order for Pacific rock-cod tacos – and Wednesdays bring live music and happy hours from 3pm to close.

Taylor Lane Farms CAFE

(☎707-634-7129; www.taylorlane.com; 6790 McKinley St, Barlow; ⊙6:30am-6pm Sun-Thu, to 7pm Fri, 7am-7pm Sat) Waking Sonoma farmers in the nicest possible way since 1993, Taylor Lane roasts organic beans fresh daily in Sonoma. A classic California third-wave coffeehouse, Taylor Lane makes coffee to order in the method of your choice – press, espresso, pour-over, you name it – and gets creative with foam art and seasonal drinks like lavender lattes.

Shopping

★Solful DISPENSARY

(☎707-596-9040; https://solful.com; 785 Gravenstein Ave; ⊙10am-6pm) Your Solful budtender introduces you to prime cannabis to suit every need: de-stressing, creative hijinks, pain relief and parties. Solful's impressive range comes from 'muddy-shoe sourcing' across California, seeking out sustainably outdoor-farmed, organic and biodynamic cannabis in every form – chocolates, joints, gummies, body butter, beer. Don't miss 'meet your cannabis farmer' events; ID required.

People's Music MUSICAL INSTRUMENTS

(☎707-823-7664; www.peoplesmusic.com; 122 N Main St; ⊙noon-6pm;) Jam sessions have kicked off at People's Music since 1973 – you might still spot Grateful Dead drummer Mickey Hart testing out the bongos. Let the music move you and your instrument choose you: ukulele, hemlock-root flute, autoharp, banjo, saxophone, guitar. Ask about lessons and check the bulletin board for fellow musicians to jump-start Sebastopol's next jam session.

Antique Society ANTIQUES

(☎707-829-1733; www.antiquesociety.com; 2661 Gravenstein Hwy S; ⊙10am-5pm;) Clear your morning schedule to browse 125 antiques vendors inside this 20,000-sq-ft industrial shed. Treasures that may still await your discovery include Victorian picnic baskets, lithographed Sonoma fruit labels, California highway signage, miracle-cure medicine bottles from the gold rush, and an entire wall of copper kitchen utensils.

Beekind FOOD, HOMEWARES

(☎707-824-2905; www.beekind.com; 921 Gravenstein Hwy S; ⊙10am-6pm Mon-Sat, to 4pm Sun) This place gets great buzz – whether you're an aspiring beekeeper or just here for the honey, the range is impressive. Taste the difference between Sonoma County wildflower and California sage honeys, and choose Sonoma beeswax candles hand-molded into a redwood tree or beehive (how meta).

Information

Sebastopol Area Chamber of Commerce & Visitors Center (Map p220; ☎707-823-3032; www.sebastopol.org; 265 S Main St; ⊙10am-5pm Mon-Fri) Offers maps, information and exhibits.

Getting There & Away

Sebastopol is about an 80-minute drive north from San Francisco.

Bikers can take the San Francisco Bay Ferry (p173) from San Francisco to Marin's Larkspur Landing, hop the SMART (p173) train to Santa Rosa, then take the Joe Rodota Trail to Sebastopol.

Hwy 116 splits downtown; southbound traffic uses Main St, northbound traffic Petaluma Ave. North of town, it's called Gravenstein Hwy N and continues toward Guerneville; south of downtown, it's Gravenstein Hwy S, which heads toward Hwy 101 and Sonoma.

Graton, Forestville & Around

Once known as Green Valley, the peaceful rolling farmland surrounding the western outposts of Graton and Forestville made its reputation with a party for the ages. After the 1906 earthquake shook up most of Western Sonoma, the residents of Green Valley pulled together to host a July 4 party to raise spirits – and thousands of people showed up. Luckily, Green Valley farmers had plenty of wine to go around, thanks to the foresight of thirsty Russian farmers, who first planted vineyards here in 1836.

Even Prohibition couldn't stop the party: the first speakeasy in Sonoma County was in Forestville. The memory of Green Valley's

WORTH A TRIP

SCENIC DRIVE: COLEMAN VALLEY ROAD

Sonoma County's most scenic drive isn't through the grapes, but along these 10 miles of winding byway from Occidental to the sea. It's best in the late morning, when the fog has lifted and the sun's filtering through the tree canopy.

Once you reach the ridgeline on Coleman Valley Rd, jog left onto Joy Rd and right onto Fitzpatrick Lane to find a hidden glory: the Grove of the Old Trees (p216). Stop to picnic or stroll the easy 1-mile loop trail winding through ancient redwoods in this designated 'Forever Wild' conservation site.

Back on Coleman Valley Rd, you'll dip into lush valleys where Douglas firs are cloaked in sphagnum moss – an eerie sight in the fog. Pass gnarled oaks and craggy rock formations as you ascend 1000ft, until finally you see the vast blue Pacific, unfurling at your feet. The road ends at coastal Hwy 1, where you can explore **Sonoma Coast State Beach**, then turn left and find your way to the tiny town of **Bodega** (not Bodega Bay) to see locales where Hitchcock shot his 1963 classic, *The Birds*.

food, wine and good times has remained – and Graton and Forestville remain Michelin-noted gourmet magnets today. Unprecedented fires forced area evacuations in 2017, 2019 and 2020, but the all-volunteer Graton Fire Department saved both towns and their residents. True to form, within months, Graton and Forestville residents resumed their roles as legendary hosts. This calls for a celebration...be sure to bring enough wine.

Sights & Activities

★Iron Horse WINERY

(Map p220; ☎707-887-1507; www.ironhorsevineyards.com; 9786 Ross Station Rd, Sebastopol; by appointment tasting $30, incl tour $50; ⏰10am-4:30pm, last tasting 4pm; P) Raise a toast or five at Iron Horse's hilltop tasting bar, where hosts keep handing you more bubbly. Celebrate your own milestones with Iron Horse sparkling wines served at White House inaugurations from Carter to Obama, and toast global changes with special cuvées celebrating LGBTQ Pride and climate resilience. Tastings refunded with six-bottle sampler purchase.

Martinelli WINERY

(Map p220; ☎707-525-0570; www.martinelliwinery.com; 3360 River Rd, Windsor; tastings $25-40, with picnic lunch $75; ⏰10am-5pm; P) Don't be fooled by this quaint red barn – the Martinellis have been bucking convention since 1887, when a young Tuscan winemaker eloped to California to grow grapes on notoriously steep, stubbornly rocky Jackass Hill. Now in their sixth generation farming the Russian River Valley, the Martinellis continue to produce award-winning zinfandels, pinots and muscat from 140-year-old Jackass Hill vines with winemaker Courtney Wagner – now making her mark in a long line of celebrated women winemakers at this trailblazing winery.

Furthermore Wines WINERY

(Map p220; ☎707-823-3040; www.furthermorewines.com; 3541 Gravenstein Hwy N, Sebastopol; tastings $20-30; ⏰10am-4:30pm; P 🐾) Start with pinot, break for bocce in Furthermore's pinot vineyards, then return to the urgent matter of pinot. Furthermore's estate is planted to pinot, with just 15 rows of chardonnay – but they also source pinot grapes from neighbors across Sonoma and Santa Barbara counties, so you can enjoy a pinot turf-war tasting ($20 to $40). Even tough guys against pink drinks should make an exception for Furthermore's mysterious rosé of pinot noir – then spend a lifetime chasing that rosé dream.

Marimar Estate WINERY

(Map p220; ☎707-823-4365; www.marimarestate.com; 11400 Graton Rd, Graton; tasting $20; ⏰by appointment 11am-4pm Mon-Wed, to 5pm Fri-Sun; 🐾) Back in 1975, Marimar Torres was the rebel of her Catalan winemaking family, and moved to California – where she quickly spotted pinot potential in these hills. Today her Marimar Estate specializes in all-organic pinot – seven different kinds – plus cool-climate chardonnay and some Iberian surprises, including a stunning albariño. The hacienda-style hilltop tasting room has a vineyard-view terrace for picnics, and offers Catalan tapas-and-wine pairings ($55). The guided tour includes a current-release bottle ($95).

Russian River Cycle Service CYCLING

(☎707-887-2453; www.russianrivercycles.com; 6559 Front St, Forestville; half-/full-day rental from $35/45, delivery $20; ⏰7am-7pm) Stop in for local riding info and/or bike rentals, which come with helmets, baskets, air pumps and locks – plus free wine-tasting passes on request. They also deliver bicycles to Russian River locations (anywhere from Forestville to Duncans Mills), with 24-hour notice ($20 for one to two bikes). Hybrids and kids bikes available; ask about discounts for multiday rentals.

Sleeping

Raford Inn B&B $$
(Map p220; ☎, 707-887-9573; www.rafordinn.com; 10630 Wohler Rd; d $225-275;) Wake up feeling on top of the world at this hilltop Victorian B&B, surrounded by swaying palm trees and rambling vineyards. Guest rooms lined with lace, floral wallpaper and antiques bring costume drama to life in this 1880 gingerbread-trimmed house. Arrive in time for wine receptions and sunsets on the veranda, and enjoy complimentary country breakfasts before wine tasting with free guest passes.

★**Farmhouse Inn** INN $$$
(Map p220; ☎707-887-3300; www.farmhouseinn.com; 7871 River Rd, Forestville; d $356-1495;) Trade up to Farmhouse living in whitewashed cottages primed for romance with soothing luxuries: four-poster feather beds, wood-burning fireplaces, well-curated wine fridges, and spa-bathrooms with soaking tubs, steam showers and heated floors. Venture beyond the heated pool and hot tub, and you'll discover the on-site winery, Michelin-starred restaurant, and a farm-to-massage-table spa putting farm honey to excellent work in facials.

Eating

★**Nightingale Breads** BAKERY $
(☎707-887-8887; www.nightingalebreads.com; 6665 Front St, Forestville; bread from $7; 11am-6pm Wed-Fri, 10am-4pm Sat & Sun;) Everyone in Forestville knows when Jessie Frost's baking – the aroma of her organic breads changes traffic patterns. Jessie bought Nightingale from her boss/mentor a couple of years ago, producing wood-fired-oven wonders and weekend specials. Friday means poppy-seed-sprinkled challah, Saturday brings Moonlight spent-grain bread – made with grains left over from Sonoma's Moonlight (p209) microbrews – and Sunday scones celebrate seasonal flavors.

★**Backyard** CALIFORNIAN $$
(☎707-820-8445; www.backyardforestville.com; 6566 Front St, Forestville; mains lunch/brunch $14-30, dinner $22-30; 11:30am-9pm Mon & Fri, 9am-9pm Sat, to 8pm Sun;) Chefs Marianna Gardenhire and Daniel Kedan met at Napa's Culinary Institute of America, married, started Bee Run Hollow farm, and opened Backyard in an old train depot, sourcing sustainable ingredients from neighbors. Every dish is a Wine Country love letter: house-brined pickles with Dungeness crab cakes, hempseed-sprinkled salads, neighbor-raised fried chicken and Sonoma-honey biscuits.

Canneti Roadhouse ITALIAN $$
(☎707-887-2232; www.cannetirestaurant.com; 6675 Front St, Forestville; mains lunch $14-30, dinner $23-45; 5:30-9pm Tue-Thu, 11:30am-3pm & 5:30-9:30pm Fri & Sat, to 8:30pm Sun;) When Tuscan-born chef Francesco Torre visited Sonoma, he found his muse – you can taste Sonoma's farm-fresh inspiration in his handmade pasta and gnocchi, grilled seafood and lamb, plus tiramisu made from scratch. Five-course Tuscan tasting menus ($65) are decadent deals; corkage is free Wednesdays and Thursdays bring three-course dinners ($40).

Underwood Bar & Bistro AMERICAN $$
(☎707-823-7023; www.underwoodgraton.com; 9113 Graton Rd, Graton; mains $16-40; 11:30am-2:30pm & 5-10pm Tue-Thu, to 11pm Fri & Sat) Imagine a Wild West saloon where the barkeeper knows exactly which Sonoma Coast chardonnay to pair with Marin Gem oysters: welcome to Underwood. Rock up to the bar for flavor-packed small plates: Hoisin-glazed ribs, harissa fries, caramelized onion and Sonoma blue-cheese flatbread – or settle into a banquette for Sonoma duck confit with lentils.

Willow Wood Market Cafe AMERICAN $$
(☎707-823-0233; www.willowwoodgraton.com; 9020 Graton Rd, Graton; mains $15-32; 8am-9pm Mon-Sat, 9am-3pm Sun) The West has clearly been won over by this general store and cafe. Anytime cowboys and wine-tasters roll into town, Willow Wood greets them with California comfort food: chicken pot pies, smoked-trout watercress salads, polenta with goat's cheese and pesto – plus Champagne cocktails cheerfully served all day. Snag a garden spot if you can, and ask for extra blackberry jam.

Farmhouse Inn Restaurant CALIFORNIAN $$$
(Map p220; ☎707-887-3300; www.farmhouseinn.com; 7871 River Rd, Forestville; 3-/4-/5-course dinner $99/119/139; 5:30-8:30pm Thu-Mon) Flavor and flair make this Farmhouse mighty fancy. Chef Steve Litke is an early Slow Food advocate, changing his menu seasonally to feature

locally raised, organic ingredients – recurring signatures include crab-stuffed squash blossoms, 'rabbit, rabbit, rabbit' (rabbit roasted, bacon-wrapped and mustard-sauced) and chocolate soufflé. For flavor without the fuss, stop by outdoor, to-go Farmstand in summer.

Shopping

Graton Gallery ARTS & CRAFTS, HOMEWARES
(707-829-8912; www.gratongallery.net; 9048 Graton Rd, Graton; 10:30am-5pm Tue-Sat, to 4pm Sun) Skip the airport souvenirs and opt for art instead, from Graton's showcase of Sonoma inspirations. Here you can pick up Rik Olsen's striking linocut prints of redwoods and Nancy Overton's collaged California quails – plus one-of-a-kind gifts of art-glass dishes, pottery mugs, table textiles and jewelry.

Mr Ryder & Co Art & Antiques ANTIQUES
(707-824-8221; www.mrryderantiques.com; 9040 Graton Rd, Graton; 11am-5pm Mon-Sat, 10am-4pm Sun) Inside Graton's 1906 post-office building, there's a gift from Sonoma with your name on it: sterling grape-cluster pins, California Rose potato-sack pillows, Victorian forget-me-not sapphire pinky rings, and a tiny paddock's worth of donkey figurines. Ten dealers searched the county for these finds and arranged them into stage-sets that spill onto the garden patio.

Occidental, Freestone & the Bohemian Highway

From the instant you turn onto the aptly named Bohemian Hwy at Freestone, you're in for a wild ride. Freestone is a former stagecoach stop where shaggy barns and sun-bleached farmsteads house a current population of 32 – yet the road is lined with cars. People flock here for organic, nutty buns, and stay for the complete Freestone immersion experience: a warm bath in soft, fermenting cedar chips.

Your adventure continues in Occidental, the lumber town that time forgot and trees reconquered – with help from visionary ecologists and back-to-the-land hippies, who started local environmental education camps and preserved the Grove of the Old Trees. Here you'll meet local artists and browse recycled, organic and women-made goods. On Fridays during summer and fall, everyone emerges from the woods for Occidental's farmers market, a free-form street party featuring local musicians, crafts and homemade food. The power of countercultural thinking is celebrated every day here, but especially during Occidental's **April Fool's Day Parade**.

Sights & Activities

★**Bohème Wines** WINERY
(Map p220; 707-874-3218; www.bohemewines.com; 3625 Main St, Occidental; tasting $15; noon-6pm Thu & Fri, to 5pm Sat & Sun) Drop by this Western frontier storefront tasting room in downtown Occidental, and taste what a difference old-growth trees can make in a bottle of wine. Dappled sunlight through Occidental's lofty tree canopy is the key to these fascinating, sun-shy pinot noirs, sublime, long-ripening chardonnays, and subtle, cool-climate syrahs. Tasting fee refunded with purchase; bottles run $36 to $65.

★**Grove of the Old Trees** FOREST
(Map p220; 707-544-7284; www.landpaths.org; 17599 Fitzpatrick Lane, Occidental; dawn-dusk;) Outside the lumber boomtown of Occidental, on a ridge off Fitzpatrick Lane, lies a peaceful, 48-acre forest once owned by families who made their living sawing timber – yet they couldn't bear to cut down these ancient giants. Environmental activists rallied to these old-growth redwoods' defense in the 1990s, and conservation nonprofits purchased the entire grove. You can still see faint blue marks on towering trees once destined for lumberyards, now thriving in this designated 'Forever Wild' conservation site.

Occidental Community Farmers Market MARKET
(Map p220; 707-874-8478; https://occidentalcommunityfarmersmarket.com; 3611 Bohemian Hwy, Occidental; 4pm-dusk Fri mid-May–Oct;) Summer means Friday-night throw-down hoedowns in Occidental, when the whole community converges in front of Howard's Station Cafe for live music and a detour-worthy local farmers market with abundant, all-local attractions: crafts, flowers, cheese, smoked salmon, organic produce and giant pans of Pacific seafood paella.

★**Osmosis** SPA
(Map p220; 707-823-8231; www.osmosis.com; 209 Bohemian Hwy, Freestone; individual bath $109, spa packages from $235; by appointment 9am-8pm Thu- Mon, to 7pm Tue & Wed) Your spa ritual begins with organic tea in the bonsai garden, then proceeds to a tub full of soft, fermenting cedar and rice bran fibers – the woodsy,

balsamic aroma is grounding, and the dry-enzyme action warms to the bone.

Sonoma Canopy Tours OUTDOORS
(Map p220; 888-494-7868; www.sonomacanopytours.com; 6250 Bohemian Hwy, Occidental; zipline tour weekday/weekend/night from $99/109/139;) Soar through the redwood canopy on interconnected ziplines at 30mph, cross sky bridges between trees, and rappel down to the forest floor. It's adrenaline-pumping fun and eco-educational for ages 10 and up – plus tour proceeds provide scholarships for low-income and at-risk kids at Alliance Redwoods' outdoor education camps. Entrance is about 2 miles north of Occidental; reservations required.

Sleeping

★Shanti Permaculture Farm FARMSTAY $
(Map p220; 707-874-2001; www.shantioccidental.com; 16715 Coleman Valley Rd, Occidental; tent & RV sites $45-80, cottage & yurt from $159;) Retreat to the redwoods off scenic Coleman Valley Rd for the ultimate NorCal farmstay. Your knowledgeable host explains ecofriendly agricultural practices like biochar (charcoal for soil regeneration) and *hugelkultur* (compost-garden beds) while introducing her chickens, sheep, goats and guard llama. The one-bedroom cottage is colorful and comfy, with wi-fi, hammocks and hot tub.

Valley Ford Hotel INN $
(707-876-1983; www.vfordhotel.com; 14415 Shoreline Hwy, Valley Ford; d $125-185;) Hold your horses and stay awhile at this 1864 stagecoach stop, 5 miles southeast of Freestone, in the remote western outpost of Valley Ford. Upstairs, seven simple, snug rooms are tucked under the eaves with patchwork quilts and white-tiled bathrooms, while the legendary roadhouse restaurant and saloon downstairs draw Sonoma ranchers from miles around.

Inn at Occidental INN $$
(707-874-1047; www.innatoccidental.com; 3657 Church St, Occidental; d $219-399;) Escape the ordinary at this 16-room Victorian inn that's a true Occidental character, with colorful heirloom quilts, collectible antiques, and everything you need to get cozy in the redwoods – gas fireplaces, deep tubs and cushy feather beds. Guest rooms with balconies overlooking the cottage garden make romantic hideaways, but you'll want to emerge for complimentary farm-to-table breakfasts and sociable wine hours.

Eating & Drinking

★Wild Flour Bread BAKERY $
(Map p220; 707-874-2938; www.wildflourbread.com; 140 Bohemian Hwy, Freestone; items from $3; 8am-6pm Fri-Mon;) The West goes wild for organic artisan breads, mushroom fougasse glossy with olive oil, and sticky buns, all hot from the brick oven. Picnic table seating here is more sought after than royal thrones – regulars loll on grassy lawns or stroll through the gardens, which are the only possible post-Wild Flour activities anyway.

Howard Station Cafe AMERICAN $
(707-874-2838; www.howardstationcafe.com; 3611 Bohemian Hwy, Occidental; mains $8-17; 8am-2:30pm Mon-Fri, 7am-3pm Sat & Sun;) Since the 1870s, Howard's has restored weary travelers and hungover ranchers alike with reliable, generous, comforting brunches. Farm eggs make Benedicts better, juices are freshly squeezed, organic quinoa bowls come turbo-loaded with sautéed vegetables, and Belgian waffles get an upgrade with real maple syrup and toasted coconut. Cash only.

Freestone Cheese CHEESE $
(Map p220; 707-874-1030; www.freestoneartisan.com; 380 Bohemian Hwy, Freestone; cheese from $4; 10am-6pm Fri-Mon, from noon Thu, winter 10am-5pm Fri-Sun;) Brake on the Bohemian Hwy for artisan cheese, local olive oil, and Shakespeare sonnets recited by cheesemonger and poetry fan Omar Mueller (he's named for poet Omar Khayyam). Tell Omar what you enjoy in life, and he'll customize a counter tasting for you that may well involve buffalo milk, volcanic ash, washed rinds, gooey centers and absolute bliss.

Bohemian Market DELI $
(707-874-3312; 3691 Main St, Occidental; 7am-9pm Mon-Fri, from 8am Sat & Sun;) Go boho for all your hippie gourmet needs: fair-trade coffee, organic kombucha, certified-humane goat's cheese and vegetarian-friendly deli, where fresh sandwiches are made to order (10am to 7pm). If you're particular about your coffee – no shame in admitting that in California – the coffee bar's open until 1pm. Save a buck or two change for local musicians performing out front.

★Hazel CALIFORNIAN $$
(707-874-6003; www.restauranthazel.com; 3782 Bohemian Hwy, Occidental; shared plates $18-36; 5-9pm Wed-Sat, 10am-2pm & 5-9pm Sun;) Whenever you arrive, you're right on

time for another fabulous dinner party at Jim and Michele Wimborough's cottage restaurant. Wine flows and *oooOooh!* choruses erupt as dishes arrive bubbling from wood-fired ovens: caramelized brussels sprouts, herb-roasted chicken, wild-mushroom pizzas and strawberry-rhubarb crisp. Dishes are generous and your hosts unfailingly delightful – all you have to do is make happy noises.

Shopping

★Hinterland & Neon Raspberry DESIGN, ARTS & CRAFTS
(☎707-599-0573; www.hinterlandempire.com; 3605 Main St, Occidental; ⏲10am-5pm Thu-Sun) Retail for the redwoods: everything here is recycled, organic and/or women-made, with punk attitude. 'The future is feral,' announces Hinterland's hoodie – meanwhile you're 'drinking beer and raising kale in Occidental' (to quote Hinterland's beer cozy) or just 'weird in the woods' (as Hinterland key chains confess). Adjoining Neon Raspberry (www.neonraspberry.com) showcases local artists, including Andy Rado's slogan-splashed pitcher: 'Pour yourself some optimism.'

Getting There & Away

Occidental and Freestone are about a two-hour drive from San Francisco. There's no good way to get here via public transportation, but cyclists will love the ride from Santa Rosa's train station via Joe Rodota Trail and Bodega Hwy.

Russian River Valley

The source of the Russian River is north in Ukiah, and the valley begins outside Healdsburg – but when locals talk about hitting 'the River,' they usually mean the stretch of the Russian River Valley starting around Guerneville, winding past Monte Rio and Duncans Mills, and heading for the Sonoma Coast, where it flows into the sea at Jenner.

This stretch of Russian River may be slow-moving, but it's full of unexpected twists. For a century this has been the summer-weekend destination for Northern Californians to splash in the river, come out and play at LGBTQ resorts, and find romance.

Dappled sunlight and cooling mists make Russian River Valley idyllic for hiking, and midday 'fogdog' sunbreaks provide enough California sunshine for sensitive grapes like pinot noir and cool-climate chardonnay. With its mysterious microclimates, Russian River Valley has become one of California's most distinctive and important wine appellations. Today there are 70-odd wineries spread across 15,000 acres, listed in the handy *Russian River Wine Road* map (www.wineroad.com) you'll find on tourist-brochure racks.

Monte Rio, Duncans Mills & Around

On the final westward stretch of Russian River, these two tiny western towns have outsized swagger. Riverfront inns, public beaches, general stores and storefront diners make Monte Rio and Duncans Mills look like old Western movie sets – but they're not faking it. These resort towns really do date from the 1800s, when this was the last stop on a Bay Area railroad system built for transporting lumber. Duncans Mills is named for two brothers who built lumber mills here in the 1870s.

Lumber trains were repurposed to transport starry-eyed bohemian San Franciscans to nature, and the river-resort scene took root. San Franciscan's elitist, men-only Bohemian Club established its **Bohemian Grove** outside Monte Rio in 1872 – and despite anti-discrimination and unfair-labor lawsuits, Bohemian Grove remains a secret all-male retreat where US presidents and industry moguls frolic nude in the woods. Monte Rio also has several resorts hiding in plain sight, and tiny Duncans Mills has a cluster of Western storefronts 8 miles west of Guerneville.

Sights

Monte Rio Beach BEACH
(Map p220; www.mrrpd.org/monteriobeach.html; under Monte Rio Bridge; ⏲late May-late Sep; P) The launching pad for summer fun is east of Monte Rio Bridge. Redwoods tower behind a pebbled beach, but summer sun shines on horseshoe pits, volleyball fields, canoe launches and barbecue grills. Events here include Saturday farmers markets (11am to 2pm) and July 4 festivities, including boat flotillas and fireworks. The beach west of the bridge is smaller, but sandy and dog-friendly.

Sleeping

Highland Dell INN $
(☎707-865-2300; www.highlanddell.com; 21050 River Blvd, Monte Rio; d $119-219; ⏲Apr-Nov; P) A grand 1906 riverfront lodge, Highland Dell was thoughtfully updated as an event center in 2006. The character of the lodge remains, with a dining room, ballroom and river-rock fireplace lobby downstairs and

12 serene upstairs guest rooms with comfy beds piled with down duvets. The best rooms are top-floor love nests with balconies over the river – but no elevator.

Village Inn INN $$
(707-865-2304; www.villageinn-ca.com; 20822 River Blvd, Monte Rio; d $155-275; P) Between towering redwoods and the Russian River sits this quaint 1906 wood-shingled inn. Four rooms with river views perch above the bar-restaurant (open Wednesday to Sunday), while six rooms in a separate lodge have private entrances – request a deck or river views. It looks like a movie set because it was: Bing Crosby sang 'White Christmas' here in 1942.

Eating & Drinking

Cape Fear Cafe SOUTHERN US $$
(707-865-9246; www.capefearcafe.net; 25191 Main St, Duncans Mills; mains lunch/brunch $9-18, dinner $15-27; 10am-3pm Mon-Wed, to 8pm Thu, to 9pm Fri, 9am-9pm Sat & Sun) Don't let the name scare you – this sunshine-yellow Western storefront diner is downright cheery. The best dishes here have a southern drawl, including oyster po'boy sandwiches and tuna remoulade – but the big draw is brunch, especially Nik's crab-cake Benedict and Sanford Benedict, with house-smoked salmon and grits.

Village Inn Restaurant AMERICAN $$
(707-865-2304; www.villageinn-ca.com; 20822 River Blvd, Monte Rio; mains $16-32; 5-8pm Wed-Sun summer-fall; P) Riverfront dining at Village Inn has been a mainstay of Russian River summers since 1906. The local wine list and full bar kick evenings off right, and all-American menu classics are served in generous portions: steaks, pork chops, chicken pot pies and beet salads. Bet you'll be back for fried chicken and waffles and Bloody Mary at brunch.

Sophie's Cellars WINE BAR
(707-865-1122; www.sophiescellars.com; 25179 Main St/Hwy 116, Duncans Mills; 11am-5pm Thu, Sat & Sun, to 7pm Fri) Detour to this all-artisan wine bar for pours of Sonoma cult wines you won't find anywhere else – winery workers and wine collectors sell their extras here. With local cheese and salami, this could become dinner as you browse the dream wine-cellar racks. Friday 'locals' happy hour' (4pm to 7pm) brings drink specials and small bites.

Shopping

★ **Kool City Surf Shop** SPORTS & OUTDOORS, ART
(707-865-9613; Quonset 13, 20396 Bohemian Hwy, Monte Rio; 10am-5pm Fri-Sun) Stop for selfies at the 'Welcome to Monte Rio, Vacation Wonderland' sign, and you'll spot a local character: a skeleton in a top hat, leaning on a surfboard with Kool City's flaming logo. Anytime you see Debbie's hot rod parked nearby, pop into the Quonset hut to score Kool City tees and hoodies, snap-back caps, custom skateboards and bowling pins reinvented as art.

Pig Alley JEWELRY, GIFTS & SOUVENIRS
(707-865-2698; www.pigalleyshop.com; 25193 Main St, Duncans Mills; 10am-5pm Mon-Fri, 9:30am-5:30pm Sat & Sun) Since 1977 this red Western storefront has stocked a vast selection of hand-crafted American-made jewelry, from entire walls of earrings to wooden eco-watches. Gift opportunities abound – and if your special someone happens to be a pet, they stock gifts for cats and dogs, too.

Guerneville & Around

The Russian River's biggest vacation destination only has about 4000 residents, but Guerneville almost doubles in size some summer weekends, with vacationers here to hike redwoods, splash in the river and hammer cocktails poolside. As if that's not enough fun for one weekend, there are 50 wineries within a 20-minute drive. This town is a good time had by all since the 1870s, and it hasn't lost its Wild West, honky-tonk reputation yet. Just ask gay partiers in town for Lazy Bear (p222), sun-worshiping lesbians here for Women's Weekend (p223), and shaggy-haired Harley straddlers along for the ride.

If you actually came to Russian River for the river, there's good river access east of Guerneville in Forestville, plus sandy beaches and swimming holes downstream toward Monte Rio. Fishing and watercraft outfitters operate on Guerneville's Johnson's Beach mid-May to early October, when winter rains swell the river and curb river activities. For picnic supplies, a **farmers market** meets in downtown Guerneville on Wednesdays, May through September, from 3pm to 7pm.

Downtown Guerneville is a year-round destination, with cafes, indie maker boutiques, straight-friendly gay bars and fun casual dining. Around the edges of Guerneville, **Armstrong Woods** is recovering after fire damage to the ancient redwoods, and

Russian River Area

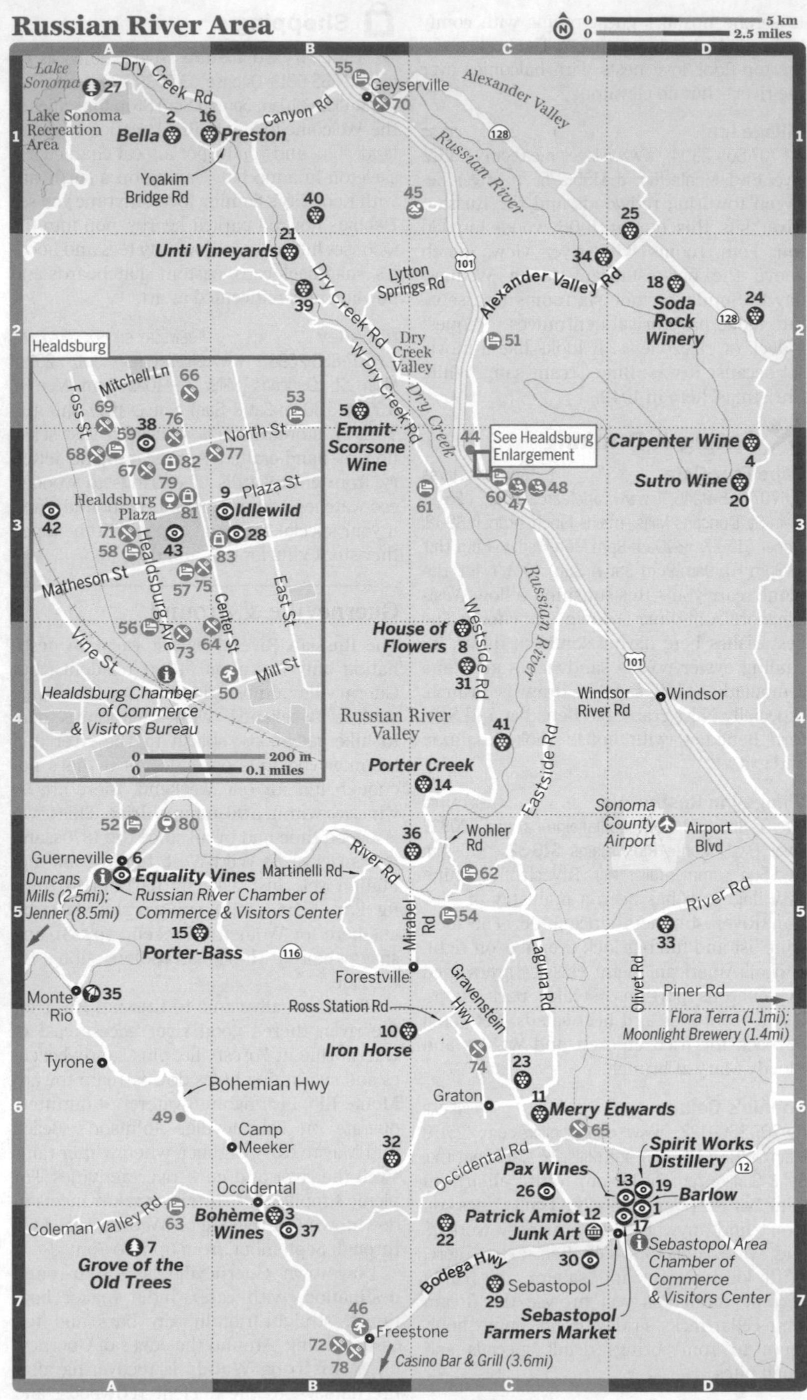

Russian River Area

Top Sights
1 Barlow D7
2 Bella A1
3 Bohème Wines B7
4 Carpenter Wine D3
5 Emmit-Scorsone Wine B2
6 Equality Vines A5
7 Grove of the Old Trees A7
8 House of Flowers C4
9 Idlewild B3
10 Iron Horse B6
11 Merry Edwards C6
12 Patrick Amiot Junk Art C7
13 Pax Wines D6
14 Porter Creek C4
15 Porter-Bass A5
16 Preston A1
17 Sebastopol Farmers Market D7
18 Soda Rock Winery D2
19 Spirit Works Distillery D6
20 Sutro Wine D3
21 Unti Vineyards B2

Sights
22 Freeman C7
23 Furthermore Wines C6
24 Hanna D2
25 Hawkes D1
26 Horse & Plow C6
27 Lake Sonoma Recreation Area A1
28 Lioco B3
29 Littorai C7
30 Luther Burbank's Gold Ridge Experiment Farm C7
31 MacRostie C4
32 Marimar Estate B6
33 Martinelli D5
34 Medlock Ames C2
35 Monte Rio Beach A5
36 Moshin C5
37 Occidental Community Farmers Market B7
38 Portalupi A3
39 Quivira B2
40 Reeve Wines B1
41 Rochioli Winery C4
42 Saturday Farmers Market A3
43 Tuesday Farmers Market on the Plaza A3

Activities, Courses & Tours
44 Breathless Wines Sabrage Session C3
45 Francis Ford Coppola Winery Swimming Pools C1
46 Osmosis B7
47 River's Edge Kayak & Canoe Trips C3
48 Russian River Adventures C3
49 Sonoma Canopy Tours A6
50 Spoke Folk Cyclery B4

Sleeping
51 Belle de Jour Inn C2
52 Boon Hotel + Spa A5
53 Camellia Inn B2
54 Farmhouse Inn C5
55 Geyserville Inn B1
56 h2hotel A4
57 Healdsburg Inn on the Plaza A3
58 Hotel Healdsburg A3
59 Hotel Les Mars A3
60 L&M Motel C3
61 Madrona Manor C3
62 Raford Inn C5
63 Shanti Permaculture Farm A7

Eating
64 Barndiva B4
65 Bohemian Creamery C6
66 Bravas Bar de Tapas A2
67 Campo Fina A3
68 Chalkboard A3
69 Costeaux French Bakery & Cafe A2
70 Diavola Pizza B1
71 Dry Creek Kitchen A3
Farmhouse Inn Restaurant (see 54)
72 Freestone Cheese B7
73 Mateo's Cocina Latina A4
74 Mom's Apple Pie C6
75 Noble Folk Ice Cream & Pie Bar A3
76 SingleThread A3
77 Valette B3
78 Wild Flour Bread B7

Drinking & Nightlife
79 Duke's Spirited Cocktails A3
80 Stumptown Brewery A5

Shopping
81 Gallery Lulo A3
82 Jam Jar A3
83 Levin & Company & Upstairs Gallery B3

the backwoods scene isn't always so fun. The local chamber of commerce has chased most tweakers off Main St, but if some off-the-beaten-path spots give you the creeps, head back to where the vibes are better. Guerneville's good-time go-tos include wine tasting at Equality Vines, plus dozens more wineries within a 15-minute drive.

Sights

★Porter-Bass WINERY

(Map p220; ☎707-869-1475; https://porter-bass.com; 11750 Mays Canyon Rd; tasting $15; ⏰10am-4pm) Mists swirl around redwoods above, while Kitchen the cow meanders sunny vineyards below: if this hidden valley seems like pure California bliss, wait until you taste the wine that perfectly captures it. Farmer Sue Bass revived this historic farm through decades of biodynamic cultivation; now flowers and chickens thrive in the vineyards. Her winemaker son Luke gently coaxes Demeter-certified sauvignon blanc, chardonnay, pinot noir and zinfandel into existence with native yeast.

★Equality Vines TASTING ROOM
(Map p220; ☎877-379-4637; https://equalityvines.com; 6215 Main St; tasting $15; ⏲1-8pm Thu, noon-8pm Fri & Sat, to 6pm Sun, to 5pm Mon) All the NorCal wines produced and sold by Equality Vines support social-justice nonprofits, so you're drinking your way to better days with tastings here – cheers to that! You choose your wine/cause: winemaker Alison Green-Doran's 'Get Your Own Damn Coffee' is a bold Russian River chardonnay supporting Equal Rights Advocates, and Stonewall old-vine zin commemorates 50 years of hard-won LGBT+ rights.

★House of Flowers WINERY
(Map p220; ☎707-723-4800; www.flowerswinery.com; 4035 Westside Rd; tasting with food pairing $55; ⏲10am-4pm; P) A fallen redwood points the way from flowering vineyards to the front door, making a dramatic introduction to Flowers' famed pinots and chardonnays grown in extreme coastal conditions. You'll be greeted by name and ushered into the Sea Ranch–styled great room for Wine Country's most inspired pairings, courtesy of winemaker Chantal Forthun and chef Jamil Peden. Start with Sonoma Coast chardonnay and fennel-pollen sprinkled *gougères*, and progress to ridge-top pinot noir with black *nori* splashed with purple beets and yellow flowers.

★Porter Creek WINERY
(Map p220; ☎707-433-6321; www.portercreekvineyards.com; 8735 Westside Rd; tasting $20; ⏲10:30am-4:30pm; P) From family vineyards originally cultivated in 1978 and Demeter-certified in 2003, Alex Davis crafts sensational, sustainable pinot noir, syrah, viognier and chardonnay. Step inside the 1930s tool shed, and try Alex's latest releases at a tasting bar made from an old bowling-alley lane. Tasting fee waived with purchase; bottles run $28 to $72.

Rochioli Winery WINERY
(Map p220; ☎707-433-2305; www.rochioliwinery.com; 6192 Westside Rd; tasting $25; ⏲by appointment 10:30am-3:30pm; P) Entering Rochioli's tasting room is like jumping a velvet rope: you're about to taste pinot noirs collectors line up to buy. Three generations of Rochiolis have farmed these prestigious vineyards. The most distinctive micro-batches become single-vineyard estate wines – to buy these, collectors join multiyear wait lists. Vineyard blends strike fine balances – Rochioli's flinty chardonnay and tart-cherry pinot noir are finessed to impress. Tasting fee refunded with two-bottle purchase; bottles $28 to $64.

MacRostie WINERY
(Map p220; ☎707-473-9303; www.macrostiewinery.com; 4605 Westside Rd; tasting $25-35, with tour $55; ⏲11am-5pm Mon-Thu, from 10am Fri-Sun; P) True, these pinots regularly rack up 90-plus points from critics, but folks at MacRostie are even more proud of one locally acknowledged fact: Wine Country cooks drink these wines at home. Relaxed, personalized sit-down tastings with cheese and charcuterie give you a chance to admire these certified-sustainable vineyards alongside the chardonnays, pinots and rosé achieved by prodigious winemaker Heidi Bridenhagen. Tasting fee waived with a three-bottle purchase; bottles $13 to $65.

Activities

Johnson's Beach WATER SPORTS
(☎707-869-2022; www.johnsonsbeach.com; 16215 & 16217 1st St; kayak & canoe rental per hour/day $15/40; ⏲10am-6pm May-Oct;) FREE Inner tubes, paddleboat rentals, beer and wine concessions make Johnson's Beach fun central. Everyone's here in summer, from Speedo-clad hipsters to bikers with toddlers. You can camp here, and buy hot dogs and burgers. Beach admission is free, but it's $7 to park. The river floods with heavy rains though, so it's closed winter through spring and in poor weather.

Pee Wee Golf & Arcade MINIGOLF
(☎707-869-9321; 16155 Drake Rd; adult/child 6-18yr/child under 6yr $9/7/free; ⏲11am-10pm Sat & Sun Jun-Sep;) Through fires and floods, this vintage 1946 course designed by minigolf pioneer Bill Koplin has remained remarkably intact – though the cannibals cooking a guy have been repainted as Romans helping him into a bath. Indoors there's a vintage arcade; outdoors are games and Ping-Pong.

Festivals & Events

★Lazy Bear Week LGBT
(www.lazybearweekend.org; ⏲Aug) The grizzlies are long gone in Guerneville, but in late summer downtown you'll see thousands of bears

NAPA & SONOMA WINE COUNTRY RUSSIAN RIVER VALLEY

– the queer community's affectionate nickname for burly, hairy men. In 2020, while pool parties and dance scenes were suspended due to COVID-19, the nonprofit organizers behind Lazy Bear organized a food drive instead – that definitely deserves a bear hug.

★**Women's Weekend** LGBT
(www.womensweekendrussianriver.com; ⌚Sep) Just when you thought summer was over in September, queer women and trans folx bring the party to Guerneville at the R3 Hotel. Pool parties, DJs, dancing, DIY workshops and drag shows have been bringing women out to play in the Russian River for 40 years and counting.

Sleeping

★**AutoCamp** RESORT $
(☎888-405-7553; https://autocamp.com; 14120 Old Cazadero Rd; trailer or tent cabin $139-239; P) For rustic splendor minus rustic accommodations, bunk in an iconic, shiny silver Airstream trailer retrofitted for modern comfort. Extra-long Airstreams come with living rooms, walk-in tiled showers and private bedrooms, with big beds and peekaboo-window views of stars and redwoods. Vast tent cabins have memory-foam mattresses and private fire pit campsites, but shared bathrooms.

Johnson's Beach Resort CABIN, CAMPGROUND $
(☎707-869-2022; www.johnsonsbeach.com; 16241 1st St; tent sites $40, cabins $135-165; P) Go retro on the river and bunk at Johnson's 1920s rustic, whitewashed wood-frame cabins on stilts. They're thin walled but clean, with en-suite bathrooms, wrought-iron beds, crisp cotton sheets and Pendleton blankets; most have kitchenettes. Johnson's also offers tent campsites with picnic tables and parking, plus coin-op hot showers and laundry. No pets or RVs; credit card only, two night minimum.

Highlands Resort CABIN, CAMPGROUND $
(☎707-869-0333; www.highlandsresort.com; 14000 Woodland Dr; tent sites $40-60, d $100-210, cabins $135-200;) Mellow out in the redwoods at Guerneville's most laid-back LGBT+ and straight-friendly resort, walking/biking distance to downtown. Cabins on the wooded hillside have sociable porches, cheerful rooms and en-suite bathrooms; some have kitchenettes or fireplaces. Campsites dot the redwood grove, with well-kept shared facilities and complimentary breakfasts. The big clothing-optional pool is a sunny, PG13 scene (weekday/weekend use $10/15).

R3 Hotel RESORT $
(Triple R; ☎707-869-8399; www.ther3hotel.com; 16390 4th St; d $99-250;) Ground zero for party-all-day gays and lesbians, Triple R (as it's known) has standard motel-style rooms surrounding a bar and pool deck that get so crowded on summer weekends that management won't allow guests to bring pets because 'they get hurt' (actual quote). Come for the scene, not for quiet. Midweek it's mellow, wintertime it's boring.

Boon Hotel + Spa BOUTIQUE HOTEL $$
(Map p220; ☎707-869-2721; www.boonhotels.com; 14711 Armstrong Woods Rd; tents $175-230, d $195-400; P) Get back to nature in style at this sleek retreat, walking/biking distance from downtown and Armstrong Woods. Between palms and redwoods, 14 spacious, modernist rooms feature wood-burning fireplaces, and platform beds piled with organic-cotton duvets. Lounge by the solar-powered, saline-clean swimming pool and Jacuzzi, and enjoy complimentary breakfast and bikes. In summer, 'glamping tents' and an Airstream trailer offer outdoorsy comfort.

Eating

Big Bottom Market MARKET, CAFE $
(☎707-604-7295; www.bigbottommarket.com; 16228 Main St; sandwiches $10-13; ⌚8am-5pm Wed-Mon;) Russian River does deli differently – Big Bottom is gourmet all day and hike-ready. Sandwiches named for famous redwoods are big on flavor, especially the Colonel Armstrong (curried chicken on brioche), but Sea Biscuit (smoked salmon, pickled onions and capers) wins top honors. Coffee and bespoke wines are wonderful.

Boon Eat + Drink CALIFORNIAN $$
(☎707-869-0780; www.eatatboon.com; 16248 Main St; mains $12-28; ⌚11am-3pm & 5-9pm Sun-Tue & Thu, to 10pm Fri & Sat;) Good vibes are the not-so-secret ingredient in this tiny, always-packed bistro. Hyperlocal flavor bombs like mycopia-mushroom mac and cheese and preserved Meyer lemon chicken satisfy lumberjack appetites, while checking environmental scorecards. Chef/owner/dynamo Crista Luedtke uses homegrown ingredients from her Boon Hotel + Spa and pours her own Big Bottom Market wines – her cooking has sustained Guerneville through firestorms and floods, not to mention first dates.

Drinking & Nightlife

R3 Hotel Pool Bar GAY & LESBIAN

(Triple R; 707-869-8399; www.ther3hotel.com; 16390 4th St; 9am-close;) The all-gay, all-day, 21-plus swimming-pool party scene at the R3 Hotel is free, provided you buy drinks and bring your own towel. The indoor-outdoor, retro redwood pool bar is party central during Women's Weekend and Lazy Bear Week. Bathing suits are mandatory, but only because state liquor-license laws require them.

Stumptown Brewery BREWERY

(Map p220; 707-869-0705; www.stumptown.com; 15045 River Rd; 11am-midnight Sun-Thu, to 2am Fri & Sat) After big days on the river, everyone washes up about a mile east of downtown at the riverside beer garden of Guerneville's gay-friendly, mostly straight brewpub for microbrews on tap with house-smoked barbecue. Their Donkey Punch pilsner lubricates boogie muscles when the jukebox booms, and Rat Bastard pale ale is liquid courage to challenge regulars at billiards.

Shopping

★**rio rio** FASHION & ACCESSORIES, ARTS & CRAFTS

(707-604-7028; https://riostore.com; 16216b Main St; 11am-4pm Sat & Sun Oct-Apr, to 6pm May-Sep) Russian River's boho-style well-spring is an essential source of NorCal necessities: nubby hand-knit sweaters for redwoods nights, ceramic pipes disguised as peaches by crafty stoners, uterus-shaped bookmarks by crafty feminists, and vintage bracelets banged out by '70s Sonoma silversmiths. Hours are limited and items unique at this upstairs micro-boutique, so snap up vintage scores and accessories when you can.

★**Guerneville Bank Club** FOOD

(707-666-9411; www.guernevillebankclub.com; 16290 Main St; 11am-9pm Sun-Thu, to 10pm Fri & Sat;) The bank went bust 30 years ago – now the front counter sells ice cream, the back office hosts wine tastings, and the vault is a photo booth. Independent local businesses have taken over Guerneville's 1921 beaux arts bank, fronted by Nimble & Finn's organic ice cream and Jam Jar's (p229) handcrafted gifts, including boho-glam macramé earrings.

Information

Russian River Chamber of Commerce & Visitors Center (Map p220; 707-869-9000; www.russianriver.com; 16209 1st St; 10am-4:45pm Mon-Sat, plus to 3pm Sun May-Oct) Information and lodging referrals.

Getting There & Away

The drive from San Francisco takes just over two hours, depending on traffic. Public transit is complicated, but you can take the SMART (p173) train to Santa Rosa. From there, you could cycle to Guerneville via Sebastopol and Forestville.

Healdsburg & Dry Creek Valley

Today Healdsburg seems to have it all – looks, style, taste, plenty of money – but its history is a real-life telenovela. It began with forbidden romance, when rebellious SoCal teenager Joséfa Carrillo fell for wise-cracking, Massachusetts-born sea captain Henry Fitch. To marry Joséfa, Henry became a citizen of Mexican California and converted to Catholicism. But California's governor had a crush on Joséfa, and blocked the wedding. Undeterred, they eloped.

This forbidden love affair was California's first big scandal, and Joséfa had to sue the governor for her marriage to be recognized. Joséfa and Henry planned to homestead 48,000-acre ranch on leased Wappo land in Sonoma – but Henry died of pneumonia in 1849, leaving Joséfa widowed at age 39, with 11 kids and a not-yet-working ranch.

Following in the footsteps of her mother María Ygnacia, founder of Santa Rosa, Joséfa packed up her kids and made the 700-mile journey north. When she arrived, she discovered her mother had died, Sonoma was US territory, and under US law, women could not own property. Joséfa fought for her rights for seven years – and meanwhile, an uninvited guest named Harmon Heald squatted on Joséfa's property. The US government decided Joséfa was obliged to pay back taxes on a ranch she might not even own, and auctioned off her property to the highest bidders, including Harmon. Disputes erupted into turf battles known as the Healdsburg Wars.

When the dust finally settled in Healdsburg in the 1860s, a Victorian village began to flourish around the Russian River bend near **Healdsburg Plaza**, the town's sun-dappled central square (bordered by Healdsburg Ave and Center, Matheson and Plaza Sts). Surrounding ranchlands were planted over with farms and vineyards, and a pioneering volunteer fire department saved the township many times over.

Today Healdsburg is a gourmet magnet, with farm-inspired bistros and wine-tasting rooms ringing the Plaza. Bicycle over to vineyard-lined **West Dry Creek Road** and **Westside Road**, where California sunshine, riverbed terrain and valley mists produce wonderfully nuanced wines. True to Healdsburg's origins, they taste of stubborn roots and undeniable romance, with a faint whiff of scandal.

Sights

★Emmit-Scorsone Wine — WINERY

(Map p220; ☎707 287 8080; www.emmittscorsone.com; 1830 Jameson Rd; tasting $25; ⊙by appointment 10am-3:30pm) Dry Creek's best find is this hidden winery, where upstart cult wines Judge Palmer and Domenica Amato are made – and between tasks, the winemaker pours sneak previews. The tiny hillside vineyard is mighty productive, yielding Judge Palmer cabernet with more character than a roomful of Napa cowboys. Don't miss Judge Palmer's unexpectedly profound sauvignon blanc, or Domenica Amato's inspired tributes to California's Italian-immigrant wines: statuesque fianos, irresistible rosés, and ingenious field blends. Three-bottle minimum purchase; tasting fee is refunded (bottles $26 to $75).

★Preston — WINERY

(Map p220; ☎707-433-3372; www.prestonvineyards.com; 9282 W Dry Creek Rd, bar tasting/private tasting/tour $20/30/40; ⊙11am-4:30pm; P 🚻) Behind a white picket fence, Lou Preston planted the seeds of revolution at a 19th-century farmstead. A pioneer in organics and biodynamic wines, Preston grows heirloom produce and raises livestock to support an integrated ecosystem – sheep handle weeding, and artichokes and radishes help with pest control. The farm store sells produce, olive oil and estate-grown-wheat bread, while the bar pours citrusy sauvignon blanc, satiny viognier, spicy zinfandel, and food-friendly barbera (bottles $22 to $46). Picnic under century-old walnut trees – joining a revolution has never been so relaxing.

★Idlewild — TASTING ROOM

(Map p220; www.idlewildwines.com; 132 Plaza St; tasting $20; ⊙noon-7pm) Italy's most fascinating wines come from the northern province of Piedmont – but several especially fascinating Piedmontese wines are quietly made in Northern California by fourth-generation winemaker Sam Bilbro. Through traditional natural winemaking practices, Sam transforms Mendocino grapes into micro-batches of gardenia-and-pearls arneis, sneaky-spicy white cortese, and a stunning, multifaceted gem nebbiolo that easily outclasses reds six times the price (bottles $25 to $50). Generous pairings of Piedmontese artisan cheeses and salumi provide excellent reasons to idle a while longer.

★Unti Vineyards — WINERY

(Map p220; ☎707-433-5590; www.untivineyards.com; 4202 Dry Creek Rd; tasting $20; ⊙by appointment 10am-4pm; 🐾) From Unti's tasting-room window, rolling Dry Creek Valley vineyards look like sun-drenched Tuscan hills – and that's exactly what you'll taste in your wineglass. Not a cab or chardonnay in sight here: Mitch Unti organically farms Mediterranean noble grapes that thrive in these conditions, including silky vermentino, crisp white fiano, coveted rosé of mourvedre and grenache, Châteauneuf-du-Pape–style grenache blends that fool French palates, and a sangiovese to rival Super Tuscans (bottles $24 to $70). Tasting fee refundable with purchase.

★Bella — WINERY

(Map p220; ☎707-395-6136; www.bellawinery.com; 9711 W Dry Creek Rd; tasting $20; ⊙11am-4:30pm; P) Under a flowering hill at the northern edge of Dry Creek Valley, there's a party in progress. Bella's caves are as pretty as the name suggests and impressively hardworking, turning grapes from 105-year-old estate vines into prize zinfandels and syrah. Duck into the cave for a tasting with Bella's upbeat winery team, and emerge blinking in the sunshine, gripping a glass (OK, bottle) of rosé of grenache to toast the enduring beauty of life (bottles $28 to $68).

Reeve Wines — WINERY

(Map p220; ☎707-235-6345; www.reevewines.com; 4551 Dry Creek Rd; tastings $35-50; ⊙11am-5pm; P) Follow a tree-lined country lane into a California oak grove, where dappled sunlight dances down the path into an old brick farmhouse. This landscape painting is an actual place, and better yet it's a winery whose small-batch wines earn rock-star followings. Patio bistro-table tastings let you admire the vineyards and sheep pastures as you sip poetry-inducing rosé of pinot noir and alluring single-vineyard sangiovese, with a stoneware platter of local cheeses and charcuterie for DIY pairing.

Saturday Farmers Market MARKET

(Map p220; www.healdsburgfarmersmarket.org; North & Vine Sts; ⊙8:30am-noon Sat Apr-Nov;) Sunny Saturdays begin with warm hellos from Sonoma farmers, inspiring cooking demos, and live music in downtown Healdsburg. Graze local food vendors – Dry Creek peaches, Lata's samosas, Volo chocolate's bean-to-bar treats, Valley Ford Creamery's award-winning Estero Gold cheeses, organic Preston olive oil – and find unique handmade gifts, including Lissa Herschleb's stamped ceramic earrings and Michael Rosen's stoneware mugs. Since 1978 the market has hosted seasonal events, from zucchini races to pumpkin-carving contests; see the website schedule.

Lioco TASTING ROOM

(Map p220; 707-395-0148; www.liocowine.com; 125 Matheson St; tastings $20-40; ⊙noon-7pm) Drink all along Northern California's coast from the comfort of your lounge seat at Lioco, specialist in cool-climate coastal chardonnays and pinot noirs. Taste the forest floor in Sonoma Coast pinots, wild berries in Anderson Valley pinots, oyster shells in Santa Cruz chardonnays, and pot gummy bears in Mendocino Indica rosé. Discerning drinkers will especially enjoy the *omokase* flight, where your bartender chooses six wines for you to try.

Quivira WINERY

(Map p220; 707-431-8333; www.quivirawine.com; 4900 W Dry Creek Rd; tastings $20-30, incl tour $40; ⊙by reservation 11am-4pm;) Sunflowers wave, pigs oink and roosters crow as you arrive at this certified-organic vineyard and biodynamic farm, with self-guided garden tours and a redwood grove beside the vines. Breathe deeply in the lavender gardens, and you might forget what brought you here: zesty zins, crowd-pleasing rosé and award-winning sauvignon blanc (bottles $22 to $60). Estate tastings on the sunny patio includes six wines plus seasonal treats, including farm-raised charcuterie.

Portalupi TASTING ROOM

(Map p220; 707-395-0960; www.portalupiwine.com; 107 North St; tasting $30, refundable with purchase; ⊙11am-6pm Sun-Thu, to 7pm Fri & Sat) Drinkers owe a debt to crafty Italian farmers, who procured special dispensation to cultivate Dry Creek grapevines through Prohibition for 'communion wine.' Highlights include sea-breezy vermentino, unexpected *méthode champenoise* sparkling barbera, and old-vine zins full of sunshine and songs. Refillable milk-bottles of rosé and Piedmont-style white blends honor family matriarch Marina Portalupi, who sold her own homemade wine at her San Jose grocery store.

Activities

Russian River Adventures CANOEING

(Map p220; 707-433-5599; www.russianriveradventures.com; 20 Healdsburg Ave; canoe rental & shuttle adult/child from $75/35;) Paddle a secluded stretch of river in comfortable inflatable canoes, stopping for rope swings, swimming holes, beaches and bird-watching in the redwoods. This ecotourism outfit points you in the right direction and gives you a choice of shuttle options: take an e-bike or car shuttle, or they'll valet your car to the pickup point. Kids are freer to play around in these stable canoes, and so are dogs ($15 per dog) – and everyone gets life jackets that fit. Reservations required.

River's Edge Kayak & Canoe Trips KAYAKING, CANOEING

(Map p220; 707-433-7247; www.riversedgekayakandcanoe.com; 1 Healdsburg Ave; kayak/canoe rental from $70, incl shuttle from $140) Hop in a canoe or kayak and paddle down a lazy stretch of Russian River, past posing egrets, playful turtles and shy deer. Take your pick of hard-sided canoes or single/double kayaks for self-guided river tours, and don't worry about portage – staff take you 5 miles upriver in a shuttle and help get you launched. After three to five hours of floating, paddling and goofing off, you'll end up at the boat dock. For less commitment, try stand-up paddleboards.

Courses

★Breathless Wines Sabrage Session WINE

(Map p220; 707-395-7300; www.breathlesswines.com; 499 Moore Lane; sabrage class incl sparkling wine $69; ⊙11am-5pm Thu-Mon) Anyone can pop a bottle of bubbly, but can they open it with a sword? Napoleon's troops did it after victories, and after a one-on-one lesson with a Breathless expert in sabrage (the art of opening wine with a saber), you too can celebrate triumphs with this surprisingly simple swashbuckling trick. Afterwards, enjoy your tasty bubbly on Breathless' sunny patio.

Festivals & Events

Wine Road Barrel Tasting WINE

(www.wineroad.com/events/barrel-tasting; ⊙Mar) Wine aficionados, mark your calendars: Sonoma wineries from Alexander Valley to

Russian River throw open wine-cave doors and let visitors sample wine directly from the barrel, before it's bottled or sold. You get a sneak peek at wines that promise to be great,and can snap up bottles in advance (called 'futures'), before collectors buy them. Prices vary by tasting.

Wine & Food Affair FOOD & DRINK
(www.wineroad.com/events/wine-food-affair; weekend/Sun only $100/70; ⏲Nov) Let your taste buds be your guide to 100 Sonoma wineries, which offer a featured dish and wine pairing. Events take place across Sonoma's Alexander, Dry Creek and Russian River Valleys – check the website for dates, maps, menus and recipes. Vegetarian and gluten-free options are available at some locations. Laws and licenses prohibit bringing kids and dogs.

Sleeping

L&M Motel MOTEL $$
(Map p220; ☎707-433-6528; www.landmmotel.com; 70 Healdsburg Ave; d $175-205; P⊖❄🛜≋🐾) A classic 1952 motor court, L&M is like an American road-movie set, with telephone tables, kitschy bedspreads and huge plastic key chains. Rooms are kept clean, and a couple have kitchenettes; bonuses include an indoor swimming pool, Jacuzzi and cedar sauna. Outdoors, Adirondack chairs, fire pits and barbecue grills dot grassy lawns. Breakfast included; two-night minimum.

Belle de Jour Inn B&B $$
(Map p220; ☎707-431-9777; www.belledejourinn.com; 16276 Healdsburg Ave; d $225-295, ste $355; ⊖❄🛜) Manicured gardens hug white-washed cottages, giving you all the country charm you could ask for without actually getting dirty. Each sunny, uncluttered guest room has its own individual character – some have terraces or jetted tubs, all have sun-dried sheets and fresh flowers grown at your doorstep. A 10-minute drive from downtown or Dry Creek wineries; two-night minimum.

Camellia Inn B&B $$
(Map p220; ☎800-727-8182, 707-433-8182; www.camelliainn.com; 211 North St; d $159-395; P⊖❄🛜≋) Good moods come naturally at this cheery pink 1871 mansion, with camellia-filled gardens, sociable parlors and upbeat, helpful innkeepers. Plush guest rooms have dreamy beds and updated bathrooms, and iPads are thoughtfully provided to eliminate TV noise. Perks include a seasonal pool, complimentary breakfasts, happy-hour wine, and wine-tasting passes at 100-plus wineries (some within walking distance).

Healdsburg Inn on the Plaza INN $$
(Map p220; ☎707-433-6991; www.healdsburginn.com; 112 Matheson St; d $230-460; ⊖❄🛜🐾) Prime location on Healdsburg Plaza and reliable service make stays at this spiffy former stagecoach stop worthwhile. Twelve modern guest rooms have gas fireplaces and comfortable beds with fine linens, but they're a bit too beige to be memorable – though a couple of bathrooms squeeze in a jetted double tub. Complimentary wine hour and breakfasts; check for deals online.

★**Hotel Healdsburg** HOTEL $$$
(Map p220; ☎707-431-2800; www.hotelhealdsburg.com; 25 Matheson St; d from $409; ⊖❄@🛜≋) Polished concrete and mood-lit minimalism may seem out of place on Healdsburg's quaint plaza, but Hotel Healdsburg's easygoing warmth works its charms even before you hit the spa (get the Meyer-lemon-sage massage). Sunny guest rooms have sumptuous beds, soaking tubs and cloudscapes by Healdsburg's own Wade Hoefer. Relaxation aids include the garden pool, complimentary bikes, on-site **Dry Creek Kitchen** (Map p220; ☎707-431-0330; www.drycreekkitchen.com; 317 Healdsburg Ave; mains $32-44, tasting menu $29, wine pairing $48; ⏲5:30-9:30pm Sun-Thu, to 10pm Fri & Sat), cocktails and weekend jazz.

★**Madrona Manor** HISTORIC HOTEL $$$
(Map p220; ☎707-433-4231; www.madronamanor.com; 1001 Westside Rd; d $295-435; P⊖❄🛜≋) Live it up at this Victorian hilltop manor like you just invented California sparkling wine. The original 1881 mansion has nine suite-sized rooms with fireplaces, plush king beds and ornate carved furnishings; two have balconies with views across the 8-acre estate. The converted carriage-house and schoolhouse offer spacious, cushy accommodations, but star attractions remain the mansion and in-house restaurant.

Hotel Les Mars BOUTIQUE HOTEL $$$
(Map p220; ☎707-433-4211; www.hotellesmars.com; 27 North St; d $490-550; ⊖❄🛜) *Mais oui,* you're still in Healdsburg – this beaux arts hotel offers gracious welcomes with francophone flourishes. Spacious guest rooms have four-poster beds you might find hard to leave, until breakfast arrives at your door – classic and timeless, if a bit stuffy for Sonoma. Local wineries provide afternoon wine-and-cheese

tastings, plus complimentary passes to winery tours. Two-night minimum on weekends.

Eating

Costeaux French Bakery & Cafe CAFE $
(Map p220; 707-433-1913; www.costeaux.com; 417 Healdsburg Ave; mains $9-17; 7am-3pm Mon-Sat, to 1pm Sun;) Serving restorative breakfasts since 1923, Healdsburg's favorite bakery-cafe provides quiches, omelets and breakfast pastries all day, with cheerful efficiency – Costeaux is repeatedly voted one of Sonoma's best places to work. For picnics, get sandwiches on fresh baguettes or award-winning multigrain. Through COVID-19 quarantine, Costeaux kept baking to supply bread for Redwood Empire Food Bank.

Noble Folk Ice Cream & Pie Bar DESSERTS $
(Map p220; 707-395-4426; www.thenoblefolk.com; 116 Matheson St; items $3-6; noon-9pm;) The plaza buzz is about Noble Folk ice cream, especially local-favorite flavors: *horchata*, passion fruit, matcha and black-sesame-coconut. That sweet taste of success is made fresh daily by partners and co-chefs/owners Ozzy Jimenez and Christian Sulberg, a dessert dream team – their Sonoma lemon-lavender cupcakes, brownie cubes and raspberry brown-butter macarons are even tastier than they look on your Insta feed.

★Mateo's Cocina Latina FUSION $$
(Map p220; 707-433-1520; www.mateoscocina latina.com; 214 Healdsburg Ave; mains $16-30; 3-8pm Mon & Wed-Sat, to 7pm Sun) Stepping up to every plate with all-organic Sonoma ingredients, Michelin-level precision and profound Yucatán flavors, owner/chef/farmer Mateo Granados is rocking Wine Country cuisine. Slow-braised dishes like *pollo alcaparrado* (chicken with olives and capers) and *cochinita pibil* are soul-satisfying with made-to-order organic masa tortillas – and perfectly paired with Sonoma pinots or small-batch mezcal.

Chalkboard CALIFORNIAN $$
(Map p220; 707-473-8030; www.chalkboard healdsburg.com; 29 North St; mains $19-26; 4:30-8:30pm Wed-Sun, from 5pm Mon & Tue) That small, seasonal, ingredient-driven bistro every chef dreams of opening has come to life at Chalkboard, a snug wine grotto with a sunny back patio where customers share plates family-style with genuine excitement. Start with shots of today's soup, progress to housemade pasta, followed by local scallops, crispy buttermilk-fried chicken, braised short ribs – and please pass that Meyer-lemon semifreddo.

Campo Fina ITALIAN $$
(Map p220; 707-395-4640; www.campofina.com; 330 Healdsburg Ave; pizza $17.50-19.50, mains $19-26; 11:30am-10pm;) In an 1884 storefront, Campo Fina maintains Healdsburg's spaghetti-Western traditions with pasta and wood-fired pizza – go classic mozzarella *di bufala* and basil, or gourmet *cardoncello* mushrooms and sausage. Recipes from *nonna* inspire tomato-braised chicken with polenta and 'old school in a skillet' meatballs with housebaked ciabatta.

Barndiva CALIFORNIAN $$
(Map p220; 707-431-0100; www.barndiva.com; 231 Center St; mains lunch $16-24, dinner $28-38; noon-2:30pm Wed-Sun, dinner from 5:30pm) Edible landscape paintings are your lunch in the garden at Barndiva, where striking, sustainable modern dishes like espresso-dusted beet-red risotto and bright-orange California salmon on black forbidden rice prove rustic can be artistic. Inside the action focuses on the bar, featuring original concoctions like the shameless Flirt: jalapeño-infused Hot Mama tequila, St Germain liqueur, lime and peach bitters.

★SingleThread CALIFORNIAN, JAPANESE $$$
(Map p220; 707-723-4646; www.singlethread farms.com; 131 North St; tasting menu per person $330; dinner from 5:30pm daily, lunch from 11:30am Sat & Sun) Once twinkly-eyed staff treat you to welcome tea, they usher you to a table seemingly set by a meticulous Pacific tsunami. A mossy log is sprinkled with meadow wildflowers and ceramic dishes of pristine Pacific seafood – all sublime, especially silken Dungeness crab *chawanmushi* (egg custard) and amberjack with purple daikon and chrysanthemum flowers. This edible Sonoma landscape is the first of 11 sensational seasonal courses, ranging from vineyard 'cover crop' grains to forest-floor foraged morel dashi – a tour de force of nature.

Valette CALIFORNIAN $$$
(Map p220; 707-473-0946; www.valettehealds burg.com; 344 Center St; tasting menu per course $15, minimum 3 courses; 5:30-9:30pm) Healdsburg-inspired describes Dustin and Aaron, the Sonoma-born brothers behind Valette, and the meals they share with friends and strangers alike. You might spot Dustin at Healdsburg Farmers Market, hauling a wagon-full of produce destined for his 'trust me'

tasting menu – recently, garden-grown nasturtium-flower salads, Duroc pork rubbed with Flying Goat espresso, Dry Creek peach pannacotta, and Valette's own-label wine (or BYOB; corkage is $20).

Bravas Bar de Tapas TAPAS $$$
(Map p220; ☎707-433-7700; www.starkrestaurants.com/stark-restaurant/bravas-bar-de-tapas; 420 Center St; tapas $7-16, family-style large plates $28-74; ⌚11:30am-9pm Sun-Thu, to 10pm Fri & Sat) Sonoma meets Spain in this bungalow tapas bar dishing up platters of classic seafood paella, Sonoma-inspired *piquillo* peppers stuffed with Dungeness crab, decadent roast cauliflower with blue cheese and dates, and namesake *patatas bravas* (spicy potatoes). When temperatures hit 72 degrees, Healdsburg converges on the back patio for sangria and deep cuts from the vast menu, including crispy pig ears and duck-meatball sliders.

Drinking & Nightlife

Duke's Spirited Cocktails COCKTAIL BAR
(Map p220; ☎707-431-1060; www.drinkatdukes.com; 111 Plaza St; ⌚4pm-midnight Mon-Thu, to 2am Fri & Sat, 2pm-midnight Sun) Keeping Healdsburg up past its bedtime since 1933, Duke's pours creative craft cocktails in good company – once the drink kicks in, so does the dance floor. Signature cocktails have cheeky names like 'Fools Paradise' (tequila, vermouth, passion fruit) and 'The Remedy' (scotch, chamomile, lemon, turmeric), but that pour is no joke and ingredients are grown, distilled and fermented by Sonoma neighbors.

Shopping

Gallery Lulo JEWELRY, ART
(Map p220; ☎707-433-7533; www.gallerylulo.com; 303 Center St; ⌚11am-5pm Mon-Thu, to 6pm Fri-Sun) Elemental glamor is Healdsburg's preferred look, and Gallery Lulo is here to see you rock it. Some of the original, handmade works on display are wearable, including Emily Bixler's crocheted chain collars and Morgania Moore's Sonoma olive-wood statement necklaces, while other artworks are inspirational totems, including Recheng Tsang's shaggy porcelain tree-bark wall hangings and Jennifer Kent's radiant energy ink drawings.

Levin & Company & Upstairs Gallery BOOKS, MUSIC
(Map p220; ☎707-433-1118; www.levinbooks.com; 306 Center St; ⌚9am-6pm Mon-Thu, to 9pm Fri & Sat, from 10am Sun; 👪) Artistic souls find their spiritual home in Healdsburg at Levin & Co, a bookseller with over 17,000 titles, plus music on vinyl and CD, including an impressive jazz selection. For 23 years the co-op gallery on the mezzanine has showcased local talents in a range of media, from blown glass to contemporary quilts.

Jam Jar ARTS & CRAFTS, GIFTS & SOUVENIRS
(Map p220; ☎707-508-6664; www.jamjargoods.com; 126 North St; ⌚11am-5pm Wed-Sat, to 2pm Sun) When you don't know what gifts to bring home from California, let Jam Jar give you a hand – maybe literally, because nothing says hello from California like Meg Meyers' rainbow-hued stained-glass hands. Bring home Sonoma style with La Donna's boho beaded shoulder-duster earrings, Local Yokel soy candles in bewitching woodsy scents, and artist Molly Perez' collage kits for blustery days.

Information

Healdsburg Chamber of Commerce & Visitors Bureau (Map p220; ☎800-648-9922, 707-433-6935; www.healdsburg.com; 217 Healdsburg Ave; ⌚10am-4pm Mon-Fri, 11am-2pm Sat & Sun) A block south of the plaza, this small but helpful office has winery maps, some two-for-one tasting passes, and information on ballooning, golf, tennis, spas and nearby farms.

Getting There & Away

Sonoma County Transit (p173) buses travel around Healdsburg and connect it to neighboring cities, with prices ranging from $1.50 to $4.80 depending on how many zones you pass through on your journey. Child prices range from $1.25 to $4.55. From Santa Rosa, SMART (p173) train and bus takes you to Marin's Larkspur Landing, from where the Bay Ferry (p173) will take you to San Francisco.

Healdsburg is about a 90-minute drive north from San Francisco.

Geyserville, Alexander Valley & Around

Welcome to Geyserville, population 862 – but where are the geysers? Wander the town's old wooden boardwalk, and you'll find genuine Wild West character, plus Diavola Pizza and wine made by Alexander Valley neighbors, but no sign of the geothermal wonders that initially attracted visitors here in 1847.

The hot springs are underground, making Geyserville an early adopter of geothermal power generation. Harnessing 350 fumaroles just uphill from Geyserville, the local power-generating operation now produces 20% of California's renewable energy. To get into hot water, reserve a spot at Coppola Winery's vast hilltop swimming pools.

Geyserville also invested in a state-of-the-art fire station that has saved the town and rescued the historic vineyards of Alexander Valley (www.alexandervalley.org). Follow Hwy 128 to Soda Rock winery's tasting room in the old fire-singed barn, and raise a toast to firefighters with signature California zinfandel. Down the road you'll find resilient Chalk Hill AVA vineyards flourishing at two indie wineries run by women. Reserve ahead to try velvety Carpenter pinots and mineral-rich Sutro sauvignon blanc. The geysers may be hidden up in the hills now, but the people power is more apparent than ever in Alexander Valley.

Sights & Activities

★Sutro Wine WINERY
(Map p220; 707-509-9695; www.sutrowine.com; 13301 Chalk Hill Rd, Healdsburg; vineyard hike with tasting per person $25; by appointment 11am-4:30pm;) Hike Sutro vineyard with brilliant young winemaker and old soul Alice Sutro, and you'll see California landscapes differently. A fifth-generation farmer on this plot, Alice could walk it with her eyes closed: here's the white volcanic outcropping that gives Chalk Hill its name, and sauvignon blanc its pearlescent beauty; there's the treeline where river mists hang, providing cabernet and merlot just enough cover to cultivate an air of dark mystery. Post-hike tastings are held in neighboring Medlock Ames' barrel room; purchase customary ($28 to $50).

★Carpenter Wine WINERY
(Map p220; 707-385-8177; www.carpenterwine.com; 14255 Chalk Hill Rd; by appointment 11am-6pm;) Under a sheltering oak surrounded by vineyards, you're having a dream picnic with some real Sonoma characters. Co-founder/sommelier Laura Carpenter Hawkes is your engaging host, introducing natural wines with distinct Sonoma personalities: the redwood-roaming boho rosé, the soulful Sonoma Coast pinot down for all-night jam sessions, the irreverent carbonic pinot noir making light of any situation. These wines love food, so Laura graciously introduces all-local treats: herb-wrapped goat cheese, spiced nuts, artisan charcuterie. Call for appointment and directions; tasting complimentary with purchase (three bottles per person; bottles $24 to $60).

★Soda Rock Winery WINERY
(Map p220; 707-433-3303; www.sodarockwinery.com; 8015 Hwy 128; tasting $15; 11am-5pm) All hail Lord Snort, Sonoma artist Bryan Tedrick's recycled-metal boar sculpture, which survived its 2016 Burning Man debut before arriving at Soda Rock – where it faced more trials by fire. Soda Rock's 1869 stone tasting room collapsed in the 2019 Kincade Fire – but Lord Snort survived, his triumphant grin a symbol of Sonoma's resurgence. Soda Rock's redwood bar was dragged from tasting-room ruins and set up in the singed barn, where tastings of big-hearted zinfandel, primitivo, merlot and cab will make you glad to be alive.

Hawkes WINERY
(Map p220; 707-433-4295; www.hawkeswine.com; 6734 Hwy 128, Healdsburg; reserve cab tasting or vineyard tour & tasting $60; 10am-5pm;) Back when this sunny valley held the dubious honor of being America's prune-producing capital, rebel farmer Stephen Hawkes started growing cabernet grapes instead. Fast-forward about 50 years, and Hawkes' big, bold, estate-grown cabs firmly established Alexander Valley as premier cab country. Second-generation winemaker Jake Hawkes upholds the family's deliciously contrarian streak with prismatic, mind-bending merlots, and a supernova cab/merlot rosé that sells out before it's bottled – taste it here, and you can score 'futures' before it's released (bottles $28 to $75).

Hanna WINERY
(Map p220; 707-431-4310; www.hannawinery.com; 9280 Hwy 128, Healdsburg; tastings $15-35, with food pairing $40-45, with lunch $50-85; 10am-4pm;) Looking westward across oak-studded hills from the veranda, you can practically taste Hanna's sunny, rustic, estate-grown chardonnay, zinfandel and cabernet. Drop-ins are welcome, but owner/winemaker/oenology professor/superhuman Christine Hanna also happens to be a gourmet chef and cookbook author – reserve ahead for her inspired charcuterie and estate cabernet pairings ($45), picnic lunches with five-wine flights under Hanna's ancient oak ($50), and hearty four-course plated meals with wine pairings ($85). Otherwise, buy a bottle and enjoy scenic DIY picnics (bottles $19 to $68).

Medlock Ames WINERY
(Map p220; 707-431-8845; www.medlockames.com; 3487 Alexander Valley Rd, Healdsberg; tasting of current releases/with cheese pairing/library wine

& cheese $20/30/50; 10am-4:30pm;) Backlit wines cast a rosy glow across the tasting room, and they work similar magic in your glass. Organically estate-grown wines hint at nostalgic pie flavors: lemon-meringue in sauvignon blanc, rhubarb in merlot rosé, and blueberry in heritage merlot, from a clone of vines grown by Thomas Jefferson. But Medlock Ames is also thinking ahead: 80% of their acreage is set aside for woodlands and wildlife, and there's room for kids and puppies to frolic here too.

Lake Sonoma Recreation Area PARK

(Map p220; www.spn.usace.army.mil/Missions/Recreation/Lake-Sonoma; 3333 Skaggs Springs Rd, Geyswerville; sunrise-sunset) A teal lake amid golden Sonoma foothills, this scenic wilderness preserve was made by the US Army. In 1983 the US Army Corps of Engineers built Warm Springs Dam for practical purposes, including flood control and irrigation – and the result was this sporting paradise, with a lake for boating and fishing, miles of trails for hiking and biking, a hillside archery range, and a fish hatchery that's helped restore Sonoma's once-endangered steelhead.

Francis Ford Coppola Winery Swimming Pools SWIMMING, WINE

(Map p220; 707-857-1471; www.francisfordcoppolawinery.com; 300 Via Archimedes, Geyserville; day pass adult/child $35/15; 11am-6pm daily Jun-Sep, Fri-Sun May & Oct;) Bask in Hollywood glamour at the hilltop winery estate of movie/wine mogul Francis Ford Coppola. Bocce ball is free (11am to 9pm), wine tastings are fun ($20 to $30), and tours ($15) and scavenger hunts ($10) include Coppola family movie memorabilia – but the best attraction on a summer's day are the pools flanked by lounge chairs.

Sleeping

Old Crocker Inn LODGE $$

(707-894-4000; www.oldcrockerinn.com; 1126 Old Crocker Inn Rd, Cloverdale; d $165-265;) Live large on the historic ranch of railroad baron Charles Crocker. The Crocker guest room is the lodge's fanciest, with a hand-carved four-poster bed and clawf-oot tub – but the most elegant is Canton Cottage, honoring California's Chinese railroad builders. For rustic atmosphere, book snug Golden Spike cottage, with pine-wood walls, heritage quilts and jetted tub.

Geyserville Inn INN $$

(Map p220; 707-857-4343; www.geyservilleinn.com; 21714 Geyserville Ave, Geyserville; d/ste from $209/299;) Drift off amid Alexander Valley vineyards 8 miles north of Healdsburg, walking distance from dinner in downtown Geyserville. Freshly renovated, well-kept modern rooms are furnished in soothing silvery tones, with big upholstered beds piled with feather pillows. Request a deluxe room with a balcony or fireplace. Outside, there's a solar-heated pool and a hot tub with those vineyard views.

Eating

Plank Coffee & Tea CAFE, BAKERY $

(707-894-6187; 227 N Cloverdale Blvd, Cloverdale; pastries $2-7; 6am-6pm;) Wine Country runs on caffeine – and discerning drinkers detour to Plank for house-roasted, single-origin espresso drinks and an impressive selection of 50 loose-leaf teas. The quiche and baked treats are housemade, including classic Bundt cakes and gluten-free brownies – but if you're on a post-wine-tasting cleanse, so are fresh-squeezed green juice and strawberry shrub (vinegar soda).

Pick's Drive-In BURGERS $

(707-894-2962; 117 S Cloverdale Blvd, Cloverdale; burgers $9-12; 11am-8pm;) An all-American classic, Pick's opened during Prohibition, hoping to convince Wine Country to switch from booze to root-beer floats. That didn't exactly work, but Pick's became a Sonoma standby for its burgers. Pull up to original counter stools for local, hormone free, humanely raised Niman Ranch beef burgers, Sonoma lamb burgers or vegetarian black-bean patties – plus tasty root-beer floats made with Sonoma's Clover ice cream.

★Diavola Pizza ITALIAN, CALIFORNIAN $$

(Map p220; 707-814-0111; www.diavolapizzeria.com; 21021 Geyserville Ave, Geyserville; mains $16-29; 11:30am-9pm;) A contender for California's best pizza, Diavola graces perfectly crispy thin-crust, wood-fired pizza with house-cured salumi and sausage. Seasonal oven-roasted beets, brussels sprouts and broccolini are positively decadent, generously drizzled with Sonoma olive oil, balsamic and parmigiano. Diavola's secret is dedication – when fires raged down the street, Diavola stayed open to make free pizza for firefighters. Anticipate waits; it's worth it.

AT A GLANCE

POPULATION
305,890

TALLEST REDWOOD TREE
Hyperion, 380.1ft

BEST OYSTERS
Humboldt Bay Provisions (p274)

BEST SMALL TOWN
Point Arena (p244)

BEST GREEN INITIATIVE
Real Goods Solar Living Center (p257)

WHEN TO GO

Jun–Jul The driest season in the Redwoods is spectacular for day hikes and big views.

Aug–Oct Warm weather and clear skies are ideal for hiking the Lost Coast.

Dec–Apr Whales migrate off the coast.

Redwood National Park (p281)
CARMEN MARTINEZ TORRON / GETTY IMAGES ©

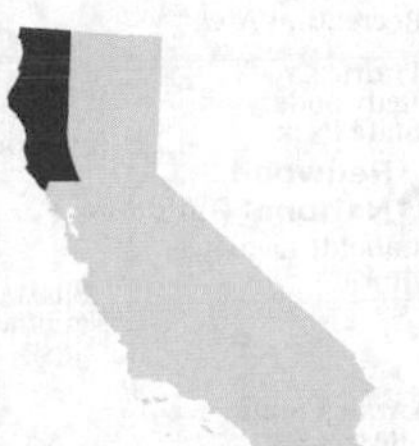

North Coast & Redwoods

This is not the legendary California of the Beach Boys' song – there are no palm-flanked beaches and very few surfboards. The jagged edge of the continent is wild, scenic and even slightly foreboding. Craggy sienna cliffs tower over windswept beaches and rocky coves. Spectral fog and an outsider spirit have fostered the world's tallest trees, most potent weed and a string of idiosyncratic two-stoplight towns.

Explore hidden coves, scan the horizon for migrating whales and retreat at night to fire-warmed Victorians. As you travel further north, you will find valleys of redwood, wide rivers and mossy, overgrown forests where elk roam. Expect cooler, damper weather too. The unlikely mélange of residents befits this clash of land and water: timber barons, tree huggers, pot farmers and radicals of every political persuasion.

INCLUDES

North Coast & Redwoods Highlights

1 Avenue of the Giants (p269) Humbling yourself on a road trip through the largest contiguous old-growth redwood forest on earth.

2 Mendocino (p247) Strolling past the wave-blasted bluffs and salt-worn cottages of this swanky seaside village.

3 Hopland (p256) Using this teensy ecofriendly town to explore America's greenest wine region.

4 Redwood National Park (p282) Hiking along meandering trails whose trees will give you a crick in your neck.

5 Whale-watching (p246) Searching for spouts atop the historic Point Arena Lighthouse.

6 Marijuana Tours (p274) Educating yourself about the burgeoning 'white market' for marijuana on a Humboldt County cannabis tour.

7 The Lost Coast (p237) Discovering why the highway bypassed this mountainous stretch on a multi-day backpacking adventure.

8 Clear Lake (p257) Paddleboarding the oldest lake in North America before taste-testing wallet-friendly wines.

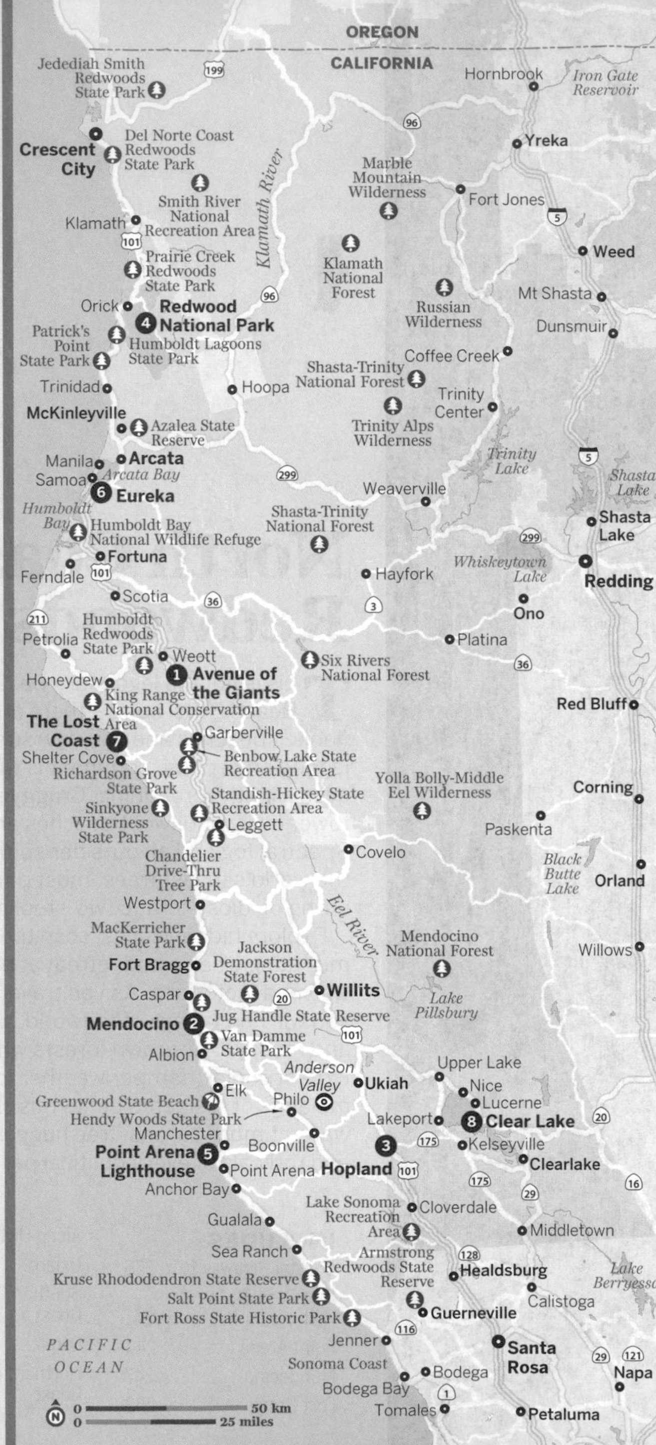

Getting Around

Although Hwy 1 is popular with cyclists and there are bus connections, you will almost certainly need a car to explore this region. Those headed to the far north and on a schedule should take Hwy 101, the faster, inland route, and then cut over to the coast. Windy Hwy 1 hugs the coast, then cuts inland and ends at Leggett, where it joins Hwy 101. Neither Amtrak nor Greyhound serve cities on coastal Hwy 1.

AIR

Arcata–Eureka Airport (p275) is located north of McKinleyville on the North Coast. It has regular services to San Francisco and Los Angeles, though flight cancellations due to fog are not uncommon. United Express (www.united.com) is currently the only commercial carrier serving this airport.

In the far north of the region, Crescent City is home to the tiny **Del Norte County Regional Airport** (CEC; Map p279; ☎707-464-7288; www.flycrescentcity.com; 1650 Dale Rupert Rd, Crescent City), which has one daily service to Oakland on Contour Airlines (www.contourair lines.com) thanks to the government's Essential Air Service program.

BUS

Brave souls willing to piece together bus travel through the region will face a time-consuming headache, but connections are possible to most (but certainly not all) towns. **Greyhound** (☎800-231-2222; www.greyhound.com; 📶) runs buses between San Francisco and Ukiah (from $32, 3¼ hours, daily), Willits (from $35, four hours, daily), Rio Dell (near Fortuna; from $35, six hours, daily), Eureka (from $35, seven hours, daily) and Arcata (from $39, 7¼ hours, daily).

The Mendocino Transit Authority (p263) operates bus 65, which travels between Fort Bragg, Willits, Ukiah, Hopland and Santa Rosa daily, with an afternoon return. Bus 95 runs between Point Arena and Santa Rosa, via Jenner, Bodega Bay and Sebastopol (daily). Bus 75 heads north every weekday from Gualala to the Navarro River junction at Hwy 128, then runs inland through the Anderson Valley to Ukiah, returning in the afternoon. The North Coast route goes north between Navarro River junction and Albion, Little River, Mendocino and Fort Bragg Monday to Friday.

North of Mendocino County, the **Redwood Transit System** (☎707-443-0826; www.redwoodtransit.org) operates buses ($3.50) daily between Scotia and Trinidad (2½ hours), stopping en route at Eureka (1¼ hours) and Arcata (1½ hours). **Redwood Coast Transit** (☎707-464-6400; www.redwoodcoasttransit.org) runs buses Monday to Saturday between Crescent City, Klamath ($2, one hour, five daily) and Arcata ($8, two hours, three daily), with numerous stops along the way

COASTAL HIGHWAY 1

Down south it's called the 'PCH,' or Pacific Coast Hwy, but North Coast locals simply call it 'Hwy 1.' However you label it, get ready for a fabulous coastal drive, which cuts a winding course on isolated cliffs high above the crashing surf. Compared to the famous Big Sur coast, the serpentine stretch of Hwy 1 up the North Coast is more challenging, more remote and more *real*, passing farms, fishing towns and hidden beaches. Drivers use roadside pullouts to scan the hazy Pacific horizon for migrating whales and explore a coastline dotted with rock formations that are relentlessly pounded by the surf. The drive between Bodega Bay and Fort Bragg takes three hours of daylight driving without stops. At night in the fog, it takes steely nerves and much, much longer. The most popular destination is the cliffside charmer of Mendocino.

Considering their proximity to the Bay Area, Sonoma and Mendocino Counties remain unspoiled, and the austere coastal bluffs are some of the most spectacular in the country. But the trip north gets more rewarding (and remote) with every mile. By the time Hwy 1 cuts inland to join Hwy 101, the land along the Pacific – called the Lost Coast – offers the state's best-preserved natural gifts.

Coastal accommodations (including campgrounds) can fill from Memorial Day to Labor Day (late May to early September) and on fall weekends, and sometimes require two-night stays, so reserve ahead. There is a good choice of places to lay your head along the highway, although the budget conscious may find a definite lack of chain motels in these parts.

Bodega Bay

Bodega Bay is the first pearl in a string of sleepy fishing towns that line the North Coast and was the setting of Hitchcock's terrifying 1963 avian psycho-horror flick *The Birds*. The skies are free from bloodthirsty gulls today (though you'd best keep an eye on your picnic); it's Bay Area weekenders who descend en masse for extraordinary beaches, tide pools, whale-watching, fishing, surfing and seafood. Mostly made up of a few restaurants, hotels and shops on both sides of Hwy 1, the downtown is not made for strolling, but it is a great base for exploring the endless nearby coves of the Sonoma Coast State Beach. Hwy 1 runs through town and along the east side of Bodega Bay. On the west side, a peninsula

HIKING & DRIVING THE LOST COAST

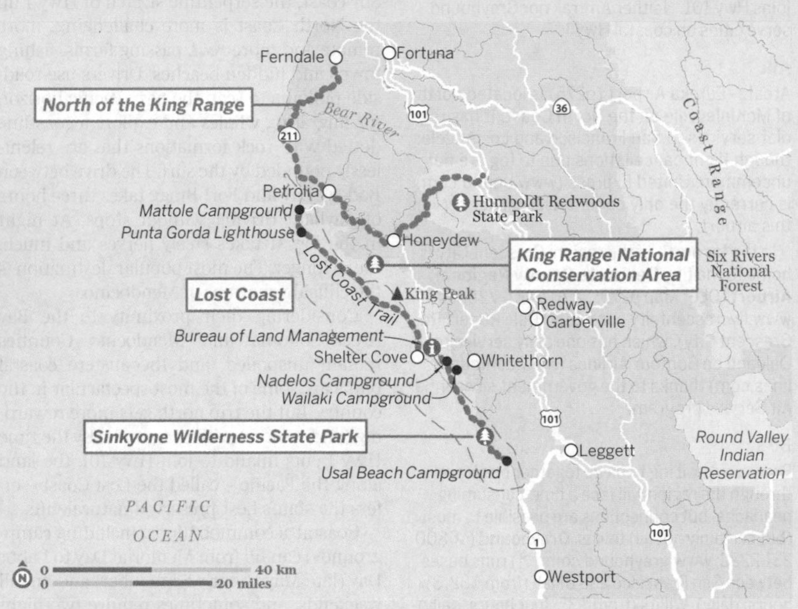

THE LOST COAST

To visit the Lost Coast is to discover volcanic beaches of black sand and ethereal mist hovering above roaring surf as majestic Roosevelt elk graze the forests. The King Range boldly rises 4000ft within 3 miles of the coast between where Hwy 1 cuts inland north of Westport to just south of Ferndale. The coast became 'lost' when the state's highway system deemed the region impassable in the mid 20th century.

In autumn, the weather is clear and cool. Wildflowers bloom from April through May and gray whales migrate from December through April. The warmest, driest months are June to September, but days are foggy and the weather can change quickly.

The best way to see the Lost Coast is to hike, but keep in mind that the area is a patchwork of government-owned land and private property. Visit the **Bureau of Land Management** (BLM; ☎707-986-5400, 707-825-2300; www.blm.gov; 768 Shelter Cove Rd; ⏰8am-4:30pm Mon-Fri) office near Shelter Cove for information, maps and tide charts (some stretches of coastal trail are inaccessible in high tides). Note that there are few circuitous routes, and rangers can advise on reliable (if expensive) shuttle services in the area.

Aside from a few one-horse villages, Shelter Cove is the only real option for food and lodging. Both Wailaki and Nadelos have developed **campgrounds** (tent sites $8) with toilets but no water. There are another two developed campgrounds around the range, as well as multiple primitive walk-in sites. Overnighters will need a bear canister and backcountry permit, both available from the Bureau of Land Management, though the latter is best acquired weeks in advance at www.recreation.gov.

The North Coast's superlative backpacking destination is a mystifying coastal stretch where narrow dirt trails ascend rugged seafront peaks.

WHERE TO HIKE

☆ Sinkyone Wilderness State Park

Named for the Sinkyone people who once lived here, this 7367-acre wilderness extends south of Shelter Cove along pristine coastline. The **Lost Coast Trail** passes through here for 22 miles, from Whale Gulch south to **Usal Beach Campground** (☎707-247-3318; www.parks.ca.gov; Sinkyone Wilderness State Park; tent sites $25). It takes about three days to walk as it meanders along high ridges, providing bird's-eye views down to deserted beaches and the crashing surf (side trails descend to water level).

To get to Sinkyone, drive west from Garberville and Redway on Briceland-Thorn Rd, 21 miles through Whitethorn to Four Corners. Turn left (south) and continue for 3.5 miles down a very rugged road to the ranch house; it takes 1½ hours. North of the Usal Beach Campground, Usal Rd is even rougher and recommended only if you have a high-clearance 4WD and a chainsaw. Seriously.

☆ King Range National Conservation Area

Stretching over 35 miles of virgin coastline, with ridge after ridge of mountainous terrain plunging to the surf, this 68,000-acre area tops out at namesake King Peak (4087ft). The wettest spot in California, the range receives between 100 to 200 inches of annual rainfall, causing frequent landslides; in winter, snow falls on the ridges. By contrast, nearby sea-level Shelter Cove gets only 69in of rain and no snow.

The 25-mile stretch of the **Lost Coast Trail** between Shelter Cove and the Mattole trailhead is one of the finest hikes in the area, though be prepared: you'll spend three days walking on sand! Highlights include an abandoned lighthouse at Punta Gorda, remnants of early shipwrecks, tidepools and abundant wildlife including sea lions, seals and some 300 bird species. Fire restrictions begin around July and last until the first soaking rain, usually in November. During this time, there are no campfires allowed outside developed campgrounds.

The prevailing northerly winds make it best to hike from north to south. Shelter Cove-based **Lost Coast Adventure Tours** (☎707-986-9895; www.lostcoastadventures.com; 210 Wave Dr; shuttle from $85; ⏲10am-2pm Mon-Fri) runs a daily shuttle service to Mattole at 7am and 1:30pm, and can carry up to 11 people. It also organizes guided hikes, ranging from one day to multiday adventures.

Those with minimal time can tackle a scenic 3-mile stretch of the Lost Coast Trail from the Mattole trailhead to Punta Gorda Lighthouse. Note that the final part is impassable at high tide.

WHERE TO DRIVE

☆ North of the King Range

Though it's less of an adventure, you can reach the Lost Coast's northern section year-round via the paved, if heavily potholed, Mattole Rd. Plan on three hours to navigate the sinuous 68 miles from Ferndale in the north to the coast at Cape Mendocino, then inland to **Humboldt Redwoods State Park** (p269) and Hwy 101. Don't expect redwoods: the vegetation is grassland and pasture. It's beautiful in spots – lined with sweeping vistas and wildflowers that are prettiest in spring.

You'll pass two tiny settlements, both 19th-century stage-coach stops. **Petrolia** has an all-in-one store that rents bear canisters, and sells supplies for the trail, as well as good beer and gasoline. **Honeydew** also has a general store. The drive is enjoyable, but the Lost Coast's wild, spectacular scenery lies further south in the more remote regions.

resembling a crooked finger juts out to sea, forming the entrance to Bodega Harbor.

Sights & Activities

Surfing, beachcombing and sportfishing are the main activities here – the latter requires advance booking. From January to April, the fishing boats host whale-watching trips, which are also good to book in advance. Almost everyone in town sells kites for flying at Bodega Head. The excellent **Farm Trails** (www.farmtrails.org) guide at the Sonoma Coast Visitor Center has suggestions for tours of ranches, orchards, farms and apiaries.

Bodega Head VIEWPOINT
(off Bay Flat Rd) At the peninsula's tip, Bodega Head rises 265ft above sea level. It's great for whale-watching, and there is also a seal colony just offshore. Landlubbers enjoy hiking above the surf, where several good trails include a 3.75-mile trek to Bodega Dunes Campground and a 2.2-mile walk to Salmon Creek Ranch. Head west from Hwy 1 onto Eastshore Rd, then turn right at the stop sign onto Bay Flat Rd.

Ren Brown Collection Gallery GALLERY
(707-875-2922; www.renbrown.com; 1781 Hwy 1; 10am-5pm Wed-Sun) The renowned collection of modern Japanese prints and California works at this small gallery is a tranquil escape from the elements. Check out the Japanese garden at the back.

Bodega Marine Laboratory & Reserve SCIENCE CENTER
(707-875-2211; https://marinescience.ucdavis.edu/bml; 2099 Westshore Rd; 2-4pm Fri; P) FREE Run by University of California (UC) Davis, this spectacularly diverse teaching and research reserve surrounds the research lab, which has studied Bodega Bay since the 1920s. The 362-acre reserve hosts many marine environments, including rocky intertidal coastal areas, mudflats and sand flats, salt marsh, sand dunes and freshwater wetlands. On most Friday afternoons docents give tours of the lab and surrounds.

Sonoma Coast Vineyards TASTING ROOM
(707-921-2860; www.sonomacoastvineyards.com; 555 Hwy 1; tastings $25; 11am-6pm) Swirl coastal pinot noirs and chardonnays in this sleek tasting room with views over the Pacific to see if you can detect the ocean's strong influence on them. Most bottles are made from small 1- or 2-acre plots (some literally in the backyards of families living within 10 miles of the coast), making it an incredibly bespoke experience.

Chanslor Ranch HORSEBACK RIDING
(707-589-5040; https://chanslorstables.com; 2660 Hwy 1; rides from $40; 9am-5pm, reduced hours Nov-Feb) Just north of town, this friendly outfit leads horseback expeditions along the coastline and the rolling inland hills. The 90-minute beach rides are justifiably popular, as are trips that combine horseback riding with kayaking.

Bodega Bay Surf Shack SURFING
(707-875-3944; www.bodegabaysurf.com; 1400 N Hwy 1, Pelican Plaza; surfboard/SUP/kayak/bike rental from $17/40/45/16) If you want to get on the water, this easygoing one-stop shop has all kinds of equipment rentals, lessons and good local information. It also rents bikes for landlubbers.

Festivals & Events

Bodega Bay Fishermen's Festival CULTURAL
(www.bbfishfest.org; Bodega Bay; Apr or May) At the end of April, or start of May, this festival culminates in a blessing of the fleet, a flamboyant parade of vessels, an arts-and-crafts fair, kite-flying and feasting.

Bodega Seafood, Art & Wine Festival FOOD & DRINK
(www.bodegaseafoodfestival.com; 16855 Bodega Hwy, Watt's Ranch, Bodega; 10am-6pm Sat, to 5pm Sun late Aug;) Held over a weekend in late August, this festival of food and drink brings together the best beer- and wine-makers of the area, tons of seafood and activities for kids. It takes place in the town of Bodega.

Sleeping

There's a wide spread of options – RV and tent camping, quaint motels, B&Bs and fancy hotels. Several have lovely views of the bay and all fill up early during peak seasons and at weekends. Campers should consider heading just north of town to the state-operated sites.

Doran Regional Park CAMPGROUND $
(www.parks.sonomacounty.ca.gov; 201 Doran Beach Rd; tent sites $7, RV sites without hookups $32;) Watch for the sign if you are approaching town from the south. There are a few campsites here and easy access to the protected 2-mile Doran Beach, which has a boat launch and picnic areas.

BLOODTHIRSTY BIRDS OF BODEGA BAY

Bodega Bay has the enduring claim to fame as the setting for Alfred Hitchcock's *The Birds*. Although special effects radically altered the actual layout of the town, you still get a good feel for the supposed site of the farm owned by Mitch Brenner (played by Rod Taylor). The once-cozy Tides Wharf & Restaurant (p240), where much avian-caused havoc occurs in the movie, is still there but since 1962 it has been transformed into a vast restaurant complex. Venture 5 miles inland to the tiny town of Bodega and you'll find two icons from the film: the Potter Schoolhouse and the St Teresa of Avila Church. Both stand just as they did in the movie – a crow overhead may make the hair rise on your neck.

Coincidentally, right after production of *The Birds* began, a real-life bird attack occurred in Capitola, the sleepy seaside town east of Santa Cruz. Thousands of sooty shearwaters ran amok, destroying property and attacking people.

Westside Park CAMPGROUND $

(☎707-565-2267; www.parks.sonomacounty.ca.gov; 2400 Westshore Rd; day use $7, RV sites without hookups $32) This park caters mainly for RVs and boaters. It has windy exposures, beaches, hot showers, fishing and boat ramps.

Chanslor Guest Ranch RANCH $$

(☎707-589-5055; www.chanslor.com; 2660 Hwy 1; r from $150; 📶) This working horse ranch a mile north of town has four rooms of varying comfort, with sweeping vistas across open grasslands to the sea. Arrange guided horseback and kayak tours onsite for the complete experience.

Bodega Bay Lodge & Spa LODGE $$$

(☎707-875-3525; www.bodegabaylodge.com; 103 Hwy 1; r $180-400; 🅿@📶🏊) Bodega's plushest option, this oceanfront resort has a sea-view swimming pool, a golf course, a Jacuzzi and a state-of-the-art fitness club. In the evenings it hosts wine tastings. The more expensive rooms have commanding views, but all have balconies. The other pluses on-site include Bodega Bay's best spa and Drakes (p240) restaurant, which is the fanciest spot in town.

Eating & Drinking

For the old-fashioned thrill of seafood by the docks, there are several options where you can enjoy sea views, along with a simple menu of clam chowder, fried fish and coleslaw. There are also fish and produce markets in town where self-caterers can pick up supplies, and a fair range of other eateries specializing in everything from fast-food hotdogs to Tex-Mex and more sophisticated offerings.

★ **Fishetarian Fish Market** CALIFORNIAN $

(☎707-875-9092; www.fishetarianfishmarket.com; 599 Hwy 1; mains from $12; ⊙11am-6pm Mon-Thu, to 7pm Fri-Sun; 📶) This fish market and deli is a great place to eat, with reggae as the soundtrack. It features an outdoor deck near the water and an expansive menu that includes colorful and imaginative organic salads, fried tofu (or calamari) with homemade fries, oysters, fish tacos, crab cakes and a fine clam chowder. Also serves craft beers on tap and decadent desserts.

★ **Spud Point Crab Company** SEAFOOD $

(☎707-875-9472; www.spudpointcrab.com; 1910 Westshore Rd; mains $8-13; ⊙9am-5pm) In the classic tradition of dockside crab shacks, Spud Point serves salty-sweet crab sandwiches and *real* clam chowder (that consistently wins local culinary prizes). You can also buy a crab to take home if you fancy. Eat at picnic tables overlooking the marina. Take Bay Flat Rd to get here.

Casino Bar & Grill CALIFORNIAN $$

(☎707-876-3185; 17000 Bodega Hwy; mains $12-22; ⊙9am-9pm, dinner from 5pm) Shhh! This is the place locals don't tell tourists about. At its heart, it's everyone's favorite dive bar. Come nightfall, however, it serves killer California cuisine at prices you won't find in Bodega Bay (it's in the town of Bodega, 5 miles inland). Menus change daily depending on what's fresh. Cash only.

Lucas Wharf Restaurant & Bar SEAFOOD $$

(☎707-875-3522; www.lucaswharfrestaurant.com; 595 Hwy 1; mains $17-32; ⊙11:30am-8:30pm) Located right on the water, this place specializes in sophisticated seafood options, with ingredients such as roasted cherry tomatoes accompanying dishes like Dungeness crab cakes and popcorn shrimp. Founded by a family of commercial fishers, the restaurant originated as a fish market, which is now located next door (along with an upmarket deli). In other words, these folks know their seafood and you can guarantee it is flapping fresh.

Tides Wharf & Restaurant SEAFOOD $$
(☎707-875-3652; www.innatthetides.com; 835 Hwy 1; breakfast $9-24, lunch $15-30, dinner $25-45; ⏲7:30am-9:30pm Mon-Thu, 7:30am-10pm Fri, 7am-10pm Sat, 7am-9:30pm Sun) Enjoy a stunning view of the bay and an upscale atmosphere. The emphasis is on seafood here, but pasta and meat dishes are also available. The black-and-white pics of the Hitchcock days add to the atmosphere and, if you're lucky, you may spy seals and dolphins from the vast picture window.

Check out the great fish market and deli adjacent to the restaurant. This is also a good place to pick up a bottle of local wine.

Terrapin Creek Cafe & Restaurant CALIFORNIAN $$$
(☎707-875-2700; www.terrapincreekcafe.com; 1580 Eastshore Rd; mains $27-45; ⏲4:30-9pm Thu-Sun;) This upscale restaurant is run by a husband-wife team who espouse the slow-food movement and serve local dishes sourced from the surrounding area. Asia-influenced plates like Hokkaido scallops and Hiramasa yellowtail also shine, while the warm service and relaxing setting make it anything but stuffy.

Drakes CALIFORNIAN $$$
(☎707-875-3525; www.drakesbodegabay.com; 103 Hwy 1, Bodega Bay Lodge & Spa; mains $24-45, appetizers $8-17; ⏲7:30am-8:30pm;) This fancy spot offers a choice of dining experiences. The Drakes Sonoma Coast menu runs from breakfast to dinner, the latter concentrating on hearty staples like braised short ribs or more intriguing creations like crab risotto. The aptly named Fireside Lounge offers a relaxed setting for lighter bites, including charcuterie plates or garlic fries.

Gourmet Au Bay WINE BAR
(☎707-875-9875; www.gourmetaubay.com; 1412 Bay Flat Rd; ⏲noon-7pm Wed-Mon;) This sophisticated wine bar offers sophisticated snacks to accompany your tipple. Head to the spacious deck where you can enjoy a salty breeze along with your wine tasting (three local glasses for $18).

Information

Sonoma Coast Visitor Center (☎707-377-4459; www.visitbodegabayca.com; 913 Hwy 1; ⏲9am-5pm) Opposite the Tides Wharf. Stop by for the best help on the coast and for a copy of the *North Coaster*, a small-press indie newspaper filled with essays and brilliant insights on local culture. Foodies should ask for flyers on regional cheese and chowder trails.

Sonoma Coast State Beach

Stretching 19 miles north from Bodega Head to Vista Trail, four miles north of Jenner, the glorious Sonoma Coast State Beach is actually a series of beaches separated by several beautiful rocky headlands. Some beaches are tiny, hidden in little coves, while others stretch far and wide. Most of the beaches are connected by vista-studded coastal hiking trails that wind along the bluffs. Bring binoculars and your camera – the views are stunning, with rock outcrops, mini islands, inlets and shifting tides. During summer there can be morning fog, which generally burns off by midday. Exploring this area makes an excellent day-long adventure, but facilities are zero, so bring water and food, as well as a fully charged cell phone, in case of emergency. Also note that the surf is often too treacherous to wade through, so keep a close eye on children.

Sights & Activities

Goat Rock Beach BEACH
(Goat Rock Rd, Jenner; P) Famous for its colony of harbor seals lazing in the sun at the mouth of the Russian River. Noted for its mystical-looking rock archway, as well.

Salmon Creek Beach BEACH
(cnr Bean Ave & Maryanna Dr, Bodega Bay; P) Situated around a lagoon, with 2 miles of hiking and good waves for surfing.

Schoolhouse Beach BEACH
(cnr Hwy 1 & Viking Strand; P) A very pleasant beach with parking (but no other facilities); can be prone to riptides, so swimmers should take care.

Duncan's Landing BEACH
(Duncan's Landing Overlook, Bodega Bay; P) Small boats unload near this rocky headland in the morning. It's also a good place to spot wildflowers in the spring.

Shell Beach BEACH
(Shell Beach Rd, Jenner; P) Just south of the small town of Jenner, a boardwalk and trail

leads out to a stretch perfect for tide-pooling and beachcombing.

Portuguese Beach BEACH
(cnr Hwy 1 & Eureka Dr; P) Very easy to access; features sheltered coves between rocky outcroppings.

Sleeping

Unless you are willing to hammer down tent pegs, you will need to base yourself in Bodega Bay or Jenner. This is no real hardship, however, as both are just a few miles away either to the south or the north.

Wright's Beach Campground CAMPGROUND $
(800-444-7275; www.parks.ca.gov; 7095 Hwy 1; tent & RV sites $35-45, day use $8) Of the precious few parks that allow camping along Sonoma Coast State Beach, this is the best, even though sites lack privacy and there are no showers. There are just 27 sites but they can be booked six months in advance, and numbers one to 10 are right on the beach. There are BBQ pits for day use and it's a perfect launch for sea kayakers.

Bodega Dunes Campground CAMPGROUND $
(800-444-7275; www.reservecalifornia.com; 2485 Hwy 1, Bodega Bay; tent & RV sites $35, day use $8) The largest campground in the Sonoma Coast State Beach system of parks with close to 100 sites; it is also closest to Bodega Bay and justifiably popular. Sites are set in high dunes and have hot showers, but be warned – the foghorn sounds all night.

Jenner

Perched on the hills looking out to the Pacific and above the mouth of the Russian River, tiny Jenner offers access to the coast and the Russian River wine region. A **harbor-seal colony** sits at the river's mouth and pups are born here from March to August. There are restrictions about getting too close to the chubby, adorable pups – handling them can be dangerous and cause the pups to be abandoned by their mothers. The best way to see them is by kayak, and most of the year you will find **Water Treks Ecotours** (707-865-2249; www.watertreks.com; 2hr kayak rental from $50, 4hr guided tours from $120; hours vary) renting kayaks on the highway. Heading north on Hwy 1 you will begin driving on one of the most beautiful, windy stretches of California highway. You'll also probably lose cell-phone service – possibly a blessing.

Sleeping & Eating

River's End Inn COTTAGE $$
(707-865-2484; www.ilovesunsets.com; 11048 Hwy 1; cottages $160-250;) Run by the same folk who own the superb River's End Restaurant, these ocean-view cottages are wood-paneled and have no TVs, wi-fi or phones; however, many do come with fireplaces, breezy decks and breathtaking ocean views, complete with harbor seals. To preserve the romantic atmosphere, bringing children under 12 years old is not recommended.

★ **Café Aquatica** CAFE $
(707-865-2251; 10439 Hwy 1; pastries & sandwiches $4-12; 8am-5pm;) This is the kind of North Coast coffee shop you've been dreaming of: fresh pastries, fog-lifting organic coffee and chatty locals. The expansive view of the Russian River from the patio and gypsy seahut decor make it hard to leave, especially at weekends when a strumming guitarist adds to the California dreamin' ambience.

River's End Restaurant CALIFORNIAN $$$
(707-865-2484; www.ilovesunsets.com; 11048 Hwy 1; lunch mains $15-35, dinner mains $20-55; 11:30am-3pm & 5-8:30pm Fri-Tue;) Unwind in style at this picture-perfect restaurant, perched on a cliff overlooking the river's mouth and a grand sweep of the Pacific Ocean. It serves world-class meals at world-class prices, but the real reward is the view.

Fort Ross State Historic Park

A curious glimpse into Tsarist Russia's exploration of the California coast, the salt-washed buildings of **Fort Ross State Historic Park** (707-847-3437; www.fortross.org; 19005 Hwy 1; per car $8; park sunrise-sunset, visitor center 10am-4:30pm) offer a fascinating insight into the pre-American Wild West. It's a quiet, picturesque place with a riveting past. If you pass by on a winter weekday when the fort is sometimes closed (due to budget cuts), you still may be able to walk down and have a peek inside if a school group is there.

In March 1812, a group of 25 Russians and 80 Alaskans (including members of the Kodiak and Aleutian communities) built a wooden fort here, near a Kashaya Pomo village. The southernmost outpost of the 19th-century Russian fur trade on America's Pacific Coast, Fort Ross was established as a base for sea-otter hunting operations and trade with Alta California, and for growing crops for Russian settlements in Alaska. The Russians dedicated the fort in August 1812 and occupied it until 1841, when it was abandoned because the sea-otter population had been decimated and agricultural production had never taken off.

Fort Ross State Historic Park, an accurate reconstruction of the fort, is 11 miles north of Jenner on a beautiful point. The original buildings were sold, dismantled and carried off to Sutter's Fort during the gold rush. The visitor center has a great museum with historical displays and an excellent bookshop on Californian and Russian history. Ask about hikes to the Russian cemetery.

During the Fort Ross Festival, the last Saturday in July, costumed volunteers bring the fort's history to life; check www.fortross.org or call the visitor center for other special events.

Sleeping

Stillwater Cove Regional Park CAMPGROUND **$**
(707-565-2267; www.sonomacountycamping.org; 22455 Hwy 1; tent & RV sites $32) Two miles north of Timber Cove, this park has hot showers and hiking under Monterey pines. Sites 1, 2, 4, 6, 9 and 10 have distant ocean views.

★**Timber Cove Resort** LODGE **$$$**
(707-847-3231; www.timbercoveresort.com; 21780 N Hwy 1; r $170-550;) A dramatic and quirky '60s-modern seaside inn that has been refurbished into a luxury lodge. The rustic architectural shell is stunning, and a duet of tinkling piano and crackling fire fills the vast open-plan lobby. Rooms have fireplaces and balconies or terraces. Prices vary according to the views. The Coast Kitchen restaurant offers a menu of well-prepared Californian cuisine.

Even those who don't bunk here should wander agape in the shadow of Benny Bufano's 93ft-tall peace statue, a spectacular totem on the edge of the sea.

Salt Point State Park

Stunning 6000-acre **Salt Point State Park** (707-847-3221; www.saltpoint.org; 25050 Hwy 1; per car $8; sunrise-sunset) has sandstone cliffs that drop dramatically into the kelp-strewn sea and hiking trails that crisscross windswept prairies and wooded hills, connecting pygmy forests and coastal coves rich with tidepools. The 6-mile-wide park is bisected by the **San Andreas Fault** – the rock on the east side is vastly different from that on the west. Check out the eerily beautiful tafonis (honeycombed-sandstone formations) near Gerstle Cove. For a good roadside photo op, there's a pullout at mile marker 45.

Though some of the day-use areas have been closed off due to budget cuts, trails lead off Hwy 1 pullouts to views of the pristine coastline. The platform overlooking Sentinel Rock is just a short stroll from the Fisk Mill Cove parking lot at the park's north end. Further south, seals laze at **Gerstle Cove Marine Reserve**, one of California's first underwater parks. Tread lightly around tidepools and don't lift the rocks: even a glimpse of sunlight can kill some critters. If you're here between April and June, you must see **Kruse Rhododendron State Reserve**. Growing abundantly in the forest's filtered light, magnificent, pink rhododendrons reach heights of more than 30ft; turn east from Hwy 1 onto Kruse Ranch Rd and follow the signs. Be sure to walk the short Rhododendron Loop Trail.

Sleeping

Ocean Cove Lodge Bar & Grill MOTEL **$**
(707-847-3158; www.oceancovelodge.com; 23255 Hwy 1; r from $99;) Just a few minutes south of Salt Point State Park is Ocean Cove Lodge Bar & Grill, a godsend for those on a budget. It's just a basic motel but the location is fabulous, with uninterrupted ocean views (and whale-watching) beyond the sweeping lawns and hot tub. There's a surprisingly good American-style restaurant on the premises.

The owner prides himself on the homemade cinnamon rolls made daily with an added hit of chili.

Salt Point State Park Campgrounds CAMPGROUND **$**
(800-444-7275; www.reservecalifornia.com; Salt Point State Park; tent & RV sites $35) Two campgrounds, Woodside and Gerstle Cove, both signposted off Hwy 1, have sites with cold water. Inland Woodside (closed December to March) is well protected by Monterey pines. Gerstle Cove's trees burned over a decade ago and have only grown halfway back, giving the gnarled, blackened trunks a ghostly look when the fog twirls between the branches.

Sea Ranch

Though not without its fans, the exclusive community of Sea Ranch is a sort of weather-beaten Stepford-by-the-Sea. The ritzy subdivision that sprawls 10 miles along the coast is connected with a well-watched network of private roads, with hiking trails leading to the sea and along the bluffs. Approved for construction prior to the existence of the watchdog Coastal Commission, the community was a precursor to the concept of 'slow growth,' with strict zoning laws requiring that houses be constructed of only weathered wood. Though there are some pleasant short-term rentals here, don't break any community rules – like throwing wild parties – or security will come knockin'. Just north of Shell Beach, you'll find the iconic nondenominational **Sea Ranch Chapel** (open dusk to dawn). This extraordinary building, designed by artist James Hubbell, features a swooping cedar roof that's accented with copper, bisected by stained-glass and topped with a bronze spire. For supplies and gasoline, go to Gualala.

Sights & Activities

Walk-On Beach BEACH
(Hwy 1, Mile 56.53; parking per day $7; 6am-sunset May-Sep, from 8am Oct-Apr) A half-mile trail passes through a large grove of cypress trees leading to a staircase down to this pristine quarter-mile beach. Walkers can follow the stunning Bluff Top Trail from here, which leads north to Gualala Point Regional Park 3 miles away.

Stengel Beach BEACH
(Hwy 1, Mile 53.96; 6am-sunset May-Sep, from 8am Oct-Apr;) One of a handful of idyllic beaches on this stretch of coastline, Stengel has a large, free car park and a short access trail lined by cypress trees that takes you to a wooden staircase leading to the beach.

Shell Beach BEACH
(Hwy 1, Mile 55.24; parking per day $7; 6am-sunset May-Sep, from 8am Oct-Apr) A lovely beach comprising two sandy coves divided by a rocky headland. You can park just south of Whale Bone Reach Rd from where there is a mile-long access trail to the beach via pine trees and meadows. Note that there are no facilities, aside from toilets at the car park.

Unbeaten Path Tours & Yoga OUTDOORS
(707-888-6121; www.unbeatenpathtours.com; tours from $70) Runs an intriguing mix of area tours focusing on everything from architecture to landscapes to meditation. The nature walks, which culminate in a yoga session, are particularly popular.

Sleeping

Depending on the season, it can be surprisingly affordable to rent a house in Sea Ranch. There are several agencies that can assist you in finding a place, including **Rams Head Realty & Rentals** (707-785-2417; www.ramshead.com; 39000 Hwy 1, Gualala; 10am-5pm) and **Sea Ranch Rentals** (707-884-4235; www.searanchrentals.com; 39200 Hwy 1, Gualala; 9am-6pm), both located in the center of nearby Gualala.

Gualala & Anchor Bay

Located at the mouth of the Gualala River on the Pacific Coast, Gualala (pronounced by most locals as 'Wah-la-la') is a Native American Pomo name meaning 'where the waters flow down.' It is a hub for weekend getaways as it sits squarely in the middle of the 'Banana Belt,' an area known for unusually sunny weather. Founded as a prosperous lumber town in the 1860s, the downtown stretches along Hwy 1 with a bustling commercial district that has a great grocery store, several spas and some cute, slightly upscale shops.

Just north, quiet Anchor Bay is the destination of choice for many visitors seeking a tranquil stay, as it is home to some exceptional accommodation choices with a string of secluded, hard-to-find beaches situated just to the north. Both Gualala and Anchor Bay are excellent jumping-off points for exploring the surrounding area.

Sights & Activities

Seven miles north of Anchor Bay, pull off at mile marker 11.41 for **Schooner Gulch**. A trail into the forest from the north end of the parking area leads down cliffs to a sandy beach with tide pools. Bear right at the fork in the trail to reach iconic **Bowling Ball Beach**, where low tide reveals rows of big, round rocks resembling bowling balls. Consult tide tables for Arena Cove. The forecast low tide must be lower than +1.5ft on the tide chart for the rocks to be visible.

Gualala Arts Center ARTS CENTER
(707-884-1138; www.gualalaarts.org; 46501 Old State Hwy, Gualala; 10am-4pm Mon-Fri, noon-4pm Sat & Sun) Inland along Old State Hwy, at the south end of town, this center was beautifully built entirely by volunteers. It hosts changing exhibitions, organizes the **Art in the Redwoods Festival** in late August, holds a range of art classes and has loads of info on local art.

Sleeping & Eating

Of the two towns, Gualala has more services than Anchor Bay, including places to stay, and is a more practical hub for exploring – there is a bunch of good motels, plus campgrounds and a handful of inns and B&Bs.

Compared to their coastal neighbors, the dining scene in both towns is rather lackluster.

★Gualala Point Regional Park CAMPGROUND $
(☎707-565-2267; www.sonomacountycamping.org; 42401 Hwy 1, Gualala; parking $7, tent & RV sites $32; P) Shaded by a stand of redwoods and fragrant California bay laurel trees, a trail connects this creekside campground to the beach. The quality of sites, including several secluded hike-in spots, makes it the best drive-in camping on this part of the coast.

Gualala River Redwood Park CAMPGROUND $
(☎707-884-3533; www.gualalapark.com; Gualala Rd, Gualala; day use $5 per person, tent/RV sites $50/60) Located inland from the Old State Hwy is this gorgeously maintained (though exceptionally pricey) private park where you can camp and do short hikes along the Gualala River. Twenty sites have river views, while amenities include a general store, fish cleaning station and laundry room.

★St Orres Inn INN $$
(☎707-884-3303; www.saintorres.com; 36601 Hwy 1, Gualala; B&B $95-135, cottages $140-445;) Famous for its striking Russian-inspired architecture, including dramatic rough-hewn timbers, stained glass and burnished-copper domes, there's no place quite like St Orres. On the property's fairytale-like, wild-mushroom-strewn 90 acres, hand-built cottages range from rustic to luxurious. The inn's fine restaurant is worth the splurge, with inspired California cuisine served in one of the coast's most romantic rooms.

North Coast Country Inn B&B $$
(☎707-884-4537; www.northcoastcountryinn.com; 34591 S Hwy 1, Anchor Bay; r $200-235;) Perched on an inland hillside beneath towering trees and surrounded by lovely gardens, the perks of this adorable place begin with the gregarious owner. The six spacious, country-style rooms are decorated with lovely prints and boast exposed beams, fireplaces, board games and private entrances.

★Mar Vista Cottages CABIN $$$
(☎707-884-3522; www.marvistamendocino.com; 35101 Hwy 1, Anchor Bay; cottages $195-320;) These elegantly renovated 1930s fishing cabins offer a simple, stylish seaside escape with a vanguard commitment to sustainability. The harmonious environment is the result of pitch-perfect details: linens are line-dried over lavender, guests browse the organic vegetable garden to harvest their own dinner and chickens cluck around the grounds laying the next morning's breakfast. It requires two-night stays.

The private walkway down to a stunner of a beach is the ultimate perk!

Trinks CAFE $
(☎707-884-1713; www.trinkscafe.com; 39140 Hwy 1, Gualala; snacks & sandwiches $12-17; ⊙7am-4pm Mon, Tue, Thu & Sat, to 8pm Wed, 8am-3pm Sun;) Tucked into the corner of a strip of shops with a seaview terrace, the overstuffed sandwiches are good value here. Be sure to leave room for a slice of fresh fruit pie; there are generally at least four to select from. Lightweights can opt for quiche and salad, while vegetarians will rejoice over the hearty veg-filled lentil bowl.

Anchor Bay Village Market MARKET $
(☎707-884-4245; 35513 S Hwy 1, Anchor Bay; ⊙8am-7pm Mon-Sat, to 6pm Sun) This grocery store specializes in organic produce and products, with a superb range including baked goods and deli items.

Information

Redwood Coast Visitors Center (www.redwoodcoastchamber.com; 39150 Hwy 1, Shoreline Hwy, Gualala; ⊙noon-5pm Thu, Fri & Sun, from 11am Sat) A well-stocked tourist office with plenty of information on the area, including a free local map. Look out for the *Lighthouse Peddler* (www.thelighthousepeddler.com), a monthly guide to music, art and events on the Mendocino Coast.

Point Arena

This laid-back little town of less than 475 residents combines creature comforts with relaxed, eclectic California living. It's the first town up the coast where the majority of residents don't seem to be retired Bay Area refugees, but are rather a young, creative bunch who tout organic food, support their local theater and sell their fair share of dream catchers. The main street is part of scenic Hwy 1, with a small harbor at one end and a clutch of arty shops, cafes and restaurants housed in pretty Victorian-era buildings running through the center of town. Peruse the shops and restaurants, then follow the sign leading to the lighthouse at the north end of Main St, or head to the docks a mile west at Arena Cove and watch surfers mingle with fisherfolk and locals.

Sights

★Point Arena Lighthouse LIGHTHOUSE
(707-882-2809; www.pointarenalighthouse.com; 45500 Lighthouse Rd; adult/child $8/1; 10am-3:30pm mid-Sep–mid-May, to 4:30pm mid-May–mid-Sep) This iconic lighthouse was constructed in 1870, destroyed in a 1906 earthquake and then rebuilt in 1908. It remains the tallest on the US West Coast (tied with nearby Pigeon Point) at 115ft. Check in at the museum and have a look at the Fresnel lens, then climb 145 steps to the top for the jaw-dropping view. You can stay nearby in keepers' homes and apartments. The turnoff is 2 miles northwest of town off Hwy 1.

Stornetta Public Lands NATURE RESERVE
(Lighthouse Rd) For fabulous bird-watching, hiking on terraced rock past sea caves and access to hidden coves, head 1 mile down Lighthouse Rd from Hwy 1 and look for the Bureau of Land Management (BLM) signs on the left indicating these 1132-acre public lands. The best, most dramatic walking trail leads along the coast for about 3.5 miles, and also begins on Lighthouse Rd from a small parking area about a quarter-mile before the lighthouse parking area.

Sleeping

Oz Farm CABIN $
(707-882-3046; www.ozfarm.com; 41601 Mountain View Rd; campsite $75, cabin from $125;) Sleep in a rustic cabin, yurt or dome on a 240-acre organic farm north of town for a real off-grid experience. The place, which runs on solar and wind power, was initially a commune of sorts and maintains a free-spirited vibe. You'll have access to nearby redwood forests, as well as the Garcia River in summer.

Point Arena Lighthouse Lodging RENTAL HOUSE $$
(707-882-2809; www.pointarenalighthouse.com; 45500 Lighthouse Rd; houses $150-375;) True lighthouse buffs should look into staying at the one- to three-bedroom former coast-guard homes at the lighthouse. They're quiet, windswept retreats, and all but one is equipped with a kitchen. Aim for the newly renovated units like Head Keeper's House 1 and Assistant Keeper's House 4.

Wharf Master's Inn HOTEL $$
(707-882-3171; www.wharfmasters.com; 785 Port Rd; r $139-210;) This is a cluster of comfortable, spacious rooms on a cliff overlooking fishing boats and a stilt pier. Most of the rooms have private balconies with uninterrupted sea views, but all are eminently comfortable with four-poster beds.

Eating & Drinking

Franny's Cup & Saucer BAKERY $
(707-882-2500; www.frannyscupandsaucer.com; 213 Main St; cakes from $2; 8am-4pm Wed-Sat) The cutest patisserie on this stretch of coast is run by Franny and her mother, Barbara (a veteran of Chez Panisse in Berkeley). The fresh berry tarts and creative housemade chocolates seem too beautiful to eat, until you take the first bite and immediately want to order another. Once a month they pull out all the stops for a farmhouse dinner ($35).

Arena Market & Cafe ORGANIC, DELI $
(707-882-3663; www.arenaorganics.org; 185 Main St; soup $6.50, sandwiches $8; 7am-7pm Mon-Sat, 8am-6pm Sun) The deli at this fully stocked organic co-op makes excellent to-go veg and gluten-free options, including sandwiches, with ingredients generally sourced from local farms. The serve-yourself soup is delicious; you can enjoy it at one of the tables out front.

★Bird Cafe & Supper Club CALIFORNIAN $$
(707-882-1600; https://birdcatepa.com; 194A Main St; small plates $5-15, supper club menu $47; 5:30-9pm Thu-Sat) Chef Aaron Peters works with farmers and ranchers to create locavore Mendocino cuisine, pairing it alongside a stellar list of Anderson Valley wines. Thursday and Friday nights it's all about small plates (think roasted oysters with Thai vinaigrette), while Saturdays are reservation-only supper club events with a prix fixe menu. Stunning avian murals by artist Nicole Ponsler set the mood.

Cove Cafe COFFEE
(707-882-2665; www.covecoffee-ptarena.com; 790 Port Rd; 7am-3pm) This quirky pier-side cafe buzzes each morning as locals pour in for espresso coffees, bagels, organic granola and smoothies. You can also pick up fishing tackle or surf accessories to use out front.

TOP WHALE-WATCHING SPOTS

Watch for spouts, sounding and breaching whales and pods. Anywhere coastal will do, but the following are some of the North Coast's best:

- Point Arena Lighthouse (p245)
- Mendocino Headlands State Park (p249)
- Point Cabrillo Light Station
- Patrick's Point State Park (p281)
- Klamath River Overlook (Map p279)

Entertainment

Arena Theater CINEMA

(707-882-3020; www.arenatheater.org; 214 Main St; movies $10) Shows mainstream, foreign and art films in a beautifully restored movie house. Sue, the ticket seller of 40 years, passed away in 2018, but her replacement Shelita is also a wealth of local knowledge. Got a question about Point Arena? Ask her.

Manchester

Follow Hwy 1 north beyond Point Arena, through bucolic fields dropping down from the hills to the blue ocean, and a turnoff leads to **Manchester State Beach**, a long, wild stretch of sand. If you visit from November to April, you may spy gray and humpback whales during their annual migration. Part of the protected **Manchester State Park** (707-882-2463; www.parks.gov.ca; Kinney Rd; tent sites $25-35; late May-early Sep), an ocean-adjacent camping park, the area around here is remote and pastoral, with grazing land for sheep and cattle further inland and two freshwater streams noted for their salmon and steelhead (anglers, take note). The population hovers around the 200 mark so there is not much here in terms of shops and facilities (only one grocery store), but it's a quick 7-mile drive south to Point Arena with its shops, restaurants and appealing places to stay.

Based inland around 8 miles to the north and actually closer to Elk, **Ross Ranch** (707-877-1834; www.rossranch.biz; 28300 Philo Greenwood Rd; 2hr rides $60;) organizes two-hour rides along Manchester Beach or in nearby woodlands and for groups of up to 10.

Toward the ocean, **Mendocino Coast KOA** (707-882-2375; www.manchesterbeachkoa.com; 44300 Kinney Rd; tent/RV sites from $42/52, cabins $75-95;) is an impressive private campground with campsites beneath enormous Monterey pines, a cooking pavilion, hot showers, a hot tub, bocce ball courts and a community campfire area. The cabins are a great option for families who want to get the camping experience without roughing it.

Elk

Itty-bitty Elk is famous for its stunning cliff-top views of 'sea stacks,' towering rock formations jutting out of the water. Otherwise, it's one of the cutest (yet gentrified-looking) villages before Mendocino. There is *nothing* to do after dinner, so bring a book if you're a night owl. And you can forget about the cell phone too; reception here is nonexistent. Elk's **visitor center** (707-877-3458; https://visitmendocino.com/listing/open-687/; 5980 Hwy 1, Shoreline Hwy; 10am-2pm) has exhibits on the town's logging past. At the southern end of town, **Greenwood State Beach** sits where Greenwood Creek meets the sea and marks the spot where ships used to stop when carrying timber to San Francisco and China. There are excellent walks along the cliffs offering dramatic ocean views combined with dense woods.

Sights

Artists' Collective in Elk GALLERY

(707-877-1128; www.artists-collective.net; 6031 S Hwy 1, Shoreline Hwy; 10am-5pm) Tucked into a tiny clapboard house looking across the road to the ocean, this gallery is run as a cooperative by 30 local artists and is a fascinating combination of everything from carvings and pottery to photography and jewelry.

Sleeping & Eating

★ **Harbor House Inn** INN $$$

(800-720-7474; www.theharborhouseinn.com; 5600 S Hwy 1; r & cottages incl breakfast $399-809;) Nestled within an old showcase home of the Goodyear Redwood Company – and with plenty of redwood paneling to show for it! – is this stunning 10-room hotel with oh-my-god views, cliff-top gardens and a private beach. The Michelin-starred restaurant on-site is a destination itself, with tasting menus of hyperlocal coastal cuisine sourced from within a 50-mile radius.

Elk Cove Inn & Spa INN $$$

(800-725-2967; www.elkcoveinn.com; 6300 S Hwy 1; r $195-425, cottages $275-355;) Several upmarket B&Bs take advantage of the views along the coast, but you simply can't beat those from Elk Cove Inn & Spa: located on a bluff, it has steps leading down to the driftwood-strewn beach below. Prices in the wide selection of rooms and cottages include breakfast, wine, champagne and cocktails, plus you can relax even further at the deluxe spa.

Elk Store DELI $
(☎707-877-3544; 6101 Hwy 1, Shoreline Hwy; sandwiches from $9; ⏲9am-6pm) Make a stop here for gourmet foods, gifts, Mendocino County wines and a great deli menu with build your own sandwiches, burritos, bagels and wraps, and an awesomely good clam chowder.

Queenie's Roadhouse Cafe DINER $
(☎707-877-3285; 6061 S Hwy 1, Shoreline Hwy; mains $10-15; ⏲8am-3pm Thu-Mon, closed Jan; 🖉) Everyone swears by this excellent, retro-chic classic diner for a creative range of breakfast (try the wild-rice waffles) and lunch treats, including a great burger and Reuben sandwich.

Van Damme State Park

Three miles south of Mendocino, this sprawling 1831-acre **park** (☎707-937-4016; www.mendoparks.org/van-damme; 8125 N Hwy 1, Little River; per car $8; ⏲hours vary; P) draws beachcombers, divers and kayakers to its easy-access beach, and hikers to its pygmy forest. The latter is a unique and precious place, where acidic soil and an impenetrable layer of hardpan have created a miniature forest of decades-old trees. The **visitor center** (☎707-937-4016; www.mendoparks.org/van-damme; 8125 N Hwy 1; ⏲hours vary) has nature exhibits and programs.

You can reach the forest on the moderate 2.5-mile **Fern Canyon Scenic Trail**, which crosses back and forth over Little River and past the Cabbage Patch, a bog of skunk cabbage that's rich with wildlife. Return 2.5 miles to where you started, or continue for another 3 miles on a loop into the pygmy forest. A separate park entrance down Little River Airport Rd leads you to the quarter-mile **Pygmy Forest Boardwalk Loop**.

Two pretty **campgrounds** (☎800-444-7275; www.reservecalifornia.com; 8125 N Hwy 1, Little River; tent & RV sites from $40; 🐾) are excellent for family car camping. They both have hot showers: one is just off Hwy 1, while the other is located in a highland meadow, which has lots of space for kids to run around.

For sea-cave kayaking tours contact **Kayak Mendocino** (☎707-813-7117; www.kayakmendocino.com; Van Damme Beach State Park, 8001 N Hwy 1, Little River; adult/child $60/40; ⏲tours 9am, 11:30am & 2pm).

Mendocino

Leading out to a gorgeous headland, Mendocino is the North Coast's perfect, salt-washed village, with B&Bs surrounded by rose gardens, white-picket fences and New England-style redwood water towers. Bay Area weekenders walk along the headland among berry bramble and wildflowers, where cypress trees stand over dizzying cliffs. The town itself is full of cute shops – no chains – and has earned the nickname 'Spendocino,' for its upscale goods.

Built by transplanted New Englanders in the 1850s, Mendocino thrived late into the 19th century, with ships transporting redwood timber from here to San Francisco. The mills shut down in the 1930s, and the town was rediscovered in the 1950s by artists and bohemians. Today the culturally savvy, politically aware, well-traveled citizens welcome visitors, but eschew corporate interlopers – don't look for a Big Mac or Starbucks. To avoid crowds, come midweek or in the low season, when the vibe is mellower – and prices more reasonable.

Sights

Mendocino is lined with all kinds of interesting galleries, which hold openings on the second Saturday of each month from 5pm to 7pm.

Point Cabrillo Light Station LIGHTHOUSE
(☎707-937-6123; www.pointcabrillo.org; 45300 Lighthouse Rd; suggested $5 donation; ⏲park sunrise-sunset, lighthouse 11am-4pm) Built in 1909, this stout lighthouse stands on a 300-acre wildlife preserve north of town, between Russian Gulch and Caspar Beach. The grounds also contain a collection of restored 1900s-era houses and a large sea-water aquarium within a former blacksmith and carpenter shop. Because the land here juts out into the sea, it's a great spot for whale-watching.

Note that it's a half-mile walk from the parking area to the lighthouse.

Kelley House Museum MUSEUM
(Map p248; ☎707-937-5791; www.kelleyhousemuseum.org; 45007 Albion St; $5; ⏲11am-3pm

Mendocino

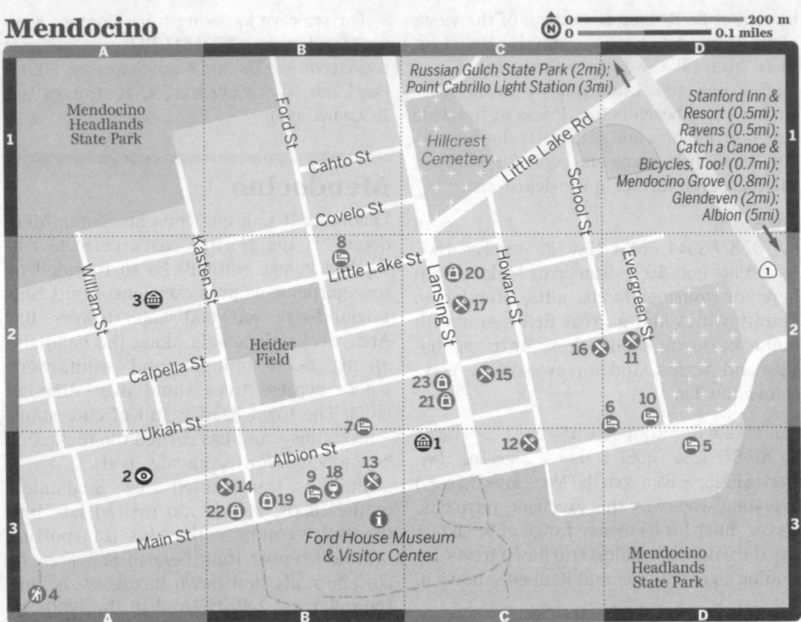

Mendocino

Sights
1 Kelley House Museum C3
2 Kwan Tai Temple A3
3 Mendocino Art Center A2

Activities, Courses & Tours
4 Mendocino Headlands State Park A3

Sleeping
5 Alegria D3
6 Didjeridoo Dreamtime Inn D2
7 MacCallum House Inn B2
8 Mendocino Coast Reservations B2
9 Mendocino Hotel B3
10 Raku House D2

Eating
11 Café Beaujolais D2
12 Farmers Market C3
13 Flow B3
14 Fog Eater Cafe B3
15 Frankie's C2
16 Luna Trattoria C2
MacCallum House Restaurant .... (see 7)
17 Patterson's Pub C2

Drinking & Nightlife
18 Dick's Place B3

Shopping
19 Gallery Bookshop B3
20 Harvest Market C2
21 Mendocino Chocolate Company C2
22 Out of This World B3
23 Village Toy Store C2

Thu-Tue Jun-Sep, Fri-Mon Oct-May) Check out the research library and changing exhibits on early California and Mendocino. The 1861 museum hosts seasonal, two-hour walking tours for $10; call for times.

Mendocino Art Center GALLERY
(Map p248; ☎707-937-5818; www.mendocinoartcenter.org; 45200 Little Lake St; ⊙11am-4pm) FREE Behind a yard of iron sculptures, the city's art center takes up a whole tree-filled block. It hosts exhibitions, nationally renowned art classes and the 81-seat Helen Schoeni Theatre, which is home to the **Mendocino Theatre Company** (www.mendocinotheatre.org). You can also pick up the *Mendocino Arts* magazine here, a biannual publication listing all the happenings and festivals in town.

Kwan Tai Temple TEMPLE
(Map p248; ☎707-937-5123; www.kwantaitemple.org; 45160 Albion St; ⊙noon-2pm Sat & Sun May-Oct or by appointment) Peering in the window of this 1852 temple reveals an old altar dedicated to the Chinese god of war. Tours are available by and provide a fascinating insight into the

history of the area's Chinese American immigrants, dating from the mid-19th century when they worked in the lumber industry.

Activities

Wine tours, whale-watching, shopping, hiking, cycling: there's more to do in the area than a thousand long weekends could accomplish. For navigable river and ocean kayaking, launch from tiny Albion, which hugs the north side of the Albion River mouth, 5 miles south of Mendocino.

Catch a Canoe & Bicycles, Too! CANOEING
(707-937-0273; www.catchacanoe.com; 10051 S Big River Rd, The Stanford Inn & Resort; 3hr kayak, canoe or bicycle rental adult/child $35/15; 9am-5pm) This friendly outfit offers seasonal guided tours and rents bikes, kayaks, stand-up paddleboards and canoes (including redwood outriggers) for trips up the 8-mile Big River tidal estuary. Northern California's longest undeveloped estuary has no highways or buildings, only beaches, forests, marshes, streams, abundant wildlife and historic logging sites.

Mendocino Headlands State Park HIKING
(Map p248; 707-937-5804; www.parks.ca.gov) FREE Mendocino Headlands State Park surrounds the village with trails that crisscross bluffs and rocky coves. Ask at the visitor center (p252) about the guided walks each Saturday at 1pm, which run the gamut from spring wildflower explorations to winter whale-watching jaunts.

Festivals & Events

For a complete list of Mendocino's many festivals, check with the visitor center or www.visitmendocino.com.

Mendocino Whale Festival WILDLIFE
(www.mendowhale.com; early Mar) Wine and chowder tastings accompany whale-watching. Regional whale festivals also take place in Fort Bragg, Little River and Westport throughout the month.

Mendocino Music Festival MUSIC
(www.mendocinomusic.com; mid-Jul) Enjoy orchestral and chamber music concerts on the headlands, including children's matinees and open rehearsals.

Mendocino Wine & Mushroom Festival FOOD & DRINK
(www.mendocino.com; early Nov) Includes guided mushroom tours and symposia.

Sleeping

Standards are high in stylish Mendocino and so are prices; two-day minimums often crop up on weekends. Fort Bragg, 10 miles north, has cheaper lodgings. All B&B rates include breakfast; only a few places have TVs. For a range of cottages and B&Bs, contact **Mendocino Coast Reservations** (Map p248; 707-937-5033; www.mendocinovacations.com; 45084 Little Lake St; 9am-4pm).

Russian Gulch State Park CAMPGROUND $
(reservations 800-444-7275; www.reservecalifornia.com; day use $8, tent & RV sites $45) Set in a wooded canyon 2 miles north of town, with secluded drive-in sites and hot showers. A moderate 2.7-mile trail leads from the campground into a fern-filled canyon with a small waterfall, or it's a quick stroll to the Devil's Punch Bowl (a collapsed sea arch).

Mendocino Hotel HISTORIC HOTEL $
(Map p248; 707-937-0511; www.mendocinohotel.com; 45080 Main St; r with/without bath from $95/75, ste from $120;) Built in 1878 as the town's first hotel, this place is like a piece of the Old West. If you can sacrifice some comforts, like a private bathroom, you can get an outstanding deal for the location. And though the rooms are a bit cramped, the character-filled ground floor almost makes up it.

★ **Alegria** B&B $$
(Map p248; 707-937-5150; www.oceanfrontmagic.com; 44781 Main St; r $149-309;) A perfect romantic hidecaway: beds have views over the coast, decks have ocean views and all rooms have wood-burning fireplaces. Outside, a gorgeous path leads to a big, amber-gray beach. Ever-so-friendly innkeepers whip up amazing breakfasts served in the sea-view dining area. Less expensive rooms are available across the street at bright and simple **Raku House** (998 Main St; r $129-189;).

Didjeridoo Dreamtime Inn B&B $$
(Map p248; 707-937-6200; www.didjeridooinn.com; 44860 Main St; r $150-199;) One of the town's more economical choices, rooms here are all different yet share the same homey, unpretentious atmosphere with tasteful artwork, antiques and, perhaps, a ghost or two. Several rooms have en suites, and a couple have mini hot tubs. The breakfast spread is excellent, while the front garden is a lovely place to sit.

MacCallum House Inn B&B $$
(Map p248; 707-937-0289; www.maccallumhouse.com; 45020 Albion St; r/cottage from $159/199, water-tower ste $259-359;) One of the more memorable B&B options in town with gardens in a riot of color. There are cheerful cottages, and a modern luxury home, but the most unique space is within one of Mendocino's iconic, historic water towers – living quarters fill the ground floor, a sauna is on the 2nd and there's a view of the coast from the top.

All accommodations have cushy extras like robes, stereos and plush linens. Those in the main building are looking a tad tired.

Mendocino Grove CAMPGROUND $$
(https://mendocinogrove.com; 9601 Hwy 1; tent from $140; May-Oct;) Sleep amid the trees, a quick stroll from town, at this hipster-friendly glamping resort. The safari-style platform tents here have proper beds with down comforters, wool blankets and cotton linens, ensuring maximum camping comfort. Sites also have fire pits, picnic tables and decks with leather butterfly chairs. The bathhouse is luxurious by camp standards.

Andiron Seaside Inn & Cabins CABIN $$
(707-937-1543; www.theandiron.com; 6051 N Hwy 1, Little River; d $124-284;) Styled with hip vintage decor, this cluster of 1950s roadside cottages is a refreshingly playful option amid the cabbage-rose and lace aesthetic of Mendocino. Each cabin houses two rooms with complementing themes: 'Read' has old books, comfy vintage chairs and retro eyeglasses, while the adjoining 'Write' features a huge chalkboard and a ribbon typewriter.

Lighthouse Inn at Point Cabrillo COTTAGE $$
(707-937-5033; www.pointcabrillo.org; Point Cabrillo Dr; cottages from $142, houses from $450;) On 300 acres, in the shadow of Point Cabrillo lighthouse, the stately lightkeeper's and assistant lightkeeper's houses, together with the staff's two turn-of-the-century cottages have been revamped into vacation rentals. All options have verandas and lush period decor but are not very private.

★**Stanford Inn & Resort** INN $$$
(707-937-5615; www.stanfordinn.com; 44850 Comptche-Ukiah Rd; r $300-500;) This masterpiece of a lodge standing on 10 lush acres has wood-burning fireplaces, knotty-pine walls, original art, stereos and top-quality mattresses in every room. Take a stroll in the organic gardens, where food is harvested for the excellent on-site restaurant, and go for a dip in the solarium-enclosed pool and hot tub; it's a sublime getaway.

Glendeven B&B $$$
(707-937-0083; www.glendeven.com; 8205 Hwy 1, Shoreline Hwy; r $225-365;) This historic 1860s estate 2 miles south of town has organic gardens, grazing llamas, chickens for those breakfast eggs, forest and oceanside trails and a wine bar serving only Mendocino wines – and that's just the start. Romantic rooms have neutral tones, soothing decor, fireplaces and top-notch linens.

Eating

With quality to rival Napa Valley, the influx of Bay Area weekenders has fostered an excellent dining scene that enthusiastically espouses organic, sustainable principles. Make reservations. Gathering picnic supplies is easy at Harvest Market organic grocery store (with deli) and the **farmers market** (Map p248; www.mcfarm.org; cnr Howard & Main St; noon-2pm Fri May-Oct).

Frankie's PIZZA $
(Map p248; 707-937-2436; www.frankiesmendocino.com; cnr Ukiah & Lansing Sts; pizza $13-18; 11am-9pm;) There is no Sicilian-style simplicity to these pizzas; they are pure California, with piled-high organic ingredients such as cremini mushrooms, Canadian bacon, roasted red peppers and pineapple (not combined, fortunately). It also serves healthy fare such as quinoa kale cakes and gluten-free falafel, plus soups, salads and Fort Bragg's famous Cowlick's ice cream.

Fog Eater Cafe VEGETARIAN $$
(Map p248; 707-397-1806; https://fogeatercafe.com; 45104 Main St; mains $13-20; 5-8:30pm Wed-Sat, 10am-2pm & 5-8:30pm Sun;) Forget everything you think you know about vegetarian food and the cuisine of the American South. Fog Eater challenges your perceptions of both by taking the hearty recipes of the American South and reframing them through a Northern California lens. The resulting plates – including heirloom grits, herb-crusted pot pie and cornbread french toast – are like a revelation.

Luna Trattoria ITALIAN $$
(Map p248; 707-962-3093; www.lunatrattoria.com; 955 Ukiah St; mains $12-29; 5-9pm Tue-Thu & Sun, to 10pm Fri & Sat) Follow the boardwalk lit with fairy lights to this cozy and casual northern Italian restaurant where the bread and

pastas are homemade, portions are generous and the service is outstanding. There's a lovely garden out back, while indoors a rock-music soundtrack amps up the mood. After a few glasses of Primitivo it all makes sense.

Ravens VEGETARIAN **$$**
(☎707-937-5615; www.ravensrestaurant.com; Stanford Inn & Resort, Comptche-Ukiah Rd; breakfast $12-17, mains $20-30; ⏰8-10:30am & 5:30-8pm; ✎) Ravens brings haute-contemporary concepts to a completely vegetarian and vegan menu. Produce comes from the idyllic organic gardens of the Stanford Inn & Resort and the bold menu takes on everything from sea-palm strudel and portabella sliders to decadent (guilt-free) desserts.

Flow CALIFORNIAN **$$**
(Map p248; ☎707-937-3569; www.mendocinoflow.com; 45040 Main St; mains $14-20; ⏰11am-10pm Mon-Fri, 9am-10pm Sat & Sun; 📶) This very busy place has the best views of the ocean in town from its 2nd-story perch, though the service can be abysmal. Brunch is a specialty, as are Mexican-inspired plates, artisan pizzas and a sublime wild rock cod chowder.

Patterson's Pub PUB FOOD **$$**
(Map p248; www.pattersonspub.com; 10485 Lansing St; mains $13-20; ⏰10am-midnight, food to 11pm) If you pull into town late and hungry, you'll thank your lucky stars for this place: it serves quality pub grub – fish and chips, burgers, dinner salads and even vegan burgers – alongside 26 taps of local beer. The only thing that spoils the traditional Irish pub ambience is the plethora of flat-screen TVs.

★ **Café Beaujolais** CALIFORNIAN **$$$**
(Map p248; ☎707-937-5614; www.cafebeaujolais.com; 961 Ukiah St; lunch mains $11-20, dinner mains $24-50; ⏰11:30am-3pm Wed-Sun, 5:30-9pm daily, closed Jan) Mendocino's iconic, beloved country-Cal-French restaurant occupies an 1893 farmhouse restyled into an urban-chic dining room. The refined, inspired cooking draws diners from San Francisco who make this the centerpiece of their trip. The menu changes with the seasons, but the dry-aged duck breast is a gourmand's delight.

MacCallum House Restaurant CALIFORNIAN **$$$**
(Map p248; ☎707-937-0289; www.maccallumhouse.com; 45020 Albion St; cafe dishes $15-20, mains $30-42; ⏰8-10am Mon-Fri, to 11am Sat & Sun, plus 5:30-9pm daily; 📶) Sit on the veranda or fireside for a romantic dinner of all-organic game, fish or risotto primavera. Chef Alan Kantor makes *everything* from scratch and his commitment to sustainability and organic ingredients is nearly as alluring as his menu. The cafe menu, served at the Grey Whale Bar, is one of Mendocino's few four-star bargains.

Drinking & Nightlife

Have cocktails at the Mendocino Hotel (p249) or the Grey Whale Bar at the MacCallum House Inn. For boisterousness and beer head to Patterson's Pub.

Dick's Place BAR
(Map p248; ☎707-937-6010; 45070 Main St; ⏰11:30am-2am) It's a bit out of place among the fancy-pants shops downtown, but this is an excellent spot to check out the *other* Mendocino and do shots with rowdy locals. Complimentary wieners on Wednesdays.

Shopping

Mendocino's walkable streets are great for shopping, and the ban on chain stores ensures unique, often upscale gifts. There are many small galleries in town where one-of-a-kind artwork is for sale.

Mendocino Chocolate Company CHOCOLATE
(Map p248; https://mendochocolateco.com; 10466 Lansing St; ⏰11am-5:30pm) This company has been around for more than 30 years in Fort Bragg, so it know its cocoa beans. This newer second outlet adds a sweet touch to Mendocino's shopping scene. Check out the exquisite handmade seashells in marbled white, milk and dark chocolate.

Harvest Market FOOD & DRINK
(Map p248; ☎707-937-5879; www.harvestmarket.com; 10501 Lansing St; ⏰7:30am-10pm) The town's biggest grocery store has legit organic credentials, an excellent cold-food bar and great cheese and meat.

Village Toy Store TOYS
(Map p248; ☎707-937-4633; 10450 Lansing St; ⏰10am-5pm) Get a kite or browse the old-world selection of wooden toys and games that you won't find in the chains – hardly anything requires batteries.

Gallery Bookshop BOOKS
(Map p248; ☎707-937-2665; www.gallerybookshop.com; 319 Kasten St; ⏰9:30am-6pm) Stocks a great selection of books on local topics, titles from California's small presses and specialized outdoor guides.

Out of This World SPORTS & OUTDOORS
(Map p248; ☎707-937-3335; www.outofthisworldshop.com; 45100 Main St; ⏰10am-5:30pm) Birders, astronomy buffs and science geeks head directly to this telescope, binocular and science-toy shop.

Information

Ford House Museum & Visitor Center (Map p248; ☎707-937-5397; www.mendoparks.org; 45035 Main St; ⏰11am-4pm) Enjoy maps, books, information and exhibits, including a scale model of 1890 Mendocino, in a historical setting with Victorian-period furniture and decor. The center runs events and activities including whale-watching walks, living-history days and soap-making workshops. Check the website to see what's happening during your visit, or pick up a copy of the *Coast Packet* for monthly events and listings.

Jug Handle State Reserve

Between Mendocino and Fort Bragg, **Jug Handle** (☎707-937-5804; www.parks.ca.gov; Hwy 1, Caspar; ⏰sunrise-sunset) FREE preserves an **ecological staircase** that you can view on a 5-mile (round-trip) self-guided nature trail. The reserve is a good spot to stroll the headlands, whale-watch or lounge on the beach; you can pick up a printed guide detailing the area's geology, flora and fauna from the parking lot. Watch for the turnoff, just north of Caspar.

Five wave-cut terraces ascend in steps from the seashore, each 100ft and 100,000 years removed from the previous one, and each with its own distinct geology and vegetation. One of the terraces has a **pygmy forest**, similar to the better-known example at Van Damme State Park, 7 miles south.

Jug Handle Creek Farm & Nature Center (☎707-964-4630; www.jughandlecreekfarm.com; 15501 N Hwy 1; tent sites $45, dm $20, r & cabins $50-55) is a nonprofit 39-acre farm with rustic cabins and hostel rooms in a 19th-century farmhouse. Drive 5 miles north of Mendocino to Caspar; the farm is on the east side of Hwy 1 across from the state reserve. Take the second driveway after Fern Creek Rd.

Fort Bragg

In the past, Fort Bragg was Mendocino's ugly stepsister, home to a lumber mill, a scrappy downtown and blue-collar locals who gave a cold welcome to outsiders. Since the mill closure in 2002, the town has started to reinvent itself, slowly warming to a tourism-based economy, with the downtown continuing to develop as a wonderfully unpretentious alternative to Mendocino (even if its southern outskirts are hideous). Unlike the *entirely* franchise-free 180-mile stretch of Coastal Hwy 1 between here and the Golden Gate, in Fort Bragg you can get a Big Mac, grande latte or any of a number of chain-store products whose buildings blight the landscape. Don't fret. Downtown you'll find better hamburgers and coffee, old-school architecture and residents eager to show off their little town.

By car, twisting Hwy 20 provides the main access to Fort Bragg from the east, and most facilities are near Main St, a 2-mile stretch of Hwy 1. The Mendocino Transit Authority (p263) operates bus 65, which travels between Fort Bragg, Willits, Ukiah and Santa Rosa daily, with an afternoon return ($23, four hours, four daily). Monday to Friday, the North Coast route 60 goes north between Navarro River junction and Albion, Little River, Mendocino and Fort Bragg ($2.25, 1½ hours, two daily).

Sights & Activities

Fort Bragg has the same banner North Coast activities as Mendocino – beachcombing, surfing, hiking, kayaking – but basing yourself here is cheaper and arguably less quaint and pretentious. The wharf lies at **Noyo Harbor** – the mouth of the Noyo River – south of downtown. Here you can find some whale-watching cruises and deep-sea fishing trips.

A fully paved **Coastal Trail** skirts the ocean edge of town from Noyo all the way to Glass Beach and beyond, offering excellent biking or strolling.

★**Mendocino Coast Botanical Gardens** GARDENS
(☎707-964-4352; www.gardenbythesea.org; 18220 N Hwy 1; adult/child/senior $15/8/12; ⏰9am-5pm Mar-Oct, to 4pm Nov-Feb) This gem of Northern California displays native flora, rhododendrons and heritage roses. The succulent display alone is amazing, and the organic garden is harvested by volunteers to feed area residents in need. The serpentine paths wander along 47 seafront acres south of town. Primary trails are wheelchair accessible.

Noyo Center for Marine Science SCIENCE CENTER
(☎707-733-6696; www.noyocenter.org; 338 N Main St; donations welcome; ⏰11am-5pm Thu-Mon; 👪)

FREE This small science center educates visitors about the climate-based threats facing the Mendocino coast, including the mass sea star die-off, explosion of invasive purple urchins and collapse of California's kelp forests over the past decade. It also has one of the largest orca skeletons on display anywhere in the world. The staff are incredibly knowledgeable and eager to share how everyday visitors can help.

Northcoast Artists Gallery GALLERY
(www.northcoastartists.org; 362 N Main St; 11am-5pm) An excellent local arts cooperative where 20 full-time members work in photography, glass, woodworking, jewelry, painting, sculpture, textiles and printmaking. Openings are on the first Friday of the month. Check www.visitmendocino.com for a comprehensive list of galleries throughout Mendocino County.

Glass Beach BEACH
(Elm St) Named for (what very little is left of) the sea-polished glass in the sand, remnants of its days as a city dump, this beach is now part of MacKerricher State Park (p255). Take the headlands trail from Elm St, off Main St, but leave the glass – visitors are not supposed to pocket souvenirs.

Be wary of the tides here, and there can be big waves and an undertow. A safer beach to swim is just north at **Pudding Creek Beach.**

Triangle Tattoo & Museum MUSEUM
(707-964-8814; www.triangletattoo.com; 356b N Main St; noon-6pm Sun-Thu, to 8pm Fri & Sat) FREE This one-off museum has an excellent exhibition of international tattoo art and explains the history in various cultures. You can also get a tattoo done here if you fancy.

★ **Skunk Train** RAIL
(707-964-6371; www.skunktrain.com; 100 W Laurel St; adult/child from $42/26; 9am-3pm) Fort Bragg's pride and joy, this vintage train got its nickname in 1925 for its stinky gas-powered steam engines, but today runs on diesel. One- or two-hour trips pass through the Pudding Creek Estuary for views of blue herons, ospreys, otters and redwood forests. Tracks run to Willits (p265), where there are also rail journeys, but you cannot travel between the two as bookings are roundtrip to either Glen Blair Junction or Crowley and back.

You can also hire two-person **rail bikes** for a seven-mile roundtrip guided tour along the same route as the train, including a short hike at the turnaround point ($90 per two-person bike). Book well in advance as it's extremely popular.

Liquid Fusion Kayaking KAYAKING
(707-962-1623; www.liquidfusionkayak.com; 32399 Basin St; tours from $49; by reservation only) From leisurely paddles down the calm waters of the Noyo River to wet and wild ocean adventures out to remote sea caves, Liquid Fusion is one of the most respected kayak outfits on this stretch of the California coast.

All-Aboard Adventures FISHING, WHALE-WATCHING
(707-964-1881; www.allaboardadventures.com; 32410 N Harbor Dr; fishing trips $80, whale-watching $40) Captain Tim leads five-hour crabbing or salmon-fishing trips and two-hour whale-watching explorations during the whale migration.

Festivals & Events

Paul Bunyan Days CARNIVAL
(www.paulbunyandays.com; Sep) Held on Labor Day weekend in September, this festival celebrates California's logging history with a logging show, fire hose fight, parade and fair.

Sleeping

Fort Bragg's lodging is cheaper than Mendocino's, but most of the motels are along noisy Hwy 1, so you'll hear traffic through your windows. The best of the motel bunch is **Colombi Motel** (707-964-5773; www.colombimotel.com; 647 E Oak St; 1-/2-bedroom units with kitchenette from $80/145;), which is in town. Most B&Bs do not have TVs and they all include breakfast.

★ **Country Inn** B&B $
(707-964-3737; www.beourguests.com; 632 N Main St; r $80-170;) This gingerbread trimmed B&B in the middle of town is an excellent way to dodge the chain motels for a good-value stay. The lovely family hosts are welcoming and easygoing and can offer good local tips. Breakfast can be delivered to your room, and at night you can soak in a hot tub out back. There is a minimum two-night stay at weekends.

Shoreline Cottages MOTEL, COTTAGE $
(707-964-2977; www.shoreline-cottage.com; 18725 Hwy 1; d $99-149, ste $141-169;) Low-key, four-person rooms and cottages with kitchens surrounding a central, tree-filled lawn. The family rooms are a good bargain, and suites feature modern artwork and clean

sight lines. All rooms have microwaves, cable TV, snacks and access to a library of DVDs, plus there's a communal hot tub.

Beachcomber Motel MOTEL $$
(707-964-2402; www.thebeachcombermotel.com; 1111 N Main St; r $119-229;) Standard motel rooms with nonstandard perks like ocean views, Jacuzzi baths, fire pits and spa services. It's right off the iconic Pudding Creek Trestle, which makes for a scenic stroll to town.

Eating & Drinking

Similar to the lodging scene, the food in Fort Bragg is less spendy than Mendocino, but there are a number of fine options, mainly located on or around Main St. Self-caterers should try the farmers market downtown or the **Harvest Market** (707-964-7000; cnr Hwys 1 & 20; 5am-11pm) for the best groceries.

★ **Piaci Pub & Pizzeria** ITALIAN $
(707-961-1133; 120 W Redwood Ave; mains $8-14; 11am-9:30pm Mon-Thu, to 10pm Fri & Sat, 4-9:30pm Sun) Fort Bragg's must-visit pizzeria is known for its sophisticated wood-fired, brick-oven pizzas as much as for its long list of microbrews. Try the 'Gustoso' – with chèvre, pesto and seasonal pears, all carefully orchestrated on a thin crust. It's tiny, loud and fun, with much more of a bar atmosphere than a restaurant. Expect to wait at peak times.

★ **Taka's Japanese Grill** JAPANESE $
(707-964-5204; 250 N Main St; mains $10-19; 11:30am-3pm & 4:30-9pm) Although it may look fairly run-of-the-mill, this is an exceptional Japanese restaurant. The owner is a former grader at the Tokyo fish market, so the quality is tops, and he makes a weekly run to San Francisco to source freshly imported seafood. Sushi, teriyaki dishes, noodle soups and pan-fried noodles with salmon, beef or chicken are just a few of the options.

Princess Seafood Market & Deli SEAFOOD $
(707-962-3123; www.fvprincess.com; 32410 N Harbor Dr; mains $11-19; 10am-6pm Sun-Thu, to 7pm Fri & Sat;) Sit at picnic tables by the docks and chow down on sustainably caught ocean-to-table delicacies, including Dungeness crab cakes, fish tacos and oysters on the half shell. There's live music on weekends and plenty of local craft beer (or kombucha) to keep you lingering long into the afternoon.

Cowlick's Handmade Ice Cream ICE CREAM $
(707-962-9271; www.cowlicksicecream.com; 250b N Main St; scoops from $2.90; 11am-9pm) Just great ice cream in fun flavors, from classics such as mocha almond fudge to the very unusual, such as ginger, chai or candy cap mushroom (tastes like maple syrup but better). The sorbets (try the pear or mango) are also delish.

Headlands Coffeehouse CAFE $
(707-964-1987; www.headlandscoffeehouse.com; 120 E Laurel St; mains $5-13; 7am-10pm Mon-Sat, to 5pm Sun;) Fort Bragg's best cafe is in the middle of the historic downtown, with high ceilings and lots of atmosphere. The menu gets rave reviews for the Belgian waffles, homemade soups, veggie-friendly salads and paninis. As a bonus, there's live music nightly.

Certified Farmers Market MARKET $
(www.mcfarm.org; cnr E Laurel & N Franklin Sts; 3-5pm Wed) This is an above-average farmers market with an excellent array of fresh produce, plus breads, preserves and locally produced cheese.

Silver's at the Wharf AMERICAN $$
(707-964-4283; www.silversatthewharf.com; 32260 N Harbor Dr; mains $10-33; 11:30am-3:30pm & 4:30-8pm;) Given its position, overlooking the docks, you would expect this to be a swanky oysters-and-champagne sort of place. Far from it. The decor is stuck in the '60s and the cuisine is well prepared but solidly traditional, with a vast selection that includes pasta, steak, Mexican fare and seafood, such as Pacific Bay shrimp and calamari steak. Ideal for families.

North Coast Brewing Company AMERICAN $$
(707-964-3400; www.northcoastbrewing.com; 444 N Main St; mains $14-22; 11:30am-9:30pm Sun-Thu, to 10:30pm Fri & Sat;) Though dishes like ceviche and seafood polenta demonstrate that this establishment takes the food as seriously as the bevvies, it's the burgers and garlic fries that soak up the fantastic selection of handcrafted brews. A great stop for serious beer lovers.

Cucina Verona ITALIAN $$$
(707-964-6844; www.cucinaverona.com; 124 E Laurel St; mains $16-42; 9am-9pm) A real-deal Italian restaurant with no-fail traditional dishes, plus a few with a California tweak, such as butternut-squash lasagne and artichoke bruschetta. The atmosphere is as

comforting as the cuisine, with dim lighting, a warm color scheme and unobtrusive live music most evenings. There is an extensive microbrew selection on offer, as well as local and imported wines.

Overtime Brewing MICROBREWERY
(☎707-962-3040; http://overtimebrewing.com; 190 E Elm St; ⊙11am-10pm Mon-Sat, from noon Sun; ☎) It may be the new kid on the craft-beer block, but Overtime outshines its stalwart neighbor, North Coast Brewing, when it comes to pushing the envelope. The brews here are far more experimental, and you can pair them with alcohol soaking mac 'n' cheese, jambalaya or burgers while playing board games or chatting with locals at the horseshoe bar.

Shopping

There's plenty of window-shopping in Fort Bragg's compact downtown, including a string of galleries along Franklin St.

Outdoor Store SPORTS & OUTDOORS
(☎707-397-7171; cnr Main & Redwood Sts; ⊙10am-5:30pm Mon-Sat, to 5pm Sun) If you're planning on camping or exploring the Lost Coast, this is the best outfitter in the region, stocking detailed maps of wilderness areas, fuel for stoves and high-quality gear. Staff can also give advice on nearby parks.

Information

Mendocino Coast Chamber of Commerce
(☎707-961-6300; www.mendocinocoast.com; 332 S Main St; ⊙9am-5pm Mon-Fri, 10am-3pm Sat; ☎) The chamber of commerce has lots of helpful information about this stretch of coast and what's on. Its online guide is also worth checking out.

MacKerricher State Park

Three miles north of Fort Bragg, the **MacKerricher State Park** (☎707-964-9112; www.parks.ca.gov; Fort Bragg) FREE preserves 9 miles of pristine rocky headlands, sandy beaches, dunes and tidepools.

The visitor center sits next to the whale skeleton at the park entrance. Hike the Coastal Trail along dark-sand beaches and see rare and endangered plant species. **Lake Cleone** is a 30-acre freshwater lake stocked with trout and visited by more than 90 species of birds. At nearby **Laguna Point** an interpretive boardwalk (accessible to visitors with disabilities) overlooks harbor seals and, from

NORTH COAST BEER TOUR

The craft breweries of the North Coast don't mess around – bold hop profiles, Belgian-style ales and smooth lagers are regional specialties, and they're produced with style. Some breweries are better than others, but the following tour makes for an excellent long weekend of beer tasting in the region.

➡ Anderson Valley Brewing Company (p262), Boonville

➡ Overtime Brewing, Fort Bragg

➡ Gyppo Ale Mill (p269), Shelter Cove

➡ Redwood Curtain Brewing (p277), Arcata

➡ Seaquake Brewing (p286), Crescent City

December to April, migrating whales. **Ricochet Ridge Ranch** (☎707-964-7669; www.horse-vacation.com; 24201 N Hwy 1; per hour/day $60/345; ⊙9am-6:30pm) offers horseback-riding trips through redwoods or along the beach.

Popular **campgrounds** (☎800-444-7275; www.reservecalifornia.com; MacKerricher State Park; tent & RV sites $40), nestled in pine forest, have hot showers and water. Ten superb, secluded walk-in tent sites (numbers 1 to 10) are first-come, first-served.

Just north of the park is **Pacific Star Winery** (☎707-964-1155; www.pacificstarwinery.com; 33000 Hwy 1, Westport; tastings $10; ⊙noon-5pm Thu-Sun), in a dramatic, rub-your-eyes-in-disbelief-beautiful location on a bluff over the sea. The wines don't get pros excited but they are perfectly drinkable, the owners are friendly and you're encouraged to picnic at one of the many coast-side tables, stroll some of the short coastal trails along the cliffs and generally enjoy yourself (which isn't hard).

Westport

If sleepy Westport feels like the peaceful edge of nowhere, that's because it is. The last hamlet before the Lost Coast, on a twisting 15-mile drive north of Fort Bragg, it is the final slice of civilization before Hwy 1 veers inland on the 22-mile ascent to meet Hwy 101 in Leggett. The population here is around 60 and the town today consists of little more than a couple of choice places to stay, a fine pub, a small grocer and deli, and a couple of gas pumps. Westport dates from 1877 when it was called Beall's Landing after a (long-gone) timber loading facility built by Samuel Beall, the town's first white settler.

Head 1.5 miles north of town for the ruggedly beautiful **Westport-Union Landing State Beach** (707-937-5804; cnr Hwy 1 & Seaview Dr; tent sites $35), which extends for 3 miles on coastal bluffs. A rough hiking trail leaves the primitive campground and passes by tidepools and streams, accessible at low tide.

Sleeping & Eating

Howard Creek Ranch CABIN $
(707-964-6725; www.howardcreekranch.com; 40501 N Hwy 1, Shoreline Hwy; r from $115, cabins from $125;) Howard Creek Ranch, sitting on 60 stunning acres of forest and farmland abutting the wilderness, has delightfully eccentric accommodations in an 1870s farmhouse. There are also some gonzo cabins, including a carriage barn, in which way-cool redwood rooms have been expertly handcrafted by the artist owner. If you can deal with a few quirks, it's truly a sight to behold. Rates include breakfast.

Westport Inn INN $
(707-964-5135; www.westportinnca.com; 37040 N Hwy 1, Shoreline Hwy; r from $89) Dating from the 1970s, this is a simple yet lovely place to stay, with beach access and extremely comfortable rooms with plush mattresses and nice artwork. The innkeepers are quite charming; toss in a continental breakfast, and it's great value.

Westport Hotel & Old Abalone Pub INN $$
(707-964-3688; www.westporthotel.us; 38921 Hwy 1, Shoreline Hwy; r $150-250; closed late Dec to mid-Feb;) Westport Hotel & Old Abalone Pub is quiet enough to have a motto that brags 'You've finally found nowhere.' The rooms are sumptuous – feather duvets, hardwood furniture, plush carpeting – with excellent views. The classy historic pub downstairs is the only option for dinner, so be thankful it's a delicious sampling of whimsical California fusions and hearty, expertly presented pub food.

ALONG HIGHWAY 101

To get into the most remote and wild parts of the North Coast on the quick, eschew winding Hwy 1 for inland Hwy 101, which runs north from San Francisco as a freeway, then as a two- or four-lane highway north of Sonoma County, occasionally pausing under the traffic lights of small towns.

Know that escaping the Bay Area at rush hour (weekdays between 4pm and 7pm) ain't easy. You might sit bumper-to-bumper through Santa Rosa or Willits, where trucks bound for the coast turn onto Hwy 20.

Although Hwy 101 may not look as enticing as the coastal route, it's faster and less winding, leaving you time along the way to detour into Mendocino County wine regions (Mendocino claims to be the greenest wine region in the country), explore pastoral Anderson Valley, splash about Clear Lake or soak at hot-springs resorts outside Ukiah – time well spent indeed!

Hopland

Apparently using the most solar power per capita in the world, Hopland flaunts its eco-geek, green-living ways at every turn with more organic produce available than you can shake a carrot stick at, plus a sustainable-living demonstration site. Hops were first grown here in 1866, but Prohibition brought the industry temporarily to a halt. Today, with its location as a gateway to Mendocino County's wine country, booze drives Hopland's economy again, with wine tasting the primary draw. Most of the tasting rooms are conveniently located right on Hwy 101, which runs through the center of town, and are generally small, boutique-style operations offering an enjoyable personalized experience.

Sights

For an excellent weekend trip, use Hopland as a base for exploring the regional wineries. More information about the constantly growing roster of wineries is available at www.destinationhopland.com. Find a map to the wine region at www.mendowine.com.

Brutocao Cellars WINERY
(800-433-3689; www.brutocaocellars.com; 13500 S Hwy 101; 10am-5pm) FREE Located in a former 1920s schoolhouse in central Hopland, this fourth-generation family-owned winery has bocce courts, bold red wines and chocolate – a perfect combo. There is also, refreshingly, no charge for wine tasting here (although there is generally a limit to how much tippling you can do!).

★ **Graziano Family of Wines** WINERY
(707-744-8466; www.grazianofamilyofwines.com; 13275 S Hwy 101; 10am-5pm) FREE The

Italian Graziano family is one of the oldest grape-growing families in Mendocino County and specializes in 'Cal-Ital' wines – including primitivo, dolcetto, barbera and Sangiovese – at some fantastic prices. Wine tasting is complimentary.

Saracina Vineyards WINERY
(707-670-0199; www.saracina.com; 11684 S Hwy 101; tasting/tour $10/25; 10am-5pm Wed-Sun) The highlight of a tour here is the descent into the cool caves (book a day in advance). Sensuous whites and rare-in-California malbecs are all biodynamically and sustainably farmed.

Real Goods Solar Living Center MUSEUM
(707-472-2456; www.solarliving.org; 13771 S Hwy 101; by donation; 10am-5pm) This progressive, futuristic 13-acre campus is largely responsible for the area's bold green initiatives. Shop at the Real Goods Store, take a self-guided tour of permaculture and aquaponics exhibits, or visit the Emerald Pharms solar-powered marijuana dispensary, which is a safe place for newbies and has a strong educational focus.

Sleeping & Eating

★Thatcher Hotel HISTORIC HOTEL $$
(707-723-0838; www.thatcherhotel.com; 13401 Hwy 101; r $145-500;) What's not to love about this newly renovated 1890s-era hotel? It's got a full bar with curated cocktails, a tempting cafe, a handsome library and a pool to enjoy all those libations in (unless the bocce court is more your scene!). The rooms are Nordic-esque with hardwood floors and a cooling color palate that tempers the warm environs. Great service, too!

Stock Farm INN $$
(707-744-1977; www.stockfarmhopland.com; 13441 S Hwy 101; ste $185-305;) Modern Californian meets Italian at this very comfortable inn where all of the spacious suites have Jacuzzis, fireplaces and private balconies. The homey taverna and pizzeria in front have big tables for communal dining and fantastic artisanal pizzas, craft beer and wine.

Bluebird Cafe DINER $
(707-744-1633; 13340 S Hwy 101; mains $10-17; 7am-2pm Wed-Mon) This classic American diner serves hearty breakfasts and homemade pie (the summer selection of peach-blueberry pie is dreamy). For a more exciting culinary adventure, try the wild-game burgers, such as elk, with a bite of horseradish.

Steep COFFEE
(707-670-6005; www.steephopland.com; 13275 Hwy 101; 6am-5pm Mon-Fri, 7am-4pm Sat & Sun;) A stylish third-wave coffee shop with a jungle-chic vibe and lots of healing crystals. The cold brew, matcha latte and pour-overs are highlights.

Clear Lake

With more than 100 miles of shoreline and 68 square miles of surface area, Clear Lake is the largest naturally occurring freshwater lake in California (Tahoe is bigger, but crosses the Nevada state line). In summer the warm water thrives with algae, giving it a murky green appearance and creating a fabulous habitat for fish, especially bass and catfish, so you can expect plenty of anglers here, particularly on weekends. Mt Konocti, a 4300ft-tall dormant volcano, lords over the scene. The lake is ringed by small, low-key resorts with budget-friendly places to stay, dine and kick back enjoying the lake views. You can also rent boats, kayaks, paddleboards and just about anything else that floats on the water at one of several marinas. On a more somber note, the area was devastated by a large wildfire in the summer of 2015 with Middletown, in particular, being badly affected. Smaller fires struck again in 2019, though the towns have all bounced back.

Locals refer to the northwest portion as 'upper lake' and the southeast portion as 'lower lake.' Likeable and well-serviced **Lakeport** (population 4695) sits on the northwest shore, a 20-mile drive east of Hopland along Hwy 175 (off Hwy 101); tiny, Old West–style **Kelseyville** (population 3353) is 7 miles south and has the largest concentration of wineries. **Clearlake**, off the southeastern shore, is the biggest town.

The old-timey village of **Upper Lake** is the most attractive place up north. Hwy 20 links it with the relatively bland north-shore hamlets of **Nice** and **Lucerne**, 4 miles southeast. **Middletown**, an historic stagecoach stop, lies 18 miles south of Clearlake at the junction of Hwys 175 and 29, 18 miles north of Calistoga.

Sights

Clear Lake State Park STATE PARK
(707-279-4293, 707-279-2267; www.clearlakestatepark.org; 5300 Soda Bay Rd, Kelseyville; per car $8; sunrise-sunset) Four miles from Kelseyville, on the lake's western shore, this park is idyllic and gorgeous, with hiking trails,

TOP CLEAR LAKE WINERIES

There are some 30 wineries of varying quality around Clear Lake. Most lie in volcanic soils more than 1300ft above sea level, and many provide grapes for neighboring Napa wineries. All are incredibly welcoming, and typically wave tasting fees if you purchase a bottle. For info on tasting rooms and events, check out www.lakecountywineries.org.

Olof Cellars (707-391-7947; www.olofcellars.com; 5616 Highland Springs Rd, Lakeport; tasting $10; 11am-5pm Sat & Sun, by appointment weekdays) If you visit one boutique winery in Lake County, make it Olof Cellars. The wines are excellent – most are reds aged for a minimum of three years – and the informative winemaker-led tastings take place in the old chicken coop. Olof produces just 500 cases annually; the bottles of nebbiolo, barbera, malbec and petit verdot are both unique and a steal.

Brassfield Estate (707-998-1895; www.brassfieldestate.com; 10915 High Valley Rd, Clearlake Oaks; tasting $15; 11am-5pm daily May-Nov, to 4pm Thu-Mon Dec-Apr) Remote, stunning Tuscan villa in the unique High Valley appellation surrounded by magnificent landscaped gardens.

Chacewater Winery & Olive Mill (707-279-2995; www.chacewaterwine.com; 5625 Gaddy Ln, Kelseyville; tasting $5; 11am-5pm) Sample a wide array of largely organic wines and then soak up the alcohol with an equally memorable olive oil tasting. Bring your favorite bottle to the picnic area out back where you can play horseshoes or bocce ball in front of the olive groves. Or, spend the night at the great-value three-bedroom farmhouse ($150, two night minimum).

Langtry Estate Vineyards (707-995-7501; www.langtryestate.com; 21000 Butts Canyon Rd, Middletown; tasting $10, tours from $65; 11am-5pm Fri-Sun, by appointment Mon-Thu) This winery has a stunning location on a hilltop overlooking the lake with picnic tables available for anyone who wants to pack a lunch. Visitors can opt for a wine tasting of six wines, a tasting plus tour, or a tour that includes a wine tasting and lunch. The late actress Lillie Langtry owned the vineyard and house from 1888 until 1906.

fishing, boating and camping. The bird-watching is extraordinary (up to 300 species!). The visitor center (open May to September) has natural history and cultural diorama exhibits.

Calpine Geothermal Visitor Center SCIENCE CENTER
(707-987-4270; www.geysers.com/Visitor-Center-and-Tours; 15500 Central Park Rd, Middletown; 11:30am-5pm Wed-Sat) The Geysers is the largest geothermal energy complex in the world, generating 850MW of clean, renewable energy. Check out operator Calpine's visitor center in Middletown, which runs occasional tours to the nearby facilities.

Sleeping & Eating

For the greatest range of places to stay, head to Lakeport, where most accommodations are conveniently located on and around Main St. Be sure to make reservations ahead on weekends and during summer, when people flock to the cool water. There are several campsites close to the lake, although be aware that they can flood if there are heavy rains, so always check in advance. For the budget conscious, Lakeport also has the most affordable options.

Clearlake

Vista del Lago CABIN $
(707-349-9768; www.vdlresort.com; 14103 Lakeshore Dr, Clearlake; cottages $75-179;) Located right on the main road, handy for shops and restaurants, these funky little cottages are a delight. Sizes and facilities vary, but all have well-equipped kitchenettes and are comfortably furnished. Other options may include hot tubs or fireplaces; one cabin even has its own pool table. There is an outside Jacuzzi, kayak rentals and barbecues right on the lake.

Lakeport & Kelseyville

There are a number of motels along the main drags in Clearlake and Lakeport, but if you want fresh air, Clear Lake State Park has four **campgrounds** (800-444-7275; www.reservecalifornia.com; State Park Rd; tent & RV sites $30; year round) with showers. The weekly **farmers market** (www.lakecountyfarmersfinest.

org; Hwy 29 & Thomas Dr, Kelseyville; 8:30am-noon Sat May-Oct) is in Kelseyville.

★Lakeport English Inn B&B $$
(707-263-4317; www.lakeportenglishinn.com; 675 N Main St, Lakeport; r $165-195; Fri-Sun only Dec-May;) The finest B&B at Clear Lake is an 1875 Carpenter Gothic with 10 impeccably furnished rooms, styled with a nod to the English countryside and with such quaint names as the Prince of Wales or (wait for it) Roll in the Hay. You'll get a $10 discount on your room if you say 'Baby Prince George' while making the reservation.

A daily afternoon-tea ritual, known as cream tea, involves scones, fresh strawberry jam and real Devonshire cream (for guests only). High tea is celebrated seasonally and is open to nonguests (make reservations).

Angelina's Bakery & Espresso CAFE $
(707-263-0391; www.angelinas365.com; 365 N Main St, Lakeport; sandwiches from $8; 7am-5pm Mon-Fri, 9am-2pm Sat;) The best baked goodies in Clear Lake, especially the giant decadent muffins and gooey cinnamon rolls. Also makes sandwiches to order and serves savory pastries. The coffee comes with a caffeine kick that should set you up for the day.

Studebakers Coffee House DELI $
(707-279-8871; 3990 Main St, Kelseyville; sandwiches from $6; 6am-4pm Mon-Fri, 7am-4pm Sat, 7am-2pm Sun) A friendly, old style diner with plenty of character, starting with the checkered ketchup-and-mustard linoleum floors. The chalkboard menu lists great sandwiches, including vegetarian options, plus Mexican fare such as quesadillas and burritos. The coffee is just alright.

★Saw Shop Bistro CALIFORNIAN $$
(707-278-0129; 3825 Main St, Kelseyville; small plates $14-16, mains $18-32; 11:30am-9pm Tue-Sat;) The best restaurant in Lake County serves a California cuisine-inspired menu of wild salmon and chili-rubbed flank steak, as well as a small-plates menu of harvest salads, pasture-raised beef burgers and flatbread pizzas. Laid-back atmosphere, too. Reservations recommended.

Park Place AMERICAN $$
(707-263-0444; www.parkplacelakeport.com; 50 3rd St, Lakeport; mains $12-30; 11am-8:30pm;) Simple but set right on the waterfront, this bright and completely unpretentious eatery serves basics like pasta, burgers and pizza made from sustainable, local produce at nice prices. A local favorite.

Northshore

★Tallman Hotel HISTORIC HOTEL $$
(707-275-2245; www.tallmanhotel.com; 9550 Main St, Upper Lake; r $185-265;) The centerpiece may be the smartly renovated historic hotel – tile bathrooms, warm lighting, thick linens – but the rest of the property, including the shady garden, walled-in swimming pool, brick patios and porches, exudes timeless elegance. Some garden rooms come with outdoor Japanese soaking tubs heated by an energy-efficient geothermal-solar system.

The connected **Blue Wing Saloon** (11:30am-9pm daily, mains $11-25) is the most atmospheric restaurant on the north shore with frequent live music.

Featherbed Railroad Co HERITAGE HOTEL $$
(707-274-8378; www.featherbedrailroad.com; 2870 Lakeshore Blvd, Nice; cabooses $175-220;) A treat for train buffs and kids, Featherbed has nine comfy, real cabooses on a grassy lawn. Some of the cabooses straddle the border between kitschy and tacky (the 'Easy Rider' has a Harley-Davidson headboard and a mirrored ceiling), but they're great fun if you keep a sense of humor. There's a tiny beach across the road, plus Jacuzzi tubs in some cabooses.

Drinking & Nightlife

Library Park, in Lakeport, has free lakeside Friday-evening summer concerts, with blues and rockabilly tunes to appeal to road-trippers.

Kelsey Creek Brewing BREWERY
(707-279-2311; www.kelseycreekbrewing.com; 3945 Main St, Kelseyville; 2-8pm Mon-Thu, noon-8pm Fri & Sat, noon 6pm Sun) A 'hop'-ping fun local's scene with excellent craft beer, peanut shells on the floor and a bring-your-own-food, bring-your-dog kind of laid-back vibe.

Entertainment

Lakeport Auto Movies CINEMA
(www.lakeportautomovies.com; 52 Soda Bay Rd, Lakeport; 2/3 people per car $20/28;) Lakeport is home to one of America's few surviving and wonderfully nostalgic drive-in movie theaters, with showings on Friday and Saturday nights in shoulder seasons and daily in summer (June to August).

OFF THE BEATEN TRACK

HARBIN HOT SPRINGS

Beloved **Harbin Hot Springs** (707-987-2477; www.harbin.org; 18424 Harbin Springs Rd, Middletown; campsite per person from $35, caravans from $155, cottages from $180;) reopened in 2019 after a devastating 2015 wildfire swept through its 1,700 acres of meadows and forestland, destroying 95% of the structures. The heart and soul of the revived retreat center is the clothing-optional pool area, with eight baths of varying temperatures, plus a sauna and sundeck offering sweeping valley views. Lodging is in creekside caravans or hilltop cottages. Budgeteers can also pitch a tent. Reserve well in advance.

Day use (Monday-Thursday adult/child $20/15, Fri-Sun $30/25) gives you up to six hours to explore the facilities and dine at the organic (and mostly vegetarian) **Dancing Bear Cafe**. At least one person in your party will have to become a member, which starts at $10 for a month.

Note that Harbin has a more youthful, no-frills vibe than the neighboring Mendocino hot springs. It's also much more hippie-dippie (don't be surprised when the bare-chested lady next to you starts groaning out mantras in the sauna!). Overnight visits feel a bit like going to adult summer camp with yoga classes, drum circles and nightly movies. If you're comfortable in the buff, it can be a revelatory experience.

Information

Lake County Visitor Information Center (707-263-5092; www.lakecounty.com; 875 Lakeport Blvd, Lakeport; 9am-5pm Mon-Fri) Offers hiking maps and guides to Lake County wineries. It's worth a visit just to check out the hilltop vista.

Getting Around

Lake Transit (707-263-3334, 707-994-3334; www.laketransit.org; 9240 Highway 53, Lower Lake) Operates weekday routes between Middletown, Calistoga and St Helena ($5, 35 minutes, four daily). Buses serve Ukiah ($8, 2 hours, four daily), from Clearlake via Lakeport ($5, 1½ hours, seven daily). Since piecing together routes and times can be difficult, it's best to phone ahead.

Anderson Valley

Rolling hills surround pocket-size Anderson Valley, a one-time redwood-logging community more famous today for the apple orchards,vineyards, pastures and its general air of tranquility.Visitors come primarily to winery-hop; the winery scene here has been compared to the Napa Valley some 30 years ago. Most of the wineries are clustered between Boonville and Navarro, but you'll also find good hiking and cycling in the hills and the chance to escape civilization (although weekends can get busy with San Franciscans fleeing the city). Other things to check out include the **Historical Society Museum** (707-895-3207; www.andersonvalleymuseum.org; 12340 Hwy 128, Boonville; 1-4pm Sat & Sun Feb-Nov) FREE – where you can learn about the local language Boontling – plus the delicious farmstead cheeses; look for signs on the roadside. Cheese is also sold at several of the vineyards and agreeably available for tasting along with the wine. Traveling through the valley is the most common route to Mendocino from San Francisco.

Boonville (population 1035) and **Philo** (population 349) are the valley's principal towns. From Ukiah, winding Hwy 253 heads 20 miles southwest to Boonville. Equally scenic Hwy 128 twists and turns 60 miles between Cloverdale on Hwy 101, south of Hopland, and Albion on coastal Hwy 1.

Sights & Activities

Philo Apple Farm FARM
(707-895-2333; www.philoapplefarm.com; 18501 Greenwood Rd, Philo; 10am-5pm) For the best fruit, skip the obvious roadside stands and head to this gorgeous farm for preserves, chutneys and organic heirloom apples and pears. For overnight guests, the farm also hosts **cooking classes** on select dates (check the website). You can make a weekend out of it by staying in one of the highly recommended **Philo Apple Farm Guest Cottages** (707-895-2333; www.philoapplefarm.com; 18501 Greenwood Rd, Philo; d $300;).

Festivals & Events

Pinot Noir Festival WINE
(707-895-9463; www.avwines.com; Philo; May) One of Anderson Valley's many wine celebrations; held over three days toward the end of May.

Sierra Nevada World Music Festival MUSIC (www.snwmf.com; Mendocino County Fairgrounds, 14400 Hwy 128, Boonville; ⏲ mid-Jun) In the middle of June, over three days, the sounds of reggae and roots fill the air, comingling with the scent of Mendocino County's *other* cash crop.

Mendocino County Fair & Apple Show FAIR (www.mendocountyfair.com; Mendocino County Fairgrounds, 14400 Hwy 128, Boonville; adult/child $10/6; ⏲ mid-Sep; 👪) A classic autumnal county fair with wine tasting, a rodeo and lively parades.

Sleeping

Overall the accommodation options are in the midrange to high-end categories, catering to San Franciscan weekenders seeking a self-pampering break with wine tasting, vineyard views and Egyptian-cotton sheets thrown in. If you are looking for somewhere more family and budget-friendly, there are some excellent campsites in the valley, some with cabin accommodation available.

Hendy Woods State Park CAMPGROUND $ (☎ office 707-895-3141, reservations 800-444-7275; www.reservecalifornia.com; Hwy 128; tent & RV sites $40, cabins $60) Bordered by the Navarro River on Hwy 128, west of Philo, this lovely redwood park has hiking, picnicking and a forested campground with hot showers.

★ **Boonville Hotel** BOUTIQUE HOTEL $$ (☎ 707-895-2210; www.boonvillehotel.com; 14050 Hwy 128, Boonville; d $165-325;) Decked out in contemporary American-country style with sea-grass flooring, pastel colors and fine linens, this historic hotel's rooms and suites are safe for urbanites who refuse to abandon style just because they've gone to the country. The rooms are all different and there are agreeable extras, including hammocks and fireplaces.

Other Place COTTAGE $$ (Sheep Dung Properties; ☎ 707-895-3979; www.sheepdung.com; 14655 CA-128, Boonville; cottages $150-375;) Located outside of town on a ridge with blissful panoramic and vineyard views, the 500 acres of ranch land here surround private, fully equipped hilltop cottages. The owners also hire out a cottage in downtown Boonville that shares access to the ranch with its picturesque views and walking trails.

Madrones HOTEL $$$ (☎ 707-895-2955; www.themadrones.com; 9000 Hwy 128, Philo; r $175-350;) Tucked off the back of the Madrones Mediterranean-inspired complex, which includes a restaurant, apothecary and three winery tasting rooms, the spacious 'guest quarters' here are modern-country-luxe, with a tinge of Tuscany. Above all, they are eminently comfortable with plush furnishings, soft carpeting and a soothing color scheme.

A stone's throw away is sister property The Brambles, which is home to a handful of more adventurous cabins tucked into a towering redwood grove.

Eating & Drinking

Boonville restaurants seem to open and close as they please, so expect hours to vary based on season and whims. There are several places along Hwy 128 which can supply a picnic with fancy local cheeses and fresh bread. Locally grown produce is the norm in these parts, so you can expect organic seasonal veg and a pleasing lack of fast-food options. Nope, gourmet burgers don't count.

Paysanne ICE CREAM $ (☎ 707-895-2210; www.sweetpaysanne.com; 14111 Hwy 128, Boonville; ice cream from $2.50; ⏲ 11am-6pm Fri-Mon Apr-Nov) Boonville's fantastic sweets shop serves the innovative flavors of Three Twins Ice Cream, whose delightful choices include Lemon Cookie and Strawberry Je Ne Sais Quoi (which has a hint of balsamic vinegar); it's the best ice cream to be found in the Anderson Valley, according to the locals – and they know best.

Lauren's AMERICAN $ (☎ 707-895-3869; www.laurensgoodfood.com; 14211 Hwy 128, Boonville; mains $10-18; ⏲ 5-9pm Tue-Sat, also 11:30am-2:30pm Thu-Sun May-Oct;) Locals pack Lauren's for eclectic homemade cookin' and a good wine list. Musicians sometimes jam on the stage by the front window, plus there are weekly quiz and trivia nights.

★ **Restaurant at the Boonville Hotel** CALIFORNIAN $$$ (☎ 707-895-2210; www.boonvillehotel.com; 14050 Hwy 128, Boonville; mains $20-30, dinner tasting menu $78; ⏲ 6-8pm Thu-Mon Apr-Nov, 6-8pm Fri & Sat, noon-2pm Sun Dec-Mar;) Food-savvy travelers love the constantly changing, adventurous tasting menus dreamed up by renowned chef Perry Hoffman. His distinctive haute cuisine is made up of seasonal produce, local seafood and meat, along with foraged greens and mushrooms. Family-style prix-fixe options make weekend dinners freewheeling, elegant

TOP ANDERSON VALLEY WINERIES

The valley's cool nights yield high-acid, fruit-forward, food-friendly wines. Pinot noir, chardonnay and dry gewürztraminer flourish. Most wineries (www.avwines.com) sit outside Philo. Many are family owned and offer free tastings; some give tours. The following are particularly noteworthy.

Toulouse Vineyards (707-895-2828; www.toulousevineyards.com; 8001 Hwy 128, Philo; tasting $10; 11am-5pm Thu-Mon) Sample standout (and organic!) pinot gris, valdiguié and pinot noir from a stunning hilltop tasting room tucked into the forest.

Navarro Vineyards (707-895-3686; www.navarrowine.com; 5601 Hwy 128, Philo; 9am-6pm Jun-Oct, to 5pm Nov-May) One of the most visitor-friendly options around, with award-winning pinot noir and dry gewürztraminer; has twice-daily free tours (10:30am and 2pm; reservations recommended) and ample picnicking facilities.

Pennyroyal Farm (707-895-2410; www.pennyroyalfarm.com; 14930 Hwy 128; tastings $10; 10am-5pm, cheese tastings until 4:30pm) You'll get the highlights reel of Anderson Valley at this sustainable farm, creamery and vineyard where you can pair small-batch cheeses with Alsatian-style wines.

Greenwood Ridge Vineyards (707-895-2002; www.greenwoodridge.com; 5501 Hwy 128, Philo; tasting $5; 10am-5pm) The best reason to come here is to view the Frank Lloyd Wright-inspired tasting room, which was built from a single fallen redwood trunk. The pinot noir is also legendary. Groups can spend the night in Greenwood Ridge's three-bedroom cottage ($200) surrounded by vines and redwoods.

social affairs, either indoors by the fireplace or outdoors at big farm tables with soft lighting.

Anderson Valley Brewing Company BREWERY
(707-895-2337; www.avbc.com; 17700 Hwy 253, Boonville; tasting from $10; 11am-8pm Sat-Thu, to 9pm Fri, tours 1pm Sat) East of the Hwy 128 crossroads, this partially solar-powered brewery crafts award-winning beers in a Bavarian-style brewhouse, and hosts a massive craft-beer festival in late April or early May. You can also toss around a Frisbee on the **disc-golf course** but, be warned, the sun can take its toll. Call ahead for tours.

Ukiah

As the county seat and Mendocino's largest city, Ukiah is mostly a utilitarian stop for travelers to refuel the car and get a bite. But, if you have to pause here for the night, you could do much worse: the town is a friendly place. There is a plethora of cookie-cutter hotel chains, some cheaper mid-century motels and a handful of very good dining options. The coolest attractions, a pair of thermal springs and a sprawling campus for Buddhist studies complete with 10,000 golden Buddha statues, lie outside the city limits. There are also some excellent wineries and tasting rooms within easy access from the center; the **Greater Ukiah Visitor Center** (707-467-5766; www.visitukiah.com; 200 S School St; 10am-5pm Mon-Fri, to 2pm Sat) can point you in the right direction. Ukiah has a pleasant, walkable shopping district along School St near the courthouse, where you can find some idiosyncratic shops.

Sights

★Grace Hudson Museum & Sun House MUSEUM
(707-467-2836; www.gracehudsonmuseum.org; 431 S Main St; $5; 10am-4:30pm Wed-Sat, from noon Sun) One block east of State St, the collection's mainstays are paintings by Grace Hudson (1865–1937). Her sensitive depictions of Pomo people and other indigenous groups complement the ethnological work and Native American baskets collected by her husband, John Hudson. The lovely 1911 Sun House, adjacent to the museum, was the former Hudson home and is typical of the arts-and-crafts style of that era; docent-led tours are available at noon.

Festivals & Events

Redwood Empire Fair FAIR
(707-462-3884; www.redwoodempirefair.com; 1055 N State St; Jun & Aug) There are two major fairs held here: the Redwood Empire Spring Fair, held over a weekend in early June, and the Redwood Empire Fair, held

over a weekend in early August. Both have loads of events, ranging from quilt exhibitions to garden expos.

Sleeping & Eating

Ukiah is a handy stop off point for those heading to the redwoods and beyond, though chain hotels are the only option. For something with more personality, hot spring resorts and campgrounds cluster around town.

It'd be a crime to eat the fast-food junk located off the highway; Ukiah has a burgeoning food scene that pairs nicely with the surrounding wine country.

Hampton Inn HOTEL **$$**
(☎707-462-6555; www.hamptoninn.com; 1160 Airport Park Blvd; r $130-200;) The best of the 'chain gang' in Ukiah, with a whiff of the Hilton about it. Expect excellent amenities, including a fitness center and comprehensive offerings for the business bunch. The rooms may still be hotel-chain bland but are comfortable, carpeted and spacious.

★ **Schat's Bakery & Cafe** CAFE **$**
(☎707-462-1670; www.schats.com; 113 W Perkins St; mains $6-11; ⏰6am-6pm Mon-Fri, to 5pm Sat) Founded by Dutch bakers, Schat's makes a dazzling array of chewy, dense breads, sandwiches, wraps, big salads, dee-lish hot mains, full breakfasts and homemade pastries.

★ **Cultivo** PIZZA **$$**
(☎707-462-7007; www.cultivorestaurant.com; 108 W Standley St; pizzas $14-19, mains $19-24; ⏰11:30am-9pm Mon-Thu, to 10pm Fri & Sat, 10am-2:30pm Sun) Yes, there are arty pizzas with toppings like braised duck and wild boar sausage, but there are also amazing salads, pastas and meat dishes – the heritage porkchop with squash and Brussels sprouts is particularly outstanding. The small-town ambience is chic but fun and informal.

Patrona MODERN AMERICAN **$$**
(☎707-462-9181; www.patronarestaurant.com; 130 W Standley St; lunch mains $13-20, dinner mains $15-34; ⏰11am-9pm) Foodies flock to excellent Patrona for earthy, flavor-packed, seasonal and regional organic cooking in superstylish surrounds. The unfussy menu includes dishes such as roasted chicken, brined-and-roasted pork chops and housemade pasta, as well as local wines. Great cocktails, too.

Taste of Nepal NEPALI **$$**
(☎707-467-9900; www.tasteofnepalukiahca.com; 1639 S State St; express lunch $11, dinner mains $13-19; ⏰11am-2:30pm & 5-9pm Tue-Sun;) This unassuming restaurant in the south of town transports you from the vineyards of Ukiah to the foothills of the Himalaya with its dark wood paneling, ornamental curtains and hard-to-find Nepali dishes, such as momo dumplings and thukpa noodle soup. Much of the menu is vegan and gluten-free. The express lunches are a real bargain.

Drinking & Nightlife

Dive bars and scruffy cocktail lounges line State St, especially to the north of town. For a wider and marginally more appealing selection, head to S State St and the surrounding streets.

Black Oak Coffee Roasters CAFE
(☎866-390-1427; www.blackoakcoffee.com; 476 N State St; ⏰6:30am-6pm;) A spacious industrial-chic coffee house that roasts its own beans and has some interesting and delicious menu items such as a *café borgia latté* with artisan chocolate and orange essence or, for tea lovers, a matcha chai. Light breakfasts and lunches are also superb.

Information

Bureau of Land Management (☎707-468-4000; www.blm.gov; 2550 N State St; ⏰8am-4:30pm Mon-Fri) Maps and information on backcountry camping, hiking and biking in wilderness areas.

Getting Around

Mendocino Transit Authority (MTA; ☎707 462-1422; www.mendocinotransit.org; 241 Plant Rd, Ukiah; most 1-way fares $1.50-6) Operates bus 65, which travels between Fort Bragg, Willits, Ukiah, Hopland and Santa Rosa daily, with an afternoon return. Bus 95 runs between Point Arena and Santa Rosa, via Jenner, Bodega Bay and Sebastopol (daily). Bus 75 heads north every weekday from Gualala to the Navarro River junction at Hwy 128, then runs inland through the Anderson Valley to Ukiah, returning in the afternoon.

The North Coast route goes north between Navarro River junction and Albion, Little River, Mendocino and Fort Bragg Monday to Friday.

Around Ukiah

Vichy Springs Resort

This **spa resort** (☎707-462-9515; www.vichysprings.com; 2605 Vichy Springs Rd; s/d $205/,$265, ste s/d $280/345, cottages from $415;) offers a tranquil retreat – that is, if you can tune out shots from the gun club across the street. There are a choice of rooms and suites in an historic 1870s inn with a shared terrace overlooking sweeping lawns. The cottages are airy with floral fabrics and fully equipped kitchens. Guests can enjoy the spa facilities as well as hiking trails on the 700-acre property, including one to a 40ft waterfall.

Vichy is the oldest continuously operating mineral-springs spa in California. The water's composition perfectly matches that of its famous namesake in Vichy, France. A century ago, Mark Twain, Jack London and Robert Louis Stevenson traveled here for the water's restorative properties, amid claims it ameliorated everything from arthritis to poison oak.

Today, the historic resort has the only warm-water, naturally carbonated mineral baths in North America. It tends to draw an older crowd and, unlike nearby hot springs, requires swimsuits (rentals $3). Day use (for guests and nonguests) costs $35 for two hours or $75 for a full day.

Facilities include a swimming pool, outdoor mineral hot tub, 14 indoor and outdoor tubs with natural 100°F (38°C) waters, and a grotto for sipping the effervescent waters. Massages and facials are available.

Orr Hot Springs

A soak in the thermal waters of the forest-clad **Orr Hot Springs** (707-462-6277; www.orrhotsprings.org; 13201 Orr Springs Rd; day use adult/child $35/25; by appointment 10am-10pm) is heavenly. While it's not for the bashful, the clothing-optional resort is beloved by locals, back-to-the-land hipsters, backpackers and liberal-minded tourists. Still, you don't have to let it all hang out. Enjoy the private tubs, a sauna, a spring-fed, rock-bottomed swimming pool, steam room, massage facilities and storybook gardens. Soaking in the rooftop stargazing tubs on a clear night is magical. Make reservations well in advance.

You can stay here in one of the elegantly rustic **accommodations** (tent sites per adult/child $75/35, r & yurt $230, cottages $300;), which includes use of the spa and communal kitchen; while some share bathrooms, cottages have their own kitchens. There are also six yurts tucked into the woods here, offering total privacy.

Orr Hot Springs can be tricky to find. Drive south on Hwy 101 and take exit 551 for N State St. Turn left and head approximately a quarter mile north, turning left onto Orr Springs Rd. Follow the paved road over the hills for 12 miles until you reach mile marker 31.31.

Montgomery Woods State Natural Reserve

Two miles west of Orr Hot Springs, this 2743-acre **reserve** (707-937-5804; www.parks.ca.gov; 15825 Orr Springs Rd) FREE protects some of the best old-growth redwood groves within a day's drive from San Francisco. A 2-mile loop **trail**, starting near the picnic tables and toilets, crosses the creek, winding through the serene forest. Visitors are likely to have it mostly to themselves.

The trees here are impressive – some up to 367ft tall – but remember to admire them from the trail, both to protect the root systems of the trees and to protect yourself from poison oak, which is all over the park.

City of Ten Thousand Buddhas

The showpiece at the **City of Ten Thousand Buddhas** (707-462-0939; www.cttbusa.org; 4951 Bodhi Way; 8am-6pm) is the ornate temple with its, you guessed it, 10,000 golden Buddha statues. Elsewhere enjoy pretty courtyards, lush landscaping and decorative peacocks. This Buddhist monastery and college is home to both nuns and monks and runs courses on Buddhism and meditation; check the website for more information. There is a small gift shop with souvenirs as well as literature on Buddhism.

The excellent **Jyun Kang Vegetarian Restaurant** (707-468-7966; www.cttbusa.org; City of Ten Thousand Buddhas; mains $5-9; 11:30am-3pm Wed-Mon;) will have vegetarians (and vegans) swooning over the superb Asian-influenced dishes.

Ukiah Wineries

You'll notice the acres of grapes stretching out in every direction on your way into town. Winemakers around Ukiah enjoy many of the same climatic conditions that made Napa so famous. Pick up a wineries map from the Greater Ukiah Visitor Center (p262). Tasting fees (around $5-$10) are generally waived if you purchase a bottle.

★ **Parducci Wine Cellars** WINERY
(800-362-9463; www.parducci.com; 501 Parducci Rd; tasting $10; 11am-5:30pm Wed-Sun)

Sustainably grown, harvested and produced, 'America's Greenest Winery' offers affordable, bold, earthy reds. The tasting room, lined in brick with low ceilings and soft lights, is a perfect little cave-like environment to get out of the summer heat, sip wine and chat about sustainability practices. Or head for the terrace overlooking the vineyards and organic gardens, complete with contented chickens.

Nelson Family Vineyards WINERY
(☎707-462-3755; www.nelsonfamilyvineyards.com; 550 Nelson Ranch Rd; tasting $5; ⏲10am-5pm) Just south of Ukiah, this winery, vineyard and pear, olive and Christmas-tree farm with wondrous views over the valley is a great place to picnic (in a small redwood grove), make friends and sip pinot grigio and luscious red blends. Just one aside – it is a popular venue for weddings, which can affect visits by the public.

Willits

Twenty miles north of Ukiah, Willits mixes NorCal dropouts with loggers and ranchers (the high school has a bull-riding team). The main drag has a small-town atmosphere with an appealing clutch of idiosyncratic shops and some solid eating choices. Though ranching, timber and manufacturing may be its mainstays, tie-dye and gray ponytails are de rigueur. For visitors, Willits has a couple of claims to fame: it is the eastern terminus of the Skunk Train and is also home to the oldest continuous rodeo in California. **Willits Frontier Days & Rodeo** (www.willitsfrontierdays.com; ⏲early Jul) attracts bucking bronco fans from all over the US. Fort Bragg is 35 miles away on the coast; allow an hour to navigate twisty Hwy 20.

Sights & Activities

Ten miles north of Willits, Hwy 162/Covelo Rd makes for a superb drive following the route of the Northwestern Pacific Railroad along the Eel River toward **Mendocino National Forest**. The trip is only about 30 miles, but plan on taking at least an hour on the winding road, passing exquisite river canyons and rolling hills. Eventually, you'll reach **Covelo**, known for its unusual round valley.

★**Mendocino County Museum** MUSEUM
(☎707-459-2736; www.mendocinocounty.org/museum; 400 E Commercial St; adult/child $4/1; ⏲10am-5pm Wed-Fri, noon-4pm Sat & Sun) Among the best community museums in this half of the state. It puts the lives of early settlers in excellent historical context – much drawn from old letters – and there's an entire 1930s soda fountain and historic dental clinic inside. You could spend an hour perusing Pomo basketry and artifacts, or reading about local scandals.

Ridgewood Ranch HISTORIC SITE
(☎reservations 707-391-3872; www.seabiscuitheritage.org; 16200 Hwy 101; tours $20 per person; ⏲9am 1st & 3rd Sat Jun-Sep) Willits' most famous resident was the champion racehorse Seabiscuit, who grew up here. Three-hour tours of his former ranch are available by reservation. There are also excellent nature walks on the property.

Jackson Demonstration State Forest STATE PARK
(☎707-964-5674; www.fire.ca.gov; Fort Bragg-Willits Rd) FREE Fifteen miles west of Willits on Hwy 20, this forest offers day-use recreational activities, including hiking trails and mountain biking. You can also camp here. A demonstration forest is so named as it is used for forestry education, research and sustainable felling techniques. Seek out the 25ft Chamberlain Creek Waterfall on the mile-long **Waterfall Grove Trail** if you can. These beautiful falls are situated in a lush canyon surrounded by redwoods and ferns.

Skunk Train HISTORIC TRAIN
(☎707-964-6371; www.skunktrain.com; 299 E Commercial St; adult/child $50/30; ⏲Mar-Dec) This heritage railroad has its depot on E Commercial St, three blocks east of Hwy 101. The two-hour roundtrip journey takes you into the lush redwood country of the Noyo River Canyon, but not all the way to Fort Bragg (p253), where a separate Skunk Train operates.

Sleeping

Quality accommodations are pretty sparse here. Some of the in-town motels – and there seems to be about a hundred of them – are overpriced dumps, so absolutely check out the room before paying. For only the most desperate campers, there are a couple of crowded, loud RV parks on the edges of town.

★**Old West Inn** MOTEL $
(☎707-459-4201; www.theoldwestinn.com; 1221 S Main St; r $90-140;) The facade looks like a mock-up of an Old West main street and each room has a theme, from the 'Stable' to the 'Barber Shop.' The decor is simple and comfy with just enough imagination to

make it interesting. Besides that this is the cleanest, friendliest and most highly recommended place in town.

Baechtel Creek Inn BOUTIQUE HOTEL **$$**
(☎707-459-9063; www.baechtelcreekinn.com; 101 Gregory Lane; d $119-189;) As Willits' only upscale option, this place draws an interesting mix: Japanese bus tours, business travelers and wine-trippers. The standard rooms are nothing too flashy, but they have top-notch linens and tasteful art. The immaculate pool and lovely egg breakfast on the patio are perks.

Eating

La Siciliana ITALIAN **$**
(☎707-459-5626; www.lasicilianawillits.com; 1611 S Main St; mains $11-16; ⊙11:30am-8:30pm;) The *sugo* (sauce) is pure Sicilian, the pesto is rich with basil and pine nuts, the olive oil is extra virgin and the pizza crust is crisp and thin. There is no dreaded ping of the microwave and everything is freshly made in-house. That said, the prices are decent and the atmosphere no-fuss and family-friendly.

Loose Caboose Cafe SANDWICHES **$**
(☎707-459-1434; www.loosecaboosewillits.com; 10 Wood St; sandwiches $10.50; ⊙10am-4pm Mon-Sat) People tend to get a bit flushed when talking about the sandwiches at the Loose Caboose, which gets jammed at lunch. The Reuben and Sante Fe chicken sandwiches are two savory delights. Look for a ramshackle entrance complete with a historic rail crossing sign.

Drinking & Nightlife

The main street through town is home to a couple of cafes, as well as a brewery, a pub with regular live music and a dimly lit bar (or two).

★ **Shanachie Pub** BAR
(☎707-459-9194; 50 S Main St; ⊙3pm-midnight Mon-Sat) The kind of intimate, make-instant-friends, small-town bar you dream of stumbling across while traveling, full of intellectual puzzle games, excellent live indie music and dark, scarlet-lit corners. It's all the best parts of Willits wrapped up in an eccentric little bow.

Entertainment

Willits Community Theatre THEATER
(☎707-459-0895; www.willitstheatre.org; 37 W Van Lane; ⊙hours vary) Stages award-winning plays, hosts concerts and has occasional comedy acts in an intimate 75-seat theater.

Shopping

JD Redhouse & Co CLOTHING, HOMEWARES
(☎707-459-1214; www.jdredhouse.com; 212 S Main St; ⊙9am-6pm Mon-Fri, 10am-5pm Sat & Sun) Family owned and operated, this central mercantile is a good reflection of Willits itself, balancing cowboy essentials – boots and grain, tools and denim – with treats for the weekend tourist. The Cowlick's counter (with excellent Mendocino-made ice cream) is a good place to cool off when the heat on the sidewalk gets intense.

SOUTHERN REDWOOD COAST

There's some real magic in the loamy soil and misty air 'beyond the redwood curtain'; it yields the tallest trees and most potent herb on the planet. North of Fort Bragg, Bay Area weekenders and antique-stuffed B&Bs give way to lumber wars, pot farmers and an army of carved bears. The 'growing' culture here is palpable and the huge profit it brings to the region has evident cultural side effects – an omnipresent population of seasonal labourers who work the harvests, a chilling respect for 'No Trespassing' signs and a political culture that is an uneasy balance between gun-toting libertarians, ultra-left progressives and typical college-town chaos. Nevertheless, the reason to visit is to soak in the magnificent landscape, which runs through a number of pristine, ancient redwood forests.

Leggett

Leggett marks the redwood country's beginning and Hwy 1's end. There's not much going on here, aside from a single gas station, a grocery store, a small restaurant and a post office; however, fear not, there is plenty to do and see close by.

Visit 1000-acre **Standish-Hickey State Recreation Area** (☎707-925-6482; www.parks.ca.gov; 69350 Hwy 101; day use per car $8, camping incl 1 car $35, extra car $8), 1.5 miles to the north, for camping, picnicking, swimming and fishing in the Eel River and hiking trails among virgin and second-growth redwoods.

Chandelier Drive-Thru Tree Park (☎707-925-6363; www.drivethrutree.com; 67402

Drive Thru Tree Rd; per car $10; 8:30am-dark;) has 200 private acres of virgin redwoods with picnicking and nature walks. And yes, there's a redwood with a square hole carved out, which cars can drive through. Only in America.

The 1949 tourist trap of **Confusion Hill** (707-925-6456; www.confusionhill.com; 75001 N Hwy 101; Gravity House adult/child $5/4, Mountain Train adult/child $10/7.50; 9am-6pm May-Sep, to 5pm Oct-Apr;) is an enduring curiosity and the most elaborate of the old-fashioned roadside attractions that line the route north.

Richardson Grove State Park

Fifteen miles to the north of Leggett, and bisected by the Eel River, serene **Richardson Grove** (707-247-3318; www.parks.ca.gov; 1600 Hwy 101, Garberville; per car $8) occupies 2000 acres of virgin forest. Many trees are more than 1000 years old and 300ft tall. There aren't many sizable hiking trails, but you can combine a few into a five-mile loop. In winter, there's decent catch-and-release fishing for salmon and steelhead. For the last few years, CalTrans has been pushing to widen the road through Richardson Grove, which has sparked an intense protest.

The park is primarily a **campground** (reservations 800-444-7275; www.reservecalifornia.com; 1600 Hwy 101; tent & RV sites $35, cabins $70-80), with three separate areas and hot showers; some remain open year-round. Summer-only Oak Flat on the east side of the river is shady and has a sandy beach. The **visitor center** (707-247-3318; www.parks.ca.gov; 1600 Hwy101, Garberville; 10am-4pm May-Sep, weekends only Oct-Apr) sells books inside a 1930s lodge, which often has a fire going during cool weather.

Garberville

The main supply center for southern Humboldt County, Garberville is also the primary jumping-off point for both the Lost Coast to the west, and the Avenue of the Giants to the north. It has an alluring laissez-faire attitude, but is not for everyone. There's an uneasy relationship here between the old-guard loggers and the hippies, many of whom came in the 1970s to grow sinsemilla (potent, seedless marijuana) after the feds chased them out of Santa Cruz. The transition to legal pot – and

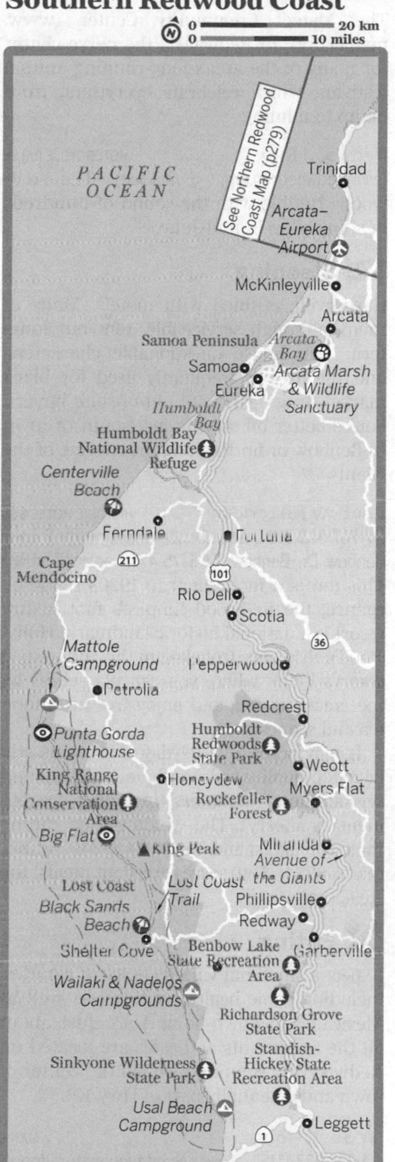

its state-mandated regulations – has been difficult for some area farmers, with weed prices down and homelessness up. Many growers have either gone out of business, or back underground. An outlaw culture persists.

Two miles west is Garberville's ragtag sister, Redway, which has fewer services.

Festivals & Events

The Mateel Community Center (www.mateel.org), in Redway, is the nerve center for many of the area's long-running annual festivals, which celebrate everything from hemp to miming.

Redwood Run MOTORCYCLE RALLY
(www.redwoodrun.org; mid-Jun) The redwoods rumble with the sound of hundreds of shiny bikes in mid-June.

Sleeping

Garberville is lined with motels. Many of them, although serviceable, rent out long-term, can house questionable characters, and the area is frequently used for black market drug deals with out-of-state buyers. You're better off staying just south of town in Benbow or north along the Avenue of the Giants.

Benbow Historic Inn HISTORIC HOTEL $$$
(707-923-2124; www.benbowinn.com; 445 Lake Benbow Dr, Benbow; d $175-475;) This inn is a monument to 1920s rustic elegance; the Redwood Empire's first luxury resort is a national historic landmark. Hollywood's elite once frolicked in the Tudor-style resort's lobby, where you can play chess by the crackling fire, and enjoy free afternoon tea and scones.

It may be past its heyday, but rooms still have top-quality beds, antique furniture and crystal sherry decanters (including complimentary sherry). The window-lined dining room (breakfast and lunch $14 to $19, dinner mains $28 to $39) serves excellent meals; the steaks earn raves.

Eating

Expect a small but varied choice of eateries, including some healthy options, as well as Mexican and down-home USA. Just about all the restaurants and cafes are located on Redwood Dr running through the center of town and essentially part of Hwy 101.

★ **Souji House** ASIAN $
(707-923-1115; www.chautauquanaturalfoods.com/souji-house; 436 Church St; mains $10-14; 11am-7pm Tue-Fri, to 4pm Sat;) This unexpectedly trendy restaurant has livened up Garberville's culinary scene with seriously delicious 'Asian soul food.' Gluten-free and vegan options shine on the menu of rice bowls, noodle soups, bountiful salads and daily sushi specials.

Woodrose Café AMERICAN $
(707-923-3191; www.thewoodrosecafe.com; 911 Redwood Dr; mains $9-18; 8am-2pm;) Garberville's beloved cafe serves organic omelets, veggie scrambles and buckwheat pancakes with *real* maple syrup in a cozy room. Lunch brings crunchy salads, sandwiches with all-natural meats and good burritos. Plenty of gluten-free options.

Cecil's New Orleans Bistro CAJUN $$
(707-923-7007; www.garbervillebistro.com; 733 Redwood Dr; mains $13-35; 5-9pm Tue-Sat) This 2nd-story eatery overlooks Main St and serves ambitious dishes that may have minted the California-Cajun style. Start with fried oysters before launching into the pork & okra gumbo. Check the website for nightly music events.

Information

Find out what's really happening by tuning in to amazing community radio KMUD FM 91.1 (www.kmud.org).

Garberville-Redway Area Chamber of Commerce (707-923-2613; www.garberville.org; 782 Redwood Dr; 8:30am-5pm Mon-Fri) Located inside the Redwood Drive Center, with plenty of information about the town including where to stay and what is on.

Shelter Cove

The only sizable community on the Lost Coast, Shelter Cove is surrounded by the King Range National Conservation Area and abuts a large south-facing cove. It's a tiny seaside subdivision with an airstrip in the middle – indeed, many visitors are private pilots. Fifty years ago, Southern California swindlers subdivided the land, built the airstrip and flew in potential investors, fast-talking them into buying seaside land for retirement. But they didn't tell buyers that a steep, winding, one-lane dirt road provided the *only* access and that the seaside plots were eroding into the sea. Today, the large number of 'For Sale' plaques are a sobering sign of the times.

There's still only one route, but now it's paved. Most use Shelter Cove as a base for hiking (a short drive brings you to the stunning Black Sands Beach stretching for miles northward). While tourism may be a mainstay of the economy, locals are strangely leery of outsiders, so don't expect a sunny California welcome. Cell phones barely work here: this is a good place to disappear.

Sleeping

★Tides Inn HOTEL $$
(707-986-7900; www.sheltercovetidesinn.com; 59 Surf Pt; r/ste from $170/220;) Perched above tide pools teeming with starfish and sea urchins, the squeaky-clean rooms here offer excellent views (go for the mini suites on the 3rd floor with fireplaces). The full-suite options are good for families, while management is refreshingly welcoming.

Oceanfront Inn INN $$
(707-986-7002; http://oceanfrontinnsc.com; 26 Seal Ct; r $150-250, ste $180-300;) The big, bright rooms here all have private balconies, fridges, microwaves, coffeemakers and phenomenal sea views. There is one apartment unit complete with a full kitchen (minimum two-night stay). The nine-hole golf course across the street is within putting distance of the sea.

Inn of the Lost Coast INN $$
(707-986-7521; www.innofthelostcoast.com; 205 Wave Dr; r from $190, ste from $325;) Shelter Cove's most family-friendly hotel has a choice of rooms and suites; the latter including options with a full kitchen, private hot tub and sauna and/or fireplace. The double rooms are spacious, with picture windows to maximize the breathtaking ocean views; most have private balconies.

Downstairs the Delgada Pizzeria & Bakery serves decent pizza, while the Fish Tank Cafe is a good stop for coffee, pastries and sandwiches.

Eating

Shelter Cove General Store SUPERMARKET $
(707-986-7733; 7272 Shelter Cove Rd; 7am-7pm) For those who are self-catering, Shelter Cove General Store is 2 miles before town. Get groceries and gasoline here.

★Gyppo Ale Mill AMERICAN $$
(707-986-7700; www.gyppo.com; 1661 Upper Pacific Dr; mains $10-20; 4-8pm Mon-Fri, noon-8pm Sat & Sun) Gyppo injects a jolt of youthful energy into this aging community, brewing a dozen of its own ales and showcasing them alongside local wines and ciders. There's all-you-can-eat popcorn, but the burgers, brats and salads are recommended. Ping-Pong, lawn games, fire pits and a serene ocean view complete the picture.

Sky's at the Cove THAI $$
(707-986-4424; www.skysatthecoverestaurant.com; 10 Seal Ct; mains $14-19; 8am-noon & 4-8pm Thu-Sun;) At the Oceanfront Inn, American breakfasts and Thai dinners are paired with sweeping sea views.

Humboldt Redwoods State Park & Avenue of the Giants

Don't miss this magical drive through California's largest redwood park, **Humboldt Redwoods State Park** (707-946-2409; www.parks.ca.gov; Hwy 101) FREE, which covers 53,000 acres – 17,000 of which are old-growth – and contains some of the world's most magnificent trees. It also boasts three-quarters of the world's tallest 100 trees. Tree huggers take note: these groves rival (and some say surpass) those in Redwood National Park, which is a long drive further north, although the landscapes here are less diverse.

Exit Hwy 101 when you see the 'Avenue of the Giants' sign, and take this smaller alternative to the interstate; it's an incredible, 32-mile, two-lane stretch. You'll find free driving guides at roadside signboards at both the avenue's southern entrance, 6 miles north of Garberville, near Phillipsville, and at the northern entrance, south of Scotia, at Pepperwood; there are access points off Hwy 101.

Three miles north of the visitor center, the **California Federation of Women's Clubs Grove** is home to an interesting four-sided hearth designed by renowned San Franciscan architect Julia Morgan in 1931 to commemorate 'the untouched nature of the forest.'

In **Founders Grove**, a mile further north, the Dyerville Giant was knocked over in 1991 by another falling tree. A walk along its gargantuan 370ft length, with its wide trunk towering above, helps you appreciate how huge these ancient trees are.

Primeval **Rockefeller Forest**, 4.5 miles west of the avenue via the incredibly picturesque Mattole Rd, appears as it did a century ago. It's the world's largest contiguous old-growth redwood forest, and contains about 20% of all such remaining trees. From June to September, when a seasonal bridge is in place, you can tackle the 8-mile **Bull Creek Loop**. You quickly walk out of sight of cars and feel like you have fallen into the time of dinosaurs. Less ambitious hikers can try the half-mile **Bull Creek Flats Loop**.

The park has more than 100 miles of trails for hiking, singletrack mountain biking and horseback riding. Easy walks include short nature trails in Founders Grove and Rockefeller Forest, as well as the 2.4-mile **Drury-Chaney Loop Trail** (with berry picking in summer). Challenging treks include the popular 14-mile roundtrip **Grasshopper Peak Trail**, south of the visitor center, which climbs to the 3379ft fire lookout.

Humboldt Redwoods State Park Campgrounds CAMPGROUND $
(information 707-946-1811, reservations 800-444-7275; www.reservecalifornia.com; tent & RV sites $35, trail/environmental campsites $5/20;) The park runs three campgrounds, along with environmental camps, trail camps and a horse camp. Year-round Burlington Campground is beside the visitor center and near a number of trailheads; Hidden Springs Campground is 5 miles south along Avenue of the Giants; and Albee Creek Campground is on Mattole Rd past Rockefeller Forest. The latter two are seasonal (generally late spring to early fall).

Miranda Gardens Resort RESORT $$
(707-943-3011; www.mirandagardens.com; 6766 Avenue of the Giants, Miranda; cottages $125-300;) The best indoor stay along the avenue. The cozy, dark, slightly rustic cottages have redwood paneling, some with fireplaces and kitchens, and are spotlessly clean. The grounds – replete with outdoor Ping-Pong, a seasonal swimming pool and a play area for kids amid swaying redwoods – have wholesome appeal for families.

Information

Humboldt Redwoods Visitor Center (707-946-2263; www.humboldtredwoods.org; Avenue of the Giants; 9am-5pm Apr-Oct, 10am-4pm Nov-Mar) Located 2 miles south of Weott, a volunteer-staffed visitor center shows videos (three in total), sells maps and also has a sizable exhibition about the local flora, fauna and human history.

Ferndale

The North Coast's most charming town is stuffed with impeccable Victorians – known locally as 'butterfat palaces' because of the dairy wealth that built them. There are so many, in fact, that the entire place is a state and federal historical landmark. Dairy farmers built the town in the 19th century and it's still run by the 'milk mafia': you're not a local till you've lived here 40 years. A stroll down Main St offers a taste of wholesome, small-town America, from galleries to old-world emporiums and soda fountains. Although Ferndale relies on tourism, it has avoided becoming a tourist trap and has no chain stores. It's a lovely place to spend a summer night, but folks close the shutters early in winter and it may be hard to find a bite to eat late evening time, let alone a pint of something frothy.

Sights

Many use Ferndale as a base for exploring the Lost Coast or Avenue of the Giants, but there are attractions right at its doorstep, too. Half a mile from downtown via Bluff St, enjoy short tramps through fields of wildflowers, beside ponds and past a mature Sitka spruce forest (rarer even than redwood) at 110-acre **Russ Park**. The **cemetery**, also on Bluff St, is amazingly cool, with graves dating to the 1800s and expansive views to the ocean.

Fern Cottage HISTORIC BUILDING
(707-786-4835; www.ferncottage.org; 2121 Centerville Rd; tours per person $10; by appointment) This 1866 Carpenter Gothic grew to a 32-room mansion. Only one family ever lived here, so the interior is completely, and charmingly, preserved.

Festivals & Events

This wee town has a packed social calendar, especially in the summer. If you're planning a visit, check the events page at www.victorianferndale.com.

Tour of the Unknown Coast SPORTS
(www.tuccycle.org; June) A challenging one-day event in early June in which participants in the 100-mile bicycle race climb nearly 10,000ft. Widely recognized as being California's toughest cycle race, there are now shorter routes for all levels.

Humboldt County Fair FAIR
(www.humboldtcountyfair.org; Humboldt County Fairgrounds; mid-Aug) Held in mid-August, it's the longest-running county fair in California.

Sleeping

There is a small and, overall, very select choice of places to stay in Ferndale. The overarching aesthetic is 'fancy Grandma's place', but it fits with the town.

Hotel Ivanhoe HISTORIC HOTEL $

(707-786-9000; www.hotel-ivanhoe.com; 315 Main St; r $95-145; closed Jan;) Ferndale's oldest hostelry opened in 1875. It has four antique-laden rooms and an Old West–style, 2nd-floor gallery, perfect for morning coffee. The adjoining saloon with dark wood and lots of brass is an atmospheric place for a nightcap, while the adjacent restaurant is a reliable choice for a meal.

★**Victorian Inn** HISTORIC HOTEL $$

(707-786-4949; www.victorianvillageinn.com; 400 Ocean Ave; r $125-250;) The bright, sunny rooms inside this venerable, two-story former bank building (1890) are comfortably furnished with thick carpeting, period-style wallpaper, fantastic linens and funky antiques. The restaurant and saloon downstairs are among the most happening spots in town, and service is wonderful across the board.

Shaw House B&B $$

(707-786-9958; www.shawhouse.com; 703 Main St; r $145-189, ste $249-289; closed late Dec to mid-Feb;) Shaw House, an emblematic 'butterfat palace,' was the first permanent structure in Ferndale, completed by founding father Seth Shaw in 1854. Today, it's California's oldest B&B, set back on extensive grounds. Original details remain, including painted wooden ceilings. Most of the rooms have private entrances.

★**Gingerbread Mansion** B&B $$$

(707-786-4000; www.gingerbread-mansion.com; 400 Berding St; r $165-425;) This is the cream of dairyland elegance, an 1894 Queen Anne–Eastlake that's unsurprisingly the town's most photographed building. And the inside is no less extravagant, with each room having its own unique (and complex) mix of floral wallpaper, patterned carpeting, grand antique furniture and perhaps a fireplace, wall fresco, stained-glass window or Greek statue thrown in for kicks.

Eating & Drinking

Tuyas MEXICAN $

(707-786-5921; www.tuyasferndale.com; 553 Main St; mains $9-18; 11:30am-8pm Sun-Thu, to 9pm Fri & Sat;) A classy Mexican spot with art-filled walls and sultry Latin music to set the mood. The elevated cuisine (think spicy-sweet *mole* and tangy shrimp ceviche) is a fine match for the superbly executed margaritas.

No Brand Burger Stand BURGERS $

(707-786-9474; 1400 Main St; burgers $5-8; 11am-4pm) Hiding near the entrance to town by an industrial building, this hole-in-the-wall turns out a juicy jalapeño double cheeseburger that ranks easily as the North Coast's best burger. The shakes – so thick your cheeks hurt from pulling on the straw – are about the only other thing on the menu.

★**Mind's Eye Coffee Lounge** COFFEE

(707-786-3393; www.mindseyemanufactory.com; 393 Main St; 6:30am-7pm;) The kind of coffee shop you dream of finding in a small town like this, with a library of intriguing books, local art on the walls and sturdy leather chairs lined up in front of the fireplace. Oh, and they also build custom-made wooden sea kayaks in the back! Check out **True North Boats** (www.facebook.com/truenorthboats) for woodworking classes if you get inspired.

Entertainment

Check the website of Ferndale Music Company (www.ferndalemusiccompany.com) to see what concerts are playing at the **Old Steeple**, an ex-church turned folk music venue.

Ferndale Repertory Theatre THEATER

(707-786-5483; www.ferndalerep.org; 447 Main St) This top-shelf community company produces excellent contemporary theater in the historic Hart Theatre Building.

Shopping

Main St is a great place to browse with several art galleries, confectionery shops and curio stores.

Blacksmith Shop & Gallery METAL GOODS

(707-786-4216; www.ferndaleblacksmith.com; 455 & 491 Main St; 10am-5pm) From wrought-iron art to sculpture and jewelry, this is the largest collection of contemporary blacksmithing in the US. Note that there are two venues here: the shop and the gallery, two doors apart, and it is well worth checking them both out.

Ferndale Arts Gallery ARTS & CRAFTS

(707-786-9634; www.ferndalearts.com; 580 Main St; 10am-5pm) This cooperative runs a large gallery space selling prints, paintings, pottery, photography and greeting cards that showcase local artists from Humboldt County.

Golden Gait Mercantile GIFTS & SOUVENIRS

(707-786-4891; www.goldengaitmercantile.com; 421 Main St; 10am-5pm Mon-Sat, noon-4pm Sun)

An eclectic old-school general store you enter just to browse – but exit carting a bourbon-scented candle, lighthouse puzzle, bag of scones and toy you haven't seen since you were a kid. It's *that* kind of place.

Humboldt Bay National Wildlife Refuge

This pristine **wildlife refuge** (707-733-5406; www.fws.gov/refuge/humboldt_bay; 1020 Ranch Rd, Loleta; 8am-5pm) FREE protects wetland habitats for more than 200 species of resident birds and their feathered friends migrating annually along the Pacific Flyway. Between the fall and early spring, when 100,000 Aleutian geese descend en masse to the area, huge numbers might be seen in a cackling gaggle outside the visitor center.

The peak season for waterbirds and raptors runs September to March; for black brant geese and migratory shorebirds, it's mid-March to late April, and again from August to September. Gulls, terns, cormorants, pelicans, egrets and herons come year-round. Look for harbor seals offshore; bring binoculars. Drive out South Jetty Rd to the mouth of Humboldt Bay for a stunning perspective.

In April, look for the Godwit Days festival (www.godwitdays.org), a celebration of the spring bird migration.

Pick up a map from the **Richard J Guadagno Headquarters & Visitor Center**, where you'll find the 1.7-mile Shorebird Loop Trail. Exit Hwy 101 at Hookton Rd, 11 miles south of Eureka, turn north along the frontage road, on the freeway's west side.

Eureka

One hour north of Garberville, on the edge of the largest bay north of San Francisco, lies the city of Eureka. With a strip-mall sprawl surrounding a lovely historic downtown, it wears its role as the county seat a bit clumsily. On one hand, it's got a diverse and interesting community of artists, writers, pagans and other freethinkers. But it's also home to a disturbingly large homeless population.

Its main draws are its serene waterfront trail, fantastic restaurants, glorious street murals, and all-around alternative edge. Make for Old Town, a small historic district with good shopping and a revitalized waterfront.

Eureka was a major logging town in the late 19th century, and many Victorian lumber-baron mansions dot the city; an impressive 150 or so of the Old Town buildings have been catalogued as important historical structures. The most famous is the hilltop **Carson Mansion** (Ingomar Club; www.ingomar.org; 143 M St, Ingomar Club), an ornate 1880s home of lumber baron William Carson that took 100 men two years to build.

Sights

The free *Eureka Visitors Map*, available at tourist offices, details walking tours and scenic drives, focusing on architecture and history. **Old Town**, along 2nd and 3rd Sts from C St to M St, was once down-and-out, but has been refurbished into a buzzing pedestrian district. The F Street Plaza and Boardwalk runs along the waterfront at the foot of F St. Gallery openings fall on the first Saturday of every month.

Sequoia Park PARK
(707-441-4263; www.sequoiaparkzoo.net; 3414 W St; park free, zoo adult/child $10/6; zoo 10am-5pm May-Sep, 10am-5pm Tue-Sun Oct-Apr) A 67-acre old-growth redwood grove is a surprising green gem in the middle of a residential neighborhood. It has biking and hiking trails, a children's playground and picnic areas, as well as a small **zoo** – the oldest in California.

Romano Gabriel Wooden Sculpture Garden PUBLIC ART
(315 2nd St) FREE The coolest thing to gawk at downtown is this collection of whimsical outsider art that's enclosed by aging glass. For 30 years, wooden characters in Gabriel's front yard delighted locals. After he died in 1977, the city moved the collection here.

Kinetic Museum Eureka MUSEUM
(707-786-3443; http://kineticgrandchampionship.com/kinetic-museum-eureka; 518 A St; admission by donation; 2:12-6:32pm Fri-Sun;) Come see the fanciful, astounding, human-powered contraptions used in the annual Kinetic Grand Championship (p276) race from Arcata to Ferndale. Shaped like giant fish and UFOs, these colorful piles of junk propel racers over roads, water and marsh during the May event.

Morris Graves Museum of Art MUSEUM
(707-442-0278; www.humboldtarts.org; 636 F St; $5; noon-5pm Wed-Sun) Across Hwy 101, this hit-or-miss museum shows rotating Californian artists and hosts performances inside the 1904 **Carnegie library**, the state's first public library. If you are around for a while,

and need something to do, it also hosts art workshops and classes for adults and kids.

Activities

Harbor Cruise CRUISE

(Madaket Cruises; ☎707-445-1910; www.humboldtbaymaritimemuseum.com; 1st St; narrated cruises adult/child $22/18; ⊙1pm, 2:30pm & 4pm Wed-Sat, 1pm & 2:30pm Sun-Tue mid-May–mid-Oct) Board the 1910 *Madaket*, the USA's oldest continuously operating passenger vessel, and learn Humboldt Bay's history. Docked at the foot of C St, it originally ferried mill workers and passengers until the Samoa Bridge opened in 1971. The $10 sunset cocktail cruise (Wednesday to Saturday) serves from the smallest licensed bar in the state. There's also a Sunday-morning wildlife cruise.

Humboats KAYAKING

(☎707-443-5157; www.humboats.com; 601 Startare Dr; kayak tours from $55, 2hr rental $30; ⊙hours vary) At Woodley Island Marina, this outfit rents kayaks and SUPs. Also offers sunset, full-moon, wildlife and river tours.

Tours

Blue Ox Millworks & Historic Park HISTORIC BUILDING

(☎707-444-3437; www.blueoxmill.com; 1 X St; adult/child 6-12yr $12/7; ⊙9am-5pm Mon-Fri year-round, plus 9am-4pm Sat Apr-Nov;) One of only a few of its kind in the US, here antique tools are used to produce authentic gingerbread trim for Victorian buildings, stained glass, decorative gemstones, hand-painted signs and other craft goods from another era. One-hour self-guided tours take you through the mill and historical buildings, including a blacksmith shop and 19th-century skid camp. Peruse the gift shop!

Workshops are regularly held if you fancy trying your hand at one of the crafts here.

Festivals & Events

Eureka Street Art Festival ART

(www.eurekastreetartfestival.com; ⊙Aug) A week-long festival where local and international artists paint murals and create street art across Old Town. Check the website for a map of murals from past events.

Sleeping

Every brand of chain hotel is located along Hwy 101. Room rates run high midsummer; you can sometimes find cheaper options in Fortuna, to the south. There is also a handful of motels that cost from $45 to $100 and have no air-conditioning; choose places set back from the road. The cheapest options are south of downtown on the suburban strip.

Inn at 2nd & C HISTORIC HOTEL $$

(☎707-444-3344; www.theinnat2ndandc.com; 139 2nd St; r/ste from $129/$199;) Formerly the Eagle House Inn, this glorious Victorian hotel has been tastefully restored to combine Victorian-era decor with every possible modern amenity. The magnificent turn-of-the-century ballroom is used for everything from theater performances to special events. There is also a yoga studio. Breakfast, tea and complimentary cocktails are additional perks.

Eureka Inn HISTORIC HOTEL $$

(☎707-497-6903; www.eurekainn.com; cnr 7th & F Sts; r/ste from $109/270;) A majestic and enormous historic hotel with a mock Tudor frontage. It is cozy, in an early-20th-century-lodge, vaguely Wild West sort of way; the staff are extremely friendly and there's a decent bar on the premises. The plush suites are the best rooms in town.

Carter House Inns B&B $$$

(☎707-444-8062; www.carterhouse.com; 301 L St; r $184-395;) Constructed in period style, this aesthetically remodeled hotel is a Victorian look-alike. Rooms have modern amenities and top-quality linens; suites have in-room Jacuzzis and marble fireplaces. The same owners operate four other sumptuously decorated lodgings: a single-level house, two honeymoon hideaway cottages and a replica of an 1880s San Francisco mansion, which the owner built himself, entirely by hand.

Eating

You won't go hungry in this town, and health-conscious folk are particularly well catered to with two excellent natural-food grocery stores – **North Coast Co-op** (☎707-443-6027; www.northcoast.coop; cnr 4th & B Sts; ⊙6am-9pm) and **Eureka Natural Foods** (☎707-442-6325; www.eurekanaturalfoods.com; 1450 Broadway St; ⊙7am-9pm) – and two weekly farmers markets – one **street market** (cnr 2nd & F Sts; ⊙10am-1pm Tue Jun-Oct) and one at the **Henderson Center** (☎707-441-9999; cnr F & Henderson Sts; ⊙10am-1pm Thu Jun-Oct). The vibrant dining scene is focused in the Old Town district and has an excellent array of foodie options and price categories.

THE BUDDING INDUSTRY OF MARIJUANA TOURISM

With an estimated one-fifth of Humboldt County's population farming its world-famous weed, a good chunk of the economy here has run, for decades, as bank-less, tax-evading and cash only. This is starting to change, albeit slowly, thanks to local incentives aimed at drawing black market farmers out of the forests and into the valleys now that recreational marijuana is – at least in California and some other US states – legal. While the transition hasn't been easy (most farmers remain in the illegal market due to high regulatory fees and plummeting legal marijuana costs) there are several safe and informative ways that visitors to the county capital Eureka can learn about the local industry.

For newbies, purchasing legal weed can be like walking into a fancy wine store and not knowing your sauvignon blanc from your cabernet sauvignon. Enter the folks at **Humboldt Cannabis Tours** (707-839-4640; www.humcannabis.com; 215 C St, Ste D1; tours from $55), who can take you on educational visits to the best local dispensaries – including **HPRC** (707-476-0450; www.hprchumboldt.com; 445 4th St; 10am-7pm Mon-Sat, 11am-6pm Sun), which sells pesticide-free cannabis products and offers free yoga classes – or out to 'white market' farms, where you'll learn about the growing cycle from the Emerald Triangle's longtime cannabis farmers.

Several other businesses around Eureka are out to defy stoner stereotypes by offering a mature and tourist-friendly look at the area's cannabis culture (for those 21 and older, of course). California's first licensed 'bud and breakfast,' for instance, is so quaint it will dispel any lingering myths about reefer madness. **Riverbar Pharms** (707-726-1170; www.riverbarpharms.com; 355 River Bar Rd; r $149-199;) is run by a husband and wife team (he's the farmer and she's the chef), and has just four rooms tucked into a refurbished butter-yellow Victorian overlooking greenhouses of marijuana. You can expect a complimentary cannabis tea blend and rolled joint atop the bed!

Cafe Nooner MEDITERRANEAN $
(707-443-4663; www.cafenooner.com; 409 Opera Alley; mains $10-17; 11am-4pm;) Exuding a cozy bistro-style ambience with red-and-white checkered tablecloths and jaunty murals, this perennially popular restaurant serves natural, organic and Med-inspired cuisine with choices that include a Greek-style meze platter, plus kebabs, salads and soups. There's a healthy kids menu, as well.

Ramone's Bakery & Cafe BAKERY $
(707-442-1336; www.ramonesbakery.com; 2297 Harrison Ave; mains $6-10; 7am-6pm Sun-Mon, to 9pm Tue-Sat;) Come here for delicious cakes, tarts, pies and pastries, as well as baguette sandwiches and salads; there are four other branches in the area.

★ **Brick & Fire** CALIFORNIAN $$
(707-268-8959; www.brickandfirebistro.com; 1630 F St; dinner mains $17-28; 11:30am-9pm Mon & Wed-Fri, 5-9pm Sat & Sun;) Tucked into an intimate, warm-hued and bohemian-tinged setting, this spot is almost always busy. Choose from thin-crust pizzas, delicious salads (try the pear, bacon and blue cheese), and an ever-changing selection of appetizers and mains that highlight local produce and wild mushrooms. There's a weighty wine list and servers are well versed in pairings.

★ **Humboldt Bay Provisions** SEAFOOD $$
(707-672-3850; www.humboldtbayprovisions.com; 205 G St; half-dozen oysters $13; 4-9pm Mon-Fri, from 1pm Sat & Sun) Sit at the long redwood bar at this rustic-chic establishment and watch as experts shuck local oysters and top them off with intriguing sauces such as habanero and peach juice. The locavore menu also includes charcuterie-style platters and regional wines and ales. If you like what you taste, be sure to ask about the two-hour **Humboldt Bay Oyster Tours** (www.humboldtbayoystertours.com).

Restaurant 301 CALIFORNIAN $$$
(707-444-8062; www.carterhouse.com; 301 L St; mains $25-39; 5-9pm) Part of the excellent Carter House Inns, romantic, sophisticated 301 serves a contemporary Californian menu, using produce from its organic gardens (tours available). The five-course tasting menu ($70, wine pairings $40) is a good way to sample local seasonal food in its finest presentation.

Drinking & Nightlife

Eureka has some fine old bars and pubs, including live-music venues, mainly located in and around the historic center. The annual jazz festival attracts some top musicians and also includes blues concerts.

Old Town Coffee & Chocolates CAFE
(☎707-445-8600; www.oldtowncoffeeeureka.com; 211 F St; ⊙7am-9pm; 📶) You'll smell roasting coffee blocks before you see this place. It's a local hangout in a historic building and has board games, local art on the wall and savory choices like bagels with hummus and wraps.

Speakeasy BAR
(☎707-444-2244; 411 Opera Alley; ⊙4-11pm Mon-Thu, to 2am Fri & Sat) Squeeze in with the locals at this New Orleans–inspired bar with regular live blues and an infectious convivial atmosphere.

2 Doors Down WINE BAR
(☎707-268-8989; www.2doorsdownwinebar.com; 1626 F St; ⊙4.30-9.30pm Wed-Mon) Wonderfully cozy and inviting, this Victorian-feeling wine bar will open any bottle on its list of 80-plus wines if you're buying two or more glasses of it. Plenty of snacks are available for order from Brick & Fire two doors down.

Shanty BAR
(☎707-444-2053; 213 3rd St; ⊙noon-2am) The coolest spot in town is grungy and fun. Play pool, pinball or Ping-Pong, or kick it on the back patio with local 20- and 30-something hipsters.

☆ Entertainment

Morris Graves Museum of Art PERFORMING ARTS
(☎707-442-0278; www.humboldtarts.org; 636 F St; $5) Hosts performing-arts events, usually on Saturday evenings and Sunday afternoons, but sometimes on other days as well.

Shopping

Eureka's streets lie on a grid: numbered streets cross lettered streets. For the best window-shopping, head to the 300, 400 and 500 blocks of 2nd St, between D and G Sts. The town's low rents and cool old spaces harbor lots of indie boutiques.

Dick Taylor Craft Chocolate CHOCOLATE
(☎707-798-6010; www.dicktaylorchocolate.com; 4 W 4th St; ⊙10am-6pm Mon-Fri, 11am-4pm Sat) This bean-to-bar company specializes in single-origin craft chocolates, most of which only have two ingredients (cacao and sugar). Everything is made on-site, and you can tour the factory on Fridays and Saturdays (check the website for timings).

ℹ Information

Eureka Visitor Center (☎707-572-4227; www.visiteureka.com; 240 E St; ⊙10am-6pm Tue-Sat, 11am-4pm Sun; 📶) The main visitor information center for the city of Eureka

Humboldt County Visitor Bureau (☎707-443-5097; www.visitredwoods.com; 322 1st St; ⊙9am-5pm Mon-Fri) Stocks flyers and magazines on the greater redwoods region. You can also order a brochure on the website to be emailed to you ahead of your trip.

ℹ Getting There & Around

Arcata–Eureka Airport (Humboldt County Airport; Map p279; ☎707-839-5401; https://humboldtgov.org/1396/Airports; 3561 Boeing Ave, McKinleyville) The Arcata–Eureka Airport, also known as California Redwood Coast – Humboldt County Airport, is located north of McKinleyville on the North Coast, signposted west of Hwy 101 and with regular services to San Francisco and Los Angeles. United Express is currently the only commercial carrier serving this airport. Flight cancellations due to fog are not uncommon.

Eureka Transit Service (Humboldt Transit Authority; ☎707-443-0826; www.eurekatransit.org; 133 V St; single fare $1.70) Runs five routes throughout Eureka: the red, gold, green, purple and rainbow routes. Fares may be paid on the bus, and day or monthly passes are also available.

Samoa Peninsula

Grassy dunes and windswept beaches extend along the half-mile-wide, 10-mile-long Samoa Peninsula. At its southern end, **Samoa Dunes Recreation Area** (☎707-825-2300; www.blm.gov; 1400 Bay St; ⊙sunrise-sunset) FREE is good for picnicking and fishing. For wildlife, head north to **Ma-le'l Dunes**; from Arcata, take Samoa Blvd west for 3 miles, then turn right at Young Ln, near Manila. Trails here pass mudflats, salt marsh and tidal channels. There are more than 200 species of birds: migrating waterfowl in spring and fall, songbirds in spring and summer, shorebirds in fall and winter, and waders year-round.

The **Samoa Cookhouse** (☎707-442-1659; www.samoacookhouse.net; 908 Vance Ave; all-you-can-eat meals per adult $14-18, child $7-8; ⊙7am-3pm & 5-8pm, closed Mon & Tue Nov-Apr; 👪) is the dining hall of an 1893 lumber camp. Hikers, hippies and lumberjacks get stuffed while sharing long, red-checked oilcloth-covered tables. There is no menu but you can guarantee that anything you order will be freshly made that day. Think fried chicken, pork ribs and bumper breakfasts. Vegetarians should call ahead.

Arcata

The North Coast's most progressive town, Arcata surrounds a tidy central square that fills with college students, campers, wanderers and tourists. Sure, it occasionally reeks of patchouli and its politics lean far left, but its earnest embrace of sustainability has fostered some of the most progressive civic action in America. Here, garbage trucks run on biodiesel, wastewater gets filtered clean in marshlands and almost every street has a bike lane. Predictably enough, organic products and produce are the norm, art-and-craft markets are rampant and vegans are well catered to.

Founded in 1850 as a base for lumber camps, today Arcata is defined as a magnet for 20-somethings looking to expand their minds: either at Humboldt State University (HSU), and/or on the local highly potent marijuana.

Sights

Around Arcata Plaza are two National Historic Landmarks: the 1857 **Jacoby's Storehouse** (☎707-826-2426; Arcata Plaza; ⊙hours vary) and the 1915 **Hotel Arcata** (☎707-826-0217; www.hotelarcata.com; 708 9th St). Another great historic building is the 1914 **Minor Theatre** (☎707-822-3456; www.minortheatre.com; 1001 H St; ⊙hours vary), which some local historians claim is the oldest theater in the US built specifically for showing films.

Arcata Marsh & Wildlife Sanctuary WILDLIFE RESERVE
(www.cityofarcata.org; 569 South G St) FREE On the shores of Humboldt Bay, this sanctuary has 5 miles of walking and biking trails, plus outstanding birding. The **Redwood Region Audubon Society** (☎707-826-7031; www.rras.org; donation welcome) offers guided walks on Saturdays at 8:30am from the parking lot at I St's south end. Friends of Arcata Marsh offer guided tours Saturdays at 2pm from the Arcata Marsh Interpretive Center (p278).

Humboldt State University UNIVERSITY
(HSU; ☎707-826-3551; https://ccat.humboldt.edu; 1 Harpst St) The university on the northeastern side of town holds the Campus Center for Appropriate Technology (CCAT), a world leader in developing sustainable technologies. On the first Friday of the month at noon and the third Friday of the month at 2pm, you can take a tour of CCAT's house, a converted residence that uses less than 5% of the energy consumed by the average American home.

Activities

Finnish Country Sauna and Tubs SPA
(☎707-822-2228; http://cafemokkaarcata.com; 495 J St; per 30min adult/child $10.25/2; ⊙11am-11pm Sun-Thu, to midnight Fri & Sat) Like some kind of Euro-crunchy bohemian dream, these private, open-air redwood hot tubs and sauna are situated around a small frog pond. The staff is easygoing and the facility is relaxing, simple and clean. Reserve ahead, especially on weekends.

Hatchet House HEALTH & FITNESS
(☎707-630-5203; www.hatchethousethrowing.com; 639 6th St; 30min/1hr $10/15; ⊙3-9pm Mon-Fri, 11am-9pm Sat, 11am-6pm Sun) Imagine a shooting range, but instead of guns, you're armed with hatchets! Welcome to lumber land's fastest-growing pastime: indoor axe throwing. Scarily, you can drink (craft) beer while you play. Apparently, it's good for stress relief...

HSU Center Activities OUTDOORS
(☎707-826-3357; https://centeractivities.humboldt.edu; Humboldt State University, 1 Harpst St; ⊙10am-5pm Mon-Fri) Located in the Recreation & Wellness Center of HSU, this department sponsors myriad workshops and is a fantastic option for sporting-gear rentals or area info. Also runs kayaking, SUP, canoe, white-water rafting, sailing, surfing and backpacking adventures. Nonstudents welcome.

Festivals & Events

Kinetic Grand Championship ART
(☎707-786-3443; www.kineticgrandchampionship.com; ⊙late May) Arcata's most famous event is held Memorial Day weekend: people on amazing self-propelled contraptions travel 42 miles from Arcata to Ferndale over a period of three days.

Arcata Bay Oyster Festival FOOD & DRINK
(www.arcatamainstreet.com; Arcata Plaza; ⊙mid-Jun) A magical celebration of oysters and beer held on a Saturday in mid-June.

North Country Fair FAIR
(www.sameoldpeople.org; Arcata Plaza; ⊙Sep) A fun September street fair, where bands with names like the Fickle Hillbillies jam.

Sleeping

Arcata has affordable but limited lodgings. A cluster of hotels – Comfort Inn, Hampton Inn etc – is just north of town, off Hwy 101's Giuntoli Lane. There's cheap camping further north at Clam Beach. One of the best situated hotels is the old-fashioned **Hotel Arcata** (707-826-0217; www.hotelarcata.com; 708 9th St; r $85-200;), right on the city's main square.

Arcata Stay ACCOMMODATION SERVICES $
(707-822-0935; www.arcatastay.com; 814 13th St; apt from $119) A network of excellent and centrally situated apartments, B&Bs and cottage rentals. There is a two-night minimum and prices go down the longer you stay.

★ **Front Porch Inn** INN $$
(916-751-6192; www.frontporchinn.net; 150 G St; d/q $150/250;) Not only does this converted motor lodge have a collection of artsy rooms – all with kitchens and quirky wooden design touches – but there's also a bathhouse behind a living wall of ferns. There, you find a striking sauna made from local river rocks, as well as open-air copper and clawfoot tubs that make civilization seem hours away.

There is no sign out front and it's self check in, so book in advance.

Lady Anne Inn INN $$
(707-822-2797; www.ladyanneinn.com; 902 14th St; r $115-220;) Dating from 1888, this eco inn is owned by the former mayor of Arcata, so he knows a fair bit about the town. The front garden is eclectic, while the rooms continue the floral theme with decorative wallpaper and pastel paintwork. Dark wood antiques complete the look.

Eating

Great food abounds in restaurants throughout Arcata, almost all casual and most promoting organic produce and ingredients; vegetarians and vegans will have no problem in this town.

There is a fantastic farmers market at the **Arcata Plaza** (www.northcoastgrowersassociation.org; btwn 8th & 9th Sts; 9am-2pm Sat Apr-Nov, from 10am Dec-Mar). Just a few blocks north of downtown, there is a cluster of the town's best restaurants on G St, near Hwy 101.

Slice of Humboldt Pie CALIFORNIAN $
(707-630-5100; 828 I St; pies $4.50-7.50; 11am-6pm Tue-Thu, to 8pm Fri & Sat, closed Sun & Mon) Pies are the mainstays here, ranging from chicken pot pie to Mexican chocolate pecan pie. Savory empanadas also shine and include everything from vegan chipotle black bean to pulled pork with green chili. Ciders are the welcome accompaniment and cover mostly local varieties. The decor is pure industrial chic with exposed pipes and soft gray paintwork.

T's Cafe CAFE $
(707-826-2133; 860 10th St; breakfast $8-15; 7am-2pm;) Housed in an early-20th-century mansion; try and grab the table on the front porch if you can. Inside, two cavernous rooms with sage walls, local art, books, toys and magazines provide an informal kick-back space for enjoying delicious breakfast classics such as eggs with corned beef hash, stuffed French toast and the specialty: seven kinds of eggs Benedict.

★ **SALT Fish House** SEAFOOD $$
(707-630-5300; www.saltfishhouse.com; 761 8th St; mains $17-32; 11:30am-10pm Tue-Fri, 4-10pm Sat & Sun;) This low-lit, nautical-themed restaurant on the plaza promises sustainably harvested seafood, locally sourced produce and thoughtfully crafted cocktails. It delivers on all three. Come for oysters, chowders, poke bowls and seafood pastas, then stick around for the killer libations.

Cafe Brio CAFE $$
(707-822-5922; www.cafebrioarcata.com; 791 G St; mains $12-22; 7am-9pm Mon-Fri, 8am-4pm Sat & Sun;) Occupying an ace position on the corner of this central square, the patisserie here serves sumptuous cakes, breakfasts are delish and the lunch salads, sandwiches and pies are a notch above the norm. There is also a coffee-cum-wine-bar for suppin'.

Drinking & Nightlife

Dive bars and cocktail lounges line the plaza's northern side. Arcata is awash with coffeehouses and brewpubs.

★ **Redwood Curtain Brewing Company** MICROBREWERY
(707-826-7222; www.redwoodcurtainbrewing.com; 550 S G St; noon-11pm Sun-Tue, to midnight Wed-Sat;) This tiny gem of a brewery has gone through a major expansion thanks to its varied collection of rave-worthy craft ales. The taproom is family-friendly, invites food trucks to park out back, and has live music or DJs some nights.

Six Rivers Brewery MICROBREWERY
(☎707-839-7580; www.sixriversbrewery.com; 1300 Central Ave, McKinleyville; ⊙11:30am-11pm Tue-Sun, from 4pm Mon) One of the first female-owned breweries in California, the 'brew with a view' kills it in every category: great beer, amazing community vibe, occasional live music and delicious hot wings. The spicy chili-pepper ale is superb. At first glance the menu might seem like ho-hum pub grub, but portions are fresh and huge. It also makes a helluva pizza.

Wrangletown Cider Company CIDER
(☎707-508-5175; www.wrangletownciderccompany.com; 1350 9th St; ⊙3-7pm Fri, 1-6pm Sat) Sonoma winemaker Pat Knittel returned home to Humboldt to open this hole-in-the-wall cidery in the Creamery District, which offers tastings of four dry ciders made with local apples. Note at the time of research that Wrangletown planned to move to the Humboldt Machine Works building and expand hours.

Cafe Mokka CAFE
(☎707-822-2228; www.cafemokkaarcata.com; cnr 5th & J Sts; ⊙11am-11pm Sun-Thu, to midnight Fri & Sat) Bohos head to this cafe at Finnish Country Sauna & Tubs (p276) for a mellow, Nordic vibe, good coffee drinks and homemade cookies.

☆ Entertainment

Center Arts PERFORMING ARTS
(☎tickets 707-826-3928; https://centerarts.humboldt.edu; Humboldt State University, 1 Harpst St; ⊙hours vary) Hosts events on campus and at the Arkley Center for the Performing Arts in Eureka. You'd be amazed at the kind of toptier talent that shows up.

Arcata Theatre CINEMA
(☎707-613-3030; www.arcatatheater.com; 1036 G St) An exquisite remodeling has revived this old-school movie house, which shows cult classics, rock documentaries, silent films and more. Plus, it serves beer!

Shopping

★**Holly Yashi** JEWELRY
(☎707-822-5132; www.hollyyashi.com; 1300 9th St; ⊙10am-6pm Mon-Sat) The renowned hometown jeweler, famed for its nature-inspired Niobium metalwork, has its headquarters in Arcata's up-and-coming Creamery District. You get free coffee or tea just for showing up to browse, and can take a 30-minute tour to watch the jewelry-making magic (11am & 2pm Mon-Fri).

ℹ Information

Arcata Humboldt Welcome Center (☎707-822-3619; www.visitarcata.com; 1635 Heindon Rd; ⊙9am-4pm Mon-Fri) Near the junction of Hwys 299 and 101; has area info.

Arcata Marsh Interpretive Center (☎707-826-2359; www.cityofarcata.org; 569 South G St; ⊙9am-5pm Tue-Sun, from 1pm Mon) Has books, maps and a small exhibition room.

ℹ Getting There & Around

The Arcata–Eureka Airport (p275) is located north of McKinleyville, signposted west of Hwy 101 and with regular services to San Francisco and Los Angeles. United Express is currently the only commercial carrier serving this airport. Flight cancellations due to fog may occur.

Greyhound (p235) serves Arcata from San Francisco ($36, seven hours, daily). Redwood Transit System (p235) serves Arcata and Eureka on the daily Trinidad–Scotia routes ($3.50, 2½ hours).

A great way to get around town is to rent a bike from **Revolution Bicycles** (☎707-822-2562; www.revolutionbicycle.com; 1593 G St; half-day rental $25; ⊙9am-6pm Mon-Fri, 5pm Sat, 10am-4pm Sun) or test out the Zagster bike-share program ($1 per 30 minutes, www.bike.zagster.com/arcata). There is a sizable network of cycle lanes in Arcata. Arcata city buses stop at the **Arcata & Mad River Transit Center** (☎707-822-3775; www.arcatatransit.org; 925 E St at 9th St; $1.75 per ride).

NORTHERN REDWOOD COAST

Congratulations, traveler, you've reached the middle of nowhere, or at least the top of the middle of nowhere. Here, the trees are so large that the tiny towns along the road seem even smaller. The scenery is pure drama: cliffs and rocks, legendary salmon runs, mammoth trees, wild elk – and RVing retirees. Leave time to dawdle and bask in the haunting natural grandeur of it all and, even though there are scores of mid-century motels, try and make an effort to sleep outdoors if possible. Then, as you gaze skywards, ponder the fact that giant redwoods once covered some 5000 square miles of coast here, before the brutal mass logging that took place around the turn of the 20th century (apparently some 95% of the trees were felled). Fortunately, conservation measures are now firmly in place to protect these magnificent trees that can live for thousands of years.

Trinidad

Cheery, tiny Trinidad perches prettily on the side of the ocean, combining upscale mid-century homes with a mellow surfer vibe. Somehow it feels a bit off-the-beaten-path even though tourism augments fishing to keep the economy going. Trinidad is also a big hit with ornithologists; it's home to one of the most diverse seabird colonies in California. The town gained its name when Spanish sea captains arrived on Trinity Sunday in 1775 and named the area La Santisima Trinidad (the Holy Trinity); later it was the site of bloody battles and raids against the local Native Americans during the Civil War. Around this period, it also experienced a boom, becoming an important port for miners. If you can, check out the superb beaches and rocky coves and stop for a seafood meal overlooking the water.

Sights & Activities

Trinidad is small; approach via Hwy 101 or from the north via Patrick's Point Dr (which becomes Scenic Dr further south). To reach town, take Main St.

A free town map available at the **Trinidad Museum** (☎707-677-3883; www.trinidadmuseum.org; 400 Janis Ct; ⊙noon-4pm Thu-Sun) FREE shows several fantastic hiking trails, most notably the 1.5-mile **Trinidad Head Trail**, which has superb coastal views and is excellent for **whale-watching** (December to April). Stroll along an exceptionally beautiful cove at **Trinidad State Beach**; take Main St and bear right at Stagecoach, then take the second turn left (the first is a picnic area) into the small lot.

Scenic Dr twists south along coastal bluffs, passing tiny coves with views back toward the bay. It peters out before reaching the broad expanses of **Luffenholtz Beach** (accessible via the staircase) and serene gold-sand **Moonstone Beach**. Exit Hwy 101 at 6th Ave/Westhaven to get there. Further south Moonstone becomes **Clam Beach County Park**.

Surfing is good year-round, but potentially dangerous: unless you know how to judge conditions and get yourself out of trouble – there are no lifeguards here – surf in better-protected Crescent City.

HSU Telonicher Marine Laboratory AQUARIUM
(☎707-826-3689; www.hsumarinelab.org; 570 Ewing St; by donation; ⊙9am-4:30pm Mon-Fri, 10am-4pm Sat & Sun; 👪) Near Edwards St, this marine lab has a self-guided tour that leads

Northern Redwood Coast

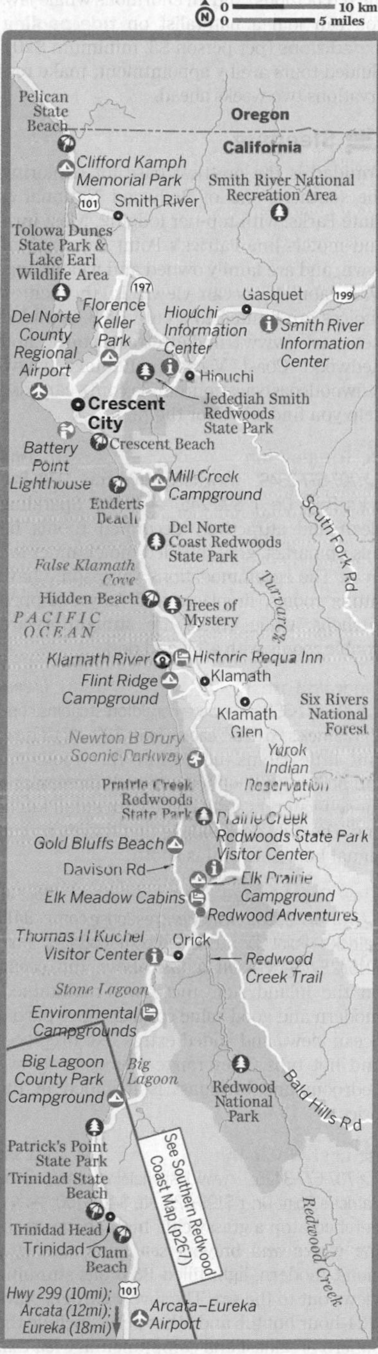

to a touch tank, several aquariums (look for the red octopus) and an enormous whale jaw. You can join a naturalist on **tide-pooling expeditions** (per person $3, minimum $20). Guided tours are by appointment; make reservations two weeks ahead.

Sleeping

Trinidad is the prettiest base for exploring the southern end of Redwood National & State Parks, with top-tier lodging. Most inns and motels line Patrick's Point Dr, north of town, and are family owned and welcoming, with fabulous ocean views. In the center, choices are limited to a cute B&B. Trinidad Retreats (www.trinidadretreats.com) and Redwood Coast Vacation Rentals (www.redwoodcoastvacationrentals.com) can also help you find a bed for the night.

★Trinidad Inn INN $
(707-677-3349; www.trinidadinn.com; 1170 Patrick's Point Dr; r $90-245;) Sparkling clean and attractively decorated rooms fill this upmarket, gray-shingled motel under tall trees. The accommodations vary; some have sitting rooms, fireplaces and fully equipped kitchens, while others are straightforward double rooms with a TV and desk.

Emerald Forest CABIN $
(707-677-3554; www.emeraldforestcabins.com; 753 Patrick's Point Dr; cabins from $89;) These cute little cabins tucked into the woods are the best budget option around, particularly for self-caterers as all come with small kitchens. The only downside is that there's no cell signal here and wi-fi is spotty.

View Crest Lodge LODGE $$
(707-677-3393; www.viewcrestlodge.com; 3415 Patrick's Point Dr; 1-/2-bedroom cottages from $115/215;) On a hill above the ocean on the inland side, these well-maintained, modern and good-value cottages have partial ocean views and added extras like fireplaces and hot tubs. They range from one to two bedroom and breakfast is included in the price.

★Lost Whale Inn B&B $$$
(707-677-3425; www.lostwhaleinn.com; 3452 Patrick's Point Dr; r $199-325, ste $408-750;) Perched atop a grassy cliff, high above crashing waves and braying sea lions, this spacious, modern, light-filled B&B has stunning views out to the sea. The lovely gardens have a 24-hour hot tub and other perks include the superb breakfast and complimentary tea that is served at 4pm. The owner is Portuguese and family antiques feature in every room.

Turtle Rocks Oceanfront Inn B&B $$$
(707-677-3707; www.turtlerocksinn.com; 3392 Patrick's Point Dr; r $185-335;) Enjoy truly stunning sea vistas from every room at this plush, modern place on three peaceful, windswept acres. Rooms are spacious with terraces; number 3 comes particularly recommended with its warm blue decor.

Trinidad Bay B&B B&B $$$
(707-677-0840; www.trinidadbaybnb.com; 560 Edwards St; r $200-350;) This light-filled Cape Cod–style home overlooks the harbor and Trinidad Head. Breakfast may be delivered to your uniquely styled room, and in the afternoon the house fills with the scent of freshly baked cookies. The Trinity Alps room has a kitchenette and is well set up for families.

Eating

Trinidad is home to superb beaches and hideaway coves where packing a picnic is always a tempting option (thankfully the town has a solid choice of delis and supermarkets). Trinidad State Beach also has excellent picnicking facilities. The restaurants here are, unsurprisingly, centered on seafood and fish; several have coastal views to enhance that ocean-inspired dining experience.

Katy's Smokehouse & Fishmarket SEAFOOD $
(www.katyssmokehouse.com; 740 Edwards St; 9am-6pm) This establishment makes its own chemical-free and amazingly delicious smoked and canned fish, using line-caught, sushi-grade seafood; the tuna has been voted number one in the US, no less. There's no restaurant – just grab some for a picnic.

Beachcomber Cafe CAFE $
(707-677-0106; www.beachcombertrinidad.com; 363 Trinity St; breakfast from $6; 7am-4pm Mon-Fri, 8am-4pm Sat & Sun;) Head here for the best breakfast in these parts, ranging from a hearty bowl of organic black beans with avocado and poached egg to moist and delicious homemade muffins. It also has plenty of newspapers and local info to peruse.

Lighthouse Grill CALIFORNIAN $
(707-677-0077; www.trinidadlighthousegrill.com; 355 Main St; mains $6-12; 11am-8pm) Across from the Chevron, this fun little arty joint makes good food fast, using mostly organic ingredients – try the creative soups, fish and

chips with hand-cut fries, local grass-fed beef burgers and homemade ice cream.

★**Larrupin Cafe** CALIFORNIAN $$$
(707-677-0230; www.thelarrupin.com; 1658 Patrick's Point Dr; mains $32-47; 5-9pm) Everybody loves Larrupin, where Moroccan rugs, chocolate-brown walls, gravity-defying floral arrangements and deep-burgundy Oriental carpets create a moody atmosphere perfect for a lovers' tryst. On the menu, expect consistently good mesquite-grilled seafood and meats – the smoked beef brisket is truly amazing. In the summer, book a table on the garden patio for live music some nights.

Patrick's Point State Park

Coastal bluffs jut out to sea at the 640-acre **Patrick's Point State Park** (Map p279; 707-677-3570; www.parks.ca.gov; 4150 Patrick's Point Dr; per car $8; sunrise-sunset), where sandy beaches abut rocky headlands. Easy access to a dramatic coastline makes this a great bet for families, but any age will find a feast for the senses as they climb rock formations, search for breaching whales, carefully navigate tide pools and listen to barking sea lions and singing birds. Get maps and info at the **visitor center** (10am-4pm).

Sumêg is an authentic reproduction of a Yurok village, with hand-hewn redwood buildings where Native Americans gather for traditional ceremonies. In the native plant garden you'll find species for making traditional baskets and medicines.

On Agate Beach look for bits of jade and sea-polished agate. Follow the signs to tide pools. The 2-mile Rim Trail, an old Yurok trail around the bluffs, circles the point with access to huge rocky outcrops. Don't miss Wedding Rock, one of the park's most romantic spots. Other trails lead around unusual formations like Ceremonial Rock and Lookout Rock.

The park's three well-tended **campgrounds** (information 707-677-3570, reservations 800-444-7275; www.reservecalifornia.com; 4150 Patrick's Point Dr; tent & RV sites $35;) have coin-operated showers and clean bathrooms. Penn Creek and Abalone campgrounds are more sheltered than Agate Beach.

Humboldt Lagoons State Park

Stretching out for miles along the coast, this state park contains long, sandy beaches and the largest lagoon system in North America. **Big Lagoon** and the even prettier **Stone Lagoon** are both excellent for bird-watching and kayaking (for the latter contact Kayak Zak's, www.kayakzak.com). Sunsets are spectacular, with no artificial structures in sight. Picnic at Stone Lagoon's north end. The Stone Lagoon Visitor Center, on Hwy 101, has been closed for years, but there's a toilet and a bulletin board displaying information.

A mile north, **Freshwater Lagoon** is also great for birding. South of Stone Lagoon, tiny **Dry Lagoon** (a freshwater marsh) has a fantastic day hike and good agate hunting. Park at Dry Lagoon's picnic area and hike north on the unmarked trail to Stone Lagoon; the trail skirts the southwestern shore and ends up at the ocean, passing through woods and marshland rich with wildlife. Mostly flat, it's about 2.5 miles one way. The trail is clearly marked on the popular Maps.me app.

You will have to sleep under canvas in these parts. All campsites are first-come, first-served. The park runs two primitive **environmental tent sites** (Map p279; Humboldt Lagoons State Park; tent sites $20); bring water. Stone Lagoon has six boat-in environmental tent sites, but you'll need to obtain a permit from the ranger at the entrance to Patrick's Point State Park.

Humboldt County Parks also operates a decent cypress-grove picnic area and campground: the **Big Lagoon County Park Campground** (Map p279; www.humboldtgov.org; off Hwy 101; tent & RV sites per vehicle $25;) beside Big Lagoon, a mile off Hwy 101, with flush toilets and coin-operated showers.

Redwood National & State Parks

Hidden away in the upper reaches of California's northwestern Pacific coast, Redwood National Park encompasses some of the world's tallest and most ancient trees, along with a luxuriantly verdant mix of coastal, riverine and prairie wildlands. The massive stands of old-growth California coastal redwoods (*Sequoia sempervirens*) here, draped in moss and ferns and towering up to 379ft tall, are managed in conjunction with three neighboring state parks – Prairie Creek Redwoods, Del Norte Coast Redwoods and Jedediah Smith Redwoods State Park (the latter famed as a backdrop in the original *Star Wars* movie).

Collectively the parks constitute an International Biosphere Reserve and World

Heritage Site, yet they remain little visited when compared to their southern brethren, like the Sequoia National Park. It is worth contemplating that some of these trees have been standing here for time immemorial, predating the Roman Empire by over 500 years. Prepare to be impressed.

Redwood National Park

This park is the southernmost of a patchwork of state and federally administered lands under the umbrella of **Redwood National & State Parks** (Map p279; ☎707-464-6101, 707-465-7335; www.nps.gov/redw; Hwy 101, Orick) FREE. After picking up a map at the **Thomas H Kuchel Visitor Center** (Map p279; ☎707-465-7765; www.nps.gov/redw; Hwy 101, Orick; ⏲9am-5pm Apr-Oct, to 4pm Nov-Mar), you'll have a suite of choices for hiking. A few miles north along Hwy 101, a trip inland on Bald Hills Rd will take you to **Lady Bird Johnson Grove**, with its 1-mile, kid-friendly loop trail, or get you lost in the secluded serenity of **Tall Trees Grove**.

To protect the Tall Trees Grove, a limited number of cars per day are allowed access; get permits at the visitor center in Orick. This can be a half-day trip in itself, but you're well rewarded after the challenging approach (a 6-mile ramble on an old logging road behind a locked gate, then a moderately strenuous 4-mile round-trip hike). Another recommended hike is to **Trillium Falls** – a 2½-mile trail leading to a small waterfall, accessed from Davison Rd at Elk Meadow.

Note that during the winter, several foot bridges crossing the Redwood Creek are removed due to the high waters. If you are hiking at this time of year, be sure to check with a ranger regarding the current situation before striding out.

Elk Meadow Cabins CABIN **$$**
(Map p279; ☎866-733-9637; www.redwoodadventures.com; 7 Valley Green Camp Rd, Orick; cabins $169-299; 📶🐾) These spotless and bright cabins with equipped kitchens and all the mod-cons are in a perfect mid-parks location – they're great if you're traveling in a group and the most comfy choice even if you're not. Expect to see elk on the lawn in the mornings. Cabins sleep six to eight people and there's an additional $65 cleaning fee.

Redwood Adventures (Map p279; ☎866-733-9637; www.redwoodadventures.com; 7 Valley Green Camp Rd, Orick; guided tour from $85, half-day bike rental $30) operates out of here, with guided tours and mountain bike rentals.

ℹ Information

Unlike most national parks, there are no fees and no highway entrance stations at Redwood National Park, so it's imperative to pick up the free map at the park headquarters in Crescent City (p286) or at the information center in Orick. Only rangers at the latter can issue permits to visit Tall Trees Grove. Both loan bear-proof containers for backpackers.

The non-profit Redwood Parks Conservancy (www.redwoodparksconservancy.org) is a great resource for pre-trip planning.

ℹ Dangers & Annoyances

There has been a spate of break-ins at parking lots in Redwood National & State Parks in recent years. Don't leave any valuables in your vehicle, and be sure to lock it before setting off.

Prairie Creek Redwoods State Park

Famous for some of the world's best virgin redwood groves and unspoiled coastline, this 14,000-acre **section** (Map p279; ☎707-488-2039; www.parks.ca.gov; Newton B Drury Scenic Pkwy) of Redwood National & State Parks has spectacular scenic drives and 75 miles of mainly shady hiking trails, many of which are excellent for children. Kids of all ages will enjoy the magnificent herd of elk here, which can generally be spied grazing at the Elk Prairie, signposted from the highway; the best times to be sure of seeing the elk are early morning and around sunset.

There are 32 **mountain-biking** and **hiking trails** through the park, from simple to strenuous. A few easy nature trails start near the **visitor center** (Map p279; ☎707-488-2039; www.parks.ca.gov; Prairie Creek Rd; ⏲9am-5pm Apr-Oct, to 4pm Nov-Mar), including Revelation Trail, Elk Prairie Trail and Prairie Creek Trail. You can also stroll the reforested logging road on the Ah-Pah Interpretive Trail at the park's north end. The most rewarding hike is a spectacular 12-mile loop from the visitor center following the James Irvine Trail to Fern Canyon and Gold Bluffs Beach. Return on Miner's Ridge Trail, rising from the coast into primordial redwoods.

Unpaved Davison Rd provides access to the park's only fee area ($8 per car). Just past the Gold Bluffs Beach Campground the severely potholed road dead-ends at Fern Canyon, the second-busiest spot in the park, where 60ft fern-covered sheer-rock walls are so unusual that they were used in scenes from Steven Spielberg's *Jurassic Park 2: The Lost World*, as well as *Return of the Jedi*. This is one of the most photographed spots on the North Coast – damp and lush, all emerald green – and totally worth getting your toes wet to see on the 1-mile loop trail. Note that two creek crossings may prevent access to the last mile of the road in the winter rainy season if you don't have four-wheel drive. There are also no footbridges in the canyon between October and April, making rubber boots the only alternative to drenched feet.

Newton B Drury Scenic Parkway DRIVING
(Map p279; Hwy 101, Orick) Just north of Orick is the turnoff for this 8-mile parkway, which runs parallel to Hwy 101 through untouched ancient redwood forests. This is a not-to-miss short detour off the freeway where you can view the magnificence of these trees. Numerous trails branch off from roadside pullouts, including family-friendly options and paved ones that fit American Disabilities Act (ADA) requirements.

★**Gold Bluffs Beach** CAMPGROUND $
(Map p279; ☎800-444-7275; www.reservecalifornia.com; Prairie Creek Redwoods State Park; tent & RV sites $35) This gorgeous campground sits between 100ft cliffs and wide-open ocean, but there are some windbreaks and solar-heated showers. Look for sites closer to the cliff under the trees.

Elk Prairie Campground CAMPGROUND $
(Map p279; ☎reservations 800-444-7275; www.reservecalifornia.com; Prairie Creek Rd; tent & RV sites $35, hike-in sites $5 per person, cabins $80; 🐾) Elk roam this popular campground, where you can sleep under redwoods or at the prairie's edge. There are hike-in sites, four six-person cabins and hot showers, plus a shallow creek to splash in. Sites 69 to 76 are on grassy prairies and get full sun; sites eight to 68 are wooded. To camp in a mixed redwood forest, book sites 20 to 25.

Del Norte Coast Redwoods State Park

Marked by steep canyons and dense woods north of Klamath, this **park** (Map p279; ☎707-464-6101; www.nps.gov/redw; Mill Creek Rd) contains 15 miles of hiking trails and several old logging roads that are a mountain biker's dream. Many routes pass by branches of Mill Creek (bring your fishing rod). The park also fronts 8 miles of rugged coastline.

Hwy 1 winds in from the coast at dramatic Wilson Beach, and traverses the dense forest, with groves stretching as far as you can see. Picnic on the sand at False Klamath Cove. Heading north, tall trees cling precipitously to canyon walls that drop to the rocky, timber-strewn coastline.

Serious hikers will be most greatly rewarded by the **Damnation Creek Trail**. It's only 4.2 miles round trip, but the 1100ft elevation change and cliff-side redwood makes it the park's best hike. The unmarked trailhead starts from a parking area off Hwy 101 at Mile 16. Don't worry about signs warning of a broken bridge near the end of the trail; the tiny creek it traverses is easily crossed any time of the year.

Crescent Beach Overlook and picnic area has superb wintertime whale-watching. At the park's north end, watch the surf pound at Crescent Beach, just south of Crescent City via Enderts Beach Rd.

Mill Creek Campground (Map p279; ☎reservations 800-444-7275; www.reservecalifornia.com; Mill Creek Rd; tent & RV sites $35; ⏲mid-May–Oct) has hot showers and 145 sites in a second-growth redwood grove, 2 miles east of Hwy 101 and 9 miles south of Crescent City. Sites 1-74 are woodsier; sites 75-145 sunnier. Hike-in sites are prettiest.

Pick up maps and inquire about guided walks at the Crescent City Information Center

THE ENDANGERED MARBLED MURRELET

Notice how undeveloped the Redwood National and State Parks have remained? Thank the marbled murrelet, a small white and brown-black auk that nests in old-growth conifers. Loss of nesting territory due to logging has severely depleted the bird's numbers, but Redwood National Park scientists have discovered that corvid predators (ravens, jays etc) are also to blame. Because corvids are attracted to food scraps left by visitors, the number of snacking, picnicking or camping humans in the park greatly affects predation on the marbled murrelet. Restrictions on development to prevent food scraps and thus protect the birds are so strict that it's nearly impossible to build anything new.

WORTH A TRIP

SMITH RIVER NATIONAL RECREATION AREA

West of Jedediah Smith Redwoods State Park, the Smith River, the state's last remaining undammed waterway, runs right beside Hwy 199. Originating high in the Siskiyou Mountains, its serpentine course cuts through deep canyons beneath thick forests. Chinook salmon (October to December) and steelhead trout (December to April) annually migrate up its clear waters. Camp (there are four developed campgrounds), hike (70 miles of trails), raft (145 miles of navigable white water) and kayak here, but check regulations if you want to fish. Stop by the **Smith River Information Center** (Map p279; ☎707-457-3131; www.fs.usda.gov/recarea/srnf; 10600 Hwy 199, Gasquet; ⏰8am-4:30pm Mon-Fri) to get your bearings. Pick up pamphlets for the **Darlingtonia Trail** and **Myrtle Creek Botanical Area**, both easy jaunts into the woods, where you can see rare plants and learn about the area's geology.

(p286) or the Thomas H Kuchel Visitor Center (p282) in Orick.

Jedediah Smith Redwoods State Park

The northernmost park, **Jedediah Smith** (Map p279; ☎707-464-6101; www.nps.gov/redw; Hwy 199, Hiouchi; ⏰sunrise-sunset), is 9 miles northeast of Crescent City (via Hwy 101 north to Hwy 199 east). The redwood stands are so thick that few trails penetrate the park, but the outstanding 11-mile **Howland Hill Road scenic drive** cuts through otherwise inaccessible areas (take Hwy 199 to South Fork Rd; turn right after crossing two bridges). It's a rough road, impassable for RVs, but if you can't hike, it's the best way to see the forest.

Stop for a half-mile stroll under enormous trees in **Simpson-Reed Grove**. There's a swimming hole and picnic area at the **campground** (☎information 707-464-6101, reservations 800-444-7275; www.reservecalifornia.com; off Hwy 199, Hiouchi; tent & RV sites $35, day use $8). An easy half-mile trail, departing from the far side of the campground, crosses the Smith River via a summer-only footbridge, leading to **Stout Grove**, the park's most famous grove, which is also accessible off Howland Hill Rd. At the time of research, the popular Mill Creek Trail was due to reopen in 2021 with a new boardwalk through Grove of Titans. The **visitor center** (Map p279; ☎707-464-6101; www.nps.gov/redw; Hwy 199, Hiouchi; ⏰9am-5pm Apr-Oct, to 4pm Nov-Mar) has hiking maps and nature guides.

Klamath

Giant metal-cast golden bears stand sentry at the bridge across the Klamath River, announcing Klamath, one of the tiny settlements that break up Redwood National & State Parks between Prairie Creek Redwoods State Park and Del Norte Coast Redwoods State Park. With a gas station/market, bar/diner and a casino, Klamath is basically a wide spot in the road with some seriously great roadside kitsch at its edges. The striking **Yurok Country Visitor Center** (☎707-482-1555; www.visityurokcountry.com; 101 Klamath Blvd; 2hr canoe tour $125; ⏰10am-2pm Thu-Fri) is in the town center, featuring cultural displays, crafts and activities, including guided canoe tours along the Klamath River. The Yuroks are the largest group of Native Americans in the state of California and the entire settlement and much of the surrounding area is the tribe's ancestral land.

Klamath is roughly an hour north of Eureka and is popular with hikers, campers and anglers; the river is famed for its wild freshwater salmon.

Sights & Activities

The mouth of the **Klamath River** is a dramatic sight. Marine, riparian, forest and meadow ecological zones all converge, and the birding is exceptional. For the best views, head north of town to Requa Rd and the **Klamath River Overlook** and picnic on high bluffs above driftwood-strewn beaches. This is one of the most spectacular viewpoints on the North Coast, and one of the best whale-watching spots in California. For a hike, head north 3 miles along the Coastal Trail and you'll have the sand to yourself at **Hidden Beach**.

Just south of the river, off Hwy 101, is the scenic **Coastal Drive Loop**, a narrow, winding country road that traces extremely high cliffs over the ocean for six photogenic miles. Sections of the loop are one-way, so do it in a clockwise direction.

Due to erosion, a 3.3-mile section of Coastal Drive south of the loop (between Carruther's

Cove trailhead and the intersection of the Coastal Drive with Alder Camp Rd) has been closed to motor traffic since 2011, but it's still walkable.

Sleeping

Woodsy Klamath is cheaper than Crescent City, but there aren't as many places to eat or buy groceries, and there's nothing to do at night but play cards. There is an overabundance of private RV parks in the area.

Flint Ridge Campground CAMPGROUND
(Map p279; ☎707-465-7335) FREE Four miles from the Klamath River Bridge via Coastal Drive, this tent-only, hike-in campground sits among a wild, overgrown meadow of ferns and moss. It's a quarter-mile walk east, uphill from the parking area. No water, plenty of bear sightings (bear boxes are provided on-site) and you have to pack out trash. Get a permit at the visitor center (p282) in Orick.

Ravenwood Motel MOTEL $
(☎707-482-5911; www.ravenwoodmotel.com; 151 Klamath Blvd; r/ste with kitchen from $65/115;) The spotlessly clean rooms are individually decorated with furnishings and flair you'd expect in a city hotel, not a small-town motel. Add in the loveliest of owners, and you've got the best value in the redwoods!

★ **Historic Requa Inn** HISTORIC HOTEL $$
(Map p279; ☎707-482-1425; www.requainn.com; 451 Requa Rd; r $130-250;) A woodsy country lodge on bluffs overlooking the mouth of the Klamath, the creaky and bright 1914 Requa Inn is a North Coast favorite and – even better – it's a carbon-neutral facility. Many of the charming, old-timey Americana-themed rooms have mesmerizing views over the misty river, as does the dining room, which serves locally sourced, organic New American cuisine.

The dinners are family-style, and served only from April to October, Tuesday through Saturday. Make reservations.

Crescent City

Crescent City is California's last big town north of Arcata. Founded as a thriving seaport and supply center for inland gold mines in the mid-19th century, its history was quite literally washed away in a massive 1964 tsunami. It was rebuilt (though mostly with the utilitarian ugliness of ticky-tacky buildings), Mother Nature struck again in 2011 with a turbo-charged wave that devastated the harbor. All told, some 35 tsunamis have washed in since records began in 1933, which may explain why such a spectacular setting is home to such a humdrum city.

The economy is heavily dependent on shrimp and crab fishing, hotel tax and on Pelican Bay maximum-security prison, just north of town, which adds tension to the air.

Hwy 101 splits into two parallel one-way streets, with the southbound traffic on L St, northbound on M St. To see the major sights, turn west on Front St toward the lighthouse. Downtown is along 3rd St.

Sights

If you're in town in August, the **Del Norte County Fair** features a rodeo, and lots of characters.

Battery Point Lighthouse LIGHTHOUSE
(Map p279; ☎707-464-3089; https://delnortehistory.org; Lighthouse Way; adult/child $5/1; ⏲10am-4pm Apr-Sep, 10am-4pm Sat & Sun Oct-Mar) This New England-style lighthouse dating to 1856 still operates on a tiny, rocky island that you can easily reach at low tide. Walking around outside is free, and with the admission fee you'll get a tour of the on-site museum and tower. Note that the listed hours are subject to change due to tides and weather.

North Coast Marine Mammal Center SCIENCE CENTER
(☎707-465-6265; www.northcoastmmc.org; 424 Howe Dr; ⏲hours vary;) Just east of Battery Point, this is the ecologically minded foil to the garish Ocean World nearby. The clinic treats injured seals and sea lions, then releases them back into the wild. Check the website for seasonally changing hours.

Beachfront Park PARK
(Howe Dr;) Between B and H Sts, this park has a harborside beach with no large waves, making it perfect for little ones. Further east on Front St, near I St, you'll come to **Kidtown**, with slides and swings and a make-believe castle.

Sleeping

Hwy 101 is lined with both chain and indie motels of mixed quality, and you will generally have no problem finding a room, whatever the season. The number of B&Bs here has dwindled. Del Norte County operates three excellent first-come, first-served campgrounds just outside of town.

Curly Redwood Lodge MOTEL $
(707-464-2137; www.curlyredwoodlodge.com; 701 Hwy 101 S; r $60-107;) This motel is a marvel: its paneling came from a single curly redwood tree that measured over 18ft thick in diameter. Progressively restored and polished into a gem of mid-20th-century kitsch, the inn is like stepping into a time capsule and is a delight for retro junkies. Rooms are clean, large and comfortable (request one away from the road).

Florence Keller Park CAMPGROUND $
(Map p279; 707-464-7230; www.co.del-norte.ca.us; 3400 Cunningham Lane; tent & RV sites $20) County-run Florence Keller Park has 50 sites in a beautiful grove of young redwoods (take Hwy 101 north to Elk Valley Cross Rd and follow the signs). There are limited facilities at this campground: toilets, but no showers.

Bay View Inn MOTEL $
(800-742-8439; www.ccbvi.com; 310 Hwy 101 S; r $55-99;) Bright, modern rooms with microwaves and refrigerators fill this centrally located, independent motel. It may seem a bit like a better-than-average highway-exit chain, but colorful bedspreads and warm hosts add homespun appeal. The rooms upstairs in the back have views of the lighthouse and the harbor.

★ **Scopa at the Sea** B&B $$$
(541-944-4156; www.scopaproperties.com; 344 N Pebble Beach Dr; r from $240;) The Cape Cod–style architecture twinned with deluxe contemporary decor make Scopa the best reason to hang around in Crescent City. Furnished in warm earth colors with a design eye for detail, the en suites have tubs, as well as showers, while the front terrace is ideally placed for whale-watching.

Eating

If Crescent City is your introduction to California, fear not: the dining scene gets better from here on south! There are tons of fast-food options, all located on Hwy 101. For fresh seafood, there are a couple of aptly located restaurants near the water.

★ **SeaQuake Brewing** AMERICAN $
(707-465-4444; www.seaquakebrewing.com; 400 Front St; mains $10-17; 11:30am-9pm Tue-Thu, to 10pm Fri & Sat;) Easily the most happening place in town thanks to its inventive pizzas, creative salads and appealing barn-like atmosphere. Oh, and did we mention the 12 taps of home-brewed ales? They're some of the best along the North Coast.

Good Harvest Cafe AMERICAN $
(707-465-6028; 575 Hwy 101 S; mains $8-20; 7:30am-9pm Mon-Sat, from 8am Sun;) This popular family-owned cafe is in a spacious location across from the harbor. It's got a bit of everything – all pretty good – from soups and sandwiches to full meals and smoothies. Fine beers, a crackling fire and loads of vegetarian options make this one of the better dining spots in town.

Enoteca ITALIAN, AMERICAN $
(707-464-2909; www.facebook.com/Enotecarestaurant; 960 3rd St; mains $10-14; 11am-8pm Mon-Thu & Sat, to 10pm Fri;) Is 'cutesy-divey' a design aesthetic? If so, these gals nailed it! Stop in for salads, pasta, sandwiches or jazz on Friday nights.

Chart Room SEAFOOD $$
(707-464-5993; www.ccchartroom.com; 130 Anchor Way; dinner mains $10-30; 7am-7pm Wed-Thu & Sun, to 8pm Fri & Sat, 11am-4pm Tue;) At the tip of the South Harbor pier, this joint is renowned far and wide for its fish and chips: batter-caked golden beauties that deliver on their reputation. It's often a hive of families, retirees, Harley riders and fisherfolk, so grab a beer at the small bar and wait for a table.

Shopping

★ **Rumiano Cheese** CHEESE
(707-465-1535; www.rumianocheese.com; 511 9th St; 9am-5pm Mon-Fri, to 3pm Sat) You'll find the non-GMO cheeses made by this 100-year-old company on the menus of high-end restaurants up and down the California coast. Be sure to stop by its headquarters to sample the signature dry jack and peek through windows into the factory to learn about the cheese-making process.

Information

Crescent City Information Center (Redwood National and State Parks Headquarters; 707-465-7306; www.nps.gov/redw; 1111 2nd St; 9am-5pm Mar-Oct, to 4pm Thu-Mon Nov-Feb) Located on the corner of K St, you'll find information about all four parks under Redwood National and State Parks' jurisdiction, as well as rangers.

Crescent City-Del Norte Chamber of Commerce (☎707-464-3174; www.visitdelnortecounty.com; 1001 Front St; ⏰9am-5pm daily May-Aug, 10am-4pm Tue-Sat Sep-Apr) Situated in a striking wooden building at the entrance to town, offering local information and maps.

Getting There & Around

Tiny Del Norte County Regional Airport (p235), located 3 miles northwest of town, has daily service to Oakland on Contour Airlines (www.contourairlines.com).

Redwood Coast Transit (p235) serves Crescent City with local buses ($1.25), and runs buses Monday to Saturday between Crescent City, Klamath ($2, one hour, five daily) and Arcata ($8, two hours, three daily), with numerous stops along the way. Be sure to carry the exact fare, as the driver carries no change.

Drivers may experience delays on Hwy 101 between Klamath and Crescent City as corrosion continues to affect the highway, particularly after heavy rains.

Tolowa Dunes State Park & Lake Earl Wildlife Area

Two miles north of Crescent City, this **state park and wildlife area** (Map p279; ☎707-464-6101; Kellogg Rd; ⏰sunrise-sunset) encompasses 10,000 acres of wetlands, dunes, meadows and two lakes – **Lake Earl** and **Lake Tolowa**. This major stopover on the Pacific Flyway route attracts more than 250 species of birds. Listen for the whistling, warbling chorus. On land, look for coyotes and deer, angle for trout, or hike or ride 20 miles of trails; at sea, spot whales, seals and sea lions.

This park and wildlife area is a patchwork of lands administered by California State Parks and the California Department of Fish and Wildlife (CDFW). The CDFW focuses on single-species management, hunting and fishing; the State Parks' focus is on ecodiversity and recreation. You might be hiking a vast expanse of pristine dunes, then suddenly hear a shotgun or a whining 4WD. Strict regulations limit where and when you can hunt and drive; trails are clearly marked.

To get here from Crescent City, take Northcrest Dr north off Hwy 101, which becomes Lake Earl Dr. Turn left on Lower Lake Rd to Kellogg Rd, which leads to the park.

TREES OF MYSTERY

It's hard to miss the giant statues of Paul Bunyan and Babe the Blue Ox towering over the parking lot at **Trees of Mystery** (Map p279; ☎707-482-2251; www.treesofmystery.net; 15500 Hwy 101; museum free, gondola adult/child $18/9; ⏰9am-4:30pm; 👪), a shameless tourist trap with a gondola running through the redwood canopy and a fun 'Tall Tales Forest' where chainsaw sculptures tell the tale of Paul Bunyan. It's perfect for families. The surprisingly wonderful **End of the Trail Museum** located behind the gift shop has an outstanding collection of Native American arts and artifacts, and it's free.

Pelican State Beach

The northernmost beach in California and the most northern spot on the California Coastal Trail, never-crowded **Pelican State Beach** (Map p279; ☎707-464-6101; Gilbert Way, Hwy 101) occupies 5 coastal acres just south of the Oregon border. There are no facilities and, due to its easy-to-miss access, this stretch of sand has been described as the loneliest beach in California. It's great for walking, beachcombing and kite-flying; pick one up from the kite specialty shops just over the border in Oregon.

Clifford Kamph Memorial Park CAMPGROUND $
(Map p279; ☎707-464-7237; 15100 Hwy 101; tent sites $20, day use $5) Pitch a tent by the ocean (no windbreaks) at Clifford Kamph Memorial Park. It's a steal for the beachside location and, even though sites are exposed in a grassy area and there isn't much privacy, all have BBQs. It's first-come, first-served. No RVs.

Casa Rubio BOUTIQUE HOTEL $$
(☎541-251-2272; www.casarubio.com; 17285 Crissey Rd; r $108-178; 📶🐾) The best reason to visit Pelican State Beach is to stay at secluded, charming Casa Rubio, where three of the four spacious ocean-view rooms have kitchens. It's surrounded by tropical gardens and a short path leads directly to the beach.

AT A GLANCE

POPULATION
994,750

AREA
7994 sq miles

BEST ROLLER-COASTER
Giant Dipper (p291)

BEST RAINY DAY FUN
Monterey Bay Aquarium (p302)

BEST ECCENTRIC ATTRACTION
Hearst Castle (p323)

WHEN TO GO

Apr–May Wildflowers bloom, temperatures are balmy, and there are fewer tourists than summer.

Jul–Aug Fog disappears as ocean waters warm up for beach season.

Sep–Oct Sunny blue skies, smaller crowds and wine-country harvest festivals.

Bixby Bridge (p317)

Central Coast

Bookended by San Francisco and LA, this stretch of California coast is packed with wild beaches, misty redwood forests and rolling golden hills of fertile vineyards.

Coastal Hwy 1 pulls out all the stops, scenery-wise. Santa Cruz and the historic port town of Monterey are gateways to the rugged and bohemian Big Sur coast. It's an epic journey past vainglorious Hearst Castle, lighthouses and edgy cliffs above which condors soar.

Get acquainted with California's agricultural heartland along inland Hwy 101, named El Camino Real (the King's Highway) by Spanish conquistadors and Franciscan friars. Colonial missions still line the route, which passes through Paso Robles' flourishing wine and craft beer country. Then soothe your nature-loving soul in collegiate San Luis Obispo, ringed by sunny beach towns and volcanic peaks.

INCLUDES

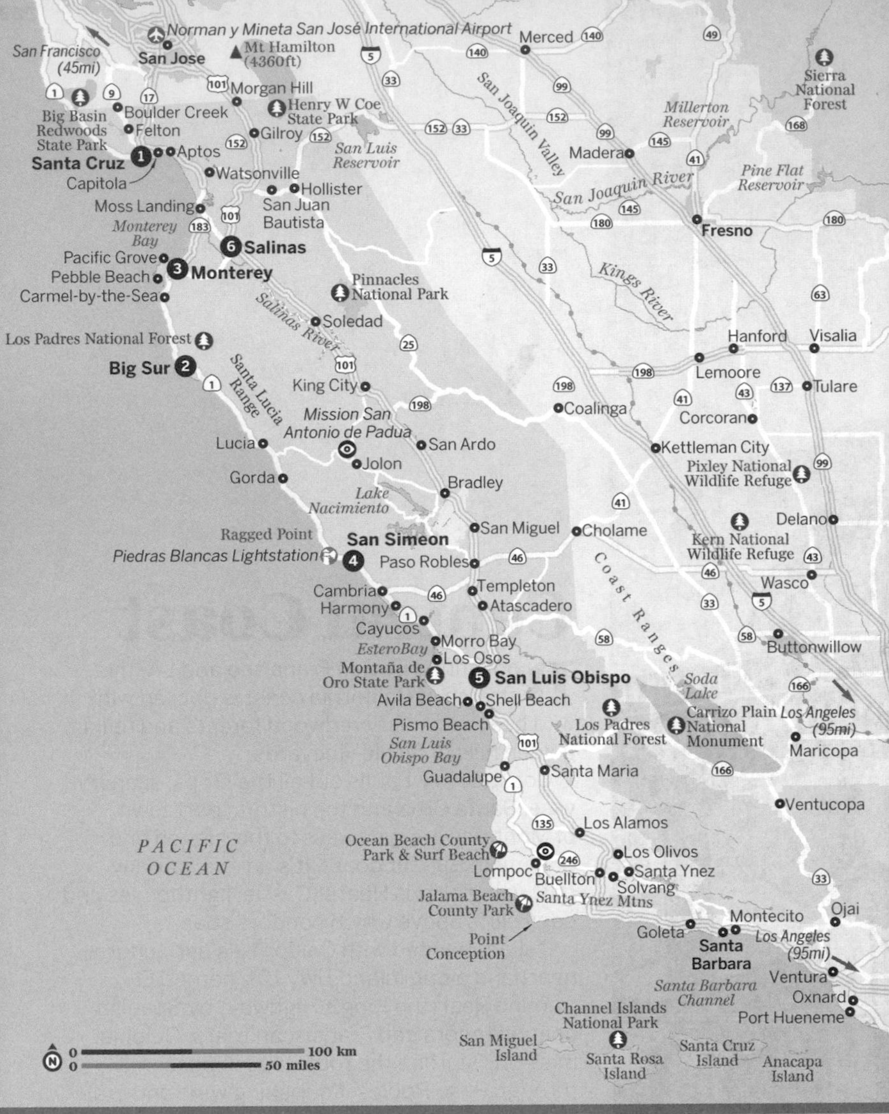

Central Coast Highlights

1 Santa Cruz (p291) Learning to surf, and scaring yourself silly on the Giant Dipper along the famed beach boardwalk.

2 Big Sur (p315) Cruising Hwy 1, where the sky touches the sea along a mystical and rocky coastline.

3 Monterey (p302) Being mesmerized by aquatic denizens of the 'indoor ocean' at the superb kid-friendly aquarium.

4 San Simeon (p322) Marveling at the astonishing grandiosity of Hearst Castle, after meeting the neighbors: ginormous elephant seals.

5 San Luis Obispo (p335) Chilling out in this easygoing college town surrounded by beaches, vineyards and mountains.

6 Salinas (p330) Exploring the blue-collar world of Nobel Prize–winning, down-to-earth novelist John Steinbeck.

ALONG HIGHWAY 1

Anchored by Santa Cruz to the north and Monterey to the south, Monterey Bay teems with richly varied marine life. Its half-moon shore is bordered by wild beaches and seaside towns that are full of character. On the 125-mile stretch south of the Monterey Peninsula, you'll snake along the jaw-dropping Big Sur coast and past Hearst Castle until Hwy 1 joins Hwy 101 in San Luis Obispo.

Santa Cruz

Santa Cruz has marched to its own beat since long before the Beat Generation of the 1950s and '60s. This is counterculture central, a new Agey city famous for its leftie-liberal politics, easygoing ideology, and a thoroughly relaxed downtown area. It's still cool to be a hippie or a stoner here, although some of the far-out-looking freaks may just be slumming trust-fund babies. With Silicon Valley a 45-minute drive away through the Santa Cruz Mountains, it's also becoming popular as a place of residence for all sorts of tech types.

Santa Cruz is a city of madcap fun, with a vibrant, chaotic downtown. On the waterfront is the famous beach boardwalk, and in the hills redwood groves embrace the University of California, Santa Cruz (UCSC) campus. Plan at least half a day here, but to appreciate the aesthetic of jangly skirts, crystal pendants and cool coffee shops, stay longer and plunge headlong into the rich local brew of surfers, students, punks and eccentric characters.

Sights

One of the best things to do in Santa Cruz is simply stroll, shop and watch the sideshow along **Pacific Avenue** downtown, a 15-minute walk from the beach and the Santa Cruz Wharf. Ocean-view **West Cliff Drive** follows the waterfront southwest of the wharf, paralleled by a paved recreational path.

★Seymour Marine Discovery Center — MUSEUM

(Map p300; ☎831-459-3800; http://seymourcenter.ucsc.edu; 100 McAllister Way; adult/child 3-16yr $9/7; ⏲10am-5pm Tue-Sun Sep-Jun, daily Jul & Aug; P 👪) This educational center is part of UCSC's Long Marine Laboratory. Interactive natural-science exhibits include tidal touch pools and aquariums, while outside you can gawk at the world's largest blue-whale skeleton.

Guided 45-minute tours run at 1pm, 2pm and 3pm (free with admission; first come, first served) and teach you about the research taking place at the lab. There's also a 30-minute family tour at 11am.

★Santa Cruz Beach Boardwalk — AMUSEMENT PARK

(Map p292; ☎831-423-5590; www.beachboardwalk.com; 400 Beach St; boardwalk free, per ride $4-7, all-day pass $40-50; ⏲daily late May-Aug, most weekends Sep-Apr, weather permitting; P 👪) The West Coast's oldest beachfront amusement park, this 1907 boardwalk has a glorious old-school Americana vibe. The smell of cotton candy mixes with the salt air, which is punctuated by the squeals of kids hanging upside down on carnival rides. Famous thrills include the **Giant Dipper**, a 1924 wooden roller coaster, and the 1911 **Looff carousel**, both National Historic Landmarks. During summer, catch free movies on Wednesdays, and Friday-night concerts by rock veterans you may have thought were already dead.

All-day parking costs $15 on weekdays and $20 on weekends.

Santa Cruz Wharf — LANDMARK

(Map p292; www.santacruzwharf.com) Seafood restaurants, gift shops and barking sea lions all compete for attention along Santa Cruz' wharf, the longest wooden wharf in the US.

University of California, Santa Cruz — UNIVERSITY

(UCSC; Map p300; www.ucsc.edu; P 👪) Check it out: the school mascot is a banana slug! Established in 1965 in the hills above town, UCSC is known for its creative, liberal bent. The rural campus has fine stands of redwoods and architecturally interesting buildings – some made with recycled materials – designed to blend in with rolling pastureland. Amble around the peaceful **arboretum** (Map p300; ☎831-502-2998; www.arboretum.ucsc.edu; cnr High St & Arboretum Rd; adult/child 6-17yr $5/2, 1st Tue of month free; ⏲9am-5pm) and picturesquely decaying 19th-century structures from Cowell Ranch, upon which the campus was built.

Museum of Art & History — MUSEUM

(MAH; Map p292; ☎831-429-1964; www.santacruzmah.org; McPherson Center, 705 Front St; adult/child 12-17yr $10/8, 1st Fri of each month free; ⏲10am-6pm Sun-Thu, to 8pm Fri, to 3pm Sat; 👪) In Santa Cruz' downtown, regular special exhibitions combine with excellent permanent displays on the city's history and culture.

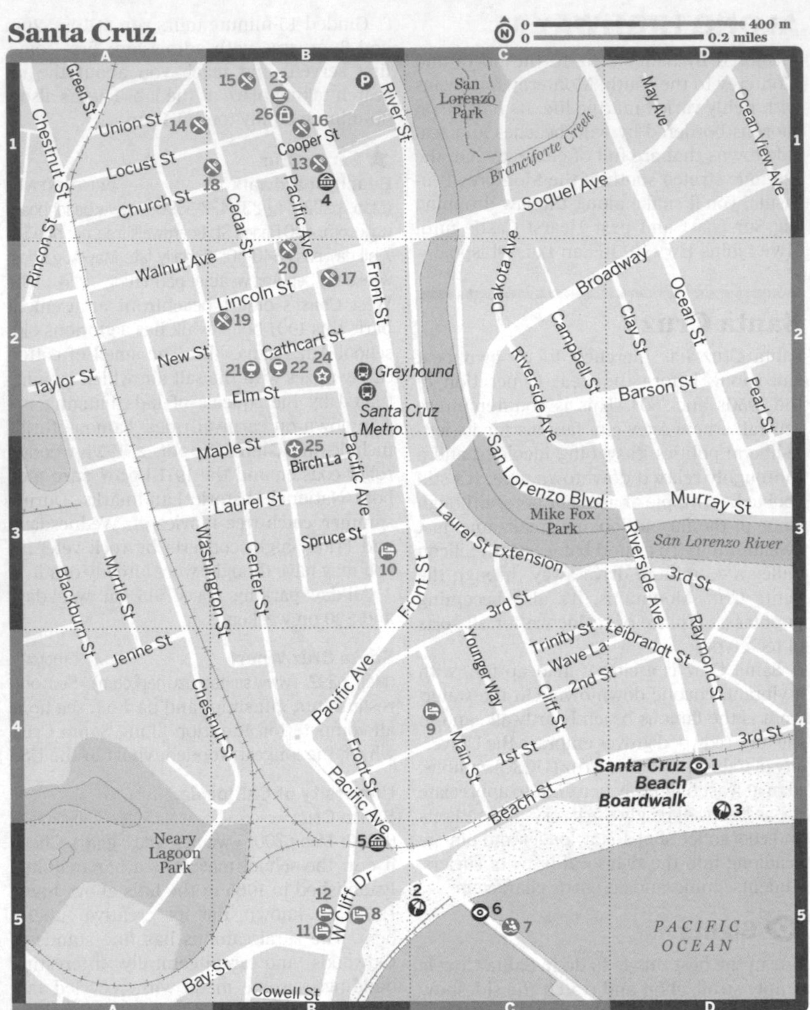

Interesting one-off exhibitions have included the history of both skateboarding and tattooing in the city, and adjacent to the museum is an excellent food market (p296) with bars and cafes. Check the museum's website for details of craft markets and live music events held in adjacent Abbott Sq.

Sanctuary Exploration Center MUSEUM
(Map p292; ☎831-421-9993; www.montereybay.noaa.gov; 35 Pacific Ave; ⏲10am-5pm Wed-Sun; P 🚻) FREE Operated by the Monterey Bay National Marine Sanctuary, this educational museum near the beach boardwalk is an interactive multimedia experience that teaches kids and adults about the bay's marine treasures, watershed conservation and high-tech underwater exploration for scientific research.

Santa Cruz Surfing Museum MUSEUM
(Map p300; ☎831-420-6289; 701 W Cliff Dr; entry by donation; ⏲10am-5pm Thu-Tue Jul 4-early Sep, noon-4pm Thu-Mon early Sep-Jul 3; P 🚻) A mile southwest of the wharf along the coast, this tiny museum inside an old lighthouse is packed with memorabilia, including vintage redwood surfboards. Fittingly, its location on Lighthouse Point overlooks two popular surf breaks.

Santa Cruz

Mystery Spot LANDMARK
(831-423-8897; www.mysteryspot.com; 465 Mystery Spot Rd; $8; 10am-4pm Mon-Fri, to 5pm Sat & Sun; P) A kitschy, old-fashioned tourist trap, Santa Cruz' Mystery Spot has scarcely changed since it opened in 1940. On a steeply sloping hillside, compasses seem to point crazily, mysterious forces push you around and buildings lean at silly angles. Book ahead online or risk not getting on a tour, and note it's cash only for walk-ins. It's about 4 miles northeast of downtown: take Water St to Market St north and continue on Branciforte Dr into the hills. Parking costs $5.

Santa Cruz Museum of Natural History MUSEUM
(Map p300; 831-420-6115; www.santacruzmuseum.org; 1305 E Cliff Dr; adult/child under 18yr $4/free,1st Fri of each month free; 11am-4pm Tue-Fri & 10am-5pm Sat & Sun; P) The collections at this pint-sized museum include stuffed-animal mounts, Native California cultural artifacts and a touch-friendly tide pool that shows off sea critters living by the beach right across the street. Look for the sculpture of a gray whale and you're in the right place.

Activities

★**Santa Cruz Food Tour** FOOD
(866-736-6343; www.santacruzfoodtour.com; per person $69; 2:25-6pm Fri & Sun Apr-Oct) These congenial walking tours are the perfect way to plug into Santa Cruz' progressive, global and sophisticated food scene. Guides also deliver a healthy serving of local knowledge and interesting insights into Santa Cruz history, culture and architecture. You'll be walking for about 2 miles and will eat enough for most people not to need dinner afterwards.

Vegetarians and gluten-free foodies can be accommodated. A second tour through Capitola runs Wednesdays from 2pm to 5pm.

Slow Adventure WALKING
(831-332-7923; www.slowadventure.us; per person $1495; Mar-Oct) Well-traveled Santa Cruz local Marle Henley arranges self-guided walking adventures around Monterey Bay. The full itinerary from Santa Cruz to Monterey takes six days and five nights, covering from 44 miles in total by walking mainly on beaches, and overnighting in comfortable ocean-view accommodations en route. Luggage is transferred independently, and highlights include birdlife, marine mammals and superb coastal views.

Shorter four-day/three-night coastal adventures to the north and south of Santa Cruz are also available (per person $995 to $1095).

DeLaveaga Disc Golf Club SPORTS
(Map p300; www.facebook.com/groups/DelaDDGC; Upper Park Rd;) FREE Touring pros and families with kids toss discs across this challenging hillside layout that peaks at Hole No 27, nicknamed 'Top of the World.' It's a couple of miles northeast of downtown Santa Cruz, off Branciforte Dr. Bring along your own disc.

DON'T MISS

TOP SANTA CRUZ BEACHES

Sun-kissed Santa Cruz has warmer beaches than San Francisco or Monterey. *Baywatch* it isn't, but 29 miles of coastline reveal a few Hawaii-worthy beaches, craggy coves, some primo surf spots and long, sandy stretches where kids will have a blast. Fog may ruin many a summer morning; it often burns off by the afternoon.

W Cliff Dr is lined with scramble-down-to coves and plentiful parking. If you don't want sand in your shoes, park yourself on a bench and watch enormous pelicans dive for fish. You'll find bathrooms and showers at the lighthouse parking lot opposite the Santa Cruz Surfing Museum.

Locals favor less-trampled E Cliff Dr beaches, which are bigger and more protected from the wind, meaning calmer waters. Except at a small metered lot at 26th Ave, parking is by permit only on weekends (buy an $8 per-day permit at 9th Ave).

Main Beach (Map p292;) This is *the* scene in Santa Cruz, with a huge sandy stretch, volleyball courts and swarms of people. Park on E Cliff Dr and walk across the *Lost Boys* trestle to the beach boardwalk (p291).

Its Beach (Map p300;) The only official off-leash beach for dogs (before 10am and after 4pm) in Santa Cruz is just west of the lighthouse. The field across the street is another good romping ground.

Natural Bridges State Beach (Map p300; 831-423-4609; www.parks.ca.gov; 2531 W Cliff Dr; day use per car $10; beach 8am-sunset, visitor center 10am-4pm;) Great for sunsets, this sandy beach fronted by a natural sandstone bridge is a family favorite and tops for wildlife viewing. Scan the bay for whales, seals and otters or, at low tide, comb tide pools for sea stars and sea anemones. Shorebirds patrol the skies, while monarch butterflies make the park their winter home, usually arriving mid-October and leaving in late January.

Seacliff State Beach (831-685-6442; www.parks.ca.gov; State Park Rd, Aptos; per car $10; 8am-sunset) Seacliff State Beach harbors a 'cement boat,' a quixotic freighter built of concrete that floated OK, but ended up here as a coastal fishing pier. During huge storms in February 2017, the boat actually broke apart but remains *in situ*.

Manresa State Beach (831-724-3750; www.parks.ca.gov; San Andreas Rd, Watsonville; per car $10; 8am-sunset) Near Watsonville, the La Selva Beach exit off Hwy 1 leads to this sparsely populated beach.

Moran Lake County Park (Map p300; E Cliff Dr; 8am-sunset) With a good surf break and bathrooms, this pretty all-around sandy spot is further east of 26th Ave off E Cliff Dr.

Cowell's Beach (Map p292) Popular Santa Cruz surfing beach off W Cliff Dr.

Sunset State Beach (831-763-7062; www.parks.ca.gov; San Andreas Rd, Watsonville; per car $10; 8am-sunset) The La Selva Beach exit off Hwy 1, near Watsonville, brings you here, where you can have miles of sand and surf almost to yourself.

SUP Shack WATER SPORTS
(Map p300; 831-464-7467; www.supshacksantacruz.com; 2214 E Cliff Dr; rental/lessons from $25/40; from 9am, last rental 3pm;) Based in the calm waters of Santa Cruz Harbor, SUP Shack offers stand-up paddleboarding (SUP) lessons and rentals. Kayaks and bodyboards are also available for rental.

Surfing

Year-round, water temperatures average under 60°F (16°C), meaning that without a wetsuit, body parts quickly turn blue. Surfing is incredibly popular, especially at experts-only **Steamer Lane** and beginners' Cowell's, both off W Cliff Dr. Other favorite surf spots include **Pleasure Point Beach**, on E Cliff Dr toward Capitola, and Manresa State Beach off Hwy 1 southbound.

O'Neill Surf Shop SURFING
(Map p300; 831-475-4151; www.oneill.com; 1115 41st Ave, Capitola; wetsuit/surfboard rental from $20/30; 9am-8pm Mon-Fri, from 8am Sat & Sun) About 4 miles east of downtown Santa Cruz in Capitola, this is one of several local outposts of the iconic surfboard brand that also sells cool fashion and accessories, and

rents boards. Other branches are on Pacific Ave and on Beach St in central Santa Cruz.

Richard Schmidt Surf School SURFING
(Map p300; ☎831-423-0928; www.richardschmidt.com; 849 Almar Ave; lessons 2hr group/1hr private $100/130;) This award-winning, time-tested surf and SUP school can get you out and up on the frigid waters of Monterey Bay, wetsuit and equipment included. Group lessons have one instructor for every four students. Lessons take place either at Cowell's Beach or at Pleasure Point in Capitola.

Summer surf camps hook adults and kids alike.

Kayaking

Kayaking lets you discover the craggy coastline and kelp beds where sea otters float.

Kayak Connection KAYAKING
(Map p300; ☎831-479-1121; www.kayakconnection.com; Santa Cruz Harbor, 413 Lake Ave; kayak rental/tour from $40/60; ⊙10am-5pm Mon, Wed & Fri, 9am-5pm Sat & Sun;) This outfit rents kayaks and offers lessons and tours, including whale-watching, sunrise, sunset and full moon trips. It also rents SUP sets (from $40), wetsuits ($10) and boogie boards ($10).

Venture Quest KAYAKING
(Map p292; ☎831-425-8445, 831-427-2267; www.kayaksantacruz.com; Santa Cruz Wharf; kayak rental/tour from $35/60; ⊙10am-7pm Mon-Fri, from 9am Sat & Sun late May-late Sep, hours vary late Sep–mid-May;) Offers convenient rentals on the wharf, plus whale watching and coastal sea-cave tours, moonlight paddles and kayak-sailing trips. Book ahead for kayak-surfing lessons. Booking rental kayaks and tours one day ahead is recommended during summer and on holiday weekends.

Whale-Watching & Fishing

Winter whale-watching trips run from December through April, though there's plenty of marine life to see on a summer bay cruise.

Many fishing trips depart from Santa Cruz' wharf, where a few shops rent fishing tackle and poles if you're keen to join locals waiting patiently for a bite.

Stagnaro's BOATING
(Map p300; ☎info 831-427-0230, reservations 888-237-7084; www.stagnaros.com; 1718 Brommer St; adult/child under 14yr cruise from $20/13, whale-watching tour from $51/36) This long-standing tour operator offers scenic and sunset cruises around Monterey Bay during spring and summer, and whale-watching tours year-round.

Festivals & Events

Woodies on the Wharf CULTURAL
(www.santacruzwoodies.com; ⊙late June) Classic-car show featuring vintage surf-style station wagons on Santa Cruz Wharf (p291).

First Friday Santa Cruz ART
(www.firstfridaysantacruz.com; ⊙1st Fri of month) The Arts Council Santa Cruz County sponsors 'First Friday' art exhibitions on the initial Friday of each month. Venues and galleries around the wider Santa Cruz region that open for the event include artists' ateliers at the heritage Tannery Arts Center located just north of downtown. Check the website to see what's scheduled.

Also involved with 'First Friday,' the Museum of Art & History (p291) offers live music in adjacent Abbott Sq on the same dates.

Sleeping

Santa Cruz does not have enough beds to satisfy demand: expect high prices at peak times for nothing-special rooms. Places near the beach boardwalk (p291) range from friendly to frightening. For a decent motel, consider Ocean St inland or Mission St (Hwy 1).

HI Santa Cruz Hostel HOSTEL $
(Map p292; ☎831-423-8304; www.santacruzhostel.com; 321 Main St; dm $36-40, r with shared bath $79-169; ⊙office 8-10am & 4-10pm;) Budget overnighters dig this cute hostel set inside five rambling Victorian cottages and surrounded by flowering gardens, just two blocks from the beach. Whip up meals in the communal kitchen or watch a movie in the funky furnished lounge with fireplace. There's one downside: the midnight curfew.

Non-Hostelling International members pay a daily surcharge of $3.

California State Park Campgrounds CAMPGROUND $
(☎800-444-7275; www.reservecalifornia.com; tent/RV sites $35/65; P) Book well ahead to camp at state beaches off Hwy 1 south of Santa Cruz or up in the foggy Santa Cruz Mountains off Hwy 9. Family-friendly campgrounds include Henry Cowell Redwoods State Park in Felton and New Brighton State Beach in Capitola.

Seaway Inn MOTEL $$
(Map p292; ☎831-471-9004; www.seawayinn.com; 176 W Cliff Dr; r $169-239; P) Goodvalue and welcoming accommodations just a short

walk uphill from Santa Cruz Wharf (p291). Try and stay on a weekday as prices surge on weekends.

Hotel Paradox HOTEL **$$**
(Map p300; ☎831-425-7100; www.thehotelparadox.com; 611 Ocean St; r from $227; P@🛜≋) This downtown boutique hotel brings the great outdoors inside, with nature prints on the walls, textured wood panels and earth-toned furnishings. Relax in a cabana by the pool or next to an outdoor fire pit. Weekday rates can be reasonable, but summer weekends are ridiculously high-priced. Parking is $10.

Mission Inn MOTEL **$$**
(Map p300; ☎831-425-5455; www.mission-inn.com; 2250 Mission St; r $129-199; P❄🛜) Perfectly serviceable two-story motel with a garden courtyard, hot tub and complimentary continental breakfast. It's on busy Hwy 1 near the UCSC campus (p291), away from the beach.

Pacific Blue Inn B&B **$$$**
(Map p292; ☎831-600-8880; www.pacificblueinn.com; 636 Pacific Ave; r $229-285; P🚭🛜🐾) 🌿 This downtown courtyard B&B is an eco-conscious gem, with water-saving fixtures and renewable and recycled building materials. Refreshingly elemental rooms have pillowtop beds, electric fireplaces and flat-screen TVs with DVD players.

Free parking and loaner bikes. Pet fee $50.

Babbling Brook Inn B&B **$$$**
(Map p300; ☎831-427-2437; www.babblingbrookinn.com; 1025 Laurel St; r $290-370; 🚭🛜) Built around a running creek amid meandering gardens and old pine and redwood trees, this wood-shingled inn has 13 cozy rooms named after impressionist painters and decorated in French-provincial style. Most have gas fireplaces, some have Jacuzzis and all have feather beds. There's afternoon wine and hors d'oeuvres, plus a full breakfast included.

Dream Inn HOTEL **$$$**
(Map p292; ☎831-740-8069; www.dreaminnsantacruz.com; 175 W Cliff Dr; r $250-576; P🚭❄@🛜≋) Proud of being Santa Cruz' only oceanfront hotel, the Dream Inn has good-sized rooms brimming with retro-chic charm and turquoise color accents. Catch hypnotic bay views from private balconies. The sleek swimming pool, fronted by sandy Cowell's Beach, is just steps away.

West Cliff Inn INN **$$$**
(Map p292; ☎831-457-2200; www.westcliffinn.com; 174 W Cliff Dr; r $205-375; P🛜) In a classy Victorian house west of the wharf (p291), this boutique inn's quaint rooms mix seagrass wicker, dark wood and jaunty striped curtains. The most romantic suites have gas fireplaces and let you spy on the breaking surf. Rates include a breakfast buffet and afternoon wine, tea and snacks.

Eating

There's some delicious dining to be done in Santa Cruz, which has seriously upped the kitchen ante in recent years. Seafood features prominently on menus, many of which are also driven by the regional-seasonal-organic trifecta. Pacific Ave in downtown has some excellent midrange to upscale options, while Mission St near UCSC, Soquel Ave east of downtown and 41st Ave in Capitola all offer cheaper eats.

★**Santa Cruz Farmers Market** MARKET **$**
(Map p292; ☎831-454-0566; www.santacruzfarmersmarket.org; cnr Lincoln & Center Sts; ⏲1-6pm Wed Apr-Oct, to 5pm Nov-Mar; 🌱👪) 🌿 Organic produce, baked goods, as well as arts-and-crafts and food booths, all give you an authentic taste of the local vibe. Shorter fall and winter hours.

Abbott Square Market FOOD HALL **$**
(Map p292; www.abbottsquaremarket.com; 725 Front St; mains $8-15; ⏲7am–10pm Sun-Thu, to midnight Fri & Sat; 🌱👪) 🌿 This multi-cuisine food market includes outlets selling pizza, sushi, Tex-Mex flavors and organic, plant-based dishes. Factor in good coffee, freshly baked pastries and a couple of after-dark bars and the Abbott Square Market is one of the city's most versatile, all-day spots. Check the website for events including live music in adjacent Abbott Sq on Friday and Saturday nights.

Penny Ice Creamery ICE CREAM **$**
(Map p292; ☎831-204-2523; www.thepennyicecreamery.com; 913 Cedar St; snacks $5-7; ⏲noon-11pm; 👪) 🌿 With a cult following, this artisan ice-cream shop crafts zany flavors such as bourbon-candied ginger, lemon-verbena blueberry and ricotta apricot all from scratch using local, organic and wild-harvested ingredients. Even plain old vanilla is special.

New Leaf Community Market SUPERMARKET **$**
(Map p292; ☎831-425-1793; www.newleaf.com; 1134 Pacific Ave; ⏲8am-9pm; 🌱) 🌿 Sells organic and local produce, natural-foods groceries and deli takeout meals in the middle of downtown Santa Cruz. Salads and sandwiches are a good option for picnics and

self-catering, and there's a very good selection of wine and beer.

★**Bad Animal** BISTRO $$

(Map p292; ☎831-900-5031; www.badanimalbooks.com; 101 Cedar St; shared plates & mains $12-23; ⏰5-10pm Wed-Sat, 11am-2pm & 5-9pm Sun; ✎) A thoroughly modern menu – including contemporary interpretations of French flavors and natural and organic wines – complements this brilliant bookshop showcasing Santa Cruz' bohemian and counter-culture roots. Try the mussel cassoulet or yuzu-tinged steak tartare for dinner, or enjoy a leisurely Sunday brunch with the duck hash.

★**Barceloneta** TAPAS $$

(Map p292; ☎831-900-5222; www.eatbarceloneta.com; 1541 Pacific Ave; shared dishes $9-21; ⏰5-10pm Wed-Mon) Spanish-style shared plates and beverages including cider, sherry and cocktails create a convivial atmosphere at Barceloneta. Highlights include grilled Monterey squid with chorizo and aioli, and smoke-infused pork spare ribs with a sticky harissa- and honey-laced sauce. Robust servings of paella are ideal for couples and groups, while ham and cheese platters are a good option for a lighter snack.

Bantam CALIFORNIAN, ITALIAN $$

(Map p300; ☎831-420-0101; www.bantam1010.com; 1010 Fair Ave; shared plates $12-26, pizza $12-22; ⏰5-9pm Mon-Thu, to 9:30pm Fri & Sat; ✎) Another excellent option amid the emerging dining scene in Santa Cruz' West End, Bantam's versatile space is often packed with SC locals enjoying wood-fired pizza, a savvy cocktail, the wine and craft-beer list, and moreish shared plates including squid, meatballs and pork belly. No reservations, but the informal and easygoing ambience means tables are turned over fairly promptly.

Laili AFGHANI $$

(Map p292; ☎831-423-4545; www.lailirestaurant.com; 101b Cooper St; mains $15-29; ⏰11:30am-2:30pm & 5-9pm Tue-Sun; ✎) A chic downtown dining oasis, family-owned Laili invites diners in with an elegant high-ceilinged dining room and garden patio. Share apricot-chicken flatbread, tart pomegranate eggplant, roasted cauliflower with saffron, succulent lamb kebabs and more. Reservations advised.

Engfer Pizza Works PIZZA $$

(Map p300; ☎831-429-1856; www.engferpizzaworks.com; 537 Seabright Ave; pizzas $11-27; ⏰4-9:30pm Tue-Sun; ✎) Detour to this old factory, where wood-fired-oven pizzas are made from scratch with love – the No Name is like a giant salad on roasted bread while the Lift Truck is a carnivore's dream. Play Ping-Pong and down local craft beers while you wait. There's also a good selection of takeout beers and desserts if you're dining off-site.

Soif CALIFORNIAN $$$

(Map p292; ☎831-423-2020; www.soifwine.com; 105 Walnut Ave; mains $26-35; ⏰5-9pm Sun-Thu, to 10pm Fri & Sat; ✎) A perennial local foodie fave, this chic and cosmopolitan lair harnesses mostly local products and turns them into triumphs of flavor pairings. Combinations could include black cod with a dashi broth or duck with a citrus-ginger gastrique. There's a perfect wine match for each dish and Soif's cocktails are also highly regarded.

Drinking & Nightlife

Santa Cruz' downtown overflows with bars, lounges and coffee shops. Heading west on Mission St (Hwy 1), craft breweries and wine-tasting rooms fill the raffish industrial ambience of the Swift and Ingalls St Courtyards.

★**Lupulo Craft Beer House** CRAFT BEER

(Map p292; ☎831-454-8306; www.lupulosc.com; 233 Cathcart St; ⏰11:30am-10pm Mon-Thu, to 11:30pm Fri & Sat, to 10pm Sun) Named after the Spanish word for hops, Lupulo Craft Beer House is an essential downtown destination for beer fans. Modern decor combines with an ever-changing tap list – often including hard-to-get seasonal brews from local breweries – and good bar snacks ($4 to $15) such as empanadas, tacos and charcuterie plates. Almost 400 bottled and canned beers create delicious panic for the indecisive drinker.

515 COCKTAIL BAR

(Map p292; ☎831-425-5051; www.515santacruz.com; 515 Cedar St; ⏰5pm-midnight Sun-Tue, to 1:30am Wed-Sat) This locally beloved cocktail parlor is the perfect place for a night of dapper drinking. Settle into a huge armchair amid the vintage-chic decor to celebrate classic and masterfully concocted libations. Le Pamplemousse, a delicious blend of vodka, Aperol and citrus, is a perennial favorite. Happy hour runs until 7pm and food is served until midnight. Reservations advised.

Verve Coffee Roasters CAFE

(Map p292; ☎831-600-7784; www.vervecoffee.com; 1540 Pacific Ave; ⏰6:30am-9pm; 📶) To sip

LOCAL KNOWLEDGE

TOP SANTA CRUZ BREWERIES & TAPROOMS

Sante Adairius Rustic Ales (Map p300; ☎831-462-1227; www.rusticales.com; 103 Kennedy Dr, Capitola; ⊙3-8pm Tue-Thu, from 1pm Fri-Sun; 🐕) This brewer is located off Hwy 1 in Capitola, around 7 miles east of Santa Cruz; its Belgian-inspired and barrel-aged beers are a beer geek's dream. There's also another **Sante Adairius** (Map p300; www.rusticales.com; 1315 Water St; ⊙noon-9pm Sun-Thu, to 10pm Fri & Sat; 🐕) taproom closer to downtown Santa Cruz on Water St. Try the excellent farmhouse ales.

Discretion Brewing (Map p300; ☎831-316-0662; www.discretionbrewing.com; 2703 41st Ave, Soquel; ⊙11:30am-9pm; 🐕) Spicy rye beers, English ales and traditional Belgian and German brews are always on tap just off Hwy 1. The raffish beer garden is dog-friendly, and foodie highlights from the on-site Kitchen at Discretion include house-cured trout sandwiches, tamarind-glazed pork ribs, and cheese and charcuterie platters. The hoppy highlight of our last visit was the Hi Citra! IPA.

Humble Sea Brewing Company (Map p300; ☎831-2431-6189; www.humblesea.com; 820 Swift St; ⊙noon-9pm Mon-Fri, 11am-8:30pm Sat, 11am-8pm Sun; 🐕) Humble Sea's hip nautical-themed taproom is a top spot to try some of the best hazy IPAs in the Santa Cruz region. Its Socks & Sandals brew is often found at local restaurants, but the full Humble Sea experience is only attained by sampling from the bar's 10 taps. Enjoy light snacks including shrimp tacos on the sunny outdoor terrace.

Santa Cruz Mountain Brewing (Map p300; ☎831-425-4900; www.scmbrew.com; 402 Ingalls St, Ingalls St Courtyard; ⊙11:30am-10pm Mon-Fri, 11am-10pm Sat & Sun; 🐕) Part of the eating and drinking scene in the Ingalls St Courtyard on Santa Cruz' Westside, Santa Cruz Mountain Brewing is a rustic spot to combine brews and a burger. Crowd into the compact tasting room or share an outside table with friendly locals and their well-behaved canine pals. Our favorite beer is the robust Truth or Dare stout.

finely roasted artisan espresso or a cup of rich pour-over coffee, join the surfers and hipsters at this high-ceilinged industrial-zen cafe. Single-origin brews and house blends rule. The mod design is a study of how to get creative with wood, and the avocado toast is a good way to kick-start the day.

Front & Cooper COCKTAIL BAR

(Map p292; www.frontandcooper.com; 725 Front St, Abbott Square Market; ⊙11am-10pm Sun-Thu, to midnight Fri & Sat) With a luxury, heritage vibe, and perhaps Santa Cruz' longest and most spectacular bar, Front & Cooper delivers on its promise of offering the city's best craft cocktails. The beer and wine lists are equally interesting, usually showcasing local brews and California varietals, and it's possible to bring in snacks and dishes from nearby food outlets in Abbott Square Market.

West End Tap & Kitchen CRAFT BEER

(Map p300; ☎831-471-8115; www.westendtap.com; 334d Ingalls St, Ingalls St Courtyard; ⊙11:30am-9:30pm Sun-Thu, to 10pm Fri & Sat) A high flyer amid the brewpubs, cafes and wine-tasting rooms in the Ingalls St Courtyard, West End Tap & Kitchen combines local Santa Cruz beers with a full menu including Mediterranean-style flatbreads and hearty steaks, pasta and burgers. Standout brews include the Double Dank Vision Double IPA from Hermitage Brewing in San Jose, and there's also a good wine list.

☆ Entertainment

Free tabloid *Good Times* (http://goodtimes.sc) covers the music, arts and nightlife scenes in Santa Cruz.

Kuumbwa Jazz Center JAZZ

(Map p292; ☎831-427-2227; www.kuumbwajazz.org; 320 Cedar St; admission varies by gig) Hosting jazz luminaries since 1975, this nonprofit theater is for serious jazz cats snapping their fingers for famous-name performers in an electrically intimate room.

Moe's Alley LIVE MUSIC

(Map p300; ☎831-479-1854; www.moesalley.com; 1535 Commercial Way; admission varies by gig) In a way-out industrial wasteland, this joint puts on live sounds almost every night: jazz, blues, reggae, roots, salsa and acoustic jams.

Catalyst LIVE MUSIC

(Map p292; ☎831-423-1338; www.catalystclub.com; 1011 Pacific Ave; admission varies by gig) Over the years, this stage for local bands has seen big-time national acts perform, from Queens of the Stone Age to Snoop Dogg, Pussy Riot and George Clinton's Parliament Funkadelic. Expect loads of energy and attitude, and look forward to gigs ranging from classic reggae acts to blues, alt country and Americana concerts.

Shopping

Stroll Pacific Ave and downtown side streets to find Santa Cruz' one-of-a-kind, locally owned boutiques. For vintage clothing and surf shops, amble 41st Ave around Portola Dr.

Bookshop Santa Cruz BOOKS
(Map p292; ☎831-423-0900; www.bookshopsantacruz.com; 1520 Pacific Ave; ⏰9am-10pm Sun-Thu, to 11pm Fri & Sat) Vast selection of new books, a few used ones, popular and unusual magazines, and 'Keep Santa Cruz Weird' bumper stickers. Check the website for regular readings, book launches and author events.

Donnelly Fine Chocolates FOOD
(Map p300; ☎831-458-4214; www.donnellychocolates.com; 1509 Mission St; ⏰10:30am-6pm Tue-Fri, from noon Sat & Sun) The Willy Wonka of Santa Cruz makes stratospherically priced chocolates on par with the big city. Try the cardamom or chipotle truffles – pricey, but worth it. The chocolate- and nut-covered ice-cream bars are pretty damn good too.

Information

Public Library (☎831-427-7707; www.santacruzpl.org; 224 Church St; ⏰10am-8pm Mon-Thu, 10am-5pm Fri & Sat, 1-5pm Sun; 📶) Free wi-fi and public internet terminals.

Santa Cruz Post Office (Map p300; ☎800-275-8777; www.usps.com; 850 Front St; ⏰9am-5pm Mon-Fri)

Santa Cruz Visitor Center (Map p300; ☎831-425-1234; www.santacruz.org; 303 Water St, Suite 100; ⏰9am-noon & 1-4pm Mon-Fri, 11am-3pm Sat & Sun) Maps and brochures.

Getting There & Around

Greyhound (Map p292; ☎831-423-4082; www.greyhound.com; 920 Pacific Ave; 📶) Greyhound runs several buses daily to San Francisco (from $16, 3½ hours), Salinas (from $12, one hour), Santa Barbara from ($39, 5½ hours), Los Angeles (from $22, nine hours) and other destinations.

Santa Cruz Shuttles (☎831-421-9883; www.santacruzshuttles.com) This locally owned outfit runs shared shuttles to/from the airports at San Jose ($55), San Francisco ($85) and Oakland ($85). Additional passengers traveling with you pay just $10 each and there's a $25 surcharge for trips originating before 7am and after 10pm.

Santa Cruz Metro (Map p292; ☎831-425-8600; www.facebook.com/SantaCruzMETRO; 920 Pacific Ave; single rides/day pass $2/6) Local and countywide bus routes converge on downtown's Metro Center. Destinations include San Jose, Capitola and Watsonville.

Around Santa Cruz

Santa Cruz Mountains

Winding between Santa Cruz and Silicon Valley, Hwy 9 is a 40-mile backwoods byway through the Santa Cruz Mountains, passing tiny towns, towering redwood forests and fog-kissed vineyards. The **Santa Cruz Mountains Winegrowers Association** (www.scmwa.com) publishes a free winery map, available at tasting rooms, including those that have opened more convenient tasting rooms in Santa Cruz.

Heading north from Santa Cruz, it's 7 miles to **Felton**, where there is forest ziplining excitement with **Mt Hermon Adventures** (☎831-430-4357; www.mounthermonadventures.com; 17 Conference Dr, Felton; zipline from $99, canopy walkway $75) and also hiking in the **Henry Cowell Redwoods State Park** (☎info 831-335-4598, reservations 800-444-7275; www.parks.ca.gov; 101 N Big Trees Park Rd, Felton; entry per car $10, tent & RV sites $35; ⏰sunrise-sunset; P 👪) 🍃. Built in 1871 and Felton's oldest building, the **Cremer House** (☎831-335-3976; www.cremerhouse.com; 6256 Hwy 3, Felton; mains $15-19; ⏰11:30am-2:30pm & 5-9pm Tue-Sun) does a fine line in seasonal American classics, local wines and craft beers. Also near Felton is the pioneer-era fun and spectacle of **Roaring Camp Railroads** (☎831-335-4484; www.roaringcamp.com; 5401 Graham Hill Rd, Felton; adult/child 2-12yr from $33/24, parking $10; 👪), and fans of cryptozoology should definitely visit the comprehensive and interesting **Bigfoot Discovery Museum** (☎831-355-4478; www.bigfootdiscoveryproject.com; 5497 Hwy 9, Felton; suggested donation $2, museum tours $5; ⏰11am-6pm Wed-Mon; P).

Follow Hwy 236 northwest for a further nine twisting miles from Boulder Creek to **Big Basin Redwoods State Park** (Map p49; ☎831-338-8860; www.parks.ca.gov; 21600 Big Basin Way, Boulder Creek; entry per car $10, tent & RV sites $35; ⏰sunrise-sunset; P 👪) 🍃 for

Around Santa Cruz

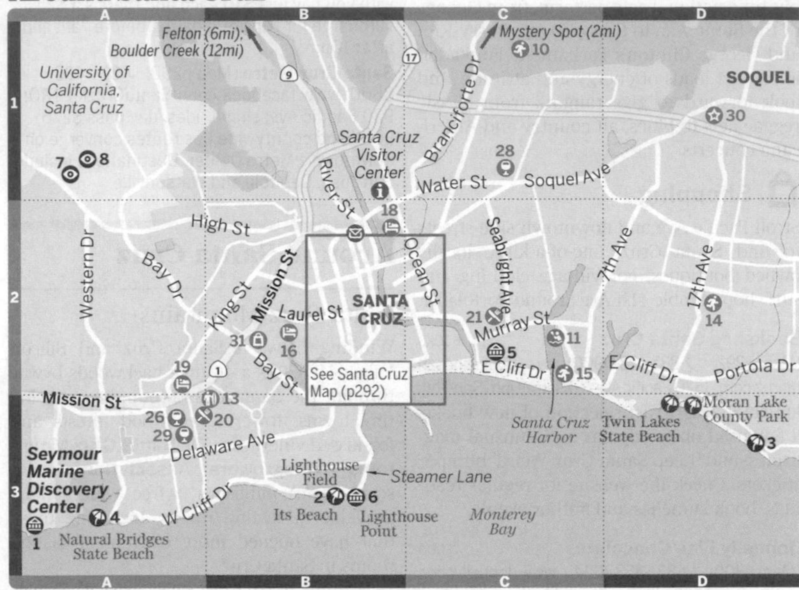

Around Santa Cruz

Top Sights

1 Seymour Marine Discovery Center A3

Sights

2 Its Beach B3
3 Moran Lake County Park D3
4 Natural Bridges State Beach A3
5 Santa Cruz Museum of Natural History C2
6 Santa Cruz Surfing Museum B3
7 UCSC Arboretum A1
8 University of California, Santa Cruz A1

Activities, Courses & Tours

9 Capitola Surf & Paddle E2
10 DeLaveaga Disc Golf Club C1
11 Kayak Connection C2
12 O'Neill Surf Shop E2
13 Richard Schmidt Surf School B3
14 Stagnaro's D2
15 SUP Shack C2

Sleeping

16 Babbling Brook Inn B2
17 Capitola Hotel E2
18 Hotel Paradox B2
19 Mission Inn A2

Eating

20 Bantam A3
21 Engfer Pizza Works C2
22 Gayle's Bakery & Rosticceria E2
23 Pretty Good Advice E1
24 Sotola Bar & Grill E2

Drinking & Nightlife

25 Discretion Brewing E1
26 Humble Sea Brewing Company A3
Santa Cruz Mountain Brewing ...... (see 20)
27 Sante Adairius Rustic Ales E1
28 Sante Adairius Santa Cruz Portal C1
29 West End Tap & Kitchen A3

Entertainment

30 Moe's Alley D1

Shopping

31 Donnelly Fine Chocolates B2

excellent hiking. A 12.5-mile one-way section of the **Skyline to the Sea Trail** ends at Waddell Beach, almost 20 miles northwest of Santa Cruz on Hwy 1. This area was severely impacted by bushfires in 2020, which saw the destruction of the park's visitor center. Check the website for the latest update regarding access and facilities. On weekends between mid-March and mid-December, you can usually ride **Santa Cruz Metro** (☎831-425-8600; www.scmtd.com) bus 35A up to Big Basin in the morning and get picked up by bus 40 at the beach in the afternoon.

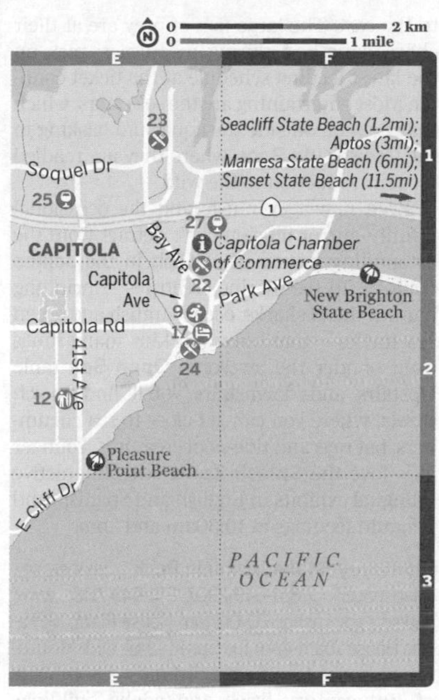

Capitola & Aptos

Six miles east of Santa Cruz, the diminutive beach town of Capitola nestles quaintly between ocean bluffs. Show up for mid-September's **Capitola Art & Wine Festival** (www.capitolaartandwine.com) or the famous **Begonia Festival** (www.begoniafestival.com), held over Labor Day weekend, with floral floats along Soquel Creek.

By the beach, downtown is laid out for strolling, and cute shops and touristy restaurants inhabit seaside houses. Drop by **Capitola Surf & Paddle** (Map p300; ☎831-435-6503; www.capitolasurfandpaddle.com; 208 San Jose Ave, Capitola; surfboard/SUP rental from $10/20, surfing & SUP lessons $60-85; ⏱10am-6pm) to rent water-sports gear or, if you book ahead, take surfing and SUP lessons. For an overnight stay, the centrally located and charming **Capitola Hotel** (Map p300; ☎831-476-1278; www.capitolahotel.com; 210 Esplanade, Capitole; d $169-279;) features 10 elegant rooms named after Caribbean islands.

Enjoy Capitola marine views with interesting salads and excellent gourmet mains at the cosmopolitan **Sotola Bar & Grill** (Map p300; ☎831-854-2800; www.sotolabarandgrill.com; 231 Esplanade, Capitola; mains $23-32; ⏱11:30am-10pm), or head inland to **Gayle's Bakery & Rosticceria** (Map p300; ☎831-462-1200; www.gaylesbakery.com; 504 Bay Ave; dishes $5-12; ⏱6:30am-8:30pm;) to stock up for a beach picnic. Around 1 mile further north **Pretty Good Advice** (Map p300; ☎831-226-2805; www.prettygoodadvicesoquel.com; 3070 Porter St, Capitola; snacks $5-8; ⏱8am-8pm;) has a fun ambience and offers modern takes on sandwiches and burgers – try the Timo Time with kimchi, a fried egg and crispy potato – and seasonal juices and soups. A few miles to the east in Aptos, **Aptos St BBQ** (☎831-662-1721; www.aptosstbbq.com; 8059 Aptos St, Aptos; mains $11-32; ⏱11am-9pm) pairs smoked tri-tip beef and pulled pork with California craft beers and live music.

The **Capitola Chamber of Commerce** (Map p300; ☎800-474-6522; www.capitolachamber.com; 716G Capitola Ave, Capitola; ⏱10am-4pm) offers travel tips. Driving downtown can be a nightmare in summer and on weekends; use the parking lot behind City Hall, off Capitola Ave by Riverview Dr.

Moss Landing & Elkhorn Slough

Hwy 1 swings back toward the coast at Moss Landing, just south of the Santa Cruz County line, almost 20 miles north of Monterey. From the working fishing harbor, **Sanctuary Cruises** (☎info 831-917-1042, tickets 831-350-4090; www.sanctuarycruises.com; 7881 Sandholdt Rd, Moss Landing; tours $40-55;) operates whale-watching and dolphin-spotting cruises year-round aboard biodiesel-fueled boats (reservations are essential). Devour dock-fresh seafood at warehouse-sized **Phil's Fish Market** (☎831-633-2152; www.philsfishmarket.com; 7600 Sandholdt Rd; mains $12-28; ⏱10am-9pm;) or, after browsing the antiques shops, lunch at **Haute Enchilada** (☎831-633-5483; www.hauteenchilada.com; 7902 Moss Landing Rd, Moss Landing; mains $13-26; ⏱11am-8:30pm Sun-Thu, to 9pm Fri & Sat) , an inspired Mexican restaurant inside an art gallery.

On the eastern side of Hwy 1, **Elkhorn Slough National Estuarine Research Reserve** (☎831-728-2822; www.elkhornslough.org; 1700 Elkhorn Rd, Watsonville; adult/child under 16yr $4/free; ⏱9am-5pm Wed-Sun;) is popular with bird-watchers and hikers, and can also be explored by cruising on an electric boat with **Whisper Charters** (☎800-979-3370; www.whispercharters.com; 2370 Hwy 1, Moss Landing; 2hr tour adult/child under 12yr $60/50;) . Kayaking and SUP are also fantastic ways to see the slough, though not on a windy day or when the tides are against you. Reserve ahead for kayak or SUP rentals, guided tours and paddling instruction with

Kayak Connection (☎831-724-5692; www.kayakconnection.com; 2370 Hwy 1, Moss Landing; kayak & SUP rental from $40, tours $65; ⊙9am-5pm; 👪) or **Monterey Bay Kayaks** (☎831-373-5357; www.montereybaykayaks.com; 2390 Hwy 1, Moss Landing; kayak & SUP rental/tour from $30/60; ⊙9am-5pm; 👪).

Around 10 miles north of Moss Landing on the edge of **Watsonville**, visit **Annieglass** (☎831-761-2041; www.annieglass.com; cnr Riverside Dr & Harvest Dr, Watsonville; ⊙10am-5pm Mon-Sat) for artful glass products designed by Annie Morhauser, and stop in at **Martinelli's Company Store Tasting Room** (☎831-768-3938; www.facebook.com/MartinellisCoStore; 345 Harvest Dr, Watsonville; ⊙9am-5pm Mon-Fri, 10am-2pm Sat) for excellent apple juices and (non alcoholic) ciders. Both are a short detour off Hwy 1.

Monterey

Life in still delightfully rough-around-the-edges Monterey revolves around the sea. The city's biggest draw is a world-class aquarium overlooking **Monterey Bay National Marine Sanctuary**, which protects dense kelp forests and a sublime variety of marine life, including seals and sea lions, dolphins and whales. The aquarium sits on the edge of Cannery Row, which made Monterey the sardine capital of the world in the 1930s. Today it's an unabashedly touristic strip lined with souvenir shops and standard eateries in faux retro buildings. For more authenticity, take a stroll past downtown's cluster of restored buildings from the Spanish and Mexican periods.

Sights

★Monterey Bay Aquarium AQUARIUM

(Map p303; ☎info 831-648-4800, tickets 866-963-9645; www.montereybayaquarium.org; 886 Cannery Row; adult/child 3-12yr/13-17yr $50/30/40, tours $15; ⊙9:30am-6pm May-Aug, 10am-5pm Sep-Apr; 👪) Monterey's most mesmerizing experience, this enormous aquarium occupies the site of a humongous sardine cannery. All kinds of aquatic creatures inhabit its halls and outside areas, from sea stars and slimy sea slugs to animated sea otters and surprisingly nimble 800lb tuna. The aquarium is much more than an impressive collection of glass tanks; thoughtful placards underscore the bay's cultural and historical contexts.

Every minute, up to 2000 gallons of seawater are pumped into the three-story **kelp forest**, recreating as closely as possible the natural conditions you see out the windows to the east. The large fish of prey are at their charismatic best during mealtimes; pick up the latest feeding schedule at the ticket counter. Most entertaining are the sea otters, which may be seen outside the aquarium basking in the **Great Tide Pool**, where they are readied for reintroduction to the wild.

Even new-agey music and the occasional infinity-mirror illusion can't detract from the astounding beauty of jellyfish in the **Jellies Gallery**. To see marine creatures – including hammerhead sharks, ocean sunfish and green sea turtles – that outweigh kids many times over, ponder the awesome **Open Sea** tank. Upstairs and downstairs you'll find **touch pools**, where you can get close to sea cucumbers, bat rays and tide-pool creatures. Younger kids love the **Splash Zone**, with interactive bilingual exhibits in English and Spanish, and penguin feedings at 10:30am and 3pm.

Monterey State Historic Park HISTORIC SITE

(Map p303; ☎831-649-2907, 831-649-7118; www.parks.ca.gov/mshp; 20 Custom House Plaza; ⊙Pacific House 10am-4pm Tue-Sun) FREE Old Monterey is home to an extraordinary assemblage of 19th-century brick and adobe buildings administered as a state park and linked by a 2-mile self-guided walking tour called the 'Path of History.' Pick up a copy at Pacific House Museum, which also doubles as the park HQ. Route highlights are the nearby Custom House and the **Old Whaling Station** (Map p303; 391 Decatur St; ⊙10am-2pm Tue-Fri).

Pacific House MUSEUM

(Map p303; ☎831-649-7118; www.parks.ca.gov; 20 Custom House Plaza; walking tour adult/child $10/free; ⊙10am-4pm Tue-Sun; 👪) Find out what's currently open at Monterey State Historic Park (p302), grab a free map and buy tickets for guided walking tours inside this 1847 adobe building, where fascinatingly in-depth exhibits cover the state's early Spanish, Mexican and American eras. Walking tours depart from Pacific House and run at 10:30am, 12:30pm and 2pm Thursday to Sunday. Tours are free on the last Sunday of the month. Displays at Pacific House also include the Monterey Museum of the American Indian.

Custom House HISTORIC BUILDING

(Map p303; ☎831-649-7111; www.parks.ca.gov; Custom House Plaza; ⊙10am-4pm; 👪) FREE In 1822 a newly independent Mexico ended the Spanish trade monopoly and stipulated that any traders bringing goods to Alta (Upper) California must first unload their cargoes here for duty to be assessed. In 1846,

Monterey

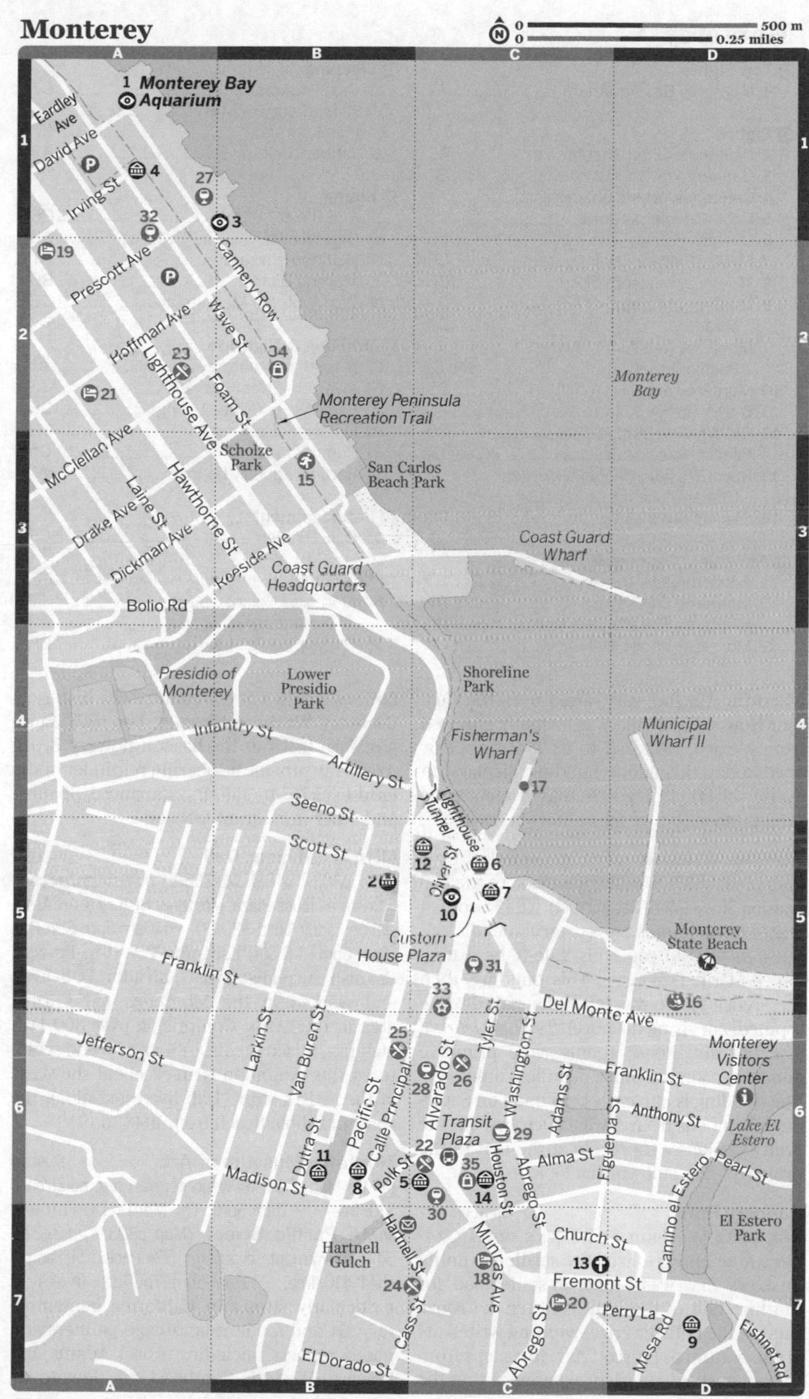

0 500 m
0 0.25 miles
1 Monterey Bay Aquarium
Eardley Ave
David Ave
Irving St
Prescott Ave
Hoffman Ave
Lighthouse Ave
Cannery Row
Wave St
Foam St
McClellan Ave
Drake Ave
Laine St
Hawthorne St
Dickman Ave
Reeside Ave
Bolio Rd
Monterey Peninsula Recreation Trail
Scholze Park
San Carlos Beach Park
Coast Guard Headquarters
Coast Guard Wharf
Monterey Bay
Presidio of Monterey
Lower Presidio Park
Shoreline Park
Infantry St
Artillery St
Fisherman's Wharf
Municipal Wharf II
Seeno St
Lighthouse Tunnel
Scott St
Oliver St
Custom House Plaza
Monterey State Beach
Franklin St
Del Monte Ave
Jefferson St
Larkin St
Van Buren St
Pacific St
Calle Principal
Alvarado St
Tyler St
Washington St
Adams St
Figueroa St
Monterey Visitors Center
Anthony St
Lake El Estero
Transit Plaza
Dutra St
Polk St
Houston St
Abrego St
Alma St
Camino el Estero
Pearl St
Madison St
Hartnell St
Munras Ave
Church St
El Estero Park
Hartnell Gulch
Fremont St
Perry La
Cass St
Mesa Rd
Fishnet Rd
El Dorado St

Monterey

when the US flag was raised over the Custom House, California was formally annexed from Mexico. Restored to its 1840s appearance, today this adobe building displays an exotic selection of goods that traders once brought to exchange for California cowhides.

Stevenson House HISTORIC BUILDING

(Map p303; ☎831-649-7118; www.parks.ca.gov; 530 Houston St; ⊙1-4pm Sat Apr-Oct) FREE Scottish writer Robert Louis Stevenson came to Monterey in 1879 to court his wife-to-be, Fanny Van de Grift Osbourne. This building, then the French Hotel, was where he stayed while reputedly devising his novel *Treasure Island*. The boarding-house rooms were primitive and Stevenson was still a penniless unknown. The building is currently only open on Saturday afternoons from April to October, but the pretty gardens – especially at the rear of the property – are still worth a look.

Cannery Row HISTORIC SITE

(Map p303; 👪) John Steinbeck's novel *Cannery Row* immortalized the sardine-canning business that was Monterey's lifeblood for the first half of the 20th century. A bronze **bust** of the Pulitzer Prize–winning writer sits at the bottom of Prescott Ave, just steps from the unabashedly touristy experience that the famous row has devolved into. The historical **Cannery Workers Shacks** (Map p303; Bruce Ariss Way) FREE at the base of flowery Bruce Ariss Way provide a sobering reminder of the hard lives led by Filipino, Japanese, Spanish and other immigrant laborers.

MHAA: Salvador Dalí GALLERY

(Map p303; ☎831-372-2608; www.mhaadali.com; 5 Custom House Plaza, Monterey History & Art Association; adult/child $20/10; ⊙10am-5pm Sun-Thu, 10am-6pm Fri & Sat) Escaping WWII in Europe, Spanish surrealist artist Salvador Dalí lived and worked in the Monterey and Carmel area in the 1940s. Comprising over 300 Dalí etchings, mixed media, lithographs and sculptures, this exhibition is an excellent showcase of the artist's work. Dalí lived just along the coast in Pebble Beach from 1943 to 1948.

Monterey Museum of Art MUSEUM

(MMA; Map p303; www.montereyart.org; adult/child $10/free; ⊙11am-5pm Thu-Mon) Downtown, **MMA Pacific Street** (Map p303; ☎831-372-5477; www.montereyart.org; 559 Pacific St; adult/child $10/free; ⊙11am-5pm Thu-Tue; P👪) is particularly strong in California contemporary art and modern landscape painters and photographers, including Ansel Adams and Edward Weston. Southeast of downtown,

MMA La Mirada (Map p303; ☎831-372-3689; www.montereyart.org; 720 Via Mirada), a silent-film star's villa, has humble adobe origins that are exquisitely concealed. It is now only used for special museum events, and not generally open to the public.

Cooper-Molera Adobe HISTORIC BUILDING
(Map p303; ☎831-223-0172; www.coopermolera.org; 525 Polk St; ⏲11am-4pm Tue-Sat, to 2:30pm Sun) FREE This stately early-19th-century adobe home was built by John Rogers Cooper, a New England sea captain, and three generations of his family resided here. Over time, the original adobe buildings were partitioned and expanded, gardens were added and later everything was willed to the National Trust for Historic Preservation. Browse the gardens and museum before grabbing a bite at Alta Bakery & Cafe (p308).

Royal Presidio Chapel & Heritage Center Museum CHURCH
(Map p303; ☎831-373-2628; www.sancarloscathedral.org; 500 Church St; donations accepted; ⏲10am-2pm Fri-Sun, to noon Wed, 1:15-3:15pm 2nd & 4th Mon of month; P) Built of sandstone in 1794, this graceful chapel is California's oldest continuously functioning parish and first stone building. The original 1770 mission church stood here before being moved to Carmel. As Monterey expanded under Mexican rule in the 1820s, older buildings were gradually destroyed, leaving behind this National Historic Landmark as the strongest reminder of the defeated Spanish colonial presence. On-site docents are happy to provide tours during opening hours.

Activities

Like its larger namesake in San Francisco, Monterey's **Fisherman's Wharf** is a tacky tourist trap, but also a jumping-off point for deep-sea fishing trips and whale-watching cruises. A short walk east at workaday **Municipal Wharf 2**, fishing boats bob and sway in the bay.

Whale-Watching

You can spot whales off the coast of Monterey Bay year-round. The season for blue and humpback whales runs from April to early December, while gray whales pass by from mid-December through March. Sanctuary Cruises (p301) tour boats depart from Fisherman's Wharf and Moss Landing. Reserve trips at least a day in advance; be prepared for a bumpy, cold ride.

Monterey Whale Watching BOATING
(Map p303; ☎831-372-2203; www.montereywhalewatching.com; 96 Fisherman's Wharf; 2½hr tour adult/child from $50/35;) This boating outfit offers several daily departures; no children under age three or pregnant women allowed.

Monterey Bay Whale Watch BOATING
(Map p303; ☎831-375-4658; www.gowhales.com; Fisherman's Wharf; 3hr tours adult/child 4-12yr $49/38;) Right on Fisherman's Wharf, this is one of the oldest whale-watching tour operators in Monterey. Morning and afternoon boat rides are led by knowledgeable marine biologists for extra insight into the animals and their habitat. Sightings are guaranteed or you get another trip for free.

Diving & Snorkeling

Monterey Bay offers world-renowned diving and snorkeling, including off **Lovers Point** in Pacific Grove and at Point Lobos State Natural Reserve (p313) south of Carmel-by-the-Sea. You'll want a wetsuit year-round. In summer, upwelling currents carry cold water from the deep canyon below the bay, sending a rich supply of nutrients up toward the surface level to feed the bay's diverse marine life. These frigid currents also account for the bay's chilly water temperatures and the summer fog that blankets the peninsula.

Aquarius Dive Shop DIVING
(☎831-375-1933; www.aquariusdivers.com; 2040 Del Monte Ave; snorkel-/scuba-gear rental $35/65, dive tours from $65; ⏲9am-6pm Mon-Thu, to 7pm Fri, 7am-7pm Sat, 7am-6pm Sun) Talk to this five-star PADI-certified operation for gear rentals, classes and guided dives of Monterey Bay.

Kayaking & Surfing

Monterey Bay Kayaks KAYAKING
(Map p303; ☎831-373-5357; www.montereybaykayaks.com; 693 Del Monte Ave; kayak & SUP rental/tour from $30/60; ⏲9am-5pm, extended hours in summer;) Rents kayaks and SUP equipment, offers paddling lessons and leads guided tours of Monterey Bay, including full-moon and sunrise trips.

Cycling & Mountain Biking

Along an old railway line, the **Monterey Peninsula Recreational Trail** travels for 18 car-free miles along the waterfront, passing Cannery Row en route to Lovers Point in Pacific Grove. Road-cycling enthusiasts and e-bike tourists can make

Monterey Peninsula

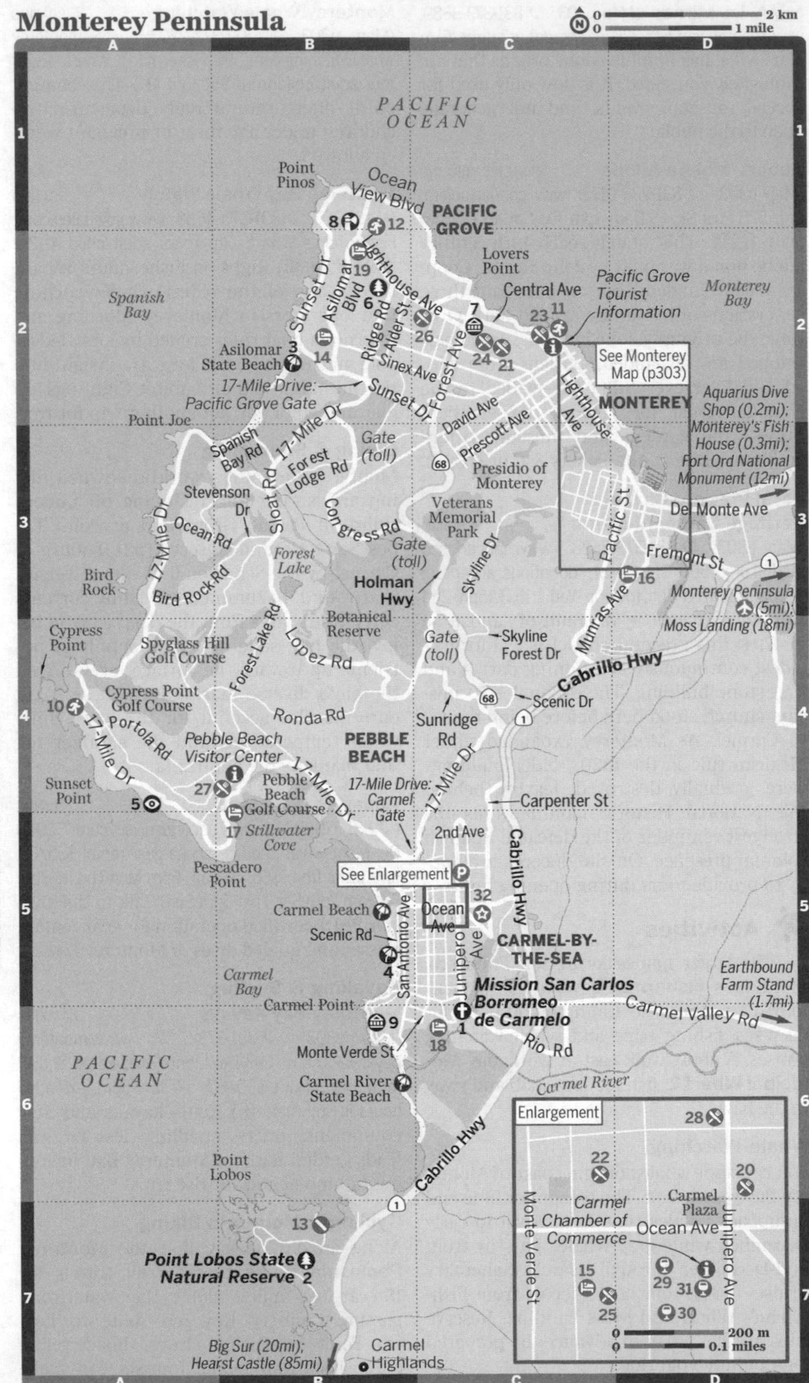

CENTRAL COAST MONTEREY

Monterey Peninsula

the round trip to Carmel along the 17-Mile Drive (p312). Mountain bikers head to **Fort Ord National Monument** to pedal over 80 miles of single-track and fire roads; the **Sea Otter Classic** (www.seaotterclassic.com) races there in mid-April.

Adventures by the Sea CYCLING, KAYAKING
(Map p303; 831-372-1807; www.adventuresbythesea.com; 299 Cannery Row; per day bicycle rental $35, e-bike tour $59, SUP from $30, 1-/2-seater kayak $35/60, kayak tours from $60; 9am-sunset) No matter if you fancy kayaking with sea otters, joining a kayak tour across the kelp-forest canopy, learning to paddleboard or exploring the area on a hybrid or e-bike, these folks can set you up. They have six locations in all, with Cannery Row being the largest and most central. Guided e-bike tours exploring 17-Mile Drive (p312) on two wheels are a popular option.

Big Sur Adventures CYCLING
(Map p306; 831-244-0169; www.bikebigsur.com; 125 Ocean View Blvd, American Tin Cannery; e-bike rental half-/full day $50/70, tours from $59; 9am-dusk) Conveniently located near the aquarium, this operation offers e-bike rental and guided bike tours of 17-Mile Drive (p312). Regular mountain bikes are half the cost of e-bikes. Tours exploring Big Sur's Old Coast Road and filming locations for *Big Little Lies* are also available.

Festivals & Events

Castroville Artichoke Food & Wine Festival FOOD & DRINK
(831-633-2465; www.artichokefestival.org; late May/early Jun) Head 15 miles north of Monterey for 3D 'agro art' sculptures, cooking demos, a farmers market and field tours. There's also a wine-and-beer garden with tasty beverages from around the region.

Monterey County Fair CARNIVAL, FOOD
(www.montereycountyfair.com; late Aug & early Sep) Old-fashioned fun, carnival rides, horseback riding and livestock competitions, wine tasting and live music.

★ **Monterey Jazz Festival** MUSIC
(www.montereyjazzfestival.org; mid-Sep) One of the world's longest-running jazz festivals (since 1958) showcases big-name headliners over a long September weekend.

Sleeping

Book ahead for special events, on weekends and in summer. To avoid the tourist congestion and jacked-up prices of Cannery Row, look to Pacific Grove. Cheaper motels line Munras Ave, south of downtown, and N Fremont St, east of Hwy 1. Prices are usually higher on Saturday nights.

HI Monterey Hostel HOSTEL $
(Map p303; 831-649-0375; www.montereyhostel.org; 778 Hawthorne St; dm $46-48, tr/q with shared bath $129/149;) Four blocks from Cannery Row and the aquarium, this simple, clean hostel houses single-sex and mixed dorms, as well as private rooms for three to five people. Days start with free make-your-own-pancake breakfasts and might conclude with barbecue parties or story-swapping in the lounge, which has a piano. Check in from 2pm to 9pm.

Take MST bus 1 from downtown's Transit Plaza (p310).

Inn by the Bay MOTEL $
(Map p306; 831-372-5409; www.innbythebaymonterey.com; 936 Munras Ave; d from $126;) An easy walk downhill to downtown Monterey, Inn on the Bay is the quiet achiever along the Munras Ave motel strip. Look forward to modernized interiors and flat-screen TVs in the rooms; a location set back from the street means it is uniformly quiet.

Hotel Abrego BOUTIQUE HOTEL $$
(Map p303; 831-372-7551; www.hotelabrego.com; 755 Abrego St; r from $212;) At this downtown Monterey boutique hotel, most of the spacious, clean-lined contemporary rooms have gas fireplaces and chaise longues. Work out in the fitness studio, take a dip in the outdoor pool or warm up in the hot tub. A fire pit is a cozy feature for cooler Monterey evenings.

Casa Munras BOUTIQUE HOTEL $$
(Map p303; 831-375-2411; www.hotelcasamunras.com; 700 Munras Ave; r from $224;) Built around an adobe hacienda once owned by a 19th-century Spanish colonial don, this hotel boasts chic modern rooms with lofty beds set inside two-story motel-esque buildings; some rooms have gas fireplaces. Splash in a heated outdoor pool, unwind at the on-site spa or enjoy modern Spanish cuisine at the property's Estéban restaurant. Pet fee $50.

★ **Jabberwock** B&B $$$
(Map p303; 831-372-4777; www.jabberwockinn.com; 598 Laine St; r $239-379;) Barely visible behind a shroud of foliage, this 1911 khaki-shingled arts-and-crafts-style house hums a playful *Alice in Wonderland* tune through seven immaculate rooms, a few with fireplaces and Jacuzzis for two. Over afternoon wine and hors d'oeuvres, ask the genial hosts about the house's many salvaged architectural elements. Weekends have a two-night minimum. Breakfast included.

Eating

For casual indie eateries, head uphill from Cannery Row to Lighthouse Ave to feast on everything from Hawaiian barbecue and Thai flavors to sushi and kebabs. For more contemporary and upscale plates, head downtown around Alvarado St.

Alta Bakery & Cafe CAFE $
(Map p303; 831-920-1018; www.altamonterey.com; 502 Munras Ave; snacks & mains $8-12; 7am-4pm;) In the restored Cooper-Molera Adobe (p305), Alta Bakery & Cafe's excellent baking is showcased with brunch options including orange marmalade and ricotta on sourdough, while daily doughnut, strudel and muffin specials are always worth trying. There's kombucha on tap and organic and fair-trade coffee, and interesting historic photos in the main dining area. In warmer weather, adjourn to the lovely gardens.

Crystal Fish SUSHI $
(Map p303; 831-649-3474; https://crystalfishmonterey.com; 514 Lighthouse Ave; sushi $5-7, mains $10-23; 11:30am-2pm & 5-9:30pm Mon-Fri, 1-9:30pm Sat & Sun;) The best sushi in town is at this perennially popular Lighthouse Ave address. Expect a short wait at the height of lunch and dinner service – a worthwhile price to pay for the superfresh seafood, udon noodle soups and good-value *bentō* boxes. There's also a decent variety of vegetarian sushi options.

Old Monterey Marketplace MARKET $
(Map p303; www.oldmonterey.org; Alvarado St btwn Del Monte Ave & Pearl St; 4-7pm Tue Sep-May, to 8pm Jun-Aug;) Rain or shine, head downtown on Tuesdays for farm-fresh fruit and veggies, artisan cheeses, international food stalls and a scrumptious 'baker's alley.'

Heirloom Pizza Co PIZZA $$
(Map p303; 831-717-4363; www.heirloompizzapie.com; 700 Cass St; pizza $21-28; 5-8:30pm Sun, Mon & Wed-Thu, to 9:30pm Fri & Sat;) In a residential neighborhood bordering downtown, Heirloom Pizza Co is a popular spot to enjoy Californian craft beers with innovative versions of Italy's favorite snack. Our preferred combo is a pizza with apple, bacon and gorgonzola cheese, and a citrusy Ten Million Flowers German-style *Kölsch* beer from Discretion Brewing. Service is relaxed but prompt and professional.

Monterey's Fish House SEAFOOD $$
(☎831-373-4647; www.montereyfishhouse.com; 2114 Del Monte Ave; mains $12-27; ⏲11:30am-2:30pm Mon-Fri & 5-9:30pm daily; Ⓟ) Watched over by photos of Sicilian fishermen, dig into oak-grilled or blackened swordfish, barbecued oysters or, for those stout of heart, the Mexican squid steak. Reservations are essential (it's *so* crowded), but the vibe is island-casual: Hawaiian shirts seem to be de rigueur for men.

★**Montrio Bistro** CALIFORNIAN $$$
(Map p303; ☎831-648-8880; www.montrio.com; 414 Calle Principal; shared plates $6.50-20, mains $20-46; ⏲4:30-10pm Sun-Thu, to 11pm Fri & Sat; 📶) With 'clouds' hanging from the ceiling and tube sculptures wriggling toward them, it's apparent that much thought has gone into the design of this dining-scene stalwart set inside a 1910 firehouse. Fortunately, the New American fare, prepared with ingredients hunted and gathered locally, measures up nicely. Drink and snack prices during happy hour (daily until 6:30pm) are practically a steal.

Drinking & Nightlife

Prowl downtown Monterey's Alvarado St, touristy Cannery Row and more local Lighthouse Ave for the best watering holes.

★**Alvarado Street Brewery** CRAFT BEER
(Map p303; ☎831-655-2337; www.alvaradostreetbrewery.com; 426 Alvarado St; ⏲11:30am-10pm Sun-Thu, to 11pm Fri & Sat) Vintage beer advertising punctuates Alvarado Street's brick walls, but that's the only concession to heritage at this craft-beer pub. Innovative brews harness new hop strains, sour and barrel-aged beers regularly fill the taps, and superior bar food includes pork belly poutine. In summer, adjourn to the alfresco beer garden with a hazy IPA and the excellent *al pastor* pizza.

Fieldwork Brewing BEER GARDEN
(Map p303; ☎831-324-0658; www.fieldworkbrewing.com; 560 Munras Ave; ⏲noon-10pm Sun-Thu, to 11pm Fri & Sat; 🐾) Headquartered further north in Berkeley, Fieldwork's downtown Monterey beer garden is a popular year-round location. During cooler months, the fire pit attracts locals and their well-behaved dogs, while summer nights are best enjoyed amid Fieldwork's shared outdoor tables. Standout brews include the Chloe Belgian Pale Ale, and it's possible to bring in takeout food from Tuesday-evening's Old Monterey Marketplace.

A Taste of Monterey WINE BAR
(Map p303; ☎831-646-5446; www.atasteofmonterey.com; 700 Cannery Row; tasting flights $20; ⏲11am-6pm Sun-Thu, to 8pm Fri & Sat) Sample medal-winning Monterey County wines from as far away as the Santa Lucia Highlands while soaking up dreamy sea views, then peruse thoughtful exhibits on barrel-making and cork production. Shared plates, including crab cakes and smoked salmon, provide a tasty reason to linger, and there's also a good selection of California craft beers.

Sardine Factory Lounge LOUNGE
(Map p303; ☎831-373-3775; www.sardinefactory.com; 701 Wave St; ⏲5pm-midnight) The legendary restaurant's fireplace lounge pours wines by the glass, delivers filling appetizers to your table and has a live pianist most nights.

East Village Coffee Lounge CAFE, LOUNGE
(Map p303; ☎831-373-5601; www.facebook.com/eastvillagemonterey; 498 Washington St; ⏲6am-10pm Mon-Fri, from 7am Sat & Sun; 📶) This downtown Monterey coffee shop on a busy corner creates brews with fair-trade, organic beans. At night, it pulls off a big-city lounge vibe with film, open-mike and live-music nights (and an all-important booze license). Check the Facebook page for event listings.

Entertainment

For comprehensive entertainment listings, browse the free tabloid *Monterey County Weekly* (www.facebook.com/MontereyCountyWeekly).

Osio Cinema CINEMA
(Map p303; ☎831-644-8171; http://osiotheater.com; 350 Alvarado St; adult $11, before 6pm $8; 📶) Downtown Monterey cinema screens indie dramas, cutting-edge documentaries and offbeat Hollywood films. Drop by its Cafe Lumiere for locally roasted coffee, loose-leaf tea and decadent cheesecake.

Puma Road LIVE MUSIC
(Map p303; ☎831-747-1911; www.facebook.com/pg/pumaroadportola; 281 Alvarado St, Portola Plaza; ⏲2-8pm Mon-Thu, noon-8pm Fri-Sun) Regular live music – usually from around 5pm on Tuesday, Friday, Saturday and Sunday – combines with French-style Bordeaux and Burgundy reds from the Santa Lucia Highlands at this popular wine bar and tasting

room on Portola Plaza. Check Facebook to see what's scheduled.

Shopping

Cannery Row is jammed with claptrap shops, while downtown Monterey's side streets hide more one-of-a-kind finds.

Monterey Peninsula Art Foundation Gallery ART
(Map p303; 831-655-1267; www.mpaf.org; 425 Cannery Row; 11am-5pm) Taking over a cozy sea-view house, more than 30 local artists sell plein-air paintings and sketches alongside contemporary works in all media.

Old Capitol Books BOOKS
(Map p303; 831-333-0383; www.oldcapitolbooks.com; 559 Tyler St; 10am-6pm Wed-Mon, to 7pm Tue) Tall shelves of new, used and antiquarian books, including rare 1st editions, California titles and John Steinbeck's works.

Information

Doctors on Duty (831-649-0770; www.doctorsonduty.com; 501 Lighthouse Ave; 7am-8pm Mon-Fri, 8am-6pm Sat & Sun) Walk-in, non emergency medical clinic.

Monterey Public Library (831-646-3933; www.monterey.org/library; 625 Pacific St; noon-8pm Mon-Wed, 10am-6pm Thu-Sat, 1-5pm Sun; wi-fi) Free wi-fi and public internet terminals.

Monterey Visitors Center (Map p303; 831-657-6400; www.seemonterey.com; 401 Camino el Estero; 10am-6pm May-Aug, to 5pm Sep-Apr) Free tourist brochures and accommodations booking service for all of Monterey County. See the website or drop by for information about filming locations for the HBO series *Big Little Lies* (2017–19).

Post Office (Map p303; 800-275-8777; www.usps.com; 565 Hartnell St; 8:30am-5pm Mon-Fri, 10am-2pm Sat) Located just south of downtown Monterey.

Getting There & Away

Monterey is 43 miles south of Santa Cruz and 177 miles north of San Luis Obispo.

AIR

A few miles east of downtown off Hwy 68, **Monterey Regional Airport** (831-648-7000; www.montereyairport.com; 200 Fred Kane Dr) has flights with United (Denver, LA, San Francisco), American (Dallas/Fort Worth, Phoenix), Alaska (Seattle, San Diego) and Allegiant Air (Las Vegas). An Uber or Lyft from downtown is around $15 (10 minutes), and to get here by public transport, catch buses 7, 56 or 93 ($2.50) from Monterey's **Transit Plaza** (Map p303; cnr Pearl & Alvarado Sts).

The **Monterey Airbus** (831-373-7777; www.montereyairbus.com; $42-52; wi-fi) shuttle service links Monterey with international airports in San Jose ($40, 1½ hours) and San Francisco ($50, 2½ hours) almost a dozen times daily; book online for discounts.

BUS

Monterey-Salinas Transit (MST; Map p303; 888-678-2871; www.mst.org; Jules Simoneau Plaza; single rides $1.50-3.50, day pass $10) operates local and countywide buses, including routes to Pacific Grove, Carmel, Big Sur (weekends only, daily in summer) and Salinas. Routes converge on downtown's Transit Plaza.

From late May until early September, MST's free trolley loops around downtown, Fisherman's Wharf and Cannery Row between 10am and 7pm or 8pm daily (weekends only, September to April).

Pacific Grove

Founded as a tranquil Methodist summer retreat in 1875, Pacific Grove (or PG) maintained its quaint, holier-than-thou attitude well into the 20th century. The selling of liquor was illegal up until 1969, making it California's last 'dry' town. Today, leafy streets are lined by stately Victorian homes and a charming, compact downtown orbits Lighthouse Ave.

Sights & Activities

Pacific Grove's aptly named **Ocean View Boulevard** affords views from Lovers Point Park west to Point Pinos, where it becomes **Sunset Drive**, offering tempting turnoffs where you can stroll by pounding surf, rocky outcrops and teeming tide pools all the way to Asilomar State Beach. This seaside route is great for cycling, too – some say it rivals the famous 17-Mile Drive (p312) for beauty and, even better, it's free.

Asilomar State Beach BEACH
(Map p306; Sunset Dr; P) Negotiate a 1-mile trail boardwalk through rugged sand dunes. Note this beach is known for riptides and unpredictable surf, and care must be taken when swimming here.

Point Pinos Lighthouse LIGHTHOUSE
(Map p306; 831-648-3176; www.pointpinoslighthouse.org; 80 Asilomar Ave; suggested donation adult/child 7-17yr $5/2; 1-4pm Thu-Mon; P) The West Coast's oldest continuously operating lighthouse has been warning ships off

the hazardous tip of the Monterey Peninsula since 1855. Inside are modest exhibits on the lighthouse's history and, alas, its failures – local shipwrecks.

Pacific Grove Museum of Natural History MUSEUM
(Map p306; ☎831-648-5716; www.pgmuseum.org; 165 Forest Ave; adult/child $9/6; ⏰10am-5pm Tue-Sun; 👪) With a gray-whale sculpture out front, this small kid-oriented museum has old-fashioned exhibits about sea otters, coastal birdlife, butterflies, the Big Sur coast and Native California tribes. Drop in before driving Big Sur.

Monarch Grove Sanctuary PARK
(Map p306; www.cityofpacificgrove.org/visiting; 250 Ridge Rd; ⏰dawn-dusk; 👪) FREE Between November and February, monarch butterflies cluster in this thicket of tall eucalyptus trees that is secreted inland. Numbers were significantly lower in 2019/20, with researchers citing the destruction of the monarch's milkweed habitat along their migratory route and the increased use of pesticides and herbicides as key reasons for the decline. Ask for the latest update at Pacific Grove Tourist Information (p312). During peak season, volunteer guides answer all of your questions between noon and 3pm, weather permitting.

Pacific Grove Golf Links GOLF
(Map p306; ☎831-648-5775; www.playpacificgrove.com; 77 Asilomar Blvd; green fees $49-69) Can't afford to play at famous Pebble Beach? This historic 18-hole municipal course, where deer freely range, has impressive sea views, and it's a lot easier (not to mention cheaper) to book a tee time here.

Sleeping

Antique-filled B&Bs have taken over many stately Victorian homes around downtown Pacific Grove and by the beach. Motels cluster at the peninsula's western end, off Lighthouse Ave and Asilomar Blvd.

Sunset Inn MOTEL $$
(Map p306; ☎831-375-3529; www.gosunsetinn.com; 133 Asilomar Blvd; r $161; P 📶) At this small motor lodge near the golf course and the beach, attentive staff hand out keys to crisply redesigned rooms that have hardwood floors, king-sized beds with cheery floral-print comforters and sometimes a hot tub and a fireplace.

Asilomar Conference Grounds LODGE $$
(Map p306; ☎831-372-8016; www.visitasilomar.com; 800 Asilomar Blvd; r from $188; P @ 📶 🏊) This state-park lodge sprawls by sand dunes in pine forest. Skip ho-hum motel rooms and opt for historic houses designed by early-20th-century architect Julia Morgan (of Hearst Castle fame) – the thin-walled, hardwood-floored rooms may be small, but they share a fireplace lounge. Head to the lodge lobby for Ping-Pong, pool tables and wi-fi. Bike rentals available.

Eating

Downtown PG teems with European-style bakeries, coffee shops and neighborhood cafes.

Happy Girl Kitchen VEGETARIAN $
(Map p306; ☎831-373-4475; www.happygirlkitchen.com; 173 Central Ave; mains $4-10; ⏰cafe 7:30am-3pm, shop 7am-5pm; ✏) On Pacific Grove's eastern edge, Happy Girl Kitchen is a versatile one-stop shop for healthy breakfasts – try the organic muesli and yogurt – and lunches, fresh home-style baking and a diverse range of restorative teas. Much of the menu is organic and sustainable, and the attached store has a good range of artisan food products from around the region.

Crema CAFE $$
(Map p306; ☎831-324-0347; www.cremapg.com; 481 Lighthouse Ave; mains $11-18; ⏰7am-4pm; ✏👪) Our pick for Pacific Grove's best coffee, with expertly prepared lattes and macchiatos complemented by delicious brunch plates guaranteed to set you up for the day. If you're planning on cycling 17-Mile Drive (p312), you could do worse than Crema's crab cakes and eggs or the waffles with spiced apple and toasted pecans. Cocktails and craft beer are particularly popular on weekends.

Jeninni Kitchen & Wine Bar MEDITERRANEAN $$
(Map p306; ☎831-920-2662; www.jeninni.com; 542 Lighthouse Ave; mains $18-29; ⏰4-9pm Sun-Tue & Thu, to 10pm Sat & Sun) Happy-hour snacks from 4pm to 6pm segue to dinner at this bistro featuring the flavors of the Med. Housemade charcuterie and shared plates, such as crispy octopus, create a convivial ambience, while larger mains featuring venison, duck or lamb partner well with an informed wine list. On balmy summer nights, dine on the front patio watching Pacific Grove's passing parade.

17-MILE DRIVE

What to See

Pacific Grove and Carmel are linked by the spectacularly scenic, if somewhat overhyped, **17-Mile Drive** (Map p306; www.pebblebeach.com; per car/bicycle $10.50/free), which meanders through Pebble Beach, a wealthy private resort. It's no chore staying within the 25mph limit – every curve in the road reveals another postcard vista, especially when wildflowers are in bloom. Cycling the drive is enormously popular: try to do it during the week, when traffic isn't as heavy, and ride with the flow of traffic from north to south.

In Monterey, both Adventures by the Sea (p307) and Big Sur Adventures (p307) can hook you up with an e-bike, and both operators also run regular 17-Mile Drive bike tours.

Using the self-guided touring map you'll receive at the toll gate, you can pick out landmarks such as **Spanish Bay**, where explorer Gaspar de Portolá dropped anchor in 1769; treacherously rocky **Point Joe**, which was often mistaken for the entrance to Monterey Bay and thus became the site of shipwrecks; and **Bird Rock**, also a haven for harbor seals and sea lions. The pièce de résistance is the trademarked **Lone Cypress** (Map p306), which has perched on a seaward rock for possibly more than 250 years.

Besides the coastal scenery, star attractions at Pebble Beach include world-famous golf courses, where a celebrity and pro tournament happens every February. The luxurious **Lodge at Pebble Beach** (Map p306; 831-624-3811; www.pebblebeach.com; 1700 17-Mile Drive; r from $800;) has a spa, bars, restaurants and designer shops.

Interactive displays at the adjacent **Pebble Beach Visitor Center** (Map p306; 831-622-6394; www.pebblebeach.com/visitor-center; 1700 17-Mile Dr; 8am-5pm) feature plenty of fascinating information on Pebble Beach's star-studded golfing heritage, and the made-to-order deli sandwiches and salads at the nearby **Pebble Beach Market** (Map p306; 831-625-8528; www.pebblebeach.com/dining/pebble-beach-market; 1700 17-Mile Drive & Cypress Ave; sandwiches $12-14; 7:30am-6pm;) are the best-value lunch options along 17-Mile Drive.

The Route

Operated as a toll road by the Pebble Beach Company, the 17-Mile Drive is open from sunrise to sunset. The toll can be refunded later as a discount on a $35 minimum food purchase at local restaurants.

Time & Mileage

There are five separate gates for the 17-Mile Drive; how far you drive and how long you take is up to you. To take advantage of the most scenery, enter on Sunset Dr in Pacific Grove and exit onto San Antonio Ave in Carmel-by-the-Sea.

Passionfish SEAFOOD **$$$**
(Map p306; 831-655-3311; www.passionfish.net; 701 Lighthouse Ave; mains $23-34; 5-9pm Sun-Thu, to 10pm Fri & Sat;) Fresh, sustainable seafood is artfully presented in any number of inventive ways, and a seasonally inspired menu also carries slow-cooked meats and vegetarian dishes spotlighting local farms. The earth-tone decor is spare, with tables squeezed conversationally close together. An ambitious world-ranging wine list is priced near retail, and there are as many Chinese teas as wines by the glass.

Reservations are strongly recommended.

Information

Pacific Grove Tourist Information (Map p306; 831-324-4668; www.pacificgrove.org; 100 Central Ave; 9:30am-5pm Mon-Fri, 10am-3pm Sat) Located at the western entrance to Pacific Grove up the hill from the Monterey Bay Aquarium. Helpful with a good range of maps and brochures.

Getting There & Around

MST (p310) bus 1 connects downtown Monterey and Cannery Row with Pacific Grove, continuing to Asilomar ($2.50, 15 minutes, every 30 to 60 minutes). Heading to Carmel from Pacific Grove, catch bus 2 ($2.50, 15 minutes, every 30 to 60 minutes).

Carmel-by-the-Sea

With borderline fanatical devotion to its canine citizens, quaint Carmel has the well-manicured feel of a country club. Watch the parade of behatted locals toting fancy-label shopping bags to lunch and dapper folk driving top-down convertibles along Ocean Ave, the village's slow-mo main drag.

Founded as a seaside resort in the 1880s – fairly odd, given that its beach is often blanketed in fog – Carmel quickly attracted famous artists and writers, such as Sinclair Lewis and Jack London, and their hangers-on. Artistic flavor survives in nearly 100 galleries that saturate downtown's immaculate streets and courtyards, but sky-high property values have long obliterated any salt-of-the-earth bohemia.

Dating from the 1920s, Comstock cottages, with their characteristic stone chimneys and pitched gable roofs, still dot the town, making it vaguely reminiscent of the English countryside. Even garbage cans and newspaper vending boxes are quaintly shingled.

Sights & Activities

Escape downtown Carmel's harried shopping streets and stroll tree-lined neighborhoods on the lookout for domiciles both charming and peculiar. The *Hansel and Gretel* houses on Torres St, between 5th and 6th Aves, are just how you'd imagine them. Another eye-catching house on Guadalupe St near 6th Ave is shaped like a ship and made from local river rocks and salvaged ship parts.

★ Point Lobos State Natural Reserve STATE PARK
(Map p306; ☎831-624-4909; www.pointlobos.org; Hwy 1; per car $10; ⊙8am-5pm, last entry 4:30pm; P ♿) They bark, they laze and bathe and they're fun to watch – sea lions are the stars in this state park some 4 miles south of Carmel, along with the dramatically rocky coastline and its excellent tide-pooling. Even a short hike through this spectacular scenery is rewarding. Note that parking inside the reserve is limited to 150 cars, and spaces fill quickly in summer. Arrive before 9:30am or after 3pm to avoid the crowds. Alternatively, park on Hwy 1 and walk in.

★ Mission San Carlos Borromeo de Carmelo CHURCH
(Map p306; ☎831-624-1271; www.carmelmission.org; 3080 Rio Rd; adult/child 7-17yr $10/7; ⊙9:30am-5pm; P) Carmel's strikingly beautiful mission is an oasis of solemnity with flowering gardens and a thick-walled basilica filled with Spanish Colonial art and artifacts. The mission was originally established by Franciscan friar Junípero Serra in 1770 in nearby Monterey, but poor soil and the corrupting influence of Spanish soldiers forced the move to Carmel two years later. The mission became Serra's home base and he died here in 1784.

Tor House HISTORIC BUILDING
(Map p306; ☎844-285-0244; www.torhouse.org; 26304 Ocean View Ave; adult/child 12-17yr $12/7; ⊙tours hourly 10am-3pm Fri & Sat) Even if you've never heard of 20th-century poet Robinson Jeffers, a pilgrimage to this house built with his own hands offers fascinating insights into both the man and the bohemian ethos of Old Carmel. A porthole in the Celtic-inspired **Hawk Tower** reputedly came from the wrecked ship that carried Napoleon from Elba. The only way to visit the property is to reserve a tour (children under 12 years old not allowed), although the tower can be glimpsed from the street.

Carmel Beach City Park BEACH
(Map p306; off Scenic Rd; ♿ 🐾) Not always sunny, Carmel Beach is a gorgeous blanket of white sand, where pampered pups excitedly run off-leash. South of 10th Ave, bonfires crackle after sunset (until 10pm Monday through Thursday only).

Whalers Cove DIVING
(Map p306; ☎831-624-8413; www.parks.ca.gov; Point Lobos State Natural Reserve; dive permits $20-30; ⊙8am-7pm) The kelp forest at Whalers Cove teems with rockfish, sea otters, seals and other underwater critters and is one of only two places in the Point Lobos State Natural Reserve where you can snorkel or dive. Permits are available online; they're essential on weekends and holidays and a good idea on weekdays. Divers must show certification.

Festivals & Events

Pebble Beach Food & Wine FOOD & DRINK
(☎866-907-3663; www.pbfw.com; ⊙mid- to late April) Excellent four-day gastronomy-focused festival sponsored by the prestigious *Food & Wine* magazine. Held in mid- to late April.

Sleeping

In summer and on weekends, shockingly overpriced boutique hotels, inns and B&Bs fill up quickly in Carmel-by-the-Sea. Ask the

Carmel Visitor Center about last-minute deals. For better-value lodgings, head north to Monterey.

Mission Ranch INN $$

(Map p306; 831-624-6436; www.missionranchcarmel.com; 26270 Dolores St; r $130-335; P) If the sight of woolly sheep grazing on green fields by the beach doesn't convince you to stay here, maybe knowing that Hollywood icon Clint Eastwood restored this historic ranch will. Accommodations are shabby-chic and rustic.

Cypress Inn BOUTIQUE HOTEL $$$

(Map p306; 831-624-3871; www.cypress-inn.com; cnr Lincoln St & 7th Ave; r/ste from $299/499; P) Done up in Spanish Colonial style, this 1929 inn was co-owned by movie star Doris Day for 20 years. Airy terracotta hallways with colorful tiles give it a Mediterranean feel, while sunny rooms face the courtyard. Pet fee $30.

Eating

Carmel's dining scene has traditionally been more about old-world atmosphere, but more recent openings have added a more modern, cosmopolitan sheen.

Bruno's Market & Deli DELI $

(Map p306; 831-624-3821; www.brunosmarket.com; cnr 6th & Junipero St; sandwiches $6-9; 7am-8pm; P) This small supermarket deli counter makes a saucy sandwich of oak-wood-grilled tri-tip beef and stocks all the accoutrements for a beach picnic, including Sparky's root beer from Pacific Grove. A good-value choice in pricey Carmel.

★**Cultura Comida y Bebida** MEXICAN $$

(Map p306; 831-250-7005; www.culturacarmel.com; Dolores St btwn 5th & 6th Aves; mains $19-33; 5:30pm-midnight daily, 10:30am-3:30pm Sat & Sun;) In a brick-lined courtyard, this vivaciously elegant restaurant pairs art and candlelight with food inspired by Oaxacan flavors and an entire library's worth of mezcal. The ambience is upscale but relaxed, and suitable both for a date night or an outing with your posse. The Cultura mole with smoked pork and saffron tortillas is a signature dish.

Yafa MEDITERRANEAN $$

(Map p306; 831-624-9232; www.yafarestaurant.com; cnr Junipero St & 5th Ave; meze $8-13, mains $20-30; 5-10pm;) Middle Eastern and Mediterranean cuisine shines at Yafa's corner location in the center of Carmel village. Share a few meze-style appetizers including ouzo-sautéed shrimp, pita bread and grilled octopus, before enjoying grilled kabobs or pasta dishes infused with the flavors of both Italy and the Levant. Plenty of vegetable-based dishes make this a good option for vegetarians.

La Bicyclette FRENCH $$$

(Map p306; 831-622-9899; www.labicyclerestaurant.com; cnr Dolores St & 7th Ave; mains lunch $21-31, dinner $21-48; 8am-10pm) Rustic French comfort food using seasonal local ingredients and an open kitchen baking wood-fired-oven pizzas packs couples into this bistro. Excellent local wines by the glass. It's also a top spot for a leisurely lunch.

Drinking & Entertainment

The best option for late-night drinks is the cool and energetic scene at Barmel.

★**Yeast of Eden** CRAFT BEER

(Map p306; 831-293-8621; www.yoebeer.com; Mission St & Ocean Ave, Suite 112m Carmel Plaza; 11:30am-9pm Sun-Thu, to 10pm Fri & Sat) Mixed fermentation beers – many harnessing wild yeasts – make this offshoot of Monterey's Alvarado Street Brewery (p309) one of coastal California's most interesting destinations for traveling beer fans. Secure a spot at the bar amid the modern decor and try a wild ale barrel-fermented with albariño grapes or a stone-fruit farmhouse ale. Good food includes tuna *tataki* and pan-roasted scallops.

Barmel BAR

(Map p306; 831-626-2095; www.facebook.com/BarmelByTheSea; San Carlos St btwn Ocean & 7th Aves; 3pm-2am Mon-Sat, to midnight Sun) Shaking up Carmel's conservative image and adding a dash of after-dark fun is this cool little Spanish-themed courtyard bar. Come for free concerts from 7pm to 9pm Thursday to Saturday, or hit the dance floor on Friday and Saturday when DJs helm the decks from 9:30pm until closing. Sundays are vinyl nights.

Scheid Vineyards WINE BAR

(Map p306; 831-656-9463; www.scheidvineyards.com; San Carlos St, at 7th Ave; tasting flights $15-25; noon-6pm Sun-Thu, to 7pm Fri & Sat) Pop into Scheid Vineyards' wine-tasting room to sip a prodigious range of grape varietals, all grown in Monterey County. Red wine varietals including merlot, pinot noir and cabernet sauvignon are local stars.

WORTH A TRIP

CARMEL VALLEY

Where sun-kissed vineyards rustle beside farm fields, Carmel Valley is a peaceful side trip, just a 20-minute drive east of Hwy 1 along eastbound Carmel Valley Rd. At organic **Earthbound Farm Stand** (805-625-6219; www.ebfarm.com; 7250 Carmel Valley Rd; 8am-6pm Mon-Sat, 9am-6pm Sun;), sample homemade soups and salads or harvest your own herbs from the garden.

An expanding number of wineries and tasting rooms further east offer tastings. Highlights include the pinot noir bottled by **Boekenoogen** (Map p316; 831-659-4215; www.boekenoogenwines.com; 24 W Carmel Valley Rd; tasting flights $15-20; 11am-5pm; P), and the Californian-, French- and Spanish-style wines at **I. Brand & Family** (Map p316; 831-298-7227; www.ibrandwinery.com; 19 E Carmel Valley Rd; tastings $20; noon-6pm Wed-Sun). A vinyl turntable and retro board games give the tasting room a hip ambience. Nearby, the tasting room at **Joyce Wine Company** (Map p316; 831-659-2885; www.joycewineco.com; 1 E Carmel Valley Rd; tastings $15-20; noon-5:30pm; P) is one of Carmel Valley's most stylish and a good place to try its well-regarded pinot noir and rosé varietals.

Afterwards, stretch your legs in the village of Carmel Valley, crammed with genteel shops and bistros. There is excellent Mediterranean cuisine including wood-fired pizza and an exceptionally cozy atmosphere at **Corkscrew Cafe** (Map p316; 831- 659-8888; www.corkscrewcafe.com; 55 W Carmel Valley Rd; mains $18-30; 11:30am-9pm Thu-Mon; P), and close by, **Roux** (Map p316; 831-659-5020; www.rouxcarmel.com; 6 Pilot Rd; tapas $12-18, mains $19-28; 11:30am-2pm & 5-8pm Fri-Mon) combines French and Spanish flavors amid a shaded garden setting. Try the 'Surf & Turf' paella for two people. Reservations are recommended for dinner.

Try and visit on a weekend for the widest selection of open tasting rooms and restaurants, and consider the centrally located **Hidden Valley Inn** (Map p316; 831-659-5361; www.visithiddenvalleyinn.com; 102 W Carmel Valley Rd; d $189-259; P) for a relaxing overnight stay in this exceptionally pleasant rural village.

Forest Theater THEATER
(Map p306; box office 831-622-0100; www.foresttheatercarmel.org; cnr Mountain View Ave & Santa Rita St) At this 1910 venue, community-theater musicals, dramas and comedies as well as film screenings take place under the stars by flickering fire pits.

Information

Carmel Visitor Center (Map p306; 831-624-2522; www.carmelchamber.org; Ocean Ave btwn Junipero & Mission Sts, 2nd fl, Carmel Plaza; 10am-5pm) Pick up maps, brochures and tips on Carmel and the surrounding area.

Getting There & Away

Carmel is about 5 miles south of Monterey via Hwy 1. There's free parking (no time limit) in a **municipal lot** (Map p306; cnr 3rd Ave & Junípero St) behind the Vista Lobos building.

MST (888-678-2871; www.mst.org) 'Grapevine Express' bus 24 ($2.50, hourly) connects Monterey's Transit Plaza with downtown Carmel, the mission and Carmel Valley. Bus 22 ($3.50) stops in downtown Carmel and at the mission en route to/from Point Lobos and Big Sur three times daily between late May and early September, and twice daily on Saturday and Sunday only throughout the rest of the year.

Big Sur

Big Sur is more a state of mind than a place to pinpoint on a map, and when the sun goes down, the moon and the stars are the area's natural streetlights. (That is, if summer's fog hasn't extinguished them.) Raw beauty and an intense maritime energy characterize this land shoehorned between the Santa Lucia Range and the Pacific Ocean, and a first glimpse of the craggy, unspoiled coastline is a special moment.

In the 1950s and '60s, Big Sur – named by Spanish settlers living on the Monterey Peninsula, who referred to the wilderness as *el país grande del sur* ('the big country to the south') – became a retreat for artists and writers, including Henry Miller and Beat Generation visionaries such as Lawrence Ferlinghetti. Today Big Sur attracts self-proclaimed artists, New Age mystics, latter-day hippies and city slickers seeking to unplug and reflect more deeply on this emerald-green edge of the continent.

Big Sur

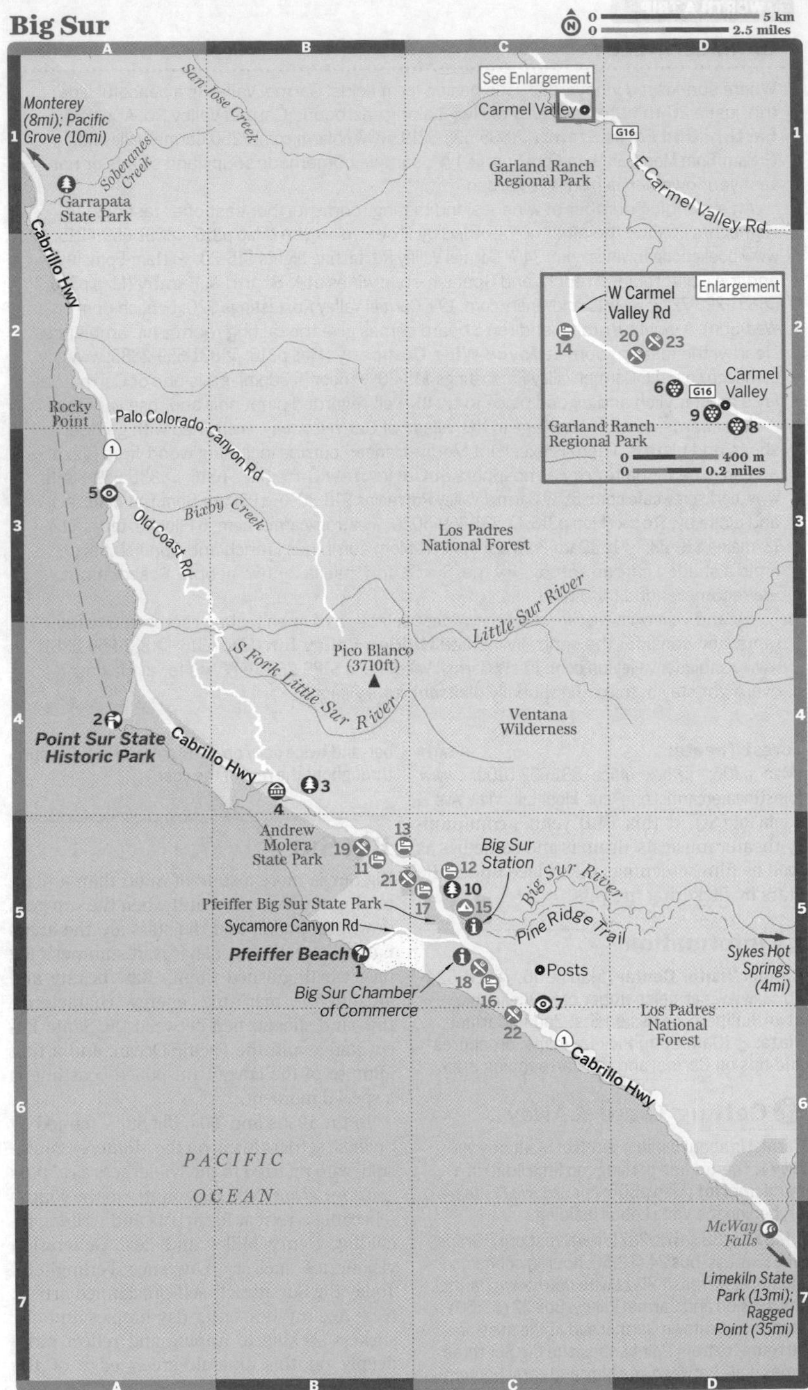
0 5 km
0 2.5 miles
See Enlargement
Carmel Valley
G16
Garland Ranch Regional Park
E Carmel Valley Rd
Monterey (8mi); Pacific Grove (10mi)
San Jose Creek
Soberanes Creek
Garrapata State Park
Cabrillo Hwy
Enlargement
W Carmel Valley Rd
14
20
23
Carmel Valley
6
G16
9
8
Garland Ranch Regional Park
0 400 m
0 0.2 miles
Rocky Point
Palo Colorado Canyon Rd
1
5
Bixby Creek
Old Coast Rd
Los Padres National Forest
Little Sur River
Pico Blanco (3710ft)
S Fork Little Sur River
Ventana Wilderness
2
Point Sur State Historic Park
Cabrillo Hwy
3
4
Andrew Molera State Park
13
19
11
12
21
10
17
Big Sur Station
Big Sur River
15
Pfeiffer Big Sur State Park
Sycamore Canyon Rd
Pine Ridge Trail
Pfeiffer Beach
1
Sykes Hot Springs (4mi)
Posts
18
16
Big Sur Chamber of Commerce
7
22
Los Padres National Forest
1
Cabrillo Hwy
PACIFIC OCEAN
McWay Falls
Limekiln State Park (13mi); Ragged Point (35mi)

Big Sur

Top Sights

1 Pfeiffer Beach ... B5
2 Point Sur State Historic Park ... A4

Sights

3 Andrew Molera State Park ... B4
4 Big Sur Discovery Center ... B4
5 Bixby Bridge ... A3
6 Boekenoogen ... D2
7 Henry Miller Memorial Library ... C5
8 I. Brand & Family ... D3
9 Joyce Wine Company ... D2
10 Pfeiffer Big Sur State Park ... C5

Sleeping

11 Big Sur Campground & Cabins ... B5
12 Big Sur Lodge ... C5
13 Glen Oaks Big Sur ... B5
14 Hidden Valley Inn ... C2
15 Pfeiffer Big Sur State Park Campground ... C5
16 Post Ranch Inn ... C5
17 Ripplewood Resort ... C5

Eating

18 Big Sur Bakery & Restaurant ... C5
Big Sur Deli & General Store ... (see 18)
19 Big Sur River Inn ... B5
Big Sur Roadhouse ... (see 13)
20 Corkscrew Cafe ... D2
21 Fernwood Tavern ... B5
22 Nepenthe ... C6
23 Roux ... D2

Drinking & Nightlife

Big Sur Taphouse ... (see 18)

Entertainment

Henry Miller Memorial Library ... (see 7)

Sights & Activities

At Big Sur's state parks, your parking fee ($10) receipt is valid for same-day entry to all except Limekiln. Note that most parks can't accept electronic payments or credit cards and you'll need to pay with cash.

Please don't skip paying the entry fee by parking illegally outside the parks along Hwy 1 – California's state parks have suffered severe budget cutbacks, and every dollar helps.

Due to the impact of COVID-19, many California state parks have had to restrict access. Check park websites carefully for the latest information before setting off.

Garrapata State Park — PARK

(Map p316; 831-624-4909; www.parks.ca.gov; off Hwy 1;) FREE Over 4 miles south of Point Lobos on Hwy 1, pull over to hike coastal headlands, where you might spot whales cruising by offshore during winter, or into canyons of wildflowers and redwood trees. *Garrapata* is Spanish for 'tick,' of which there are many in the canyon and woods, so wearing long sleeves and pants is smart. Leashed dogs are allowed on the beach only.

Bixby Bridge — LANDMARK

(Map p316) Less than 15 miles south of Carmel, this landmark spanning Rainbow Canyon is one of the world's highest single-span bridges. Completed in 1932, it was built by prisoners eager to lop time off their sentences. Off-road parking is limited and can create a traffic hazard. Consider stopping instead at other safer lay-bys taking in equally stellar coastal scenery at many other places further south along Hwy 1. If you do stop at the bridge, early morning is the safest option.

★ Point Sur State Historic Park — LIGHTHOUSE

(Map p316; 831-625-4419; www.pointsur.org; off Hwy 1; adult/child 6-17yr from $15/5; tours 10am & 2pm Wed & Sat, 10am Sun Apr-Sep, 1pm Wed, 10am Sat & Sun Oct-Mar) FREE Around 6 miles south of Bixby Bridge, Point Sur rises like a green fortress from the sea. It looks like an island, but is connected by a sandbar. Atop the volcanic rock sits an 1889 stone light station, staffed until 1974. Three-hour guided tours include ocean views and engrossing tales of the facility's importance in tracking Soviet submarines during the Cold War. Tours are first come, first served and meet at the locked farm gate 0.25-miles north of Point Sur Naval Facility.

Andrew Molera State Park — STATE PARK

(Map p316; 831-667-2315; www.parks.ca.gov; Hwy 1; day use per car $10, cash only; 30min before sunrise-30min after sunset;) Named after the farmer who first planted artichokes in California, this oft-overlooked park is a trail-laced, patchwork quilt of grassy meadows, ocean bluffs and rugged sandy beaches offering excellent wildlife-watching. Look for the entrance just more than 8 miles south of Bixby Bridge. Occasional floods can sometimes close some trails. Check the website for current conditions.

South of the parking lot, you can learn all about endangered California condors as well as long-term species recovery and monitoring programs inside the **Big Sur Discovery Center** (Map p316; ☎831-620-0702; www.ventanaws.org/discovery_center; Andrew Molera State Park; ⏰10am-4pm Sat & Sun late May-early Sep; P 👪) FREE. The center also arranges two-hour condor tours at 10:30am on occasional Saturdays from June to November (per person $75, register online). Check the website for confirmed dates.

Pfeiffer Big Sur State Park PARK
(Map p316; ☎831-667-2315; www.parks.ca.gov; 47225 Hwy 1; per car $10; ⏰30min before sunrise-30min after sunset; P 👪) Big Sur's largest state park was named after the area's first European settlers. It has hiking trails looping through stately redwood groves. Traditionally, the most popular trail has been a 2-mile round trip to 60ft-high **Pfeiffer Falls** (usually flowing from December to May), but this was closed temporarily at the time of writing. Also popular is a 0.7-mile **nature walk** and the **Buzzard's Roost** trail, a 3-mile moderate loop following the Big Sur River to views of the Pacific.

★**Julia Pfeiffer Burns State Park** PARK
(☎831-667-2315; www.parks.ca.gov; Hwy 1; day use per car $10, cash only; ⏰30min before sunrise-30min after sunset; P 👪) If you're chasing waterfalls, swing into this state park named for a Big Sur pioneer. From the parking lot, the 1.3-mile round-trip **Waterfall Overlook Trail** rushes downhill toward the ocean, offering photogenic views of the 80ft-high **McWay Falls**, which tumbles year-round over granite cliffs and free-falls into the sea. Note there is no trail access to the beach and it is strictly forbidden to explore the cliff areas beyond the fenced boundaries.

★**Pfeiffer Beach** BEACH
(Map p316; ☎805-434-1996; www.campone.com; Sycamore Canyon Rd; day use per car $12, cash and credit cards; ⏰9am-8pm; P 👪 🐾) This phenomenal crescent-shaped beach is known for its huge double-rock formation, through which waves crash with life-affirming power. Dig down into the wet sand – it's purple! That's because manganese garnet washes down from the craggy hillsides above. It's often windy, and the surf is too dangerous for swimming.

Henry Miller Memorial Library ARTS CENTER
(Map p316; ☎831-667-2574; www.henrymiller.org; 48603 Hwy 1; donations accepted; ⏰11am-5pm Wed-Sun) FREE Novelist Henry Miller was a Big Sur denizen from 1944 to 1962. More of a beatnik memorial, alt-cultural venue and bookshop, this community gathering spot was never Miller's home. The house belonged to Miller's friend, painter Emil White, until his death and is now run by a nonprofit group. Stop by to browse and relax on the deck. Concerts are held on a stage in the garden. Check online for listings. The library is 0.4 miles south of Nepenthe restaurant (p321).

Partington Cove BEACH
(off Hwy 1) FREE This is a raw, breathtaking spot where crashing surf salts your skin. On the steep, half-mile dirt hike down to the cove, you'll cross a cool bridge and go through an even cooler tunnel. The cove's water is unbelievably aqua and within it grow tangled kelp forests. Look for the unmarked trailhead turnoff inside a hairpin turn on the ocean side of Hwy 1, about 6 miles south of Nepenthe restaurant (p321) and 2 miles north of Julia Pfeiffer Burns State Park.

Limekiln State Park PARK
(☎831-434-1996; www.parks.ca.gov; 63025 Hwy 1; per car $10, cash only; ⏰8am-sunset) Two miles south of Lucia, this park gets its name from the four remaining wood-fired kilns originally built here in the 1880s to smelt quarried limestone into powder, a key ingredient in cement-building construction from Monterey to San Francisco. Tragically, pioneers chopped down most of the steep canyon's old-growth redwoods to fuel the kilns' fires. A 1-mile round-trip trail leads through a redwood grove to the historic site, passing a creekside spur trail to a delightful 100ft-high waterfall.

Los Padres National Forest FOREST
(☎805-968-6640; https://fs.usda.gov/lpnf; Hwy 1; 🐾) The tortuously winding 40-mile stretch of Hwy 1 south of Lucia to Hearst Castle is sparsely populated, rugged and remote, mostly running through national forest lands. Around 5 miles south of **Kirk Creek Campground** (☎805-434-1996, reservations 877-444-6777; www.recreation.gov; Hwy 1; tent & RV sites $35) and Nacimiento-Fergusson Rd, almost opposite **Plaskett Creek Campground** (☎reservations 877-477-6777; www.recreation.gov; Hwy 1; tent & RV sites $35), is **Sand Dollar Beach** (http://campone.com; Hwy 1; per car $10, free with local USFS campground fee; ⏰9am-8pm; 🐾). From the picnic area, it's a five-minute walk to southern Big Sur's longest sandy beach, a crescent-shaped strip of sand protected from winds by high bluffs. Nearby is **Jade Cove**

WORTH A TRIP

VENTANA WILDERNESS

The 240,000-acre Ventana Wilderness is Big Sur's wild backcountry. It lies within the northern Los Padres National Forest, which straddles the Santa Lucia Range running parallel to the coast. Most of this wilderness is covered with oak and chaparral, though canyons cut by the Big Sur and Little Sur Rivers support virgin stands of coast redwoods and the rare endemic Santa Lucia fir, which grows on steep, rocky slopes too.

Still slowly regenerating after devastating wildfires in 2008, Ventana Wilderness is popular with adventurous backpackers. A popular overnight destination is **Sykes Hot Springs**, natural 100°F (35°C) mineral pools framed by redwoods. It's a moderately strenuous 10-mile, one-way hike along the **Pine Ridge Trail**, starting from Big Sur Station (p321), where you can get free campfire permits and pay for overnight trailhead parking ($5). Don't expect solitude on weekends during peak season (April through September) and always follow Leave No Trace (www.lnt.org) principles.

(http://campone.com; Hwy 1; sunrise-sunset;) FREE and it's a short drive south to Salmon Creek Falls (p319).

Ragged Point LANDMARK
(19019 Hwy 1) Your last – or first – taste of Big Sur's rocky grandeur comes at this craggy cliff outcropping with fabulous views of the coastline in both directions, about 15 miles north of Hearst Castle (p323). Once part of the Hearst empire, Ragged Point is now taken over by a sprawling, ho-hum lodge with a pricey gas station. Heading south, the land grows increasingly windswept as Hwy 1 rolls gently down to the water's edge.

Salmon Creek Falls WATERFALL
(https://visitsansimeonca.com/what-to-do/salmon-creek-falls; Hwy 1;) FREE Take a short hike to splash around in the pools at the base of this double-drop waterfall, tucked uphill in a forested canyon. The falls usually run from December through May, and the trail is dog-friendly. In a hairpin turn of Hwy 1, the roadside turnoff is marked only by a small brown trailhead sign, about 8 miles south of Gorda.

Esalen Hot Springs HOT SPRINGS
(831-667-3047; www.esalen.org; 55000 Hwy 1; per person $30; by reservation only) At the private **Esalen Institute** (831-667-3000; www.esalen.org; 55000 Hwy 1; per person $35; 1am-3am), clothing-optional baths fed by a natural hot spring sit on a ledge above the ocean. We're confident you'll never take another dip that compares scenery-wise, especially on stormy winter nights. Only two small outdoor pools perch directly over the waves, so once you've stripped and taken a quick shower, head outside immediately. Credit cards only.

Sleeping

With few exceptions, Big Sur's lodgings do not have TVs and rarely have telephones. This is where you come to escape the world. There aren't a lot of rooms overall, so demand often exceeds supply and prices can be steep. Bigger price tags don't necessarily buy you more amenities either. In summer and on weekends, reservations are essential everywhere, from campgrounds to deluxe resorts.

Ripplewood Resort CABIN $$
(Map p316; 831-667-2242; www.ripplewoodresort.com; 47047 Hwy 1; cabins $110-275;) North of Pfeiffer Big Sur State Park, Ripplewood supports fiscal equality by charging the same rates year-round. Most of the throwback Americana style cabins have kitchens and sometimes even wood-burning fireplaces. Quiet riverside cabins are surrounded by redwoods, but roadside cabins can be noisy. There's a small general store and a popular cafe that serves breakfast and lunch (8am to 2pm). Wi-fi is available in the cafe only.

★**Glen Oaks Big Sur** BOUTIQUE HOTEL $$$
(Map p316; 831-667-2105; www.glenoaksbigsur.com; 47080 Hwy 1; d $310-660;) At this 1950s redwood-and-adobe motor lodge, rooms and cabins are rustic yet exude effortless chic. Dramatically transformed by eco-conscious design, each of these romantic hideaways has a gas fireplace and unique design features. For more space, book into the woodsy cottages in a redwood grove that come with kitchenettes and shared fire pits.

Post Ranch Inn LUXURY HOTEL $$$
(Map p316; 831-667-2200; www.postranchinn.com; 47900 Hwy 1; d from $1095;)

(📶🐕) The last word in luxurious coastal getaways, this adult-only ranch retreat pampers guests with private hot tubs, wood-burning fireplaces, decks and a free minibar. Enjoy dreamy sunset views from the ocean-facing units or fall asleep 9ft off the forest floor in a tree house. The clifftop infinity pool invites chilling, perhaps after a shamanic-healing session or yoga class. Breakfast included.

Treebones Resort CABIN $$$
(☎805-927-2390; www.treebonesresort.com; 71895 Hwy 1; tent sites $95, yurts with shared bath from $320; P⊖📶🐕) 🍃 Don't let the word 'resort' mislead you. Yes, it has an ocean-view hot tub, a heated pool and massage treatments. But a unique woven 'human nest' and canvas-sided yurts with polished pine floors, quilt-covered beds, sink vanities and redwood decks offer an experience more akin to glamping, with little privacy. Communal bathrooms and showers are a short stroll away.

Public Campgrounds

Camping is currently available at two of Big Sur's state parks and two United States Forest Service (USFS) campgrounds along Hwy 1.

Pfeiffer Big Sur State Park Campground CAMPGROUND $
(Map p316; ☎reservations 800-444-7275; www.reservecalifornia.com; 47225 Hwy 1; tent & RV sites $35-50; P🐕) These 169 campsites (without hookups) nestle in a redwood-shaded valley and are good for novice campers and families with young kids. Facilities include toilets, drinking water, fire pits and coin-operated hot showers.

Limekiln State Park Campground CAMPGROUND $
(☎reservations 800-444-7275; www.reservecalifornia.com; 63025 Hwy 1; tent & RV sites $35; 🐕) In southern Big Sur, this quiet state park has two dozen campsites huddled under a bridge next to the ocean. Drinking water, fire pits and coin-operated hot showers are available.

Big Sur Campground & Cabins CABIN, CAMPGROUND $$
(Map p316; ☎831-667-2322; www.bigsurcamp.com; 47000 Hwy 1; tent/RV sites from $70/80, cabins $185-440; P⊖) Situated on the Big Sur River and shaded by redwoods, cozy cabins sport full kitchens and fireplaces, while canvas-sided tent cabins share bathroom facilities. The riverside campground, where neighboring sites have little privacy, is popular with RVers. There are hot showers and a coin-operated laundry, a playground and a general store.

Eating

Like Big Sur's lodgings, some restaurants and cafes alongside Hwy 1 can be overpriced and underwhelming, but stellar views at some locations do offset any mediocrity.

Big Sur Roadhouse CALIFORNIAN $
(Map p316; ☎831-667-2370; www.glenoaksbigsur.com/big-sur-roadhouse; 47080 Hwy 1; snacks & mains $8-16; ⊙8am-2:30pm; 📶👪) This modern roadhouse glows with color-splashed artwork and an outdoor fire pit. At riverside tables, tuck into upscale California-inspired bar food such as spicy wings, pork sliders and gourmet burgers, with craft beer on tap. It's also a top spot for coffee and cake.

DRIVING HIGHWAY 1

Driving this narrow two-lane highway through Big Sur and beyond is slow going. Allow at least three hours to cover the 140 miles between the Monterey Peninsula and San Luis Obispo, more if you stop to explore the coast. Don't travel Hwy 1 at night as it's too risky and you'll also miss out on the terrific views. Watch out for cyclists, and avoid stopping at Bixby Bridge. Make use instead of safer signposted roadside pullouts for photographs and to let faster-moving traffic pass.

Traffic along the route can get congested so try and avoid overtouristed weekends – accommodations are also usually cheaper mid-week – and park at state park lots instead of along crowded roadsides.

Future plans to alleviate Highway 1's surging popularity are detailed at www.sustainablehighway1.com. Ideas being considered include increasing public transit via an integrated series of shuttles, applying a parking reservation system at the most popular stops, and creating more paved viewpoints and pullouts.

Big Sur Deli & General Store SANDWICHES $

(Map p316; 831-667-2225; www.bigsurdeli.com; 47520 Hwy 1, Big Sur Village; sandwiches $5-11; 7am-8pm;) Put together a picnic of freshly made sandwiches from this family-owned deli and pair them with drinks and chips from the attached store, which also carries other essentials from beer to batteries. The best-value food along this part of Hwy 1.

Fernwood Tavern PUB FOOD $$

(Map p316; 831-667-2422; www.fernwoodbigsur.com; 47200 Hwy 1; mains $12-20; 11am-11pm Sun-Thu, to 1am Fri & Sat;) Hearty burgers, burritos and build-your-own pizzas combine with regular weekend live music at this laid-back and welcoming tavern. Adjourn to the rear deck to cozy up to the fire pits or take on your traveling companions at the table tennis table. Check the website to see what's scheduled – usually on Friday and Saturday nights.

Nepenthe CALIFORNIAN $$$

(Map p316; 831-667-2345; www.nepenthebigsur.com; 48510 Hwy 1; mains lunch $18-25, dinner $18-53; 11:30am-10pm;) Nepenthe comes from a Greek word meaning 'isle of no sorrow,' and indeed it's hard to feel blue while sitting by the fire pit on this aerial terrace. Just-OK California cuisine (try the renowned Ambrosia burger) takes a back seat to the views and Nepenthe's history – Orson Welles and Rita Hayworth briefly owned a cabin here in the 1940s. Kids menu available.

Downstairs, casual Café Kevah serves coffee, baked goods, light brunches and the same head-spinning ocean views on its deck (closed during winter and bad weather).

Big Sur Bakery & Restaurant CALIFORNIAN $$$

(Map p316; 831-667-0520; www.bigsurbakery.com; 47540 Hwy 1; bakery items $5-12, mains $22-38; bakery from 8am daily, restaurant 9:30am-2pm Mon-Fri, 10am-2:30pm Sat & Sun, 5:30pm-late Wed-Sat) Behind the Shell station, this warmly lit, funky house has seasonally changing menus, on which wood-fired pizzas share space with rustic dishes like grilled swordfish or wood-roasted chicken. Fronted by a pretty patio, the bakery makes addictive cinnamon buns and stuffed sandwiches. Expect occasional longish waits. Dinner reservations are essential.

Big Sur River Inn AMERICAN $$$

(Map p316; 831-667-2700; www.bigsurriverinn.com; 46840 Hwy 1; mains breakfast & lunch $12-28, dinner $21-32; 8am-9pm;) Woodsy restaurant with a deck, overlooking a creek teeming with throaty frogs. The food is standard American – burgers, steak, sandwiches, roast chicken and salads – and there are a few vegetarian dishes. Breakfast features breakout options such as the utterly irresistible carrot-cake French toast with maple-caramel sauce. Great apple pie, too.

Rooms (starting at $150), a general store and gas station are also available.

Drinking & Entertainment

Californian craft beers are a Big Sur highlight at the Big Sur Taphouse while there are excellent wine lists at clifftop restaurants with rugged Pacific Ocean vistas.

Big Sur Taphouse BAR

(Map p316; 831-667-2197; www.bigsurtaphouse.com; 47520 Hwy 1, Big Sur Village; noon-10pm;) Down California craft beers and regional wines on the back deck or by the fireplace inside this high-ceilinged wooden bar. There are board games, sports on the TVs and balance-restoring pub grub from tacos to artisanal cheeses (dishes $7 to $19).

Henry Miller Memorial Library LIVE PERFORMANCE

(Map p316; 831-667-2574; www.henrymiller.org; 48603 Hwy 1; 11am-5pm Wed-Sun;) FREE Henry Miller lived in Big Sur for 17 years, some 5 miles south of this now nonprofit alternative art space and community center in the home of his late best friend Emil White. Eclectic sculptures line a tree-shaded path leading to a bookshop and an outdoor stage hosting concerts, readings, screenings and other cultural fodder.

Information

Visitors often wander into businesses along Hwy 1 and ask, 'How much further to Big Sur?' In fact, there is no town of Big Sur as such, though you may see the name on maps. Commercial activity is concentrated along the stretch north of Pfeiffer Big Sur State Park (p318). Sometimes called 'the Village,' this is where you'll find most of the lodgings, restaurants and shops.

Big Sur Chamber of Commerce (Map p316; 831-667-2100; www.bigsurcalifornia.org; Hwy 1; 9am-1pm Mon, Wed & Fri)

Big Sur Station (Map p316; 831-667-2315; 47555 Hwy 1; 9am-4pm;) This multiagency ranger station has information about hiking, camping, backpacking, road conditions and more. It also sells trail maps and guidebooks. Cellphone coverage is decent. It's about 1 mile north of Big Sur village.

Getting There & Around

Big Sur is best explored by car, since you'll be itching to stop frequently and take in the rugged beauty and vistas that reveal themselves after every hairpin turn. Even if your driving skills are up to these narrow switchbacks, others' aren't: expect to average 35mph or less along the route. Parts of Hwy 1 are battle-scarred, evidence of a continual struggle to keep them open after landslides and washouts. Check current highway conditions with **CalTrans** (CalTrans; ☎800-427-7623; www.dot.ca.gov) and fill up your gas tank beforehand.

MST (☎888-678-2871; www.mst.org) bus 22 ($3.50, 1¼ hours) travels from Monterey via Carmel and Point Lobos as far south as Nepenthe restaurant (p321), stopping en route at Andrew Molera State Park (p317) and the Big Sur River Inn (p321). Buses run three times daily between late May and early September, and twice daily on Saturdays and Sundays only the rest of the year. On southbound journeys only, bus drivers will stop on request for photographs of Bixby Bridge.

Point Piedras Blancas

Many lighthouses still stand along California's coast, but few offer such a historically evocative seascape. Federally designated an outstanding natural area, the jutting, windblown grounds of this 1875 **light station** (☎805-927-7361; www.piedrasblancas.org; Hwy 1, San Simeon; tours adult/child 6-17yr $10/5; ⏲tours 9:45am Mon, Tue & Thu-Sat mid-Jun–Aug, 9:45am Tue, Thu & Sat Sep–mid-Jun) have been replanted with native flora. Everything looks much the way it did when the first lighthouse keepers helped ships find safe harbor at San Simeon Bay. Guided tours meet at the old Piedras Blancas Motel, 1.5 miles north of the light house gate on Hwy 1. No reservations are taken; call ahead to check tour schedules.

At a signposted vista point, around 4.5 miles north of Hearst Castle, you can observe a colony of northern elephant seals bigger than the one at Año Nuevo State Reserve near Santa Cruz. During peak winter season, about 18,000 seals seek shelter in the coves and beaches along this stretch of coast. Interpretative panels along a beach boardwalk and blue-jacketed Friends of the Elephant Seal (www.elephantseal.org) guides demystify the behavior of these giant beasts.

San Simeon

Little San Simeon Bay sprang to life as a whaling station in 1852, by which time California sea otters had been hunted almost to extinction by Russian fur traders. Shoreline whaling was practiced to catch gray whales migrating between Alaskan feeding grounds and birthing waters in Baja California. In 1865 Senator George Hearst purchased 45,000 acres of ranch land and established a small settlement beside the sea. Designed by architect Julia Morgan, the historic 19th-century houses today are rented to employees of the Hearst Corporation's 82,000-acre free-range cattle ranch.

Sights

William Randolph Hearst Memorial State Beach BEACH
(www.parks.ca.gov; Hwy 1; ⏲dawn-dusk; P 🚻) FREE Across from Hearst Castle, this bayfront beach is a pleasantly sandy stretch punctuated by rock outcroppings, kelp forests, a wooden pier (fishing permitted) and picnic areas with barbecue grills.

Hearst Ranch Winery WINERY
(☎805-927-4100; www.hearstranchwinery.com; 442 SLO-San Simeon Rd; tasting fee $15-20; ⏲11am-5pm; P) Currently operating from a new farm-style building with ocean views, the Hearst Ranch Winery's tasting room also includes many heritage black-and-white photographs of the area and the farming history of the Hearst family.

Sleeping

Modern San Simeon is nothing more than a strip of unexciting motels and lackluster restaurants. There are better-value places to stay and eat in Cambria and beach towns further south, such as Cayucos and Morro Bay.

Hearst San Simeon State Park Campground CAMPGROUND $
(☎805-772-6101; www.reservecalifornia.com; Hwy 1; tent/RV sites $20/35; P) About 2 miles north of Cambria, this bluff-top state park encompasses two campgrounds: **San Simeon Creek**, just steps from the beach, and the undeveloped **Washburn**, about 1 mile inland on a plateau. Both have tent and RV sites with fire pits and picnic tables, and the former has drinking water, chemical flush toilets and coin-operated showers.

CALIFORNIA'S COMEBACK CONDORS

When it comes to endangered species, one of the state's biggest success stories is the California condor (*Gymnogyps californianus*). These gigantic, prehistoric birds weigh more than 20lb with a wingspan of up to 10ft, letting them fly great distances in search of carrion. They're easily recognized by their naked pink head and large white patches on the underside of each wing.

This big bird became so rare that in 1987 there were only 27 left in the world, and all were removed from the wild to special captive-breeding facilities. Read the whole gripping story in journalist John Moir's book *Return of the Condor: The Race to Save Our Largest Bird from Extinction*.

There are more than 500 California condors alive today, with increasing numbers of captive birds being released back into the wild. It's hoped they will begin breeding naturally, although it's an uphill battle. Wild condors are still dying of lead poisoning caused by hunters' bullets in the game carcasses that the birds feed on.

The Big Sur coast and Pinnacles National Park (p331) offer excellent opportunities to view this majestic bird. In Big Sur, the Ventana Wildlife Society (www.ventanaws.org) occasionally leads two-hour guided condor-watching tours ($75) using radio telemetry to track the birds; for sign-up details, check the website or ask at the Big Sur Discovery Center (p318).

Hearst Castle

Hearst Castle (reservations 800-444-4445; www.hearstcastle.org; 750 Hearst Castle Rd; tours adult/child 5-12yr from $25/12; from 9am, last tour departs 4pm; P) is a wondrous, historic, over-the-top homage to material excess, perched high on a hill. The estate sprawls across acres of lushly landscaped gardens, accentuated by shimmering pools and fountains, statues from ancient Greece and Moorish Spain, and the ruins of what was in Hearst's day the world's largest private zoo (look for zebras grazing on the hillsides of neighboring Hearst Ranch). To see anything of this historic monument, you have to take a tour (try to book ahead).

The most important thing to know about William Randolph Hearst (1863–1951) is that he did not live like Citizen Kane. Not that Hearst wasn't bombastic, conniving and larger than life, but the moody recluse of Orson Welles' movie? Definitely not. Hearst also didn't call his 165-room estate a castle, preferring its official name, La Cuesta Encantada ('The Enchanted Hill'), or more often calling it simply 'the ranch.'

From the 1920s into the '40s, Hearst and Marion Davies, his longtime mistress (Hearst's wife refused to grant him a divorce), entertained a steady stream of the era's biggest movers and shakers. Invitations were highly coveted, but Hearst had his quirks – he despised drunkenness, and guests were forbidden to speak of death.

California's first licensed female architect, Julia Morgan based the main building, Casa Grande, on the design of a Spanish cathedral, and over the decades she catered to Hearst's every design whim, deftly integrating the spoils of his fabled European shopping sprees, including artifacts from antiquity and pieces of medieval monasteries.

Much like Hearst's construction budget, the castle will devour as much of your time and money as you let it. In peak summer months, show up early enough and you might be able to get a same-day tour ticket, but it's always better to make reservations in advance.

Tours usually depart starting at 9am daily, with the last leaving the visitor center for the 10-minute ride to the hilltop by 4pm (later in summer). There are three main tours: the guided portion of each lasts about an hour, after which you're free to wander the gardens and terraces and soak up the views. Best of all are Christmas holiday and springtime evening tours, featuring living-history reenactors who escort you back in time to the castle's 1930s heyday. For holiday and evening tours, book at least two weeks to a month beforehand.

Dress in plenty of layers: gloomy fog at the sea-level visitor center can turn into sunny skies at the castle's hilltop location, and vice versa. At the visitor center, a five-story theater shows a 40-minute historical film (free admission included with daytime tour tickets) about the castle and the Hearst family. Other facilities are geared for industrial-sized mobs of visitors. Before you leave, take a moment to visit the often-overlooked museum area at the back of the center.

It's closed on Thanksgiving, Christmas and New Year's Day, and closing time varies throughout the year. On Saturdays and Sundays, **RTA** (RTA; Map p337; ☎805-541-2228; www.slorta.org; single-ride fares $1.75-3.25) bus 15 makes a few daily round trips to the Hearst Castle Visitor Center via Cambria and Cayucos from Morro Bay ($3.25, 55 minutes), where you can transfer to/from bus 12 ($2.50, 25 minutes) to San Luis Obispo. A regional day pass for return day trips to Hearst Castle is $5.50. Outside of weekends, an Uber or Lyft one way from Cambria is around $25 but can be hard to secure.

Note that a full restoration of the famed Neptune Pool was completed in 2018, and the stunning pool is once again full of water.

Cambria

With a whopping dose of natural beauty, the coastal idyll of Cambria is a lone pearl cast along the coast. Built on lands that once belonged to Mission San Miguel, one of the village's first nicknames was Slabtown, after the rough pieces of wood that pioneer buildings were constructed from. Today, just like at neighboring Hearst Castle, money is no object in this wealthy community, whose motto 'Pines by the Sea' is affixed to the back of BMWs that cruise around town.

Sights & Activities

Although its milky-white moonstones are long gone, Moonstone Beach still attracts romantics to its oceanfront boardwalk and truly picturesque rocky shoreline. For more solitude, take the Windsor Blvd exit off Hwy 1 and drive down to where the road dead-ends, then follow a 2-mile round-trip bluff-top hiking trail across Fiscalini Ranch Preserve.

A 10-minute drive south of Cambria, past the Hwy 46 turnoff to Pasa Robles' wine country, tiny **Harmony** (population 18) is a privately owned collection of historic buildings awash with heritage charm. It's an easygoing slice of Americana where an 1865 creamery houses artists' workshops, and the delightful **Harmony Cellars winery** (☎805-927-1625; www.harmonycellars.com; 3255 Harmony Valley Rd, Harmony; tastings $15, refundable with purchase; ⏲10am-5pm, to 5:30pm Jul & Aug) sits on a nearby hillside. Don't miss the artisan ice cream from the Harmony Valley Creamery food truck.

A few miles further south there's good hiking at **Harmony Headlands State Park** (www.parks.ca.gov; Hwy 1; ⏲6am-sunset) FREE.

Sleeping

Cambria's choicest motels and hotels line Moonstone Beach Dr, while quaint B&Bs cluster around East Village.

Bridge Street Inn GUESTHOUSE $

(☎805-215-0724; www.bsicambria.com; 4314 Bridge St, East Village; r $50-100, cottage $125-200; P) Inside a 19th-century parsonage, surrounded by a garden, this European-style guesthouse has a quaint, raffish charm. There's a communal kitchen and five rooms with shared bathroom facilities, and the BBQ area is well used by international guests. One additional room has a separate toilet and washbasin, and there's an adjacent cottage with two compact bedrooms and a kitchenette.

Blue Dolphin Inn MOTEL $$

(☎805-927-3300; www.cambriainns.com; 6470 Moonstone Beach Dr; r $189-429; P) This sand-colored inn may not impress at first glance, but behind the ho-hum exterior are 20 supremely comfortable rooms with fireplaces, pillowtop mattresses and Tivoli radios. Rates include a satisfying picnic breakfast that you can take to the beach.

Eating & Drinking

It's a short walk between relaxed cafes and interesting restaurants in Cambria's East Village. Around 1 mile away, the West Village is developing as a hub for wine-tasting rooms.

Linn's Easy as Pie Cafe AMERICAN $

(☎805-924-3050; www.linnsfruitbin.com; 4251 Bridge St, East Village; dishes $10-15; ⏲10am-7pm Mon-Thu, to 8pm Fri & Sat;) If you don't have time to visit Linn's original farm stand on Santa Rosa Creek Rd (a 20-minute drive east via Main St), fork into its famous olallieberry pie at this takeout counter. There's a deck where you can devour dishes such as soulful chicken pot pie, meat loaf and clam chowder or bite into hearty wraps and panini.

Cambria Farmers Market MARKET $

(www.cambriafarmersmarket.com; 1000 Main St, Veteran's Hall parking lot; ⏲2:30-5:30pm Fri) Featuring plenty of local and seasonal produce.

Robin's INTERNATIONAL $$$

(☎805-927-5007; www.robinsrestaurant.com; 4095 Burton Dr, East Village; lunch $15-22, dinner $25-42; ⏲11am-9pm Sun-Thu, to 9:30pm Fri &

Sat; ✎) Global flavors from Asia and India feature on the wide-ranging menu at Robin's. Relax under the shaded arbor canopy in the rustic courtyard and graze on Indian flatbreads or Vietnamese spring rolls, or tuck into surprising lamb-curry burritos. A stellar wine list is equally cosmopolitan, with labels from Australia, New Zealand, Spain and France complementing California favorites.

Madeline's INTERNATIONAL $$$
(☎805-927-4175; www.madelinescambria.com; 788 Main St, West Village; dinner mains $26-37, lunch snacks $10-18; ⊙tasting room 11am-5pm, dinner 5-9pm, lunch 11am-3pm Sat & Sun) Madeline's own wines – including chardonnay and cabernet franc – are partnered with well-executed European classics at this combination restaurant and tasting room. Highlights of the dinner menu include rabbit crepes and Spanish octopus, while weekend lunches are a more informal affair featuring salads and savory tarts. Choose a bottle while tasting and then segue directly to dinner. Reservations recommended.

Information

Cambria Chamber of Commerce (☎805-927-3624; www.cambriachamber.org; 767 Main St; ⊙9am-5pm Mon-Fri, noon-4pm Sat & Sun) Staffed by a friendly crew ready to dispense maps and information.

Getting There & Away

Cambria is 140 miles south of Monterey and 39 miles north of San Luis Obispo. From Morro Bay, RTA (p340) bus 15 heads north via Cayucos to Cambria ($3.25, 35 minutes), stopping along Main St and Moonstone Beach Dr. On Saturdays and Sundays, buses continue north to Hearst Castle (p323). A regional day pass is $5.50 for return day trips to Hearst Castle.

Cayucos

With its historic storefronts housing antiques shops and eateries, the main drag of amiable, slow-paced Cayucos recalls an Old West frontier town. Just one block west of Ocean Ave, surf's up alongside the heritage wooden pier.

Sights & Activities

Fronting a broad white-sand beach, Cayucos' long wooden pier is popular with fishers. It's also a sheltered spot for beginner surfers.

Estero Bluffs State Park PARK
(☎805-772-7434; www.parks.ca.gov; Hwy 1; ⊙sunrise-sunset) FREE Ramble along coastal grasslands and pocket beaches at this small state park, accessed from unmarked roadside pulloffs north of Cayucos. Look among the scenic sea stacks to spot harbor seals hauled out on tide-splashed rocks.

Good Clean Fun WATER SPORTS
(☎805-995-1993; www.goodcleanfunusa.com; 136 Ocean Front Lane; group surfing lesson or kayak tour from $75; ⊙9am-6pm; 👪) By the beach, this friendly surf shop has all kinds of rental gear – wetsuits, bodyboards, surfboards, SUP sets and kayaks. Book in advance for surfing lessons and kayak (or kayak-fishing) tours.

EYEING ELEPHANT SEALS

The elephant seals that visit coastal California each year follow a precise calendar. In November and December, bulls (adult males) return to their colony's favorite California beaches and start the ritual struggles to assert superiority. Only the largest, strongest and most aggressive 'alpha' males gather a harem of females. In January and February, adult females, already pregnant from last year's beach antics, give birth to pups and soon mate with the dominant males, who promptly depart on their next feeding migration.

At birth an elephant seal pup weighs about 75lb; while being fed by its mother, it puts on about 10lb a day. Female seals leave the beach in March, abandoning their offspring. For up to two months the young seals, now known as 'weaners,' lounge around in groups, gradually learning to swim, first in tidal pools, then in the ocean. The weaners depart by May, having lost 20% to 30% of their weight during a prolonged fast.

Between June and October, elephant seals of all ages and both sexes return in smaller numbers to the beaches to molt. Always observe elephant seals from a safe distance (minimum 25ft) and do not approach or otherwise harass these unpredictable wild animals, who surprisingly can move faster on the sand than you can!

Cayucos Surf Company SURFING
(805-995-1000; www.surfcompany.com; 95 Cayucos Dr; board rentals from $19; 10am-5pm Mon-Fri, to 6pm Sat & Sun;) Near the pier, this landmark local surf shop rents surfboards, bodyboards, paddleboards and wetsuits. It also has a great line of own-brand surf apparel.

Sleeping

Cayucos doesn't lack for motels or beachfront inns. If there's no vacancy or prices look too high, head 6 miles south to Morro Bay.

Seaside Motel MOTEL $$
(805-995-3809; www.seasidemotel.com; 42 S Ocean Ave; d $120-200;) Expect a super-warm welcome at this vintage motel, which has a pretty cottage garden with Cape Cod chairs and ocean views. Some of the lovingly decorated country-kitsch rooms may be on the small side, so get a suite or a unit with kitchenette if you're a space craver. There's also a barbecue, complete with charcoal and tongs, available to guests.

★**Cass House Inn** INN $$$
(805-995-3669; www.casshousecayucos.com; 222 N Ocean Ave; d $265-385;) Inside a charmingly renovated 1867 Victorian inn, five boutique rooms beckon, some with ocean views, deep-soaking tubs and antique fireplaces to ward off chilly coastal fog. All rooms have plush beds, flat-screen TVs with DVD players, and tasteful, romantic accents.

Eating & Drinking

The dining scene stretches from excellent barbecue and fish tacos to local favorites, such as Cayucos cookies and sausages.

★**Cayucos Sausage Company** DELI $
(805-900-5377; www.facebook.com/CayucosSausageCompany; 12 N Ocean Ave; snacks $10-15; 10am-6pm Wed-Mon;) You'll need to wait around 20 minutes for your order, but be confident that the lovingly assembled grilled sausage sandwiches are definitely worth the wait. First choose your sausage – seasonal flavors could include bratwurst or hot Italian – and then settle on dressings and fixings. Deli sandwiches, including one with tender tri-tip steak, are also available. Canine customers are welcomed with outdoor treats.

Brown Butter Cookie Co BAKERY $
(805-995-2076; www.brownbuttercookies.com; 98 N Ocean Ave; snacks from $3; 9am-6pm;) Seriously addictive cookies are baked in all sorts of flavors including almond, citrus, cocoa, coconut-lime and original butter. Buy a bagful to provide tasty sustenance as you negotiate a stroll along Cayucos' restored 1872 pier. Special seasonal flavors could include cinnamon or lemon-citrus.

Ruddell's Smokehouse SEAFOOD $
(805-995–5028; www.smokerjim.com; 101 D St; dishes $6-15; 11am-6pm;) 'Smoker Jim' puts fresh-off-the-boat salmon, albacore tuna, ahi tuna and shrimp through the smoker before packing toasted tacos and french roll sandwiches. You might need to squeeze yourself in the door to order. If you're lucky, you may chance upon the Ruddell's food truck on summer weekends at craft breweries around the region. Dogs are allowed at the sidewalk tables.

Cayucos Coffee CAFE
(805-995-1617; www.cayucoscoffee.com; 155 N Ocean Ave; 6:30am-3pm) The best coffee in town. There's also kombucha on tap and superfood bowls and smoothies.

Getting There & Away

Cayucos is 15 miles south of Cambria and 19 miles north of San Luis Obispo. **RTA** (805-541-2228; www.slorta.org) bus 15 travels three to five times daily from Morro Bay ($1.75, 15 minutes) to Cayucos, continuing north to Cambria ($2.25, 20 minutes). On Saturdays and Sundays it also continues to the Hearst Castle Visitor Center ($2.25, 35 minutes).

Morro Bay

Home to a commercial fishing fleet, Morro Bay's biggest claim to fame is Morro Rock, a volcanic peak jutting dramatically from the ocean floor. It's one of the Nine Sisters, a 21-million-year-old chain of rocks stretching all the way south to San Luis Obispo. The town's less boast-worthy landmark comes courtesy of the power plant, whose three cigarette-shaped smokestacks mar the bay views. Along this humble, working-class stretch of coast you'll find fantastic opportunities for kayaking, hiking and camping.

Sights & Activities

This town harbors natural riches that are easily worth a half-day's exploration. The bay itself is a deep inlet separated from the ocean by a 5-mile sand spit. South of Morro Rock is the **Embarcadero**, a small waterfront boulevard jam-packed with souvenir shops and eateries.

Morro Rock LANDMARK
Chumash tribespeople are the only people legally allowed to climb this volcanic rock, now the protected nesting ground of peregrine falcons. You can laze at the small beach on the rock's north side, but you can't drive all the way around it. Instead, rent a kayak to paddle the giant estuary, inhabited by two dozen threatened and endangered species, including brown pelicans, snowy plovers and sea otters.

Morro Bay Whale Watching WHALE WATCHING
(☎805-772-9463; www.morrobaywhalewatching.com; 699 Embarcadero; adult/child $50/35; ⌚tours 9am; 👪) Humpback whales visit the Morro Bay area from May to October, and then from December to May more than 20,000 gray whales pass by on their annual migration. Other species often seen include minke whales, dolphins, porpoises, sea lions and sea otters. Bring along binoculars for coastal and pelagic birdlife. Excursions take place on an open catamaran, so dress warmly. Tours require a minimum of six passengers.

Kayak Shack WATER SPORTS
(☎805-772-8796; www.morrobaykayakrental.com; 10 State Park Rd; kayak/SUP/canoe rental from $16/16/20; ⌚9am-5pm daily late May-Sep, 9am-4pm Fri-Sun Oct-late May; 👪) No one gets you out on the water faster than this laid-back kayak, canoe and SUP rental spot by the marina in Morro Bay State Park. A no-frills DIY operation, this is a calmer place to start paddling than the Embarcadero. Guided kayak tours are also offered in conjunction with Central Coast Outdoors.

Tours

Sub-Sea Tours BOATING
(☎805-772-9463; www.morrobaywhalewatching.com/sub-sea-tour; 699 Embarcadero; 45min tour adult/child $17/8; ⌚departures noon & 2pm; 👪) For pint-sized views of kelp forests and schools of fish, take the kids on a spin around the bay in a yellow semi submersible with underwater viewing windows.

Central Coast Outdoors TOURS
(☎805-528-1080; www.centralcoastoutdoors.com; tours from $60; 👪) 🍃 Leads kayaking tours (including sunset and full-moon paddles), guided hikes and cycling trips along the coast and to Paso Robles and Edna Valley vineyards. Also available are guided hikes and biking tours along the Big Sur coast.

Festivals & Events

Morro Bay Winter Bird Festival OUTDOORS
(☎805-234-1170; www.morrobaybirdfestival.org; ⌚Jan) Bird-watchers flock here for guided hikes, kayaking tours and naturalist-led field trips, during which more than 200 species can be spotted along the Pacific Flyway.

Sleeping

Dozens of motels cluster along Hwy 1 and around Harbor and Main Sts, between downtown Morro Bay and the Embarcadero.

Morro Bay State Park Campground CAMPGROUND $
(☎reservations 800-444-7275; www.reservecalifornia.com; campsites/RV sites $35/50; 🐾) In Morro Bay State Park, more than 240 campsites with fire pits, picnic tables and food lockers are fringed by eucalyptus and cypress trees; amenities include coin-operated hot showers, flush toilets and an RV dump station.

Morro Strand State Beach Campground CAMPGROUND $
(☎reservations 800-444-7275; www.reserveamerica.com; tent & RV sites $35-50) At the north end of town off Hwy 1, Morro Strand State Beach has 75 simple oceanfront campsites.

456 Embarcadero Inn & Suites HOTEL $$
(☎805-772-2700; www.embarcaderoinn.com; 456 Embarcadero; r from $139; P 📶) Located at the quieter southern end of the Embarcadero, this modern property features 33 chic and spacious rooms, some with excellent views of the estuary and Morro Rock. Decor is more contemporary than in other local accommodations, and online midweek discounts are good value. Ease into the Jacuzzi after an afternoon's kayaking.

Pleasant Inn Motel MOTEL $$
(☎805-772-8521; www.pleasantinnmotel.com; 235 Harbor St; r $149-229; P 📶 🐾) Two blocks uphill from the Embarcadero, this spiffy motel has nautical-esque rooms (some with compact kitchens) sporting sailboat photos on the walls, open-beam wooden ceilings and blue-and-white rugs underfoot. It's one of the most welcoming places in town, and the team at reception has plenty of good restaurant advice. Pet fee $25.

★ **Anderson Inn** INN $$$
(☎805-772-3434; www.andersoninnmorrobay.com; 897 Embarcadero; d $299-429; P 📶) Like a

small boutique hotel, this waterfront inn has just a handful of spacious, soothingly earth-toned rooms. If you're lucky, you'll get a gas fireplace, spa tub and harbor views. The friendly owners infuse the whole property with an easygoing Californian cool. Weekday rates offer the best value.

Eating & Drinking

Seafood shacks line the Embarcadero, and a few more local cafes and restaurants are scattered uphill around Main St.

Giovanni's Fish Market & Galley SEAFOOD **$**
(805-772-2123; www.giovannisfishmarket.com; 1001 Front St; mains $6-15; market 9am-6pm, restaurant 11am-6pm;) At this family-run been-here-forever joint on the Embarcadero, folks line up at the window for batter-fried fish and chips and killer garlic fries along with novelties such as 'fish on a stick' and $3 tacos on Tuesdays. Inside there's a market with all the fixings for a beach campground fish-fry.

House of JuJu CALIFORNIAN **$$**
(805-225-1828; www.houseofjuju.com; 945 Embarcadero; mains $12-18; 11am-9:30pm Sun-Thu, to 10:30pm Fri & Sat) Friendly service lifts this waterfront spot above other nearby bars and eateries. House of JuJu's signature gourmet burgers are deservedly world-famous-in-Morro Bay. Our favorite is the JuJu Bleu with caramelized onions, bacon and blue cheese. Salads and wraps are good options for smaller appetites. Ask for a table with views of Morro Rock.

Galley Seafood Grill & Bar SEAFOOD **$$$**
(805-772-7777; www.galleymorrobay.com; 899 Embarcadero; mains $26-50; 11am-2:30pm & 5-10pm) The Galley's waterfront location serves expert renditions of classic American dishes with a briny touch of the ocean. There's definitely nothing groundbreaking about the menu, but when you're hankering for crab cakes and fresh oysters, or perfectly grilled fish and a glass of white wine, this is where to come.

Three Stacks & A Rock Brewing CRAFT BEER
(805-771-9286; www.threestacksandarockbrewing.com; 3118 Main St; 4-9pm Wed-Fri, noon-9pm Sat, noon-6pm Sun;) Located around 2.5 miles north of central Morro Bay, the excellent beers here are served in a rustic wood-lined taproom. Its own brews include the very quaffable Marine Layer hazy IPA, and beers from other Californian breweries complete the rotating tap list. Snack on free popcorn or oven-baked pretzels.

Siren LOUNGE
(805-772-8478; www.thesirenmorrobay.com; 900 Main St; noon-2am Mon-Thu, 11:30am-2am Fri-Sun) A laid-back spot for a quiet drink or game of pool during the week, the Siren is transformed into a rockin' live-music venue on Friday and Saturday nights. Beats range from blues and Americana through to yacht rock revivalists, and dancing is definitely encouraged after a few six-buck shooters, ten-buck cocktails or tasty craft brews. Bar snacks complete the picture.

Information

Morro Bay Visitor Center (805-225-1633; www.morrobay.org; 695 Harbor St; 10am-5pm) Located a few blocks uphill from the Embarcadero, in the less touristy downtown area. Note that at the time of writing, a move to the waterfront was mooted, but not yet confirmed. Check the website for the up-to-date location.

Getting There & Away

Morro Bay is 142 miles south of Monterey and 13 miles northwest of San Luis Obispo. From San Luis Obispo, **RTA** (805-541-2228; www.slorta.org) bus 12 travels hourly on weekdays and a few times daily on weekends along Hwy 1 to Morro Bay ($2.50, 25 minutes). Three to five times daily, bus 15 heads north to Cayucos ($2, 15 minutes), Cambria ($2, 35 minutes) and Hearst Castle ($2, 55 minutes).

From late May through early October, a **trolley** (single ride $1, day pass $3) loops around the waterfront, downtown and north Morro Bay, operating varying hours (no service Tuesday to Thursday).

Montaña de Oro State Park

In spring the hillsides are blanketed by bright native poppies, wild mustard and other wildflowers, giving this **park** (805-772-6101; www.parks.ca.gov; 3550 Pecho Valley Rd, Los Osos; 6am-10pm;) FREE its Spanish name, meaning 'mountain of gold.'

Wind-tossed coastal bluffs with wild, wide-open sea views make this a favorite spot with hikers, mountain bikers and horseback riders. The northern half of the park features sand dunes and an ancient marine terrace visible due to seismic uplifting.

Once used by smugglers, **Spooner's Cove** is now a postcard-perfect sandy beach and picnic area. If you go tide-pooling, avoid disturbing the marine creatures and never remove them from their aquatic homes. You can hike along the grassy ocean bluffs, or drive uphill past the visitor center inside a historic ranch house to the start of the exhilarating 7-mile loop trail tackling **Valencia Peak** (1346ft) and **Oats Peak** (1347ft).

Montaña de Oro State Park Campground CAMPGROUND $
(Map p49; ☎reservations 800-444-7275; www.reservecalifornia.com; Montaña de Oro State Park; tent & RV sites $25; P) Tucked into a small canyon, this minimally developed campground has pleasantly cool drive-up and environmental walk-in sites. Limited amenities include vault toilets, drinking water and fire pits.

Getting There & Away

To reach Montaña de Oro State Park by private car from the north, exit Hwy 1 in Morro Bay at South Bay Blvd; after 4 miles, turn right onto Los Osos Valley Rd (which runs into Pecho Valley Rd) for 6 miles. From the south, exit Hwy 101 in San Luis Obispo at Los Osos Valley Rd, then drive northwest for around 16 miles.

ALONG HIGHWAY 101

Driving inland along Hwy 101 is a quicker way to travel between the Bay Area and Southern California. Although it lacks the striking scenery of coastal Hwy 1, the historic El Camino Real (King's Highway), established by Spanish conquistadors and missionaries, has a beauty of its own. Along the way are plenty of sights worth stopping for – from oak-dappled golden hills and ghostly missions to jaw-dropping sights in Pinnacles National Park and sprawling wineries.

San Juan Bautista

In atmospheric old San Juan Bautista, where you can practically hear the whispers of the past, California's 15th mission is fronted by the state's only remaining original Spanish plaza. In 1876 the railroad bypassed the town, which has been a sleepy backwater ever since. Along 3rd St, evocative historic buildings mostly shelter antiques shops and petite garden restaurants. San Juan Bautista features a few B&Bs and is conveniently visited as a day trip from Santa Cruz or Monterey. Visit from Friday to Sunday for the best range of shopping, eating and drinking opportunities.

Sights

Mission San Juan Bautista CHURCH
(☎831-623-4528; www.oldmissionsjb.org; 406 2nd St; adult/child 5-17yr $4/2; ⏰9:30am-4:30pm; P) Founded in 1797, this mission claims the largest church among California's original 21 missions. Unknowingly built directly atop the San Andreas Fault, the mission has been rocked by earthquakes. Bells hanging in the tower today include chimes that were salvaged after the 1906 San Francisco earthquake toppled the original mission. Scenes from Alfred Hitchcock's thriller *Vertigo* were shot here, although the bell tower in the movie's climactic scene was just a special effect.

San Juan Bautista State Historic Park PARK
(☎831-623-4881; www.parks.ca.gov; 2nd St btwn Mariposa & Washington Sts; museum adult/child $3/free; ⏰10am-4:30pm; P) Buildings around the old Spanish plaza opposite the mission anchor this small historical park. Cavernous **stables** hint at San Juan Bautista in its 1860s heyday as a stagecoach stop. The 1858 **Plaza Hotel**, which started life as a single-story adobe building, now houses a little historical **museum**. Next door to the hotel, the **Castro-Breen Adobe** once belonged to Mexican general and governor José Castro. In 1848 it was bought by the Breen family, survivors of the Donner Party disaster.

Eating & Drinking

Lolla CAFE $
(☎831-593-5064; www.lollasjb.com; cnr 3rd & Washington Sts; snacks $7-9; ⏰11am-4pm Tue-Sat;) Seasonal soup, salad and sandwich specials make Lolla's sunny corner location the best place in SJB for a well-priced lunch. Everything is made from scratch with many ingredients sourced locally. Try the Mission Melt ciabatta sandwich, oozing with fontina and mozzarella cheese, and served with an olive dipping sauce.

Vertigo Coffee CAFE $
(☎831-623-9533; www.facebook.com/vertigocoffee; 81 4th St; mains $6-9, pizza $13-17; ⏰7am-3pm Mon-Wed, to 9pm Thu-Sun) Rich espresso and pour-over brews, breakfast and brunch classics, and wood-fired pizzas (from 2pm Thu-Sun only) make this coffee-roaster's shop a real find. Rotating exhibitions from local artists often fill the whitewashed walls, and sev-

en taps of craft beer feature surprising brews from around the central Californian coast.

18th Barrel Tasting Room BAR
(☎831-623-4049; www.18thbarrel.com; 322 3rd St; ⏰3-8pm Wed & Thu, noon-10pm Fri & Sat, noon-5pm Sun) With two heritage wooden bars – one serving 17 taps of craft beer and cider and the other focused on local wines – the friendly, family-owned 18th Barrel is often the social hub of San Juan Bautista. Ask if any beers from locally based Brewery Twenty Five are available. Wines are sometimes sourced from the nearby Santa Lucia Highlands wine region.

Getting There & Away

San Juan Bautista is on Hwy 156, a few miles east of Hwy 101, about a 20-minute drive south of Gilroy. Public transport is very limited, and the town is best visited with your own transport. Further south, Hwy 101 enters the sun-dappled eucalyptus grove that James Stewart and Kim Novak drove through in *Vertigo*.

Salinas

Best known as the birthplace of John Steinbeck and nicknamed the 'Salad Bowl of the World,' Salinas is a working-class agricultural center with down-and-out streets. It makes a thought-provoking contrast with the affluence of the Monterey Peninsula, a fact of life that helped shape Steinbeck's novel *East of Eden*. Historic downtown stretches along Main St, with the National Steinbeck Center capping off its northern end.

Around 20 miles southeast of Salinas are the vineyards and tasting rooms of the River Road Wine Trail (www.riverroadwinetrail.com). This area can also be visited from Monterey as a day trip.

Sights

★National Steinbeck Center MUSEUM
(☎831-775-4721; www.steinbeck.org; 1 Main St; adult/child 6-17yr $13/7; ⏰10am-5pm, to 9pm first Friday of month; 👪) This museum will interest almost anyone, even if you don't know anything about Salinas' Nobel Prize–winning native son, John Steinbeck (1902–68), a Stanford University dropout. Tough, funny and brash, he portrayed the troubled spirit of rural, working-class Americans in novels like *The Grapes of Wrath*. Interactive exhibits and short video clips chronicle the writer's life and works in an engaging way. Gems include Rocinante, the camper in which Steinbeck traveled around the USA while researching *Travels with Charley*.

Steinbeck House HISTORIC BUILDING
(☎831-424-2735; www.steinbeckhouse.com/about-us; 132 Central Ave; ⏰restaurant 11:30am-2pm Tue-Sat, gift shop to 3pm) Steinbeck was born and spent much of his boyhood in this house, four blocks west of the museum. It's now a twee lunch cafe, which we're not sure he'd approve of. Guided tours are given on select summer Sundays; check online for details.

Festivals & Events

Steinbeck Festival CULTURAL
(www.steinbeck.org; ⏰early May) This three-day festival features films, lectures, live music, and guided bus and walking tours.

California International Airshow OUTDOORS
(www.salinasairshow.com) Professional stunt-flying and vintage and military aircraft take wing. Timing varies from year to year; check the website for the most up-to-date information.

Sleeping

Salinas has plenty of motels off Hwy 101, including at the Market St exit.

Howard Johnson Inn BUSINESS HOTEL $
(☎831-757-1020; www.wyndhamhotels.com; 131 John St; d $130; P❄📶) Sure, it's part of a chain, but a warm welcome at reception and surprisingly stylish rooms lift this HoJo's ahead of the pack. And it's just a half-mile walk to restaurants and bars along Main St. A basic breakfast is complimentary, but you're better off grabbing something at a downtown cafe.

Eating & Drinking

Cafes, pubs and restaurants feature in downtown Salinas, especially in the heritage shop fronts along Main St.

First Awakenings AMERICAN $
(☎831-784-1125; www.firstawakenings.net; 171 Main St; mains $8-13; ⏰7am-2pm; 👪) Dig into diner-style breakfasts of fruity pancakes, crepes and egg skillets, or turn up later in the day for handcrafted sandwiches and market-fresh salads. Try the Sonoran frittata, an open-faced omelet crammed with spicy chorizo.

Villa Azteca MEXICAN $$
(☎831-256-2669; www.facebook.com/VillaAztecaRestaurant; 157 Main St; mains $12-19; ⏰11am-4pm & 5:30-9pm Tue-Fri, 5-9:30pm Sat, 10am-4pm Sun; 🍷) 🌿 Oaxacan flavors are expertly showcased at one of the region's best Mexican restaurants. Interesting seasonal menus could include dishes like squash flower enchiladas with chicken or lobster, while classics like tacos al pastor are enlivened with grilled salmon. Service can be slightly leisurely, but everything is prepared from scratch. Just relax with a cocktail and enjoy the wait.

Patria EUROPEAN $$
(☎831-424-5555; www.facebook.com/PatriaOldtownSalinas; 228 Main St; pizzas $12-15, mains $16-38; ⏰11:30am-2pm Tue-Fri, 5-9pm Tue-Sun) There's a distinct European vibe to Patria's cozy, wood-lined interior, and the diverse menu features flavors from across the continent. Cheese and charcuterie platters, wood-fired pizzas and housemade pasta all come with an Italian accent, while German cuisine is represented by spaetzle noodles and hearty plates of schnitzel. Be sure to order a delicious side dish of potatoes au gratin.

Alvarado Street Brewery & Tasting Room CRAFT BEER
(☎831-800-3332; www.alvaradostreetbrewery.com/salinas-brewery; 1315 Dayton St; ⏰3-8pm Tue-Fri, from 1pm Sat & Sun) This Salinas production facility of the Monterey-based craft brewery is an integral part of the beer scene around Monterey Bay. Location-wise, it's in an industrial park around 3 miles south of downtown. Food trucks regularly drop by, and the beers on tap are often unique to this location.

Farmers Union Pour House CRAFT BEER
(☎831-975-4890; www.facebook.com/FarmersUnionPourHouse; 217 Main St; ⏰3-10pm Mon-Thu, to midnight Fri & Sat) Brick-lined walls and wooden floors combine with a thoroughly modern big screen displaying the 24 different beers on tap. Up to 15 Californian wines are also available.

ℹ Information

Salinas 411 (☎831-594-1799; www.salinas411.org; 222 Main St; ⏰11am-8pm) Integrated with a gift and souvenir shop. Touring maps of the River Road Wine Trail are available.

ℹ Getting There & Away

Salinas is 106 miles south of San Francisco and 126 miles north of San Luis Obispo.

Amtrak (☎800-872-7245; www.amtrak.com; 11 Station Pl) runs daily *Coast Starlight* trains north to Oakland (from $23, three hours) and south to Paso Robles (from $21, two hours), San Luis Obispo (from $29, 3¼ hours), Santa Barbara (from $43, 6¼ hours) and LA ($61, 9¼ hours).

Greyhound (☎800-231-2222; www.greyhound.com; Station Pl) has a few daily buses heading north to Santa Cruz (from $13, 65 minutes) and San Francisco (from $21, 3½ to five hours), and south to Santa Barbara (from $24, 4¾ hours). Buses depart from the Salinas railway station.

From the nearby **Salinas Transit Center** (110 Salinas St), **MST** (☎888-678-2871; www.mst.org) bus 20 goes to Monterey ($3.50, one hour, every 30 to 60 minutes).

Pinnacles National Park

Named for the towering rock spires that rise abruptly out of the chaparral-covered hills east of Salinas Valley, this off-the-beaten-path **park** (☎831-389-4486; www.nps.gov/pinn; 5000 Hwy 146, Paicines; weekly pass per car $30; ⏰park 24hr, east visitor center 9:30am-5pm, west visitor center 9am-4:30pm; 🅿👪) 🌿 protects one of California's most unique landscapes. Formed by the movements of tectonic plates over millions of years, the rocky spires at the heart of the park are the eroded remnants of a long-extinct volcano that originated in present-day Southern California before getting sheared in two and moving nearly 200 miles north along the San Andreas Fault.

Initially established as a national monument in 1908, Pinnacles earned national park designation in 2013. The park, divided into eastern and western sections with no through road connecting them, preserves forests of oak, sycamore and buckeye, wildflower-strewn meadows, caves and dramatic rock formations. Endangered California condors still soar overhead, and the park's remote beauty makes it popular with hikers and climbers.

Spring and fall are the best seasons to visit. Try to avoid weekends and holidays when the park is extremely popular.

👁 Sights & Activities

Besides rock climbing (for route information, visit www.pinnacles.org), the park's biggest attractions are its two talus caves, formed by piles of boulders. **Balconies Cave** is almost always open for exploration. Scrambling through it is not an exercise recommended for claustrophobes, as it's pitch-black inside, making a flashlight essential. Be prepared to get lost a bit too. The cave is found along a 2.5-mile hiking loop from the west entrance. Nearer the east entrance, **Bear Gulch Cave** is closed seasonally, so as not to disturb a resident colony of Townsend's big-eared bats.

To really appreciate Pinnacles' stark beauty, you need to hike. Moderate loops of varying lengths and difficulty ascend into the **High Peaks** and include thrillingly narrow clifftop sections. In the early morning or late afternoon, you may spot endangered California condors soaring overhead. Get an early start to tackle the 9-mile round-trip trail to the top of **Chalone Peak**, granting panoramic views.

Rangers lead guided full-moon hikes and star-gazing programs on weekend nights, usually in spring or fall. Reservations are required: call 831-389-4485 in advance or check for last-minute vacancies at the visitor center.

Sleeping & Eating

The **Pinnacles Campground Store** (831-389-4538; 2400 Pinnacles Hwy; 9:30am-5pm Mon-Thu, to 6:30pm Fri, 8:30am-6:30pm Sat, to 5pm Sun) sells water, drinks, basic snacks and supplies, but it's best to stock up for self-catering in supermarkets in King City or Salinas.

Pinnacles National Park Campground CAMPGROUND $
(831-389-4538; www.recreation.gov; 5000 Hwy 146; tent/RV sites $35/45; P) On the park's east side, this popular family-oriented campground has over more than 130 sites (some with shade), drinking water, coin-operated hot showers, fire pits and an outdoor pool (usually closed from October to March).

Information

Pinnacles National Park Visitor Center
(831-389-4485; www.nps.gov/pinn; 9:30am-5pm Mon-Thu, to 6:30pm Fri, 8:30am-6:30pm Sat, to 5pm Sun) Information, maps and books are available on the park's east side from the small NPS visitor center inside the campground store.

Getting There & Away

There is no road connecting the two sides of Pinnacles National Park. To reach the less-developed **west entrance** (7:30am-8pm), exit Hwy 101 at Soledad and follow Hwy 146 northeast for 14 miles. The **east entrance** (24hr), where you'll find the visitor center and campground, is accessed via lonely Hwy 25 in San Benito County, southeast of Hollister and northeast of King City.

San Miguel

Founded in 1797, **Mission San Miguel Arcángel** (805-467-3256; www.missionsanmiguel.org; 775 Mission St; adult/child 5-17yr $5/3; 10am-4:30pm) suffered heart-breaking damage during a 2003 earthquake. Although repairs are still underway, the church, cemetery, museum and gardens are open. An enormous cactus out front was planted during the early days of the mission.

Hungry? Look for a couple of no-name Mexican delis, where the limited options include massive shrimp burritos.

Paso Robles

In northern San Luis Obispo County, Paso Robles is the heart of a historic agricultural region where grapes are now the biggest money-making crop. Scores of wineries along Hwy 46 produce a brave new world of more-than-respectable bottles. The Mediterranean climate and laid-back lifestyle are yielding other bounties as well, and olive oil, craft beer and artisan distilleries are growing in popularity. Paso's historic downtown centers on Park and 12th Sts, where boutique shops and wine-tasting rooms await.

Sights & Activities

Studios on the Park GALLERY
(805-238-9800; www.studiosonthepark.org; 1130 Pine St; noon-4pm Mon-Wed, to 6pm Thu & Sun, to 9pm Fri & Sat) Artists from around the Central Coast work and display their art at this collection of open studios on the eastern edge of Paso Robles' town square. Up to 15 different artists work from six studios, and other facilities include art galleries and an excellent fine-art shop. Check the website for interesting special exhibitions and a class schedule.

Sensorio ARTS CENTER
(805-226-4287; www.sensoriopaso.com; 4380 Hwy 46 E; P) Originally the location of the **Field of Light**, a spectacular outdoor art installation, Sensorio is Paso Robles' new destination for traveling art fans. An official 2021 opening is envisaged, including new galleries and buildings that will host exhibitions, events and displays blending art, technology, music and nature. Check the website for progress on the project or ask Paso's tourist information team (p335) for an update. Sensorio is located around five miles northeast of town along Hwy 46.

Eastside Wineries

Around Paso Robles, you could spend days wandering country back roads off Hwy 46, running east and west of Hwy 101. Most wineries have tasting rooms and a few offer vineyard tours. For more wineries and olive-oil farms to visit, browse www.pasowine.com.

Field Recordings WINERY
(☎805-503-9660; www.fieldrecordingswine.com; 3070 Limestone Way, Suite C, Tin City; ⏰11am-5pm; P) Our pick for Paso's most interesting urban winery, Field Recordings sources grapes from a range of small holding vineyards around the Central Coast. Winemaker Andrew Jones makes both single- and multi-vineyard wines, often in very limited volumes, to reflect a diverse range of different terroirs. Check out the Wonderwall label for surprising pinot noir and chardonnay crafted from exposed coastal sites.

J Lohr Vineyards & Wines WINERY
(☎805-239-8900; www.jlohr.com; 6169 Airport Rd; tastings $15; ⏰10am-5pm; P) A Central Coast wine pioneer, J Lohr owns vineyards in Napa Valley, Monterey's Santa Lucia Highlands and Paso's pastoral countryside. Knowledgeable staff guide you through a far-reaching wine list. The tasting fee is waived with a purchase.

Eberle Winery WINERY
(☎805-238-9607; www.eberlewinery.com; 3810 E Hwy 46; tastings free-$25; ⏰10am-6pm Apr-Oct, to 5pm Nov-Mar; P) Offers lofty vineyard views and tours of its wine caves every half hour from 10:30am to 5pm. Sociable tastings run the gamut of white and red varietals and Rhône blends. Food trucks sometimes swing by on weekends from April to October.

Westside Wineries

Tablas Creek Vineyard WINERY
(☎805-237-1231; www.tablascreek.com; 9339 Adelaida Rd; tastings from $15; ⏰10am-5pm; P) Breathe easy at this organic estate vineyard reached via a pretty, winding drive up into the hills. Known for Rhône varietals, the signature blends also rate highly. Vineyard tours (per person $15) include a tasting and depart at 10:30am and 2pm daily (online reservations necessary).

Castoro Cellars WINERY
(☎805-238-0725; www.castorocellars.com; 1315 N Bethel Rd; tastings $10; ⏰10am-5:30pm; P) This husband-and-wife team produces 'dam fine wine' (the mascot is a beaver, get it?), including vintages made from custom-crushed and organic grapes. Outdoor vineyard concerts happen during the summer and there's also a Frisbee-golf course ($5).

Thacher Winery WINERY
(☎805-237-0087; www.thacherwinery.com; 8355 Vineyard Dr; tastings $20; ⏰11am-5pm) Breathe deeply as you drive up the dirt road to this historic ranch that makes memorable Rhône blends – 'Controlled Chaos' is a perennial fave.

Festivals & Events

★**Wine Festival** WINE, FOOD
(www.pasowine.com; ⏰mid-May) Oenophiles come for Paso's premier Wine Festival in mid-May, but the Vintage Paso weekend, focusing on zinfandel wines, held in mid-March, and the Harvest Wine Weekend (mid-October) are just as much fun.

California Mid-State Fair CARNIVAL, MUSIC
(www.midstatefair.com; ⏰mid-Jul) Twelve days of live rock and country-and-western concerts, farm exhibits, carnival rides and a rodeo draw huge crowds.

Sleeping

Melody Ranch Motel MOTEL $
(☎805-238-3911; www.melodyranchmotelca.com; 939 Spring St; r $80-100; P ❄ 🛜 🏊) At this superfriendly, family-owned, 1950s motor court downtown, comfortable rooms go for prices that are almost as small as the compact outdoor pool. Location-wise it's just a short walk to great eating and drinking options.

★**Summerwood Inn** B&B $$$
(☎805-227-1111; www.summerwoodwine.com; 2175 Arbor Rd; d from $300; P 🚭 🛜) Located along Hwy 46 within an easy drive of dozens of wineries, this gorgeous inn renovated in cool neutral tones mixes vintage and modern elements. Each of the nine rooms is named after a wine varietal and has a gas fireplace and balcony overlooking the vineyards. Indulge with the chef's gourmet breakfasts, afternoon hors d'oeuvres and evening desserts.

★**Hotel Cheval** BOUTIQUE HOTEL $$$
(☎805-226-9995; www.hotelcheval.com; 1021 Pine St; d $380-480; P 🚭 🛜 🏊) Near downtown Paso, this European-style boutique hotel has 16 rooms arrayed around a sheltered inner courtyard. Spacious guest accommodations

DON'T MISS

JAMES DEAN MEMORIAL

In Cholame, about 25 miles east of Paso Robles via Hwy 46, there's a memorial near the spot where *Rebel Without a Cause* star James Dean fatally crashed his Porsche on September 30, 1955, at the age of 24. Ironically, the actor had recently filmed a public-safety campaign TV spot, in which he implored motorists to drive slowly and safely.

Look for the shiny stainless-steel memorial wrapped around an oak tree outside the truck-stop Jack Ranch Cafe, which has old photographs and movie-star memorabilia inside.

feature flat-screen TVs and fireplaces, and rates include breakfast. Stylish shared spaces incorporate a library and the Pony Bar, serving Californian wine and featuring live music from 5pm on Friday and Saturday. A pool and luxury spa were added in 2020.

Inn Paradiso B&B $$$
(805-239-2800; www.innparadiso.com; 975 Mojave Lane; ste $250-350, apt $795;) An intimate B&B pulls off no-fuss luxury with suites decorated with art and antiques, and perhaps a fireplace, a deep-soaking tub, a canopy king-sized bed or French balcony doors. Breakfast is generously laden with local and organic produce. The larger Paradiso apartment accommodating up to four is also available. Pet fee $50.

Eating

Restaurants and wine-tasting rooms surround downtown's grassy central square, off Spring St between 11th and 12th Sts.

brunch CAFE $
(805-762-4960; www.brunchpaso.com; 840 13th St; mains $10-16; 9am-2pm Mon, Thu & Fri, to 3pm Sat & Sun;) Definitely doing what it says on the tin, with a singular focus on tasty ways to kick off the morning – especially recommended if you're planning on hitting Paso's vineyard tasting rooms later in the day. Our favorite dish is the eggs Benedict with crab cakes. Mimosas and sparkling wine are both available to fuel more leisurely dining occasions.

Hatch Rotisserie & Bar AMERICAN $$
(805-221-5727; www.hatchpasorobles.com; 835 13th St; mains $17-30; 4:30-9pm Mon-Wed, to 10pm Thu, to 11pm Fri & Sat) Wood-fired treats in this heritage location, which combines shimmering chandeliers and rustic bricks, include grilled octopus, rotisserie chicken and creamy bone marrow. It adds a sly sophistication to American comfort food including shrimp and grits and buttermilk fried chicken. Craft beer, cocktails and local wines are all tasty diversions. Check the website for nightly dinner specials.

Paso Market Walk FOOD HALL $$
(www.pasomarketwalk.com; 1803 Spring St; mains $10-25; hours vary;) Around 800 yd north of downtown Paso, this purpose-built collection of eating and drinking establishments includes ramen noodles, vegan and plant-based flavors, artisan ice cream, a craft brewery and a wine-tasting room. Altogether there are around 15 different places where visitors can refuel and relax. Check the website to compile your own foodie hit list.

★ **Les Petites Canailles** FRENCH $$$
(805-296-3754; www.lpcrestaurant.com; 1215 Spring St; mains $18-40; 5-9pm Sun-Tue & Thu, to 10pm Fri & Sat) Co-owned by a US-French couple, Les Petites Canailles' excellent seasonal menus blend Central Coast ingredients with the best of Gallic and European culinary traditions. Rabbit Two Ways combines spaetzle noodles with a mustard sauce, while octopus is served with a fennel and citrus salad. The warm and welcoming ambience of the dining room encourages family-style sharing of the various dishes.

Fish Gaucho MEXICAN, SEAFOOD $$$
(805-239-3333; www.fishgaucho.com; 1244 Park St; mains $17-39; kitchen 3-9:30pm, from 11:30am Fri-Sun, bar to midnight daily;) Hand-made furnishings, antiques and decor imported from Mexico fill this Baja-style seafood joint and tequila bar. Smoky, spicy and fruity cocktails wash down stuffed poblano chilis, braised short-rib tacos and oyster shooters with chorizo and *cotija* (white, crumbly Mexican cheese) crumbles. Reservations recommended.

Drinking & Nightlife

Paso Robles is home to excellent craft breweries, and the Tin City area south of the city also features cider bars, urban distilleries and wine-tasting rooms.

See www.brewpaso.com for information on the brewing, distilling and coffee-roasting scenes in and around the city.

Kilokilo Brewing CRAFT BEER

(☎805-296-3670; www.kilokilobrewing.com; 3340 Ramada Dr; ⊙3-8pm Wed & Thu, 2-9pm Fri, 11am-9pm Sat, to 7pm Sun) A surprising smaller craft brewery, Kilokilo turns out an excellent range of beers, including some delicious IPAs made with citrusy New Zealand hops. Friendly head brewer and co owner Steve Stewart is always keen to chat with fellow beer fans, and the brewery is named for Steve's wife, Pam, who is originally from Hawaii. Ask if the Helluva Ride Hazy IPA is available.

Silva Brewing CRAFT BEER

(☎805-369-2337; www.silvabrewing.com; 525 Pine St; ⊙2-7pm Wed-Fri, noon-7pm Sat, to 5pm Sun) Chuck Silva was previously with San Diego's Green Flash Brewing and is now crafting his own brews in a compact space in Paso Robles. Look forward to bold, hop-forward styles as well as Belgian-influenced beers. Just through an adjoining door (literally!) is a separate craft-beer pub, so make a night of it. Silva's excellent brews also feature in restaurants around town.

BarrelHouse Brewing Co BREWERY

(☎805-296-1128; www.barrelhousebrewing.com; 3055 Limestone Way, Tin City; ⊙11am-9pm; 👪🐾) Detour south of downtown, where locals chill in the dog- and family-friendly outdoor beer garden with ales, stouts and zingy sour beers. Live bands frequently play, and most afternoons there's a local food truck in attendance. Try the ironically named Gym Membership Double Hazy IPA.

Tin City Cider Co CIDER

(☎805-293-6349; www.tincitycider.com; 3005a Limestone Way, Tin City; ⊙11am-8pm Sun-Wed, to 9pm Thu-Sat) Joining the tangle of breweries, distilleries and wine-tasting rooms in Paso Robles' Tin City neighborhood, Tin City Cider's thoroughly modern tasting room showcases tart and tangy tipples crafted from apples. Its standard range is crisp and refreshing, and more complex flavors underpin innovative variations fermented with Belgian brewers yeast, enlivened with passion fruit, or aged in bourbon barrels or French oak.

Re:Find Distillery DISTILLERY

(☎805-239-9456; www.refinddistillery.com; 2725 Adelaida Rd; ⊙11am-5pm) Paso Robles' first micro-distillery makes crisp botanical brandy (gin) and also whiskey and flavored vodkas. Scores of lemons were being zested when we dropped by. Try all the spirits in the rustic and rural tasting room.

For more on the growing Paso Robles distillery scene, see www.pasoroblesdistillerytrail.com, and download a touring map listing 10 different distilleries.

Wine Shine DISTILLERY

(☎805-286-4453; www.wineshine.com; 3064 Limestone Way, Tin City; ⊙1-5pm Fri-Sun) Grape juice sourced from Paso Robles wineries is the versatile basis for the innovative spirits crafted by Wine Shine. Sample brandies tinged with mango, ginger or cinnamon and aged in oak barrels, or try Wine Shine's Manhattan Project whiskey that is a tribute to the classic days of American cocktails.

Shopping

Around Paso Robles' downtown square, side streets are full of wine-country boutiques.

Pasolivo FOOD & DRINKS

(☎805 227 0186; www.pasolivo.com; 8530 Vineyard Dr; ⊙11am-5pm) Located on a pleasantly winding back road in Paso Robles wine country, Pasolivo's olive-oil tasting room features bold and earthy oils flavored with basil, citrus and rosemary. The laid-back ranch-style surroundings make a pleasant break from wine tasting, and the attached shop sells excellent artisan foods and olive oil–based soaps and beauty products.

Paso Robles General Store FOOD GIFTS

(☎805-226-5757; www.generalstorepr.com; 841 12th St; ⊙10am-7pm) 🍃 Stock up on picnic provisions such as California-made pistachio butter, fresh local baguettes, fruit jams and more, plus home goods like lavender soap. Many of the products are locally sourced, organic and sustainable. Also an excellent source of gifts and homewares.

Information

Paso Robles Chamber of Commerce (☎805-238-0506; www.travelpaso.com; 1225 Park St; ⊙8:30am-5pm Mon-Fri, 9am-5pm Sat, 10am-2pm Sun) Run by a very helpful and friendly team.

Geting There & Away

From an unstaffed **Amtrak station** (☎800-872-7245; www.amtrak.com; 800 Pine St), daily *Coast Starlight* trains head north to Salinas (from $21, two hours) and Oakland (from $33, 4¾ hours), and south to Santa Barbara (from $30, 4¼ hours) and LA (from $45, 7½ hours). Several daily Thruway buses link to more-frequent regional trains, including the *Pacific Surfliner*.

RTA (☎805-541-2228; www.slorta.org) bus 9 travels between San Luis Obispo and Paso Robles ($3.25, 70 minutes) hourly Monday to Friday, and a few times daily on weekends.

San Luis Obispo

Almost midway between LA and San Francisco, at the junction of Hwys 101 and 1, San Luis Obispo (SLO) is a popular overnight stop for road-trippers. It also makes a handy base from which to explore the coastal towns of Pismo Beach, Avila Beach and Morro Bay, as well as Hearst Castle. SLO may not have any big-ticket sights, unless you count the Spanish-Colonial mission and the kooky Madonna Inn. But this refreshingly low-key city does have an enviably high quality of life, helped along by Cal Poly university students who inject a healthy dose of hubbub into the streets, bars and cafes. Thursday is a great day to be in SLO – the farmers market turns downtown's Higuera St into a party with live music and sidewalk BBQs. There's also excellent eating and drinking courtesy of local chefs, craft breweries and the vineyards of the nearby Edna Valley.

Sights

San Luis Obispo Creek, once used to irrigate mission orchards, flows through downtown. Uphill from Higuera St, **Mission Plaza** is a shady oasis with restored adobe buildings and fountains overlooking the creek. Look for the **Moon Tree**, a coast redwood grown from a seed that journeyed on board *Apollo 14*'s lunar mission.

Mission San Luis Obispo de Tolosa CHURCH
(Map p337; ☎805-543-6850; www.missionsanluisobispo.org; 751 Palm St; suggested donation $5; ⏲9am-5pm late Mar-Oct, to 4pm Nov–mid-Mar; 👪) Those reverberatory bells heard around downtown emanate from this fifth California mission, founded by Padre Junípero Serra in 1772 and named for a 13th-century French saint. Cradled by bountiful gardens, the modest church has an unusual L-shape and whitewashed walls decorated with Stations of the Cross. The friars' former residential quarters house an old-fashioned **museum** with artifacts illustrating life during the Chumash tribal and Spanish colonial periods. Interesting guided tours run most days at 1:15pm.

Madonna Inn HISTORIC BUILDING
(☎805-543-3000; www.madonnainn.com; 100 Madonna Rd; ⏲cafe 7am-10pm, bar 10am-midnight; P 👪) The fantastically campy Madonna Inn is a garish confection visible from Hwy 101. Curious international tourists and irony-loving hipsters adore the 110 themed rooms, but it's also worth visiting to experience the over-the-top decor of the hotel's cafes and restaurants. Settle in for brunch at the Copper Cafe, while the Silver Bar Cocktail Lounge is a riot of bright pink rose-adorned carpet. Order a Madonna Cadillac, an in-house variation on a margarita, and relax into SLO's glorious theater of kitsch.

San Luis Obispo Museum of Art MUSEUM
(Map p337; ☎805-543-8562; www.sloma.org; 1010 Broad St; ⏲11am-5pm Thu-Mon) FREE By the creek, this small gallery showcases the work of local painters, sculptors, printmakers and fine-art photographers, as well as traveling California art exhibitions.

Activities & Tours

For hiking with ocean views, head to Montaña de Oro State Park (p328) or the Pismo Preserve (p343), high above Pismo Beach. The SLO visitor center (p340) can advise on local hikes including Cerro San Luis near downtown, and the more challenging Bishop Peak.

Margarita Adventures ZIPLINING, KAYAKING
(☎805-438-3120; www.margarita-adventures.com; 22719 El Camino Real, Santa Margarita; adult/child zipline tour $119/89; ⏲8am-4:30pm; 👪) Whoosh down six ziplines across the vineyards beneath the Santa Lucia Mountains at this historic ranch, about a 10-mile drive northeast of SLO via Hwy 101. Reservations are required and trips leave from Margarita Adventures' office in the main street of sleepy Margarita. Ziplining experiences are 10 bucks cheaper from Monday to Friday. Kayaking on Santa Margarita Lake and nature tours at Santa Margarita Ranch are also on offer.

Hop On Beer Tours FOOD & DRINK
(☎855-554-6766; www.hoponbeertours.com; per person $40-50) Jump aboard these sociable minibus tours to explore the San Luis Obispo and Paso Robles craft-beer scenes. Tours visit up to four different breweries. Check the website for timings of 'Social Tours' open to the public – usually on Friday, Saturday or Sunday nights, two to four times per month – as Hop On also runs private tours. Weekend walking tours of beer venues in downtown SLO are also available.

San Luis Obispo

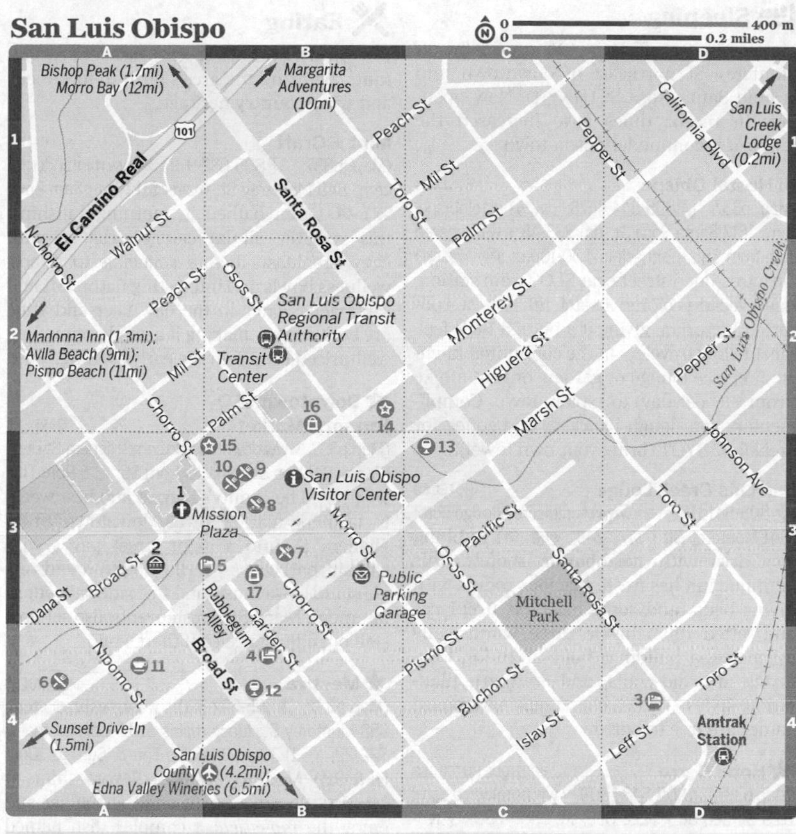

San Luis Obispo

Sights

1 Mission San Luis Obispo de Tolosa A3
2 San Luis Obispo Museum of Art A3

Sleeping

3 HI Hostel Obispo D4
4 Hotel Cerro B4
5 SLO Brew Lofts B3

Eating

6 Bear & the Wren A4
Creamery Marketplace .... (see 6)
7 Downtown SLO Farmers' Market B3
8 Giuseppe's Cucina Rustica B3
9 Mestiza B3
10 Mint + Craft B3

Drinking & Nightlife

11 Kreuzberg A4
12 Libertine Brewing Company B4
13 Luis Wine Bar C3

Entertainment

14 Fremont Theater B2
15 Palm Theatre B3

Shopping

16 Boo Boo Records B2
17 Hands Gallery B3

Festivals & Events

SLO International Film Festival FILM

(www.slofilmfest.org; mid-Mar) This annual six-day celebration of film has been a mainstay of the SLO cultural calendar since 1993. Events and screenings are held around the greater San Luis Obispo County area, including in Paso Robles and Pismo Beach.

Concerts in the Plaza MUSIC, FOOD

(www.downtownslo.com; 4:30-8pm Fri, Jun-Sep) Downtown's Mission Plaza rocks out with local bands and food vendors.

Sleeping

Motels cluster off Hwy 101, especially off Monterey St northeast of downtown and around Santa Rosa St (Hwy 1). New openings in recent times have increased the range of accommodations in town.

HI Hostel Obispo HOSTEL **$**
(Map p337; 805-544-4678; www.hostelobispo.com; 1617 Santa Rosa St; dm $33-45, r with shared bath from $65; check-in 4:30-10pm;) On a tree-lined street near SLO's train station, this avocado-colored hostel inhabits a converted Victorian, giving it a bit of a B&B feel. Meet fellow travelers in the communal kitchen, fireplace lounge or garden, or rent a bike (from $10 per day) to explore town. Complimentary sourdough pancakes and coffee for breakfast. BYOT (bring your own towel).

San Luis Creek Lodge HOTEL **$$**
(805-541-1122; www.sanluiscreeklodge.com; 1941 Monterey St; r $179-249;) Rubbing shoulders with neighboring motels, this boutique inn has fresh, spacious rooms with divine beds (and some have gas fireplaces and jetted tubs) inside three whimsically mismatched buildings built in Tudor, California arts-and-crafts, and Southern plantation styles. DVDs, chess sets and board games are free to borrow.

★**Hotel Cerro** BOUTIQUE HOTEL **$$$**
(Map p337; 805-548-1000; www.hotelcerro.com; 1125 Garden St; r $228-399, ste $380-630; restaurant 7:30am-9:30pm Mon-Sat, to 3pm Sun;) Hotel Cerro combines luxury boutique style with a significant commitment to sustainable design. The hotel has been constructed around a restored heritage brick facade, and suites look over an inner garden enlivened with fresh herbs used by the on-site Brasserie SLO. There's a spa and wellness center, and the hotel's own compact distillery crafts artisan spirits for its cocktail bar.

SLO Brew Lofts APARTMENT **$$$**
(Map p337; 805-305-2168; www.slobrewlofts.com; 738 Higuera St; apts from $250;) Located above a popular creek-side restaurant, SLO Brew Lofts offer a unique urban stay in downtown. Apartments range from one to three bedrooms – the lofts are suitable for families or friends – and stylish decor is partnered by cool touches like a refrigerator stocked with SLO Brew's fine products, and record players with stacks of vintage vinyl.

Eating

Downtown SLO has several excellent restaurants, befitting the area's farm-to-fork focus and wine-country heritage.

Mint + Craft CAFE **$**
(Map p337; 805-632-9191; www.mintandcraft.com; 848 Monterey St; mains $11-16; 8am-8pm;) Often bathed in morning sunshine, this versatile all-day eatery kicks off with eggy breakfasts before segueing to salads, wellness bowls and interesting flatbreads and sandwiches later in the day. Beer and wine are both served, making it a good option for a well-priced dinner in the early evening.

★**Downtown SLO Farmers' Market** MARKET **$**
(Map p337; www.downtownslo.com; Higuera St btwn Nipomo & Osos Sts; snacks from $5; 6-9pm Thu;) The county's biggest and best weekly farmers market turns downtown SLO's Higuera St into a giant street party, with smokin' barbecues, overflowing fruit and veggie stands, live music and free sidewalk entertainment. Many SLO restaurants also set up a stall outside. Canceled if there's rain.

★**Mestiza** MEXICAN **$$**
(Map p337; 805-592-3201; www.mestizaslo.com; 858 Monterey St; lunch mains $10-16, dinner mains $22-29; 11:30am-9pm Tue-Thu & Sun, to 10pm Fri & Sat) Modern Mexican flavors shine at Mestiza. Secure a booth or sit at the bar and enjoy the *molcajete*, a complex dish named after a traditional Mexican mortar and pestle and crammed with steak, chorizo, rice and shrimp. It's definitely a dish for sharing; for a lighter end-of-day snack pair shrimp *taquitos* with a smoky mezcal cocktail.

Creamery Marketplace FOOD HALL **$$**
(Map p337; www.creameryslo.com; 570 Higuera St; snacks & mains from $5; hours vary;) This spacious open-air food hall includes outlets dishing up artisan ice cream, European-style baked goods and modern Peruvian flavors. A standout destination is **Bear & the Wren** (Map p337; 805-439-0326; www.bearandthewren.com; 570 Higuera St, Creamery Marketplace; pizza $14-18; 5-10pm Tue-Sat;), a popular SLO food truck that's graduated to a bricks-and-mortar location serving superb wood-fired pizza.

Giuseppe's Cucina Rustica ITALIAN **$$**
(Map p337; 805-541-9922; www.giuseppesrestaurant.com; 849 Monterey St; pizzas from $16, mains $17-39; 11:30am-3pm daily, 4:30-9:30pm

Sun-Thu, to 10:30pm Fri & Sat;) Visit garlic-perfumed Giuseppe's for a leisurely lunch of toothsome salads, pizza and antipasti starring produce harvested on the owner's farm. Out the back, the facade of the heritage Sinsheimer Brothers building overlooks a shaded courtyard that's perfectly suited to languid dinners of chicken parmigiana and a glass of hearty SLO County red.

Drinking & Nightlife

Higuera St is littered with bars jammed with college students. Craft-beer fans have plenty to look forward to, while grape-lovers will have no trouble finding places to sample regional wines.

There Does Not Exist MICROBREWERY
(www.theredoesnotexist.com; 4070 Earthwood Lane, Suite 110; 3-9pm Tue-Fri, noon-9pm Sat, to 6pm Sun;) Brilliant European-style beers including elegant pilsners and bone-dry farmhouse ales served in a modern taproom enlivened with pop art renditions of Fidel Castro and Chairman Mao. Located around 3 miles south of downtown SLO.

Libertine Brewing Company CRAFT BEER
(Map p337; 805-548-2337; www.libertinebrewing.com; 1234 Broad St; 11am-10pm Sun-Thu, to 11pm Fri & Sat) Wild and sour beers are the standout brews at this sprawling bar on the edge of downtown SLO. Saisons, kettle sours and grisettes all appeal to the traveling beer geek, and the full tap list of more than 70 beers covers all the bases. Pub food is decent and there's a good selection of bottled seasonal releases for takeout purchase.

SLOBrew Rock BAR
(805-543-1843; www.slobrew.com; 855 Aerovista Pl; 11:30am-9pm Sun-Thu, to 10pm Fri & Sat;) SLOBrew Rock's sprawling setup incorporates an on-site brewery and excellent Mexican-infused food and barbecue, and it's also a rocking live-music venue with regular gigs. Check the website for what's scheduled. Our favorite brews are the Cali Squeeze Blood Orange wheat beer and the punchy Still Frothy Double IPA. Lots of outdoor games make it a good option for families too.

Luis Wine Bar WINE BAR
(Map p337; 805-762-4747; www.luiswinebar.com; 1021 Higuera St; 3-11pm Sun-Thu, to midnight Fri & Sat) This downtown wine bar is an urbane but unpretentious alternative to SLO's more raucous student-heavy drinking dens. About half of the roughly 60 wines on the list are available by the glass, and there's also a solid craft-beer selection, along with cheese and charcuterie platters.

Kreuzberg CAFE
(Map p337; 805-439-2060; www.kreuzbergcalifornia.com; 685 Higuera St; 7:30am-10pm;) This shabby-chic coffeehouse and roaster has earned a fervent following with its comfy couches, sprawling bookshelves and local art. Look forward to occasional live music partnered with craft beer and comfort food in the adjacent lounge. Drop by and see what's scheduled.

Entertainment

Sunset Drive-In CINEMA
(805-544-4475; www.facebook.com/sunsetdrivein; 255 Elks Lane; adult/child 5-11yr $10/4;) Recline your seat, put your feet up on the dash and munch on bottomless bags of popcorn at this classic American drive-in. Sticking around for the second feature (usually a B-list Hollywood blockbuster) doesn't cost extra. It's about 2 miles southwest of downtown SLO off Higuera St. Check the Facebook page for screening times.

Fremont Theater THEATER
(Map p337; www.fremontslo.com; 1035 Monterey St) This Streamline Moderne theater opened in 1942 and now hosts a wide variety of live concerts including indie, Americana and rap gigs. Tickets are usually sold across the road at the excellent Boo Boo Records. Check the website for what's coming up.

Palm Theatre CINEMA
(Map p337; 805-541-5161; www.thepalmtheatre.com; 817 Palm St; tickets $6-10) This small-scale movie house showing foreign and indie flicks just happens to be the USA's first solar-powered cinema. Seats are a bargain $6 on Mondays. Look for the SLO International Film Festival (p337) in March.

Shopping

For shopping fans visiting San Luis Obispo, downtown Higuera and Marsh Sts, along with all of the arcades and cross streets in between, are full of unique boutiques.

Boo Boo Records MUSIC
(Map p337; 805-541-0657; www.booboorecords.com; 978 Monterey St; 10am-8pm Mon-Wed, to 9pm Thu-Sat 11am-6pm Sun) An excellent music shop crammed with vinyl, CDs, books and T-shirts. Also sells tickets to most local gigs.

Hands Gallery ARTS & CRAFTS
(Map p337; ☎805-543-1921; www.handsgallery.com; 777 Higuera St; ⏰10am-6pm Mon-Wed, to 8pm Thu-Sat, 11am-5pm Sun) This brightly lit downtown shop sells vibrant contemporary pieces by California artisans, including jewelry, fiber arts, sculptures, ceramics and blown glass.

Information

San Luis Obispo Visitor Center (Map p337; ☎805-781-2777; www.visitslo.com; 895 Monterey St; ⏰9:30am-5pm Sun-Wed, to 6pm Thu-Sat)

Mission San Luis Obispo Post Office (Map p337; ☎800-275-8777; www.usps.com; 893 Marsh St; ⏰10am-5pm Mon-Fri, to 2pm Sat) Centrally located in downtown SLO.

San Luis Obispo Library (☎805-781-5991; www.slolibrary.org; 995 Palm St; ⏰10am-6pm Mon-Thu, to 5pm Fri & Sat, noon-4pm Sun; 📶) Free wi-fi and public internet terminals.

French Hospital (☎805-543-5353; www.frenchmedicalcenter.org; 1911 Johnson Ave; ⏰24hr) Emergency-room services.

Getting There & Away

Amtrak (☎800-872-7245; www.amtrak.com; 1011 Railroad Ave) runs daily Seattle–LA *Coast Starlight* trains and twice-daily SLO–San Diego *Pacific Surfliner* trains. Both routes head south to Santa Barbara (from $29, 2½ hours) and Los Angeles (from $44, 5½ hours). The *Coast Starlight* connects north via Paso Robles to Salinas (from $29, three hours) and Oakland (from $43, six hours). Several daily Thruway buses link to more regional trains.

Off Broad St, more than 3 miles southeast of downtown, **San Luis Obispo County Regional Airport** (☎805-781-5205; www.sloairport.com; 903 Airport Dr) has scheduled flights with United (San Francisco, Denver, LA), American Airlines (Phoenix, Dallas/Fort Worth) and Alaska Airlines (Seattle, Portland, San Diego).

There's no public bus transport to the airport. An Uber or Lyft from downtown costs around $15.

SLO Regional Transit Authority (p324) operates county-wide bus routes, including to the Hearst Castle Visitor Center (weekends only), Pismo Beach and Morro Bay. All routes converge on downtown's **transit center** (Map p337; cnr Palm & Osos Sts).

Avila Beach

Quaint, sunny Avila Beach lures crowds with its strand of golden sand and a shiny seafront commercial district of restaurants, cafes and shops. Explore the arcades behind Front St for art galleries and winery tasting rooms. Two miles west of downtown, Port San Luis is a working fishing harbor with a rickety old pier.

Sights & Activities

For a lazy summer day at Avila Beach, you can rent beach chairs and umbrellas, surfboards, boogie boards and wetsuits underneath **Avila Pier**, off downtown's waterfront promenade. Over by the port, the beach has bonfire pits and the barking of sea lions accompanies your stroll atop **Harford Pier**, one of the Central Coast's most authentic fishing piers.

★**Point San Luis Lighthouse** LIGHTHOUSE
(Map p342; ☎guided hike reservations 805-528-8758, trolley tour reservations 805-540-5771; www.pointsanluislighthouse.org; Wild Cherry Canyon parking area, Avila Beach Dr; lighthouse $5, trolley tours incl lighthouse adult/child 3-12yr $25/20; ⏰guided hikes 8:45am-1pm Wed & Sat, trolley tours noon, 1pm & 2pm Wed & Sat; 👪) Just getting to this scenic 1890 lighthouse, overshadowed by Diablo Canyon nuclear power plant, is an adventure. You can either join a free docent-led hike on the 3.75-mile round trip along a rocky, crumbling trail or take it easy by riding out on a two-hour trolley tour. Reservations are required for both tours. Inside the lighthouse you can inspect an original Fresnel lens and Victorian period furnishings.

Avila Valley Barn FARM
(Map p342; ☎805-595-2816; www.avilavalleybarn.com; 560 Avila Beach Dr; ⏰9am-6pm May-Sep, to 5pm Apr, Oct & Nov, to 5pm Thu-Mon Dec-Mar; P 👪) At this rural farm stand and pick-your-own berry farm, you can park alongside the sheep and goat pens, lick an ice-cream cone, then grab a basket and walk out into the fields to harvest jammy olallieberries in late spring and early summer, peaches and nectarines in mid-summer, or apples and pumpkins in autumn. During summer, kids can enjoy rides on tractors or ponies. There's also home-style baking on offer, including excellent pies crammed with seasonal fruit.

Sycamore Mineral Springs SPA
(Map p342; ☎805-595-7302; www.sycamoresprings.com; 1215 Avila Beach Dr; 1hr per person $17.50-22.50; ⏰8am-midnight, last reservation 10:30pm) Make time for a therapeutic soak in thermal mineral-spring water in private redwood hot tubs discreetly laddered up a woodsy hillside. Call in advance for reservations, especially during summer and after dark on weekends.

DON'T MISS

EXPLORING THE EDNA VALLEY WINE SCENE

To the north, the vineyard scene around Paso Robles has recently been growing in national popularity, but the bucolic and rural wine-making scene in the Edna Valley near SLO remains pleasantly low-key and under the radar. Pinot noir and chardonnay are the stars of the local terroir.

See www.slocoastwine.com or pick up a touring map at the SLO visitor center.

Malene Wines (☎805-235-3338; www.malenewines.com; 7767 Orcutt Rd; tastings $20; ⏰11am-5pm Fri-Sun; P) Serving excellent rosé wine on tap from a vintage 1969 Airstream caravan, Malene is a hip and popular addition to the traditionally conservative Edna Valley wine scene. Look for the bright pink plastic flamingos at the driveway entrance and you're in the right place.

Sextant Wines (Old Edna Tasting Room; ☎805-542-0133; www.sextantwines.com; 1653 Old Price Canyon Rd; tastings $20; ⏰10am-4pm Mon-Fri, to 5pm Sat & Sun; P) Pinot noir and chardonnay are the standouts at this heritage tasting room pouring different varietals from Edna Valley and Paso Robles. There's also a gourmet deli with panini and salads (from $13), making it one of the few local vineyards with a place to eat on-site.

Chamisal Vineyards (☎805-541-9463; www.chamisalvineyards.com; 7525 Orcutt Rd; tasting flights from $25; ⏰10am-5pm) In a rust-colored barn tasting room, taste hand-crafted, small-lot wines grown mostly organically. Exceptional pinot noir and chardonnay are Chamisal's perennial favorites.

Tolosa Winery (☎805-782-0500; www.tolosawinery.com; 4910 Edna Rd; tasting flights from $25; ⏰11am-6pm; P) No Oak Chardonnay, barrel-selected pinot noir and bold estate syrah are all highlights at this well-established and architecturally spectacular winery.

Niven Family Wine Estates (☎805-269-8200; www.nivenfamilywines.com; 5828 Orcutt Rd; tastings $15-30; ⏰10am-5pm; P) Tastings from the Baileyana, Tangent, Zocker and True Myth labels are offered inside a sunny, early-20th-century wooden schoolhouse, with two bocce ball courts outside. Outdoor seating is available amid the property's fragrant gardens.

Edna Valley Vineyard (☎805-544-5855; www.ednavalleyvineyard.com; 2585 Biddle Ranch Rd; tastings from $25; ⏰10am-5pm) Sip a glass of Reserve Chardonnay by panoramic windows overlooking fields of grapes, quite probably the best view in all of the Edna Valley. From Friday to Sunday the Perfect Pairing Wine & Food Experience ($50) partners four select wines with small tasting plates of local produce. Booking ahead online is recommended.

Kynsi Winery (☎805-544-8461; www.kynsi.com; 2212 Corbett Canyon Rd, Arroyo Grande; tastings $15; ⏰11am-5pm) This small, family-run vineyard pours cult-worthy pinot noir and chardonnay inside a cozy brick tasting room.

Sleeping

Accommodations in Avila Beach range from simple RV parking at nearby Port San Luis to a very comfortable boutique hotel. There are also public laundry and shower facilities at Port San Luis.

★**Avila La Fonda** INN $$$
(Map p342; ☎805-595-1700; www.avilalafonda.com; 101 San Miguel St; d from $279; P@) Downtown, this small boutique hotel is a harmonious mix of Mexican and Spanish colonial styles, with hand-painted tiles, stained-glass windows, wrought iron and rich wood. Gather around the fireplace for nightly wine and hors d'oeuvres. Complimentary beach gear to borrow for guests.

Avila Lighthouse Suites HOTEL $$$
(Map p342; ☎805-627-1900; www.avilalighthousesuites.com; 550 Front St; ste from $359; P@) Any closer to the ocean and your bed would actually be sitting on the sand. With families in mind, this apartment-style hotel offers suites and villas with kitchenettes, but it's the giant heated outdoor pool, Ping-Pong tables, putting green and life-sized checkers board that keep kids amused. Ask about steep off-season discounts. Reception is off 1st St.

San Luis Obispo Bay

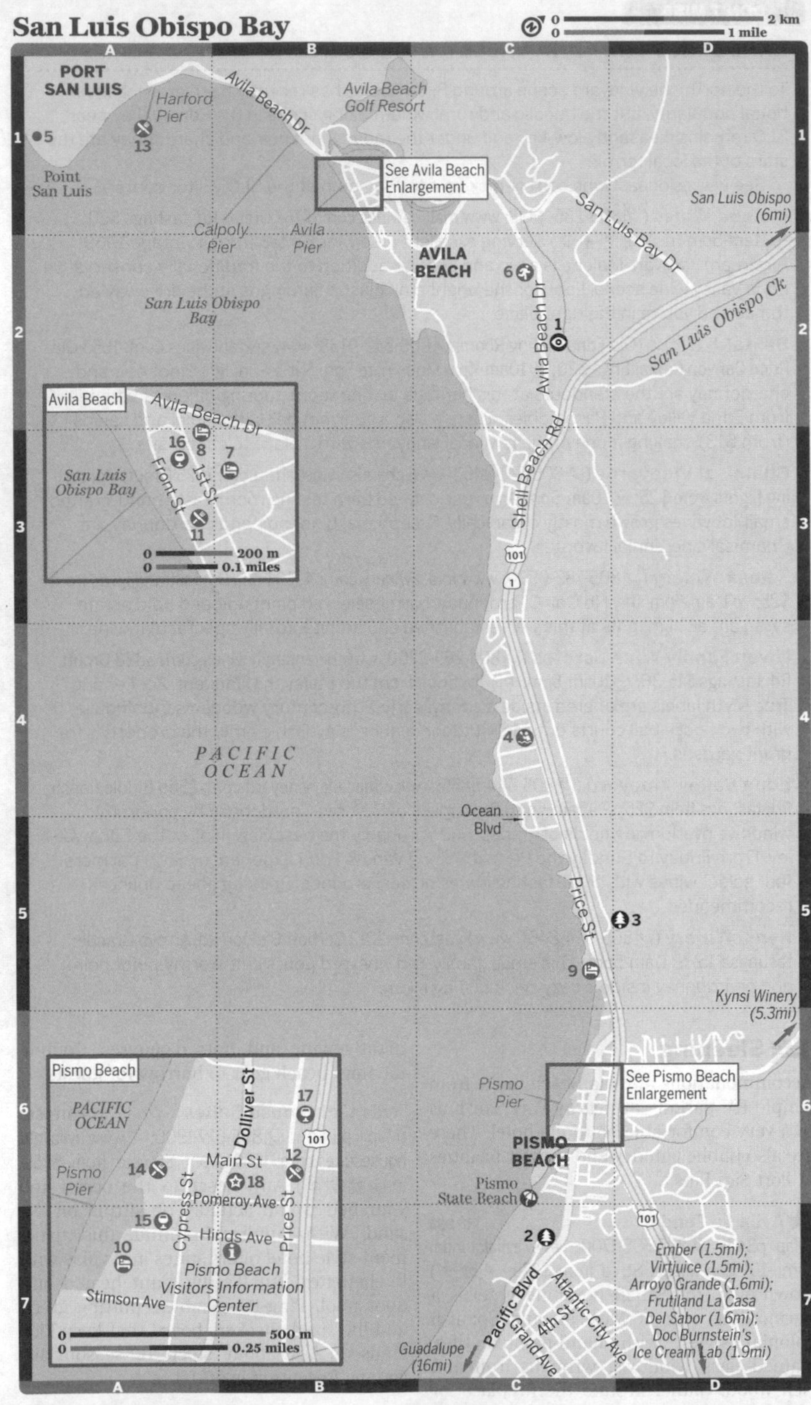

San Luis Obispo Bay

Eating & Drinking

Avila's Front St promenade features cafes and upscale restaurants. At Port San Luis, Harford Pier is home to a good restaurant and seafood shops selling fresh catch right off the boats.

Avila Beach Farmers Market MARKET $
(Map p342; www.avilabeachpier.com; Front St; 4-8pm Fri early Apr-late Sep) With local farmers, food booths and rockin' live music, this street party takes over downtown's oceanfront promenade weekly from spring to fall.

Mersea's SEAFOOD $
(Map p342; 805-548-2290; www.merseas.com; 3985 Avila Beach Dr, Harford Pier; mains $10-16; 11am-8pm;) A brilliant pier-side location combines with the freshest of seafood at Mersea's. Factor in family-friendly pricing and it's no surprise it can get busy. There's nothing innovative on a menu offering chowder, fish and chips and crab cakes, but paired with a gentle sea breeze and the occasional bark of nearby sea lions, it all makes perfect sense.

PierFront Wine & Brew WINE BAR
(Map p342; 805-439-3400; www.pierfrontwine.com; 480 Front St; noon-8pm Mon-Thu, to 9pm Fri & Sat, 11am-7pm Sun;) California craft beers and West Coast wines come with a side order of stellar sunset views of Avila's pier at this cosmopolitan eatery. Relax on a sofa in the eclectic interior or secure a sun-dappled spot under market umbrellas on the compact patio. Well-behaved dogs are welcomed as regulars, and PierFront's concise food menu includes flatbreads and cheese boards.

Getting There & Away

Avila is around 10 miles south of San Luis Obispo and 8 miles northwest of Pismo Beach.

Between 10am and 4pm on Saturdays and Sundays from late March until mid-October, a free **trolley** (SCT; 805-781-4472; www.slorta.org) loops from Pismo Beach around downtown Avila Beach to Port San Luis; from early June to early September, extended hours are 10am to 6pm Thursday through Sunday. There's no public transportation offered between mid-October and late March.

Pismo Beach

Backed by a wooden pier that stretches toward the setting sun, Pismo Beach is where James Dean once trysted with Pier Angeli. Fronted by an invitingly wide, sandy beach, this 1950s-retro town feels like somewhere straight out of *Rebel Without a Cause* or *American Graffiti*. If you're looking for a sand-and-surf respite from coastal road tripping, break your journey here.

Pismo traditionally called itself the 'Clam Capital of the World,' but over the last 20 years the beach has largely been bereft of the mollusk. In 2018, however, it was reported that clams are making a comeback at Pismo, but they are still very undersized and it's forbidden to gather them. You'll have better luck catching something fishy off the pier, where you can rent rods. To rent a wetsuit, bodyboard or surfboard, cruise nearby surf shops. For stellar coastal views, negotiate the hilltop walking trails at the Pismo Preserve.

Sights & Activities

Pismo Preserve NATURE RESERVE
(Map p342; www.lcslo.org; Mattie Rd; 6am-9:30pm Mar-Oct, to 7pm Nov-Apr;) FREE Inaugurated in early 2020, this 880-acre land conservancy high above Pismo Beach offers more than 11 miles of hiking

trails traversing oak woodlands and hilltop ridges with superb coastal views. Trails range in length from 1300yd to 5.2 miles. Download trail maps from the website. There's limited parking on-site so try and get an early start and avoid weekends.

Pismo Beach Monarch Butterfly Grove PARK
(Map p342; ☎805-773-5301; www.monarchbutterfly.org; Hwy 1; ⏲10am-4pm late Oct-Feb; P 👪) FREE Numbers have been dwindling but, for now, thousands of black-and-orange monarch butterflies still make their winter home in this eucalyptus grove just south of the North Beach Campground. Look closely: the dense clusters in the treetops might easily be mistaken for leaves. To learn more, study the information boards or join a free docent tour daily at 11am and 2pm.

Central Coast Kayaks KAYAKING
(Map p342; ☎805-773-3500; www.centralcoastkayaks.com; 1879 Shell Beach Rd, Shell Beach; kayak or SUP set rental $20-30, classes $65-75, tours from $80; ⏲9am-5pm mid-Jun–Sep, noon-5pm Mon-Thu & 9am-5pm Fri-Sun Oct-Dec & Apr–mid-Jun, 9am-5pm Fri-Mon Jan-Mar; 👪) Paddle out among sea otters and seals and through mesmerizing sea caves, rock grottos, arches and kelp forests. Wetsuits, paddle jackets and booties available (small surcharge applies) with kayak rentals.

Festivals & Events

Taste of Pismo FOOD & DRINK
(www.pismochamber.com; Dinosaur Caves Park; per person $75; ⏲late Apr) Annual celebration of the food and wine scene of the Central Coast. Held in a clifftop park with excellent ocean views. Restricted to those 21 years and older.

Classic at Pismo Beach CULTURAL
(www.theclassicatpismobeach.com; ⏲late May) Look forward to a spectacular display of hot rods and muscle cars roaring in off Hwy 1.

Clam Festival FOOD & DRINK
(www.pismochamber.com; 100 Pomeroy Ave, Pismo Beach Pier Parking; ⏲mid-Oct) Celebrate the tasty mollusk slowly making a comeback with a chowder cook-off, food vendors and live music.

Sleeping

Pismo Beach has dozens of motels, but rooms fill up quickly and prices skyrocket in summer, especially on weekends. Resorts and hotels roost on cliffs north of town via Price St and Shell Beach Rd, while motels cluster near the beach and along Hwy 101.

Pismo Lighthouse Suites RESORT $$
(Map p342; ☎805-773-2411; www.pismolighthousesuites.com; 2411 Price St; ste $157-499; P @ 🛜 🏊 🐾) This rambling cliffside compound about 1 mile north of town is a winner with families thanks to its many diversions: a pool, a playground, a giant chessboard and badminton courts. The cheapest suites are more functional than stylish, but all come with balconies and kitchenettes. For extra comfort, book one of the newly upgraded waterfront units. Pet fee $50.

Sandcastle Inn HOTEL $$
(Map p342; ☎805-773-2422; www.sandcastleinn.com; 100 Stimson Ave; r from $209; P 🛜) Many of these Eastern Seaboard–styled rooms are mere steps from the sand. The top-floor ocean-view patio is perfect for cracking open a bottle of wine at sunset or after dark by the fireplace.

Eating

Good restaurants – including cheaper seafood joints – feature in downtown Pismo Beach, especially along Price St, and the nearby adjoining town of Arroyo Grande also has good eating.

Virtjuice VEGETARIAN $
(☎805-994-7076; www.virtjuice.com; 1200 E Grand Ave, Arroyo Grande; juices & smoothies $6-11; ⏲7:30am-5pm Mon-Sat; P 🌿 👪) Superfood smoothies, fresh juices and wellness bowls are all good reasons to refuel at this organic, plant-based cafe in Arroyo Grande. Kick-start another day on the road with a Fireball shot combining lemon, orange, coconut water and cayenne pepper.

Doc Burnstein's Ice Cream Lab ICE CREAM $
(☎805-474-4068; www.docburnsteins.com; 114 W Branch St, Arroyo Grande; snacks from $5; ⏲11am-9:30pm Sun-Thu, to 10:30pm Fri & Sat, reduced hours in winter; 👪 🐾) In Pismo's neighboring Arroyo Grande, Doc's scoops up fantastical flavors like merlot raspberry truffle and the 'Elvis Special' (peanut butter with banana swirls). Also popular are Doc's delicious range of chocolates and doggy treats for well-behaved canine companions. From Hwy 101 southbound, exit at Grand Ave. Ask about seasonal flavors like sour blue raspberry sorbet.

Frutiland La Casa Del Sabor MEXICAN $
(805-541-3663; www.facebook.com/frutiland.frutiland; 803 E Grand Ave, Arroyo Grande; mains $10-15; 10am-6pm;) Oversized, overstuffed Mexican *tortas* (sandwiches) will feed two, and there are two dozen varieties to choose from. Or order a platter of blue-corn-tortilla fish tacos with a mango or papaya *agua fresca* (fruit drink). To find this taco shack in Arroyo Grande, exit Hwy 101 southbound at Halcyon Rd.

Cracked Crab SEAFOOD $$
(Map p342; 805-773-2722; www.crackedcrab.com; 751 Price St; mains $16-61; 11am-9pm Sun-Thu, 11am-10pm Fri & Sat;) Fresh seafood and regional wines are staples at this super-casual family-owned grill. When the famous Big Bucket – a messy bonanza of crab, clams, shrimp and mussels accompanied by Cajun sausage, red potatoes and cob corn – gets dumped on your butcher-paper-covered table, make sure you're wearing one of those silly-looking plastic bibs. No reservations, but the wait is worth it.

★Ember CALIFORNIAN $$$
(805-474-7700; www.emberwoodfire.com; 1200 E Grand Ave, Arroyo Grande; shared dishes $13-26, mains $28-45; 4-9pm Wed, Thu & Sun, to 10pm Fri & Sat;) Chef Brian Collins, who once cooked at Alice Waters' revered Chez Panisse, has returned to his roots in SLO County. Out of this heartwarming restaurant's wood-burning oven come savory flatbreads, harissa-smoked meatballs and hearty red-wine-braised beef cheeks. No reservations, so show up at 4pm or after 7:30pm, or be prepared for a very long wait for a table.

Oyster Loft CALIFORNIAN, SEAFOOD $$$
(Map p342; 805-295-5104; www.oysterloft.com; 101 Pomeroy Ave; mains $20-45; 5-9pm Sun-Thu, to 10pm Fri & Sat) Delve into the appetizers menu – including crab cakes and orange-glazed octopus – or kick off with tuna *tataki* or fresh oysters from the crudo raw bar. Mains including pan-fried halibut are still seafood heavy, but they do venture successfully into steak and chicken. Look forward to excellent views of the surf and the Pismo Beach pier from the restaurant's elevated position.

Drinking & Entertainment

Pismo Beach has a standout craft beer bar, and downtown Arroyo Grande along W Branch St has welcoming pubs, bistros and wine-tasting rooms.

The Boardroom BAR
(Map p342; 805-295-6222; www.theboardroompismobeach.com; 160 Hinds Ave; 2-10pm Mon-Wed, noon-10pm Sun & Thu, to midnight Fri & Sat;) An exemplary range of craft beers – mainly from the West Coast – is served by knowledgeable and friendly bartenders at this easygoing bar with a surfing ambience. Get to know the locals over a game of darts, maximize your travel budget during happy hour from 4pm to 6pm, and fill up on pizza, salad and panini.

Tastes of the Valleys WINE BAR
(Map p342; 805-773-8466; 911 Price St; noon-9pm Mon-Sat, to 8pm Sun) Inside a wine shop stacked floor to ceiling with hand-picked vintages from around California and beyond, ask for a taste of anything the staff has open, or sample from a quite astounding list of more than 1000 wines poured by the glass.

Pismo Bowl BOWLING
(Map p342; 805-773 2482; www.pismobeachbowl.com; 277 Pomeroy Ave; game per person $4.75, shoe rental $3.75; noon-10pm Sun-Thu, to midnight Fri & Sat;) Epitomizing Pismo Beach's retro vibe, this old-fashioned bowling alley is just a short walk uphill from the pier. Black-light 'cosmic' and karaoke bowling rule on Friday and Saturday nights.

Information

Pismo Beach Visitors Information Center (Map p342; 805-556-7397; www.experiencepismobeach.com; 581 Dolliver St; 9am-5pm Mon-Fri, 10am-2pm Sat) Free maps and brochures. A smaller kiosk on the pier is open from 11am to 4pm on Sunday.

Getting There & Around

Hourly from Monday to Friday, and a few times daily on weekends, **RTA** (805-541-2228; www.slorta.org) bus 10 links San Luis Obispo with Pismo's Premium Outlets mall ($2.25, 30 minutes), a mile from the beach, before continuing to downtown Arroyo Grande ($1.75, 15 minutes).

AT A GLANCE

POPULATION
448,370

NUMBER OF WINERIES
275

BEST WINE TOUR
Sustainable Wine Tours (p369)

BEST GOURMET DINING
Bouchon (p364)

BEST CRAFT BEERS
Figueroa Mountain Brewing (p364)

WHEN TO GO

Apr Balmy temperatures, fewer tourists than in summer. Wildflowers bloom on Channel Islands.

Jun Summer vacation and beach season begin. Summer Solstice Celebration parade.

Oct Sunny blue skies and smaller crowds. Wine country harvest festivities.

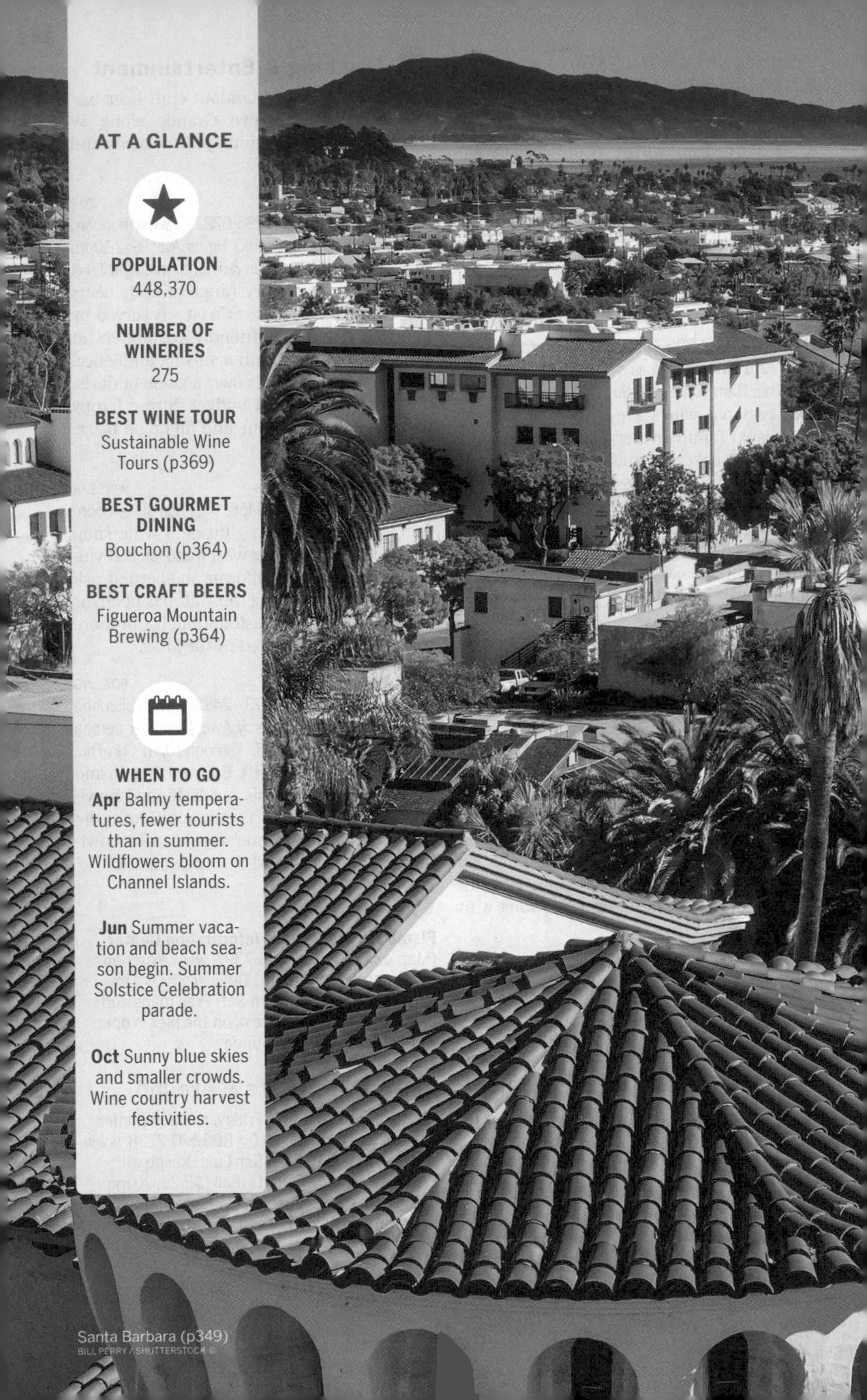

Santa Barbara (p349)

Santa Barbara County

Frankly put, this area is damn pleasant to putter around. Low-slung between lofty mountains and the shimmering Pacific, chic Santa Barbara's red-tiled roofs, white stucco buildings and Mediterranean vibe give credence to its claim of being the 'American Riviera.' It's an enticing place to loll on the beach, eat and drink extraordinarily well, shop a bit and push all your cares off to another day. The city's car-free campaign has brought electric shuttle buses, urban bike trails and earth-friendly wine tours. Mother Nature returns the love with hiking, biking, surfing, kayaking, scuba-diving and camping opportunities galore. Meanwhile, winemaking is booming in the bucolic Santa Ynez Mountains, west of Santa Barbara, where over 100 wineries vie for your attention.

INCLUDES

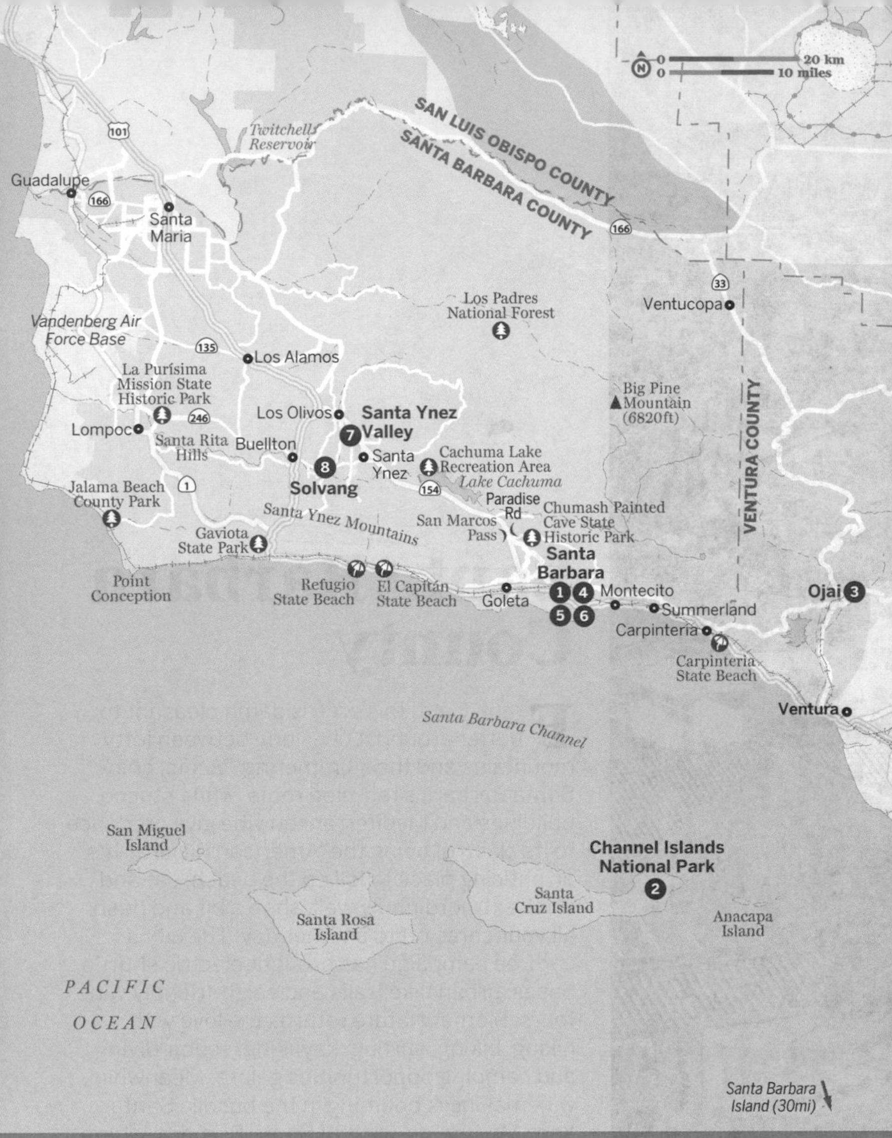

Santa Barbara County Highlights

❶ **Santa Barbara County Courthouse** (p349) Surveying 360-degree panoramic views atop the *Vertigo*-esque clock tower.

❷ **Channel Islands National Park** (p382) Kayaking sea caves and watching for whales.

❸ **Ojai** (p377) Rejuvenating body and soul.

❹ **Stearns Wharf** (p355) Strolling out to sea along California's oldest pier.

❺ **Funk Zone** (p349) Ambling between wine-tasting rooms, galleries and unique shops in Santa Barbara's favorite neighborhood.

❻ **Mission Santa Barbara** (p349) Exploring a rich vein of Spanish-colonial history.

❼ **Santa Ynez Valley** (p351) Pedaling past vineyards and organic farms.

❽ **Solvang** (p371) Eating *aebleskivers* (pancake popovers) in this Danish-themed village.

SANTA BARBARA

Perfect coastal weather, beautiful Spanish Colonial architecture, an easy-to-stroll downtown, excellent bars and restaurants, and activities for all tastes and budgets make Santa Barbara a great place to live (as the locals will proudly tell you) and a must-see place for visitors to Southern California. Check out the Santa Barbara Mission first, then see where the day takes you.

History

For hundreds of years before the arrival of the Spanish, Chumash tribespeople thrived in this region, setting up trade routes between the mainland and the Channel Islands, and constructing redwood canoes known as *tomols*. In 1542 explorer Juan Rodríguez Cabrillo sailed into the channel and claimed it for Spain – then quickly met his doom (from a gangrenous leg injury) on a nearby island.

The Chumash had little reason for concern until the permanent return of the Spanish in the late 18th century. Catholic priests established missions up and down the coast, ostensibly to convert Native Americans to Christianity. Spanish soldiers often forced the Chumash to construct the missions and presidios (military forts) and provide farm labor; they also rounded up and removed the tribespeople from the Channel Islands. Back on the mainland, the indigenous population shrank dramatically, as many Chumash died of European diseases and ill treatment.

Mexican ranchers arrived after their country won independence in 1821. Easterners began migrating en masse after California's gold rush kicked off in 1849. By the late 1890s, Santa Barbara was an established SoCal vacation spot for the wealthy. After a massive earthquake in 1925, laws were passed requiring much of the city to be rebuilt in a faux-but-attractive Spanish Colonial style, with white-stucco buildings and red-tiled roofs.

Sights

★MOXI MUSEUM

(Wolf Museum of Exploration & Innovation; Map p352; 805-770-5000; www.moxi.org; 125 State St; adult/child $16/12; 10am-5pm;) This next-gen science museum is an interactive treasure trove of exhibits and experiences related to sound, technology, speed, light and color that are sure to delight and enlighten little ones. On three floors they can learn about music (by stepping inside a giant guitar), build a race car, or recreate sound effects from famous movie scenes. Don't miss the views from the Sky Garden roof terrace and a nerve-challenging walk across a glass ceiling.

Weekends get very busy, with waits for many of the exhibits, so try to come during the week when it's quieter.

★Santa Barbara County Courthouse HISTORIC BUILDING

(Map p352; 805-962-6464; http://sbcourthouse.org; 1100 Anacapa St; 8am-5pm Mon-Fri, 10am-5pm Sat & Sun) FREE Built in Spanish Colonial Revival style in 1929, the courthouse features hand-painted ceilings, wrought-iron chandeliers and tiles from Tunisia and Spain. On the 2nd floor, step inside the hushed Mural Room depicting Spanish-colonial history, then head up to El Mirador, the 85ft clock tower, for arch-framed panoramas of the city, ocean and mountains. Explore on your own or join a free hour-long tour offered at 2pm daily and 10:30am Monday to Friday, starting in the Mural Room.

★Old Mission Santa Barbara CHURCH

(805-682-4713; www.santabarbaramission.org; 2201 Laguna St; adult/child 5-17yr $15/10; 9am-4:15pm Sep-Jun, to 5:15pm Jul & Aug; P) California's 'Queen of the Missions' reigns above the city on a hilltop perch more than a mile north of downtown. Its imposing Ionic facade, an architectural homage to an ancient Roman chapel, is topped by an unusual twin bell tower. Inside the mission's 1820 stone church, notice the striking Chumash artwork. In the cemetery the elaborate mausoleums of early California settlers stand out, while the graves of thousands of Chumash lie largely unremarked.

The self-guided tour starts in the pretty garden before heading to the cemetery (where Juana María, the Chumash girl made famous in Scott O'Dell's 1960 children's novel *Island of the Blue Dolphins,* was buried behind the tower). Next up is the church itself, followed by a series of rooms turned into a museum, which exhibit Chumash baskets, a missionary's bedroom, a recreated 17th-century kitchen, and time-capsule black-and-white photos showing the last Chumash residents of the mission and the damage done to the buildings after the 1925 earthquake. Docent-guided tours are usually run at 11am on weekdays, 10:30am on

SANTA BARBARA WINE COUNTRY

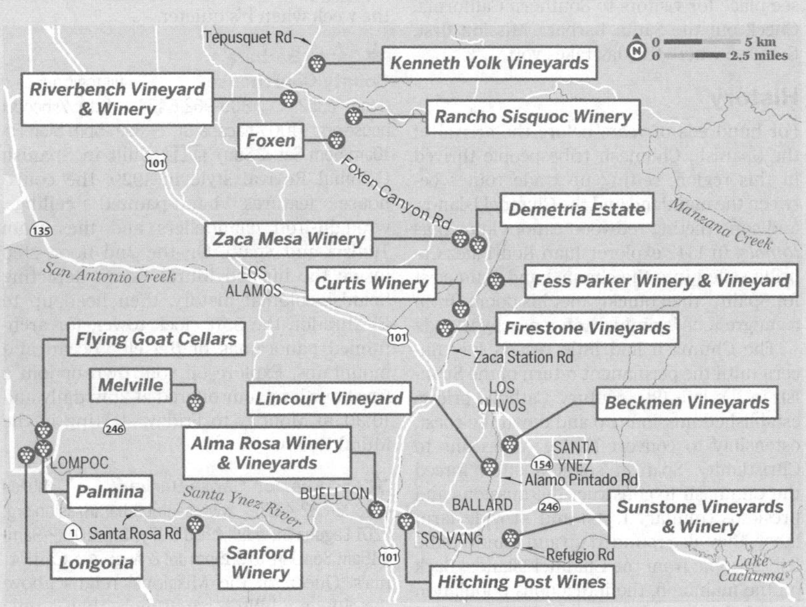

WINE TRAILS

☆ Los Alamos

If you've only got half a day, one option for a quick, satisfying hit of wine country is to breeze up Hwy 101 beyond Buellton to Los Alamos, 15 miles further north.

Begin with exactingly made coffee and pastries at **Bob's Well Bread** (☎805-344-3000; www.bobswellbread.com; 550 Bell St; mains $8.50-20; ⏲7am-6pm Thu-Sun, to 4pm Mon). From there, take a ramble to one of the diverse tasting rooms including **Lo-Fi Wines** (☎805-344-0179; https://lofi-wines.com; 448 Bell St; ⏲noon-7pm Thu-Sat, to 5pm Sun) and **Babi's Beer Emporium** (☎805-344-1900; www.babisbeeremporium.com; 388 Bell St; ⏲noon-4pm Mon, to 8pm Thu, 11am-8pm Fri & Sat, 11am-6pm Sun). For more sustenance, **Full of Life Flatbread's** (☎805-344-4400; http://fulloflifefoods.com; 225 Bell St; mains $9-23; ⏲4:30-9pm Thu, to 10pm Fri, 11:30am-10pm Sat, to 8pm Sun) wood-fired goodness takes advantage of local bounty, as does the sublime French food at **Bell's** (www.bellsrestaurant.com; 406 Bell St; mains $21-27; ⏲11am-9pm Thu-Mon).

☆ Foxen Canyon Wine Trail

Taking Foxen Canyon Rd (just west of Los Olivos off Hwy 154), start at **Demetria Estate** (Map p370; ☎805-686-2345; www.demetriaestate.com; 6701 Foxen Canyon Rd, Los Olivos; tastings $25; ⏲by appointment; P) . Sample biodynamically farmed chardonnay, syrah and viognier, plus Rhône-style red blends here. Tastings are by appointment only.

Follow Foxen Canyon Rd to **Foxen** (Map p370; ☎805-937-4251; www.foxenvineyard.com; 7200 & 7600 Foxen Canyon Rd, Santa Maria; tastings $15-20; ⏲11am-4pm; P) , which crafts full-fruited pinot noir, warm syrah, chardonnay and rich Rhône-style wines.

Continue a few miles to **Rancho Sisquoc Winery** (Map p370; ☎805-934-4332; www.ranchosisquoc.com; 6600 Foxen Canyon Rd, Santa Maria; tastings $15; ⏲10am-4pm Mon-Thu, to

Oak-dotted hillsides, winding country lanes, rows of grapevines stretching as far as the eye can see – it's hard not to gush about Santa Barbara's Wine country.

5pm Fri-Sun) for small-batch reds and whites. Picnic outdoors at **Riverbench Vineyard & Winery** (Map p370; 805-937-8340; www.riverbench.com; 6020 Foxen Canyon Rd, Santa Maria; tastings $15; 10am-4pm).

Other notable wineries along this route include **Zaca Mesa Winery** (Map p370; 805-688-9339; www.zacamesa.com; 6905 Foxen Canyon Rd, Los Olivos; tastings $15-25, tours $30; 10am-4pm daily year-round, to 5pm Fri & Sat late May-early Sep;), **Firestone Vineyards** (Map p370; 805-688-3940; www.firestonewine.com; 5017 Zaca Station Rd, tastings $10-15, incl tour $20; 11am-5pm; P), **Kenneth Volk Vineyards** (Map p370; 805-938-7896; www.volkwines.com; 5230 Tepusquet Rd, Santa Maria; tastings $15; 10:30am-4:30pm Thu-Mon) and **Fess Parker Winery & Vineyard** (Map p370; 800-841-1104; www.fessparkerwines.com; 6200 Foxen Canyon Rd; tastings $15-25; 10am-5pm).

☆ Santa Rita Hills Wine Trail

Begin in Buellton at **Hitching Post Wines** (p374), which had a boost from the 2004 film *Sideways*. Sample a few of its great pinot noirs. Next, cross Hwy 101 to make a left on Industrial Way, heading to **Alma Rosa Winery & Vineyards** (Map p370; 805-691-9395; www.almarosawinery.com; 181-C Industrial Way, Buellton; tastings $20; 11am-5:30pm Mon-Thu, to 6pm Fri-Sun; P) to taste Burgundian varietals, as well as pinot blanc and pinot gris.

If it's open, **Industrial Eats** (p374) is the obvious next stop for culinary brilliance before heading on Santa Rosa Rd to **Sanford Winery** (Map p370; 800-426-9463; www.sanfordwinery.com; 5010 Santa Rosa Rd, Lompoc; tastings $20-30; 10am-4pm Wed-Sun, by appointment Mon & Tue).

Alternatively, take Hwy 246 from Buellton to **Melville** (Map p370; 805-735-7030; www.melvillewinery.com; 5185 E Hwy 246, Lompoc; tastings $15-20; 11am-4pm Sun-Thu, to 5pm Fri & Sat; P) for some syrah, chardonnay and pinot noir.

Both Hwy 246 and Santa Rosa Rd bring you into Lompoc. Taste some of the region's best wines at **Ampelos** (805-736-9957; www.ampeloscellars.com; 312 N 9th St, Lompoc; tastings $10; 11am-5pm Thu-Sun, to 4pm Mon) , **Palmina** (805-735-2030; www.palminawines.com; 1520 E Chestnut Ct, Lompoc; 11am-5pm Thu-Sun), **Longoria** (805-736-9700; https://longoriawine.com; 415 E Chestnut Ave, Lompoc; 11am-4:30pm) and **Flying Goat Cellars** (805-736-9032; https://flyinggoatcellars.com; 1520 E Chestnut Ct, Suite A, Lompoc; 11am-4pm Thu-Mon).

☆ Santa Ynez Valley

Estate wineries scattered between Solvang and the town of Santa Ynez invite relaxed visits in the valley.

Heading out of Solvang on Hwy 154, turn left on Alamo Pintado Rd to **Lincourt Vineyard** (Map p370; 805-688-8554; www.lincourtwines.com; 1711 Alamo Pintado Rd, Solvang; tastings $15; 11am-5pm) for chardonnay and pinot noir and a dry French-style rosé.

Continue north into the heart of Los Olivos. Start at **Los Olivos Tasting Room** (Map p370; 805-688-7406; http://site.thelosolivostastingroom.com; 2905 Grand Ave, Los Olivos; tastings $10; 11am-5pm) to sample from wineries or tasting rooms like **Liquid Farm** (Map p370; 805-697-7859; www.liquidfarm.com; 2445 Alamo Pintado Ave, Suite 101, Los Olivos; tasting $20; 11am-5pm Mon-Thu, to 7pm Fri-Sun), **Story of Soil** (Map p370; 805-686-1302; http://storyofsoilwine.com; 2362 Alamo Pintado Ave; 11am-5pm Thu-Mon, noon-5pm Tue & Wed) and **Blair Fox Cellars** (Map p370; 805-691-1678; www.blairfoxcellars.com; 2477 Alamo Pintado Ave, Los Olivos; noon-5pm Thu-Mon).

Loop onto Hwy 154 heading south and detour on Ontiveros Rd to chill in a gazebo at **Beckmen Vineyards** (Map p370; 805-688-8664; www.beckmenvineyards.com; 2670 Ontiveros Rd, Los Olivos; tastings $20; 11am-5pm; P) , where estate-grown Rhône varietals flourish.

Or take Refugio Rd south to cross Hwy 246 and check out **Sunstone** (Map p370; 805-688-9463; www.sunstonewinery.com; 125 N Refugio Rd, Santa Ynez; tastings $20; 11am-5pm) and its Bordeaux-style wines.

Wind down your day with Italian cuisine at **SY Kitchen** (Map p370; 805-691-9794; https://sykitchen.com; 1110 Faraday St, Santa Ynez; mains $18-38; 11:30am-2pm & 5-9pm Sun-Thu, 5-9:45pm Fri & Sat) in Santa Ynez.

Downtown Santa Barbara

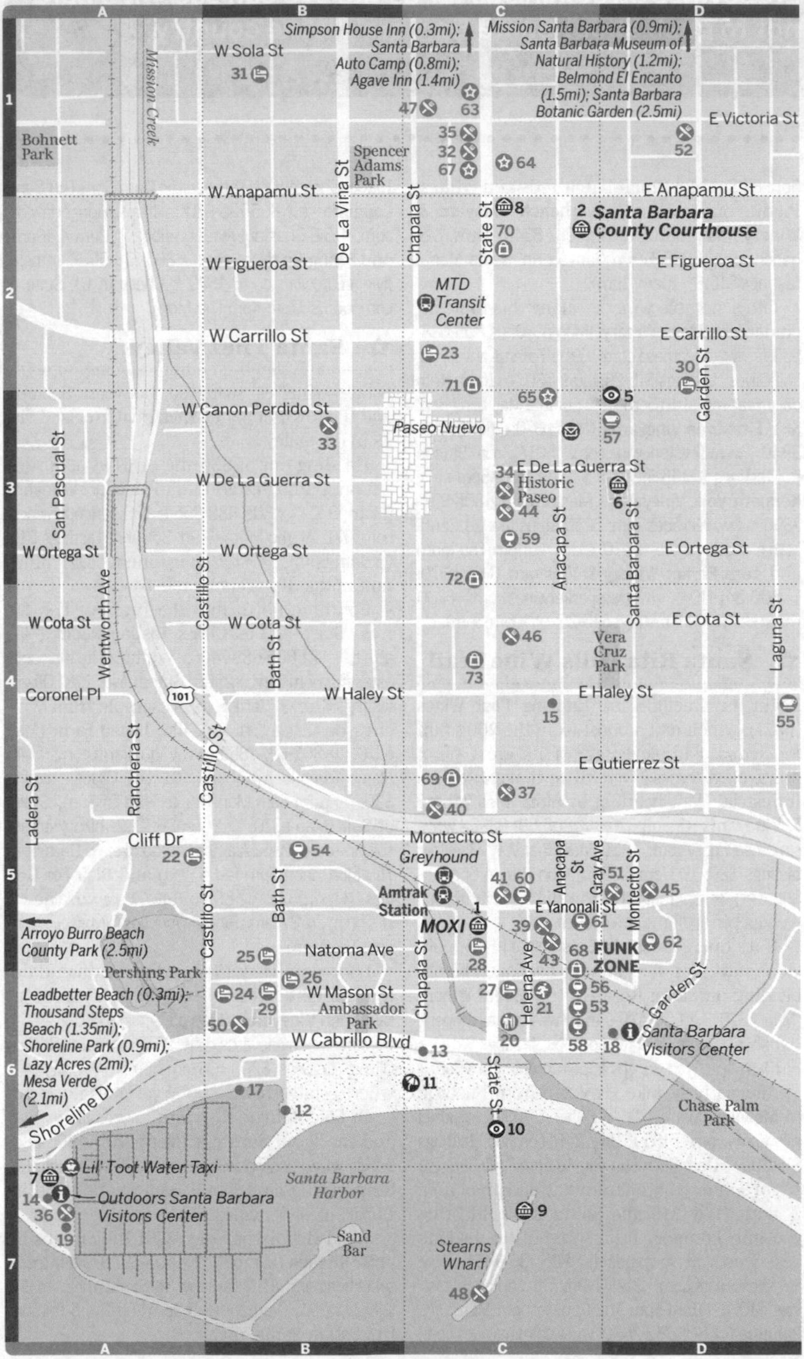

A B C D
1 2 3 4 5 6 7

Simpson House Inn (0.3mi); Santa Barbara Auto Camp (0.8mi); Agave Inn (1.4mi)
Mission Santa Barbara (0.9mi); Santa Barbara Museum of Natural History (1.2mi); Belmond El Encanto (1.5mi); Santa Barbara Botanic Garden (2.5mi)
W Sola St
31
Mission Creek
47
63
E Victoria St
35
32
67
64
52
Bohnett Park
Spencer Adams Park
W Anapamu St
E Anapamu St
De La Vina St
Chapala St
State St
8
70
2 **Santa Barbara County Courthouse**
W Figueroa St
E Figueroa St
MTD Transit Center
W Carrillo St
E Carrillo St
23
30
Garden St
71
65
5
W Canon Perdido St
33
Paseo Nuevo
57
San Pascual St
E De La Guerra St
34
Historic Paseo
44
6
W De La Guerra St
59
Anacapa St
Santa Barbara St
W Ortega St
W Ortega St
E Ortega St
Wentworth Ave
Castillo St
72
W Cota St
W Cota St
E Cota St
46
Vera Cruz Park
Laguna St
Bath St
73
Coronel Pl
101
W Haley St
E Haley St
15
55
Rancheria St
Castillo St
E Gutierrez St
Ladera St
69
37
40
Cliff Dr
Montecito St
22
54
Greyhound
Bath St
Amtrak Station
41
60
Anacapa St
Gray Ave
51
Montecito St
45
1
MOXI
E Yanonali St
39
61
Arroyo Burro Beach County Park (2.5mi)
Natoma Ave
Chapala St
43
68 **FUNK ZONE**
62
25
28
Pershing Park
26
Helena Ave
Leadbetter Beach (0.3mi); Thousand Steps Beach (1.35mi); Shoreline Park (0.9mi); Lazy Acres (2mi); Mesa Verde (2.1mi)
24
29
W Mason St
Ambassador Park
27
21
56
53
Garden St
50
20
58
18
Santa Barbara Visitors Center
W Cabrillo Blvd
13
State St
11
17
Shoreline Dr
12
10
Chase Palm Park
7
Lil' Toot Water Taxi
Santa Barbara Harbor
14
36
19
Outdoors Santa Barbara Visitors Center
9
Sand Bar
Stearns Wharf
48

Saturdays and 12:30pm on Sundays; no reservations are taken.

The mission was established on December 4 (the feast day of St Barbara), 1786, as the 10th California mission. Of California's original 21 Spanish-colonial missions, it's the only one that escaped secularization under Mexican rule. Continuously overseen by Franciscan friars since its founding, the mission is still an active parish church.

From downtown, take MTD bus 6 or 11, then walk five blocks uphill.

Santa Barbara Museum of Natural History MUSEUM

(805-682-4711; www.sbnature.org; 2559 Puesta del Sol; adult/child 2-12yr/13-17yr $15/9/12, incl planetarium show $16/12/12; 10am-5pm; P) The blue-whale skeleton by the entrance whets the appetite for the city's natural-history museum. The usual dioramas of stuffed animals are on display (the bird collection is especially good on local species). But the joy of this place is that once you've learned about nature inside, you can head outside to the 'Museum Backyard,' a trail through woods along Mission Creek, and engage with the real thing.

Uniquely local exhibits include a cast of the intact pygmy-mammoth skeleton found on Santa Rosa Island in 1994, and the gallery on Chumash life, which features recordings of the last native speakers of the area's indigenous languages. From 2pm to 4pm daily (except Tuesdays), meet the museum's resident birds of prey up close – all of these wildlife ambassadors were rescued and rehabbed but can no longer survive in the wild.

Santa Barbara Botanic Garden GARDENS

(805-682-4726; www.sbbg.org; 1212 Mission Canyon Rd; adult/child 2-12yr/13-17yr $14/8/10; 9am-6pm Mar-Oct, to 5pm Nov-Feb; P) Take a soul-satisfying jaunt around this 40-acre botanic garden, devoted to California's native flora. Miles of partly wheelchair-accessible trails meander past cacti, redwoods and wildflowers and by the old mission dam, originally built by Chumash tribespeople to irrigate the mission's fields. Guided tours (included with admission) depart at 11am and 2pm on Saturday and Sunday, and 2pm on Monday. Leashed, well-behaved dogs are welcome.

If you're driving, head north from the mission to Foothill Blvd/Hwy 192, turn right

Downtown Santa Barbara

Top Sights
1 MOXI ... C5
2 Santa Barbara County Courthouse ... C2

Sights
3 Chase Palm Park ... E6
4 East Beach ... E7
5 El Presidio de Santa Barbara State Historic Park ... D3
6 Santa Barbara Historical Museum ... D3
7 Santa Barbara Maritime Museum ... A7
8 Santa Barbara Museum of Art ... C2
9 Sea Center ... C7
10 Stearns Wharf ... C6
11 West Beach ... C6

Activities, Courses & Tours
12 Condor Express ... B6
13 Land & Sea Tours ... C6
14 Paddle Sports Center ... A7
15 Santa Barbara Adventure Company ... C4
16 Santa Barbara Bikes To-Go ... F6
17 Santa Barbara Sailing Center ... B6
18 Santa Barbara Trolley ... D6
19 Sunset Kidd's Sailing Cruises ... A7
20 Surf-n-Wear's Beach House ... C6
21 Wheel Fun Rentals ... C6

Sleeping
22 Brisas del Mar ... A5
23 Canary Hotel ... C2
24 Castillo Inn ... B6
25 Franciscan Inn ... B5
26 Harbor House Inn ... B6
27 Hotel Californian ... C6
28 Hotel Indigo ... C5
29 Marina Beach Motel ... B6
30 Spanish Garden Inn ... D2
31 White Jasmine Inn ... B1

Eating
32 Arigato Sushi ... C1
33 Barbareño ... B3
34 Bibi ji ... C3
35 Bouchon ... C1
36 Brophy Brothers ... A7
Corazon Cocina ... (see 47)
37 Dawn Patrol ... C5
38 La Super-Rica Taquería ... F3
39 Lark ... C5
40 Lilly's Taquería ... C5
41 Loquita ... C5
42 Los Agaves ... F4
43 Lucky Penny ... C5
44 McConnell's Fine Ice Creams ... C3
45 Metropulos ... D5
46 Palace Grill ... C4
47 Santa Barbara Public Market ... C1
48 Santa Barbara Shellfish Company ... C7
49 The Shop ... F3
50 Toma ... B6
51 Tyger Tyger ... D5
52 Yoichi's ... D1

Drinking & Nightlife
53 Brass Bear ... C6
54 Brewhouse ... B5
55 Cajé ... D4
56 Corks n' Crowns ... C6
Cutler's Artisan Spirits ... (see 39)
Figueroa Mountain Brewing Co ... (see 39)
Good Lion ... (see 64)
57 Handlebar Coffee Roasters ... D3
58 Municipal Winemakers ... C6
59 Press Room ... C3
Riverbench Winery Tasting Room ... (see 39)
60 Test Pilot ... C5
61 Valley Project ... C5
62 Waterline ... D5

Entertainment
63 Arlington Theatre ... C1
64 Granada Theatre ... C1
65 Lobero Theatre ... C3
66 Santa Barbara Bowl ... F2
67 Soho ... C1

Shopping
68 Channel Islands Surfboards ... C5
69 Chocolate Maya ... C5
70 La Arcada ... C2
71 Plum Goods ... C2
72 Santa Barbara Artisans ... C3
73 Santa Barbara Farmers Market ... C4

and then left to continue on Mission Canyon Rd; the road is well signed.

Santa Barbara Zoo ZOO
(805-962-6310; www.sbzoo.org; 500 Ninos Dr; adult/child under 13yr $19.95/11.95; 10am-5pm; P) Small (so it's perfect for young kids) Santa Barbara Zoo has 146 species great and small, including several not found in many other zoos. Popular residents include the Western lowland gorilla brothers, and the adorable meerkats. If you can't make it to the Channel Islands, check out the diminutive native island foxes. Don't miss the chance to see endangered California condors – probably your best bet for seeing them in the whole state – and giant anteaters.

Information panels give details on the animals and their habitats, plus tips for visitors on how to help preserve the creatures' natural environments (don't buy unsustainable palm oil, for example).

Parking is available ($11), or take the Waterfront shuttle for just 50¢.

Shoreline Park PARK
(Shoreline Dr; 8am-sunset; P 🐾) FREE For great views across the city, mountains and ocean (with the chance to spot whales in season and dolphins year-round), come to Shoreline Park, west of the harbor. There are restrooms, picnic tables and a children's playground, and dogs are welcome.

Santa Barbara Historical Museum MUSEUM
(Map p352; 805-966-1601; www.sbhistorical.org; 136 E De La Guerra St; 10am-5pm Tue-Sat, from noon Sun) FREE Embracing a romantic cloistered adobe courtyard, this peaceful little museum tells the story of Santa Barbara. Its endlessly fascinating collection of local memorabilia ranges from the simply beautiful, such as Chumash woven baskets and Spanish colonial-era textiles, to the intriguing, such as an intricately carved coffer that once belonged to Junípero Serra. Learn about the city's involvement in toppling the last Chinese monarchy, among other interesting lessons in local history.

Stearns Wharf PIER
(Map p352; www.stearnswharf.org; 8am-10pm; P) FREE The southern end of State St gives way to Stearns Wharf, a rough wooden pier lined with souvenir shops, snack stands and seafood shacks. Built in 1872, it's the oldest continuously operating wooden wharf in California, although the actual structure has been rebuilt more than once. During the 1940s it was co-owned by tough-guy actor Jimmy Cagney and his brothers. If you have kids, don't miss the **Sea Center** (Map p352; 805-962-2526; www.sbnature.org; 211 Stearns Wharf; adult/child 2-12yr/13-17yr $10/7/8; 10am-5pm; P).

Santa Barbara Maritime Museum MUSEUM
(Map p352; 805-962-8404; www.sbmm.org; 113 Harbor Way, Suite 190; adult/child 6-17yr $8/5; 10am-5pm Sun-Tue, Thu & Fri, 9am-3pm Sat; P) On the harborfront, this jam-packed two-story exhibition celebrates Santa Barbara's briny history with nautical artifacts, memorabilia and hands-on exhibits both fun and educational. Virtual experiences include sustainable fishing in a kelp forest, raising a sail, sorting trash into world gyres, visiting a tattoo parlor and going diving. Enjoy deep-sea-diving documentaries in the theater, and don't miss the awesome harbor view from the 4th floor, which also has a visitor center (11am to 4pm).

There's 90 minutes of free parking in the public lot, or take the Lil' Toot water taxi (p368) from Stearns Wharf.

Santa Barbara Museum of Art MUSEUM
(Map p352; 805-963-4364; www.sbma.net; 1130 State St; adult/child 6-17yr $10/6, 5-8pm Thu free; 11am-5pm Tue, Wed & Fri-Sun, to 8pm Thu;) This thoughtfully curated bite-size art museum displays the work of European and American masters – including Monet, Van Gogh and Degas – along with photography, classical antiquities, Asian artifacts and thought-provoking temporary exhibits.

Highlight tours of current exhibitions start at 1pm Tuesday through Sunday and are included with admission; additional tours start at 2pm Friday through Sunday. It also has an interactive children's space, a museum shop and a cafe.

El Presidio de Santa Barbara State Historic Park HISTORIC SITE
(Map p352; 805-965-0093; www.sbthp.org/presidio; 123 E Canon Perdido St; adult/child under 17yr $5/free; 10:30am-4:30pm) Founded in 1782 to defend the mission, this adobe-walled fort built by Chumash laborers was Spain's last military stronghold in Alta California. But its purpose wasn't solely to protect – the presidio also served as a social and political hub, and as a stopping point for traveling Spanish military. Today this small urban park harbors some of the city's oldest structures. On a self-guided walking tour, be sure to stop at the chapel, its interior radiant with rich hues.

Activities

Cycling

A paved **recreational path** stretches 3 miles along the waterfront in both directions from Stearns Wharf, west to Leadbetter Beach beyond the harbor and east just past East Beach. Find route ideas for a spectrum of skills and cycling styles at https://santabarbaraca.com/itinerary/popular-bike-trails-in-santa-barbara.

Wheel Fun Rentals CYCLING
(Map p352; 805-966-2282; http://wheelfunrentalssb.com; 24 E Mason St; 8am-8pm Apr–mid-Oct, to 6pm mid-Oct–Mar;) This well-established local outfit has hourly rentals of beach cruisers ($11), e-bikes ($20), mountain bikes ($13) and two-/four-person surreys ($30/40), with discounted half-day and full-day rates.

TOP 10 BEACHES IN SANTA BARBARA

Although Santa Barbara's beaches are beauty-pageant prize winners, don't expect sunsets over the ocean: most of this coast faces south.

East Beach (Map p352; E Cabrillo Blvd;) Santa Barbara's largest and most popular beach is a long, sandy stretch sprawling east of Stearns Wharf, with volleyball nets for pickup games, a children's play area and a snack bar. On Sunday afternoon, around 200 local artists set up booths along the sidewalk, near the bike path.

Butterfly Beach (Channel Dr) No facilities, but quite a high chance of celebrity spotting (the nearby Four Seasons Biltmore hotel is a popular destination for the rich and famous) at this small beach.

West Beach (Map p352; W Cabrillo Blvd;) Central, palm-tree-backed stretch of sand, right next to Stearns Wharf and the harbor (swimming isn't advisable). It's also the setting for large outdoor city events such as Fourth of July celebrations.

Leadbetter Beach (805-564-5418; Shoreline Dr, cnr Loma Alta Dr; per vehicle per hour $2; P) One of Santa Barbara's most popular beaches, always busy with surfers, wind- and kitesurfers, joggers and sunbathers. Facilities include reservable picnic areas and showers.

Goleta Beach County Park (www.countyofsb.org/parks/day-use/goleta-beach.sbc; Sandspit Rd, Goleta; 8am-sunset; P) Good beach for sunbathing, swimming and picnicking (nab a prized shaded spot if you can), or strolling the 1500ft-long pier for views out to the Channel Islands.

Arroyo Burro Beach County Park (Hendry's; 805-568-2460; www.countyofsb.org/parks/day-use/arroyo-burro-beach.sbc; Cliff Dr, at Las Positas Rd; 8am-sunset; P) Swim (lifeguards on duty), stroll or just picnic on this gem of a place, also known as Hendry's Beach, 5 miles southwest of Santa Barbara. It's flat, wide, away from tourists and great for kids, who can go tide-pooling. It's also a popular local surf spot and the eastern section is dog-friendly (there's even a dog wash in the parking lot).

El Capitán State Beach (805-968-1033; www.parks.ca.gov/?page_id=601; El Capitan State Beach Rd, Goleta; per vehicle $10; 8am-sunset; P) Head down from the low cliffs to enjoy swimming (confident bathers only), surfing and fishing from this pebbly beach, overlooked by native sycamore and oak trees. The seasonal beach store opens April to mid-September and sells basic groceries and camping supplies.

Thousand Steps Beach (Shoreline Dr, southern end of Santa Cruz Blvd; sunrise-10pm) Descend the cliffs on a historic staircase (don't worry, there are only 150 steps) for some windy beachcombing and tide-pooling (only at low tide), but no swimming. The beach is also accessible from Shoreline Park (p355) – head west along Shoreline Dr from the park and take a left on Santa Cruz Blvd.

Carpinteria State Beach (p376) Calm waters and tide pools make this idyllic stretch of beach an ideal spot for families. Also a good location to see harbor seals and sea lions during winter.

Also at the Hilton Santa Barbara Beachfront Resort.

Santa Barbara Bikes To-Go CYCLING
(Map p352; 805-628-2444; www.sbbikestogo.com; 736 Carpinteria St; bike rental per day $35-105; 9am-5pm) Offers top-quality beach cruisers and road, mountain and hybrid bikes to rent by the hour or day. Complimentary delivery available for road bikes, multi-day or multi-bike rentals. Rentals include helmets and emergency-kit saddle bags. Also offers two- to three-hour guided bike tours on people-powered or electric bikes ($75 or $95 per person). Discounts for multi-day, weekly and monthly rentals; reservations essential.

Kayaking & Boating

Paddle the calm waters of Santa Barbara's harbor or the coves of the Gaviota coast, or hitch a ride to the Channel Islands for awesome sea caves.

Some tour companies offer year-round whale-watching boat trips, mostly to see grays in winter and spring, and humpbacks and blues in summer.

Santa Barbara Adventure Company KAYAKING
(Map p352; ☎805-884-9283; www.sbadventureco.com; 32 E Haley St; ⏰office 8am-5pm Mon-Sat; 👪) The name says it all: if you want a company that provides a whole host of well-organized adventures then you've come to the right place. It offers everything from Channel Island kayaking (from $149) to surf and stand-up paddleboarding (SUP) lessons ($89) to bike tours (from $119).

Paddle Sports Center KAYAKING
(Map p352; ☎805-617-3425; http://paddlesportsca.com; 117 Harbor Way, Suite B; SUP/kayak rental from $25/15; ⏰8am-5pm) Long-established, friendly outfitter offering year-round kayak and SUP rentals from Santa Barbara harbor and Goleta Beach, as well as tours from $60. Walk-ins are welcome, but reduced rates are available if you book online in advance.

Santa Barbara Sailing Center CRUISE
(Map p352; ☎805-962-2826; www.sbsail.com; Marina 4, off Harbor Way; ⏰9am-6pm, to 5pm winter; 👪) Climb aboard the *Double Dolphin*, a 50ft sailing catamaran, for a two-hour coastal or sunset cruise ($45); join a whale-watching trip ($50), offered from mid-February to mid-May; or hop on for a one-hour spin around the harbor to view marine life ($25). The outfit also offers kayak and SUP rentals and tours.

Condor Express CRUISE
(Map p352; ☎805-882-0088; https://condorexpress.com; 301 W Cabrillo Blvd; 150/270min cruises adult from $50/99, child 5-12yr from $30/50; 👪) Take a whale-watching excursion aboard the high-speed catamaran *Condor Express*. Whale sightings are guaranteed, so if you miss out the first time, you'll get a free voucher for another cruise.

Sunset Kidd's Sailing Cruises CRUISE
(Map p352; ☎805-962-8222; www.sunsetkidd.com; 125 Harbor Way; cruises $50) Float in an 18-passenger sailboat on a 2½-hour whale-watching trip or a two-hour morning, afternoon, sunset-cocktail or full-moon cruise. Reservations recommended.

Surfing

Unless you're a novice, conditions are too mellow in summer – come back in winter, when ocean swells kick back up. Santa Barbara's **Leadbetter Point** is best for beginners. Legendary **Rincon Point** awaits just outside Carpinteria.

Surf-n-Wear's Beach House SURFING
(Map p352; ☎805-963-1281; www.surfnwear.com; 10 State St; rental per hour/day wetsuit $4/16, bodyboard $4/16, surfboard $10/35, SUP set per day $50; ⏰9am-6pm Sun-Thu, to 7pm Fri & Sat) Not far from Stearns Wharf, you can rent soft (foam) boards, bodyboards, wetsuits and SUP sets from this 1960s surf shop. It also sells modern and vintage surfboards, unique T-shirts and hoodies, colorful bikinis, shades, beach bags and flip-flops.

Hiking

Gorgeous day hikes await in the foothills of the Santa Ynez Mountains and elsewhere in the Los Padres National Forest. Most trails cut through rugged chaparral and steep canyons – sweat it out and savor jaw-dropping coastal views. Spring and fall, when temperatures are moderate, are the best seasons for hiking. Always carry plenty of extra water and watch out for poison oak.

To find even more local trails to explore, browse Santa Barbara Hikes online (www.santabarbarahikes.com) or visit the Los Padres National Forest Headquarters (p368), west of the airport.

Tours

★ Architectural Foundation of Santa Barbara WALKING
(☎805-965-6307; www.afsb.org; adult/child under 12yr $10/free; ⏰10am Sat & Sun weather permitting) Take time out of your weekend for a fascinating two-hour guided walking tour of downtown's art, history and architecture.

DIY WALKING TOURS

Santa Barbara's self-guided, 12-block **Red Tile walking tour** is a convenient introduction to downtown's historical highlights. The tour's name comes from the half-moon-shaped red clay tiles covering the roofs of many Spanish Revival–style buildings. You can download a free map of this walking tour, as well as other paths including along the waterfront, from Santa Barbara Car Free (https://santabarbaraca.com/itinerary/red-tile-walking-tour). For a lazy stroll between wine-tasting rooms, follow the city's Urban Wine Trail (p365).

SANTA BARBARA COUNTY IN...

One Day

Spend your first morning exploring Santa Barbara's historic mission (p349) before visiting downtown's museums, landmarks and shops along **State Street**, stopping at the county courthouse (p349) for 360-degree views from its clock tower. Grab lunch on State St and then soak up some rays at the city's East Beach (p356), walking out onto Stearns Wharf (p355) and down by the **harbor** for sunset. After dark, head to the **Funk Zone** for dinner and drinks in Santa Barbara's coolest neighborhood.

Two Days

Head up to Santa Barbara's Wine Country. Enjoy a do-it-yourself vineyard tour by car, motorcycle or bicycle along a scenic wine trail – **Foxen Canyon** (p350) and the **Santa Rita Hills** (p351) are exceptionally beautiful. Pack a picnic lunch or grab a bite in charming Los Olivos (p369) or Danish-inflected Solvang (p371).

Three Days

Spend the morning cycling along the coast, surfing or sea kayaking on the Pacific, or hiking in the Santa Ynez foothills. In the afternoon, drive to posh Montecito (p375) for shopping and people-watching, or hang loose in the chill little beach town of Carpinteria (p376).

Four Days

Head east for a stop in arty Ojai (p377), up in the mountains and known for its hot springs and spas, or book a day trip from Ventura (p380) by boat to explore one of the rugged Channel Islands (p382).

No reservations required; call or check the website for meet-up times and places.

Santa Barbara Trolley BUS
(Map p352; ☎805-965-0353; www.sbtrolley.com; adult/child 3-12yr $25/8; ⊙10am-3pm; 👪) Biodiesel-fueled trolleys make a narrated 90-minute one-way loop stopping at 14 major tourist attractions around the city, including the mission and the zoo. They start from the visitor center (hourly departures 10am to 3pm), and the hop-on, hop-off tickets are valid all day (and one consecutive day) – pay the driver directly, or buy discounted tickets online in advance.

Land & Sea Tours TOURS
(Map p352; ☎805-683-7600; www.out2seesb.com; 99 W Cabrillo Blvd; adult/child 2-9yr $30/20; ⊙noon & 2pm year-round, plus 4pm May-Oct; 👪) If you dig James Bond–style vehicles, take a narrated tour of the city on the *Land Shark*, an amphibious vehicle that drives right into the water. Trips depart from Stearns Wharf; buy tickets on board (no reservations).

Festivals & Events

To find out what's happening now, check the event calendars at www.santabarbaraca.com and www.independent.com.

Santa Barbara International Film Festival FILM
(☎805-963-0023; http://sbiff.org; 1528 Chapala St, Suite 203; from $60; ⊙late Jan-early Feb) Film buffs and Hollywood A-list stars show up for screenings of more than 200 independent US and foreign films.

I Madonnari Italian Street Painting Festival ART, FOOD
(www.imadonnarifestival.com; ⊙Memorial Day weekend; 👪; 🚌6, 11) FREE Benefitting local children's arts education, this street painting festival echoes back to 16th-century Italian folk art. A patchwork of colorful chalk drawings adorns Mission Santa Barbara's sidewalks over Memorial Day weekend (generally the last weekend in May), with Italian-food vendors and arts-and-crafts booths to accompany the viewing of artists at work and their transient masterpieces.

★**Summer Solstice Celebration** FESTIVAL
(☎805-965-3396; www.solsticeparade.com; ⊙late Jun) FREE Kicking off summer, this wildly popular and quintessentially Santa Barbarian parade features floats, dance troupes and inventive miscellany sashaying down State St – established in 1974, it's like a living prequel of Burning Man. Live music, kids activities, food stands, a wine-and-beer

garden and an art-and-craft show happen all weekend long in Alameda Park.

French Festival CULTURE, ART
(805-963-8198; www.frenchfestival.com; Oak Park; mid-Jul; ; 3) FREE California's biggest Francophile celebration has lots of food and wine, world music and dancing, a mock Eiffel Tower and Moulin Rouge, and even a poodle parade.

★**Old Spanish Days Fiesta** CULTURE, ART
(www.oldspanishdays-fiesta.org; late Jul-early Aug) FREE The entire city fills up for this long-running festival celebrating Santa Barbara's Spanish and Mexican colonial heritage. Also known simply as 'Fiesta,' its attractions include outdoor bazaars and food markets, live music, dance performances of flamenco and *folklórico*, horseback and rodeo events, and a big ole parade (plus a cuter children's parade complete with tiny señoritas, and caballeros with penciled on mustaches).

Sleeping

Prepare for sticker shock: even basic motel rooms by the beach command more than $200 in summer. Don't arrive without reservations and expect to find something reasonably priced, especially not on weekends. A good selection of renovated motels is tucked between the harbor and the 101 freeway, just about walking distance to everything. Cheaper motels cluster along upper State St and Hwy 101 northbound to Goleta and southbound to Carpinteria, Ventura and Camarillo.

★**Santa Barbara Auto Camp** CAMPGROUND $$
(9am-6pm Mon-Sat 888-405-7553; https://autocamp.com/guides/location/santa-barbara; 2717 De La Vina St; d from $251; P) Ramp up the retro chic and bed down with vintage style in one of six shiny silver Airstream trailers next to a historic RV park near upper State St, north of downtown. Sporting crisp mid-century-modern looks, all come with TV, fancy bedding and bath products, as well as a basic kitchen, a patio with electric barbecue, and two cruiser bikes.

Book ahead; two-night minimum may apply. Pet fee $25.

Agave Inn MOTEL $$
(805-687-6009; www.agaveinnsb.com; 3222 State St; r from $139; P) While it's still just a motel at heart, this property's 'Mexican pop meets modern' motif livens things up with a color palette from a Frida Kahlo painting. Flat-screen TVs, microwaves, mini fridges and air-conditioning add a welcome level of comfort. Family-size rooms have a kitchenette and pullout sofa beds. Light breakfast included.

It's a little north of downtown, so a car is a necessity, or good walking shoes.

Castillo Inn MOTEL $$
(Map p352; 800-965-8570; www.sbcastilloinn.com; 22 Castillo St; r from $199; P@) Minutes from West Beach (p356), the harbor and Stearns Wharf (p355), the Castillo Inn offers the best-priced accommodations of this quality in central Santa Barbara. The simply decorated rooms at this spruced-up motel are large and bright, and a continental breakfast (just fruit and muffins) is included in the rate. Some rooms have terraces.

Harbor House Inn INN $$
(Map p352; 805-962-9745; www.harborhouseinn.com; 104 Bath St; r from $224; P) Two blocks from the beach, this meticulously run inn offers bright, individually decorated sandy-hued studios with hardwood floors, small kitchens, and amenities such as smart TVs with free Netflix and Hulu. If you're staying two nights or more, rates include a welcome basket of breakfast goodies. Make use of free loaner beach towels, chairs, umbrellas and three-speed bicycles.

Hotel Indigo BOUTIQUE HOTEL $$
(Map p352; 805-966-6586; www.indigosantabarbara.com; 121 State St; r from $204; P@) Poised between downtown and the beach, this petite Euro-chic boutique hotel has all the right touches:

SANTA BARBARA ART WALKS

Prime time for downtown gallery hopping is **First Thursday** (www.santabarbaradowntown.com), from 5pm to 8pm on the first Thursday of every month, when art galleries on and off State St throw open their doors for new exhibitions, artists' receptions, wine tastings and live music, all free. Closer to the beach but similar in aim is the **Funk Zone Art Walk** (http://funkzone.net), happening on a bimonthly basis from 5pm to 8pm and featuring free events and entertainment at offbeat art galleries, bars and restaurants.

curated contemporary-art displays, terraces and ecofriendly green-design elements. Peruse local-interest and art-history books in the library nook. Take Amtrak to town and get 20% off the rate Sunday through Thursday, except in July and August. Parking $48 per night; pet fee $40.

Marina Beach Motel MOTEL **$$**
(Map p352; 805-307-7764; https://marinabeachmotel.com; 21 Bath St; r from $180; P ❄ 📶 🐾) Family owned since 1942, this whitewashed, one-story motor lodge that wraps around a grassy courtyard is worth a stay just for the location. Right by the beach, tidy remodeled rooms are comfy enough and some have kitchenette. There are complimentary beach-cruiser bikes to borrow. Dogs and cats OK (fee $15).

Franciscan Inn MOTEL **$$**
(Map p352; 805-963-8845; www.franciscaninn.com; 109 Bath St; r $171-225, ste $261-297; P ❄ 📶 🏊) Settle into the relaxing charms of this Spanish Colonial two-story motel just over a block from the beach. Rooms differ in shape and decor, but some have kitchenette and all evince French-country charm. Embrace the friendly vibe, afternoon cookies and outdoor pool.

★**Hotel Californian** BOUTIQUE HOTEL **$$$**
(Map p352; 805-882-0100; www.thehotelcalifornian.com; 36 State St; r from $400; P ⊖ ❄ 📶 🏊) Hotel Californian is the new kid on the once-run-down block that is the lower end of State St. It would be worth staying here just for the prime location (next to the beach, Stearns Wharf and the Funk Zone), but the appeal goes way beyond geography. A winning architectural mix of Spanish Colonial and North African Moorish styles sets a glamorous tone.

★**Spanish Garden Inn** BOUTIQUE HOTEL **$$$**
(Map p352; 805-564-4700; www.spanishgardeninn.com; 915 Garden St; r from $489; P ⊖ ❄ @ 📶 🏊) At this cloistered yet central Spanish-style inn, casual elegance, first-rate service and a romantic central courtyard will have you feeling like the don(na) of your own private villa. Rooms front a balcony or patio; beds are draped in luxurious linens; and bathrooms come with oversized tubs. Chill by the small outdoor pool, or unwind with a massage in your room.

★**Belmond El Encanto** LUXURY HOTEL **$$$**
(805-845-5800; www.elencanto.com; 800 Alvarado Pl; r/ ste from $575/811; P ❄ @ 📶 🏊 🐾) This 1918 icon of Santa Barbara style is a hilltop hideaway for travelers who demand the very best of everything. An infinity pool gazes out at the Pacific, while flower-filled gardens, fireplace lounges, a full-service spa and private bungalows with sun-drenched patios concoct the glamorous atmosphere perfectly fitted to SoCal socialites.

Pacific Crest Hotel BOUTIQUE HOTEL **$$$**
(805-966-3103; www.pacificcresthotel.com; 433 Corona del Mar Dr; r from $235; P 📶 🏊) 🍃 Wonderfully friendly Greg and Jennifer make sure all guests feel at home at their boutique motel, close to East Beach and the zoo. Remodeled rooms at this family-run hotel are spotless, spacious and come in cool, neutral tones that provide a soothing retreat.

Simpson House Inn B&B **$$$**
(805-963-7067; www.simpsonhouseinn.com; 121 E Arrellaga St; r $386-476; P ❄ 📶) Whether

CAMPING & CABINS AROUND SANTA BARBARA

You won't find a campground anywhere near downtown Santa Barbara, but just 15 minutes southbound on Hwy 101 is the beachfront Carpinteria State Beach Campground (p376) – book early – and 30 minutes northbound, also right on the ocean, are **El Capitán** (reservations 800-444-7275; www.reserveamerica.com; tent & RV drive-up sites $35, hike-&-bike tent sites $10; P 🐾) and **Refugio State Beaches** (reservations 800-444-7275; www.reserveamerica.com; tent & RV drive-up sites $35-45, hike-&-bike tent sites $10; P 🐾). If glamping is more your speed, check out **El Capitan Canyon** (reservations 866-352-2729; www.elcapitancanyon.com; 11560 Calle Real; safari tents $180, yurts $235, cabins $255-795; P ⊖ 📶 🏊) 🍃. You'll also find family-friendly campgrounds with varying amenities in the mountainous **Los Padres National Forest** (877-444-6777; www.recreation.gov; Paradise Rd; campsites $30) and at **Cachuma Lake Recreation Area** (info 805-686-5055, reservations 805-568-2460; http://reservations.sbparks.org; 2225 Hwy 154; campsites $25-45, yurts $65-90, cabins $110-140; P 🐾), closer to Santa Barbara's Wine Country.

you book an elegant room with a claw-foot bathtub or a sweet cottage with a fireplace, you'll be pampered at this Victorian-era estate ensconced in English-style gardens. From gourmet vegetarian breakfasts through to evening wine, hors d'oeuvres and sweets receptions, you'll be well fed, too. In-room luxuries include Netflix. Complimentary bicycles and beach gear to borrow.

The hotel is perfect for a romantic break and is for adults only.

Canary Hotel BOUTIQUE HOTEL $$$

(Map p352; ☎805 884-0300; www.canarysantabarbara.com; 31 W Carrillo St; r/ste from $340/521; P ❄ @ 📶 🏊 🐾) 🌿 On a busy block downtown, this grand multistory hotel has a rooftop pool and sunset-watching perch for cocktails. Stylish accommodations show off four-poster beds and all the usual amenities. In-room spa services, Saturday yoga classes and bathroom goodies will soothe away stress, but ambient street noise may leave you sleepless (ask for an upper floor). Complimentary fitness-center access and cruiser bicycles.

Hungry? Taste local farm goodness at the hotel's downstairs restaurant, Finch & Fork.

Parking $38; there's a 50% discount for electric vehicles. Pets are welcome and stay for free.

White Jasmine Inn B&B $$$

(Map p352; ☎805-966-0589; www.whitejasmineinnsantabarbara.com; 1327 Bath St; r $170-350; P 📶) Tucked behind a jasmine-entwined wooden fence, this cheery inn stitches together an arts-and-crafts bungalow and two quaint cottages. Rooms all have private bath and fireplace; most are air-conditioned and come with Jacuzzi. A full European-style buffet breakfast spread awaits every morning. No children under 12 years old allowed.

Brisas del Mar HOTEL $$$

(Map p352; ☎805-966-2219; http://brisasdelmarinn.com; 223 Castillo St; r from $249; P ❄ @ 📶 🏊) Kudos for all the freebies (DVDs, continental breakfast, afternoon wine and cheese, evening milk and cookies), the newer Mediterranean-style front section and the helpful staff. The outdoor pool and mountain-view sun decks are great for winding down after a day of sightseeing. It's on a noisy street three blocks north of the beach, so ask for a room in the back.

Eating

Restaurants abound along downtown's State St, and even the wharf and harbor have a few local faves among the touristy fare. More creative kitchens are found in the Funk Zone, while east of downtown, Milpas St has great taquerias. Book a week or two ahead for popular places or somewhere you're particularly keen to eat, especially on summer weekends.

★ **Corazon Cocina** MEXICAN $

(Map p352; ☎805-845-0282; https://corazoncocinash.com; 38 W Victoria St; mains $5.50-16.50; ⏰11am-9pm Mon-Fri, 10am-9pm Sat & Sun) Mexican regional favorites, elevated: *al pastor* tacos with pineapple and habanero salsa, delicate wild-shrimp ceviche laden with chili-spiked mango and cucumber, grilled Oaxacan quesadillas featuring local veggies – *sí, por favor.* Head into the Santa Barbara Public Market and prepare to get food drunk (and to wait a while – it's popular for very good reason).

★ **La Super-Rica Taqueria** MEXICAN $

(Map p352; ☎805-963-4940; 622 N Milpas St; dishes $1.55-6.80; ⏰11am-9pm Sun, Mon & Thu, to 9:30pm Fri & Sat; 👪) Although there's plenty of good Mexican food in town, La Super-Rica is deluged daily by locals and visitors keen on tasting the dishes once so loved by the late culinary queen Julia Child. Join the line to tuck into tacos, tamales and other Mexican staples, and see for yourself what the fuss is about.

★ **McConnell's Fine Ice Creams** DESSERTS $

(Map p352; ☎805-324-4402; www.mcconnells.com; 728 State St; scoops from $5.25; ⏰11am-10pm Sun-Thu, to 11pm Fri & Sat; 👪) Just try walking past this place on State St if you have a sweet tooth. A Santa Barbara institution since 1949, McConnell's uses local milk and other ingredients to produce an array of flavors, from the classic such as chocolate and vanilla to the adventurous like Turkish coffee and cardamom and gingersnaps.

★ **Lucky Penny** PIZZA $

(Map p352; ☎805-284-0358; www.luckypennysb.com; 127 Anacapa St; pizzas $10-16; ⏰11am-9pm Sun-Thu, to 10pm Fri & Sat; 🖉) Shiny exterior walls covered in copper pennies herald a brilliant pizza experience inside this Funk Zone favorite, right beside the Lark (p363). Always jam-packed, it's worth the wait for a crispy pizza topped with a variety of fresh ingredients, many vegetarian-friendly, or a wood-oven-fired lamb-and-pork-meatball sandwich. The coffee is taken seriously too.

Metropulos DELI $
(Map p352; ☎805-899-2300; www.metrofinefoods.com; 216 E Yanonali St; dishes $2-10; ⏲8:30am-5pm Mon-Fri, 10am-5pm Sat) Before a day at the beach, pick up custom-made specialty sandwiches (the Harissa Bomb doesn't disappoint), gyros and fresh salads at this perennially popular gourmet deli in the Funk Zone. Artisan crackers, imported cheeses, cured meats, and California olives and wines will be bursting out of your picnic basket.

Tyger Tyger SOUTHEAST ASIAN $
(Map p352; ☎805-880-4227; 121 E Yanonali St; mains $13-18; ⏲11am-3pm & 5-9pm Mon-Thu, to 10pm Fri & Sat) This low-slung, cheery space in the Funk Zone is a combo platter of Southeast Asian cafe, ice-cream shop and coffee bar, Tyger Tyger being the main course. Start with Thai-style noodles, Vietnamese banh mi and other Southeast Asian dishes, and head to the ice-cream counter for lychee-lemongrass soft serve.

The Shop BREAKFAST $
(Map p352; ☎805-845-1696; www.shopbrunch.com; 730 N Milpas St; breakfast $8-16; ⏲8am-3pm; 🐾) Away from the hustle of State St, the Shop still gets crowded thanks to its top-quality breakfast offerings. The poached eggs on toast are at the healthier end of the menu spectrum. In the opposite direction are the YOLO (fried chicken, biscuit and gravy) and the Tugboat (eggs Benedict on a biscuit with your choice of protein).

Lilly's Taquería MEXICAN $
(Map p352; ☎805-966-9180; http://lillystacos.com; 310 Chapala St; tacos $2; ⏲10:30am-9pm Wed-Mon, to 10pm Fri & Sat) There's almost always a line roping around this downtown taco shack at lunchtime. But it goes fast, so you'd best be snappy with your order – the *adobada* (marinated pork) and *lengua* (beef tongue) are standout choices. Second location in Goleta, west of the airport, off Hwy 101.

Dawn Patrol BREAKFAST $
(Map p352; ☎805-962-2889; www.dawnpatrolsb.com; 324 State St; breakfast $7-14.50; ⏲7:30am-2pm; 🖉) Bright and colorful decor helps wake you up, and the option to build your own hash breakfast ($14.50) sets you up for exploring Santa Barbara. Bread is housemade and other ingredients are locally sourced. Add a coffee, smoothie or mimosa (go on, you're on vacation) and you have a great start to the day.

Santa Barbara Public Market FOOD HALL $
(Map p352; ☎805-770-7702; http://sbpublicmarket.com; 38 W Victoria St; ⏲7:30am-11pm Mon-Fri, 8am-11pm Sat, 8am-10pm Sun; P) 🍃 Noodles, cupcakes, ice cream and Mexican magic from Corazon Cocina (p361) are just some of the tempting dining options available at this central market, handy for a break from sightseeing. Stop by too for coffee and wine, and have a break at the Garden, with more than 40 beers on tap.

Lazy Acres SUPERMARKET $
(☎805-564-4410; www.lazyacres.com/santa-barbara; 302 Meigs Rd; ⏲7am-11pm Mon-Sat, to 10pm Sun; P🖉) 🍃 High-quality supermarket standards with an emphasis on natural and organic food, plus a salad and soup bar. It's a short drive southwest of town; follow W Carrillo St, which turns into Meigs Rd.

★**Loquita** TAPAS $$
(Map p352; ☎805-880-3380; http://loquitasb.com; 202 State St; mains $11-29; ⏲5-9pm Sun-Thu, to 10pm Fri & Sat; 🖉) Spanish tapas done the Spanish way – simply and with top-quality ingredients. The wine list is a curated best-of-Spain selection, too, so pair your *pulpo* (octopus) with a crisp albariño and eat with a smile on your face. Or loosen your belt for one of the best paellas (from $35) this side of the Atlantic.

★**Arigato Sushi** JAPANESE $$
(Map p352; ☎805-965-6074; www.arigatosb.com; 1225 State St; rolls from $7; ⏲5:30-10pm Sun-Thu, to 10:30pm Fri & Sat; ❄🖉) Phenomenally popular Arigato Sushi always has people milling around waiting for a table (no reservations taken), but it's worth the wait. Traditional and more unusual sushi, including lots of vegetarian options, plus salads and a dizzying array of hot and cold starters will make you order a sake pronto just to help you get through the menu.

It's noisy and bustling, so not the place for a romantic dinner, unless you nab a table on the small patio on State St.

Bibi ji INDIAN $$
(Map p352; ☎805-560-6845; www.bibijisb.com; 734 State St; mains $16-30) Starting with Santa Barbara's super-fresh local produce, fish

and other seasonal ingredients, Bibi ji takes traditional Indian favorites and makes them inventively, multiculturally contemporary. As one of the restaurant's partners is local master sommelier Rajat Parr, the wine list is phenomenal and complements the cuisine beautifully.

Los Agaves MEXICAN $$
(Map p352; ☎805-564-2626; www.los-agaves.com; 600 N Milpas St; mains $11.75-21.95; ⏲11am-9pm) In the heart of east Santa Barbara's Mexican culinary scene, Los Agaves stands out for its well-cooked food and hacienda-style decor. Start with the zucchini-blossom quesadillas if they're in season and then take your pick from the mostly seafood and meat dishes. There's always a wait (no reservations taken), but that allows you time to peruse the menu carefully.

Toma MEDITERRANEAN $$
(Map p352; ☎805-962-0777; www.tomarestaurant.com; 324 W Cabrillo Blvd; mains $17-35; ⏲5pm-close) Enjoy a glass of wine or a cocktail before tucking into some tasty pasta, flatbreads or meat and seafood dishes at one of Santa Barbara's most popular restaurants. The decor's not the most exciting, but the food more than compensates. Book well in advance.

Santa Barbara Shellfish Company SEAFOOD $$
(Map p352; ☎805-966-6676; http://shellfishco.com; 230 Stearns Wharf; dishes $4-24; ⏲11am-9pm;) 'From sea to skillet to plate' sums up this end-of-the-wharf seafood shack that's more of a buzzing counter joint than a sit-down restaurant. Chase away the seagulls as you chow down on garlic-baked clams, crab cakes and coconut-fried shrimp at wooden picnic tables outside. Awesome lobster bisque, ocean views and the same location for almost 40 years.

Brophy Brothers SEAFOOD $$
(Map p352; ☎805-966-4418; www.brophybros.com; 119 Harbor Way; mains $11.50-20; ⏲11am-10pm; P) A longtime favorite for its fresh-off-the-dock fish and seafood, rowdy atmosphere and salty harborside setting. Slightly less claustrophobic tables on the upstairs deck are worth the long wait – they're quieter and have the best ocean views. Or skip the lines and start knocking back oyster shooters and Bloody Marys with convivial locals at the bar.

Palace Grill CAJUN, CREOLE $$
(Map p352; ☎805-963-5000; http://palacegrill.com; 8 E Cota St; mains lunch $11-26, dinner $24-39; ⏲5:30-10pm Mon-Thu, 11:30am-3pm & 5:30-10pm Fri-Sun;) With all the exuberance of Mardi Gras, this N'awlins-style grill makes totally addictive baskets of housemade muffins and breads, and ginormous (if so-so) plates of jambalaya, gumbo ya-ya, blackened catfish and pecan chicken. Stiff cocktails and indulgent desserts make the grade. Act unsurprised when the staff leads the crowd in a rousing sing-along.

Boathouse CALIFORNIAN $$
(☎805-898-2628; http://boathousesb.com; 2981 Cliff Dr; mains from $14; ⏲7:30am-close;) Water views and ocean air accompany your healthy dining at the Boathouse, right on Arroyo Burro Beach (also known as Hendry's Beach). The patio is great for enjoying a cocktail and fancy salad with other beachgoers, while the walls inside display photos paying homage to the area's surfing and rowing heritage.

Mesa Verde VEGAN $$
(☎805-963-4474; http://mesaverderestaurant.com; 1919 Cliff Dr; shared plates $10-18; ⏲11am-9pm Tue-Fri, 11am-3:30pm & 5-9pm Sat & Sun;) A top pick for plant-based dining, Mesa Verde has so many delicious, innovative all-vegan sharing plates on the menu that meat-avoiding procrastinators will be in torment. If in doubt, pick a selection and brace yourself for flavor-packed delights. Meat eaters welcome (and may be converted).

★Barbareño CALIFORNIAN $$$
(Map p352; ☎805-963-9591; www.barbareno.com; 205 W Canon Perdido St; mains $21-45; ⏲5-9:30pm Wed-Mon) The terroir of Santa Barbara encapsulated in an eatery that prepares thoughtfully creative cuisine and does so playfully. The seasonally changing menu sources as many ingredients as possible locally, which in this region means abundance and novelty from sea and land. Its wine list is wide-ranging, and its off-State location makes for an intimate and quietly palate-blowing dining experience.

★Lark CALIFORNIAN $$$
(Map p352; ☎805-284-0370; www.thelarksb.com; 131 Anacapa St; mains $16-38; ⏲5-9pm Sun-Thu, to 10pm Fri & Sat; P) A top spot to savor SoCal's bountiful farm and fishing goodness, chef-run Lark was named after an antique Pullman railway car and is based

at a former fish market transformed into a buzzy casual-urban restaurant in the Funk Zone. The menu morphs with the seasons, presenting inspiring flavor combinations such as crispy brussels sprouts with dates or juniper-smoked duck breast. Make reservations.

Just as much imagination goes into the craft cocktails. Try the Green Goddess, starring chili vodka, arugula, matcha, Suze bitters and ginger beer.

★Yoichi's JAPANESE **$$$**
(Map p352; ☎805-962-6627; www.yoichis.com; 230 E Victoria St; 5-/7-course set menu $80/125; ⊙5:30-9pm Tue-Sun) Headline: *kaiseki* (traditional Japanese multicourse dining) comes to Santa Barbara and wows locals. It might have limited hours, take a chunk out of your wallet and need to be booked way in advance, but none of that has stopped Yoichi's from being hailed as one of Santa Barbara's best (and slightly hidden away) eating experiences.

The set menu consists of seven courses (five-course menu also available Tuesday through Thursday), divided into different types of dish (soup, sashimi, grilled and so on), each of which delivers on both flavor and presentation thanks to chef Yoichi's culinary skills and the beautiful handmade ceramic plates on which he serves his creations. And of course there's top-quality and some unusual sakes to try too. It's tucked away on a quiet residential road a few blocks northeast of State St.

★Bouchon CALIFORNIAN **$$$**
(Map p352; ☎805-730-1160; www.bouchonsantabarbara.com; 9 W Victoria St; mains $26-36; ⊙5-9pm) The perfect, unhurried follow-up to a day in the wine country is to feast on the bright, flavorful California cooking at pretty Bouchon (meaning 'wine cork'). A seasonally changing menu spotlights locally grown farm produce and ranched meats that marry beautifully with almost three dozen regional wines available by the glass. Lovebirds, book a table on the candlelit patio.

Drinking & Nightlife

On lower State St, most of the boisterous watering holes have happy hours, tiny dance floors and rowdy college nights. The Funk Zone's eclectic mix of bars and wine-tasting rooms provides a more on-trend, sophisticated alternative.

★Good Lion COCKTAIL BAR
(Map p352; ☎805-845-8754; www.goodlioncocktails.com; 1212 State St; ⊙4pm-1am) Grab a cocktail at the beautiful blue-tiled bar, then grab a book from the shelves and settle into a leather banquette in this petite place that has a cool turn-of-the-20th-century-Montmartre feel (candles on the tables and absinthe in many of the cocktails help create the Parisian atmosphere).

★Waterline BREWERY
(Map p352; ☎805-845-1482; www.waterlinesb.com; 116-120 Santa Barbara St; ⊙hours vary; 🐾) Not sure if your palate can take any more wine after a Funk Zone tasting tour? The Waterline is a repurposed warehouse space combining two taprooms (Topa Topa and Lama Dog), a restaurant (the Nook) serving elevated bar food, and a wine-tasting room (Fox Wine). Wander through the maze of rooms to decide which itch you want to scratch.

★Municipal Winemakers WINE BAR
(Map p352; ☎805-931-6864; www.municipalwinemakers.com; 22 Anacapa St; tastings $12; ⊙1-8pm Thu & Sun, 1-9pm Fri & Sat; 🐾) Muni's winemaker, Dave, studied the oenological arts in Australia and France before applying his knowledge in this industrially decorated tasting room. His fun, accessible blends are hugely popular – enjoy a bottle on the large patio. For food, you can't beat the cheese plate; on weekends, pair your wine selection with East Coast–style lobstah rolls and sea-urchin crudo.

★Figueroa Mountain Brewing Co CRAFT BEER
(Map p352; ☎805-324-4461; www.figmtnbrew.com; 137 Anacapa St, Suite F; ⊙11am-11pm Sun-Thu, to midnight Fri & Sat) Father-and-son brewers have brought their gold-medal-winning hoppy IPA, Danish red lager and potent stout from Santa Barbara's Wine Country to the Funk Zone. Knowledgeable staff will help you choose. Clink glasses below vintage-style posters in the 'surf-meets-Old-West' taproom or on the open-air patio while acoustic acts play.

Enter on Yanonali St. Happy hour runs from 3pm to 6pm Monday to Friday.

Brass Bear CRAFT BEER
(Map p352; ☎805-770-7651; www.brassbearbrewing.com; 28 Anacapa St, Suite E; ⊙noon-9pm Sun-Wed, to 10pm Thu, to 11pm Fri & Sat; 👪🐾) Large

DON'T MISS

URBAN WINE TRAIL

No wheels to head up to Santa Barbara's Wine Country? No problem. Ramble between over three dozen wine-tasting rooms (and microbreweries) throughout downtown and in the Funk Zone near the beach. Pick up the Urban Wine Trail (www.urbanwinetrailsb.com) anywhere along its route. Most tasting rooms are open every afternoon or sometimes into the early evening. On weekends, join the beautiful people rubbing shoulders as they sip outstanding glasses of regional wines and listen to free live music.

For a sociable scene, start at Municipal Winemakers or Corks n' Crowns, both on Anacapa St. Then head up to Yanonali St, turning left for Riverbench Winery Tasting Room; Cutler's Artisan Spirits distillery, a storefront where you can sample bourbon whiskey, vodka and apple liqueur; and Figueroa Mountain Brewing Co . Walk further west to find more wine-tippling spots.

Or turn right on Yanonali St and stop at the Valley Project for a liquid education about Santa Barbara's five distinct wine-growing regions. A couple of blocks east, on Santa Barbara St, Waterline has the Fox Wine tasting room, housed in a cool, multipurpose complex that offers beer and food too.

glasses of wine and beer and a great grilled cheese make this cozy place, located up an alley off Anacapa (follow the murals), a worthy detour. Friendly staff add to the convivial atmosphere. Parents, take note: Saturday and Sunday from 1pm to 7pm it hosts a supervised play area for kids so parents can eat and drink in peace (!).

Cajé COFFEE

(Lab Social; Map p352; https://cajé.com; 416 E Haley St; 8am-1pm & 5:30pm-12:30am Tue-Sat) When is a coffeehouse not a coffeehouse? When night falls, the shades are drawn and Cajé turns into Lab Social, a speakeasy serving cocktails. To say its coffee concoctions and cocktails are creative is an understatement; suffice to say, most components are painstakingly housemade. You can't enter Lab Social through the front door, naturally; look for the not-so-secret side entrance.

Cajé walks the sustainability talk: if you don't bring your own cup for to-go drinks, you can take a ceramic cup for $5, refundable when you return, or yours to keep.

Test Pilot COCKTAIL BAR

(Map p352; 805-845-2518; www.testpilotcocktails.com; 211 Helena Ave; 4pm-1am Mon-Thu, 2pm-2am Fri & Sat, 2pm-1am Sun) Any actual test pilot would be grounded after one of the strong but delicious cocktails at this tiki bar in the Funk Zone. The decor follows a nautical theme; the drinks ($9 to $12) keep it simple with interesting twists on traditional concoctions. Expect foliage in your piña colada.

Riverbench Winery Tasting Room WINE BAR

(Map p352; 805-321-4100; www.riverbench.com; 137 Anacapa St; tastings $10; 11am-6pm) Beautiful pinot noirs and sparkling wines by winemaker Clarissa Nagy showcase the best of the eponymous Santa Maria Valley vineyard. Knowledgeable staff at this Funk Zone tasting room can help you choose a tasting or glass.

Valley Project WINE BAR

(Map p352; 805-453-6768; www.thevalleyprojectwines.com; 116 E Yanonali St; tastings $12; noon-7pm) From the sidewalk, passersby stop just to peek through the floor-to-ceiling glass windows at a wall-size, digestibly informative map of Santa Barbara's Wine Country, all hand drawn in chalk. Inside, wine-lovers lean on the tasting bar while sipping flights of favorite local Rhône and Burgundian varietals.

Corks n' Crowns BAR

(Map p352; 805-845-8600; www.corksandcrowns.com; 32 Anacapa St; tastings $7-20; 11am-7pm, last call for tastings 6pm;) Sit on the sunny porch or inside the rustic-feel hut by the fire and try out the wines and beers from Santa Barbara in general and a few international destinations too. Tastings come in a flight of three for wine and four for beer – pours are generous. Board games are available – try Jenga after a tasting for added fun.

Cutler's Artisan Spirits DISTILLERY

(Map p352; 805-845-4040; http://cutlersartisan.com; 137 Anacapa St, Suite D; tastings $12; 1-6pm Sun, Wed & Thu, to 9pm Fri & Sat) Family-run craft distillers producing whiskey, vodka, gin and apple pie (liqueur) since before (and during) Prohibition. The spirits are hard to find in stores, so this is your chance to taste and then purchase up to three bottles (the maximum under local law) of the specialty liquors. The gin in particular is highly prized.

Press Room PUB
(Map p352; ☎805-963-8121; 15 E Ortega St; ⏰11am-2am) This tiny pub can barely contain the college students, European travelers and random locals who cram the place to its seams. Pop in to catch soccer games, stuff the jukebox with quarters and banter with the bartender.

Handlebar Coffee Roasters CAFE
(Map p352; www.handlebarcoffee.com; 128 E Canon Perdido St; ⏰6:30am-5pm; 🐾) Bicycle-themed coffee shop brewing rich coffee and espresso drinks from small-batch roasted beans. Sit and sip yours on the sunny patio.

Brewhouse BREWERY
(Map p352; ☎805-884-4664; www.sbbrewhouse.com; 229 W Montecito St; ⏰11am-midnight, brunch 10am-1pm Sat & Sun; 📶🐾) Down by the railroad tracks, the boisterous Brewhouse crafts its own unique small-batch beer (Saint Barb's Belgian-style ales rule), serves wines by the glass, dishes up surprisingly good bar food and has cool art and rockin' live music Wednesday to Saturday nights.

☆ Entertainment

Santa Barbara's appreciation of the arts is evidenced not only by the variety of performances available on any given night but also by its gorgeous, often historic venues. For a current calendar of live music and special events, check www.independent.com or www.newspress.com/category/scene.

Santa Barbara Bowl LIVE MUSIC
(Map p352; ☎805-962-7411; http://sbbowl.com; 1122 N Milpas St; most tickets $35-145) Built by Works Progress Administration (WPA) artisans during the Great Depression, this naturally beautiful outdoor stone amphitheater has ocean views from the highest cheap seats. Kick back in the sunshine or under the stars for live rock, jazz and folk concerts in summer. Headliners like Joni Mitchell, Bob Marley and local graduate Jack Johnson have all taken the stage here.

Arlington Theatre THEATER
(Map p352; ☎805-963-4408; https://thearlingtontheatre.com; 1317 State St; ⏰box office 11am-6pm Fri & Sat, noon-6pm Sun-Thu) Harking back to 1931, this Mission Revival–style movie palace has a Spanish courtyard and a star-spangled ceiling. It's a drop-dead

SANTA BARBARA FOR CHILDREN

Santa Barbara abounds with family-friendly fun for kids of all ages, from tots to tweens.

MOXI (p349) Santa Barbara's newest hands-on, kid-friendly attraction.

Santa Barbara Museum of Natural History (p353) Giant skeletons, an insect wall and a pitch-dark planetarium captivate kids' imaginations. It's a 0.5-mile drive uphill from the mission.

Santa Barbara Maritime Museum (p355) Peer through a periscope, reel in a virtual fish, watch underwater films or check out the model ships.

Santa Barbara Sailing Center (p357) Short sails around the harbor let young 'uns see sea lions up close.

Sea Center (p355) From touch tanks full of tide-pool critters and crawl-through aquariums to whale sing-alongs, it's interactive and educational. Hourly parking on the wharf costs $2.50.

Lil' Toot water taxi (p369) Take a joyride along the waterfront on this tiny yellow boat.

Chase Palm Park (Map p352; www.santabarbaraca.gov/gov/depts/parksrec; 323 E Cabrillo Blvd; ⏰sunrise-10pm; 👪) FREE Has a shipwreck-themed playground decked out with seashells and a miniature lighthouse.

Arroyo Burro Beach County Park (p356) A wide, sandy beach, away from the tourists but not too far from downtown.

gorgeous place to attend a film-festival screening, and has a series of high-profile performers throughout the year.

Granada Theatre THEATER, LIVE MUSIC
(Map p352; ☎805-899-2222; www.granadasb.org; 1214 State St; ⊙box office 10am-5:30pm Mon-Sat, noon-5pm Sun) This beautifully restored 1930s Spanish Moorish–style theater is home to the city's symphony, ballet and opera, as well as touring Broadway shows and big-name musicians.

Lobero Theatre THEATER, LIVE MUSIC
(Map p352; ☎805-963-0761; www.lobero.org; 33 E Canon Perdido St; ⊙box office 10am-5pm Mon-Fri, noon-5pm Sat) One of California's oldest theaters (founded in 1873) presents modern dance, chamber music, jazz and world-music touring acts and stand-up comedy nights. This lovely venue hosts the Sings Like Hell concert series, featuring emerging musicians you can say you discovered before everyone else did.

Soho LIVE MUSIC
(Map p352; ☎805-962-7776; www.sohosb.com; 1221 State St, Suite 205; most tickets $8-50) One unpretentious brick room plus live music almost nightly equals Soho, upstairs inside a downtown office complex behind McDonald's. Lineups range from indie rock, jazz, folk and funk to world beats. Some all-ages shows.

Shopping

Downtown's **State Street** is packed with shops of all kinds, and even chain stores conform to the red-roofed architectural style. The lower (beach) end has budget options, with quality and prices going up as the street does. For more local art galleries and indie shops, dive into the **Funk Zone**, east of State St, tucked in south of Hwy 101.

Plum Goods GIFTS & SOUVENIRS
(Map p352; ☎805-845-3900; www.plumgoodsstore.com; 909 & 911 State St; ⊙10am-5pm Mon-Thu, to 6pm Fri, to 7pm Sat, 11am-5pm Sun) A go-to shop for ethically and locally made gifts, Plum Goods curates a playful and quality array of upcycled art, jewelry, skincare, books and homewares. Its newer shop next door is more sartorially focused.

Santa Barbara Artisans ARTS & CRAFTS
(Map p352; sbartisans@gmail.com; 619a State St; ⊙11am-6pm Mon-Thu, to 7pm Fri & Sat, noon-6pm Sun) Support local artists at this gallery collective, staffed by the artists themselves. Take home a handmade souvenir from its collection of textiles, jewelry, ceramics, lotions and potions as well as more unique paper and mosaic art.

Santa Barbara Farmers Market MARKET
(Map p352; ☎805-962-5354; www.sbfarmersmarket.org; 500 & 600 blocks of State St; ⊙4-7:30pm Tue mid-Mar–early Nov, 3-6:30pm Tue mid-Nov–mid-Mar, 8:30am-1pm Sat year-round; 👪) 🌿 Pick up picnic provisions year-round at this twice-weekly market. Local farmers sell everything from organic avocados, cherimoyas and dates to wildflower honey, grass-fed beef, smoked pistachios and artisan cheese. Tuesday-afternoon markets set up on lower State St, while Saturday mornings take place at the corner of Santa Barbara and Cota Sts for now (check the website for current location).

Chocolate Maya CHOCOLATE
(Map p352; ☎805-965-5956; www.chocolatemaya.com; 15 W Gutierrez St; tastings $25; ⊙10am-6pm Mon-Fri, to 5pm Sat, to 4pm Sun) Personally sourced, fair-trade cacao from around the world means the chocolates on offer here not only taste good but make you feel good about yourself for buying them. Truffles are a specialty and ingredients are sometimes unusual (tarragon and pineapple, anyone?). Make reservations for private tastings ($25; two-person minimum).

Channel Islands Surfboards SPORTS & OUTDOORS
(Map p352; ☎805-966-7213; www.cisurfboards.com; 36 Anacapa St; ⊙10am-7pm Mon-Sat, 11am-5pm Sun) The flagship store of surfboard shaper Al Merrick is the place for innovative pro-worthy board designs, as well as surf-style threads, swimsuits and flip-flops.

La Arcada MALL
(Map p352; www.laarcadasantabarbara.com; 1114 State St; ⊙hours vary) Filled with specialty boutiques, restaurants and whimsical art galleries, this historic red-tile-roofed passageway was designed by Myron Hunt (builder of Pasadena's Rose Bowl) in the 1920s. Savor handmade French candies from Chocolats du Calibressan as you wander around, or grab lunch at the Santa Barbara branch of **Jeannine's** (☎805-966-1717; http://jeannines.com; 15 E Figueroa St; mains $8-16; ⊙7am-1:30pm Wed-Sun; 🌶👪). There are entrances on State and Figueroa Sts.

GO GREEN IN SANTA BARBARA

Santa Barbara's biggest eco-travel initiative is **Santa Barbara Car Free** (https://santabarbaraca.com/itinerary/red-tile-walking-tour). Browse the website for tips on seeing the city without your car, plus valuable discounts on accommodations, vacation packages, rail travel and more. Still don't believe it's possible to tour Santa Barbara without a car? Let us show you how to do it.

From LA, hop aboard the *Pacific Surfliner* or *Coast Starlight* for a memorably scenic, partly coastal ride to Santa Barbara's Amtrak station (around 2½ hours), a few blocks from the beach and downtown. Then hoof it or catch one of the electric shuttles that zips north–south along State St and east–west along the waterfront. MTD buses 6 and 11 connect with the shuttle halfway up State St and will get you within walking distance of the famous mission (get off at Los Olivos St and walk uphill). For a DIY cycling tour, Wheel Fun Rentals (p355) is a short walk from the train station.

Even Santa Barbara's Wine Country is getting into the sustainable swing of things. More and more vineyards are implementing biodynamic farming techniques and following organic guidelines. Many vintners and oenophiles are starting to think that the more natural the growing process, the better the wine, too. **Sustainable Wine Tours** (☎805-698-3911; www.sustainablewinetours.com; tours from $165) whisks you around family-owned sustainable vineyards. Minimize your carbon footprint even further by following Santa Barbara's Urban Wine Trail (www.urbanwinetrailsb.com) on foot. If you love both wine and food, *Edible Santa Barbara* magazine (http://ediblecommunities.com/santabarbara) publishes insightful articles about vineyards and restaurants that are going green. It's available free at many local markets, restaurants and wineries.

Santa Barbara County abounds with ecofriendly outdoor activities, too. Take your pick of hiking trails, cycling routes, ocean kayaking, swimming, surfing or stand-up paddle boarding (SUP). If you're going whale-watching, ask around to see if there are any alternative-fueled tour boats with trained onboard naturalists.

Information

Los Padres National Forest Headquarters (☎805-968-6640; www.fs.usda.gov/lpnf; 6750 Navigator Way, Suite 150, Goleta; ⏰8am-noon & 1-4:30pm Mon-Fri) HQ for the whole Los Padres National Forest. Pick up maps, recreation passes etc.

Outdoors Santa Barbara Visitors Center (Map p352; ☎805-456-8752; http://outdoorsb.sbmm.org; 113 Harbor Way, 4th fl; ⏰11am-5pm Sun-Fri, 9am-3pm Sat) On the 4th floor above the Maritime Museum, this volunteer-staffed visitor center offers info on Channel Islands National Park and has a harbor-view deck.

Santa Barbara Central Library (☎805-962-7653; www.sbplibrary.org; 40 E Anapamu St; ⏰10am-7pm Mon-Thu, to 5:30pm Fri & Sat, 1-5pm Sun; 📶) Free internet access for up to two hours (photo ID required). Reserve in advance or try a walk-in.

Santa Barbara Visitors Center (Map p352; ☎805-965-3021; www.santabarbaraca.com; 1 Garden St; ⏰9am-5pm Mon-Sat, to 5:30pm Sun) Drop by for maps and brochures and consult the helpful staff about how to get the most out of your stay. The website has handy downloadable DIY maps and itineraries, from food-and-drink routes to wine trails, art galleries and outdoors fun.

Getting There & Away

Santa Barbara Airport (SBA; ☎805-683-4011; www.flysba.com; 500 James Fowler Rd, Goleta; 📶) Nine miles west of downtown Santa Barbara, off Hwy 101. SBA has direct flights to 12 destinations, including Denver, San Francisco, Phoenix, Las Vegas and Chicago. A taxi to downtown or the waterfront costs $35 to $40 plus tip. Car-rental agencies with airport lots include Alamo, Avis, Budget, Enterprise, Hertz and National; reserve in advance in summer.

Santa Barbara Airbus (☎805-964-7759; www.sbairbus.com) Shuttles between Los Angeles International Airport (LAX) and Santa Barbara (one way/round trip $55/100, 2½ hours, eight daily each way). The more people in your party, the cheaper the fare. For more discounts, prepay online at least 24 hours in advance.

Amtrak (☎800-872-7245; www.amtrak.com; 209 State St) Trains run south to LA (from $31, 2¾ hours) via Carpinteria, Ventura and Burbank's airport, and north to San Luis Obispo (from $34, 2¾ hours) and Oakland (from $57, 8¾ hours), with stops in Paso Robles, Salinas and San Jose.

Greyhound (Map p352; ☎805-965-7551; www.greyhound.com; 224 Chapala St; ⏰8-11am & 2-5pm Mon-Fri; 📶) Operates a few direct buses daily to LA (from $14, three hours), Santa Cruz (from $42, six hours) and San Francisco (from $42, nine hours).

If you're driving on Hwy 101, take the Garden St or Carrillo St exits for downtown.

Ventura County Transportation Commission (VCTC; ☎800-438-1112; www.goventura.org) Runs frequent daily Coastal Express commuter buses between Santa Barbara and Carpinteria ($1.75, 15 to 30 minutes) and Ventura ($4, 60 to 70 minutes); check online for schedules.

Getting Around

Local buses operated by the **Metropolitan Transit District** (MTD; ☎805-963-3366; www.sbmtd.gov) cost $1.75 per ride (exact change, cash only). Equipped with front-loading bike racks, these buses travel all over town and to adjacent communities; ask for a free transfer upon boarding. **MTD Transit Center** (Map p352; ☎805-963-3366; www.sbmtd.gov/passenger-information/transit-center.html; 1020 Chapala St; 6am-7pm Mon-Fri, 9am-5pm Sat & Sun) has details about routes and schedules.

Bus	Destination	Frequency
5	Arroyo Burro Beach	hourly
11	State St, UCSB campus	every 30min
20	Montecito, Summerland, Carpinteria	hourly

MTD's electric **Downtown Shuttle** buses run every 10 to 15 minutes, 10am to 6pm, along State St down to Stearns Wharf. There they connect with the **Waterfront Shuttle**, which travels from Stearns Wharf west to the harbor and east to the zoo. Between Memorial Day (late May) and Labor Day (early September), both routes run until 9pm on Friday and Saturday. The fare is 50¢ per ride; transfers between routes are free.

Lil' Toot water taxi (Map p352; ☎805-465-6676; www.celebrationsantabarbara.com; 113 Harbor Way; one way adult/child $5/2; noon-sunset Apr-Oct, hours vary Nov-Mar;) provides a fun and ecofriendly way to make the quick journey between the harbor and Stearns Wharf. It leaves from the harbor on the hour and half hour, and from Stearns Wharf at quarter past and quarter to the hour.

For bicycle rentals, Wheel Fun Rentals (p355) has a handy location in the Funk Zone near Stearns Wharf.

Taxis are metered, costing around $3 flagfall plus $3 to $4 per mile.

Downtown street parking or parking in any of a dozen municipal lots is free for the first 75 minutes; each additional hour costs $1.50.

SANTA BARBARA WINE COUNTRY

Los Olivos

The posh ranching town of Los Olivos is many visitors' first stop when exploring Santa Barbara's Wine Country. Its four-block-long main street has rustic wine-tasting rooms, bistros and boutiques seemingly airlifted straight out of Napa.

Clairmont Farms FARM
(Map p370; ☎805-688-7505; www.clairmontfarms.com; 2480 Roblar Ave; 11am-5pm Wed-Mon; P) Natural beauty awaits just outside Los Olivos at this friendly, organic, family-owned farm, where purple lavender fields bloom like a Monet masterpiece, usually peaking mid-June to late July. Cruise the olive-tree-lined drive to the tiny shop selling bath and body products, and enjoy a lavender-scented picnic outside.

Sleeping & Eating

Options are limited and choices aren't cheap around these parts, but the quality is high.

Fess Parker Wine Country Inn & Spa SPA HOTEL $$$
(Map p370; ☎805-688-7788; www.fessparkerinn.com; 2860 Grand Ave; r from $436;) Spacious rooms and suites with calming, contemporary design set the scene at this luxurious spa hotel in the center of Los Olivos. Fireplaces are standard, there's a heated pool and a decent-size gym, and breakfast and a wine tasting are included in the price.

Los Olivos Grocery DELI $
(Map p370; ☎805-688-5115; www.losolivosgrocery.com; 2621 W Hwy 154; 7am-9pm;) Eat in for breakfast or lunch (grab a table on the covered porch) or get sandwiches, artisan breads, salads, specialty cheeses, pickles and everything else you'll need for a vineyard picnic to go. Everything's produced in-house or locally. It's a couple of minutes southeast of central Los Olivos, just off Hwy 154.

Panino SANDWICHES $
(Map p370; ☎805-688-9304; www.paninorestaurants.com; 2900 Grand Ave; sandwiches $12-13.50; 10am-4pm;) Take your pick from a huge range of gourmet deli sandwiches and salads: curry chicken is a perennial

Santa Barbara Wine Country

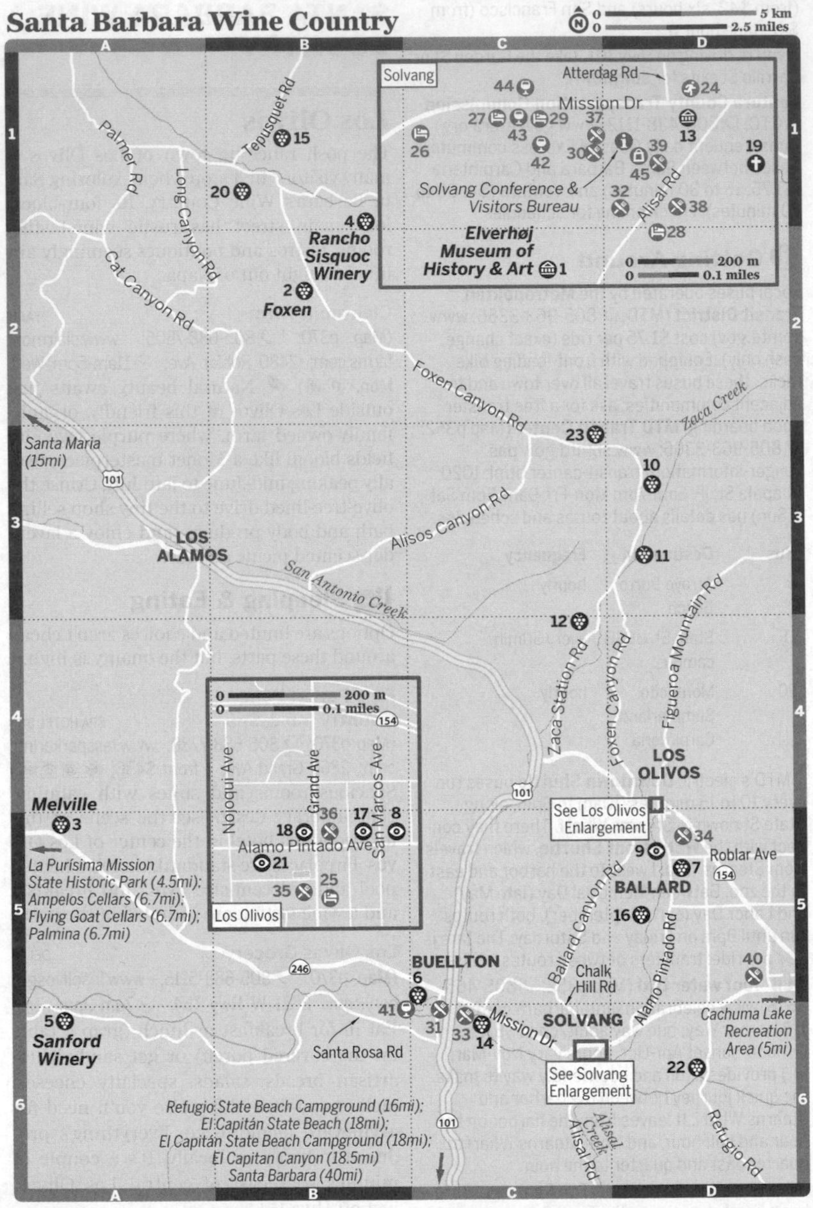

fave, but there are robust vegetarian options too. Order at the counter, then eat outside at an umbrella-covered table. There are other branches around Santa Barbara County, including in nearby Solvang and Santa Ynez.

Los Olivos Wine Merchant & Café CALIFORNIAN **$$**
(Map p370; ☎805-688-7265; www.winemerchantcafe.com; 2879 Grand Ave; mains $15-28; ⏰11:30am-8pm Mon-Thu, to 8:30pm Fri, 11am-8:30pm Sat, 11am-8pm Sun) This wine-country landmark (seen in the film *Sideways*) swirls

Santa Barbara Wine Country

Top Sights
1 Elverhøj Museum of History & Art C2
2 Foxen B2
3 Melville A5
4 Rancho Sisquoc Winery B1
5 Sanford Winery A6

Sights
6 Alma Rosa Winery & Vineyards C5
7 Beckmen Vineyards D5
8 Blair Fox Cellars B5
9 Clairmont Farms D5
10 Demetria Estate D3
11 Fess Parker Winery & Vineyard D3
12 Firestone Vineyards C4
13 Hans Christian Andersen Museum D1
14 Hitching Post Wines C6
15 Kenneth Volk Vineyards B1
16 Lincourt Vineyard D5
17 Liquid Farm B5
18 Los Olivos Tasting Room B5
19 Old Mission Santa Ínes D1
20 Riverbench Vineyard & Winery B1
21 Story of Soil B5
22 Sunstone Vineyards & Winery D6
23 Zaca Mesa Winery C3

Activities, Courses & Tours
24 Dr J's Bicycle Shop D1

Sleeping
25 Fess Parker Wine Country Inn & Spa ... B5
26 Hadsten House C1
27 Hamlet Inn C1
28 Hotel Corque D2
29 Landsby C1

Eating
30 Aly's C1
31 Ellen's Danish Pancake House C6
32 First & Oak D1
33 Hitching Post II C6
Industrial Eats .... (see 6)
34 Los Olivos Grocery D5
35 Los Olivos Wine Merchant & Café B5
36 Panino B5
Paula's Pancake House .... (see 27)
37 Ramen Kotori C1
38 Root 246 .... D1
39 Solvang Restaurant D1
Succulent Café .... (see 43)
40 SY Kitchen D5

Drinking & Nightlife
41 Figueroa Mountain Brewing Co B6
42 Lost Chord Guitars C1
43 Solvang Brewing Company C1
44 The Backroom C1

Shopping
Book Loft .... (see 13)
45 Copenhagen House D1

up a casual-chic SoCal ambience with its wisteria-covered trellis entrance. The food is bold, complex and addictive, prepared with organic ingredients from Los Olivos' own farm and harmoniously paired with its exceptional wine selection. Sit inside in the elegant dining room or outside on the covered patio.

Solvang

Statues of the Little Mermaid and Hans Christian Andersen in the middle of wine country can only mean one thing: Solvang. A Danish village founded in 1911 beside a 19th-century Spanish-colonial mission, this Santa Ynez Valley town holds tight to its Danish heritage. With its knickknack stores and cutesy motels, the town is almost as cloying as the Scandinavian pastries for which it's famed. But some newer establishments are toning down the kitsch and upping the coolness factor; plus, Solvang has the most sleeping and eating options in the valley, making it a great base for exploration.

Sights

★Elverhøj Museum of History & Art MUSEUM
(Map p370; ☎805-686-1211; www.elverhoj.org; 1624 Elverhoy Way; suggested donation adult $5, child under 13yr free; ⏲11am-4pm Wed-Sun; 👪) South of downtown, tucked away on a residential side street, this delightful little museum has pristine, thoughtful exhibits on Solvang's Danish heritage and philosophy, as well as Danish culture, art and history. Housed in one of Solvang's original structures that was modeled on an 18th-century Danish design, complete with tongue-and-groove construction (no nails involved), custom wrought iron and sculptures made by the couple who built it, the building itself is a work of art.

Hans Christian Andersen Museum MUSEUM
(Map p370; ☎805-688-2052; www.solvangca.com/museum; 1680 Mission Dr, 2nd fl; ⏲10am-5pm; 👪) FREE If you remember childhood fairy tales with fondness, stop by this tiny two-room museum. A larger-than-life bust of Denmark's favorite storyteller welcomes

WORTH A TRIP

MISSION LA PURÍSIMA

One of the most evocative of Southern California's missions, La Purísima was founded in 1787 and completely restored in the 1930s by the Civilian Conservation Corps (CCC). Today it's a **state historic park** (805-733-3713; www.lapurisimamission.org; 2295 Purísima Rd, Lompoc; per car $6; park 9am-5pm, visitor center 10am-4pm Tue-Sun year-round, 11am-3pm Mon Jul & Aug; P) with buildings furnished just as they were during Spanish-colonial times. The mission's fields still support livestock, while gardens are planted with medicinal plants and trees once used by Chumash tribespeople.

Start in the excellent visitor center, where exhibits tell stories of the Chumash, the Spanish missionaries and the work of the CCC. Self-guided visits are the usual way to explore the buildings themselves, though guided tours, lasting 1½ to two hours, are available too. The mission is just outside Lompoc, about 16 miles west of Hwy 101 (take Hwy 246 west from Buellton).

you to a mix of original letters, 1st-edition copies of his illustrated books, and a model of Andersen's childhood home. It's upstairs in the Book Loft (p374) building.

Old Mission Santa Ínes CHURCH
(Map p370; 805-688-4815; www.missionsantaines.org; 1760 Mission Dr; adult/child under 12yr $6/free; 9am-5pm, closed for services; P) The 19th of 21 California missions was founded by Franciscan friars in 1804 and remains an active parish. A self-guided tour takes you through a small, dated museum, into the restored church, and through the pretty gardens to the cemetery. Of special note are the painting of archangel Raphael in the museum and the brightly hued Chapel of the Madonnas.

Activities

Solvang is best known by cyclists for the **Solvang Century races** (www.bikescor.com) in March. For self-guided cycling tours, visit www.solvangusa.com and www.bike-santabarbara.org and rent a bike from **Dr J's Bicycle Shop** (Map p370; 805-688-6263; www.drjsbikeshop.com; 1693 Mission Dr; day rates $45-85; 9am-6pm Mon-Fri, to 5pm Sat, to 4pm Sun).

Sleeping

Choices are the best in the region, but sleeping in Solvang isn't cheap, not even at modest motels with ersatz-Danish decor. On weekends, rates skyrocket and rooms fill fast, so book ahead.

★**Landsby** BOUTIQUE HOTEL $$
(Map p370; 805-688-3121; www.thelandsby.com; 1576 Mission Dr; r from $159; @) Forget Solvang's cheesy Danish side: the Landsby is all about slick contemporary Scandinavian style. The principal decorative themes in this new arrival on the town's sleeping scene are white and wood, but cool design doesn't mean there's not a warm atmosphere. Start your day with the complimentary breakfast and finish it with a drink at the popular lobby bar.

The in-house Mad & Vin ('food and wine' in Danish) restaurant has similarly chic surroundings and a good menu of classic American dishes (mains $16 to $34).

Hamlet Inn MOTEL $$
(Map p370; 805-688-4413; www.thehamletinn.com; 1532 Mission Dr; r $99-229; P) This remodeled motel is to wine-country lodging what IKEA is to interior design: a budget-friendly, trendy alternative. Crisp, modern rooms have bright Danish-flag bedspreads and iPod docking stations. Free loaner bicycles and a super-central location add to the appeal. Rates include coffee and a pastry from Olsen's Bakery across the street.

Hadsten House BOUTIQUE HOTEL $$
(Map p370; 805-688-3210; www.hadstenhouse.com; 1450 Mission Dr; r $197-297; P) This revamped motel has luxuriously updated just about everything, except for its routine exterior. Inside, rooms are surprisingly plush, with flat-screen TVs, comfy duvets and high-end bath products. Spa suites come with jet tubs. There's a good in-house restaurant (Tuesday to Saturday). Pet fee $50.

Hotel Corque BOUTIQUE HOTEL $$$
(Map p370; 805-688-8000; www.hotelcorque.com; 400 Alisal Rd; r $179-409; @) This clean-lined hotel is a relief from all things Scandinavian. Overpriced rooms may look

anonymous, but they're quite spacious. Amenities include an outdoor swimming pool and hot tub, plus access to the next-door fitness center.

Eating

Though it might seem like every other eatery here is a Danish bakery, little Solvang is packed with high-quality, creative restaurants. The best of the bunch make stellar use of the diverse, often organic local produce.

Ramen Kotori RAMEN $

(Map p370; ☎805-691-9672; https://ramenkotori.com; 1618 Copenhagen Dr; mains $8-16; ⊙noon-2:30pm & 5:30-9pm Wed-Sun) Although the rich, complex broth and chewy ramen are obviously the main attraction here, the menu also offers an array of small bites like kimchi, pot stickers, *shishito* peppers and Japanese-style fried chicken. It's run by husband and wife team Francisco and Erica (who hails from Kyoto), who worked in a Michelin-starred kitchen together and bring authenticity and local goodness into every dish.

Paula's Pancake House DANISH ¢

(Map p370; ☎805-688-2867; www.paulaspancakehouse.com; 1531 Mission Dr; mains from $8.50; ⊙6am-3pm;) *God morgen!* Start the day Danish-style with a hearty breakfast in which, clue in the name, pancakes feature heavily – over 30 years beating batter means Paula knows her stuff. The lunch menu ventures into burger and sandwich territory, but with breakfast served all day there's no wrong time to put away some Danish pancakes with real maple syrup.

It's hugely popular and lines are long, so arrive early or expect to wait.

Solvang Restaurant BAKERY $

(Map p370; ☎805-688-4645; www.solvangrestaurant.com; 1672 Copenhagen Dr; mains $8.50-11; ⊙6am-3pm Mon-Fri, to 5pm Sat & Sun;) Duck around the Danish-inscribed beams with decorative borders to order *aebleskivers* – round pancake popovers covered in powdered sugar and raspberry jam. They're so popular there's even a special takeout window, and if you develop a fondness for them you can buy all the ingredients (and the special pan) to make your own.

★**Succulent Café** CALIFORNIAN $$

(Map p370; ☎805-691-9444; www.succulentcafe.com; 1555-1557 Mission Dr; mains breakfast & lunch $6-15, dinner $18-37; ⊙10am-3pm Mon & Wed-Fri, 8:30am-3pm Sat & Sun, 5-9pm Wed-Mon;) An inspired, if meat-centric, menu allows farm-fresh ingredients to speak for themselves at this family-owned gourmet cafe and market. For breakfast and lunch, order at the counter, then stake out a spot in the woodsy dining room or on the cheerful patio (dogs welcome). At dinner time, go 'the whole hog' with the signature Three Little Pigs (bacon-wrapped pork tenderloin).

★**First & Oak** CALIFORNIAN $$$

(Map p370; ☎805-688-1703; www.firstandoak.com; Mirabelle Inn, 409 1st St; 3/4/5-course set menu $59/74/89; ⊙5:30-8:45pm) Rich, innovative small plates in an elegant but cozy setting make First & Oak Solvang's best dining experience. The menu changes with the seasons, but you can expect unusual takes on California cuisine, such as baked beets with bee pollen and whipped goat's cheese or linguine with soft-shell crab and yuzu emulsion. Inventive desserts round off a memorable meal.

Aly's AMERICAN $$$

(Map p370; ☎805-697-7082; http://alysbyalebru.com; 451 2nd St; mains $30-46; ⊙5-8:45pm Thu-Mon) Fine cuisine isn't usually associated with Solvang, but Aly's meat- and fish-focused dishes hit the mark. The low-lit, simply furnished dining room complements the rich, flavorful food that is sourced locally and prepared with skill. If you're struggling to choose, go with the chef's tasting menu and pair it with carefully selected wines.

Root 246 AMERICAN $$$

(Map p370; ☎805-686-8681; www.root-246.com; 420 Alisal Rd; mains $16-42; ⊙5-9pm Tue-Thu, to 12:30am Fri & Sat) Headed by chef Crystal DeLongpré, the creative farm-to-table cuisine at Root 246 shows an artful touch with ingredients sourced from local farmers and fishers – from its fennel pollen and pea shoots to the pasture-raised pork. Excellent wine list and a late-night lounge open until 2am on weekends.

Drinking & Nightlife

After dinner this town is deader than an ancient Viking, with a few notable exceptions.

Solvang Brewing Company BREWERY

(Map p370; ☎805-688-2337; http://solvangbrewing.com; 1547 Mission St; ⊙11am-midnight or later) If you're done with wine but down for beer then the Brewing Company is the place to head. A decent selection of beers (including a stout and a couple of wheat ales) is complemented by filling pub grub and live music (usually Wednesday to Sunday). Plus it's one of the few places in town that stays open past sundown.

Backroom BEER GARDEN
(Valley Brewers; Map p370; ☎805-691-9160; www.valleybrewers.com/the-backroom; 515 4th Pl; ⊙1-6pm Sun & Mon, to 8pm Wed-Sat) It looks like your friendly neighborhood brewers' supply store – which it is – but push open the false bookshelf in back and you enter a wondrous speakeasy where the rotating beer list is curated by owners Sandy and Chris. Taps flow with fascinating picks from near and far to please a range of palates, and the taproom opens onto a cozy enclosed patio.

Lost Chord Guitars BAR
(Map p370; ☎805-242-1041; www.lostchordguitars.com; 1576 Copenhagen Dr; ⊙5-9pm Sun & Wed-Thu, to 10pm Fri & Sat) If there's live music here, come in for a listen as it's bound to be high caliber. On non-performance nights, it's a chill spot to have a glass of the house-label wine, made locally by **Hitching Post** (Map p370; ☎805-688-0676; www.hpwines.com; 420 E Hwy 246, Buellton; tastings $20; ⊙11am-5pm Sun-Thu, to 8pm Fri & Sat), or a Santa Barbara–brewed beer. And if you're a guitar player you can drool over the Bedell and McPherson beauties behind the bar.

Shopping

Downtown Solvang's notoriously kitschy shops cover a half-dozen blocks south of Mission Dr/Hwy 246 between Atterdag Rd and Alisal Rd. For Danish cookbooks, handcrafted quilts and other homespun items, visit the Elverhøj Museum (p371).

Copenhagen House DESIGN
(Map p370; ☎805-693-5000; http://thecopenhagenhouse.com; 1660 Copenhagen Dr; ⊙10am-5:30pm Mon-Fri, to 6pm Sat & Sun) The name stays true to Solvang's Danish roots, but the eclectic mix of top-quality design goods, all from the motherland, couldn't be further from the town's usual tourist tat. Keep kids happy with some Lego, treat yourself to exquisite Pandora jewelry or a Bering watch, or buy some stylish home- and kitchenwares that make you feel cooler just looking at them.

Book Loft BOOKS
(Map p370; ☎805-688-6010; www.bookloftsolvang.com; 1680 Mission Dr; ⊙9am-6pm Sun-Thu, to 8pm Fri & Sat) Long-running independent bookshop carrying antiquarian and Scandinavian titles and children's storybooks. The Hans Christian Andersen Museum (p371) is upstairs.

Information

Solvang Conference & Visitors Bureau (Map p370; ☎805-688-6144; www.solvangusa.com; 1639 Copenhagen Dr; ⊙9am-5pm) Pick up free tourist brochures and winery maps at this kiosk in the town center, by the municipal parking lot and public restrooms.

Getting There & Away

Santa Ynez Valley Transit (☎805-688-5452; www.syvt.com; per ride $1.50; ⊙6:30am-7pm Mon-Sat) runs local buses equipped with bike racks on a loop around Buellton, Solvang, Santa Ynez, Ballard and Los Olivos. Buses operate roughly between 7am and 7pm Monday through Saturday; one-way rides cost $1.50 (exact change only).

Buellton

Tiny Buellton was once best known for Andersen's Pea Soup Restaurant, and you can still get heaping bowls of the green stuff, a tradition going back almost 100 years. If split-pea soup doesn't appeal, then the growing drinking (beer as well as wine) and eating scene on **Industrial Way**, just south of Hwy 246, should do the trick instead.

★**Industrial Eats** AMERICAN $
(Map p370; ☎805-688-8807; http://industrialeats.com; 181 Industrial Way; mains $9-15; ⊙10am-9pm) Hugely and justifiably popular locals' hangout, housed in an eclectically decorated warehouse on Buellton's coolest street. Pizzas have traditional to what-the? toppings (eg duck and pistachio); the small plates are huge, innovative and eminently shareable; and the wine and beer are top notch. The seasonally morphing menu includes imaginative combinations of texture and flavor utilizing the best of local bounty.

Ellen's Danish Pancake House BREAKFAST $
(Map p370; ☎805-688-5312; 272 Ave of Flags; mains $8.50-15; ⊙6am-8pm, to 2pm Mon; P) West of Hwy 101, just off Hwy 246, this old-fashioned, always-busy diner is where locals congregate for friendly service and the wine country's best Danish pancakes and sausages. Breakfast served all day.

Hitching Post II STEAK $$$

(Map p370; ☎805-688-0676; www.hitchingpost2.com; 406 E Hwy 246; mains $29-61; ⊙5-9:30pm Mon-Fri, from 4pm Sat & Sun;) As seen in the movie *Sideways,* this dark-paneled chophouse offers oak-grilled steaks, pork ribs, smoked duck breast and rack of lamb. Every old-school meal comes with a veggie tray, garlic bread, shrimp cocktail or soup, salad and potatoes. The Hitching Post makes its own pinot noir, and it's damn good (wine tastings at the bar start at 4pm).

Figueroa Mountain Brewing Co BREWERY

(Map p370; ☎805-694-2252; www.figmtnbrew.com; 45 Industrial Way; ⊙11am-9pm;) Fig Mountain's original brewpub gives you a break from the wine with its award-winning, house-brewed beers; Hoppy Poppy, Danish Red lager and Davy Brown ale are three favorites. Soak them up with some great pub grub and enjoy the frequent live music and comedy nights. Or sit outside in the pet-friendly beer garden

Getting There & Around

Central Coast Shuttle (☎805-928-1977; www.cclax.com; prepaid one way/round trip LA-Buellton $75/140; ⊙info line 7am-7pm Mon-Fri, 9:30am-5:30pm Sat & Sun) will bus you from LAX to Buellton (book in advance online to avoid a non-prepaid small additional cost). Amtrak provides a couple of daily connecting Thruway buses to and from Solvang, but only if you're catching a train (or arriving on one) in Santa Barbara.

Santa Ynez Valley Transit runs local buses equipped with bike racks on a loop around Buellton, Solvang, Santa Ynez, Ballard and Los Olivos. You'll need exact change for the fare.

AROUND SANTA BARBARA

Can't quit your day job to follow your bliss? Don't despair: a long weekend in the mountains, valleys and beaches between Santa Barbara and LA will keep you inspired until you can. In this land of daydreams, perfect waves beckon off Ventura's coast, shady trails wind skyward in the Los Padres National Forest and spiritual Zen awaits you in Ojai Valley. Surf, stroll, seek – if outdoor rejuvenation is your goal, this is the place.

And then there's Channel Islands National Park, a biodiverse chain of islands shimmering just off the coast where you can kayak majestic sea caves, scuba dive in wavy kelp forests, wander fields of wildflower blooms or simply disappear from civilization at a remote wilderness campsite.

Montecito

Well-heeled, leafy Montecito, just east of Santa Barbara in the Santa Ynez foothills, is home not just to the rich and famous but to the obscenely rich and the uber-famous.

Though many homes hide behind manicured hedges these days, a taste of the Montecito lifestyle of yesteryear can be experienced by taking a tour of **Casa del Herrero** (☎805-565-5653; http://casadelherrero.com; 1387 E Valley Rd; 90min tour $25; ⊙10am & 2pm Wed & Sat, reservations 9am-5pm Mon-Sat; P). The town's cafe- and boutique-filled main drag is Coast Village Rd (exit Hwy 101 at Olive Mill Rd).

Most visitors base themselves in Santa Barbara and visit Montecito (a 10-minute drive away) as a day trip. Upmarket, beachside Four Seasons Biltmore is an option if money is no object.

From Santa Barbara, MTD (p368) buses 14 and 20 run to and from Montecito ($1.75, 20 minutes, every 40 to 60 minutes); bus 20 also connects Montecito with Summerland and Carpinteria.

Summerland

This drowsy seaside community was founded in the 1880s by HL Williams, a real-estate speculator. Williams was also a spiritualist whose followers believed in the power of mediums to connect the living with the dead. Spiritualists were rumored to keep hidden rooms for séances – a practice that earned the town the indelicate nickname of 'Spookville.'

Today, those wanting to connect to the past wander the town's antique shops, where you won't find any bargains, but you can ooh and aah over beautiful furniture, jewelry and art from decades or even centuries gone by.

To find the beach, turn south off exit 91 and cross the railroad tracks to cliffside **Lookout Park** (www.countyofsb.org/parks/day-use/lookout.sbc; Lookout Park Rd; ⊙8am-sunset;) FREE, which has a kids playground, picnic tables, barbecue grills and access to a wide, relatively quiet stretch of sand (leashed dogs OK).

Grab breakfast or brunch at the Victorian seaside–style **Summerland Beach Café** (805-969-1019; www.summerlandbeachcafe.com; 2294 Lillie Ave; mains $9-14; 7am-3pm Mon-Fri, to 4pm Sat & Sun;), known for its fluffy omelets, and enjoy the ocean breezes on the patio. Or walk over to **Tinker's** (805-969-1970; 2275 Ortega Hill Rd; items $5-10; 11am-8pm;), an eat-out-of-a-basket burger shack that delivers seasoned curly fries and old-fashioned milkshakes.

From Santa Barbara, MTD (p368) bus 20 runs to Summerland ($1.75, 25 minutes, hourly) via Montecito, continuing to Carpinteria.

Carpinteria

Lying 11 miles east of Santa Barbara, the laid-back beach town of Carpinteria was named for the Chumash carpenters who built seafaring canoes here. You could easily spend a day sunning at the beach, then wandering into the antiques shops and beachy boutiques along Linden Ave, downtown's main street, and rounding things off with a few intriguing nanobrews in the town's tiny industrial zone.

Sights & Activities

Experienced surfers will want to check **Rincon Point** for its long, glassy, right point-break waves. It's about 3 miles southeast of downtown, off Hwy 101 (exit Bates Rd).

Carpinteria State Beach BEACH
(805-968-1033; www.parks.ca.gov/?page_id=599; end of Linden Ave; per car $10; 7am-sunset;) An idyllic, mile-long strand where kids can splash around in calm waters and go tide-pooling along the shoreline. In winter, hike over a mile south along the coast to a bluff-top overlook to view harbor seal pups and parents hauled out on the sand at the protected rookery below.

Surf Happens SURFING
(805-966-3613; http://surfhappens.com; 3825 Santa Claus Lane; 2hr private lesson from $160;) Welcoming families, beginners and 'Surf Happens Sisters,' these highly reviewed classes and camps led by expert staff incorporate the Zen of surfing. In summer you'll begin your spiritual wave-riding journey. Make reservations in advance. Find the office on Santa Claus Lane (just north of Carpinteria).

Festivals & Events

California Avocado Festival FOOD & DRINK
(www.avofest.com; 800 Linden Ave; early Oct) FREE Still going strong after 30 years, the annual California Avocado Festival is one of the state's largest free events, held in downtown Carpinteria. Bands play, avocado recipes are judged and the world's largest vat of guacamole makes a guest appearance. Tacos, tri-tip steak and beer fuel Carp's biggest party of the year.

Sleeping

Carpinteria's cookie-cutter chain motels and hotels are unexciting, but they're usually less expensive than those in nearby Santa Barbara.

Carpinteria State Beach Campground CAMPGROUND $
(reservations 800-444-7275; www.reservecalifornia.com; 205 Palm Ave; tent & RV drive-up sites $45-70, hike-&-bike tent sites $10) Often crowded, this oceanfront campground offers lots of family-friendly amenities including flush toilets, hot showers, picnic tables and barbecue grills. Book ahead (reservations are taken up to seven months in advance).

Eating & Drinking

The Spot BURGERS $
(805-684-6311; 389 Linden Ave; burgers from $4.70, tacos from $3.50; 10am-4pm Mon, to 6:30pm Sun & Tue-Thu, to 7pm Fri & Sat) This scrappy little shack three blocks from the beach has been slinging burgers and Mexican favorites for more than 50 years. Order at the window and eat on the patio, or post up under the shade of the towering eucalyptus in the park across the street.

Delgado's MEXICAN $$
(805-684-4822; https://delgadoscarp.com; 4401 Carpinteria Ave; mains $9.75-19.25; 11:30am-8:30pm Mon, from 11am Tue-Fri, 11am-9pm Sat, 7:30am-8:30pm Sun) This family-run Mexican restaurant has been serving Carpinteria for over 50 years, with sit-down dining inside and out, as well as a bar, in a bustling, friendly atmosphere. All the classics are offered, plus *sopes*, seafood specialties and menudo. The margaritas are strong and complement the Mexican comfort food.

Rincon Brewery CRAFT BEER
(805-684-6044; http://rinconbrewery.com; 5065 Carpinteria Ave; 11am-9pm Sun-Thu, to

DON'T MISS

LOTUSLAND

In 1941 the eccentric opera singer and socialite Madame Ganna Walska bought the 37 acres that make up **Lotusland** (☎ info 805-969-3767, reservations 805-969-9990; www.lotusland.org; 695 Ashley Rd; adult/child 3-18yr $50/25; ⏱ tours by appointment 10am & 1:30pm Wed-Sat mid-Feb–mid-Nov; P) with her lover and yoga guru Theos Bernard. After marrying and then divorcing Bernard, she retained control of the gardens and spent the next four decades tending and expanding this incredible collection of rare and exotic plants from around the world; there are over 140 varieties of aloe alone. Come in summer when the lotuses bloom, typically during July and August.

Reservations are required for tours, but the phone is only attended from 9am to 5pm weekdays and to 1pm Saturday.

10pm Fri & Sat) Swap ocean waves for 'waves of grain' (Rincon's words) and knock back Belgian-style craft beers (among others) and a long menu of standard but tasty pub grub that keeps this place busy most nights of the week.

brewLAB BREWERY
(☎ 507-319-5665; https://brewlabcraft.com; 4191 Carpinteria Ave, No 8; ⏱ 4-9pm Wed & Thu, to 10pm Fri & Sat, noon-8pm Sun; 🐾) Experimental nanobrewery deeply connected with the community – these heart driven brewers source super-local herbs, fruits and veggies to make their sustainable tiny-batch sours, stouts and all styles in between while fostering a taproom that welcomes strangers as friends. On weekends, pair your brew with an Argentine empanada from the pop-up next door.

Apiary BREWERY
(☎ 805-684-6216; www.theapiary.co; 4191 Carpinteria Ave, No. 10; ⏱ 2-8pm Mon-Wed, to 10pm Thu & Fri, noon-10pm Sat, noon-8pm Sun) Unique to the Santa Barbara area, the Apiary is a sweet spot brewing interesting small-batch meads, ciders and *jun* (low-alcohol fermented honey beverage) that incorporate herbs and fruit grown by local farmers. Sample a tasting flight amid the backdrop of live music and fun folk in this cozy, rustic warehouse space.

Island Brewing Co BREWERY
(☎ 805-745-8272; www.islandbrewingcompany.com; 5049 6th St; ⏱ noon-9pm Mon-Thu, to 10pm Fri, 11am-10pm Sat, 11am-9pm Sun; 🐾) Wanna hang with friendly beach bums and drink bourbon-barrel-aged brews? Find this local-fave industrial space with an outdoor, dog-friendly patio by the railroad tracks – look for the sign pointing off Linden Ave.

Getting There & Away

Carpinteria is 11 miles east of Santa Barbara via Hwy 101 (southbound exit Linden Ave, northbound Casitas Pass Rd). From Santa Barbara, take MTD (p368) bus 20 ($1.75, 40 minutes, at least hourly) via Montecito and Summerland.

Amtrak (☎ 800-872-7245; www.amtrak.com; 475 Linden Ave) has an unstaffed platform downtown; buy tickets online or by phone before catching one of five daily *Pacific Surfliner* trains west to Santa Barbara ($8, 13 minutes) or south to Ventura ($11, 20 to 30 minutes) or LA ($30, 2½ hours).

Ojai

Hollywood director Frank Capra chose the Ojai Valley to represent the mythical Shangri-La in his 1937 movie *Lost Horizon*. Today Ojai ('*OH*-hi,' from the Chumash word for 'moon') attracts artists, organic farmers, spiritual seekers and anyone ready to indulge in day-spa pampering. Bring shorts and flip-flops: Shangri-La sure gets hot in summer.

Sights & Activities

Ojai Olive Oil Company FARM
(☎ 805-646-5964; www.ojaioliveoil.com; 1811 Ladera Rd; ⏱ 10am-4pm) FREE Outside town, family-owned Ojai Olive Oil Company has a tasting room open six days a week, and offers free talks and tours on Wednesday (1pm to 4pm) and Saturday (10am to 4pm). It also sells at the Ojai Farmers Market (p380) on Sunday. Dip bread into the various oils (and balsamic vinegars from Modena, its home) – the milder Provençale variety is the most popular.

Ojai Vineyard Tasting Room WINERY
(☎ 805-649-1674; www.ojaivineyard.com; 109 S Montgomery St; tastings $15; ⏱ noon-6pm) Inside

downtown's historic firehouse, Ojai Vineyard pours tastes of its delicate small-batch wines. It's best known for standard-bearing chardonnay, pinot noir and syrah, but the crisp sauvignon blanc, dry riesling and zippy rosé are also worth sampling.

Ojai Valley Trail HIKING
(www.traillink.com/trail/ojai-valley-trail.aspx) FREE Running beside the highway, the 9-mile Ojai Valley Trail, converted from defunct railway tracks, is popular with walkers, runners, cyclists and equestrians. Pick it up downtown two blocks south of Ojai Ave, off Bryant St, then head west through the valley.

Mob Shop CYCLING
(805-272-8102; www.themobshop.com; 110 W Ojai Ave; bicycle rental per hour/day from $17/29; 10am-5pm Mon & Wed-Fri, 9am-5pm Sat, 9am-4pm Sun) Bike rental (including electric and kids' versions) for DIY two-wheel exploration of Ojai, plus organized tours of the city and surrounding area. Mountain bikers can sign up for a descent of nearby Sulphur Mountain.

Spa Ojai SPA
(855-697-8780; www.ojairesort.com/spa-ojai; Ojai Valley Inn & Spa, 905 Country Club Rd) For the ultimate in relaxation, book a day at top-tier Spa Ojai at the Ojai Valley Inn, where non-resort guests pay an extra $35 to access swimming pools, a workout gym and mind/body fitness classes.

Day Spa of Ojai SPA
(805-640-1100; www.thedayspa.com; 209 N Montgomery St; treatments $21-190; 10:30am-5:30pm) Soothing everyday cares away for two decades now, this family-run operation is the place to come for facials, body wraps and hot-rock treatments for men and women. It specializes in Swedish massages, starting from $68.

Sleeping

Pricey but excellent quality would best describe the local accommodations scene. Book well in advance, especially for weekends. Almost all places in town provide free bikes for guests.

★ **Lavender Inn** B&B $$
(805-646-6635; http://lavenderinn.com; 210 E Matilija St; r from $165;) For a central location in a historic 1874 schoolhouse building, you can't beat the Lavender Inn. Room decor ranges from quaint to modern; a hearty, healthy breakfast can be enjoyed on the porch overlooking the pretty garden; and the evening tapas and wine are nice touches.

An on-site spa sees to your relaxation needs, while the in-house cookery courses can satisfy any culinary aspirations. Just remember you *are* allowed to leave to explore Ojai itself, a short walk away.

Ojai Retreat & Inn B&B $$
(805-646-2536; www.ojairetreat.com; 160 Besant Rd; r $95-315;) On a hilltop on the outskirts of town, this peaceful place has a back-to-nature collection of 12 country arts-and-crafts-style guest rooms and cottage suites, all perfect for unplugging. Find a quiet nook for reading or writing (no TVs), ramble through the wonderful grounds, or practice your downward dog in a yoga class.

Capri Hotel HOTEL $$
(805-646-4305; http://hotelojai.com; 1180 E Ojai Ave; r from $180;) Another hip, revamped property in the local Shelter Social Club empire, the Capri hits the mark with its modern interpretation of the motel's mid-century roots. Clean but playful design in warm neutrals, a great location just outside the busy stretch of Ojai Ave, and a pool and lawn conspire to create a relaxing stay.

Blue Iguana Inn INN $$
(805-646-5277; www.blueiguanainn.com; 11794 N Ventura Ave; r/ste from $139/169;) Artsy iguanas lurk everywhere at this funky architect-designed inn – on adobe walls, around Mediterranean-tiled fountains and anywhere else that reptilian style could bring out a smile. Roomy bungalow and cottage suites are unique, and the pool is a social scene for LA denizens. Rates include continental breakfast; two-night minimum stay on weekends. Some pets allowed with prior approval only.

For a more central location and romantic atmosphere, try the sister **Emerald Iguana Inn** (805-646-5277; www.emeraldiguana.com; 108 Pauline St; r/ste from $179/249;), just north of downtown.

Ojai Rancho Inn MOTEL $$
(805-646-1434; http://ojairanchoinn.com; 615 W Ojai Ave; r from $180;) At this low-slung motel next to the highway, pine-paneled rooms each have a king bed. Cottage rooms come with fireplaces, and some have Jacuzzis and kitchenettes. Besides competitive rates, the biggest bonuses

of staying here are a small pool and sauna, shuffleboard, a fire pit, and bicycles to borrow for the half-mile ride to downtown. Pet fee $20.

Caravan Outpost CARAVAN PARK $$
(805-836-4891; www.caravanoutpostojai.com; 317 Bryant St; caravans/tiny houses from $194/219;) These glamping-style Airstreams are peak Ojai, kitted out with all the modern comforts and a Southwestern aesthetic. There are communal showers and toilets if you don't want to wait 30 minutes for your caravan's water to heat up, a fire pit for grilling, an on-trend boutique and a fun community vibe in this cozy spot. Two-night minimum on weekends.

Ojai Valley Inn & Spa RESORT $$$
(855-697-8780, 805-646-1111; www.ojairesort.com; 905 Country Club Rd; r from $459;) At the west end of town, this pampering resort has landscaped gardens, tennis courts, swimming pools, a championship golf course and a fabulous spa. Luxurious rooms are outfitted with all mod cons, and some sport fireplace and balcony. Recreational activities run the gamut from kids camps and complimentary bikes to full-moon yoga and astrological readings. Nightly 'service' surcharge is $40.

If the resort's size puts you off, don't worry – a free golf-cart shuttle will whisk you to wherever you want to be.

On-site restaurant Olivella (p380) is one of the best in town.

Eating & Drinking

First-rate organic, sustainable and local ingredients are part of everyday culinary life here, and in keeping with the city's bohemian, hippie vibe, vegetarians and vegans will revel in the options available. The main drag, Ojai Ave, has plenty of places serving excellent food, but there are equally good choices a bit more out of the way.

Hip Vegan VEGAN $
(805-669-6363; https://hipvgn.square.site; 201 N Montgomery St; mains $12-15; 11am-9pm;) On a sunny corner with plenty of space inside and a tree-shaded patio outside, this locals' kitchen stays true to Ojai's granola-crunching hippie roots with delicious Mexican- and Asian-influenced salads, sandwiches, bowls and classic SoCal date shakes and teas. The interior is spartan, so grab a shaded picnic table outside.

Topa Topa Brewing Company CRAFT BEER
(Sama Sama Kitchen; 805-798-9079; www.topatopa.beer; 345 E Ojai Ave; dishes $5-16; noon-9pm Mon-Wed, to 10pm Thu-Sat, 11:30am-8pm Sun;) Though Topa Topa and Sama Sama might sound nonsensical, their partnership is brilliant. Ventura's brewery and Santa Barbara's catery share a light-flooded space in Ojai so that you can thrill your palate by pairing pints of excellent microbrew with Southeast Asian noshes. Order dishes to share so you can sample *jidori* wings, *okonomiyaki*-sauced tots and fresh, veggie-forward noodles and salads.

Bonnie Lu's Country Cafe BREAKFAST $
(805-646-0207; www.facebook.com/bonnielus; 328 E Ojai Ave; mains $8-15; 7am-2:30pm Thu-Tue) Central, and therefore busy (expect to wait at weekends), diner where all your breakfast favorites are available, including a variety of eggs Benedict, pancakes and biscuits with gravy. Not the place for a light start to the day.

Farmer & the Cook MEXICAN, VEGETARIAN $
(805-640-9608; www.farmerandcook.com; 339 W El Roblar Ave; mains $8.50-14.50; 8am-8:30pm;) Flavorful, organic, vegetarian (some vegan) homemade Mexican cooking bursts out of this roadside market, which has its own farm nearby. Come for the squash and goat's-cheese tacos or the highly rated *huarache* (tortilla, potatoes, onions, pepper, feta and more) or, at dinner Thursday to Sunday, creative pizzas and a salad bar. Smoothies are available throughout the day.

Sage Ojai INTERNATIONAL $$
(805-646-9204; www.sageojai.com; 217 E Matilija St; 11am-9pm Wed-Thu, to 11pm Fri, 9am-11pm Sat, 9am-4pm Sun) Run by the owners of the long-standing Rainbow Bridge health-food store, Sage Ojai is rooted in the same values of local, nourishing and sustainable food. With a bakery counter facing E Matilija St, the Asian-leaning restaurant occupies a space that opens onto a patio next to a grassy courtyard, plus a chic lounge branching off to the side for cocktails and other elixirs.

Boccali's ITALIAN $$
(805-646-6116; http://boccalis.com; 3277 E Ojai Ave; mains $11-19; 4-9pm Mon & Tue, from 11:45am Wed-Sun;) This roadside farm stand with red-and-white-checkered tablecloths does simple, big-portion Italian cooking. Much of the produce is grown behind

the restaurant and the fresh tomato salad is often still warm from the garden. The real draws are the wood-oven pizzas and the seasonal strawberry shortcake. It's over 2 miles east of downtown via Ojai Ave.

Olivella CALIFORNIAN $$$
(☎855-697-8780; www.ojairesort.com/dining/olivella-restaurant; 905 Country Club Rd; mains $39-68; ⊙5:30-9pm Wed-Sun; ☑) In the Ojai Valley Inn & Spa (p379), this worth-getting-dressed-up-for (though you don't have to) restaurant is *the* place in Ojai for a special meal. Meat and pasta are the stars of the menu (the Bolognese sauce is a 19th-century chef-family recipe), but salads and fish dishes are equally tasty. Or push the boat out (and loosen the belt) with the four-course experience.

Service is friendly but can be disorganized.

Beacon Coffee COFFEE
(www.beaconcoffee.com; 211 W Ojai Ave; coffee $3-4.50; ⊙6am-4pm) Ethically and sustainably grown beans, sourced directly by the owners, have coffee-lovers lining up at this spacious repurposed restaurant space. While the coffee is indeed excellent, the well-executed pastries – savory and sweet, with gluten-free and vegan options – are a treat.

Ojai Beverage Company CRAFT BEER
(☎805-646-1700; www.ojaibevco.com; 655 E Ojai Ave; ⊙11am-9pm Sun, noon-9pm Mon, 11am-10pm Tue & Wed, 11am-11pm Thu-Sat) Along with about a dozen wide-ranging, interesting beers on tap at a time, OBC is also a popular brewpub and insanely well-stocked bottle shop featuring walls of beer and wine, from hyper-local sips to obscure international finds. Best to dine during off-peak hours, as it gets crowded, but cruise in and choose a bottle to try on the spot anytime.

Shopping

★Bart's Books BOOKS
(☎805-646-3755; www.bartsbooksojai.com; 302 W Matilija St; ⊙9:30am-sunset) One block north of Ojai Ave, this charming, unique indoor-outdoor space sells new and well-loved tomes. It's been going for well over a half century so demands at least a 30-minute browse and a purchase or two – just don't step on the lurking but surprisingly nimble cat.

Ojai Farmers Market MARKET
(☎805-698-5555; www.ojaicertifiedfarmersmarket.com; 300 E Matilija St; ⊙9am-1pm Sun) It's no surprise in this agriculturally blessed region that Ojai's farmers market is a beauty. There are the usual high-quality fruit and vegetables on offer each Sunday, plus seafood, meat, bread, chocolate, flowers and plants. It's worth a Sunday-morning roam to mingle with Ojai denizens in their natural habitat.

Fig ARTS & CRAFTS
(☎805-646-6561; www.figojai.com; 327 E Ojai Ave; ⊙10am-5pm Mon-Thu, to 6pm Fri & Sat, 11am-5pm Sun) Down a long corridor lined with organically shaped ceramic and glass planters, rolled-up rugs and air plants, you'll find an interior shop containing more thoughtfully curated objects to explore. Delicate jewelry, olive-wood charcuterie boards, books, handmade prints and novel housewares draw your eye around the room. You can't go wrong with a gift here – it's all handmade, local and/or fair trade.

Information

Ojai Library (☎805-646-1639; www.vencolibrary.org/locations/ojai-library; 111 E Ojai Ave; ⊙10am-8pm Mon-Thu, noon-5pm Fri-Sun; 📶) Free online computer terminals and wi-fi for public use.

Ojai Ranger Station (☎805-646-4348; www.fs.usda.gov/detail/lpnf; 1190 E Ojai Ave; ⊙8am-4:30pm Mon-Fri) Camping tips and trail maps for hiking to hot springs, waterfalls and mountaintop viewpoints in the Los Padres National Forest.

Ojai Visitor Information (☎805-640-3606; www.ojaivisitors.com; 150 W Ojai Ave; ⊙9am-4pm Mon-Fri) Provides brochures and other material to visitors.

Getting There & Away

Ojai is around 33 miles east of Santa Barbara via scenic Hwy 150, or 15 miles inland (north) from Ventura via Hwy 33. **Gold Coast Transit** (☎805-487-4222; www.goldcoasttransit.org) bus 16 runs from Ventura (including a stop near the Amtrak station) to downtown Ojai ($1.50, 45 minutes, hourly).

Ventura

The primary launch point for Channel Island boat trips, the beach town of Ventura (officially the city of San Buenaventura) may not look to be the most enchanting coastal city, but it has its low-key seaside charm, especially on the historic pier and downtown along Main St.

Sights & Activities

South of Hwy 101 via Harbor Blvd, **Ventura Harbor** is the main departure point for boats to Channel Islands National Park.

Museum of Ventura County MUSEUM
(805-653-0323; www.venturamuseum.org; 100 E Main St; adult/child 6-17yr $5/1; 11am-5pm Tue-Sun;) This tiny downtown museum has an excellently eclectic collection that includes exhibits on the local Chumash people and rotating exhibitions of local artists' work. The highlight, though, is the George Stuart Historical Figures gallery. An Ojai resident, Stuart made models of famous people from the past to help bring to life historical lectures he gave around the country. Look out for emperor Nero, Vlad Tepes (aka Dracula), Henry VIII (with, sadly, just two of his wives), Hitler and Putin.

San Buenaventura State Beach BEACH
(805-968-1033; www.parks.ca.gov; per car $10; dawn-dusk;) Along the waterfront off Hwy 101, this long white-sand beach is ideal for swimming, surfing or just lazing on the sand. A recreational cycling path connects to nearby **Emma Wood State Beach**, another popular spot for swimming, surfing and fishing. Enter San Buenaventura off San Pedro St.

Mission San Buenaventura CHURCH
(805-643-4318; www.sanbuenaventuramission.org; 211 E Main St; adult/child $4/2; 10am-5pm Sun-Fri, from 9am Sat) Ventura's Spanish-colonial roots go back to this 1782 mission, the last to be founded by Junípero Serra. A stroll around the mellow parish church leads you through a garden courtyard and a small museum, past statues of saints, centuries-old religious paintings and unusual, unique wooden bells.

Eating

In downtown Ventura, Main St is chockablock with taquerias, casual cafes and globally flavored kitchens.

★ **Paradise Pantry** DELI $
(805-641-9440; www.paradisepantry.com; 222 E Main St; sandwiches $12-16; 11am-8:30pm Tue-Thu, to 9:30pm Fri & Sat, 11am-3pm Sun;) On the cafe side of Paradise Pantry you can grab a sandwich, soup, or cheese or meat plate in a quietly buzzing atmosphere. On the deli side you can stock up on supplies for a beach or Channel Island picnic (sandwiches can be made to go) and even grab some wine or beer to wash it all down.

Beach House Tacos TACOS $
(805-648-3177; www.beach-house-tacos.com; 668 Harbor Blvd; tacos $3.25-5; 11am-8pm Mon-Fri, 8:30am-8:30pm Sat & Sun) The location doesn't get much better than this, perched on the Ventura Pier with views down the beach and out to the Channel Islands on the horizon. Choose from various seafood or the usual meat fillings and eat at the tables there or carry them up to MadeWest Brewery next door to wash them down with a local brew.

Harvest Cafe VEGETARIAN $
(805-667-8386; www.harvestcafeventura.com; 175 S Ventura Ave; mains $8-15; 8am-4pm Mon-Thu, to 8pm Fri & Sat, 9am-3pm Sun) With an emphasis on – you guessed it – local, sustainable and organic ingredients, Harvest Cafe offers a little respite from all the seafood. Vegetarians, vegans and gluten-free diners have lots of choices here, from hearty bowls to pizzas to smoothies. The industrial-style space gets a lot of natural light, but there's also a small patio out front.

Lure Fish House SEAFOOD $$$
(805-567-4400; www.lurefishhouse.com; 60 S California St; mains $17-43; 11:30am-9pm Sun-Thu, to 10pm Fri & Sat;) For seafood any fresher, you'd have to catch it yourself off Ventura Pier. Go nuts ordering off a stalwart menu of sustainably caught seafood, organic regional farm produce and California wines. Make reservations or turn up at the bar during happy hour (4pm to 6pm Monday to Friday, 11:30am to 6pm Sunday) for strong cocktails, fried calamari and charbroiled oysters.

Drinking & Nightlife

You'll find plenty of rowdy dives down by the harbor and a bunch of excellent craft-beer places around town.

★ **Topa Topa Brewing Company** CRAFT BEER
(805-628-9255; http://topatopa.beer; 104 E Thompson Blvd; noon-9pm Mon-Wed, noon-10pm Thu-Sat, 11am-8pm Sun;) Between the freeway and downtown Ventura is not exactly the most salubrious location, but the beer here makes up for the surroundings. Chief Peak IPA takes the medal, but all the quality brewed-on-site options are worth trying. Food trucks (a different one

every night; see the website for details) feed the hungry.

MadeWest Brewing Co BREWERY
(☎805-947-5002; https://madewest.com/pages/ventura-pier-taproom; 668 E Harbor Blvd, 2nd fl; ⏲11am-9pm Sun-Thu, to 10pm Fri & Sat) The satellite taproom of this Ventura brewery snagged this sweet location upstairs on the Ventura Pier. It's a minimalist space, highlighting the natural beauty around it and letting the beer speak for itself. Bringing in outside food is okay; tacos from Beach House Tacos (p381) next door are highly recommended.

Surf Brewery BREWERY
(☎805-644-2739; http://surfbrewery.com; 4561 Market St, Suite A; ⏲4-9pm Tue-Thu, from 1pm Fri, noon-9pm Sat, noon-7pm Sun) Operating since 2011, Surf Brewery makes big waves with its hoppy and black IPAs and rye American pale ale. Beer geeks and food trucks gather at the sociable taproom in an industrial area, about 5 miles from downtown (take Hwy 101 southbound, exit Donlon St).

Shopping

★**Copperfield's** GIFTS & SOUVENIRS
(☎805-667-8198; www.copperfields.biz; 242 E Main St; ⏲10am-6pm Mon-Sat, from 11am Sun) Part standard gift shop, part what can only be described as emporium of ephemera, this is the kind of place where you can buy a birthday card one day and an infra-compunctive resonance perversion ray gun the next (your guess is as good as ours). Quirky souvenirs don't come better than this.

B on Main GIFTS & SOUVENIRS
(☎805-643-9309; www.bonmain.com; 446 E Main St; ⏲10:30am-6pm Mon-Thu, 10am-9pm Fri & Sat, 11am-6pm Sun) For coastal living, B sells nifty reproductions of vintage surf posters, shabby-chic furnishings, SoCal landscape art, locally made jewelry and beachy clothing for women.

Real Cheap Sports CLOTHING
(☎805-648-3803; www.realcheapsports.com; 36 W Santa Clara St; ⏲10am-6pm Mon-Sat, to 5pm Sun) Patagonia's flagship store is just down the street, but you can get theirs and other outdoor brands' past-season styles here at a discount. It may not be truly 'real cheap' unless you luck into a sale, but you can find decent deals on hiking, climbing and camping gear, or a jacket if the sunny SoCal weather turns on you.

ARC Foundation Thrift Store VINTAGE
(☎805-650-861; www.arcvc.org; 265 E Main St; ⏲9am-6pm Mon-Sat, 10am-5pm Sun) Loads of thrift stores, antiques malls and secondhand and vintage shops cluster downtown. Most are on Main St, west of California St, where ARC is always jam-packed with bargain hunters.

Information

Ventura Visitors & Convention Bureau
(☎805-648-2075; www.ventura-usa.com; 101 S California St; ⏲9am-5pm Mon-Sat, 10am-4pm Sun) Downtown visitor center handing out free maps and tourist brochures. It also contains a gift shop.

Getting There & Away

Ventura is about 30 miles southeast of Santa Barbara via Hwy 101. **Amtrak** (☎800-872-7245; www.amtrak.com; Harbor Blvd) operates five daily trains north to Santa Barbara ($15, 45 minutes) via Carpinteria and south to LA ($24, 2¼ hours). Amtrak's platform station is unstaffed; buy tickets in advance online or by phone. **VCTC** (Ventura County Transportation Commission; ☎800-438-1112; www.goventura.org) runs several daily 'Coastal Express' buses between downtown Ventura and Santa Barbara ($3, 40 to 70 minutes) via Carpinteria; check online or call for schedules.

Channel Islands National Park

Don't let this off-the-beaten-path **national park** (☎805-658-5730; www.nps.gov/chis; 1901 Spinnaker Dr, Ventura; ⏲visitor center 8:30am-5pm) FREE loiter for too long on your lifetime to-do list. It's easier to access than you might think, and the payoff is immense. Imagine hiking, kayaking, scuba diving, camping and whale-watching, and doing it all amid a raw, edge-of-the-world landscape. Rich in unique flora and fauna, tide pools and kelp forests, the islands are home to 145 plant and animal species found nowhere else in the world, earning them the nickname 'California's Galapagos.'

Geographically, the Channel Islands are an eight-island chain off the Southern California coast, stretching from Santa Barbara to San Diego. Five of them – San Miguel, Santa Rosa, Santa Cruz, Anacapa and tiny Santa Barbara – compose Channel Islands National Park.

Originally the Channel Islands were inhabited by Chumash tribespeople, who were forced to move to mainland Catholic missions by Spanish military forces in the early 1800s. The islands were subsequently taken over by Mexican and American ranchers during the 19th century and the US military in the 20th, until conservation efforts began in the 1970s and '80s.

Sights & Activities

Anacapa and Santa Cruz, the park's most popular islands, are within an hour's boat ride of Ventura. Both are doable day trips, though much larger Santa Cruz is a good overnight camping option. Bring plenty of water, because none is available on either island except at Scorpion Campground on Santa Cruz.

Most visitors arrive during summer, when island conditions are hot, dusty and bone dry. Better times to visit are during the spring wildflower bloom or in early fall, when the fog clears. Winter can be stormy, but it's also great for wildlife-watching, especially whale-watching.

Before you shove off from the mainland, stop by Ventura Harbor's NPS Visitor Center (p385) for educational natural-history exhibits, a free 25-minute nature film and, on weekends and holidays, family-friendly activities and ranger talks.

Santa Cruz ISLAND

(www.nps.gov/chis/planyourvisit/santa-cruz-island.htm) Santa Cruz, the Channel Islands' largest at 96 sq miles, claims two mountain ranges and the park's tallest peak, Mt Diablo (2450ft). The western three-quarters is mostly wilderness, managed by the Nature Conservancy and only accessible with a permit (www.nature.org/cruzpermit). The rest, managed by the National Park Service, is ideal for an action-packed day trip or laid-back overnight stay. Boats land at either Prisoners Harbor or Scorpion Anchorage, a short walk from historic Scorpion Ranch.

You can swim, snorkel, dive and kayak here, and there are plenty of hiking options too, starting from Scorpion Anchorage. It's a 1-mile climb to captivating Cavern Point. Views don't get much better than from this windy spot. For a longer jaunt, continue 1.5 miles west, along the North Bluff Trail, to Potato Harbor. The 4.5-mile Scorpion Canyon Loop heads uphill to an old oil well and fantastic views, then drops through Scorpion Canyon to the campground. Alternatively, follow Smugglers Rd all the way to the pebble beach at Smugglers Cove, a strenuous 7.5-mile round-trip. From Prisoners Harbor there are several more strenuous trails, including the 18-mile round trip China Pines hike – your efforts will be rewarded by the chance to see the rare bishop pine.

There's little shade on the island, so avoid midday summer walks and bring plenty of water (available at Scorpion Anchorage only). Make sure you're at the harbor in plenty of time to catch your return boat, otherwise you'll be stuck overnight.

Anacapa ISLAND

(www.nps.gov/chis/planyourvisit/anacapa.htm) Actually three separate islets totaling just over 1 sq mile, Anacapa gives a memorable introduction to the Channel Islands' ecology. It's also the best option if you're short on time. Boats dock year-round on the East Island, where, after a short climb, you'll find 2 miles of trails offering fantastic views of island flora, a historic lighthouse, and rocky Middle and West Islands. You're bound to see western gulls too – the world's largest breeding colony is here.

Kayaking, diving, tide-pooling and watching seals and sea lions are popular outdoor activities, while inside the museum at the small visitor center, divers with video cameras occasionally broadcast images to a TV monitor you can watch during spring and summer.

Santa Rosa ISLAND

(www.nps.gov/chis/planyourvisit/santa-rosa-island.htm) The indigenous Chumash people called Santa Rosa 'Wima' (driftwood) because of

ISLAND OF THE BLUE DOLPHINS

For bedtime reading around the campfire, pick up Scott O'Dell's Newbery Medal–winning *Island of the Blue Dolphins*. This young-adult novel was inspired by the true-life story of a woman from the Nicoleño tribe who was left behind on San Nicolas Island during the early 19th century, when her people were forced off the Channel Islands. Incredibly, the woman survived mostly alone on the island for 18 years, before being discovered and brought to the mainland by a hunter in 1853. However, fate was not on her side, and she died just seven weeks later.

the redwood logs that often came ashore here, with which they built plank canoes called *tomols*. This 84-sq-mile island has rare Torrey pines, sandy beaches and hundreds of plant and bird species. Beach, canyon and grasslands hiking trails abound, but high winds can make swimming, diving and kayaking tough for anyone but experts.

San Miguel ISLAND

(www.nps.gov/chis/planyourvisit/san-miguel-island.htm) While 14-sq-mile San Miguel can guarantee solitude and a remote wilderness experience, its westernmost location in the Channel Islands chain means it's often windy and shrouded in fog. Some sections are off-limits to protect the island's fragile ecosystem, which includes a caliche forest (hardened calcium-carbonate castings of trees and vegetation) and seasonal colonies of seals and sea lions. Peregrine falcons have been reintroduced, and some of the archeological sites from when the Chumash lived here date back almost 12,000 years.

Santa Barbara ISLAND

(www.nps.gov/chis/planyourvisit/santa-barbara-island.htm) Santa Barbara, only 1 sq mile and the smallest of the islands, is a jewel box for nature-lovers. Big, blooming coreopsis, cream cups and chicory are just a few of the island's memorable plant species. You'll also find the humongous northern elephant seal here, as well as Scripps's murrelets, a bird that nests in cliff crevices.

Get more information from the island's small visitor center. For the latest information on when it might open, check the website.

 Tours

Most trips require a minimum number of participants, and may be canceled due to high surf or weather conditions. Santa Barbara Adventure Company (p357) also runs kayaking day trips to Santa Cruz Island.

Raptor Dive Charters DIVING

(805-650-7700; www.raptordive.com; 1559 Spinnaker Dr, Ventura) Certified and experienced divers can head out for some underwater action, including night dives, off Anacapa and Santa Cruz Islands. Prices start at $130; equipment rentals are available for a surcharge; and plenty of snacks, sandwiches and drinks are available on board.

Island Packers Cruises CRUISE

(805-642-1393; http://islandpackers.com; 1691 Spinnaker Dr, Ventura; Channel Island day trips from $59, wildlife cruises from $38) Main provider of boats for visits to the Channel Islands, with day trips and overnight camping excursions available. Boats mostly set out from Ventura, but a few go from nearby Oxnard. Also offers wildlife cruises year-round, including seasonal whale-watching from late December to mid-April (gray whales) and mid-May through mid-September (blue and humpback whales).

Channel Islands Kayak Center KAYAKING

(805-984-5995; www.cikayak.com; 1691 Spinnaker Dr, Ventura; by appointment) Book ahead to rent kayaks ($35) and SUPs ($25 per hour; harbor only) or arrange a private guided kayaking tour of Santa Cruz or Anacapa Island (from $180 per person; two-person minimum).

CALIFORNIA'S CHANNEL ISLANDS: PARADISE LOST & FOUND

Human beings have left a heavy footprint on the Channel Islands. Erosion was caused by overgrazing livestock, and rabbits fed on native plants. The US military even used San Miguel as a practice bombing range. In 1969 an offshore oil spill engulfed the northern islands in an 800-sq-mile slick, killing thousands of seabirds and mammals. Meanwhile, deep-sea fishing has caused the destruction of three-quarters of the islands' kelp forests, which are key to the marine ecosystem.

Despite past abuses, the future isn't all bleak. Brown pelicans – decimated by the effects of DDT and reduced to one surviving chick in 1970 – have rebounded and are now off the endangered list, with healthy populations on West Anacapa and Santa Barbara Islands. On San Miguel Island, native vegetation has returned a half century after overgrazing sheep were removed. On Santa Cruz Island, the National Park Service and the Nature Conservancy have implemented multiyear plans to eliminate invasive plants and feral pigs.

CHANNEL ISLANDS NATIONAL PARK CAMPGROUNDS

CAMPGROUND	NUMBER OF SITES	ACCESS FROM BOAT LANDING	DESCRIPTION
Anacapa	7	0.5-mile walk with over 150 stairs	High, rocky, sun exposed and isolated
Santa Cruz (Scorpion Ranch)	31	Flat 0.5-mile walk	Popular with groups, often crowded and partly shady
Santa Barbara	10	Steep 0.25-mile walk uphill	Large, grassy and surrounded by trails
San Miguel	9	Steep 1-mile walk uphill	Windy, often foggy with volatile weather
Santa Rosa	15	Flat 1.5-mile walk	Eucalyptus grove in a windy canyon

Sleeping

Each island has a primitive year-round **campground** (reservations 877-444-6777; www.recreation.gov; tent sites $15) with pit toilets and picnic tables. Water is only available on Santa Cruz Island. You must pack everything in and out, including trash. Due to fire danger, campfires aren't allowed, but enclosed gas camp stoves are OK. Advance reservations are required for all island campsites.

Information

Channel Islands National Park Visitor Center (Robert J Lagomarsino Visitor Center; 805-658-5730; www.nps.gov/chis; 1901 Spinnaker Dr, Ventura; 8:30am-5pm;) Trip-planning information, books and maps are available on the mainland at the far end of Ventura Harbor. A free 25-minute video, *A Treasure in the Sea*, gives some background on the islands, and weekends and holidays see free ranger-led tidepool talks at the center at 11am and 3pm.

Getting There & Away

You can access the national park by taking a boat from Ventura or Oxnard or a plane from Camarillo. Trips may be canceled anytime due to high surf or weather conditions. Reservations are essential for weekends, holidays and summer trips.

The open seas on the boat ride out to the Channel Islands may feel choppy to landlubbers. To avoid seasickness, sit outside on the lower deck, keep away from the diesel fumes in the back, and focus on the horizon. The outbound trip is typically against the wind and a bit bumpier than the return. Over-the-counter motion-sickness pills (eg Dramamine) can make you drowsy. Boats usually brake when dolphins or whales are spotted – always a welcome distraction from any nausea.

AIR

If you're prone to seasickness or just want a memorable way to get to the Channel Islands, you can take a scenic flight to Santa Rosa or San Miguel with **Channel Islands Aviation** (805-987-1301; www.flycia.com; 305 Durley Ave, Camarillo). Half-day packages include hiking or a guided 4WD tour, while overnight camping excursions are more DIY.

BOAT

Island Packers offers regularly scheduled boat services to all the islands, mostly from Ventura, but with a few sailings from Oxnard too. Anacapa and Santa Cruz are closer to the mainland and so less expensive to visit than other islands. Day trips are possible; overnight campers pay an additional surcharge. Be forewarned: if you do camp and seas are rough the following day, you could get stuck for an extra night or more.

AT A GLANCE

POPULATION
10.1 million

NUMBER OF CARS
6,567,187

BEST FOOD MARKET
Grand Central Market (p410)

BEST GARDENS
Huntington Library, Art Museum & Botanical Gardens (p404)

BEST OUTDOOR MUSIC VENUE
Hollywood Bowl (p417)

WHEN TO GO

Dec–Feb Good hotel deals, though demand is high in February due to the Academy Awards.

Mar–May An ideal time to visit. Decent hotel deals are still available.

Sep–Nov The summer crowds have thinned, though temperatures remain warm.

Venice beach (p400)
TREKANDSHOOT / SHUTTERSTOCK

Los Angeles

LA runs deeper than its blond beaches, bosomy hills and ubiquitous Beemers would have you believe. It's a myth. A beacon for countless small-town dreamers, rockers and risk-takers; an open-minded angel who encourages its people to live and let live without judgment or shame. It has given us Quentin Tarantino, Kim Kardashian, and Serena and Venus Williams. Spawned skateboarding and gangsta rap, popularized implants, Botox and spandex, and nurtured not just great writers, performers and directors, but also the groundbreaking yogis who first brought Eastern wisdom to the Western world.

LA is best defined by those simple life-affirming moments. A cocktail on Sunset Blvd, a hike into the Hollywood Hills, a pink-washed sunset over Venice Beach, the perfect taco. And the night music. There is always night music.

INCLUDES

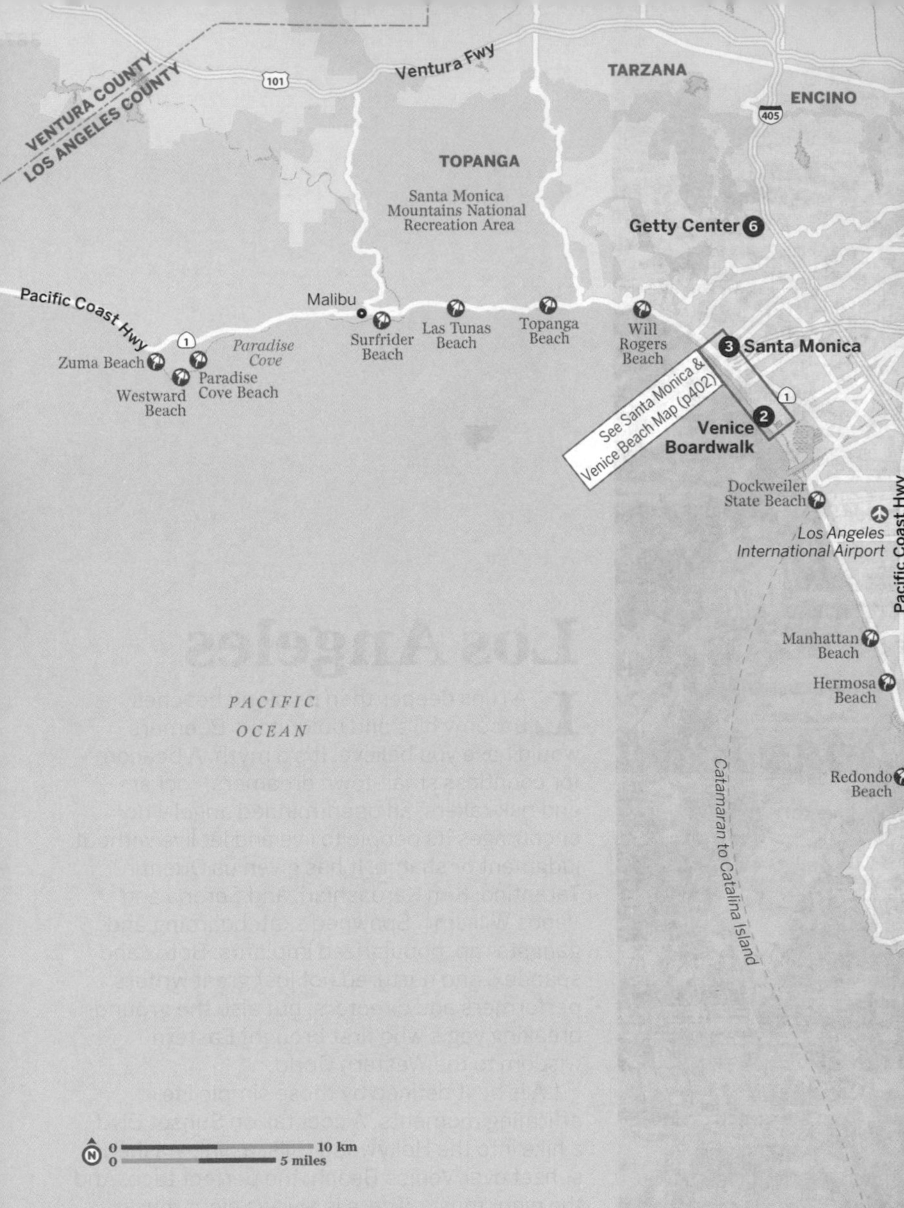

Los Angeles Highlights

1 Downtown LA (p390) Taking in iconic architecture, artworks and a plethora of hot-spot hangouts in Los Angeles' booming birthplace.

2 Venice Boardwalk (p401) Getting your freak on strutting down LA's most eccentric oceanside strip.

3 Santa Monica (p399) Soaking up sun, surf and boho-chic vibes at the end of America's Route 66.

4 Hollywood (p392) Channeling Tinseltown's Golden Age ghosts in veteran

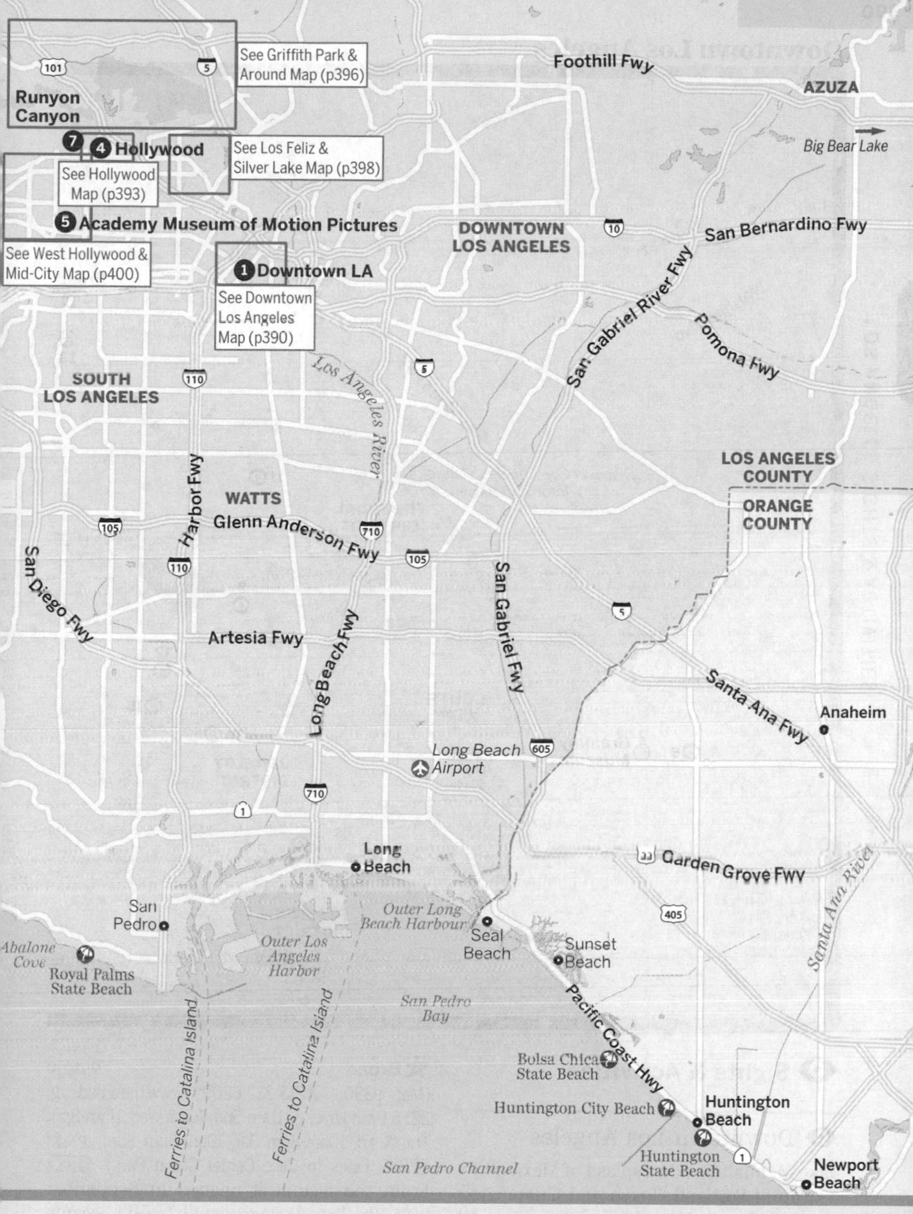

bars, hidden streets and a maverick make-up studio.

5 Academy Museum of Motion Pictures (p396)
Immersing yourself in the magic of cinema at Renzo Piano's state-of-the-art film museum.

6 Getty Center (p397)
Finding inspiration in culture and LA's natural beauty at Richard Meier's luminous hilltop art hub.

7 Runyon Canyon (p394)
Joining the buff and the famous on a hike through this Hollywood Hills park.

Downtown Los Angeles

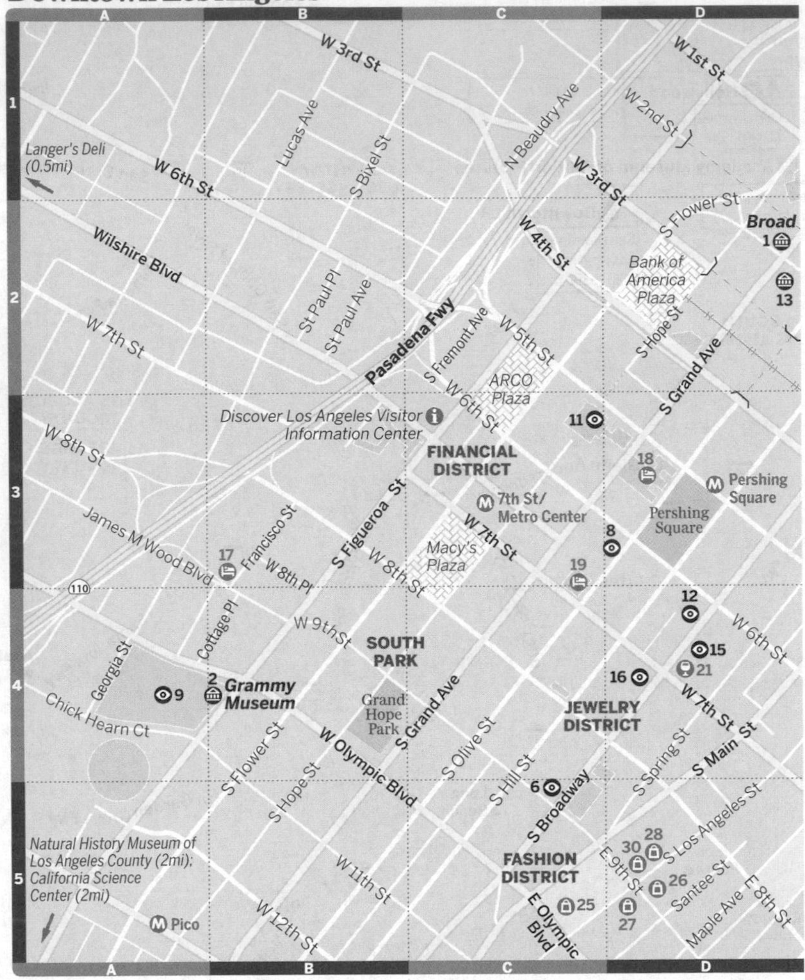

Sights & Activities

Downtown Los Angeles

Take Manhattan, add a splash of Mexico City, a drop of Portland, Tokyo and Guangzhou, shake and pour. Your drink: Downtown LA (DTLA). Effortlessly hip, ever-evolving yet stubbornly gritty, this is the city's historic and cultural heart, a place where the space-age silhouettes of modern-art museums and concert halls contrast with the crumbling opulence of Broadway theaters, the Spanish curves of historic Olvera St and the hulking warehouses of the booming Arts District.

★Broad MUSEUM

(Map p390; ☎213-232-6200; www.thebroad.org; 221 S Grand Ave; ⏱11am-5pm Tue & Wed, 11am-8pm Thu & Fri, 10am-8pm Sat, 10am-6pm Sun; P 🚸; M B/D Lines to Civic Center/Grand Park) FREE

From the instant it opened in September 2015, the Broad (rhymes with 'road') became a must-visit for contemporary-art fans. It houses the world-class collection of local philanthropist and billionaire real-estate honcho Eli Broad and his wife, Edythe, with more than 2000 postwar pieces by dozens of heavy hitters, including Cindy Sherman, Jeff Koons, Andy Warhol, Roy Lichtenstein, Robert Rauschenberg, Keith Haring and Kara Walker.

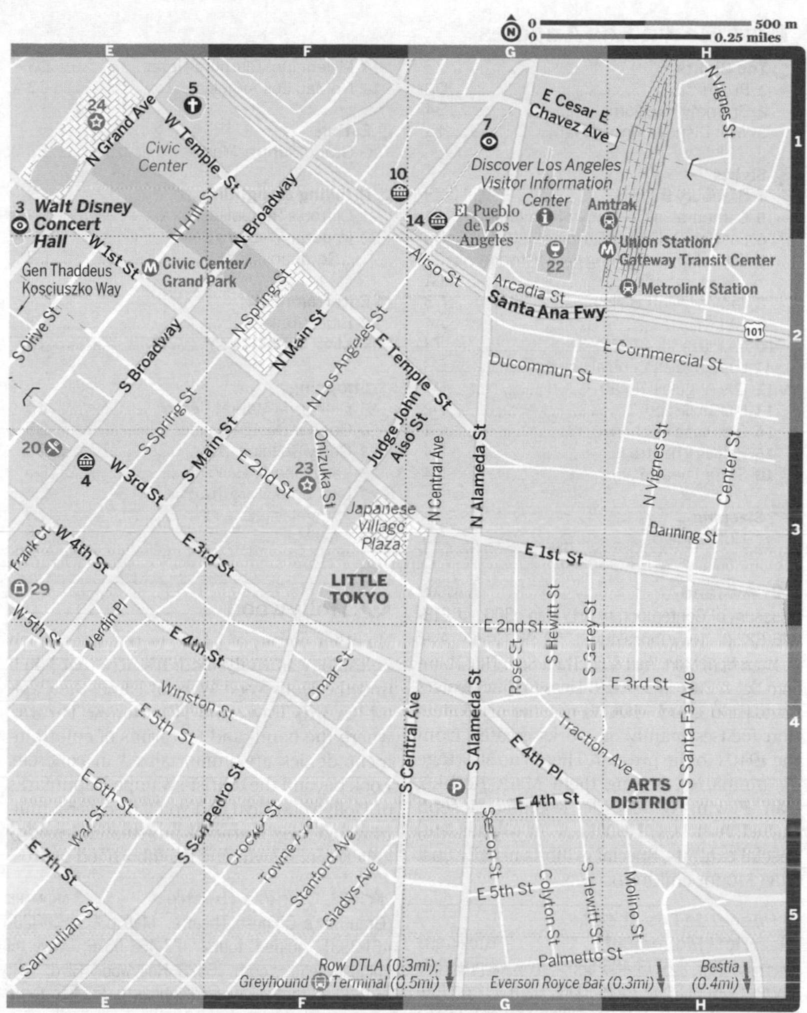

★Walt Disney Concert Hall

NOTABLE BUILDING

(Map p390; ☎323-850-2000; www.laphil.org; 111 S Grand Ave; P; M B/D Lines to Civic Center/Grand Park) FREE A molten blend of steel, music and psychedelic architecture, this iconic concert venue is the home base of the Los Angeles Philharmonic, but has also hosted contemporary bands such as Phoenix, and classic jazz musicians such as Sonny Rollins. The 2003 concert hall's visionary architect, Frank Gehry, pulled out all the stops for this building, a gravity-defying sculpture of heaving and billowing stainless steel.

★Grammy Museum

MUSEUM

(Map p390; ☎213-765-6800; www.grammymuseum.org; 800 W Olympic Blvd; adult/child $15/13; ⏲10:30am-6:30pm Sun, Mon, Wed & Thu, 10am-8pm Fri & Sat; P 👪; M A/E Lines to Pico) The highlight of **LA Live** (Map p390; ☎213-763-5483; www.lalive.com; 800 W Olympic Blvd; P 👪; M A/E Lines to Pico), this museum explores the evolution of the world's most famous music awards, as well as defining, differentiating and linking musical genres. Its rotating treasures might include iconic threads from the wardrobes of Michael Jackson, Whitney Houston and Beyoncé, and instruments once used by world-renowned rock legends.

Downtown Los Angeles

Top Sights
1 Broad ... D2
2 Grammy Museum ... B4
3 Walt Disney Concert Hall ... E1

Sights
4 Bradbury Building ... E3
5 Cathedral of Our Lady of the Angels ... E1
6 Eastern Columbia Building ... C5
7 El Pueblo de Los Ángeles Historical Monument ... G1
8 James Oviatt Building ... D3
9 LA Live ... A4
10 LA Plaza ... F1
11 Los Angeles Central Library ... C3
12 Los Angeles Theatre ... D4
13 MOCA Grand ... D2
14 Old Plaza Firehouse ... G1
15 Palace Theatre ... D4
16 State Theatre ... D4

Sleeping
17 Hotel Indigo ... B3
18 Millennium Biltmore Hotel ... D3
19 NoMad Los Angeles ... C3

Eating
20 Grand Central Market ... E3

Drinking & Nightlife
21 Clifton's Republic ... D4
22 Imperial Western Beer Company ... G2

Entertainment
23 Blue Whale ... F3
24 Mark Taper Forum ... E1

Shopping
25 California Market Center ... C5
26 Cooper Design Space ... D5
27 Gerry Building ... D5
28 Lady Liberty Building ... D5
29 Last Bookstore in Los Angeles ... E3
30 New Mart ... D5

MOCA Grand MUSEUM

(Museum of Contemporary Art; Map p390; ☎213-626-6222; www.moca.org; 250 S Grand Ave; ⏰11am-6pm Mon, Wed & Fri, 11am-8pm Thu, 11am-5pm Sat & Sun; ; Ⓜ B/D Lines to Civic Center/Grand Park) FREE MOCA's notable art collection focuses mainly on works created from the 1940s to the present. There's no shortage of luminaries, among them Mark Rothko, Dan Flavin, Willem de Kooning, Joseph Cornell and David Hockney, in regular and special exhibits. Special exhibits usually cost $18 ($10 for children).

El Pueblo de Los Ángeles Historical Monument HISTORIC SITE

(Map p390; ☎213-485-6855; www.elpueblo.lacity.org; Olvera St; ⏰tours 10am, 11am & noon Tue-Sat; ; Ⓜ B/D/L Lines to Union Station) FREE This compact, colorful district is where LA's first colonists settled in 1781. Wander through narrow Olvera St's vibrant Mexican-themed stalls and check out the area's free museums, the best of which is **LA Plaza** (La Plaza de Cultura y Artes; Map p390; ☎213-542-6200; www.lapca.org; 501 N Main St; ⏰noon-5pm Mon & Wed-Fri, 10am-5pm Sat & Sun; ; Ⓜ B/D/L Lines to Union Station) FREE, offering snapshots of the Mexican-American experience in Los Angeles. Free guided tours of the area leave from beside the **Old Plaza Firehouse** (Map p390; ☎213-485-8437; 134 Paseo de la Plaza; ⏰10am-3pm Tue-Sun; Ⓜ B/D/L Lines to Union Station) FREE; no reservations necessary.

Hollywood

No other corner of LA is steeped in as much mythology as Hollywood. It's here that you'll find the Hollywood Walk of Fame, the Capitol Records Tower and TCL Chinese Theatre, where the hand- and footprints of entertainment deities are immortalized in concrete. Look beyond the tourist-swamped landmarks of Hollywood Blvd and you'll discover a multifaceted neighborhood punctuated by edgy galleries and swinging neighborhood bistros.

★ **TCL Chinese Theatre** LANDMARK

(Grauman's Chinese Theatre; Map p393; ☎323-461-3331, guided tours 323-463-9576; www.tclchinesetheatres.com; 6925 Hollywood Blvd; ; Ⓜ B Line to Hollywood/Highland) FREE Ever wondered what it's like to be in George Clooney's shoes? Find his foot- and handprints alongside dozens of other stars', forever set in the concrete forecourt of this world-famous movie palace, opened in 1927. Join the throngs to find out how big Arnold's feet really are, or search for Betty Grable's legs, Whoopi Goldberg's braids, Daniel Radcliffe's wand or R2-D2's wheels.

★ **Hollywood Museum** MUSEUM

(Map p393; ☎323-464-7776; www.thehollywoodmuseum.com; 1660 N Highland Ave; adult/senior & student/child $15/12/5; ⏰10am-5pm Wed-Sun; ; Ⓜ B Line to Hollywood/Highland) For a genuine taste of Old Hollywood, do not miss

Hollywood

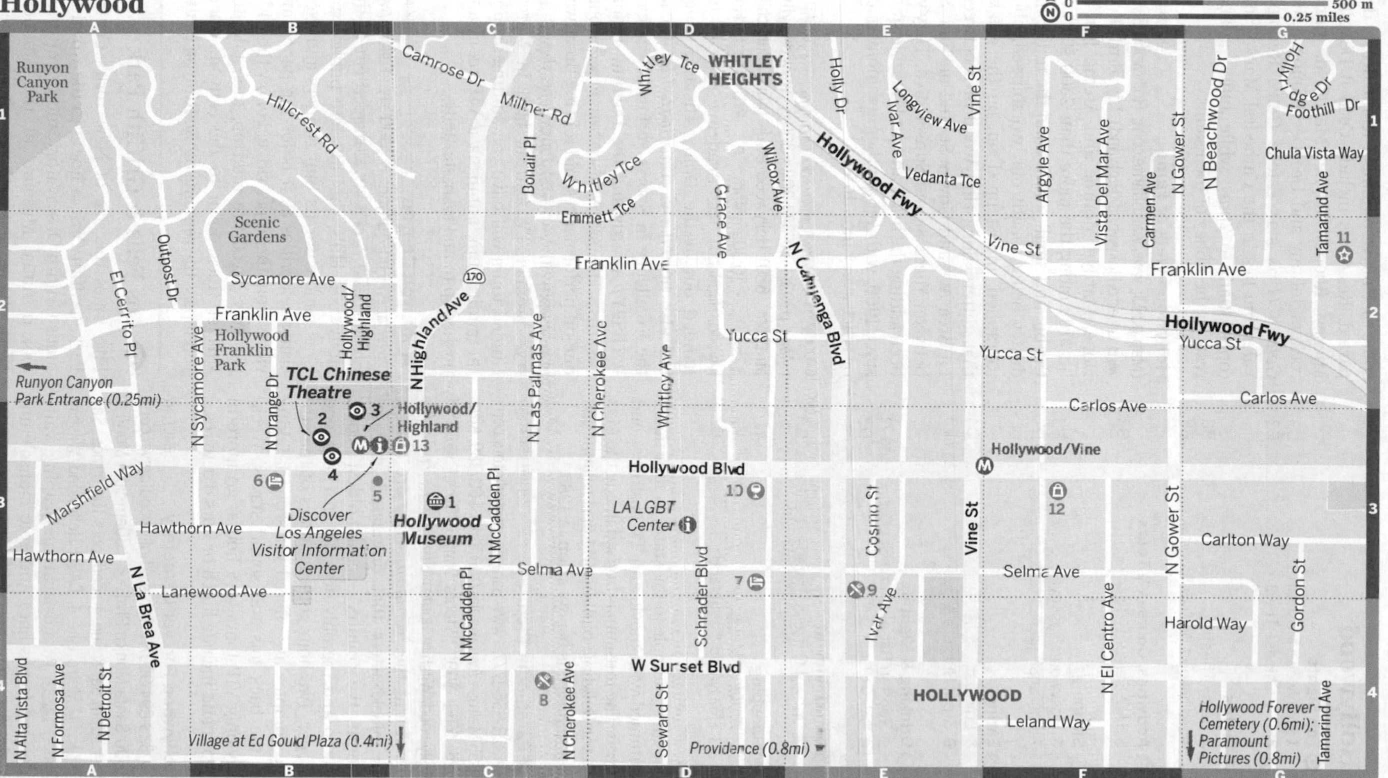

500 m
0.25 miles
Runyon Canyon Park
WHITLEY HEIGHTS
Scenic Gardens
Hollywood Franklin Park
Runyon Canyon Park Entrance (0.25mi)
TCL Chinese Theatre
Hollywood/Highland
Hollywood Museum
Discover Los Angeles Visitor Information Center
LA LGBT Center
Hollywood/Vine
HOLLYWOOD
Village at Ed Gould Plaza (0.4mi)
Providence (0.8mi)
Hollywood Forever Cemetery (0.6mi); Paramount Pictures (0.8mi)
Hollywood Fwy
Hollywood Blvd
W Sunset Blvd
N Highland Ave
N Cahuenga Blvd
N La Brea Ave
Vine St
Franklin Ave
Yucca St
Selma Ave
Carlos Ave

Hollywood

this musty temple to the stars, its four floors crammed with movie and TV costumes and props. The museum is housed inside the Max Factor Building, built in 1914 and relaunched as a glamorous beauty salon in 1935.

★Paramount Pictures FILM LOCATION
(☎323-956-1777; www.paramountstudiotour.com; 5555 Melrose Ave; regular/VIP tours $60/189, After Dark tours $99; ⊙tours 9am-3:30pm; DASH Hollywood/Wilshire Route) *Star Trek, Indiana Jones* and the *Ironman* series are among the blockbusters that originated at Paramount, the country's second-oldest movie studio and the only one still in Hollywood proper. Two-hour golf-cart tours of the studio complex are offered year-round, taking in the back lots and sound stages. Weekday-only VIP tours (4½ hours) go more in depth and include lunch or hors d'oeuvres.

Hollywood Forever Cemetery CEMETERY
(☎323-894-9507; https://hollywoodforever.com; 6000 Santa Monica Blvd; ⊙8:30am-5pm Mon-Fri, to 4:30pm Sat & Sun, guided tours 10am most Sat; P; Metro Line 4, DASH Hollywood/Wilshire Route) FREE Paradisiacal landscaping, vainglorious tombstones and epic mausoleums make for an appropriate resting place for some of Hollywood's most iconic dearly departed. Residents include Cecil B DeMille, Mickey Rooney, Jayne Mansfield, punk rockers Johnny and Dee Dee Ramone, and *Golden Girls* star Estelle Getty. Rudolph Valentino lies in the Cathedral Mausoleum (open 10am to 2pm), while Judy Garland rests in the Abbey of the Psalms.

Hollywood Walk of Fame LANDMARK
(Map p393; www.walkoffame.com; Hollywood Blvd; M B Line to Hollywood/Highland) Big Bird, Bob Hope, Marilyn Monroe and Aretha Franklin are among the more than 2600 stars of the big and small screens and the music industry being sought out, worshipped, photographed and stepped on, on the galaxy that glitters along Hollywood Blvd between La Brea Ave and Gower St, and on Vine St between Yucca St and Sunset Blvd. They've been adding the brass and pink-marble stars since 1960, with yet another ceremony once or twice every month.

Dolby Theatre THEATER
(Map p393; ☎323-308-6300; www.dolbytheatre.com; 6801 Hollywood Blvd; tours adult/child $25/19; ⊙10:30am-4pm; P; M B Line to Hollywood/Highland) The Academy Awards are handed out at the Dolby Theatre, which has also hosted the *American Idol* finale, the Excellence in Sports Performance Yearly (ESPY) Awards and the Daytime Emmy Awards. The stage also hosts occasional one-off performances and touring Broadway shows, plus the annual PaleyFest, the country's premier TV festival, held in March. Guided tours will have you sniffing around the auditorium, admiring a VIP room and nosing up to an Oscar statuette.

★Runyon Canyon HIKING
(www.laparks.org/runyon; 2000 N Fuller Ave; ⊙dawn-dusk) A chaparral-draped cut in the Hollywood Hills, this 130-acre public park is as famous for its buff runners and exercising celebrities as it is for the panoramic views from the upper ridge. Follow the wide, partially paved fire road up, then take the smaller track down to the canyon, where you'll pass the remains of the Runyon estate.

Los Feliz & Griffith Park

Five times the size of New York's Central Park, Griffith Park is home to the world-famous Griffith Observatory and the oft-overlooked Autry Museum of the American West. Rising above the southern edge of

Los Feliz, Barnsdall Art Park is crowned by architect Frank Lloyd Wright's Californian debut, the World-Heritage listed **Hollyhock House** (Map p398; ☎323-913-4031; https://barnsdall.org/hollyhock-house; Barnsdall Art Park, 4800 Hollywood Blvd, Los Feliz; adult/student/child $7/3/free; ⊙self-guided tours 11am-4pm Thu-Sun; P; M B Line to Vermont/Sunset).

★Griffith Observatory MUSEUM
(Map p396; ☎213-473-0890; www.griffithobservatory.org; 2800 E Observatory Rd, Griffith Parj; admission free, planetarium shows adult/student & senior/child $7/5/3; ⊙noon-10pm Tue-Fri, 10am-10pm Sat & Sun; P 👪; 🚌DASH Observatory/Los Feliz Route) FREE LA's landmark 1935 observatory opens a window onto the universe from its perch on the southern slopes of Mt Hollywood. Its planetarium claims the world's most advanced star projector, while its astronomical touch displays explore some mind-bending topics, from the evolution of the telescope and the ultraviolet and x-ray techniques used to map our solar system to the cosmos itself.

★Autry Museum of the American West MUSEUM
(Map p396; ☎323-667-2000; www.theautry.org; 4700 Western Heritage Way, Griffith Park; adult/senior & student/child $14/10/6, 2nd Tue of month free; ⊙10am-4pm Tue-Fri, 10am-5pm Sat & Sun; P 👪; 🚌Metro Line 96) Established by singing cowboy Gene Autry, this expansive museum offers contemporary perspectives on the history and people of the American West. Permanent exhibitions span Native American traditions to 19th-century cattle drives, daily frontier life to costumes and artifacts from Hollywood Westerns. Blockbuster temporary exhibits include the annual Autry Masters Art Exhibition and Sale, showcasing the work of contemporary artists exploring Western themes.

Silver Lake & Echo Park

Pimped with stencil art, inked skin and skinny jeans, Silver Lake and Echo Park are the epicenter of LA hipsterdom.

Neutra VDL House ARCHITECTURE
(www.neutra-vdl.org; 2300 Silver Lake Blvd, Silver Lake; adult/senior/child $15/10/free; ⊙guided tours 11am-3pm Sat, last tour commences 2:30pm; 🚌Metro Line 92) Built in 1932, burnt to a crisp in 1963 then rebuilt, the light-washed former home and laboratory of modernist architect Richard Neutra is a leading example of mid-century Californian design. Indeed, the site was declared a National Historic Landmark in 2017. Thirty-minute guided tours of the property run most Saturdays, shedding light on the Austrian-born architect's theories and stylistic evolution. Reservations not required.

West Hollywood & Mid-City

LA rainbows lead to West Hollywood (WeHo), an independent city with way more personality (some might say frivolity) than its 1.9-sq mile frame might suggest. Home to legendary comedy clubs, Hollywood lore

UNIVERSAL STUDIOS HOLLYWOOD

Although **Universal** (Map p396; ☎800-864-8377; www.universalstudioshollywood.com; 100 Universal City Plaza, Universal City; 1-/2-day from $109/149, child under 3yr free; ⊙daily, hours vary; P 👪; M B Line to Universal City) is one of the world's oldest continuously operating movie studios, the chances of seeing any filming action here, let alone a star, are slim to none. But never mind. This theme park on the studio's back lot presents an entertaining mix of thrill rides, live-action shows and a tram tour.

First-timers should head straight for the 60-minute **Studio Tour** narrated by *Tonight Show* host Jimmy Fallon, aboard a multi-car tram that drives around the sound stages (some may be in active use) and back lot – take in the crash site from *War of the Worlds*, vehicles from *The Fast and the Furious* and the spooky Bates Motel from *Psycho*. Also prepare to brave a flash flood, survive a shark attack, a spitting dino and an 8.3-magnitude earthquake, before facing down King Kong in a 3-D experience created by Peter Jackson, director of the *Lord of the Rings* trilogy. It's a bit hokey but fun.

The phenomenally popular **Wizarding World of Harry Potter** is the park's biggest attraction. Climb aboard the Flight of the Hippogriff roller coaster and the signature ride, Harry Potter and the Forbidden Journey.

General parking costs from $28 per day. If you're arriving by Metro subway, a free shuttle connects the park with Universal City station.

Griffith Park & Around

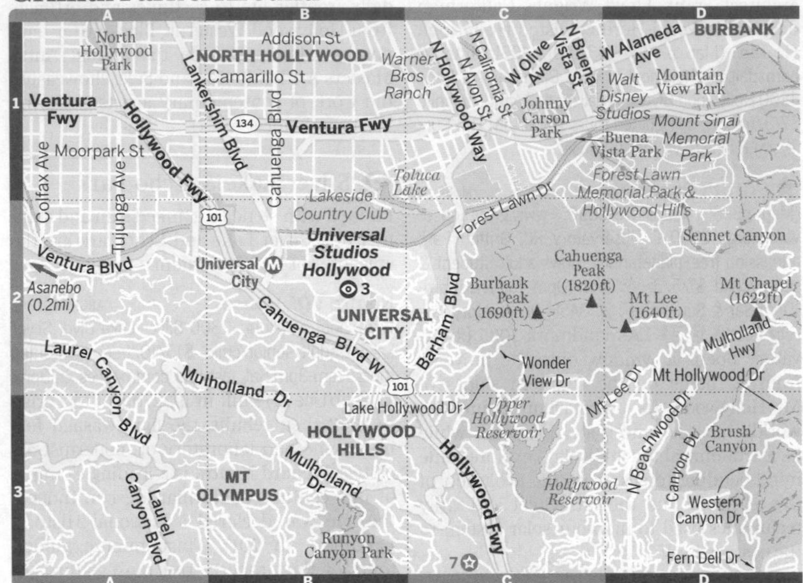

Griffith Park & Around

hotels and a renowned design district, it's also the city's gay heartland.

To the south and east, Mid-City encompasses the Miracle Mile (flanked by some of the best museums in the west), the Orthodox-Jewish-meets-hipster Fairfax district and the legendary rock, punk and vintage shopping strip of Melrose Ave.

★ Academy Museum of Motion Pictures MUSEUM

(Map p400; ☎323-930-3000; www.academymuseum.org; cnr Wilshire Blvd & Fairfax Ave, Mid-City; ; Metro Lines 20, 217, 720, 780, DASH Fairfax Route) Designed by Italian starchitect Renzo Piano, this 300,000-sq-ft blockbuster celebrates LA's greatest passion: movies. The museum's permanent exhibition offers an immersive, state-of-the-art journey through cinema's evolution, with priceless props and costumes that include Dorothy's ruby slippers from *The Wizard of Oz*. Temporary exhibitions explore diverse aspects and figures of the industry, while daily screenings include anything from world movies to weekend children's matinees. The museum's Dolby Family Terrace offers a suitably cinematic panorama of the world's entertainment capital.

★ Los Angeles County Museum of Art MUSEUM

(LACMA; Map p400; ☎323-857-6000; www.lacma.org; 5905 Wilshire Blvd, Mid-City; adult/senior/student/child $25/21/21/free, 2nd Tue of month free; ⊙11am-5pm Mon, Tue & Thu, 11am-8pm Fri, 10am-7pm Sat & Sun; P; Metro Lines 20, 217, 720, 780, DASH Fairfax Route) The depth and wealth of the collection at the largest art museum in the western US is stunning. LACMA holds all the major players – Rembrandt, Cézanne, Magritte, Mary Cassatt, Ansel Adams – plus millennia's worth of Chinese, Japanese, pre-Columbian and ancient Greek, Roman and Egyptian sculpture. Due to major redevelopment works (due for completion in 2024), only the Broad Contemporary

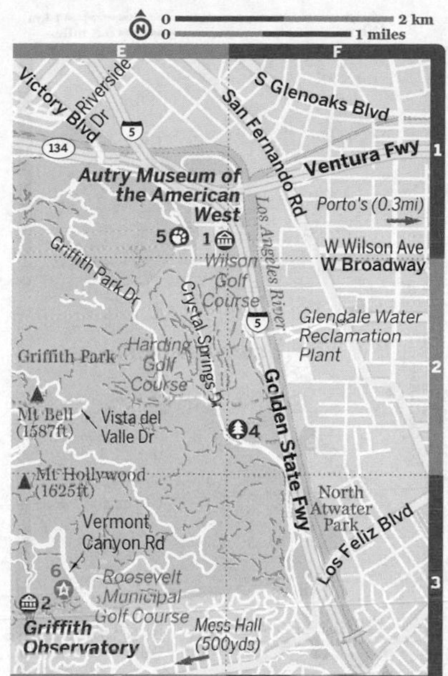

Art Museum (BCAM) and Resnick Pavilion galleries are currently open, hosting world-class temporary exhibitions and a reduced selection of its permanent hoard.

★Petersen Automotive Museum MUSEUM
(Map p400; ☎323-930-2277; www.petersen.org; 6060 Wilshire Blvd, Mid City; adult/senior/student/child $16/14/14/11; ⊙10am-5pm Mon-Fri, to 6pm Sat & Sun; P 👪; 🚌Metro Lines 20, 217, 720, 780, DASH Fairfax Route) A four-story ode to the auto, this is a treat even for those who can't tell a piston from a carburetor. A headlights-to-brake-lights futuristic makeover (by Kohn Pederson Fox) in 2015 saw the museum swag the prestigious American Architecture Award for significant new buildings. While we love its skin of undulating bands of stainless steel on a hot-rod-red background, it's what's inside that counts: four gripping, themed floors exploring the history, industry and artistry of motorized transportation.

La Brea Tar Pits & Museum MUSEUM
(Map p400; ☎213-763-3499; https://tarpits.org; 5801 Wilshire Blvd, Mid-City; adult/student/senior/child $15/12/12/7, every Tue in Sep & 1st Tue of month Oct-Jun free; ⊙9:30am-5pm; P 👪; 🚌Metro Line 20, DASH Fairfax Route) Mammoths, saber-toothed cats and dire wolves roamed LA's savanna in prehistoric times. We know this because of an archaeological trove of skulls and bones unearthed here, at one of the world's most fecund and famous fossil sites. Generations of young dino hunters have come to seek out fossils and learn about paleontology from docents and demonstrations in on-site labs at the museum that now sits here.

Beverly Hills, Bel Air, Brentwood & Westwood

A quadruplet of megamansions, luxury wheels and tweaked cheekbones, Beverly Hills, Bel Air, Brentwood and Westwood encapsulate the LA of international fantasies.

★Getty Center MUSEUM
(☎310-440-7300; www.getty.edu; N Sepulveda Blvd & Getty Center Dr, off I-405 Fwy; ⊙10am-5:30pm Tue-Fri & Sun, 10am-9pm Sat; P 👪; 🚌Metro Lines 234, 734) FREE In its billion-dollar, in-the-clouds perch, high above the city grit and grime, the Getty Center presents triple delights: an engaging art collection (everything from medieval triptychs to baroque sculpture and impressionist brushstrokes), Richard Meier's cutting-edge architecture, and the visual splendor of seasonally changing gardens. Admission is free, but parking is $20 ($15 after 3pm).

★Hammer Museum MUSEUM
(☎310-443-7000; https://hammer.ucla.edu; 10899 Wilshire Blvd, Westwood; ⊙11am-8pm Tue-Fri, 11am-5pm Sat & Sun; P; 🚌Metro Lines 2, 234, 302, Big Blue Bus Lines 1, 2, 8) FREE Originally a vanity project of the late oil tycoon Armand Hammer, this expanding, UCLA-affiliated museum is one of LA's most underrated cultural highlights. The museum really shines in cutting-edge contemporary exhibits featuring local, under-represented and controversial artists. The Made in LA biennial, showcasing a diverse spectrum of LA-area artists in even-numbered years, is headquartered here. It all stands in counterpoint to Armand Hammer's personal collection of Renaissance to early-20th-century European and American art. All that, and it's free.

Museum of Tolerance MUSEUM
(☎reservations 310-772-2505; www.museumoftolerance.com; 9786 W Pico Blvd; adult/senior/student/child $15.50/12.50/11.50/11.50, Anne Frank Exhibit $15.50/13.50/12.50/12.50; ⊙10am-5pm Sun-Wed & Fri, 10am-9:30pm Thu Apr-Oct, 10am-5pm Sun-Wed, 10am-9:30pm Thu, 10am-3:30pm Fri Nov-Mar, closed Sat; P 👪; 🚌Big Blue Bus Line 7)

Los Feliz & Silver Lake

Run by the Simon Wiesenthal Center, this powerful, deeply moving museum uses interactive technology to engage visitors in discussion and contemplation around racism and bigotry. Particular focus is given to the Holocaust, with a major basement exhibition that examines the social, political and economic conditions that led to the Holocaust as well as the experience of the millions persecuted. On the museum's 2nd floor, another major exhibition offers an intimate look into the life and impact of Anne Frank.

Malibu & Pacific Palisades

Malibu enjoys near-mythical status thanks to its large celebrity population and the incredible beauty of its 27 miles of coastal mountains, pristine coves, wide sweeps of golden sand and epic waves. Despite its star quotient, the best way to appreciate

DON'T MISS

SOUTH BAY BEACHES

When you've had all the Hollywood ambition, artsy pretension, velvet ropes and mind-numbing traffic you can take, head south of the airport, where this string of money-eyed beach towns will soothe that mess from your psyche in one surf- and volleyball-infused sunset.

It all starts with **Manhattan Beach**, just 15 minutes from LAX. A bastion of surf music and the birthplace of beach volleyball, Manhattan Beach has also gone chic. Its downtown area along Manhattan Beach Blvd has seen an explosion of trendy restaurants, boutiques and hotels. Yet, even with this Hollywood-ification, it remains a serene seaside enclave with prime surf on either side of the pier.

To its south, **Hermosa Beach** is indeed *muy hermosa* (Spanish for 'very beautiful') – long, flat and dotted with permanent volleyball nets – and probably the funkiest of the three towns. Next up, **Redondo Beach** is a working-class beach town and the most culturally diverse of the three.

As the coast winds to the south end of Santa Monica Bay you can follow it uphill to the **Palos Verdes Peninsula**. It's a revelation of sand-swept silver bays and the shadows of Catalina Island whispering through a fog rising from cold Pacific blue. Long, elegant and perfectly manicured lawns front sprawling mansions, and to the north, south and east there's nothing but layered jade hills forming the headland that cradles the bay's southernmost reach, before it turns a corner east toward Long Beach.

Malibu is through its natural assets, so grab your sunscreen and a towel and head to the beach, or lace up for an idyllic hike.

Closer in to LA, Pacific Palisades is a well-to-do bedroom community with a couple of star-power sites of its own.

★El Matador State Beach — BEACH

(☎818-880-0363; www.parks.ca.gov; 32215 Pacific Coast Hwy, Malibu; P) At arguably Malibu's most stunning beach (known as the place swimsuit-model photo shoots take place), you park on the bluffs and stroll down a trail to sandstone rock towers that rise from emerald coves. Sunbathers stroll through the tides, and dolphins breech the surface beyond the waves. It's been impacted by coastal erosion, but you can still find a sliver of dry sand tucked against the bluffs.

★Getty Villa — MUSEUM

(☎310-430-7300; www.getty.edu; 17985 Pacific Coast Hwy, Pacific Palisades; ⏰10am-5pm Wed-Mon; P 👪; 🚌Metro Line 534 to Coastline Dr) FREE Stunningly perched on an ocean-view hillside, this museum in a replica 1st-century Roman villa is an exquisite, 64-acre showcase for Greek, Roman and Etruscan antiquities. Dating back 7000 years, they were amassed by oil tycoon J Paul Getty. Galleries, peristyles, courtyards and lushly landscaped gardens ensconce all manner of friezes, busts and mosaics, along with millennia-old cut, blown and colored glass and brain-bending geometric configurations in the Hall of Colored Marbles. Other highlights include the Pompeii fountain and Temple of Herakles.

★Mishe Mokwa Trail & Sandstone Peak — HIKING

(www.nps.gov/samo; 12896 Yerba Buena Rd, Malibu) On warm spring mornings, when the snowy blue ceonothus perfumes the air with honeysuckle, there's no better place to be than this 6-mile loop trail beyond the end of Malibu. It winds through a red-rock canyon dotted with climbers, into the oak oasis at **Split Rock** and up to Mt Allen (aka Sandstone Peak), the tallest peak in the Santa Monica Mountains.

Santa Monica

Santa Monica is LA's cute, alluring, hippie-chic little sister, its karmic counterbalance and, to many, its salvation. Here, real-life Lebowskis sip white Russians next to martini-swilling Hollywood producers, celebrity chefs dine at family-owned taquerias, and soccer moms and career bachelors shop at abundant farmers markets.

Once the very end of the mythical Route 66, and still a tourist love affair, the **Santa Monica Pier** (Map p402; ☎310-458-8901; www.santamonicapier.org; 👪) dates back to 1908. It's stocked with rides and arcade games, blessed with spectacular views, and is the city's most compelling landmark. After a stroll on the pier, hit the **beach** (Map p402; ☎310-458-

West Hollywood & Mid-City

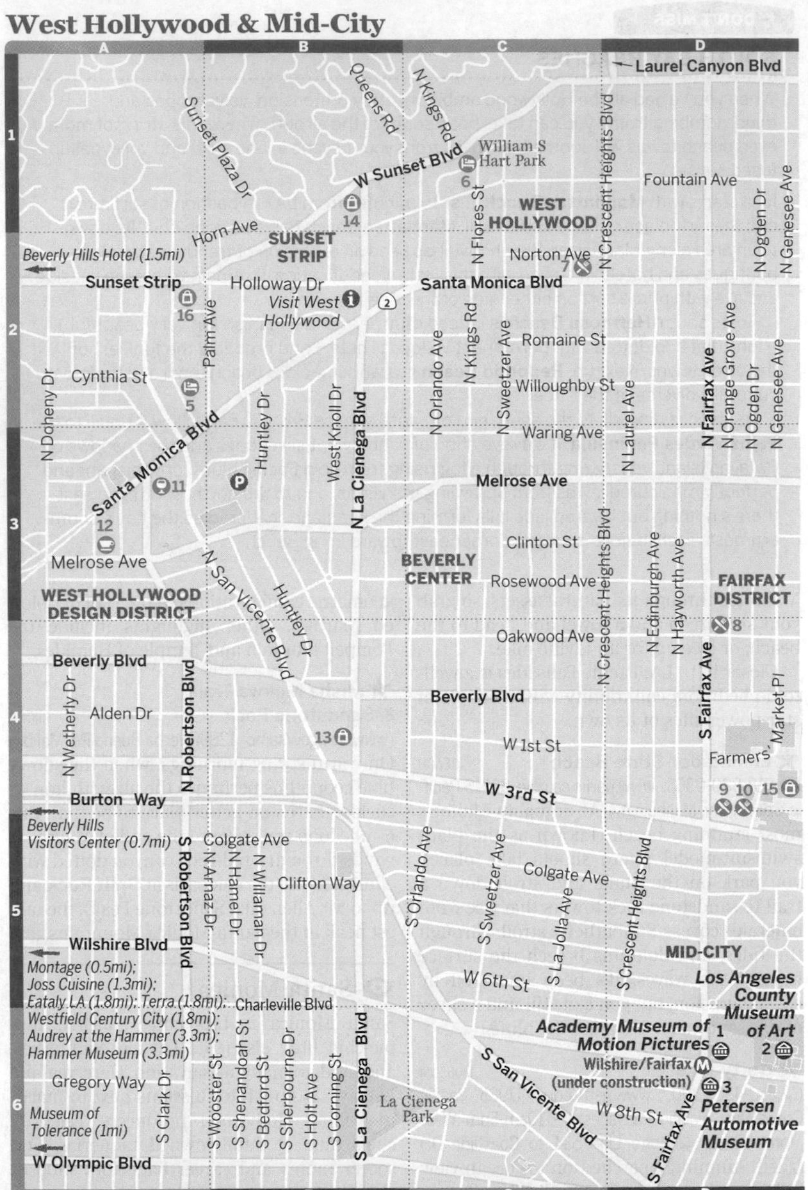

8411; www.smgov.net/portals/beach; 🚌 Big Blue Bus 1). We like the stretch just north of Ocean Park Blvd. Or rent a bike or some skates from **Perry's Café** (Map p402; ☎310-939-0000; www.perryscafe.com; Ocean Front Walk; per hour/day from $10/35, boogie boards $7/20, surfboards $15/45; ⏰9am-7:30pm Mon-Fri, 8:30am-7:30pm Sat & Sun) and explore the 22-mile **South Bay Bicycle Trail** (Map p402; ⏰sunrise-sunset; 👪).

👁 Venice

If you were born too late, and have always been a little jealous of the hippie heyday,

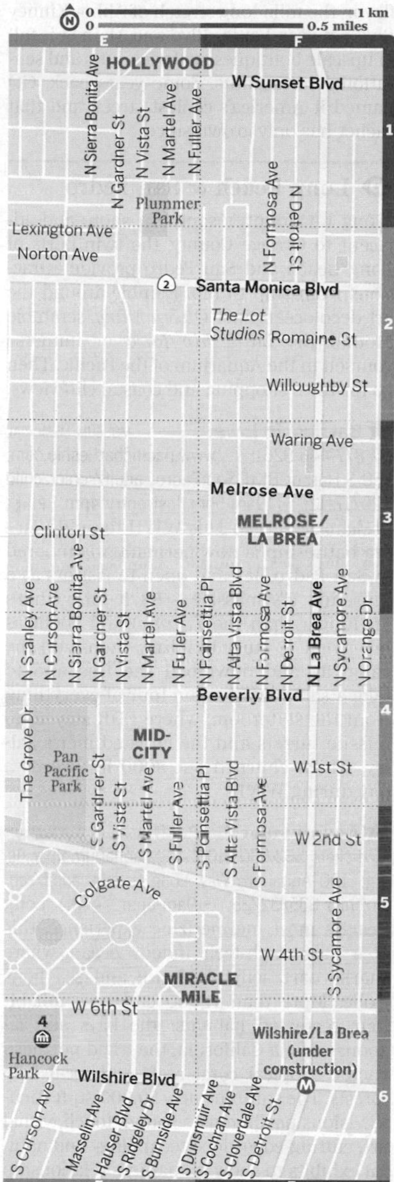

West Hollywood & Mid-City

Top Sights

1 Academy Museum of Motion Pictures D6
2 Los Angeles County Museum of Art.. D6
3 Petersen Automotive Museum D6

Sights

4 La Brea Tar Pits & Museum E6

Sleeping

5 Petit Ermitage A2
6 Sunset Tower Hotel C1

Eating

7 Connie & Ted's C2
8 Jon & Vinny's D4
9 Original Farmers Market D4
10 Pampas Grill D4

Drinking & Nightlife

11 Abbey A3
12 Verve Coffee Roasters A3

Shopping

13 Beverly Center B4
14 Fred Segal B1
15 Grove D4
16 Mystery Pier Books A2

come down to the Boardwalk and inhale a (not just) incense-scented whiff of Venice, a boho beach town and longtime haven for artists, New Agers, road-weary tramps, freaks and free spirits.

★ **Venice Boardwalk** WATERFRONT

(Ocean Front Walk; Map p402; Venice Pier to Rose Ave) Life in Venice moves to a different rhythm and nowhere more so than on the famous Venice Boardwalk, officially known as Ocean Front Walk. It's a freak show, a human zoo and a wacky carnival alive with Hula-Hoop magicians, old-timey jazz combos, solo distorted garage rockers and artists (good and bad) – as far as LA experiences go, it's a must.

★ **Venice Skatepark** SKATEBOARDING

(Map p402; www.veniceskatepark.com; 1500 Ocean Front Walk; dawn-dusk; Metro line 733, Big Blue Bus Line 1) Long the destination of local skate punks, the concrete at this skate park has now been molded and steel-fringed into 17,000 sq ft of vert, tranny and street terrain with unbroken ocean views. The old-school-style skate run and the world-class pool are most popular for high flyers and gawking spectators. Great photo ops, especially as the sun sets.

★ **Abbot Kinney Boulevard** AREA

(Map p402; Big Blue Bus Line 18) Abbot Kinney, who founded Venice in the early 1900s, would probably be delighted to find that one of Venice's best-loved streets bears his name. Sort of a seaside Melrose with a Venetian

flavor, the mile-long stretch of Abbot Kinney Blvd between Venice Blvd and Main St is full of upscale boutiques, galleries, lofts and sensational restaurants. Some years back, GQ named it America's coolest street, and that cachet has only grown since.

Long Beach & San Pedro

Along LA County's southern shore and adjacent to Orange County, the twin ports of Long Beach and San Pedro provide attractions from ship to hip. Ramble around the art deco ocean liner *Queen Mary,* scramble around the *Battleship Iowa* or immerse yourself in the Aquarium of the Pacific. Then go for retro shopping and coastal cliff views.

★Battleship Iowa MUSEUM, MEMORIAL
(☎877-446-9261; www.pacificbattleship.com; 250 S Harbor Blvd, San Pedro; adult/senior/child $20/17/12; ⏰10am-5pm, last entry 4pm; P 👪; 🚌Metro Silver Line) This WWII to Cold War–era battleship is now permanently moored in San Pedro Bay and open to visitors as a museum. It's massive – 887ft long (that's 5ft longer than the *Titanic*) and about as tall as an 18-story building. Step onto the gangway and download the free app to take a self-guided audio tour of everything from the stateroom, where FDR stayed, to missile turrets and the enlisted men's galley, which churned out 8000 hot meals a day during WWII.

★Aquarium of the Pacific AQUARIUM
(☎tickets 562-590-3100; www.aquariumofpacific.org; 100 Aquarium Way, Long Beach; adult/senior/child $35/32/25; ⏰9am-6pm; P 👪) Long Beach's most mesmerizing experience, this is a vast, high-tech indoor ocean where sharks dart, jellyfish dance and sea lions frolic. More than 11,000 creatures inhabit four recreated habitats: the bays and lagoons of Baja California, the frigid northern Pacific, tropical coral reefs and local kelp forests. The stunning new 29,000-sq-ft Pacific Visions pavilion uses sound, touch, visual art, cutting-edge video technology and natural exhibits to show humanity's relationship with the ocean and sustainability.

★Museum of Latin American Art MUSEUM
(☎562-437-1689; www.molaa.org; 628 Alamitos Ave, Long Beach; adult/senior & student/child Wed-Sat $10/7/free, Sun free; ⏰11am-5pm Wed & Fri-Sun, 11am-9pm Thu; P) This gem of a museum is the only one in the US to present art

Santa Monica & Venice Beach

Top Sights
1 Abbot Kinney Boulevard ... B6
2 Santa Monica Pier ... A3
3 Venice Boardwalk ... A6

Sights
4 Palisades Park ... A1
5 Santa Monica State Beach ... A2

Activities, Courses & Tours
6 Gold's Gym ... B5
7 Perry's Café & Rentals ... A2
8 South Bay Bicycle Trail ... A3
9 Venice Skatepark ... A6

Sleeping
10 HI Los Angeles – Santa Monica ... A2
11 Hotel Erwin ... A6
12 Samesun ... A6
13 Shutters on the Beach ... A3

Eating
14 Cassia ... B2
15 Gjelina ... B7
16 Rose ... B5
17 Santa Monica Farmers Markets ... B2

Drinking & Nightlife
18 Basement Tavern ... B4
19 Bungalow ... A2
High ... (see 11)

Shopping
20 Aviator Nation ... B6
21 Waraku ... B6

created since 1945 in Latin America and in Latino communities in the US through temporary exhibits. Recent thought-provoking shows included Caribbean art, Day of the Dead art, tattoo art and works by LA's own Frank Romero and Robert Graham, the Mexico City–born Angeleno whose monumental sculptures include the image of Mary at the **Cathedral of Our Lady of the Angels** (Map p390; ☎213-680-5200; www.olacathedral.org; 555 W Temple St, Downtown; ⏰6:30am-6pm Mon-Fri, 9am-6pm Sat, 7am-6pm Sun, Mass 7am & 12:10pm Mon-Fri, 8am, 10am & 12:30pm Sun; P; M B/D Lines to Civic Center/Grand Park).

Exposition Park & South Los Angeles

The massive area south of the I-10 Fwy and straddling the I-110 Fwy comprises dozens of neighborhoods collectively called South LA. On its north end are Exposition Park, home to some of LA's most visited natural history and science museums, and the University of Southern California (USC). A couple miles west, Leimert Park is the thriving, beating heart of LA's African American community, and east of the 110 is Watts, known for Watts Towers, a masterpiece of folk art.

Expect increased focus on South LA as a new Metro light-rail line opens along Crenshaw Blvd in 2021.

★ Watts Towers — LANDMARK

(☎213-847-4646; www.wattstowers.org; 1761-1765 E 107th St, Watts; ⏰tours 11am-3pm Thu & Fri, 10:30am-3pm Sat, noon-3pm Sun; P; M A Line to 103rd St) The three 'Gothic' spires of the fabulous Watts Towers rank among the world's greatest monuments of folk art. In 1921 Italian immigrant Simon Rodia set out to 'make something big' and then spent 33 years cobbling together this whimsical free-form sculpture from concrete, steel and a motley assortment of found objects: green 7Up bottles to seashells, tiles, rocks and pottery.

California Science Center — MUSEUM

(☎film schedule 213-744-2019, info 323-724-3623; www.californiasciencecenter.org; 700 Exposition Park Dr, Exposition Park; IMAX movie adult/student/senior/child $8.95/7.95/7.95/6.75; ⏰10am-5pm; 👪) FREE Top billing at the Science Center goes to the Space Shuttle *Endeavour*, one of only four space shuttles nationwide. But there's plenty else to see at this large, multistory, multimedia museum filled with buttons to push, lights to switch on and knobs to pull. That and a simulated earthquake bring out the kid in everyone. Admission is free, but special exhibits, experiences and IMAX movies cost extra.

Natural History Museum of Los Angeles — MUSEUM

(☎213-763-3466; www.nhm.org; 900 Exposition Blvd, Exposition Park; adult/student/senior/child $15/12/12/7; ⏰9:30am-5pm; P 👪; M E Line to Expo/Vermont) Dinos to diamonds, bears to beetles, hissing roaches to African elephants – this museum will take you around the world and back, through millions of years in time. It's all housed in a beautiful 1913 Spanish Renaissance–style building that stood in for Columbia University in the first Tobey Maguire *Spider-Man* movie – yup, this was where Peter Parker was bitten by the radioactive arachnid. There's enough to see here to fill several hours.

LA County residents get free entry 3pm to 5pm Monday to Friday.

Pasadena & the San Gabriel Valley

One could argue that there's more blue-blood, meat-eating, robust Americana in Pasadena than in all other LA neighborhoods combined. Here you'll find a community with a preppy old soul, a historical perspective, an appreciation for art and jazz, a progressive undercurrent and two of the US's top universities. The annual **Tournament of Roses Parade** (www.tournamentofroses.com; viewing stands from $80, sidewalk viewing free; Jan 1) and **Rose Bowl** (626-577-3100; www.rosebowlstadium.com; 1001 Rose Bowl Dr, Pasadena) football game may have given Pasadena its long-lasting fame, but it's the spirit of this genteel city and its location beneath the lofty San Gabriel Mountains that make it a charming and attractive place to visit year-round.

Head just east and southeast, further into the San Gabriel Valley, and a huge influx of immigrants from Asia, principally China, is changing the demographics and bringing a new cultural energy.

★Huntington Library, Art Museum & Botanical Gardens — MUSEUM, GARDEN

(626-405-2100; www.huntington.org; 1151 Oxford Rd, San Marino; adult weekday/weekend & holidays $25/29, student & senior $21/24, youth 4-11yr $13; 10am-5pm Wed-Mon; P) One of the most delightful, inspirational spots in LA, the century-old Huntington is rightly a highlight of any trip to California, thanks to a world-class mix of art, literary history and over 120 acres of themed gardens (any one of which would be worth a visit on its own), all set amid stately grounds. There's so much to see and do that it's hard to know where to begin; allow three to four hours for even a basic visit.

The first Thursday of each month is free with advance ticket.

Norton Simon Museum — MUSEUM

(626-449-6840; www.nortonsimon.org; 411 W Colorado Blvd, Pasadena; adult/senior/student/child $15/12/free/free; noon-5pm Mon, Wed & Thu, 11am-8pm Fri & Sat, 11am-5pm Sun; P) Rodin's *The Burghers of Calais* standing guard by the entrance is only a mind-teasing overture to the full symphony of art in store at this exquisite museum. Norton Simon (1907–93) was an entrepreneur with a Midas touch and a passion for art who parlayed his millions into an admirable collection of Western art and Asian sculpture. Meaty captions really help tell each piece's story.

San Gabriel Mission — LANDMARK

(626-457-3035; www.sangabrielmission.org; 428 S Mission Dr, San Gabriel; adult/child 6-17yr $6/3; 9am-4:30pm Tue-Sat, 10am-4pm Sun; P 👪) In 1771 Spanish *padres* founded the Mission San Gabriel Arcángel, the fourth in the chain of 21 missions in California and one of the prettiest and best preserved. Its church boasts Spanish Moorish flourishes, a copper baptismal font, carved statues of saints and a 1790 altar made in Mexico City. Ten years later, settlers embarked from here to found a village called El Pueblo de Nuestra Señora la Reina de los Ángeles (p392), which we now call LA.

Tours

★Glitterati Tours — BUS

(310-720-3809; https://glitteratitours.com; tours per hour 1-2/3-4/5-7 people $149/179/209; 👪) This highly regarded outfit offers a string of engaging private tours, covering numerous pockets of LA, from celeb-studded Beverly Hills and Hollywood, to Downtown and the beach communities of Santa Monica, Malibu and Venice. Tours are conducted in luxury SUVs, complete with multimedia iPad presentations, wi-fi and snacks.

★Esotouric — BUS

(www.esotouric.com; tours $64) Discover LA's lurid and fascinating underbelly on these offbeat, insightful and entertaining walking and bus tours themed around famous crime sites (Black Dahlia, anyone?), film locations, literary lions including Chandler and Bukowski, and more.

★Los Angeles Conservancy — WALKING

(213-623-2489; www.laconservancy.org; adult/child $15/10; 👪) Downtown LA's intriguing historical and architectural gems – from an art deco penthouse to a beaux arts ballroom and dazzling silent-movie theater – are revealed on this nonprofit group's 1¾- to 2¾-hour walking tours. To see some of LA's grand historic movie theaters from the inside, the conservancy also offers an annual Last Remaining Seats season, screening classic films in gilded movie palaces.

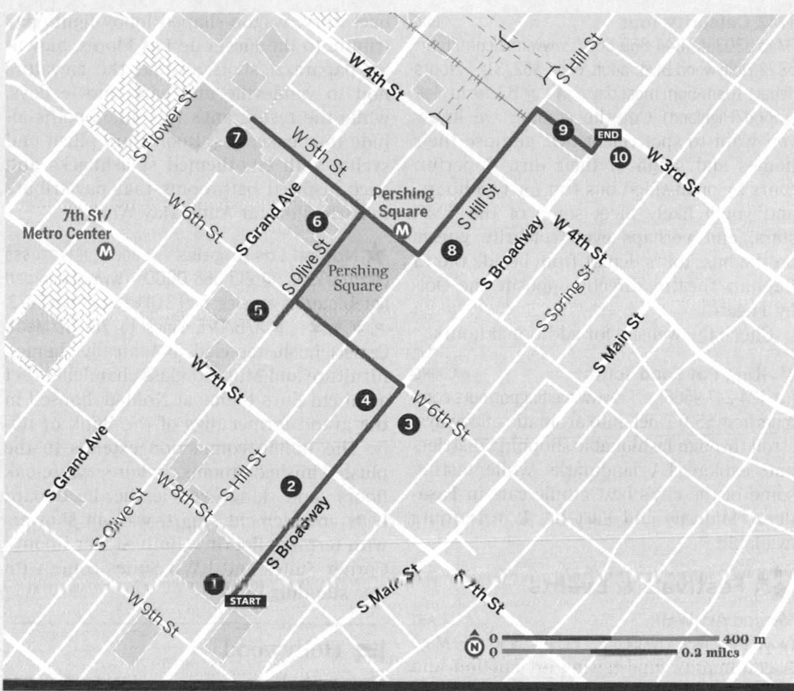

City Walk Downtown Revealed

START EASTERN COLUMBIA BUILDING
END BRADBURY BUILDING
LENGTH 1.5 MILES; TWO TO THREE HOURS

Start your saunter on 9th St and Broadway. Dominating the intersection is the turquoise-and-gold **1 Eastern Columbia Building** (Map p390; www.easterncolumbiahoa.com; 849 S Broadway; M B/D Lines to Pershing Sq), an art deco beauty with a spectacular vestibule.

Head north on Broadway through the old theater district. Its mishmash of beaux-arts architecture, retro marquees, discount jewelers and trendy new enterprises sums up Downtown's ongoing renaissance. Take note of the **2 State Theatre** (Map p390; 703 S Broadway), **3 Palace Theatre** (Map p390; ☎213-629-2939; www.facebook.com/palace.theatre.la; 630 S Broadway) and **4 Los Angeles Theatre** (Map p390; ☎213-629-2939; www.losangelestheatre.com; 615 S Broadway).

Turn left onto 6th St, then left onto Olive St to marvel at the art deco lobby forecourt of the **5 James Oviatt Building** (Map p390; 617 S Olive S). Backtrack and cross 5th St to reach the **6 Millennium Biltmore Hotel** (Map p390; ☎213-624-1011; www.thebiltmore.com; 506 S Grand Ave); its Historic Corridor harbors a fascinating photograph of the 1937 Academy Awards.

Cross Grand Ave and slip inside the **7 Los Angeles Central Library** (Map p390; ☎213-228-7000; www.lapl.org/branches/central-library; 630 W 5th St), its magnificent, 2nd-floor rotunda framed by large-scale murals dating from 1933. The 48 light bulbs of its zodiac chandelier represent the number of US states upon its completion in 1926.

Southeast, on the corner of 5th and Hill, admire the handsome **8 Pershing Square Building**, topped by panoramic rooftop bar Perch, then head northeast on Hill to **9 Grand Central Market** (p410), once home to Frank Lloyd Wright's LA office. Make your way through its sea of vendors to reach Broadway and the breathtaking atrium of the **10 Bradbury Building** (Map p390; www.laconservancy.org/locations/bradbury-building; 304 S Broadway; ⏲lobby 7am-6pm Mon-Fri, 9am-5pm Sat & Sun; M B/D Lines to Pershing Sq).

TMZ Celebrity Tour BUS
(Map p393; 844-869-8687; www.tmz.com/tour; 6822 Hollywood Blvd; adult/child $52/31; tours depart 10am-5pm most days; ; B Line to Hollywood/Highland) Cut the shame; we know you want to spot celebrities, glimpse their homes and laugh at their dirt. Superfun tours by open-sided bus run for two hours, and you'll likely meet some of the TMZ stars…and perhaps even celebrity guests on the bus. Tours depart from beside the El Capitan Theatre, directly opposite the Dolby Theatre.

Check the website for additional hours.

Melting Pot Food Tours WALKING
(424-247-9666; www.meltingpottours.com; tours from $50) Duck into aromatic alleyways, stroll through fashionable shopping districts and explore LA landmarks while tasting some of the city's best ethnic eats in Pasadena, Mid-City and East LA. Private tours available.

Festivals & Events

Venice Art Walk ART
(www.theveniceartwalk.org; tickets $50; May) A community fund-raising art auction and studio tour in Venice, with entry into dozens of local studios featuring hundreds of artworks to bid for or simply admire.

Off the 405 MUSIC
(www.getty.edu; May-Sep) From May to September, the Getty Center courtyard fills with evening crowds for a collision of art, top-notch live music and beat-pumping DJ sets.

Sleeping

From rock-and-roll Downtown digs to fabled Hollywood hideaways and beachside escapes, LA serves up a dizzying array of slumber options. The key is to plan well ahead. Do your research and find out which neighborhood is most convenient for your plans and best appeals to your style and interests. Trawl the internet for deals, and consider visiting between January and April, when room rates and occupancy are usually at their lowest (Oscars week aside).

Downtown Los Angeles

Hotel Indigo HOTEL $$
(Map p390; 877-270-1392; www.ihg.com; 899 Francisco St; d from $190; P; A/B/D/E Lines to 7th St/Metro Center) This 350-room property celebrates Downtown's colorful backstory: wagon-shaped lobby lights pay tribute to the Fiesta de Las Flores, blown-up paparazzi shots around the elevators nod to vaudeville and early movie days, while the restaurant's tube-like booths allude to speakeasies. Rooms are plush and svelte, with city-themed splashbacks and deco-inspired bathrooms that pay tribute to early film star Anna May Wong.

★**NoMad Los Angeles** BOUTIQUE HOTEL $$$
(Map p390; 213-358-0000; www.thenomadhotel.com/los-angeles; 649 S Olive St; r from $272; P; A/B/D/E Lines to 7th St/Metro Center) Lush, tasseled, botanically themed furniture and Murano-glass chandeliers set a chi chi Euro theme at NoMad, housed in the grand former digs of the Bank of Italy. The Italian connection extends to the plush, hushed rooms, where white-oak floors and king-size, leather-headboard beds complement smart, walk-in showers with terrazzo flooring. Both Atelier Rooms, Corner Suites and RWB Suites come with free standing tubs.

Hollywood

Mama Shelter BOUTIQUE HOTEL $$
(Map p393; 323-785-6666; www.mamashelter.com; 6500 Selma Ave; r from $189; P@; B Line to Hollywood/Vine) Hip, affordable Mama Shelter keeps things playful with its lobby gumball machines and foosball table. Standard rooms are small but cool, with quality, king-size beds and linen, and subway-tiled bathrooms with decent-size showers. Quirky in-room touches include movie scripts and *Star Wars*–themed lights, with tech specs including Apple TVs. The **rooftop bar** (Map p393; 323-785-6600; www.mamashelter.com/en/los-angeles/restaurants/rooftop; noon-1am Mon-Thu, 11am-2pm Fri & Sat, 11am-1am Sun) offers killer views of LA.

★**Hollywood Roosevelt** HISTORIC HOTEL $$$
(Map p393; 323-856-1970; www.thehollywoodroosevelt.com; 7000 Hollywood Blvd; d from $318; P@; B Line to Hollywood/Highland) At the heart of the action, the Roosevelt heaves with Hollywood lore: Shirley Temple learned to tap dance on the stairs off the lobby, Marilyn Monroe shot her first print ad by the pool (later decorated by artist David Hockney) and it's said that the ghost of actor Montgomery Clift can still be heard playing the bugle.

Silver Lake & Echo Park

★Silver Lake Pool & Inn BOUTIQUE HOTEL **$$**
(Map p398; 323-486-7225; www.palisociety.com/hotels/silverlake; 4141 Santa Monica Blvd, Silver Lake; r from $235; P ❄ ☎ ≋; Metro Lines 2, 4, 302, 704) Channeling Palm Springs, this re-imagined 1980s motel is the slumber pad Silver Lake deserves. Effortlessly hip, chilled and awash in SoCal light, its design credentials include locally produced art and bright, crisp rooms adorned with low-slung leather-and-timber chairs, bespoke terrazzo nightstands and Nespresso coffee machines. Cacti flank the sun-drenched pool, with a simple, solid list of coastal-Italian plates at the slinky, Modernist trattoria-bar.

West Hollywood & Mid-City

Petit Ermitage BOUTIQUE HOTEL **$$$**
(Map p400; 310-854-1114; www.petitermitage.com; 8822 Cynthia St, West Hollywood; ste from $256; P ❄ @ ☎ ≋; Metro Lines 2, 30, 105, 330) Turkish rugs, antiques and an impressive art collection set apart this secret, boho-chic retreat. No two of its sultry 79 suites are the same, but all feature Venetian-style plaster walls, eclectic curios and luxurious linens. Some even come with wet bar and kitchenette. At the heart of the action is the Riviera-spirited, panoramic rooftop, complete with a small, heated saltwater pool and flawless cocktails.

★Sunset Tower Hotel HISTORIC HOTEL **$$$**
(Map p400; 323-654-7100; www.sunsettowerhotel.com; 8358 W Sunset Blvd, West Hollywood; r from $416; P @ ☎ ≋; Metro Line 2) Art deco veteran Sunset Tower evokes the romance of Hollywood's Golden Age, when Errol Flynn, Truman Capote and Marilyn Monroe resided here. Still a good spot for celebrity spotting, its chi chi, pastel-hued rooms come with floor-to-ceiling windows, good work desks and bathrooms clad in playful, Cali-inspired gold wallpaper by pop artist Donald Robertson.

Beverly Hills, Bel Air, Brentwood & Westwood

★Montage LUXURY HOTEL **$$$**
(855-691-1162; www.montagebeverlyhills.com; 225 N Cañon Dr, Beverly Hills; r/ste from $595/1075; P @ ☎ ≋; Metro Lines 14, 37) Drawing on-point eye candy and serious wealth, the 201-room Montage balances elegance with warmth and affability. Models and moguls lunch by the gorgeous rooftop pool, while the property's sprawling five-star spa is a Moroccan-inspired marvel, with both single-sex and unisex plunge pools. Rooms are classically styled, with custom Sealy mattresses, dual marble basins, spacious showers and deep-soaking tubs.

Beverly Hills Hotel LUXURY HOTEL **$$$**
(310-276-2251; www.dorchestercollection.com; 9641 Sunset Blvd, Beverly Hills; r/bungalows from $820/1339; P ❄ @ ☎ ≋; Metro Lines 2, 302) The revered 'Pink Palace' packs more Hollywood lore than any other hotel in town. Slumber in one of 208 elegantly appointed hotel rooms or – if money isn't an issue – live like the stars in one of 23 discreet, self-contained bungalows. Interiors in the latter are inspired by the stars who've stayed there, from Liz Taylor in number 5 to Frank Sinatra in 22.

Malibu & Pacific Palisades

★Malibu Beach Inn INN **$$$**
(310-651-7777; www.malibubeachinn.com; 22878 Pacific Coast Hwy, Malibu; r from $595; P ⊖ ❄ ☎; Metro Line 534) This intimate, adult-oriented hacienda was recently given a four-star upgrade by Waldo Hernandez, a celebrity designer who has done work for the likes of the former Brangelina. The look is ocean-friendly grays and blues, and you might just find yourself face-to-face with well-curated art pieces by the likes of Jasper Johns, Robert Indiana and Andy Warhol.

Santa Monica

HI Los Angeles – Santa Monica HOSTEL **$**
(Map p402; 310-393-9913; www.hilosangeles.org; 1436 2nd St; dm $30-50, r with shared bath $130-150, with private bath $180-220; ⊖ ❄ @ ☎; M E Line to Downtown Santa Monica) Near the beach and promenade, this hostel has an enviable location and modernized facilities that rival properties charging much more. Its approximately 275 beds in single-sex dorms are clean and safe, private rooms are decorated with hipster chic, and public spaces (courtyard, library, TV room, dining room, communal kitchen) let you lounge and surf.

★Shutters on the Beach HOTEL **$$$**
(Map p402; 310-458-0030; www.shuttersonthebeach.com; 1 Pico Blvd; r $708; P @ ☎;

Where to Stay in Los Angeles

Malibu & Pacific Palisades
27 miles of ocean vistas with high celebrity quotient and hills for hiking.

Best For Luxury, escapists, beachgoers

Transport Ride-hail recommended to DTLA

Price Mid-range to top end

West Hollywood & Mid-City
Celeb-spangled rstaurants and gay bars in WeHo, must-see museums and cult-status shopping in Mid-City.

Best For Musum lovers, shoppers, revelers, LGBT+

Transport Ride-hail recommended to DTLA

Price Mostly midrange to top end

Hollywood
Historical movie-industry landmarks and lots of buzz; packed with tourists and tourist traps.

Best For Families and showbiz fans

Transport DTLA 20 minutes by metro

Price Mosztly midrange to top end

Santa Monica
Big-ticket sights; vibrant nightlife; top hotels, restaurants and farmers' markets, though expensive and touristy.

Best For Weekenders, luxury travelers, backpackers, foodies

Transport DTLA 50 minutes by metro

Price Mostly top end

Beverly Hills, Bel Air, Brentwood & Westwood
Fabled home of the rich and famous, with luze dining, shopping and Hollywood-lore hotels; can feel pretentious and beige.

Best For Well-heeled travelers, star spotters

Transport Ride-hail recommended to DTLA

Price Mostly top end

Venice, Marina Del Rey & Playa Del Rey
Alternative meets uber-hip by the ocean; top restaurants; clever boutiques; crowded on summer weekends; significant homeless population.

Best For Beach people, shoppers, hipsters

Transport Ride-hail recommended to DTLA

Price Midrange to top end

South Bay Beaches
Beach towns with endless summer vibes; piers, surf, volleyball and yuppies; downtown bars and clubs.

Best For Summer vacay, compact nightlife districts

Transport Ride-hail recommended to DTLA

Price Midrange to top end

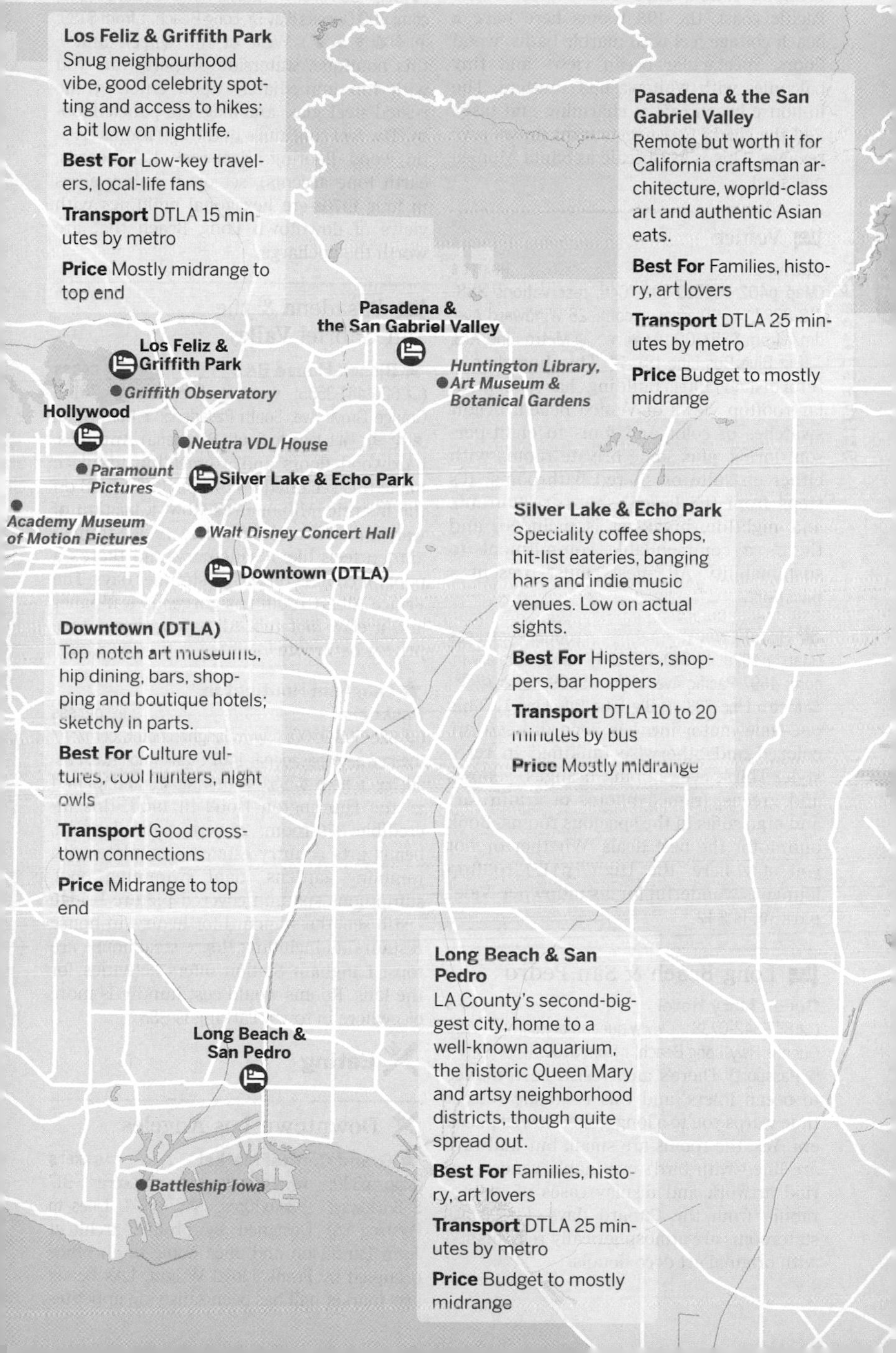

Los Feliz & Griffith Park
Snug neighbourhood vibe, good celebrity spotting and access to hikes; a bit low on nightlife.

Best For Low-key travelers, local-life fans

Transport DTLA 15 minutes by metro

Price Mostly midrange to top end

Pasadena & the San Gabriel Valley
Remote but worth it for California craftsman architecture, woprld-class art and authentic Asian eats.

Best For Families, history, art lovers

Transport DTLA 25 minutes by metro

Price Budget to mostly midrange

Silver Lake & Echo Park
Speciality coffee shops, hit-list eateries, banging bars and indie music venues. Low on actual sights.

Best For Hipsters, shoppers, bar hoppers

Transport DTLA 10 to 20 minutes by bus

Price Mostly midrange

Downtown (DTLA)
Top notch art museums, hip dining, bars, shopping and boutique hotels; sketchy in parts.

Best For Culture vultures, cool hunters, night owls

Transport Good cross-town connections

Price Midrange to top end

Long Beach & San Pedro
LA County's second-biggest city, home to a well-known aquarium, the historic Queen Mary and artsy neighborhood districts, though quite spread out.

Best For Families, history, art lovers

Transport DTLA 25 minutes by metro

Price Budget to mostly midrange

(Metro Line 733, Big Blue Bus Lines 1, 7) Bringing classic Cape Cod charm to the Pacific coast, the 198 rooms here have a beach-cottage feel with marble baths, wood floors, spectacular ocean views and tiny balconies with whitewashed shutters. The in-house beach cafe is charming and tasty, and the chichi Coast restaurant draws rave reviews. This is as upscale as Santa Monica nests get.

Venice

Samesun HOSTEL $
(Map p402; 310-399-7649, reservations 888-718-8287; www.samesun.com; 25 Windward Ave; dm/r from $35/100; ; Metro Line 733, Big Blue Bus Line 18) This hostel in a refurbished 1904 building has spectacular rooftop views of Venice Beach, bright swatches of color and four- to eight-person dorms, plus some private rooms with either en suite or shared bathrooms. It's steps from the beach, shops, restaurants and nightlife, breakfast is included, and there's a commendable commitment to sustainability. All guests must present a passport.

★**Hotel Erwin** BOUTIQUE HOTEL $$$
(Map p402; 310-452-1111; www.hotelerwin.com; 1697 Pacific Ave; r from $269; ; Metro Line 733, Big Blue Bus Line 1) This one-time motor inn has been dressed up, colored and otherwise funkified in retro style. Think eye-popping oranges, yellows and greens, framed photos of graffiti art and ergo sofas in the spacious rooms. Book online for the best deals. Whether or not you stay here, the High (p417) rooftop lounge is wonderful for a sundowner. Valet parking is $42.

Long Beach & San Pedro

Queen Mary Hotel SHIP $
(877-342-0738; www.queenmary.com; 1126 Queens Hwy, Long Beach; r from $102; ; Passport) There's an irresistible romance to ocean liners, and this nostalgic retreat time warps you to a long-gone, slower-paced era. Yes, the rooms are small, but hallways are lined with bird's-eye maple veneer, period artwork and display cases of memorabilia from the Cunard days. First-class staterooms are atmospherically refurbished with original art deco details.

★**Hotel Maya** BOUTIQUE HOTEL $$
(562-435-7676; https://hotelmayalongbeach.com; 700 Queens Way Dr, Long Beach; r from $189;) West of the *Queen Mary*, this boutique, waterside property hits you with hip immediately upon entering the rusted-steel, glass and magenta-paneled lobby. The feel continues in the 199 rooms (rustic wood flooring, river-rock headboards, earth tone accents), set on 11 palmy acres in four 1970s-era hexagonal buildings with views of downtown Long Beach that are worth the upcharge.

Pasadena & the San Gabriel Valley

★**Bissell House B&B** B&B $$
(626-441-3535; www.bissellhouse.com; 201 S Orange Grove Ave, South Pasadena; r from $199; ; L Line to South Pasadena) Antiques, hardwood floors and a crackling fireplace make this secluded Victorian (1887) B&B on the historic 'Millionaire's Row' a bastion of warmth and romance. The hedge-framed garden feels like a sanctuary, and there's a pool for cooling off on hot summer days. The Prince Albert room has gorgeous wallpaper and a claw-foot tub. All seven rooms have private bathrooms.

★**Langham Huntington Pasadena** RESORT $$$
(626-568-3900; www.langhamhotels.com/en/the-langham/pasadena; 1401 S Oak Knoll Ave, Pasadena; r from $295;) Opened as the Huntington Hotel in 1906, this incredible 379-room, 23-acre, palm-dappled, beaux arts country estate – complete with rambling gardens, giant swimming pool, sumptuous spa and covered picture bridge – still sets the standard for luxury. In-house restaurants including Royce steakhouse are tops. Langham Station offers activities for the kids. Rooms would cost hundreds more elsewhere in town. Parking is $35.

Eating

Downtown Los Angeles

★**Grand Central Market** MARKET $
(Map p390; www.grandcentralmarket.com; 317 S Broadway; 8am-10pm; ; B/D Lines to Pershing Sq) Designed by prolific architect John Parkinson and once home to an office occupied by Frank Lloyd Wright, LA's beaux arts market hall has been satisfying appetites

since 1917 and today is DTLA's gourmet mecca. Lose yourself in its bustle of neon signs, stalls and counters, peddling everything from fresh produce and nuts, to sizzling Thai street food, hipster breakfasts, modern deli classics, artisanal pasta and specialty coffee.

★M.Georgina CALIFORNIAN $$$
(☎213-334-4113; www.mgeorgina.com; B1 Suite 114, 777 S Alameda St, Row DTLA; mains $22-34; ⏲5-9pm Tue-Thu, 5-10pm Fri & Sat, 3-9pm Sun; P; Metro Lines 60, 62, 760) San Francisco's Michelin-starred Melissa Perello is the talent behind this outstanding eatery-bar, part of the Row DTLA complex. Modern, Italo-influenced menus rotate around impeccable produce and the kitchen's wood-burning oven, translated into textured revelations such as semolina pasta with gorgonzola dolce, pickled treviso and candied walnuts, and wood-baked black cod with creamed escarole. Also worth trying: the coal-baked potato.

Bestia ITALIAN $$$
(☎213-514-5724; https://bestiala.com; 2121 7th Pl, Arts District; pizzas $19-21, pasta $21-32, mains $39-135; ⏲5-11pm Sun-Thu, to midnight Fri & Sat; P; Metro Lines 18, 60, 62) A boisterous, convivial Arts District 'it kid,' Bestia remains one of the most sought-after reservations in town; book at least a week ahead. The draw remains Chef Ori Menashe's clever, produce-driven take on Italian flavors, from charred pizzas topped with housemade *'nduja* (spicy Calabrian paste), to rigatoni with sultry duck ragù, parmesan, star anise, pink peppercorn and dry seaweed.

Hollywood

Luv2eat THAI $
(Map p393; ☎323-498-5835; www.luv2eatthai.com; 6660 W Sunset Blvd; mains $12-21; ⏲11am-3:30pm & 4:30-11pm; P; Metro Lines 2, 302, M B Line to Hollywood/Highland) Don't let the odd name put you off; strip-mall Luv2eat is a virtual temple for local Thai foodies. Cordon Bleu–trained Chef Fern and Thailand-raised Chef Pla offer generous serves of dishes not normally seen on LA's Thai menus, from a non-negotiable Phuket-style crab curry to tangy *moo-ping* (grilled pork skewers). They nail the standards, too, among them a phenomenal papaya salad.

Stout Burgers & Beers BURGERS $
(Map p393; ☎323-469-3801; www.stoutburgersandbeers.com; 1544 N Cahuenga Blvd; burgers $12-15, salads $8-12; ⏲11:30am-4am; P; M B Line to Hollywood/Vine) Woody, pub-inspired Stout flips gourmet burgers and pours great craft brews. The beef is ground in-house, the chicken is free range and the veggie patties are made fresh daily. The Six Weeker burger (brie, fig jam and caramelized onions) and onion rings are standouts, while the hugely popular happy hour (4pm to 6pm weekdays) slashes food prices in half.

★Found Oyster SEAFOOD $$$
(Map p398; ☎323-486-7920; www.foundoyster.com; 4880 Fountain Ave; dishes $7-28; ⏲4-10pm Tue-Thu, 4-11pm Fri, noon-11pm Sat, noon-10pm Sun; DASH Hollywood Route, Metro Lines 2, 175) Bonhomie and exceptional seafood are on the menu at this tiny, always-packed clam shack. Squeeze in among foodies and East Hollywood hipsters for straightforward, produce-driven offerings including Littleneck clams, live Maine scallops, New England–style chowder, lobster bisque rolls and a daily-changing selection of East and West Coast oysters. Head in early (by 5pm in the evenings) or midweek to minimize any wait.

★Providence AMERICAN $$$
(☎323-460-4170; www.providencela.com; 5955 Melrose Ave; lunch tasting menus $130-190, dinner tasting menus $190-265; ⏲noon-2pm Fri, 6-10pm Mon-Fri, 5:30-10pm Sat, 5:30-9pm Sun; P; Metro Line 10) A modern classic, chef Michael Cimarusti's James Beard–winning, two-Michelin starred darling is known for turning superlative seafood into revelatory creations that never feel experimental for the sake of it. Whether it's kampachi paired with black truffle, burdock gelée and Meyer lemon, or Santa Barbara spot prawns with sweet pea and mint, flavors conspire in unexpected, memorable ways worth the hefty price tag.

Los Feliz & Griffith Park

HomeState TEX-MEX $
(Map p398; ☎323-906-1122; www.myhomestate.com; 4624 Hollywood Blvd, Los Feliz; tacos $3.50, dishes $7-11; ⏲8am-10pm; M B Line to Vermont/Sunset) Texan expat Briana Valdez is behind this rustic ode to the Lone Star State, where locals queue patiently for authentic breakfast tacos such as the Trinity, a handmade flour tortilla topped with organic egg, bacon, potato and cheddar. Then there's the *queso* (melted cheese) and our lunchtime

favorite, the brisket sandwich, a coaxing combo of shredded meat, cabbage slaw, guacamole and pickled jalapeños.

Mess Hall PUB FOOD $$
(☎323-660-6377; www.messhallkitchen.com; 4500 Los Feliz Blvd, Los Feliz; mains $17-32; ⊙9am-10pm Sun-Thu, to 11pm Fri & Sat; P; Metro Lines 180, 181) What was formerly The Brown Derby, a swing dance spot made famous by the film *Swingers,* is now a wonderfully convivial, cabin-style hangout with snug booths, TV sports and a comfy, neighborly vibe. The feel-good factor extends to the menu, with standouts that include comforting mac 'n' cheese and smoky baby-back ribs with slaw and house fries.

★**Atrium** CALIFORNIAN $$$
(Map p398; ☎323-607-6944; www.atriumlosfeliz.com; 1816 N Vermont Ave, Los Feliz; dishes $12-29; ⊙4-11pm Mon-Wed, 4pm-midnight Thu & Fri, 10am-midnight Sat, 10am-11pm Sun; ; M B Line to Vermont/Sunset) A narrow pathway leads to this lofty, greenhouse-inspired eatery-bar, adorned with bespoke wallpaper, plush banquettes and a horseshoe centerpiece bar. Here, LA's multiculti makeup is translated into unforgettable bites such as caramelized kimchi burrito and decadent chicken and waffles with Oklahoma caviar, sake-kasu crema and smoked maple syrup. Exceptional cocktails exude a light, bright, Cali vibe.

Silver Lake & Echo Park

★**Sqirl** CAFE $
(Map p398; ☎323-284-8147; www.sqirlla.com; 720 N Virgil Ave; dishes $8-16; ⊙6:30am-4pm Mon-Fri, 8am-4:30pm Sat & Sun; ; M B Line to Vermont/Santa Monica) Despite its somewhat obscure location, this tiny, subway-tiled cafe is forever pumping thanks to its top-notch, out-of-the-box breakfast and lunch offerings. Join the queue to order made-from-scratch wonders such as long-cooked chicken and rice porridge served with dried lime, ginger, turmeric, cardamon ghee and tomato, or the cult-status ricotta toast, a symphony of velvety house-made ricotta, thick-cut brioche and Sqirl's artisanal jams.

★**Night + Market Song** THAI $$
(Map p398; ☎323-665-5899; www.nightmarketla.com; 3322 Sunset Blvd, Silver Lake; dishes $8-15; ⊙noon-3pm Mon-Fri, 5-11pm Mon-Sat; ; Metro Lines 2, 4) After cultivating a cult following in WeHo, this gleefully garish temple to real-deal Thai and Cambodian street food expanded to the hipster heartlands. Years later, it's still killing it with zingy, palate-pleasing dishes such as spicy *larb* (minced-meat salad), proper pad Thai and harder-to-find specialties such as Isaan-style fermented pork sausage. To minimize the wait, head in early (before 7pm).

★**Pine & Crane** TAIWANESE $$
(Map p398; ☎323-668-1128; www.pineandcrane.com; 1521 Griffith Park Blvd, Silver Lake; dishes $5-14; ⊙noon-10pm Wed-Mon; ; Metro Lines 2, 4) You'll be licking chopsticks at this hip, unfussy hot spot for Taiwanese-inspired small plates, noodles and rice-based dishes. Feast on spicy shrimp wontons, nutty Dan Dan noodles and the unmissable beef roll, a burrito-like concoction packed with tender beef, cucumber, cilantro, scallions and piquant hoisin sauce. It gets crazy busy, especially at night, so consider heading in for an early lunch.

West Hollywood & Mid-City

★**Original Farmers Market** MARKET $
(Map p400; ☎323-933-9211; https://farmersmarketla.com; 6333 W 3rd St; ⊙9am-9pm Mon-Fri, 9am-8pm Sat, 10am-7pm Sun; P; Metro Lines 217, 218, DASH Fairfax Route) The Farmers Market is an atmospheric spot for a casual meal any time of day, especially if the rug rats are tagging along. Its narrow walkways are lined with choices: gumbo and diner classics to tacos and pizza, sit-down or takeout. One of the better foodie options is cafeteria-style **Pampas Grill** (Map p400; ☎323-931-1928; www.pampas-grill.com; Stall 618; combination platters per pound $12.65; ⊙10:30am-9pm Mon-Sat, 10:30am-8pm Sun;), a Brazilian *churrascaria* specializing in barbecued meats.

★**Jon & Vinny's** ITALIAN $$
(Map p400; ☎323-334-3369; www.jonandvinnys.com; 412 N Fairfax Ave, Mid-City; breakfast $10-21, lunch & dinner pasta $15-24, mains $18-26; ⊙8am-10pm; ; Metro Lines 217, 218, DASH Fairfax Route) It might look like a Finnish sauna, but this oak-clad evergreen is all about simple, modern Italian cooked smashingly. Charred pizzas and the housemade pastas are the standouts, with soul-soothing meatballs also worth an encore. If it's breakfast, start right with

olive-oil fried eggs with grilled kale, crispy potato, *'nduja* and preserved Meyer lemon. Reserve well ahead, especially for dinner.

★**Connie & Ted's** SEAFOOD **$$$**
(Map p400; ☎323-848-2722; www.connieandteds.com; 8171 Santa Monica Blvd, West Hollywood; mains $15-46; ⊙4-10pm Mon & Tue, 11:30am-10pm Wed & Thu, 11:30am-11pm Fri, 10am-11pm Sat, 10am-10pm Sun; P; Metro Lines 4, 218) Acclaimed chef Michael Cimarusti is behind this buzzing, homely take on the New England seafood shack. Freshness and sustainability underscore the offerings, with up to a dozen oyster varieties at the raw bar, as well as superb, authentic renditions of northeast classics such as lobster rolls (served cold with mayo or hot with drawn butter), clam cakes, chowder and steamers.

Beverly Hills, Bel Air, Brentwood & Westwood

★**Eataly LA** FOOD HALL **$$**
(☎213-310-8000; www.eataly.com/us_en/stores/los-angeles; 10250 Santa Monica Blvd, Westfield Century City; pizzas $13-29, pasta $14-39, fish mains $28; ⊙8am-10pm Sun-Thu, 8am-11pm Fri & Sat, individual eateries vary; P; Metro Lines 4, 16, 28, 316, 704, 728, Big Blue Bus Line 5) Part of Westfield Century City, the LA branch of this Italian gastronomic Disneyland features a dedicated wine store; bakery, cheese, charcuterie and fresh produce sections; plus both quick-service counters and sit-down restaurants peddling everything from cannoli and wood-fired pizzas to proper pasta and responsibly sourced seafood dishes. If you love your gin, grab a pre-dinner G&T at its rooftop restaurant-bar **Terra** (pasta $19-38, dinner mains $30-47; ⊙11:30am-2:30pm & 5-10pm Mon-Thu, 10:30am-2:30pm Sat & Sun, 5-10:30pm Fri & Sat, 5-9:30pm Sun; P), but dine at the better-value Eataly options downstairs.

★**Joss Cuisine** CHINESE **$$**
(☎310-277-3888; www.josscuisine.com; 9919 S Santa Monica Blvd, Beverly Hills; mains $16.50-48; ⊙noon-3pm Mon-Fri, 5:30-10pm daily; Metro Lines 4, 16, 316, 704) With fans including Barbra Streisand, Gwyneth Paltrow and Jackie Chan, this warm, intimate restaurant serves up superlative, MSG-free Chinese cuisine at noncelebrity prices. Premium produce drives everything from the flawless dim sum and ginger fish broth, to crispy mustard prawns and one of the finest Peking ducks you'll encounter this side of China. Reservations recommended.

★**Audrey at the Hammer** CALIFORNIAN **$$**
(☎310-443-7037; www.audreyatthehammer.com; Hammer Museum, 10899 Wilshire Blvd, Westwood; lunch $12-28, dinner mains $18-65; ⊙11am-11pm Tue-Sat, 11am-6pm Sun; P; Metro Lines 2, 234, 302, Big Blue Bus Lines 1, 2, 8) Leagues ahead of most museum restaurants, indoor-outdoor Audrey serves bright, polished SoCal cuisine in a svelte, mid-century-inspired fit-out. Join lunching ladies and hip art fiends for a midday salad of bitter endive, anchovy, aged pecorino and soft-boiled egg, or perhaps an evening heritage pork porterhouse with broccoli di cicco and dates. Both the craft cocktails and specialty coffee are exemplary.

Malibu & Pacific Palisades

Malibu Farm CALIFORNIAN **$$**
(☎310-456-1112; www.malibu-farm.com; 23000 Pacific Coast Hwy, Malibu Pier, Malibu; mains breakfast $14-20, lunch & dinner $17-38; ⊙7am-9pm Sun-Fri, to 10pm Sat; Metro Line 534) A lovely antidote to the seafood and burger shacks that dominate piers up and down California's coast, this suite of whitewashed dining rooms is beachy keen and a perfect place to munch on farm-to-table brunches, pizzas (try the ones with cauliflower crust) and skirt-steak sandwiches. It also operates a cafe at the end of the pier.

★**Saddle Peak Lodge** AMERICAN **$$$**
(☎818-222-3888; www.saddlepeaklodge.com; 419 Cold Canyon Rd, Calabasas; appetizers $14-25, mains $39-62; ⊙5-9pm Mon-Fri, 5-10pm Sat, 10:30am-2pm & 7-9pm Sun; P) Rustic as a Colorado mountain lodge, and tucked into the Santa Monica Mountains with a creek running beneath, Saddle Peak Lodge serves up elk, venison, buffalo and other game in a setting watched over by mounted versions of the same. Though the furnishings are rustic timber, this is fine dining, so don't come here after a day on the trail.

★**Nobu Malibu** JAPANESE **$$$**
(☎310-317-9140; www.noburestaurants.com/malibu; 22706 Pacific Coast Hwy, Malibu; dishes $18-78; ⊙noon-10pm Mon-Thu, 9am-11pm Fri & Sat, 9am-10pm Sun; P; Metro Line 534) Chef Nobu Matsuhisa's empire of luxe Japanese restaurants began in LA, and the Malibu outpost

is consistently one of LA's hot spots. East of the pier, it's a cavernous, modern wood chalet with long sushi bar and a dining room that spills onto a patio overlooking the swirling sea. Remember, it's the cooked food that built the brand.

Santa Monica

★ Santa Monica Farmers Markets MARKET $
(Map p402; www.smgov.net/portals/farmers-market; Arizona Ave btwn 2nd & 3rd Sts; 8:30am-1:30pm Wed, 8am-1pm Sat;) You haven't really experienced Santa Monica until you've explored one of its outdoor farmers markets stocked with organic fruits, vegetables, flowers, baked goods and freshly shucked oysters. The mack daddy is the Wednesday market, around the intersection of 3rd and Arizona – it's the biggest and arguably the best for fresh produce, and is often patrolled by leading local chefs.

★ Milo & Olive ITALIAN $$
(310-453-6776; www.miloandolive.com; 2723 Wilshire Blvd; mains breakfast $11-15, lunch & dinner $17-24; 7am-11pm) We love this place for its small-batch wines, incredible pizzas, terrific breakfasts (creamy polenta and poached eggs, anyone?), breads and pastries, all of which you may enjoy at the marble bar or shoulder to shoulder with new friends at one of two communal tables. It's a cozy neighborhood joint so it doesn't take reservations.

★ Cassia SOUTHEAST ASIAN $$$
(Map p402; 310-393-6699; www.cassiala.com; 1314 7th St; appetizers & sides $16-24, mains $37-39; 5-10pm Sun-Thu, 5-11pm Fri & Sat; P) Open, airy Cassia has made about every local and national 'best' list of LA restaurants. Chef Bryant Ng draws on his Chinese-Singaporean heritage in dishes such as *kaya* toast (with coconut jam, butter and a slow-cooked egg), 'sunbathing' prawns, and the encompassing Vietnamese pot-au-feu: short-rib stew, veggies, bone marrow and delectable accompaniments.

Venice

★ Night + Market Sahm THAI $
(310-301-0333; www.nightmarketsong.com/nm-sahm; 2533 Lincoln Blvd; mains $12-18; 5-11pm Wed-Mon; Big Blue Bus Line 3, Metro Line 33, 733, Culver City Bus Line 1) The Venice outpost of chef-owner-wunderkind Kris Yenbamroong's mini-empire specializes in take-no-prisoners spicy Thai dishes such as *nam khao tod* (crispy rice salad with soured pork, raw ginger and peanuts) and *larb gai* (spicy minced chicken), alongside standard-heat curry, noodle and veggie dishes. Pastrami *pad kee mao* is pure LA fusion: spicy 'drunken' noodles with pastrami from landmark **Langer's Deli** (213-483-8050; www.langersdeli.com; 704 S Alvarado St, Westlake; hot pastrami sandwiches $18-20, mains $14-33; 8am-4pm Mon-Sat; P; M B/D Lines to Westlake/MacArthur Park) in Westlake.

★ Gjelina AMERICAN $$
(Map p402; 310-450-1429; www.gjelina.com; 1429 Abbot Kinney Blvd; mains $10-35; 8am-midnight; Big Blue Bus Line 18) If one restaurant defines the new Venice, it's this. Carve out a spot on the communal table between the hipsters and yuppies, or get your own slab of wood on the elegant stone terrace, and dine on imaginative small plates (raw yellowtail spiced with chili and mint and drenched in olive oil and blood orange) and sensational thin-crust, wood-fired pizza.

★ Rose CALIFORNIAN $$
(Map p402; 310-399-0711; www.rosecafevenice.com; 220 Rose Ave; brunch $10-20, lunch mains $14-30, dinner mains $17-45; 7am-10pm Sun-Thu, 7am-11pm Fri & Sat; P) This airy Venice institution dates from 1979 yet is as current as ever, serving a diverse, all-day menu to a crowd of laptop-toting writers, tech geeks and beefcakes from nearby **Gold's Gym** (Map p402; 310-392-6004; www.goldsgym.com/veniceca; 360 Hampton Dr; day pass $25; 4am-midnight Mon-Fri, to 11pm Sat & Sun; Big Blue Bus Lines 1, 18, Metro line 733). Fun, sophisticated and tasty treats span elegant pastries to farmers-market-fresh salads, pastas, pizzas, lunchtime sandwiches and bowls, and mains that are not afraid to be veggie-forward.

Long Beach & San Pedro

★ Steelcraft FOOD HALL $
(www.steelcraftlb.com; 3768 Long Beach Blvd, Long Beach; prices vary by shop; 7am-10pm, individual shop hours vary; P; Long Beach Transit line 51) About 6 miles north of central Long Beach, shipping containers have been repurposed with mini-kitchens churning out burgers (at Pig Pen Delicacy),

pizzas (DeSano), ramen (Tajima), waffles (Waffle Love), Coffee (Steel Head), craft beer (Smog City Brewing Co) etc. Order at the counters, grab a communal table seat in the AstroTurf courtyard – covered or not, your choice – and get grazing.

★ San Pedro Fish Market & Restaurant SEAFOOD **$$**

(☎310-832-4251; www.sanpedrofish.com; 1190 Nagoya Way, San Pedro; burgers & sandwiches $5.50-15, mains $12-22, trays from $46.50; ⏲8am-8pm; P 👪; 🚌Metro Silver Line) Seafood feasts don't get more decadent, or divey, than at this family-run, harbor-view institution. Buy fresh fish or seafood at the counter and the price includes cooking. You'll see entire families gathered around plastic trays piled high with plump shrimp (the house specialty), meaty crabs, fresh oysters, melty yellowtail and tender halibut, spiced and cooked with potatoes, tomatoes and peppers.

San Fernando Valley

★ Porto's CUBAN, BAKERY **$**

(☎818-956-5996; www.portosbakery.com; 315 N Brand Blvd, Glendale; ⏲6:30am-8pm Mon-Sat, 7am-6pm Sun; 👪) Locals obsess over Porto's. There always seems to be a queue somewhere in this sprawling bakery-cafe, where different stations dispense hearty sandwiches, luscious cakes and obsession-worthy *pasteles* (small pastries). Deep-fried potato balls filled with meat or cheese and jalapeño define comfort food, as do flaky guava-cheese pastries and meaty sandwiches such as *medianoche* and Cuban. There's simple cafeteria-style seating. Olé, y'all!

★ Mizlala MIDDLE EASTERN **$**

(☎818-783-6698; 4515 Sepulveda Blvd, Sherman Oaks; small plates $5-14, mains $12-18; ⏲noon-10pm Tue-Sat, noon-9pm Sun; P; 🚌Metro line 750) Chef Danny Emaleh runs one of LA's gourmet faves out of a strip mall storefront just off the 405 Fwy. Inside, you'll see why it's so loved when you taste the artichoke hummus, Moroccan fried chicken, kebabs and tagines, which make an impressive presentation.

★ Asanebo SUSHI **$$$**

(☎818-760-3348; www.asanebo-restaurant.com; 11941 Ventura Blvd, Studio City; sushi $6-24; ⏲noon-2pm & 6-10:30pm Tue-Fri, 6-10:30pm Sat, 6-10pm Sun; P; 🚌Metro lines 150, 240) Although it's in a strip mall (welcome to the Valley), Asanebo is a Sushi Row standout thanks to dishes such as halibut sashimi with fresh truffle, and *kanpachi* (amberjack) with miso and serrano chilies. Chef Tetsuya Nakao has a Michelin star under his belt and helped launch chef Nobu Matsuhisa toward his Nobu Japanese restaurant empire.

Pasadena & the San Gabriel Valley

★ Din Tai Fung CHINESE **$**

(☎626-574-7068; www.dintaifungusa.com; 1108 S Baldwin Ave, Arcadia; dishes $3-14.75; ⏲11am-9am Mon-Fri, 10am-9pm Sat & Sun; P) It's a testament to the SGV's ethnic Chinese community that Taiwan's most esteemed dumpling house opened its first US outpost here. The menu of dumplings, greens, noodles, desserts, teas and smoothies is as long as the phone directory at a medium size corporation, but everyone orders pork *xiaolongbao* – steamed dumplings juicy with rich broth; get them with truffles for $24.25.

NBC Seafood DIM SUM **$**

(☎626-282-2323; www.nbcrestaurant.com; 404-A Atlantic Blvd, Monterey Park; dim sum $3.38-8.38, mains $10-17; ⏲8am-10pm, dim sum until 4pm; P) Behind the rotunda facade, this SGV dim-sum institution can seat 388 at a time. At peak hours (roughly 10am to 1pm on weekends) all seats are full, with a line out the door. Shrimp *har gao,* pan-fried leek dumplings and addictive shrimp on sugarcane are worth the wait, as are dozens of other small plates wheeled around on carts.

La Grande Orange CALIFORNIAN **$$**

(☎626-356-4444; www.lgostationcafe.com; 260 S Raymond Ave, Pasadena; pizzas $16-18, lunch mains $15-25, dinner mains $18-34, steaks $41-52; ⏲11am-10pm Mon-Thu, 11am-11pm Fri, 10am-11pm Sat, 9am-9pm Sun; P; M L Line to Del Mar) Pasadena's original train station (c 1911) has been handsomely renovated into this cheery, popular dining room beneath lovingly aged wooden beams. The kitchen in the former ticket booth serves a menu of New American cooking: mesquite-grilled burgers and seafood, salads and pricier Midwestern aged steaks. Watch today's light-rail trains go by from the generous bar.

Drinking

Downtown Los Angeles & Boyle Heights

★Clifton's Republic COCKTAIL BAR

(Map p390; ☎213-613-0000; https://thenevarlands.com/cliftons-republic; 648 S Broadway; ⏲6pm-2am Fri & Sat; 📶; Ⓜ B/D Lines to Pershing Sq) Opened in 1935 and back after a $10-million renovation, multilevel, mixed-crowd Clifton's defies description. Order drinks from a Gothic church altar amid taxidermied forest animals, watch burlesque performers shimmy in the shadow of a 40ft faux redwood, or slip through a glass-paneled door to a luxe tiki paradise where DJs spin in a repurposed speedboat.

Everson Royce Bar COCKTAIL BAR

(☎213-335-6166; www.erbla.com; 1936 E 7th St, Arts District; ⏲11:30am-2am Mon-Fri, from 5pm Sat, 2pm-midnight Sun; 🚌 Metro Lines 18, 60, 62) Don't be fooled by the unceremonious gray exterior. Behind that wall lies a hopping Arts District hangout, with a buzzy, bulb-strung outdoor patio. The barkeeps are some of the city's best, using craft liquor to concoct drinks such as the prickly-pear Mateo Street Margarita. Bar bites are equally scrumptious, with standouts including the buttermilk biscuits and roast-pork steamed buns.

Imperial Western Beer Company MICROBREWERY

(Map p390; ☎213-270-0035; www.imperialwestern.com; Union Station, 800 N Alameda St, Downtown; ⏲3pm-midnight Mon-Thu, 3pm-2am Fri, noon-2am Sat, noon-midnight Sun; 📶; Ⓜ B/D/L Lines to Union Station) Even New York's Grand Central Terminal can't claim an in-house craft brewery, but that's exactly what awaits at Union Station. Occupying a glorious hall with Navajo-inspired floor tiles, the fun, sprawling space pours everything from single-hop and unfiltered IPAs, to ales, dubbels, oyster stouts and goses. Bonuses include decent $1 happy-hour oysters (3pm to 7pm weekdays).

Hollywood

★Harvard & Stone BAR

(☎747-231-0699; www.harvardandstone.com; 5221 Hollywood Blvd; ⏲8pm-2am; 📶; Ⓜ B Line to Hollywood/Western) With daily rotating craft whiskey, bourbon and cocktail specials, Harvard & Stone lures hipsters with its solid live bands, DJs and burlesque troops working their saucy magic on Fridays and Saturdays. Think Colorado ski lodge meets steampunk factory, with a blues and rockabilly soul. Note the dress code, which discourages shorts, shiny shirts, baggy clothes, sports gear and flip-flops.

★Sayers Club CLUB

(Map p393; ☎323-871-8233; www.facebook.com/TheSayersClub; 1645 Wilcox Ave; cover varies; ⏲10pm-2am Wed, Fri & Sat, 9pm-2am Thu; 📶; Ⓜ B Line to Hollywood/Vine) When established stars such as the Black Keys, and even movie stars such as Joseph Gordon-Levitt, decide to play secret shows in intimate environs, they come to the back room at this brick-house, speakeasy-style Hollywood nightspot. Dress to impress.

Tabula Rasa WINE BAR

(☎213-290-6309; www.tabularasabar.com; 5125 Hollywood Blvd; ⏲5pm-1am Mon-Thu, 2pm-2am Fri & Sat, 2pm-1am Sun; 📶; 🚌 180, 181, 217, 780, Ⓜ B Line to Hollywood/Western) Thai Town's Tabula is everything one could want in a neighborhood wine bar: eclectic drops, unpretentious barkeeps, well-picked tunes on the turntable and regular live gigs (including Sunday jazz). Offerings by the glass are short, sharp and engaging, touching on anything from qvevri-aged Georgian reds to funky Italian orange vino. Beers are equally intriguing and the Cuban sandwich is a knockout.

Silver Lake & Echo Park

★Virgil BAR

(Map p398; ☎323-660-4540; www.thevirgil.com; 4519 Santa Monica Blvd, Silver Lake; ⏲7pm-2am; 🚌 Metro Line 4) A vintage-inspired hangout with farm-to-bar cocktails and a stocked calendar of top-notch comedy, live music and DJs. Highlights include Monday's Hot Tub variety show, hosted by Kurt Braunohler and Kristen Schaal (the latter of *Flight of the Conchords* fame) and featuring an eclectic lineup of oft-irreverent stand-up comics.

Ototo BAR

(☎213-784-7930; www.ototo.la; 1360 Allison Ave, Echo Park; ⏲5:30-11pm Mon-Sat, 2-9pm Sun; 📶; 🚌 Metro Lines 2, 4, 302, 704) This intimate sake bar pours a rotating selection of Japanese rice wines, thoughtfully categorized by flavor profile. Enthusiastic barkeeps are knowledgeable and generous with tastings, and the Japanese bar food includes commendable *okonomiyaki* (Japanese savory pancake) and chicken *katsu* sandwiches.

Sunset Beer Company BAR
(☎213-481-2337; www.sunsetbeerco.com; 1498 Sunset Blvd, Echo Park; ⊙4-11pm Mon-Thu, 2pm-midnight Fri, 1pm-midnight Sat, 1-10pm Sun; 📶; 🚇Metro Lines 2, 4) What's better than a beer store? One with a bar. That's what you get here, where clued-up, attitude-free staffers are happy to help you decide between that Swing Flare IPA from Mumford, the Blood Orange White Ale from Telegraph, or perhaps the Torrential Hop Pour from Smog City. It's a snug, low-key spot and always a good bet before a Dodgers game.

West Hollywood & Mid-City

★**Abbey** GAY & LESBIAN
(Map p400; ☎310-289-8410; www.theabbeyweho.com; 692 N Robertson Blvd, West Hollywood; ⊙11am-2am Mon-Thu, from 10am Fri, from 9am Sat & Sun; 📶; 🚇Metro Lines 4, 704) It's been called the best gay bar in the world, and who are we to argue? Once a humble coffeehouse, the chi chi Abbey has expanded into the bar/club/restaurant of record in WeHo. It has so many different-flavored martinis and mojitos that you'd think they were invented here, plus a menu of upscale pub food (brunch $14 to $22, dinner mains $16 to $22).

Verve Coffee Roasters COFFEE
(Map p400; ☎310-385-9605; www.vervecoffee.com; 8925 Melrose Ave, West Hollywood; ⊙7am-8pm; 📶👶; 🚇Metro Line 4) With an airy interior and see-and-be-seen patio, specialty roaster Verve pours high-quality coffee for discerning palates. Kick back with a pour-over Ethiopian, a creamy nitro flash brew or perhaps a well-chosen tea. The food menu includes all-day-breakfast chia pudding, organic poached-egg biscuits and avocado toast.

Santa Monica

★**Bungalow** LOUNGE
(Map p402; www.thebungalowsm.com; 101 Wilshire Blvd, Fairmont Miramar Hotel; ⊙5pm-2am Mon-Fri, noon-2am Sat, noon-10pm Sun) A Brent Bolthouse nightspot, the indoor-outdoor lounge at the Fairmont Miramar remains one of the hottest nights out in LA. Like most Westside spots, it can be too dude-centric late in the evening, but the setting is elegant, and there's still beautiful mischief to be found here.

★**Basement Tavern** BAR
(Map p402; www.basementtavern.com; 2640 Main St; ⊙5pm-2am) A creative speakeasy housed in the basement of the Victorian beach club, and our favorite well in Santa Monica. We love it for its craft cocktails, cozy booths, island bar and nightly live-music calendar that features blues, jazz, bluegrass and rock bands. It gets way too busy on weekends, but weeknights can be special.

Venice

★**High** ROOFTOP BAR
(Map p402; ☎424-214-1062; www.highvenice.com; 1697 Pacific Ave, Hotel Erwin; ⊙3-10pm Mon-Thu, 3pm-midnight Fri, noon-midnight Sat, noon-10pm Sun) Venice's only rooftop bar is quite an experience, with 360-degree views from the shore to the Santa Monica Mountains – if you can take your eyes off the beautiful people. High serves creative seasonal cocktails (blood-orange julep, lemon apple hot toddy, Mexican hot chocolate with tequila) and dishes including beef or lamb sliders, meze plates and crab dip. Reservations recommended.

☆ Entertainment

★**Hollywood Bowl** CONCERT VENUE
(Map p396; ☎323-850-2000; www.hollywoodbowl.com; 2301 N Highland Ave; rehearsals free, performance costs vary; ⊙late May–mid-Oct; 🚇Metro Line 237) Summers in LA just wouldn't be the same without alfresco melodies under the stars at the Bowl, a huge natural amphitheater in the Hollywood Hills. Its annual season – which usually runs from late May to September – includes symphonies, jazz bands and iconic acts such as Bob Dylan, Diana Ross, the B52s and Pet Shop Boys. Bring a sweater or blanket as it gets cool at night.

★**Greek Theatre** LIVE MUSIC
(Map p396; ☎844-524-7335; www.lagreektheatre.com; 2700 N Vermont Ave; ⊙late Apr–mid-Oct; 🚇DASH Observatory/Los Feliz Route) The 'Greek' in the 2010 film *Get Him to the Greek* is this 5900-capacity outdoor amphitheater, tucked into a woodsy Griffith Park hillside. A more intimate version of the Hollywood Bowl, it's much loved for its vibe and variety – recent acts include Gladys Knight, Alicia Keys, John Legend and Adam Ant.

★**Mark Taper Forum** THEATER
(Map p390; ☎213-628-2772; www.centertheatregroup.org; 135 N Grand Ave, Downtown; Ⓜ B/D Lines to Civic Center/Grand Park) Part of the Music Center, the Mark Taper is one of the three venues used by the Center Theatre Group, SoCal's leading resident ensemble and producer of Tony-, Pulitzer- and Emmy-winning plays. It's an intimate space with only 15 rows of seats arranged around a thrust stage, so you can see every sweat pearl on the actors' faces.

★**Comedy & Magic Club** LOUNGE
(☎310-372-1193; www.comedyandmagicclub.com; 1018 Hermosa Ave, Hermosa Beach; ⏱Tue-Sun) Live music and comedy right on the Hermosa strip. It has something going almost every night, including some big names: David Spade, Paul Reiser, Helen Hong, Alonzo Bodden, Maz Jobrani, and 10 – count 'em, 10! – comedians most Fridays and Saturdays. The legendary Jay Leno (former *Tonight Show* host) often performs live and up close on Sundays.

★**Upright Citizens Brigade Theatre** COMEDY
(Map p393; ☎323-908-8702; https://franklin.ucbtheatre.com; 5919 Franklin Ave; tickets $5-12; 🚌Metro Line 207) Founded in New York by *Saturday Night Live* alums Amy Poehler and Ian Roberts along with Matt Besser and Matt Walsh, this sketch-comedy group cloned itself in Hollywood in 2005. With numerous nightly shows spanning anything from stand-up comedy to improv and sketch, it's arguably the best comedy hub in town. Valet parking costs $7.

LGBT+ LOS ANGELES

LA is one of the country's gayest cities and has made many contributions to gay culture. Your gaydar may well be pinging throughout the county, but the rainbow flag flies especially high in Boystown, along Santa Monica Blvd in West Hollywood, flanked by dozens of high-energy bars, cafes, restaurants, gyms and clubs. Most cater to gay men, although there's plenty for lesbians, trans and mixed audiences. Thursday through Sunday nights are prime time.

Beauty reigns supreme among the buff, bronzed and styled of Boystown. Elsewhere the scene is considerably more laid-back and less body conscious. The crowd in Silver Lake and Downtown is more mixed age and runs from cute hipsters to leather-and-Levi's, counterculture types and business folk. Long Beach has the most relaxed, neighborly scene.

If nightlife isn't your bag, there are plenty of other ways to meet, greet and engage. Outdoor options include the **Frontrunners** (www.lafrontrunners.com) running club and the **Great Outdoors** (https://greatoutdoors.wildapricot.org/la) hiking club. The latter runs day and night hikes, as well as neighborhood walks and camping trips. For insight into LA's fascinating queer history, download the free **Pride Explorer** (www.thelavendereffect.org/tours) app, which offers self-guided walking tours of Hollywood and Downtown LA.

There's gay theater all over town, but the multi-venue **Celebration Theatre** (☎323-957-1884; www.celebrationtheatre.com; 6760 Lexington Ave, Hollywood) ranks among the nation's leading companies for LGBT+ plays. Silver Lake's **Cavern Club Theater** (Map p398; www.cavernclubtheater.com; 1920 Hyperion Ave, Silver Lake; 🚌Metro Line 175) pushes the envelope, particularly with uproarious drag performers; it's downstairs from Casita del Campo restaurant. If you're lucky enough to be in town when the **Gay Men's Chorus of Los Angeles** (☎424-239-6514; http://gmcla.org) is performing, don't miss out: this world-class ensemble has been doing it since 1979.

The **LA LGBT Center** (Map p393; ☎323-993-7400; https://lalgbtcenter.org; 1625 Schrader Blvd; ⏱9am-8pm Mon-Fri; 🚌Metro Lines 212, 217, 222, 312) is a one-stop service and health agency, and its affiliated **Village at Ed Gould Plaza** (☎323-993-7400; https://lalgbtcenter.org; 1125 N McCadden Pl; ⏱6-10pm Mon-Fri, 9am-5pm Sat; Ⓟ; 🚌Metro Lines 4, 237) offers art exhibits, theater and other cultural events throughout the year.

The festival season kicks off in mid-May with **Long Beach Pride** (☎562-987-9191; https://longbeachpride.com; 450 E Shoreline Dr, Long Beach; ⏱mid-May) and continues with the three-day **LA Pride** (https://lapride.org; ⏱Jun) in mid-June with a parade down Santa Monica Blvd. On Halloween (October 31), the same street brings out 500,000 outrageously costumed revelers of all persuasions.

Blue Whale JAZZ
(Map p390; ☎213-620-0908; www.bluewhalemusic.com; 123 Onizuka St, Suite 301, Little Tokyo; prices vary; ⊙8pm-2am; Ⓜ L Line to Little Tokyo/Arts District) An intimate space on the top floor of Weller Court in Little Tokyo, Blue Whale serves top-notch jazz nightly from 9pm to around midnight. The crowd is eclectic, the beers craft and the spirits focused on small batch. Acts span from emerging and edgy to established, and the acoustics are excellent. The cover charge varies, but is generally between $15 and $30.

Shopping

Downtown Los Angeles

★**Last Bookstore in Los Angeles** BOOKS
(Map p390; ☎213-488-0599; http://lastbookstorela.com; 453 S Spring St; ⊙10am-10pm Sun-Thu, 10am-11pm Fri & Sat; 👪; Ⓜ B/D Lines to Pershing Sq) What started as a one-person storefront is now California's largest new-and-used bookstore. And what a bookstore! Across two sprawling levels of an old bank building, you'll find everything from cabinets of rare books to an upstairs horror-and-crime book vault, book tunnel and smattering of art galleries. The store also houses a terrific vinyl collection and cool store-themed merch.

★**Row DTLA** SHOPPING CENTER
(☎213-988-8890; https://rowdtla.com; 1320 E 7th St; ⊙8am-10pm, individual shops & eateries vary; 📶👪; 🚌Metro Lines 60, 62, 760) Row DTLA has transformed a sprawling industrial site into a sharp edit of specialty retail and dining. It's like Tribeca, with better weather. Saunter pedestrianized streets for discerning apparel and accessories, designer homewares, niche fragrances, even Japanese bicycles. Top picks include stationery purveyor **Hightide Store DTLA** (☎213-935-8135; www.hightidestoredtla.shop; Garage Retail, Shop 140; ⊙11am-7pm Mon-Sat, 11am-5pm Sun), affordable design store **Poketo** (☎213-372-5686; www.poketo.com; Shop 174; ⊙11am-5pm) and progressive unisex fashion label **Shades of Grey** (www.shadesofgreyclothing.com; Suite 110; ⊙noon-5pm Mon-Fri, 11am-6pm Sat & Sun).

Hollywood

Amoeba Music MUSIC
(Map p393; ☎323-245-6400; www.amoeba.com; 6200 Hollywood Blvd; ⊙10:30am-11pm Mon-Sat, 11am-10pm Sun; Ⓜ B Line to Hollywood/Vine) When a record store not only survives but thrives in this techno age, you know it's doing something right. Flip through 500,000 new and used CDs, DVDs, videos and vinyl at this cult-status music hub, which also stocks band-themed T-shirts, music memorabilia, books and comics. Handy listening stations and the store's outstanding *Music We Like* booklet keep you from buying lemons.

West Hollywood & Mid-City

WeHo and Mid-City are shopping hot spots. Melrose Ave, between N Poinsettia Pl and Fairfax Ave, gets a lot of the buzz, thanks to the boutiques stuck together like block-long hedgerows. Most of their gear is rather low-end, so if you're after the hipper, higher-end stuff, explore the long stretch between N Crescent Heights Blvd and N Almont Dr, or hit 3rd St.

Both Beverly Blvd (west of San Vincente Blvd) and N Robertson Blvd (south of Melrose Ave) are stocked with gorgeous interiors showrooms and galleries, with the occasional fashion boutique mixed in. Fairfax Ave, between Beverly and Melrose, is where street, skate and hip-hop culture collide.

For a mall trawl, hit the **Grove** (Map p400; ☎323-900-8080; www.thegrovela.com; 189 The Grove Dr; ⊙10am-9pm Mon-Thu, to 10pm Fri & Sat, to 8pm Sun; 📶👪; 🚌Metro Lines 217, 218, DASH Fairfax Rte) or **Beverly Center** (Map p400; ☎310-854-0070; https://beverlycenter.com; 8500 Beverly Blvd; ⊙10am-9pm Mon-Fri, 10am-8pm Sat, 11am-6pm Sun; 📶👪; 🚌Metro Lines 14, 16, 17, 105, 218, 705, DASH Fairfax Route).

★**Fred Segal** FASHION & ACCESSORIES
(Map p400; ☎310-432-0560; www.fredsegal.com; 8500 Sunset Blvd, West Hollywood; ⊙10am-7pm Mon-Sat, 11am-6pm Sun; 🚌Metro Lines 2, 302) No LA shopping trip is complete without a stop at Fred's. This is its flagship store, 21,000-sq-ft of chic, Cali-casual threads, accessories, beauty products and homewares hip enough for cashed-up celebs. The space also hosts regular product drops, trunk shows and live music.

★**Mystery Pier Books** BOOKS
(Map p400; ☎310-657-5557; www.mysterypierbooks.com; 8826 W Sunset Blvd, West Hollywood; ⊙11am-6pm Mon-Sat, noon-5pm Sun; 🚌Metro Lines 2, 302) The charming Louis and Harvey have no shortage of fans (including famous ones) thanks to their remarkable

WeHo bookstore. Famed for stocking signed shooting scripts from blockbusters, it also sells rare and obscure 1st editions, from Shakespeare ($3500 to $9000) and Salinger ($10,000) to JK Rowling ($30,000 and up).

Beverly Hills & the Westside

Downtown Beverly Hills bursts with well-known and more obscure luxury brands. The most famous (and most expensive) strip is Rodeo Dr, with boutiques also on the surrounding streets. Among these is N Beverly Dr, dotted with higher-end midrange fashion and lifestyle boutiques. To the west of Beverly Hills lies Westfield Century City, one of LA's best malls.

★**Westfield Century City** MALL

(310-277-3898; www.westfield.com/centurycity; 10250 Santa Monica Blvd, Century City; 10am-9pm Mon-Sat, 11am-7pm Sun, individual restaurant and movie theater hours vary; Metro Lines 4, 16, 28, 316, 704, 728, Big Blue Bus Line 5) This is West LA's best mall, a buzzing, sun-dappled, indoor-outdoor wonderland of midrange and high-end retail. Major draws include Italian gourmet temple Eataly LA (p413), impressive branches of department-store giants Bloomingdale's, Macy's *and* Nordstrom, plus a state-of-the-art, 15-screen AMC multiplex. When pooped, refuel at one of the quality restaurants or in the food court, home to outposts of numerous top LA casual eateries.

Venice

Abbot Kinney Blvd has become one of LA's top shopping destinations. Bargains are few and far between, but there's a lot of tantalizing stuff – clothing, gifts, accessories and more. As rents have risen here, more well-financed national and international brands, including online retailers (Adidas, Allbirds, John Fluevog, Robert Graham, Le Labo, Warby Parker, Will, etc), have opened flagship stores, and some local retailers have closed or moved to less expensive locations.

Waraku SHOES

(Map p402; 310-452-5300; www.warakuusa.com; 1225 Abbot Kinney Blvd; 10am-7pm; Big Blue Bus Line 18) Waraku is a compact, Japanese-owned shop with a curated, stylish selection of shoes (mostly athletic) and Japanese streetwear for men and women. It blends Far East couture with mainstream street brands such as Puma and Converse. Some 60% of the shoes are imported from Japan; the rest are domestic limited editions.

Aviator Nation CLOTHING

(Map p402; 310-396-9100; www.aviatornation.com; 1224 Abbot Kinney Blvd; 10am-6pm; Big Blue Bus Line 18) This beachwear brand's flagship and original store sells coastal-chic hoodies, tees and blankets, even guitar picks emblazoned with the signature stripes of yellow, orange and red. Behind the store is an awesome space with a DJ station, Ping-Pong table and plenty of couches to chill and listen to the bands it sometimes brings in.

Information

INTERNET ACCESS

Free wi-fi is relatively common at coffee shops, restaurants, malls, museums and major tourist areas. These include LAX, Pershing Sq and Grand Central Market in Downtown, Echo Park Lake, the Griffith Observatory, the Hollywood & Highland mall and Santa Monica.

TOURIST INFORMATION

Beverly Hills Visitors Center (310-248-1015; www.lovebeverlyhills.com; 9400 S Santa Monica Blvd, Beverly Hills; 9am-5pm Mon-Fri, from 10am Sat & Sun;) Sightseeing, activities, dining and accommodations information focused on the Beverly Hills area.

Discover Los Angeles Visitor Information Center (Map p390; www.discoverlosangeles.com; Union Station, 800 N Alameda St, Downtown; 9am-5pm) Maps and general tourist information in the lobby of Union Station. Other locations include the **Intercontinental Los Angeles Downtown** (Map p390) and **Hollywood & Highland** (Map p393; 6801 Hollywood Blvd; 9am-10pm Mon-Sat, 10am-7pm Sun;).

Long Beach Transit & Visitor Center (562-436-7700; www.visitlongbeach.com; 130 East 1st St, Long Beach; 11:30am-4:30pm) Tourist office located in downtown Long Beach.

Marina del Rey (310-305-9545; www.visitmarinadelrey.com; 4701 Admiralty Way, Marina del Rey; 9am-5pm Mon-Fri, 10am-4pm Sat & Sun) Maps and information on sights, activities, events and accommodations in the Marina del Rey area.

Santa Monica Visitor Center (Map p402; 800-544-5319; www.santamonica.com; 2427 Main St, Santa Monica) The main tourist information center in Santa Monica, with free guides, maps and helpful staff.

Visit West Hollywood (Map p400; 800-368-6020, 310-289-2525; www.visitwesthollywood.com; 1017 N La Cienega Blvd, Ste 400, West Hollywood; 9am-5pm Mon-Fri;) Informa-

LA'S FASHION DISTRICT DEMYSTIFIED

Bargain hunters love the frantic, 100-block warren of fashion in southwestern Downtown that is the Fashion District. Deals can be amazing, but first-timers are often bewildered by the district's size and immense selection. For orientation, check out www.fashiondistrict.org.

Basically, the area is subdivided into several distinct retail areas, with womens wear and accessories constituting the bulk of the offerings.

Women Santee St between 9th and 14th Sts, Pico Blvd between Main and Santee Sts, and Wall and Maple Sts between Olympic Blvd and 12th St.

Children Pico Blvd between Maple Ave and San Julian St, as well as Wall St between 12th St and Pico Blvd.

Men Maple Ave between 11th and 14th Sts, Main St between 14th St and Pico Blvd, as well as Santee St between 12th and 15th Sts and between 9th St and Olympic Blvd.

Textiles The blocks bordered by 8th St, Olympic Blvd, Maple Ave and San Julian St. Avoid the sketchy stretch of San Julian St between 9th St and Olympic Blvd and the relatively empty block of Olympic Blvd between Wall and San Julian Sts.

Jewelry and accessories Santee Alley and 11th St between Los Angeles and Santee Sts.

Shops are generally open from 10am to 5pm daily, with Saturday being the busiest day because that's when many wholesalers open to the public. Around a third of the shops are closed on Sunday. Cash is king and haggling may get you 10% or 20% off, especially when buying multiple items. Refunds or exchanges are a no-no, so choose carefully and make sure items are in good condition. Most stores don't have dressing rooms. Sample sales are usually held on the last Friday of every month from 9am to 3pm, with popular showrooms including the **California Market Center** (Map p390; ☎213-630-3600; www.californiamarketcenter.com; 155 E Olympic Blvd), **Cooper Design Space** (Map p390; ☎213-627-3754; www.cooperdesignspace.com; 860 S Los Angeles St), **Gerry Building** (Map p390; ☎213-228-1988; www.gerrybuilding.com; 910 S Los Angeles St), **Lady Liberty Building** (Map p390; ☎310-276-2282; www.theladylibertybuilding.com; 843 S Los Angeles St) and **New Mart** (Map p390; ☎213-627-0671; www.newmart.net; 127 E 9th St). Upcoming sales are posted on the LA Fashion District Instagram account (www.instagram.com/lafashiondistrict) and website (https://fashiondistrict.org/explore/calendar).

tion on attractions, accommodations, tours and more in the West Hollywood area.

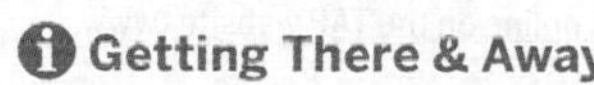

Getting There & Away

AIR

The main LA gateway is Los Angeles International Airport (p779), one of the world's busiest. Its nine terminals are linked by the free LAX Shuttle A, leaving from the lower (arrival) level of each terminal. Hotel and car-rental shuttles stop here as well. A free minibus for travelers with disabilities can be ordered by calling ☎310-646-6402. Ticketing and check-in are on the upper (departure) level.

The hub for most international airlines is the Tom Bradley International Terminal.

Some domestic flights operated by Alaska, American, American Eagle, Delta, Delta Connection, JetBlue, JSX, Southwest, Spirit and United also arrive at **Hollywood Burbank Airport** (BUR, Bob Hope Airport; https://hollywood-burbankairport.com; 2627 N Hollywood Way, Burbank), which is handy if you're headed for Hollywood, Downtown LA or Pasadena.

To the south, on the border with Orange County, the small **Long Beach Airport** (www.longbeach.gov/lgb; 4100 Donald Douglas Dr, Long Beach) is convenient for Disneyland, offering a handful of domestic routes operated by American, Delta, Hawaiian, JetBlue and Southwest.

BUS

The main bus terminal for **Greyhound** (☎213-629-8401; www.greyhound.com; 1716 E 7th St, Downtown) is in an industrial part of Downtown, so try not to arrive after dark. Take bus 18, 60, 62 or 760 to the 7th St/Metro Center metro station, from where metro trains head to Hollywood (Red Line), Koreatown (Purple Line), Culver City and Santa Monica (Expo Line) and Long Beach (Blue Line). Both the Red and Purple Lines reach Union Station, from where you can catch the Metro Gold Line (for Highland Park and Pasadena).

CAR & MOTORCYCLE

If you're driving into LA, there are several routes by which you might enter the metropolitan area.

From San Francisco and Northern California, the fastest route to LA is on I-5 through the San Joaquin Valley. Hwy 101 is slower but more picturesque, while the most scenic – and slowest – route is via Hwy 1 (Pacific Coast Hwy, or PCH).

From San Diego and other points south, I-5 is the obvious route. Near Irvine, I-405 branches off I-5 and takes a westerly route to Long Beach and Santa Monica, bypassing Downtown LA entirely and rejoining I-5 near San Fernando.

From Las Vegas or the Grand Canyon, take I-15 south to I-10 then head west into LA. I-10 is the main east–west artery through LA and continues to Santa Monica.

TRAIN

Amtrak (www.amtrak.com) trains roll into Downtown LA's historic **Union Station** (☎ Amtrak 800-872-7245; www.unionstationla.com; 800 N Alameda St, Downtown). Interstate trains stopping in the city are the daily *Coast Starlight* to Seattle (via Oakland and Portland), the daily *Southwest Chief* to Chicago and the thrice-weekly *Sunset Limited* to New Orleans. The *Pacific Surfliner* travels numerous times daily between San Diego, Santa Barbara and San Luis Obispo via LA.

ℹ Getting Around

TO/FROM THE AIRPORT

LAX FlyAway (☎ 714-507-1170; www.lawa.org/FlyAway) buses travel nonstop for $9.75 to Downtown's Patsaouras Transit Plaza at Union Station (35 minutes), Hollywood (1 hour), Van Nuys (40 minutes) and Long Beach (55 minutes). Trip times are subject to traffic conditions.

For scheduled bus services, catch the free shuttle bus (labeled 'Lot South/City Bus Center') from the airport terminals to the LAX City Bus Center. From here, local buses serve all of LA County. For Santa Monica or Venice, change to the Santa Monica Big Blue Bus Line 3 or Rapid 3 ($1.25). If you're headed for Culver City, catch Culver City bus 6 ($1). For Manhattan, Hermosa or Redondo Beaches, hop aboard Beach Cities Transit 109 ($1).

Taxis and ride-sharing vehicles (including Lyft, Opoli and Uber) are located at the LAX-it (pronounced 'LA Exit') stand, about a three-minute walk east of Terminal 1. A free, frequent shuttle bus connects all terminals to LAX-it.

BICYCLE

Most buses have bike racks, and bikes ride for free, although you must securely load and unload them yourself. Bicycles are also allowed on Metro Rail trains at all times.

LA has a number of bike-sharing programs.

Metro Bike Share (https://bikeshare.metro.net) Has more than 60 self-serve bike kiosks in the Downtown area, including Chinatown, Little Tokyo and the Arts District. Pay using your debit or credit card ($3.50 per 30 minutes) or TAP card, though you will first need to register it on the Metro Bike Share website. The smartphone app offers real-time bike and rack availability.

CAR & MOTORCYCLE

Unless time is no factor – or money is extremely tight – you're going to want to spend some time behind the wheel, although this means contending with some of the worst traffic in the country.

Parking at motels and cheaper hotels is usually free, while fancier ones charge anywhere from $8 to around $45 for the privilege.

The usual international car-rental agencies have branches at LAX and throughout LA. For Harley rentals, go to Route 66 (p502). Rates start from $149 per six hours, or $185 for one day. Discounts are available for longer rentals.

PUBLIC TRANSPORTATION

Most public transportation is handled by **Metro** (☎ 323-466-3876; www.metro.net), which offers maps, schedules and trip-planning help through its website.

To ride Metro trains and buses, buy a reusable TAP card. Available from TAP vending machines at Metro stations with a $2 surcharge, the cards allow you to add a preset cash value or day passes. The regular base fare is $1.75 per boarding, or $7/25 for a day/week pass with unlimited rides. Both single-trip tickets and TAP cards loaded with a day pass are available on Metro buses (ensure you have the exact change). When using a TAP card, tap the card against the sensor at station entrances and aboard buses.

TAP cards are accepted on DASH and municipal bus services and can be reloaded at vending machines or online on the TAP website (www.taptogo.net).

Metro Buses

Metro operates about 200 bus lines across the city and offers numerous types of bus services:

- Metro Local buses (painted orange) make frequent stops along major thoroughfares throughout the city.
- Metro Rapid buses (painted red) stop less frequently and have special sensors that keep traffic lights green when a bus approaches.
- Commuter-oriented Metro Express buses (painted blue) connect communities with Downtown LA and other business districts and usually travel via the city's freeways.

Metro Rail

The Metro Rail network consists of two subway lines, four light-rail lines and two express bus lines. Six lines converge in Downtown.

A Line (Blue) Light-rail running from Downtown to Long Beach; connects with the B, D and E Lines at 7th St/Metro Center station and the C Line at Willowbrook/Rosa Parks station.

B Line (Red) The most useful for visitors. A subway linking Downtown's Union Station to North Hollywood (San Fernando Valley) via central Hollywood and Universal City; connects with the A, D and E Lines at the 7th St/Metro Center station in Downtown, the L Line at Union Station and the G Line express bus at North Hollywood.

C Line (Green) Light-rail between Norwalk and Redondo Beach; connects with the A Line at Willowbrook/Rosa Parks.

D Line (Purple) Subway between Downtown LA, Westlake and Koreatown; shares six stations with the B Line. The line's extension will see it reach Beverly Hills in 2023, Century City in 2025 and Westwood in 2027.

E Line (Expo) Light-rail linking USC and Exposition Park with Culver City and Santa Monica to the west and Downtown LA to the northeast, where it connects with the B and D Line at 7th St/Metro Center station.

G Line (Orange) Express bus linking the west San Fernando Valley to North Hollywood, from where the Red Line subway shoots south to Hollywood and Downtown LA.

J Line (Silver) Express bus linking the El Monte regional bus station to the Harbor Gateway Transit Center in Gardena via Downtown LA. Some services continue to San Pedro.

L Line (Gold) Light-rail running from East LA to Little Tokyo/Arts District, Chinatown and Pasadena via Union Station, Mt Washington and Highland Park; connects with the B and D Lines at Union Station.

Crenshaw/LAX Line Opening in 2021, this light-rail will connect the C and E lines. A people-mover is expected to run between the line's Aviation/Century station and LAX from 2023.

Most lines run from around 4:30am to 1am Sunday to Thursday, and until around 2:30am on Friday and Saturday nights. Frequency ranges from up to every five minutes in rush hour to every 10 to 20 minutes at other times (up to 45 minutes for the G and J express bus lines). Schedules for all lines are available at www.metro.net.

Municipal Buses

Santa Monica–based **Big Blue Bus** (☎310-451-5444; www.bigbluebus.com) serves much of western LA, including Santa Monica, Venice, Westwood and LAX ($1.25). Its weekday express bus 10 runs from Santa Monica to Downtown.

The **Culver City Bus** (☎310-253-6510; www.culvercity.org/how-do-i/find/culver-city-bus) runs services throughout Culver City and the Westside.

Long Beach Transit (☎562-591-2301; https://ridelbt.com; per ride $1.25) serves Long Beach and surrounding communities.

All three municipal bus companies accept payment by TAP card.

AROUND LOS ANGELES

Ditch the congestion, crowds and smog, and use LA as a hub to all the natural glory of California. Get an early start to beat the traffic, and point the compass across the ocean or up into the mountains.

Catalina Island

Mediterranean-flavored Santa Catalina Island is a popular getaway for harried Angelenos drawn by fresh air, seemingly endless sunshine, seaside fun and excellent hiking.

Originally the home of Tongva Nation, Catalina has gone through stints as a hangout for Spanish explorers, Franciscan friars, sea-otter poachers, smugglers and Union soldiers. In 1919 it was snapped up by chewing-gum magnate William Wrigley Jr (1861–1932), who had buildings constructed in the Spanish Mission style and for years sent his Chicago Cubs baseball team here for spring training. Apart from its human population (about 4100), Catalina's highest-profile residents are a herd of bison that were brought here for a 1924 movie shoot.

Today most of the island is owned by the **Catalina Island Conservancy** (☎310-510-2595; www.catalinaconservancy.org; 125 Clarissa Ave, Avalon; biking/hiking permits $35/free), and 88% of the island's 75 sq miles is a nature preserve requiring (easily available) permits for access to hiking and cycling.

Even if Catalina sinks under the weight of day-trippers in summer, if you stay overnight you may well feel the ambience go from frantic to, as the song says, 'romance, romance, romance, romance.'

Commercial activity is concentrated in the town of **Avalon** (population about 3730), which is small enough to be explored in an hour or two, so there's plenty of time for hiking, swimming and touring.

The only other settlement is **Two Harbors** (population about 300) on the remote west coast, which has a general store, a dive and kayak center, a snack bar and a lodge.

Catalina boasts hotels that have been recently upgraded while preserving the

Around Los Angeles

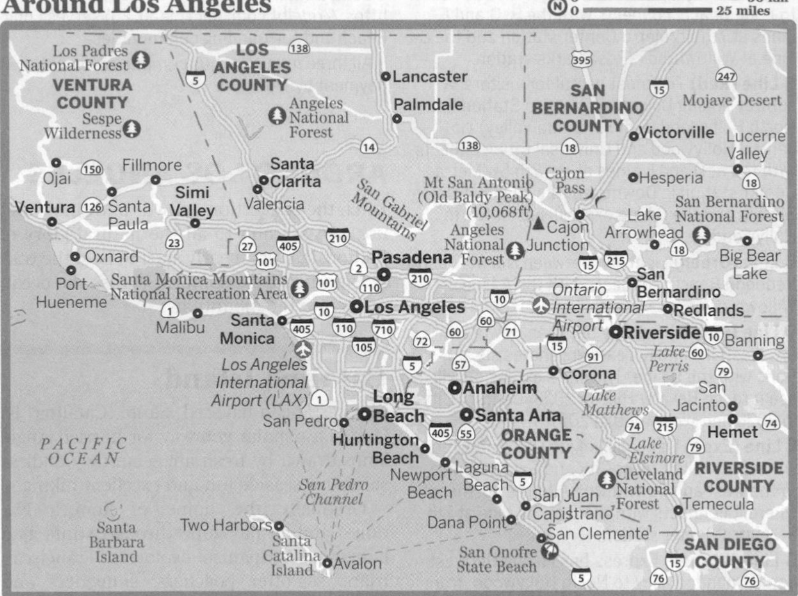

island's traditional charm. For camping information, see www.visitcatalinaisland.com/avalon/camping.php.

Activities

There are plenty of activities right in Avalon and on the harbor, as well as hiking, mountain biking and ziplining inland with the chance to spot eagles and bison. If you're going into the backcountry, there's very little shade, so take a hat, sunscreen and plenty of water.

In Avalon you can hang out on the privately owned **Descanso Beach** (☎310-510-7410; www.visitcatalinaisland.com/descanso-beach-club; 1 St Catherine Way, Avalon). There's good snorkeling at **Lovers' Cove** and at **Casino Point (Avalon Underwater Park)**, a marine reserve that's also the best shore dive. Another way to escape the throngs is by kayaking to the quiet coves along Catalina's rocky coastline. **Catalina Island Expeditions** (Descanso Beach Ocean Sports; ☎310-510-1226; www.kayakcatalinaisland.com; Descanso Beach Club; single/double kayak rental per hour $22/30, per day $60/72, SUP per hour/day from $25/75) rents snorkeling gear, stand-up paddleboarding (SUP) kits and kayaks, and also runs guided kayaking tours and kayak camping trips.

To get into the protected backcountry, you must get a permit (and maps) from the Catalina Island Conservancy (p423) if you're going to be hiking or mountain biking.

Alternatively, you could just hop on an air-conditioned tour bus and let someone else show you around. Both **Catalina Adventure Tours** (☎877-510-2888; www.catalinaadventuretours.com; Green Pier, Avalon; tours adult/child/senior from $16/12/14 to $79/59/69) and the **Catalina Island Company** (☎800-626-1496; www.visitcatalinaisland.com; 10 Island Plaza, Avalon; tours $19-124) operate historical Avalon itineraries and jaunts further out with memorable views of the rugged coast, deep canyons and sandy coves, and possible encounters with eagles and bison.

Snorkelers and certified scuba divers can rent equipment at Descanso Beach to glimpse local shipwrecks and kelp forests. **Two Harbors Dive and Recreation Center** (☎310-510-4272; www.visitcatalinaisland.com/activities-adventures/two-harbors/dive-recreation-center; 1 Banning House Rd, Two Harbors; kayaks or mountain bikes per hour from $24 , snorkeling gear $35/day; ⏲10am-5pm, longer in summer) offers access to pristine dive sites off the island's less developed coast.

Getting There & Away

A few companies operate ferries to Avalon and Two Harbors. Reservations are recommended at any time and especially during summer. The use of cars on Catalina is restricted, so there are no vehicle ferry services.

Catalina Express (☎800-613-1212; www.catalinaexpress.com; round trip adult/senior/child $74.50/67.50/59 from Long Beach & San Pedro, $76.50/69.50/61 from Dana Point) Ferries to Avalon from San Pedro and Long Beach and Dana Point in Orange County, and to Two Harbors from San Pedro. The ride takes one to 1½ hours each way. Ferry schedules vary seasonally and by day of the week, with generally the most departures on weekends. You'll ride free on your birthday...true story.

Catalina Flyer (☎949-673-5245; https://catalinainfo.com; 400 Main St, Newport Beach; round trip adult/senior/under 12yr $70/65/53; ⏰departs Newport Beach/Avalon 9am/4:30pm daily) Operates one daily round trip to Avalon (about 75 minutes each way) from Balboa Harbor in Newport Beach in Orange County.

Big Bear Lake

About 110 miles northeast of LA, Big Bear Lake is a family-friendly year-round mountain resort (elevation 6750ft) centered on the 7-mile-long namesake lake. Snowy winters lure scores of ski bunnies and boarders to its two mountains, while the warmer seasons bring hikers, mountain bikers and watersports enthusiasts wishing to escape the stifling heat down in the basin. A beautified and revitalized downtown area, called the Village, has elevated the range of dining, shopping and drinking options.

Big Bear's two ski mountains are jointly managed by **Big Bear Mountain Resort** (☎844-462-2327; www.bigbearmountainresorts.com; 👪). The higher of the two, **Bear Mountain** (8805ft) is nirvana for freestyle freaks with more than 150 jumps, 80 jibs, and two pipes including a 580ft in-ground superpipe. **Snow Summit** (8200ft) is more about traditional downhill and has trails for everyone. Altogether the mountains are served by 26 lifts and crisscrossed by more than 55 runs.

On snowy winter weekends, demand may exceed Big Bear's capacity, so plan ahead. Campgrounds and two hostels offer the cheapest digs, private villas are the priciest and in between you'll find plenty of aging motels along the main highway and around 2000 private cabins tucked into the woods. For a wide range of options, check www.bigbear.com/places-to-stay.

For cheap sleeps tuck into the clean and friendly **Big Bear Hostel** (☎909-866-8900; www.bigbearhostel.com; 527 Knickerbocker Rd; dm $20-40, d $39-239; P@📶). **Switzerland Haus** (☎909-866-3729; https://switzerlandhaus.com; 41829 Switzerland Dr; r from $125; P📶) offers comfy rooms with mountain-view patios and a Nordic sauna. **Himalayan** (☎909-878-3068; www.himalayanbigbear.com; 672 Pine Knot Ave; mains $10-21; ⏰11am-9pm Sun-Thu, 11am-10pm Fri & Sat; 🌶👪) is a popular Nepali and Indian kitchen with speedy service.

Information

Big Bear Discovery Center (☎909-382-2790; http://mountainsfoundation.org; 40971 N Shore Dr/Hwy 38, Fawnskin; ⏰9am-4pm Thu-Mon) Nonprofit visitor center dispensing information and maps on all outdoor-related activities around Big Bear, including camping. Also sells the National Forest Adventure Pass.

Big Bear Visitors Center (☎800-424-4232, 909-866-7000; www.bigbear.com; 40824 Big Bear Blvd; ⏰9am-5pm Sun-Thu, 9am-7pm Fri & Sat; 📶) Has lots of free flyers, maps and wi-fi, and sells trail maps and the National Forest Adventure Pass.

Getting There & Away

Big Bear is on Hwy 18, an offshoot of Hwy 30 in San Bernardino. A quicker approach is via Hwy 330, which starts in Highland and intersects with Hwy 18 in Running Springs. If you don't like serpentine mountain roads, pick up Hwy 38 near Redlands, which is longer, but easier on the queasy. It has less traffic too, handy on peak weekends.

Mountain Transit (☎909-878-5200; https://mountaintransit.org) Route 5 buses connect Big Bear Lake with the Greyhound and Metrolink stations in San Bernardino twice on weekdays ($10, 1¼ hours). Buses are wheelchair accessible and have bike racks.

AT A GLANCE

POPULATION
3.2 million

ATTRACTIONS AT DISNEYLAND
55

BEST NOODLE SOUP
Pho 79 (p435)

BEST ALTERNATIVE SHOPPING
Lab (p449)

BEST DISNEYLAND RESTAURANT
Napa Rose (p433)

WHEN TO GO

May Visitation dips. Mostly sunny, balmy temperatures.

Jul & Aug Beach season peak. Surfing and art festivals by the coast.

Sep Blue skies, cooler temperatures inland, fewer crowds.

Laguna Beach (p449)

Disneyland & Orange County

Orange County sits between California's two biggest cities, LA and San Diego, but it hardly rests in their shadows. Once a hotbed of conservatism, the county has in recent times embraced a more progressive stance. Mickey Mouse and surfers, thriving immigrant communities, office parks and artist colonies, luxury shopping extravaganzas and 'anti malls' give 'the OC' an identity all its own.

The Disneyland Resort dominates tourism in northern Orange County, but if that's all you see, you're missing out. Take time to get off the beaten path and into the communities to see what makes Orange County residents thrive. Forty-two miles of coast promise endless summer in their broad beaches and coastal coves, and from Seal Beach to San Clemente the towns offer many different lifestyles.

INCLUDES

Disneyland & Orange County Highlights

❶ Disneyland Resort (p429) Meeting Mickey and screaming your head off on Space Mountain before catching the fireworks show.

❷ Huntington Beach (p439) Building a beach bonfire after a day of surfing killer waves.

❸ Balboa Peninsula (p443) Cycling past the as-seen-on-TV sands of Newport Beach.

❹ Laguna Beach (p450) Watching the sun dip below the horizon from the art-filled bluff-tops.

❺ Old Towne Orange (p433) Shopping for vintage treasures and slurping soda-fountain milkshakes.

❻ Costa Mesa (p448) Discovering high culture, luxe shopping and Orange County's alternative side at 'anti-malls.'

❼ Mission San Juan Capistrano (p454) Being awed by Spanish-colonial history and beauty.

DISNEYLAND RESORT

Mickey is one lucky guy. Created by animator Walt Disney in 1928, this irrepressible mouse caught a ride on a multimedia juggernaut (film, TV, publishing, music, merchandising and theme parks) that rocketed him into a global stratosphere of recognition, money and influence. Plus, he lives in Disneyland, the 'Happiest Place on Earth,' an 'imagineered' hyper-reality where the streets are always clean, employees – called 'cast members' – are always upbeat and there are parades every day.

Sure, every ride seems to end in a gift store, prices are sky-high and there are grumblings that management could do more about affordable housing and health insurance for employees – but even determined grouches should find reason to grin. For the more than 18 million kids, grandparents, honeymooners and international tourists who visit every year, the Disneyland Resort remains a magical experience.

> **DISNEY DETAILS**
>
> For lots of practical tips for managing your Disneyland Resort vacation, the resort's website (https://disneyland.disney.go.com) and app cover every attraction.

Sights

Disneyland Park

Spotless, wholesome Disneyland is still largely laid out according to Walt's original 1955 plans: Main Street USA, Sleeping Beauty Castle, Frontierland, Adventureland and Tomorrowland now coexist with newer 'lands' like Mickey's Toontown and Star Wars: Galaxy's Edge.

Main Street USA AREA

(Map p430) Fashioned after Walt's hometown of Marceline, Missouri, bustling Main Street USA resembles the classic turn-of-the-20th-century, all-American town. It's an idyllic, relentlessly upbeat representation, complete with barbershop quartet, penny arcades, ice-cream shops and a steam train. The music playing in the background is from American musicals, and there's a flag-retreat ceremony every afternoon.

★Star Wars: Galaxy's Edge AREA

(Map p430) Disneyland's newest and largest land (14 acres) is dedicated to the *Star Wars* saga. The top-billed **Millennium Falcon: Smugglers Run** puts you in the cockpit of the 'fastest hunk of junk in the galaxy' on an exhilarating blast-off through hyperspace. In **Star Wars: Rise of the Resistance**, you and other 'members of the Resistance' are captured by fearsome stormtroopers and must escape from a Star Destroyer; encountering Rey, BB-8, Kylo Ren and more along the way.

Tomorrowland AREA

(Map p430) How did 1950s imagineers envision the future? As a galaxy-minded community filled with monorails, rockets and Googie style architecture, apparently. In 1998 this 'land' was revamped to honor three timeless futurists: Jules Verne, HG Wells and Leonardo da Vinci. **Space Mountain**, Tomorrowland's signature attraction and one of the USA's best roller coasters, hurtles you into complete darkness at frightening speed. *Star Wars*-themed attractions (separate from the **Star Wars: Galaxy's Edge** land) include **Star Wars Launch Bay**, showing movie props and memorabilia.

Meanwhile, **Star Tours – The Adventures Continue** clamps you into a Starspeeder shuttle for a wild and bumpy 3D ride through the desert canyons of Tatooine on a space mission.

If it's retro high-tech you're after, the **monorail** glides to a stop in Tomorrowland, its rubber tires traveling a 13-minute, 2.5-mile round-trip route to Downtown Disney. Just outside Tomorrowland station, kiddies will want to shoot laser beams on **Buzz Lightyear Astro Blaster** and drive their own miniature cars in the classic **Autopia** ride. Then jump aboard the **Finding Nemo Submarine Voyage** to look for the world's most famous clownfish and rumble through an underwater volcanic eruption.

Fantasyland AREA

(Map p430) Fantasyland is filled with the characters of classic children's stories. If you only see one attraction here, visit **it's a small world**, a boat ride past hundreds of audio-animatronic children from different cultures, interspersed with Disney characters, all singing that earworm of a theme song.

Frontierland AREA

(Map p430) This Disney 'land' is a salute to old Americana: the Mississippi-style paddle-wheel **Mark Twain Riverboat**, the 18th-century replica **Sailing Ship Columbia**,

Disneyland Resort

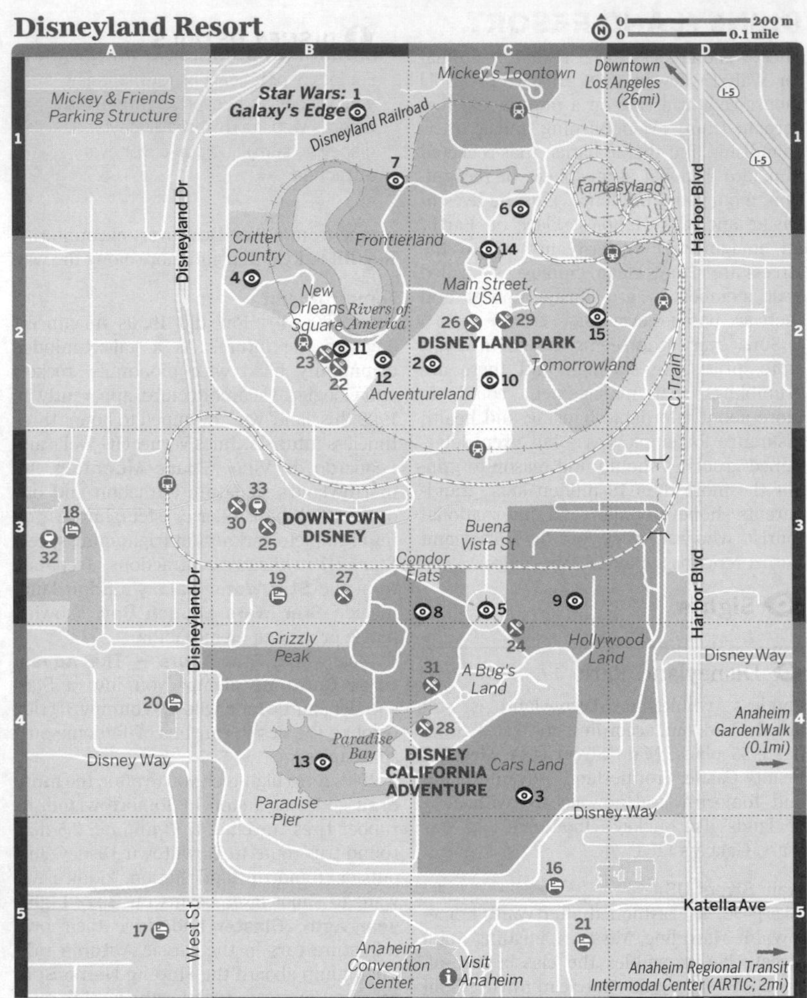

a rip-roarin' Old West town with a shooting gallery and the **Big Thunder Mountain Railroad**, a mining-themed roller coaster. The former Tom Sawyer Island – the only attraction in the park personally designed by Uncle Walt – has been reimagined in the wake of the *Pirates of the Caribbean* movies and renamed the **Pirate's Lair on Tom Sawyer Island**.

Adventureland AREA

(Map p430;) Loosely deriving its jungle theme from Southeast Asia and Africa, Adventureland has a number of attractions, but the hands-down highlight is the safari-style **Indiana Jones Adventure**. Nearby, little ones love climbing the stairways of **Tarzan's Treehouse**. Cool down on the **Jungle Cruise**, viewing exotic audio-animatronic animals from rivers of South America, India, Africa and Southeast Asia. And the classic **Enchanted Tiki Room** features carvings of Hawaiian gods and goddesses, and a show of singing, dancing audio-animatronic birds and flowers.

New Orleans Square AREA

(Map p430;) New Orleans Square has all the charm of the eponymous city's French Quarter but none of the marauding drunks. New Orleans was the favorite city of Walt and his wife, Lillian, and he paid tribute to it

Disneyland Resort

Top Sights
1 Star Wars: Galaxy's Edge B1

Sights
2 Adventureland C2
3 Cars Land C4
4 Critter Country B2
5 Disney California Adventure C3
6 Fantasyland C1
7 Frontierland B1
8 Grizzly Peak C3
9 Hollywood Land C3
10 Main Street USA C2
11 New Orleans Square B2
12 Pirates of the Caribbean B2
13 Pixar Pier B4
14 Sleeping Beauty Castle C2
15 Tomorrowland C2

Sleeping
16 Alpine Inn C5
17 Best Western Plus Stovall's Inn A5
18 Disneyland Hotel A3
19 Disney's Grand Californian Hotel & Spa B3
20 Paradise Pier Hotel A4
21 Residence Inn Anaheim Resort/Convention Center C5

Eating
22 Blue Bayou B2
23 Café Orleans B2
24 Carthay Circle C4
25 Catal Restaurant B3
26 Jolly Holiday Bakery Cafe C2
27 Napa Rose B3
28 Pacific Wharf C4
29 Plaza Inn C2
30 Ralph Brennan's New Orleans Jazz Kitchen B3
31 Wine Country Trattoria C4

Drinking & Nightlife
32 Trader Sam's Enchanted Tiki Lounge A3
33 Uva Bar B3

by building this stunning square lined with restaurants and attractions.

Pirates of the Caribbean is the longest ride in Disneyland (17 minutes) and provided 'inspiration' for the popular movies. You'll float through the subterranean haunts of tawdry pirates, where dead buccaneers perch atop their mounds of booty and Jack Sparrow pops up occasionally. Over at the **Haunted Mansion**, 999 'happy haunts' – spirits, goblins, shades and ghosts – appear and evanesce while you ride in a cocoon-like 'Doom Buggy' through web-covered graveyards of dancing skeletons.

Critter Country AREA

(Map p430;) Critter Country's main attraction is **Splash Mountain**, a flume ride through the story of Brer Rabbit and Brer Bear, based on the controversial 1946 film *Song of the South*. Just past Splash Mountain, hop in a mobile beehive on the **Many Adventures of Winnie the Pooh**. Nearby on the Rivers of America, you can paddle **Davy Crockett's Explorer Canoes**.

Disney California Adventure

Across the 'esplanade' from Disneyland is **Disney California Adventure** (DCA; Map p430; 714-781-4565; https://disneyland.disney.go.com; 1313 Harbor Blvd, Anaheim; 1-day pass adult $104-149, child 3-9yr $96-141, 2-day pass adult/child 3-9yr $225/210; P), an ode to California's geography, history and culture – or at least a sanitized, G-rated version. DCA, opened in 2001, covers more acres than Disneyland and feels less crowded. It has more modern rides and attractions inspired by coastal amusement parks, inland mountains and redwood forests, the magic of Hollywood (especially Pixar animation), and automotive culture by way of the movie *Cars*.

Cars Land AREA

(Map p430;) This land gets kudos for its incredibly detailed design based on the popular Disney Pixar *Cars* movies. Top billing goes to the wacky **Radiator Springs Racers**, a race-car ride that bumps and jumps around a track painstakingly decked out like the Great American West.

Grizzly Peak AREA

(Map p430;) Grizzly Peak is broken into sections highlighting California's natural and human achievements. Its main attraction, **Soarin' Around the World**, is a virtual hang-gliding ride using Omnimax technology that 'flies' you over famous landmarks. Enjoy the light breeze as you soar, keeping your nostrils open for aromas blowing in the wind.

Pixar Pier AREA

(Map p430;) If you like carnival rides, you'll love Pixar Pier, designed to look like all the beachside amusement piers in California. The state-of-the-art **Incredicoaster** glides along a smooth-as-silk track. Just as popular is **Toy Story Midway Mania!** – a 4-D ride where you earn points by shooting at targets while your carnival car swivels and careens through an oversize, old-fashioned game arcade.

Hollywood Land AREA

(Map p430; 👪) California's biggest factory of dreams is presented here in miniature, with soundstages, movable props and – of course – a studio store. Top billing goes to **Guardians of the Galaxy – Mission: BREAKOUT!**, a literally hair-raising journey of rapid ups and downs on a gigantic elevator. For a different kind of thrill, there's a one-hour live stage version of *Frozen*, at the **Hyperion Theater**.

Learn how to draw like Disney in the **Animation Academy** or simply be amazed by the interactive **Sorcerer's Workshop**, both housed inside the **Animation Building**.

Children can navigate a taxicab through 'Monstropolis' on the **Monsters, Inc: Mike & Sulley to the Rescue!** ride heading back toward the street's beginning.

Sleeping

★Disney's Grand Californian Hotel & Spa RESORT $$$

(Map p430; info 714-635-2300, reservations 714-956-6425; https://disneyland.disney.go.com/grand-californian-hotel; 1600 S Disneyland Dr; r from $586; P ❄ @ ☰ ≋) Soaring timber beams rise above the cathedral-like lobby of the six-story Grand Californian, Disney's homage to the arts-and-crafts architectural movement. Cushy rooms have triple-sheeted beds, down pillows, bathrobes and all-custom furnishings. Outside there's a faux-redwood waterslide into the pool.

Disneyland Hotel HOTEL $$$

(Map p430; 714-778-6600; www.disneyland.com; 1150 Magic Way, Anaheim; r from $445; P @ ☰ ≋) Though built in 1955, the year Disneyland opened, the park's original hotel has been rejuvenated with a dash of bibbidi-bobbidi-boo. There are three towers with themed lobbies (adventure, fantasy and frontier), and the 972 good-sized rooms boast Mickey-hand wall sconces in bathrooms and headboards lit like the fireworks over **Sleeping Beauty Castle** (Map p430; https://disneyland.disney.go.com/attractions/disneyland/sleeping-beauty-castle-walkthrough; 👪).

Paradise Pier Hotel HOTEL $$$

(Map p430; info 714-999-0990, reservations 714-956-6425; http://disneyland.disney.go.com/paradise-pier-hotel; 1717 S Disneyland Dr, Anaheim; r from $339; P ❄ @ ☰ ≋) Sunbursts, surfboards and a giant superslide are all on deck at the Paradise Pier Hotel, the smallest (472 rooms), cheapest and maybe the most fun of the Disney hotel trio. Kids will love the beachy decor and game arcade, not to mention the pool and the tiny-tot video room filled with mini Adirondack chairs.

Eating

Disneyland Park

Jolly Holiday Bakery Cafe AMERICAN $

(Map p430; https://disneyland.disney.go.com/dining/disneyland/jolly-holiday-bakery-cafe; Main Street USA; mains $6-11; breakfast, lunch & dinner; 👪) At this Mary Poppins–themed restaurant, the satisfying Jolly Holiday combo (grilled cheese and tomato basil soup for $10) is a decent deal. Other sandwiches on the sophisticated side include the mozzarella caprese or turkey on ciabatta. Great people-watching from outdoor seating.

Café Orleans CAJUN $$

(Map p430; https://disneyland.disney.go.com/dining/disneyland/cafe-orleans; New Orleans Square; mains $20-25; hours vary; 👪) This restaurant is famous for its three-cheese Monte Cristo sandwiches, plus Southern favorites like shrimp and grits. Breakfast is served seasonally.

Plaza Inn AMERICAN $$

(Map p430; https://disneyland.disney.go.com/dining/disneyland/plaza-inn; Main Street USA; mains $15-19, breakfast buffet adult/child 3-9yr $34/19; breakfast, lunch & dinner; 👪) Finger-lickin' good fried chicken platter and pot roast come with mashed potatoes, buttermilk biscuits and veggies at this 1950s original. There's a fun breakfast buffet with Disney characters. The rest of the day, if you can snag an outdoor table you'll also enjoy great people-watching at the crossroads of Main Street USA.

Blue Bayou SOUTHERN US $$$

(Map p430; 714-781-3463; https://disneyland.disney.go.com/dining/disneyland/blue-bayou-restaurant; New Orleans Sq; mains lunch $29-48, dinner $30-52; lunch & dinner; 👪) Surrounded by the 'bayou' inside the Pirates of the Caribbean attraction, this is the top choice for sit-down dining in Disneyland Park and is famous for its jambalaya and lunchtime Monte Cristo sandwich.

Disney California Adventure

Pacific Wharf FOOD HALL $

(Map p430; https://disneyland.disney.go.com/destinations/disney-california-adventure/pacific-wharf; mains $9-14.50; breakfast, lunch & dinner;) This counter-service collection of restaurants shows off some of California's ethnic cuisines (Chinese, Mexican etc) as well as hearty soups in sourdough-bread bowls, farmers-market salads and deli sandwiches. Eat at umbrella-covered tables by the water.

Wine Country Trattoria ITALIAN $$

(Map p430; https://disneyland.disney.go.com/dining/disney-california-adventure/wine-country-trattoria; Pacific Wharf; mains $18-38; lunch & dinner;) If you can't quite swing the Napa Rose or Carthay Circle, this sunny Cal-Italian terrace restaurant is a fine backup. Fork into Italian pastas and salads. Or a rib-eye, potatoes and roasted brussels sprouts with bacon and honey, washed down with Italian or California wines.

★ **Carthay Circle** AMERICAN $$$

(Map p430; https://disneyland.disney.go.com/dining/disney-california-adventure/carthay-circle-restaurant; Buena Vista St; mains lunch $26-40, dinner $34-51; lunch & dinner;) Decked out like a Hollywood country club, Carthay Circle is the best dining in either park, with seasonal steaks, seafood, pasta, smart service and a good wine list. Order fried biscuits, stuffed with white cheddar, bacon and jalapeño, and served with apricot honey butter.

Downtown Disney & Disneyland Resort

Ralph Brennan's New Orleans Jazz Kitchen CAJUN $$

(Map p430; 714-776-5200; http://rbjazzkitchen.com; Downtown Disney; mains $17-32; 8am-10pm Sun-Thu, to 11pm Fri & Sat;) Hear live jazz combos on the weekends and piano on weeknights at this resto-bar with NOLA-style Cajun and Creole dishes: gumbo, po-boy sandwiches, jambalaya, plus a (less adventurous) kids menu and specialty cocktails. There's breakfast and lunch express service if you don't have time to linger.

★ **Napa Rose** CALIFORNIAN $$$

(Map p430; 714-300-7170; https://disneyland.disney.go.com/dining; Grand Californian Hotel & Spa; mains $38-58; 5:30-10pm;) High-back arts-and-crafts-style chairs, leaded-glass windows and towering ceilings befit Disneyland Resort's top-drawer restaurant. On the plate, seasonal 'California Wine Country' (read: NorCal) cuisine is as impeccably crafted as the Sleeping Beauty Castle. Kids menu available, and there's a great bar. Reservations essential.

> **WORTH A TRIP**
>
> **OLD TOWNE ORANGE**
>
> One of the most rewarding visits in the OC, 7 miles southeast of Disneyland, the city of Orange retains its charming historical center. It's where locals go, and visitors will find it well worth the detour for antiques and vintage clothing shops, smart restaurants and pure SoCal nostalgia.

Catal Restaurant MEDITERRANEAN $$$

(Map p430; 714-774-4442; https://disneyland.disney.go.com/dining/downtown-disney-district/catal-restaurant; Downtown Disney; mains breakfast $10-15, lunch $10-30, dinner $27-46; hours vary, to 10pm Fri & Sat;) The chef cooks up a fusion of Californian and Mediterranean cuisines (steelhead salmon, paellas, lunchtime sandwiches, plus a kids menu) at this airy two-story restaurant decorated in a sunny Mediterranean-Provençal style with exposed beams and lemon-colored walls. Sit on the balcony. It's attached to **Uva Bar** (Map p430; 714-774-4442; www.patinagroup.com/uva-bar-cafe; Downtown Disney; 8am-11pm Sun-Thu, to midnight Fri & Sat) and does great happy hours upstairs, from 3pm to 5pm daily.

Entertainment

See the Disneyland resort's website (https://disneyland.disney.go.com) and app for details on parades, stage shows and fireworks.

ANAHEIM & NEARBY CITIES

There's a whole other 'world' outside of the parks. It's called Anaheim and the surrounding towns of north-central Orange County. They don't have Disney magic per se, but these communities do have their own sort of interest: shops from funky to luxury, food and craft beer halls, ethnic neighborhoods, and even some high culture.

Sights

★Knott's Berry Farm AMUSEMENT PARK
(714-220-5200; www.knotts.com; 8039 Beach Blvd, Buena Park; adult/child 3-11yr $84/54; from 10am, closing hours vary 5-11pm; P) Old West–themed Knott's Berry Farm often teems with packs of speed-crazed adolescents testing their mettle on an intense lineup of thrill rides. Gut-wrenchers include the wooden GhostRider and the '50s-themed Xcelerator; the single-digit-aged can find tamer action at Camp Snoopy.

In 2020 the park celebrated the 100th anniversary of the actual, 20-acre farm owned by Walter and Cordelia Knott. During the Great Depression, Walter cultivated a new blackberry-raspberry hybrid he named the boysenberry, and Cordelia's fried-chicken dinners attracted crowds of local farmhands. By 1940 Walter had built an imitation ghost town to keep the customers entertained, and eventually built carnival rides and charged admission. Cordelia kept frying the chicken, but the rides and Old West buildings became the main attraction.

GhostRider is the West Coast's tallest, fastest and longest wooden roller coaster. The **Sierra Sidewinder** roller coaster rips through banks and turns while rotating on its axis. Nearby, the suspended, inverted **Silver Bullet** screams through a corkscrew, a double spiral and an outside loop. From the ground, look up to see the dirty socks and bare feet of suspended riders who've removed their shoes just for fun.

Knott's Soak City WATER PARK
(714-220-5200; www.knotts.com/play/soak-city; 8039 Beach Blvd, Buena Park; adult/child 3-11yr $53/43; 10am-5pm, 6pm or 7pm mid-May–mid-Sep; P) Next door to Knott's Berry Farm is this water park, boasting a 750,000-gallon wave pool, dozens of high-speed slides, tubes and flumes, and one of the world's longest lazy river attractions. You must have a bathing suit without rivets or metal pieces to go on some slides. Bring a beach towel and a change of dry clothes.

★Bowers Museum MUSEUM
(714-567-3600; www.bowers.org; 2002 N Main St, Santa Ana; Tue-Fri adult/child 12-17yr & senior $13/10, Sat & Sun $15/12, special exhibit surcharge varies; 10am-4pm Tue-Sun; 53, 83) From its stately, Spanish Colonial–style shell, the Bowers Museum explodes onto the scene every year or so with remarkable exhibits that remind LA-centric museum-goers that the Bowers, too, is a local and national power player. Permanent exhibits are equally impressive, a rich collection of pre-Columbian, African, Chinese and Native American art, plus California art from the missions to Laguna Beach–style *plein air* painting. Our favorite: the Spirits and Headhunters gallery, showing jewelry, armaments, masks and religious articles of the Pacific Islands.

★Discovery Cube MUSEUM
(714-542-2823; www.discoverycube.org; 2500 N Main St, Santa Ana; adult/child 3-14yr/senior $20/15/17, 4-D movies $3 extra; 10am-5pm; P) Follow the giant 10-story cube – balanced on one of its points – to the county's best educational kiddie attraction. About 100 hands-on displays await, covering everything from dinosaurs to robotics, rockets to the water supply, the environment to hockey. In the **Grand Hall of Science**, you might learn the science of tornadoes or the physics of pulleys, while the **Discovery Theater** screens 4D movies.

Richard Nixon Presidential Library & Museum MUSEUM
(714-993-5075; www.nixonfoundation.org; 18001 Yorba Linda Blvd, Yorba Linda; adult/child 5-11yr/student/senior $16/6/10/12; 10am-5pm; P) The Nixon Library offers a fascinating walk through America's modern history and that of this controversial native son of Orange County (1913–94), who served as president 1969–74. Noteworthy exhibits include a full-size replica of the White House East Room, recordings of conversations with Apollo 11 astronauts on the moon, access to the ex-presidential helicopter – complete with wet bar and ashtrays – and excerpts from landmark TV appearances including the Kennedy–Nixon debates and Nixon's famous self-parody on the *Laugh-In* comedy show.

Sleeping

Anaheim

Hotels and motels in Anaheim proper generally have better rates than the Disneyland Resort hotels and offer packages combining lodging with theme-park tickets; most have family rooms or suites that sleep four to six people. Some operate complimentary guest shuttles to Disneyland. Otherwise, consider staying within walking distance of the parks or along the public shuttle routes operated by Anaheim Resort Transportation (p437).

WORTH A TRIP

LITTLE SAIGON

About 7 miles southwest of Anaheim, Little Saigon is America's largest community of expat ethnic Vietnamese, population around 190,000, who began arriving here around the Vietnam War in the 1970s, carving out a vibrant commercial district. Even if it looks like the essence of suburban sprawl – strip malls and small homes on a grid of wide, multilane roads with no discernible center – there's a lot going on. The massive **Asian Garden Mall** (9200 Bolsa Ave, Westminster; 10am-7pm) is a good place to see this community in action in shops selling everything from jewelry to medicinal herbs and clothing, plus a food court.

But the best reason to visit Little Saigon is the food. Newbies might start at **Lee's Sandwiches** (714-636-2288; www.leessandwiches.com; 13991 Brookhurst St, Garden Grove; sandwiches from $4.35; 24hr; P) serving tasty, wallet friendly Vietnamese banh mi sandwiches on French baguette rolls, plus Vietnamese-style coffees and teas and East-meets-West pastries. Another great, inexpensive casual eatery is **Pho 79** (714-531-2490; www.pho79.com; 9941 Hazard Ave, Garden Grove; mains $7-13; 7am-9pm Wed-Mon; P), which dishes up another Vietnamese staple, pho noodle soups, and more.

For a wider menu of rice, noodle and stir-fried dishes, visit **Brodard** (657-247-4401; www.brodard.net; 16105 Brookhurst Ave, Fountain Valley; mains $8-16; 8am-9pm), known for its addictive rice-paper spring rolls and large bakery, or its fancier sister, **Brodard Chateau** (714-899-8273; www.brodard.net; 9100 Trask Ave, Garden Grove; mains $9-35; 10:30am-9:30pm Mon-Thu, to 10pm Fri-Sun), while **Garlic & Chives** (714-591-5196; www.garlicandchives.com; 9892 Westminster Ave, Garden Grove, Mall of Fortune; mains $8-12, hotpots $22-32; 11am-10pm Mon-Thu, from 10am Fri-Sun; P) is a Vietnamese fusion experience like none other. Vegans will be thrilled by the varied Vietnamese menu of **Au Lac** (714-418-0658; www.aulac.com; 16563 Brookhurst St, Fountain Valley; 11:33am-3:33pm & 5:33-9:33pm Tue-Sun; P).

Little Saigon lies south of Hwy 22 (Garden Grove Fwy, connecting to Orange) and east of I-405 (San Diego Fwy).

Alpine Inn MOTEL $

(Map p430; 714 535-2186, 800-772-4422; www.alpineinnanaheim.com; 715 W Katella Ave; r $99-399; P) Connoisseurs of kitsch will hug their Hummels over this 42-room, snow-covered chalet facade on an A-frame exterior and icicle-covered roofs – framed by palm trees, of course. Bordering Disney California Adventure, the inn also has Ferris-wheel views. It's circa 1958, and air-con rooms are well kept and have fridges and microwaves. Grab 'n' go breakfast is served in the lobby.

Best Western Plus Stovall's Inn MOTEL $$

(Map p430; 714-778-1880; www.stovallsinn.com; 1110 W Katella Ave; r $114-210; P) Generations of guests have been coming to this 289-room motel about 15 minutes' walk to Disneyland. Around the side are two pools, two Jacuzzis, a fitness center, kiddie pool and a garden of topiaries (for real). The remodeled sleek and modern-design rooms sparkle; all have air-con, a microwave and mini-fridge. Rates include breakfast and there's a guest laundry.

Ayres Hotel Anaheim HOTEL $$

(714-634-2106; www.ayreshotels.com/ayres-hotel-anaheim; 2550 E Katella Ave; r $139-269; P; ARTIC, Amtrak to ARTIC) This well-run mini-chain of business hotels delivers solid-gold value. The 133 regularly renovated rooms have microwaves, minifridges, safes, wet bars, pillow-top mattresses and contemporary European-inspired design. Fourth-floor rooms have extra-high ceilings. Rates include a full breakfast buffet and evening social hours Monday to Thursday with craft beer, wine and snacks.

Residence Inn Anaheim Resort/ Convention Center HOTEL $$

(Map p430; 714-782-7500; www.marriott.com; 640 W Katella Ave; r from $179; P) This hotel near the convention center, yet only 10 minutes on foot to Disneyland, shines with sleek linens, marble tables and glass walls within in-room kitchens, big windows and a rooftop pool deck with Jacuzzi and a splash zone for kids. Rates include full breakfast, and there's also a gym and laundry machines. Overnight parking is $24.

WORTH A TRIP

ANAHEIM PACKING DISTRICT & CENTER STREET

The **Anaheim Packing District** (www.anaheimpackingdistrict.com; S Anaheim Blvd) is a smart, attractive renewal project of a long-shuttered 1925 Packard dealership and a 1919 orange-packing house a couple of miles from Disneyland, near Anaheim's downtown.

It's home to trendy restaurants like **Umami Burger** (714-991-8626; www.umamiburger.com; 338 S Anaheim Blvd; mains $10.50-17.50; 11am-11pm Sun-Thu, to midnight Fri & Sat; P), the **Anaheim Brewery** (714-780-1888; www.anaheimbrew.com; 336 S Anaheim Blvd; 5-9pm Tue-Thu, to 11pm Fri, noon-11pm Sat, 1-7pm Sun), an evolving collection of shops and a park for events.

About a quarter-mile away is **Center Street** (www.centerstreetanaheim.com; W Center St), a quietly splashy redeveloped neighborhood with an ice rink designed by Frank Gehry, and a couple of blocks packed with hipster-friendly shops selling everything from casual clothing and accessories to comic books. Among the many dining offerings is a mini food court where you might indulge in healthy junk at, um, **Healthy Junk** (714-772-5865; www.thehealthyjunk.com; 201 Center St Promenade; mains $9-14; 10am-9pm;).

Knott's Berry Farm

Knott's Berry Farm Hotel HOTEL $

(714-995-1111; www.knotts.com/stay/knotts-berry-farm-hotel; 7675 Crescent Ave, Buena Park; r from $109; P@) Say 'good night,' not 'good grief,' in a Snoopy-themed room at this nine-story, 320-room hotel bordering Knott's Berry Farm (p434) and its beloved Camp Snoopy. In fact, while your kids are hugging the beagle at breakfast or dinner in the hotel's restaurant, you'll be hugging yourself for finding a low-cost room that's not too far from that *other* park.

Eating & Drinking

Most restaurants surrounding Disneyland are informal chains, although **Anaheim GardenWalk** (www.anaheimgardenwalk.com; 400 W Disney Way; 11am-9pm;) has some nicer ones, about a 10-minute walk from Disneyland's main gate. A short drive away are some of the OC's most interesting independent restaurants, while adventurous palates can drive further afield to **Little Arabia**, or Little Saigon (p435).

Anaheim

Anaheim Packing House FOOD HALL $

(714-533-7225; www.anaheimpackingdistrict.com; 440 S Anaheim St; prices vary; opens 9am, closing hours vary; P) This 1919 former Sunkist orange packing house has a fabulous new life. Over 20 stalls and restaurants sell both sit-down and stroll-around eats and drinks: fish dinners to ramen, cocktails to shaved ice, adventurous ice-cream pops to waffles. It's all airy and modern on the inside, with lots of spaces to hang out.

★**Blind Rabbit** COCKTAIL BAR

(www.theblindrabbit.com; Anaheim Packing House, 440 S Anaheim Blvd; reservations 10:30pm Mon-Fri, from noon Sat & Sun) This chill, dimly lit, atmospheric speakeasy carves its own ice, makes its own juice, does regularly changing (but always creative) cocktails and has live music four nights a week. Reserve online (until 2pm on the same day) and they'll tell you where to show up. A dress code means no flip-flops, shorts or ball caps.

Knott's Berry Farm

Mrs Knott's Chicken Dinner Restaurant SOUTHERN US $$

(714-220-5055; 8039 Beach Blvd, Buena Park; chicken dinner lunch $17, dinner $22; 11am-9pm Mon-Fri, 8am-10pm Sat, 7am-9pm Sun;) The restaurant that launched a theme park. Classic, button-busting fried chicken and mashed potato dinners are served in this restaurant from 1934, remodeled in country style with distressed white wooden furniture. The **Chicken-to-Go** (714-220-5083; www.knotts.com/play/drinks-dining/chicken-to-go; 8039 Beach Blvd, Buena Park; meals/buckets from $11/29; 11am-7pm Mon-Fri, to 8pm Sat & Sun) counter does takeout. Validated parking for three hours with purchase.

Old Towne Orange

Rutabegorz CALIFORNIAN $

(714-633-3260; www.rutabegorz.com; 264 N Glassell St; mains $7-13.25; 10:30am-9pm Mon-Sat;) Known by locals as just Ruta's, this flowering cottage north of the plaza puts a healthy spin on breakfast or lunch. Cal-Mexican, vegetarian and Middle Eastern snacks all jostle on the tables alongside comfort-food sandwiches, wraps, salads, soups and fruit smoothies. Kids menu available.

Burger Parlor BURGERS $
(☎714-602-8220; www.burgerparlor.com; 149 N Glassell St; mains $8-13.50; ⏰11am-9pm Sun-Wed, to 10pm Thu, to 11pm Fri & Sat; 👪) Chef Joseph Mahon has parlayed his work at a Michelin starred restaurant into gourmet burgers that have been named the OC's best. The cheerily contemporary counter-service Orange location dishes up the same award-winning Smokey and Parlor burgers, plus fries and onion rings.

Filling Station Cafe DINER $
(☎714-289-9714; www.fillingstationcafe.com; 201 N Glassell St; mains breakfast $5-17, lunch $8-13.50, dinner $8-19; ⏰6:30am-3pm Mon & Tue, until 8:30pm Sun, Wed & Thu, until 9:30pm Fri & Sat; 🐾) For breakfast, not much beats this former gas station now serving *haute* pancakes, chorizo eggs and shiitake mushroom scramblers. Lunch brings Cobb salads and patty melts. Check out the vintage SoCal photographs on the walls. There's a dog-friendly outdoor patio, or grab a counter stool or booth inside. Breakfast all day, lunch from 11am.

★**Watson Soda Fountain Café** DINER $$
(☎714-202-2899; www.watsonscafe.com; 116 E Chapman Ave; mains $8-20; ⏰8am-9pm Mon-Thu, to midnight Fri, 7am-midnight Sat, 7am-9pm Sun) Established in 1899, this former drugstore was refurbished to a period design (check out the old safe, apothecary cabinets and telephone switchboard). It offers old-fashioned soda-fountain treats such as malts, milkshakes and sundaes, as well as burgers, fries, fried pickle chips and breakfast all day. Bonus: beer and wine list, and tall cakes in the adjacent Rockwell Bakery.

ℹ Information

Visit Anaheim (Map p430; ☎855-405-5020; http://visitanaheim.org; 800 W Katella Ave, Anaheim Convention Center, Anaheim) The city's official tourism bureau has information on lodging, dining and transportation, during events at the Convention Center.

Anaheim Urgent Care (☎714-533-2273; https://urgentmednetwork.com/anaheimeuclidurgentcare; 831 S State College Blvd, Anaheim; ⏰8am-8pm Mon-Fri, 9am-5pm Sat & Sun) Walk-in nonemergency medical clinic.

Anaheim Global Medical Center (☎714-533-6220; www.anaheim-gmc.com; 1025 S Anaheim Blvd, Anaheim; ⏰24hr) Hospital emergency room.

ℹ Getting There & Away

Anaheim's transit center, **ARTIC** (Anaheim Regional Transportation Intermodal Center; 2150 E Katella Ave, Anaheim), connects trains and buses from out of town with local transport. ARTIC is about 3 miles east of the Disneyland Resort.

AIR

Most international travelers arrive at Los Angeles International Airport (LAX) or San Diego (SAN), but for easy-in, easy-out domestic travel, nothing beats nearby **John Wayne Airport** (SNA; www.ocair.com; 18601 Airport Way, Santa Ana) in Santa Ana, served by all major US airlines and Canada's WestJet. The airport is about 14 miles south of Disneyland, near the junction of Hwy 55 and I-405 (San Diego Fwy). Ride-hailing services cost about $20 each way to Anaheim.

If you do arrive at LAX, it's barely an hour by road. **Super Shuttle** (www.supershuttle.com; LAX/SNA to Disneyland hotels one way $17/11) operates from LAX to Disney resort hotels from $17 each way (more expensive to Disneyland proper).

BUS

Anaheim Resort Transportation (ART; ☎888-364-2787; www.rideart.org; adult/child fare $3/1, day pass $6/2.50, multiple-day passes available) ART connects the Disney resorts with hotels and other locations around Anaheim and nearby. Day passes can be purchased at hotels or via the ART Ticketing app (www.rideart.org/fares-and-passes).

Greyhound (☎714-999-1256; www.greyhound.com; 2626 E Katella Ave, Anaheim, ARTIC) has several daily buses between ARTIC and Downtown LA (from $6, 40 minutes) and San Diego (from $7, 2¼ hours).

The **Orange County Transportation Authority** (OCTA; ☎714-560-6282; www.octa.net; ride/day pass $2/5) operates throughout the county. Buy tickets onboard (cash only) or via the app.

TRAIN

Amtrak (☎800-872-7245; www.amtrak.com; 2626 E Katella Ave, ARTIC) has almost a dozen daily trains to/from LA's Union Station ($15.60, 40 minutes) and San Diego ($30.45, 2¼ hours). Less frequent **Metrolink** (☎800-371-5465; www.metrolinktrains.com; 22150 E Katella Ave, Anaheim, ARTIC) commuter trains connect Anaheim to LA's Union Station ($8.75, 50 minutes), Orange ($2.50, six minutes), San Juan Capistrano ($8.50, 40 minutes) and San Clemente ($10, 50 minutes).

ORANGE COUNTY BEACHES

You'll find gorgeous sunsets, prime surfing and just-off-the-boat seafood when traveling the OC's blissful 42 miles of surf and sand. But it's also the unexpected, serendipitous discoveries you'll remember: learning to surf the waves in Seal Beach, playing volleyball at Huntington Beach, piloting your own boat around Newport Harbor, wandering around eclectic art displays in Laguna Beach, or spotting whales on a cruise from Dana Point.

Seal Beach

First stop out of LA County, 'Seal' is one of the last great California beach towns and a refreshing alternative to the more crowded coast further south. Its 1.5 miles of pristine beach sparkle like a crown, and its three-block Main St is a stoplight-free zone with mom-and-pop restaurants and indie shops low on 'tude and high on charm.

Sights & Activities

Seal Beach Pier PIER

Where Main St ends, Seal Beach Pier begins, extending 1865ft over the ocean. The 1906 original fell victim to winter storms in the 1930s and has since been rebuilt three times with a wooden boardwalk. It's splintery in places, so wear shoes (no high heels!). Snap a picture of the playful bronze seal standing guard at the pier's east entrance – he may be the only one you see.

M&M Surfing School SURFING

(☎714-846-7873; www.surfingschool.com; 802 Ocean Ave; 1/3hr group lesson $80/90; ⌚lessons 8am-noon early Sep–mid-Jun, Sat & Sun year round, to 2pm Mon-Fri mid-Jun–early Sep; 👪) Offers group and private lessons that include surfboard and wet suit rental, for students age five and up. Look for its van in the parking lot just north of the pier, off Ocean Ave at 8th St. Book lessons via register.sealbeachca.gov.

Eating

Paradis ICE CREAM $

(☎562-936-0196; www.paradis-icecream.com; 205 Main St; ice cream $4.75-8.75; ⌚noon-9pm Mon-Thu, to 10pm Fri, 11am-10pm Sat, 11am-9:30pm Sun) Paradis makes about 200 (whoa!) flavors of ice cream, of which it serves about 16 on any given day, so there's always a reason to come back. They also do creative combos of ice cream with coffee: latte, *affogato* (ice cream in espresso) and signature hot cocoa.

Crema Café CAFE $

(☎562-493-2501; www.cremacafe.com; 322 Main St; mains $9.25-17; ⌚6:30am-3pm Mon-Fri, 7am-4pm Sat & Sun; 👪🐾) Brunch rules at this indoor-outdoor, Euro-inspired cafe; think sweet and savory French crepes – artichoke and chicken; chocolate; Nutella and banana – and satisfying omelets and Benedicts. In a hurry? The made-from-scratch pastries and muffins are fab, as are the garden-fresh salads and toasted panini. There's a kids menu, and Crema has been voted one of the OC's most pet-friendly restaurants.

★**Walt's Wharf** SEAFOOD $$$

(☎562-598-4433; www.waltswharf.com; 201 Main St; mains lunch $13-29, dinner $18-42; ⌚11am-9pm) Everybody's favorite for fresh fish (some drive in from LA), Walt's packs them in on weekends. You can't make reservations for dinner (though they're accepted for lunch), but it's worth the wait for the oak-fire-grilled seafood and steaks in the many-windowed ground floor or upstairs in captain's chairs. Otherwise, eat at the bar.

★**Mahé** FUSION $$$

(☎562-431-3022; www.eatatmahe.com; 1400 Pacific Coast Hwy; mains $15-55; ⌚opens 4pm Mon-Thu, 3pm Fri, 11:30am Sat, 10am Sun, closing hours vary; 🅿) Raw-fish fans gather barside at this beach-chic sushi bar with live bands some nights in the back room. Sake salmon, ahi *tataki* wraps, and filet mignon with Gorgonzola cream sauce all hang out on the Cal-Japanese menu. It's about five blocks from Main St but worth the walk.

Drinking & Entertainment

On Main St you'll find a surprising number of Irish pubs, alongside coffee bars; we're particularly fond of cozy Bogart's. Jazz, folk and bluegrass bands play by the pier at the foot of Main St from 6pm to 8pm every Wednesday during July and August for the annual **Summer Concerts in the Park**. The rest of the time, Main St is the kind of place where you'll find sidewalk musicians.

If dive bars are your thing, head a couple miles south to Sunset Beach, home of the biker hangout **Mother's Tavern** (☎562-592-2111; www.motherstavernsunsetbeach.com; 16701 Pacific Coast Hwy; ⌚11am-10pm Mon & Tue, to midnight Wed-Sun) and 1953-vintage **Turc's** (☎562-592-2311; 16321 Pacific Coast Hwy; ⌚11am-2am).

Bogart's Coffee House CAFE
(☎562-431-2226; www.bogartscoffee.com; 905 Ocean Ave; ⏰6am-9pm Mon-Thu, to 10pm Fri, 7am-10pm Sat, 7am-9pm Sun; 📶) At this award-winning coffeehouse around the corner from Main St, sip organic espresso drinks on leopard-print armchairs and play Scrabble as you watch the surf roll in on the beach across the street. Food includes crepes, panini and pastries, and Bogart's hosts live music Friday and Saturday nights.

Shopping

Be sure to walk the full three blocks of Main St and browse the eclectic shops.

Harbour Surfboards SPORTS & OUTDOORS
(☎562-430-5614; www.harboursurfboards.com; 329 Main St; ⏰9am-7pm Mon-Sat, to 6pm Sun) This place has been making surfboards since 1959, but it's also about the surf-and-skate lifestyle, man. Eavesdrop on local surfers talking about their wax as you pillage the racks of hoodies, wetsuits, T-shirts and beanie hats.

Anderson Brothers & Tankfarm FASHION & ACCESSORIES
(☎562-735-2320; www.tankfarmco.com; 212 Main St; ⏰10am-6pm Sun-Thu, to 8pm Fri & Sat) On a street dominated by women's clothing and beachwear, this Seal Beach–based brand carries duds for dudes craving the outdoor lifestyle: board shorts, hoodies, flannels and blankets from brands like Herschel and Deus Ex Machina, plus its own cool tees, woven shirts and accessories.

Up, Up & Away GIFTS & SOUVENIRS
(☎562-596-7661; http://upupandawaykites.com; 139 1/2 Main St; ⏰10am-7pm Sun-Thu, to 8pm Fri & Sat) This shop's specialty is kites in every color of the rainbow and tons of decorative flags: lighthouses, sailboats, sports-team logos, frogs wearing sunglasses – if you want to wave it, there's a flag for it. There are badass beach kites, nostalgic toys like Gumby and Mr Bill, and Moo Poppers that shoot balls from their mouths.

Endless Summer CLOTHING
(☎562-430-9393; 124 Main St; ⏰11am-6pm) Teenie Wahine, Roxy and Billabong jostle for attention at this bustling store for girly tweens to college-age beach babes. It's packed with bikinis, beach bags, shades and loads more.

COASTAL OC TIPS

Sleeping

Accommodations along the coast span campgrounds to intimate motels and massive resort hotels. There are few budget options near the water, and especially during summer vacation season. For a cheaper stay, look to motels around I-405 and I-5, which parallel the coast a few miles inland.

Bus

Orange County Transportation Authority (p437) bus line 1 runs along Pacific Coast Hwy (CA-1) from Long Beach in southern LA county to San Clemente in southern Orange County. The one-way fare/day pass is $2/5 (exact change). Alternatively, download the OC Bus app to buy tickets and discounted day passes ($4.50).

Parking

Read parking signage carefully. With luck, you may find a free parking spot. Otherwise, metered parking starts at $1-$1.50 per hour, and parking lots by the ocean range from about $5 per day in Dana Point to $20 in Laguna Beach.

Huntington Beach

'No worries' is the phrase you'll hear over and over in Huntington Beach, the town that goes by the trademarked nickname 'Surf City USA.' In 1910 real-estate developer and railroad magnate Henry Huntington hired Hawaiian-Irish surfing star George Freeth to give demonstrations. When legendary surfer Duke Kahanamoku moved here in 1925, that solidified its status as a surf destination. Buyers for major retailers come here to see what surfers are wearing, then market the look.

Sights

Huntington Beach Pier HISTORIC SITE
(cnr Main St & Pacific Coast Hwy; ⏰5am-midnight) The 1853ft Huntington Pier is one of the West Coast's longest. It has been here – in one form or another – since 1904, though the mighty Pacific has damaged giant sections or completely demolished it multiple times since then. The current concrete structure was built in 1983 to withstand 31ft waves or a 7.0-magnitude earthquake, whichever hits HB first. On the pier you can rent fishing

gear from **Let's Go Fishing** (714-960-1392; 21 Main St, Huntington Beach Pier; fishing sets per hour/day $6/15; hours vary) bait and tackle shop.

Huntington City Beach BEACH
(www.huntingtonbeachca.gov; 5am-10pm; P) One of SoCal's best beaches, the sand surrounding the pier at the foot of Main St gets packed on summer weekends with surfers, volleyball players, swimmers and families. Bathrooms and showers are located north of the pier at the back of the snack-bar complex. In the evening volleyball games give way to beach bonfires.

International Surfing Museum MUSEUM
(714-960-3483; www.huntingtonbeachsurfing museum.org; 411 Olive Ave; admission $3; noon-5pm Tue-Sun) Look for the world's biggest surfboard next to this small museum, an entertaining stop for surf-culture enthusiasts. Temporary exhibits chronicle the sport's history with photos, vintage surfboards, movie memorabilia and surf music. For the best historical tidbits, spend a minute chatting with the all-volunteer staff. That surfboard? It's 42ft long, 1300lbs, holds 66 people and the Guinness World Record.

Activities

Huntington is a one-stop shop for outdoor pleasures by OC beaches. If you forgot to pack beach gear, head to Zack's or Dwight's Beach Concession. Huntington Surf & Sport (p442) rents boards and wetsuits.

Surfing

For newbie surfers, Zack's offers lessons. If you're an experienced surfer, keep in mind that surfing in HB is competitive. Control your longboard or draw ire from local dudes who pride themselves on being 'aggro.' Surf north of the pier.

Zack's SURFING
(714-536-0215; www.zackssurfcity.com; 405 Pacific Coast Hwy; group lessons $85, surfboard rentals per hour/day $12/35, wetsuits $5/15) This well-established outfit by the pier offers surfing lessons and rents all sorts of beach equipment, including umbrellas, beach chairs, bikes and volleyballs. Lessons include equipment rental for the day.

Dwight's Beach Concession SURFING
(714-536-8083; www.dwightsbeachconcession.com; 201 Pacific Coast Hwy; surfboard rentals per hour/day $10/40, bicycle rentals from $10/30; 9am-5pm Mon-Fri, to 6pm Sat & Sun) Rents surfboards, bodyboards, bikes and other beach gear at competitive rates. It's HB's oldest longest running business, since 1932.

Cycling & Skating

Explore the coast while cycling or skating along the 8.5-mile **paved recreational path** running from Huntington State Beach in the south to Bolsa Chica State Beach in the north.

Vans Off the Wall Skatepark OUTDOORS
(714-379-6666; www.vans.com/skateparks-hb.html; 7471 Center Dr; helmet & pad set rentals $5; 9am-8pm) FREE This custom-built facility by the OC-based sneaker and skatewear company has plenty of ramps, bowls, dips, boxes and rails for boarders to catch air. BYOB (board). Helmets and pads required for visitors under 18.

Festivals & Events

Every Tuesday night brings street fair and farmers market **Surf City Nights** (www.surfcityusa.com/things-to-do/attractions/surf-city-nights/; 1st 3 blocks Main St; 5-9pm Tue). Car buffs get up early on Saturday mornings for the **Donut Derelicts Car Show** (www.donutderelicts.com; cnr Magnolia St & Adams Ave), a weekly gathering of woodies, beach cruisers and pimped-out street rods, 2.5 miles inland from Pacific Coast Hwy. The **4th of July celebration** (www.hb4thofjuly.org) is said to be the largest west of the Mississippi.

Huntington Harbor Cruise of Lights CHRISTMAS
(www.cruiseoflights.org; 16889 Algonquin St; adult/child $21/14; mid-late Dec) If you're here for the Christmas holidays, don't miss the evening boat tour past harborside homes twinkling with holiday lights. Run by the Philharmonic Society, cruise proceeds go to support youth music education programs.

Vans US Open of Surfing SURFING
(www.usopenofsurfing.com; Huntington Beach Pier; late Jul & early Aug) This six-star competition lasts more than a week and draws more than 600 world-class surfers, skateboarders and BMX competitors. Other festivities include beach concerts and movie premieres.

GIMME MORE!

Want even more surf and sand? **Huntington State Beach** (714-536-1454; www.parks.ca.gov/huntington; 21601 Pacific Coast Hwy; 6am-10pm; P) extends 2 miles from Beach Blvd (Hwy 39) to the Santa Ana River and Newport Beach boundary. All-day parking costs $15. Meanwhile, dogs can romp in the surf at **Huntington Dog Beach** (714-841-8644; www.dogbeach.org; Pacific Coast Hwy btwn Goldenwest & Seapoint Sts; 5am-10pm; P), north of Huntington City Beach. Nearly a mile long, it's a postcard-perfect place to play with your pooch. Parking meters cost 25¢ every 10 minutes.

Stretching alongside Pacific Coast Hwy between Huntington Dog Beach to the south and Sunset Beach to the north, **Bolsa Chica State Beach** (714-377-5691; www.parks.ca.gov/bolsachica; Pacific Coast Hwy btwn Seapoint & Warner Aves; parking $15; 6am-10pm; P) is a 3-mile-long strip of sand favored by surfers, volleyball players and fishers. Even though it faces a monstrous offshore oil rig, Bolsa Chica (meaning 'little pocket' in Spanish) gets mobbed on summer weekends. You'll find picnic tables, fire rings and beach showers, plus a bike path running north to Anderson Ave in Sunset Beach and south to Huntington State Beach.

Sleeping

Huntington Surf Inn MOTEL $$

(714-536-2444; www.huntingtonsurfinn.com; 720 Pacific Coast Hwy; r $120-250; P) You're paying for location at this two-story 1960s-era motel just north of Main St and across from the beach. Its 9 smallish rooms are individually decorated with surf and skateboard art – cool, brah – with firm mattresses and fridges, and microwaves on request. There's a small common deck area with a beach view.

★Paséa RESORT $$$

(855-622-2472; http://meritagecollection.com/paseahotel; 21080 Pacific Coast Hwy; r May-Aug from $359, rest of year from $280; P@) This hotel is slick and serene, with tons of light and air. Floors are themed for shades of blue from denim to sky and each of its 250 shimmery, minimalist, high-ceilinged rooms has an ocean-view balcony. As if the stunning pool, gym, Balinese-inspired spa and Pacific City–adjacent location weren't enough, *USA Today* named it America's most pet-friendly hotel.

Parking $40.

★Shorebreak Hotel BOUTIQUE HOTEL $$$

(714-861-4470; www.shorebreakhotel.com; 500 Pacific Coast Hwy; r from $269; P@) Stow your surfboard (lockers provided) as you head inside HB's hippest hotel, a stone's throw from the pier. The Shorebreak has 'surf ambassadors,' a wet suit mural in the lobby, pseudo-steampunk fitness center with climbing wall, and surfboard headboards in geometric-patterned rooms. Minibars stock temporary tattoos and surfboard wax, in case you forgot yours.

Waterfront Beach Resort RESORT $$$

(714-845-8000; www.waterfrontresort.com; 21100 Pacific Coast Hwy; r $279-390; P@) The lounge-chair-filled poolside may recall Vegas, until you see the backdrop: miles and miles of gorgeous deep-blue sea. Tiny surfers adorn the lobby fountain, and each of the 437 plush rooms (in two towers) has a balcony with ocean view, or watch the sunset from the rooftop Offshore 9 lounge. Bicycle rentals available. Parking $42.

Eating

Main St has been Huntington's restaurant strip for decades, and at **Pacific City** (www.gopacificcity.com; 21010 Pacific Coast Hwy; hours vary) shopping center, high-flying restaurants have unimpeded ocean views and food to match.

★Lot 579 FOOD HALL $

(www.gopacificcity.com/lot579; Pacific City, 21010 Pacific Coast Hwy; hours vary; P) The food court at HB's ocean-view mall offers some unique and fun restaurants for pressed sandwiches (Burnt Crumbs – the spaghetti grilled cheese is so Instagrammable), Vietnamese street food (Phans 55), coffee (Portola) and ice cream (Hans'). For the best views, take your meal to the deck, or eat at American Dream (brewpub) or Bear Flag Fish Company.

★Sancho's Tacos MEXICAN $

(714-536-8226; www.sanchostacos.com; 602 Pacific Coast Hwy; mains $6-10.75; 11am-8pm Mon-Fri, from 10am Sat & Sun; P) There's no shortage of taco stands in HB, but locals are fiercely dedicated to the original location of this local mini-chain, across from the beach.

This two-room shack with patio grills flounder, shrimp and tri-tip to order. Trippy Mexican-meets-skater art.

Sugar Shack CAFE $

(714-536-0355; www.hbsugarshack.com; 213½ Main St; mains $4.25-14; 6am-2pm Mon, Tue, Thu & Fri, to 8pm Wed, to 3pm Sat & Sun) Expect a wait at this HB institution, or get here early to see surfer dudes don their wetsuits. Breakfast is served all day on the bustling Main St patio and inside, where you can grab a spot at the counter or a two-top. Photos of surf legends plastering the walls raise this place almost to shrine status.

Cucina Alessá ITALIAN $$

(714-969-2148; http://cucinaalessarestaurants.com; 520 Main St; mains lunch $16-20, dinner $16-35; 11am-10pm) Every beach town needs its favorite go-to Italian kitchen. Alessá wins hearts and stomachs with classics like Neapolitan lasagna, butternut-squash ravioli and chicken marsala. Lunch brings panini, pizzas and pastas, plus breakfasts including 'famous' French toast. Get sidewalk seating, or sit behind big glass windows.

Duke's HAWAIIAN $$

(714-374-6446; www.dukeshuntington.com; 317 Pacific Coast Hwy; mains lunch $15-19, dinner $17-49; 11:30am-8:30pm Mon, to 9pm Tue-Sat, 10am-8:30pm Sun, bar open later) It may be touristy, but this Hawaiian-themed restaurant – named after surfing legend Duke Kahanamoku – is a kick. With unbeatable views of the beach, fresh fish and sassy cocktails, it's a primo spot to relax and show off your tan. For drinks and appetizers, the Barefoot Bar is open between lunch and dinner.

Drinking & Nightlife

It's easy to find a bar in HB: just walk up Main St.

★Bungalow CLUB

(714-374-0399; www.thebungalow.com/huntington-beach; Pacific City, 21058 Pacific Coast Hwy, Suite 240; 5pm-2am Mon-Fri, noon-2am Sat, noon-10pm Sun) The second location of this Santa Monica landmark of cool is in Pacific City, and with its combination of lounge spaces, outdoor patio, cozy, rustic-vintage design, specialty cocktails, DJs who know how to get the crowd going and – let's not forget – ocean views, it's setting new standards for the OC. The food menu's pretty great too.

Main Street Wine Company WINE BAR

(www.mainstreetwinecompany.com; 301 Main St, Suite 105; 4-9pm Mon, noon-10pm Tue-Thu, noon-11pm Fri, 1-11pm Sat, 1-9pm Sun) Boutique California-wine shop with a sleek bar, generous pours and meet-your-(wine)maker nights.

Huntington Beach Beer Co BAR

(714-960-5343; www.hbbeerco.com; 2nd fl, 201 Main St; from 11am, closing times vary;) Cavernous brewpub specializing in ales brewed in a half-dozen giant, stainless-steel kettles on-site, like the HB Blonde, Brickshot Red and seasonal beers flavored with sage to cherry. Try the sampler. DJs and dancing Thursday to Saturday nights.

Shopping

You'll find lots of one-off shops in central HB and some big, mostly chain stores in the Pacific City (p441) shopping center.

Huntington Surf & Sport SPORTS & OUTDOORS

(www.hsssurf.com; 300 Pacific Coast Hwy; 8am-9pm Sun-Thu, to 10pm Fri & Sat) Towering behind the statue of surf hero Duke Kahanamoku, this massive store supports the Surf City vibe with vintage surf photos, the **Surfers' Hall of Fame** (www.hsssurf.com/shof; 300 Pacific Coast Hwy) and lots of tiki-themed decor. You'll also find rows of surfboards to buy or rent, beachwear and surfing accessories.

Information

Visit Huntington Beach Information Kiosk

(714-969-3492; www.surfcityusa.com; Pier Plaza, 325 Pacific Coast Hwy; 10:30am-7pm Mon-Fri, from 10am Sat & Sun, shorter hours in winter) Visitor information kiosk by the pier.

Newport Beach

There are really three Newport Beaches: paradise for wealthy Bentley- and Porsche-driving yachtsmen and their trophy wives; perfect waves and beachside dives for surfers and stoners; and glorious sunsets and seafood for everyone else living the day-to-day. Somehow, these diverse communities all seem to live – mostly – harmoniously.

For visitors, the pleasures are many: just-off-the-boat seafood, boogie-boarding the human-eating waves, and the ballet of yachts in the harbor. You'll find more lifestyles of the rich and famous in Newport's shopping districts.

Sights

Newport is best known for its beach, and the Balboa Peninsula (p443) has some of the best access to both beaches, historic architecture and retro-cool amusements.

Balboa Peninsula AREA
(Map p444) Four miles long but less than a half-mile wide, Balboa Peninsula has a white-sand beach on its ocean side and countless stylish homes, including the 1926 landmark **Lovell Beach House** (Map p444; 1242 W Ocean Front) by noted architect Rudolf Schindler. Hotels, restaurants and bars cluster around the peninsula's two famous piers: **Newport Pier** near the western end and **Balboa Pier** at the eastern end. The two-mile oceanfront strip between them teems with beachgoers; people-watching is great.

Balboa Fun Zone AMUSEMENT PARK
(Map p444; www.thebalboafunzone.com; 600 E Bay Ave; Ferris wheel $4; ⏲ Ferris wheel 11am-6pm Sun-Thu, to 9pm Fri, to 10pm Sat; 👪) On the harbor side of Balboa Peninsula, the Fun Zone has delighted locals and visitors since 1936. There's a small Ferris wheel, arcade games, touristy shops and restaurants, and frozen banana stands (just like the one in the TV sitcom *Arrested Development*). Nearby the landmark 1906 **Balboa Pavilion** (Map p444; www.balboapavilion.com; 400 Main St) is beautifully illuminated at night. The Fun Zone is also the place to catch a harbor cruise, fishing or a whale-watching expedition, or the Balboa Island Ferry (p446) just across the channel.

Activities

Surfers flock to the breaks at the small jetties surrounding the Newport Pier between 18th and 56th streets. Word of warning: locals can be territorial. For lessons, try Huntington Beach or Laguna Beach instead. Rent equipment from **15th Street Surf & Supply** (Map p444; ☎949-751-7867; https://15thstsurfsupply.com; 103 15th St; boogie boards per hour/day $7/15, surfboards $15/40; ⏲ 8am-8pm summer, 9am-6pm rest of year).

Besides the beach, the best thing about Newport Beach is its harbor. Go full-on Newport and rent a flat-bottomed, canopied, electric **Duffy Boat** (Map p444; ☎949-577-8926; www.duffyofnewportbeach.com; 2001 W Coast Hwy; first 2hr $219; ⏲ 10am-8pm), a local institution that you pilot yourself around the harbor; bring tunes, food and drinks, and cruise with up to 12 friends. **Balboa Boat Rentals** (Map p444; ☎855-690-0794; http://boats4rent.com; 510 E Edgewater Pl; kayaks 2hr $25, powerboats 1/2hr $85/130, electric boats 1/2hr $95/160; ⏲ 10am-7pm, extended hrs in summer) can outfit you with powerboats, pontoon boats, kayaks and stand-up paddleboards (SUPs). For nature tours, try operators **Davey's Locker** (Map p444; ☎949-673-1434; www.daveyslocker.com; 400 Main St; per adult/child 3-12yr & senior 2½hr whale-watching cruise from $34/28, half-day sportfishing $45.50/38) and **Fun Zone Boat Co** (Map p444; ☎949-673-0240; www.funzoneboats.com; 700 Edgewater Pl; 45min cruise per adult/child 5-11yr from $15/5).

To experience fabulous ocean views, rent a bicycle from one of many shops and ride along the paved recreational path that encircles almost the entire Balboa Peninsula. Inland cyclists like the paved scenic loop around Upper Newport Bay Ecological Preserve (p449).

WORTH A TRIP

WETLAND WONDER: BOLSA CHICA ECOLOGICAL RESERVE

You'd be forgiven for overlooking **Bolsa Chica Ecological Reserve** (☎714-846-1114; http://bolsachica.org; 18000 Pacific Coast Hwy; ⏲ sunrise-sunset; 🅿) , at least on first glance. Against a backdrop of nodding oil derricks, this flat expanse of wetlands doesn't exactly promise the unspoiled splendors of nature. However, more than 200 bird species aren't so aesthetically prejudiced, either making the wetlands their home throughout the year, or dropping by mid-migration. Simply put, the restored salt marsh is an environmental success story.

Festivals & Events

Christmas Boat Parade CHRISTMAS
(www.christmasboatparade.com; ⏲ Dec) The week before Christmas brings thousands of spectators to Newport Harbor to watch a century-old tradition. The 2½-hour parade features up to 150 boats, including some fancy multimillion-dollar yachts all decked out with Christmas lights and holiday cheer.

Newport Beach Film Festival FILM
(www.newportbeachfilmfest.com; ⏲ Aug) Roll out the red carpet for screenings of over 350 mostly new independent and foreign films. Some films shown here, such as *Crash*, *Waitress*, *(500) Days of Summer* and *Chef*

Newport Beach

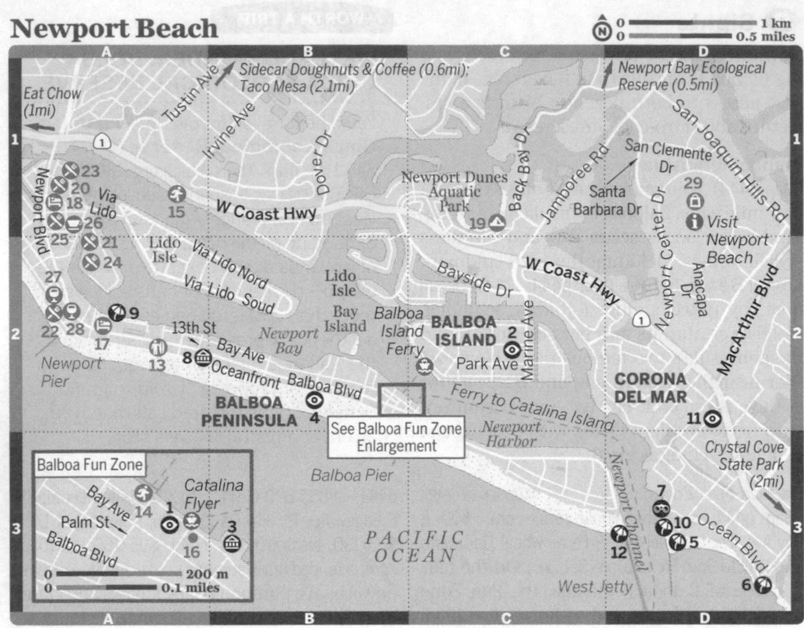

Newport Beach

Sights

1 Balboa Fun Zone ... A3
2 Balboa Island ... C2
3 Balboa Pavilion ... B3
4 Balboa Peninsula ... B2
5 Corona del Mar State Beach ... D3
6 Little Corona Beach ... D3
7 Lookout Point ... D3
8 Lovell Beach House ... A2
9 Mothers Beach ... A2
10 Pirate's Cove ... D3
11 Sherman Library & Gardens ... D2
12 The Wedge ... D3

Activities, Courses & Tours

13 15th Street Surf & Supply ... A2
14 Balboa Boat Rentals ... A3
Davey's Locker ... (see 3)
15 Duffy Electric Boat Rentals ... A1
16 Fun Zone Boat Co ... A3

Sleeping

17 Bay Shores Peninsula Hotel ... A2
18 Lido House ... A1
19 Newport Dunes Waterfront Resort ... C1

Eating

20 Bear Flag Fish Company ... A1
21 Buddha's Favorite ... A2
22 Dory Deli ... A2
23 Malibu Farm Lido ... A1
24 Sabatino's ... A2
25 Wild Taco ... A1

Drinking & Nightlife

26 Alta Coffee Warehouse ... A1
27 Mutt Lynch's ... A2
28 Stag Bar ... A2

Shopping

29 Fashion Island ... D1

have gone on to become classics, while earlier classics like *Sunset Boulevard* get anniversary screenings.

Newport Beach Wine and Food FOOD & DRINK
(www.newportwineandfood.com; late Sep-early Oct) Flashy food-and-wine fest shows off local restaurateurs, top chefs, prestigious winemakers and brewmasters with live rock concerts staged near Fashion Island (p446).

Sleeping

Newport Dunes Waterfront Resort CAMPGROUND $
(Map p444; 949-729-3863; www.newportdunes.com; 1131 Back Bay Dr; campsite from $67, cottage/1-bedroom cottage from $95/159; P @) RVs and tents aren't required

for a stay at this upscale campground: two dozen tiny, well-kept A-frames and picket-fenced one-bedroom cottages are available, all within view of Newport Bay. A fitness center and walking trails, kayak rentals, board games, family bingo, ice-cream socials, horseshoe and volleyball tournaments, outdoor pool and playground, and summertime movies on the beach await. Wheelchair-accessible.

Bay Shores Peninsula Hotel HOTEL **$$$**
(Map p444; 949-675-3463; www.thebestinn.com; 1800 W Balboa Blvd; r incl breakfast $175-300; P ❄ @ ☎) With a 50-plus-year history, this family-run, three-story hotel flexes some surf-themed muscle. From complimentary fresh-baked cookies to free rental movies, it's beachy, casual and customer-focused with surf-themed murals in each room. Complimentary parking, beach gear and continental breakfast buffet, best enjoyed on the 360-degree-view sun deck. Coin-op laundry available.

★Lido House HOTEL **$$$**
(Map p444; 949-524-8500; www.lidohousehotel.com; 3300 Newport Blvd; P ❄ @ ☎) Newport's newest lodging (opened in 2018) is also one of its coolest. There's a beach-house feel of nautical blues and whites enhanced by works by local artists and panoramic views from Topside, the town's only rooftop bar. Other fun touches: ice-cream shop, beach kits, bike, surfboard and bodyboard rentals, a beach shuttle, and great shopping across the street.

Eating

Dozens of Newport restaurants and pubs offer fish dinners (as you'd expect), plus nouveau Japanese and modern Mexican.

★Bear Flag Fish Company SEAFOOD **$**
(Map p444; 949-673-3474; www.bearflagfishco.com; 3421 Via Lido; mains $11-17; 11am-9pm Tue-Sat, to 8pm Sun & Mon;) This is *the* place for generously sized, grilled and *panko*-breaded fish tacos, ahi burritos, spankin' fresh ceviche and oysters. Pick out what you want from the ice-cold display cases, then grab a picnic-table seat. About the only way this seafood could be any fresher is if you caught and hauled it off the boat yourself!

Wild Taco MEXICAN **$**
(Map p444; 949-673-9453; www.facebook.com/wildtaconewport; 407 31st St; tacos $4.50, mains and combo meals $6-16; 11am-9pm Sun & Mon, to 10pm Tue-Sat; P) This nifty, Baja-inspired cantina makes salsas, *aguas frescas* (fruit drinks) and tortillas inhouse and serves them with tacos of grilled meats (*al pastor*), pork carnitas, shrimp and some delectable veggie options like grilled kale and feta. Mexican and Californian beers on tap, and margaritas are a steal. It's in a simple glass-fronted, concrete-floored room that can get loud.

Dory Deli DELI **$**
(Map p444; 949-220-7886; www.dorydeli.com; 2108 W Oceanfront; mains $8-13; 6am-8pm Sun-Thu, to 9pm Fri & Sat) This hip beachfront storefront does hot and cold sandwiches like the Rubinstein, Lifeguard Club and the steak-filled Rocky Balboa, plus fresh-caught fish and chips. For breakfast, you could be good and get the yoga pants burrito, or sin a little with chicken and waffles. Full bar too! Sure, we'll stop in after surfing...

★Malibu Farm Lido CALIFORNIAN **$$**
(Map p444; www.malibu-farm.com; 3420 Via Oporto, Lido Marina Village; small plates $13-20, large plates $20-31; P) Coastal chic rules at this whitewashed, indoor-outdoor *boîte* facing the yachts on the harbor. Cauliflower crust pizzas, Newport nachos, branzino fish tacos and Swedish mini-pancakes just taste better with a view this good.

Eat Chow CALIFORNIAN **$$**
(949-423-7080; www.eatchownow.com; 211 62nd St; mains $10-20; 8am-9pm Mon-Thu, to 10pm Fri, 7am-10pm Sat, 7am-9pm Sun) Hidden a block behind W Coast Hwy, Eat Chow's crowd is equal parts tatted hipsters and ladies who lunch, which makes it very Newport indeed. They all queue happily for rib-eye Thai beef salads, warm chicken curry salad, and the BBQ burger with homemade barbecue sauce, smoked Gouda, crispy onions and more.

Buddha's Favorite JAPANESE **$$**
(Map p444; 949-723-4203; www.buddhasfavorite.com; 634 Lido Park Dr; mains $9-29.50; 5:30-9pm Mon-Wed, to 10:30pm Thu & Fri, 2-10:30pm Sat, 2-9pm Sun) Who are we to disagree with the Enlightened One? This dockside sushi joint has a hipster following for creative hot and cold appetizers like sashimi 'candy,' *saikyo* miso black cod or *donburi* rice bowls. Snag a table outside on the heated deck and enjoy the twinkling harbor lights.

DON'T MISS

BALBOA ISLAND

In the middle of the harbor sits the **island** (Map p444; http://explorebalboaisland.com; P) that time forgot. Its streets are lined with tightly clustered cottages built in the 1920s and '30s when this was a summer getaway from LA. The 1.5-mile promenade that circles the island makes a terrific car-free stroll or jog. Departing from the Balboa Fun Zone (p443) on the Balboa Peninsula, the ferry lands at Agate Ave, about 0.6 miles west of Marine Ave, lined with swimwear boutiques, Italian trattorias and cocktail bars.

Sabatino's ITALIAN $$
(Map p444; 949-723-0621; www.sabatinoschicagosausage.com; 251 Shipyard Way; mains lunch $11-27, dinner $16-35; 9am-9pm) The claim to fame of this authentic Italian place on Lido Island is its handmade Chicago-style sausage, blended with Sicilian goat cheese for that cholesterol double-whammy. Family-size deli sandwiches, shrimp scampi and stuffed and baked pastas keep the locals coming back for more.

Drinking

The area around Newport Beach Pier is chock-a-block with drinking establishments, mostly pretty casual.

★ **Alta Coffee Warehouse** COFFEE
(Map p444; www.altacoffeeshop.com; 506 31st St; 6am-10pm Mon-Fri, from 7am Sat & Sun) Hidden on a side street, this cozy coffeehouse in a beach bungalow with a covered patio lures locals with live music and poetry readings, art on the brick walls and honest baristas who dish the lowdown on the day's soups, savories, popular comfort food and baked goods like carrot cake and cheesecake.

Mutt Lynch's BAR
(Map p444; 949-675-1556; www.muttlynchs.com; 2301 W Oceanfront; 7am-2am) By the beach, this rowdy dive (beer can chandelier, anyone?) offers schooners filled with dozens of beers on tap and cocktails made with *soju* (Korean vodka). Food from a huge menu comes in huge portions, especially at breakfast (mains $9- $15). Best on 'Sunday Fundays.'

Stag Bar BAR
(Map p444; 949-673-4470; www.stagbar.com; 121 McFadden Pl; 8am-2am) This giant space with a *looooong* bar reels them in for billiards, darts, creative cocktails and a chill vibe. Pub grub punches above its weight too, like skillet pancakes or breakfast pizza on weekend mornings, and daytime meatballs, salads and pizzas like the Meat Coma and Dirty Hippie.

Shopping

Fashion Island (Map p444; 949-721-2000; www.shopfashionisland.com; 401 Newport Center Dr; 10am-9pm Mon-Fri, to 7pm Sat, 11am-6pm Sun), inland from the beach, is Newport's biggest, most established shopping center (over 200 shops). The new **Lido Marina** district is small-scale upscale: about two dozen establishments including stylish boutiques and casual indoor-outdoor dining. On Balboa Island, **Marine Avenue** is lined with old-fashioned villagey shops, a good place to pick up something for the kids, unique gifts and beachy souvenirs, or jewelry, art and antiques.

Information

Visit Newport Beach (Map p444; 855-563-9767; www.visitnewportbeach.com; 401 Newport Center Dr, Fashion Island, Atrium Court; 10am-9pm Mon-Fri, to 7pm Sat, to 6pm Sun) The city's official visitor center hands out free brochures and maps.

Getting There & Around

BOAT

The West Coast's largest passenger catamaran, the **Catalina Flyer** (Map p444; 949-673-5245; www.catalinainfo.com; 400 Main St; round trip adult/child 3-12yr/senior $70/53/65, per bicycle $7), makes a daily round trip to Catalina Island, taking 75 minutes each way. It leaves Balboa Pavilion around 9am and returns before 6pm; check online for discounts.

Balboa Island Ferry (Map p444; www.balboaislandferry.com; 410 S Bay Front; adult/child $1/50¢, car incl driver $2; 6:30am-midnight Sun-Thu, to 2am Fri & Sat)

Around Newport Beach

Corona del Mar

Part of Newport Beach, south of Balboa Peninsula, Corona del Mar is a ritzy bedroom community with plenty of upscale stores and restaurants, some of SoCal's most celebrated ocean views from the bluffs, and postcard-perfect beaches with rocky coves and child-friendly tide pools.

Sights

Corona del Mar State Beach BEACH

(Big Corona Beach, Main Beach; Map p444; 949-644-3151; www.newportbeachca.gov; off E Shore Ave; 6am-10pm;) This half-mile-long beach lies at the foot of rocky cliffs and offers restrooms and fire rings (arrive early to snag one). It's popular for swimming, surfing and volleyball.

Lookout Point VIEWPOINT

(Map p444; 3001 Ocean Blvd) Locals enjoy impromptu, though not quite legal, cocktail parties at Lookout Point, perched above Corona del Mar State Beach (p447), with views of Pirate's Cove (p447) and the Balboa Peninsula (p443). Street parking only.

Pirate's Cove BEACH

(Map p444;) Take the stairs off the north end of the Corona del Mar State Beach (p447) parking lot down to hideaway Pirate's Cove, a waveless beach that's great for families. Scenes from the classic TV sitcom *Gilligan's Island* were shot here.

Little Corona Beach BEACH

(Map p444; 3100 Ocean Blvd;) FREE If you're seeking an escape, head down the steep hill to this secluded beach known for its tide pools. Kids love the tide pools, but be aware that the pools are being loved to death. Don't yank anything from the rocks and tread carefully: light, oxygen and heavy footsteps can kill the critters.

Sherman Library & Gardens NOTABLE BUILDING

(Map p444; 949-673-2261; www.slgardens.org; 2647 E Pacific Coast Hwy; adult/12-18yr/child under 12yr $5/3/free; free Mon; 10:30am-4pm, library closed Sat & Sun;) A variety of lush gardens awaits at Corona del Mar's prize attraction. On 2.2 acres, the profuse orchids, a rose garden, a koi pond and even a desert garden are worth a wander. The small, non-lending research library holds some 15,000 historical documents from California, Arizona, Nevada and Baja.

CRYSTAL COVE STATE PARK

A few miles of open beach and 2400 acres of undeveloped woodland at this **state park** (949-494-3539; www.parks.ca.gov; 8471 N Coast Hwy; per car $15; 6am-sunset;) let you forget you're in a crowded metropolitan area, at least once you get past the parking lots and stake out a place on the sand. Overnight guests can stay in the dozens of vintage cottages (reserve well in advance), and anyone can stop for a meal or cocktails at the Beachcomber restaurant.

Crystal Cove is also an underwater park. Scuba enthusiasts can check out two historic anchors dating from the 1800s as well as the crash site of a Navy plane that went down in the 1940s. Alternatively you can just go tide-pooling, fishing, kayaking and surfing along the undeveloped shoreline. On the park's inland side, miles of hiking and mountain-biking trails await.

Sleeping & Eating

★ **Crystal Cove Beach Cottages** CABIN $$

(reservations 800-444-7275; www.crystalcovealliance.org; 35 Crystal Cove, Crystal Cove State Park Historic District; dm with shared bath from $38, cottages from $269; check-in 4-9pm;) Right on the beach, these two dozen preserved cottages (circa 1930s to '50s) now host guests for a one-of-a-kind stay. Each cottage is different, sleeping between two and nine people in a variety of private or dorm-style accommodations. To snag one, book six months before your intended stay – or pray for cancellations.

Crystal Cove Shake Shack AMERICAN $

(949-464-0100; 7703 E Coast Hwy; mains $5-9; 7am-8pm;) At this 1946-vintage wooden snack stand, the shakes – and the ocean views – are as good as ever. Don't fear the date shake; it's delish. They also serve snacks ,and simple meals (sandwiches, burgers, fries, chili, etc) and a kids menu. Expect lunchtime waits during summer and on weekends.

Beachcomber Café AMERICAN $$

(949-376-6900; www.thebeachcombercafe.com; 15 Crystal Cove; mains breakfast $9-19, lunch $14-21, dinner $20-47; 7am-9pm Sun-Thu, to 10pm Fri & Sat) The much-loved seaside joint lets you soak up the vintage 1950s beach vibe as you tuck into macadamia-nut pancakes, roasted turkey club sandwiches or more serious surf-and-turf. Sunset is the magic hour for Polynesian tiki drinks by the sea.

Costa Mesa

Northeast of Newport Beach and so close that they're often lumped together, Costa Mesa at first glance looks like just another landlocked suburb transected by I-405, but top venues attract some 24 million visitors each year. South Coast Plaza (p449) is SoCal's largest mall – properly termed a 'shopping resort.' Steps away the performing-arts venues **Segerstrom Center for the Arts**

(☎714-556-2787; www.scfta.org; 600 Town Center Dr) and **South Coast Repertory** (☎714-708-5555; www.scr.org; 655 Town Center Dr) lend the city's nickname, City of the Arts, and the **Orange County Museum of Art** is scheduled to open in its new location here in 2021. **California Scenario** (Noguchi Garden; http://henrysegerstrom.com/home/philanthropy/public-art/california-scenario; 611 Anton Blvd; ⊙8am-midnight) FREE is a stone sculpture garden designed by renowned artist Isamu Noguchi.

If that all sounds rather hoity-toity, a pair of 'anti-malls' bring hipster cool, while strip malls throughout town reveal surprisingly tasty dishes and ethnic-food holes-in-the-wall. There's some driving among these destinations, but combined they make Costa Mesa one of the OC's most interesting communities.

Sleeping

Crowne Plaza Costa Mesa HOTEL $$
(☎714-557-3000; www.cpcostamesa.com; 3131 Bristol St; r from $129; P) A decently priced, central stay with generous rooms, friendly staff, and pool, fitness and laundry facilities. Rooms facing the inner courtyard are quieter. It's about halfway between South Coast Plaza and the Camp and Lab areas, each about 10 minutes on foot along busy Bristol St, or a hotel shuttle can take you (it also serves the airport).

Avenue of the Arts Hotel HOTEL $$$
(☎714-751-5100; www.avenueoftheartshotel.com; 3350 Avenue of the Arts; from $209; P) Costa Mesa's poshest stay is in the cultural district and walking distance to South Coast Plaza. Rooms are sleek and modern, and our favorites have balconies overlooking a courtyard with a relaxing lagoon. There's a fitness center, pool and sauna, and the Silver Trumpet restaurant and bar. Parking is $27, and there's a free airport shuttle.

Eating

Taco Mesa MEXICAN $
(☎949-642-0629; www.tacomesa.net; 647 W 19th St; mains $3-13; ⊙7am-11pm;) Brightly painted in Mexican Day of the Dead art, this out-of-the-way stand is a local institution for fresh, healthy tacos of sustainably farmed steak, beer-battered fish and more, with an awesome salsa bar. We like the tacos blackened, with cheese, chipotle sauce, cabbage relish and *crema fresca*. The kids menu offers quesadillas and such.

Native Foods VEGAN $
(www.nativefoods.com; The Camp, 2937 Bristol St; mains $8-12; ⊙11am-10pm; P) Lunch in a yurt? In Orange County? Them's the digs at this vegan spot serving organic salads, veggie burgers, Nashville-style hot 'chicken' sandwiches, rice bowls like the Soul Bowl (imitation chicken, beans and rice with ranch and BBQ sauce) and ooey-gooey desserts. The kids menu includes vegan mac 'n' cheese and faux chicken strips.

Sidecar Doughnuts & Coffee DESSERTS $
(☎949-873-5424; www.sidecardoughnuts.com; 270 E 17th St; doughnuts from $3.50; ⊙6:30am-6pm Sun-Thu, to 9pm Fri & Sat; P) Tucked away in a nondescript strip mall, Sidecar's a pilgrimage for doughnut lovers. Weekend crowds queue out the door for a frequently changing lineup of one-of-a-kind flavors like Saigon cinnamon crunch, maple bacon, huckleberry, and butter and salt.

★**Taco María** MEXICAN $$
(☎714-538-8444; www.tacomaria.com; The OC Mix, 3313 Hyland Ave; a la carte tacos $15-18, prix-fixe dinner $84; ⊙11am-2:30pm Tue-Sun, 5:30-8:30pm Tue, prix-fixe dinner 5:30-9:30pm Wed-Sat; P) One of the county's two Michelin-starred restaurants, Taco María is the brainchild of OC-raised chef Carlos Salgado. He incorporates farmers market produce into tacos of chicken, pork belly, fried black cod and *arrachera* (hanger steak) on housemade tortillas, for two-to-a-plate taste explosions. Most nights are pricy prix-fixe dinners, while Sunday brunch spans pancakes to *huevos pescador* (like an elaborate seafood benedict).

Habana LATIN AMERICAN $$
(☎714-556-0176; www.habanacostamesa.com; The Lab, 2930 Bristol St; mains lunch $13-20, dinner $20-30; ⊙11am-1am Sun-Thu, 11:30am-2am Fri & Sat) With its flickering votive candles, ivy-covered courtyard and spicy Cuban, Mexican and Jamaican specialties, this sultry cantina whispers rendezvous. Paella, *ropa vieja* (shredded flank steak in tomato sauce), rum pepper shrimp and salmon *a la parilla* (grilled) come with plantains and black beans on the side. On weekends, the bar gets jumpin' late-night.

Drinking

Milk + Honey CAFE
(☎714-708-0092; www.milkandhoneycostamesa.com; the Camp, 2981 Bristol St; ⊙7am-10pm Mon-Thu, to 11pm Fri, 8am-11pm Sat, 8am-10pm Sun;)

This minimalist cool cafe takes fair-trade and organic coffee a little further with unusual flavor combinations that (mostly) work: Spanish latte, lavender latte, plus chai tea, fruit smoothies, seasonal froyo flavors and Japanese-style shave ice with flavors like strawberry, red bean and almond. There's a small menu of sandwiches and snacks.

Ruin BAR
(714-884-3189; http://theruinbar.com; The Lab, 2930 Bristol St; 5:30-11pm Mon-Wed, 2pm-2am Thu, noon-2am Fri & Sat, noon-midnight Sun) This intimate, eclectic bar is decorated kind of like grandma's attic...if grandma collected faux buffalo heads, piano fronts and a ski gondola, and crocheted her trees in yarn. There's a constantly changing selection of cocktails and beers on tap. It's on the southern side of the Lab.

Wine Lab WINE BAR
(714-850-1780, www.winelabcamp.com; The Camp, 2937 Bristol St, Suite A101B; noon-10pm Tue-Thu, to 11pm Fri & Sat, to 7pm Sun, 4-9pm Mon) This friendly wine and cheese bar and shop offers New World wine and craft-beer tasting flights, plus small plates of artisan cheeses and charcuterie.

Shopping

Shopping in Costa Mesa runs two extremes: luxury for the well-heeled at South Coast Plaza, and trendy 'anti-malls' the Camp and the Lab.

South Coast Plaza MALL
(800-782-8888; www.southcoastplaza.com; 3333 Bristol St; 10am-9pm Mon-Fri, to 8pm Sat, 11am-6:30pm Sun) The stats at SoCal's premier luxury shopping destination speak for themselves: about $2 billion in annual sales, over 250 boutiques, 46 restaurants, five department stores, three valet stations and 10,000 parking spaces. It's been in business since 1967, yet it still feels current. Grab a map (you'll need it) from a concierge desk.

★Camp MALL
(714-966-6661; www.thecampsite.com; 2937 Bristol St; 11am-8pm Mon-Sat, to 5pm Sun, individual shop hours vary) Vegans, tree huggers and rock climbers, lend me your ears. The Camp offers one-stop shopping for all your outdoor and natural-living needs. **Seed People's Market** for fair-trade home goods and the Japan-based **2nd Street** for name-brand secondhand fashion are among the stores clustered along a leafy outdoor walkway. Parking spaces are painted with inspirational quotes like 'Show Up for Life.'

WORTH A TRIP

UPPER NEWPORT BAY NATURE PRESERVE

The brackish water of this 752-acre **preserve** (949-923-2290; www.ocparks.com/parks/newport; 2301 University Dr; 7am-sunset; P) FREE, where runoff from the San Bernardino Mountains meets the sea, supports more than 200 species of birds. This is one of the few estuaries in Southern California that has been preserved and it's an important stopover on the Pacific Flyway migration route. There are also trails for jogging and cycling. For guided tours with naturalists and weekend kayak tours of the Back Bay, contact the Newport Bay Conservancy (http://newportbay.org).

★Lab MALL
(714-966-6661; www.thelab.com; 2930 Bristol St; 10am-9pm Sun-Thu, to 10pm Fri & Sat, individual shop hours vary;) Sister property to the Camp across the street, this outdoor, ivy-covered 'anti-mall' is the original, 1995, in-your-face alternative to South Coast Plaza, even if nowadays more (cool) national chains have moved in. Sift through vintage clothing, unique sneakers and trendy duds for teens, tweens and 20-somethings. For short attention spans, contemporary art exhibitions are displayed in shipping containers at ARTery.

Getting There & Away

Costa Mesa starts immediately inland from Newport Beach via Hwy 55. South Coast Plaza is off Bristol St, north of the intersection of I-405, toll road Hwy 73 and Hwy 55, about 6 miles northeast of Pacific Coast Hwy.

Several OCTA (p437) routes converge on South Coast Plaza, including bus 57 running along Bristol Ave south to Newport Beach's Fashion Island ($2, 20 minutes, every half hour).

Laguna Beach

It's easy to love Laguna: secluded coves, romantic cliffs, azure waves and waterfront parks imbue the city with a Riviera-like feel. But nature isn't the only draw. From public sculptures and renowned art festivals to free shuttle buses, the city has taken thoughtful

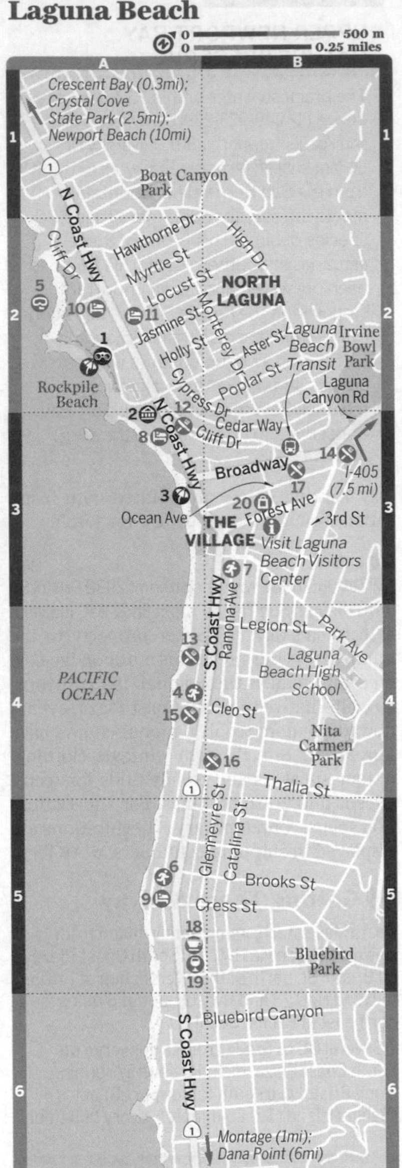

Laguna Beach

Sights

Activities, Courses & Tours

Sleeping

Eating

Drinking & Nightlife

Shopping

steps to promote tourism while discreetly maintaining its moneyed quality of life.

Sights

With 30 public beaches sprawling along 7 miles of coastline, there's always another stunning view or hidden cove just around the bend. A good local map or sharp eye will take you to stairways leading from the Pacific Coast Hwy down to the beach. Just look for the 'beach access' signs, and be prepared to pass through people's backyards to reach the sand. Rent beach chairs, umbrellas and boogie boards from **Main Beach Toys** (Map p452; ☎949-494-8808; 150 Laguna Ave; chairs/umbrellas/boards per day $15/15/25; ⏰10am-6pm, until sunset summer).

Laguna Art Museum MUSEUM

(Map p452; ☎949-494-8971; www.lagunaartmuseum.org; 307 Cliff Dr; adult/student & senior/child under 13yr $7/5/free, 5-9pm 1st Thu of month free; ⏰11am-5pm Fri-Tue, to 9pm Thu) This breezy museum has changing exhibitions featuring contemporary California artists, and a permanent collection heavy on California landscapes, vintage photographs and works by early Laguna bohemians. Free guided tours are usually given at 11am, and there's a unique gift shop.

Pacific Marine Mammal Center NATURE CENTER

(☎949-494-3050; www.pacificmmc.org; 20612 Laguna Canyon Rd; donations welcome; ⏰10am-

4pm; P) FREE A nonprofit organization dedicated to rescuing and rehabilitating injured or ill marine mammals, this center northeast of town has a small staff and many volunteers who help nurse Orange County's rescued pinnipeds – mostly sea lions and seals – before releasing them back into the wild. Visitors can view outdoor pools and holding pens – but remember, this is a rescue center, not SeaWorld. Still, it's educational and heartwarming.

Activities

Diving & Snorkeling

With its coves, reefs and rocky outcroppings, Laguna is one of the best SoCal beaches for diving and snorkeling. One of the most famous spots is **Divers Cove** (Map p452) just below Heisler Park. It's part of the **Glenn E Vedder Ecological Reserve**, an underwater park stretching to the northern border of Main Beach. Also popular is **Shaw's Cove**. Check weather and surf conditions with the city's **marine safety forecast line** (949-494-6573) beforehand, as drownings have happened. The visitors bureau has tide charts.

Kayaking

Take a guided kayaking tour of the craggy coves of Laguna's coast with **La Vida Laguna** (Map p452; 949-275-7544; www.lavidalaguna.com; 1257 S Coast Hwy; 2hr guided tour from $95) and you might just see a colony of sea lions. Make reservations in advance.

Hiking

Surrounded by a green belt – a rarity in So Cal – Laguna has great nature trails for hikes. If you love panoramic views, take the short, scenic drive to locals-only **Alta Laguna Park**, up-canyon from town. There, the moderate **Park Avenue Nature Trail**, a 1.25-mile one-way hike, takes you through fields of spring wildflowers. Open to hikers and mountain bikers, the 2.5-mile **West Ridge Trail** follows the ridgeline of the hills above Laguna. Both trails are in-and-out trips, not loops. To reach the trailheads, take Park Ave to its end at Alta Laguna Blvd then turn left to the park, which has restrooms and a drinking fountain.

Sleeping

Laguna has plenty of high-quality accommodations, most on busy Pacific Coast Hwy, so expect traffic noise; bring earplugs or ask for a room away from the road.

La Casa del Camino HISTORIC HOTEL $$
(Map p452; 949-497-6029, 855-634-5736; www.lacasadelcamino.com; 1289 S Coast Hwy; r from $134; P) A bargain for downtown Laguna, this 1929 Spanish-style hotel has 36 rooms and inspiring views from the **Rooftop Lounge** (Map p452; www.rooftoplagunabeach.com; 1289 S Coast Hwy; 11:30am-9pm Mon-Thu, to 10pm Fri & Sat, 10:30am-9pm Sun) bar. No two rooms are the same and the Casa surf rooms feature hip design by local surf-gear companies.

Tides Inn MOTEL $$
(Map p452; 949-494-2494, 888-777-2107; www.tideslaguna.com; 460 N Coast Hwy; r $130-200 off season, $210-400 Jul & Aug; P) A bargain for Laguna, especially considering its convenient location just three long blocks north of the village. The feel is understated refinement: plush bedding, beachy-keen decor and inspirational quotes painted into each room. Each room is different; some have kitchenettes and many have wooden floors. Shared facilities include a heated saltwater pool, barbecue grill and fireplace for toasting marshmallows.

★ **Ranch at Laguna Beach** RESORT $$$
(949-499-2271, reservations 800-223-3309; www.theranchlb.com; 31106 S Coast Hwy; r from $349; P) This lovely resort is secluded away in Aliso Creek Canyon on the south side of town. Ninety-seven rooms, suites and a standalone tree house are in multiple buildings spread across 87 acres, sporting a subtle, rustic refinement with board-and-batten construction and hand-painted tile bathrooms.

TIDE POOL EXPLORATIONS

North of downtown Laguna, off Cliff Dr north of **Heisler Park** (Map p452; 375 Cliff Dr), **Shaw's Cove** provides the best tide-pooling around. Volunteers are often on duty to answer questions and give you tide-pooling tips. Further on, **Crescent Bay** has big hollow waves good for bodysurfing, but parking is difficult; try the bluffs atop the beach; the views here are reminiscent of Italy's Amalfi Coast.

Tread lightly on dry rocks only and don't pick anything up that you find living in the water or on the rocks.

TOP BEACHES IN ORANGE COUNTY

Seal Beach (p438)

Bolsa Chica State Beach (p441)

Huntington City Beach (p440)

Balboa Peninsula (p443)

Crystal Cove State Beach (p447)

Aliso Beach County Park (949-923-2280; http://ocparks.com/beaches/aliso; 31131 S Pacific Coast Hwy; parking per hour $1; 6am-10pm; P)

Doheny State Beach (p455)

★**Laguna Beach House** HOTEL **$$$**
(Map p452; 949-497-6645; www.thelagunabeachhouse.com; 475 N Coast Hwy; r $205-419; P) Be it good feng shui, friendly staff or proximity to the beach, this 36-room courtyard inn feels right. From the surfboards in the lobby to colorful throw pillows and clean white walls and linens, the decor is contemporary, comfy and clean, around a heated pool and fire pit.

Inn at Laguna Beach HOTEL **$$$**
(Map p452; 949-497-9722; www.innatlagunabeach.com; 211 N Coast Hwy; r & suites $250-700; P) Pride of place goes to this three-story white, modern hotel, at the north end of **Main Beach** (Map p452;). Its 70 keen rooms feature rattan furniture, blond woods, marble, French blinds and pillow-top beds. Some have balconies overlooking the water. Extras include smart TVs, bathrobes, beach gear to borrow and nightly ocean-view wine reception.

★**Montage** RESORT **$$$**
(949-715-6000; www.montagelagunabeach.com; 30801 S Coast Hwy; r from $795; P@) You'll find nowhere more indulgent on the OC's coast than this luxury waterside resort, especially if you hide away with your lover in a secluded bungalow. Even the most basic of its 259 rooms are plush and generous, offering California arts-and-crafts style, marble bathrooms, lemon verbena bath products and unobstructed ocean views. Staff could not be more attentive.

Eating

Laguna's dining scene will tickle foodies' fancies. Vegetarians will be happy, too, especially at the weekly **farmers market** (Map p452; 949-301-9180; www.facebook.com/lagunabeachfm; 505 Forest Ave; 8am-noon Sat) in the Lumberyard parking lot, near City Hall.

Orange Inn DINER **$**
(Map p452; 949-494-6085; www.orangeinncafe.com; 703 S Coast Hwy; mains $7-13; 5:30am-5:30pm) Birthplace of the smoothie (it's in the *Guinness World Records*), this little 1931 shop continues to pack in surfers fueling up before hitting the waves. It also serves date shakes, big omelets and breakfast burritos, homemade muffins and deli sandwiches on whole-wheat or sourdough bread.

Stand VEGAN **$**
(Map p452; 949-494-8101; www.thestandnaturalfoods.com; 238 Thalia St; mains $8-15.50; 7am-8pm;) With its friendly, indie-spirited vibe comes this tiny tribute to healthy cuisine. From hummus and guac sandwiches to sunflower-sprout salads and black-beans-and-rice burritos, the menu is both long and soul satisfying. Try a smoothie or an all-natural shake. Order at the counter in the red minibarn, then cross your fingers for an outdoor patio table.

Zinc Cafe & Market CALIFORNIAN **$**
(Map p452; www.zinccafe.com; 350 Ocean Ave; mains $7-14; market 7am-5pm, cafe to 4pm;) This gourmet market has a lovely, minimalist patio where you can munch on tasty, vegetarian (though not vegan) Cali-classic breakfasts and lunches: avocado or poached eggs on toast, Mediterranean omelets, asparagus sandwiches with cauliflower purée, garden-fresh salads, pizzas and burgers.

★**Driftwood Kitchen** AMERICAN **$$$**
(Map p452; 949-715-7700; www.driftwoodkitchen.com; 619 Sleepy Hollow Lane; mains lunch $15-37, dinner $25-44; 9-10:30am & 11am-2:30pm Mon-Fri, 5-9:30pm Sun-Thu, to 10:30pm Fri & Sat, 9am-2:30pm Sat & Sun) Ocean views and ridiculous sunsets alone ought to be enough to bring folks in, but gourmet Driftwood steps up the food with seasonal menus centered around fresh, sustainable seafood, plus options for landlubbers. Inside it's all beachy casual, whitewashed and pale woods. And the cocktails are smart and creative.

242 Cafe Fusion Sushi JAPANESE **$$$**
(Map p452; 949-494-2444; www.fusionart.us; 242 N Coast Hwy; dishes $12-26, sushi market price; 4:30-10pm Sun-Thu, to 10:30pm Fri & Sat) One of the most renowned sushi chefs in Orange

County, Miki Izumisawa slices and rolls organic rice into Laguna's most creative, artfully presented sushi, sashimi and cooked dishes. For a real feast, splurge on the eight-course (plus dessert) *omakase* menu ($70). It's first come, first served, so arrive early or expect a wait.

Drinking & Nightlife

There are almost as many watering holes in downtown's village as there are art galleries. Most cluster along S Coast Hwy and Ocean Ave, making for an easy pub crawl. If you drink, don't drive; local cops take driving under the influence (DUI) very seriously.

Koffee Klatch COFFEE
(Map p452; 949-376-6867; 1440 S Coast Hwy; 7am-8pm Sun-Thu, to 9pm Fri & Sat;) About a mile south of downtown, this cozy coffee shop draws an eclectic gay/straight/hipster crowd for coffees, breakfasts served all day, salads and ginormous cakes.

Main Street GAY
(Map p452; 949-494-0056; www.mainstreet-bar.com; 1460 S Coast Hwy; 4pm-2am, closing hours may vary) Although Laguna has historically had one of SoCal's largest gay populations, this Tudor-style house is the last gay bar standing. The lineup includes a mix of DJs, disco and the OC's best drag shows. Check the website for calendar listings and drink specials.

Shopping

Downtown's village is a shopper's paradise, with hidden courtyards and little bungalows that beg further exploration. Forest Ave has the highest concentration of chic boutiques, but south of downtown, Pacific Coast Hwy has its fair share of fashionable and arty shops where you can balance your chakras or buy vintage albums and posters.

Hobie Surf Shop SPORTS & OUTDOORS
(Map p452; 949-497-3304; www.hobiesurfshop.com; 294 Forest Ave; 9am-7pm) Hobart 'Hobie' Alter started his internationally known surf line in his parents' Laguna Beach garage in 1950. Today, this is one of only a handful of logo retail shops where you can stock up on surfboards and beachwear (love those flip-flops in rainbow colors!) for babes and dudes.

Information

Visit Laguna Beach Visitors Center (Map p452; 949-497-9229; www.lagunabeachinfo.com; 381 Forest Ave; 10am-5pm;) Helpful staff, bus schedules, restaurant menus and free brochures on everything from hiking trails to self-guided walking tours.

Getting There & Away

From I-405, take Hwy 133 (Laguna Canyon Rd) southwest. If you're coming from along the coast via Hwy 1, know that it changes names in Laguna Beach: south of Broadway, it's called South Coast Hwy; north of Broadway it's North Coast Hwy.

Getting Around

BUS

Laguna Beach Transit (Map p452; www.lagunabeachcity.net; 375 Broadway) has its central bus depot in downtown's village. Buses operate on three routes at hourly intervals (no service from 12:30pm to 1:30pm or on Sundays or public holidays). Routes are color-coded and are easy to follow. For tourists, the most important bus route is the red route that runs south of downtown along Pacific Coast Hwy. Rides cost 75¢ (exact change). All routes are free during July and August.

FESTIVALS & THE CITY

Laguna's **Festival of Arts** (www.foapom.com; 650 Laguna Canyon Rd; admission adult/child/student & senior $10-15/5/7-11; noon-11:30pm Mon-Fri, from 10am Sat & Sun Jul & Aug;) is a two-month celebration of original artwork in almost all its forms by about 140 OC-based artists displaying paintings and handcrafted furniture to scrimshaw. Begun in the 1930s, the festival now attracts international patrons. In addition to the art show, there are kid-friendly art workshops and live music and entertainment daily. Across the road, look for the slightly more independent-minded **Sawdust Festival** (949-494-3030; www.sawdustartfestival.org; 935 Laguna Canyon Rd; adult/child 6-12yr/senior $9/4/7; 10am-10pm late Jun-early Aug, to 6pm Sat & Sun late Nov–mid-Dec), which also hosts a more limited festival in late fall.

The most thrilling part of the main festival – that will leave you rubbing your eyes in disbelief – is the **Pageant of the Masters** where human models blend seamlessly into recreations of famous paintings. Tickets are hard to get (order them months in advance) but you may be able to snag last-minute cancellations at the gate.

DON'T MISS

FIRST THURSDAYS

Once a month, downtown Laguna Beach gets festive during the **First Thursdays Gallery Art Walk** (949-683-6871; www.firstthursdaysartwalk.com; 6-9pm 1st Thu of month). Free shuttles make the rounds of over 30 local galleries and the Laguna Art Museum.

Around Laguna Beach

San Juan Capistrano

Famous for its swallows that fly back to town every year on March 19 (though sometimes they're just a bit early), San Juan Capistrano is home to the 'jewel of the California missions,' Roman Catholic outposts established in the late 18th and early 19th centuries. Amid that photogenic mission streetscape of adobe, tile-roofed buildings, and historic wood-built cottages, there's enough history and charm here to make almost a day of it.

'San Juan Cap' is a little town, just east of Dana Point and just over 10 miles southeast of downtown Laguna Beach.

Sights

★Mission San Juan Capistrano CHURCH

(949-234-1300; www.missionsjc.com; 26801 Ortega Hwy; adult/child $10/7; 9am-5pm;) Plan on spending at least an hour poking around the sprawling mission's tiled roofs, covered arches, lush gardens, fountains and courtyards – including the padre's quarters, soldiers' barracks and the cemetery. Admission includes an audio tour with interesting stories narrated by locals. Check out the towering remains of the Great Stone Church, almost completely destroyed by a powerful 1812 earthquake. The Serra Chapel – whitewashed outside with restored frescoes inside – is believed to be the oldest existing building in California (1782).

Los Rios Historic District HISTORIC SITE

One block southwest of the mission, next to the Capistrano train depot, this peaceful assemblage of a few dozen historic cottages and adobes now mostly houses cafes and gift shops. To see 1880s-era furnishings and decor, as well as vintage photographs, stop by the tiny **O'Neill Museum** (949-493-8444; https://sjchistoricalsociety.com/content/oneill-museum; 31831 Los Rios St; adult/child $1/50¢; 9am-noon & 1-4pm Tue-Fri, noon-3pm Sat & Sun).

Eating & Drinking

★El Campeon MEXICAN $

(31921 Camino Capistrano, El Adobe Plaza; items $2-9; 6:30am-9pm;) For real-deal Mexican food, in a strip mall south of the mission, try this multiroom restaurant, *panadería* (bakery) and *mercado* (grocery store). Look for tacos, tostadas and burritos in freshly made tortillas, *pozole* (hominy stew), pork carnitas, and *aguas frescas* in flavors like watermelon, strawberry and grapefruit.

★Ramos House Café CALIFORNIAN $$

(949-443-1342; www.ramoshouse.com; 31752 Los Rios St; weekday mains $16-21, weekend brunch $35; 8:30am-3pm Thu-Tue) The best spot for breakfast or lunch in Los Rios Historic District, this Old West–flavored, wood-built house from 1881 (with brick patio) does organically raised comfort food flavored with herbs grown on-site: banana-Nutella *pain perdu* (French toast), apple-cinnamon beignets, basil-cured salmon lox, huevos rancheros, and duck mac and cheese.

El Adobe de Capistrano MEXICAN $$

(949-493-1163; www.eladobedecapistrano.com; 31891 Camino Capistrano; mains $14-36; 11am-9pm Mon-Thu, to 10pm Fri & Sat, 10am-9pm Sun) In a building that traces its origins to 1797, this sprawling 'Mexican steakhouse' and bar does a big business in the standards (enchiladas, fajitas) through to prime rib, garlic shrimp and honey-chipotle salmon. It was a favorite of President Nixon, who lived in nearby San Clemente.

Coach House CLUB

(949-496-8930; www.thecoachhouse.com; 33157 Camino Capistrano; tickets from $20; hours vary) Long-running live-music venue featuring a roster of local and national rock, indie, alternative and tribute bands, like Jonny Lang and the Young Dubliners, plus comedians like Alonzo Bodden.

Getting There & Away

From Laguna Beach, ride OCTA (p437) bus 1 south to Dana Point. At the intersection of Pacific Coast Hwy and Del Obispo St, catch bus 91 northbound toward Mission Viejo, which drops you near the mission. Buses run every 30 to 60 minutes. The trip takes about an hour and costs $2 (exact change only) each way.

Drivers should take I-5 exit 82 (Ortega Hwy). There's free three-hour parking on streets and in municipal lots.

The **Amtrak** (☎800-872-7245; www.amtrak.com; 26701 Verdugo St) depot is one block south and west of the mission. Trains serve LA ($20.45, 75 minutes) and San Diego ($23.85, 90 minutes). A few daily **Metrolink** (☎800-371-5465; www.metrolinktrains.com) commuter trains link San Juan Capistrano to Orange ($8.50, 45 minutes), with limited connections to Anaheim.

Dana Point

Dana Point was once called 'the only romantic spot on the coast.' Too bad that quote dates from seafarer Richard Dana's voyage here in the 1830s. Its built-up, parking-lotted harbor detracts from the charm of neighboring towns, but it still gets a lot of visitors to its lovely beaches and port for ocean activities like whale-watching and sportfishing.

Sights & Activities

Most attractions cluster in and around artificial Dana Point Harbor, at the foot of Golden Lantern St, just south of Pacific Coast Hwy off Dana Point Harbor Dr.

Rent bicycles at **Wheel Fun Rentals** (☎949-496-7433; www.wheelfunrentals.com; 25300 Dana Point Harbor Dr; cruiser rental per hour/day $12/32; ⏲9am-sunset daily late May-early Sep, Sat & Sun early Sep-late May) at Doheny State Beach. Off Dana Point Harbor Dr, **Capo Beach Watercraft Rentals** (☎949-661-1690; www.capobeachwatercraft.com; 34512 Embarcadero Pl; jet ski before/after 11:30am per hour Mon-Fri $104/120, Sat & Sun $115/135) and **Pure Watersports Dana Point** (☎949-661-4947; www.danapointjetski.com; 34671 Puerto Pl; rentals per hour kayak and SUP from $15, jet ski from $95; ⏲10am-6pm Mon-Fri, from 9am Sat & Sun) both rent kayaks for harbor paddling. For boat dive trips, try **Beach Cities Scuba** (☎949-443-3858; www.beachcitiesscuba.com; 34283 Pacific Coast Hwy; boat dive trips from $125; ⏲hours vary).

Doheny State Beach BEACH
(Map p49; ☎949-496-6171; www.dohenystatebeach.org; 25300 Dana Point Harbor Dr; per car $15; ⏲park 6am-10pm, visitor center 10am-4pm Wed-Sun; P 👪) Just south of Dana Point Harbor, California's first state beach was immortalized in the Beach Boys' hit 'Surfin' USA.' This mile-long beach is great for swimmers, surfers, surf fishers and tide-poolers. At the 62-acre coastal park you'll find picnic tables with grills, and volleyball courts, and spot migratory whales and butterflies in season. The park's **visitor center** has aquariums and other natural history exhibits.

Ocean Institute MUSEUM
(☎949-496-2274; www.ocean institute.org; 24200 Dana Pt Harbor Dr; adult/child 2-12yr $10/7.50; ⏲10am-4pm Mon-Fri, to 3pm Sat & Sun, last entry 2:15pm; P 👪) 🌿 This child-friendly educational center encompasses four separate ocean-centric 'adventures.' It is mostly reserved for school groups on weekdays, so it's best to come on weekends to enjoy the interactive marine-focused exhibits. On Sundays, admission includes the opportunity to discover what life was like aboard an early-19th-century tall ship, the brig **Pilgrim**. Guided tours of this full size replica of the ship sailed by Richard Dana during his journey around Cape Horn to California are offered hourly.

Salt Creek Beach BEACH
(☎949-923-2280; www.ocparks.com/beaches/salt; 33333 S Pacific Coast Hwy, off Ritz Carlton Dr; ⏲5am-midnight; P) Just south of the Laguna Beach boundary, this 18-acre county-run park is popular with surfers, sunbathers, bodysurfers and tide poolers. Families make the most of the park's picnic tables, grills, restrooms and showers – all sprawling beneath the elegant bluff-top Ritz-Carlton (p456) resort. Open in summer, a beach concession stand rents boogie boards, beach chairs and umbrellas. Pay-and-display parking costs $1 per hour.

Tours

In Mariner's Village off Dana Point Harbor Dr, Dana Wharf is the starting point for most boat tours and trips to Catalina Island. For more kid-friendly whale-watching tours and cruises, book ahead with the Ocean Institute.

FESTIVAL OF THE SWALLOWS

The famous swallows return to nest in the walls of Mission San Juan Capistrano every year around March 19, the feast of St Joseph, after wintering in South America. Their flight covers about 7500 miles each way. The highlight of the month-long **Festival of the Swallows** (Fiesta de las Golondrinas; ☎949-493-1976; www.swallowsparade.com; ⏲mid-Mar) is one of the largest nonmotorized parades in the country, which first took place in the 1930s.

Capt Dave's Dolphin & Whale Safari BOATING
(☎949-488-2828; www.dolphinsafari.com; 34451 Ensenada Pl; adult/child 3-12yr from $65/45) This popular outfit runs year-round dolphin- and whale-watching trips on a catamaran equipped with underwater viewing pods and a listening system for you to hear what's going on below the surface.

Dana Wharf Sportfishing BOATING
(☎888-224-0603; www.danawharf.com; 34675 Golden Lantern St; sportfishing trips adult/child 3-12yr/senior from $51/32/46, whale-watching tours from $49/29/39) Half-day sportfishing trips are best for beginners. Family whale-watching tours in winter and summer.

Festivals & Events

Doheny Blues Festival MUSIC
(https://dohenybluesfestival.com; Doheny State Beach; ⊙mid-May) Blues, rock and soul legends perform alongside up-and-comers over a weekend of funky live-music performances and family fun at Doheny State Beach. Headliners have included Blues Traveler, Buddy Guy, Melissa Etheridge, Mavis Staples and Chris Isaak.

Festival of Whales FAIR
(http://festivalofwhales.com; ⊙early–mid-Mar) For two weekends, a parade, street fair, nature walks and talks, canoe races, surfing clinics, art exhibitions, live music, and surf 'woody' wagon and hot-rod show make up the merriment.

Tall Ships Festival SAILING
(www.tallshipsfestival.com; ⊙early Sep;) The Ocean Institute (p455) hosts the West Coast's largest gathering of tall ships, with living-history encampments, themed meals (mermaid breakfast, anyone?), scrimshaw carving demonstrations and lots more family-friendly marine-themed activities.

Sleeping & Eating

There are plenty of midrange chain motels near Dana Point Harbor, along Pacific Coast Hwy. At the top end of the spectrum is the oceanfront stunner, the **Ritz-Carlton Laguna Niguel** (☎949-240-2000; www.ritzcarlton.com; 1 Ritz-Carlton Dr; r from $599;), well positioned for catching sunsets at Salt Creek Beach. For budget motels, head inland along I-405 (San Diego Fwy) back toward Irvine.

Turk's GRILL $
(☎949-496-9028; 34683 Golden Lantern St; mains $6-16; ⊙8am-2am, shorter hours winter) At Dana Wharf, this dive bar is so dark it feels like you're drinking while jailed in the brig of a ship, but never mind. There's plenty of good pub grub (including burgers and fish and chips), Bloody Marys and beers, a mellow crowd and a groovy jukebox.

Jon's Fish Market SEAFOOD $$
(☎949-496-2807; 34665 Golden Lantern; mains $10.50-18.50; ⊙11am-7pm Sun-Thu, to 8pm Fri & Sat, open 1hr later in summer;) This counter-service fish market does large, hearty portions of deep-fried ocean goodness: famous fish and chips, scallops, clams, shrimp and calamari, all with fries and coleslaw. Eat inside or on the dock.

Information

Dana Point Chamber of Commerce & Visitor Center (☎949-248-3501; www.danapoint.org; cnr Golden Lantern & Dana Point Harbor Dr; ⊙9am-4pm Fri-Sun late May-early Sep) Stop at this tiny booth for tourist brochures and maps. Gung-ho volunteers sure love their city.

Getting There & Away

From the harbor, **Catalina Express** (☎800-481-3470; www.catalinaexpress.com; 34675 Golden Lantern St, Dana Wharf Sportfishing; round trip adult/child 2-11yr/senior $76.50/70/61) makes daily round trips to Catalina Island, 90 minutes each way.

Four-hour public parking at the harbor is free, or pay $5 per day (overnight $10).

San Clemente

Just before reaching San Diego County, Pacific Coast Hwy (PCH) slows down and rolls past the laid-back surf town of San Clemente. Home to surfing legends, top-notch surfboard companies and the Surfing Heritage & Culture Center, this unpretentious enclave may be one of the last spots in the OC where you can authentically live the surf lifestyle.

The city center is also one of SoCal's most picturesque as the sun glimmers off the ocean. Head south off PCH and follow **Avenida del Mar** as it curves downhill toward the ocean.

Further south along the coast, at the foot of Trafalgar St, **T-Street** is a popular surf break, as is Trestles Beach.

Sights

San Clemente Pier PIER
(611 Avenida Victoria; ⏰4am-midnight; P) San Clemente City Beach stretches alongside this historic 1296ft-long, wood-built pier. The original 1928 pier, where Prohibition-era bootleggers once brought liquor ashore, was rebuilt most recently in 1985. Surfers go north of the pier, while swimmers and bodysurfers take the south side.

Surfing Heritage & Culture Center MUSEUM
(☎949-388-0313; www.facebook.com/surfingheritage; 110 Calle Iglesia; suggested donation $5; ⏰11am-5pm Tue-Sun; P) FREE This foundation gives a timeline of surfing history by exhibiting surfboards ridden by the greats, from Duke Kahanamoku to Kelly Slater. Its photo archive has some 100,000 photos (a tiny fraction may be on display at any one time). Temporary exhibits (photos, skateboarding, surf-shop culture and more) change approximately every three months.

Sleeping & Eating

There's lovely lodging right across from the pier, worthwhile campgrounds at San Onofre State Beach and chain motels further inland, closer to the 5 Freeway.

Bagel Shack BREAKFAST $
(☎949-388-0745; www.thebagelshack.com; 777 S El Camino Real; bagel sandwiches $3.25-11; ⏰5:30am-2:30pm) Wetsuit-clad crowds frequent this long-standing, tiki-inflected breakfast and lunch place, which serves both OG breakfast sandwiches (lox and cream cheese) to new-style Cali creations like the Upper (steak, eggs, caramelized onions and pepper jack cheese). Lunch sandwiches are more predictable. They blend fruit smoothies, too. It's directly uphill from T-Street.

Fisherman's Restaurant & Bar SEAFOOD $$$
(☎949-498-6390; www.thefishermansrestaurant.com; 611 Avenida Victoria; breakfast $11-22, mains lunch $17-29, dinner $18-64; ⏰8am-9:30pm Sun-Thu, to 10pm Fri & Sat) Right on the pier, Fisherman's chowders, fish and chips and mesquite-grilled fresh catches come with a side of incomparable ocean views. Generous four-course Fisherman's Feasts ($32-$62 per person, minimum two people) offer clams, chowder, salad and your choice of fish. Sure, you'll be with tourists, but hey, you're a tourist too, right? Embrace it.

DON'T MISS

TRESTLES

Surfers won't want to miss world-renowned Trestles, in protected **San Onofre State Beach** (☎949-492-4872; www.parks.ca.gov/sanonofre; parking per day $15; ⏰6am-10pm Apr 15-Sep, until 8pm Oct-Apr 14; P), just southeast of San Clemente and famous for its natural surf break that consistently churns out perfect waves, even in summer. There are also rugged bluff-top walking trails, swimming beaches and a developed inland **campground** (☎reservations 800-444-7275; www.reservecalifornia.com; San Mateo Campground, 830 Cristianitos Rd, San Onofre State Beach; primitive/hookup sites from $28/48; P).

Trestles is also a great success story for environmentalists and surfers, who for over a decade fought the extension of a nearby toll road. Visit savetrestles.surfrider.org to learn more.

To reach the beach, exit I-5 at Basilone Rd, then hoof it along the nature trail.

Shopping

The highlight of San Clemente's shopping scene is Avenida del Mar as it slopes downhill from city hall southwest toward the beach. The tree lined street has a low-to-the-ground feel with little boutiques selling clothing, crafts, furniture and shoes, plus cafes and specialty shops. Bargain shoppers will want to head to the outlet mall just north of central San Clemente off I-5.

Getting There & Away

OCTA (p437) bus 1 heads south from Dana Point every 30 to 60 minutes. At San Clemente's **Metrolink station** (☎800-371-5465; www.metrolinktrains.com), transfer to OCTA bus 191, which runs hourly to San Clemente Pier. Unless you have a bus pass, you'll need to pay the one-way fare ($2, exact change) twice.

At least two daily **Amtrak** (☎800-872-7245; www.amtrak.com) trains between San Diego ($21, 75 minutes) and LA ($23, 90 minutes), via San Juan Capistrano and Anaheim, stop at San Clemente Pier.

AT A GLANCE

POPULATION
3,379,160

AREA
4526 sq miles

BEST FISH TACOS
Oscars Mexican Seafood (p477)

BEST SUNSET VIEWS
Sunset Cliffs (p471)

BEST NON-BALBOA PARK MUSEUM
USS Midway Museum (p466)

WHEN TO GO

Jun–Aug High season: temperatures and hotel rates are highest, June has cloudy skies.

Sep–Oct, Mar–May Shoulder seasons: moderate rates, warm with blue skies.

Nov–Feb Low season but far from cold during the day, and it's whale season.

San Diego Museum of Man (p463)

San Diego & Around

New York has its cabbie, Chicago its blues musician and Seattle its coffee-drinking boho. San Diego has its surfer dude, with tousled hair, great tan and gentle enthusiasm. They look like they're on a perennial vacation, and when they wish you welcome, they mean it.

San Diego calls itself 'America's Finest City,' and its breezy confidence and sunny countenance filter down to its people. It feels like a collection of villages each with its own personality, but it's the nation's eighth-largest city, and for its size, there's probably no place more laid-back on earth.

San Diego bursts with world-famous attractions, including the zoo and the museums of Balboa Park. Then there's the excellent seafood, a buzzing Downtown and beautiful hikes for all. Plus, more than 60 beaches and the USA's most perfect weather.

INCLUDES

CENTRAL & COASTAL SAN DIEGO

Whoosh – here comes a skateboarder. And there goes a wetsuited surfer, board under the arm. In parallel, there's a Chanel-clad diner lifting a dainty porcelain cup off its saucer. The city of San Diego and the city's coastal neighborhoods exude the kind of freewheeling spirit that embraces people from all walks of life.

San Diego's Downtown is the region's main business, financial and convention district. It may not have the energy of San Francisco or New York, but what Downtown lacks it makes up for in fun shopping, dining and nightlife in the historic Gaslamp Quarter, and the hipster havens of East Village and North Park. The

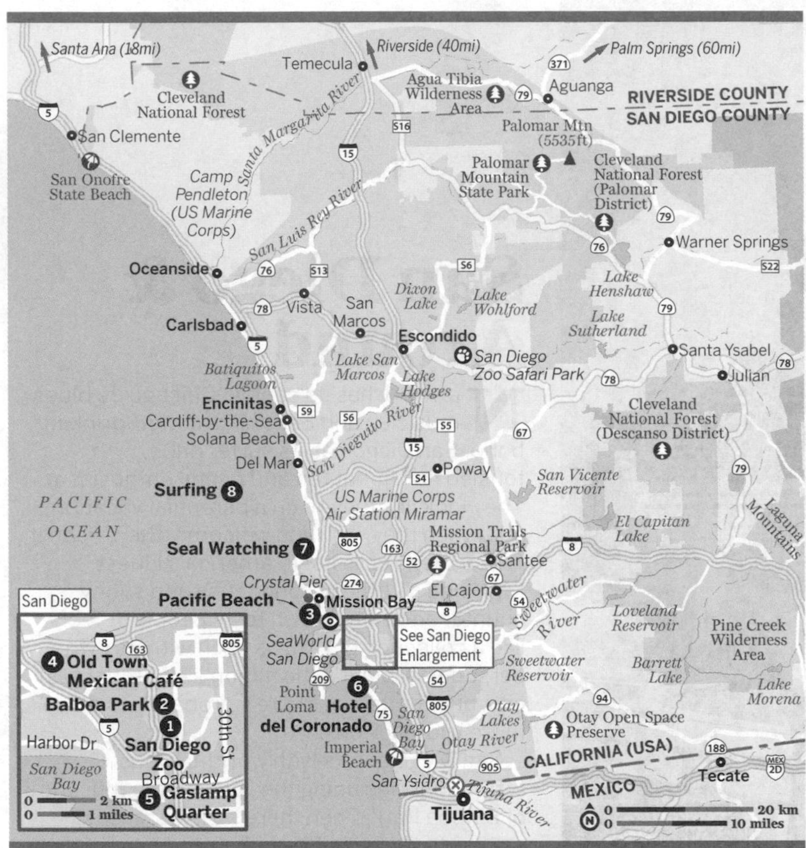

San Diego & Around Highlights

1. **San Diego Zoo** (p461) Cooing at koalas and pandering to pandas.
2. **Balboa Park** (p461) Museum hopping along an avenue of historic architecture.
3. **Pacific Beach** (p467) Promenading along the boardwalk with an epic sunset.
4. **Old Town Mexican Café** (p475) Eating tortillas and swilling margaritas in a legendary spot.
5. **Gaslamp Quarter** (p479) Pub-crawling and Downtown catching a dueling piano show at Shout House.
6. **Hotel del Coronado** (p467) Marveling at history and architecture.
7. **La Jolla** (p483) Spotting sealsat La Jolla's seal rock and ecological reserve.
8. **Surfing** (p468) Ripping at many excellent wave-riding beaches.

waterfront Embarcadero is great for a stroll. In the northwestern corner of Downtown, vibrant Little Italy brims with progressive eats, while Old Town is a hub of local history.

The city of Coronado, with its landmark 1888 Hotel del Coronado (p467) and top-rated beach, sits across San Diego Bay from Downtown. At the entrance to the bay, Point Loma has sweeping views across sea and city from the Cabrillo National Monument (p467). Mission Bay, northwest of Downtown, has lagoons, parks and recreation, from water skiing to camping and SeaWorld. The nearby coastal neighborhoods – Ocean Beach, Mission Beach and Pacific Beach – epitomize the SoCal beach scene.

Sights

San Diego Zoo & Balboa Park

San Diego Zoo is a highlight of any trip to California and should be a high priority for first-time visitors. The zoo occupies some prime real estate in Balboa Park, which itself is packed with museums and **gardens** (Map p464; ☎619-239-0512; www.balboapark.org/in-the-park/Gardens; Balboa Park). To visit all the park's sights would take days; plan your trip at the **Balboa Park Visitor Center** (Map p464; ☎619-239-0512; www.balboapark.org; House of Hospitality, 1549 El Prado; ⏰9:30am-4:30pm). Pick up or view a park map (www.balboapark.org/map) and study the latest opening schedule.

Discount admission coupons are widely available in local publications and at hotels and information-center kiosks. The **multiday explorer pass** (adult/child $103/68) covers admission to 16 of Balboa Park's museums and one day at the zoo; it's valid for seven days. A **one-day pass** (adult/child $48/29) excludes zoo entry, but includes five museums in one day. The **one-week pass**, excluding zoo entry (adult/child $59/32), is great value.

The **Go San Diego** (https://gocity.com) card offers up to 55% off big-ticket attractions. The three-day pass (adult/child $207/189) includes one premium attraction (SeaWorld), plus San Diego Zoo, Legoland and many of Balboa Park's museums.

Free tours depart from Balboa Park Visitors Center. To uncover the park's architectural heritage nature, and history, led by volunteers and rangers, see www.balboapark.org/explore/tours for timings.

Balboa Park is easily reached from Downtown on bus 7 along Park Blvd. By car, Park Blvd provides easy access to free parking. El

> **RESOURCES**
>
> **Lonely Planet** (www.lonelyplanet.com/usa/san-diego) Destination information, hotel bookings, traveler forum and more.
>
> **San Diego Tourism** (www.sandiego.org) Search hotels, sights, dining, rental cars and more, and make reservations.

Prado is a pedestrian road running through the park and between museums; visitors can access it via Laurel St, then cross Cabrillo Bridge with the Cabrillo Fwy (CA 163) 120ft below. Hanging greenery makes it look like a rainforest gorge.

The free **Balboa Park Tram** bus makes a continuous loop around the park; however, it's easiest and most enjoyable to walk.

★ San Diego Zoo ZOO
(Map p464; ☎619-231-1515; https://zoo.sandiegozoo.org; 2920 Zoo Dr; day pass adult/child 3-11yr from $58/48, 2-visit pass zoo &/or safari park adult/child 3-11yr $92.80/82.80; ⏰9am-9pm mid-Jun–early Sep, to 5pm or 6pm rest of year; P 👪) One of SoCal's biggest attractions, San Diego's justifiably famous zoo has more than 4000 animals representing more than 650 species in a beautifully landscaped setting. Typically enclosures replicate a species' natural habitat. Its sister park, San Diego Zoo Safari Park (p491), focuses on free-range big game enclosures and is in northern San Diego County. Arrive early at both, as many of the animals are most active in the morning – though some perk up again in the afternoon.

★ New Children's Museum MUSEUM
(Map p472; ☎619-233-8792; www.thinkplaycreate.org; 200 W Island Ave; admission $15.50, parking Mon-Thu $10, Fri-Sun $15; ⏰10am-5pm Mon-Sat, 9:30am-4pm Sun; 👪) This interactive children's museum offers endless activities for kids. Installations are designed by artists, so the future generation can learn the principles of movement and physics while simultaneously being exposed to art and working out the ants in their pants. Exhibits change every 18 months or so, so there's always something new. Workshops rotate daily and include clay and paint sessions.

Balboa Park Museums MUSEUM
(Map p464; ☎800-310-7106; www.balboapark.org/explorer/museums; Balboa Park; multi-entry tickets adult/child 3-12yr from $48/29; P 👪)

Metropolitan San Diego

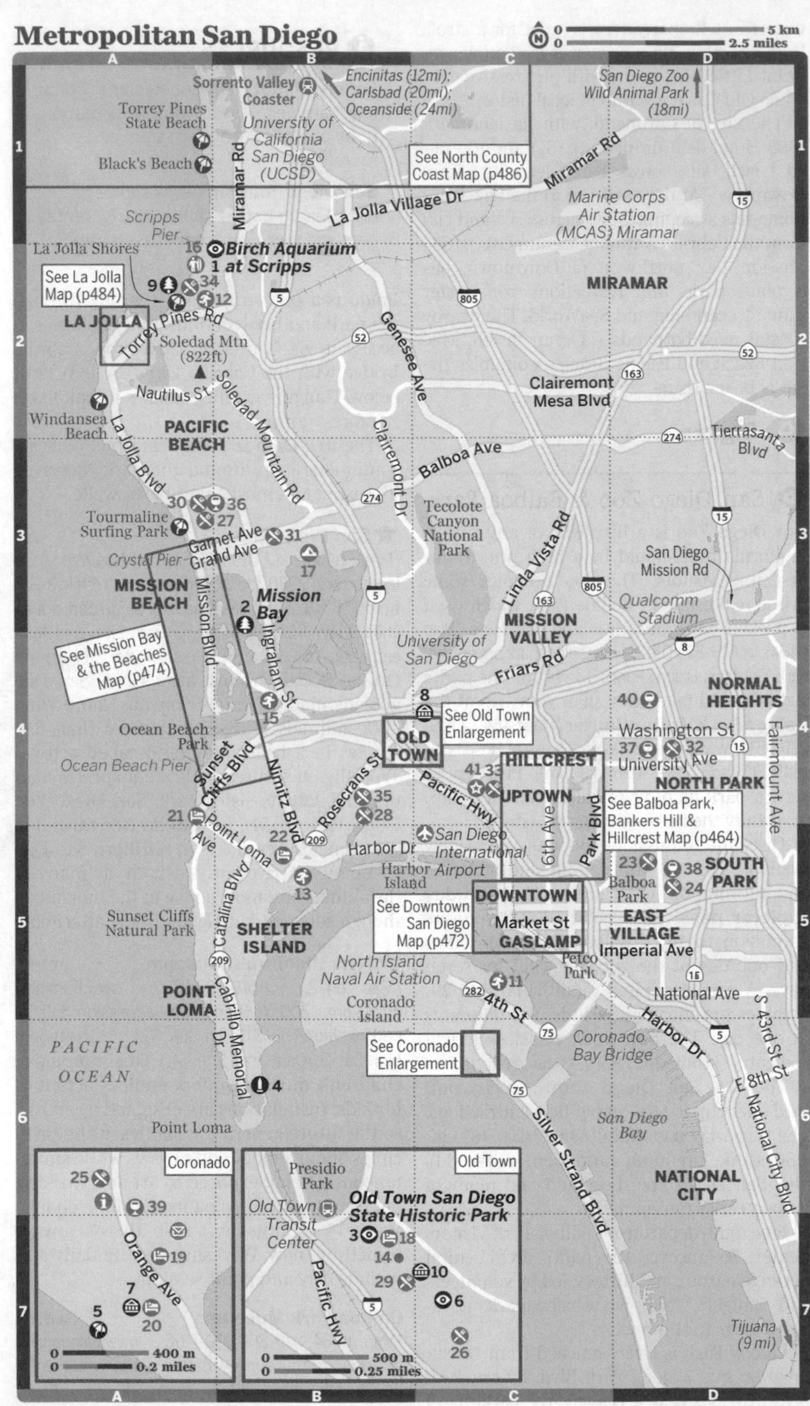

Metropolitan San Diego

Top Sights
1 Birch Aquarium at Scripps B2
2 Mission Bay B3
3 Old Town San Diego State Historic Park B7

Sights
4 Cabrillo National Monument B6
5 Coronado Municipal Beach A7
6 El Campo Santo C7
7 Hotel del Coronado A7
8 Junípero Serra Museum C4
9 San Diego-La Jolla Underwater Park Ecological Reserve A2
10 Whaley House Museum C7

Activities, Courses & Tours
11 Bikes & Beyond C5
12 Everyday California A2
13 H&M Landing B5
14 Old Town Trolley Tours & Seal Tours B7
Point Loma Sportfishing .... (see 22)
15 Seaforth Sportfishing B4
16 Surf Diva A2

Sleeping
17 Campland on the Bay B3
18 Cosmopolitan Hotel B7
19 El Cordova Hotel A7
20 Hotel del Coronado A7
21 Inn at Sunset Cliffs A4
22 Pearl Hotel B5

Eating
23 Big Kitchen D5
24 Buona Forchetta D5
25 Clayton's Coffee Shop A6
26 El Agave C7
27 Fig Tree Cafe A3
28 Liberty Public Market B4
29 Old Town Mexican Café B7
30 Oscars Mexican Seafood A3
31 Pacific Beach Fish Shop B3
Point Loma Seafoods .... (see 22)
32 Poke One N Half D4
33 Saffron C4
Seréa .... (see 20)
Shakespeare Pub & Grille .... (see 33)
34 Shore Rider A2
35 Stone Brewing World Bistro & Gardens B4

Drinking & Nightlife
36 Cafe Bar Europa B3
37 Coin-Op Game Room D4
38 Kindred D5
39 McP's Irish Pub A6
40 Polite Provisions D4

Entertainment
41 National Comedy Theatre C4

Balboa Park is a 1200-acre space with more than 16 museums and cultural institutions, including key attractions **San Diego History Center** (Map p464; ☎619-232-6203; www.sandiegohistory.org; 1649 El Prado, Suite 3; $5 donation recommended; ⊙10am-5pm) FREE, San Diego Air & Space Museum, **San Diego Museum of Art** (SDMA; Map p464; ☎619-232-7931; www.sdmart.org; 1450 El Prado, Balboa Park; adult/student/child under 17yr $15/8/free; ⊙10am-5pm Mon, Tue, Thu & Sat, 10am-8pm Fri, noon-5pm Sun), San Diego Museum of Man, San Diego Natural History Museum and San Diego Zoo (p461). All attractions are easily walkable, or jump aboard the park's tram to whizz around them all at speed.

★ San Diego Museum of Man — MUSEUM

(Map p464; ☎619-239-2001; www.museumofman.org; Plaza de California, 1350 El Prado, Balboa Park; adult/child under 5yr $13/free; ⊙10am-5pm; 👪) Inside the iconic 1915 California Building, this anthropological museum is packed with exhibits hopscotching from ancient Egypt to local Kumeyaay people, and from beer to monsters and the long-running (and particularly good!) cannibals exhibition. The latter has many interactive features and games; operate for your survival on a life-size operation game (lift out body parts without sounding the alarm, and check their calories).

★ San Diego Air & Space Museum — MUSEUM

(Map p464; ☎619-234-8291; www.sandiegoairandspace.org; 2001 Pan American Plaza, Balboa Park; adult/child 3-11 yr/child under 2yr $20/11/free; ⊙10am-5pm, last entry 4:30pm; 👪) This circular museum is a shrine to all things aviation – it houses around 50 life-size aircraft and spacecraft (originals, replicas and models), including a hot-air balloon from 1783, an Apollo command module and a Vietnam-era Cobra helicopter. In the Space Age zone, there's a mercury capsule you can sit in, a spacesuit you can wear while someone takes a picture of you and you, can pretend to be a NASA controller on retro computers.

San Diego Natural History Museum — MUSEUM

(The Nat; Map p464; ☎619-232-3821; www.sdnhm.org; 1788 El Prado, Balboa Park; adult/child 3-17yr/child under 2yr $19.95/11.95/free; ⊙10am-5pm;

Balboa Park, Bankers Hill & Hillcrest

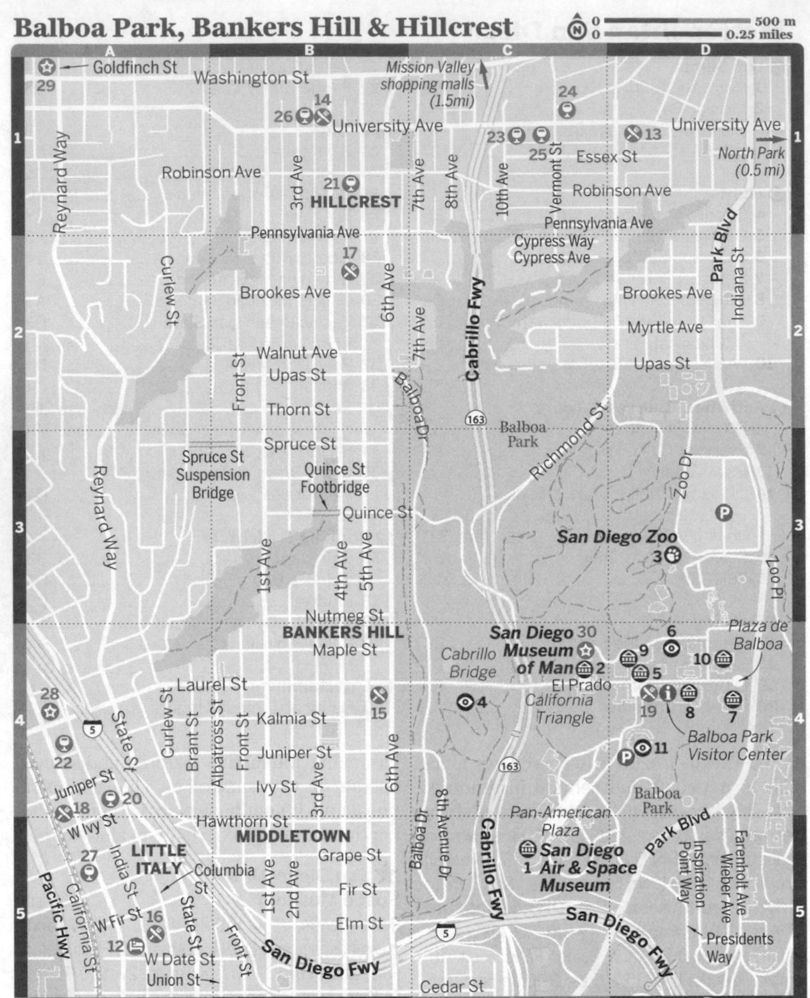

) The 'Nat' houses 7.5 million specimens, including rocks, minerals, fossils (many, including a walrus skull, are tens of millions of years old!) and taxidermied animals over four floors. It has an impressive dinosaur skeleton and a living lab with snakes, lizards and creepy-crawlies. Exhibitions range from those on Hidden Gems to Climate Change, and are laid out in beautiful spaces. 2D and 3D cinemas show educational movies on a giant screen.

Fleet Science Center MUSEUM

(Map p464; 619-238-1233; www.rhfleet.org; 1875 El Prado, Balboa Park; adult/child 3-12yr incl IMAX film $22/19, VR ride $8; 10am-5pm Mon-Thu, 10am-6pm Fri-Sun;) This hands-on museum features awesome fun interactive displays that will get you and your kids seriously excited about science. Inside, lively gaggles of kids pull levers, press buttons and run enthusiastically to the next interactive display. Exhibition subjects range from those on electrics to the environment, with illusions, things to build, games to tease your brain and, most importantly, lots of learning opportunities. One of the biggest draws is the **Giant Dome Theater**, which presents several different films and planetarium shows.

Balboa Park, Bankers Hill & Hillcrest

Top Sights
1 San Diego Air & Space Museum C5
2 San Diego Museum of Man C4
3 San Diego Zoo D3

Sights
4 Balboa Park Gardens C4
5 Balboa Park Museums D4
6 Botanical Building D4
7 Fleet Science Center D4
8 San Diego History Center D4
9 San Diego Museum of Art D4
10 San Diego Natural History Museum D4
11 Spreckels Organ Pavilion D4

Sleeping
12 La Pensione Hotel A5

Eating
13 Baja Betty's D1
14 Bread & Cie B1
15 Cucina Urbana B4
16 Filippi's Pizza Grotto A5
17 Hash House a Go Go B2
18 Juniper & Ivy A4
19 Prado D4

Drinking & Nightlife
20 Ballast Point Tasting Room & Kitchen A4
21 Brass Rail B1
22 El Camino A4
23 Flicks C1
24 Gossip Grill C1
25 Rich's C1
26 Urban Mo's B1
27 Waterfront A5

Entertainment
28 Casbah A4
29 Cinema Under the Stars A1
30 Old Globe Theaters C4

The hemispherical, wraparound screen and 152-speaker state-of-the-art sound system create sensations ranging from pretty cool to mind-blowing. Kid's City is for children under five, who can build skills and senses in a safe and colorful environment. At the entrance, there's a cafe serving snacks and drinks, plus beer and wine for the parents.

Little Italy

Little Italy was settled in the mid-19th century by Italian immigrants, mostly fishing families, who lived off a booming fish industry and whiskey trade.

Over the past few years, the Italian community has been joined by exciting contemporary architecture, and an influx of galleries and gourmet restaurants. Design and architecture businesses have transformed Little Italy into one of the hippest places to live, eat and shop in Downtown San Diego.

Gaslamp Quarter

Gaslamp Museum & William Heath Davis House MUSEUM
(Map p472; ☎619-233-4692; www.gaslampquarter.org; 410 Island Ave; admission $5, audio tour adult/senior/student $10/8/5, walking tour $20/15/10; ⊙10am-4:30pm Tue-Sat, noon-3:30pm Sun) This house, a prefab affair brought from Maine in 1850, has a small museum with 19th-century furnishings, plus historic newspaper clippings in the basement. From here, the Gaslamp Quarter Historical Foundation leads a weekly, 90 minute **walking tour** of the neighborhood on Thursdays at 1pm ($20 per person), which includes admission to the house.

Old Town

Under the Mexican government, which took power in San Diego in 1821, any settlement with a population of 500 or more was entitled to become a *pueblo* (village) and the area below the Presidio became the first official civilian Mexican settlement in California – the Pueblo de San Diego.

In 1968 the area was named **Old Town San Diego State Historic Park** (Map p462; ☎619-220-5422; www.parks.ca.gov; 4002 Wallace St; ⊙visitor center & museums 10am-5pm May-Sep, 10am-4:30pm Oct-Apr; P ♿) FREE, archaeological work began, and the few surviving original buildings were restored. Now it's a pedestrian district of shade trees, a large open plaza, and shops and restaurants.

There's the park visitor center and an excellent history museum in the Robinson-Rose House at the southern end of the plaza. The **Whaley House** (Map p462; ☎619-297-7511; www.whaleyhouse.org; 2476 San Diego Ave; adult/child before 5pm $10/8, after 5pm $13/8, children under 5yr free; ⊙10am-9:30pm daily summer, 10am-4:30pm Sun-Tue, 10am-9:30pm Thu-Sat rest of year) is the city's oldest brick building and nearby is **El Campo Santo** (Map p462; San Diego Ave, btwn Arista & Conde Sts), a notable 1849 cemetery. The **Junípero Serra Museum** (Map p462; ☎619-232-6203;

https://sandiegohistory.org/serramuseum; 2727 Presidio Dr; suggested donations $5; ⏲10am-4pm Sat & Sun Oct-Apr, 10am-5pm Fri-Mon May-Sep; P) is named for the Spanish padre who established the first Spanish settlement in California, in 1769, and has artifacts of the city's mission and rancho periods.

Embarcadero & the Waterfront

South and west of the Gaslamp Quarter, San Diego's well-manicured waterfront **promenades** stretch along Harbor Dr and are perfect for strolling or jogging. Southwest of the ship museums is **Seaport Village** (Map p472; ☎619-530-0704; www.seaportvillage.com; 849 West Harbor Dr; ⏲10am-10pm Jun-Aug, 10am-9pm Sep-May; 👪), with restaurants and gift shops, and the convention center, with its sail-inspired roof that stretches for a half-mile. Another gathering place is the former **police headquarters** (Map p472; ☎619-235-4013; www.theheadquarters.com; 789 W Harbor Dr; ⏲10am-9pm Mon-Sat, 10am-8pm Sun), since turned into a shopping center.

★USS Midway Museum MUSEUM
(Map p472; ☎619-544-9600; www.midway.org; 910 N Harbor Dr; adult/child 6-12yr/child under 6yr $26/12/free; ⏲10am-5pm, last admission 4pm; P 👪) The hulking aircraft carrier USS *Midway* was one of the Navy's flagships from 1945 to 1991, last playing a combat role in the First Gulf War. On the flight deck, walk right up to some two dozen restored aircraft, including an F-14 Tomcat and F-4 Phantom jet fighter. Admission includes an audio tour along the narrow confines of the upper decks to the bridge, the admiral's war room, and below deck to the sick bay, galley and engine room.

Maritime Museum MUSEUM
(Map p472; ☎619-234-9153; www.sdmaritime.org; 1492 N Harbor Dr; adult/child 3-12yr/child under 3yr $20/10/free; ⏲9am-9pm late May-early Sep, 9am-8pm rest of year; 👪) Next to the new Waterfront Park, this collection of 11 historic sailing ships, steam boats and submarines is easy to spot: just look for the 100ft-high masts of the iron-hulled square-rigger *Star of India*, a tall ship launched in 1863 to ply the England–India trade route. Also moored here is a replica of the *San Salvador* that brought explorer Juan Rodríguez Cabrillo to San Diego's shore in 1542. It's easy to spend hours looking at exhibits and clambering around vessels.

Coronado

Across the bay from Downtown San Diego, Coronado is a civilized escape from the jumble of the city and the chaos of the beaches. After crossing the bay by ferry or via the elegantly curved 2.12-mile-long Coronado Bay Bridge, follow the manicured median strip of Orange Ave a mile or so toward the commercial center, Coronado Village. Then park your car; you won't need it again until you leave.

FREE STUFF

Balboa Park Gardens (p461) Balboa Park includes a number of gardens, reflecting different horticultural styles and environments.

Hotel del Coronado (p467) Forever associated with Marilyn Monroe and *Some Like It Hot*.

Old Town San Diego State Historic Park (p465) Surrounded by trees and period buildings housing museums, shops and restaurants.

Spreckels Organ Pavilion (Map p464; ☎619-702-8138; http://spreckelsorgan.org; Balboa Park; ⏲concerts 2-3pm Sun) FREE Said to be the world's largest outdoor musical instrument.

Botanical Building (Map p464; ☎619-232-5762; www.balboapark.org/tours/botanical-bldg; 1549 El Prado; ⏲10am-4pm, tours 11am every 3rd Friday) FREE Each season gives this stunning structure a different look.

Mission & Pacific Beaches (p467) Home to Ocean Front Walk and plenty of other distractions.

Coronado Municipal Beach (p467) This beach is consistently ranked in the US's top 10.

As an alternative to ferries, water taxis and bike rentals, bus 901 from Downtown San Diego runs along Orange Ave to the Hotel del Coronado. The Old Town Trolley (p469) tour stops in front of **Mc P's Irish Pub** (Map p462; 619-435-5280; www.mcps-pub.com; 1107 Orange Ave; 11am-late;).

The story of Coronado is in many ways the story of the **Hotel del Coronado** (Map p462; 619-435-6611, tours 619-522-8100; www.hoteldel.com; 1500 Orange Ave; tours $40; tours 10am daily plus 2pm Sat & Sun; P) FREE. It was opened in 1888 by John D Spreckels, the millionaire who bankrolled the first rail line to San Diego, took over Coronado and turned the island into one of the West Coast's most fashionable getaways.

Point Loma

On maps Point Loma looks like an elephant's trunk guarding the entrance to San Diego Bay. Highlights are the Cabrillo National Monument (at the end of the trunk), the shopping and dining of Liberty Station (at its base) and harborside seafood meals.

Cabrillo National Monument MONUMENT
(Map p462; 619-557-5450; www.nps.gov/cabr; 1800 Cabrillo Memorial Dr; per car/walk-in/motorcycle $20/10/15; 9am-5pm, tide pools to 4:30pm, bayside trail to 4pm; P) Atop a steep hill at the tip of the peninsula, this is San Diego's finest locale for history, views and nature walks. It's also one of the best places in town to see the gray whale migration (January to March) from land. It's easy to forget you're in a major metropolitan area. The **visitor center** has a comprehensive old-school presentation on Portuguese explorer Juan Rodríguez Cabrillo's 1542 voyage up the California coast, plus exhibits on early California Native inhabitants and the area's natural history.

Ocean Beach

San Diego's most bohemian seaside community is a place of endearingly scruffy haircuts, facial hair and body art. You can get tattooed, shop for antiques and walk into some eateries barefoot and shirtless without anyone batting an eyelid. **Newport Avenue**, the main drag, runs perpendicular to the beach through a compact business district of bars, surf shops, music stores, used-clothing stores and antique stores.

Mission Bay, Mission Beach & Pacific Beach

The big ticket attraction around Mission Bay is SeaWorld, while the nearby Mission, Ocean and Pacific Beaches are the SoCal of the movies.

★**Mission & Pacific Beach Boardwalks** BEACH
(Map p474; Parallel to Mission Blvd) FREE Central San Diego's best beach scene is concentrated in a narrow strip of land between the ocean and Mission Bay. There's great people-watching along the **Ocean Front Walk**, the boardwalk running from South Mission Beach Jetty to the Pacific Beach pier. It's crowded with joggers, in-line skaters and cyclists any time of the year. On warm summer weekends, the beaches are packed with oiled bodies frolicking in sand and sea.

While there's lots to do, perhaps the best use of your time is to walk along the boardwalk, then spread a blanket in the sand, or kick back over cocktails and take in the scenery.

A block off Mission Beach, Mission Blvd (the main north–south road) is lined with surf, smoke and swimwear shops. **Cheap Rentals** (Map p474; 858-488-9070; https://cheap-rentals.com; 3689 Mission Blvd, Pacific Beach; surfboards/bicycles per day from $20/15; 10am-5pm) loans bikes, skates and surfboards.

In Pacific Beach, to the north, activity extends inland, particularly along Garnet (pronounced gar-*net*) Ave, lined with bars, restaurants and shops, mostly targeted at a 20-something crowd. At the ocean end of Garnet Ave, **Crystal Pier** is a mellow place to fish or gaze out to sea.

At peak times these beaches can get super-crowded: get there before noon if you hope to find parking.

★**Mission Bay** PARK
(Map p462; www.sandiego.gov/park-and-recreation; P) Just east of Mission and Pacific Beaches is this 7-sq-mile playground, with 27 miles of shoreline and 90 acres of parks on islands, coves and peninsulas. Sailing, windsurfing and kayaking dominate northwest Mission Bay, while water-skiers zip around **Fiesta Island**. Kite flying is popular in **Mission Bay Park**, beach volleyball is big on Fiesta Island, and there's delightful cycling and inline skating on the miles of bike paths.

Although hotels, boatyards and other businesses dot about one-quarter of the land, it feels wide open. Fun fact: Spanish explorers called this expanse at the mouth of the San Diego River 'False Bay' – it formed a shallow bay when the river flowed and a marshy swamp when it didn't. After WWII, a combination of civic vision and coastal engineering turned it into a recreational area.

Activities

There are plenty of hikes in and around San Diego, but most outdoor activities involve the ocean, which is a dream playground for surfers, stand-up paddleboarder (SUPs)s, kayakers and boaters.

Surfing

A good number of residents moved to San Diego just for the surfing, and boy, is it good. Even beginners will understand why surfing is so popular here.

Fall brings strong swells and offshore Santa Ana winds. In summer, swells come from the south and southwest, and in winter from the west and northwest. Spring brings more frequent onshore winds, but the surfing can still be good. For the latest beach, weather and surf reports, call **San Diego County Lifeguard Services** (☎619-221-8824; www.sandiego.gov/lifeguards).

Beginners should head to Mission or Pacific Beach (p467) for beach breaks (soft-sand bottomed). About a mile north of Crystal Pier, **Tourmaline Surfing Park** is a crowded but good improvers' spot for those who are comfortable surfing a reef break.

Rental rates vary depending on the quality of the equipment, but figure on soft boards from around $10/20 per hour/day or $15/35 including a wetsuit. Packages are available from Cheap Rentals (p467) and **Pacific Beach Surf Shop** (Map p474; ☎858-373-1138; www.pbsurfshop.com; 4208 Oliver Ct; 90min private lessons 1/2/3 people $90/80/75, surfboard rental per hour from $10; ⏲9am-5:30pm Oct-Apr, 9am-7:30pm May-Sep).

Diving & Snorkeling

Off the coast of San Diego County, divers will find kelp beds, shipwrecks (including a thrilling 60ft to 80ft dive to the *Yukon,* a WWII destroyer sunk off Mission Beach in 2000) and canyons deep enough to host bat ray, octopus and squid. For current conditions, call San Diego County Lifeguard Services.

Fishing

The most popular public fishing piers in San Diego are Imperial Beach Pier, Embarcadero Fishing Pier, Shelter Island Fishing Pier, Ocean Beach Pier and Crystal Pier at Pacific Beach. Generally, the best pier fishing is from April to October, and no license is required. Offshore fishing catches can include barracuda, bass and yellowtail and, in summer, albacore tuna. A state fishing license is required for offshore fishing; visit www.wildlife.ca.gov for details or book a daily fishing trip around Coronado or Point Loma with a tour company such as **Point Loma Sportfishing** (Map p462; ☎619-223-1627; www.pointlomasportfishing.com; 1403 Scott St, Point Loma; half-day from $45) and **H&M Landing** (Map p462; ☎619-222-1144; www.hmlanding.com; 2803 Emerson St, Point Loma; fishing/crab netting/whale trips from $52/65/34; ⏲5am-10pm). For trips along the Baja coast and Coronado Islands, book with **Seaforth Sportfishing** (Map p462; ☎619-224-3383; www.seaforthlanding.com; 1717 Quivira Rd, Mission Bay; half-day trips $36-50, full $155-230; ⏲shop 5am-6pm).

Boating & Kayaking

San Diego offers rental of pedal, catamaran and power boats (per hour from $20/35/140) and kayaks. Rent SUPs (per hour from $18) and canoes at Mission Bay from **Mission Bay Sportcenter** (Map p474; ☎858-488-1004; www.missionbaysportcenter.com; 1010 Santa Clara Pl; kayak and SUP rental from $18, pedal boats from $20 catamaran from $35; ⏲10am-5pm Mon-Fri, 9am-5pm Sat & Sun).

Sailing

Experienced sailors are able to charter boats ranging from catamarans to yachts. Other charter operators can be found around Shelter and Harbor Islands (on the west side of San Diego Bay near the airport). Or to simply float around on the water head to the calm waters of Mission Bay where you can rent kayaks and a floating hot tub.

Whale-Watching

Gray whales pass San Diego from mid-December to late February on their way south to Baja California, and again in mid-March on their way back up to Alaskan waters. Their 12,000-mile round-trip journey is the longest migration of any mammal on earth.

Cabrillo National Monument (p467) is the best place to see the whales from land and has a shelter from which to watch the whales breach (bring binoculars). You'll also find exhibits and whale-related ranger programs.

Half-day whale-watching boat trips are offered by most of the companies that run daily fishing trips, such as Seaforth Sportfishing. Half-day trips generally cost around $35 per adult excursion, sometimes with a guaranteed sighting or a free ticket. Look for coupons and special offers at tourist kiosks and online.

Tours

Brewery Tours of San Diego BREWERY
(619-961-7999; www.brewerytoursofsandiego.com; per person from $85) San Diego has one of the US's best craft-brew scenes, with dozens of small breweries. To leave the driving to someone else, this outfit offers a variety of bus tours each week to an assortment of breweries. Price varies by amount and type of drink and food provided. Tours leave from Old Town and Downtown; times vary.

San Diego Food Tours FOOD & DRINK
(619-233-8687; http://sodiegotours.com/san-diego-food-tours; from $65) Walking tours run daily at various times, showcasing the city's gastronomic treasures from Gaslamp, Little Italy and the Old Town, with some enthusiastic native San Diegan guides. Come hungry.

Old Town Trolley Tours & Seal Tours TOURS
(Map p462; 619-298-8687; www.trolleytours.com; 4010 Twiggs St; adult/child $42/25; 9am-5pm) Not to be confused with the municipal San Diego Trolley, this outfit operates hop-on hop-off, open-air buses decorated like old-style streetcars, looping around the main attractions of Downtown and Coronado in about two hours, leaving every 30 minutes or so. The main trolley stand is in Old Town, but you can start or stop at any of the well-marked trolley-tour stops. Look out for discounts on their website.

It also operates 90-minute amphibious **Seal Tours**, which depart from Seaport Village (p466) and the Embarcadero and tour the bay via Shelter Island.

Festivals & Events

San Diego Crew Classic SPORTS
(www.crewclassic.org; Mission Bay Park; late Mar/early Apr) The national college rowing regatta takes place in Mission Bay.

Ocean Beach Kite Festival OUTDOORS
(https://oceanbeachkiwanis.org/kite-festival; Robb Athletic Field, 2525 Bacon St; May;) Kite making, decorating and flying, as well as competitions.

San Diego Rock 'n' Roll Marathon SPORTS
(www.runrocknroll.com/Events/San-Diego; end May/early Jun) Running for more than 20 years, this 26.2-mile race has live bands performing at each mile mark and a big concert at the finish line.

San Diego County Fair FAIR
(www.sdfair.com; Del Mar Fairgrounds; early Jun-early Jul) More than a million people watch headline acts, enjoy hundreds of carnival rides and shows, and pig out on 'fair fare' (plus some healthier options).

San Diego LGBT Pride LGBT
(www.sdpride.org; Balboa Park; one day/weekend from $15/20; mid-Jul) The city's gay community celebrates in Hillcrest and Balboa Park with parades, parties, performances, art shows and more.

Opening Day at Del Mar Racetrack SPORTS
(www.dmtc.com; 2260 Jimmy Durante Blvd; from $20; mid-late Jul) Outrageous hats, cocktails and general merriment kick off the horse-racing season, 'where the turf meets the surf.' Racing through early September.

★**Comic-Con International** FESTIVAL
(www.comic-con.org; San Diego Convention Center; late Jul) The USA's largest event for collectors of comic, pop-culture and movie memorabilia attracts more than 150,000 people annually, and has gone from geek chic to trend-maker. It has panel talks with writers and actors plus seminars and workshops with comic book creators. Many professionals from the genre choose to preview or launch their coveted work at the event.

Fleet Week FESTIVAL
(www.fleetweeksandiego.org; Oct/Nov) The US military shows its pride in events including a sea and air parade, special tours of US Navy and US Coast Guard ships, the Miramar Air Show (the world's largest) and the Coronado Speed Festival (featuring vintage cars). Events happen in different parts of San Diego (from Broadway Pier to SDCCU Stadium).

San Diego Beer Week BEER, FOOD & DRINK
(http://sdbw.org; early Nov) Celebrating all things hoppy: take part in beer-tasting breakfasts and dinners with beer pairing, and roam around the giant beer garden with dozens of San Diego's best breweries and chefs.

San Diego Bay Wine & Food Festival FOOD & DRINK
(www.sandiegowineclassic.com; ⏲ mid-Nov) Cooking classes, wine-tasting parties, gourmet food stands and more.

Harbor Parade of Lights FESTIVAL
(www.sdparadeoflights.org; San Diego Bay; ⏲ Dec) Dozens of decorated, illuminated boats float in procession on San Diego's harbor on two Sunday evenings in December.

December Nights CHRISTMAS
(www.balboapark.org/decembernights; ⏲ early Dec) This festival in Balboa Park includes crafts, carols, food stalls and a candlelight parade.

Sleeping

We list high-season (June to September) rates for single- or double-occupancy rooms. Prices drop significantly between September and June, but whatever the time of year, ask about specials, suites and package deals. The San Diego Tourism Authority runs a room **reservation line** (☎ 800-350-6205; www.sandiego.org).

For camping try **Campland on the Bay** (Map p49; ☎ 858-581-4260; www.campland.com; 2211 Pacific Beach Dr, Mission Bay; RV & tent sites Jun-Aug $60-473, Sep-May $55-364; P 📶 🏊 🐾) in Mission Bay, or **KOA** (☎ 619-427-3601; https://koa.com/campgrounds/san-diego; 111 N 2nd Ave, Chula Vista; tent/RV with hookup sites from $60/90, camping cabin without bathroom from $109, std/deluxe cabins from $120/200; ⏲ office 8am-8pm Sun-Thu, 8am-9pm Fri & Sat; P @ 📶 🏊 🐾), about 8 miles south. Book months ahead of time; both are popular full-service resorts geared towards families and groups.

Downtown San Diego

Downtown is San Diego's most convenient place to stay, for its wealth of restaurants and hotels and easy access to transit. It's also one of the pricier areas.

HI San Diego Downtown Hostel HOSTEL $
(Map p472; ☎ 619-525-1531; www.hiusa.org/hostels; 521 Market St; dm with shared bath from $34, r from $84; ❄ @ 📶) Location, location, location. This Gaslamp Quarter HI facility is steps from public transportation, restaurants and big-city fun, and it has a wide range of rooms, including some with private bathrooms. If the local nightlife doesn't suffice, there is a games room with arcades and a pool table. Free beach equipment rental; continental breakfast included; 24-hour access.

La Pensione Hotel BOUTIQUE HOTEL $$
(Map p464; ☎ 619-236-8000; www.lapensionehotel.com; 606 W Date St, Little Italy; r from $160; P ❄ 📶) Despite the name, Little Italy's La Pensione isn't a pension but an intimate hotel of 67 modern and tasteful, carpeted rooms with blackout blinds and one or two queen-size beds, plus vintage black-and-white photos of San Diego. Days start with coffee and pastries at downstairs Caffe Italia, and there are other hip cafes, restaurants, bars and galleries just steps away.

Parking is $20.

★**US Grant Hotel** LUXURY HOTEL $$$
(Map p472; ☎ 619-232-3121; www.starwood.com; 326 Broadway; r from $290; P ❄ @ 📶) This 11-story-high 1910 hotel was built as the fancy-city counterpart to the Hotel del Coronado (p467). Its chandelier-lit rooms, now decorated in classic monotones and original artwork, have hosted everyone from Albert Einstein to Harry Truman. It's owned by members of the Sycuan tribe of Native Americans but managed by Marriott Hotels & Resorts. Parking costs $52.

★**Pendry San Diego** BOUTIQUE HOTEL $$$
(Map p472; ☎ 619-738-7000; www.pendry.com/san-diego; 550 J St; r from $277) San Diego's hippest digs include 12 design-oriented floors dressed in chic art deco design. The 317 rooms cater toward moneyed millennials, with walk-in showers, and tasteful surfers, swirl and palm tree wallpaper. The heated rooftop pool has become a city destination. Meanwhile, onsite Provisional Kitchen is superb: it serves classy cocktails, plus Moët & Chandon Champagne from a vending machine.

Old Town

Base yourself in San Diego's atmospheric Old Town and you may not need a car. Many lodgings offer free airport shuttles and there are convenient transit links on the other side of the state park.

★**Cosmopolitan Hotel** B&B $$
(Map p462; ☎ 619-297-1874; http://oldtowncosmopolitan.com; 2660 Calhoun St; r $119-210; ⏲ front desk 9am-9pm; P 🚭 📶) Right in Old Town State Park, this creaky, 10-room hotel has been restored to its 1870 glory and has oodles of charm, antique furnishings and is possibly haunted (!). There's a **restaurant**

downstairs for lunch and dinner, with regular live music and afternoon tea. Breakfast is a simple affair centered on coffee and scones. Free wi-fi and free parking.

Coronado

A stay in Coronado Village – around the Hotel del Coronado – puts you close to the beach, shops and restaurants. The northern end is an easy walk to the ferry. Or get away from it all near the deserted **Silver Strand Beach**; a car is advisable here if you're looking to explore further afield.

El Cordova Hotel HISTORIC HOTEL **$$**
(Map p462; ☎619-435-4131; www.elcordovahotel.com; 1351 Orange Ave; r $189-309;) This exceedingly cozy Spanish-style former mansion from 1902 has 13 plush rooms and 30 suites (with kitchens) around an outdoor courtyard of shops, restaurants, pool, hot tub and barbecue grills. Rooms are charming with leather headboards and colorful Spanish-Mexican-style tiles in the bathrooms, though they are homey more than fancy.

★**Hotel del Coronado** LUXURY HOTEL **$$$**
(Map p462; ☎619-435-6611; www.hoteldel.com; 1500 Orange Ave; r from $382;) Now managed by Hilton, San Diego's iconic hotel provides the essential Coronado experience: more than a century of history (p467), a pool, full-service spa, well-equipped gym, shops, restaurants, manicured grounds and a pristine white-sand beach. Even the most basic of the 757 rooms have luxurious marbled bathrooms. Book a room in the main Victorian-era hotel, not in the adjacent seven-story 1970s tower.

Note that there's a $35 per day resort fee and a daily $40 self-parking fee.

Point Loma Area

Although it's a bit out of the way, Point Loma boasts some fun accommodations. Head to **Shelter Island** for tiki-style hotels.

Pearl Hotel BOUTIQUE HOTEL **$$**
(Map p462; ☎619-226-6100; www.thepearlsd.com; 1410 Rosecrans St, Point Loma; r $169-290;) This 1959 gem was showing its age, which is why the new owners have given it a big-bucks face-lift while preserving its mid-century-modern bone structure. New rooms are tasteful and modern with light tones, hardwoods and beachy design-touches. Abodes wrap around a heated peanut-size swimming pool where guests mingle during 'dive-in movies' on Wednesday nights.

Ocean Beach

Ocean Beach (OB) is a happening hippy 'hood, like a mini Haight-Ashbury district, with independent stores, cafes, bars and an excellent farmers market with live music on Wednesdays.

Ocean Beach International Hostel HOSTEL **$**
(Map p474; ☎619-223-7873; www.californiahostel.com; 4961 Newport Ave; dm/r from $34/120;) Central OB's cheapest option is also the most psychedelic building in town, with its rainbow-colored exterior and peace sign on the top of the building. Only a couple of blocks from the ocean, it's a simple but friendly and fun place reserved for international travelers, with free wi-fi and breakfast. Entertainment comes in the form of free yoga, walks and boogie-board rental.

Inn at Sunset Cliffs HOTEL **$$**
(Map p462; ☎619-222-7901; www.innatsunsetcliffs.com; 1370 Sunset Cliffs Blvd; r/ste from $200/315;) Wake up to the sound of surf crashing onto the rocky shore at this privately owned 1950s charmer wrapped around a flower-bedecked courtyard with a heated pool. Spiffed up in 2018, the 24 rooms and suites (some with full kitchens) now sparkle in shiny white and blue hues, and sport laminate flooring, blond furniture and attractive bathrooms. Suites have kitchens.

Mission Bay, Mission Beach & Pacific Beach

Surfers and college kids favor this super laid-back area, with a happening boardwalk and gorgeous sunsets. Just east of Mission Beach, Mission Bay has waterfront lodging at slightly lower prices than on the ocean.

Beach Bungalow HOSTEL **$**
(Map p474; ☎858-412-5878; 707 Reed Ave, Pacific Beach; dm/r from $33/89; ; 30) Right on Pacific Beach, the Bungalow has a top location, a beach-party atmosphere, communal terrace right on the boardwalk. It's reasonably clean but lackluster, very basic, gets crowded, and there's no air-conditioning. Shared rooms are mixed-gender. Breakfast is free and wi-fi is included, as are free bodyboard rentals. Rates change depending on room availability.

Downtown San Diego

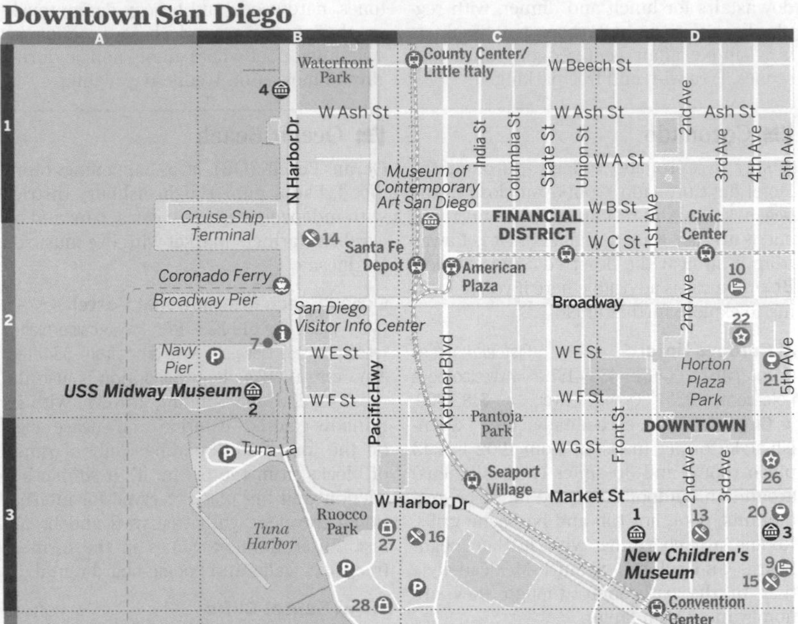

Downtown San Diego

Top Sights
1 New Children's Museum D3
2 USS Midway Museum B2

Sights
3 Gaslamp Museum & William Heath Davis House D3
4 Maritime Museum B1
5 Petco Park E4
6 San Diego Main Library F4

Activities, Courses & Tours
7 Flagship Cruises B2

Sleeping
8 HI San Diego Downtown Hostel E3
9 Pendry San Diego D3
10 US Grant Hotel D2

Eating
11 Basic E3
12 Brian's 24 .... E2
13 Café 222 .... D3
14 Carnitas' Snack Shack B2
15 Oceanaire D3
16 Puesto at the Headquarters C3

Drinking & Nightlife
17 Bang Bang E3
18 East Village Tavern & Bowl E3
19 Noble Experiment E3
20 Prohibition Lounge D3
21 Star Bar D2

Entertainment
22 Arts Tix D2
23 House of Blues E2
24 Quartyard F3
25 San Diego Symphony E1
26 Shout House D3

Shopping
27 Headquarters at Seaport District B3
28 Seaport Village B3

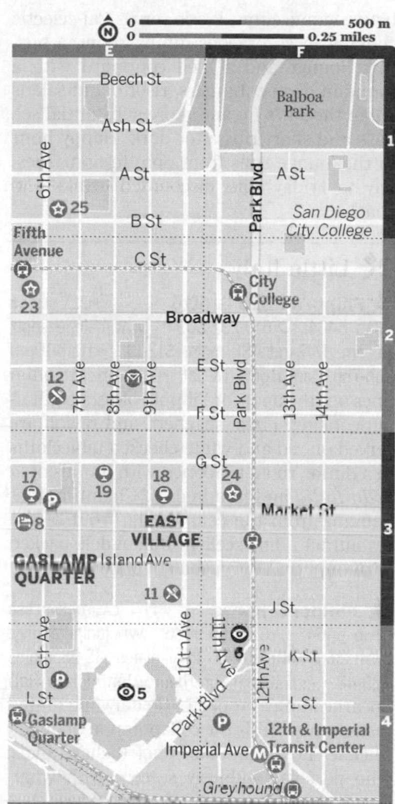

Catamaran Resort Hotel RESORT $$
(Map p474; ☎858-488-1081; www.catamaranresort.com; 3999 Mission Blvd; r $169-349; P@🛜🏊) Tropical landscaping and tiki decor fill this resort backing onto Mission Bay (there's a luau on some summer evenings!). A plethora of activities make it a perfect place for families (sailing, kayaking, tennis, biking, skating, spa-ing, etc), or board the **Bahia Belle** (Map p474; www.bahiahotel.com/bahia-belle-cruises; 998 W Mission Bay Dr; 1½ hour cruises $10) here. Room decor is slightly dated but some have views and full kitchens. There's a daily resort fee of $30.

Tower 23 BOUTIQUE HOTEL $$$
(Map p474; ☎866-869-3723, 858-270-2323; www.t23hotel.com; 723 Felspar St, Pacific Beach; r from $287; P❄@🛜🐾) If you like your oceanfront stay with contemporary cool style, this modernist place is in an awesome location on Pacific Beach boardwalk, with minimalist decor, lots of teals and mint blues, water features and a sense of humor. There's no pool but, dude, you're right on the beach. Discounts available if you book on the website.

Crystal Pier Hotel & Cottages COTTAGE $$$
(Map p474; ☎858-483-6983; www.crystalpier.com; 4500 Ocean Blvd, Pacific Beach; cottages $225-600; P⊖🛜) Hear the waves crashing below while you sleep in one of the charming 1930s cottages on San Diego's wooden Crystal Pier – in a fabulous location in the center of Pacific Beach boardwalk. The dreamy ocean views and sunsets from spacious decks don't get much better than this. Most have small kitchens, and newer, larger cottages sleep up to six.

Eating

San Diego has a thriving dining culture, with an emphasis on Mexican and Californian cuisine and seafood. San Diegans eat dinner early, usually around 6pm or 7pm, and most restaurants are ready to close by 10pm. Breakfast is a big affair. There's a burgeoning farm-to-table and gourmet scene all over the county.

Balboa Park & Around

★**Big Kitchen** BREAKFAST $
(Map p462; ☎619-234-5789; www.bigkitchencafe.com; 3003 Grape St, South Park; mains $7-14; ⏰7:30am-2:30pm; 👪) Here since the '70s, this neighborhood joint is decorated with bric-a-brac, progressive bumper stickers, homages to the Beatles and pictures of Whoopi Goldberg – she once worked here as a dishwasher. The kitchen serves American classic breakfasts and 'One Big Buttermilk Pancake' (if you can eat two the second is half price). Plus big bowls of chili and mac 'n' cheese. Cash only.

★**Buona Forchetta** ITALIAN $$
(Map p462; ☎619 381 4844; www.buonaforchettasd.com; 3001 Beech St; small plates $7-15, pizzas $9-19; ⏰noon-3pm Tue-Fri, 5-10pm Mon-Thu, 5-11pm Fri, noon-11pm Sat, noon-10pm Sun; 🐾) A gold-painted brick wood-fired oven imported from Italy delivers authentic Neapolitan pizzas straight to jammed-together family-size tables at this South Park trattoria with a dog-friendly patio. No reservations can mean long waits.

Prado CALIFORNIAN $$$
(Map p464; ☎619-557-9441; www.pradobalboa.com; 1549 El Prado, Balboa Park; mains lunch $10-19, dinner $24-37; ⏰11:30am-3pm Mon-Fri, 11am-3pm Sat & Sun, 5-9pm Tue-Sun) A stylish pit stop

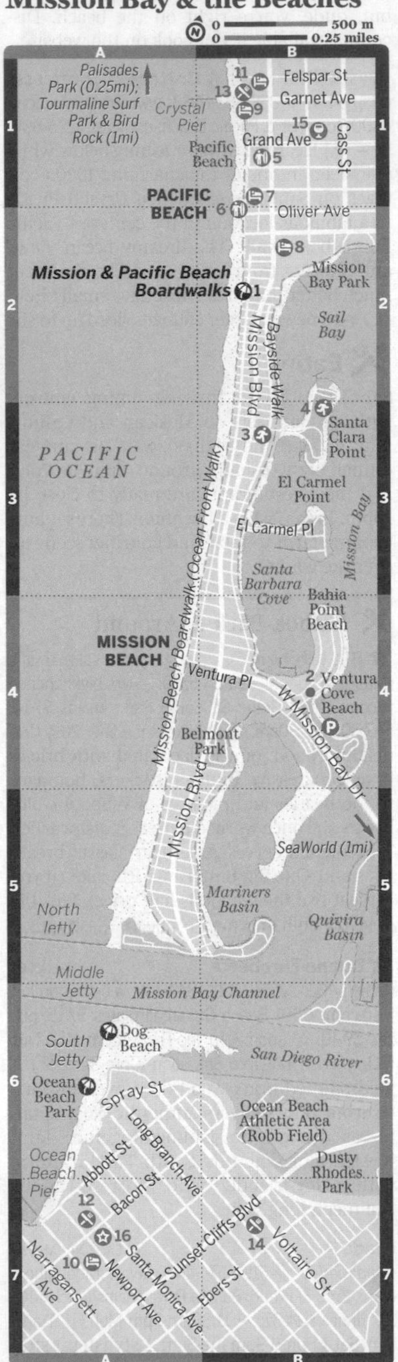

between museums, Prado serves Cal-eclectic cooking in a gorgeous dining room, a bustling lounge and a tiled courtyard with a fountain. Expect burgers, risotto and salads when the sun's up and more substantial sea bass and short ribs after dark. Happy hour in the lounge runs from 4pm to 6pm Tuesday to Friday with discounted drinks and snacks.

Little Italy

★Filippi's Pizza Grotto — PIZZA, DELI $$

(Map p464; ☎619-232-5094; www.realcheesepizza.com; 1747 India St; mains $12-19; ⏰11am-10pm Sun-Thu, 11am-11pm Fri & Sat; 👪) There are often lines out the door for Filippi's old-school Italian cooking. Pizza, spaghetti and ravioli are served on red-and-white-checked tablecloths in a dining room festooned with murals of *la bella Italia* and hundreds of Chianti bottles hanging from the ceiling. The front of the restaurant is an excellent Italian deli, packed with imported European goodies.

★Juniper & Ivy — CALIFORNIAN $$$

(Map p464; ☎619-269-9036; www.juniperandivy.com; 2228 Kettner Blvd; small plates $15-28, mains $20-48; ⏰5-10pm Sun-Thu, 5-11pm Fri & Sat) Spearheading a crop of Little Italy fine-dining restaurants, J&I is the collaboration of owner Michael Rosen and star chef Richard Blais, who performs culinary sorcery with whatever is fresh, in season and locally available. While the menu is always in flux, the sharing concept and creative dishes are constants. It's all beautifully presented in the spacious setting of an open-beamed warehouse.

Gaslamp Quarter

Café 222 — BREAKFAST $

(Map p472; ☎619-236-9902; www.cafe222.com; 222 Island Ave; mains $8-16; ⏰7am-1:45pm) Downtown's favorite breakfast place serves renowned peanut-butter-and-banana-stuffed French toast; buttermilk, orange-pecan or granola pancakes; and eggs in scrambles or Benedicts. It also sells lunchtime sandwiches and salads, but most go for the ace breakfast (available until closing).

Brian's 24 — BREAKFAST $

(Map p472; ☎619-702-8410; https://brians24.com; 828 6th Ave; mains $12-22; ⏰24hr) Smart art deco-esque diner open all day and night, serving comfort food to soak up the party. Order every breakfast you can imagine from

Mission Bay & the Beaches

Top Sights
1 Mission & Pacific Beach Boardwalks ... B2

Activities, Courses & Tours
2 Bahia Belle ... B4
3 Cheap Rentals ... B3
4 Mission Bay Sportcenter ... B3
5 Mission Surf ... B1
6 Pacific Beach Surf Shop ... B2

Sleeping
7 Beach Bungalow ... B1
8 Catamaran Resort Hotel ... B2
9 Crystal Pier Hotel & Cottages ... B1
10 Ocean Beach International Hostel ... A7
11 Tower 23 ... B1

Eating
12 Hodad's ... A7
JRDN ... (see 11)
13 Kono's Surf Club ... B1
14 Ocean Beach People's Market ... B7

Drinking & Nightlife
15 Grass Skirt ... B1

Entertainment
16 Winston's ... A7

the enormous menu – from roast beef hash and eggs to chorizo burritos, breakfast tacos, hotcakes, pancakes and waffles. Wash it down with a bloody Mary, beer or mimosa.

Oceanaire SEAFOOD $$$
(Map p472; 619-858-2277; www.theoceanaire.com; 400 J St; oysters $4, mains $32-75; 5-10pm Sun-Thu, 5-11pm Fri & Sat) The look is art deco ocean liner, and the service is just as elegant, with an oyster bar and creations including chicken-fried lobster with truffled honey, California seabass and Alaska red king crab meat. If you don't feel like a total splurge, look out for happy-hour deals with bargain-priced oysters and fish tacos in the bar (times vary).

East Village

Basic PIZZA $$
(Map p472; 619-531-8869; www.barbasic.com; 410 10th Ave; small/large pizzas from $11/15, toppings from $1; 11:30am-2am;) East Village hipsters feast on thin-crust brick-oven-baked pizzas under Basic's high ceiling (it's in a former warehouse). Make your own red or white basic pie (with either parmesan or mozzarella), and cover it with toppings spanning the usual to the brilliantly bizarre – the mashed potato topping is an unexpected delight. Wash it down with a craft beer or cocktail.

Bankers Hill & Old Town

★ **Old Town Mexican Café** MEXICAN $
(Map p462; 619-297-4330; www.oldtownmexcafe.com; 2489 San Diego Ave, Old Town; mains $5-17; 7-10pm Sun-Thu, 7-11pm Fri & Sat;) In business since the 1970s, this vibrant Mexican joint delivers authentic south-of-the-border fare despite the clichéd folkloric look. Marvel at staff churning out fresh tortillas at lightning speed while you sip a margarita and anticipate the arrival of menu stars such as crispy carnitas and succulent ribs.

Cucina Urbana CALIFORNIAN, ITALIAN $$
(Map p464; 619-239-2222; www.urbankitchengroup.com/cucina-urbana-bankers-hill; 505 Laurel St, Bankers Hill; dinner mains $16-43; 5-9pm Mon, 11am-10pm Tue-Fri, 5-10pm Sat, 4:30-9:30pm Sun) In this corner place with modern rustic ambience, business gets done, celebrations get celebrated and friends gather over refined yet affordable Cal-Ital cooking. Look for short-rib pappardelle, pizzas like spicy coppa pork and pineapple or pear and Gorgonzola with caramelized onion, and smart cocktails and local 'brewskies.' Reservations recommended.

El Agave MEXICAN $$$
(Map p462; 619-220-0692; www.elagave.com; 2304 San Diego Ave, Old Town; dishes from $12, dinner mains $22-39; 11am-10pm; P) Candlelight flickers in this romantic 2nd-floor, white-tablecloth, high-end place catering to cognoscenti. The mole is superb (there are seven types to choose from), and there are a whopping 2000 tequilas covering just about every bit of wall space and in racks overhead – enough that it calls itself a 'tequila museum.'

North Park & Hillcrest

★ **Hash House a Go Go** AMERICAN $
(Map p464; 619-298-4646; www.hashhouseagogo.com; 3628 5th Ave, Hillcrest; mains $9-24; 7:30am-2pm & 5:30-9pm Thu-Sun, 7:30am-2:30pm Mon-Wed) This buzzing bungalow, with its old-school dining room, busy bar and breezy patio, dishes up rib-sticking 'twisted farm food' straight from the American Midwest. Towering Benedicts, sage-fried chicken, large-as-your-head pancake stacks and – wait for it – hash six different ways will keep you going for the better part of the day.

Poke One N Half HAWAIIAN $
(Map p462; ☎619-497-0697; www.onenhalf.com; 3030 University Ave, North Park; poke bowls from $11; ⏲11am-10pm Mon-Sat, noon-10pm Sun) There's nowhere better in town to get a heaping bowl of poke. At the express counter, choose white/brown rice, salad or chips. Pile with free toppings such as avocado, edamame, sesame, ginger and cilantro. Then pick your fresh fish; from salmon and tuna to albacore and shrimp. Slather your protein with a tasty house sauce (the citrusy ponzu is sublime).

Baja Betty's MEXICAN $
(Map p464; ☎619-269-8510; http://bajabettyssd.com; 1421 University Ave, Hillcrest; mains $11.50-17; ⏲11am-midnight Sun-Thu, 11am-1am Fri & Sat) Gay-owned and straight-friendly, this restaurant-bar is always a party with more than 30 margaritas to choose from, plus dozens of tequilas, alongside dishes such as fish tacos, loaded burritos and bowls, and tasty combo plates. There are drinks or food specials every night – like Thirsty Thursdays with discounted pitchers, and $4 tequila shots on Fridays to get the weekend started.

Bread & Cie BAKERY, CAFE $
(Map p464; ☎619-683-9322; www.breadandcie.com; 350 University Ave, Hillcrest; sandwiches $9.75, mains $7-13; ⏲7am-6:30pm Mon-Fri, 7am-6pm Sat, 7:30am-6pm Sun; Ⓟ) Aside from crafting some of San Diego's best artisan breads (including anise and fig, black olive, and walnut and raisin), this wide-open bakery-deli makes fabulous sandwiches with fillings such as curried-chicken salad or ham and Swiss cheese. Great pastries and cakes too.

Mission Hills

Saffron THAI $
(Map p462; ☎619-574-7737; www.saffronsandiego.com; 3731 India St; mains $7-15; ⏲10:30am-10pm Mon-Sat, 11am-10pm Sun) You can't go wrong with this express Asian joint, serving tasty broths such as tom yum noodle soup, plus plates of stir-fried noodles (pad Thai, *pad esann* spicy noodles and the like). The hunger-busting fried-rice dishes are satisfying. If you've still got room, pair with an egg roll or Cambodian salad in a light lime dressing.

Shakespeare Pub & Grille PUB FOOD $$
(Map p462; ☎619-299-0230; www.shakespearepub.com; 3701 India St; dishes $9-17; ⏲10:30am-11pm Mon, 10:30am-midnight Tue-Thu, 10:30am-1am Fri, 8am-1am Sat, 8am-midnight Sun) One of San Diego's most authentic English alehouses, Shakespeare is the place for darts, soccer by satellite, beer on tap and legit pub grub. Get classic fish and chips, bangers and mash, and Sunday roasts. One thing they don't have in Britain: a year-round sundeck. On weekends, load up with a British breakfast: bacon, mushrooms, black and white pudding and more.

Embarcadero & the Waterfront

Carnitas' Snack Shack CALIFORNIAN, MEXICAN $
(Map p472; ☎619-696-7675; http://carnitassnackshack.com; 1004 N Harbor Dr; mains $8-13; ⏲11am-9pm Mon-Thu, 11am-10pm Fri, 9am-1pm Sat & Sun) Eat honestly priced, pork-inspired slow food on a cute outdoor patio on the Embarcadero. The tangy triple-threat pork sandwich comes with schnitzel, pepperoncini, pickle relish, shack aioli and a brioche bun. Wash it down with local craft ales. Look out for regular events on the website, including pigs 'n' pups (for dog lovers) and live music on Taco Tuesdays.

★ **Puesto at the Headquarters** MEXICAN $$
(Map p472; ☎610-233-8880; www.eatpuesto.com; 789 W Harbor Dr; mains from $14; ⏲11am-10pm) In the old San Diego Police Headquarters, this vibrant eatery serves modern Mexican street food that will knock your *zapatos* off. Start with some creamy guacamole before moving on to innovative tacos, such as chicken in hibiscus-chipotle sauce with avocado and pineapple-habanero salsa in a blue-corn tortilla. Sit on the spacious patio or inside amid murals and floating potted plants.

Coronado

★ **Clayton's Coffee Shop** DINER $
(Map p462; ☎619-435-5425; www.claytonscoffeeshop.com; 979 Orange Ave; mains $6-16; ⏲6am-10pm; 👪) Most diners just look old-fashioned; this one is the real deal from the 1940s. It has vintage red leatherette swivel stools and booths with mini jukeboxes. It does famous all-American breakfasts and Mexican specialties such as *machaca* with eggs and cheese, plus burgers, sandwiches and dogs. For dessert: mile-high pie from the counter. Chase with an orange soda float.

Seréa CALIFORNIAN $$$
(Map p462; ☎619-435-6611; https://sereasandiego.com; Hotel del Coronado, 1500 Orange Ave; mains $36-84; ⏲5-10pm; Ⓟ) It's hard to beat the romance of supping at the Hotel del Corona-

do (p467), especially at a table overlooking the sea at Seréa, decorated in upmarket/casual beachy California-chic decor, with portraits of palm trees, cactuses and sandy scenes all around. The menu is all about clean, quality, sustainable seafood. You may spend a pretty penny here, but it's a dining 'experience.'

Point Loma Area

★Liberty Public Market MARKET $

(Map p462; 619-487-9346; www.bluebridgehospitality.com; 2820 Historic Decatur Rd, Point Loma; dishes $5-20; 11am-9pm;) The culinary heart of a 1920s-era naval training center turned artistic urban playground, this hip food hall presents around 30 local artisan vendors who sling everything from ramen and bulging tacos to lobster sandwiches, pasta and poke bowls. Pick your fave, then follow it up with craft beer or innovative cocktails in the bustling bar in the former mess hall.

★Point Loma Seafoods SEAFOOD $

(Map p462; 619-223-1109; www.pointlomaseafoods.com; 2805 Emerson St, Point Loma; mains $10-17; 9am-7pm Mon-Sat, 10am-7pm Sun) From California spiny lobster to harpoon-caught swordfish, the seafood at this been-there-forever fish market is off-the-boat-fresh and finds its destiny in sandwiches, salads, fried dishes and sushi. Order at the counter, then devour at a picnic table on the upstairs marina-view deck. Superb value for money.

Ocean Beach

★Hodad's BURGERS $

(Map p474; 619-224-4623; www.hodadies.com; 5010 Newport Ave; burgers $5-15; 11am-9pm Sun-Thu, 11am-9:30pm Fri & Sat) Since the flower-power days of 1969, OB's legendary burger joint has served great shakes, massive baskets of onion rings and succulent hamburgers wrapped in paper. The walls are covered in license plates; grunge/surf-rock plays (loud!); and your bearded, tattooed server might sidle into your booth to take your order. No shirt, no shoes, no problem, dude.

★Ocean Beach People's Market VEGETARIAN $

(Map p474; 619-224-1387; www.obpeoplesfood.coop; 4765 Voltaire St; dishes around $8, salads per pound from $8.49; 8am-9pm;) For strictly vegetarian groceries and fabulous prepared meals and salads north of central Ocean Beach, this organic cooperative does bulk foods and excellent (incredibly good value) counter-service soups, sandwiches, salads and mains by weight. Order dishes such as cashew cranberry quinoa, vegan Greek salad or dhal curry and rice, plus tasty chocolate and coconut cookies to finish.

Pacific Beach

★Oscars Mexican Seafood MEXICAN $

(Map p462; 858-488-6392; www.oscarsmexicanseafood.com; 703 Turquoise St; tacos/ceviche from $2.25/6.75) This phenomenal California-Mexican hole-in-the-wall joint is lauded by locals in the know. The perfectly tangy mixed fish and shrimp ceviche (served with fresh avocado and crispy tortillas) is probably the best we've ever tasted. The fish soup is also seriously good, and all heaped tacos are super fresh. Smother them with the punchy housemade green hot sauce.

★Fig Tree Cafe CAFE $

(Map p462; 858-274-2233; http://figtreeeatery.com; 5119 Cass St; mains $8-14; 8am-2:30pm Mon-Fri, 8am-3pm Sat & Sun;) There will be lines at the weekend to enjoy breakfast here. Locals and surfers tuck into the hearty breakfasts and specialty eggs Benedicts in a pleasant courtyard and garden. Everything on the menu is good. We absolutely love the veggie scramble with feta, sun-dried tomatoes, spinach and house potatoes, but the lobster and blue crab cake Benedict is something special.

Kono's Surf Club CAFE $

(Map p474; 858-483-1669; www.konoscafe.com; 704 Garnet Ave; mains $5.50-12; 7am-3pm Mon-Fri, 7am-4pm Sat & Sun;) This place makes five kinds of breakfast burritos that you eat out of a basket in view of Crystal Pier (patio seating available), alongside pancakes, eggs and Kono potatoes. Burgers and sandwiches for lunch. It's always crowded but well worth the wait.

★Pacific Beach Fish Shop SEAFOOD $$

(Map p462; 858-483-1008; www.thefishshoppb.com; 1775 Garnet Ave; tacos/fish plates from $6/16.50; 11am-10pm) You can't miss this fishy-themed joint with its enormous swordfish hanging outside. Inside, it's a casual, communal bench affair. Line up at the counter and choose from more than 10 types of fresh fish, from ahi to yellowtail. Pick your marinade (garlic butter to chipotle glaze) and your style – fish plate with rice and salad, taco or sandwich. Great value.

JRDN CALIFORNIAN **$$$**

(Map p474; 858-270-2323; www.t23hotel.com/dine; Tower 23 Hotel, 723 Felspar St; breakfast & lunch dishes $11-21, dinner mains $28-49; 9am-9pm Sun-Thu, 9am-9:30pm Fri & Sat;) A heaping dose of chic amid PB's surfer-digs feel. There's an ocean view and a futuristic interior (and most excellent happy hour 4pm to 6pm Monday to Friday with discounts on beer and wine). Fresh, clean Californian dishes, with sustainably farmed meats and seafood join local veggies to create festivals on the plate. Order from the raw bar or mains such as lobster pasta.

Drinking & Nightlife

Little Italy

★**Waterfront** BAR

(Map p464; 619-232-9656; www.waterfrontbarandgrill.com; 2044 Kettner Blvd; 6am-2am) San Diego's first liquor license was granted to this place in the 1930s (it was on the waterfront until the harbor was filled and the airport built). The city's oldest tavern has a room full of historic bric-a-brac and big windows looking onto the street, and is always a good time.

El Camino LOUNGE

(Map p464; 619-685-3881; www.elcaminosd.com; 2400 India St; 5pm-late Mon-Sat, from 11am Sun) This buzzy watering hole illuminated in pink neon has a Día de los Muertos (Mexican Day of the Dead holiday) theme and sits in the flight path of San Diego Airport – you can watch planes land from the outdoor patio. The clientele is cool, the design mod, the margaritas strong and the Mexican victuals *fabulosos*.

Ballast Point Tasting Room & Kitchen PUB

(Map p464; 619-255-7213; www.ballastpoint.com; 2215 India St; 11am-11pm) This San Diego–based brewery does 4oz tasters of its beers for $2.50 each or a flight of four for just $9, one of the best deals in town. Enjoy them with a full menu including housemade pretzels, beer-steamed mussels, salads or a spicy burger.

Gaslamp Quarter

★**Prohibition Lounge** COCKTAIL BAR

(Map p472; 619-501-1919; http://prohibitionsd.com; 548 5th Ave; 8pm-1:30am Tue-Sun) Find the unassuming doorway on 5th Ave with 'Eddie O'Hare's Law Office' on it, then flip the light switch on to alert the door staff, who'll guide you into a sensuously lit basement exuding a 1920s Prohibition vibe. Enjoy live jazz and blues while sipping innovative craft cocktails. Dress nicely and keep that cell phone off.

Star Bar BAR

(Map p472; 619-234-5575; 423 E St; 6am-2am) When you've had it with Downtown's gentrified bars and you're looking for a historic dive, head to this old-school bar (decorated year-round with Christmas lights) for possibly the cheapest drinks in Gaslamp. It's open seriously early, 20 hours a day, 365 days a year.

Bang Bang CLUB

(Map p472; 619-677-2264; www.bangbangsd.com; 526 Market St; cover $10-30; 5pm-midnight Wed, Thu & Sun, 5pm-2am Fri & Sat) This Gaslamp hot spot serves sushi and Asian bites five nights a week and turns into a steamy dance club (EDM, minimal, deep house) on Fridays and Saturdays. Enter via a tiled Tokyo subway-style staircase to mingle with shiny happy people or share a giant punch bowl with your posse. Cocktails $15.

East Village

Noble Experiment BAR

(Map p472; 619-888-4713; http://nobleexperimentsd.com; 777 G St; 6pm-2am Tue-Sun) This 'speakeasy' is so well known you need to make advance reservations. Once inside the 30-seat lair, order a Dealer's Choice and study the brass skulls and oil paintings while the bartender whips up a bespoke potion according to your tastes. Enter via a secret door on 8th Ave.

East Village Tavern & Bowl SPORTS BAR

(Map p472; 619-677-2695; www.tavernbowl.com; 930 Market St; Wed-Sat 4-10pm, Sun 9am-9pm) This large sports bar a few blocks from baseball stadium **Petco Park** (Map p472; 619-795-5000; www.mlb.com/padres/ballpark/tours; 100 Park Blvd; tours adult/child under 13yr/senior $22/19/19; tours 10:30am, 12:30pm & 3pm;) has six bowling lanes (thankfully, behind a wall for effective soundproofing; per hour from $30). Pub menu (dishes $6 to $20 from bacon-jam sliders to mac 'n' cheese balls) is served all day.

South Park

★**Kindred** COCKTAIL BAR

(Map p462; 619-546-9653; https://barkindred.com; 1503 30th St; 4pm-midnight Mon-Thu,

4pm-1am Fri, 10am-1am Sat, 10am-midnight Sun) An entirely vegan cocktail lounge, with killer craft creations in an upmarket heavy metal-cum–mystic apothecary setting with a large marble bar at its center. There are hundreds of rare liquors to try, all of them at a steeper price point.

North Park & Hillcrest

★Coin-Op Game Room BAR

(Map p462; ☎619-255-8523; www.coinopsd.com; 3926 30th St, North Park; ⊙4pm-2am Mon-Fri, noon-2am Sat & Sun) Dozens of classic arcade games on rotation – from pinball and Mortal Kombat, Pac-Man and Big Buck Safari to Beer Pong Master – line the walls of this hipster bar in North Park. All the better to quaff craft beers and cocktails like the Rum DMC (white rum, Averna, allspice and lemon) and chow on truffle-parm tots, fried pickle spears and fried Oreos.

★Polite Provisions COCKTAIL BAR

(Map p462; ☎619-677-3784; www.politeprovisions.com; 4696 30th St, North Park; ⊙3pm-2am Mon-Thu, 11:30am-2am Fri-Sun) With a French-bistro feel and plenty of old-world charm, Polite Provisions' has a hip clientele who sip cocktails at the marble bar, under a glass ceiling, and in a beautifully designed space, complete with a vintage cash register, wood-paneled walls and tiled floors. Many cocktail ingredients, syrups, sodas and infusions are homemade and displayed in apothecary-esque bottles.

Pacific Beach

Grass Skirt COCKTAIL BAR

(Map p474; ☎858-412-5237; http://thegrassskirt.com; 910 Grand Ave; ⊙5pm-2am Mon-Sat, 11am-2am Sun) Through a secret doorway, disguised as a refrigerator in the next-door **Good Time Poke** cafe, you'll step into a lost Hawaiian world with Polynesian wood carvings, thatched verandas, fire features and tiki-girl figurines made into lamps. Sip your daiquiri or mai tai and wait for more surprises to come…listen out for immersive weather sounds and lighting effects.

Cafe Bar Europa BAR

(Map p462; ☎858-488-4200; http://theturquoise.com; 873 Turquoise St; ⊙6pm-midnight Tue-Thu, 6pm-2am Fri &Sat, 5-10:30pm Sun) A Bohemian bar with frescoes on the walls, chandeliers overhead, an old piano and fire pits on the patio. Sip on craft cocktails or absinthe and listen to live jazz in the European-style setting. Cocktail hour, with discounted drinks and tapas, runs 6pm to 7pm.

SURF & SUDS

There is a serious independent craft brewery scene in San Diego. The **San Diego Brewers Guild** (www.sandiegobrewersguild.org) counts more than 120 listed establishments. Go to the guild's website for a map or pick up one of its pamphlets around town and start planning your brewery-hopping tour. To leave the driving to someone else, Brewery Tours of San Diego (p469) offers bus tours to different breweries for a variety of tastes. Tour price varies by timing and whether a meal is served.

See also **Stone Brewing** (Map p462; ☎619-269-2100; www.stonebrewing.com/visit/bistros/liberty-station; Liberty Station, 2816 Historic Decatur Rd; mains $13-26; ⊙11:30am-9pm Mon-Fri, 11:30am-10pm Sat & Sun; P 🛜) and Ballast Point Tasting Room & Kitchen .

☆ Entertainment

Check out the San Diego *CityBeat* or *San Diego Union Tribune* for the latest movies, theater, galleries and music gigs around town. **Arts Tix** (Map p472; ☎858-437-9850; www.sdartstix.com; Horton Plaza Park, South Pavilion; ⊙10am-4pm Tue-Thu, to 6pm Fri & Sat, to 2pm Sun), in a kiosk on Horton Plaza, has discounted tickets (up to half-price) for same-day evening or next-day matinee performances; it also offers regular and discounted tickets to other events. Ticketmaster (www.ticketmaster.com) also sells tickets to gigs around the city.

★Shout House LIVE MUSIC

(Map p472; ☎619-231-6700; www.facebook.com/TheShoutHouseSanDiego; 655 4th Ave; Mon-Wed free, Thu & Sun after 8pm $5, Fri $10, Sat $12; ⊙7pm-late Sun-Thu, 6pm-late Fri & Sat) Good, clean fun at this cavernous Gaslamp bar with dueling pianos. Talented players have an amazing repertoire, including classics, rock and more. We once heard a dirty version of 'Part of Your World' from *The Little Mermaid* (OK, maybe the fun's not so clean). The lively crowd ranges from college age to conventioneers. Requests encouraged.

House of Blues LIVE MUSIC

(Map p472; ☎619-299-2583; www.houseofblues.com/sandiego; 1055 5th Ave; ⊙4-10pm Tue-Thu, 4-11pm Fri, 10am-11pm Sat, 10am-10pm Sun, concerts usually 7pm) This Gaslamp venue presents an eclectic lineup of concerts (some free), a good-mood-inducing Sunday Gospel brunch, raucous party nights and other events. Come early for the daily happy hour (4pm to 6pm).

San Diego Symphony CLASSICAL MUSIC

(Map p472; ☎619-235-0804; www.sandiegosymphony.com; 750 B St, Jacobs Music Center; $20-100; ⊙show times vary) This accomplished orchestra presents classical and family concerts at Jacobs Music Center. Look out for special concerts from Celtic to jazz.

Quartyard LIVE PERFORMANCE

(Map p472; ☎619-432-5303; www.quartyardsd.com; 1102 Market St; ⊙8am-10pm Sun-Thu, 8am-midnight Fri & Sat) FREE Reimagined colorful containers make up this new outdoor community space and stage in East Village, a short walk from Gaslamp. Home to a coffee shop, beer garden, restaurant and live venue all in one, it's a great summer hangout spot when open-air performances, DJ sets, comedy and screenings take place. Note that events may be ticketed.

Old Globe Theater THEATER

(Map p464; ☎619-234-5623; www.theoldglobe.org; Balboa Park) Balboa Park's Old Globe Theater dates from the 1935 Exposition, and in the 1970s the main stage was rebuilt *à la* the 17th-century Globe in England, where Shakespeare's works were originally performed. This Globe puts on around a dozen main productions each year, plus the annual Dr Seuss' *How the Grinch Stole Christmas!* musical, honoring the famed children's book writer who lived and died in nearby La Jolla.

Cinema Under the Stars OUTDOOR CINEMA

(Map p464; ☎619-295-4221; www.topspresents.com; 4040 Goldfinch St; $18-20) This unique venue screens mostly classic American films in the open air in Mission Hills; during winter months the area is covered and the patio heated, and guests are given cozy blankets.

Casbah LIVE MUSIC

(Map p464; ☎619-232-4355; www.casbahmusic.com; 2501 Kettner Blvd; $5-45) Bands from Smashing Pumpkins to Death Cab for Cutie all rocked the Casbah on their way up the charts. This divey venue is still a great place to catch tomorrow's headliners. Check the website for upcoming gigs.

National Comedy Theatre COMEDY

(Map p462; ☎619-295-4999; www.nationalcomedy.com; 3717 India St, Mission Hills) Performances and improv classes in Mission Hills and a regular 'Whose Line Is It Anyway?'- type show Thursday to Saturday (tickets from $20).

Winston's LIVE MUSIC

(Map p474; ☎619-222-6822; www.winstonsob.com; 1921 Bacon St, Ocean Beach; cover charges vary; ⊙1pm-2am) Bands play most nights at this top grungy neighborhood dive venue. Each night is different: open mic, karaoke, comedy, game day matches. Cover bands range from local legends to Grateful Dead and Red Hot Chili Peppers tributes. Check the website for schedules.

Information

INTERNET ACCESS

All public libraries and most coffeehouses and hotel lobbies in San Diego offer free wi-fi. Libraries usually offer computer terminals for access.

LGBT+ SAN DIEGO

San Diego's main gay-friendly area is Hillcrest, which has a large concentration of bars, restaurants, cafes and shops flying the rainbow flag. The scene is more casual, friendly and unpretentious than neighboring LA or in San Francisco. The premier lesbian bar is **Gossip Grill** (Map p464; ☎619-260-8023; www.thegossipgrill.com; 1220 University Ave, Hillcrest; ⊙noon-midnight Mon & Tue, noon-2am Wed-Fri, 10am-2am Sat, 10am-midnight Sun; 🐾), while **Flicks** (Map p464; ☎619-297-2056; www.sdflicks.com; 1017 University Ave, Hillcrest; ⊙2pm-2am Mon-Sat noon-2am Sun), **Rich's** (Map p464; ☎619-295-2195; www.richssandiego.com; 1051 University Ave, Hillcrest; ⊙10pm-2am Wed-Sun), **Urban Mo's** (Map p464; ☎619-491-0400; www.urbanmos.com; 308 University Ave, Hillcrest; ⊙10am-midnight Mon-Thu, 9am-1:30am Fri & Sat, 9am-midnight Sun) and **Brass Rail** (Map p464; ☎619-298-2233; www.thebrassrailsd.com; 3796 5th Ave; ⊙4-10pm Mon, 11am-midnight Thu, 11am-2am Fri-Sun) are mixed, host various themed nights and are always lively spots to grab a drink.

San Diego Main Library (Map p472; ☎619-236-5800; www.sandiego.gov/public-library; 330 Park Blvd; ⏰9:30am-7pm Mon-Thu, 9:30am-6pm Fri & Sat, noon-6pm Sun) The city's main library is an architectural dazzler and has free wi-fi.

MEDIA

Free listings magazines *San Diego Citybeat* (http://sdcitybeat.com) and *San Diego Reader* (www.sdreader.com) cover the active music, art and theater scenes. Find them in shops and cafes.

KPBS 89.5 FM (www.kpbs.org) National public radio station.

San Diego Magazine (www.sandiegomagazine.com) Glossy monthly.

San Diego Union Tribune (www.sandiegouniontribune.com) The city's major daily.

POST

For post-office locations, call ☎800-275-8777 or log on to www.usps.com.

Coronado Post Office (Map p462; ☎800-275-8777; www.usps.com; 1320 Ynez Pl; ⏰8:30am-5pm Mon-Fri, 9am-noon Sat)

Downtown Post Office (Map p472; ☎800-275-8777; www.usps.com; 815 E St; ⏰9am-5pm Mon-Fri)

TOURIST INFORMATION

Coronado Visitor Center (Map p462; ☎866-599-7242; http://coronadovisitorcenter.com; 1100 Orange Ave; ⏰10am-4pm)

San Diego Visitor Info Center (Map p472; ☎619-236-1242; www.sandiegovisit.org; 996 N Harbor Dr; ⏰9am-4pm) Across from the B St Cruise Ship Terminal; helpful staff offer very detailed neighborhood maps, sell discounted tickets to attractions and maintain a hotel-reservation hotline.

ℹ Getting There & Away

AIR

Most flights arriving at **San Diego International Airport** (SAN; Map p462; ☎619-400-2400; www.san.org; 3325 N Harbor Dr; 📶) are domestic. The airfield conveniently sits just 3 miles west of Downtown; plane-spotters will thrill watching jets come in over Balboa Park for landing.

Nonstop flights arrive from Frankfurt, Zurich, London and Tokyo. Travelers from other international destinations will need to change flights – and clear US customs – at one of the major US gateway airports, such as LA, San Francisco, Chicago, New York or Miami.

All major US airlines serve San Diego, as do Air Canada, British Airways, Lufthansa, Japan Airlines and the Canadian carrier WestJet.

BUS

Greyhound (Map p472; ☎619-515-1100; www.greyhound.com; 1313 National Ave; ⏰5am-11:45pm; 📶) links San Diego with cities across North America from its Downtown location. Inquire about discounts and special fares, many available only online.

Buses depart frequently for LA; the standard fares (one way/round trip) start at $14 and the trip takes 2½ to four hours. There are several daily departures to Anaheim (singles from $12, about 2¼ hours).

Buses to San Francisco (from $59, 12 hours, about seven daily) require a transfer in Los Angeles; round-trip airfares often cost about the same. Most buses to Las Vegas (one way from $23, eight to nine hours, about eight daily) require a transfer in LA or San Bernardino.

CAR & MOTORCYCLE

Allow at least two hours to drive the 125 miles between San Diego and LA downtowns in off-peak traffic. With peak traffic, it's anybody's guess. If your car has two or more passengers, you can use the high-occupancy vehicle lanes, which may shave off a fair amount of time in heavy traffic.

TRAIN

Amtrak runs the *Pacific Surfliner* several times daily to Anaheim (two hours), LA (three hours) and Santa Barbara (5¾ hours) from the historic **Santa Fe Depot** (Amtrak Station; ☎800-872-7245; www.amtrak.com; 1050 Kettner Blvd). Some trains continue north to San Luis Obispo (8½ hours). Within San Diego County, trains stop in Solana Beach, Oceanside, San Clemente and San Juan Capistrano. Fares start from around $31 and the coastal views are glorious.

ℹ Getting Around

While most people get around San Diego by car, it's possible to have an entire vacation here using your own two feet along with municipal buses and trolleys run by the **Metropolitan Transit System** (www.sdmts.com). Most buses/trolleys cost adult/senior $2.50/1.25 per ride. Transfers are not available, so purchase a day pass ($6) if you're going to be taking more than two rides in a day. You will need a rechargeable **Compass Card** ($2 one-time purchase) available from ticket-vending machines at trolley stations and the **MTS Transit Store** (☎619-234-1060; www.sdmts.com; 1255 Imperial Ave; one way adult/child $2.50/1.25; ⏰8am-5pm Mon-Fri), which also has route maps.

BICYCLE

While in San Diego, mostly flat Pacific Beach, Mission Beach, Mission Bay and Coronado are all great places to ride a bike. Visit **iCommute** (www.icommutesd.com) for maps and information about biking in the region. Public buses are equipped with bike racks.

A few outfits , including **Bikes & Beyond** (Map p462; ☎619-435-7180; www.bikes-and-beyond.com; 1201 1st St, Coronado; per hour/day from $8/30; ⏲9am-sunset), rent bicycles, from mountain and road bikes to kids bikes and cruisers. In general, expect to pay about $8 per hour, and $25 to $30 per day.

BOAT

Flagship Cruises (Map p472; ☎619-234-4111; www.flagshipsd.com; 990 N Harbor Dr; 2hr harbor tours adult/child $33/16.50) operates the hourly **Coronado Ferry** (Map p472; ☎800-442-7847; www.flagshipsd.com; 990 N Harbor Dr; one way $5; ⏲4.50am-9:30pm Sun-Thu, 9am-10:30pm Fri & Sat) shuttling between San Diego's **Broadway Pier** (1050 N Harbor Dr; ⏲sunrise-sunset) on the Embarcadero and the ferry landing at the foot of B Ave in Coronado, two blocks south of Orange Ave. Bikes are permitted onboard at no extra charge.

BUS

MTS (p481) covers most of San Diego's metropolitan area, North County, La Jolla and the beaches. It's most convenient if you're based Downtown and not staying out late.

There's a new Compass Cloud mobile ticketing app for easy online purchases and tickets delivered right to your phone.

Bus route	Stops in San Diego
3	Balboa Park, Hillcrest, UCSD Medical Center
7	Gaslamp, Balboa Park, Zoo, Hillcrest, North Park
8/9	Old Town, Pacific Beach, SeaWorld
30	Gaslamp, Little Italy, Old Town, Pacific Beach, La Jolla, University Town Center
35	Old Town, Ocean Beach
901	Gaslamp, Coronado, Imperial Beach

CAR

All the big-name car-rental companies have desks at the San Diego airport (p481); lesser-known companies may be cheaper. Shop around – prices vary widely, even from day to day within the same company. The airport has free direct phones to a number of car-rental companies. Rental rates tend to be comparable to LA ($30 to $80 per day plus insurance fees). Most San Diego neighborhoods are only 20 minutes apart by car, and it's easy to drive and park in most areas. There's usually little to no traffic compared to nearby LA.

METROPOLITAN TRANSIT SYSTEM (MTS)

The Metropolitan Transit System runs buses and trolleys throughout central San Diego and beyond. For route and fare information, call ☎619-233-3004; operators are available 5:30am to 8:30pm Monday to Friday, and 8am to 5pm Saturday and Sunday. For 24-hour automated information, call ☎619-685-4900. Visit www.sdmts.com/schedules-real-time to plan your route online.

One paying adult may travel with up to two children aged 5 and under for free on buses with a valid MTS ticket.

TAXI & RIDESHARE

Taxi fares vary, but plan on about $12 to $15 for a 3-mile journey. Companies include **Yellow Cab** (www.driveu.com). App-based companies such as **Uber** (www.uber.com) and **Lyft** (www.lyft.com) are established in the market with competitive fares.

TROLLEY

Municipal trolleys, not to be confused with Old Town Trolley tourist buses (p469), operate on three main lines in San Diego. From the transit center across from the Santa Fe Depot, **Blue Line** trolleys go south to **San Ysidro** (☎619-690-8900; www.cbp.gov/contact/ports/san-ysidro-class; 720 E San Ysidro Blvd; ⏲24hr), (on the Mexico border), and north to **Old Town Transit Center** (Map p462; www.amtrak.com/stations/olt; 4009 Taylor St). The **Green Line** runs from Gaslamp to Old Town east through Mission Valley. The **Orange Line** connects the Convention Center and Seaport Village with Downtown, but otherwise, it's less useful for visitors. Trolleys run between about 4:15am and 1am daily at 15-minute intervals during the day, and every 30 minutes in the evening (check www.sdmts.com for a full up-to-date timetable). Fares are adult $2.50 per ride, valid for two hours from the time of purchase at vending machines on the station platforms. A day pass for adult/child aged 6 to 18 years is $6/3. Children aged five and under ride free.

LA JOLLA & NORTH COUNTY COAST

With landscaped parks, white-sand coves, upscale boutiques, top restaurants, and cliffs above deep, clear-blue waters, it's no wonder La Jolla (pronounced la-*hoy*-yah) is thought to be named after Spanish phrase *la joya*, meaning 'the jewel.' The name may actually date from Native Americans who inhabited the area from 10,000 years ago to the mid-19th century, and called the place 'mut la hoya, la hoya' – the place of many caves.

Northward from La Jolla, North County's coast evokes the San Diego of 40 years ago. Pretty Del Mar continues through low-key Solana Beach, Encinitas and Carlsbad (home of Legoland), before hitting Oceanside, home to Camp Pendleton Marine Base. All the beaches are terrific, and the small seaside towns are great for soaking up the laid-back SoCal scene and working on your tan.

La Jolla

Sights

★Children's Pool WILDLIFE RESERVE

(Map p484; 850 Coast Blvd; 24hr;) FREE Built in the 1930s behind a wave-cutting seawall, La Jolla's Children's Pool was created as a family beach but has since been invaded by herds of seals and sea lions. Tourists come in droves to see them larking around, swimming, fighting and mating, viewed from the plaza above the cove. The pinnipeds don't seem to mind – but there's strictly no touching, feeding or selfies to be taken with the residents.

★Birch Aquarium at Scripps AQUARIUM

(Map p462; 858-534-3474; www.aquarium.ucsd.edu; 2300 Expedition Way; adult/child 3-17yr/child under 2yr $19.50/15/free; 9am-5pm;) This state-of-the-art aquarium is a wondrous underwater world home to 5000 fish. Visitors can watch sharks dart, see kelp forests sway, and even meet a rescued loggerhead turtle. The Hall of Fishes has more than 60 fish tanks, simulating marine habitats from the Pacific Northwest to tropical seas. The Tide Pool Plaza, with its fabulous ocean views, is the place to get touchy-feely with sea stars, hermit crabs, sea cucumbers, lobsters and tidal-zone critters. Don't miss the new Seadragons & Seahorses exhibit.

★Sunny Jim Sea Cave Store CAVE

(Map p484; 858-459-0746; www.cavestore.com; 1325 Coast Blvd; adult/child $5/3; 10am-5:30pm, cave entry 5pm;) Waves have carved a series of caves into the sandstone cliffs east of La Jolla Cove. The one below this store of curios is named the Sunny Jim Cave and is 200,000 years old. Watch your head as you descend into the (artificial) tunnel from the store and down 145 steps to the natural cave. During 1920s prohibition, the cave was used to smuggle alcohol into La Jolla.

Activities

Some of the county's best beaches are north of the Shores in **Torrey Pines City Park**, between the Salk Institute and Torrey Pines State Natural Reserve. Hang gliders and paragliders launch into the sea breezes rising over the cliffs at **Torrey Pines Gliderport** (Map p486; 858-452-9858; www.flytorrey.com; 2800 Torrey Pines Scenic Dr; tandem paragliding/hang gliding per person $175/225), at the end of Torrey Pines Scenic Dr. It's a beautiful sight – tandem flights are available if you can't resist trying it.

La Jolla Shores and Black's Beach are popular surfing spots, the former being a top family hangout.

★Torrey Pines State Natural Reserve HIKING

(Map p486; 858-755-2063; https://torreypines.org; 12600 North Torrey Pines Rd; visitor center 9am-6pm) FREE Walkers and hikers explore 8 miles of hillside sandy trails in a wilderness oasis of 2000 acres. Choose from routes of varying difficulties in this well trodden coastal state park. The 0.7-mile Guy Fleming Trail has panoramic sea views and paths through wildflowers, ferns and cacti. Meanwhile, the 1.4-mile Razor Point Trail offers a good whale-spotting lookout during winter months.

Everyday California ADVENTURE SPORTS

(Map p462; 858-454-6195; www.everydaycalifornia.com; 2246 Avenida de la Playa; kayak tours from $44; 9am-6pm Mon-Fri, 8:30am-6pm Sat & Sun) This welcoming and competent adventure outfit offers paddleboard hire, kayak hire (during summer), snorkel sets and kayaking tours year-round along La Jolla's coastline and ecological reserve. On the 90-minute tours there's a good chance of spotting sea lions and seals in the water and, if you're lucky, dolphins and whales (in winter).

San Diego-La Jolla Underwater Park SNORKELING, DIVING

(Map p484; 619-525-8213; 8302 Camino Del Oro) Some of California's best and most accessible diving is in this reserve, accessible from La Jolla Cove and La Jolla Shores. With an average depth of 20ft, the 6000 acres of look-but-don't-touch underwater real estate are great for snorkeling, too. Ever-present are the spectacular bright-orange garibaldi fish – California's official state fish and a protected species (there's a hefty fine for poaching one).

La Jolla

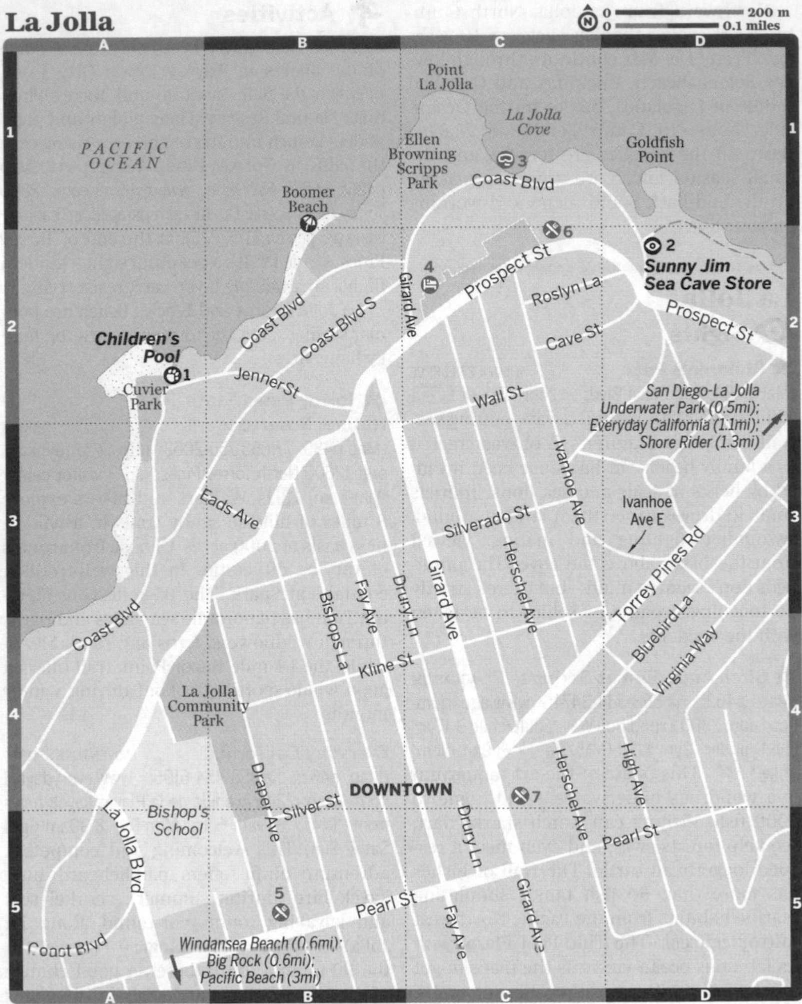

La Jolla

Top Sights
1 Children's Pool A2
2 Sunny Jim Sea Cave Store D2

Activities, Courses & Tours
3 San Diego-La Jolla Underwater Park C1

Sleeping
4 La Valencia C2

Eating
5 El Pescador B5
6 George's at the Cove C2
7 Harry's Coffee Shop C4

Sleeping

★La Valencia HISTORIC HOTEL **$$$**
(Map p484; ☎855-476-6870; www.lavalencia.com; 1132 Prospect St; r from $345; P ❄ @ 🛜 ≋ 🐾) This atmospheric 1926 pink-walled, Mediterranean-style landmark was designed by William Templeton Johnson. Rooms in the main building are rather compact while the villas are spacious. All are romantic and beautifully decorated with European features combined with an Old Hollywood charm. Raise

a glass – and a pinkie – to the sunset from its Spanish Revival lounge, La Sala. Resort fee $35; includes valet parking.

Lodge at Torrey Pines LUXURY HOTEL $$$

(Map p486; ☎858-453-4420; www.lodgetorreypines.com; 11480 N Torrey Pines Rd; r from $419; P@☒) Inspired by the architecture of Greene & Greene, the turn-of-the-20th-century arts-and-crafts masters who designed the **Gamble House** (☎bookstore 626-449-4178, info 626-793-3334, tickets 844-325-0812; https://gamblehouse.org; 4 Westmoreland Pl, Pasadena; tours adult/student/senior/child $15/12.50/12.50/free; ⊙tours 10:30am, 11am, 11:30am, noon & 1pm Tue, 11:40am-3pm Thu-Sat, noon-3pm Sun; P) in Pasadena, this lodge has discreetly luxurious rooms with Mission oak-and-leather furniture, Tiffany-style lamps, en plein air paintings and basket-weave bathroom-floor tiling in marble. There's a stellar full-service spa and a croquet lawn.

Eating

★Shore Rider CALIFORNIAN $

(Map p462; ☎858-412-5308; www.shoreridersd.com; 2168 Avenida de la Playa; dishes $9-15; ⊙11am-10pm Mon-Thu, 11am-11pm Fri, 9am-11pm Sat, 9am-10pm Sun) For tasty eats in a surf vibe right near the beach, head to this cafe-cum-bar with a mellow open-air patio. California rock plays, beer is on tap, and lunch plates including fish and chips, Baja chicken and cheese melts and seafood ceviche are served. For weekend brunch (until 1pm Saturday and Sunday), try the yummy big breakfast burrito.

★Harry's Coffee Shop DINER $

(Map p484; ☎858-454-7381; http://harryscoffeeshop.com; 7545 Girard Ave; mains $10-14; ⊙6am-3pm; 👪) This classic 1960s coffee shop, with retro brown booths and historic photographs, has a posse of regulars from blue-haired socialites to sports celebs. The food is American at its best – pancakes, tuna melts, burgers (and a local concession, breakfast burritos). Wash it down with mimosas, Greyhound cocktails, Bloody Marys or beer, and soak up the special aura of the place.

★El Pescador SEAFOOD $$

(Map p484; ☎858-456-2526; www.elpescadorfishmarket.com; 634 Pearl St; sandwiches/salads/plates from $10/15/18, mains $7-25; ⊙11am-9pm) You could pay three times as much for seafood with the tourists at fancier restaurants in town; meanwhile, the locals will be at this fish market and restaurant on the edge of La Jolla Village. Order your catch from refrigerator cases and it'll be made into a sandwich, salad or plate (the latter is served with salad and rice).

★George's at the Cove CALIFORNIAN $$$

(Map p484; ☎858-454-4244; www.georgesatthecove.com; 1250 Prospect St; mains $20-56; ⊙11am-10pm Sun-Thu, 11am-11pm Fri & Sat) The Euro-Cal cooking is as dramatic as the oceanfront location, thanks to the bottomless imagination of chef Trey Foshee. George's has graced just about every list of top restaurants in California – and, indeed, the USA. Three venues allow you to enjoy the food in different atmospheres and at different price points: Ocean Terrace, George's California Modern and the no-reservations Level 2.

Getting There & Away

Bus number 30 connects La Jolla with Bird Rock, Pacific Beach, Mission Bay Park and the Old Town Transit Center (p482). There's a bus stop at Silverado St and Herschel St in La Jolla. The full journey takes around 45 minutes and costs $2.50 one way.

By car, via I-5 from Downtown San Diego, take the La Jolla Pkwy exit and head west toward Torrey Pines Rd, from where it's a right turn onto Prospect St.

Del Mar

The ritziest of North County's seaside suburbs is north of La Jolla, with a Tudor aesthetic that somehow doesn't feel out of place. Del Mar boasts good (if pricey) restaurants, unique galleries, high-end boutiques and, north of town, the West Coast's most renowned horse-racing track, also the site of the annual county fair. Downtown Del Mar (sometimes called 'the village') extends for about a mile along Camino Del Mar. At its hub, where 15th St crosses Camino Del Mar, the tastefully designed **Del Mar Plaza** (Map p486; ☎858-847-2284; http://delmarplaza.com; 1555 Camino Del Mar) shopping center has restaurants, boutiques and upper-level terraces that look out to sea.

Activities

★Los Penasquitos Canyon Trail HIKING

(Map p486; ☎county ranger 858-538-8066; www.sandiego.gov/park-and-recreation/parks/osp/lospenasquitos; entry via Park Village Rd & Celome Way; ⊙sunrise-sunset) FREE A 20-minute drive inland finds a series of wonderful,

North County Coast

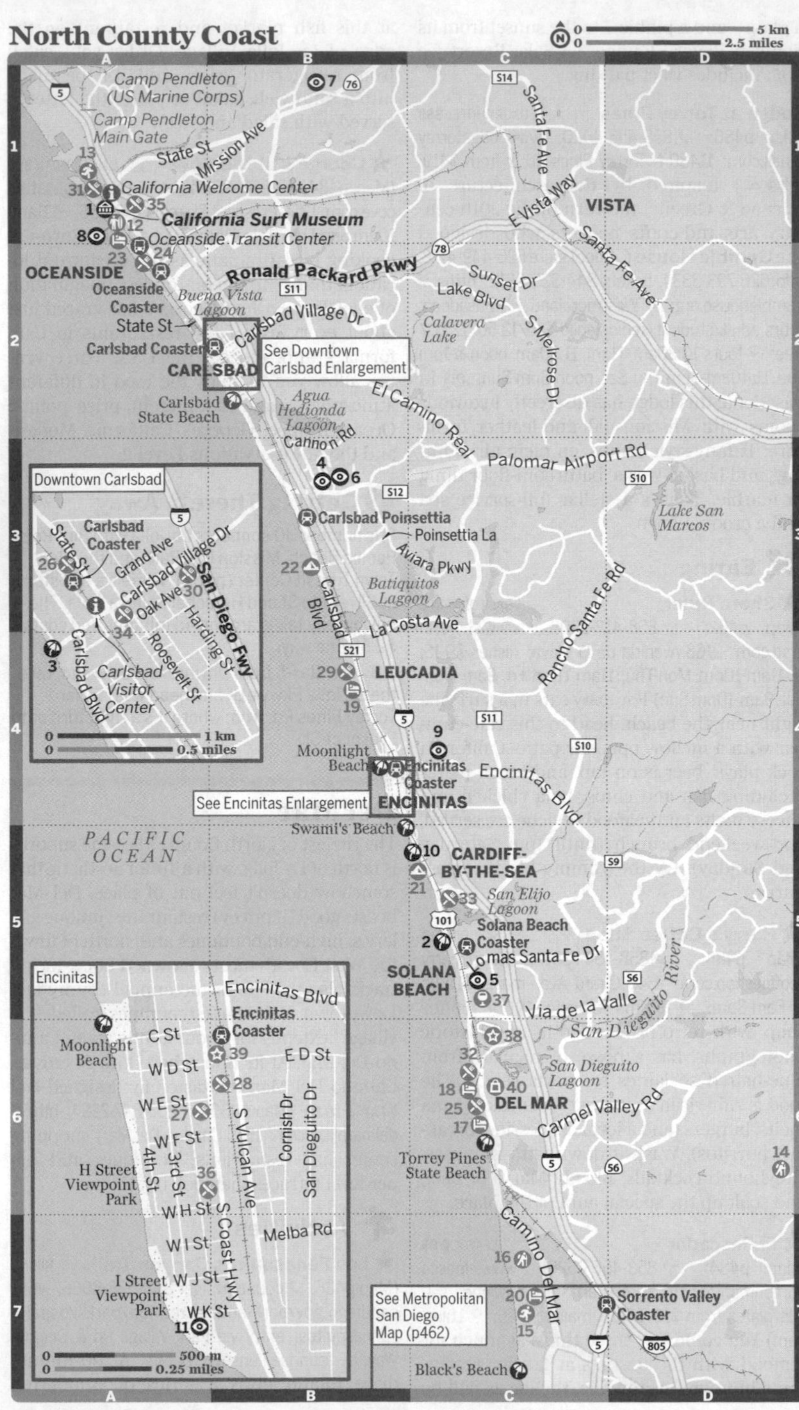

SAN DIEGO & AROUND DEL MAR

North County Coast

mostly flat, shady and sunny paths snaking through a lush valley and past a cascading waterfall surrounded by volcanic rock. The main 7-mile pathway is moderately trafficked with runners, walkers and mountain bikers. Look out for butterflies, mule deer and bobcats. Stay alert when exploring – rattlesnakes also favor these arid pathways. Download the very useful (and free!) Easy-2Hike app before you set off, for maps and trail info.

Sleeping & Eating

Hotel Indigo San Diego Del Mar BOUTIQUE HOTEL $$
(Map p486; 858-755-1501; www.hotelindigossddelmar.com; 710 Camino Del Mar; r from $198; P) This collection of whitewashed buildings with gray clay-tiled roofs has two outdoor heated pools, a spa, and new fitness and business centers. Tasteful rooms feature hardwood floors, mosaic-tile accents and beach-inspired motifs, and some units have kitchenettes and distant ocean views. The hotel's **Ocean View Bar & Grill** serves breakfast and dinner. Free parking.

L'Auberge Del Mar Resort & Spa RESORT $$$
(Map p486; 844-875-5256, 858-259-1515, www.laubergedelmar.com; 1540 Camino Del Mar; r from $377; P) Rebuilt in the 1990s on the grounds of the historic Hotel Del Mar, where 1920s Hollywood celebrities once frolicked, L'Auberge continues a tradition of European-style elegance with luxurious linens, a spa and lovely grounds. It feels intimate and the service is so individual, you'd never know there are 121 rooms. The daily resort fee ($42) includes valet parking.

Americana MODERN AMERICAN $$
(Map p486; 858-794-6838; 1454 Camino Del Mar; dishes breakfast from $10, dinner $17-27; 7am-10pm Tue-Sat, 7am-3pm Sun & Mon) This quietly chichi and much-loved local landmark serves a diverse lineup of regional American cuisine, from eggs Benedict and cheesy grits to turkey meatloaf, beer-battered fish and chips and herbed Jidori chicken for dinner. Wash it down with an artisan cocktail amid checkerboard linoleum floors, giant windows and homey wainscoting.

Jake's Del Mar SEAFOOD $$$
(Map p486; 858-755-2002; www.jakesdelmar.com; 1660 Coast Blvd; lunch $14-22, dinner $16-39; 11:30am-2:30pm Tue-Sat, 4:30-9pm Sun-Thu, 4:30-9:30pm Fri & Sat) Head to this beachside classic for ocean views. The atmosphere is chic and the food imaginative, such as truffle flatbread with oyster mushrooms, burrata cheese, arugula, apple cider vinaigrette and parmesan, plus jumbo lump crab cake and 'surfing steak' with herb-grilled jumbo shrimp and chimichurri. Valet parking $6, or use the metered street parking bays outside.

☆ Entertainment

Del Mar Racetrack & Fairgrounds HORSE RACING
(Map p486; 858-792-4242; www.dmtc.com; 2260 Jimmy Durante Blvd; from $6; race season mid-Jul–early Sep) Del Mar's biggest draw during summer months was founded in 1937 by a prestigious group that included Bing Crosby. It's worth trying to brave the crowds on opening day (tickets from $20), if nothing else to see the amazing spectacle of women in over-the-top hats. The rest of the season, enjoy the visual perfection of the track's lush gardens and pink, Mediterranean-style architecture.

Getting There & Away

The 101 bus runs between La Jolla and Oceanside, stopping at Camino Del Mar and 15th St. The route takes approximately one hour, single fares $2.50.

By car, N Torrey Pines Rd from La Jolla is the most scenic approach from the south. Heading north, the road (S21) changes name from Camino Del Mar to Coast Hwy 101 to Old Hwy 101. If you're in a hurry or headed out of town, the faster I-5 parallels it to the east. Traffic can snarl everywhere during rush hour and in race or fair season.

Underground parking is free for two hours at Del Mar Plaza (p485) with a purchase, so ask vendors to validate your ticket. From then on it's $2 every 30 minutes ($20 daily maximum).

Solana Beach

Solana Beach is the next town north from Del Mar – it's not as posh, but it has good beaches and lots of contemporary style. Don't miss the **Cedros Design District** (Map p486; www.cedrosavenue.com; Cedros Ave), four blocks on Cedros Ave where interior designers from all over the region come for inspiration and merchandise from buttons to bathrooms, paint to photographs and even garden supplies.

Belly Up (Map p486; 858-481-8140; www.bellyup.com; 143 S Cedros Ave; tickets $10-55; show times vary) is a converted warehouse and bar that consistently books good bands from jazz to funk, and big names from Jimmy Buffett and Aimee Mann to Merle Haggard and tribute bands. There's also a microbrewery, **Culture Brewery** (Map p486; 858-345-1144; https://culturebrewingco.com; 111 S Cedros Ave, Suite 200; noon-10pm), a few doors down.

Getting There & Away

The 101 bus route (running from La Jolla to Oceanside roughly every hour) stops at Hwy 101 and Lomas Santa Fe Drive. The route takes around one hour and costs $2.50 per journey.

It takes roughly 25 minutes by car to reach Solana from Downtown San Diego, heading north on I-5.

Coaster (www.gonctd.com) commuter trains run several times a day in the morning and evening during weekdays, stopping at Solana Beach on the way to either Oceanside or Downtown San Diego. Four trains run on Saturday and Sunday via Solana Beach, with one-/two-/three-zone fares from $5/5.75/6.50. Amtrak *Surfliner* (www.amtrak.com) trains run through Solana Beach with fares starting from $11 from Oceanside and $13 from San Diego's Old Town. Trains south to San Diego city and north to Los Angeles leave several times a day. Check the websites for timetables.

Cardiff-by-the-Sea

Beachy Cardiff is good for surfing and popular with a laid-back crowd. The town center has the perfunctory supermarkets and everyday shops along San Elijo Ave, about 0.25 miles from the ocean and across the railroad tracks, but the real reasons to visit are the miles of restaurants, cafes and surf shops along Hwy 101.

The best option if you want to spend the night is the **San Elijo State Beach Campground** (Map p486; 760-753-5091, reservations 800-444-7275; www.parks.ca.gov/sanelijo; 2050 S Coast Hwy 101; inland tent/RV sites from $35/60, ocean-side tent/RV $50/75; P). Sitting right next to the beach, it has the best views in town.

For dinner, head for **Las Olas** (Map p486; 760-942-1860; www.lasolasmex.com; 2655 S Coast Hwy 101; dishes $6.50-20; 11am-8:30pm Mon-Thu, 11am-9:30pm Fri, 10am-9pm Sat, 10am-

8:30pm Sun;), which serves fish tacos with a sea view. Lobster is served in the style of legendary Baja California lobster village Puerto Nuevo. House cocktails include pineapple and chili margaritas and drinks made with RIP (rum infused with pineapple). **Ki's Restaurant** (Map p486; 760-436-5236; www.kisrestaurant.com; 2591 S Coast Hwy 101; mains breakfast $6-12, lunch $9-16, dinner $15-27; 8am-8:30pm Sun-Thu, 8am-9:30pm Fri & Sat;) is also a solid option: upstairs, there's a great ocean view from the sit-down restaurant and bar, where from 4:30pm daily fancier dishes such as Jidori chicken or macadamia-coated mahimahi with Thai peanut sauce are served with ingredients from nearby family farms.

Getting There & Away

The easiest way to reach Cardiff is by car, as it's a short 20- to 30-minute drive from central San Diego. However, the North County Transit District (p491) runs bus route 101, connecting UC San Diego with Torrey Pines, Del Mar, Cardiff and Encinitas. In Cardiff, it stops near **San Elijo State Beach** (Map p486; 760-753-5091; www.parks.ca.gov; 2050 S Coast Hwy 101; 24hr, parking closes at 10pm;) and the adjacent campground. There's another stop further south in Cardiff, outside Ki's Restaurant and **Cardiff State Beach** (Map p486; 760-753-5091; www.parks.ca.gov; off Hwy 101; 7am-sunset;). It runs roughly every hour and takes an hour from start to finish. Fares $2.50.

Encinitas

Peaceful Encinitas has a decidedly down-to-earth surf vibe and a laid-back, beach-town main street, perfect for a relaxing day trip or weekend escape. North of central Encinitas, yet still part of the city, is **Leucadia**, a leafy stretch of N Hwy 101 with a hippie vibe of used-clothing stores and taco shops.

Sights

Self-Realization Fellowship Retreat RELIGIOUS SITE
(Map p486; 760-436-7220; http://encinitastemple.org; 215 K St; meditation garden 9am-5pm Tue-Sat, from 11am Sun) FREE Yogi Paramahansa Yogananda founded his center here in 1937, and the town has been a magnet for holistic healers and natural-lifestyle seekers ever since. The gold lotus domes of the hermitage – conspicuous on South Coast Hwy 101 – mark the southern end of Encinitas and the turn-out for **Swami's Beach**, a powerful reef break surfed by territorial locals. The fellowship's compact but lovely **Meditation Garden** is a tranquil place to unwind, with wonderful ocean vistas, a stream and a koi pond.

San Diego Botanic Garden GARDENS
(Map p486; 760-436-3036; www.sdbgarden.org; 230 Quail Gardens Dr; adult/child 3-17yr/senior $18/10/12; 9am-5pm;) This 37-acre garden has a large collection of California native plants as well as flora from different regions of the world, including Australia and Central America. There are often special activities for children; check the website for a full schedule. Parking $2 (free on Tuesdays).

Sleeping

Leucadia Beach Inn MOTEL $
(Map p486; 760-943-7461; www.leucadiabeachinn.org; 1322 N Coast Hwy; r $79-149;) All the sparkling-clean homey rooms in this charming 1920s courtyard motel have tile floors and bright paint jobs, and many have kitchenettes. The beach is a few blocks' walk. It's across Hwy 101 from the train tracks, so light sleepers should pack earplugs.

Eating

★**Fish 101** SEAFOOD $
(Map p486; 760-634-6221; www.fish101restaurant.com; 1468 N Coast Hwy 101; mains $11-14; 11:30am-9pm Tue-Sun) In this casual grown-up fish shack, order at the counter, sidle up to a butcher-block table, sip craft beer or Mexican Coke from a mason jar and tuck into albacore-tuna poke, clam chowder, shrimp po'boy or fish and chips. Simple grilling techniques allow the catch's natural flavors to show through, and healthy rice-bran oil is used for frying. On Thursdays, oysters are $1.25 from 4pm.

East Village Asian Diner FUSION $
(Map p486; 760-753-8700; www.eateastvillage.com; 628 S Coast Hwy 101; mains $10-13; 11:30am-2:30pm daily, 5-9pm Sun-Tue, 5-10pm Wed-Sat;) This cool diner-decorated eatery fuses mostly Korean cooking with Western and other Asian influences (witness the 'super awesome' beef-and-kimchi burrito). Try noodle dishes (Thai peanut, beef and broccoli etc), or build your own 'monk's stone pot,' a superheated rice bowl to which you can add ingredients from pulled pork to salmon. Sauces are made in-house.

★Eve VEGAN $$

(Map p486; ☎760-230-2560; www.eveencinitas.com; 575 S Coast Hwy 101; buddha bowls from $12; ⏰10am-10pm Mon-Fri, 8am-10pm Sat, 8am-9pm Sun; ☎) One part coffee shop, one part lounge and one part restaurant, this excellent vegan eatery serves super fresh and hearty Buddha bowls, heaped with good ingredients. Our fave is the Legendary Hero flavor with braised kale, sprouts, beets, carrots, brown rice, hemp seed, walnuts, cranberries and tahini sauce. Or go for a superfood smoothie, flatbread, Beyond Meat burger or burrito.

★Trattoria I Trulli ITALIAN $$

(Map p486; ☎760-943-6800; www.trattoriaitrullisd.com; 830 S Coast Hwy 101; mains $7-29; ⏰11am-2:30pm daily, 5-9:30pm Sun-Thu, 5-10pm Fri & Sat) Country-style seating indoors and great people-watching on the sidewalk. Just one taste of the homemade ravioli or lasagna, salmon with arugula, capers and red onion, or *pollo uno zero uno* (101; chicken stuffed with cheese, spinach and artichokes in mushroom sauce) and you'll know why this mom-and-pop Italian trattoria is always packed. Reservations are recommended.

☆ Entertainment

La Paloma Theatre CINEMA

(Map p486; ☎760-436-7469; www.lapalomatheatre.com; 471 S Coast Hwy 101; tickets $10) Built in 1928, this historic landmark looks like it did nearly 100 years ago. The central Encinitas movie theater shows art-house films nightly and stages occasional concerts. Bring warm clothes for sitting in the auditorium during winter months.

ℹ Getting There & Away

The 101 bus ($2.50 for a single one-zone fare) travels between La Jolla and Oceanside, stopping at **Encinitas Station** (25 E D St) roughly every 45 minutes. The entire bus route takes around one hour, depending on traffic. It takes half an hour to drive to Encinitas by car from Downtown San Diego. The NCTD *Coaster* (www.gonctd.com) runs commuter trains in the morning and evening, plus four trains on Saturday and Sunday stopping at Encinitas, one-/two-/three-zone fares from $5/5.75/6.50.

Carlsbad

Most visitors come to Carlsbad for Legoland and head right back out. That's too bad because they've missed the charming, intimate Carlsbad Village with shopping, dining and beaching nearby.

Sights

Legoland California Resort AMUSEMENT PARK

(Map p486; ☎760-203-3604; www.legoland.com/california; 1 Legoland Dr; adult/child 3-12yr from $101/95, parking $25; ⏰10am-5pm; P 👪) A fantasy environment built largely of those little colored plastic blocks from Denmark. Many rides and attractions are targeted to elementary schoolers: a junior 'driving school,' a jungle cruise lined with Lego animals, wacky 'sky cruiser' pedal cars on a track, and fairytale-, princess-, pirate-, adventurer- and dino-themed escapades. If you have budding scientists (age nine and over) with you, sign them up on arrival at the park for an appointment for **Mindstorms**, where they can make computerized Lego robots.

Carlsbad Coast BEACH

(Map p486; off Carlsbad Blvd; ⏰6am-11pm; P) Carlsbad's 3-mile-long, sandy beach is great for walking and searching for seashells. Good access from Carlsbad Blvd, two blocks south of Carlsbad Village Dr, where there's a boardwalk, restrooms and parking.

Carlsbad Ranch Flower Fields GARDENS

(Map p486; ☎760-431-0352; www.theflowerfields.com; 5704 Paseo del Norte; adult/child 3-10yr $18/9; ⏰usually 9am-6pm Mar–mid-May; P 👪) During spring, the 50-acre flower fields of Carlsbad Ranch are ablaze in a sea of the carmine, saffron and snow-white blossoms of giant *tecolote ranunculus*. It's best in mid-April, when the full field is in bloom. Find it next to the Armstrong Flower Shop.

Sleeping

South Carlsbad State Park Campground CAMPGROUND $

(Map p49; ☎760-438-3143, reservations 800-444-7275; www.reserveamerica.com; 7201 Carlsbad Blvd; ocean-/streetside tent & RV sites $50/35, ocean/inland tent & RV sites with hookups $75/60; P) Three miles south of town and sandwiched between Carlsbad Blvd and the beach, this campground has more than 200 tent and RV sites. All spaces accommodate both tents and RVs.

Legoland Hotel HOTEL $$$

(Map p486; ☎760-918-5346, 760-786-0034; www.legoland.com/california; 5885 The Crossings Dr; r

WORTH A TRIP

SAN DIEGO ZOO SAFARI PARK

Since the early 1960s, the San Diego Zoological Society has been developing this 1800-acre, open-range **zoo** (☎760-747-8702, 619-231-1515; www.sdzsafaripark.org; 15500 San Pasqual Valley Rd, Escondido; day pass adult/child 3-11yr from $58/48, 2-visit pass safari park &/or zoo adult/child $92.80/82.80; ⏱9am-5pm; P 👪) where herds of giraffes, zebras, rhinos and other animals roam the open valley floor. For an instant safari feel, board the Africa Tram ride, which tours you around the second-largest continent in under half an hour.

Elsewhere, animals are in enclosures so naturalistic it's as if the humans are guests, and there's a petting kraal and animal shows; pick up a map and schedule. Additional 'safaris,' including ziplining, a balloon safari from 400ft, and even sleepovers (yowza!), are available with reservations and additional payment.

The park's just north of Hwy 78, 5 miles east of I-15 from the Via Rancho Parkway exit. Plan on 45 minutes transit by car from San Diego, except in rush hour when that figure can double. For bus information contact **North County Transit District** (NCTD; ☎760-966-6500; www.gonctd.com; from $2.50).

from $396; P ⊖ ❄ @ 🛜 ≋) Lego designers were let loose on this hotel, just outside Legoland's main gate, and boy is it fun. Thousands of Lego models populate the property, and the elevator turns into a disco between floors. Each floor has its own theme (pirate, adventure, kingdom), down to the rooms' wallpaper, props (Lego cannonballs – cool!), even the shower curtains.

Eating & Drinking

French Bakery Cafe BAKERY, CAFE $
(Map p486; ☎760-729-2241; www.carlsbadfrenchpastrycafe.com; 1005 Carlsbad Village Dr; bread/pastries from $2.50/4.25; ⏱7am-7pm Mon-Sat, 7:30am-5pm Sun; 🛜) Its location may be in a drab-looking shopping center just off I-5, but it's the real deal for croissants and brioches (baked daily) and kick-start espresso, plus omelets, salads and sandwiches.

★Campfire AMERICAN $$
(Map p486; ☎760-637-5121; https://thisiscampfire.com; 2725 State St; small plates from $11, mains $23-31; ⏱5-10pm Mon, 11:30am-11pm Tue-Thu, 11:30am-1am Fri, 10am-1am Sat, 10am-11am Sun) Inside an effortlessly cool converted air hangar, shared plates, wood-fired mains and craft cocktails are served in a lively atmosphere. Order honest food inspired by the wild, such as roasted whole fish or smoked half chicken. A covered patio and cushioned banquette are ideal for brunch, while a 12ft-tall tipi keeps kids intrigued.

Pizza Port PIZZA $$
(Map p486; ☎760-720-7007; www.pizzaport.com; 571 Carlsbad Village Dr; slices from $2, pizza pies from $9-24; ⏱11am-11pm Sun-Thu, 11am-midnight Fri & Sat; 👪) Rockin' and raucous local brewpub chain with a huge beer hall setting, surf art, rock music and 'anti-wimpy' pizzas to go with a choice of two dozen beers brewed on-site, including the excellent signature Sharkbite Red Ale. Look out for the $5.99 two slices and a soda deal. Multiple locations.

Information

Carlsbad Visitor Center (Map p486; ☎760 434-6093; www.visitcarlsbad.com; 400 Carlsbad Village Dr; ⏱9am-5pm Mon-Fri, 9am-4pm Sat, 9am-3pm Sun) Housed in the original 1887 Santa Fe train depot, with maps and lots of local info on the area.

Getting There & Away

The 101 bus route runs between La Jolla's Westfield UTC shopping center and Oceanside, stopping at Carlsbad Village Station en route. Fares are $2.50 one way; the full bus journey takes roughly one hour.

Coaster trains (www.gonctd.com) run from Downtown's Santa Fe Depot (p481) along the breadth of the coastline, stopping at **Carlsbad Village Station** (☎800-872-7245; 2775 State St). They run nearly every hour in the morning and evenings with zoned fares; one/two/three-zone from $5/5.75/6.50 for a single journey.

Oceanside

The largest North County town, Oceanside is home to many who work at giant Camp Pendleton Marine Base just to the north. The huge military presence mixes with an attractive natural setting, surf shops and a downtown that's slowly revitalizing.

Little remains from the 1880s streetscape, when the new Santa Fe coastal railway came through Oceanside, but a few buildings designed by Irving Gill and Julia Morgan still stand. Stop in at the Welcome Center for details on self-guided walks of the local area.

Sights & Activities

★California Surf Museum MUSEUM

(Map p486; ☎760-721-6876; www.surfmuseum.org; 312 Pier View Way; adult/student/child under 12yr $5/3/free, 1st Tue of month $1; ⏰10am-4pm Fri-Wed, 10am-8pm Thu; 👪) It's easy to spend an hour in this heartfelt museum of surf artifacts, from a timeline of surfing history to surf-themed art and a radical collection of boards, including the one chomped by a shark when it ate the arm of surfer Bethany Hamilton. Exhibits change frequently; previous themes have included Women of Surfing, Adaptive Surfing and Surfers of the Vietnam War.

Mission San Luis Rey de Francia HISTORIC SITE

(Map p486; ☎760-757-3651; www.sanluisrey.org; 4050 Mission Ave; adult/senior/child 6-18yr/ child under 6yr $7/5/3/free; ⏰9:30am-5pm Mon-Fri, 10am-5pm Sat & Sun, Mass 7am Sun) About 4.5 miles inland from central Oceanside was the largest California mission and the most successful in recruiting Native American converts. At one point some 3000 neophytes lived and worked here. After the Mexican government secularized the missions, San Luis fell into ruin; the adobe walls of the church, from 1811, are the only original parts left. Inside are displays on work and life in the mission, with some original religious art and artifacts, plus a tranquil cemetery.

Oceanside Pier PIER

(Map p486; south of Pier View Way) This wooden pier extends more than 1942ft out to sea. Bait-and-tackle shops rent poles to the many anglers who line its wooden fences (per

TEMECULA WINE REGION

Temecula has become a popular short-break destination for its Old West Americana main street, nearly two dozen wineries and California's largest casino, Pechanga.

Temecula means 'Place of the Sun' in the language of the native Luiseño people, who were present when the first Spanish missionary, Father Fermín Lasuén, visited in 1797. In the 1820s the area became a ranching outpost for the Mission San Luis Rey, in present-day Oceanside. Later, Temecula became a stop on the Butterfield stagecoach line (1858–61) and the California Southern railroad.

But it's Temecula's late-20th-century growth that's been most astonishing, from 2700 people in 1970 – the city didn't get its first traffic light until 1984 – to around 115,000 residents today. Between Old Town and the wineries is an off-putting, 3-mile buffer zone of suburban housing developments and shopping centers. Ignore that and you'll do fine.

Sample plenty of creative wines in the Temecula area, including the almond champagne at **Wilson Creek** (www.wilsoncreekwinery.com; 35960 Rancho California Rd; 6 wine tastings $20; ⏰10am-5pm; 🅿). Get a designated driver to ferry you around the vineyards during the afternoon (many tasting rooms close at 5pm) or book a tasting tour with **Grapeline Temecula** (☎951-693-5755; www.gogrape.com; tours from $79).

Of an evening, artisan restaurant and bar **Crush & Brew** (☎951-693-4567; www.crushnbrew.com; 28544 Old Town Front St, Suite 103; ⏰4-10pm Mon-Thu, 11:30am-2am Fri & Sat, 11.30am-10pm Sun) serves hand-crafted cocktails, and line-dancing dive the **Temecula Stampede** (☎951-695-1761; www.thetemeculastampede.com; 28721 Old Town Front St; cover $5-10; ⏰Mon, Fri & Sat 6pm-2am, Thu 8pm-2am) is open for a late-night drink. Check at the visitor center (p491) for upcoming events.

Temecula is just off the I-15 freeway, which begins in San Diego. Either of the Rancho California Rd or Rte 79 exits will take you to Old Town Front St. Allow at least 60 minutes from Downtown San Diego, 70 minutes from Anaheim, 80 minutes from Palm Springs or 90 minutes from LA.

Greyhound (☎800-231-2222; www.greyhound.com; 28464 Old Town Front St; 📶) routes head to central San Diego twice daily (from $19 one way, when purchased in advance online). Journeys take roughly 1½ hours with no traffic.

hour/day $5/15 with a $35 deposit). Two major surf competitions – the WSA West Coast Championships and the National Scholastic Surf Association (NSSA) – take place on this coastline each May and June.

Asylum Surf SURFING
(Map p486; 760-722-7101; www.asylumboardshop.com; 310 Mission Ave; surfboards 3hr/day $17/25, wetsuits $12/17; 10am-6pm Sun-Thu, 10am-7pm Fri & Sat) Surfers can rent equipment here.

Helgren's BOATING
(Map p486; 760-722-2133; www.helgrensportfishing.com; 315 Harbor Dr S; charter fishing half-day from $48; half-day trips 10am-3pm) At the northern end of town, Oceanside's extensive harbor is home to hundreds of boats. This outfit leads a variety of charter trips for sportfishing and rod rental (from $16 per day). Phone for details and reservations.

Sleeping & Eating

★Springhill Suites Oceanside Downtown HOTEL $$$
(Map p486; 760-722-1003; www.shsoceanside.com; 110 N Myers St; r from $236;) Awash in summery yellows and sea blues in the lobby, this modern, six-story hotel has gorgeous ocean views. Rooms have crisp linens and distressed-wood headboards, some have balconies or patios. Best views are from the pool and hot tub on the top floor, where there's also a fitness center and an outdoor fire pit of an evening. Hot breakfast buffet included.

Parking is $26.

101 Café DINER $
(Map p486; 760-722-5220; 631 S Coast Hwy; mains $6-10; 7am-2pm Mon-Thu, 7am-3pm Fri-Sun;) This tiny, streamlined modern diner (1928) serves all-American classics from omelets and burgers to corned beef hash or stacked pancakes. Check out the local historic photos on the wall. At the time of research, the diner had just been sold after 30 years, and while there may be slight changes, the new owner intends to keep the vintage all-American feel.

Harbor Fish & Chips SEAFOOD $
(Map p486; 760-722-4977; www.harborfishandchips.net; 276 Harbor Dr S; fish and chips from $9.50; 11am-7pm Sun-Thu, 11am-8pm Fri & Sat;) Decorated in taxidermied catches and old fishing photos, there's nothin' fancy about this harborside chippie from the '60s, but the fish is fried to a deep crackle. The 'chips' are most definitely American fries rather than authentic chunky English chips (you can switch them out for salad or coleslaw). Eat at a wooden booth or picnic table on the dock.

That Boy Good BARBECUE $
(TBG; Map p486; 760-433-4227; www.tbgbbq.com; 326 N Horne St; mains $7-13; 11am-8pm Tue-Sun;) Situated inside a converted factory where North Pine Brewery makes its beer, this shrine to the Mississippi Delta serves belly-busting portions of pulled pork and chopped brisket slathered in delicious house BBQ sauce. Or order up baby back ribs and chicken wings with a side of dirty fries and wash it all down with a craft beer.

Ruby's Diner DINER $
(Map p486; 760-433-7829; www.rubys.com/locations/oceanside; 1 Oceanside Pier; mains $10-15; 7am-9pm Sun-Thu, 7am-10pm Fri & Sat;) This '50s-style diner has good burgers and milkshakes, big breakfasts and a full bar. Yes, it's a chain, but you can't get views like this elsewhere – it's right at the end of the pier.

Information

California Welcome Center (Map p486; 760-721-1101, 800-350-7873; www.visitoceanside.org; 928 N Coast Hwy; 9am-5pm) Helpful, informative staff dispense coupons for local attractions, maps and information for the San Diego area. Also helps book lodgings in Oceanside and sells discounted tickets to local attractions. It's just off the freeway exit.

Getting There & Away

Local buses and trains stop at the **Oceanside Transit Center** (Map p486; 800-872-7245; www.amtrak.com/stations/osd; 235 S Tremont St).

Coaster (www.gonctd.com) trains run almost an hour apart in the morning and evenings and a single journey costs from $5/5.75/6.50 for one/two/three zones. There are around three *Surfliner* (https://tickets.amtrak.com) trains a day, with fares from $18 from Downtown San Diego (Santa Fe Depot) to Oceanside.

The 101 bus route (running from La Jolla to Oceanside) runs approximately every hour. It costs $2.50 per single, and takes roughly an hour from the start of the route to the end.

Traveling by car via I-5 from Downtown San Diego, take the La Jolla Pkwy exit and head west toward Torrey Pines Rd, from where it's a right turn to Oceanside's Prospect St.

AT A GLANCE

POPULATION
2,458,089

AREA
38,500 sq miles

BEST OFF-BEAT ATTRACTION
Slab City (p528)

BEST SUNRISE SPOT
Mesquite Flat Sand Dunes (p531)

BEST HIKE
Lost Palm Oasis Trail (p517)

WHEN TO GO

Dec–Apr Moderate temperatures lure in 'snowbirds' and LA weekend-trippers.

May–mid-Jun, mid-Sep–Nov Crowds thin out as temperatures arc during shoulder season.

Jun–Sep Some inns and restaurants close in summer's heat; many of the rest offer great deals.

Palm Springs Aerial Tramway (p507)
JEFF WHYTE / SHUTTERSTOCK ©

Palm Springs & the Deserts

There's something undeniably artistic in the way the landscape unfolds in the California desert. Weathered volcanic peaks stand sentinel over singing sand dunes and mountains shimmering in hues from mustard yellow to vibrant pink. Hot mineral water spurts from the earth's belly to feed palm oases and soothe aching muscles in stylish spas. Wildflowers push up from the baked soil to celebrate springtime.

The riches of the desert soil have lured prospectors and miners, while its beauty and spirituality have tugged at the hearts of artists, visionaries and wanderers. Hipsters and celebs come for the climate and retro flair, especially in unofficial desert capital, Palm Springs. Through it all threads iconic Route 66, lined with moodily rusting roadside relics. No matter what your trail, the desert will creep into your consciousness and never fully leave.

INCLUDES

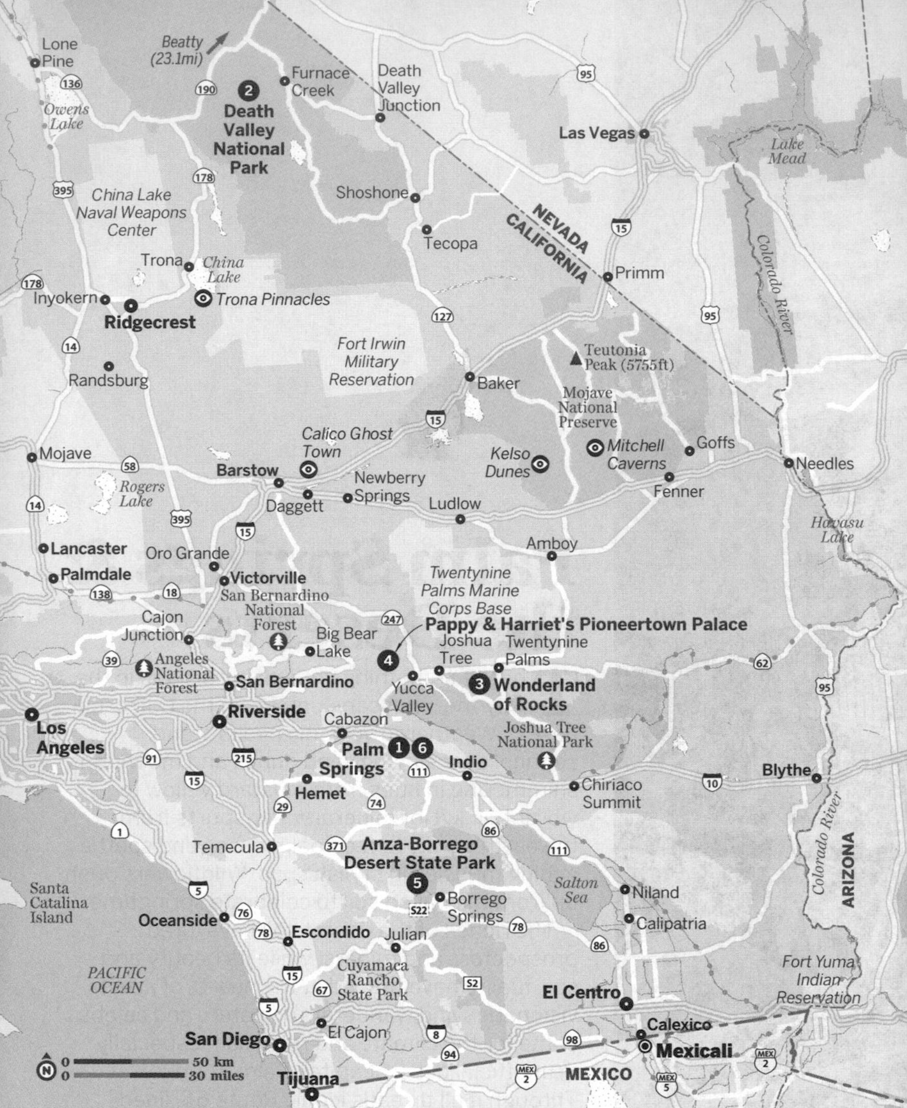

Palm Springs & the Deserts Highlights

❶ **Palm Springs** (p497) Feeling fabulous in this revitalized mid-century modern Rat Pack hangout.

❷ **Death Valley National Park** (p529) Traversing ethereal landscapes to the lowest point in the western hemisphere.

❸ **Wonderland of Rocks** (p516) Marveling at whimsically eroded rock formations on a hike through Joshua Tree National Park.

❹ **Pappy & Harriet's Pioneertown Palace** (p121) Spending a rollickin' evening in a quintessential honky-tonk.

❺ **Anza-Borrego Desert State Park** (p523) Exploring canyons, oases and mystical wind caves.

❻ **Palm Springs Aerial Tramway** (p507) Ascending through five distinct zones in 10 minutes.

PALM SPRINGS & THE COACHELLA VALLEY

The Rat Pack is back, baby, or at least its hangout is. In the 1950s and '60s, Palm Springs, some 100 miles east of LA, was the swinging getaway of Frank Sinatra, Elvis Presley and other Hollywood stars. Once the Rat Pack packed it in, Palm Springs surrendered to golfing retirees. However, since the mid-1990s, new generations have rediscovered the city's retro-chic vibe and elegant mid-century modern structures built by famous architects. Today, retirees and snowbirds mix comfortably with hipsters, hikers and celebs on getaways from LA and from across the globe. Perhaps surprisingly, Palm Springs is also one of the nation's gayest towns with roughly half of the population being part of the LGBTIQ+ community. In 2019 it elected the first all-LGBTIQ+ city council in the US.

Palm Springs is the principal city of the Coachella Valley, a string of desert towns ranging from ho-hum Cathedral City to glamtastic Palm Desert and Coachella, the latter home of the star-studded music festival, all linked by Hwy 111. North of Palm Springs, scruffy Desert Hot Springs draws visitors with chic boutique hotels built on top of soothing mineral springs.

History

Cahuilla (ka-wee-ya) tribespeople have lived in the canyons on the southwest edge of the Coachella Valley for over 1000 years. Early Spanish explorers called the hot springs beneath Palm Springs *agua caliente* (hot water), which later became the name of the local Cahuilla tribe.

In 1876 the federal government carved the valley into a checkerboard of various interests. The Southern Pacific Railroad received odd-numbered sections, while the Agua Caliente were given even-numbered sections as their reservation. Casinos have made the tribes quite wealthy today.

In the town of Indio, about 20 miles southeast of Palm Springs, date palms were imported from French-held Algeria in 1890 and have become the valley's major crop, along with citrus and table grapes.

Sights

Most sights are in Palm Springs proper but a few blue-chip destinations such as Sunnylands (p512) and the Living Desert Zoo & Gardens (p509) are worth the drive down valley.

Palm Springs

Downtown Palm Springs has been undergoing a slow-paced urbanization that has brought in retailers like H&M and MAC Cosmetics, a sleek hotel tower and new restaurants and cafes. Two recreational spaces – Downtown Park and the Agua Caliente Cultural Plaza – are expected to open in 2021.

★ Palm Springs Art Museum MUSEUM

(Map p506; ☎760-322-4800; www.psmuseum.org; 101 Museum Dr; adult/student/child under 18 $14/6/free; ⏲10am-5pm Fri-Tue, noon-8pm Thu; P) Art fans should not miss this museum and its changing exhibitions drawn from a stellar collection of international modern and contemporary painting, sculpture, photography and glass art. The permanent collection includes works by Henry Moore, Ed Ruscha, Mark di Suvero, Frederic Remington and many more heavy hitters. Other highlights are glass art by Dale Chihuly and William Morris, and a collection of pre-Columbian figurines. Free entry from 4pm to 8pm Thursdays.

Palm Springs Art Museum, Architecture & Design Center MUSEUM

(Map p506; ☎760-423-5260; www.psmuseum.org/architecture-design-center; 300 S Palm Canyon Dr; adult/child under 18 $5/free; ⏲noon-8pm Thu, 10am-5pm Fri-Tue) FREE Showcasing changing exhibits drawn from the Palm Springs Art Museum's architecture and design collection, the center occupies an iconic and spiffily restored 1961 mid-century modern bank building by E Stewart Williams.

Enjoy grand views of the San Jacinto Mountains through floor-to-ceiling windows, then browse for souvenirs in the bank vault turned gift shop.

McCallum Adobe Museum MUSEUM

(Map p506; ☎760-323-8297; www.pshistoricalsociety.org; 221 S Palm Canyon Dr; ⏲10am-4pm) FREE The town's oldest building, the 1884 McCallum Adobe, is the former home of the McCallum family, the first permanent white settlers in Palm Springs. Today, the Palm Springs Historical Society presents an engaging parade of photographs and memorabilia to chronicle the region's storied past and the people who shaped it.

Agua Caliente Cultural Museum MUSEUM

(Map p506; ☎760-778-1079; www.accmuseum.org; cnr E Tahquitz Cyn & S Indian Canyon Dr; P) Scheduled to open in 2021, this museum will showcase the history and culture of the

HIKING IN ANZA-BORREGO DESERT STATE PARK

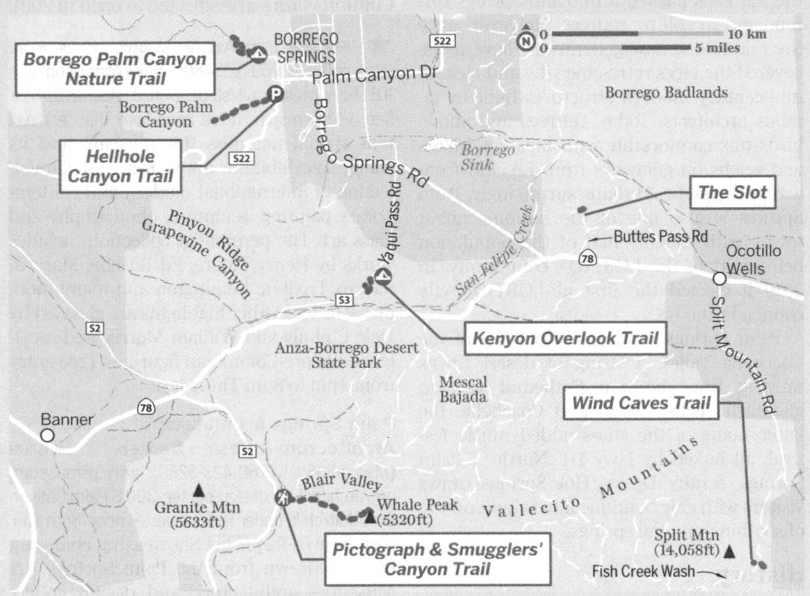

BORREGO PALM CANYON NATURE TRAIL

START/END BORREGO PALM CANYON CAMPGROUND
DURATION 2 HOURS
DISTANCE 3 MILES
DIFFICULTY EASY

This popular loop trail travels through a rocky canyon to a grove of shaggy fan palms and little waterfalls. Birds love it here and even the elusive bighorn sheep might come down for a drink. Pick up the self-guided brochure at the trailhead to learn more about the native flora and fauna.

Unfortunately, a fire in 2020 burned about a third of the grove and resulted in the trail's temporary closure. Check at the visitor center to see if it has reopened. It will take some time but, happily, most palms are expected to make a comeback. Note that there is a $10 day-use fee for this trail.

PICTOGRAPH & SMUGGLERS' CANYON TRAIL

START/END BLAIR VALLEY
DURATION 90 MINUTES
DISTANCE 3 MILES
DIFFICULTY EASY

Aside from contemplative desert landscape, this in-and-out trail delivers two big payoffs. About a mile in on the gently climbing sandy path, you'll reach a massive boulder with ancient, rust-colored Native American Kumeyaay pictographs. Keep going to narrow Smuggler's Canyon, which ends at the edge of a dry waterfall with the geologic wonderland of the Vallecito Valley unfolding below you.

This is one of three easy trails weaving through the southern Blair Valley, some 25 miles south of Borrego Springs. Turn off on County Rte S2 and follow the dirt road for about 3.6 miles.

Much of the rugged and remote terrain of California's largest state park can only be sampled on foot. Expect close-ups of winding canyons, soul-stirring viewpoints, lush palm oases and whimsical geological formations.

KENYON OVERLOOK TRAIL

START/END YAQUI PASS CAMPGROUND
DURATION 30–45 MINUTES
DISTANCE 1 MILE
DIFFICULTY EASY TO MODERATE

This in-and-out trail meanders past cactus and creosote, and rewards you with humbling vistas over the Vallecito Mountains and the overlapping alluvial fans of the Mescal Bajada. Views are at their golden-hued best at sunset.

Return the same way (recommended) or turn the hike into a loop by continuing to Yaqui Pass Rd and walking a quarter mile along the road back to your car.

THE SLOT

START/END OFF BUTTES PASS RD
DURATION 1 HOUR
DISTANCE 1.5 MILES
DIFFICULTY MODERATE

One of the top hikes in Anza-Borrego, the short but memorable Slot trail threads through a siltstone canyon that, at one point, narrows so much that you have to squeeze through sideways. The winding canyon ends just past a rock bridge wedged into the towering eroded walls above. Backtrack (recommended) or climb up and return via the longer and less scenic dirt road.

To get to the trailhead, drive east on Hwy 78, turn left on Buttes Pass Rd, left again at the Y junction and park at the mouth of the canyon after another mile.

WIND CAVES TRAIL

START/END FISH CREEK WASH
DURATION 1–1½ HOUR
DISTANCE 2 MILES
DIFFICULTY MODERATE

This fairly steep and rocky 2-mile in-and-out trail in the park's remote eastern reaches leads up to delicate wind caves carved into sculpted sandstone outcrops. Aside from playing hide-and-seek in this natural playground, you also get to savor the spirit-lifting expanse of undulating badlands stretching out toward the horizon.

Getting there is half the adventure and usually requires high-clearance 4WD. From Borrego Springs, head east on Hwy 78 for about 6.5 miles east to Ocotillo Wells, then turn south for 8 miles on Split Mountain Rd. When the pavement ends, turn right and follow the Fish Creek Wash dirt road for about 4 miles. Check road conditions with the visitor center.

HELLHOLE CANYON TRAIL

START/END HELLHOLE CANYON PARKING AREA
DURATION 4–5 HOURS
DISTANCE 6 MILES
DIFFICULTY STRENUOUS

This plucky 6-mile round-trip trail packs open desert, an untamed canyon, palm groves and a seasonal waterfall (usually in early spring) that supports birdlife and a variety of plants into one neat package. It starts at the Hellhole Canyon Trailhead on County Rte 22, close to Borrego Springs. Wear sturdy shoes as some rock scrambling is required.

From the parking lot, the trail starts out wide and easy and arrives at the canyon mouth in about 1.5 miles. As the ravine narrows, the designated trail peters out into several faint ones made by other hikers that all run parallel to a stream bed – it's impossible to get lost. About half a mile in, a couple of small palm oases will tempt you with their shade: resist and plough on even though the final stretch will have you tackling boulders and underbrush. Soon you'll reach a smaller waterfall but keep going a bit longer to the much more rewarding 20ft Maidenhair Falls, named for its fern- and moss-draped cliffs. Take a dip before heading back out.

HIKING IN JOSHUA TREE NATIONAL PARK

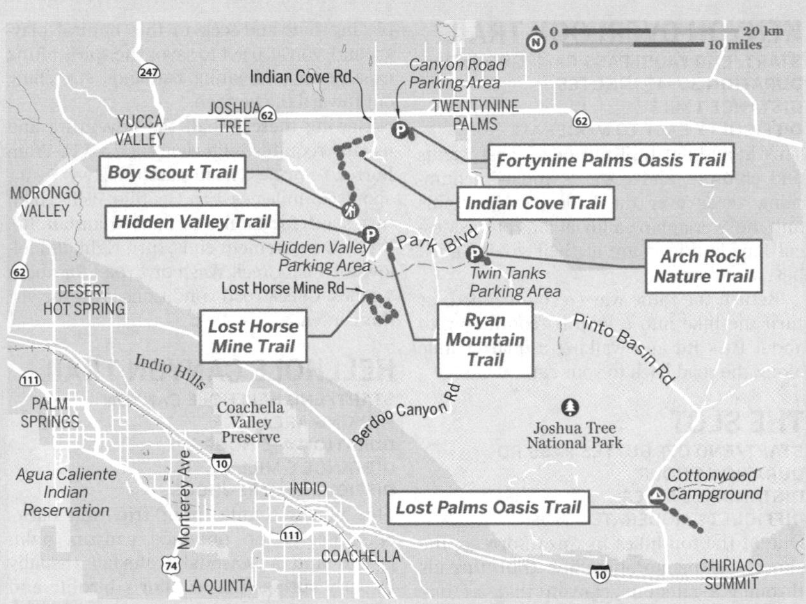

HIDDEN VALLEY TRAIL

START/END HIDDEN VALLEY PARKING AREA
DURATION 1 HOUR
DISTANCE 1 MILE
DIFFICULTY EASY

This easy 1-mile loop trail meanders between dramatic rock clusters to a hidden valley where cattle rustlers once hid their hoard. Feel free to veer off the beaten path and clamber over the piles of smoothly rounded boulders for different perspectives and more solitude. It's a lovely hike for families. The trailhead is just south of Park Blvd, near the Hidden Valley picnic area.

ARCH ROCK NATURE TRAIL

START/END TWIN TANKS PARKING AREA
DURATION 1 HOUR
DISTANCE 1.2 MILES
DIFFICULTY EASY

For the quintessential Joshua Tree photo-op, take this short and easy trail to an amazing 30ft-wide arch behind the White Tank Campground. There are plenty more formations around here, including the equally impressive 'Heart Rock,' so keep clambering to discover other hidden gems.

INDIAN COVE TRAIL

START/END INDIAN COVE WEST RD
DURATION 30–45 MINUTES
DISTANCE 0.6 MILES
DIFFICULTY EASY

Rock hounds love Indian Cove's hulking caramel-colored formations, while birders are drawn by feathered friends hiding out among the yuccas and shrubs along the half-mile Indian Cove nature trail. Access is via Indian Cove Rd, which veers off Hwy 62/29 Palms Hwy between Joshua Tree and Twentynine Palms. There's also a campground with over 100 sites for tenters and RVs.

Leave the car behind to appreciate Joshua Tree's trippy lunar landscapes, epic vistas, warped geological features, Old West history, and fascinating flora and fauna.

FORTYNINE PALMS OASIS TRAIL

START/END CANYON RD PARKING AREA
DURATION 2–3 HOURS
DISTANCE 3 MILES
DIFFICULTY MODERATE

Escape the crowds on this well-maintained 3-mile round-trip trek to a fan-palm oasis scenically cradled by a canyon. It goes up and down, mostly gently but with some sections likely to get your heart pumping. The trailhead is at the end of Canyon Rd off 29 Palms Hwy/Hwy 62, just east of the Indian Cove turnoff.

LOST HORSE MINE TRAIL

START/END LOST HORSE MINE RD
DURATION 2–3 HOURS
DISTANCE 4 MILES
DIFFICULTY MODERATE

This moderately tough in-and-out 4-mile climb visits the remains of one of the most productive of the 300 gold and silver mines on park land. Between 1894 and 1931, it yielded more than 10,000 ounces of gold and 16,000 ounces of silver. Joshua trees and yucca occasionally flank the trail to the mill and the tunnels. The old mine area is fenced off, but there's enough left to see to kindle your imagination.

To get to the trailhead, head south of Park Blvd on Keys View Rd, then turn left onto Lost Horse Mine Rd and follow it for a mile to the parking area.

BOY SCOUT TRAIL

START BOY SCOUT TRAILHEAD, PARK BLVD
END INDIAN COVE
DURATION 6 HOURS
DISTANCE 8 MILES
DIFFICULTY STRENUOUS

For an immersion into Joshua Tree flora and topography, embark on this tough 8-mile one-way trail cutting through canyons, washes and mountains along the western edge of the Wonderland of Rocks. Most hikers prefer to launch from Park Blvd near the Quail Springs picnic area and head north to Indian Cove, but it can just as easily be done the other way around. Arrange for pick-up at the other end, although camping overnight and backtracking the next day has its rewards. Note that part of the trail is unmarked, so ask for detailed directions at a visitor center, bring a topo and get ready to harness those scouting skills.

LOST PALM OASIS TRAIL

START/END COTTONWOOD SPRING CAMPGROUND
DURATION 5–6 HOURS
DISTANCE 7.5 MILES
DIFFICULTY STRENUOUS

This rewarding 7.5-mile round-trip trek leads to a hidden desert-fan palm oasis from Cottonwood Spring near the park's southern edge. The path starts out fairly moderate, weaving through various washes, before descending steeply into a canyon to an overlook and from there down into the oasis. Enjoy the shady palms before embarking on the tough slog back out of the canyon.

For an additional challenge and killer views of the Eagle Mountains and the Salton Sea, add the 2-mile detour to the top of 3371ft-high **Mastodon Peak** on your way back.

RYAN MOUNTAIN TRAIL

START/END PARK BLVD, 2 MILES EAST OF KEYS VIEW RD
DURATION 1½–2½ HOURS
DISTANCE 3 MILES
DIFFICULTY STRENUOUS

Short but tough, this trail pays peak baggers back with some of the most stunning views in the park. Feel free to pause frequently to take in iconic Wonderland of Rocks formations, the Ryan Ranch ruins and the alien desertscape beyond as you tackle this well-trodden 3-mile in-and-out hike up 5458ft-high Ryan Mountain. Be sure to pack water, sunscreen and stamina – the 1000ft elevation gain will likely make your thighs burn.

ROUTE 66 – THE 'MOTHER ROAD' IN CALIFORNIA

For generations of Americans, California, with its sparkling waters and sunny skies, was the promised land for road-trippers on Route 66. Follow their tracks through the gauntlet of Mojave Desert ghost towns, railway whistle-stops like Barstow and Victorville, and across the Cajon Pass. Finally, wind through the LA Basin and put your vehicle in park near the crashing ocean waves in Santa Monica.

1 Needles

At the Arizona border, the arched 1916 **Old Trails Bridge** (Needles-Topock; no public access; P) marked the Mother Road's entrance to California until 1948. In the movie version of John Steinbeck's novel *The Grapes of Wrath*, the Joad family used it to cross the Colorado River. For the best vantage point, head to the Route 66 Welcome

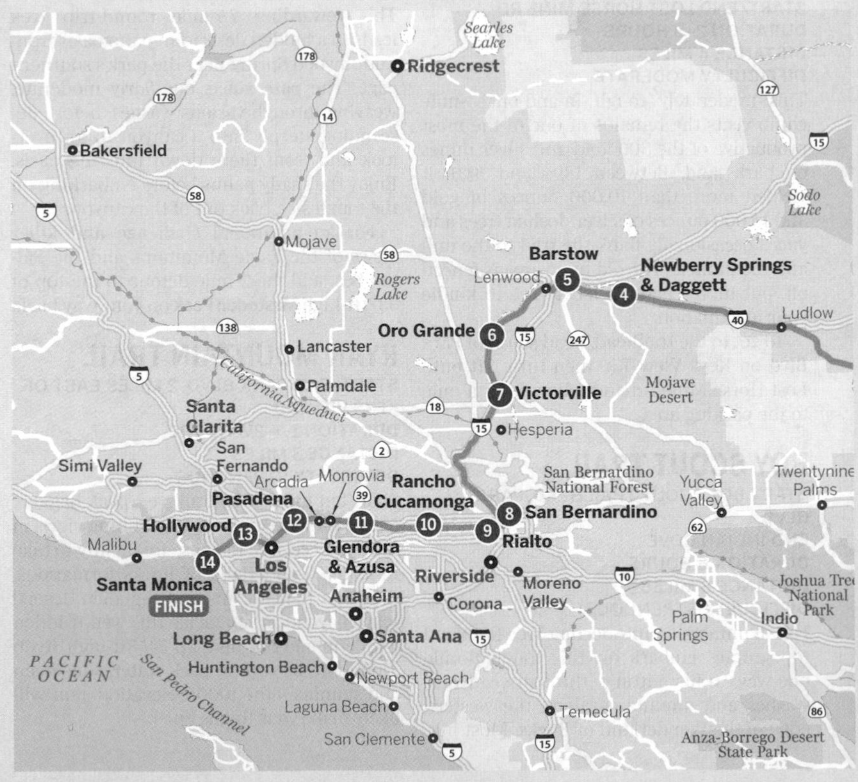

3–4 Days 350 miles / 565km

Great For... History & Culture

Best Time to Go Spring and fall for cooler days.

Sign off National Trails Hwy about a quarter mile south of I-40 (exit 153).

About 14 miles north, the jewel of the railroad town of Needles is the restored **El Garces train depot**. It's one of only a few remaining 'Harvey Houses,' a chain of early-20th-century railway hotels and restaurants managed by the Fred Harvey Company. They were famous for employing traveling waitresses, as portrayed in the 1946 MGM musical *The Harvey Girls*.

The Drive > Drive west on I-40 for about 15 miles, take exit 133 and follow Hwy 95 north for 6 miles. Turn left and follow Goffs Rd (Historic Route 66) for another 15 miles. You'll inevitably be running alongside a long train – this is a primary rail shipping route to the West Coast.

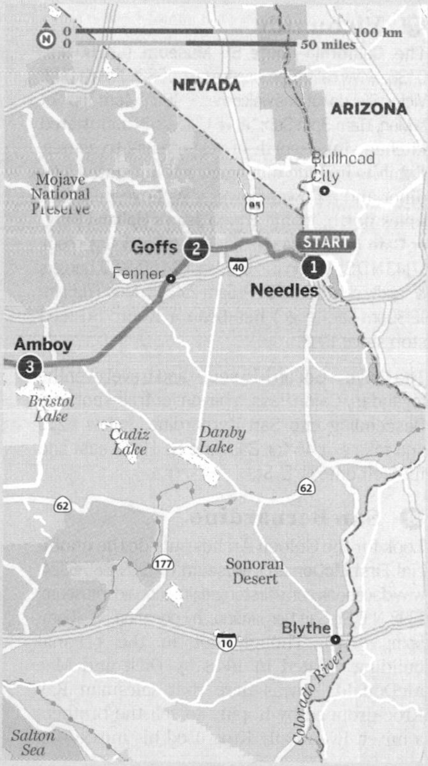

2 Goffs

The 1914 Spanish Mission–style **schoolhouse** (760-733-4482; www.mdhca.org; 37198 Lanfair Rd, Essex; 9am-4pm Sat-Mon Oct-Jun, outdoor 24hr; P) FREE in Goffs (population 12) is a fun stop along this stretch of highway. In the old classroom historic photographs illustrate the tough life on the edge of the Mojave. Outside you're free to wander around a graveyard of rusting vintage cars, gas pumps and even a bullet-riddled old yellow school bus.

The Drive > Until the flood damaged Route 66 stretch between Fenner and Amboy reopens, you need to detour 30 miles west on I-40 and cut 12 miles south on Kelbaker Rd before rejoining the National Trails Hwy. Just before reaching Amboy, keep an eye out for a pair of gleaming white, massive Chinese guardian lion sculptures incongruously perched in the sunbaked emptiness.

3 Amboy

In the near-ghost town of Amboy, **Roy's Motel & Cafe** (www.visitamboy.com; National Old Trails Hwy, Amboy; 7am-8pm, seasonal variations; P) FREE has been a popular pit stop since 1938. If you believe the lore, Roy once cooked his Route 66 double cheeseburger on the hood of a '63 Mercury. Although closed, Roy's iconic neon sign kicked back into glimmering glory in 2019.

Two miles west, **Amboy Crater** (760-326-7000; www.blm.gov/visit/amboy-crater; Crater Rd; sunrise-sunset; P) FREE is a 250ft-high, almost perfectly symmetrical volcanic cinder cone. It's a 3-mile round-trip hike to the top for great views over the lava fields where NASA engineers field-tested the Mars Rover.

The Drive > Travel 28 miles along National Trails Hwy to Ludlow. Turn right onto Crucero Rd and pass under I-40, then follow the north frontage road west for 8 miles before it makes a sharp left and crosses under I-40 on Lavic Rd. Take the first right to get back on National Trails Hwy and travel past Lavic Lake volcanic field.

DETOUR TO CALICO GHOST TOWN

Not only kids will love the 6-mile detour north from Daggett to **Calico Ghost Town** (☎800-862-2542; www.calicotown.com; 36600 Ghost Town Rd, Yermo; adult/child $8/5; ⏲9am-5pm; P 👪 🐾), a park with a cluster of reconstructed pioneer-era buildings amid ruins of a late-19th-century silver-mining town. Pan for gold, explore a mine or ride a narrow-gauge railway, but skip the food and instead head down the road to **Peggy Sue's** (☎760-254-3370; www.peggysuesdiner.com; 35654 Yermo Rd, Yermo; mains $10-15; ⏲6am-10pm; P ❄ 👪), an authentic 1950s diner.

4 Newberry Springs & Daggett

Near Newberry Springs, Route 66 passes by the grizzled **Bagdad Cafe** (☎760-257-3101; 46548 National Trails Hwy, Newberry Springs; ⏲7am-7pm; P) FREE, the main filming location of Percy Adlon's 1987 cult flick starring CCH Pounder and Jack Palance. It is chockablock with posters, movie stills and memorabilia.

The highway passes under I-40 and 12 miles later reaches windswept **Daggett**, site of the harsh California inspection station faced by Dust Bowl refugees in *The Grapes of Wrath*. Pay your respects to such early desert adventurers as Sierra Nevada naturalist John Muir at the long-shuttered **Stone Hotel**.

The Drive > Return to Daggett, then drive west to Nebo Rd, turn left and rejoin I-40. You'll drive about 4 miles before exiting at E Main St, which runs through Barstow, a railroad settlement and historic crossroads, where murals adorn empty buildings downtown. Turn right on N 1st St.

5 Barstow

After 1926, Barstow became a major rest stop for motorists and is still lined with chain motels today. Follow N 1st St to the beautifully restored 1911 Harvey House, nicknamed **Casa del Desierto**, designed by Western architect Mary Colter. Inside is the **Route 66 Mother Road Museum** (☎760-255-1890; www.route66museum.org; 681 N 1st St; ⏲10am-4pm Fri & Sat, 11am-4pm Sun, or by appointment; P 👪) FREE with B&W photographs, a 1915 Ford Model T and odds and ends from the heyday of Route 66. At the building's other end is a collection of historic locomotives, a bright-red caboose and other **railroad relics**.

The Drive > Leaving Barstow via Main St, rejoin the National Trails Hwy heading west as it meanders alongside the Mojave River through Lenwood. This rural byway is like a scavenger hunt for Mother Road ruins, including antique filling stations and tumbledown motor courts. After 25 miles you'll arrive in Oro Grande.

6 Oro Grande

Elmer's Bottle Tree Ranch (24266 National Trails Hwy, Oro Grande; ⏲24hr; P) FREE in Oro Grande is a quirky piece of roadside folk-art with over 200 'bottle trees.' It's the work of Elmer Long, a cracked artistic genius who died in 2109. Elmer used bottles in all sorts of colors, shapes and sizes to build this offbeat sculpture garden, incorporating telephone poles, railroad signs and other bric-a-brac.

The Drive > Continue south on National Trails Hwy and cross over the Mojave River on a 1930s steel-truss bridge, then roll into downtown Victorville, a trip of 12 miles.

7 Victorville

The **California Route 66 Museum** (☎760-951-0436; www.califrt66museum.org; 16825 South D St, Victorville; donations welcome; ⏲10am-4pm Thu-Sat & Mon, 11am-3pm Sun; P 👪) FREE is a cluttered kitchen sink's worth of yesteryear's treasures. Exhibits include old signs, a selfie-suited '50s diner and a flower-power VW 'Love Bus.' Two miles north, iconic **Emma Jean's Holland Burger Cafe** (☎760-243-9938; www.hollandburger.com; 17143 N D St, Victorville; breakfast $4.50-9.50, burgers & sandwiches $6-8.60; ⏲5am-2:45pm Mon-Fri, 6am-12:30pm Sat; P ❄) has been a Route 66 feed stop since 1947.

The Drive > Get on I-15 south and travel over the legendary Cajon Pass, a haven for trainspotters. Descending into San Bernardino, follow I-215 and take exit 45 for Baseline St. Head east and turn left onto N 'E' St.

8 San Bernardino

Look for the Golden Arches outside the unofficial **First McDonald's Museum** (☎909-885-6324; www.facebook.com/firstoriginalmcdonaldsmuseum; 1398 N E St, San Bernardino; by donation; ⏲10am-5pm; P 👪). Though not in the original building created in 1948 by Dick and Mac McDonald, it was here that salesman Ray Kroc dropped by hoping to sell the brothers a mixer. Eventually Kroc used his moxie – as portrayed by Michael Keaton in *The Founder* (2016) – to buy the rights to the McDonald's name and build an empire.

The Drive > Turn west on 5th St, leaving San Bernardino via Foothill Blvd, which continues straight into the urban sprawl of Greater Los Angeles. It's a long haul west to Pasadena (over 50 miles), with stop-and-go traffic most of the way, but there are some gems to uncover en route.

9 Rialto

In Rialto, swing by the **Wigwam Motel** (☎909-875-3005; www.wigwammotel.com; 2728 W Foothill Blvd, Rialto; d with bath $107-159; P ❄ 📶 🏊 🐕), a cluster of 32ft-tall tipis that have welcomed travelers since 1950. Cruising through **Fontana**, birthplace of the Hells Angels biker club, pause for a photo by the **Giant Orange**, a 1930s juice stand of the kind that was once a fixture alongside SoCal's citrus groves. Find it in the parking lot of **Bono's Italian Restaurant** (☎909-441-4036; www.bonsitalia.com; 15395 E Foothill Blvd, Fontana; pizza & pasta $11-14; ⏱11am-10pm Wed-Sun; P ❄), a historic Route 66 diner that was reimagined as a pizza parlor in 2019.

The Drive > Continue west on Foothill Blvd to Rancho Cucamonga.

10 Rancho Cucamonga

Rancho Cucamonga is home to two old-school steakhouses with a Route 66 pedigree. First up is the **Magic Lamp Inn**, easily recognized by its fabulous neon Aladdin's lamp. A bit further on, storied **Sycamore Inn** (☎909-982-1104; www.thesycamoreinn.com; 8318 Foothill Blvd, Rancho Cucamonga; mains $28-59; ⏱5-9pm Mon-Thu, to 10pm Fri & Sat, 4-8:30pm Sun; P ❄) has fed its juicy steaks to generations of meat-lovers, including Marilyn Monroe.

The Drive > Continue driving west on Foothill Blvd.

11 Glendora & Azusa

A key stop in Glendora is **The Hat**, which has been serving its famous hot pastrami sandwiches since 1951. Route 66 continues as Huntington Dr in Duarte. Turn right on Magnolia Ave and rejoin Foothill Blvd in Azusa, whose supposedly haunted 1925 **Aztec Hotel** (☎626-358-3231; 311 W Foothill Blvd, Monrovia) FREE sports a striking Mayan Revival–style facade.

The Drive > Continue west on Foothill Blvd, then turn left (south) on Santa Anita Ave, right (west) on Huntington Dr and right again on Colorado Pl past the 1930s Santa Anita Park horseracing track. It's where the Marx Brothers filmed *A Day at the Races* (1937) and where legendary thoroughbred Seabiscuit once ran.

12 Pasadena

Colorado Blvd leads straight into Old Pasadena, where boutiques and cafes are housed in restored historic Spanish Colonial Revival–style buildings. Follow Fair Oaks Ave south to the nostalgic 1915 **Fair Oaks Pharmacy** (☎626-799-1414; www.fairoakspharmacy.net; 1526 Mission St, South Pasadena; sundaes $7-10; ⏱9am-9pm Mon-Sat, 10am-7pm Sun; P ❄ 👪), where 'soda jerks' still dish out 'phosphates' (flavored syrup, soda water and 'secret potion'), banana splits and other sugary kicks.

The Drive > Rejoin the modern world on the Pasadena Fwy (Hwy 110), which streams south into LA. One of the first freeways in the US, it's a truck-free state historic freeway. Take exit 24B and follow Sunset Blvd northwest to Santa Monica Blvd westbound.

13 Hollywood

The exact track that Route 66 ran through Tinseltown isn't possible to follow these days (it changed several times). Start exploring at the **Hollywood & Highland** (Map p393; www.hollywoodandhighland.com; 6801 Hollywood Blvd; ⏱10am-10pm Mon-Sat, to 7pm Sun; 📶 👪; M B Line to Hollywood/Highland) shopping, dining and entertainment complex in the center of the action. Travelers looking for a creepy fun communion with stars of yesteryear should stroll the **Hollywood Forever Cemetery** (p394) next to Paramount Pictures.

The Drive > Follow Santa Monica Blvd west for 13 miles to reach the end of the road – it meets Ocean Ave at Palisades Park. Hwy 1 is downhill from Ocean Ave heading north. The pier is a few blocks to the south.

14 Santa Monica

This is the end of the line: Route 66 reaches its finish, over 2400 miles from its starting point in Chicago, on an ocean bluff in **Palisades Park** (Map p402; ☎800-544-5319; Ocean Ave btwn Colorado Ave & San Vicente Blvd; ⏱5am-midnight) FREE, where a Will Rogers Hwy memorial plaque marks the official end of the Mother Road. Celebrate on **Santa Monica Pier** (p399), where you can ride a 1920s carousel featured in *The Sting* (1973) and enjoy other attractions and carnival rides. With the glittering Pacific as a backdrop, take a selfie with the 'Santa Monica 66 End of Trail' sign. Then hit the beach.

Palm Springs

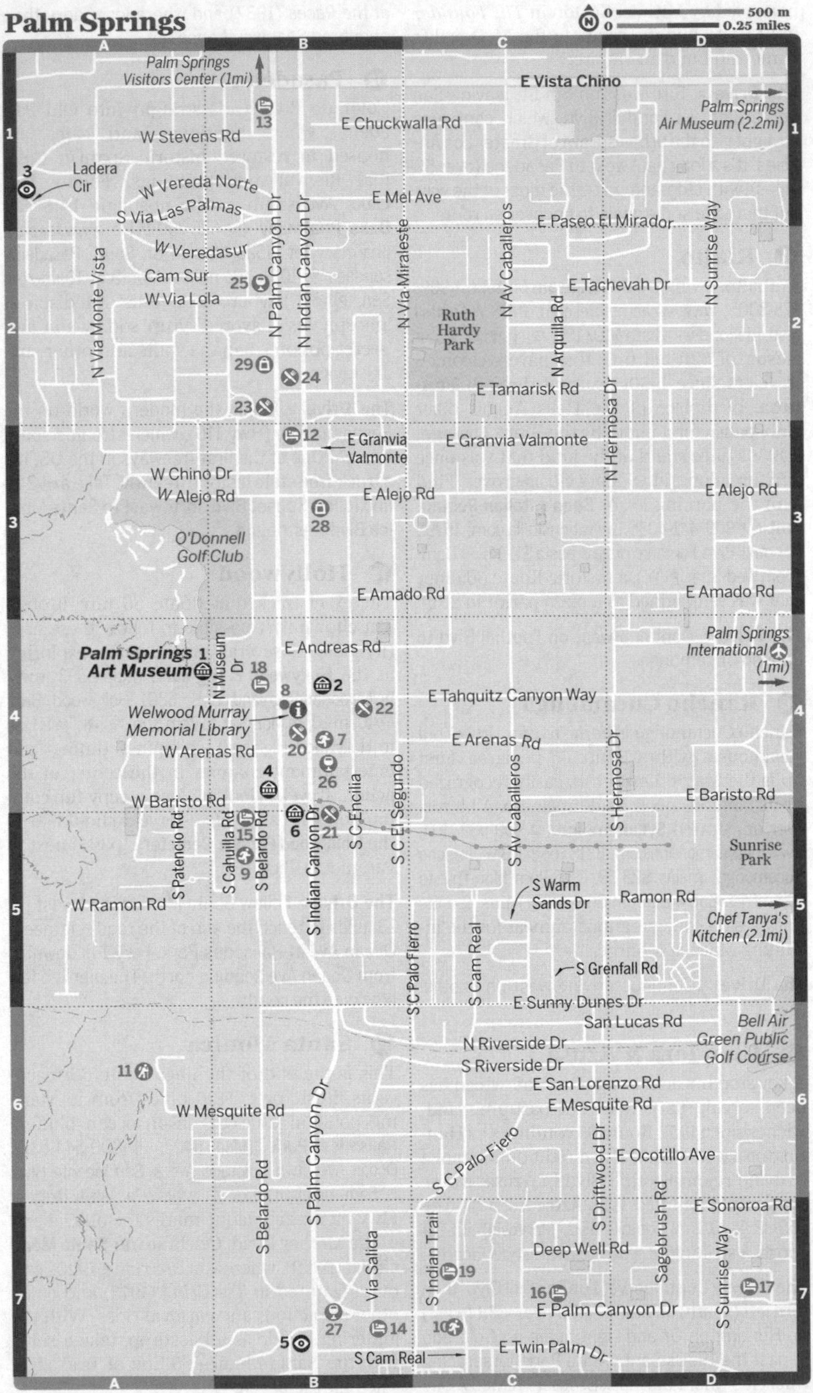

0 — 500 m
0 — 0.25 miles

Palm Springs Visitors Center (1mi)
E Vista Chino
Palm Springs Air Museum (2.2mi)
W Stevens Rd
E Chuckwalla Rd
Ladera Cir
W Vereda Norte
S Via Las Palmas
E Mel Ave
E Paseo El Mirador
W Veredasur
Cam Sur
W Via Lola
N Via Monte Vista
N Palm Canyon Dr
N Indian Canyon Dr
N Via Miraleste
Ruth Hardy Park
N Av Caballeros
N Arquilla Rd
E Tachevah Dr
N Sunrise Way
E Tamarisk Rd
N Hermosa Dr
E Granvia Valmonte
W Chino Dr
W Alejo Rd
E Alejo Rd
O'Donnell Golf Club
E Amado Rd
E Andreas Rd
Palm Springs International (1mi)
Palm Springs Art Museum
N Museum Dr
E Tahquitz Canyon Way
Welwood Murray Memorial Library
W Arenas Rd
E Arenas Rd
W Baristo Rd
E Baristo Rd
S Patencio Rd
S Cahuilla Rd
S Belardo Rd
S Indian Canyon Dr
S C Encilia
S C El Segundo
S Av Caballeros
S Hermosa Dr
Sunrise Park
W Ramon Rd
S Warm Sands Dr
Ramon Rd
Chef Tanya's Kitchen (2.1mi)
S C Palo Fierro
S Cam Real
S Grenfall Rd
E Sunny Dunes Dr
San Lucas Rd
Bell Air Green Public Golf Course
N Riverside Dr
S Riverside Dr
E San Lorenzo Rd
W Mesquite Rd
E Mesquite Rd
S Palm Canyon Dr
S C Palo Fiero
S Driftwood Dr
E Ocotillo Ave
E Sonoroa Rd
Sagebrush Rd
S Sunrise Way
Via Salida
S Indian Trail
Deep Well Rd
E Palm Canyon Dr
E Twin Palm Dr
S Cam Real

Palm Springs

Agua Caliente Band of Cahuilla people. It will be part of a cultural plaza designed to evoke tribal traditions and the desert landscape while also integrating a spa fed by the Agua Caliente hot mineral spring and an interpretive walking trail.

Ruddy's 1930s General Store Museum MUSEUM

(Map p506; ☎760-327-2156; www.palmsprings.com/points/heritage/ruddy.html; 221 S Palm Canyon Dr, Palm Springs; adult/child 95¢/free; ⏰10am-4pm Thu-Sun Oct-Jun, Sat & Sun Jul-Sep) In a cabin within the Village Green Heritage Center, this meticulously recreated 1930s general store takes you on a nostalgic trip back in time with its 6000 preserved original products from groceries to medicines, beauty aids to clothing and hardware.

Palm Springs Air Museum MUSEUM

(Map p508; ☎760-778-6262; www.palmspringsairmuseum.org; 745 N Gene Autry Trail; adult/child $18.50/11.50; ⏰10am-5pm; P) Adjacent to the airport, this vast museum has an exceptional collection of WWII aircraft (many still flyable) and flight memorabilia along with a movie theater and interactive stations, including an F-16 flight simulator. A highlight for many is a clamber around the WWII-era Boeing B-17 Flying Fortress bomber. There's also a hangar with aircraft and exhibits from the wars in Korea and Vietnam.

Moorten Botanical Gardens GARDENS

(Map p506; ☎760-327-6555; http://moortenbotanicalgarden.com; 1701 S Palm Canyon Dr; adult/child $5/2; ⏰10am-4pm Thu-Tue Sep 22-Jun 20, 9am-1pm Fri-Sun Jun 21-Sep 21; P) This petite private garden was created in 1938 by silent movie actor Chester 'Cactus Slim' Moorten and his wife, Patricia, and is now overseen by their son, Clark. A stroll through this enchanting symphony of cacti, agaves and other succulents and desert flora is balm for eyes and soul and also takes you past 'Cactus Castle', the Spanish-style family home.

Coachella Valley

★ Palm Springs Aerial Tramway CABLE CAR

(Map p508; ☎760-325-1391; www.pstramway.com; 1 Tram Way, Palm Springs; adult/child $27/17, parking $8; ⏰1st tram up 10am Mon-Fri, 8am Sat & Sun, last tram up 8pm, last tram down 9:45pm, varies seasonally; P) Since 1963, the 2.5-mile ride aboard the Palm Springs Aerial Tramway's rotating gondolas has been the coolest trip in town. Enjoy uplifting views as you're whisked through five vegetation zones – dusty Sonoran desert floor to pine-scented Mt San Jacinto State Park (p509) – in just 10 minutes. It's

Coachella Valley

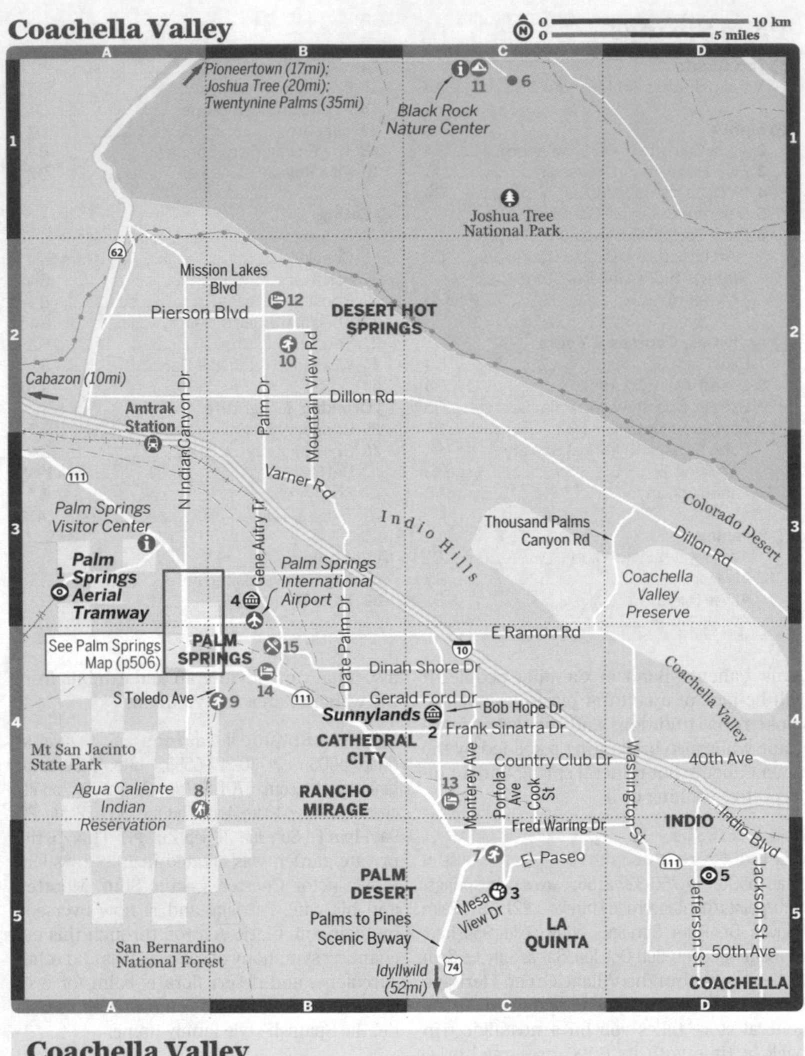

Coachella Valley

Top Sights

1 Palm Springs Aerial Tramway A3
2 Sunnylands C4

Sights

3 Living Desert Zoo & Gardens C5
4 Palm Springs Air Museum B3
5 Shields Date Garden D5

Activities, Courses & Tours

6 Covington Flat C1
7 Funseekers/Palm Desert Bike C5
8 Indian Canyons A4
9 Smoke Tree Stables B4
10 Two Bunch Palms Resort & Spa B2

Sleeping

11 Black Rock Campground C1
12 El Morocco Inn & Spa B2
13 Omni Rancho Las Palmas Resort & Spa C4
14 Parker Palm Springs B4
Two Bunch Palms .... (see 10)

Eating

15 Chef Tanya's Kitchen B4

about 30°F to 40°F (up to 22°C) cooler at the mountain station (8561ft), so don't go up in flip-flops and tank top, especially if you plan on hitting a trail.

There are exhibits, food, viewing platforms and gift shops at both ends. Good-value Ride 'n' Dinner deals are available after 4pm.

The valley station is 3.5 miles off Hwy 111; the turnoff is about 3 miles north of downtown Palm Springs. Cable cars depart at least every 30 minutes. Online tickets are available from six weeks to 24 hours in advance and are highly recommended to avoid often horrendous wait times. A contingent of on-site tickets is available on a first-come, first-served basis.

Living Desert Zoo & Gardens ZOO
(Map p508; ☎760-346-5694; www.livingdesert.org; 47900 Portola Ave, Palm Desert; adult/child $25/15; ⌚8am-5pm Oct-May, 7am-1:30pm Jun-Sep; P ♿) This popular park showcases desert plants and animals alongside exhibits on regional geology and Native American culture. Camel encounters, giraffe feeding, the butterfly garden, a spin on the endangered species carousel, and a hop-on, hop-off shuttle cost extra. Allow for a visit of two to three hours and avoid weekends if you don't like crowds.

Shields Date Garden GARDENS
(Map p508; ☎760-347-7768; www.shieldsdategarden.com; 80-225 Hwy 111, Indio; gardens $5; ⌚9am-5pm; P ♿) In business since 1924, this roadside attraction is where you can watch the 15-minute documentary, *Romance and Sex Life of the Date*, sip a creamy date shake, stock up on plump dates in the gift shop and, incongruously, tour a garden accented with biblical statuary.

Activities

Indian Canyons HIKING
(Map p508; ☎760-323-6018; www.indian-canyons.com; 38520 S Palm Canyon Dr, Palm Springs; adult/child $9/5; ⌚8am-5pm daily Oct-Jun, Fri-Sun Jul-Sep, last entry 4pm year-round) Sacred to the Agua Caliente Band of Cahuilla Indians, these canyons sustain rich plant life fed by seasonal streams flowing from the San Jacinto Mountains. The most famous is the 15-mile-long Palm Canyon, where you can picnic, meditate or hike beneath a canopy of magnificent fan palms. Quiz the folks at the trading post for other hiking ideas such as the 4.7-mile Murray Canyon trail to a seasonal waterfall or the 1.2-mile Andreas Canyon loop trail past photogenic rock formations.

★ **Tahquitz Canyon** HIKING
(Map p506; ☎760-416-7044; www.tahquitzcanyon.com; 500 W Mesquite Ave, Palm Springs; adult/child $12.50/6; ⌚7:30am-5pm Oct-Jun, Fri-Sun only Jul-Sep, last entry 3:30pm) Considered historic and sacred by the Agua Caliente people, this gorgeous canyon can be explored via a fairly steep and rocky 1.8-mile (round-trip) hike culminating at a 60ft waterfall. An interpretive trail guide available at the visitor center points out rock art, viewpoints and native plant life. The center also has natural- and cultural-history exhibits and screenings of *The Legend of Tahquitz* video about an evil Cahuilla shaman.

Mt San Jacinto State Park HIKING
(Map p518; ☎951-659-2607; www.parks.ca.gov/msjsp) FREE The wilderness beyond the Palm Springs Aerial Tramway mountain station extends for 14,000 acres and is crowned by Mt San Jacinto (10,384ft). Except for the easy but still rewarding nature trails around Long Valley right below the station, hikers need to obtain a free day-use permit from the nearby ranger station. The most popular wilderness hike is the 4.5-mile Round Valley loop, while the most challenging is the 11-mile round trip up Mt San Jacinto (summer only). Expect snow from November to April.

Applications for wilderness camping permits ($5 per person, check or money order only) can be mailed up to eight weeks, but no fewer than 10 days, in advance. See the website for the form and instructions.

Smoke Tree Stables HORSEBACK RIDING
(Map p508; ☎760-327-1372; www.smoketreestables.com; 2500 S Toledo Ave, Palm Springs; guided rides 60/100min $60/120; ⌚1hr rides hourly 8am-2pm Fri-Tue, 100min tours 9am, 11am & 1pm Fri-Tue; ♿) This well-established outfit offers public one-hour guided horse rides along the base of the mountains and 100-minute tours from Andreas Canyon to palm-lined Murray Canyon and back. Both are geared toward novice riders. Reservations are not needed but call to confirm departure times and show up 30 minutes beforehand. Private tours available by arrangement.

Tours

★ **Desert Tasty Tours** TOURS
(Map p506; ☎760-870-1133; www.deserttastytours.com; tours $75; ⌚11am Mon-Sat Sep-May) Get the inside scoop on Palm Springs' tasty dining scene on a three-hour walking tour of

Palm Canyon Dr. A snack is served at each of the seven stops set within 1 mile.

Palm Springs Historical Society Walking Tours TOURS
(Map p506; ☎760-323-8297; www.pshistoricalsociety.org; 221 S Palm Canyon Dr, Palm Springs; tours $25) The Palm Springs Historical Society (PSHS) runs this bouquet of seven tours lasting between one and 2½ hours and covering history, architecture, Hollywood stars and more. Check the website for the schedule and to purchase advance tickets. Tickets are also sold at the PSHS office.

Festivals & Events

Palm Springs and the other Coachella cities have a busy schedule of events and festivals, especially in winter. Room rates and demand skyrocket during the biggest ones such as the Coachella Valley Music & Arts Festival and the Stagecoach Festival.

Palm Springs Villagefest FOOD & DRINK
(http://villagefest.org; S Palm Canyon Dr, Palm Springs; ⊙6-10pm Thu Oct-May, from 7pm Jun-Sep) FREE Every Thursday night locals and visitors alike flock to downtown Palm Springs for this street fair with food stalls, craft vendors, music and entertainment. It runs for three blocks south of Tahquitz Canyon Way.

Palm Springs International Film Festival FILM
(☎tickets 760-778 8979; www.psfilmfest.org; ⊙Jan) January brings a Hollywood-star-studded two-week film festival, showing more than 200 films from around the world at various venues in town. A short-film festival follows in June. Tickets available online and by phone.

Modernism Week CULTURAL
(www.modernismweek.com; ⊙mid-Feb) Ten-day celebration of all things mid-century modern: architecture and home tours, films, lectures, design show and lots of parties. There are more than 250 events but tickets to some sell out quickly.

★**Coachella Valley Music & Arts Festival** MUSIC
(☎855-771-3667; www.coachella.com; 81800 Ave 51, Indio; general/VIP $429/999; ⊙Apr) The mother of all indie-music and art fests, Coachella takes over the Empire Polo Club in Indio over two three-day weekends in April. The line up features both major headliners and the stars of tomorrow. The

TIME OUT FOR SPA TIME

Palm Springs is famous for its luxe spas. Here's a shortlist of our fave pampering shrines to work out the kinks and turn your body into a glowing lump of tranquility. Reservations are essential.

Estrella Spa at Avalon Palm Springs (Map p506; ☎760-318-3000; www.avalon-hotel.com/palm-springs/estrella-spa; 415 S Belardo Rd, Palm Springs; 60/90min massage from $155/225; ⊙10am-3pm Mon-Fri, from 9am Sat & Sun) A tranquil vibe permeates this stylish retreat that's big on natural options, including such next-gen treatments as a CBD Spa Experience, a Vichy shower (massage shower with multiple shower heads) and the Milky Way manicure/pedicure that starts with a warm fresh-milk soak (vegan version available).

Two Bunch Palms Resort & Spa (Map p508; ☎760-288-7801; www.twobunchpalms.com/spa; 67425 Two Bunch Palms Trail, Desert Hot Springs; day pass $125, treatments from $95; ⊙day pass valid 10am-6pm) Tim Robbins enjoyed a mud bath at this whisper-only oasis retreat in Robert Altman's film *The Player*, but the spa's treatment menu actually offers more intriguing sessions to propel you into a state of bliss. How about an Ayurvedic consultation, a sonic meditation or a chakra-balancing massage? Non-resort guests should call ahead for day passes.

Feel Good Spa (Map p506; ☎760-866-6188; www.acehotel.com/palmsprings/feel-good-spa; 701 E Palm Canyon Dr, Palm Springs; 60/90min massage $145/195; ⊙by appointment 9am-6pm Sun-Thu, to 8pm Fri & Sat) At the hip Ace Hotel & Swim Club, this low-key spa offers the gamut of treatments to guests and the public, including a glow-restoring crystal facial or the detoxifying Deep Goodness massage to make you feel less guilty when bellying up to the pool bar afterwards.

website has the low-down on how to score one of those sizzling-hot tickets.

Stagecoach Festival MUSIC
(www.stagecoachfestival.com; 81800 Ave 51, Indio; general/VIP passes $349/1299; ⌚Apr) Top-of-the-line country-music artists and the people that love them make the pilgrimage to Indio's Empire Polo Club for this three-day festival every April.

It's organized by the same promoter as the Coachella Valley Music & Arts Festival held later that month.

Splash House MUSIC
(☎888-833-1031; www.splashhouse.com; general/after-hour/combo pass $125/45/160; ⌚Jun & Aug) Three weekends and three locations: Splash House is the ultimate pool party dance-a-thon that takes over the Renaissance, the Saguaro and the Riviera resorts with big-name DJs and acts from around the globe. After-hours the action moves to the Palm Springs Air Museum at the airport for more beats under the stars.

DON'T MISS

ELVIS HONEYMOON HIDEAWAY

Elvis slept at the **Elvis Honeymoon Hideaway** (Map p506; ☎760-322-1192; www.elvishoneymoon.com; 1350 Ladera Circle, Palm Springs; adult/child $35/15; ⌚tours 1pm & 3:30pm Mon, Wed, Fri-Sun or by appointment) with Priscilla no less, kicking off their honeymoon on May 1, 1967 at the Alexander Estate. Their daughter, Lisa Marie, reportedly saw the light of day precisely nine months later. Today, you can channel the king on tours of this 1960 modernist icon nicknamed 'House of Tomorrow' thanks to its futuristic design. Expect four circles arranged over three floors, floor-to-ceiling windows, a rock wall and a suspended fireplace. Elvis memorabilia has been added throughout.

Sleeping

Palm Springs and the Coachella Valley offer the gamut of lodging options, from vintage-flair boutique hotels and full-on luxury resorts to plain-Jane motels. Many properties add a hefty daily 'resort fee' to your room bill. Some places are adults-only (21 and over). Most are entirely nonsmoking in rooms and outside areas. Campers should head to Joshua Tree National Park or into the San Jacinto Mountains (via Hwy 74).

Villa Royale BOUTIQUE HOTEL $$
(Map p506; ☎760-327-2314; https://villaroyale.com; 1620 S Indian Trail, Palm Springs; d/ste $190/285; P⊖❄🛜≋🐾) 🍃 Built in 1947, adult-only Villa Royale retains the original Spanish Mission exterior and lush plantings. Renovated rooms flaunting custom-made built-ins, select pieces of mid-century modern furniture and contemporary art depicting Hollywood stars are a soothing antidote to a day on the tourist track. The Del Rey restaurant feels like a speakeasy serving adventurous cocktails and small-plate Med-style dishes.

Arrive Hotel HOTEL $$
(Map p506; ☎760-227-7037; www.arrivehotels.com; 1551 N Palm Canyon Dr, Palm Springs; studios $190-390; P⊖❄🛜≋🐾) 🍃 Rusted steel, wood and concrete are the main design ingredients of this high-octane lair where the bar doubles as reception. The 32 spacious, phone-less rooms, some with enclosed patio, tick such hipster boxes as rain shower, Apple TV and fancy bath products. At weekends the pool, bar and restaurant turn into a lively party zone for both guests and locals. No resort fee.

Ace Hotel & Swim Club HOTEL $$
(Map p506; ☎760-325-9900; www.acehotel.com/palmsprings; 701 E Palm Canyon Dr, Palm Springs; d $160-210, ste $280-660; P❄🛜≋🐾) Palm Springs goes Hollywood – with all the sass, *sans* the attitude – at this former Howard Johnson motel turned hipster hangout. The 176 rooms (many with patio) sport a sophisticated cabin look and such mood-enhancers as a fireplace, a vintage record player or an MP3 docking station. Happening pool scene, low-key spa, and an on-site restaurant and bar to boot.

Del Marcos Hotel BOUTIQUE HOTEL $$
(Map p506; ☎760-325-6902; www.delmarcoshotel.com; 225 W Baristo Rd, Palm Springs; d $200-350; P⊖❄🛜≋🐾) At this 1947 adults-only gem, designed by William F Cody, groovy lobby tunes usher you to a saltwater pool and ineffably chic mid-century modern rooms. The pricier ones have such bonus touches as an Eames-style kitchen, a private redwood deck, a tiki bar or an oversized shower.

DON'T MISS

SUNNY DAYS AT SUNNYLANDS

One of America's 'first families' of the 20th century, industrialist/diplomat/philanthropist couple Walter (1908–2002) and Leonore (1918–2009) Annenberg entertained seven US presidents, royalty, Hollywood celebrities and heads of state at their 200-acre winter retreat, **Sunnylands** (Map p508; ☎760-202-2222; www.sunnylands.org; 37977 Bob Hope Dr, Rancho Mirage; visitor center & gardens free; ⏰house tours Wed-Sun, birding tours 8:45am Thu & Sat, visitor center & gardens 8:30am-4pm Wed-Sun mid-Sep–early Jun; P), in Rancho Mirage, about 10 miles east of downtown Palm Springs. The estate's art-filled main home, a 1966 mid-century modern masterpiece by A Quincy Jones, is accessible only by 90-minute guided tour; book online far in advance. No reservations are required for the exhibits and documentary on view at the architecturally stunning **visitor center** or to stroll the magnificent, sustainably designed **gardens**, inspired by impressionist paintings.

Tickets for the Historic House Tour ($48, no children under 10) and Birding on the Estate ($38) are released at 9am on the 15th of the preceding month and sell out quickly. Tickets for the 45-minute Open-Air Experience, a shuttle tour of the grounds and golf course that runs from September to April ($21), are sold first come, first served at the visitor center (credit cards only). Neither the Birding nor the Open-Air tour give access to the house.

Saguaro HOTEL $$

(Map p506; ☎760-323-1711; www.thesaguaro.com; 1800 E Palm Canyon Dr, Palm Springs; d $135-230, ste $215-330; P❄📶🏊🐾) 🍃 Hot yellow, pink, red and orange reminiscent of a desert blooming with wildflowers animate this updated mid-century modern hotel (pronounced Sah-wa-ro). Three stories of rooms with patio or balcony look over a generous pool deck flanked by spiffy new cabanas. The restaurant bar does great tacos and other south-of-the-border munchies.

Omni Rancho Las Palmas Resort & Spa RESORT $$

(Map p508; ☎760-568-2727; www.omnihotels.com/hotels/palm-springs-rancho-las-palmas; 41000 Bob Hope Dr, Rancho Mirage; d $200; P❄📶🏊🐾) Kids hit the entertainment mother lode at this sprawling, full-service resort with its lazy river, waterslides, a sandy beach and even a Mermaid University. Grown-ups, meanwhile, can leave the daily grind behind on two dozen tennis courts, a 27-hole championship golf course and a big spa.

Alcazar BOUTIQUE HOTEL $$

(Map p506; ☎760-318-9850; www.alcazarpalmsprings.com; 622 N Palm Canyon Dr; d from $160; P❄@📶🏊🐾) A fashionable (but not party) crowd make new friends poolside before retiring to one of the 34 bright white rooms set around a saltwater pool. Some have Jacuzzi, patio, fireplace or all three. Must be 21 to check in.

Caliente Tropics MOTEL $$

(Map p506; ☎760-327-1391; www.calientetropics.com; 411 E Palm Canyon Dr, Palm Springs; d from $150; P🚭❄📶🏊🐾) Frank Sinatra and the Rat Pack once frolicked poolside at this joyful 1964 tiki-style motor lodge. Although the glamour quotient has faded a lot, it's still a comfortable pit stop where you can wrap up the day with a tropical potion in the dimly lit Reef Bar before drifting off to dreamland on quality mattresses in basic but spacious rooms decorated with Polynesian posters.

★El Morocco Inn & Spa BOUTIQUE HOTEL $$$

(Map p508; ☎760-288-2527; http://elmoroccoinn.com; 66810 4th St, Desert Hot Springs; d from $250; ⏰check-in 8:30am-7pm or by arrangement; P🚭❄📶🏊) Heed the call of the casbah at this drop-dead gorgeous hideaway where the scene is set for romance. Twelve exotically furnished rooms wrap around a pool deck where your enthusiastic hosts serve free 'Morocco-tinis' during happy hour. The on-site spa offers tempting treatments; the Moroccan Mystical Ritual includes a 'Moroccan Rain' massage that uses seven detoxifying essential oils.

★L'Horizon Hotel & Spa BOUTIQUE HOTEL $$$

(Map p506; ☎760-323-1858; http://lhorizonpalmsprings.com; 1050 E Palm Canyon Dr, Palm Springs; d from $360; P❄📶🏊🐾) The intimate William F Cody–designed 1952 retreat that saw celebs such as Marilyn Monroe and Ronald Reagan lounging poolside has been rebooted as a desert-chic adults-only resort, with 25 low-slung bungalows scattered across generous grounds for maximum privacy. Exposed stone, rich woods and floor-to-ceiling windows characterize each unit, while the spa menu features such tasty treats as a lemongrass mimosa scrub.

Two Bunch Palms SPA HOTEL **$$$**
(Map p508; 760-676-5000; www.twobunchpalms.com; 67525 Two Bunch Palms Trail, Desert Hot Springs; d $225-295;) This legendary grown-ups-only retreat is quite literally an oasis built atop mineral springs and famous for its unrelentingly soothing spa where you can 'take the waters.' Refreshed rooms and villas are perfect for privacy cravers and connect to nature through eco friendly wood and stone accents. Nice touch: the free reusable water bottles handed out at check-in.

The Rowan Palm Springs HOTEL **$$$**
(Map p506; 760-904-5015; www.rowanpalmsprings.com; 100 W Tahquitz Canyon Way, Palm Springs; d from $300;) Topping out at seven stories, the Rowan is not only the newest but the tallest kid on the downtown Palm Springs hotel circuit. Expect memorable views from the upper floor rooms and the rooftop pool deck with a restaurant and swinging bar scene. Spacious rooms are more sleek international contemporary than mid-century modern, fitted out with Frette bathrobes and yoga mats.

The resort fee is $40.

Parker Palm Springs RESORT **$$$**
(Map p508; 760-770-5000; www.theparkerpalmsprings.com; 4200 E Palm Canyon Dr, Palm Springs; d from $309;) Comfortably decadent, the Parker packs plenty of Jonathan Adler's whimsical design cachet into a rambling estate with a spa, multiple pools and lodging options like poolside bungalows or a private villa once owned by Gene Autry. Stroll the lovely gardens, kick back in a hammock or try your hand at croquet and pétanque.

Avalon Hotel BOUTIQUE HOTEL **$$$**
(Map p506; 760-320-4117; www.avalon-hotel.com/palm-springs; 415 S Belardo Rd, Palm Springs; d $170-900;) Wear a Pucci dress and blend right in at this Spanish-style mini resort with 13 bungalows done up in sleek black-and-white Hollywood Regency style. After a day of lounging by the pool or getting pummeled in the spa, unwind on the patio or by the gas-burning fireplace. The on-site restaurant serves spirited California cuisine.

Eating

A lineup of zeitgeist-capturing restaurants has seriously elevated the level of dining in Palm Springs. The most exciting, including several with eye-catching design, flank N Palm Canyon Dr in the Uptown design district.

★ **Rooster & the Pig** VIETNAMESE **$**
(Map p506; 760-832-6691; www.roosterandthepig.com; 356 S Indian Canyon Dr, Palm Springs; plates $7-19; 5-9pm Wed-Mon;) A vibe of understated cool permeates this popular progressive-Vietnamese place tucked away in a strip mall. Boundary-pushing dinner winners like jasmine-tea-leaf salad, lemongrass meatballs or green papaya spring rolls are good for sharing, while season-linked specials keep the menu in flux. Eccentric cocktails, craft beer and wine, but no reservations or cash.

★ **Cheeky's** CALIFORNIAN **$**
(Map p506; 760-327-7595; www.cheekysps.com; 622 N Palm Canyon Dr, Palm Springs; mains $9-15; 8am-2pm;) Waits can be long at this hip breakfast and lunch spot, but the farm-to-table dishes dazzle with witty inventiveness. The offerings change on a weekly basis but faves such as custardy scrambled eggs, grass-fed burger with pesto fries, and bacon flights never rotate off the list. No reservations.

Chef Tanya's Kitchen VEGAN **$**
(Map p508; 760-832-9007; www.cheftanyaskitchen.com; 706 S Eugene Rd, Palm Springs; mains $11-15; 11am-8pm;) Teensy and cheerful, this plant-based kitchen-cum-grocery store brightens up a ho-hum industrial street south of the airport. Despite its obscure location, it's a point of pilgrimage for vegetarian sandwiches, tempeh burgers, colorful bowls and toothsome sides like the Fleetwood macaroni or the Moroccan cauliflower. There are a few seats but most people come for takeaway.

Sherman's Deli & Bakery DELI **$**
(Map p506; 760-325-1199; www.shermansdeli.com; 401 E Tahquitz Canyon Way, Palm Springs; sandwiches $8-13; 7am-9pm;) Every community with a sizable retired contingent needs a good kosher-style deli. In Palm Springs, Sherman's is it. With a breezy sidewalk patio, it pulls in an all-ages crowd

with its 40 sandwich varieties (great hot pastrami!), finger-lickin' rotisserie chicken and tasty lox and bagels. Kids menu available. The in-house bakery whips up awesome cakes and pies daily.

★Farm FRENCH **$$**
(Map p506; ☎760-322-2724; www.farmpalmsprings.com; 6 La Plaza, Palm Springs; breakfast & lunch mains $7-18, dinner prix-fixe $56; ⏰8am-2pm daily, 6-9pm Fri & Sat;) Farm is so fantastically Provençal, you expect to see lavender fields pop up in the desert. Greet the day with fluffy crepes or omelets, tuck into a salad or sandwich for lunch or book ahead for the three-course prix-fixe surprise dinner. It's in the heart of Palm Springs, yet secluded thanks to its country-style courtyard.

Trio CALIFORNIAN **$$**
(Map p506; ☎760-864-8746; www.triopalmsprings.com; 707 N Palm Canyon Dr, Palm Springs; mains lunch $14-24, dinner $18-36; ⏰11am-10pm Mon-Thu, to 11pm Fri, 10am-11pm Sat, 10am-10pm Sun;) The winning formula in this '60s modernist space: updated American comfort food (awesome Yankee pot roast) surrounded by eye-catching artwork and picture windows. The $25 prix-fixe three-course dinner (served between 3pm and 6pm) is a steal, while happy hour from 3pm to 7pm lures a rocking after-work crowd with bar bites and bargain drinks.

Birba ITALIAN **$$**
(Map p506; ☎760-327-5678; www.birbaps.com; 622 N Palm Canyon Dr, Palm Springs; mains $13-23; ⏰5-11pm Tue-Sun Nov-May, 6-10pm Wed-Sun Jun-Oct;) On a balmy night, Birba's hedge-fringed patio with twinkle lights and a sunken fire pit brings a dolce vita vibe to the desert. Unwind with a glass of *frizzante* and casual-elegant Italian fare, from inventive pizzas to pork milanese.

★Workshop Kitchen + Bar AMERICAN **$$$**
(Map p506; ☎760-459-3451; www.workshoppalmsprings.com; 800 N Palm Canyon Dr, Palm Springs; small plates $12-22, mains $32-42; ⏰5-10pm Mon-Thu & Sun, to 11pm Fri & Sat, 10am-2pm Sun;) Hidden away in the back of the ornate 1920s El Paseo building, a large patio with olive trees leads to this starkly beautiful space. At its center is a long, communal table flanked by mood-lit booths. The kitchen crafts market-driven American classics, mostly from locally hunted and foraged ingredients, and injects them with 21st-century sassiness. Matching liquid treats from the bar.

Drinking & Nightlife

Drinking has always been in style in Palm Springs and many bars and restaurants have popular happy hours that sometimes run all day. A handful of speakeasy bars spice up the cocktail scene and craft beer continues to be a draw. Friday is the big night out for the LGBTIQ+ crowd, especially along Arenas Rd between S Indian Canyon Dr and S Calle Encilia.

★Bootlegger Tiki COCKTAIL BAR
(Map p506; ☎760-318-4154; www.bootleggertiki.com; 1101 N Palm Canyon Dr, Palm Springs; ⏰4pm-2am) Crimson light bathes even pasty-faced hipsters with a healthy glow in this bat cave of a tiki bar in the original 1953 Don the Beachcomber restaurant. Beware: after a couple of their pretty but potent cocktails, those blowfish lamps may look downright trippy.

Truss & Twine COCKTAIL BAR
(Map p506; ☎760-699-7294; www.trussandtwine.com; 800 N Palm Canyon Dr, Palm Springs; ⏰4pm-12:30am Sun-Thu, to 1:30am Fri & Sat) This libation station with exposed rafters and back-lit bar is a go-to spot for serious drinkers. The menu covers the gamut of potions listed by period. Sample a playful Golden Age gimlet, a potent Prohibition-era Hanky Panky or a contempo concoction like the mind-altering absinthe-based Green Philter. Quality nibbles (may) help keep your brain in check.

Seymour's COCKTAIL BAR
(Map p506; ☎760-892-9000; https://seymoursps.com; 233 E Palm Canyon Dr, Palm Springs; ⏰6pm-midnight Sun & Tue-Thu, to 2am Fri & Sat;) This furtive booze parlor behind a steakhouse is decked out in clubby vintage decor that delivers plenty of fodder to fuel any conversation. Order one of their boundary-pushing 'originals' like the badass Big Trouble in Little TJ and make new friends at the intricately tiled bar or while couchsurfing on the breezy patio.

Del Rey BAR
(Map p506; ☎760-327-2314; https://villaroyale.com/food-and-drink; 1620 S Indian Trail, Palm Springs; ⏰4-11pm Sun-Thu, to midnight Fri & Sat;) A shooting star on Palm Springs' fancy drinking circuit, Del Rey hides out at the historic Villa Royale boutique hotel. Dim lighting, a coffered ceiling, sleek oak-and-marble bar and a tiled fireplace provide the kind of refined setting that appeals to crouched conversationalists keen on quality

cocktails or Spanish wines. Tapas provide sustenance.

Chill Bar GAY & LESBIAN

(Map p506; ☎760-696-9493; www.chillbarpalmsprings.com; 217 E Arenas Rd, Palm Springs; ⊙noon-2am Mon-Thu, from 10am Fri-Sun; 📶) More high-energy than relaxed, Chill Bar is an essential stop on Palm Springs' main LGTBIQ+ strip. Make new friends with people of all ages, races and proclivities at the rectangular bar or on the wraparound patio. Friendly bartenders sling reasonably priced cocktails, while drag shows, karaoke nights and dance parties keep the octane levels up.

Shopping

Central Palm Springs has two main shopping districts along N Palm Canyon Dr. The Uptown Design District north of Alejo Rd brims with galleries and furniture, fashion and design boutiques. South of Alejo Rd, the rejuvenated downtown now sports big-city chains like H&M and Sephora along with old-school souvenir shops. Thrift shops and high-end vintage stores are dotted around town.

Desert Hills Premium Outlets MALL

(☎951-849-6641; www.premiumoutlets.com/outlet/desert-hills; 48400 Seminole Dr, Cabazon; ⊙11am-7pm Mon-Sat, noon-6pm Sun; 📶) Bargain hunters should wear comfortable shoes when tackling this rambling but attractive outlet mall with views of the snow-capped San Jacinto Mountains. Some 180 designer stores – Gap to Gucci, Polo to Prada, Bose to Burberry – vie for your dollars.

It's off I-10 (exit 104, Morongo Trail), 20 miles west of Palm Springs.

Trina Turk FASHION & ACCESSORIES

(Map p506; ☎760-416-2856; www.trinaturk.com; 891 N Palm Canyon Dr, Palm Springs; ⊙10am-6pm Mon-Sat, 11am-5pm Sun) California style icon Trina Turk has designed her boldly pigmented and patterned fashions for about a quarter century. After an expansion and boho-sophisticated makeover of the original flagship boutique in a low-slung 1960s Albert Frey building, the space now also showcases her line of menswear, swimming fashions and whimsical housewares.

Angel View Resale Store THRIFT SHOP

(Map p506; ☎760-320-1733; www.angelview.org; 462 N Indian Canyon Dr, Palm Springs; ⊙9am-8pm Mon-Sat, 10am-7pm Sun) At the most central branch of this local thrift store chain, hipsters can shop for clothes and accessories as cool today as when they were first worn a generation or two ago. Prices are rock bottom.

Information

Palm Springs Visitor Center (Map p508; ☎760-778-8418; www.visitpalmsprings.com; 2901 N Palm Canyon Dr, Palm Springs; ⊙9am-5pm) The visitor center is in a 1965 Albert Frey–designed gas station, 3 miles north of downtown. Lots of souvenirs, little information.

Welwood Murray Memorial Library (Map p506; ☎760-323-8296; www.facebook.com/welwoodlibrary; 100 S Palm Canyon Dr, Palm Springs; ⊙9am-9pm; 📶) This renovated 1941 library doubles as a small visitor center and has free public computers and wi-fi.

Getting There & Away

Ask if your hotel provides free airport transfers. Otherwise, a taxi to downtown Palm Springs costs about $12 to $15, including a $2.50 airport surcharge. Uber and Lyft pick up at the south end of the terminal across from WestJet.

SunLine (☎760-343-3451; www.sunline.org; tickets $1) bus 24 stops by the airport and goes most (though, frustratingly, not all) of the way to downtown Palm Springs.

AIR

Palm Springs International Airport (PSP; Map p508; ☎760-318-3800; www.palmspringsairport.com; 3400 E Tahquitz Canyon Way, Palm Springs; 📶) is a regional airport served year-round from throughout North America by 11 airlines, including United, American, Alaska and WestJet.

WHAT THE...?

Driving along I-10, about 20 miles west of Palm Springs, you may do a double take when glimpsing 'Dinny the Dinosaur' and 'Mr Rex' on the north side of the freeway at **World's Biggest Dinosaurs** (☎951-922-8700; www.cabazondinosaurs.com; 50770 Seminole Dr, Cabazon; adult/child $13/11; ⊙9am-6pm Mon-Fri, to 7pm Sat & Sun; P 👪) . Starting in the 1960s, theme park sculptor Claude K Bell spent more than two decades crafting these concrete behemoths to draw customers to his adjacent restaurant. Even more bizarre, the beasts are now owned by creationists who promote their anti-evolution world view in a museum. You can also pan for dino fossils, climb inside Rex's mouth and stock up on dino souvenirs in the gift shop.

CAR & MOTORCYCLE

Palm Springs is just over 100 miles east of Los Angeles via I-10, and 140 miles northeast of San Diego via I-15 and I-10.

Getting Around

BICYCLE

Palm Springs and the Coachella Valley are pancake-flat, and more bike lanes are being built all the time. Many hotels have loaner bicycles, or try **Bike Palm Springs** (Map p506; ☎760-832-8912; www.bikepsrentals.com; 194 S Indian Canyon Dr, Palm Springs; standard/kids/ebike/tandem bikes per day $35/20/60/50; ⊙8am-5pm Oct-May, 8-10am Jun-Sep; 👪) or Palm Desert–based **Funseekers** (Map p508; ☎760-340-3861; http://4funseekers.com; 73-865 Hwy 111, Palm Desert; bicycle per 24hr/3 days/week from $25/60/75; ⊙9:30am-6pm Mon-Fri, to 5pm Sat & Sun; 👪) for rental chariots, including electric bikes.

BUS

SunLine (p515) alternative-fuel-powered public buses travel around the valley, albeit slowly. Bus 111 links Palm Springs with other Coachella Valley communities via Hwy 111. Buses have air-conditioning, wheelchair lifts and a bicycle rack. Cash only; no change given.

Buzz Trolley (www.sunline.org; ⊙noon-10pm Thu-Sat) This free downtown Palm Springs shuttle runs more or less every 20 minutes on a loop covering N Palm Canyon Dr from Via Escuela as far as Smoketree on E Palm Canyon and then back up Indian Canyon Dr.

CAR & MOTORCYCLE

You can walk to most sights in downtown Palm Springs. Travel on Hwy 111 linking the Coachella Valley towns can be extremely slow thanks to myriad traffic lights. Depending on where you're headed, it may be quicker to take I-10.

Major rental-car companies have airport desks. Also consider two-wheelers as an alternative to getting around. For now, electric scooters are banned throughout the Coachella Valley.

Eaglerider (☎442-222-6979; www.eaglerider.com; 19465 N Indian Canyon Dr, Palm Springs; Harley per day from $129; ⊙9:30am-5:30pm Tue-Fri, to 4:30pm Sat)

JOSHUA TREE NATIONAL PARK

Looking like something from Dr Seuss, the whimsical Joshua trees welcome visitors to this 794,000-acre **national park** (Map p518; ☎760-367-5500; www.nps.gov/jotr; 7-day pass per car $30; Ⓟ👪) right where the low and dry Colorado Desert bumps into the higher, moister and cooler Mojave Desert. Rock climbers know 'JTree' as the best place to climb in California, hikers are hypnotized by desert vistas and hidden fan-palm oases, while mountain bikers find solitude on dusty back roads.

The mystical quality of this stark, boulder-strewn landscape has inspired many artists and musicians, including the band U2's 1987 *Joshua Tree* album. More recently, the communities along the park's northern perimeter – Yucca Valley, Joshua Tree and Twentynine Palms – have drawn a wave of city slickers keen on ditching go-go for slo-mo under starry desert skies. The town of Joshua Tree in particular is a hub of creativity with a plethora of galleries, live music venues, quirky boutiques, a coffee roastery, artistic lodging options and other fun spots.

Sights

If you're short on time, a drive along Park Blvd through the northern half will take you past most of the attractions, including all the Joshua trees.

★Wonderland of Rocks NATURAL FEATURE
(Map p518; ☎760-367-5500; www.nps.gov/jotr; Ⓟ) This striking labyrinth of eroded rocks and boulders extends roughly from Indian Cove in the north to Hidden Valley on Park Blvd and is predictably a popular rock climbers' haunt. For a quick but satisfying impression, saunter along the 0.6-mile **Indian Cove Trail** (Indian Cove Rd) or the 1-mile **Hidden Valley Trail** (Map p518; ☎760-367-5500; www.nps.gov/jotr; Park Blvd; 👪).

The 8-mile (one way) **Boy Scout Trail** (Palm Blvd) presents a greater challenge and should not be attempted in hot weather.

★Keys View VIEWPOINT
(Map p518; ☎760-367-5500; www.nps.gov/jotr; Keys View Rd; Ⓟ) From Park Blvd, it's an easy 20-minute drive up to Keys View (5185ft) for a panoramic gander at the entire Coachella Valley as far as the shimmering Salton Sea. Best at sunrise and sunset.

Skull Rock LANDMARK
(Map p518; ☎760-367-5500; www.nps.gov/jotr; Park Blvd; Ⓟ) Much-photographed Skull Rock stares out over Park Blvd from eye-sockets hollowed out by rainwater over eons of time. A 1.7-mile loop trail starting at this roadside

attraction runs past more rock formations and the **Jumbo Rocks Campground** (per site $15; P).

Oasis of Mara OASIS

(Map p518; ☎760-367-5500; www.nps.gov/jotr; Utah Trail, Twentynine Palms; P) FREE A half-mile, wheelchair-accessible loop trail behind the Oasis Visitor Center leads to the original 29 palm trees that gave Twentynine Palms its name. They were planted by native Serranos who named the area Mara, meaning 'the place of little springs and much grass.'

Cholla Cactus Garden NATURAL FEATURE

(Map p518; ☎760-367-5500; www.nps.gov/jotr; Pinto Basin Rd; P) A dense grove of 'teddy bear' cholla cactus and ocotillo plants, this 'garden' delivers a welcome break from the forboding harshness of the Colorado Desert in the park's southern reaches. A quarter-mile loop trail threads through the patch – wear sturdy shoes to guard against cactus spines.

Cottonwood Spring NATURAL FEATURE

(Map p518; ☎760-367-5500; www.nps.gov/jotr; P) This oasis is a natural spring that Cahuilla tribespeople depended on for centuries. Look for *morteros* – rounded depressions in the rocks used for grinding seeds. Miners came searching for gold here in the late 19th century. It's a promising birding spot and launchpad of such hikes as the 7.5-mile round-trip slog to the **Lost Palms Oasis** (Cottonwood Springs Rd).

Activities

Cycling

Bikes are only allowed on public paved and backcountry roads that are also open to vehicles. They are not permitted on hiking trails. Popular routes include the challenging 20-mile **Pinkham Canyon Road** starting south of the Cottonwood visitor center and the long-distance **Black Eagle Mine Road**, which begins 6.5 miles further north. **Queen Valley** has a gentler set of trails with bike racks found along the way, so you can lock up and go hiking. It tends to be busy with cars, though, as is the bumpy, sandy and steep Geology Tour Rd (p518). There's also a wide-open network of dirt roads around Covington Flat (p518).

Rock Climbing

JT is considered California's rock-climbing hub with over 10,000 routes in quartz monzonite granite that's famous for its rough, high-friction surfaces. Trad climbing is tops here, although there are also bouldering and sport-climbing routes. Some of the most popular climbs are in the Hidden Valley area.

Shops providing climbers with quality gear, advice and tours include **Joshua Tree Outfitters** (Map p518; ☎760-366-1848; www.joshuatreeoutfitters.com; 61707 29 Palms Hwy/Hwy 62, Joshua Tree; ⏰9am-5pm Thu-Tue), **Nomad Ventures** (Map p518; ☎760-366-4684; www.nomadventures.com; 61795 29 Palms Hwy/Hwy 62, Joshua Tree; ⏰8am-6pm Mon-Fri year-round, to 8pm Sat & Sun Oct-May) and **Coyote Corner** (Map p518; ☎760-366-9683; www.jtcoyotecorner.com; 6535 Park Blvd, Joshua Tree; ⏰9am-6pm Mon-Fri, to 7pm Sat & Sun).

Joshua Tree Rock Climbing School (Map p518; ☎760-366-4745; www.joshuatreerockclimbing.com; 63439 Doggie Trail, Joshua Tree; 1-day course from $195), **Vertical Adventures** (☎800-514-8785, 949-322-6108; www.verticaladventures.com; courses from $155; ⏰Sep-May) and **Uprising Adventure Guides** (Map p518; ☎888-254-6266; www.joshuatreeuprising.com; 8332 Fleur Dr, Joshua Tree; 4/6/8hr-course from $115/125/145; ⏰8am-5pm) offer guided climbs and climbing instruction starting at $120 for a one-day introduction.

Tours

Keys Ranch Tour HISTORY

(Map p518; ☎reservations 877-444-6777; www.nps.gov/jotr; tours adult/child 6-11yr $10/5, plus park admission; ⏰tours Oct-May; 👪) Time travel back to the rough-and-tumble Old West during the 90-minute ranger-led tour of this ranch named after William Keys and his family. They built a homestead here in 1917 and turned it into a full working ranch, school, store and workshop. The buildings

SO WHAT'S A JOSHUA TREE?

Only found in the Mojave Desert, the Joshua tree (*yucca brevifolia*) is a member of the agave family and easily recognized by its prickly branches reaching toward the sky. It was Mormon settlers who named the whimsical plant, which reminded them of the biblical prophet Joshua pointing the way to the promised land. If conditions are right, the Joshua trees send up a huge single cream-colored flower in springtime.

Joshua Tree National Park

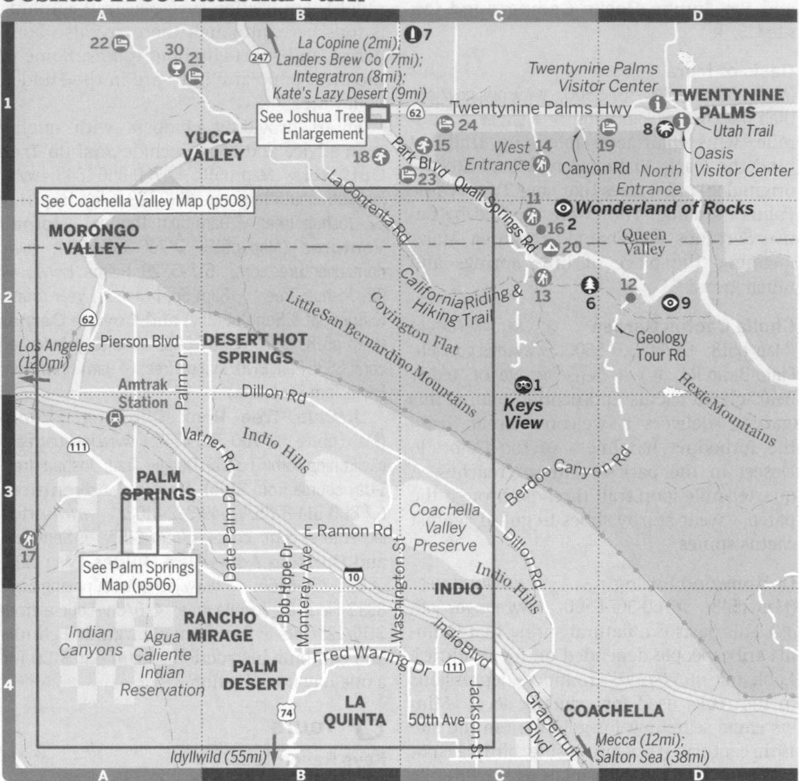

stand much as they did when Keys died in 1969. Tickets must be booked as early as possible by phone or via www.recreation.gov.

The ranch is about 2 miles northeast of **Hidden Valley Campground** (Map p518; ☎760-367-5500; www.nps.gov/jotr; Park Blvd; per site $15), up a dirt road. Drive as far as the locked gate, where your guide will meet you.

Geology Tour Rd DRIVING TOUR
(Map p518; ☎760-367-5500; www.nps.gov/jotr; off Park Blvd) On this 14-mile backcountry drive around Pleasant Valley, the forces of erosion, earthquakes and ancient volcanoes have played out in stunning splendor. There are 16 markers along the route – pick up a self-guided interpretive brochure and an update on road conditions at any park visitor center. The turnoff from Park Blvd is about 2 miles west of the Jumbo Rocks Campground.

Covington Flat DRIVING
(Map p508; ☎760-367-5500; www.nps.gov/jotr; La Contenta Rd) Joshua trees grow throughout the northern park, but some of the biggest trees are found in this Covington Flats area accessed via La Contenta Rd, which runs south off Hwy 62 between Yucca Valley and Joshua Tree. For killer views as far as Palm Springs, head up to Eureka Peak (5516ft) from the picnic area. Most passenger cars can usually handle this network of dirt roads, but check at a park visitor center to be safe.

Sleeping

Unless you're day-tripping from Palm Springs, set up camp inside the park or base yourself in the desert communities linked by 29 Palms Hwy/Hwy 62. Twentynine Palms and Yucca Valley have mostly national chain motels, while pads in Joshua Tree are generally smaller, privately run and brimming with charm and character. Also check Airbnb for

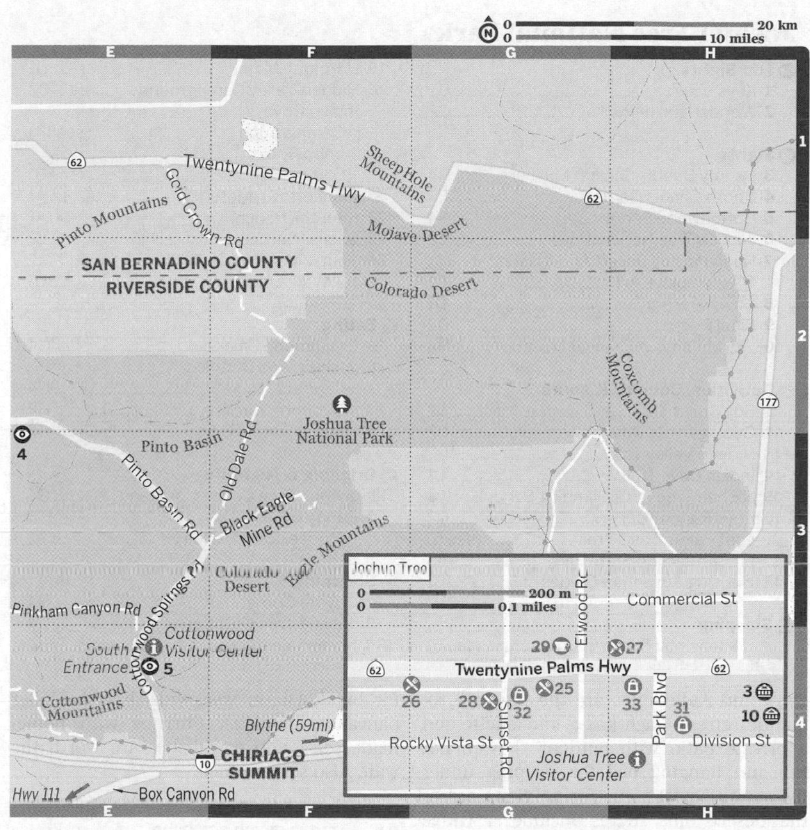

atmospheric homesteads, cabins and other middle-of-nowhere listings.

Harmony Motel MOTEL $

(Map p518; ☎760-401-1309, 760-367-3351; www.harmonymotel.com; 71161 29 Palms Hwy/Hwy 62, Twentynine Palms; d $90-95; P ❄ ☎ ≋) This immaculately kept 1950s motel, run by the charming Ash, was where U2 stayed while working on the *Joshua Tree* album. It has a small pool and seven large, cheerfully painted and handsomely decorated rooms (some with kitchenette) set around a tidy desert garden with serene views. Free coffee and tea are available in the communal guest kitchen.

★ Kate's Lazy Desert CABIN $$

(☎845-688-7200; www.lazymeadow.com; 58380 Botkin Rd, Landers; Airstreams Mon-Thu $175, Fri & Sat $200; P ❄ ☎ ≋ 🐾) Owned by Kate Pierson of the band B-52s, this desert glampcamp has a coin-sized pool (May to October) and half a dozen artist-designed Airstream trailers to sleep inside. Sporting names such as 'Tinkerbell,' 'Planet Air' and 'Hot Lava,' each is kitted out with matching fantasia-pop design, a double bed and a kitchenette.

Spin & Margie's Desert Hide-a-Way INN $$

(Map p518; ☎760-774-0850, 760-366-9124; www.deserthideaway.com; 64491 29 Palm Hwy/Hwy 62, Joshua Tree; d $160-200; P ❄ ☎ ≋) This handsome hacienda style inn is perfect for restoring calm after a long day on the road. The five boldly colored suites with kitchens are an eccentric symphony of corrugated tin, old license plates and cartoon art. Two are in separate buildings. Knowledgeable, gregarious owners ensure a relaxed visit. Pool access with day pass only (per person $20).

★ Sacred Sands GUESTHOUSE $$$

(Map p518; ☎760-424-6407, 760-974-2353; www.sacredsands.com; 63155 Quail Springs Rd, Joshua Tree; Jade/Onyx ste $339/369; P ❄ ☎) 🌿 In an isolated, pin-drop-quiet spot, the desert-chic

Joshua Tree National Park

Onyx and Jade suites are the ultimate romantic retreat. Each has a kitchenette and a private patio with outdoor shower, hot tub and hanging bed for sleeping under the stars. Expect soul-stirring views across the desert hills. Rates include a fridge stocked with breakfast supplies. Two-night minimum.

Eating

There's no food available inside the park but you can stock up at supermarkets and convenience stores along Hwy 62/29 Palms Hwy (especially in Yucca Valley). Restaurants range from greasy spoons to organic delis, funky diners to pizza parlors. On Saturday mornings, locals gather for gossip and groceries at the **farmers market** (Map p518; www.joshuatreefarmersmarket.com; 61705 29 Palms Hwy/Hwy 62, Joshua Tree; 8am-1pm Sat) in Joshua Tree.

JT Country Kitchen AMERICAN $
(Map p518; 760-366-8988; www.facebook.com/JTCountryKitchen; 61768 29 Palms Hwy/Hwy 62, Joshua Tree; mains $6-11; 6:30am-3pm Wed-Mon;) This been-here-forever roadside shack gets a big thumbs up for its scrumptious home cookin'. Lines can be extra-long for breakfast on weekends, but the killer pancakes, breakfast burritos with homemade salsa and egg dishes are worth the wait. Also serves lunch.

Natural Sisters Cafe VEGETARIAN $
(Map p518; 760-366-3600; www.thenaturalsisterscafe.com; 61695 29 Palm Hwy/Hwy 62, Joshua Tree; dishes $8-14; 7am-7pm;) Fuel up for a day in the park with a Killer Bee smoothie, a veggie-and-hummus wrap or a big bowl of organic greens at this cute hippie-vibe cafe in downtown Joshua Tree.

Crossroads Cafe AMERICAN $
(Map p518; 760-366-5414; www.crossroadscafejtree.com; 61715 29 Palms Hwy/Hwy 62, Joshua Tree; mains $8-17; 7am-9pm;) Before hitting the trail, rocks or road, fuel up at this JT institution with a carb-loaded breakfast, garden salad or fresh sandwiches that make both omnivores (burgers, Reuben) and vegans ('Fake Philly' with seitan) happy. Also a chill spot to unwind with a cold one at the end of the day.

Kids menu available.

★La Copine INTERNATIONAL $$
(760-289-8537; www.lacopinekitchen.com; 848 Old Woman Springs Rd, Flamingo Heights; dishes

$8-19; ⌚noon-6pm Thu-Mon Sep-Jun; P ❄) 🍃 It's a long road from Philadelphia to the high desert, but that's where Nikki and Claire decided to take their farm-to-table cuisine from pop-up to roadside bistro. Now loyal locals and clued-in travelers book way ahead for a chance to gobble up the globally inspired dishes in the perky dining room or on the breezy patio.

It's 9 miles north of Hwy 62 via Rte 247.

Drinking & Nightlife

Joshua Tree has a couple of artsy watering holes, often with live music featuring local and regional talent, although the most atmospheric place to steer toward after dark is Pappy & Harriet's (p513) in Pioneertown. Bars in Twentynine Palms cater mostly to marines. The best place to fill your travel mug with organic and locally roasted coffee is **Joshua Tree Coffee Company** (Map p518; ☎760-974-4060; www.jtcoffeeco.com; 61738 29 Palms Hwy/Hwy 62, Joshua Tree; ⌚7am-6pm; 📶).

Landers Brew Co PUB
(☎760-596-7819; 1388 Golden Slipper Lane, Landers; ⌚5-10pm Tue-Thu, noon-2am Fri & Sat, noon-10pm Sun; 📶) Out in the boonies near the Integratron (p522), Landers Brew Co has a big local following for its roster of craft beers on tap, convivial beer garden and local musicians in concert on Saturday night. Also serves beer and sake. It's about 15 miles north of 29 Palms Hwy/Hwy 62.

Shopping

Vintage and antiques lovers should head to the cluster of well-curated shops around the Pioneertown Rd turnoff on Hwy 62. Otherwise, Yucca Valley has mostly national chain supermarkets and big box stores along Hwy 62.

Joshua Tree plays up its artistic pedigree with quirky shops and galleries in the blocks flanking Park Blvd. The **East Village** in particular brims with unique merchants, art installations and funky outdoor performance spaces.

Information

MEDICAL SERVICES

Hi-Desert Medical Center (☎760-366-3711; www.desertcarenetwork.com; 6601 White Feather Rd, Joshua Tree; ⌚24hr) The main hospital along Hwy 62, north of the national park, has 24-hour emergency care and is fine if you can't get down to Palm Springs.

TELEPHONE

Cell-phone reception is extremely spotty inside the park – don't count on it! Emergency phones are available at the ranger station in Indian Cove, in the Intersection Rock parking area near Hidden Valley Campground and at Cottonwood Spring.

SETTING UP CAMP IN JT

Camping under the stars inside Joshua Tree National Park is truly a special experience. There are eight campgrounds, but only **Cottonwood** (Map p518; ☎760-367-5500, reservations 877-444-6777; www.nps.gov/jotr; Pinto Basin Rd; tent & RV sites $20; P) and **Black Rock** (Map p508; ☎760-367-5500, reservations 877-444-6777; www.nps.gov/jotr; Black Rock Canyon Rd, Yucca Valley; tent & RV sites $20; P) have potable water, flush toilets and dump stations. The two also accept reservations, as do **Indian Cove** (Map p518; ☎760-362-4367, reservations 877-444-6777; www.nps.gov/jotr; Indian Cove Rd, Twentynine Palms; tent & RV sites $20; P) and Jumbo Rocks (p517). The other four are first come, first served and have pit toilets, picnic tables and fire grates. None have showers, but there are some at Coyote Corner (p517) in Joshua Tree. Details are available at www.nps.gov/jotr or by calling 760-367-5500.

Between October and May, campsites fill by Thursday noon, especially during the springtime bloom. If you arrive too late, there's overflow camping on Bureau of Land Management (BLM) land north and south of the park as well as in private campgrounds. For details, see www.nps.gov/jotr/planyourvisit/camping-outside-of-the-park.htm.

Backcountry camping is allowed outside of day-use areas and at least 1 mile from any road or 500ft from any trailhead. There is no water in the park, so bring 1 to 2 gallons per person per day for drinking, cooking and personal hygiene. Campfires are prohibited to prevent wildfires and damage to the fragile desert floor. Free self-registration must be made at a backcountry board inside the park, where you can also leave your car. For full details, see www.nps.gov/jotr/planyourvisit/backpacking.htm.

TOURIST INFORMATION

Entry permits ($30 per vehicle) are valid for seven days and come with a map and the seasonally updated *Joshua Tree Guide* newspaper. For an insightful blog on happenings in the town of Joshua Tree, turn to www.joshuatree.guide.

Joshua Tree Visitor Center (Map p518; ☎760-366-1855; www.nps.gov/jotr; 6554 Park Blvd, Joshua Tree; ⊙8am-5pm; 📶)

Oasis Visitor Center (Map p518; ☎760-367-5500; www.nps.gov/jotr; 74485 National Park Dr, Twentynine Palms; ⊙8:30am-5pm)

Black Rock Nature Center (Map p508; ☎760-367-3001; www.nps.gov/jotr; 9800 Black Rock Canyon Rd, Yucca Valley; ⊙8am-4pm Sat-Thu, to 8pm Fri Oct-May; 👪)

Cottonwood Visitor Center (Map p518; www.nps.gov/jotr; Cottonwood Spring Rd; ⊙8:30am-4pm; 👪)

Twentynine Palms Visitor Center (Map p518; ☎760-358-6324; www.visit29.org; 73484 29 Palms Hwy/Hwy 62, Twentynine Palms; ⊙10am-4pm; 📶)

ℹ Getting There & Around

Joshua Tree has three park entrances. The main access point is the west entrance via Park Blvd from the town of Joshua Tree. To avoid long wait times on busy weekends, arrive well before noon or enter the park via the north entrance from Twentynine Palms or the south entrance from I-10.

Local transportation is provided by the **Morongo Basin Transit Authority** (☎760-366-2395; www.mbtabus.com). Bus 12 links Palm Springs and Yucca Valley on weekdays twice in the morning and once in the afternoon (one way/round trip $7/11). In Yucca Valley, change to Bus 1, which travels along Hwy 62/29 Palms Hwy to Joshua Tree and Twentynine Palms. Bus 15 links Twentynine Palms and the airport, but only once in the morning on Fridays and in the morning and afternoon on weekends (one way/round trip $17/21). Buses are equipped with bike racks. Cash only, exact fare required.

TOP FOUR OFFBEAT ATTRACTIONS NEAR JT

The California desert is full of bizarre roadside attractions and hidden surprises, but the area along and north of 29 Palms Hwy/Hwy 62 harbors a disproportionate share, including these kooky gems

Noah Purifoy Desert Art Museum of Assemblage Art (Map p518; www.noahpurifoy.com; 63030 Blair Lane, Joshua Tree; ⊙dawn-dusk; 🅿) The 'Junk Dada' assemblage sculptures of African American artist Noah Purifoy (1917–2004) are collected by the world's finest museums, but some of his coolest works can be seen for free at his former outdoor desert studio about 6 miles north of Joshua Tree. Toilets, tires, monitors, bicycles and beds are among the eclectic castoffs Purifoy turned variously into political statements, social criticism or just plain nonsense. Pick up a pamphlet for a self-guided tour.

The website has directions.

Integratron (☎760-364-3126; www.integratron.com; 2477 Belfield Blvd, Landers; sound baths weekdays/weekends $40/45; ⊙Wed-Sun Feb-Jul & Sep-Dec; 🅿) It may look just like a white-domed structure, but in reality it's an electrostatic generator for time travel and cell rejuvenation. Yup! At least that's what its creator, aerospace engineer George Van Tassel (1910–78), believed when building the place in the 1950s after receiving telepathic instructions from extraterrestrials. Today, you can pick up on the spacey vibes during a one-hour 'sound bath' (book months ahead) below the wooden dome.

Beauty Bubble Salon & Museum (Map p518; ☎760-366-9000; www.facebook.com/beautybubblesalonandmuseum; 61855 29 Palms Hwy/Hwy 62, Joshua Tree; museum free; ⊙10am-6pm Tue-Thu & Sat; 🅿) Jeff Hafler loves hair and everything to do with it, which is why his *Steel Magnolias*–type home salon brims with related vintage beauty paraphernalia he's collected for about a quarter century. If you wish, he can even do your tresses up in a beehive – naturally surrounded by quaint perm machines, curlers and wigs, some over 100 years old.

World-Famous Crochet Museum (Map p518; www.sharielf.com/museum.html; 61855 29 Palms Hwy/Hwy 62, Joshua Tree; ⊙24hr) A vintage lime-green photo booth is the home of Bunny, Buddy and hundreds of their crocheted friends collected by Shari Elf. Remarkably, the artist, singer, fashion designer, raw-food chef and life coach has not mastered the art of crocheting herself, but you can buy some of her creations in the adjacent gallery/shop.

DON'T MISS

TURN BACK THE CLOCK AT PIONEERTOWN

Turn north off Hwy 62 onto Pioneertown Rd in Yucca Valley and drive 5 miles straight into the past. Looking like an 1880s frontier town, **Pioneertown** (Pioneertown Rd; 24hr; P) FREE was actually built in 1946 as a Hollywood Western movie set. Gene Autry and Roy Rogers were among the original investors, and more than 50 movies were filmed here in the 1940s and '50s. These days, it's fun to stroll down 'Mane St,' perhaps popping into the little shops, the film museum or the honky-tonk. Weekends are best for visiting; weekday hours are erratic. Mock gunfights and a Wild West show kick up their spurs at 2:30pm on alternate Saturdays, October to June.

For local color, mesquite-wood BBQ, cold beer and kick-ass live music, drop by legendary **Pappy & Harriet's Pioneertown Palace** (Map p518; 760-365-5956; www.pappyandharriets.com; 53688 Pioneertown Rd; mains $11-18, steaks $22-42; 11am-2am Thu-Sun, from 5pm Mon;), a textbook honky-tonk. Monday's open-mike nights (admission free) often bring out astounding talent. From Thursday to Saturday, local and national performers take over the stage.

Within staggering distance is the atmospheric **Pioneertown Motel** (Map p518; 760-365-7001; www.pioneertown-motel.com; 5040 Curtis Rd; d from $195; P), where yesteryear's silver-screen stars once slept during filming and whose rooms are now filled with Western-themed memorabilia and modern creature comforts.

Some movie stars also stayed in the knotty-pine cabins reimagined as **Rimrock Ranch** (Map p518; 760-228-0130; www.rimrockranchpioneertown.com; 50857 Burns Canyon Rd; cabins $120-220, 2-day minimum on weekends; P), a soulful desert hideaway 4.5 miles north of Pioneertown. All have Old West decor, kitchen facilities and a private patio.

ANZA-BORREGO DESERT STATE PARK

Shaped by an ancient sea, wind, water and seismic forces, Anza-Borrego is California's largest state park. It's a majestic quilt of creased mountains rising from parched badlands and cool palm oases cocooned within narrow canyons. There's an abundance of wildlife and wildflowers as well as traces of thousands of years of Native American habitation. With just one town – Borrego Springs – most of the park's 1000 sq miles encompass untamed terrain. Its 500 miles of dirt roads and hiking trails are a serene playground for backcountry explorers. At nighttime, stargazing is a favorite pastime in this designated International Dark Sky Park. Anza-Borrego gets its name from 18th-century Spanish explorer Juan Bautista de Anza and the Spanish name for bighorn sheep. Today only a few hundred of these shy and elusive *borregos* survive due to drought, disease, poaching and off-highway driving.

Sights & Activities

Anza-Borrego's commercial hub, **Borrego Springs** (population 2328) centers on a roundabout called Christmas Circle and has restaurants, lodgings, stores, ATMs, gas stations and a handsome new public library with free wi-fi. Nearby are the park visitor center and easy-to-reach attractions, such as Borrego Palm Canyon and Fonts Point, that are fairly representative of the park as a whole. The Split Mountain area, east of Ocotillo Wells, is popular with off-highway vehicles (OHVs), but also contains interesting geology and wind caves. The desert's southernmost region is the least visited and, aside from Blair Valley, has few developed trails and facilities.

The park is prettiest (and busiest) during wildflower season, which usually runs from mid-February through March. Call the **Wildflower Hotline** (760-767-4684) for the latest updates.

Many of the trailheads are accessible only by dirt roads requiring high-clearance or 4WD vehicles. Be sure to check conditions with the park visitor center (p527) before setting out.

★ **Fonts Point** VIEWPOINT

(Map p526; 760-767-4205; www.parks.ca.gov; Anza-Borrego Desert State Park, off County Rte S22; P) FREE East of Borrego Springs, a 4-mile dirt road, sometimes passable without 4WD, diverges south from County Rte S22 out to Fonts Point (1249ft). From up here unfolds a spectacular panorama of the otherworldly, wind-and-water-chiseled Borrego Valley to

OFF THE BEATEN TRACK

SALTON SEA: THE DISAPPEARING LAKE

Driving along Hwy 111 southeast of Indio, you'll come across a most unexpected sight: the Salton Sea – California's largest lake in the middle of its largest desert. As you can quickly tell by the postapocalyptic mood hanging over the place, it's a troubled spot with a fascinating past, complicated present and uncertain future.

The Salton Sea is very much an 'accidental sea,' created in 1905 when high spring flooding breached irrigation canals built to bring water from the Colorado River to the farmland in the Imperial Valley. The water rushed uncontrollably into the nearest low spot – the Salton Sink – for 18 months until 1500 workers and 500,000 tons of rock managed to put a halt to the flooding. With no natural outlet, the water was here to stay: the Salton Sea – about 35 miles long and 15 miles wide – was born.

By mid-century the desert lake was stocked with fish and marketed as the 'California Riviera;' vacation homes lined its shores. The fish, in turn, attracted birds, and the sea became a prime bird-watching spot. In fact, the Salton Sea is one of the most important stopovers along the Pacific Flyway. Since its inception it has provided habitat for hundreds of feathered species, including eared grebes, ruddy ducks, white and brown pelicans and snowy plovers.

Their survival, however, is threatened by decreasing water levels and rising salinity from decades of agricultural runoff bloated with fertilizers. With hardly any rainfall and little freshwater inflow, salinity has increased to 56g per liter (versus 35g in the Pacific Ocean), making it impossible for most fish species to survive, tilapia being an exception. Fewer fish, in turn, make the area less attractive for birds and numbers have been declining steadily. Humans, too, are suffering as dust storms triggered by an increasingly exposed shoreline contributes to poor air quality and sends up the rate of respiratory problems.

Lawmakers have for decades made only half-hearted attempts to rescue the Salton Sea, much to the frustration of local residents. The current administration under Governor Gavin Newson has promised a renewed focus on remediation to prevent the sea from turning into an even greater environmental nightmare. Locals are hopeful but not holding their breath.

the west and the Borrego Badlands to the south. Best at sunset.

Borrego Art Institute GALLERY
(Map p526; ☎760-767-5152; www.borregoartinstitute.org; 665 Palm Canyon Dr, Borrego Springs; ⏲10am-4pm Tue-Sun; P) FREE This nonprofit outfit in a glass-fronted modernist bungalow in central Borrego Springs showcases desert-themed paintings, sculpture and crafts created by local artists. It also operates pottery workshops, kids programs, and a hip pizza and craft beer parlor next door.

Tours

California Overland Desert Excursions OUTDOORS
(Map p526; ☎760-767-1232; www.californiaoverland.com; 1233 Palm Canyon Dr, Borrego Springs; tours $85-275) If you don't have a 4WD or the idea of driving off-road is giving you the jitters, sign up with this local outfit for a rumble around Anza-Borrego's backcountry in a van or jeep. Options ranges from a 2½-hour spin around the badlands to overnight camping under the stars.

Private tours are also available.

Sleeping

A handful of motels and hotels cluster in and around Borrego Springs, but not all are open year-round. Otherwise, camping is the only way to spend the night in the park. In addition to developed campgrounds inside and near the park, free roadside camping is permitted anywhere as long as you park no more than one vehicle length off the road; all campfires must be in metal containers. Gathering vegetation (dead or alive) is strictly prohibited.

Borrego Palm Canyon Campground CAMPGROUND $
(Map p526; ☎park 760-767-5311, reservations 800-444-7275; www.reservecalifornia.com; 200 Palm Canyon Dr, Borrego Springs; tent/RV sites $25/35, day-use $10; P) About 2.5 miles northwest of central Borrego Springs, this campground

has over 100 sites and is a handy base from which to explore the park. Despite its size, it fills up quickly on weekends, thanks in part to such amenities as drinking water, flush toilets and coin-operated hot showers. Some sites have shade ramadas.

Tamarisk Grove Campground CAMPGROUND $
(Map p526; reservations 800-444-7275; www.parks.ca.gov; 5960 Yaqui Pass Rd County Rte S3; tent & RV $25, cabins $60, day-use $10;) On the site of a 1930s prison camp, this campground's 16 sites and 11 rustic cabins with sleeping lofts get plenty of shade from tall and wispy tamarisks and shade ramadas. Some 12 miles south of Borrego Springs, it has coin-operated showers but no drinking water.

Stanlunds Inn & Suites MOTEL $
(Map p526; 760-767-5501; https://stanlunds.com; 2771 Borrego Springs Rd, Borrego Springs; d $75-125, ste $150,) This low-slung classic 1960s motel is a good-value exploratory base with a variety of room configurations, including a family-friendly suite with full kitchen and patio. The owners take great pride in keeping the place neat and tidy, and a small communal pool and barbecue area invite post-hike relaxation.

Palms at Indian Head HOTEL $$
(Map p526; 760-767-7788; www.thepalmsatindianhead.com; 2200 Hoberg Rd, Borrego Springs; d $100-250;) This former desert getaway of Cary Grant, Marilyn Monroe and other Old Hollywood celebs has been reborn as a chic mid-century modern retreat. Connect with the era over martinis and filet mignon at the on-site steakhouse while enjoying dreamy desert views. Get an upstairs rooms for grand views of the big pool, clover-shaped Jacuzzi and rugged mountains.

Borrego Valley Inn INN $$
(Map p526; 760-767-0311; www.highwaywestvacations.com; 405 Palm Canyon Dr, Borrego Springs; d $170-330;) It's grown-ups only at this rustically elegant 15-unit inn where you can wind down in oversized rooms enlivened by Southwestern knickknacks and orbiting a courtyard with a pool and desert plants; some have kitchenette, a private patio or a fireplace. Between October and May, rates include breakfast and there's a two-night minimum.

★La Casa del Zorro Resort & Spa RESORT $$$
(Map p526; 760-767-0100; www.lacasadelzorro.com; 3845 Yaqui Pass Rd, Borrego Springs; d from $280 Oct-Apr, $110-153 May-Oct;) This venerable 1937 resort captures the desert magic and is the region's grandest stay. The ambience speaks of romance and relaxation in 63 elegantly rustic poolside rooms and family-sized casitas sporting vaulted ceilings and marble bathtubs. Two restaurants and a bar provide sustenance, while five pools, tennis courts, a fitness center and a yoga studio help keep the love handles at bay.

Eating

Borrego Springs has a few restaurants, from spit-and-sawdust Mexican joints to fine dining. The best-stocked supermarket is **Center Market** (Map p526; 760-767-3311; 590 Palm Canyon Dr, Borrego Springs; 8am-8pm;), also in Borrego Springs. In summer many places keep shorter hours or have closing days. From November to April, a small **farmers market** sets up at Christmas Circle on Fridays from 8am to noon.

Carmelita's Mexican Grill & Cantina MEXICAN $
(Map p526; 760-767-5666; www.facebook.com/carmelitasborrego; The Mall, 575 Palm Canyon Dr, Borrego Sprigs; mains $6-17; 10am-9pm;) This lively joint with cheerful decor serves the best Mexican food in town, including delicious *huevos rancheros* and

LOCAL KNOWLEDGE

SKY ART: ANZA-BORREGO'S QUIRKY SCULPTURE GARDEN

They pop up alongside Borrego Springs Rd like a desert mirage – mammoths, saber-toothed cats, giant camels and other long-extinct critters that once prowled the Anza-Borrego region. Today's specimens are part of a Jurassic menagerie created by artist Richard Becerra who has welded dozens of these rust-red metal sculptures with intricate detail down to the eyelashes on the camels and 'fur' on the ground sloths. He later expanded his portfolio to represent humans that shaped the area, such as a gold miner, a Native American and a Spanish missionary. Many sculptures can be spotted roadside just north and south of central Borrego Springs. For a free basic map go to http://borregospringsartmap.com or pick up a more comprehensive laminated guide at stores in town.

Anza-Borrego Desert State Park

0 — 10 km
0 — 5 miles

Enlargement
Anza-Borrego Desert State Park Visitor Center
Hoberg Rd
Palm Canyon Dr
S22
5
12
10
Christmas Circle
11
2
13
Borrego Springs Rd
0 — 1 km

Borrego Palm Canyon
BORREGO SPRINGS
S3
Borrego Valley Rd
Coyote Creek
Peg Leg Rd
S22
San Ysidro Peak (6147ft)
4
7
See Enlargement
Palm Canyon Dr
3
8
Borrego Palm Canyon
Hellhole Canyon trail
Borrego Springs Rd
Borrego Sink
6
Fonts Point
1
Salton Sea (20mi)
Borrego Badlands
Ocotillo Wells State Vehicular Recreation Area
Pinyon Ridge
Grapevine Canyon
Pacific Crest Trail
Yaqui Pass Rd
9
San Felipe Creek
78
Ocotillo Wells
Old Kane Springs Rd
Split Mountain Rd
S2
Julian (8mi)
Mescal Bajada
Pinyon Mtn Rd
Blair Valley
Granite Mtn (5633ft)
Whale Peak (5320ft)
Vallecito Mountains
Split Mtn (14,058ft)
Carrizo Badlands
Garnet Peak (5905ft)
Vallecito Creek
Pacific Crest Trail
S1
Carrizo Creek
Canyon Sin Nombre
Carrizo Badlands Overlook
San Diego (50mi)
Jacumba Mountains
I-8 (8mi)
8

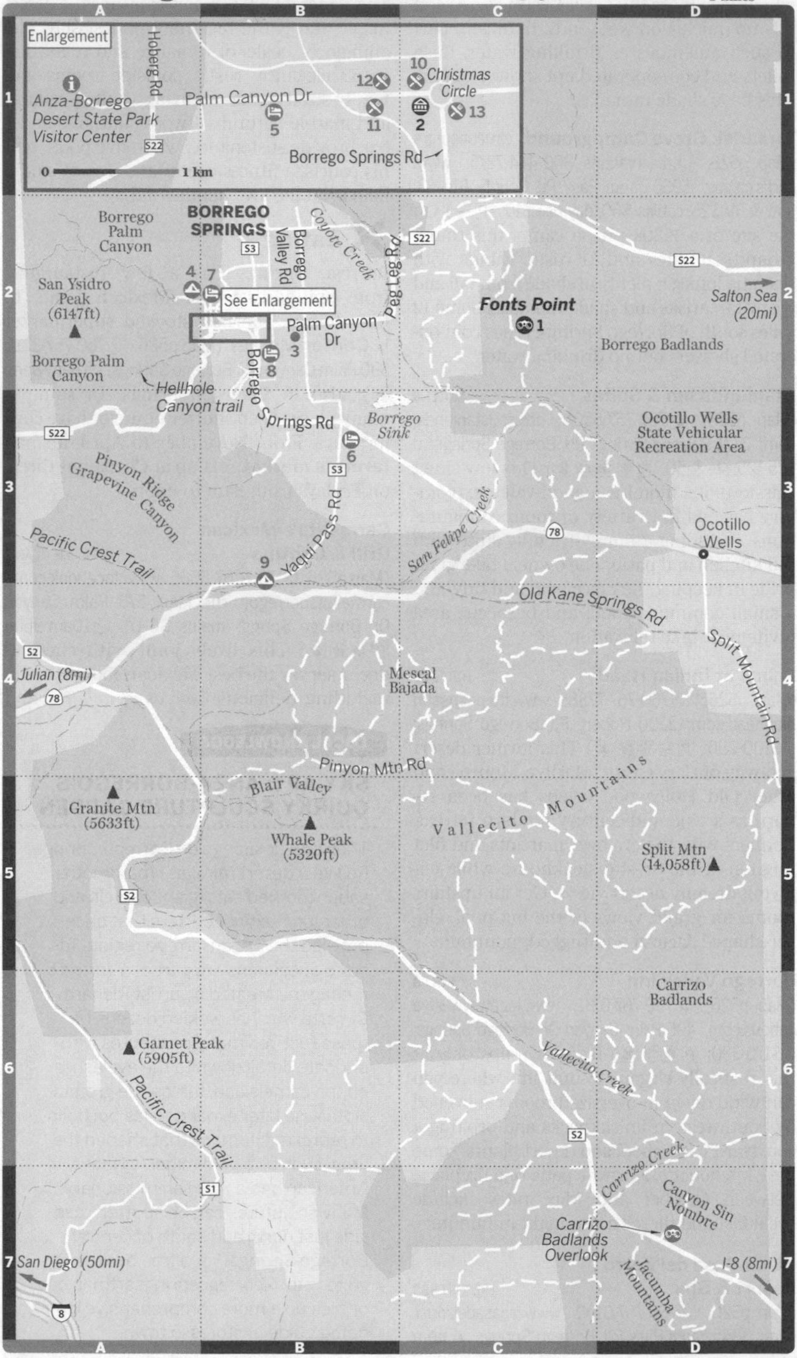

Anza-Borrego Desert State Park

fajitas. The bar staff knows how to whip up a good margarita. It's at the back of the Mall.

Kesling's Kitchen MEDITERRANEAN $
(Map p526; 760-767-7600; www.keslingskitchen.com; 665 Palm Canyon Dr, Borrego Springs; mains $14-15; 11am-9pm Nov-Mar, noon-8:30pm Apr-Oct;) Sharing space with the Borrego Art Institute in a restored mid-century modern building by William Kesling, this casual but stylish outpost has injected a dose of hipness into this tiny desert town. The big menu draw is the Neapolitan-style pizza, tickled to crispy perfection in a wood-fired oven. The integrated bar serves rotating taps of craft brews and wine.

Red Ocotillo AMERICAN $$
(Map p526; 760-767-7400; http://redocotillo.com; 721 Avenida Sureste, Borrego Springs; breakfast $8-17, mains $13-21; 7am-8:30pm;) Empty tables are as rare as puddles in the desert at this artily painted charmer in a central Borrego Springs bungalow. Fuel up for a day on the trail with the smoked salmon eggs Benedict breakfast, tuck into fresh salads or sandwiches at lunch or wrap up the day with classics from burgers to short ribs.

Carlee's AMERICAN $$
(Map p526; 760-767-3262; www.carleesplace.com; 660 Palm Canyon Dr, Borrego Springs; mains lunch $9-19, dinner $18-30; 11am-9pm, bar to 10pm Sun-Thu, to midnight Fri & Sat;) The menu is as long as a Tolstoy novel but the choices (and the decor) are good-old-fashioned Americana, hopscotching from burgers to pizza, steak to ribs, salads to pasta, all served in waist-expanding portions. It's popular with locals and visitors alike, not least for its full bar, pool table and live music on Saturdays.

Information

Anza-Borrego Desert State Park Visitor Center (Map p526; 760-767-4205; www.parks.ca.gov; 200 Palm Canyon Dr, Borrego Springs; 9am-5pm daily Oct-May, Sat, Sun & holidays only Jun-Sep) Built partly underground, the park visitor center has stone walls that blend beautifully with the mountain backdrop. Inside are top-notch displays and audiovisual presentations. The center is surrounded by a desert garden with a pupfish pond. It's 1.5 miles west of central Borrego Springs.

Getting There & Away

Approximate driving distances to Borrego Springs are 86 miles from Palm Springs, 150 miles from LA and 130 miles from Anaheim. Coming from San Diego (90 miles), I-8 to County Rte S2 is easiest, but for a more scenic ride, take twisty Hwy 79 from I-8 north through Cuyamaca Rancho State Park and into Julian, then head east on Hwy 78.

Buses 891 and 892, operated by San Diego Metropolitan Transit System, travel between Borrego Springs and El Cajon Transit Center on Thursdays and Fridays only ($8, three hours).

MOJAVE NATIONAL PRESERVE

If you're on a quest for the 'middle of nowhere,' you'll find it in the wilderness of the **Mojave National Preserve** (760-252-6100; www.nps.gov/moja; btwn I-15 & I-40; P) FREE, a 1.6-million-acre jumble of sand dunes, Joshua trees, volcanic cinder cones and pinyon-juniper forest. Its lifeless looks are deceiving for critters from coyotes and jackrabbits to desert tortoises and elusive bighorn sheep make their habitat here. Solitude and serenity draw hikers and mountain bikers. Daytime temperatures hover above 100°F (37°C) during summer, then plummet to around 50°F (10°C) in

OFF THE BEATEN TRACK

SLAB CITY & SALVATION MOUNTAIN

About 8 miles east of the Salton Sea, a mighty strange sight rises from the rugged desert floor: **Salvation Mountain** (☎760-624-8754; www.salvationmountaininc.org; 603 E Beal Rd, Niland; donations accepted; ⏰dawn-dusk; P), a 100ft-high pile of hand-mixed adobe and straw slathered in paint and decorated with flowers, waterfalls, birds and religious messages. This work of Leonard Knight (1931–2014), a passionately religious man from Vermont, was 28 years in the making and is a fabulous piece of American folk art.

Just as colorful as Salvation Mountain is the population of **Slab City** (Beal Rd; P), the off-grid community that's sprung up around Knight's artwork on top of the concrete remains of a former military base (hence the name). Dubbed 'the last free place on earth,' it attracts society dropouts, survivalists, retirees, snowbirds and just plain kooky folks – thousands in the winter, a few hardened souls year-round. It's more organized than it seems, with street names, individual 'neighborhoods' and even a library and a hostel. Feel free to walk around in the daytime, but be mindful of people's privacy.

On the Slabs northern edge, the artist collective called **East Jesus** (www.eastjesus.org) keeps the creative spirit going with an outdoor 'museum' whose eccentric installations are pure Insta-gold.

You'll find the Slabs about 3 miles east of Hwy 111 in Niland, via Main St/Beal Rd and past train tracks and trailer parks.

winter, when snowstorms are not unheard of. Strong winds will practically knock you over in spring and fall. No gas, drink or food are available within the preserve.

Sights

Kelso Dunes DUNES

(☎760-252-6100; www.nps.gov/moja; off Kelbaker Rd; P) FREE Rising to 700ft, the honey-colored Kelso Dunes are among the country's tallest sand piles. The trailhead is about 3 miles on a gravel road (no 4WD needed) west of Kelbaker Rd, 7 miles south of the Kelso Depot Visitor Center. The hike will have you mopping your brow, especially when you reach the sands, but once you're on top, all pain is forgotten. Best after sunrise or in the afternoon.

Hole-in-the-Wall NATURAL FEATURE

(☎760-252-6108; www.nps.gov/moja; Black Canyon Rd; P) FREE These rhyolite cliffs, riddled with holes like Swiss cheese, were created by a volcanic eruption millions of years ago. The area has a visitor center, picnic tables and access to four hiking trails, including the fun Rings Loop Trail.

Hole-in-the-Wall is about 20 miles north of I-40 (exit at Essex Rd).

Cima Dome VOLCANO

(☎760-252-6100; www.nps.gov/moja; Cima Rd; P) FREE Visible to the south from I-15, Cima Dome is a 1500ft hunk of granite spiked with volcanic cinder cones and crusty outcrops of basalt left by lava. Its foothills are smothered in Joshua trees that collectively make up the largest and densest such forest in the world. The dome is best seen from a distance but if you want some exercise, tackle the 3-mile round-trip Teutonia Peak Trail.

Activities

★Rings Loop Trail HIKING

(☎760-252-6100; www.nps.gov/moja; Black Canyon Rd) FREE This fun and easy 1.5-mile trail delivers close-ups of the Swiss-cheese-like cliffs of the Hole-in-the-Wall area. Starting at the south end of the parking lot, it passes petroglyphs before entering an increasingly narrow canyon that you have to scramble out of using metal rings. You'll emerge at a picnic area and follow a paved road back to the parking lot. For a shorter experience (0.5 miles), use the rings to descend straight into the canyon and climb back out the same way.

Mitchell Caverns CAVE

(Providence Mountains State Recreation Area; ☎760-928-2586; www.parks.ca.gov; 38200 Essex Rd; park per vehicle $10, tours adult/child $10/5; ⏰park 8am-5pm Fri-Sun, cavern tours 11am & 2pm Fri-Sun Oct-May, 10am Fri-Sun Jun-Sep) Part of the Providence Mountains State Recreation Area, the impressive limestone Mitchell Caverns are known for their drip-like stalactites and stalagmites. Guided tours can only be reserved by phone on Mondays between 8am and 5pm and book out fast. Wear layers and sturdy shoes for the 1.5-mile round-trip hike with great views plus a one-hour spin around the caverns.

Teutonia Peak Trail HIKING
(☎760-252-6100; www.nps.gov/moja; Cima Rd, Mojave National Preseve) FREE A lovely and moderate path, Teutonia Peak Trail meanders 1.5 miles up through dense Joshua tree forest and culminates near the top of Teutonia for unobstructed views of the volcanic Cima Dome. Head back the same way. The trailhead is off Cima Rd, 5 miles northwest of Cima or 11 miles south of I-15 (exit 272).

Sleeping & Eating

Camping is the only way to overnight in the Mojave National Preserve. First-come, first-served sites with pit toilets are available at Mid Hills and Hole-in-the-Wall campgrounds (per night $12); only the latter has potable water. Backcountry camping is not permitted within 0.25 miles of paved roads. Use existing sites, also if roadside camping. Check www.nps.gov/moja for locations and full guidelines, or ask for details and directions at the visitor centers.

Even outside the preserve, overnight picks are pretty slim and mostly confined to national chain motels. Baker is a classic stop on I-15, while Primm across the Nevada border has a trio of badly aging casino-hotels. Travelers on I-40 will find some options in Needles and Barstow.

The only place in the preserve selling a few snacks and beverages is the bookstore in the Kelso Visitor Center. Baker is the closest town with restaurants and grocery stores.

Information

Kelso Depot Visitor Center (☎760-252-6108; www.nps.gov/moja; Kelbaker Rd, Kelso; 9am-5pm) The Mojave National Preserve's main visitor center is in a gracefully restored 1920s Spanish Mission–style railway depot. You can watch a 20-minute introductory film, ask the rangers to help you plan your day, peruse natural- and cultural-history exhibits or browse a small bookshop that also sells snacks and beverages. Water and restrooms are available.

Hole-in-the-Wall Visitor Center (☎760-252-6104, 760-928-2572; Black Canyon Rd; 9am-3pm Fri-Sun) Has seasonal ranger programs, backcountry information, water, picnic tables and a restroom. Find it about 20 miles north of I-40 via Essex Rd.

Getting There & Away

There is no public transport to or within Mojave National Preserve, which is hemmed in by I-15 in the north and I-40 in the south. The main entrance off I-15 is at Baker. From there it's 35 miles south to the central Kelso Depot Visitor Center via Kelbaker Rd, which links to I-40 after another 23 miles. Cima Rd and Morning Star Mine Rd near Nipton are two other northern access roads. From I-40, Essex Rd leads to the Mitchell Caverns as well as to Black Canyon Rd and Hole-in-the-Wall.

DEATH VALLEY NATIONAL PARK

The very name evokes all that is harsh, hot and hellish – a punishing, barren and lifeless place of Old Testament severity. Yet closer inspection reveals that in **Death Valley** (Map p532; ☎760-786-3200; www.nps.gov/deva; 7-day pass per car $30; P) nature is indeed putting on a lively show: sensuous sand dunes, water-sculpted canyons, rocks moving across the desert floor, extinct volcanic craters, palm-shaded oases, stark mountains rising to 11,000ft and plenty of endemic wildlife. This is a land of superlatives, holding the US records for hottest temperature (134°F/57°C), lowest point (Badwater, 282ft below sea level) and largest national park outside Alaska (more than 5300 sq miles).

Furnace Creek is Death Valley's commercial hub, home to the national park visitor center, a gas station, ATM, post office and lodging. There's also a Mission-style 'town square' with a general store, restaurant, saloon and ice-cream and coffee parlor. Facilities at Stovepipe Wells Village and Panamint Springs also include gas, food and lodging.

Park entry permits ($30 per vehicle) are valid for seven days and available from self-service pay stations along the park's access roads and at the visitor center.

Sights & Activities

Kids can earn a junior ranger badge by completing the tasks and activities outlined in the *Junior Ranger Activity Booklet* available for free at the Furnace Creek visitor center (p535).

Furnace Creek & Around

Borax Museum MUSEUM
(Map p532; Date Grove Rd, Furnace Creek; dawn-dusk; P) FREE On the grounds of the

Ranch at Death Valley (p534), this outdoor museum illustrates Death Valley's connection to borax mining, the most profitable mineral ever extracted here. Behind an 1883 office building relocated from Twenty Mule Team Canyon, you can poke around a jumble of pioneer-era transportation equipment, including an original 'Twenty Mule Team' wagon and a steam tractor.

Harmony Borax Works HISTORIC SITE
(Map p532; ☎760-786-3200; www.nps.gov/deva; Hwy 190; P) FREE Just north of Furnace Creek, a 0.5-mile interpretive trail follows in the footsteps of late-19th-century Chinese laborers and through the adobe ruins of Harmony Borax Works, which operated from 1883 until 1888. It was from here that Twenty Mule Team wagons kicked off their 165-mile slog to the nearest train station in Mojave.

Ranch at Furnace Creek Swimming Pool SWIMMING
(Map p532; ☎760-786-2345; www.oasisatdeathvalley.com; Ranch at Furnace Creek, Hwy 190; nonguests $5; ⏰8am-11pm) This huge spring-fed pool is kept at a steady 84°F (29°C) and cleaned with a nifty flow-through system that uses minimal chlorine. It's primarily for Ranch at Furnace Creek guests, but a limited number of visitor passes are available at the reception.

Furnace Creek Golf Course GOLF
(Map p532; ☎760-786-3373; www.oasisatdeathvalley.com/furnace-creek-golf-course; Hwy 190, Furnace Creek; greens fees 9/18 holes from $30/60; ⏰year-round) For novelty's sake, play a round amid palms and tamarisks at the world's lowest-elevation golf course (214ft below sea level, 18 holes, par 70), redesigned by Perry Dye in 1997. It's also been certified by the Audubon Society for its environment-friendly management. Discounts for tee times five hours before sunset.

South of Furnace Creek

★Zabriskie Point VIEWPOINT
(Map p532; ☎760-786-3200; www.nps.gov/deva; Hwy 190; P) Early morning is the best time to visit Zabriskie Point for spectacular views across ethereally glowing, golden badlands eroded into waves, pleats and gullies. The spot was named for a manager of the Pacific Coast Borax Company and also inspired the title of Michelangelo Antonio's 1970s movie. The cover of U2's *Joshua Tree* album was also shot here.

★Artists Drive & Palette SCENIC DRIVE
(Map p532; ☎760-786-3200; www.nps.gov/deva; Badwater Rd) About 10 miles south of Furnace Creek is the turn-off for the 9-mile, one-way Artists Drive that offers 'wow' moments around every turn. About 5 miles in, you'll pass the main stop called **Artists Palette**, where oxidized metals tinge the mountains into hues from rose to green and purple; view them at their luminous best right before sunset. The road is well paved but windy with the occasional fun roller-coaster-style dip.

Badwater Basin NATURAL FEATURE
(Map p532; ☎760-786-3200; www.nps.gov/deva; Badwater Rd; P) The lowest point in North America (282ft below sea level) is an eerily beautiful landscape of crinkly salt flats. A boardwalk takes you out over a constantly evaporating bed of salty, mineralized water that's otherworldly in its beauty. It's about 17 miles south of Furnace Creek.

Dante's View VIEWPOINT
(Map p532; ☎760-786-3200; www.nps.gov/deva; Dante's View Rd, off Hwy 190; P) At 5475ft, the view of the entire southern Death Valley basin from the top of the Black Mountains is absolutely brilliant, especially at sunrise or sunset. On very clear days, you can simultaneously see the highest (Mt Whitney) and lowest (Badwater) points in the contiguous USA.

Golden Canyon HIKING
(Map p532; ☎760-786-3200; www.nps.gov/deva; Badwater Rd) Whether a short stroll or strenuous trek – don't miss a spin around this winding wonderland of golden canyons between Badwater Rd and Zabriskie Point. The most popular route is a 3-mile in-and-back trek from the main trailhead off Badwater Rd to the oxidized iron cliffs of **Red Cathedral**. Combining it with the **Gower Gulch Loop** adds another mile. Alternatively, kick off at Zabriskie Point for the 2.7-mile **Badlands Loop**.

Devil's Golf Course NATURAL FEATURE
(Map p532; ☎760-786-3200; www.nps.gov/deva; Salt Pool Rd, off Badwater Rd; P) Some 12 miles south of Furnace Creek is the turnoff to the otherworldly Devil's Golf Course where salt has piled up into saw-toothed miniature mountains in what was once a major lake that evaporated about 2000 years ago. A 1.3-mile gravel road takes you right into this

OFF THE BEATEN TRACK

THE 'MAGIC' OF NIPTON

Just northeast of the Mojave National Preserve, isolated Nipton (population 15, or so) started out as a gold-mining camp in the late 1800s and got connected to the railroad in 1905. To this day, passing freight trains still shatter the silence.

For Mojave travelers, the teensy settlement is an offbeat and off-the-beaten-track outpost to spend the night, grab a meal or a cold pint in the earthy saloon, or stock up on basics at the general store presided over by self-appointed 'mayor' Jim Eslinger. Wacky art invites picture-snapping. Energy comes from a nearby solar plant.

Nipton made headlines in 2017 when it was purchased by American Green, a cannabis technology company, with the goal to develop it into a 'marijuana resort.' Plans fizzled quickly and it was sold again in 2018, this time to an oil and gas company. Nipton did, however, gain fame in the gaming community as the setting for the video game Fallout: New Vegas.

In the real world, you can hang your hat in the cute **Hotel Nipton** (☎760-856-2335; www.nipton.com; 107355 Nipton Rd; r $95, tipis and eco-cabins from $79; check-in 3-7pm; P Wi-Fi), an Old West inn with wraparound porch, five small and basic rooms sharing two bathrooms and a large communal lounge. For more unconventional lodging, try the furnished and solar-powered tipis or the free standing huts ('eco-cabins') with wood-burning stove and outdoor shower. There's also space for tents and RVs.

bizarre landscape from Badwater Rd. You're free to walk around on the jagged surface, but don't expect to tee up.

Stovepipe Wells & Around

★Mesquite Flat Sand Dunes NATURAL FEATURE
(Map p532; ☎760-786-3200; www.nps.gov/deva; Hwy 190; P) The most accessible dunes in Death Valley are a gracefully curving sea of sand rising up to 100ft close to the highway just east of Stovepipe Wells Village. They are at their most photogenic at sunrise or sunset when bathed in soft light and accented by long, deep shadows. Keep an eye out for animal tracks. Full-moon nights are especially magical.

Mosaic Canyon Trail HIKING
(Map p532; ☎760-786-3200; www.nps.gov/deva; Mosaic Canyon Rd, off Hwy 190) West of Stovepipe Wells Village, a 2.3-mile gravel road dead-ends at the mouth of Mosaic Canyon, from where a 4-mile in-and-out trail meanders past polished marble walls carved from 750-million-year-old rocks. About 0.25 miles past the trailhead, the canyon narrows dramatically; about 1.3 miles in, a pile of boulders blocks the passage but it's possible to squeeze by on the left and continue the trek.

Northern Park

Titus Canyon Rd SCENIC DRIVE
(Map p532; ☎760-786-3200; www.nps.gov/deva; off Daylight Pass Rd/Hwy 374) Check road conditions at the visitor center (p535) before tackling grandiose but tricky Titus Canyon Rd by vehicle or mountain bike. For a rough 28 miles, it climbs, dips and winds to a crest in the Grapevine Mountains, then slowly descends back to the desert floor past a ghost town, petroglyphs and canyon narrows. The turnoff is about 2.5 miles northeast of the park boundary.

Ubehebe Crater NATURAL FEATURE
(Map p532; ☎760-786-3200; www.nps.gov/deva; Ubehebe Crater Rd; P) One of the most impressive geological features in the northern park, 600ft-deep Ubehebe Crater is believed to have formed some 2100 years ago in a single eruptive event by the meeting of fiery magma and cool groundwater. Its Martian beauty is easily appreciated from the parking lot, but for closer inspection embark on the 1.5-mile trek along the rim (not recommended if you're vertigo-prone).

Racetrack Playa NATURAL FEATURE
(Map p532; ☎760-786-3200; www.nps.gov/deva; Racetrack Rd; P) Beyond the northern end of Hwy 190, it's slow going for 27 miles on a tire-shredding dirt road (high-clearance and 4WD usually required) to the lonesome Racetrack Playa. Here, hundreds of sizable rocks have etched tracks into the dry lake bed. In 2014 a group of researchers finally lifted the mystery when they observed the stones being pushed by winds across thin sheets of ice that had formed overnight. Read all about it at www.racetrackplaya.org.

Death Valley & Around

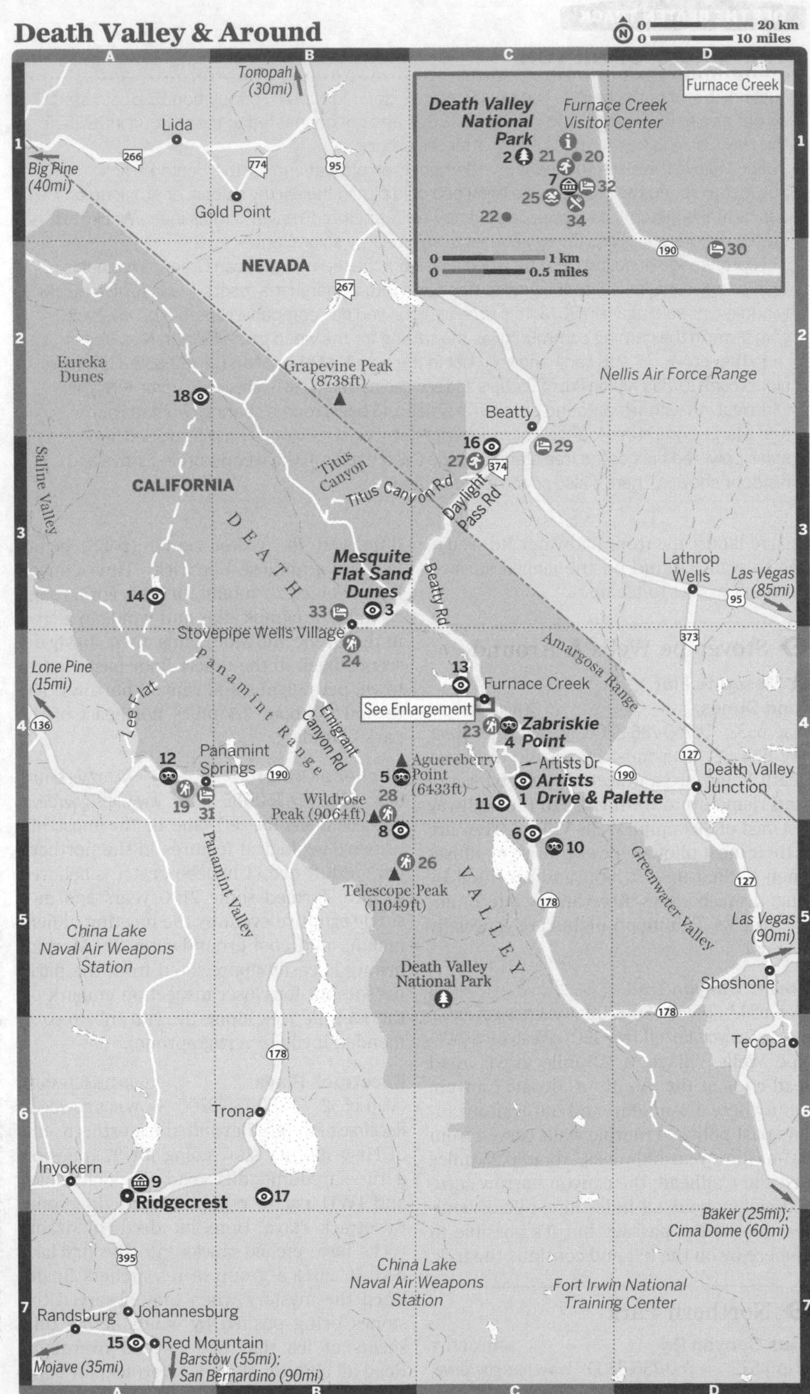

Death Valley & Around

Panamint Springs & Emigrant Canyon Rd

Aguereberry Point VIEWPOINT

(Map p532; ☎760-786-3200; www.nps.gov/deva; off Emigrant Canyon Rd; P) Named for a lucky French miner who struck gold at the nearby Eureka Mine, Aguereberry Point sits at a lofty 6433ft above the desert floor and delivers fantastic views into the valley and out to the colorful Funeral Mountains. The best time to visit is late afternoon. The 6.5-mile road off Emigrant Canyon Rd is quite rough and best done in a high-clearance vehicle.

Charcoal Kilns HISTORIC SITE

(Map p532; ☎760-786-3200; www.nps.gov/deva; Wildrose Canyon Rd) Emigrant Canyon Rd climbs steeply over Emigrant Pass to the turnoff on gravel-topped Wildrose Canyon Rd. After about 2 miles, you'll come upon a lineup of 10 large beehive-shaped charcoal kilns made of stone and once used by miners to make fuel for smelting silver and lead ore. The landscape is subalpine, with forests of piñon pine and juniper; it can be covered with snow, even in spring.

Wildrose Peak HIKING

(Map p532; ☎760-786-3200; www.nps.gov/deva; Wildrose Canyon Rd) This 8.4-mile round-trip hike with a sweat-inducing 2200ft elevation gain begins near the charcoal kilns off Wildrose Canyon Rd and threads past piñon pines and juniper to a lofty 9064ft. Grand views of the Panamint Valley, Badwater Basin and all of Death Valley National Park start about halfway. It's best in spring or fall.

Telescope Peak HIKING

(Map p532; ☎760-786-3200; www.nps.gov/deva; Wildrose Canyon Rd) The park's highest summit is Telescope Peak (11,049ft), with views that plummet to the desert floor, which is as far below as two Grand Canyons deep! The 14-mile round-trip trail clocks a 3000ft elevation gain from its trailhead at the Mahogany Flat campground. Summiting in winter requires an ice-axe, crampons and winter-hiking experience. By June, the trail is usually free of snow.

Get full details from the visitor center (p535) before setting out.

Father Crowley Vista VIEWPOINT

(Map p532; ☎760-786-3200; www.nps.gov/deva; off Hwy 190, Panamint Springs; P) This viewpoint peers deep into Rainbow Canyon, aka Star Wars Canyon, created by lava flows and scattered with multihued volcanic cinders. It's worth a quick stop on your way in or out of Death Valley. With any luck, you get to witness US Air Force and Navy fighter jets zooming through the canyon on training

THE TIMBISHA: CALLING DEATH VALLEY HOME

Timbisha Shoshone tribespeople lived in the Panamint Range for centuries, visiting the valley every winter to gather acorns, hunt waterfowl, catch pupfish in marshes and cultivate small areas of corn, squash and beans. After the federal government created Death Valley National Monument in 1933, the tribe was forced to move several times and was eventually restricted to a 40-acre village site near Furnace Creek, where it still lives. In 2000 President Clinton signed an act transferring 7500 acres of land back to the Timbisha Shoshone tribe, creating the first Native American reservation inside a US national park.

Today, a few dozen Timbisha live in the Indian Village near Furnace Creek. Pop by to sample the filling and tasty **Timbisha Taco** ($10 to $12), made with fry bread in place of a tortilla.

runs. The parking lot is about 8 miles west of Panamint Springs.

Darwin Falls HIKING
(Map p532; ☎760-786-3200; www.nps.gov/deva; Hwy 190, Panamint Springs) This natural-spring-fed year-round cascade plunges into a gorge, embraced by willows that attract migratory birds in the spring. Look for the (unmarked) turnoff about 0.75 miles west of Panamint Springs, then follow the dirt road for 2.5 miles to the parking area. The 1-mile hike to the waterfalls requires some rock scrambling and crossing small streams.

Tours

Farabee Jeep Rentals & Tours DRIVING
(Map p532; ☎760-786-9872; www.farabeejeeps.com; Hwy 190, Furnace Creek; tours from $105, 2-person minimum; ⊙Sep-May) This local outfit rents Jeeps for off-road trips (from $265 per day, minimum age 25) and also organizes Jeep tours for those who don't want to go it alone. Options include a ride down Titus Canyon ($145), out to Racetrack Playa ($280), into Echo Canyon ($105) or the more general Death Valley Experience ($195).

Furnace Creek Stables HORSEBACK RIDING
(Map p532; ☎760-614-1018; www.furnacecreekstables.net; Hwy 190, Furnace Creek; 1/2hr rides $55/70; ⊙Oct–mid-May;) Saddle up to see what Death Valley looks like from the back of a horse on guided trail rides. The one-hour ride stays on the sunbaked desert floor while the two-hour rides venture into the foothills of the Funeral Mountains for sweeping valley views. The most popular rides are at sunrise, sunset and during the full moon.

Sleeping

Camping is plentiful but if you're looking for a place with a solid roof, in-park options are limited, pricey and often fully booked in springtime. Alternative bases are the gateway towns of Beatty (40 miles from Furnace Creek), Lone Pine (40 miles), Death Valley Junction (30 miles), Shoshone (60 miles) and Tecopa (70 miles). Options a bit further afield include Ridgecrest (120 miles) and Las Vegas (140 miles).

Ranch at Death Valley RESORT $$
(Map p532; ☎760-786-2345; www.oasisatdeathvalley.com; Hwy 190, Furnace Creek; d from $180; P) Tailor-made for families, this rambling resort consists of 224 rooms with patios or balconies in one- and two-story buildings that flank lawns and lanes. Upgrades have resulted in a welcoming Spanish Colonial town square with a general store, a buffet restaurant and a saloon bar. The grounds also encompass a playground, a spring-fed swimming pool, tennis courts, a golf course and a small museum.

The daily resort fee is $22 per room.

Stovepipe Wells Village Hotel MOTEL $$
(Map p532; ☎760-786-2387; www.deathvalleyhotels.com; 51880 Hwy 190, Stovepipe Wells; RV sites $40, d $144-226; P) The 83 rooms at this private resort have beds draped in quality linens and accented with cheerful Native American–patterned blankets. The small pool is cool and the on-site cowboy-style restaurant serves breakfast and dinner daily, with lunch available in the next-door saloon. Limited wi-fi in public areas only.

Panamint Springs Resort MOTEL $$
(Map p532; ☎775-482-7680; www.panamintsprings.com; Hwy 190, Panamint Springs; d $115-215, cabins $130-290, tent cabins $50-75; P) On the western edge of Death Valley, this off-grid, family-run compound offers not just lodging and camping, but also a low-key restaurant-bar, a gas station and a general store, not to mention fantastic views of the muscular Panamint Range. Aside from rustic motel rooms, it also has nine free stand-

ing wooden cabins with air-con as well as basic tent cabins with cots.

★Inn at Death Valley HOTEL $$$
(Map p532; ☎760-786-2345, reservations 800-236-7916; www.oasisatdeathvalley.com; Hwy 190 Furnace Creek; d from $390; P ⊖ ❄ ☕ ≋) Roll out of bed, pull back the curtains and count the colors of the desert at this 1927 Spanish Mission-style hotel brimming with all the expected 21st-century comforts. After a day of sweaty touring, languid valley views await as you relax by the spring-fed swimming pool with a spa and pool bar, in the warmly furnished lounge or in the library. A class act throughout.

Eating & Drinking

The are restaurants and stores for stocking up on basic groceries and camping supplies in Furnace Creek, Stovepipe Wells Village and Panamint Springs. With few exceptions, restaurants are overpriced and mediocre. Hours vary seasonally; some close in summer.

Panamint Springs Resort AMERICAN $
(Map p532; ☎775-482-7680; www.panamintsprings.com; Hwy 190, Panamint Springs; burgers $12-16; ⊙7am-9pm; P ❄ ☕) It may look funky but this outback cafe serves some mighty fine burgers along with salads, soups and snacks. Toast the panoramic views of the Panamint Range from the front porch with a cold one from its vast selection of craft beers on tap and in the bottle.

Toll Road Restaurant AMERICAN $$
(Map p532; ☎760-786-7090; www.deathvalleyhotels.com; 51880 Hwy 190, Stovepipe Wells Village; mains $12.50-31; ⊙7-10am & 5:30-9pm; P ❄) Above-par cowboy cooking happens at this ranch house, which gets Old West flair from a rustic fireplace and rickety wooden chairs and tables. Many of the mostly meaty mains are made with local ingredients, such as mesquite honey, prickly pear and piñons. If they're closed, the same menu – and cold beer on tap – is usually available at the adjacent Badwater Saloon.

Inn Dining Room INTERNATIONAL $$$
(Map p532; ☎760-786-2345; www.oasisatdeathvalley.com; Inn at Furnace Creek, Hwy 190; breakfast $15-21, mains lunch $14-28, dinner $32-71; ⊙7-10:30am, 11:30am-2:30pm year-round, 5-9pm Oct-Apr, 6-10pm May-Sept; P ❄ ☕) This formal restaurant delivers continental cuisine with stellar views of the Panamint Mountains. Reservations are key for dinner when a 'no shorts or tank tops' policy kicks in.

Ranch 1849 Buffet AMERICAN $$
(Map p532; ☎760-786-2514; www.oasisatdeathvalley.com; Town Sq, Ranch at Furnace Creek; breakfast/dinner $16/30; ⊙7-10am, 11am-2pm & 5-8pm; P ❄ ☕) With its wooden booths, Old West paintings and paraphernalia, the revamped buffet restaurant at the Ranch at Furnace Creek offers a pleasing enough setting that, sadly, is not matched by the quality or variety of the food.

Last Kind Words Saloon AMERICAN $$$
(Map p532; ☎760-786-3335; www.oasisatdeathvalley.com; Town Sq, Ranch at Furnace Creek; mains lunch $19-25, dinner $24-105; P ❄ ☕) Despite the name, the Saloon at the Ranch at Death Valley is actually more restaurant than drinking hole. The menu is meat-centric Americana, from chili and burgers to steaks and ribs. Devour it in the high-ceilinged Disney-esque dining den amid stuffed animals, vintage guns and signs, oil paintings and other Wild West trappings.

Information

MONEY

You'll find ATMs at the Ranch at Furnace Creek, in Stovepipe Wells Village and in Panamint Springs.

TELEPHONE

Cell towers provide service at Furnace Creek and Stovepipe Wells Village but there's little to no coverage elsewhere in the park.

TOURIST INFORMATION

Furnace Creek Visitor Center (Map p532; ☎760-786-3200; www.nps.gov/deva; Furnace Creek; ⊙8am-5pm; ☕) The modern visitor center has engaging exhibits on the park's ecosystem and indigenous tribes as well as a gift shop, flush toilets, (slow) wi-fi, and friendly rangers to answer questions and help you plan your day. First-time visitors should not miss the gorgeously shot 20-minute movie. Check the daily schedule for ranger-led activities.

Getting There & Away

The park's main roads (Hwys 178 and 190) are paved and in great shape, but if your travel plans include dirt roads, a high-clearance vehicle and off-road tires are highly recommended and essential on many routes. A 4WD is often necessary after rains. Always check with the visitor center for current road conditions, especially before heading to remote areas.

Gas is available 24/7 at Furnace Creek and Stovepipe Wells Village and from 7am to 9:30pm in Panamint Springs. Prices are much higher than outside the park.

DEATH VALLEY GATEWAYS

Given Death Valley's limited and expensive non-camping lodging options, staying in one of the communities surrounding the park and driving in for day trips is worth considering. While not major destinations, some towns even have respectable sights in their own right.

Beatty

Across the Nevada border, about 40 miles northeast of Furnace Creek via Hwys 190 and 374, the old railroad town of Beatty has a cute main street with restaurants and bars, an ATM, gas station, general store and casino in case you fancy a date with Lady Luck.

Sights

Goldwell Open Air Museum SCULPTURE
(Map p532; Rhyolite Rd, off Hwy 374; 24hr; P) FREE En route to the ghost town of Rhyolite, some 5.5 miles south of Beatty, a prospector accompanied by a penguin, a ghostly plaster-cast version of Da Vinci's *Last Supper* and other surreal sculptures rise up from the dusty desert floor. The bizarre 'museum'

CAMPING IN DEATH VALLEY

The **National Park Service** (www.nps.gov/deva; campsites free-$22) operates nine campgrounds, including four tucked into the Panamint Mountains. Only Furnace Creek accepts reservations and only from mid-October to mid-April. All other campgrounds are first come, first served. At peak times, such as weekends during the spring wildflower bloom, campsites fill by midmorning. On those days, vast Sunset campground is your best bet for snagging a last-minute spot, plus there's always the option of free backcountry camping.

Private campgrounds catering mostly to RVers can be found in Furnace Creek, Stovepipe Wells Village and Panamint Springs.

Stovepipe Wells Village offers public showers ($5, including swimming-pool access). Pay at reception.

CAMPGROUND	SEASON	LOCATION	FEE	CHARACTERISTICS
Furnace Creek	year-round	valley floor	$22	pleasant grounds, some shady sites
Sunset	Oct-Apr	valley floor	$14	huge, RV-oriented
Texas Spring	Oct-Apr	valley floor	$16	decent for tents
Stovepipe Wells	Oct-Apr	valley floor	$14	parking-lot style, close to dunes
Mesquite Springs	year-round	1800ft	$14	near Ubehebe Crater
Emigrant	year-round	2100ft	free	tents only
Wildrose	year-round	4100ft	free	remote
Thorndike	Mar-Nov	7400ft	free	may need 4WD, no water, remote
Mahogany Flat	Mar-Nov	8200ft	free	may need 4WD, no water

Backcountry Camping

Free backcountry camping (no campfires) is allowed along dirt roads at least 1 mile away from paved roads and developed and day-use areas, and 100yd from any water source. Park your car next to the roadway and pitch your tent on a previously used campsite to minimize your impact. For a list of areas that are off-limits to backcountry camping, as well as additional regulations, check www.nps.gov/deva or stop by the visitor center (p535), where you can also pick up a free voluntary permit.

was begun in 1984 by the late Belgian artist Albert Szukalski and added to over the years by fellow creatives.

Rhyolite GHOST TOWN
(Map p532; Rhyolite Rd, off Hwy 374; 24hr;) FREE Rhyolite epitomizes the hurly-burly, boom-and-bust story of Western gold-rush mining towns. After the first nugget was discovered in 1904, the population soared to 8000 by 1908, only to plummet a couple of years later when the mines began petering out. The remaining ruins, including a school, store, bank and railway station, reflect the high standard of living created for such a short period. A much-photographed curiosity is a house made of thousands of beer bottles.

Atomic Inn MOTEL $
(Map p532; 775-553-2250; https://atomicinnbeatty.com; 350 S 1st St, Beatty; d $65-79;) A housing complex built for defense contractors working in Area 51 has been upcycled into a comfortable motel-style pit stop where rates include a good continental breakfast. It's in the town center with easy access to bars and restaurants.

Shady Lady Inn B&B $$
(775-553-2500; Hwy 95, Mile Marker 92; d $134-237;) The name hints at this darling B&B's former incarnation as a brothel, which still sports some quirky touches, including a room with a heart-shaped bath. Super friendly owners Jen and Nigel cook up a mean breakfast. The only downside is that it's 30 miles north of Beatty itself.

Shoshone

On the southern stoop of Death Valley, about 60 miles from Furnace Creek, blink-and-you-miss-it Shoshone stakes its existence on being an early-20th-century railroad stop. The railroad disappeared in 1941, but the village still caters to travelers with a gas station, general store, restaurant, lodging and small tourist office.

Shoshone Museum MUSEUM
(760-852-4524; Hwy 127; by donation; 9am-3pm Sun-Wed, to 5pm Fri & Sat) A rusted Chevy parked next to antique gas pumps and exhibits on bootlegging and the railroad evoke yesteryear's Old West spirit. Curators of this modest museum are especially proud of the display of mammoth bones found in the area. Staff also dispense tourist information.

Shoshone RV Park & Campground CAMPING $
(760-852-4569; http://shoshonevillage.com; Hwy 178; tent/RV site with full hookup $30/45;) This well-kept RV park has 25 full hookup sites as well as shaded tent spaces. Facilities include flush toilets, showers, a spring-fed pool and a laundromat.

Shoshone Inn MOTEL $$
(760-852-4335; www.shoshonevillage.com; 113 Old State Hwy 127; d $145-165; reception 8am-10pm;) This roadside motel has 17 contemporary rooms with dark furniture, laminate flooring and comfy beds set around a shaded courtyard. Five come with kitchenettes and there's also a bungalow with a full kitchen. Bonus: the warm mineral-spring-fed pool.

Crowbar Cafe & Saloon AMERICAN $$
(760-852-4224; www.shoshonevillage.com; 112 Old State Hwy 127; mains $13-31; 8am-9:30pm;) Shoshone's only restaurant has fed locals and travelers since 1920. Its main stock-in-trade is burgers and sandwiches, but it also serves breakfast, Mexican dishes and something called 'rattlesnake' chili (sorry, there are no actual snakes in it). The attached saloon can get lively on weekend nights.

Information

Visitor Center (760-852-4524; Main St; 9am-3pm Sun-Thu, to 5pm Fri & Sat;) Inside the Shoshone Museum, friendly staff dispenses free maps and handy tips about Death Valley National Park and its surrounds.

Tecopa

The old mining town of Tecopa was named after a peacemaking Paiute chief. Its desolate looks belie an artistic undercurrent and an unexpected number of fun spots. Soak in hot natural mineral springs, explore a hidden date-palm oasis, fuel up at excellent restaurants and get toasted at not one, but two craft breweries. It's about 70 miles from here to Furnace Creek.

Sights & Activities

China Ranch Date Farm FARM
(760-852-4415; www.chinaranch.com; China Ranch Rd; 9am-5pm;) Fed by the mostly

OFF THE BEATEN TRACK

LIFE AT DEATH VALLEY JUNCTION

An opera house in the middle of nowhere? Yes, thanks to the vision of New York dancer Marta Beckett, who fell in love with a 1920s colonnaded adobe building when her car broke down in Death Valley Junction in 1967. Until her death at age 92 in 2017, she entertained the curious with dance, music and mime shows at the **Amargosa Opera House** (☎760-852-4441; www.amargosaoperahouse.org; Hwy 127 & State Line Rd, Death Valley Junction; tours/shows $5/20; ⊙tours 9:30am-4pm, shows 7pm Fri & Sat, 2pm Sun Oct-May, call to confirm; P). Visiting performers, inspired by Marta, continue to keep her legacy alive in fall and winter. A simple roadside memorial stone honors the accomplishments of this intrepid woman.

Inquire at the adjacent hotel about tours of the auditorium whose walls Marta personally adorned with fanciful murals showing an audience she imagined might have attended an opera in the 16th century, including nuns, gypsies and royalty.

Should you choose to spend the night, don't come looking for luxury. With no TV or wi-fi, sunsets and starry skies are the only nighttime entertainment provided by the 16-room **Amargosa Hotel** (☎760-852-4441; www.amargosaoperahouse.org; Hwy 127 & State Line Rd, Death Valley Junction; r from $90; ⊙reception 8am-8pm; P @), built in 1925 by the Pacific Coast Borax Company. Today, the vintage gem delivers buckets of kookiness thanks to eccentric staff, muraled rooms and a resident ghost or two. New mattresses have raised comfort levels, and all guests are welcome to use the communal kitchenette – bring supplies as there is no store. The attached farm-to-table **cafe** (☎760-852-4432; http://amargosaoperahouse.org/cafe; Hwy 127 & State Line Rd, Death Valley Junction; mains $8.50-18, pie per slice $5; ⊙8am-3pm Fri-Mon; P) serves scrumptious breakfasts, strong coffee and healthy sandwiches but has limited hours. For more information, check www.destinationdvj.com.

belowground Armagosa River and at the end of a narrow canyon, this family-run, organic date farm is a lush oasis in the middle of the blistering desert. You can go hiking or bird-watching, stock up on luscious dates or try the yummy date-nut bread. The location is about 5 miles south of Tecopa and well signed.

Tecopa Hot Springs Campground & Pools HOT SPRINGS
(☎760-852-4377; www.tecopahotspringscampground.com; 400 Tecopa Hot Springs Rd; per 24hr $9; ⊙24hr) Men and women 'take the waters' separately in two bathhouses where nude bathing is compulsory. Private baths are available for modest types (per hour $20). Facilities are also used by guests of the affiliated campground (RVs and tents) across the street.

Delight's Hot Springs Resort HOT SPRINGS
(☎760-852-4343; www.delightshotspringsresort.com; 368 Tecopa Hot Springs Rd; day pass $15-25; ⊙8am-10pm) This place has four private soaking pools – two enclosed, two open to the sky – filled with water bubbling up from the local mineral springs and adorned with endearing desert-themed murals. Faux Roman sculptures and fountains enliven the communal patio for sunning or lounging. There are also some charm-free motel rooms and cabins (from $100), should you wish to spend the night.

Tecopa Hot Springs Resort HOT SPRINGS
(☎760-852-4420; www.tecopahotsprings.org; 860 Tecopa Hot Springs Rd; bathing $10; ⊙1-5pm year-round) There are only two lockable skylit soaking tubs in this hilltop bathhouse. The water is clean but the facilities are pretty grubby. Guests at the 'resort' campground have free 24-hour access and there are basic motel rooms with three more pools as well. The lobby doubles as an art gallery.

Sleeping

Tecopa has plenty of camping spaces, basic motel rooms and even an artsy inn.

Villa Anita B&B **$$**
(☎760-852-4595; www.villaanitadv.com; 10 Sunset Rd; r from $160; P) Staying at this artist-run three-room B&B feels much like bunking with good friends. Using recycled materials whenever possible, Carlo and David have fashioned one room from two boats and used bottles to build another, creating eccentric but supremely comfortable spaces to relax and reflect in.

Their wacky sculptures decorate the garden where their lovely dogs like to romp. All art is also for sale.

Eating & Drinking

Note that hours listed here only serve as a guideline. Call before you go.

Tecopa Brewing Company BARBECUE $
(760-852-4343; http://delightshotspringsresort.com; 420 Tecopa Springs Rd; breakfast $3-8, mains $7-21; noon-10pm Thu-Sat, to 8pm Sun & Mon Oct-Apr; P) Yes, they operate a nanobrewery, but the main reason to pop by TBC is for the finger-lickin' barbecue. Choose from beef brisket, pulled pork or pork ribs and load up on sides of coleslaw, smoked beans or cornbread, all homemade. Also serves breakfast and a wicked Tecopa Mary.

Steaks and Beer STEAKS $$
(702-334-3431; 79 Old Spanish Trail; mains $9-42; 4-10pm Fri-Sun Oct-Apr; P) A Las Vegas transplant, Eric Scott combines big-city sophistication with down-home ambience in his ramshackle lair with an intimate deck above a pond. Meat fanciers will devour the two-fisted half-pounders made from grass-fed beef or the massive Black Angus filet mignon. Vegetables are locally grown and organic, and there's an excellent wine list, bottled craft beer and fresh suds from the adjacent microbrewery.

The Bistro AMERICAN $$
(760-852-1011; www.tecopabistro.com; 860 Tecopa Hot Springs Rd; mains $7-21; 8am-9pm Thu-Sun Oct-Apr; P) Based at the Tecopa Hot Springs Resort, this funky pit stop serves up American classics with contemporary twists. Breakfast might bring French toast with caramelized peaches, lunch a made-to-order Alaskan salmon burger and dinner a feistily flavored Louisiana gumbo. Culinary adventurers should order the Scorpion Challenge for dessert!

★ **Death Valley Brewing** MICROBREWERY
(760-298-7014; www.deathvalleybrewing.com; 59 Old Spanish Trail Hwy; noon-6pm Fri-Sun Nov-Apr) The first craft brewery in the dusty desert outpost of Tecopa is not a mirage but the pint-sized operation of artist and beermeister Jon Zellhoefer in a restored railroad tie house. Brewmaster Dan uses water from the local mineral spring to whip up small-batch cold ones, from IPAs to Belgian ales, stouts to wheat beers.

Ridgecrest & Around

Some 70 miles southwest of the edge of Death Valley National Park (120 miles from Furnace Creek), Ridgecrest is a ho-hum service town. Its main raison d'être is the Naval Air Weapons Station China Lake that sprawls across a million desert acres north of town. The base is not open to the public but the China Lake Museum chronicles some of its military milestones. Gas stations, supermarkets and chain motels line up for miles along China Lake Blvd, Ridgecrest's main artery.

China Lake Museum MUSEUM
(Map p532; 760-677-2866; www.chinalakemuseum.org; 130 Las Flores Ave, Ridgecrest; adult/concession $5/3; 10am-4pm Mon-Sat; P) Pose with a 'Fat Man' (atomic bomb, that is) or a Sidewinder (the first air to air guided missile) at this small museum likely to fascinate technology, flight, history and military buffs. It's run by volunteers (mostly veterans from the nearby Naval Air Weapons Station China Lake), who are happy to play an outdated 15-minute video about the base or to provide a personal tour of the exhibits.

Trona Pinnacles NATURAL FEATURE
(Map p532; Pinnacle Rd, Trona; P) FREE What do the movies *Battlestar Galactica, Star Trek V: the Final Frontier* and *Planet of the Apes* have in common? They were all filmed at Trona Pinnacles, an eerily beautiful natural landmark where some 500 calcium carbonate spires (tufa) rise up to 140ft out of an ancient lake bed in otherworldly fashion. Find the site at the end of a 6-mile dirt road off Hwy 178 in Trona, a hard-scrabble mining town partly abandoned after suffering severe earthquake damage in 2019. It's about 25 miles east of Ridgecrest en route to Death Valley. Check locally for road conditions.

Randsburg GHOST TOWN
(Map p532; P) FREE About 20 miles south of Ridgecrest via US Hwy 395, Randsburg is a 'living ghost town,' an abandoned and now (somewhat) reinhabited gold-mining town circa 1895. Soak up Old West flair on a stroll down Main St or pop into the tiny historical museum, antiques shops, saloon, jailhouse or general store with soda fountain. Most places are open weekends only.

LAS VEGAS

Vegas, baby! An oasis of indulgence dazzling in the desert, The Strip shimmers hypnotically, promising excitement, entertainment, fortune and fame. Where else can you spend the night partying in ancient Rome, wake up for brunch next to the Eiffel Tower or take a gondola ride through Venetian canals? All in Sin City. It's yours for the taking!

Sights

Vegas' sights are primarily concentrated along the Strip, the 4.2-mile stretch of Las Vegas Blvd between Mandalay Bay to the south and the Stratosphere to the north, as well as in Downtown around the intersection of N Las Vegas Blvd and Fremont St. The 2-mile section between Downtown and the Strip's northern end is of little interest to visitors.

The Strip

★Mandalay Bay CASINO

(Map p542; 702-632-7700; www.mandalaybay.com; 3950 S Las Vegas Blvd; 24hr; P; Deuce) Mandalay Bay has anchored the southern Strip since 1999 and still impresses with its tropical theme and 135,000-sq-ft casino. Its standout attractions include the multilevel **Shark Reef Aquarium** (702-632-4555; www.sharkreef.com; 3950 S Las Vegas Blvd; adult/child $22/15; 10am-8pm Sun-Thu, to 10pm Fri & Sat; P), the Michael Jackson ONE by Cirque du Soleil spectacle, oodles of big-name-chef-associated restaurants and the family-friendly **Mandalay Bay Beach** (Map p542; 702-632-4760; www.mandalaybay.com/en/amenities/beach.html; 3950 S Las Vegas Blvd; hotel guests free, nonguests adult/child $20/10; pool 8am-7pm, Moorea Beach Club from 10am; P) with wave pool and lazy river.

In 2017 the hotel made headlines when a gunman killed 58 and wounded 413 people from his 32nd-floor suite in what went down as the deadliest mass shooting in modern US history.

★Cosmopolitan CASINO

(Map p542; 702-698-7000; www.cosmopolitanlasvegas.com; 3708 S Las Vegas Blvd; 24hr; P; Deuce) Hipsters who think they're too cool for Vegas finally have a place to go where they don't need irony to endure – or enjoy – the aesthetics of the Strip. Like the new Hollywood 'It' girl, the Cosmopolitan casino looks absolutely fabulous at all times. A steady stream of ingenues and entourages parade through the lobby (with some of the coolest design elements we've seen), along with anyone else who adores contemporary art and design.

★Bellagio CASINO

(Map p542; 702-693-7111; www.bellagio.com; 3600 S Las Vegas Blvd; 24hr; P; Deuce) The Bellagio experience transcends its decadent casino floor of high-limit gaming tables and in excess of 2300 slot machines; locals say odds here are less than favorable. A stop on the World Poker Tour, Bellagio's tournament-worthy poker room offers kitchen-to-gaming-table delivery around the clock. Most, however, come for the property's stunning architecture, interiors and amenities, including the **Conservatory & Botanical Gardens** FREE, **Gallery of Fine Art** (Map p542; 702-693-7871; adult/child under 12yr $16/free; 10am-8pm, last entry 7:30pm; P), unmissable **Fountains of Bellagio** (shows every 30min 3-7pm Mon-Fri, noon-7pm Sat, 2:30-7pm Sun, every 15min 7pm-midnight Mon-Sat, 11am-2:30pm & 7pm-midnight Sun; P) FREE and the 2000-plus hand-blown glass flowers embellishing the hotel (p544) lobby.

★Aria Fine Art Collection PUBLIC ART

(Map p542; 702-590-7111; www.aria.com; 3730 S Las Vegas Blvd; 24hr; P; Deuce, Crystals) FREE Fifteen large-scale art installations, contemporary sculptures and abstract paintings by some of the world's top artists add a dab of substance to the glitzy Aria Campus. Key works include Maya Lin's 84ft-long reclaimed-silver cast of the Colorado River overhanging the front desk, Tony Cragg's stainless-steel towers and a giant LED installation by Jenny Holzer.

★Paris Las Vegas CASINO

(Map p542; 877-796-2096; www.caesars.com/paris-las-vegas; 3655 S Las Vegas Blvd; 24hr; P; Deuce) This mini version of the French capital might lack the charm of the City of Light, but its efforts to emulate Paris' landmarks, including the Eiffel Tower, the Hotel de Ville and facades from the Opera House and Louvre, make it a fun stop for families and anyone yet to see the real thing. Its vaulted casino ceilings simulate sunny skies above myriad tables and slots, while its high-limit, authentic French roulette wheels, sans 0 and 00, slightly improve your odds.

★Caesars Palace CASINO

(Map p542; ☎866-227-5938; www.caesars.com/caesars-palace; 3570 S Las Vegas Blvd; ⏰24hr; P 🚻; 🚌Deuce) Caesars Palace claims that more players have won million-dollar slots than anywhere in the world, but its claims to fame are far more numerous than that. Entertainment heavyweights perform at the massive **Colosseum** (Map p542; ☎866-227-5938; www.thecolosseum.com; tickets $55-500; 🚌) theater, fashionistas saunter around **Forum Shops** (Map p542; ☎702-893-4800; www.simon.com/mall/the-forum-shops-at-caesars-palace; 3500 Las Vegas Blvd S; ⏰10am-11pm Sun-Thu, to midnight Fri & Sat; 📶; 🚌Deuce), while Caesars' hotel guests quaff cocktails in the Garden of the Gods Pool Oasis. By night, megaclub Omnia (p546) is one of the best places to get off your face this side of Ibiza.

LINQ Promenade STREET

(Map p542; ☎800-634-6441; www.caesars.com/linq; 3545 S Las Vegas Blvd; ⏰24hr; P 🚻; 🚌Deuce, 🚝Harrah's/The Linq) This outdoor pedestrian promenade exudes a jazzy fun vibe. Browse hip LA fashions, gorge yourself on cupcakes or on fish and chips (by Gordon Ramsay), go bowling, ride the **High Roller** (Map p542; ☎702-322-0593; www.caesars.com/linq/high-roller; adult/child $25/10, after 5pm $37/20; ⏰11:30am-2am; P 🚻) – the world's tallest observation wheel – or the **Fly Linq** zipline, get an eyeful of ink at **Tattoo'd America**, rock out to live music, or sip pints beneath the desert sun.

★Venetian CASINO

(Map p542; ☎702-414-1000; www.venetian.com; 3355 S Las Vegas Blvd; ⏰24hr; P; 🚌Deuce) The Venetian's regal casino has marble floors, hand-painted ceiling frescoes and 285 table games, including a high-limit lounge and an elegant nonsmoking poker room, where women are especially welcome (unlike at many other poker rooms in town). When combined with its younger, neighboring sibling **Palazzo** (Map p542; ☎702-607-7777; www.palazzo.com; 3325 S Las Vegas Blvd; ⏰24hr; P; 🚌Deuce), the properties claim the largest casino space in Las Vegas. A highlight of this miniature replica of Venice is a **gondola ride** (Map p542; ☎702-414-4300; www.venetian.com/resort/attractions/gondola-rides.html; shared ride per person $29, private 2-passenger ride $116; ⏰indoor rides 10am-11pm Sun-Thu, to midnight Fri & Sat, outdoor rides 11am-9:45pm, weather permitting; 🚻) down its Grand Canal.

👁 Downtown & Off-Strip

★Mob Museum MUSEUM

(☎702-229-2734; www.themobmuseum.org; 300 Stewart Ave; adult/student/under 10yr $30/17/free; ⏰9am-9pm; P; 🚌Deuce) The myth and mystique of mobsters from Bugsy Siegel to Tony Soprano get the museum treatment inside a hulking Downtown courthouse where real gangsters sat for federal hearings in 1950–51. Thoughtfully curated exhibits chart the history of organized crime in America and feature hands-on FBI equipment and mob-related artifacts. An extra fee provides access to a firearm training simulator, a crime lab or a Prohibition-era distillery tour.

★National Atomic Testing Museum MUSEUM

(Map p542; ☎702-409-7366; www.nationalatomictestingmuseum.org; 755 E Flamingo Rd; adult/child $22/16; ⏰10am-5pm Mon-Sat, from noon Sun; P; 🚌202) This affiliate of the Smithsonian is likely to fascinate even science and history luddites. Using video, documents, interactive stations and original objects, it weaves a detailed narrative of America's nuclear weapons testing program at the Nevada Test Site, a mere 90 miles from Las Vegas. A memorable highlight is the simulation of an above-ground atomic test in the Ground Zero Theater.

★Fremont Street Experience STREET

(☎702-678-5600; www.vegasexperience.com; Fremont St Mall; ⏰24hr, shows hourly dusk-midnight or 1am; P 🚻; 🚌Deuce, SDX) FREE A five block pedestrian entertainment strip, between Main St and N Las Vegas Blvd, topped by an arched steel canopy and filled with computer-controlled lights, the Fremont Street Experience was the catalyst for Downtown's rejuvenation. Every evening, the canopy turns into a 1375ft-long video screen showering revelers with dazzling light-and-sound shows powered by 600,000 watts and over 49 million LEDs.

Whoosh below the canopy on ziplines from **SlotZilla** (☎844-947-8342; www.vegasexperience.com/slotzilla-zip-line; lower/upper line $29/49; ⏰1pm-1am Sun-Thu, to 2am Fri & Sat; 🚻), an 11-story-high slot-machine. Garish, yes. Fun, yes. Busy: always.

Las Vegas Strip

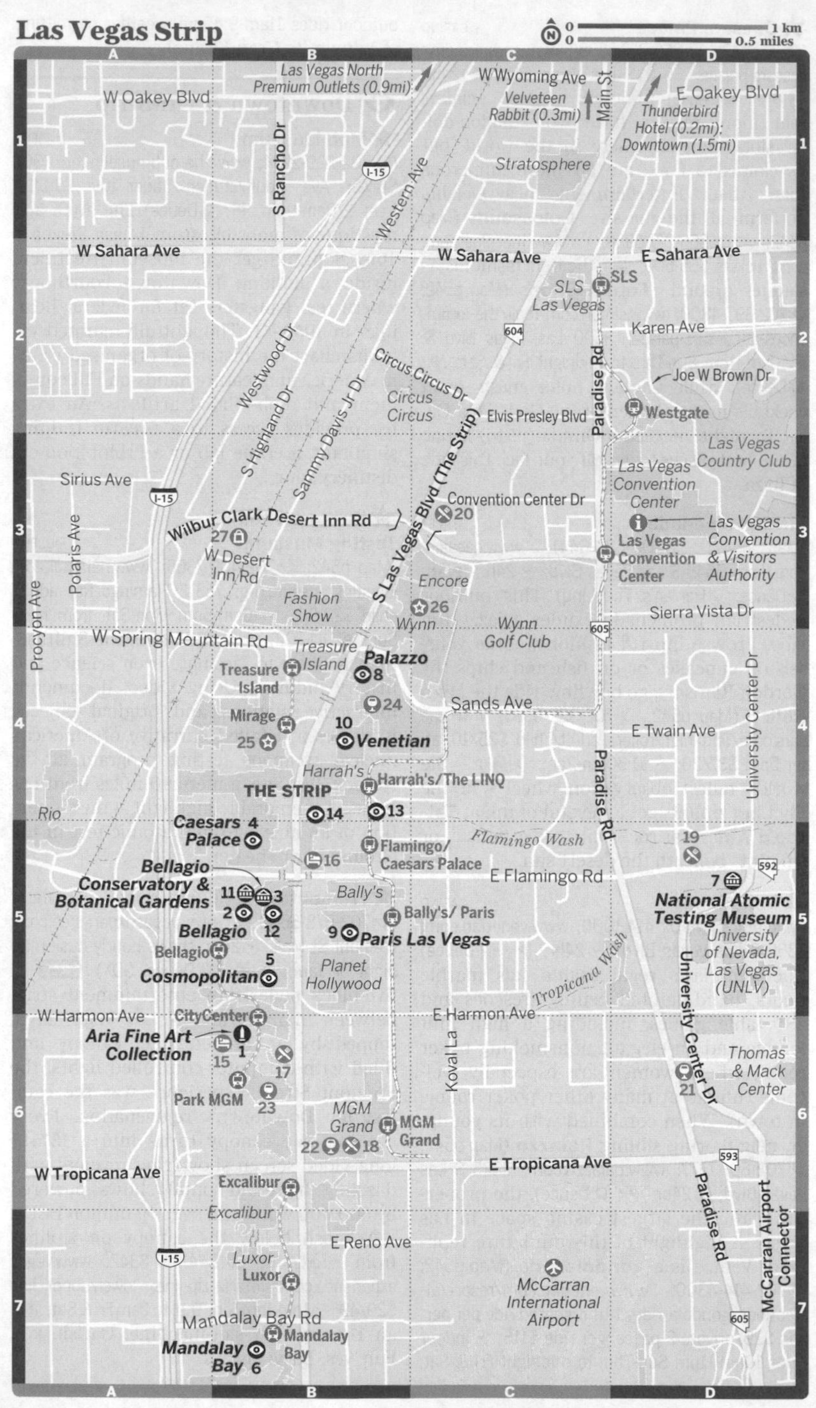

Las Vegas Strip

Neon Museum MUSEUM

(☎702-387-6366; www.neonmuseum.org; 770 N Las Vegas Blvd; tickets $20; ⏰4pm-midnight; P 👪; 🚌113) FREE A cowboy on horseback, Aladdin's genie lamp and a glowing martini glass are among the iconic Vegas neon signs to get a new lease of life at the Neon Boneyard of this nonprofit Downtown museum. You're free to wander around the alfresco exhibit (download the free app) or join a one-hour guided tour, preferably after dark. Check-in is inside the rescued lobby of the salvaged La Concha Motel, a shell-shaped jewel by Paul Revere Williams.

Downtown Container Park MALL

(☎702-359-9982; www.downtowncontainerpark.com; 707 Fremont St; ⏰11am-9pm, food & drink to 11pm Sun-Thu, to 1am Fri & Sat; 📶; 🚌Deuce) Say hi to the giant praying mantis art installation at this outdoor complex built from decommissioned shipping containers and steel-framed cubes. Inside are mostly indie boutiques, bars, restaurants, galleries and even a pole-dancing studio. A small theater called The **Dome** screens ultra-HD, 360-degree shows set to music by Pink Floyd or Led Zeppelin.

Golden Nugget CASINO

(☎702-385-7111; www.goldennugget.com; 129 Fremont St E; ⏰24hr; P 👪; 🚌Deuce, SDX) The Golden Nugget is Downtown's poshest casino address and home to the **Hand of Faith**, the world's largest gold nugget still in existence (named for its mitten shape). Its other claim to fame is the **Tank**, an outdoor pool featuring a three-story waterslide through a 200,000-gallon shark tank.

Sleeping

With more than 150,000 hotel rooms and consistently high occupancy rates, prices in Vegas fluctuate constantly. Sometimes the best deals are found in advance; other times, at the last minute. Most properties add a daily resort fee of up to $50 to the room rate.

The Strip

★**Cosmopolitan** CASINO HOTEL $$

(Map p542; ☎702-698-7000; www.cosmopolitanlasvegas.com; 3708 S Las Vegas Blvd; d weekday/weekend from $105/138; P ❄ @ 📶 🏊 🐾; 🚌Deuce) With at least eight distinctively different and equally stylish room types to choose from, Cosmo's digs are the hippest on the Strip. Ranging from oversized to decadent, about

2200 of its 2900 or so rooms have balconies (all but the entry-level category), many sport sunken Japanese tubs, and all feature plush furnishings and design quirks you'll delight in uncovering. The food options too are tops.

★Bellagio CASINO HOTEL **$$**
(Map p542; 702-693-7111; www.bellagio.com; 3600 S Las Vegas Blvd; d weekday/weekend from $139/199; ; Deuce) When it opened in 1998, Bellagio was the world's most expensive hotel. Aging gracefully, it remains one of America's finest. Its sumptuous oversized rooms fuse classic style with modern amenities and soothing color palettes. Cashmere pillow-top mattresses, mood lighting and automatic drapes complete the experience.

★Aria Resort & Casino CASINO HOTEL **$$**
(Map p542; 702-590-7111; www.aria.com; 3730 S Las Vegas Blvd; d weekday/weekend from $129/179; ; Deuce, Crystals) This sleek resort hotel has no theme and is a class act all around. Its 4000-plus cocoon-like rooms and 560 tower suites are all about soothing design, spaciousness, and luxuries like triple-sheeted linens and high-tech tablet-controlled lights and temperature.

★Cromwell Las Vegas BOUTIQUE HOTEL **$$$**
(Map p542; 702-777-3777; www.caesars.com/cromwell; 3595 S Las Vegas Blvd; d from $239; ; Deuce) Rooms at the Cromwell channel Belle Epoque Paris with their antique-style furniture, shiny hardwood floors and burgundy leather headboards. Still, they are also solidly rooted in the here and now with all the expected mod-cons and tech touches. With only 188 of them, staying here feels intimate by Vegas standards. It's popular with party-hardy millennials and home to top beach and night club **Drai's** (Map p542; 702-777-3800; www.draisgroup.com/las-vegas; nightclub cover women $20-50, men $30-100; nightclub 10:30pm-4am Fri-Sun, beach club 11am-6pm Fri-Sun, after-hours 2am-10am).

GETTING AROUND LAS VEGAS

Walking The Strip is 4.2 miles long – don't assume you can walk easily between casino hotels, even those that appear to be close together.

Bus Day passes on the 24-hour Deuce and faster (though not 24-hour and not servicing all casinos) SDX buses are an excellent way to get around.

Monorail Expensive, inconveniently located on the east side of the Strip and with a limited route, but great views and regular services.

Ride-share Ride-share where possible – rates are great and you'll never wait long.

Tram Three driverless trams link some casinos. Free but slow.

Taxi Expensive. Tips are expected.

Downtown & Off-Strip

Golden Nugget CASINO HOTEL **$**
(702-385-7111; www.goldennugget.com; 129 Fremont St E; d from $49; ; Deuce) Relive the fabulous heyday of 1950s Vegas at this swank Fremont St address. Rooms in the Rush Tower are the best in the house.

Thunderbird Hotel BOUTIQUE HOTEL **$**
(702-489-7500; www.thunderbirdhotellasvegas.com; 1215 S Las Vegas Blvd; d from $30; ; Deuce) Despite a location in the no man's land between the north Strip and Fremont St, this renovated retro-style landing pad is still an instant winner with its great rates, funky fresh rooms with chunky, reclaimed-wood furniture, youthful vibe and retro-flavored bar. It's not a hostel or a boutique hotel, but lies somewhere in between.

El Cortez CASINO HOTEL **$**
(702-385-5200; www.elcortezhotelcasino.com; 600 Freemont St E; d weekday/weekend from $25/81; ; Deuce) A wide range of rooms from old-school to contemporary cool Tower Premium rooms are available at this fun, retro property close to the Fremont St action. Bonus: free parking.

Eating

The Strip has been studded with celebrity chefs for years. All-you-can-eat buffets and $10 steaks still exist, but today's visitors demand ever more sophisticated dining experiences, with meals designed – although not personally prepared – by famous global taste-makers.

The Strip

★Tacos El Gordo MEXICAN **$**
(Map p542; 702-331-1160; www.tacoselgordobc.com; 3041 S Las Vegas Blvd; dishes $2.60-5; 10am-2am Sun-Thu, to 4am Fri & Sat; ;

(Deuce) This Tijuana-style taco shop from SoCal is just the ticket when it's way late, you've got almost no money left and you're desperately craving *carne asada* (beef) or *adobada* (chili-marinated pork) tacos in hot, handmade tortillas.

Bobby's Burger Palace BURGERS $
(Map p542; 702-598-0191; http://bobbysburgerpalace.com; 3750 S Las Vegas Blvd; burgers $6-10; 11am-midnight Sun-Thu, to 1am Fri & Sat; ; Deuce) It's no palace, but Bobby Flay's fist-sized patties are half the price of other star chefs' burger joints on the Strip. The signature is the Crunchburger with potato chips folded into the bun, but we're partial to the Green Chili with roasted green chilies, pickled red onions and queso sauce. Choose from beef, turkey, chicken or veggie patties.

Find it in front of the Waldorf Astoria.

Milk Bar DESSERTS $
(Map p542; 702-698-2662; www.cosmopolitanlasvegas.com; Eastside Tower, 3708 S Las Vegas Blvd, Cosmopolitan; soft serve from $6; 1-10pm Mon-Fri, 9am-10pm Sat & Sun; ; Deuce) Momofuku dessert program wunderkind Christina Tosi has brought her Milk Bar concept to Las Vegas, inspiring rapture and adoration. Try her cereal-milk soft serve, corn cookies or (and?) cake truffles and feel smug.

★**Wicked Spoon Buffet** BUFFET $$$
(Map p542; 877-893-2001; www.cosmopolitanlasvegas.com; Chelsea Tower, 2708 S Las Vegas Blvd, Cosmopolitan; brunch/dinner from $29/42; 8am-9pm Sun-Thu, 8am-10pm Fri & Sat; ; Deuce) Wicked Spoon gives casino buffets a contemporary feel, with freshly prepared temptations served on individual plates to encourage portion control. The spread has the expected meat, sushi, seafood and desserts, but with upgrades – think roasted bone marrow and a gelato bar. Add unlimited champagne, mimosas or Bloody Marys for $17.

★**Joël Robuchon** FRENCH $$$
(Map p542; 702-891-7925; www.mgmgrand.com; 3799 S Las Vegas Blvd, MGM Grand; tasting menus $130-445; 5:30-10pm; ; Deuce) Joël Robuchon, the acclaimed 'Chef of the Century,' leads the pack in the French culinary invasion of the Strip. His eponymous art deco–inspired dining room, done up in leather and purple velvet, exudes the sophistication of a dinner party at a 1930s Paris mansion. Complex seasonal tasting menus promise the meal of a lifetime – and they often deliver.

Downtown & Off-Strip

eat CAFE $
(702-534-1515; https://eatdtlv.chefnatalieyoung.com; 707 Carson Ave; mains $8-15; 8am-3pm Mon-Fri, to 2pm Sat & Sun; ; Deuce, BHX) Community spirit and creative cooking with mostly local products provide reason enough to venture off Fremont St for this breakfast and lunchtime gem. With a concrete floor and spare decor, it can get loud while folks treat themselves to truffled egg sandwiches, cinnamon biscuits with strawberry compote, shrimp po'boy sandwiches or bowls of green chili chicken posole.

★**VegeNation** VEGAN $
(702-366-8515; https://vegenationlv.com; 616 E Carson Ave; mains $13; 8am-9pm Sun-Thu, to 10pm Fri & Sat; ; Deuce, BHX) Faced with a health crisis, veteran chef Donald Lemperle adopted a plant-based diet and used his newfound culinary wisdom to open one of Downtown's most exciting zeitgeist-capturing cafes. His kitchen sends out insanely delicious plant-based tacos, sandwiches, pizzas and desserts made from local products to an adoring local fan base. Try the CBD kombucha.

★**Lotus of Siam** THAI $$
(Map p542; 702-735-3033; www.lotusofsiamlv.com; 620 E Flamingo Rd; mains $9-30; 11am-2:30pm Mon-Fri, 5:30-10pm daily; ; 202) Saipin Chutima's authentic northern Thai cooking has won almost as many awards as her geographically diverse wine cellar. One bite of her garlic prawns or crispy duck, and you'll be hooked. Although the strip-mall hole-in-the-wall may not look like much, those in the know flock here. Reservations essential.

★**Carson Kitchen** AMERICAN $$
(702-473-9523; www.carsonkitchen.com; 124 S 6th St; tapas & mains $8-22; 11:30am-11pm Thu-Sat, to 10pm Sun-Wed; ; Deuce) This tiny eatery with industrial-themed exposed beams, bare bulbs and chunky tables hops with downtowners looking to escape the mayhem of Fremont St or the Strip's high prices. Excellent shared plates include rainbow cauliflower, brussels sprout caesar, and baked mac 'n' cheese.

Drinking & Nightlife

You don't need us to tell you that Las Vegas is party central – the Strip is home to some of the country's hottest clubs and most happening bars, where you never know who you'll rub shoulders with. What you might not know is that Downtown's Fremont East Entertainment District is the go-to place for Vegas' coolest non-mainstream haunts.

The Strip

★Hakkasan CLUB

(Map p542; ☎702-891-3838; http://hakkasannightclub.com; 3799 S Las Vegas Blvd, MGM Grand; cover women/men from $20/30; ⌚10:30pm-4am Thu-Sun; 🚌Deuce) At this lavish Asian-inspired nightclub, international EDM jet-set DJs such as Tiësto and Steve Aoki rule the packed main dance floor bordered by VIP booths and floor-to-ceiling LED screens. More offbeat sounds spin in the intimate Ling Ling Club, with leather sofas and backlit amber glass.

★Omnia CLUB

(Map p542; ☎702-785-6200; www.omniaclubs.com/las-vegas; 3570 S Las Vegas Blvd, Caesars Palace; cover women/men from $20/30; ⌚10:30pm-4am Tue & Thu-Sun; 🚌Deuce) Hakkasan group's Caesars megaclub exudes a Miami Beach vibe and has residencies by top spinners like Calvin Harris and Martin Garrix. Dance the night away to high-octane Top 40/hip-hop beneath a kinetic chandelier whose eight circles create ever-changing visual effects.

Chandelier Lounge COCKTAIL BAR

(Map p542; ☎702-698-7979; www.cosmopolitanlasvegas.com; 3708 S Las Vegas Blvd, Cosmopolitan; ⌚24hr; 🚌Deuce) Towering high in the Cosmopolitan (p540), this ethereal cocktail bar is inventive yet beautifully simple, with three levels connected by curved staircases, draped with glowing glass beads. The second level is headquarters for experimental concoctions, while the third specializes in floral and fruit infusions.

Rosina Cocktail Lounge COCKTAIL BAR

(Map p542; ☎702-607-1945; www.venetian.com; 3325 S Las Vegas Blvd, Palazzo; ⌚5pm-3am; 🚌Deuce) The Venetian's offering to the craft cocktail gods. The attentive bar staff create meticulously mixed potions in classic fashion or, if you prefer, with their own creative twist. The art deco–leaning decor has a grown-up feel and sets the stage for civilized drinking. Neat touch: the Champagne call button.

NoMad Bar COCKTAIL BAR

(Map p542; ☎702-730-7000; www.thenomadhotel.com; 3772 S Las Vegas Blvd, NoMad Hotel; ⌚5-11pm Tue-Thu & Sun, to 2am Fri & Sat; 🚌Deuce) You have to walk across the same-name restaurant to check in with the hostess at this bar – all the better for checking out the gorgeous decor (and people) at this sumptuous craft cocktail scene contender. This place isn't just beautiful though – the drinks are truly out of this world, and there are sophisticated munchies to keep your brain in balance.

Downtown & Off-Strip

★Downtown Cocktail Room LOUNGE

(☎702-880-3696; www.downtowncocktailroom.com; 111 S Las Vegas Blvd; cocktails $12-13; ⌚4pm-2am Mon-Sat; 🚌Deuce) With a serious list of classic cocktails, this low-lit drinking den is a local darling beloved by creative types and off-duty barstaff and a top spot in the Fremont East district. The entrance is ingeniously disguised: the door looks like just another part of the wall until you discover the sweet spot you have to push to get in. Happy hour runs 4pm to 7pm Monday to Saturday.

★Commonwealth BAR

(☎702-445-6400; www.commonwealthlv.com; 525 Fremont St; ⌚7pm-late Tue-Sat, 10pm-late Sun; 🚌Deuce) It might be a little too cool for school but, whoa, that sumptuous Prohibition-style interior is worth a look: plush booths, softly glowing chandeliers, Victorian-era bric-a-brac and a saloon bar. There's dancing and imbibing with a view of the Fremont Street scene on the rooftop patio and a secret speakeasy within the bar (ask for the Laundry Room).

Double Down Saloon BAR

(Map p542; ☎702-791-5775; www.doubledownsaloon.com; 4640 Paradise Rd; ⌚24hr; 🚌108, 202) This dark, psychedelic dive bar is the gritty antithesis to Vegas glam. It never closes, there's never a cover charge, the house drink is called 'ass juice' and it claims to be the birthplace of the bacon martini. When live bands aren't terrorizing the crowd, the jukebox vibrates with New Orleans jazz, British punk, Chicago blues and the late, great surf-guitar king Dick Dale.

Velveteen Rabbit COCKTAIL BAR

(☎702-685-9645; http://velveteenrabbitlv.com; 1218 S Main St; ⌚5pm-1am Mon-Wed, to 2am Thu-Sat, 5pm-midnight Sun; 🚌108) Las Vegas wasn't always a shining neon star of craft cocktailery, but in recent years next-gen lounges like Velveteen Rabbit have put the city on the mixology map. Located in the smoothly beautified Arts District, it's a lively warren of artsy decor with imaginative cocktails, a dozen craft beers on tap and a patio for mingling alfresco.

☆ Entertainment

The gigantic casino hotels on the Strip all flashily compete to lure you with larger-than-life production shows, celebrity-filled nightclubs, burlesque cabarets and other titillating diversions.

★Le Rêve – The Dream THEATER
(Map p542; ☎702-770-9966; http://boxoffice.wynnlasvegas.com; 3131 S Las Vegas Blvd, Wynn; tickets $127-175; ⊙shows 7pm & 9:30pm Fri-Tue; ; Deuce) Acrobatic feats on, in and above water are the ammo of this spectacular show in this 'aqua-theater-in-the-round' with its million-gallon swimming pool. A crowd favorite since 2005, elements of the show have been revamped but devotees can still gasp at a thrilling 80ft dive and be charmed by the underwater tango and synchronized swimmers.

★O THEATER
(Map p542; ☎702-693-8866; www.cirquedusoleil.com/o; 3600 S Las Vegas Blvd, Bellagio; tickets $90-215; ⊙7pm & 9:30pm; ; Deuce) Phonetically speaking, 'O' is the French word for water *(eau)*, which is *très apropos* given that the show is a water-based spectacle featuring a lithe international cast telling the tale of theater through the ages. It's a stunning feat of imagination and engineering.

Beatles LOVE THEATER
(Map p542; ☎702-792-7777; www.cirquedusoleil.com/beatles-love; 3400 S Las Vegas Blvd, Mirage; tickets $60-185; ⊙7pm & 9:30pm Tue-Sat; ; Deuce) Another smash hit from Cirque du Soleil, *Beatles LOVE* started as the brainchild of the late George Harrison. Using *Abbey Road* master tapes, the show psychedelically fuses the musical legacy of the Beatles with Cirque's high-energy dancers and signature aerial acrobatics. Come early to photograph the trippy, rainbow-colored entryway.

Absinthe THEATER
(Map p542; ☎702-534-3419; https://spiegelworld.com/absinthe; Spiegeltent, 3570 S Las Vegas Blvd, Caesars Palace; tickets $100-250; ⊙8pm & 10pm; Deuce) An experimental breed of raucous variety show, Absinthe mixes bawdy and surreal comedy with burlesque, cabaret and classy acrobatics, all roped together by the foul-mouthed emcee Gazillionaire. It has an explicit erotic vibe: no one under 18 years is allowed inside the big-top tent set up outside Caesars Palace (p541).

Shopping

Las Vegas North Premium Outlets MALL
(☎702-474-7500; www.premiumoutlets.com/vegasnorth; 875 S Grand Central Pkwy; ⊙11am-7pm Mon-Sat, noon-6pm Sun; ; 207) Vegas' biggest-ticket outlet mall features 175 brands including high-end names such as Armani, Brooks Brothers, Calvin Klein and Kate Spade, alongside casual favorites such as Banana Republic, Gap, Diesel, Nike and Adidas.

Planet 13 DISPENSARY
(Map p542; ☎702-815-1313; www.planet13lasvegas.com; 2548 W Desert Inn Rd; ⊙24hr; ; Deuce) This self-described 'cannabis superstore and entertainment complex' is an emporium the size of several city blocks devoted to all things weed. Your personal concierge walks you through the myriad products, from flower, seeds and edibles to CBD products and accessories. Picture ID required.

Information

Las Vegas Convention & Visitors Authority (LVCVA; Map p542; ☎702-892-7575; www.visitlasvegas.com; 3150 Paradise Rd; ⊙8am-5pm Mon-Fri; ; Las Vegas Convention Center) In the convention center complex.

Getting There & Away

McCarran International Airport (LAS; ☎702-261-5211; www.mccarran.com; 5757 Wayne Newton Blvd;)

The easiest and cheapest way to get to your hotel is by airport shuttle (round trip from $17.50) or a ride-share service like Lyft and Uber (from $14).

AT A GLANCE

POPULATION
250,900

HIGHEST PEAK
Mt Shasta (14,179ft)

BEST SCENIC DRIVE
Feather River Scenic Byway (p563)

BEST CAVERNS
Lake Shasta Caverns (p555)

BEST SPIRITUAL EXPERIENCE
Shasta Vortex Adventures (p568)

WHEN TO GO

Jul–Sep Warm weather and snow-free passes are ideal for backcountry camping.

Oct–Nov & Apr–May Shoulder seasons; scattered showers and snow at the high elevations.

Nov–Jan Skiing Mt Shasta is the main draw. Prices drop outside ski areas.

Lassen Volcanic National Park (p556)
IULIIA SHELIEPOVA / SHUTTERSTOCK ©

Northern Mountains

Hidden California gets bandied around fairly casually, but here you have an entire corner of the state that does seem forgotten. Prepare yourself for something completely different: vast expanses of wilderness – some 24,000 protected acres – divided by rivers and streams, dotted with cobalt lakes, horse ranches and alpine peaks.

Further east is a stretch of shrubby, high desert cut with amber gorges, caves and dramatic light. Much of it doesn't look the way people envision California – the topography resembles the older mountains of the Rockies. The towns are tiny and friendly, with few comforts; come to get lost in vast remoteness and to mine this era's gold – space and tranquility. Even the two principal attractions, Mt Shasta and Lassen Volcanic National Park, remain uncrowded at the peak of summer.

INCLUDES

Northern Mountains Highlights

1 Lassen Volcanic National Park (p556) Gaping at geothermal spectacles.

2 Lava Beds National Monument (p575) Exploring deep caves and examining ancient petroglyphs.

3 Mt Shasta (p566) Hiking, skiing and basking in the vibes of NorCal's most majestic mountain.

4 Castle Crags State Park (p572) Marveling at the granite spires rising from the forest.

5 Weaverville (p577) Enjoying small-town charm and trout-filled water nearby.

6 Quincy (p563) Chilling out in this adorable mountain town.

7 Shasta Lake (p555) Floating with a dozen pals on a lake houseboat.

8 McArthur-Burney Falls State Park (p574) Getting misted by these unique spring-fed falls.

REDDING & AROUND

North of Red Bluff the dusty central corridor along I-5 starts to give way to panoramic mountain ranges on either side. Redding is the last major outpost before the small towns of the far north, and the surrounding lakes make for easy day trips or overnight camps. If you get off the highway – way off – this can be an exceptionally rewarding area of the state to explore.

Redding

Originally called Poverty Flats during the gold rush for its lack of wealth, Redding today has a whole lot of new money – malls, big-box stores and large housing developments surround its core. A tourist destination it is not, though it is the major gateway city to the northeast corner of the state and a useful spot for restocking before long jaunts into the wilderness. Recent constructions like the Sundial Bridge and Turtle Bay Exploration Park are enticing lures and worth a visit...but not a long one. A surge of good eating and drinking spots makes it an excellent pit stop for a meal if you're taking a long road trip on I-5. Downtown is bordered by the Sacramento River to the north and east. Major thoroughfares are Pine and Market Sts and there's often lots of traffic.

Sights & Activities

★Sundial Bridge BRIDGE

(Map p552; http://turtlebay.org/sundial-bridge) Resembling a beached cruise ship, the shimmering-white 2004 Sundial Bridge spans the river and is one of Redding's marquee attractions, providing an excellent photo op. The glass-deck pedestrian overpass connects the Turtle Bay Exploration Park to the north bank of the Sacramento River and was designed by renowned Spanish architect Santiago Calatrava.

The bridge/partially working sundial attracts visitors from around the world, who come to marvel at this unique feat of engineering artistry. It is accessed from the park and connects to the Sacramento River Trail. The surrounding scenery is beautiful.

Turtle Bay Exploration Park MUSEUM

(Map p552; 530-243-8850; www.turtlebay.org; 844 Sundial Bridge Dr; adult/child $16/12, after 2:30pm $11/7; 9am-5pm Mon-Sat, from 10am Sun late Mar-Oct, 9am-4:30pm Wed-Fri, from 10am Sat & Sun Nov-late Mar;) Situated on 300 meandering acres, this is an artistic, cultural and scientific center for visitors of all ages, with an emphasis on the Sacramento River watershed. The complex houses art and natural-science museums, with fun interactive exhibits. There are also extensive arboretum gardens, a butterfly house (open seasonally) and a 22,000-gallon, walk-through river aquarium full of regional aquatic life (yes, including turtles).

Courthouse Museum MUSEUM

(530-243-8194; www.parks.ca.gov; 15312 CA 299; $2; 10am-5pm Thu-Sun;) This building was the courthouse for over 30 years in the late 1800s and now houses a fun and informative museum and visitor center.

Redding Trails HIKING

(Map p552; www.reddingtrails.com) Eighty miles of trails loop through parks, along rivers and up hills for strolling, hiking and mountain biking. Check the website for maps or pick up the pamphlet at almost any hotel. The star is the Sacramento River Trail, which meanders along the river all the way to Shasta Dam. There are several access points, including the Sundial Bridge.

WaterWorks Park WATER PARK

(www.waterworkspark.com; 151 N Boulder Dr; day pass adult/child $24/20; usually late May-Sep;) Redding gets really hot, and although most hotels and motels have pools, you'll have more fun splashing around at this water park, including on the four-story-high, Avalanche, a simulated white-water river, and giant waterslides, plus there's a 'Lazy Lagoon' and kiddie pool. Great for kids or kid-like adults.

Sleeping

Redding's many motels and hotels (most large chains are represented and have swimming pools) huddle around noisy thoroughfares and some downtown options have photogenic, retro neon signs. Aim for the ones on less busy N Market St.

★Desmond House B&B $

(Map p552; 530-921-2158; https://thedesmondhouse.com; 1449 Riverside Dr; d $125;) Filled with exquisite antique furniture, fascinating Victorian-era details and views of the Sacramento River, this B&B is the prettiest in Redding. There are only two rooms, the location is close to downtown but quiet and the price is right so book in advance. Greg

Redding

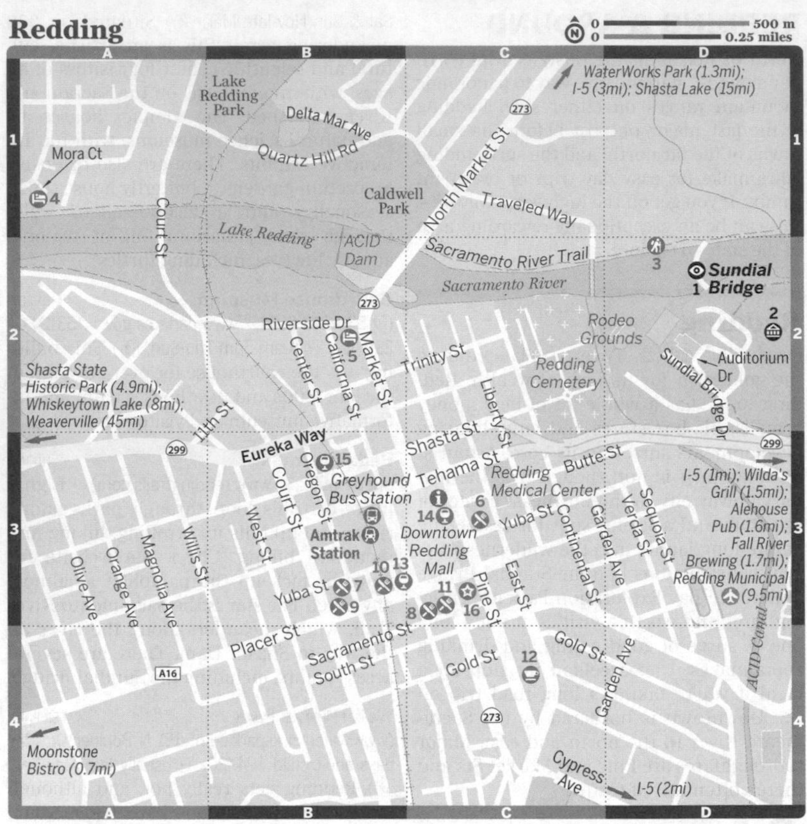

Redding

Top Sights
1 Sundial Bridge ... D2

Sights
2 Turtle Bay Exploration Park ... D2

Activities, Courses & Tours
3 Redding Trails ... D2

Sleeping
4 Apples' Riverhouse B&B ... A1
5 The Desmond House ... B2

Eating
6 Cafe Paradisio ... C3
7 Carnegie's ... B3
8 Jack's Grill ... C3
9 Ma Der Ma Der Sap House & Grill ... B3
10 The Park ... B3
11 Vintage Public House ... C3

Drinking & Nightlife
12 Evergreen ... C4
13 Final Draft Brewing Company ... B3
14 Wildcard Brewing Company ... C3
15 Woody's Brewing Co. ... B3

Entertainment
16 Cascade Theatre ... C3

the owner will entertain you with his stories or give you privacy if you prefer.

Apples' Riverhouse B&B B&B **$**
(Map p552; ☎530-243-8440; www.applesriverhouse.com; 201 Mora Ct; d $105-120; 📶) Just steps from the Sacramento River Trail, this modern, ranch-style home has three comfortable upstairs rooms, two with decks. It's a bit suburban, but it's the best independent stay in Redding. In the evening the sociable hosts invite you for cheese and wine. Bikes are yours to borrow.

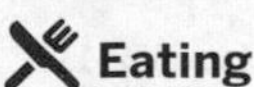

Eating

While it's certainly not a foodie hub, Redding has some surprisingly good places to eat, including for those on a budget.

The Park STREET FOOD $
(Map p552; www.facebook.com/theparkredding; 1552 Placer St; mains $8-15; ⏲5-9pm Thu-Sat & sometimes Sun;) Head to this outdoor, family-friendly spot on a warm evening to dine from a rotating collection of food trucks. There's a grassy area for kids to play, often games like cornhole or life-sized checkers, and maybe live music. Regular carts include crepes and pizza.

Ma Der Ma Der Sap House & Grill LAOTIAN $
(Map p552; ☎530-691-4194; 1718 Placer St; dishes $7-10; ⏲10am-7pm Mon-Thu, to 5pm Fri) Try the 'Sappritto,' a Laotian-inspired burrito with meat, eggs, veggies, sticky rice and a choice of hot sauce. Or go with pad Thai, Lao-sausage tacos, cheesesteak sub or Lao-style wings. Sap means 'delicious' in Lao and we agree. Everything from the hot sauces to the sausage are housemade daily. Call for to-go orders or eat in.

Wilda's Grill HOT DOGS $
(☎530-246-3502; www.wildasgrill.com; 1712 Churn Creek Rd; mains $6-8; ⏲11am-7pm Mon-Sat;) The combo sounds weird but it works: big, excellent hot dogs with toppings from roasted garlic to homemade chili or blue cheese – or go vegetarian with outrageously delicious falafel or the much-lauded Buddha Bowl, made from rice, veggies and yummy, spicy sauces. Expect a line at peak hours.

Carnegie's CALIFORNIAN $
(Map p552; ☎530-246-2926; 1600 Oregon St; mains $13; ⏲10am-3pm Mon & Tue, to 7pm Wed-Fri;) This hip and homey, split-level cafe serves up yummy sandwiches and big fresh salads. There's a good selection of beer and wine too. Friday nights get a little rowdy, and there can be a wait.

Vintage Public House CALIFORNIAN $$
(Map p552; ☎530-229-9449; www.vintageredding.com; 1790 Market St; mains $12-31; ⏲11am-9pm Mon-Fri, 5-10pm Sat) A lively pub serving well-prepared Californian fare alongside craft beers on tap, creative cocktails and excellent wines by the glass. There's also live music many nights and the outdoor patio is one of the more sublime spots downtown to spend a summer evening in Redding.

Cafe Paradisio MEDITERRANEAN $$
(Map p552; ☎530-215-3499; www.cafeparadisio.com; 1270 Yuba St; mains lunch $10-16, dinner $17-34; ⏲11am-2:30pm & 5-9pm Mon, Wed, Thu & Fri, 11:30am-2:30pm Tue, 5-10pm Sat;) Take Mediterranean food and give it a bit of Asian flair and you have the comforting fare of this casual and friendly little nook. Start with the baked brie platter then continue with salmon with coconut curry or three-cheese lasagne. The portions are huge and there are lots of vegetarian choices.

Moonstone Bistro CALIFORNIAN $$$
(☎530-241-3663; www.moonstonebistro.com; 3425 Placer St; mains lunch $14-26, dinner $23-46; ⏲11am-9pm Tue-Thu, to 10pm Fri & Sat, 10am-2pm Sun;) Organic, local, free range, line-caught, you name it – if the word is associated with sustainable food, you can use it to describe this place. Try the fish tacos at lunch and the pork chops on mashed yams with caramelized Fuji apples for dinner. And don't skip dessert – the chocolate soufflé is to die for. Top it off with a microbrew.

Jack's Grill STEAK $$$
(Map p552; ☎530-241-9705; www.jacksgrillredding.com; 1743 California St; mains $21-46; ⏲4-10pm Mon-Sat) This funky little place doesn't look so inviting – the windows are blacked out and it's dark as a crypt inside – but its popularity with locals starts with its stubborn ain't-broke-don't-fix-it ethos and ends with its steak – a big, thick, charbroiled decadence.

Regulars start lining up for dinner at 4pm when cocktail hour begins. There are no reservations, so it easily takes an hour to get a seat.

Drinking & Entertainment

★ Evergreen CAFE
(Map p552; www.evergreen.coffee; 2085 Pine St; ⏲7am-5pm;) Possibly the hippest place in Redding, this modern cafe serves the best coffee in town alongside a small menu of waffles, yogurts and thick sliced sourdough toast served with a variety of toppings. The protein bowl with veggies, meats cheese and an egg on top is the more filling option. There are also two B&B rooms available upstairs (from $140 per night).

Alehouse Pub PUB
(☎530-221-7990; www.reddingalehouse.com; 2181 Hilltop Dr; ⏲3pm-midnight Mon-Thu, to 1:30am Fri & Sat) Too bad for fans of the cheap stuff, this

local pub keeps a selection of highly hopped beers on tap and sells T-shirts emblazoned with 'No Crap on Tap.' It's a fun local place that gets packed after Redding's young professionals get out of work.

Cascade Theatre LIVE MUSIC
(Map p552; ☎530-243-8877; www.cascadetheatre.org; 1733 Market St) Try to catch some live music downtown at this refurbished 1935 art deco theater. Usually it hosts second-tier national acts, but if nothing else, take a peek inside; this is a neon-lit gem.

Information

California Welcome Center (☎530-365-1180; www.shastacascade.org; 1699 Hwy 273, Anderson; ⌚9am-5pm Mon-Fri, from 10am Sat & Sun) About 10 miles south of Redding, in Anderson's Prime Outlets Mall. It's an easy stop for northbound travelers, who are likely to pass it on the I-5 approach. It stocks maps for hiking and guides to outdoor activities, and the website has an excellent trip-planning section for the region.

Redding Visitors Bureau (Map p552; ☎530-225-4100; www.visitredding.com; 1448 Pine St; ⌚9am-5pm Mon-Fri, 10am-4pm Sat & Sun) Right in the heart of downtown Redding.

Shasta-Trinity National Forest Headquarters (☎530-226-2500; 3644 Avtech Pkwy; ⌚8am-4:30pm Mon-Fri) South of town, in the USDA Service Center near the airport. Has maps and free camping permits for all seven national forests in Northern California.

Getting There & Away

Redding Municipal Airport (RDD; http://ci.redding.ca.us/transeng/airports/rma.htm; 6751 Woodrum Circle, Redding) is 9.5 miles southeast of the city, just off Airport Rd. United Express flies to San Francisco.

The **Greyhound bus station** (Map p552; 1321 Butte St), adjacent to the Downtown Redding Mall, never closes. Destinations include San Francisco ($41, 8½ hours, four daily) and Reno, Nevada ($25, 7 hours, one daily). The Redding Area Bus Authority (RABA; www.rabaride.com) operates a dozen city routes until around 6pm Monday to Saturday. Fares start at $1.50 (exact change only).

The **Amtrak station** (www.amtrak.com; 1620 Yuba St), one block west of the Downtown Redding Mall, is not staffed. For the *Coast Starlight* service, make advance reservations by phone or via the website, then pay the conductor when you board the train. Amtrak travels once daily to Oakland ($45, six hours), Sacramento ($28, four hours) and Dunsmuir ($24, 1¾ hours).

Around Redding

Shasta State Historic Park

On Hwy 299, 6 miles west of Redding, this **state historic park** (☎520-243-8194; www.parks.ca.gov; 15312 CA 299; museum entry adult/child $3/2; ⌚10am-5pm Thu-Sun) preserves the ruins of an 1850s gold rush mining town called Shasta – not to be confused with Mt Shasta City. When the gold rush was at its height, everything and everyone passed through here. But when the railroad bypassed it to set up in Poverty Flats (present-day Redding), poor Shasta lost its raison d'être.

An 1861 courthouse contains the excellent museum, the best in this part of the state. With its amazing gun collection, spooky holograms in the basement and gallows out back, it's a thrill ride. Pick up walking-tour pamphlets from the information desk and follow trails to the beautiful Catholic cemetery, brewery ruins and other historic sites.

GETTING CRAFTY & DRAFTY IN REDDING

A handful of craft breweries, all making their own very unique brews, have opened in the last few years, giving folks more of a reason to veer off I-5 to stay in Redding a night. **Woody's Brewing Co.** (Map p552; ☎530-768-1034; www.woodysbrewing.biz; 1257 Oregon St; bar snacks from $3, meals $12-14; ⌚11am-10pm Tue-Thu, to 11pm Fri & Sat, to 9pm Sun) and **Fall River Brewing** (☎530-605-0230; www.fallriverbrewing.com; 1030 E Cypress Ave D; ⌚noon-10pm Mon-Thu, to midnight Fri & Sat, to 8pm Sun) were the two earliest, serving the more classic styles of beer, while the newer **Final Draft Brewing Company** (Map p552; ☎530-338-1198; www.finaldraftbrewingcompany.com; 1600 California St; ⌚11am-10pm Sun-Thu, to 11pm Fri & Sat) offers barrel-aged, sour beers and more. **Wildcard Brewing Company** (Map p552; ☎530-255-8582; www.wildcardbrewingco.com; 1321 Butte St; ⌚2-9pm Sun-Thu, to 10pm Fri & Sat) is the happy in-betweener with a little of everything and a convivial downtown location.

Whiskeytown Lake National Recreation Area

Sparkling **Whiskeytown Lake** (☎530-242-3400; www.nps.gov/whis; off Hwy 299, Whiskeytown; 7-day pass per car $10; P 🚻) takes its name from an old mining camp. When the lake was created in the 1960s by the construction of a 263ft dam, designed for power generation and Central Valley irrigation, the few remaining buildings of old Whiskeytown were moved and the camp was submerged.

The lake's serene 36-mile forested shoreline was the perfect place to camp while enjoying nonmotorized water sports until the 2018 Carr Fire burned 38,000 of the recreation area's 39,000 acres (this fire burned over 174,000 acres in total). The main trails and campsites have started to reopen but it will take years for the work to finish. It's still beautiful here with green regrowth contrasting with the sienna charred trees.

The **visitors center** (☎530-246-1225; www.nps.gov/whis; 14412 Kennedy Memorial Dr, Whiskeytown; ⏰10am-4pm) has knowledgeable staff that can answer your questions and let you know which areas are open. Look for ranger-led interpretive programs and guided walks. The hike to roaring **Whiskeytown Falls** (3.4 miles round-trip) follows a former logging road, opened in 2020, and is a good quick trip.

On the western side of the lake, the **Tower House Historic District** contains the El Dorado mine ruins and the pioneer Camden House, open for summer tours. In winter it's an atmospheric place to explore.

On the southern shore of the lake, Brandy Creek is ideal for swimming. Just off Hwy 299, on the northern edge of the lake, Oak Bottom Marina rents boats.

The nice but tightly packed **Oak Bottom Campground** (☎800-365-2267; www.whiskeytownmarinas.com; tent/RV sites $24/21; 🐾) is near the shore of Whiskeytown Lake. There's a parking lot for tent campers and you have to walk in a short distance to the campsites.

Shasta Lake

About 15 minutes north of Redding, Shasta Lake (www.shastalake.com) was created in the 1940s when Shasta Dam flooded towns, railways and 90% of the local Wintu tribal lands to make the largest reservoir in California. Today it's home to the state's biggest population of nesting bald eagles. Surrounded by hiking trails and campgrounds, the lake gets packed in summer. The lake is also home to more than 20 different kinds of fish, including rainbow trout.

DETOUR AROUND THE I-5 DOLDRUMS

A good alternative for travelers heading north and south on I-5 is to drive along Hwy 3 through the Scott Valley, which rewards with world-class views of the Trinity Alps. Compared to rushing along the dull highway, this scenic detour will add an additional half-day of driving.

Sights & Activities

The lake is known as the 'houseboat capital of the world,' and is very popular with boaters of all kinds. **Packer's Bay** is the best area for leg-stretcher hikes with easy access off I-5 (follow the Packer's Bay signs), but the prettiest trail (outside of summer months when the lack of shade can make it intensely hot) is the 7.5-mile loop of the **Clikapudi Trail**, which is also popular with mountain bikers and horseback riders. To get there, follow Bear Mountain Rd several miles until it dead-ends.

Lake Shasta Caverns CAVE

(☎530-238-2341; www.lakeshastacaverns.com; 20359 Shasta Caverns Rd, Lakehead; 2hr tour adult/child 3-15yr $30/18; ⏰tours every 30min 9am-4pm late May-early Sep, hourly 9am-3pm Apr-late May & early-late Sep, 10am, noon & 2pm Oct-Mar; P 🚻) High in the limestone megaliths at the north end of the lake hide these impressive caves. Tours through the many chambers dripping with massive formations operate daily and include a boat ride across Lake Shasta. Bring a sweater as the temperature inside is 58°F (14°C) year-round. With over 600 stairs, a decent level of fitness is required. On Friday and Saturday evenings in summer the company also runs sunset buffet dinner cruises on the lake.

To get there, take the Shasta Caverns Rd exit from I-5, about 15 miles north of Redding, and follow the signs for 1.5 miles.

Shasta Dam DAM

(☎530-247-8555; www.usbr.gov/mp/ncao/shasta-dam.html; 16349 Shasta Dam Blvd; ⏰visitor center 8am-5pm; P 🚻) FREE On scale with the enormous natural features of the area, this colossal, 15-million-ton concrete dam is second only in size to Grand Coolie Dam in

Washington state and second in height only to Hoover Dam in Nevada. The dam is located at the south end of the lake on Shasta Dam Blvd.

Built between 1937 and 1949, its 487ft spillway is nearly three times as high as the drop of Niagara Falls. Woody Guthrie wrote 'This Land Is Your Land' while he was here entertaining dam workers. The Shasta Dam visitors center offers a 21-minute video shown on request. Check the website to see if guided tours are available (they were halted in 2020 due to construction).

Sleeping & Eating

Hike-in camping and recreational vehicle (RV) parks are sprinkled around the lakeshore, and houseboats are popular. Most houseboats require a two-night minimum stay. Reserve as far in advance as possible, especially in summer. RV parks are often crowded and lack shade, but have on-site restaurants. For exploring the area on a day trip, stay in Redding.

Holiday Harbor Resort CAMPGROUND $
(530-238-2383; www.lakeshasta.com; Holiday Harbor Rd; tent & RV sites $48.50, houseboat per 2 nights from $1137;) Primarily an RV campground, it also rents houseboats (off-season rates are almost 50% lower) and the busy marina offers parasailing and fishing-boat rentals. A little café sits lakefront. It's off Shasta Caverns Rd, next to the lake.

Antlers RV Park & Campground CAMPGROUND $
(530-238-2322; www.shastalakevacations.com; 20679 Antlers Rd; tent & RV sites $35-50, trailer rentals $113-152;) East of I-5 in Lakehead, at the north end of the lake, this very popular, family-oriented campground has cabins, a country store and a marina renting watercraft and houseboats.

Lakeshore Inn & RV CAMPGROUND $
(530-238-2003; www.shastacamping.com; 20483 Lakeshore Dr; RV sites $25-40, cabins $100-225;) On the western side of I-5, this lakeside vacation park has a restaurant and tavern, horseshoes and basic cabins.

US Forest Service Campgrounds CAMPGROUND $
(info 530-275-1587, reservations 877-444-6777; www.recreation.gov; tent sites free-$46; P) About half of the campgrounds around Shasta Lake are open year-round. The lake's many fingers have a huge range of camping, with lake and mountain views, and some of them are very remote. Free boat-in sites are first-come, first-served – sites without boat launches will be far less busy.

MT LASSEN REGION

The dramatic crags, volcanic formations and alpine lakes of Lassen Volcanic National Park seem surprisingly untrammeled when you consider they are only a few hours from the Bay Area. Snowed in through most of winter, the park blossoms in late spring. While it is only 50 miles from Redding, and thus close enough to be enjoyed on a day trip, to really do it justice you'll want to invest a few days exploring the area along its scenic, winding roads. From Lassen Volcanic National Park you can take one of two very picturesque routes: Hwy 36, which heads east past Chester, Lake Almanor and historic Susanville; or Hwy 89, which leads southeast to the cozy mountain town of Quincy.

Lassen Volcanic National Park

The dry, smoldering, treeless terrain within this 106,000-acre **national park** (530-595-4480; www.nps.gov/lavo; 38050 Hwy 36 E, Mineral; 7-day entry per car mid-Apr–Nov $30, Dec–mid-Apr $10; P) stands in stunning contrast to the cool, green conifer forest that surrounds it. That's in summer; in winter tons of snow ensures you won't get too far inside its borders without some serious gear. Still, entering the park from the southwest entrance is to suddenly step into another world. The lavascape offers a fascinating glimpse into the earth's fiery core. In a fuming display the terrain is marked by roiling hot springs, steamy mud pots, noxious sulfur vents, fumaroles, lava flows, cinder cones, craters and crater lakes.

In earlier times the region was a summer encampment and meeting point for the Atsugewi, Yana, Yahi and Maidu Native American tribes. They hunted deer and gathered plants for basketmaking here. Some indigenous people still live nearby and work closely with the park to help educate visitors on their ancient history and contemporary culture.

Sights & Activities

Lassen Peak, the world's largest lava-dome volcano, rises 2000ft over the surrounding landscape to 10,463ft above sea level. Classified as an active volcano, its most recent,

DRIVING TOUR: THE LASSEN SCENIC BYWAY

Even in the peak of summer, the Lassen Scenic Byway is rarely busy. The long loop though Northern California wilderness skirts the edge of Lassen Volcanic National Park and circles Lassen Peak, one of the largest (arguably) dormant volcanoes on the planet. It mostly covers the big green patches on the map: expansive areas perfect for hiking, fishing, camping or just getting lost. This is a place where few people venture, and those who do come back with stories.

The launching point for this big loop could be either Redding or Sacramento, but there are few comforts for travelers along this course. The only cities in this neck of the woods – little places like Chester and Susanville – aren't all that exciting on their own; they're mostly just places to gas up, buy some beef jerky and enjoy the week's only hot meal. But the banner attractions are visible in every direction – the ominous, dormant volcanic peak of Lassen, the windswept high plains and the seemingly endless wilderness of the Lassen and Plumas National Forests.

This loop is formed by Hwy 36, Hwy 44 and Hwy 89. (See the map and some of the highlights at www.byways.org/explore/byways/2195.) It's best to do the drive between late June and mid-October. At other times some of these roads close due to snow.

sizeable eruption was in 1915, when it spewed a giant cloud of smoke, steam and ash 7 miles into the atmosphere. The national park was created the following year to protect the newly formed landscape. Some areas destroyed by the blast, including the aptly named **Devastated Area** northeast of the peak, are recovering impressively.

Hwy 89, the road through the park, wraps around Lassen Peak on three sides and provides access to dramatic geothermal formations, pure lakes, gorgeous picnic areas and remote hiking trails.

In total, the park has 150 miles of **hiking trails**, including a 17-mile section of the **Pacific Crest Trail**. Experienced hikers can attack the **Lassen Peak Trail**; it takes at least 4½ hours to make the 5-mile round-trip but the first 1.3 miles up to the Grandview viewpoint is suitable for families. The 360-degree view from the top is stunning, even if the weather is a bit hazy. Early in the season you'll need snow and ice-climbing equipment to reach the summit. Near the Kom Yah-mah-nee visitor facility, a gentler 2.3-mile trail, leads through meadows and forest to **Mill Creek Falls**. Further north on Hwy 89 you'll recognize the roadside **sulfur works** by its bubbling mud pots, hissing steam vent, fountains and fumaroles. At **Bumpass Hell** a moderate 1.5-mile trail and boardwalk leads to an active geothermal area, with bizarrely colored pools and billowing clouds of steam.

The road and trails wind through cinder cones, lava and lush alpine glades, with views of Juniper Lake, Snag Lake and the plains beyond. Most of the lakes at higher elevations remain partially and beautifully frozen in summer. Leave time to fish, swim or boat on **Manzanita Lake**, a slightly lower emerald gem near the northern entrance.

Sleeping & Eating

From the north on Hwy 89, you won't see many gas/food/lodgings signs after Mt Shasta City. Aside from the eight developed **campgrounds** (☎518 885 3639, reservations 877-444-6777; www.recreation.gov; tent & RV sites $12-26; P) in the park, there are many more in the surrounding Lassen National Forest. The nearest hotels and motels are in Chester, which accesses the south entrance of the park. There are some basic services near the split of Hwy 89 and Hwy 44, in the north.

You'll find a few modest places to eat in the small towns surrounding the park but for the most part you'll want to pack provisions.

North Entrance of the Park

Manzanita Lake Camping Cabins CABIN $
(☎May-Oct 530-779-0307, Nov-Apr 877-622-0221; www.lassenlodging.com; Hwy 89, near Manzanita Lake; cabins $71-95; ⏰May-Oct; P) These log cabins enjoy a lovely position on one of Lassen's lakes, and come in one- and two-bedroom options and slightly more basic eight-bunk configurations (a bargain for groups). They all have bear boxes, propane heaters and fire rings, but no bedding, electricity or running water. Shared bathrooms and coin-op hot showers are nearby.

Those who want to get a small taste of Lassen's more rustic comforts can call ahead to arrange a 'Camper's Amenity Package,'

Lassen Volcanic National Park

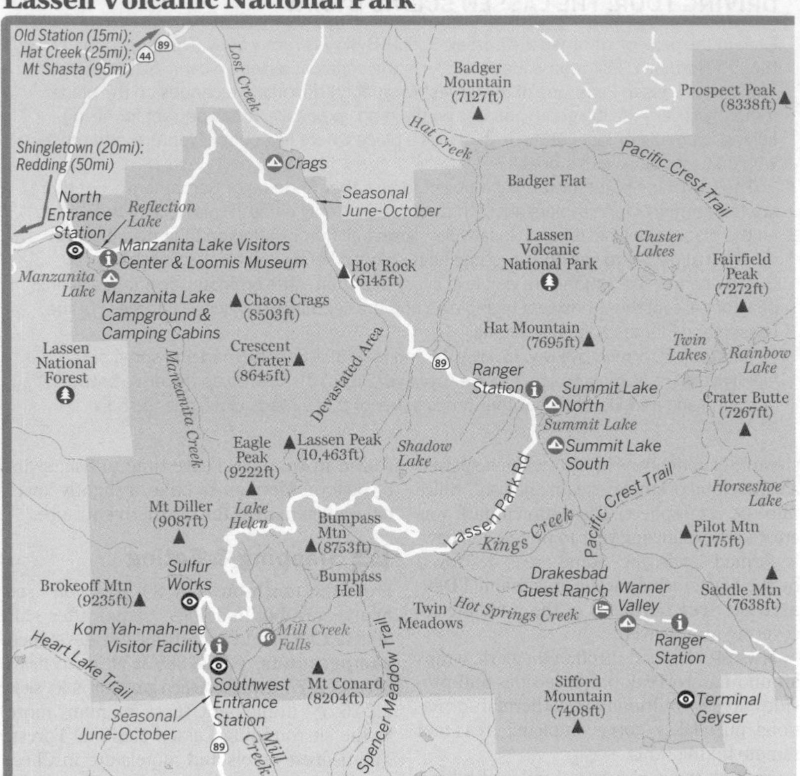

which includes basic supplies for a night under the stars (starting at $150, it includes a s'mores kit with graham crackers, chocolate and marshmallows).

Manzanita Lake Campground CAMPGROUND $
(☎ reservations 877-444-6777; www.recreation.gov; tent & RV sites $15-26; 🐾) The biggest camping area in these parts has lake access, views of Lassen, and 160 campsites with fire rings, picnic tables and bear boxes. There's a store, hot pay showers and kayak rentals here too.

Hat Creek Resort & RV Park CAMPGROUND $
(☎ 530-335-7121; www.hatcreekresortrv.com; 12533 Hwy 44/89, Old Station; tent sites $23-46, RV sites from $41, yurts $99-149, d $94-229, cabins $159-204; ⊙ Apr 15-Oct 31; 📶🐾) Outside the park, this place makes a decent stop before entering and is an OK choice. It sits along a fast-moving, trout-stocked creek. Some simple motel rooms and cabins have full kitchens. Stock up at the convenience store and deli, then eat on a picnic table by the river.

South Entrance of the Park

Mt Lassen/Shingletown KOA CAMPGROUND $
(☎ 530-474-3133; www.koa.com; 7749 KOA Rd; tent sites $40, RV sites from $61, cabins $82-301; ⊙ mid-Mar–Nov; 📶🏊🐾) Enjoy all the standard KOA amenities: a playground, a deli and laundry facilities. It's off Hwy 44 in Shingletown, about 20 miles west of the park.

Village at Childs Meadow CABIN $
(☎ 530-595-3383; www.thevillageatchildsmeadow.com; 41500 E Hwy 36, Mill Creek; tent/RV sites from $30/45, motel rooms from $164; 📶🐾) At the edge of a spectacularly lush mountain meadow, 9 miles outside the park's southwest entrance, sits this recently remodeled yet still old fashioned-feeling mountain-resort. Campsites are well spaced out and good value plus a new cafe at the entrance serves breakfast and lunch.

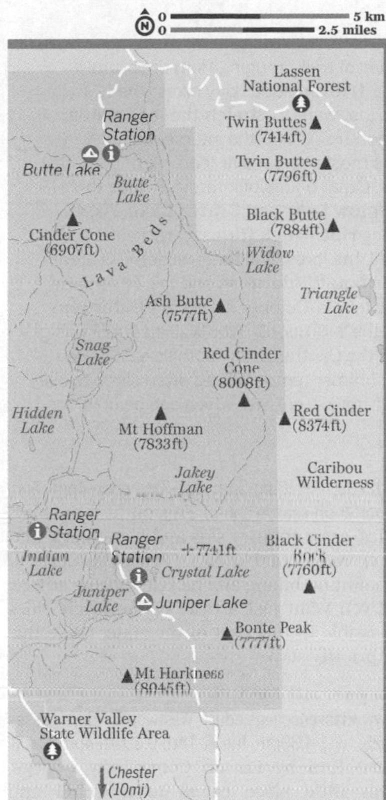

Drakesbad Guest Ranch RESORT $$$
(☎530-529-1512, ext 120; www.lassenlodging.com; Warner Valley Rd; s/d from $220/394; ⊙Jun-early Oct;) Seventeen miles northwest of Chester, this fabulously secluded place lies inside the park's boundary. Guests, often repeat visitors, use the hot-springs-fed swimming pool or go horseback riding. There's limited electricity (think kerosene lamps and campfires). Rates include three country-style meals (vegetarian options available) per day, kids under six stay free and seven- to 14-year-olds are $75 per day.

This is one of the few places in the region to book up solidly, so make advance reservations.

Information

Whether you enter at the north or southwest entrance, you'll be given a free map with general information.

Kom Yah-mah-nee Visitor Facility (☎530-595-4480; www.nps.gov/lavo; 21820 Lassen National Park Hwy, Mineral; ⊙9am-5pm, closed Mon & Tue Nov-Apr;) About half a mile north of the park's southwest entrance, this handsome center is certified at the highest standard by the US Green Building Council. Inside there are educational exhibits (including a cool topographical volcano), a bookstore, an auditorium, a gift shop and a restaurant. Visitor information and maps available.

Manzanita Lake Visitors Center & Loomis Museum (☎530-595-4480; ⊙9am-5pm Jun-Sep) Just past the entrance-fee station at the park's northern boundary, you can see exhibits and an orientation video inside this museum. During summer, rangers and volunteers lead programs on geology, wildlife, astronomy and local culture. Visitor information and maps available.

Getting There & Away

There's virtually no way to visit this park without a car, though all the two-lane roads around the park and the ample free national-forest camping options make for excellent, if fairly serious, cycle touring.

The park has two entrances. The northern entrance, at Manzanita Lake, is 50 miles east of Redding via Hwy 44. The southwest entrance is on Hwy 89, about 5 miles north of the junction with Hwy 36. From this junction it is 5 miles west on Hwy 36 to Mineral and 44 miles west to Red Bluff. Heading east on Hwy 36, Chester is 25 miles away and Susanville about 60 miles. Quincy is 65 miles southeast from the junction on Hwy 89.

Lassen National Forest

The vast Lassen National Forest (www.fs.fed.us/r5/lassen) surrounding Lassen Peak and Lassen Volcanic National Park is so big that it's hard to comprehend: it covers 1.2 million acres (1875 sq miles) of wilderness in an area called the Crossroads, where the granite Sierra, volcanic Cascades, Modoc Plateau and Central Valley meet. It's largely unspoiled land, though if you wander too far off the byways surrounding the park, you'll certainly see evidence of logging and mining operations that still happen within its borders.

The Lassen National Forest supervisor's office is in Susanville. Other ranger offices include **Eagle Lake Ranger District** (☎530-257-4188; 477-050 Eagle Lake Rd, Susanville), **Hat Creek Ranger District** (☎530-336-5521; 43225 E Hwy 299, Fall River Mills; ⊙Mon-Fri) and **Almanor Ranger District** (Lassen National Forest; ☎530-258-2141; www.fs.usda.gov; 900 CA 36, Chester; ⊙8am-4:30pm Mon-Fri), about a mile west of Chester.

LASSEN NATIONAL FOREST HIKES

The forest has some serious hikes, with 460 miles of trails, ranging from the brutally challenging (120 miles of the **Pacific Crest Trail**) to ambitious day hikes (the 12-mile Spencer Meadows National Recreation Trail), to just-want-to-stretch-the-legs-a-little trails (the 3.5-mile Heart Lake National Recreation Trail). Near the intersection of Hwys 44 and 89, visitors to the area will find one of the most spectacular features of the forest, the pitch-black 600yd **Subway Cave** lava tube. Other points of interest include the 1.5-mile volcanic **Spattercone Crest Trail**, **Willow Lake** and **Crater Lake**, 7684ft **Antelope Peak** and the 900ft-high, 14-mile-long **Hat Creek Rim** escarpment.

For those seeking to get far off the beaten trail, the forest has three wilderness areas. Two high-elevation wilderness areas are the **Caribou Wilderness** and the **Thousand Lakes Wilderness**, best visited from mid-June to mid-October. The **Ishi Wilderness** (named after Ishi, the last surviving member of the Yahi people, who walked out of this wilderness in 1911), at a much lower elevation in the Central Valley foothills east of Red Bluff, is more comfortable in spring and fall, as summer temperatures often climb to over 100°F (37°C). It harbors California's largest migratory deer herd, which can be upwards of 20,000 head.

Lake Almanor Area

Calm, turquoise Lake Almanor lies south of Lassen Volcanic National Park via Hwys 89 and 36. This human-made lake is a crystalline example of California's sometimes awkward conservation and land-management policy: the lake was created by the Great Western Power Company and is now ostensibly owned by the Pacific Gas & Electric Company. The lake is surrounded by lush meadows and tall evergreens and was once little-visited. A 3000-acre ski resort sits on the hills above, with properties continually being developed near its shore and power boats zipping across its surface. The northeastern section has become particularly ritzy and there are even a few gated communities. On the rugged southern end you'll find miles with nothing but pine trees.

The main town near the lake, Chester (population 2144, elevation 4528ft), isn't a looker, but plans are in the works for a makeover that includes a town plaza. Though you could whiz by and dismiss it as a few blocks of nondescript roadside storefronts, this little community has a fledgling art scene hidden along the back roads. It also offers some comfy places to stay but none as exciting or woodsy as you'll find along the lake.

Activities

You can rent boats and water-sports equipment at many places around the lake.

Bodfish Bicycles & Quiet Mountain Sports CYCLING
(530-258-2338; www.bodfishbicycles.com; 149 Main St, Chester; bicycle rental per hour/day $12/35; 10am-5pm Tue-Sat, noon-4pm Sun, shorter off-season hours) This outfit rents bicycles, cross-country skis and snowshoes, and sells canoes and kayaks. It's a great source of mountain-biking and bicycle-touring advice. If you want just a taste of the lovely rides possible in this part of the state, make this a priority stop.

Coppervale Ski Hill SKIING
(www.lassencollege.edu; Westwood; day passes $25; 1-4:30pm Tue & Thu, 9:30am-4pm Sat & Sun) Run by Lassen Community College, this little place caters to downhill and cross-country skiers as well as snowboarders. There are eight trails and 740ft of vertical drop.

Sleeping & Eating

The best sleeping options for campers are in the surrounding national forest.

Chester

Along Chester's main drag you'll find a scattering of 1950s-style inns and a few chain lodgings (the nicest of which is the fairly overpriced Best Western Rose Quartz Inn). Many of these places keep seasonal hours, and when you live in a place where it can snow in mid-June, the season is short.

St Bernard Lodge B&B $
(530-258-3382; www.stbernardlodge.com; 44801 E Hwy 36, Mill Creek; d without bath from $102;) Located 10 miles west of Chester, this old-world charmer has seven B&B rooms with views to the mountains and forest. All have knotty-pine paneling and

quilted bedspreads. There are stables where those traveling with a horse can board them and have access to the nearby network of Lassen's trails. The tavern is good too, serving meaty American-style fare.

Bidwell House B&B B&B **$$**
(☎ 530-258-3338; www.bidwellhouse.com; 1 Main St; d $125-260, without bath $80-175, cottage $175-285;) Set back from the street, this historic summer home of pioneers John and Annie Bidwell is packed with antiques. The classic accommodations come with all the modern amenities (including a spa in some rooms) – no roughing it here. Enjoy goodies like a three-course breakfast, home-baked cookies and afternoon sherry.

★**Cravings** AMERICAN **$**
(☎ 530-258-2229; 278 Main St; mains $8-16; 8am-2pm Thu-Sun;) You'll get cravings for this place once you're gone. Think fresh, home-made classics like crispy waffles or rustic Reuben sandwiches made to big-city-worthy standards. They make their own delectable pastries and pump out quality espresso with small-town smiles. The historic-building location includes a dedicated cafe, bookstore/visitor center and creekside dining. Gluten-free and vegetarian-friendly.

Around the Lake

Book ahead for lakefront lodgings in summer. There are restaurants at the resorts.

PG&E Recreational Area Campgrounds CAMPGROUND **$**
(☎ 916-386-5164; http://recreation.pge.com; tent & RV sites from $23; May-Sep;) A favorite for tents and RVs, Rocky Point Campground is right on the lake, with some sites basically on the beach. For something more remote, try Cool Springs Campground or Ponderosa Flat Campground, both at Butt Reservoir near the lake's south shore, at the end of Prattville Butt Reservoir Rd.

Lake Almanor Campgrounds CAMPGROUND **$**
(☎ 877-444-6777; www.recreation.gov; tent sites $15-18, RV sites $29-36; late May-early Sep) Large wooded campground on the lake. RVs can camp here, but there are no hookups.

North Shore Campground CAMPGROUND **$**
(☎ 530-258-3376; www.northshorecampground.com; 541 Catfish Beach Rd; tent sites $40, RV sites $50-60, cabins $170-279; May-Oct;) Two miles east of Chester on Hwy 36, these expansive, forested grounds stretch for a mile along the water, and get filled up with mostly RVs. Ranch-style cabins have kitchens and are great for families. This place is fine if you want to spend all your time doing water sports on the lake, but those seeking the solitude of nature should look elsewhere.

Knotty Pine Resort & Marina CABIN **$$**
(☎ 530-596-3348; www.knottypine.net; 430 Peninsula Dr; d $165, 2-bedroom cabins with kitchen $180-230;) This full-service lakeside alternative, 7 miles east of Chester, has simple cabins, rents boats, kayaks and canoes, and is open year-round.

Tantardino's ITALIAN **$$**
(☎ 530-596-3902; www.tantardinos.com; 401 Ponderosa Dr, Lake Almanor Peninsula; mains $16-21, pizzas $12-26; 11:30am-8:30pm Tue-Sat) This is hands down the locals' favorite place to eat in the region – even folks from Susanville drive the 32 miles to get here, with pleasure, for the excellent Sicillian-style lasagna, yummy pizzas and meatball or caprese sandwiches at lunchtime. It's lively, friendly and you can eat and drink outside in summer. Reserve ahead for dinner.

★**Red Onion Grill** MODERN AMERICAN **$$$**
(☎ 530-258-1800; www.redoniongrill.com; 303 Peninsula Dr, Westwood; mains $16-39; 11am-9pm, Wed-Sun, shorter hours Oct-Apr) The finest dining on the lake with upscale New American, Italian-influenced cuisine (like the simply prepared shrimp scampi), and bar food that's executed with panache.

Information

Get information about lodging and recreation around the lake, in Lassen National Forest and in Lassen Volcanic National Park at **B&B Booksellers** (☎ 530-258-2150; 278 Main St, Chester; 9am-4pm) that acts as the visitor center.

KNOW ABOUT THE SNOW

Lassen Volcanic National Park has a very short season from around the beginning of June to the beginning of September. Lower elevations open up earlier but you can expect many services to be shut between October and May. That said, the winter is an incredibly peaceful time to visit as long as the roads are open!

WORTH A TRIP

WILD HORSE SANCTUARY

Since 1978 the **Wild Horse Sanctuary** (530-474-5770; www.wildhorsesanctuary.com; 5796 Wilson Hill Rd, Shingletown; free; 10am-4pm Wed & Sat) FREE has been sheltering horses and burros that would otherwise have been destroyed. You can visit its humble visitor center on Wednesdays and Saturdays to see these lovely animals or even volunteer for a day, with advance arrangement. To see them on the open plains, take a one-day or multiday ride (contact the sanctuary for availability). Shingletown lies 20 miles to the west of Lassen Volcanic National Park.

Getting There & Away

Plumas Transit (530-283-2538; www.plumastransit.com; fares $1-4) runs buses to Quincy ($4) while Lassen Rural Bus has services to Susanville ($4).

Susanville

Though it sits on a lovely high desert plateau, the Lassen County seat isn't much of a charmer; it's a resupply post with a Wal-Mart, a few stop lights and two prisons. Although not a tourist destination in itself, it provides good services for travelers passing through. It lies 35 miles east of Lake Almanor and 85 miles northwest of Reno – and is home to a couple of modest historic sites. The town's oldest building, **Roop's Fort** (1853), is named after Susanville's founder, Isaac Roop. The fort was a trading post on the Nobles Trail, a California emigrant route. The town itself was named after Roop's daughter, Susan.

Beside Roops Fort is the friendly **Lassen Historical Museum** (530-257-3292; 75 N Weatherlow St; admission by donation; 10am-2pm Tue-Sat), with well-presented displays of clothing and memorabilia from the area, which are worth a 20-minute visit.

The restored **Railroad Depot Visitors Center** (530-257-3252; 601 Richmond Rd; 10am-4pm May-Oct), beside the Bizz Johnson Trail terminus, rents bicycles and has brochures on mountain-biking trails in the area. The best event in town is the **Lassen County Fair** (530-251-8900; www.lassencountyfair.org; $8; Jul), which swings into gear in July.

Motels along Main St average $70 to $100 per night. **Red Lion Inn & Suites** (530-257-3450; www.redlion.com; 3015 Riverside Dr; r $87-159;) is the best of these. For more character, try **Roseberry House B&B** (530-257-5675; www.roseberryhouse.com; 609 North St; r/ste $140/165;). This sweet 1902 Victorian house is two blocks north of Main St. Striking darkwood antique headboards and armoires combine with rosebuds and frill. There are nice little touches, like bath salts and candy dishes. Expect homemade muffins and jam as part of the full breakfast.

To eat, head to **Lassen Ale Works** (530-257-7666; www.lassenaleworks.com; 724 Main St; mains $10-25; 4-10pm Mon-Thu, 11am-midnight Fri & Sat). In the renovated c 1862 Pioneer Saloon, this place looks like nothing from the outside but opens up to a big and bustling space. It's known for its fish-and-chips but everything from steaks to Reuben sandwiches are fresh and as good as the service. Try one of the seven signature brews like the Pioneer Porter or Almanor Amber.

For local information visit the **Lassen County Chamber of Commerce** (530-257-4323; www.lassencountychamber.org; 1516 Main St; 9am-4pm Mon-Fri), while the **Lassen National Forest supervisor's office** (530-257-2151; 2550 Riverside Dr; 8am-4:30pm Mon-Fri) has maps and recreation information for getting into the surrounding wilds.

Sage Stage (530-233-6410; www.sagestage.com) runs buses to Redding via Alturas ($25) and south to Reno ($16.50). **Lassen Rural Bus** (530-252-7433; www.lassentransportation.com; fares $1-4) runs local buses (fare $1) and buses to nearby destinations like Chester ($4) and the Eagle Lake area ($2-3).

Eagle Lake

Those who have the time to get all the way out to Eagle Lake, California's second-largest natural lake, are rewarded with a stunningly blue jewel on the high plateau. From late spring until fall this lovely lake, about 15 miles northwest of Susanville, attracts a smattering of visitors who come to cool off, swim, fish, boat and camp. On the south shore, you'll find a pristine 5-mile **recreational trail** and several busy **campgrounds** (information 530-257-4188, reservations 877-444-6777; www.recreation.gov; tent/RV sites from $20/30) administered by Lassen National Forest and the **Bureau of Land Management** (BLM; 530-257-0456; www.blm.gov; 2550 Riverside Dr, Susanville; 7:45am-4:30pm Mon-Fri). **Eagle Lake Marina** (530-825-3454; www.eaglelakerecreationarea.

com), close by, has shower and laundry facilities, and can help you get out onto the lake with a fishing license.

Eagle Lake RV Park (☎530-825-3133; www.eaglelakeandrv.com; 687-125 Palmetto Way; tent/RV sites $25/40, cabins $40-200; ⏲May-Oct;), on the western shore, and **Eagle Lake Resort** (☎530-251-6770; www.eaglelakerv.com; Stones Landing; RV sites $33;), on the quieter northern shore, both rent boats.

Quincy

Idyllic Quincy is nestled in a high valley in the northern Sierra, southeast of Lassen Volcanic National Park via Hwy 89. It's a lovely and happy little place, endowed with just enough edge by the student population of the local Feather River College. Nearby Feather River, Plumas National Forest, Tahoe National Forest and their oodles of open space make Quincy an excellent base from which to explore.

Just about everything you need is on or close to two one-way streets: Main St with traffic heading east, and Lawrence St heading west. Jackson St runs parallel to Main St, one block south, and is another main artery, making up Quincy's low-key commercial district.

Sights & Activities

Pick up free hiking-, biking- and driving-tour pamphlets from the Plumas National Forest Headquarters (p564) to guide you through the gorgeous surrounding **American Valley**. The **Feather River Scenic Byway** (Hwy 70) leads into the Sierra. In summer the icy waters of county-namesake **Feather River** (*plumas* is Spanish for 'feathers') are excellent for swimming, kayaking, fishing and floating in old inner tubes. The area is also a wonderland of winter activities, especially at Bucks Lake.

Plumas County Museum MUSEUM
(☎530-283-6320; www.plumasmuseum.org; 500 Jackson St, at Coburn St; adult/child $5/free; ⏲10am-4pm Tue-Sat & sometimes Sun;) Behind the courthouse, this multifloor county museum has flowering gardens, as well as hundreds of historical photos and relics from the county's pioneer and Maidu days, its early mining and timber industries, and construction of the Western Pacific Railroad. For the price, it's definitely worth the stop.

Plumas County Courthouse HISTORIC BUILDING
(www.plumascourt.ca.gov; 520 Main St) Pop into the 1921 Plumas County Courthouse, at the west end of Main St, to see enormous interior marble posts and staircases, and a 1-ton bronze-and-glass chandelier in the lobby.

Big Daddy's Guide Service FISHING
(☎530-283-4103; www.bigdaddyfishing.com; trips per person from $200) Captain Bryan Roccucci is Big Daddy, the best-known fishing guide in Northeast California. He knows the lakes well and leads trips for all levels.

Festivals & Events

★**High Sierra Music Festival** MUSIC
(www.highsierramusic.com; ⏲Jul) On the first weekend in July, quiet Quincy is host to this blowout festival, renowned statewide. The four-day extravaganza brings a five-stage smorgasbord of art and music from a spectrum of cultural corners (indie rock, classic blues, folk and jazz). Past acts include Thievery Corporation, Lauryn Hill, Primus, Ben Harper and Neko Case.

Sleeping

Ranchito Motel MOTEL $
(☎530-286-2265; www.ranchitomotel.com; 2020 E Main St; d from $76;) With antique timber pillars, white-painted brick walls, old barn-style doors and the occasional wagon wheel for decoration, this friendly motel (in the eastern half of town) definitely has a Mexican ranch feel. Inside, rooms are modern, freshly painted and very comfortable for the price. The motel offers plenty more choices on the wooded land that extends back a few acres.

Pine Hill Motel MOTEL $
(☎530-283-1670; www.pinehillmotel.com; 42075 Hwy 70; s/d/cabins from $75/80/160;) A mile west of downtown Quincy, this little hotel is fronted by a manicured, flower-bedecked lawn dotted with white tables and chairs. The units are simple but clean and country cosy with knotty pine walls and colorful quilts on the beds. Each is equipped with microwave, coffeemaker and refrigerator; some cabins have full kitchens.

Feather River Canyon Campgrounds CAMPGROUND $
(☎reservations 877-444-6777; www.fs.usda.gov; tent/RV sites $25/32) Area campgrounds are administered through the Mt Hough Ranger District Office (p564). They are in a cluster along the north fork of the Feather River west of Quincy – five are no-fee, but also have no piped water. All are first-come, first-served.

Open season ranges from April or May through September or October depending on the location.

★Quincy Courtyard Suites APARTMENT $$
(☎530-283-1401; www.quincycourtyardsuites.com; 436 Main St; apt $149-189; P ⊖ ≈) Staying in this beautifully renovated 1908 Clinch building, overlooking the small main drag of Quincy's downtown, feels just right, like renting the village's cutest apartment. The warmly decorated rooms are modern – no fussy clutter – and apartments have spacious, modern kitchens, claw-foot tubs and gas fireplaces.

Ada's Place Motel Cottages MOTEL $$
(☎530-283-1954; www.adasplace.com; 562 Jackson St; cottages $130-160; ❄ ≈) Even though it feels like a B&B, without breakfast, Ada's is just an excellent B and calls itself a motel. No problem, as each of the three brightly painted garden units has a full kitchen. Ada's Cottage is worth the slight extra charge, as its skylights offer an open feel. It's very quiet and private, yet right in town.

Greenhorn Guest Ranch RANCH $$$
(☎800-334-6939; www.greenhornranch.com; 2116 Greenhorn Ranch Rd; all inclusive per person per day incl meals and trail rides from $268; ⊙May 15th-Oct 31st; ≈ ≋ 🐾) Not a 'dude' ranch but rather a 'guest' ranch: instead of shoveling stalls, guests are pampered with mountain-trail rides, riding lessons, even rodeo practice. Or you can just fish, hike, square-dance and attend evening bonfires, cookouts and frog races – think of it as a cowboy version of the getaway resort in *Dirty Dancing*.

Eating & Drinking

★Pangaea Cafe & Pub CAFE $
(☎530-283-0426; www.pangaeapub.com; 461 W Main St; mains $11-14; ⊙11am-9pm Mon-Fri; ≈ ✎ 👪) This earthy spot is all the more lovable when you consider its commitment to serving local produce. Choose from regional beef burgers, salmon sushi, a slew of sandwiches (many veggie), quesadillas and rice bowls. It's hopping with locals drinking craft brews, kids running around and lots of hugging.

Farmers Market MARKET $
(www.quincyfarmersmarket.org; 530 W Main St; ⊙9am-2pm Sun mid-Jul–mid-Sep) Everything from fruits and veggies to handmade soaps, crafts and more. Enjoy it all to live music.

Morning Thunder Café BREAKFAST $
(☎530-283-3300; 557 Lawrence St; mains $9-17; ⊙7am-2pm; ✎) Homey and hip, this is the best place in town for breakfast, and the vine-shaded patio is a lovely way to start the day. The menu has plenty of meaty or vegetarian options and portions are huge. Try the 'vegetaters' (roasted veg and potatoes smothered in cheese). The restaurant is a no-cellphone zone so bring a friend or a book.

Sweet Lorraine's CALIFORNIAN $$
(384 Main St; mains $18-27; ⊙11:30am-2pm Mon-Fri, 5-8pm Tue-Sat) On a warm day – or, better yet, evening – the patio here is especially sweet. The menu features basic Californian cuisine (ribs, pork chops, half a roast chicken, soups and salads) and the ambience is woodsy and local. Finish things off with the delicious whiskey bread pudding.

Moon's ITALIAN $$
(☎530-283-0765; www.moons-restaurant.com; 497 Lawrence St; mains $13-29; ⊙5-9pm daily Jun-Oct, Tue-Sun Nov-May) Follow the aroma of garlic to this welcoming little chalet with a charming ambience. Dig into choice steaks and Italian-American classics, including excellent pizza and rich lasagna.

Quintopia Brewing Co BREWERY
(☎530-289-6530; www.quintopiabrewing.com; 541 Main St; ⊙3-9pm Wed-Fri, noon-9pm Sat & Sun) A great addition to Quincy, the easy-drinking, crowd-pleasing beers here are even better when paired with a bar snack like lemon, garlic, parmesan fries or a falafel salad. Add the friendly local crowd, plus events including live music or trivia, and you'll want to hang out here every night.

Drunk Brush WINE BAR
(☎530-283-9380; www.facebook.com/TheDrunkBrush; 436 Main St; ⊙2-7pm Mon-Wed, to 10pm Thu & Fri, to 8pm Sat) A sweet little courtyard wine bar that pours 25 wines and a few beers. Sample delicious appetizer pairings in a welcoming, arty atmosphere and sometimes to live music.

Information

Mt Hough Ranger District Office (☎530-283-0555; www.fs.usda.gov; 39696 Hwy 70; ⊙8am-4:30pm Mon-Fri) Five miles northwest of town. Has maps and outdoors information.

Plumas National Forest Headquarters (☎530-283-2050; www.fs.usda.gov; 159 Lawrence St; ⊙8am-4:30pm Mon-Fri) For maps and outdoors information.

Bucks Lake

This clear mountain lake is cherished by locals in the know. Surrounded by pine forests, it's excellent for swimming, fishing and boating. It's about 17 miles southwest of Quincy, via the white-knuckle roads of Bucks Lake Rd (Hwy 119). The region is lined with beautiful **hiking trails**, including the **Pacific Crest Trail**, which passes through the adjoining 21,000-acre Bucks Lake Wilderness in the northwestern part of Plumas National Forest. In winter, the last 3 miles of Bucks Lake Rd are closed by snow, making it ideal for cross-country skiers.

Bucks Lake Lodge (☎530-283-2262; www.buckslakecabinrentals.com; 16525 Bucks Lake Rd; d $99-109, cabins $145-195;) is right on the lakeshore and its restaurant is popular with locals. **Haskins Valley Inn** (☎530-283-9667; www.haskinsvalleyinn.com; 1305 Haskins Circle; r $129-149;) is actually a B&B just across the street from the lake, with cozily overstuffed furnishings, woodsy paintings, Jacuzzis, fireplaces and a deck.

Five first-come, first-served campgrounds (www.fs.usda.gov) are open from June to September. Get a map at the Plumas National Forest Headquarters or Mt Hough Ranger District Office, both in Quincy.

Aside from the lodge and B&B, you'll need to bring your own grub to this rustic area.

MT SHASTA AREA

'Lonely as God, and white as a winter moon,' wrote poet Joaquin Miller about this lovely mountain. The sight of it is so awe-inspiring that the new-age claims about its power as an 'energy vortex' sound plausible even after a first glimpse.

There are a million ways to explore the mountain and surrounding Shasta-Trinity National Forest – take scenic drives or get out and hike, mountain bike, raft, ski or snowshoe. At Mt Shasta's base sit three excellent little towns: Dunsmuir, Mt Shasta City and McCloud. Each has a distinct personality, but all hold a wild-mountain sensibility and first-rate amenities. Find the snaggle-toothed peaks of Castle Crags just 6 miles west of Dunsmuir.

A long drive northeast of Mt Shasta and a world away is eerily beautiful Lava Beds National Monument, a blistered badland of petrified fire. The contrasting wetlands of Klamath Basin National Wildlife Refuges lie just west.

Many services and some roads close in winter so summer is a far easier time to visit. However, winter is a peaceful and beautiful time to come here.

Mt Shasta

'When I first caught sight of it I was 50 miles away and afoot, alone and weary. Yet all my blood turned to wine, and I have not been weary since,' wrote naturalist John Muir of Mt Shasta in 1874. Mt Shasta's beauty is intoxicating, and the closer you get to her the headier you begin to feel. Dominating the landscape, the mountain is visible for more than 100 miles from many parts of Northern California and southern Oregon. Though not California's highest peak (at 14,179ft it ranks fifth), Mt Shasta is especially magnificent because it rises alone on the horizon, unrivaled by other mountains.

Mt Shasta is part of the vast volcanic Cascade chain that includes Lassen Peak to the south and Mt Rainier to the north in Washington state. Thermal hot springs indicate that Mt Shasta is dormant, not extinct. The last eruption was about 200 years ago.

History

The story of the first settlers here is a sadly familiar one. European fur trappers arrived in the area in the 1820s, encountering several Native American tribes, including the Shasta, Karuk, Klamath, Modoc, Wintu and Pit River people. By 1851, hordes of gold-rush miners had arrived and steamrolled the place, destroying the tribes' traditional life and nearly causing their extinction. Later, the newly completed railroad began to import workers and export timber for the booming lumber industry. And since Mt Shasta City (called Sisson at the time) was the only non-dry town around, it became *the* bawdy, good-time hangout for lumberjacks.

The lumberjacks have now been replaced by middle-aged mystics and outdoor-sports enthusiasts. While the slopes have immediate appeal for explorers, spiritual seekers are attracted to the peak's reported cosmic properties. In 1987, about 5000 believers from around the world convened here for the Harmonic Convergence, a communal meditation for peace. Reverence for the mountain is nothing new; for centuries Native Americans have honored the mountain as sacred,

Mt Shasta Area

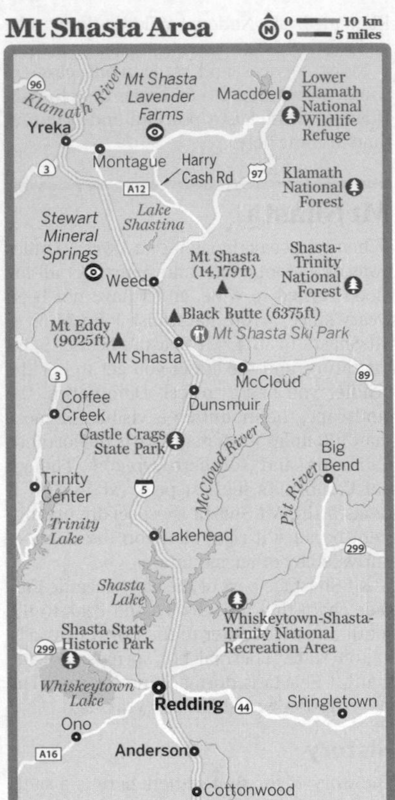

considering it to be no less than the Great Spirit's wigwam.

Sights & Activities

The Mountain

You'll come across views of **Mt Shasta** (530-926-4511; www.fs.usda.gov/stnf; Everitt Memorial Hwy; P) either peaking over a ridge or completely dominating the landscape, from the Oregon border and even into the east toward Tule Lake. The mountain has two cones: the main cone has a crater about 200yd across, and the younger, shorter cone on the western flank, called Shastina, has a crater about half a mile wide.

You can drive almost the whole way up the mountain via the Everitt Memorial Hwy (Hwy A10) and see exquisite views at any time of year. Simply head east on Lake St from downtown Mt Shasta City, then turn left onto Washington Dr and keep going. **Bunny Flat** (6860ft), which has a trailhead for Horse Camp and the Avalanche Gulch summit route, is a busy place with parking spaces, information signboards and a toilet. The section of highway beyond Bunny Flat is only open from about mid-June to October, depending on snow, but if it's clear, it's worth the trouble. This road leads to **Lower Panther Meadow**, where trails connect the campground to a Wintu sacred spring, in the upper meadows near the **Old Ski Bowl** (7800ft) parking area. Shortly thereafter is the highlight of the drive, **Everitt Vista Point** (7900ft), where a short interpretive walk from the parking lot leads to a stone-walled outcrop affording exceptional views of Lassen Peak to the south, the Mt Eddy and Marble Mountains to the west and the whole Strawberry Valley below.

Climbing the summit is best done between May and September, preferably in spring and early summer, when there's still enough soft snow on the southern flank to make footholds easier on the nontechnical route. Although the elements are occasionally volatile and the winds are incredibly strong, the round-trip could conceivably be done in one day with 12 or more hours of solid hiking. A more enjoyable trip takes at least two days with one night on the mountain. How long it actually takes depends on the route selected, the physical condition of the climbers and weather conditions (for weather information, call the recorded message of the Forest Service Mt Shasta climbing advisory on 530-926-9613).

The hike to the summit from Bunny Flat follows the **Avalanche Gulch Route**. Although it is only about 7 miles, the vertical climb is more than 7000ft, so acclimatizing to the elevation is important – even hearty hikers will be short of breath. Additionally, this route requires crampons, an ice axe and a helmet, all of which can be rented locally. Rock slides, while rare, are also a hazard. If you want to make the climb without gear, the only option is the **Clear Creek Route** to the top, which leaves from the east side of the mountain. In late summer, this route is usually manageable in hiking boots, though there's still loose scree, and it should be done as an overnight hike. Novices should contact the Mt Shasta Ranger Station (p570) for a list of available guides.

There's a charge to climb beyond 10,000ft: a three-day summit pass costs $25; an annual pass is $30. Contact the ranger station for details. You must obtain a free wilderness permit any time you go into the wilderness, whether on the mountain or in the surrounding area.

Mt Shasta Ski Park SNOW SPORTS
(☎ snow reports 530-926-8686; www.skipark.com; 4500 Ski Park Hwy, McCloud; full-day weekend lift tickets adult/child $69/49; ⏰ 9am-4pm Sun-Fri, to 6pm Sat) On the south slope of Mt Shasta, off Hwy 89 heading toward McCloud, this winter skiing and snowboarding park opens depending on snowfall. The park has a 1435ft vertical drop, 32 alpine runs and 18 miles of cross-country trails. These are all good for beginner and intermediate skiers, and are a less-crowded alternative to the slopes around Lake Tahoe.

The Lakes

There are a number of pristine mountain lakes near Mt Shasta. Some of them are accessible only by dirt roads or hiking trails and are great for getting away from it all.

The closest lake to Mt Shasta City is lovely **Lake Siskiyou** (also the largest), 2.5 miles southwest on Old Stage Rd, where you can peer into **Box Canyon Dam**, a 200ft-deep chasm. Another 7 miles up in the mountains, southwest of Lake Siskiyou on Castle Lake Rd, lies **Castle Lake**, an unspoiled gem surrounded by granite formations and pine forest. Swimming, fishing, picnicking and free camping are popular in summer; in winter folks ice-skate on the lake. **Lake Shastina**, about 15 miles northwest of town, off Hwy 97, is another beauty.

Mt Shasta City

Comfortable and practical Mt Shasta City glows in the shadow of the white pyramid of Mt Shasta. The downtown is charming; you can spend hours poking around crystal shops and galleries. Orienting yourself is easy with the mountain looming over the east side of town and you may get a kink in your neck from admiring it. The downtown area is a few blocks east of I-5. Take the Central Mt Shasta exit, then drive east on Lake St past the visitor center, up to the town's main intersection at Mt Shasta Blvd, the principal drag.

Sights & Activities

To head out hiking on your own, first stop by the ranger station or the visitors center for excellent free trail guides, including several access points along the **Pacific Crest Trail**. The 10-mile **Sisson-Callahan National Recreation Trail**, a partially paved trail that affords great views of Mt Shasta and the jagged Castle Crags, follows a historic route established in the mid-1800s by prospectors, trappers and cattle ranchers to connect the mining town of Callahan with the town of Sisson, now called Mt Shasta City.

Mt Shasta City Park & Sacramento River Headwaters PARK
(http://msrec.org; Nixon Rd) FREE Off Mt Shasta Blvd, about a mile north of downtown, the headwaters of the Sacramento River gurgle up from the ground in a large, cool spring. It's about as pure as water can get – so bring a bottle and have a drink. The park also has walking trails, picnic spots, sports fields and courts, and a children's playground.

Sisson Museum MUSEUM
(http://mtshastamuseum.com; 1 Old Stage Rd; suggested donation $1; ⏰ 10am-4pm Jun-Sep, variable hours Mar 29-Jun & Sep-mid-Dec) A half-mile west of the freeway, this former hatchery headquarters is full of curious mountaineering artifacts and old pictures. The changing exhibitions highlight history – geological and human – but also occasionally showcase local artists. Next door, the oldest operating hatchery in the West maintains outdoor ponds teeming with rainbow trout that will eventually be released into lakes and rivers.

Siskiyou Ice Rink SKATING
(www.siskiyourink.org; cnr Rockfellow & Adams Drs; adult/child $10/7; ⏰ hours dependent on weather late-Nov-mid-Mar) East of downtown, this immense outdoor skating rink is open to ice-skaters in winter and has skating and hockey lessons available.

River Dancers Rafting & Kayaking RAFTING
(☎ 530-227-5202; www.riverdancers.com; 308 S Mount Shasta Blvd; half-day trips from $80) Excellent outfit run by active environmentalists who guide one- to five-day white-water-rafting excursions down the area's rivers: the Klamath, Sacramento, Salmon, Trinity and Scott. Choose from half-day to multiday adventures.

Shasta Mountain Guides CLIMBING
(☎ 530-926-3117; http://shastaguides.com; 230 N Mt Shasta Blvd; 2-day climbs per person from $895) Offers multiday climbs of Mt Shasta, between April and September (depending on conditions), with all gear and meals included. Some of the climbs include ski descents, and these experienced mountaineers also offer rock climbing, custom trips and seminars on

avalanches. They've been operating in Shasta for more than 30 years.

Mt Shasta Mountaineering School CLIMBING
(☎888-797-6867; www.swsmtns.com; 210a E Lake St; 2-day summit climbs $795) Conducts clinics and courses for serious climbers, or those looking to get more hardcore on Mt Shasta.

Tours

Note that hiking Mt Shasta doesn't require an operator, but those wanting one have plenty of options; ask at the visitor center.

Shasta Vortex Adventures OUTDOORS
(☎530-926-4326; www.shastavortex.com; 400 Chestnut St) For a uniquely Mt Shasta outdoor experience, Shasta Vortex offers low-impact trips accented with the spiritual quest as much as the physical journey. The focus of the trips includes guided meditation and an exploration of the mountain's metaphysical power. Half/full-day tours for two people cost $320/540; larger groups get a significant discount per person.

Sleeping

Shasta has it all, from free rustic camping to plush boutique B&Bs. If you're planning to stay at the upper end of the spectrum, make reservations well in advance, especially on weekends, holidays and during ski season.

Many modest motels stretch along S Mt Shasta Blvd (costing $60 to $140 depending on how recently they were remodeled). Most offer discount ski packages in winter and lower midweek rates year-round.

★Historic Lookout & Cabin Rentals CABIN $
(☎information 530-994-2184, reservations 877-444-6777; www.fs.usda.gov/stnf; q $75; ⏱May/Jun–mid-Oct; 🐕) What better way to rough it in style than to bunk down in a fire lookout on forested slopes? Built from the 1920s to '40s, cabins come with cots, tables, chairs, panoramic views and can accommodate four people. Details about Little Mt Hoffman, Girard Creek and other lookouts can be found on the national forest website.

Panther Meadows CAMPGROUND $
(www.fs.usda.gov; tent sites free; ⏱usually Jul-Nov) Ten walk-in tent sites (no drinking water) sit at the timberline, right at the base of the mountain. They're a few miles up the mountain from other options, but are still easily accessible from Everitt Memorial Hwy. No reservations; arrive early to secure a site.

McBride Springs CAMPGROUND $
(tent sites $10; ⏱Memorial Day-late Oct, depending on weather) Easily accessible from Everitt Memorial Hwy, this campground has running water and pit toilets, but no showers. It's near mile marker 4, at an elevation of 5000ft. It's no beauty – a recent root disease killed many of the white fir trees that shaded the sites – but it's convenient. Arrive early in the morning to secure a spot (no reservations).

WEED & STEWART MINERAL SPRINGS

Just outside Weed, **Stewart Mineral Springs** (☎530-938-2222; http://stewartmineralsprings.com; 4617 Stewart Springs Rd, Weed; sauna/mineral baths $18/30; ⏱10am-6pm Thu-Sun, from noon Mon) is a popular clothing-optional hangout on the banks of a mountain stream. Henry Stewart founded these springs in 1875 after Native Americans revived him from a near-death experience. He attributed his recovery to the properties of the mineral waters, said to draw toxins from the body.

Today you can soak in a private claw-foot tub or steam in the dry-wood sauna. Other perks include massage, meditation, a Native American sweat lodge and a riverside sunbathing deck. Call ahead to be sure there's availability. Dining and **accommodations** (☎530-938-2222; http://stewartmineralsprings.com; 4617 Stewart Springs Rd, Weed; tent & RV sites $40, tipis $50, d $95-200, cabins $120-140; Ⓟ🐕) are on-site. To reach the springs, go 10 miles north of Mt Shasta City on I-5, past Weed to the Edgewood exit, then turn left at Stewart Springs Rd and follow the signs.

While in the area, tickle your nose at **Mt Shasta Lavender Farms** (☎530-926-2651; www.mtshastalavenderfarms.com; 9706 Harry Cash Rd, Montague; ⏱9am-4pm mid-Jun–early Aug; Ⓟ), or drink up the tasty porter at the **Mt Shasta Brewing Company Alehouse** (☎530-938-2394; www.weedales.com; 360 College Ave, Weed; mains $11-20; ⏱noon-9pm or 10pm).

Lake Siskiyou Beach & Camp CAMPGROUND $
(☎888-926-2618; www.lakesiskiyouresort.com; 4239 WA Barr Rd; tent/RV sites from $34/40, trailer from $100, cabins $137-252; ⌚Apr-Nov;) Tucked away on the shore of Lake Siskiyou, this sprawling place has a summer-camp feel (there's an arcade and an ice-cream stand). Hardly rustic, it has a swimming beach, and kayak, canoe, fishing-boat and paddleboat rentals. Lots of amenities make it a good option for families on an RV or camping trip.

Horse Camp HUT $
(www.sierraclubfoundation.org; per person with/without tent $5/3) This 1923 alpine abode run by the Sierra Club is a 2-mile hike uphill from Bunny Flat, at 8000ft. The stone construction and natural setting are lovely. Caretakers staff the hut from May to September only. No campfires allowed.

★**LOGE Mt Shasta** LODGE $
(☎530 926 5596; www.logecamps.com/mt-shasta; 1612 S Mt Shasta Blvd; campsites $35-40, dm $50, d $72, q $92;) An excellent choice geared towards active folks who want to mingle after exploring the mountain all day. Dorms are spacious with gear lockers, shared bathrooms and a kitchen, while there's space for après-hike yoga in the modern rooms and all have indoor hammocks. Covered camping sites have access to an outdoor kitchen and hot shower bathrooms.

Everything is geared towards energy efficiency and the company donates to several environmental organizations. The on-site Finlandia Cafe & Taproom is cool enough to be popular with locals as well as guests.

Strawberry Valley Inn MOTEL $$
(☎530-926-2052; http://strawberryvalleyinn.com; 1142 S Mt Shasta Blvd; d $119-179;) The cosy motel rooms here have some B&B-like touches like country quilts on the beds. The good Continental breakfast is served in a beautiful early 20th-century stone house and service is down-to-earth and friendly, also reminiscent of a B&B. Very convenient downtown location.

Swiss Holiday Lodge MOTEL $$
(☎530-926-3446; www.swissholidaylodge.com; 2400 S Mt Shasta Blvd; d $90-160;) Very friendly, you get a peek of the mountain from the back windows of these clean, well-priced rooms. It's a bit out of town by the exit to McCloud.

★**Shasta MountInn** B&B $$
(☎530-261-1926; www.shastamountinn.com; 203 Birch St; d $150-175;) Only antique on the outside, this bright Victorian 1904 farmhouse is all relaxed minimalism, bold colors and graceful decor on the inside. Each airy room has a great bed and exquisite views of the luminous mountain. Enjoy the expansive garden, the wraparound deck, the outdoor hot tub and sauna. Not relaxed enough yet? Chill on the perfectly placed porch swings.

Mt Shasta Resort RESORT $$
(☎530-926-3030; www.mountshastaresort.com; 1000 Siskiyou Lake Blvd; d from $129, 1-/2-bedroom chalets from $189/249;) Divinely situated away from town, this upscale golf resort and spa has arts-and-crafts-style chalets nestled in the woods around the shores of Lake Siskiyou. They're a bit soulless, but they're immaculate, and each has a kitchen and gas fireplace. Basic lodge rooms are near the golf course, which boasts some challenging greens and amazing views of the mountain.

Eating

Trendy restaurants and cafes here come and go with the snowmelt, but there are still some tried-and-true places, favored by locals and visitors alike. For more options head 6 miles south to Dunsmuir, an unexpected hot spot for great food. A **farmers market** (400 block of N Mt Shasta Blvd; ⌚3:30-6pm Mon mid-May–mid-Oct) sets up on Mt Shasta Blvd during summer.

Poncho & Lefkowitz FOOD TRUCK $
(445 S Mt Shasta Blvd; meals $5-9; ⌚11am-4pm Tue-Sat;) Surrounded by a picnic table or three, this classy, wood-sided food cart turns out juicy Polish sausage, bratwurst and hot dogs, and big plates of nachos, tamales and burritos (including vegetarian options). It's a good bet for food on the go.

Berryvale Grocery MARKET $
(☎530-926-1576; www.berryvale.com; 305 S Mt Shasta Blvd; cafe items from $3; ⌚store 8am-8pm, cafe to 7pm;) This market sells groceries and organic produce to health-conscious eaters. The excellent cafe serves good coffee, fresh juices and an array of tasty – mostly veggie – salads, sandwiches and wraps.

Mount Shasta Pastry BAKERY $
(☎530-926-9944; www.mountshastapastry.com; 610 S Mt Shasta Blvd; mains $5-12; ⌚7am-1pm

Wed-Mon;) Walk in hungry and you'll be plagued with an existential breakfast crisis: the feta spinach quiche or the Tuscan scramble? The flaky croissants or a divine apricot turnover? It also serves terrific sandwiches, gourmet pizza, Peet's coffee and mimosas.

Bistro 107 BURGERS **$$**
(530-918-5353; www.bistro107.com; 107 Chestnut St; mains $13-19; 11am-9pm Mon & Thu-Sat, from noon Sun) Get excellent burgers and hearty hot sandwiches at this homey yet classy little joint. Veggie options are available too and pair it all with a microbrew, wine, cocktail or sake.

Lily's CALIFORNIAN **$$**
(www.lilysrestaurant.com; 1013 S Mt Shasta Blvd; mains breakfast & lunch $9-18, dinner $14-30; 8am-2pm & 5-9pm;) Enjoy quality Californian cuisine – Asian- and Mediterranean-touched salads, fresh sandwiches and all kinds of veg options – in a cute clapboard house. Outdoor tables overhung by flowering trellises are almost always full, especially for breakfast. A Shasta classic, you can expect vegan and gluten-free options.

Drinking

Seven Suns Coffee & Cafe CAFE
(530-926-9701; 1011 S Mt Shasta Blvd; 6am-4pm;) This snug little hangout serves organic, locally roasted coffee, light meals (around $10) and is consistently busy. There's live acoustic music some evenings.

Yaks Mt Shasta Koffee & Eatery CAFE
(530-918-5569; www.yaksmtshasta.com; 333 N Mt Shasta Blvd; light meals $6-13; 7am-4pm;) Funky in a scattered and colorful college cafe sense, this is where to get the best coffee in town. Pair your caffeine with a bagel sandwich, panini, salad or healthy Buddha bowl.

Handsome John's Speakeasy BAR
(316 Chestnut St #2213; 2-11pm Mon-Thu, to midnight Fri & Sat) So local that people may look at you in surprise when you walk in, Handsome John's serves up 11 beers on tap, wine, cider and hard seltzers. It's known for its sushi but you can also nosh on pizza, sausages and tacos. There are games from darts to checkers and a dog-friendly outdoor courtyard, weather permitting.

Shopping

Looking for an imported African hand drum, some prayer flags or a nice crystal? You've come to the right place. The downtown shopping district has a handful of cute little boutiques to indulge a little shopping for the spiritual seeker.

Fifth Season Sports SPORTS & OUTDOORS
(530-926-3606; http://thefifthseason.com; 300 N Mt Shasta Blvd; 8am-6pm) A favorite outdoor store in Shasta, this place selsl camping, mountain-climbing, skiing and backpacking gear, and has staff familiar with the mountain. It also rents skis, snowshoes, snowboards, mountaineering equipment and electric mountain bikes.

Information

Mt Shasta Ranger Station (530-926-4511; www.fs.usda.gov/stnf; 204 W Alma St; 8am-4:30pm Mon-Fri) Issues wilderness and mountain-climbing permits, good advice, weather reports and all you need for exploring the area. It also sells topographic maps. The website offers lots of useful information on Shasta-Trinity National Forest.

Mt Shasta Visitors Center (530-926-4865; www.mtshastachamber.com; 300 Pine St; 10am-4pm) Detailed information on recreation and lodging across Siskiyou County.

Getting There & Away

Greyhound (www.greyhound.com) buses heading north and south on I-5 stop at the **depot** (175 E Vista Dr) in Weed, 8 miles north on I-5. Services include Redding ($22, one hour and 20 minutes, three daily), Sacramento ($40, 5½ hours, three daily) and San Francisco ($50, 10½ hours, two or three times daily).

The **STAGE** (530-842-8295; www.co.siskiyou.ca.us; fares $1.75-8) bus includes Mt Shasta City in its local I-5 corridor route (fares $2.50 to $8, depending on distance), which also serves McCloud, Dunsmuir, Weed and Yreka several times each weekday. Other buses connect at Yreka.

Dunsmuir

In 1886 Canadian coal baron Alexander Dunsmuir came to Pusher (named after the 'pusher' train engines) and was so enchanted that he promised the people a fountain if they would rename the town after him. The fountain stands in the park today. Stop there for a drink; it could easily be – as locals claim – 'the best water on earth.'

This town has survived avalanche, fire, flood, even a toxic railroad spill in 1991. Long since cleaned up, the river has been restored to pristine levels and the community has a plucky spirit.

Home to a spirited set of artists, naturalists, urban refugees and native Dunsmuirians, the residents here are rightly proud of the fish-stocked rivers around their little community. Its downtown streets – once a bawdy gold rush district – hold cafes, restaurants and galleries.

Sights & Activities

The Dunsmuir Chamber of Commerce (p572) stocks maps of **cycling trails** and **swimming holes** on the Upper Sacramento River.

Dunsmuir City Park PARK

(www.dunsmuirparks.org; dawn-dusk) FREE As you follow winding Dunsmuir Ave north over the freeway, look for this park with its local native **botanical gardens** and a **vintage steam engine** in front. A forest path from the riverside gardens leads to a small waterfall but **Mossbrae Falls** are the larger and more spectacular of Dunsmuir's waterfalls.

It's actually illegal to walk to the falls since the trail is partially on the railroad tracks and a woman was hit by a train here in 2011. Still, plenty of people go. Be extremely careful of trains as you walk by the tracks – the river's sound can make it impossible to hear them coming and to escape a train you'll have to run for it or jump in the river. Park by the railroad tracks (there's no sign), then walk north along the right-hand side of the tracks for a half hour until you reach a railroad bridge built in 1901. Backtracking slightly from the bridge, you'll find a little path going down through the trees to the river and the falls. The community is discussing making a safer trail, so ask around.

California Theater HISTORIC BUILDING

(5741 Dunsmuir Ave) At downtown's north end stands what was the town's pride. This once-glamorous venue opened in 1926 and hosted stars such as Clark Gable, Carole Lombard and the Marx Brothers. Today the sporadic lineup includes second-run films, musical performances and yoga classes.

Sleeping

Dunsmuir Lodge MOTEL $

(530-235-2884; www.dunsmuirlodge.com; 6604 Dunsmuir Ave; d $68-185;) Toward the south entrance of town, the simple but tastefully renovated rooms have hardwood floors, big chunky blond-wood bed frames and tiled baths. A grassy communal picnic area overlooks the canyon slope. It's a peaceful little place and very good value.

Cave Springs CABIN $

(530-235-2721; www.cavesprings.com; 4727 Dunsmuir Ave; d from $84, cabins $104-258;) These creekside cabins seem unchanged since the 1920s, but fortunately there have been some updates since then. They are rustic – *very* rustic – but their location, nestled on a piney crag above the Sacramento River, is lovely and ideal for anglers. At night the sound of rushing water mingles with the haunting whistle of trains.

Dunsmuir Inn & Suites MOTEL $

(530-235-4395; www.dunsmuirinn.com; 5400 Dunsmuir Ave; d $79-159;) Straightforward, immaculately clean motel rooms make a good, no-fuss option. Great location in the main part of town.

Railroad Park Resort INN $$

(530-235-4440; www.rrpark.com; 100 Railroad Park Rd; tent/RV sites from $29/37, d $135-200;) About 2 miles south of town, off I-5, visitors can spend the night inside refitted vintage railroad cars and cabooses. The grounds are fun for kids, who can run around the engines and plunge in a pool and hot tub. A Deluxe boxcar is furnished with antiques and a claw-foot tub, although the cabooses and cabins are a bit less expensive.

Eating

★ **Dunsmuir Brewery Works** PUB FOOD $

(530-235-1900; www.dunsmuirbreweryworks.com; 5701 Dunsmuir Ave; mains $13-15; 11am-9pm Sun-Thu, to 10pm Fri & Sat, extended hours Apr-Sep;) It's hard to describe this little microbrew pub without veering into hyperbole. Start with the beer: the crisp ales and porters are perfectly balanced and the IPA is pretty good too – patrons are always drinking it dry. Soak it up with awesome bar food: baked wings, bratwurst, or a thick Angus or perfect veggie nut burger.

Cornerstone Bakery & Café CAFE $

(www.cornerstonedunsmuir.com; 5759 Dunsmuir Ave; mains $9-15; 8am-2pm Fri-Tue;) Smack in the middle of town, this homey place serves strong coffee, espresso and friendly service. It's more of a diner than a bakery and the offerings – omelettes, French toast and some fun specials like chai sweet-potato waffles – are consistently delicious. The baked goods, including gooey cinnamon rolls, are often warm from the oven.

Yaks on the 5 AMERICAN $

(www.yaks.com; 4917 Dunsmuir Ave; mains $8-20; noon-8pm Thu-Tue;) Hiding under the Hitching Post sign just off I-5, this is the place to come to blow your diet. Breakfast means Cuban pepper-steak hash or perhaps home-baked cinnamon-roll French toast with your choice of house syrups like Baileys-and-bourbon. Lunch offers a huge range of burgers (try the one with the house-roasted coffee rub). There's also a take-out counter.

Wheelhouse CAFE $

(530-235-0754; www.thewheelhousedunsmuir.com; 5841 Sacramento Ave; mains $8-20; 7am-3pm Wed-Sun;) This casual, high-ceilinged, brick-walled hangout (originally the town mercantile) serves organic, healthy yet hefty and delicious New American–style breakfasts. If you're not feeling like bacon and eggs, try the Zephyr, ciabatta bread in a custard batter, grilled and topped with pineapple, brown sugar and brandied caramel syrup. There's a board game library too!

Railroad Park Dinner House CALIFORNIAN $$

(530-235-4611; www.rrpark.com; Railroad Park Resort, 100 Railroad Park Rd; breakfast $8-19, dinner $12-32; 8-11am & 5-8pm Sun-Thu, to 9pm Fri & Sat;) Set inside a vintage railroad car with views of Castle Crags, this popular restaurant-bar offers trainloads of dining-car ambience and Californian cuisine. Think prime-rib and fried chicken with a few veggie options thrown in for good measure. There's a good kid's menu too.

★Café Maddalena EUROPEAN $$$

(530-235-2725; www.cafemaddalena.com; 5801 Sacramento Ave; mains $21-36; 5-9pm Thu-Sun Feb 14-Dec 31) Simple and elegant, this cafe put Dunsmuir on the foodie map. The menu was designed by chef Brett LaMott (of Trinity Cafe fame) and changes seasonally to feature dishes from southern Europe and northern Africa. Some highlights might include sautéed quail with amontillado sherry sauce or braised, spiced shoulder of lamb over rice, chickpeas and roasted carrots.

Information

Dunsmuir Chamber of Commerce (530-235-2177; www.dunsmuir.com; 5915 Dunsmuir Ave; 10am-3pm Tue-Sat) Free maps, walking-guide pamphlets and excellent information on outdoor activities.

Getting There & Away

Amtrak Station (www.amtrak.com; 5750 Sacramento Ave) Dunsmuir's Amtrak station is the railroad hub for the region and bus connections are available to the surrounding towns.

STAGE (530-842-8220; www.co.siskiyou.ca.us) This local bus service covers the Shasta region, including Shasta City and Weed.

Castle Crags State Park

The stars of this glorious **state park** (530-235-2684; www.parks.ca.gov; 20022 Castle Creek Rd; per car $8; sunrise-sunset) alongside Castle Crags Wilderness Area are its soaring spires of ancient granite formed some 225 million years ago, with elevations ranging from 2000ft along the Sacramento River to more than 6500ft at the peaks. The crags are similar to the granite formations of the eastern Sierra. Castle Dome resembles Yosemite's famous Half Dome.

Rangers at the park entrance station have information and maps covering nearly 28 miles of **hiking trails**. There's also **fishing** in the Sacramento River at the picnic area on the opposite side of I-5.

If you drive past the campground, you'll reach **Vista Point** (a quarter mile hike from the parking lot) near the start of the strenuous 2.7-mile **Crags Trail**, which rises through the forest past the Indian Springs spur trail, then clambers up to the base of **Castle Dome**. You're rewarded with unsurpassed views of Mt Shasta, especially if you scramble the last 100yd or so up into the rocky saddle gap. The park also has gentle **nature trails** and 8 miles of the **Pacific Crest Trail**, which passes through the park at the base of the crags.

You can camp anywhere in the Shasta-Trinity National Forest surrounding the park if you get a free campfire permit, issued at park offices. At the time of writing, the future of this state park was uncertain because of budget issues.

The **campground** (reservations 800-444-7275; www.reservecalifornia.com; tent & RV sites $25) is one of the nicer public campgrounds in this area, and very easily accessible from the highway. It has running water, hot showers and three spots that can accommodate RVs but have no hookups. Sites are shady, but suffer from traffic noise.

McCloud

This tiny, historic mill town sits at the foot of the south slope of Mt Shasta, and is an alternative to staying in Mt Shasta City. Quiet streets retain a simple, easygoing charm. It's the closest settlement to Mt Shasta Board & Ski Park and is surrounded by abundant natural beauty. Hidden in the woods upriver are woodsy getaways for the Western aristocracy, including mansions once owned by the Hearst and Levi Strauss estates.

Sights & Activities

The **McCloud River Loop**, a gorgeous, 6-mile, partially paved road along the Upper McCloud River, begins at Fowlers Camp, 5.5 miles east of town on Hwy 89, and reemerges about 11 miles east of McCloud. Along the loop, turn off at Three Falls for a pretty trail that passes...yep, three lovely falls and a riparian habitat for bird-watching in the Bigelow Meadow. The loop can easily be done by car, bicycle or on foot, and has five first-come, first-served campgrounds.

Other good hiking trails include the **Squaw Valley Creek Trail** (not to be confused with the ski area near Lake Tahoe), an easy 5-mile loop trail south of town, with options for swimming, fishing and picnicking. Also south of town, **Ah-Di-Na** is the remains of a Native American settlement and historic homestead once owned by the William Randolph Hearst family. Sections of the **Pacific Crest Trail** are accessible from Ah-Di-Na, Paystreak Brewing (p581), off Squaw Valley Rd, and also up near Bartle Gap, offering head-spinning views.

Fishing and swimming are popular on remote **Lake McCloud** reservoir, 9 miles south of town on Squaw Valley Rd, signposted in town as Southern. You can also go fishing on the Upper McCloud River (stocked with trout) and at the Squaw Valley Creek.

McCloud Mercantile HISTORIC BUILDING
(www.mccloudmercantile.com; 222-245 Main St) The huge McCloud Mercantile anchors the downtown. There's a hotel upstairs and it hosts a couple of restaurants that warrant a longer stay, but those just passing through can get a bag of licorice at the old-world candy counter or browse the main floor. The collection of dry goods is very NorCal: Woolrich blankets, handmade soap and interesting gifts for the gardener, outdoors person or chef.

McCloud Heritage Junction Museum MUSEUM
(☎530-964-2604; 320 Main St; ⏲11am-3pm Mon-Sat, 1-3pm Sun May-Sep) FREE The tiny historical museum sits opposite the McCloud Chamber of Commerce and could use a bit of organization – it has the feel of a cluttered, messy thrift store. But tucked in the nooks and crannies are plenty of worthwhile curiosities from the town's past.

Sleeping & Eating

Lodging in McCloud is excellent and reservations are recommended. For camping, the McCloud Ranger District Office (p574) has information on the half-dozen campgrounds nearby. Fowlers Camp is the most popular. The campgrounds have a range of facilities, from primitive (no running water and no fee) to developed (hot showers and fees $15-$30 per site). Ask about nearby fire-lookout cabins for rent for amazing, remote views of the area.

McCloud's eating options are few. For more variety, make the 10-mile trip over to Mt Shasta City.

Stoney Brook Inn B&B $
(☎530-964-2300; www.stoneybrookinn.com; 309 W Colombero Dr; d $70-99, s/d without bath $58/85, ste with kitchen $107-170; 📶🐾) Smack in the middle of town, under a stand of pines, this alternative B&B also sponsors group retreats. Creature comforts include an outdoor hot tub, a sauna, a Native American sweat lodge and massage by appointment. Downstairs rooms are nicest. Vegetarian breakfast available.

McCloud Dance Country RV Park CAMPGROUND $
(☎530-964-2252; www.mccloudrvpark.com; 480 Hwy 89, at Southern Ave; RV sites $43-47, cabins $145-180; ⏲May 1-Oct 31; 📶🐾) Chock-full of RVs, with campsites under the trees and a small creek, this is a good option for families. The view of the mountain is breathtaking and there's a large, grassy picnic ground. Cabins are basic but clean.

★**McCloud River Mercantile Hotel** INN $$
(☎530-964-2330; www.mccloudmercantile.com; 241 Main St; d $139-275; P🚭📶🐾) Stroll into McCloud's second story Mercantile Hotel and try not to fall in love; it's all high ceilings and exposed brick done in modern preservationist class. All rooms have sublime antique furnishings and an open floor plan. Guests

drift to sleep on feather beds after soaking in claw-foot tubs. A pet-friendly two bedroom cabin is also available nearby.

McCloud Hotel HISTORIC HOTEL **$$**
(☎530-964-2822; www.mccloudhotel.com; 408 Main St; d $169-284;) Regal, butter-yellow and a whole block long, this grand hotel opened in 1916 and has been a destination for Shasta's visitors ever since. The elegant historic landmark has been restored to a luxurious standard and Sage, the on-site restaurant, serves the most upscale meals in town. Many rooms have Jacuzzis; one room is accessible for travelers with disabilities and there are a few family-sized rooms too.

McCloud River Inn B&B **$$**
(☎530-964-2130; www.mccloudriverinn.com; 325 Lawndale Ct; r $140-199;) Rooms in this rambling, quaint Victorian are fabulously big – the bathrooms alone could sleep two. In the morning look out for the frittatas; in the evening have a bottle of wine delivered to your room. There's also an on-site day spa. The relaxed and familial atmosphere guarantees that it books up quickly. Special fishing packages are also available.

White Mountain Cafe AMERICAN **$**
(☎530-964-2005; 241 Main St; mains $5-16; ⊙8am-3pm Wed-Sun) In the window-lined corner of the Mercantile, this old-fashioned yet classy diner serves classic American breakfasts, hot or cold sandwiches, burgers and shakes.

Drinking & Entertainment

Axe & Rose Public House PUB
(☎530-408-8322; 424 Main St; ⊙11am-8pm Mon-Thu, till 9pm Fri, 8am-9pm Sat & Sun;) This cosy, modern pub in the historic McCloud Hotel complex serves up local beers on tap, ciders and original cocktails alongside a very good menu of soups, salads, sandwiches and fancier mains like glazed salmon or ribeye steaks. There's a great outdoor patio for when the weather is warm.

Siskiyou Brew Works BREWERY
(☎530-925-5894; www.siskiyoubrewworks.com; 110 Squaw Valley Rd; ⊙4-8pm Wed-Fri & Sun, from 12:30pm Sat) In a not-obvious spot in the McCloud Dairy Barn just off Hwy 89, this rustic spot churns out the town's first craft beers and decent, heavily topped pizzas. Get a beer sampler to find your favorite.

★ **McCloud Dance Country** DANCE
(☎530-524-6922; www.mcclouddancecountry.com; cnr Broadway & Pine Sts; packages from $299 per couple) Dust it up on the 5000-sq-ft maple dance floor in the 1906 Broadway Ballroom. Square dancing, round dancing, ballroom dancing – they do it all. Multiday packages include lessons and evening dances. It's a worthwhile centerpiece to a weekend getaway. Visit the website to see what's on and to sign up.

Information

McCloud Chamber of Commerce (☎530-964-3113; www.mccloudchamber.com; 205 Quincy St; ⊙10am-4pm Mon-Fri, shorter hours in winter) Has basic info and friendly staff.

McCloud Ranger District Office (☎530-964-2184; 2019 Forest Rd; ⊙8am-4:30pm Mon-Sat summer, 8am-4:30pm Mon-Fri rest of year) A quarter-mile east of town. Detailed information on camping, hiking and recreation.

McArthur-Burney Falls Memorial State Park & Around

This beautiful **state park** (☎530-335-2777; www.parks.ca.gov; Hwy 89, Burney; per car $10;) lies southeast of McCloud, near the crossroads of Hwys 89 and 299 from Redding. Fed by a spring, the splashing 129ft-tall waterfalls flow at the same temperature, 42°F (6°C), year-round. Rangers are quick to point out that it might not be California's highest waterfall, but it may be the most beautiful (Teddy Roosevelt considered it the eighth wonder of the world). Clear, lava-filtered water surges over the top and also from springs in the waterfall's face.

Hiking trails include a portion of the **Pacific Crest Trail**, which continues north to Castle Crags State Park. The 1.3-mile **Burney Falls Trail** is the one you shouldn't miss. Upgraded with guardrails, it's an easy loop for families and allows close-up views of water rushing right out of the rock. You can **camp** (☎information 530-335-2777, summer reservations 800-444-7275; www.reserveamerica.com; off Hwy 89, Burney; tent & RV sites $35, cabins $94-116;) here.

A visit to nearby **Ahjumawi Lava Springs State Park** (☎530-335-2777; www.parks.ca.gov; ⊙sunrise-sunset) comes with serious bragging rights as the abundant springs, aquamarine bays and islets, and jagged flows of black basalt lava are truly off the beaten path, and can be reached only by boat. After you paddle out, the hikes are glorious: there are basalt outcroppings, lava tubes, cold springs bubbling and all kinds of volcanic features.

Lava Beds National Monument

A wild landscape of charred volcanic rock and rolling hills, this remote **national monument** (☎530-667-8113; www.nps.gov/labe; 1 Indian Well HQ, Tulelake; 7-day entry per car $25; P 👪) is reason enough to visit the region. Off Hwy 139, immediately south of Tule Lake National Wildlife Refuge, it's a truly remarkable 72-sq-mile landscape of volcanic features – lava flows, craters, cinder cones, spatter cones, shield volcanoes and amazing lava tubes.

Lava tubes are formed when the surface of hot, spreading lava cools and hardens upon exposure to cold air. The lava inside is insulated and stays molten, flowing away to leave an empty tube of solidified lava. Over 800 such tubular caves have been found in the monument, and many more are expected to be discovered. Approximately two dozen are currently open for exploration.

On the park's south side, the **visitors center** (☎530-667-8113; www.nps.gov/labe; Tulelake; ⏲10am-4pm with extended but varying hours in summer, spring & fall) has free maps, activity books for kids, and information about the monument, its volcanic features and history.

From the visitors center rangers loan mediocre flashlights (and sell helmets and kneepads in the summer season only) for cave exploration and lead summer interpretive programs, including campfire talks and guided cave walks. To explore the caves it's essential you use a high-powered flashlight, wear good shoes and long sleeves (lava is sharp), and do not go alone.

Near the visitors center, a short, one-way **Cave Loop** drive provides access to many lava-tube caves. **Mushpot Cave**, the one nearest the visitors center, has lighting and information signs and is beautiful, besides being a good introductory hike. There are a number of caves that are a bit more challenging, including Labyrinth, Hercules Leg, Golden Dome and Blue Grotto. Each one of these caves has an interesting history – visitors used to ice skate by lantern light in the bottom of Merrill Cave, and when Ovls Cave was discovered, it was littered with bighorn sheep skulls. There are good brochures with details about each cave available from the visitors center. We found Sunshine Cave and Symbol Bridge Cave (the latter is reached via an easy 0.8-mile hike) to be particularly interesting. Rangers are stern with their warnings for new cavers, though, so be sure to check in with the visitors center before exploring to avoid harming the fragile geological and biological resources in the park.

The tall black cone of **Schonchin Butte** (5253ft) has a magnificent outlook accessed via a steep 1-mile hiking trail. Once you reach the top, you can visit the fire-lookout staff between June and September. **Mammoth Crater** is the source of most of the area's lava flows.

The weathered Modoc **petroglyphs** at the base of a high cliff at the far northeastern end of the monument, called Petroglyph Point, are thousands of years old, but unfortunately the cliffside is now sheltered behind a cyclone fence because of vandalism. There's also a short trail at the top of the hill that offers amazing views over the plains and Lower Klamath Lake. At the visitors center, be sure to take the leaflet explaining the origin of the petroglyphs and their probable meaning. Look for the hundreds of nests in holes high up in the cliff face, which provide shelter for birds that sojourn at the wildlife refuges nearby.

Also at the north end of the monument, be sure to go to the labyrinthine landscape of **Captain Jack's Stronghold**, the Modoc Indians' very effective ancient wartime defense area. A brochure will guide you through the breathtaking Stronghold Trail.

Forty-three first-come first-served sites are available at **Indian Well Campground** (www.nps.gov/labe/planyourvisit/campgrounds.htm; tent & RV sites $10; 🐾) 0.5 miles from the visitors center. Each has a picnic table and a fire ring and there are communal flush toilets and sinks. It's legal to collect dead wood for fires in the nearby Modoc National Forest.

Klamath Basin National Wildlife Refuges

Of the six stunning national wildlife refuges in this group, Tule Lake and Clear Lake refuges are wholly within California, Lower Klamath refuge straddles the California–Oregon border, and the Upper Klamath, Klamath Marsh and Bear Valley refuges are across the border in Oregon. Bear Valley and Clear Lake (not to be confused with the Clear Lake just east of Ukiah) are closed to the public to protect their delicate habitats, but the rest are open during daylight hours.

These refuges provide habitats for a stunning array of birds migrating along the Pacific Flyway. Some stop over only briefly; others stay longer to mate, make nests and raise their young. The refuges are always packed with birds, but during the spring and fall migrations, populations can rise into the hundreds of thousands.

The **Klamath Basin National Wildlife Refuge Complex Visitor Center** (☎530-667-2231; www.klamathbasinrefuges.fws.gov; 4009 Hill Rd, Tulelake; ⊙9am-4pm) sits on the west side of the Tule Lake refuge, about 5 miles west of Hwy 139, near the town of Tulelake. Follow the signs from Hwy 139 or from Lava Beds National Monument. The center has an interesting video program, as well as maps, information on recent bird sightings and updates on road conditions. It rents photo blinds. Be sure to pick up the excellent, free *Klamath Basin Birding* Trail brochure for detailed lookouts, maps, color photos and a species checklist.

The spring migration peaks during March, and in some years more than a million birds fill the skies. In April and May the songbirds, waterfowl and shorebirds arrive, some to stay and nest, others to build up their energy before they continue north. In summer ducks, Canada geese and many other water birds are raised here. The fall migration peaks in early November. In and around February, the area hosts the largest wintering concentration of bald eagles in the lower 48 states, with 1000 in residence (but only expect to see one to a dozen at a time). The eagles prey on migrating geese, and yes, seeing an eagle catch and eat a goose is very dramatic. The Tule Lake and Lower Klamath refuges are by far the best places to see eagles and other raptors.

The Lower Klamath and Tule Lake refuges attract the largest numbers of birds year-round, and **auto trails** (driving routes) have been set up; a free pamphlet from the visitor center shows the routes. Self-guided canoe trails have been established in three of the refuges. Those in the Tule Lake and Klamath Marsh refuges are usually open from July 1 to September 30; canoe rentals are available for free from the Visitor Center. Canoe trails in the Upper Klamath refuge are open year-round. Here, canoes can also be rented at **Rocky Point Resort** (☎541-356-2287; 28121 Rocky Point Rd, Klamath Falls, OR; canoe & kayak rental per hour/half-day/day $20/45/60; ⊙Apr-Oct; 👪🐾), on the west side of Upper Klamath Lake.

Camp at nearby Lava Beds National Monument. Alternatively, a couple of RV parks and budget motels cluster along Hwy 139 near the tiny town of Tulelake (4035ft), including the friendly **Ellis Motel** (☎530-667-5242; 2238 Hwy 139; d with/without kitchen $95/75; 📶) and **Winema Lodge** (☎530-667-5158; www.winemalodge.com; 5215 Hill Rd, Tulelake; d $75, lodge rooms $90 all incl breakfast; 📶) which is located right on Tule Lake. **Wild Goose Lodge** (☎541-331-2701; www.wildgoosemotel.com; 105 E Court Dr, Merrill, OR; RV sites/r/cabins $30/57/115; ❄📶🐾) – a good-value, locally owned motel with country charm – is the best option near Lava Beds National Monument outside of Klamath Falls. Klamath Falls, OR, 29 miles from Tulelake, is the closest real town, and there are lots of lodging options there.

Modoc National Forest

This enormous national forest (www.fs.usda.gov/modoc) covers almost two million spectacular, remote acres of California's northeastern corner. Fourteen miles south of Lava Beds National Monument, on the western edge of the forest, **Medicine Lake** is a stunning crater lake in a caldera (collapsed volcano), surrounded by pine forest, volcanic formations and campgrounds. The enormous volcano that formed the lake is the largest in area in California. When it erupted it ejected pumice followed by flows of obsidian, as can be seen at **Little Glass Mountain**, east of the lake.

Pick up the *Medicine Lake Highlands: Self-Guided Roadside Geology Tour* pamphlet from the McCloud ranger district office to find and learn about the glass flows, pumice deposits, lava tubes and cinder cones throughout the area. Roads are closed by snow from around mid-November to mid-June, but the area is still popular for winter sports, and accessible by cross-country skiing and snowshoeing.

Congratulations are in order for travelers who make it all the way to the **Warner Mountains**. This spur of the Cascade Range in the east of the Modoc National Forest is probably the least visited range in California. With extremely changeable weather, it's also not so hospitable; there have been snowstorms here in every season of the year. The range divides into the North Warners and South Warners at **Cedar Pass** (elevation 6305ft), east of Alturas. Remote **Cedar Pass Snow Park** (☎530-233-

3323; www.facebook.com/NCCPSP; all-day pass $35; ⏲10am-4pm Sat, Sun & holidays during ski season) offers downhill and cross-country skiing. The majestic **South Warner Wilderness** contains 77 miles of hiking and riding trails, which are best to used from July to mid-October.

Maps, campfire permits and information are all available at the **Modoc National Forest supervisor's headquarters** (☎530-233-5811; 225 W 8th St, Alturas; ⏲8am-5pm Mon-Fri) in Alturas.

If you're heading east into Nevada from the forest, you'll pass through **Alturas**, the pancake-flat, eerily quiet seat of Modoc County. The town was founded by the Dorris family in 1874 as a supply point for travelers, and it serves the same function today, providing basic services, motels and family-style restaurants.

WEST OF I-5

The wilderness west of I-5 is right in the sweet spot: here are some of the most rugged towns and seductive wilderness areas in the entire state of California – just difficult enough to reach to discourage big crowds. The Trinity Scenic Byway (Hwy 299) winds spectacularly along the Trinity River and beneath towering cliffs as it makes its way from the plains of Redding to the coastal redwood forests around Arcata. It provides a chance to cut through some of the northern mountains' most pristine wilderness and passes through the vibrant gold rush town of Weaverville.

Heavenly Hwy 3 (a highly recommended – although slower and windier – alternative route to I-5) heads north from Weaverville. This mountain byway transports you through the Trinity Alps – a stunning granite range dotted with azure alpine lakes – past the shores of Lewiston and Trinity Lakes, over the Scott Mountains and finally into emerald, mountain-rimmed Scott Valley. Rough-and-ready Yreka awaits you at the end of the line.

Weaverville

In 1941 a journalist asked James Hilton, the British author of *Lost Horizon:* 'In all your wanderings, what's the closest you've found to a real-life Shangri-La?' Hilton's response? 'A little town in northern California. A little town called Weaverville.'

Cute as a button, Weaverville's streets are lined with flower boxes in the summer and banks of snow in the winter. The seat of Trinity County, it sits amid an endless tract of mountain and forest. At almost 3300 sq miles, the county is roughly the size of Delaware plus Rhode Island, yet has a population of only 13,600 and not one freeway.

This gem of a town is on the National Register of Historic Places and has a laid-back, bohemian feel (thanks in part to the back-to-landers and marijuana-growing subculture). You can spend the day here strolling around the quaint storefronts and visiting art galleries or hit the great outdoors.

Sights & Activities

There are 40 miles of hiking and mountain-biking trails in the Weaverville Basin Trail System, or you can cast a line along the Trinity River, Trinity Lake or Lewiston Lake for steelhead, salmon and trout.

★Weaverville Joss House State Historic Park HISTORIC BUILDING
(☎530-623-5284; www.parks.ca.gov; 630 Main St; tour adult/child $4/2; ⏲tours hourly 10am-5pm Thu-Sun; P) The walls here basically talk – they're papered inside with 150-year-old donation ledgers from the once-thriving Chinese community, the immigrants who built Northern California's infrastructure, a rich culture that has all but disappeared. It's a surprise that the oldest continuously used Chinese temple in California (and an exceptionally beautiful one at that), dating from 1874, is in Weaverville.

JJ Jackson Memorial Museum & Trinity County Historical Park MUSEUM
(www.trinitymuseum.org; 780 Main St; donation requested; ⏲10am-5pm May-Oct, 11am-4pm Nov-Dec 24, 11am-4pm Tue & Sat only Jan-Apr) Next door to the Joss House you'll find gold-mining and cultural exhibits, plus vintage machinery, memorabilia, an old miner's cabin and a blacksmith shop.

Highland Art Center GALLERY
(www.highlandartcenter.org; 691 Main St; ⏲10am-5pm Tue-Sat) Stroll through this large central gallery showcasing local artists.

Coffee Creek Ranch FISHING
(☎530-266-3343; www.coffeecreekranch.com; 4310 Coffee Creek Rd, Coffee Creek; all-inclusive per-person adult/child rates per day from $279/148; 👪) In Trinity Center, these guys run a dude ranch and lead fishing, hunting and fully outfitted pack trips into the Trinity Alps Wilderness. There are also fly-fishing and

horseback riding lessons and cowboy-style children's programs for ages three to 17.

Sleeping

There are a few basic motels at the edge of town in addition to the inn and hotel. The ranger station has information on many United States Forest Service (USFS) campgrounds in the area, especially around Trinity Lake. Commercial RV parks, some with tent sites, dot Hwy 299.

Red Hill Motel & Cabins MOTEL $
(☎530-623-4331; 116 Red Hill Rd; d $60, cabins with/without kitchen $78/68;) This very quiet and rustic motel is tucked under ponderosa pines at the west end of town, just off Main St. It's a set of red wooden cabins built in the 1940s and they're equipped with kitchenettes and minifridges. The rooms are simple and good value. It sometimes fills with visiting groups, so book ahead.

Whitmore Inn HISTORIC HOTEL $$
(☎530-623-2509; www.whitmoreinn.com; 761 Main St; d $105-165;) Settle into plush, cozy rooms in this downtown Victorian with a wraparound deck and abundant gardens. One room is accessible for travelers with disabilities. Only kids over five years old are welcome.

Weaverville Hotel HISTORIC HOTEL $$
(☎800-750-8957, 530-623-2222; www.weavervillehotel.com; 481 Main St; d $110-285;) Play like you're in the Old West at this upscale hotel and historic landmark, refurbished in grand Victorian style. It's luxurious but not stuffy, and the very gracious owners take great care in looking after you. Guests may use the local gym, and a $10 credit at local restaurants is included in the rates. Kids under 12 years are not allowed.

Eating

Downtown Weaverville caters to all, from hungry hikers to foodies. There's also a fantastic **farmers market** (www.weavervilletailgate.org; Lowden Park; ⏲4-7pm Wed May-Oct), which takes over Main St in the warmer months. In winter the tourist season dries up and opening hours can be hit or miss.

Trinideli DELI $
(☎530-623-5856; www.trinideli.com; 160 Nugget Ln; sandwiches $9-12; ⏲6:30am-4pm Mon-Fri, 10am-3pm Sat;) Get decadent sandwiches stuffed with fresh goodness at the back of Tangle Blue, the most hopping bar in town. The 1.5lb 'Trinideli' with four types of meat and three types of cheese will fill the ravenous, while simple turkey and ham standards explode with fresh veggies and tons of flavor. Breakfast burritos are perfect for a quick pre-hike fill up.

Mountain Marketplace MARKET $
(☎530-623-2656; 222 S Main St; ⏲9am-6pm Mon-Sat;) Stock up on natural foods or hit its juice bar and vegetarian deli.

Cafe on Main CALIFORNIAN $$
(520 Main St; mains $14-35; ⏲5-9pm Tue-Sat) The chefs from the popular Cafe at Indian Creek have moved their fine and creative cuisine to this new location in town. It serves the best meals in the area, set in a cosy, revamped Main St classic. Its varied international menu features everything from pasta to duck confit, plus there are veggie options and a kids' meal.

Drinking & Entertainment

★ **Tangle Blue Saloon** BAR
(☎530-623-4436; 160 Nugget Ln; ⏲9am-2am) Come here to find the most people in one place you'll see in Weaverville. Dark, lively and with a roadhouse feel, you can play billiards, check out live music or even get a meal, including pizza at night ($14) and biscuits and gravy for a bar breakfast. There are tons of events from open mike nights to taco Tuesdays. Check its Facebook page for details.

Trinity County Brewing Company BREWERY
(www.trinitycountybrewery.com; 301 Main St; ⏲11am-8pm Thu-Sun) This seven-barrel brewery and pub opened in 2020 and serves up 10 craft beers alongside good grub made with local ingredients.

Mamma Llama CAFE
(www.mammallama.com; 490 Main St; breakfasts & sandwiches $5-9; ⏲7:30am-4pm Mon-Fri, 10am-3pm Sat;) A local institution, this coffeehouse is a roomy and relaxed chill spot. The espresso is well made, there's a selection of comic books and CDs, and there are couches for lounging. The small menu does breakfasts, wraps and sandwiches, and microbrew beer is available by the bottle. Live folk music (often including a hand drum) takes over occasionally.

Trinity Theatre CINEMA
(www.trinitytheatre.us; 310 Main St; adult/child $9.50/8) This old time-y and inviting theater plays first-run movies.

Information

Trinity County Chamber of Commerce (☎530-623-6101; www.trinitycounty.com; 509 Main St; ⏰10am-5pm) Knowledgeable, friendly staff with lots of useful information.

Weaverville Ranger Station (☎530-623-2121; www.fs.usda.gov/stnf; 360 Main St; ⏰8am-4:30pm Mon-Fri) A homey little office with maps, information and permits for all lakes, national forests and wilderness areas in and near Trinity County.

Getting There & Away

A local **Trinity Transit** (☎530 623 5438; www.trinitytransit.org; fares $1-10) bus makes a Weaverville–Lewiston loop via Hwy 299 and Hwy 3, to/from Redding and a few other local communities, mostly with morning and afternoon commute hours, Monday through Friday.

Lewiston Lake

Adorable Lewiston is little more than a collection of rickety historic buildings beside a crossroad, 26 miles west of Redding. It's right beside the Trinity River, and the locals here are in tune with the environment – they know fishing spots on the rivers and lakes, where to hike and how to get around.

The lake is about 1.5 miles north of town and is a serene alternative to the other area lakes because of its 10mph boat speed limit.

Sights & Activities

Migrating bird species sojourn here – early in the evening you may see ospreys and bald eagles diving for fish. The **Trinity River Fish Hatchery** (☎530-778-3931; www.wildlife.ca.gov/Fishing/Hatcheries/Trinity-River; 1000 Hatchery Rd; ⏰7am-3pm Mon-Fri) FREE traps juvenile salmon and steelhead and holds them until they are ready to be released into the river. The only marina on the lake, **Pine Cove Marina** (☎530-778-3878; www.pine-cove-marina.com; 9435 Trinity Dam Blvd; ⏰7am-3pm closed Tue), has free information about the lake and its wildlife, boat and canoe rentals and guided off-road tours.

Sleeping & Eating

Several commercial campgrounds dot the rim of the lake. For information on USFS campgrounds, contact the ranger station in Weaverville. Two of these campgrounds are on the lake: the wooded **Mary Smith** (☎877-444-6777; www.fs.usda.gov/recarea/stnf/recarea/?recid=6489; tent sites $11; ⏰April-Oct), which is more private; and the sunny **Ackerman** (☎877-444-6777; www.fs.usda.gov; tent sites $20-35; ⏰Apr-Oct), which has more grassy space for families. If there's no host, both have self-registration options. There are also all kinds of RV parks, cabins for rent and motels in Lewiston.

★Lewiston Hotel HISTORIC HOTEL $
(☎530-778-3823; www.lewistonhotelca.com; 125 Deadwood Rd; d without bath $85-95; ⏰restaurant 4-8pm Tue-Fri, from noon Sat, 11.30am-7:30pm Sun; P ⊖ 📶) This 1862 rambling, ramshackle hotel has small, rustic rooms with quilts, historic photos and river views – all have tons of character but none have attached bathrooms. Ask (or don't ask) for the room haunted by George. Explore the building to find giant stuffed moose heads, old girly calendars, rusty saws and so much more.

Old Lewiston Inn B&B $
(☎480-506-2186; www.theoldlewistoninn.com; 71 Deadwood Rd; d $110-125; ❄📶🐾) The prettiest place in town and right beside the river, this B&B is in an 1875 house. Enjoy the hot tub, or ask about fly-fishing trips. There's one two-bedroom suite, which is great for families.

Old Lewiston Bridge RV Resort CAMPGROUND $
(☎530-778-3894; www.lewistonbridgerv.com; 8460 Rush Creek Rd; tent/RV sites $15/30, trailers $65; 🐾) A pleasant place to park the RV, with campsites beside the river bridge. It also rents travel trailers that sleep four people (bed linens not included).

Lakeview Terrace Resort CABIN $
(☎530-778-3803; www.lakeviewterraceresort.com; 9001 Trinity Dam Rd; RV sites $35, cabins $110-210; ❄📶🏊🐾) Five miles north of Lewiston, this is a woodsy Club Med with a swimming pool, horseshoe pit and boat rental.

Shopping

Country Peddler ANTIQUES
(☎530-778-3325; 4 Deadwood Rd; ⏰May-Oct, hours vary; 🐾) Impossible to miss, this funky old barn welcomes you with vintage gas pumps (no gas) and beckons you in to see its wondrous collections of junk and treasures.

Trinity Lake

Placid Trinity Lake, California's third-largest reservoir, sits beneath dramatic snowcapped alps north of Lewiston Lake. In the off season it is serenely quiet, but it attracts multitudes in the summer, who come for swimming, fishing and other water sports. Most of the campgrounds, RV parks, motels, boat rentals and restaurants line the west side of the lake.

Even if you're just driving through, it's worthwhile detouring to little-known, utterly picturesque **Alpen Cellars** (☎530-266-9513; www.alpencellars.com; East Fork Rd, Trinity Center; ⊙10am-4pm summer, by appointment Oct-May). Specializing in riesling, gewürztraminer, chardonnay and pinot noir, the vineyard is open for tours, tastings and picnicking on its idyllic riverside grounds.

Spreads over 22 acres on the shore of Trinity Lake, **Pinewood Cove Resort** (☎530-286-2201; www.pinewoodcove.com; 45110 Hwy 3; tent/RV sites $34/54, cabins $150-190; ⊙Apr 1-Oct 31; ❄) offers quality camping, cabins and marina facilities.

Klamath & Siskiyou Mountains

A dense conglomeration of rugged coastal mountains gives this region the nickname 'the Klamath Knot.' Coastal, temperate rainforest gives way to moist inland forest, creating an immense diversity of habitats for many species, some found nowhere else in the world. Around 3500 native plants live here. Local fauna includes the northern spotted owl, the bald eagle, the tailed frog, several species of Pacific salmon and carnivores like the wolverine and the mountain lion. One theory for the extraordinary biodiversity of this area is that it escaped extensive glaciation during recent ice ages. This may have given species refuge and longer stretches of relatively favorable conditions during which to adapt.

The region also includes the largest concentration of wild and scenic rivers in the US: the Salmon, Smith, Trinity, Eel and Klamath, to name a few. The fall color change is magnificent.

Five main wilderness areas dot the Klamath Knot. The **Marble Mountain Wilderness** in the north is marked by high rugged mountains, valleys and lakes, all sprinkled with colorful geological formations of marble and granite, and a huge array of flora. The **Russian Wilderness** is 8000 acres of high peaks and isolated, beautiful mountain lakes. The **Trinity Alps Wilderness**, west of Hwy 3, is one of the area's most lovely regions for hiking and backcountry camping, and has more than 600 miles of trails that cross passes over its granite peaks and head along its deep alpine lakes. The **Yolla Bolly-Middle Eel Wilderness** in the south is less visited, despite its proximity to the Bay Area, and so affords spectacular, secluded backcountry experiences. The **Siskiyou Wilderness**, closest to the coast, rises to heights of 7300ft, from where you can see the ocean. An extensive trail system crisscrosses the wilderness, but it is difficult to make loops.

The **Trinity Scenic Byway** (Hwy 299) follows the rushing **Trinity River** to the Pacific coast and is dotted with lodges, RV parks and blink-and-you'll-miss-'em burgs.

Scott Valley

North of Trinity Lake, Hwy 3 climbs along the gorgeous eastern flank of the Trinity Alps Wilderness to Scott Mountain Summit (5401ft) and then drops down into verdant Scott Valley, a bucolic agricultural area nestled between towering mountains. There are good opportunities for hiking, cycling, mountain biking, or taking horse trips to mountain lakes. For a bit of history, pick up the *Trinity Heritage Scenic Byway* brochure from the Weaverville ranger station (p579) before taking this world-class drive.

Etna (population 720), toward the north end of the valley, is known by its residents as 'California's Last Great Place,' and they might be right. Folks are uncommonly friendly, birdsong is more prevalent than road noise and if you're in town in summer and see lots of dirty people with backpacks, these are hard-core hikers taking a break from the nearby **Pacific Crest Trail** – Etna is a favorite pit stop.

Beyond Etna, **Fort Jones** (population 692) is just 18 miles from Yreka. The small stone **museum** (☎530-468-5568; www.fortjonesmuseum.com; 11913 Main St; donation requested; ⊙10am-4pm Mon-Fri, from 1pm Sat Memorial Day-Labor Day) is on the main drag and houses Native American artifacts.

There are a few places to stay in the valley, from family-run motels to bucolic B&Bs. The clean, family-run **Motel Etna** (☎530-467-5338; www.theetnahotel.com; 317 Collier Way; s/d/tw $64/74/84; ❄📶), on the outskirts of town, is a favorite with Pacific Crest Trail hikers and a good choice for anyone on a budget. The storybook-perfect 1877 mansion **Alderbrook Manor B&B** (☎530-467-3917; 836 Sawyers Bar Rd; r $135, without bathroom $110-120, dm $35,; 📶🐾) has a handful of pretty and bright antique-decorated rooms and a hikers' hut with dorm beds.

People talk about the **Etna Brewing Company** (www.etnabrew.com; 131 Callahan St; burgers $12-15; ⏲noon-8pm Fri-Mon) from Redding to Yreka. Don't miss a stop for a meal and one of its beers on tap if you're in Etna. It has some competition however with the ultra-friendly **Paystreak Brewing** (https://paystreakbrewing.business.site/; 449 Main St; ⏲11am-10pm;) that's hoping to expand its one unique beer on offer each week, to three or more, and **Denny Bar Co** (www.dennybarcompany.com; tours free; ⏲half-hour tours at noon & 2pm Fri-Sun;), a flashy distillery that offers craft spirits, cocktails, tours, tastings and great food.

Yreka

Inland California's northernmost town, Yreka (wy *ree* kah) was once a booming gold rush settlement and has the gorgeous turn-of-the-century architecture to prove it. Most travelers only pass through en route to or from Oregon, but the new-age-tinged yet authentically Wild West–feeling historic downtown makes a good spot to stretch, eat and refuel before heading out into the hinterlands of the Scott Valley or the northeastern California wilderness.

Sights & Activities

Siskiyou County Museum MUSEUM
(☎530-572-1099; www.siskiyoucountyhistoricalsociety.org; 910 S Main St; adult/child $3/1; ⏲9am-3pm Tue-Sat) Several blocks south of Yreka's downtown grid, this exceptionally well-curated museum brings together pioneer and Native American history. The native basketry collection is particularly impressive. An outdoor section contains historic buildings brought from around the county.

Yreka Creek Greenway WALKING
(www.yrekagreenway.org) Behind the museum, the Yreka Creek Greenway has an ever-expanding network of walking and cycling paths winding through the trees.

Sleeping & Eating

Motels, motels and more motels: budget travelers can do lots of comparison shopping along Yreka's Main St for mid-century motels galore. Klamath National Forest runs several campgrounds; the supervisor's office has information. RV parks cluster on the edge of town.

Klamath Motor Lodge MOTEL $
(☎530-842-2751; www.klamathmotorlodge.net; 1111 S Main St; d from $57;) Folks at this motel are especially friendly, the rooms are clean and – bonus for those headed in from the wilderness – it has an on-site laundry. Of all the motels in Yreka, this is tops. Book by phone for the best rates.

★ **Nature's Kitchen** HEALTH FOOD $
(☎530-842-1136; 412 S Main St; dishes $8-16; ⏲8am-5:30pm Mon-Fri, 9am-4pm Sat;) Friendly and quirky natural-foods store and bakery, serving healthy and tasty vegetarian and nonvegetarian dishes, fresh juices and good espresso. The adjoining store has all kinds of fairies, crazy socks, herbal supplements and new-agey trinkets.

Klander's Deli DELI $
(☎530-842-3806; 211 S Oregon St; sandwiches $7-11; ⏲9am-3pm Mon-Fri) Local to the core, this deli's long list of yummy sandwiches is named after regulars. Bob is a favorite, named for the first owner and stacked with ham, turkey, roast beef and Swiss cheese.

Drinking & Nightlife

Etna Brewery & Taphouse BREWERY
(☎530-841-0370; www.etnabrew.com; 231 W Miner St; ⏲11am-8pm Tue-Thu, to 8:30pm Fri & Sat) Serving delicious Etna brews on tap, come here for the beer more than the ambience or food (mains $12-15, mostly burgers).

Information

Klamath National Forest Supervisor's Office (☎530-842-6131; www.fs.usda.gov/klamath; 1711 S Main St; ⏲8am-4:30pm Mon-Fri) Has the lowdown on recreation and camping.

Yreka Chamber of Commerce (☎530-842-1649; www.yrekachamber.com; 310 S Broadway St; ⏲9am-5pm Mon-Fri;) Has information about Yreka and surrounding areas.

Getting There & Away

STAGE buses (☎530-842-8295; www.co.siskiyou.ca.us; 190 Greenhorn Rd; fares $1.75-6) run throughout the region from a few different stops in Yreka. There are several daily services on weekdays along the I-5 corridor to Weed, Mt Shasta, McCloud and Dunsmuir. Other buses depart daily for Fort Jones (25 minutes), Greenview (35 minutes) and Etna (45 minutes) in the Scott Valley. On Monday and Friday only, buses go out to Klamath River (40 minutes) and Happy Camp (two hours).

AT A GLANCE

POPULATION
6.7 million

CROPS GROWN
230

BEST UNDERGROUND EXPLORATION
Forestiere Underground Gardens (p608)

BEST RIDE
Tubing the Sacramento River (p599)

BEST FARMERS MARKET
Davis Farmers Market (p595)

WHEN TO GO

Feb–Mar Stop for pie and a glass of wine along the technicolor Blossom Trail.

May–Sep The peak of harvest time brings farmers markets and food festivals aplenty.

Nov–Feb Catch the return of millions of migratory waterfowl in Sacramento.

Delta King (p591)

Sacramento & Central Valley

The Central Valley is visible from space – a vast expanse of green between the Sierra Nevada and Pacific Ocean. The area is divided in two parts: the Sacramento Valley in the north and the San Joaquin Valley in the south. For millennia, the rivers cutting through these valleys flooded seasonally, creating extremely fertile soil. Today, those waterways are tamed by public works projects that support massive agricultural endeavors. Half the produce in the US is grown in these valleys – including almost every almond, olive and bulb of garlic.

Most travelers are just passing through – zipping along the highway to more popular parts of the state. But those who linger are rewarded with stately Victorian-era mansions, thriving craft beer and wine scenes, uniquely scenic byways and quirky small towns.

INCLUDES

Sacramento & Central Valley Highlights

❶ **Sacramento breweries** (p593) Strolling between breweries in Sacramento, the self-proclaimed mecca of beer.

❷ **California State Fair** (p595) Driving bumper cars, eating fried Twinkies and checking out blue-ribbon livestock.

❸ **Lodi** (p586) Uncorking the region's emerging fine-wine scene.

❹ **Bidwell Park** (p599) Hiking or biking through the miles of trails at one of the country's biggest municipal parks.

❺ **Blossom Trail** (p609) Cruising through orchards exploding with blossoms in February and March, stopping at fruit stands and small indie wineries.

❻ **Buck Owens' Crystal Palace** (p614) Sipping cold beer and listening to country music in Bakersfield.

❼ **Kern River** (p614) Rushing down world-class rapids on this mighty river.

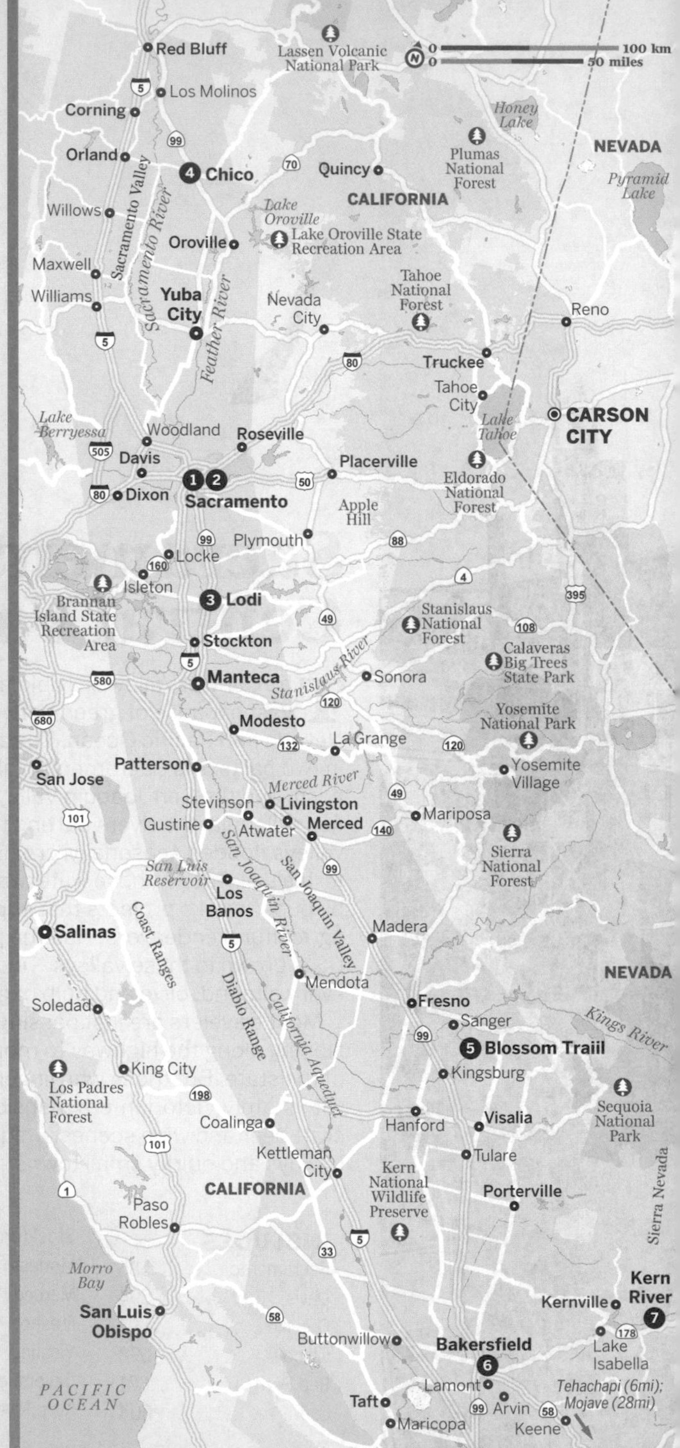

SACRAMENTO VALLEY

The Sacramento River, California's largest, rushes out of the northern mountains from Shasta Lake before hitting the Sacramento Valley basin above Red Bluff. It snakes south across grassy plains and orchards before skirting the state capital, fanning across the delta and draining into San Francisco Bay.

The valley is most beautiful in the bloom of spring, when delicate flowers bejewel the orchards and hillsides. If you're driving through the region to one of California's marquee attractions, make time for a pit stop in Sacramento, which has a plucky food and beer scene, or swing north to Chico to ramble through one of the country's largest municipal parks.

Sacramento

Sacramento is a city of contrasts. It's a former cow town where state legislators' SUVs go bumper-to-bumper with farmers' muddy, half-ton pickups at rush hour. It has sprawling suburbs, but also new lofts and upscale boutiques squeezed between aging mid-century storefronts.

The people of 'Sac' are a resourceful lot that have fostered small but energetic food, art and nightlife scenes. A whopping 50 breweries keep this town well stocked with award-winning suds, and the city's ubiquitous farmers markets and farm-to-fork fare are another point of pride.

History

The history of the state is contained in this city. Paleo-era peoples fished the rivers and thrived before colonists arrived. By the 1800s, the native communities were largely wiped out by colonizers. Control changed from Spanish to Mexican to American hands when, in 1847, a Swiss man named John Sutter came seeking fortune. Recognizing the strategic importance of the major rivers, Sutter built an outpost and raised a militia. This soon became a safe haven for traders, and Sutter expanded his operations in all directions, at the expense of the people who occupied the land before he did.

It was at his lumber mill near Coloma that something glittered in the river in 1848. Eureka! Gold rushers stampeded to the trading post, which was christened 'Sacramento.' Though plagued by fires and relentless flooding, the riverfront settlement prospered and became the state capital in 1850.

After the discovery of gold, a quarter of a million Chinese people arrived in California, often traveling through Sacramento. Although many were indentured servants who traded passage to the US in return for years of labor, they developed a thriving Chinatown and left an indelible mark on the region. These communities literally built the infrastructure of the city – as well as the levees and roads in the surrounding valley.

Chinese also built much of the Transcontinental Railroad, though you won't see any among the faces of the 'Big Four' – Leland Stanford, Mark Hopkins, Collis P Huntington and Charles Crocker. These men founded Central Pacific Railroad, which began construction here in 1863, and connected to the Union Pacific in Promontory, UT, in 1869.

Sights

Sacramento's sights range from rows of gold-rush-era historical buildings to cutting-edge art museums. As it's roughly halfway between San Francisco and Lake Tahoe, some of the state's most popular destinations are easily accessible. Head a bit out of town for gorgeous outdoor spaces along the nearby rivers.

The Grid

In the middle of the city is the Grid, where numbered streets run north–south and lettered streets run east–west (Capitol Ave replaces M). One-way J St is a main drag east from downtown to Midtown. It's easy finding sights along the Grid, but everything is spread out.

★Golden 1 Center STADIUM
(Map p588; ☎box office 916-840-5700; www.golden1center.com; 500 David J Stern Walk) This gleaming arena of the future, home to the Sacramento Kings, is one of the most advanced sports facilities in the country. Made with the highest sustainability standard, it's built from local materials, powered by solar and cooled by five-story airplane hangar doors that swing open to capture the pleasant delta breeze.

The building is also pushing the envelope of interactivity, with a free app that allows fans to monitor bathroom lines, order concessions (which follow a farm-to-fork philosophy, of course) and watch replays of the action on the court.

LODI VALLEY WINERIES

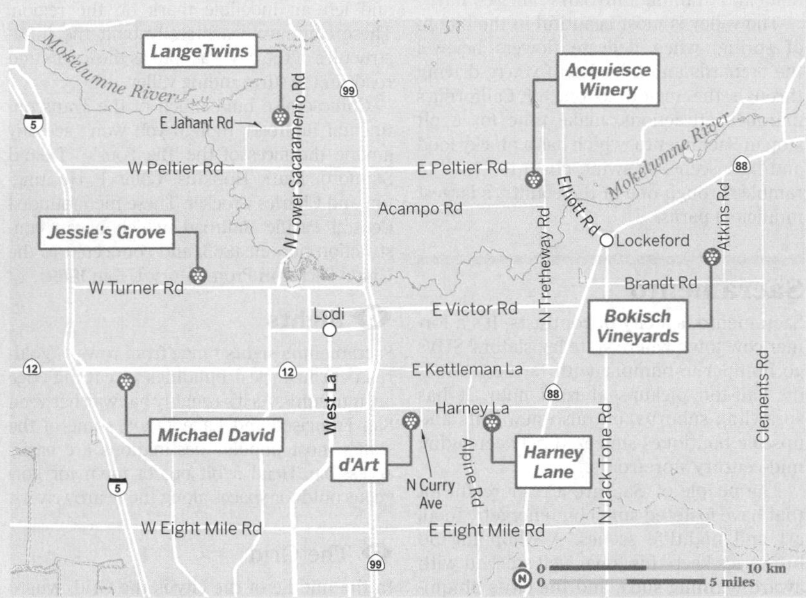

JESSIE'S GROVE

Jessie's Grove (209-368-0880; www.jessiesgrovewinery.com; 1973 W Turner Rd; noon-5pm) With its summer concert series and very long history, this is an anchor of Lodi wine producers. The winery grounds, punctuated with gnarled oaks, picnic tables and a vine-covered tasting room, make a perfect wine-drinking setting. There's also a tasting room downtown on E Locust St.

HARNEY LANE

Harney Lane (209-365-1900; www.harneylane.com; 9010 E Harney Lane; tasting $10; 11am-5pm) A sweet family outfit that's been around Lodi forever; their tempranillo is an overachiever. Enjoy a glass on their tree-covered patio in a chair made from a wine barrel.

BOKISCH VINEYARDS

Set on the easternmost edge of Lodi's wine circuit, **Bokisch** (209-642-8880; www.bokischvineyards.com; 18921 Atkins Rd; tasting $10; 11am-5pm Thu-Mon;) offers a high-quality take on Spanish varietals in a peaceful country setting – the winery lawn, dotted with cherry red Adirondack loungers, sits on a hill overlooking the vines, and hosts live music and social evenings around the fire pit.

ACQUIESCE WINERY

In zinfandel country, **Acquiesce** (209-333-6102; 22353 N Tretheway Rd; tasting $10; 11am-5pm Thu-Mon; P) delivers something different – a bright selection of white wines that buck Lodi wine tradition. The picpoul blanc and the roussanne are particularly wonderful. Tastings come with food pairings and fees are waived with bottle purchase.

Lodi's underrated wineries – easily accessed from I-5 or Hwy 99 – make a fun, budget-friendly escape from the Bay Area, and the high-quality grapes will delight true oenophiles.

MICHAEL DAVID

Michael David (☎209-368-7384; www.michaeldavidwinery.com; 4580 W Hwy 12; tasting $10; ⏲10am-5pm; P) These brothers have built an enthusiastic following with their oaky, fruity wines. The winery is a veritable campus featuring two tasting bars, a cafe and farm stand and an expansive outdoor area with water features and bocce balls courts. Tasting fee refunded with purchase; last entry is at 4:30pm. Be aware, it gets crowded.

D'ART

d'Art (☎209 334 9946; www.dartwines.com; 13299 N Curry Ave; tasting $10; ⏲noon-5pm; 🐾) Helen and Dave Dart's bold-yet-smooth cabernet sauvignon is as fun and inviting as the tasting room, which doubles as a local art gallery. Tasting fee refunded with purchase.

LANGETWINS

LangeTwins (www.langetwins.com; 1525 East Jahant Rd, Acampo; tasting $20; ⏲By appointment 11am, 1pm, 3pm Sun-Thu, walk-ins 1-5pm Fri & Sat) The fruity Nero D'Avola and the reserve blends are worth the 7-mile drive north of town to this state-of-the-art steel-and-redwood tasting room. Staff are knowledgeable and extremely happy to tell you about every detail that goes into their wines. Ask about the wine bottle designs.

MAGJEY IMAGES / GETTY IMAGES ©

Grape harvest, Lodi

Downtown Sacramento

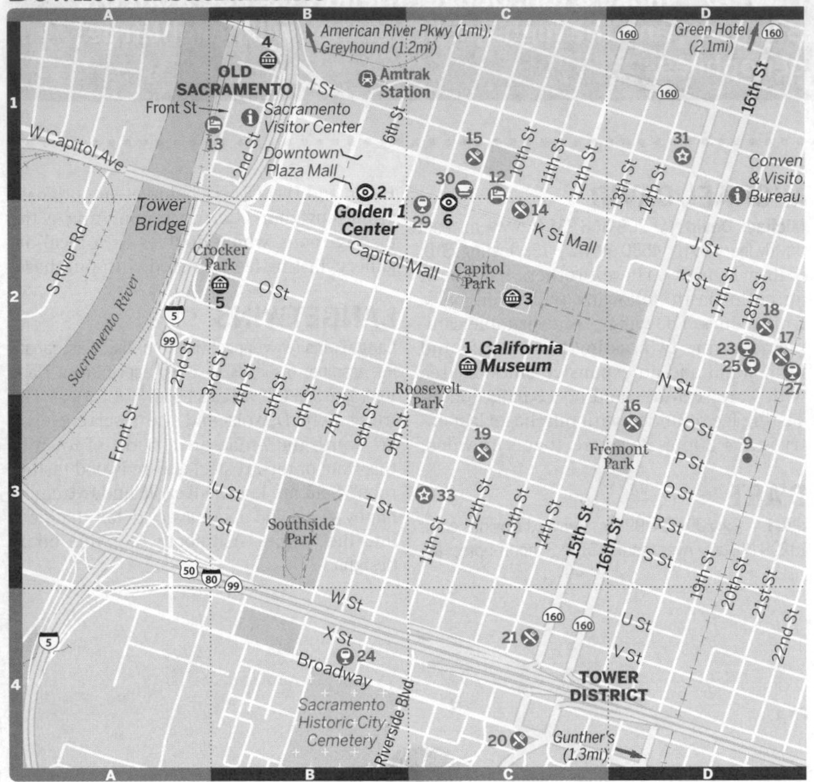

★ California Museum MUSEUM

(Map p588; ☎916-653-7524; www.californiamuseum.org; 1020 O St; adult/child $9/6.50; ⊙10am-5pm Tue-Sat, from noon Sun; 👪) This modern museum is home to the California Hall of Fame and the only place to simultaneously encounter César Chávez, Mark Zuckerberg and Amelia Earhart. The Native American exhibit is a highlight, with artifacts and oral histories of more than 10 tribes.

The museum has plans to move to the California Indian Heritage Center in West Sacramento, but as with most government projects, progress is slow-moving.

K Street Mall PLAZA

(Map p588) Known by locals as 'The Kay,' this formerly blighted neighborhood has undergone a major redevelopment effort that has transformed it into a weekend hot spot. The pedestrian mall draws a party on weekends.

State Indian Museum MUSEUM

(Map p588; www.parks.ca.gov; 2618 K St; adult/child $5/3; ⊙10am-4pm) It's with some irony that this museum sits in the shadow of Sutter's Fort. The excellent exhibits and handicrafts on display – including the intricately woven and feathered baskets of the Pomo – are traces of cultures nearly stamped out by the fervor Sutter ignited. Knowledgeable docents can provide first-hand commentary on California's native cultures and point you to other resources around the state.

Sutter's Fort State Historic Park HISTORIC SITE

(Map p588; www.suttersfort.org; 2701 L St; adult/child $5/3; ⊙10am-5pm) Originally built by John Sutter, this park was once the only trace of white settlement for hundreds of miles. Stroll within its walls, where furniture, medical equipment and a blacksmith shop are straight out of the 1850s.

Sutter dreamed of creating an 'agricultural utopia,' which he worked to achieve by enslaving the local Native American

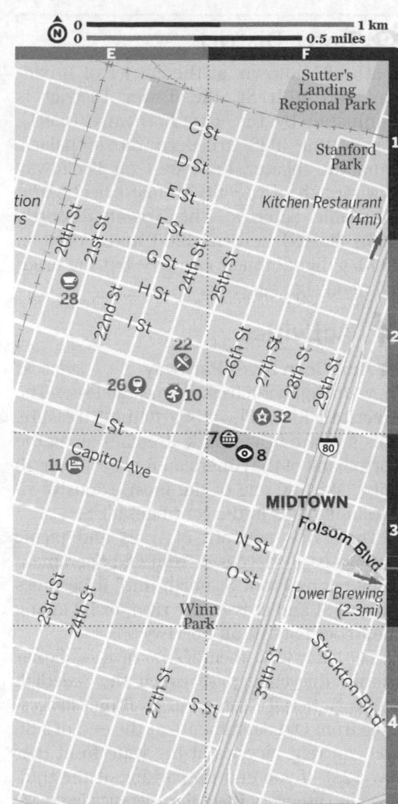

Downtown Sacramento

Top Sights
1 California Museum C2
2 Golden 1 Center B1

Sights
3 California State Capitol C2
4 California State Railroad Museum B1
5 Crocker Art Museum B2
6 K Street Mall C2
Sacramento History Museum .... (see 4)
7 State Indian Museum F3
8 Sutter's Fort State Historic Park F3

Activities, Courses & Tours
9 Sac Brew Bike D3
10 Trek Bicycles Sacramento E2

Sleeping
11 Amber House E3
12 Citizen Hotel C1
13 Delta King B1

Eating
14 Empress Tavern C2
Grange Restaurant & Bar .... (see 12)
15 La Bonne Soupe Cafe C1
16 Magpie D3
17 Mulvaney's B&L D2
18 Saigon Alley Kitchen + Bar D2
19 Shoki II Ramen House C3
20 Tower Cafe C4
21 Urban Roots Brewery & Smokehouse C4
22 Veg Cafe E2

Drinking & Nightlife
23 58 Degrees and Holding Co D2
24 Bike Dog Brewing Company B4
25 Fieldwork Brewing Company D2
26 Flamingo House Social Club E2
27 Mercantile Saloon D2
28 Old Soul E2
29 Ruhstaller BSMT C2
30 Temple Coffee Roasters C1

Entertainment
31 Broadway Sacramento D1
Crest Theatre .... (see 14)
32 Harlow's F2
33 Old Ironsides C3
Tower Theatre .... (see 20)

population; his efforts would be thwarted, however, when gold was discovered on his land, spurring the gold rush.

California State Capitol HISTORIC BUILDING
(Map p588; 916-324-0333; http://capitolmuseum.ca.gov; 1315 10th St; 7:30am-6pm Mon-Fri, 9am-5pm Sat & Sun;) FREE The gleaming dome of the California State Capitol is Sacramento's most recognizable structure. A painting of Arnold Schwarzenegger hangs in the West Wing along with the other governors' portraits. Some will find Capitol Park, the gardens and memorials surrounding the building more interesting than what's inside. Tours run hourly from 9am to 4pm.

Old Sacramento

This historic river port by Downtown remains the city's stalwart tourist draw. The aroma of river mud and restored buildings give Old Sac the vibe of a second-rate Frontierland, but it's good for a stroll on summer evenings, when boomers on Harleys rumble through the brick streets, and tourists and natty legislative aides stroll the promenade. This is California's largest concentration of buildings on the National Register of Historic Places. Most now peddle gold-rush trinkets and fudge. There are a few quality

OFF THE BEATEN TRACK

The **River Bend Park** (https://regionalparks.saccounty.net; 2300 Rod Beaudry Dr; parking $5; 7am-8pm;), snuggled into a curve of the American River, is a real treat for those looking for some green space in Sacramento. Trails crisscross remarkably peaceful riparian landscapes defined by twisted oak trees, grassy meadows and rocky river shorelines. Deer, jackrabbits, and big ol' turkeys frequent the place, making for an idyllic afternoon by the river.

attractions, but the restaurant scene is a bust – head to Midtown.

Crocker Art Museum MUSEUM
(Map p588; 916-808-7000; https://crockerartmuseum.org; 216 O St; adult/child $12/6; 10am-5pm Tue, Wed & Fri-Sun, to 9pm Thu;) Housed in the ornate Victorian mansion (and sprawling additions) of a railroad baron, this museum has striking architecture and excellent collections. Works by California painters and European masters hang beside an enthusiastically curated collection of contemporary art. The museum also hosts concerts, film series, art festivals and a monthly themed party called ArtMix.

California State Railroad Museum MUSEUM
(Map p588; 916-323-9280; www.csrmf.org; 125 I St; adult/child $12/6; 10am-5pm;) Train enthusiasts will delight in this incredible collection of vintage locomotives (even if history buffs will question the candy-coated presentation about the plight of workers who built the rails). You can also hop aboard a restored passenger train from the Sacramento Southern Railroad for a 45-minute jaunt along the river – the price is included in the ticket.

Weather permitting, train rides run hourly from 11am to 4pm on weekends from April to September.

Sacramento History Museum MUSEUM
(Map p588; www.historicoldsac.org/museum; 101 I St; adult/child $10/5, Underground Tour $18/12; 10am-5pm;) Exhibits, stories and artifacts of some of Sacramento's most fascinating citizens, though much of the information is focused on the gold rush. Get tickets here for the **Underground Tour**, a 45-minute look at what's under Old Sac's streets.

Tower District

South of Midtown, at the corner of Broadway and 16th St, the Tower District is dominated by the Tower Theatre (p594), a beautiful 1938 art deco movie palace. From the theater, head east on Broadway to a stretch of the city's most eclectic and affordable eateries. The **Tower Records** chain started here in 1960 and closed in 2006, a digital music casualty, but the original neon sign survives.

Activities

★**American River Parkway** OUTDOORS
(www.arpf.org; north bank of American River) The American River Pkwy is a natural treasure. This massive urban park stretches along the north bank of the American River for over 20 miles, skirting one of the most extensive riparian habitats in the continental US.

The park's network of trails and picnic areas is easily accessed from Old Sacramento by taking Front St north until it becomes Jiboom St and crosses the river, or by taking the Jiboom St exit off I-5/Hwy 99.

The parkway includes a nice walking/running/bicycling path called the Jedediah Smith National Recreation Trail that's accessible from Old Sacramento at the end of J St. You can rent bicycles at the waterfront (per day $25). If you end up parking at the trailhead at Discovery Park, the entrance fee is $5.

Trek Bicycles Sacramento CYCLING
(Map p588; 916-447-2453; www.facebook.com/TrekBicycleSacramento; 2419 K St; per day $40-100; 10am-7pm Mon-Fri, to 6pm Sat, 11am-5pm Sun) The perfect spot to get a bike for cruising the amazing American River Parkway for a couple of hours. Road bikes, mountain bikes and hybrids are in good condition and the staff is enthusiastic and helpful. The store also offers awesome group rides; the info on these is regularly posted on the Facebook page events calendar.

Tours

Sac Brew Bike BREWERY
(Map p588; 916-952-7973; www.sacbrewbike.com; tours depart from 1519 19th St; 15-person tour from $320, individual pricing available) Pedal your way between the city's best breweries on the multi-peddler 'Brew Bike' – you can join a mixed tour with random beer-and-bike-loving strangers for about $30 per person, but tours are ideal for groups. The

whole bike accommodates 15 people and rates increase on the weekends.

Festivals & Events

Sacramento Central Farmers Market FOOD & DRINK
(www.california-grown.com; cnr 8th & W St, under Hwy 80 overpass; 8am-noon Sun;) You're never far from a mind-blowing farmers market in Sacramento. They're hosted all year round and every day of the week in the summer and fall. Most will have food trucks and street performers.

Sleeping

The capital is a magnet for business travelers, so Sacramento doesn't lack hotels. Many have good deals during legislative recesses. Unless you're in town for something at Cal Expo, stay Downtown or Midtown, where there's plenty to do within walking distance.

Greens Hotel BOUTIQUE HOTEL $
(916-921-1736; www.thegreenshotel.com; 1700 Del Paso Blvd; d from $109;) This updated mid-century motel is a fun alternative to the city's workaday business travel hotels. The area is charming, with a cute coffee shop next door and a brewery across the street. Secure parking, pool and spacious grounds make this an ideal place for families to stop en route to or from Tahoe.

★**Citizen Hotel** BOUTIQUE HOTEL $$
(Map p588; 916-442-2700; www.thecitizenhotel.com; 926 J St; d from $180;) After an elegant upgrade, this long-vacant 1924 beaux arts tower became downtown's coolest place to stay. The details are spot-on: luxe linens, wide-striped wallpaper and an atmospheric reception area evoking the building's past. There's an upscale farm-to-fork **restaurant** (Map p588; 916-492-4450; www.grangerestaurantandbar.com; 926 J St; mains $27-56; 6:30am-10pm Mon-Thu, 8am-11pm Sat, 8am-9pm Sun;) on the ground floor.

Wi-fi costs an additional $9.95 per day.

Delta King B&B $$
(Map p588; 916-444-546; www.deltaking.com; 1000 Front St; d from $145;) It's a kitschy treat to sleep aboard the *Delta King*, a 1927 paddle wheeler docked on the river in Old Sacramento. It lights up like a Christmas tree at night.

The attached bar and grill is a nice place to grab a drink, either in the atmospheric interior or on the boat deck.

Amber House B&B $$
(Map p588; 916-444-8085; www.amberhouse.com; 1315 22nd St; r $188-250;) This Dutch Colonial home in Midtown has been transformed into a B&B, where rooms have Jacuzzis, fireplaces and lots of frill. The Lord Byron room has been updated and remodeled with accessibility needs in mind, but the upstairs rooms remain a bit dated. The warm common area is a nice place to enjoy a glass of wine with other guests.

Eating

Skip the overpriced fare in Old Sacramento or by the capitol and head to lively Midtown or to the Tower District. A cruise up J St or Broadway passes a number of creative-but-affordable restaurants where tables spill onto the sidewalks in the summer. Many source farm-fresh ingredients.

Shoki II Ramen House JAPANESE $
(Map p588; 916-441-0011; www.shokiramenhouse.com; 1201 R St; mains $8-13; 11am-2pm & 5-9pm Mon-Thu, 11am-3pm & 5-11pm Fri & Sat, 11am-10pm Sun) This cozy ramen house under the direction of Yasushi Ueyama makes amazing housemade noodles that live up to the motto of 'a bowl of dreams.' The fresh spinach, grass-fed beef and shiitake are organic and local.

Gunther's ICE CREAM $
(916-457-6646; www.gunthersicecream.com; 2801 Franklin Blvd; sundaes $4; 10am-10pm;) Look for 'Jugglin Joe' – a cheerful, ice-cream-slinging neon giant – towering above this 1940s soda fountain. Gunther's makes its own ice cream and frozen novelties in classic favors like Fudge Brownie, Pistachio Nut and Toasted Almond.

La Bonne Soupe Cafe DELI $
(Map p588; 916-492-9506; 980 9th St; items $5-10; 11am-2pm Mon-Fri) This beloved French cafe continues to serve divine soup and sandwiches, assembled with such care that the line of downtowners snakes out the door. In a hurry? Skip it. This humble lunch counter is focused on quality that predates drive-through haste.

Don't confuse it with the similarly named spot next door, La Bou Bakery & Cafe.

Veg Cafe VEGAN $
(Map p588; 916-448-8768; www.vegmidtown.com; 2431 J St, 2nd fl; $9-14; 11am-9pm Tue-Sat, 11am-3pm Sun;) A sunny spot tucked away above a Thai restaurant, Veg enchants the

DON'T MISS

THE GREAT MIGRATION

The Sacramento Valley serves as a rest stop for countless migrating species that arrive in such great numbers they are a spectacle even without binoculars.

October to February Four million waterbirds winter in the warm tules (marshes) on their way along the Great Pacific Flyway. Tours available at Sacramento National Wildlife Refuge (p597).

October to January Endangered chinook and steelhead fight their way upstream to spawn. Spot them along the American River Parkway (p590) and the Red Bluff Recreation Area (p601).

March to June Cabbage white, painted lady and Western tiger swallowtail butterflies come to party. Their offspring will gorge and then grow wings to fly north. Sacramento National Wildlife Refuge (p597) has details.

June to August Hundreds of thousands of Mexican free-tailed bats shelter under the Yolo Causeway. Tours (www.yolobasin.org) catch them alighting at twilight.

second you walk in: a disco ball dangles in a modern boho space, and patrons enthusiastically dig in to veggie staples like scrambled tofu and potato hash for breakfast and buffalo cauliflower momo for dinner. The drink menu features numerous tempting teas (including kombucha), as well as beer and cocktails.

Tower Cafe BREAKFAST **$**
(Map p588; ☎916-441-0222; www.towercafe.com; 1518 Broadway; mains $7-18; ⏰8am-10pm Sun-Thu, to midnight Fri & Sat; 👪) Best bet for big breakfasts – custardy French toast, chorizo sausage with eggs – next to the iconic art deco movie theater. Be prepared for a long line on weekends, when the space gets packed. The cozy patio is shrouded in foliage.

Saigon Alley Kitchen + Bar VIETNAMESE **$$**
(Map p588; ☎916-758-6934; www.saigonalley.com; 1801 L St #70; $10-15; ⏰11am-3pm, 4pm-midnight Sun-Wed, to 2am Fri & Sat; ❄) This sleek restaurant puts a modern spin on Vietnamese cuisine – the Pho-rench Dip, a flaky bahn mi that you dip *in* pho broth, is the dish you never knew you needed. Happy hour runs from 4pm to 7pm and includes a $3 food menu that doesn't skimp on portions; there's a 'reverse happy hour' from 9pm to close daily with $3 pho.

Magpie AMERICAN **$$**
(Map p588; ☎916-452-7594; http://magpiecafe.com; 1601 16th Street; mains $15-42; ⏰5-9pm Tue, 11am-9pm Wed-Thu, 11am-10pm Fri, 9am-10pm Sat, 9am-3pm Sun; ❄👪) In a town where the term 'farm-to-fork' is used so much it loses its meaning, Magpie delivers inventive dishes full of local ingredients that defy the convention. For breakfast, try the surprisingly flavorful chia pudding with coconut milk, pecan, orange, pomegranate, lavender mint and aged balsamic.

Urban Roots Brewery & Smokehouse BARBECUE **$$**
(Map p588; ☎916-706-3741; www.urbanrootsbrewing.com; 1322 V St; mains $13-19; ⏰11am-10pm Tue-Sun) This brewery/BBQ joint feels like a community gathering point. Don't miss the brisket or the rib tips, washed down with its well-rounded Mexican lager. Also hosts craft fairs and movie nights in its barrel room, and the large patio is perfect for enjoying beautiful days with a beer in hand.

★**Empress Tavern** NEW AMERICAN **$$$**
(Map p588; ☎916-662-7694; www.empresstavern.com; 1013 K St; mains $24-41; ⏰11:30am-9pm Mon-Thu, to 10pm Fri, 5-10pm Sat) In the catacombs under the historic Crest Theater, this gorgeous restaurant hosts a menu of creative, meat-focused dishes (including beef-cheek stroganoff and grilled pork chop). The space itself is just as impressive as the food: the arched brick ceilings and glittering bar feel like a speakeasy supper club from a bygone era.

Kitchen Restaurant CALIFORNIAN **$$$**
(☎916-568-7171; www.thekitchenrestaurant.com; 2225 Hurley Way; prix-fixe dinner $155; ⏰6:30-10pm Wed & Thu, 7-11pm Fri & Sat, 5-9pm Sun) Husband-and-wife team Randall Selland and Nancy Zimmer's cozy dining room in the northeast 'burbs is the pinnacle of Sacramento's food experience. Their demonstration dinners focus on – what else? – local, seasonal, organic food, immaculately prepared before

your eyes. Reservations far in advance are essential.

Mulvaney's B&L MODERN AMERICAN $$$
(Map p588; ☎916-441-6022; www.mulvaneysbl.com; 1215 19th St; dinner mains $33-45; ⊙11:30am-2:30pm & 5-10pm Tue-Fri, 5-10pm Sat) With effortless class and obsessive commitment to seasonality, this converted 19th-century firehouse offers delicate pastas and grilled local meats on a menu that changes daily. As one of the area's farm-to-table pioneers, it's also deeply invested in community programs and sustainable food production.

Drinking & Nightlife

Sacramento has a split personality when it comes to drinking – upscale joints where bartenders shake up sophisticated cocktails, and dive bars with vintage neons, the perfect amount of grunge and menus that begin and end with a-shot-ana-beer. Both options dot the Grid. If you're looking to party, head to the K Street Mall (p588), which has booming clubs and great restaurants.

★**Ruhstaller BSMT** BREWERY
(Map p588; ☎916-447-1881; https://ruhstallerbeer.com/basement; 726 K St; ⊙11:30am-9pm Sun-Wed, to 10pm Thu-Sat) Somehow, Ruhstaller makes the basement bar concept seem new and fresh – this comfortable space features cozy couches, a pool table and wood-accented decor, and information on Sacramento's beer-brewing heyday at the turn of the century. Bartenders serve up red ales and kolsch alongside experimental brews like their rosemary ale and beet pale ale.

Old Soul CAFE
(Map p588; ☎916-443-6340; https://oldsoulco.com; 812 21st St; ⊙6am-11pm; 📶) Old Soul roasts its coffee and bakes its bread in multiple locations around Sac, but this one is a favorite. The restored horse barn feels warm and intimate, and is the perfect spot to down one of the smooth lattes and nosh on a hot sandwich ($10-$13) framed in exceptional artisanal bread. Also has a spacious patio for sunny California days.

Flamingo House Social Club BAR
(Map p588; ☎916-409 7500; www.flamingohousesac.com; 2315 K St; ⊙3pm-2am Mon-Thu, from noon Fri-Sun) Party people, this is where you want to be. The vibe-y building evokes bright Florida kitsch and the bar inside feels like a tropical fever dream, with flowers on the ceiling and neon lights in all the places. There's a front and back patio, and the clientele is young, stylish and ready to drink.

Temple Coffee Roasters COFFEE
(Map p588; www.templecoffee.com; 1010 9th St; ⊙6am-11pm; 📶) This steel and concrete space echoes many coffeehouses, but take a moment to actually ask the staff about coffee and they'll blow you away with their encyclopedic knowledge. Everyone goes through extensive training before they begin, and the pour-overs really are things of beauty.

There are also locations on S Street and 16th Street.

SACTOWN BEER HEAVEN

In the past few years, Sacramento has developed one of California's best craft beer scenes. A number of excellent breweries are clustered on the Grid, and some of the most promising newer spots are just a bit further afield. If you want to taste all that Sacramento has to offer, pedal your way from one brewery to the next on a 15-person human-powered contraption from Sac Brew Bike (p590). If you're going it alone, these are some of our favorites.

Fieldwork Brewing Company (Map p588; ☎916-329-8367; www.fieldworkbrewing.com/sacramento; 1805 Capitol Ave; ⊙noon-10pm Mon-Thu, 11am-11pm Fri & Sat, to 10pm Sun; 👪🐕)

Ruhstaller BSMT (p593)

New Glory (☎916-451-9355; www.newglorybeer.com; 8251 Alpine Ave; ⊙noon-9pm Sun-Wed, to 10pm Thu-Sat; 👪🐕)

Tower Brewing (☎916-272-4472; www.towerbrewingcompany.com/; 1210 66th St; ⊙4-10pm Mon-Thu, 2-11pm Fri, noon-11pm Sat, to 8pm Sun)

Track 7 Brewing (www.track7brewing.com; 3747 W Pacific Ave, Ste F; ⊙3-9pm Mon-Thu, noon-10pm Fri & Sat, to 9pm Sun)

Bike Dog Brewing Company (Map p588; www.bikedogbrewing.com/west-sacramento-brewery; 915 Broadway, Ste 200; ⊙3-10pm Tue-Thu, noon-11pm Fri & Sat, to 9pm Sun)

Mercantile Saloon GAY

(Map p588; ☎916-447-0792; 1928 L St; ⊙10am-2am) In a yellow Victorian, this bar peddles stiff drinks for less than $5. Personal space is nil in this rowdy dive, though there is a somewhat spartan patio to spill onto. Start here before touring the four-block radius of gay bars and clubs that locals call 'Lavender Heights.'

58 Degrees and Holding Co WINE BAR

(Map p588; ☎916-442-5858; www.58degrees.com; 1217 18th St; ⊙11am-10pm Mon, Wed & Thu, to 11pm Fri & Sat, to 9pm Sun) A wide selection of California and European reds and a refined bistro menu make this a favorite for oenophiles who may feel a bit left out in this beer town.

☆ Entertainment

Pick up a copy of the free weekly *Sacramento News & Review* (www.newsandreview.com) for a list of current happenings around town.

Harlow's LIVE MUSIC

(Map p588; ☎916-441-4693; www.harlows.com; 2708 J St; ⊙5pm-midnight) Quality jazz, R&B and the occasional salsa or indie act in a classy joint. Just beware of the potent martinis. In addition to the main venue, you'll find the Starlet Room upstairs, which also hosts live-music acts.

Broadway Sacramento PERFORMING ARTS

(Map p588; www.broadwaysacramento.com; 1419 H St) This top-notch company hosts touring shows and local productions at its two locations.

Crest Theatre CINEMA

(Map p588; ☎916-476-3356; www.crestsacramento.com; 1013 K St) A classic old movie house that's been restored to its 1949 splendor. Hosts indie and foreign films, as well as comedy acts, concerts and film talks.

Old Ironsides LIVE MUSIC

(Map p588; ☎916-443-9751; www.theoldironsides.com; 1901 10th St; cover $5-10; ⊙10am-1am Mon, 10-2am Tue-Fri, from 6pm Sat) The tiny back room of this cool dive hosts some of the best indie bands that come through town.

Tower Theatre CINEMA

(Map p588; ☎916-442-0985; www.ReadingCinemasUS.com; 2508 Land Park Dr) Classic, foreign and indie films screen at this historic 1938 movie house with a digital upgrade.

ℹ Information

Convention & Visitors Bureau (Map p588; www.visitsacramento.com; 1608 I St; ⊙8am-5pm Mon-Fri) Local information, including event and bus schedules.

Sacramento Visitor Center (Map p588; ☎916-808-7777; www.visitsacramento.com; 1002 2nd St; ⊙10am-6pm) A great local resource with information and suggestions for travelers.

ℹ Getting There & Away

Sacramento is at the intersection of major highways, and you'll likely pass through en route to other California destinations. The Sacramento International Airport (p779) is one of the nearest options for those traveling to Yosemite National Park.

Davis

Much of Davis' energy comes from the free-spirited students who flock to the University of California, Davis (UCD), which boasts one of the nation's leading viticulture departments. Bikes outnumber cars two-to-one, and students make up half the population. It makes a good pit stop when traveling in or out of the Bay Area.

Strolling the downtown grid, you'll pass family-operated businesses (city council has forbidden any store over 50,000 sq ft – sorry, Wal-Mart), public art projects and affordable international restaurants.

I-80 skirts the south edge of town, and you can reach downtown via the Richards Blvd exit. UCD is southwest of downtown, bordered by A St, 1st St and Russell Blvd.

◉ Sights & Activities

UC Davis Arboretum PARK

(http://arboretum.ucdavis.edu; 1 Shields Ave; 👪) FREE With well-marked botanical collections, picnic grounds and family tours, the 100-acre 'Arb' is a welcome spot of green slicing through campus. Follow the peaceful 3.5-mile loop along one of the state's oldest reservoirs, dug in the 1860s.

Jan Shrem and Maria Manetti Shrem Museum of Art MUSEUM

(☎530-752-8500; https://manettishremmuseum.ucdavis.edu; 254 Old Davis Rd; ⊙noon-6pm Tue, Wed & Fri, to 9pm Thu, 11am-5pm Sat & Sun; P) FREE This gallery on UC Davis' campus features contemporary artists working across a wide range of mediums in a dreamy modern space. The staff is friendly and helpful, and the museum hosts artist talks, Art Studio Labs and weekly drop-in workshops.

Pence Gallery GALLERY
(www.pencegallery.org; 212 D St; 11:30am-5pm Tue-Sun) The Pence Gallery exhibits contemporary art and hosts classes, lectures and films. It offers a free reception 6pm to 9pm on the second Friday of each month as part of Davis' Art About event.

Davis Transmedia Art Walk WALKING
(http://davisartwalk.com;) FREE This two-hour walking tour winds through Davis' public art collection, mostly clustered on D and G Sts. There's a free smartphone app with audio and interactive media. If you're low-tech, get a map at the Yolo County Visitors Bureau (p596) or **John Natsoulas Center for the Arts** (530-756-3938; www.natsoulas.com; 521 1st St; 11am-5pm Wed Thu, to 9pm Fri, noon-5pm Sat-Sun) FREE.

Sleeping

Hotel rates are stable until graduation or special campus events, when they skyrocket and sell out fast. Worse, the trains that roll through the town will infuriate a light sleeper. For a utilitarian (if bland) stay, look for chains along the highway.

University Park Inn & Suites HOTEL $
(530-756-0910; www.universityparkinn.com; 1111 Richards Blvd; d $127;) Right off the highway, this independent hotel isn't the Ritz, but it's clean, serves breakfast and offers free bikes for guests.

Aggie Inn HOTEL $$
(530-756-0352; www.aggieinn.com; 245 1st St; d $180;) Across from UCD's east entrance, the Aggie is neat, modern and unassuming. Cottages have a bright, clean interior, but are not much more than regular rooms with kitchenettes and Jacuzzis.

Eating

College students love to eat and drink cheaply, and downtown has a decent selection of lively spots for a quick plate of pad Thai or slice of pizza. The Davis Farmers Market is renowned for being one of the best in the country, and features food vendors, picnic supplies and buskers. More excellent self-catering options can be found at the **Davis Food Co-op** (http://davisfood.coop; 620 G St; 7am-10pm).

DON'T MISS

CALIFORNIA STATE FAIR

For two weeks in late July, the **California State Fair** (916-263-3247; www.castatefair.org; 1600 Exposition Blvd; adult/child $14/10; Jul;) fills the Cal Expo, east of I-80 on the north side of the American River, with a small city of cows and carnival rides. It's likely the only place on earth where you can plant a redwood tree, watch a pig give birth, ride a roller coaster, catch some barrel racing and taste exquisite Napa vintages within one (exhausting) afternoon. See some of the auctions ($500 for a dozen eggs!) and the interactive agricultural exhibits run by the University of California, Davis. Hotels near Cal Expo run regular shuttles to the event.

★ **Davis Farmers Market** MARKET $
(www.davisfarmersmarket.org; cnr 4th & C Sts; 8am-1pm Sat year-round, 4:30-sunset Wed Apr-Oct) With more than 150 vendors and an awe-inspiring selection of local produce, meat, flowers and baked goods, this market forms the vibrant heart of Davis. It's justly considered among the best farmers markets in the nation.

On Wednesday evenings in summer, browse for provisions for a dreamy dinner picnic in the park.

Sophia's Thai Kitchen THAI $
(530-758-4333; www.sophiasthaikitchen.com; 129 E St; mains $12-25; 11:30am-2pm & 5-9pm Sun-Thu, to 9:30 Fri & Sat;) This peppy evening spot whips up tasty Thai curries, rice and noodle dishes – for those who can't choose, the curry noodles are exceptional. Sophia's also has a popular bar in a separate building that stays open late and offers modified main plates as pub grub.

Sam's Mediterranean Cuisine MIDDLE EASTERN $
(530-758-2855; http://sams-mediterranean-cuisine.cafe-inspector.com; 301 B St; shawarma $6.99; 11:30am-7:30pm Mon-Sat) Delicious and cheap shawarma (get the beef with tangy yogurt and chili sauce) makes this little spot a university institution. Cash only.

Burgers and Brew PUB FOOD $
(530-750-3600; 403 3rd St; burgers $12-15; 11:30am-3am;) It's all in the name; the brilliantly simple formula of this buzzing

brewpub makes it a charming local favorite. The 30 craft beers on tap include the best of the region and a delicious house IPA. When you're a few deep, the 'Beast Mode Fries' (caramelized onions, cheese, and spicy sauce) are a fantastic idea.

Woodstock's PIZZA $
(☎530-757-2525; www.woodstocksdavis.com; 219 G St; slice $3.50, pizzas $8-30; ⊙11am-1am Mon-Wed, to 2am Thu-Sat, to midnight Sun; ☎) Every college town has a pizza place like Woodstock's – this friendly pizza joint serves slices at lunch and gets boisterous at happy hour. Besides the usual combos, it has a fun selection of gourmet pizzas. (Sriracha, bacon, pineapple and green onions? Or maybe carnitas? Yes, please.)

Drinking & Nightlife

During the school year, downtown bars lure students with every trick in the book – drink specials, open mike nights, karaoke and trivia. Things are a bit quieter in the summer, but the downtown grid is the place to wander if you're thirsty.

Three Mile Brewing Company MICROBREWERY
(☎530-564-4351; www.threemilebrewing.com; 231 G St, Ste 3; ⊙3-10pm Mon-Thu, to 11pm Fri, noon-11pm Sat, noon-9pm Sun; ☎) This microbrewery has a fantastic flight of crisp, hoppy beer made from local ingredients. Get a flight of four for $9. The list is always changing, but if you're lucky, it will have the Lemon Bar Hazy IPA, which adds a citrusy twist to the trendy favorite.

Miskha's Cafe COFFEE
(☎530-759-0811; www.mishkascafe.com; 610 2nd St; ⊙7am-9:30pm Mon-Fri, from 7:30am Sat, from 8am Sun; ☎☎) Mishka's is a quintessential university cafe with a homey twist, and its wooden tables are always packed with students, professors and families. Its drink menu is fun and varied – the rose-and-lavender-infused lattes are house favorites, and their Jolted Thai Tea is a refreshing, buzzy treat.

Davis Beer Shoppe BEER HALL
(☎530-756-5212; 211 G St; ⊙11am-10pm Mon-Sat, to 8pm Sun) This mellow beer hall and shop stocks 650 varieties of craft beer, bottled and on tap, import and brewed down the block. Pull any bottle from the back or order one of its daily changing draft flights. BYO food.

TULE FOG

As thick as the proverbial pea soup, tule (too-lee) fog causes chain collisions each year on area roads. In 2007, more than 100 cars and big rigs collided on a stretch of Hwy 99. At its worst, these dense, immobile clouds can limit visibility up to a foot.

Tule fog, named after a marsh grass common here, is thickest from November to March, when cold mountain air settles on the warm valley floor and condenses. The fog burns off for a few afternoon hours, just long enough for the ground to warm again and perpetuate the cycle. Interestingly, though, the amount of fog has decreased in recent years (scientists credit less pollution and less moisture), though it still can create challenging travel conditions from time to time.

If you find yourself driving in fog, turn on your low beams, give other cars extra distance and maintain an easy, constant speed. Avoid passing.

☆ Entertainment

The college has fostered a flourishing cultural scene – bulletin boards around town will announce readings and performances galore. For tickets and information to UC Davis' arts events, call the Mondavi Center. For athletic events, call the **UC Davis Athletic Ticket office** (☎530-752-2471; http://campusrecreation.ucdavis.edu; Aggie Stadium, off La Rue Rd; ⊙10am-5pm).

Mondavi Center for the Performing Arts CONCERT VENUE
(www.mondaviarts.org; 523 Mark Hall Dr; ☎) Major theater, music, dance and other performances take place at this state-of-the-art venue on the UCD campus.

Varsity Theatre FILM
(www.davisvarsity.net; 616 2nd St) Davis' beloved art house movie theater has discerning programming and occasional Q&As with filmmakers.

ℹ Information

The exhaustive www.daviswiki.org is fascinating.

Yolo County Visitors Bureau (☎530-297-1900; www.visityolo.com; 132 E St, Suite 200; ⊙9am-5pm Mon-Fri) Free bike maps, travel brochures and transit info.

Getting There & Away

Amtrak (530-758-4220; 840 2nd St) Davis' station is on the southern edge of downtown. Trains connect with Sacramento ($9, 28 minutes) or San Francisco ($31, 1½ hours) throughout the day.

Yolobus (530-666-2877; www.yolobus.com; 5am-11pm) Routes 42A and B ($2.25) loop between Davis and the Sacramento International Airport. The route also connects Davis with Woodland and Downtown Sacramento.

Getting Around

Ken's Bike, Ski, Board (www.kensbikeski.com; 650 G St; 9am-7pm Mon-Fri, noon-6pm Sat) Rents basic bikes (from $21 per day), as well as serious road and mountain bikes.

Unitrans (530-752-2877; http://unitrans.ucdavis.edu; one-way $1.25) If you're not biking, this student-run outfit shuttles people around town and campus in red double-deckers.

Oroville

North of Sacramento's bustle, the quiet town of Oroville has seen quite a reversal. In the mid-19th century the lust for gold brought a crush of white settlers, who drove out the native community. Today, a somewhat quieter persona prevails, with the local economy relying on tourists headed to the rugged northern reaches of the Sierra Nevada.

Oroville's most enduring attraction, aside from the nearby lake, is an excellent museum established by descendants of a long-dispersed Chinese community. Other historic attractions revolve around the gold rush.

Hwys 162 and 70 head northeast from Oroville into the mountains and on to Quincy. Hwy 70 snakes along the magnificent **Feather River Canyon**, an especially captivating drive in autumn.

Sights & Activities

Lake Oroville State Recreation Area LAKE

(530-538-2219; www.parks.ca.gov; 917 Kelly Ridge Rd; park 8am-8pm, visitor center 9am-5pm; P) This artificial lake was formed by the USA's tallest earth-filled dam, which rises 770ft above the Feather River. Boat-in, floating campsites are available. The **visitor center** (530-538-2219; www.parks.ca.gov; 917 Kelly Ridge Rd; 9am-5pm) has exhibits on the California State Water Project and local Native American history, plus a viewing tower and loads of recreational information.

The area surrounding Lake Oroville is also full of hiking trails, and a favorite is the 9-mile round-trip walk to 640ft Feather Falls. The Brad Freeman Bicycle Trail is a 41-mile, off-road loop that takes cyclists to the top of the Oroville Dam, then follows the Feather River back to the Thermalito Forebay and Afterbay storage reservoirs, east of Hwy 70. The ride is mostly flat, but the dam ascent is steep. The Forebay Aquatic Center rents non-motorized watercraft to get out on the water.

Chinese Temple & Museum Complex MUSEUM

(530-538 2496; 1500 Broderick St; adult/child $3/free; noon-4pm Tue, Wed, Sat & Sun, Mar-Nov; P) This restored temple and museum offers a fascinating glimpse into Oroville's Chinese legacy. Constructed in 1863, it served the Chinese community, which built the area's levees and at its peak numbered 10,000. Inside is an unrivaled collection of 19th-century stage finery, religious shrines and a small garden with fine Qing-era relics

Bolt's Antique Tool Museum MUSEUM

(530-538-2528; www.boltsantiquetools.com; 1650 Broderick St; $3; 10am-3:35pm Mon-Sat, from 11:45am Sun; P) Started by Bud Bolt, a former tool salesman, this humble showroom exhibits over 12,000 hand tools stretching all the way back to ancient Rome and ranging from farm equipment to blacksmith tools to old-school medical utensils. The friendly docents spin a good yarn.

Sacramento National Wildlife Refuge BIRDWATCHING

(530-934-2801; www.fws.gov; 752 County Road 99W; $6; 1hr before sunset-1hr after sunset) Serious bird-watchers sojourn here in winter, when millions of migratory waterfowl settle into the marshland. The visitor center (p598) is off I-5 near Willows; a splendid 6-mile driving trail and walking trails are open daily. Wildlife frequently spotted include red-tailed hawks, spectacularly plumed pheasants, black-tailed jackrabbits and even otters.

Forebay Aquatic Center BOATING

(www.forebayaquaticcenter.com; 930 Garden Dr; kayaks per day from $44; 10am-8pm Fri-Sun May-Sep) This outfitter has a pair of docks and a beach for easy water access for canoeing, kayaking, rowing, pedal boats, hydro bikes, paddleboarding or just swimming in a motor-boat-free area of the Thermalito Forebay. Rentals and lessons available.

DON'T MISS

NORTH TABLE MOUNTAIN ECOLOGICAL RESERVE

The land north of Oroville is resoundingly volcanic, a series of rolling buttes and hills formed by ancient basalt lava flows. North Table Mountain Ecological Reserve is an astounding example of this geology, a 3,300-acre stretch of rock punctuated by volcanic outcroppings, fissures and several seasonal waterfalls. In spring, the area is covered in a kaleidoscope of wildflowers that include purple sky lupines, sherbet foothill poppies and pink bitterroot blooms.

There are no formal trails here and hikers will undoubtedly cross paths with cows. For guidance, refer to hiking trail apps or inquire at the California Department of Fish and Wildlife.

All visitors are required to have a CDFW Land Pass, which is easily obtainable online or by phone (800-565-1458) and costs about $5.

Sleeping

Lake Oroville State Recreation Area Campgrounds CAMPGROUND $
(☎information 530-538-2219, reservations 800-444-7275; www.reservecalifornia.com; tent & RV sites $20-45; P) Drive-in campgrounds aren't the most rustic choice, but there are good primitive campsites if you're willing to hike or – perhaps the coolest feature of the park – boat. There's a cove of floating platform sites (per night $175). There are six campgrounds to choose from.

Drinking & Nightlife

Keg Room BAR
(☎530-534-1394; 3035 Oro Dam Blvd E; ⏲6am-2am) A favorite Oroville's no-frills watering hole and an amiable spot that serves very cold beer and spicy Bloody Marys and has a shuffleboard table.

Information

For road conditions, phone 800-427-7623.

Feather River Ranger District (Plumas National Forest; ☎530-534-6500; www.fs.usda.gov; 875 Mitchell Ave; ⏲8am-4:30pm Mon-Fri) This US Forest Service (USFS) office has maps and brochures.

Oroville Area Chamber of Commerce (www.orovillechamber.net; 1789 Montgomery St; ⏲9am-3pm Mon-Fri) A source for free trail maps and information about other area activities.

Sacramento National Wildlife Refuge Visitor Center (☎530-934-2801; 752 County Rd, Willows; ⏲8am-4pm Mon-Fri, from 9am Sat-Sun) An Audubon Society bookstore and exhibits on all things birds. Pick up maps for self-guided wetland walks at this well-run visitor center.

Getting There & Away

Although **Greyhound buses** (☎800-231-2222; www.greyhound.com; 420 Richards Blvd) stop near the **Valero gas station** (555 Oro Dam Blvd E) a few blocks east of Hwy 70, a car is far and away the simplest and most cost effective way to reach the area. There are two buses daily between Oroville and Sacramento ($20, 1½ hours).

Chico

With its huge student population, Chico has the wild energy of a college kegger during the school year, and a lethargic hangover during summer. An oak-shaded downtown and university make it one of Sacramento Valley's more attractive hubs. Folks mingle late in the restaurants and bars here, which open onto patios when it's warm.

Though Chico wilts in the summer heat, the swimming holes in impressive Bidwell Park offer an escape, as does floating down the gentle Sacramento River. The Sierra Nevada Brewing Company's brews are another of Chico's refreshing blessings.

It's ironic a town so widely celebrated for its beer was founded by John Bidwell, a California pioneer who made a bid for US president with the Prohibitionist Party. In 1868, Bidwell and his philanthropist wife, Annie Ellicott Kennedy Bidwell, moved to the mansion that is now the Bidwell Mansion State Historic Park.

Sights

Chico's sights revolve around nature and beer – not a bad combo for travelers looking to relax in the shadow of the Sierras. Nearly all the sights are downtown, west of Hwy 99, easily reached via Hwy 32 (8th St). Main St and Broadway are the central downtown streets; from there, Park Ave stretches south and the tree-lined Esplanade heads north.

★**Sierra Nevada Brewing Company** BREWERY
(☎530-899-4776; www.sierranevada.com; 1075 E 20th St; ⏲tours 11am-4pm Sun-Thu, to 5:30pm Fri & Sat) Hordes of beer fans gather at the birthplace of the nationally distributed Sierra Nevada Pale Ale and Schwarber,

a Chico-only black ale. You can also stock up on eccentric 'Beer Camp' collaborations, short-run craft beers brewed by uber beer nerds at invitation-only seminars. Free brewhouse tours are given regularly.

Tours include a self-guided option, but true beerheads will want to book the three-hour Beer Geek tour (advance reservations required). There's also a tour of the brewery's cutting-edge sustainable practices – its operations are 99.8% zero waste, its rooftop solar fields are among the largest privately owned solar fields in the US, and the brewery extended a spur of local railroad to increase transportation efficiency. Recharge in the pub and restaurant (p600).

Bidwell Mansion State Historic Park HISTORIC BUILDING
(☎530-895-6144; www.parks.ca.gov; 525 Esplanade; adult/child $6/3; ⊙11am-5pm Sat-Mon) Chico's most prominent landmark, the opulent 26-room Victorian home was built for Chico's founders, John and Annie Bidwell, between 1865 and 1868. It hosted many US presidents and John Muir, who was a personal friend of Annie. Tours start every hour from 11am to 4pm.

Chico Creek Nature Center SCIENCE CENTER
(www.chicorec.com/chico-creek-nature-center; 1968 E 8th St; adult/child $4/2; ⊙9am-noon Wed-Sat; 👪) If you plan on spending the afternoon in Bidwell Park, stop here first for displays on local plants and animals and excellent hands-on science programs for families.

Activities

In summer you can cool off by tubing the Sacramento River. Inner tubes can be rented at grocery stores and other shops along Nord Ave (Hwy 32) for $7 to $12. Tubers enter at the Irvine Finch Launch Ramp on Hwy 32, a few miles west of Chico, and come out at Washout Beach, off River Rd.

★Bidwell Park HIKING
(www.bidwellpark.org) Growing out of downtown, the 3670-acre Bidwell Park is the state's third-largest municipal park. It stretches 10 miles northwest along Chico Creek with lush groves and miles of trails. Several classic movies have been shot here, including parts of *Gone with the Wind* and *The Adventures of Robin Hood.*

The upper part of the park is an untamed oasis, with miles of trails weaving along creek banks, between basalt rock formations and across meadows dusted in spring wildflowers. Bidwell is also full of swimming spots, great for hot Chico days. You'll find pools at One-Mile and Five-Mile recreation areas and swimming holes (including Bear Hole, Salmon Hole and Brown Hole) in Upper Bidwell Park, north of Manzanita Ave.

Adventure Outing OUTDOORS
(☎530-898-4011; https://as.csuchico.edu/index.php/adventure-outings; 2nd & Chestnut Sts, Bell Memorial Union basement; ⊙9am-5pm Mon-Fri) The CSU-run outfitter rents equipment like life jackets, rafts and even coolers at very reasonable prices by the weekend or week. It also leads popular trips further afield.

Festivals & Events

With the students out of town, family-friendly outdoor events take over each summer. The Thursday Night Market fills several blocks of Broadway from April to September. At the **City Plaza** (www.downtownchico.com; W 4th & Broadway Sts), you'll find free Friday night concerts starting in May.

Sleeping

There are decent independent motels with swimming pools, some of them along the shaded Esplanade north of downtown. Chico State's graduation and homecoming mania (May and October, respectively) send prices skyward.

Hotel Diamond HOTEL $$$
(☎866-993-3100; www.hoteldiamondchico.com; 220 W 4th St; r $150-599; P ❄ @ ☎) is the most luxurious place to stay, with high thread counts and attentive room service. The Diamond Suite, with its spacious top-floor balcony, is a-*maz*-ing. There's also a swanky bar and restaurant, **Diamond Steakhouse**, downstairs.

Eating

Downtown Chico is packed with fun places to eat, many of them catering to a student budget. The outdoor farmers market (p600) draws from the plentiful surrounding valley.

The Banshee PUB FOOD $
(☎530-895-9670; www.thebansheechico.com; 134 W 2nd Street; mains $13-16; ⊙11am-2am; P ❄ ☎) Besides having the coolest name for a restaurant ever, this seemingly nondescript spot happens to hawk some of the tastiest burgers in town, and the website promises that they 'won't be served on a damn cutting board.'

The Aussie Burger with bacon, fried egg and pickled beets is gooey, delicious heaven.

Rawbar Restaurant & Sushi SUSHI $
(☎ 530-897-0626; www.rawbarchico.com; 346 Broadway St; mains $6-17; ⏰11:30am-9pm Mon-Thu, to 10pm Fri, noon-10pm Sat, 5-9pm Sun; ❄ 👪) The mod Rawbar serves up surprisingly fresh sushi that takes some creative risks without being over-the-top – the Lemon Hamachi roll featuring yellowtail, cucumber, serrano pepper, crispy garlic and lemon is a bright spot on the menu. Hot plates are also highly rated.

Shubert's Ice Cream & Candy ICE CREAM $
(☎ 530-342-7163; www.shuberts.com; 178 E 7th St; ⏰9:30am-10pm Mon-Fri, from 11am Sat & Sun) Five generations of Shuberts have produced delicious homemade ice cream, chocolates and confections for more than 75 years at this beloved pastel-colored Chico landmark. The flavors change with the season; consider yourself lucky to get the boysenberry sundaes or a scoop of the Mt Shasta (chocolate with coconut and marshmallow swirl).

OM Foods VEGAN $
(☎ 530-965-5263; www.iloveomfoods.com; 142 Broadway St; mains $6.50-13; ⏰11am-7pm Mon-Sat; ❄ 🌿) This boho-chic eatery offers up extensive organic vegan and vegetarian fare in an inviting space. The menu sports options like dill slaw tempeh burgers, several interesting takes on avocado toast and the ever-popular vegan nachos.

Chico Certified Farmers Market MARKET $
(☎ 530-893-3276; www.chicofarmersmarket.com; 305 Wall St, Chico Municipal parking lot; ⏰7:30am-1pm Sat) Rain or shine, this excellent open-air market brings in the best from the valley, artisanal baked goods and coffee.

El Paisa Taco Truck MEXICAN $
(129 Walnut St; mains $1.50-5; ⏰10:30am-8pm) Debate about which of Chico's taco trucks is best can quickly lead to fisticuffs, but the smoky carnitas tacos served at this mobile kitchen are a dream.

Sin of Cortez CAFE $
(☎ 430-879-9200; http://sinofcortezchico.com; 2290 Esplanade; mains $10-16; ⏰7am-2pm; 🌿) The service won't win awards for speed, but this local favorite draws both vegetarian and omnivorous mobs with its burly breakfast plates. Order anything with the soy chorizo. Parking is somewhat limited for its popularity, however, so try to avoid busy times.

Sierra Nevada Taproom & Restaurant PUB FOOD $$
(www.sierranevada.com; 1075 E 20th St; mains $14.50-40; ⏰11am-9pm Sun-Thu, to 10pm Fri & Sat; 🌿) The suds on tap are the main draw at the on-site restaurant of the Sierra Nevada Brewery Company (p598). This genuine Chico destination is great for downing brews but lacks ambience. Still, it does have better-than-average pub food and superbly fresh ales and lagers, some not available elsewhere.

Drinking & Nightlife

Given Chico's party-school rep, you won't be thirsty. There's a strip of bars on Main St if you want to go hopping.

Naked Lounge COFFEE
(☎ 530-895-0676; 118 W 2nd St; ⏰7am-8pm; 📶) With excellent coffee, mellow music and a choice selection of beer on tap, this inviting downtown cafe is perfect for an easygoing morning. The Thai coffee and the chai latte are sure bets.

Madison Bear Garden BAR
(☎ 530-891-1639; www.madisonbeargarden.com; 316 W 2nd St; ⏰11am-1:45am; 📶) This spacious brick building with adjoining big beer garden isn't only the most reliable scene in Chico – it's an institution. The walls and ceilings are loaded with kitsch, and students pack the place for big burgers and cold pints.

Secret Trail Brewing BREWERY
(☎ 530-487-8151; www.secrettrailbrewing.com; 132 Meyers St #120; ⏰3-7pm Tue-Thu, noon-7pm Fri-Sun) This unassuming brewery tucked away from Chico's downtown has a small but energetic tap room, plus food trucks in the parking lot. The Nacht Hund Schwarzbier is particularly delicious, as is the dessert-y Choconut Baltic Porter.

Panama Bar & Cafe BAR
(☎ 530-895-8817; www.panamabarcafeinchico.com; 177 E 2nd St; iced tea from $3; ⏰11:30am-10pm Tue & Wed, to 1:30am Thu-Sat, 10am-9pm Sun) The house specializes in 31 variations of Long Island iced teas (most of which are around $3), so brace yourself. The faded palm tree wallpaper and the friendly bartender make the space feel like a timeworn coastal haunt where many hours are easily lost.

Entertainment

For entertainment options, pick up the free weekly *Chico News & Review* (www.newsandreview.com). For theater, films, concerts, art exhibits and other cultural events at the CSU campus, contact the **CSU Box Office** (530-898-6333; www.csuchico.edu/boxoffice; Sierra Hall, cnr 3rd & Chestnut; 10am-6pm Mon-Fri).

Pageant Theatre CINEMA
(www.pageantchico.com; 351 E 6th St; tickets $8) Screens international and alternative films. Monday is 'cheap skate night,' with all seats just $4.

1078 Gallery ARTS CENTER
(530-433-1043; www.1078gallery.org; 1710 Park Avenue; 12-4pm Thu-Sun) Chico's contemporary gallery exhibits artworks and hosts boundary-pushing literary readings, music and theater.

Shopping

Upper Park Clothing CLOTHING
(530-487-7118; https://upperparkclothing.com; 122 W 3rd St; 10am-5:30pm Mon-Sat, 11am-4pm Sun) This design shop started as a T-shirt printer, eventually introducing its own original art and launching a new, Chico-loving brand dedicated to outdoor and activewear. The printed shirts, sweatshirts and hats are smart and modern – many touting the natural marvels close to the city – and the shop gives back to the community via design campaigns.

Information

Chico Chamber of Commerce & Visitor Center (530-891-5556; www.chicochamber.com; 180 E 4th St Suite 120; 10am-4pm Mon-Fri) Local information including bike maps.

Getting There & Around

Greyhound (www.greyhound.com) buses stop multiple times a day at the **Amtrak station** (www.amtrak.com; 450 Orange St) heading to San Francisco ($44, five hours), Reno ($70, eight hours), Los Angeles ($50, 11½ hours) and points between. The platform is unattended so purchase tickets in advance or from the driver.

Amtrak trains on the *Coast Starlight* line depart Chico in the middle of the night for Redding ($18, 1½ hours) and Sacramento ($18, 2½ hours). Amtrak's connecting buses travel through the region as well, but require booking a connecting train.

B-Line (Butte Regional Transit; 530-342-0221; www.blinetransit.com; W 2nd St at Salem; adult/child $1.75/1.25) handles all buses throughout Butte County, and can get you around Chico and down to Oroville in 50 minutes.

Car is the easiest way to get around, but Chico is one of the best biking towns in the country. Rent from **Campus Bicycles** (www.campusbicycles.com; 247 Main St; rental half/full day $20/35; 10am-6pm Mon-Sat, 11am-4pm Sun).

Red Bluff

The smoldering streets of Red Bluff – one of California's hottest towns due to the hot-air trap of the Shasta Cascades – aren't much of a draw on their own. But a glimpse toward the mountainous horizon reveals what brings most travelers this way.

Peter Lassen laid out the town site in 1847 and it grew into a key port along the Sacramento River. Now it's a pit stop on the way to the national park that bears his name.

Cowboy culture is alive and well here. Catch it in action the third weekend of April at the **Red Bluff Round-Up** (www.redbluffroundup.com; tickets $16-35), a major rodeo event dating back to 1918, or in any of the dive bars where the jukeboxes are stocked with country and plenty of cowboys belly up to the bar. You can also stock up on your own Western wear from one of several historic storefronts in the business district.

Sights

Sacramento River Discovery Center SCIENCE CENTER
(530-527-1196; www.sacramentoriverdiscoverycenter.com; 1000 Sale Lane; admission by donation; 11am-3pm Tue-Sat;) This kid-friendly center has exhibits on the river and the Diversion Dam just outside its doors, which has been permanently opened to allow endangered chinook and green and white sturgeon to migrate. Though the fish aren't visible, up to 264 species of birds are. Bird walks along the 4.2 miles of wheelchair-accessible trails start the first Saturday of each month at 8am.

Red Bluff Recreation Area PARK
(530-527-2813; www.fs.usda.gov;) This sprawling park of meadows on the east bank of the Sacramento River has interpretive trails, bicycle paths, boat ramps, a wildlife-viewing area with excellent bird-watching, and a salmon and steelhead ladder (most active July to September).

William B Ide Adobe State Historic Park HISTORIC SITE
(☎530-529-8599; https://www.parks.ca.gov; 21659 Adobe Rd; per car $6; ⊙8am-6pm) Set on a beautiful, shaded piece of land overlooking a languorous section of the Sacramento River, this park preserves the original one-room adobe house, old forge and grounds of pioneer William B Ide, who 'fought' in the 1846 Bear Flag Revolt at Sonoma. He became president of the California Bear Republic, which lasted 25 days.

Sleeping & Eating

Sycamore Grove Camping Area CAMPGROUND $
(☎530-527-2813; www.recreation.gov; tent/RV sites $16/30) Beside the river in the Red Bluff Recreation Area is this quiet USFS campground. Campsites for tents and RVs are first-come, first-served, and offer shared showers and flush toilets. You can reserve a large group campground, Camp Discovery, which has basic screened-in cabins that must be booked as a block ($175 for all 11 cabins per night).

From The Hearth CAFE $
(☎530-727-0616; www.fthcafe.com; 638 Washington St; sandwiches $11-13; ⊙7am-8pm Mon-Sat, to 6pm Sun) Pastries and expert coffee drinks in the morning, crispy, overloaded hot sandwiches on just-baked bread for lunch and dinner. Everything is very fresh, made to order and deeply satisfying, especially the Reuben. This no-fuss cafe is a dream for travelers who want to get a quick bite and get back on the road.

Los Mariachis MEXICAN $
(☎530-529-5154; www.redblufflosmariachis.com; 604 Main St; mains $10-14; ⊙9am-9pm Mon-Fri, to 9:30pm Sat & Sun;) This bright, family-run Mexican spot overlooks the central junction of Red Bluff. It has great salsa and staples big enough to satisfy hungry campers.

Thai House THAI $
(☎530-529-1217; 248 S Main St; mains $5-14; ⊙11am-3pm & 4-9pm; P) A remarkably solid Thai restaurant with good curries and soups.

Drinking & Nightlife

Cedar Crest Brewing BREWERY
(☎530-727-9016; https://cedarcrestbrewing.com; 615 Main St; ⊙11am-8pm Tue-Thu, to 10pm Fri & Sat, 2-7pm Mon & Sun) Situated inside a local specialty food spot called Enjoy The Store, this craft brewery pours floral IPAs and a delicious Dark Matter Porter. The surrounding store is great for stocking up on fancy snacks, such as local cheese, olives and nuts. There's also a wine shop in the back serving up a tasty house cab franc.

E's Locker Room BAR
(☎530-527-4600; 1075 Lakeside Dr; ⊙4pm-close Wed-Fri, from 3pm Sat & Sun) Framed photos of local legends and sports heroes clutter the walls of this friendly, casual Red Bluff bar. Take your pint to the patio that overlooks a lazy bend of the Sacramento River.

Information

Red Bluff Chamber of Commerce (☎530-527-6220; www.redbluffchamber.com; 100 Main St; ⊙9am-4pm Mon-Fri) To get your bearings and a stack of brochures, find this white building just south of downtown.

Getting There & Away

Most visitors pull into Red Bluff to take a break from the busy I-5. By highway, the town is three hours north of San Francisco and two hours north of Sacramento. **Amtrak** (www.amtrak.com; cnr Rio & Walnut Sts) and **Greyhound** (www.greyhound.com; 22700 Antelope Blvd) connect it with other California cities via bus.

SAN JOAQUIN VALLEY

The southern half of California's Central Valley – named for the San Joaquin River – sprawls from Stockton to the Tehachapi Mountains, southeast of Bakersfield. Everything stretches to the horizon in straight lines – railroad tracks, two-lane blacktop and long irrigation channels.

The tiny towns scattering the region meld their Main St Americana appeal with the cultural influence of the Latino labor force.

This is a place of seismic, often contentious, development. Arrivals from the coastal cities have resulted in unchecked urban sprawl. What were once actual ranches and vineyards are now nostalgically named developments, and water rights is *the* issue on everyone's minds.

At its northwestern corner sits the Sacramento–San Joaquin Delta, a riparian oasis fed by runoff from the Cascade and Sierra Nevada mountains. This unique wetland ecosystem is one of the most important water supplies in the state.

Sacramento–San Joaquin River Delta

The Sacramento Delta is a sprawling web of waterways and one-stoplight towns plucked out of the 1930s. This wetland area encompasses a huge swath of the state – from the San Francisco Bay to Sacramento, and all the way south to Stockton and the edge of the San Joaquin Valley. On weekends, locals gun powerboats on the wandering rivers and cruise winding levy roads beneath twisted oak canopies. If you have the time to smell the grassy delta breezes on the slow route between San Francisco and Sacramento, travel the iron bridges of winding Hwy 160. You'll lazily make your way past orderly vineyards, vast orchards, sandy swimming banks and little towns with long histories.

The region's best-known winery, **Bogle** (916-744-1092; www.boglewinery.com; 37783 Country Rd 144, Clarksburg; 10am-5pm Mon-Fri, from 11am Sat & Sun; P) FREE, is a few miles southwest of Clarksburg via the winding County Rds 141 and 144. It's set among vineyards on a sixth-generation family farm, and is very proud of its sustainable practices.

The **Old Sugar Mill** (916-744-1615; www.oldsugarmill.com; 35265 Willow Ave, Clarksburg; 11am-5pm; P) is the hub of a thriving community of local winemakers. The wines of the Clarksburg region have developed a lot over the last decade, benefiting from the blazing sun and cool delta breezes. Peruse the tasting rooms and enjoy a bottle on the outdoor patio overlooking vineyards.

Brannan Island State Park Recreation Area Campgrounds (800-444-7275; www.reservecalifornia.com; 17645 Hwy 160, Rio Vista;

THE DELTA DETOUR

Locke (916-776-1661; www.locketown.com; 13916 Main St, Walnut Grove; tours adult/student $5/3; visitors center noon-4pm Tue & Fri, 11am-3pm Sat & Sun), on Hwy 160, is the most fascinating of the Sacramento Delta towns, founded by Chinese laborers who also built the levees that ended perpetual flooding and allowed agriculture to flourish here. After a malicious fire wiped out the settlement in 1912, a group of community leaders approached land baron George Locke for a leasehold; at the time, California didn't allow people of Chinese descent to own property. Locke became the only freestanding town built and managed by Chinese people in the US, most of whom spoke the Chungsan dialect of Cantonese. Tucked below the levee, Locke's main street feels like a ghost town these days, but the weather-beaten buildings are protected on the National Register of Historic Places.

The colorful **Dai Loy Museum** (916-776-1661; www.locke-foundation.org; 13951 Main St, Locke; donations appreciated; noon-4pm Fri-Sun;), housing dusty *pai gow* (a Chinese gambling game played with dominoes) tables and an antique safe, is the main stop. Nearby is **Al's Place** (916-776-1800; 13943 Main St, Walnut Grove; mains $7-21; 11am-9pm), a saloon that's been pouring since 1915. Below are creaking floorboards; above, the ceiling's covered in crusty dollar bills and more than one pair of undies.

Hwy 160 also passes through Isleton, so-called Crawdad Town USA, whose main street has more shops, restaurants, bars and buildings that reflect the region's Chinese heritage. Isleton's Cajun Festival, at the end of June, draws folks from across the state, but you can get very lively crawdads year round at **Bob's Bait Shop** (916-777-6666; http://themasterbaiter.tripod.com; 302 2nd St, Isleton; 6am-4pm Thu & Fri, to 5pm Sat, to 3pm Sun).

Further west on Hwy 160 you'll see signs for the Delta Loop, a drive that passes boater bars and marinas where you can rent something to take on the water. At the end is the **Brannan Island State Recreation Area** (916-777-6671; www.parks.ca.gov; 17645 Hwy 160, Rio Vista; per car $10; sunrise-sunset; P), which has boat-in, drive-in and walk-in campsites.

In the 1930s the Bureau of Reclamation issued an aggressive water-redirection program – the Central Valley and California State Water Projects – that dammed California's major rivers and directed 75% of their supply through the Central Valley for agriculture and Southern California. The siphoning affected the delta, its wetlands and estuaries, and sparked debate. Learn about the area's unique legacy by bus or on a self-guided tour with **Delta Heartbeat Tours** (916-776-4010; www.deltaheartbeattours.com), which also has leads on boat rides. If you have a car, taste the fruits of the delta on the **Delta Grown Farm Trail** (916-775-1166; www.sacriverdeltagrown.org).

DON'T MISS

SAN JOAQUIN ASPARAGUS FESTIVAL

Of all the Central Valley food celebrations, perhaps none pay such creative respect to the main ingredient as the **San Joaquin Asparagus Festival** (https://sanjoaquinasparagusfestival.net; 1658 S Airport Way; adult/child $13/free; Apr;), which brings together more than 500 vendors to serve these green stalks – more than 10 tons of them! – every way imaginable. It sprouts at the San Joaquin County Fairgrounds at the end of April.

tent & RV sites $36-49, cabin $56;) is a tidy facility in a protected wetland marsh that provides drive-in and walk-in campsites. There's a hike-in log cabin with electricity that sleeps four; bring sleeping bags.

In nearby Isleton, **Rogelio's** (916-777-5878; www.rogelios.net; 34 Main St, Isleton; mains $8-17; 4-8pm Tue & Wed, 11am-8pm Thu & Sun, to 9pm Fri & Sat) makes the most of the delta's multiethnic history, serving a mash-up of Mexican and Chinese dishes, with a few Italian and American standards mixed in. But nothing beats the carnitas.

Lodi

Although Lodi was once the 'Watermelon capital of the world,' today, full-bodied wine rules this patch of the valley. Breezes from the Sacramento River Delta soothe the area's hot vineyards, where some of the world's oldest zinfandel vines grow. Lodi's diverse soil is sometimes rocky, sometimes fine sandy loam, giving its grapes a range of distinctive characteristics that allow for experimentation with some less common varietals.

Lodi is an ideal destination for those looking for a low-key, budget-friendly wine trip. The town also hosts a slew of festivals dedicated to their famous export, including the **Wine & Chocolate Weekend** in February and **ZinFest** in May.

Sights & Activities

Micke Grove Regional Park & Zoo ZOO
(209-331-2010; www.mgzoo.com; 11793 N Micke Grove Rd; zoo entry adult/child $5/3, parking $5; 10am-5pm;) For the seriously underage, Lodi's Micke Grove Regional Park and Zoo is a good stop, home to a water play area, hissing cockroaches and some barking sea lions. There are also kiddie rides in a section called Fun Town. The park houses an exceptional **Japanese Garden** (www.sjparks.com; 11793 N Micke Grove Rd; 9am-2pm Mon-Thu, to 1pm Fri-Sun) FREE.

Headwaters Kayak KAYAKING
(209-224-8367; www.headwatersKayak.com; 847 N Cluff Ave, Suite A-6; hourly/day rental from $16/40; 10am-5pm;) This small outfit rents kayaks and stand-up paddleboards for use on nearby Lodi Lake. It regularly organizes community paddles – Full Moon, Ladies Only and Wildlife excursions are all on the roster.

Sleeping & Eating

★ **Poppy Sister Inn** B&B $$
(209-401-2502; www.poppysisterinn.com; 533 W Oak St; r $150) This buttercream-yellow Victorian house is a welcoming, atmospheric base for vineyard exploring. The home has four cozy rooms (each with a private bathroom), and your stay includes breakfast and wine social hours in the afternoon. The wraparound porch makes an ideal spot for relaxing after a long day.

Wine & Roses HOTEL $$$
(209-334-6988; http://winerose.com; 2505 W Turner Rd; d $249, ste from $299;) Surrounded by a vast rose garden, this is one of the more luxurious offerings to spring up amid Lodi's vineyards. Tasteful and romantic, the rooms have slate bathrooms, high-quality toiletries and lots of square footage. There's an acclaimed restaurant and spa too.

Dancing Fox Winery & Bakery AMERICAN $
(209-366-2634; www.dancingfoxwinery.com; 203 S School St; mains $11-14; 11am-9pm Tue-Thu, to 10pm Fri & Sat, 9am-3pm Sun) Everything here celebrates grapes – from the Lewis Family Estate's own wines to the bread cultures created from the vineyard's petite sirah grapes. Menu highlights include the grilled sandwiches stuffed to max capacity (the tri tip green chili melt is choice) and a tasty cabernet franc.

Hollywood Family Cafe DINER $
(209-369-4065; www.lodicafe.com; 315 S Cherokee Ln; mains $10-14; 6am-3pm) Originally a truck stop in the 1940s, the Hollywood Cafe is a proper blast from the past – red vinyl

seating, checkerboard floors and a roster of regulars make it feel authentically vintage. The menu includes diner staples like burgers, sandwiches and huge breakfasts. The Elvis French Toast (stuffed with peanut butter and banana) is perfection.

Towne House Restaurant CALIFORNIAN $$$
(☎209-371-6160; https://winerose.com/the-restaurant; 2505 W Turner Rd; mains $24-53; ⏰11am-2pm & 5-9pm Mon-Fri, 9am-2pm & 5-9pm Sat & Sun) The bright, crisply designed on-site restaurant of Wine & Roses draws on locally sourced ingredients in an elegant preparation. There's often live jazz in the evening in the adjoining lounge, which pours cocktails and local wines.

Drinking & Nightlife

Lodi Beer Company PUB
(☎209-368-9931; www.lodibeercompany.com; 105 S School St; ⏰11am-9pm Sun-Thu, to 10pm Fri & Sat) Beerheads, despair not! This convivial gastropub is a beer oasis in wine country, pouring solid suds that keep the bar packed. The space itself is warm, with exposed brick, a tiled ceiling and large copper brewing tanks in the middle of the room, and the friendly bartenders are happy to make recommendations – try their Oktoberfest brew. Also serves up a lengthy menu of pub grub.

Blend Ultra Lounge COCKTAIL BAR
(☎209-331-2036; www.blendlodi.com; 115 S School St, Suite 13; ⏰7pm-2am Fri & Sat) Patrons sip colorful cocktails while bathed in blue neon at this (almost) swanky lounge. When the Giants are on, it takes on the vibe of a (almost) swanky sports bar.

Shopping

Cheese Central FOOD
(☎209-368-3033; www.cheesecentrallodi.com; 11 N School St; ⏰10am-6pm Mon-Sat, 1-5pm Sun) Ask Cindy the cheesemonger for thoughtful pairings with Lodi wines. If you want to make a weekend out of Lodi's wine region, try one of the cooking classes.

Stockton

Stockton has had its share of ups and downs – including challenges with the housing crisis and large civic debt – but the waterfront redevelopment is one of the valley's more promising grassroots efforts. Slightly north of downtown you'll find 'Miracle Mile', a second hub of bars and restaurants.

The city has an interesting past just under the surface of its checkered facades. It is a major inland port and was once the main supply hub for gold rushers. During WWII it became a major center of American shipbuilding, and remains home to a few maritime transportation facilities.

A block east of Weber Point, the **Department of Tourism** (☎209-938-1555; www.visitstockton.org; 125 Bridge Pl, 2nd Fl; ⏰7:30am-4:30pm Mon-Fri) has information about the goings-on in town.

Sights & Activities

Weber Point Events Center LANDMARK
(ww1.stocktonca.gov; 221 N Center St) Downtown on the McLeod Lake waterfront, the modern white edifice standing in the middle of a grassy park looking rather like a pile of sailboats is the Weber Point Events Center.

Haggin Museum MUSEUM
(www.hagginmuseum.org; 1201 N Pershing Ave; adult/child $8/5; ⏰1:30-5pm Wed-Fri, from noon Sat & Sun, 1:30-9pm 1st & 3rd Thu; P 👪) This city gem houses galleries dedicated to Stockton's history with unique pieces like a 26ft boat by Stockton's own Stephens Bros company and vintage firefighting equipment. It also has an excellent collection of American landscape and 'Golden Age' paintings.

Banner Island Ballpark STADIUM
(☎209-644-1900; www.stocktonports.com; 404 W Fremont St) The beautiful Banner Island Ballpark is where the minor-league Stockton Ports play ball April to September.

Sleeping & Eating

University Plaza Waterfront Hotel HOTEL $
(☎209-944-1140; www.universityplazawaterfronthotel.com; 110 W Fremont St; d $139; 📶) If you're spending the night here, the best option is University Plaza Waterfront Hotel, where business travelers mingle with University of the Pacific students who live in the lofts on the upper floors. The modern building overlooking the harbor and historic park is walkable from other locations in the city center, unlike the highway chains.

Stockton Farmers Market MARKET $
(www.stocktonfarmersmarket.org; 333 E Washington St; ⏰5:30-11am Sat) You can find fresh fish and a huge variety of Asian vegetables each Saturday, under the elevated freeway.

Papa Urb's Grill FILIPINO $
(☎209-227-8144; www.papaurbsgrill.com; 331 E Weber Ave; mains $5-10; ⏰11am-7:30pm Mon-Sat) Filipino flavors drive the menu of fusion fast food at this bright cafe: there's adobo and *longanisa* (Filipino pork sausage) in many of the Mexican presentations. If you want to expand your horizons, go for the *sisig* fries, a savory mess of pork, yams and tangy cilantro dipping sauce.

Smitty's Wings & Things CHICKEN $
(☎209-227-7479; 5654 N Pershing Ave; mains $10-19; ⏰11am-8pm) This neighborhood joint is run by a former NFL player and his wife, who turn out perfectly crispy wings and pizzas. They have daily specials and a selection of cold beer on tap. The sauces for the wings are all amazing, but we love the tingling spice of the 'damn hot' and garlic chili.

On Lok Sam CANTONESE $$
(www.newonlocksam.com; 333 S Sutter St; mains $10-25; ⏰11am-8pm) Venture south of the Crosstown Freeway to (New) On Lok Sam, established in 1895 in the center of Stockton's lively Chinese settlement. The garlic chicken and spicy, deep-fried green beans are delicious.

Drinking & Nightlife

Black Rabbit BAR
(☎209-323-5141; 2353 Pacific Ave, Ste B; ⏰4pm-midnight Tue-Thu, to 12:30am Fri & Sat) Marked only by a sign depicting its signature geometric rabbit, this tiny gastropub feels like a well-kept secret. The moody interior complements its simple but effective drink list, and the kitchen produces solid pub-inspired small plates.

AVE on the Mile BAR
(☎209-462-5283; 2333 Pacific Ave; ⏰3:30pm-midnight Mon-Thu, to 1am Fri, 4:30pm-1am Sat, 10am-2pm Sun) Exposed brick and a glittering wall of bottles make this the most elegant option on the block, with a club-like atmosphere in the evenings. It has a full menu of upscale pub food and Sunday brunch comes with bottomless mimosas.

Getting There & Away

By train, boat or car, Stockton is easy to reach; it sits between I-5 and Hwy 99. You can also take Amtrak's San Joaquin line or the regional **Altamont Commuter Express** (☎800-411-7245; www.acerail.com; 949 East Channel St; one-way tickets $4.75-15.50) from the **Robert J Cabral Station** (☎800-872-7245; 949 East Channel St), or float from the downtown marina to the Sacramento–San Joaquin River Delta.

Modesto

Cruising was banned in Modesto in 1993, but the town still touts itself as the 'cruising capital of the world.' The pastime's notoriety stems mostly from homegrown George Lucas' 1973 film *American Graffiti*. You'll still see hot rods and flashy wheels around town, but they no longer clog thoroughfares on Friday nights.

This is a good spot for getting off the dusty highway. Old oaks arch over the city's streets, and downtown is a good spot to stretch your legs and grab a good bite to eat.

Classic car shows and rock and roll fill the streets every June for **Graffiti Summer** (www.visitmodesto.com; ⏰Jun). Amid all the 1950s nostalgia, the sparkling Gallo Center for the Arts brings huge acts to the valley. For details, check the **Modesto Convention & Visitors Bureau** (☎888-640-8467; www.visitmodesto.com; 1150 9th St; ⏰8am-5pm Mon-Fri).

Eating & Drinking

Thailand Restaurant THAI $
(☎209-544-0505; www.facebook.com/ThailandRestaurantModesto; 950 10th St, Ste 17; mains $9-15; ⏰10:30am-3pm & 4:30-9pm Mon-Fri, 11am-9pm Sat; 🌱) Go for the spicy noodles and green papaya salad at this friendly, spotless Thai restaurant.

Brighter Side SANDWICHES $
(1125 K St; sandwiches $6-7.25; ⏰11am-3:30pm Mon-Fri; 🌱) An earthy little sandwich shop housed in a wood-shingled former gas station that serves up sandwiches such as the Larry (Polish sausage, mushrooms, green onions on rye) or the veggie Christine (avocado, sprouts, tomato on dark rye) on the sunny patio. The vibe is a unique blend of boho-Americana.

A&W Drive-In AMERICAN $
(www.awrestaurants.com; 1404 G St; cheeseburger $4.30, float $5; ⏰10am-7pm Sat-Thu, to 9pm Fri) A vintage burger stand (part of a chain founded in nearby Lodi), where carhops still move a lot of root beer floats. George Lucas supposedly cruised here as a youth.

Commonwealth AMERICAN $$
(☎209-248-7451; www.commonwealthmodesto.com; 1022 11th St; mains $11-30; ⏲11am-10pm Mon-Wed, to midnight Thu & Fri, 9am-midnight Sat, 9am-10pm Sun) Modern and artsy yet welcoming, Commonwealth is a popular downtown stop with a great selection of local wine and beer, and indulgent sandwiches (try the M80, which unites jalapeño fried chicken and thick bacon). In the morning, it serves picture-perfect waffles.

Churchkey BEER HALL
(☎209-422-3128; www.churchkeymodesto.com; 910 12th St; pizzas $12-16; ⏲11am-9pm Sun-Wed, to 11pm Thu-Sat) This bright, subway-tile-lined industrial hall is a cheery spot for a drink and an oven-fired pizza. Depending on your mood, choose from one of its thirty rotating taps, its extensive wall of whiskey or its fresh-pressed juices.

Queen Bean Coffee House CAFE
(☎209-521-8000; 1126 14th St; ⏲7:30am-6:30pm Mon, to 8pm Tue & Wed, to 7pm Thu & Fri, to 10pm Sun) Tucked away in a house on the edge of downtown, Queen Bean is a homey spot where folks settle in to work, read, play chess, drink coffee or nom on cafe goodies like breakfast burritos, chicken salad sandwiches and BLTs. The decor reads Victorian tinged with Alice in Wonderland, and the cafe has a spacious shaded patio. Sundays are Open Mic Night.

Tiki Cocktail Lounge GAY & LESBIAN
(☎209-577-9969; 932 McHenry Ave; ⏲5pm-2am) Campy decor, friendly bartenders and an indoor fire pit give this gay hangout lots of cozy atmosphere.

Entertainment

Gallo Center for the Arts PERFORMING ARTS
(☎209-338-2100; www.galloarts.org; 1000 I St; ⏲10am-6pm Mon-Fri, from noon Sat) This huge, state-of-the-art performing-arts complex in downtown Modesto brings great musical, dance and theater acts to town.

State Theatre THEATER
(www.thestate.org; 1307 J St) This historic theater has stood here since 1934 and continues to put on films, live-music concerts, comedy shows and movie series.

Merced

You can jog over to Yosemite from many of the small towns in this part of the valley, but this is a convenient staging area, right on Hwy 140. Urban development has not been particularly kind to Merced, as it suffers more than its share of strip malls. Still, you'll find tree-lined streets, historic Victorian homes and a magnificent 1875 courthouse at the city's core. The downtown business district is a work in progress, with 1930s movie theaters, antique stores and a few casual eateries undergoing constant renovation. University of California, Merced injects a youthful contingent into the population, and the diverse student body continues to shape the city.

Sights

Castle Air Museum MUSEUM
(☎209-723-2178; www.castleairmuseum.org; 5050 Santa Fe Dr, Atwater; adult/child $20/15; ⏲9am-4pm) Aerospace buffs will enjoy strolling down the rows of vintage military aircraft, ranging from pre-WWII to the present, on former Air Force base grounds. Military mechanics volunteer their time restoring these planes and are often on-site to answer questions. The museum also hosts Open Cockpit Days for you to get an even closer look at these behemoth machines.

The museum is home to a gigantic Douglas RA-3 Skywarrior, a reconnaissance bomber with a wingspan of 72ft. It is the largest, heaviest jet to ever land on an aircraft carrier. More than 1200 wing bolts had to be unscrewed just to move it to the museum.

Merced Multicultural Arts Center GALLERY
(☎209-388-1090; www.artsmerced.org; 645 W Main St; ⏲11am-6pm Tue-Fri, 10am-2pm Sat) This friendly gallery space serves as one of Merced's best art hubs, hosting a variety of exhibits in all mediums. Check its calendar for show openings, arts programs and performances at its 'black box' theater.

Eating & Drinking

Little Oven Pizza PIZZA $
(https://littleovenmerced.com; 433 W Main St; slices $3-4; ⏲11:30am-9pm Mon-Thu, to 11pm Fri, noon-11pm Sat, noon-9pm Sun; 📶) Turning out picture-perfect, New York–style thin crust, this tidy downtown spot offers daily specials and makes a quick, cheap option. The Bee Thousand – an inventive combination of salami, honey and chili oil – is delicious. Like everything else on the menu, the ingredients are sourced from the Central Valley.

New Thai Cuisine THAI $
(209-726-1048; 909 W 16th St; mains $10-16; 11am-8pm) It's hardly the fanciest digs in town, but this downtown Thai restaurant makes an excellent combination pho soup, sweet-and-savory honey sesame wings and a nice duck curry.

Branding Iron STEAK $$
(www.thebrandingiron-merced.com; 640 W 16th St; mains lunch $9-11, dinner $10-37; 11:30am-2pm Mon-Fri, 5-9pm Sun-Thu, to 9:30pm Fri & Sat) The Branding Iron roadhouse, a favorite of ranchers in the area, has been spruced up a bit for the tour buses, but locals still dig the hearty steak platters and Western atmosphere. Presiding over the dining room is 'Old Blue,' a massive stuffed bull's head from a local dairy farm.

17th Street Public House BAR
(209-354-4449; 315 W Main St; noon-10pm Sun-Wed, to midnight Thu & Fri) This haven for serious beer drinkers has an excellent and often-updated rotation of taps and a huge selection of bottles.

Getting There & Away

Greyhound (710 W 16th St) also operates from the Transpo Center (Los Angeles $21, 6½ hours, four times daily)

YARTS (Yosemite Area Regional Transportation System; 209-388-9589; www.yarts.com) buses depart three (winter) to five (summer) times daily for Yosemite Valley from several Merced locations, including the **Merced Transpo Center** (www.mercedthebus.com; cnr 16th & N Sts) and the **Amtrak station** (www.amtrak.com; 324 W 24th St). The trip takes about 2½ hours and stops include Mariposa, Midpines and the Yosemite Valley Visitors Center. A round-trip costs $38 and includes park entry and one free child ride (6-12) – quite a bargain! There's limited space for bicycles, so show up early if you have one.

Fresno

Smack in the arid center of the state, Fresno is the Central Valley's biggest city. It's hardly scenic, but beautifully situated, just an hour and a half from four national parks (Yosemite, Sierra, Kings Canyon and Sequoia), making it the ideal last stop for expeditions.

Fresno's agriculture-based economy has suffered from droughts and plummeting food prices, but a local farm movement seeks to revolutionize food production through organic, sustainable practices and fair wages. The city's proximity to these progressive farms has fostered a food renaissance – make time to explore the orchards, wineries and restaurants surrounding town, where you'll find some of the freshest food in the state.

Like many valley cities, Fresno is home to diverse Hmong, Mexican, Chinese and Basque communities, which arrived in successive waves. The longstanding Armenian community is famously represented by author and playwright William Saroyan, who was born, lived and died in this city he loved.

Sights

One of the most bustling parts of town is the Tower District, north of downtown, an oasis of gay-friendly bars, book and record stores, music clubs and a handful of popular restaurants. Many of the historic buildings are along the Santa Fe railroad tracks and downtown, including the 1894 **Fresno Water Tower** and the 1928 **Pantages (Warnors) Theatre**. The crowds gather at the sprawling **Convention Center** and **Chukchansi Park**, home of Fresno's Triple-A baseball team, the Grizzlies.

Downtown lies between Divisadero St, Hwy 41 and Hwy 99. Two miles north, the Tower District sits around the corner of E Olive and N Fulton Aves.

Forestiere Underground Gardens GARDENS
(559-271-0734; www.undergroundgardens.com; 5021 W Shaw Ave; adult/child $19/9; tours 10am-4pm hourly Wed-Sun Apr-Oct, reduced hours Nov-Mar) If you see only one thing in Fresno, make it this intriguing historic landmark, two blocks east of Hwy 99. The gardens were built by Sicilian immigrant Baldassare Forestiere, who dug out some 70 acres beneath the hardpan soil to plant citrus trees, starting in 1906. This utterly fantastical accomplishment took 40 years to complete.

With a unique skylight system, Forestiere created a beautiful subterranean space for commercial crops and his own living quarters. The tunnel system includes bedrooms, a library, patios, grottos and a fishpond. Check the website for tour times.

Woodward Park PARK
(www.fresno.gov; 7775 Friant Rd; per vehicle $5; 7am-10pm Apr-Oct, to 7pm Nov-Mar) The city's largest park has 300 acres of barbecue facilities, lakes and ponds, a **Japanese garden** (adult/child $5/1, cash only), and a huge amphitheater for Shakespeare and other

performances. A 6-mile network of bike trails connects to the **Lewis S Eaton Trail**, which runs 22 miles from the northeast corner along Friant Rd to Friant Dam.

Cedar View Winery WINERY

(☎559-787-9412; www.cedarviewwinery.com; 1384 S Frankwood Ave, Sanger; tastings $7; ⊙noon-5pm Sat & Sun) On the easternmost reaches of the Blossom Trail, Cedar View Winery is a comfy place to enjoy a glass of wine and Sierra views from the back patio. Known for its bouschet, an unusual choice in these parts. There's also an on-site bed and breakfast.

Simonian Farms FARM

(☎559-237-2294; www.simonianfarms.com; 2629 S Clovis Ave; ⊙9am-6pm Mon-Sat, to 5:30pm Sun) This farm stand is more than a stand: it's a kitsch museum, monument, orchard and general store rolled into one. Skip the hokey made-for-tour-buses barn and wander the parking lot dotted with vintage tractors, trains and more (all labeled with dates) before ducking into the store to purchase any variation of dried fruit you could dream of. This is an ideal spot to begin your loop through Fresno's Blossom Trail.

One of the property's more poignant features is a stark wooden tower in the middle of the lot, a monument built by the owner to commemorate the Japanese American families who taught him how to farm, and honor the hardships they faced during WWII and after; the structure is built from wood taken from a Japanese internment camp.

Roeding Park PARK

(www.fresno.gov; 890 W Belmont Ave; per vehicle $5; ⊙7am-10pm Apr-Oct, to 7pm Nov-Mar) Just east of Hwy 99, this large and shady park is home to the small **Fresno Chaffee Zoo** (☎559-498-5910; www.fresnochaffeezoo.org; 894 W Belmont Ave; adult/child $14.95/8.95; ⊙9am-6pm; 👪). Adjacent to it are **Storyland** (☎559-486-2124; https://storylandfresno.com/; 890 W Belmont Ave; adult/child $6/4; ⊙10am-4pm Sat & Sun; 👪), a kitschy children's fairy-tale world dating from 1962, and **Playland** (www.playlandfresno.com; 890 W Belmont Ave; unlimited rides $20; ⊙10am-4pm Wed-Sun; 👪), which has kiddie rides and games.

Fresno Art Museum MUSEUM

(☎559-441-4221; www.fresnoartmuseum.org; 2233 N 1st St; adult/child $10/7; ⊙11am-5pm Wed-Sun; 👪) This museum has rotating exhibits of contemporary art – including work by local artists – that are among the most intriguing in the valley.

Sleeping & Eating

Fresno has room to grow when it comes to accommodations, but those using it as a launchpad for visiting Sequoia and Kings Canyon National Parks have plenty of options in the cluster of chains near the airport or a couple of high-rise offerings downtown.

Trendy eateries and breweries are in the Tower District and hidden among abandoned storefronts downtown, while farm-fresh restaurants and wineries dot the countryside right outside the city limits. Food trucks circle up every Thursday accompanied by live music in front of Fresno Brewing Company. For fantastic raw ingredients, Fresno's excellent farmers markets are abundant all year round.

Hotel Piccadilly HOTEL $

(☎559-348-5520; www.piccadillyinn.com; 2305 W Shaw Ave; d $100-110, ste from $339;) This is Fresno's nicest option, with a lovely pool, big rooms and good amenities.

Sam's Italian Deli & Market DELI $

(☎559-229-9346; www.samsitaliandeli.com; 2415 N 1st St; mains $7-13; ⊙10am-6pm Tue-Sat) This Italian market and deli is the real deal, stacking

FRESNO'S BLOSSOM TRAIL

When the Central Valley fruit and nut trees are in bloom, the winding roads around Fresno and Visalia make for a lovely, leisurely afternoon drive. The 62-mile **Fresno County Blossom Trail** (www.gofresnocounty.com) is especially stunning between February and March, when the orchards are awash in the pastel petals of apricot, almond, peach, nectarine, apple and citrus. Come back in May to taste the results.

Route maps are available at the Fresno/Clovis Convention & Visitors Bureau (p610), though DIY is possible if you don't mind taking occasional detours on the back roads between Sanger, Reedley, Orange Cove, Selma, Fowler and Kingsburg.

On your rounds, don't miss lunch at School House Restaurant (p610) and a glass of wine on the patio of Cedar View Winery.

up the 'New Yorker' pastrami and some mean prosciutto and mozzarella. It also has a variety of housemade pastas, sauces and soups to choose from, as well as a wall of wine to pair with your selection.

Rocket Dog Gourmet Brats & Brew BREW PUB $
(☎559-283-8096; www.rocketdogbratsandbrew.com; 88 E Shaw Ave; hot dogs $9; ⏰11am-9pm Sun-Thu, to 10pm Fri & Sat) Sure, something like 'Hansel's Heaven' – a bratwurst served on a pretzel roll and covered in mac 'n' cheese – isn't health food, but this excellent brewpub is the perfect highway pit stop if you're on the way in or out of Yosemite. It has a long list of elaborate hot dogs and local beer on tap.

Vineyard Farmers Market MARKET $
(☎559-222-0182; www.vineyardfarmersmarket.com; ⏰3-6pm Wed, 7am-noon Sat) Local booths sell the freshest seasonal food from surrounding farms beneath wood arches covered in vines. Choices include organic mushrooms, microgreens, fresh bread and more.

CartHop FAST FOOD $
(Mariposa Plaza; ⏰11am-2pm Thu) Every Thursday, a fleet of independent food trucks from around the valley gather, serving grab-and-go lunch options from every corner of the globe.

★ **School House Restaurant** AMERICAN $$
(☎559-787-3271; www.schoolhousesanger.com; 1018 S Frankwood Ave, Sanger; mains $14-35; ⏰11:30am-8pm Wed & Thu, to 11pm Fri & Sat, 11am-8pm Sun; P ❄) Housed in a characterful school house dating from 1921 at the base of the Sierras, this restaurant serves elevated New American cuisine in a unique setting – fans powered by pulleys cool patrons as they dive into meatloaf, duck stroganoff and venison filet. If you're in for lunch, don't miss the chicken sandwich with triple cream cheese, basil and strawberry jam.

Drinking & Nightlife

Goldstein's Mortuary & Delicatessen BAR
(1279 N Wishon Ave; ⏰3-11pm Mon, to midnight Tue-Thu, 1pm-midnight Fri, to 12:30am Sat, to 11pm Sun) This industrial bar incorporates the perfect amount of weird for a night out. While you sip on a beer from its extensive list, have a seat in a chair made from a shopping cart, pet the bar cat and listen to whatever live music is on that night – in our case, bluegrass.

Revue COFFEE
(☎559-981-2021; www.therevuefresno.com; 620 E Olive Ave; ⏰7am-8pm Mon-Sat, 8am-8pm Sun) This bright shop lures you in with its tidy, mod-deco space and keeps you there with a solid lists of coffees, teas and pastries. Come from 3pm-7pm for its Mocktail Happy Hour, which features a special menu of creative, booze-free concoctions.

☆ Entertainment

Tower Theatre for the Performing Arts PERFORMING ARTS
(www.towertheatrefresno.com; 815 E Olive Ave) In the center of Fresno's most artsy and happening neighborhood, it's hard to miss the neon deco palace that opens its stage to touring rock and jazz acts and seasonal cultural events.

ℹ Information

Fresno/Clovis Convention & Visitors Bureau (☎559-981-5500; www.visitfresnocounty.org; 1550 E Shaw Ave, Suite 201; ⏰8am-5pm Mon-Fri) Visitor information in a nondescript office complex. Brochures are also stocked in the Water Tower and airport. Its website is a good place to look for comprehensive listings about local farmers markets and events.

ℹ Getting There & Around

Greyhound (☎559-268-1829; 2660 Tulare St) Multiple regular/express rides daily to Los Angeles ($20, 4½ hours) and San Francisco ($22, 4½ hours)

Amtrak (Santa Fe station; ☎559-486-7651; 2650 Tulare St; ⏰5:30am-10pm) The most scenic way to travel these parts, the San Joaquin service stops in a white Mission building in downtown Fresno on its way to other destinations, including Yosemite ($32, four hours) and San Francisco ($37, five hours).

Fresno Yosemite International Airport (FAT; www.flyfresno.com; 5175 E Clinton Way) In the Central Valley..

Fresno Area Express (FAX; ☎559-621-7433; www.fresno.gov; 1 way $1.25) The local service that has daily buses to the Tower District (bus 22 or 28) from the downtown transit center at Van Ness Ave and Fresno St.

Visalia

Its agricultural prosperity and well-maintained downtown make Visalia a convenient stop en route to Sequoia and Kings Canyon National Parks or the Sierra Peaks.

Stroll downtown, with its old-town charm and plenty of restaurants and shops.

Sights & Activities

The original Victorian and arts-and-crafts-style homes in Visalia are architectural highlights worth viewing on foot. Maps for many **self-guided tours** are available via the of the **Visalia Convention & Visitor's Bureau** (559-334-0141; www.visitvisalia.org; 112 E Main St; 8am-5pm Mon-Fri).

Outside of the parks, the main natural draw in the area is the **Kaweah Oak Preserve** (www.sequoiariverlands.org; 29979 Rd 182, Exeter; donation adult/child $3/1; sunrise-sunset), about 7 miles east of town. With 324 acres of majestic oak trees, it's a gorgeous setting for easy hikes.

Sleeping

Lamp Liter Inn INN $

(559-732-4511; www.lampliter.net; 3300 W Mineral King Ave; d from $86;) This family-owned establishment has clean, if dated, rooms and country cottages facing an outdoor pool. The **Sequoia Shuttle** (877-287-4453; www.sequoiashuttle.com; round-trip incl park entry fee $20; late May-late Sep) stops here.

Eating & Drinking

Sol Bol HEALTH FOOD

(559-733-7902; https://solbol.com; 211 W Main St, #B; bowls $8.50-10; 8:30am-4:30pm Mon-Fri, from 9am Sat;) If you're looking to fuel up on some healthy eats before hitting the parks, Sol Bol has you covered with acai bowls generously topped with fresh fruit, granola and fun ingredients like chia seeds, hemp hearts and peanut butter. It also serves loaded toasts, bagels and paninis.

Brewbakers Brewing Company AMERICAN $$

(559-627-2739; www.brewbakersbrewingco.com; 219 E Main St; mains $12-22; 11:30am-10pm Mon-Thu, from 11am Fri-Sun;) Always jam-packed, Brewbakers beckons thirsty hikers with housemade sodas and craft beers (don't miss its Sequoia Red Ale). A huge menu of burgers, pizzas, pastas and salads promises more than it delivers, but it's a great place to refuel after a few days in the mountains.

Barrelhouse Brewing Co. BREWERY

(559-713-6690; www.barrelhousebrewing.com/locations-visalia; 521 E Main St; 2-9pm Mon-Wed, to 10pm Thu, 11am-11pm Fri & Sat, to 8pm Sun) This spacious taproom may not have the most personality around, but it's good for groups and carries some fun beers on tap, including a mango IPA. Hosts live music on weekends (and sometimes Thursday).

Entertainment

Visalia Fox Theatre CINEMA, LIVE MUSIC

(559-625-1369; www.foxvisalia.org; 308 W Main St) A 1930s 'talkie' movie palace, the Fox has an East Indian temple-themed interior and hosts film screenings, live music concerts, stand-up comedy and special events; phone the info line for the lineup.

Cellar Door LIVE MUSIC

(www.cellardoor101.com; 101 W Main St; cover $5; 8am-2am Tues, Thu & Fri, to 1am Wed, 3pm-2am Sat) Cellar Door serves wine with live music, and the events are all over the place – a Metallica cover band one night, salsa dancing the next. There's always something going on.

Shopping

Big 5 Sporting Goods SPORTS & OUTDOORS

(559-625-5934; www.big5sportinggoods.com; 1430 S Mooney Blvd; 10am-9pm Mon-Thu, 9:30am-9:30pm Fri, 9am-9pm Sat, 9:30am-8pm Sun) Stock up on camping, fishing and outdoor-sports equipment at this chain store, less than a mile south of Hwy 198.

Getting There & Around

Visalia's transit options, including direct access to **Sequoia National Park** (Map p700; 559-565-3341; www.nps.gov/seki; 7 day entry per car $35;), all funnel through the **Visalia Transit Center** (425 E Oak Ave). **Amtrak** (800-872-7245; www.amtrak.com; 425 E Oak Ave) shuttles run between the Transit Center and Hanford station a half hour away by reservation only (use local buses as an alternative). From Hanford, you can connect to all other Amtrak routes in the state, including the San Joaquin, which travels to Sacramento ($33, four hours) or south to Bakersfield ($21.50, three hours).

The convenient, bike-rack equipped Sequoia Shuttle ($20 round trip, including park entry, roughly five buses a day between May and September) picks up from major hotels and takes two hours to reach the Giant Forest Museum (p705) in Sequoia National Park.

Bakersfield

Nearing Bakersfield, the landscape has evidence of California's *other* gold rush: rusting rigs burrow into Southern California's vast oil fields. Black gold was discovered here in the late 1800s, and Kern County, the southernmost along Hwy 99, still pumps more than some OPEC countries.

This is the setting of Upton Sinclair's *Oil!*, which was adapted into the 2007 Academy Award–winning film, *There Will Be Blood*. In the 1930s the oil attracted a stream of 'Okies' – farmers who migrated out of the Great Plains – to work the derricks. The children of these tough-as-nails roughnecks put the 'western' in country and western by creating the 'Bakersfield Sound' in the mid-1950s, with heroes Buck Owens and Merle Haggard waving a defiant middle finger at the silky Nashville establishment.

Downtown Bakersfield is making moves to fancy-up, evident in the upbeat mix of restored buildings and new restaurants, theaters and clubs.

Sights

The Kern River flows along Bakersfield's northern edge, separating it from its blue-collar neighbor, Oildale, and a host of oil fields. Truxtun and Chester Aves are the main downtown thoroughfares. The mountains themselves are only a short hop away and offer an escape from Bakersfield's concrete sprawl.

César E Chávez National Monument HISTORIC SITE
(661-823-6134; www.nps.gov/cech; 29700 Woodford-Tehachapi Rd, Keene; 10am-4pm; P) FREE Located within the undulating Tehachapi Mountains, this national monument, Nuestra Señora Reina de la Paz, is the national headquarters of the United Farmworkers of America and was the home of civil rights leader César Chávez from 1971 until his death in 1993. On view are exhibits on Chávez's work, his office and grave. Keene is 27 miles southeast of Bakersfield down Hwy 58.

Chávez was born near Yuma, AZ, in 1927, and was 11 when his family lost their farm and became migrant farm workers in California. At 14, he left school to labor in the fields. Eventually, he became a champion of nonviolent social change, negotiating for better wages and access to water and bathrooms in the fields. His work resulted in numerous precedents, including the first union contracts requiring safe use of pesticides and the abolition of short-handled tools that had injured generations of farm workers.

Kern County Museum MUSEUM
(www.kerncountymuseum.org; 3801 Chester Ave; adult/child $10/5; 10am-4pm Tue-Sun; P) This museum brings local history to life with a pioneer village of more than 50 restored and replicated buildings (including Merle Haggard's childhood home) and courtyard with beautifully restored vintage neon signs. The main structure has a large (and fairly disturbing) display of taxidermy wildlife and pristine memorabilia from Bakersfield's musical heyday.

Five & Dime Antique Mall LANDMARK
(661-321-0061; 1400 19th St, Woolworth Bldg; 10am-5pm Mon-Sat, from noon Sun) Three stories hold vintage wares that date back to at least the same era as the Woolworth building they're housed in – it would take hours to peruse all the trinkets and treasures (take a moment to scope out the old car in the front of the store!). Try to go when the Woolworth Diner is open.

Sleeping & Eating

Chain motels sprout like weeds off the highways near Bakersfield. Old-school budget motels, starting from about $50, line Union Ave heading south from Hwy 178, but can be a little seedy.

★Padre Hotel BOUTIQUE HOTEL $$
(661-427-4900; www.thepadrehotel.com; 1702 18th St; d $159, ste from $419) A stylish update revived this century-old hotel, adding an upscale restaurant, two bars and a rooftop lounge that instantly became *the* places for cocktails in town. The service is excellent and the rooms have lavish details: thick mattresses, plush sheets and designer furniture. The two themed suites – the 'Oil Baron' and 'Farmer's Daughter' – have playful decor and showers for two.

Keep your eyes peeled for ghosts, rumor is this place is the most haunted in Bakersfield.

Arizona Cafe MEXICAN $
(661-324-3866; 809 Baker St; mains $9-14; 8:30am-7pm Mon-Sat, from 8am Sun;) Arizona Cafe's teal vinyl seats welcome visitors in to enjoy so-tender-you-could-cry chicken and beef incorporated into perfect Mexican staples. Perch at the bar and enjoy a drink while you dig into the huge portions – even the sides come with sides!

Mama Roomba's CARIBBEAN $
(661-322-6262; www.mamaroomba.com; 1814 Eye Street; small plates $10-15; 11am-10pm

WORTH A TRIP

A LITTLE SWEDEN IN THE VALLEY

The quiet hamlet of Kingsburg has a vibrant ethnic heritage. Around 1873, when it was established as a rail stop called 'Kings River Switch,' two Swedes arrived. Their countrymen soon followed, and by 1921, 94% of Kingsburg's residents, as it had become known, were of Swedish heritage. Today, the Swedish past mixes with more recent Mexican immigrants who drive the agricultural economy.

Draper St, the main drag, is decked out in Swedish Dala horses and crests of Swedish regions. Inside the cutesy Tudor buildings are gift shops and little bakeries stocked with buttery pastries. Pick up Nordic decor and insight on the town from June, town icon and proprietor of **Svensk Butik** (559-897-5119; https://business.facebook.com/svenskbutikswedishgifts; 1465 Draper St; 9am-5pm Mon-Sat). Sure, the town plays up its heritage for visitors, but there is genuine pride in every 'Valkommen!'

The town has gone through pains to preserve its oldest structures. Under the coffee-pot water tower, the **city jail** (www.kingsburghistoricalpark.org; 1400 Marion St; 24hr) FREE is a quick stop.

Good times to visit are during the Santa Lucia Festival (first Saturday of December) and the Swedish Festival (parades, maypole dancing and a real smorgasbord) in May.

Mon-Fri, from 5pm Sat;) A green and yellow beacon amidst the concrete buildings of Bakersfield's downtown, Mama Roomba's is a family-run Caribbean restaurant serving up a variety of small plates – try the skillet shrimp in spicy cream sauce – and mains like the Cuban classic ropa vieja and fried chicken with mango-chili sauce. Wash it down with a sangria or rum based cocktail.

Cafe Smitten CAFE $

(661-843-7305; www.cafesmitten.com; 909 18th St; mains $9-11; 6:30am-7pm Mon-Thu, to 9pm Fri, 8am-5pm Sat & Sun) This bright cafe in the heart of downtown serves lighter fare – the savory 'avocado smash' sandwich with chili flakes and pumpkin seeds is a good choice – pastries, good coffee and some wine and beer. The vibe is great too; a sunny patio attracts a fun crowd for after-work drinks.

Luigi's ITALIAN $

(661-322-0926; www.shopluigis.com; 725 E 19th St; mains $8-18; 11am-2:30pm Tue-Sat;) Lined with black-and-white photos of sporting legends, this lunch spot has been around for over 100 years. Dishes range from hot pastrami sandwiches to housemade truffle sacchetti, and the excellent bakery turns out soft, buttery rolls and an exceedingly rich Butterfinger Pie. The adjacent bar and deli stay open until 4pm.

Dewar's Candy Shop ICE CREAM $

(661-322-0933; www.dewarscandy.com; 1120 Eye St; sundaes from $5.25; 10am-9pm;) Perched on the pink stools at the counter, families dig into homemade ice cream with ingredients sourced from surrounding farms since 1930. Epic banana splits are big enough for two (maybe three), and the dreamy flavors – like the creamy, decadent lemon flake – change seasonally.

Woolworth Diner DINER $

(661-321-0061; 1400 19th St, Five & Dime Antique Mall; burger combo $7; 11am-4pm Mon-Sat, from noon Sun;) The soda jerks flip fantastic cheeseburgers and pour thick shakes at the store's original soda counter, buffed to its former glory.

★ **Noriega's** BASQUE $$

(661-322-8419; www.noriegahotel.com; 525 Sumner St; breakfast $13, lunch $20, dinner $25; breakfast 7am-9am, lunch at noon, dinner from 7pm Tue-Sun) Surly Basque gentlemen pass the wine carafes at Bakersfield's family style Basque institution. The fixed menu includes a procession of dishes leading to silky oxtail stew, ribs and amazing garlic fried chicken (check online for the day's menu). The communal ambience and the food earned a prestigious James Beard Award. Reserve in advance; seating hours are strict.

Wool Growers BASQUE $$

(661-327-9584; www.woolgrowers.net; 620 E 19th St; lunch $16.50, dinner mains $19-34; 11:30am-2pm & 6-8pm Mon-Sat) A simple Basque eating hall loaded with character – sit at the mid-century-esque bar and enjoy a drink or head to a table to dig into family-style meals that feature a main dish and nine – yes nine – sides.

Drinking & Nightlife

Dionysus Brewing Company BREWERY
(☎661-833-6000; www.dionysusbrewing.com; 6201 Schirra Ct, Ste 13; ⊙4-9pm Mon-Fri, from noon Sat, 11am-8pm Sun) Beer nerds should go out of their way for a snifter at this exceptional small brewery. It specializes in adventurous sours, but has something for every palette, from the Super Funkadelic sour aged with guava and pomegranate to the crisp, clean Berliner Weisse. They've managed to turn this small storage space into a comfy tasting room, so settle in for a flight.

Temblor Brewing Company BREWERY
(☎661-489-4855; www.temblorbrewing.com; 3200 Buck Owens Blvd; ⊙11am-10pm Sun-Thu, to midnight Fri & Sat;) Housed in a cavernous, sleekly renovated industrial space, this brewpub has plenty of space for groups to sprawl out and enjoy one of its brews, such as the refreshing Belgian with a hint of blood orange. Temblor also serves pub grub ($9 to $15) and hosts comedy and live music.

Entertainment

★**Buck Owens' Crystal Palace** LIVE MUSIC
(☎661-328-7560; www.buckowens.com; 2800 Buck Owens Blvd; ⊙shows Wed-Sat) For fans of the Bakersfield Sound, this is the first stop – just look for the huge neon homage to Buck's famous red, white and blue guitar. Part museum, honky-tonk and steakhouse (dinner from 5pm, brunch 9:30am to 1pm Sunday), it hosts top-drawer country acts. Locals in snap-button shirts, shiny boots and pressed jeans tear up the dance floor.

Bakersfield Music Hall of Fame ARTS CENTER
(☎661-864-1701; www.bakersfieldmusichalloffame.com; 2231 R St; ⊙10am-6pm Mon-Fri) Housing a small theater, recording studios and displays on local legends, this space celebrates the icons and fosters new talent. Check the schedule for local up-and-comers who perform homages to musical heroes past.

Information

Greater Bakersfield Convention & Visitors Bureau (☎661-852-7282; www.visitbakersfield.com; 515 Truxtun Ave; ⊙8am-5pm Mon-Fri) A modern building with maps and brochures.

Getting There & Around

Airport Valet Express (☎661-363-5000; www.airportvaletexpress.com; 201 New Stine Rd, Ste 120; 1 way $59; ⊙to LAX 3am, 10am, 6pm) Buses travel between Bakersfield and LAX (2½ hours, three daily). Book in advance for a discount.

Greyhound (☎661-327-5617; 1820 18th St at G St) Cheap rides from downtown Bakersfield to Los Angeles ($13, two hours).

Amtrak Station (☎800-872-7245; 601 Truxtun Ave at S St) Trains travel north from here to Sacramento ($45 to $65, 5½ hours, two direct trains). Buses head to LA, but fares must be purchased in combination with a train ticket.

Golden Empire Transit (GET; www.getbus.org; 1830 Golden State Ave, Transit Center; fares from $1.65) The efficient local bus system's Route 22 runs north on Chester Ave to the Kern County Museum (p612) and Oildale (22 minutes).

Kern River Area

A half-century ago, Kern River originated on the slopes of Mt Whitney and journeyed close to 170 miles before finally settling into the Central Valley. Now, after its wild descent from the high country – 60ft per mile – the Kern is dammed in several places and almost entirely tapped for agricultural use.

Its pristine upper reaches, declared wild and scenic by the Secretary of the Interior, makes for world-class rafting – it's nicknamed 'Killer Kern' for its occasionally lethal force.

If you're looking for a more relaxed Kern Canyon experience, there are many hiking trails through the mountainous terrain that are especially lovely in spring when the wildflowers are blooming. Head to the USFS Ranger Station in **Kernville** (☎760-376-3781; www.fs.usda.gov; 11380 Kernville Rd; ⊙8am-4:30pm Mon-Fri;) for hiking and camping information, maps and wilderness permits.

Activities

This part of the state is all about white water, and rafting is the banner attraction. The town of **Lake Isabella** is a dreary strip of local businesses on the south end of the lake, but Hwy 155 runs north to **Kernville**, a cute little town straddling the Kern River that is *the* hub for local water sports. While the lake is popular for cooling off, note that the river's currents can be extremely dangerous.

The Upper Kern and Forks of the Kern (both sections of the river north of Kernville) yield Class IV and V rapids during spring runoff and offer some of the most awe-inspiring white-water trips in the country. You'll need experience before tackling these sections, though there are still opportunities for novices. Below Lake Isabella, the Kern is tamer and steadier.

Kernville's rafting outfitters offer competitive prices and run trips from May to August, depending on conditions. Excursions include popular one-hour runs (from $40), daylong Lower Kern trips (from $150) and multiday Wild Forks of the Kern experiences (from $750). Walk-ins are welcome and experience is not necessary. Kids ages six and up can usually participate.

Rafting

Mountain & River Adventures RAFTING
(760-376-6553; www.mtnriver.com; 11113 Kernville Rd;) Besides rafting, this outfit offers combo kayak and rafting trips, mountain-biking and climbing excursions. It also has a campground right on the banks of the Kern with a volleyball court, showers and bathrooms.

Kern River Outfitters RAFTING
(800-323-4234; www.kernrafting.com; 6602 Wofford Heights Blvd, Wofford Heights; 8:30am-5:30pm Mon-Fri) Offers the staple menu of short, one-day and two-day trips.

Sierra South RAFTING
(800-457-2082, 760-376-3745; www.sierrasouth.com; 11300 Kernville Rd;) Rafting or, for something calmer, paddleboarding on Lake Isabella.

Whitewater Voyages RAFTING
(800-400-7238; www.whitewatervoyages.com; 11006 Kernville Rd) The first outfitter to dare guide clients down the entire Wild and Scenic Forks of the Kern back in 1980.

Hiking

The areas around Isabella Lake and Kernville offer a number of opportunities for exploring on foot. **Whiskey Flat Trail** (12.4 miles) runs along the river and has two trailheads right outside Kernville, and **Cannell Trail** (20 miles) is a local favorite for its wildflower meadows and mountain biking opportunities. Head further north on Mountain Hwy 99 and you'll find numerous trails and campsites in the Sequoia National Forest.

Sleeping

USFS Campgrounds CAMPGROUND $
(877-444-6777; www.recreation.gov; campsite $26) These campgrounds line the 10-mile stretch between Lake Isabella and Kernville, and several more lie north of Kernville on Mountain Hwy 99. Rangers recommend the Fairview and Limestone (marked on the map) for their seclusion. Campgrounds without running water and electricity are free.

Piazza's Pine Cone Inn MOTEL $
(760-376-6669; https://piazzas-pinecone.com; 13383 Sierra Way; d $145;) Walking onto this property feels like traveling back to the 1950s – originally opened in 1955, the Pine Cone Inn retains its retro feel while offering spotless rooms to rest your head after a long day on the water.

Whispering Pines Lodge B&B $$
(760-376-3733; www.pineskernville.com; 13745 Sierra Way; r $195-270;) This B&B, blending rustic character with creature comforts, sits on the north edge of town. Rooms with kitchens book up quickly in the summer, and some have river views. The pool *almost* feels like an infinity pool.

Drinking & Nightlife

★ **Kern River Brewing Company** BREWERY
(760-376-2337; www.kernriverbrewing.com; 13415 Sierra Way, Kernville; 11am-10pm Sun-Thu, to 11pm Fri & Sat) A hub for local rafting guides and outdoor types, this brewery has a rotation of award-winning seasonal beers. The Isabella Blonde is light and refreshing in hot weather and the Chuuurch! IPA has the perfect balance of citrus and hops. It also has a reliably tasty menu with pulled pork tacos, hot wings and sandwiches.

Big Blue Bear Cafe CAFE
(760-376-2442; www.bigbluebearcafe.com; 101 Piute Dr; 7am-4pm) This country-chic cafe serves as a one-stop-shop: in the mornings, grab a coffee and breakfast sandwich, and at lunch dive into the sandwiches and salads, or start drinking early with its wine and beer selection. Brunchers will enjoy the Bloody Marys and mimosas.

AT A GLANCE

POPULATION
756,350

GOLD EXTRACTED
750,000 pounds

BEST WINE REGION
Amador County Wine Region (p632)

BEST MINING RELIC
Malakoff Diggins State Historic Park (p624)

BEST PLACE TO FEEL SMALL
Calaveras Big Trees State Park (p636)

WHEN TO GO

Apr–May Pan for gold after the snow-melt washes the treasure into Jamestown's hills.

Jul As temperatures soar, plunge into a refreshing South Yuba swimming hole.

Sep–Oct When crisp heritage apples are ripe for the picking, head to Apple Hill's ranches.

...bia (p637)

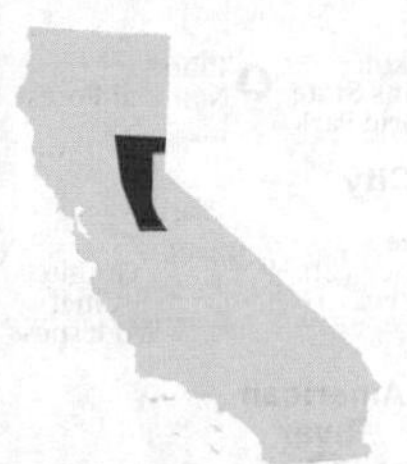

Gold Country

Hollywood draws the dreamers and Silicon Valley lures fortune-hunters, but aspiring young folk have previously streamed into the Golden State. After a sparkle in the American River caught James Marshall's eye in 1848, prospectors started digging for gold in the Sierra foothills. Soon California entered statehood with the official motto 'Eureka' solidifying its place as the land of opportunity.

The miners are gone, but a ride along Hwy 49 through sleepy hill towns, past clapboard saloons and oak-lined byways is a return to the unprecedented ride that was California's founding: historical markers tell tales about the gold rush, and others share details about its devastating impact on the indigenous people. Beyond the history, an influx of young creatives and entrepreneurs has re-energized the region. The wine-tasting scene is booming.

INCLUDES

Gold Country Highlights

❶ **Marshall Gold Discovery State Historic Park** (p628) Witnessing the birthplace of modern California at this park.

❷ **Downieville** (p625) Rumbling down the premier bike trails above this gold rush town.

❸ **Plymouth** (p630) Tasting wines made from grapes grown in the Sierra foothills.

❹ **Columbia State Historic Park** (p637) Stepping back in time at the 'Gem of the Southern Mines.'

❺ **Nevada City** (p622) Wandering the historic streets of this jewel of a town.

❻ **American River** (p627) Riding the white-water thrills on the state's top rafting river.

❼ **Indian Grinding Rock State Historic Park** (p633) Discovering rock art created by the Miwoks who once thrived near this sacred area.

❽ **Murphys** (p635) Checking out local caves and then wine tasting on Main St.

NEVADA COUNTY & NORTHERN GOLD COUNTRY

The forty-niners hit it big in Nevada County – the richest score in the region known as the Mother Lode – and their wealth built one of the most picturesque and well-preserved boomtowns, Nevada City. Get out of town and you'll find lovely, remote wilderness areas, a clutch of historic parks and fascinating remnants of the long-gone miners, including a ghost town. This is also a magnet for adrenaline junkies looking to race down single tracks on mountain bikes or plunge into swimming holes remote enough for skinny-dipping.

Auburn

Look for the big man: a 45-ton effigy of French gold panner Claude Chana marks your arrival in Placer County's Gold Country. Its gold country hallmarks are all here – ice-cream shops, strollable historic districts and antiques. A major stop on the Central Pacific's transcontinental route, Auburn still welcomes trains on the Union Pacific's main line to the east and is a popular stop for those rushing along I-80 between the Bay Area and Lake Tahoe. You'll have to venture along Hwy 49 for a deeper taste of Gold Country, but those who want just a sample will enjoy this accessible town.

Sights & Activities

The fact that Auburn is sometimes called the 'Endurance Sport Capital of the World' will give you a sense of how good the area is for cycling, trail running and other heart-pounding activities. See www.auburnendurancecapital.com for events.

For descriptions of nearby trails, visit www.canyonkeepers.org. Many are in the nearby Auburn State Recreation Area (p620).

Placer County Museum MUSEUM
(☎530-889-6500; www.placer.ca.gov; 101 Maple St; ⏰10am-4pm; P) FREE The 1st floor of the domed 1898 Placer County Courthouse has Native American artifacts and displays of Auburn's transportation heritage, including a classic 1877 stage coach. It's the easiest museum to visit and gives a good overview of area history; there's also the glitter of the museum's gold collection with huge chunks of unrefined gold on display.

Bernhard Museum Complex MUSEUM
(☎530-889-6500; www.placer.ca.gov; 291 Auburn-Folsom Rd; entry by donation; ⏰11am-4pm Tue-Sun; P) This museum, built in 1851 as the Traveler's Rest Hotel and later serving as the home of the Bernhard family, exhibits depictions of typical 19th-century farm family life. Volunteers in period garb show you around, and the concept is that the family has just left the house. Tours take about 45 minutes.

Gold Rush Museum MUSEUM
(☎530-889-6500; www.placer.ca.gov; 601 Lincoln Way; ⏰10:30am-4pm Thu-Sun; P 👪) FREE In the old Auburn depot, this museum includes a reconstructed mine and gold panning, both great for kids. Don't miss the wall of Twitter-style 'tweets' from some of Auburn's most notable gold-rush-era citizens.

Joss House MUSEUM
(☎530-823-0373; 200 Sacramento St; entry by donation; ⏰10:30am-2:30pm Sat) Built by the Yue family in the 1920s, this clapboard residence stands on 'Chinese Hill,' one of many Chinese communities established during the gold rush. After a 'mysterious' fire ripped through the settlement, the family converted their home into a public space for worship, seasonal boarders and a school.

Sleeping

Most visitors will want to head north to Nevada City or south to Placerville to find a more enticing spot to stay: Auburn is very much a gateway town. For an affordable place to sleep, look to the highway exits where there's every brand of chain hotel.

Powers Mansion Inn B&B $$
(☎916-425-9360; www.powersmansioninn.com; 195 Harrison Ave; r $119, ste $129-169; 📶) An unabashedly chintzy option, with much Victoriana – floral drapes, wrought-iron beds and clawfoot baths – as well as Jacuzzis and satellite TV. The rambling mansion was built in 1884 by gold-mining magnate Harold T Power. You can play games in the parlor and enjoy anecdotes courtesy of the friendly, voluble owner.

Eating & Drinking

Lincoln Way toward the Chamber of Commerce (p620) has several restaurants popular with locals, and there's plenty of outdoor eating right around Sacramento St.

Ikedas DINER $
(☎530-885-4243; www.ikedas.com; 13500 Lincoln Way; sandwiches & burgers $7-13; ⏰11am-7pm Mon-

Thu, 10am-8pm Fri-Sun;) If you're cruising this part of the state without time to explore, the best pit stop is this expanded farm stand – now a diner/market – off I-80 a few miles north of downtown. Thick, grass-fed beef burgers, homemade sweet and savory pies and the seasonal fresh-peach shake are deliriously good. A slice of pie is $5.

Katrina's BREAKFAST $
(530-888-1166; www.katrinas-cafe.com; 456 Grass Valley Hwy; mains $9-13; 7am-2:30pm Wed-Sat, 7am-2pm Sun) Fantastic breakfast and good service are highlights at Katrina's, where lemon yogurt or banana nut pancakes, great omelets and all manner of hot sandwiches are dished up in a homey atmosphere. Cash only with ATM on-site.

Auburn Alehouse BREWERY
(530-885-2537; www.auburnalehouse.com; 289 Washington St; mains $12-17; 11am-9pm Mon-Wed, 11am-10pm Thu, 11am-11pm Fri, 10am-11pm Sat, 10am-10pm Sun) One of those rare brewpubs with excellent craft beer *and* food – patrons dig into burgers, sweet-potato fries, 'adult mac 'n' cheese' and sweet-and-savory salads. The beer sampler is a great deal, as Auburn brings home tons of medals for its ales and pilsners. The setting, with swirly stucco and a pressed-metal ceiling, is impressive. Solo diners will feel welcome at the bar.

Information

Auburn Area Chamber of Commerce (530-885-5616; www.auburnchamber.net; 1103 High St; 10am-4pm Tue-Fri) In the Southern Pacific railroad depot at the north end of Lincoln Way, it has lots of useful local info and a monument to the Transcontinental Railroad nearby.

Auburn State Recreation Area Office (530-885-4527; 501 El Dorado St; 9am-4pm Mon-Thu) Information on sights and outdoor activities in the area.

California Welcome Center (Placer County Visitors Center; 530-887-2111; www.visitplacer.com; 1103 High St; 9am-4:30pm Mon-Sat, 11am-4:30pm Sun) Great information on Gold Country and eastward.

Getting There & Away

Amtrak (800-872-7245; www.amtrak.com; 277 Nevada St) runs one train daily along the Capital Corridor route (http://capitolcorridor.org) linking Auburn with Sacramento ($16, one hour); other destinations require connecting with Thruway buses. There is also one train daily east to Reno ($109, eight hours), which requires a change in Sacramento. Amtrak's *California Zephyr* stops in Auburn on its daily run between the Bay Area and Chicago via Reno and Denver.

The **Gold Country Stage Bus Service** (530-477-0103 ext 1003; www.goldcountrystage.com; adult $1.50-3, child under 6yr free) links Auburn, including its Amtrak station, with Grass Valley and Nevada City five times a day on weekdays (limited service on Saturdays). Kids and bikes ride free. **Placer County Transit** (530-885-2877; www.placer.ca.gov/transit; one-way fare $1.25) also runs bus services in the Auburn area.

Auburn State Recreation Area

This is a **park** (530-885-4527; www.parks.ca.gov; 501 El Dorado St, Auburn; per car $10; 7am-sunset) of deep gorges cut by the rushing waters of the North and Middle Forks of the American River, which converge below a bridge on Hwy 49, 4 miles south of Auburn. In early spring this is immensely popular for white-water rafting, as the rivers are Class II to V runs. Late summer, calmer waters allow for sunning and swimming. Trails are shared by hikers, bikers and horses.

For trail descriptions visit www.canyonkeepers.org. The easy **Lake Clementine Trail** follows a pretty 1.9-mile path along the North Fork of the American River near its confluence with the Middle Fork. The **Quarry Trail** takes a level path from Hwy 49, just south of the bridge, along the Middle Fork. Several side trails reach the river. Self-pay parking near the confluence is $10 although you may find free spots along Hwy 49 heading south, just after crossing the confluence.

One of the most popular hikes is the **Western States Pioneer Express Trail**, which connects Auburn State Recreation Area to **Folsom Lake State Recreation Area** and Folsom Lake. It's the site of the **Western States 100-Mile Endurance Run** (www.wser.org), and the **Tevis Cup** (www.teviscup.org), an endurance race on horseback.

The best tours of the American, Tuolumne and Stanislaus Rivers are offered spring through fall by the family-run **All-Outdoors California Whitewater Rafting** (925-932-8993; www.aorafting.com; trips from $124; generally Apr-Oct). Its single- and multiday wilderness rafting excursions include breaks for hiking among the boulders and historically significant sights in the canyons. Meals are provided. Check online for discounts.

For camping, there are three primitive campgrounds: two first come, first served along the Middle Fork and one boat-in only campground on Lake Clementine, which can be reserved at www.parks.ca.gov.

Grass Valley

From the margins, Grass Valley is the ugly utilitarian sister to Nevada City, a place to stock up on supplies, not necessarily vacation in. But there are treasures if you dig, including a dense cluster of Victorian and art deco buildings, some great independent boutiques and cafes, and a few surprisingly rowdy bars.

Historic Mill and W Main Sts mark the town center. E Main St leads north to modern shopping centers and mini-malls and into Nevada City, which is just 4 miles north. On Thursday nights in late June through late July, Mill St closes to traffic to serve up farmstead food, arts and crafts and music during its Thursday Night Market. On the town's outskirts are some of the state's oldest shaft mines. Being the first to exploit lode-mining (tunneling to find veins of gold in hard rock) rather than placer techniques (sifting debris carried by waterways), these were among the most profitable claims.

Sights

Empire Mine State Historic Park HISTORIC SITE
(☎530-273-8522; www.parks.ca.gov; 10791 Empire St; adult/child 6-16yr $7/3; ⏲10am-5pm Mar-Oct, 10am-4pm Nov-Feb; P) Atop 367 miles of mine shafts tunneling almost a vertical mile beneath the surface, Gold Country's best-preserved gold-quartz-mining operation is worth a solid half-day's exploration. From 1850 to 1956 the miners here, mostly Cornish, produced 5.8 million troy ounces of gold (worth about $8 billion today). The visitor center has maps and leads guided tours (schedules vary). It also houses an intricate scale model of the Empire-Star Mine from 1938. Detailing all the tunnels and connections, it was a closely guarded secret. See the website for events.

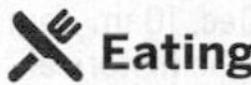

Eating

The menus around here don't vary much but the quality is good. There are several good brunch spots and bars around downtown, and every imaginable chain among the strip malls by the highway.

Lazy Dog Chocolateria ICE CREAM $
(☎530-274-0774; 111 Mill St; 1 scoop $5; ⏲10am-9pm Sun-Thu, 10am-10pm Fri & Sat) This colorful ice-cream and candy shop explodes with sugar in all its forms. Besides scoops, there are hand-dipped bars, chocolates and old-timey candies from 'juicy wax sticks' to swirly suckers. The sea salt peanut butter cups are a delight.

Tofanelli's ITALIAN $$
(☎530-272-1468; www.tofanellis.com; 302 W Main St; mains $8-19; ⏲8am-9pm) Hugely popular with locals in the know, this creative restaurant has everything from salads to hearty steaks and seasonal specials such as summer squash ravioli. Portions are burly and the patio is a treat.

Entertainment

Center for the Arts ARTS CENTER
(☎530-274-8384; http://thecenterforthearts.org; 314 W Main St) Grass Valley punches above its weight with this excellent arts center. The

TRIBAL HISTORY IN GOLD COUNTRY

A few dedicated museums tell part of the stories of the Miwok, Maidu, Konkow, Monache, Nisenan, Tubatulabal, Washo and Foothill Yokuts – the people who called this region home way before the rush for gold.

➡ The **Maidu Museum & Historical Site** (☎916-774-5934; www.roseville.ca.us; 1970 Johnson Ranch Dr, Roseville; adult/child $5/4; ⏲9am-4pm Sat, by appointment Mon-Fri) is built on the edge of an ancient Maidu village, occupied for over 3000 years.

➡ The roundhouse museum in **Indian Grinding Rock State Historic Park** (p633) has a variety of artifacts representing different tribes of the area. The limestone outcrop outside is dimpled with mortar holes for grinding acorns.

➡ The **State Indian Museum** (p588) in Sacramento features the most varied collections, with a redwood canoe and extraordinary beaded garments.

A fair number of history museums across the Gold Country supplement their Old West 'glory days' exhibits with informative displays describing the devastating impact of the gold rush on native populations – you might just have to look around a bit to find them.

program includes local and international music, dance, visual arts, comedy and literary events.

Information

Greater Grass Valley Visitor Center (☎530-273-4667; www.grassvalleychamber.com; 128 E Main St; ⊙10am-4pm Apr–mid-Dec, 10am-3pm mid-Dec–Mar; 🐾) In the thick of the historical sights stands this brick livery stable, which is stocked with maps and brochures covering the county and more. There's a very comprehensive walking-tour map.

Getting There & Away

Transit in Grass Valley is by **Gold Country Stage Bus Service** (☎530-477-0103; www.mynevadacounty.com; 13083 John Bauer Ave), which links to Nevada City hourly from 7am to 7pm weekdays, 8am to 4pm Saturday. Fares are $1.50 to $3 for adults. Kids and bikes ride free. Check the website for connections to Auburn and schedule changes.

Amtrak (p620) stops in Colfax, 12 miles south, on the *California Zephyr* route.

Nevada City

Nevada City knows it's charming, but it doesn't like to brag. The shops sell prayer flags and chia smoothies, while the drinking holes sling all manner of liquid enlightenment. The person browsing the history museum with you is just as liable to be a crusty old-timer, a road-weary backpacker or a mystical folk artist. In the midst of all this are the Victorian and gold rush tourist attractions – an elegantly restored town center and frilly B&Bs.

This is the gateway to Tahoe National Forest, but linger to experience inviting NorCal culture and the energetic, youthful vibe. The theater companies, alternative film houses, bookstores and venues put on shows almost every night; tune into radical local radio station kvmr.org at 89.5FM to hear what's on.

Sights & Activities

The main attraction is the town itself – its restored buildings, all brick and wrought-iron trimmings, wear their history proudly. There are intriguing (if pricey) boutiques, galleries and places for food and drink everywhere, all with exhaustive posted histories.

Firehouse No 1 Museum MUSEUM
(☎530-265-3937; www.nevadacountyhistory.org; 214 Main St; by donation; ⊙1-4pm Wed-Sun May-Oct, by appointment Nov-Apr) This small, painstakingly curated museum is run by the Nevada County Historical Society from a unique white wooden building with a tall bell tower. From stunning Nisenan baskets to preserved Victorian bridal wear, its collections tell the story of the local people. The prize exhibits are relics from the Chinese settlers who often built but seldom profited from the mines.

Nevada City Winery WINERY
(☎530-265-9463; http://ncwinery.com; 321 Spring St; tastings $9-15; ⊙tasting room 2-6pm Mon-Thu, noon-8pm Fri & Sat, noon-6pm Sun) This popular winery excels with syrah and zinfandel varietals, which you can savor while touring the production facility in the old Miners' Foundry Garage or sitting on the inviting back deck.

Deer Creek Tribute Trail HIKING
(www.nevadacitychamber.com; Champion Mine Rd; 🐾) Easily reached from downtown, this woodsy, multi-part trail drops to Deer Creek, where a photogenic suspension bridge honors the Nisenan people, the original inhabitants of the area. The bridge links to the Environs Trail, which connects back to downtown via Jordan St and Pine St for a pleasant 3.5-mile loop. The Chinese Tribute Bridge is another site further along the Tribute Trail.

Sleeping

Weekends, Nevada City fills up with urban refugees who inevitably weigh themselves down with real-estate brochures. There are B&Bs everywhere. The cheapest options are the National Forest campgrounds.

In the heart of downtown, the 1850s National Hotel claimed to be the oldest continuously operating hotel west of the Rocky Mountains. Closed for major renovations in 2019, it planned to reopen in 2021 as the **National Exchange Hotel** (211 Broad St; www.thenationalexchangehotel.com). The new incarnation will keep the building's best architectural aspects but spiff things up with mod cons and a breezy style.

★**Outside Inn** INN, COTTAGE $$
(☎530-265-2233; http://outsideinn.com; 575 E Broad St; r $99-175, cabin $180, cottage $230; P❄📶🐾) The best option for active explorers, this is an unusually friendly and fun inn, with 13 rooms, one cabin and one cottage maintained by staff who love the outdoors. Some rooms have a patio overlooking a small creek; all have nice quilts and access to BBQ grills. There's a small unheated outdoor pool.

Broad Street Inn INN $$
(☎530-265-2239; www.broadstreetinn.com; 517 W Broad St; r $140, carriage house $195; ❄📶) This six-room inn in the heart of town is a favorite because it keeps things simple. The good-value rooms are modern, brightly but soothingly furnished and elegant. There's also a lovely apartment within a carriage house out back. No breakfast.

Eating & Drinking

In a town of holistic thinkers, it's no surprise most menus emphasize organic and seasonal ingredients. The options are mostly clustered in a three-block radius on Commercial and Broad Sts.

★**South Pine Cafe** BREAKFAST $
(☎520-265-0260; www.southpinecafe.com; 110 S Pine St; mains $9-18; ⊙8am-3pm) It may not be Instagram-pretty, but the lobster scramble here was the best thing we ate for breakfast across the Gold Country: chunks of lobster, jack cheese, mushrooms, scrambled eggs and hollandaise sauce. All breakfast options are equally decadent. Enjoy a Bloody Mary or beer with your meal.

Ike's Quarter Cafe CREOLE, BREAKFAST $
(☎530-265-6138; www.ikesquartercafe.com; 401 Commercial St; mains $11-20; ⊙8am-2:30pm Thu-Mon;) Right out of New Orleans' Garden District, Ike's serves splendid brunch fare with a sassy charm. Sit outside under the cherry tree or in the cluttered, funky interior. There's eggs Sardou, jambalaya, vegetarian po'boy sandwiches and more. It's an excellent place to get 'Hangtown Fry' – a cornmeal-crusted mess of oysters, bacon, caramelized onions and spinach. Cash only.

Three Forks Bakery & Brewing Co CAFE $
(☎530-470-8333; www.threeforksnc.com; 211 Commercial St; pizzas $12-16, pastries $2-5, cakes per slice $5; ⊙7am-10pm Mon, Wed & Thu, 7am-11pm Fri, 8am-11pm Sat, 8am-10pm Sun) An open-plan modern place, serving cakes, pizzas and beer brewed on-site. It has a generic look compared to some of the quirky options in town, but it's got a fun and convivial youthful vibe.

★**New Moon Cafe** CALIFORNIAN $$$
(☎530-265-6399; www.thenewmooncafe.com; 203 York St; mains lunch $18-20, dinner $25-44; ⊙11:30am-2pm Tue-Fri, 5-8pm Tue-Sun) Pure elegance, Peter Selaya's organic- and local-ingredient menu changes with the seasons. If you visit during spring or summer, go for the line-caught fish or the housemade, moon-shaped fresh ravioli. The wine list is excellent.

Crazy Horse Saloon Grill BAR
(☎530-265-4000; http://crazyhorsenc.com; 230 Commercial St; ⊙11:30am-1:30am Mon-Fri, 11am-1:30am Sat & Sun) A fantastic saloon with a long convivial bar where you can eat burgers and nachos, shoot the breeze with the friendly staff, then hit the dance floor. The little raised stage, wreathed in lanterns, hosts almost nightly live music, with jazz, funk, indie pop and rock, plus trivia night on Wednesday.

Entertainment

This little village has a vibrant arts scene, with two theater-cinemas and an ambitious arts center. The entertainment section of the *Union* newspaper (www.theunion.com) comes out on Thursday, and lists what's going on throughout the county.

Miners Foundry ARTS CENTER
(☎530-265-5040; http://minersfoundry.org; 325 Spring St; ⊙9am-4pm, plus evenings for events) As the name suggests, this was once an industrial building, constructed in 1856 and used to manufacture Pelton wheels. It has been brilliantly converted into an eclectic arts center, hosting music workshops, youth theater, dance classes and gigs.

★**Onyx Theatre** CINEMA
(☎showtimes 530-265-8262; www.theonyxtheatre.com; 107 Argall Way) This beloved and adorably quirky theater screens a matchless lineup of unusual films and is about a mile south of downtown Nevada City. It serves organic popcorn, baked goods, and beer and wine.

Nevada Theatre THEATER, CINEMA
(☎530-265-6161; www.nevadatheatre.com; 401 Broad St) This brick fortress is one of California's first theaters (1865) and has welcomed the likes of Jack London, Emma Nevada and Mark Twain to its stage. Now it's home to a number of small, top-notch theater companies and an off-beat indie film series.

Shopping

Indie boutiques are scattered across downtown. Check out nature-themed gifts, toys and apparel at **Earth Store** (☎530-265-0448; 310 Broad St; ⊙11am-5pm) and ecofriendly clothing at **Mama Madrone's Eco-Emporium** (www.facebook.com/mamamadrones; 307 Broad St; ⊙9am-5pm).

Information

Nevada City Chamber of Commerce (530-265-2692; www.nevadacitychamber.com; 132 Main St; 9am-5pm Mon-Fri, 11am-4pm Sat, noon-3pm Sun) Ideally located at the east end of Commercial St, this has two welcome traveler comforts – expert local advice and public toilets.

Tahoe National Forest Headquarters (530-265-4531; www.fs.usda.gov/tahoe; 631 Coyote St; 9am-4:30pm Mon-Fri) A useful and friendly resource for trail and campground information, covering the area from here to Lake Tahoe. It sells topographical maps.

Getting There & Away

Nevada City is served by the **Gold Country Stage Bus Service** (530-477-0103; www.mynevadacounty.com; fares $1.50-3), which links it with Grass Valley (adult $1.50, 30 minutes) hourly from 6:30am to 7:30pm weekdays and 7:30am to 4:30pm Saturdays. Kids and bikes ride free. Check the website for connections to Auburn and schedule changes.

Amtrak (p620) stops in Colfax, 15 miles south, on the *California Zephyr* route.

South Yuba River State Park

Cool off with a dip at **South Yuba River State Park** (530-432-2546; www.parks.ca.gov; 17660 Pleasant Valley Rd, Penn Valley; parking Jun-Aug $10, Sep-May $5; park sunrise-sunset, visitor center 11am-4pm May-Sep, 11am-3pm Thu-Sun Oct-Apr; P), which has popular swimming holes and hiking trails.

This area's growing network of trails includes including the wheelchair-accessible **Independence Trail**, which starts from the south side of the South Yuba River bridge on Hwy 49 and continues for a couple of miles with canyon overlooks. June is best, when the rivers are rushing and the wildflowers are out.

The longest, single-span, wood-truss covered bridge in the USA, all 251ft of it, crosses the South Yuba River at **Bridgeport**, a 30-minute drive northwest of Nevada City or Grass Valley (temporarily closed for restoration). It's easy to spend a whole day hiking and swimming here, where crowds can be left behind with little effort. The **Buttermilk Bend Trail** skirts the South Yuba for 1.4 miles, offering river access and bountiful wildflowers around April.

Maps and park information are available from the state park headquarters in Bridgeport, or from the Tahoe National Forest Headquarters in Nevada City. The South Yuba River Park Association (www.southyubariverstatepark.org) is another great resource.

Malakoff Diggins State Historic Park

A testament to the mechanical determination of the gold hunt, **Malakoff Diggins** (530-265-2740; www.parks.ca.gov; 23579 N Bloomfield Rd; per car Jun-Aug $10, Sep-May $5; sunrise-sunset; P) is a place to get lost on fern-lined trails and take in the raw beauty of a landscape recovering from hydraulic mining. There is a mesmerizing ghost town here, abandoned and now frozen in time. Join a tour of the town at the **museum** (530-265-2740; www.parks.ca.gov; 23579 North Bloomfield Rd; per car May-Sep $10, Oct-Apr $5; 9am-5pm Jun-Oct, noon-4pm Thu, 10am-4pm Fri-Sun Nov-May, tours 1:30pm Jun-Oct) or stay at the **campground** (800-444-7275; www.reserveamerica.com; North Bloomfield Rd; tent sites $35, cabins $45; May-Sep; P) or in one of three humble miners' cabins.

California's largest hydraulic mine left behind massive gold and crimson cliffs and small mountains of tailings, which were carved from the land by mighty streams of water. The forestland has recovered since the legal battles between mine owners and downstream farmers shut down the mine in 1884.

In 1852 French miner Anthony Chabot channeled the Yuba through a canvas hose to blast away at the bedrock. To reach the veins of gold inside, miners eventually carved a canyon 600ft deep. To speed up the sorting process, they mixed the slurry of gravel with quicksilver (mercury) to recover the gold, and then washed all the leftovers into the Yuba River. A few decades later, when 20ft-high glaciers of tailings and toxic waste choked the rivers and caused deadly flooding, farmers and miners collided in the courtroom. In 1884 the Sawyer Decision set a critical precedent: a profitable industry can be stopped for the public good. Most fortune hunters moved on. North Bloomfield, the mining community at the center of Malakoff's operation, is the eerie ghost town within the park's limits.

Tours of the town – which had a population of 1229 back in 1880 – provide the chance to see some impressive gold nuggets. The 1-mile **Diggins Loop Trail** is the quickest way to get a glimpse of the scarred moonscape.

Access Tyler-Foote Crossing Rd, the turnoff for the park, 10 miles northwest of Nevada City on Hwy 49. This route is paved the whole way. Although N Bloomfield Rd may be suggested by some GPS services as a 'shorter' route, know that it is a dirt road for 7 miles.

North Yuba River

The northernmost segment of Hwy 49 follows the North Yuba River through some stunning, remote parts of the Sierra Nevada, known for a tough, short season of white water and great fly-fishing. An entire lifetime outdoors could hardly cover the trail network that hikers, mountain bikers and skiers blaze every season. In summer, snow remains at the highest elevations and many places have roaring fireplaces year-round. The best source of trail and camping information is the **Yuba River Ranger Station** (☎530-288-3231; 15924 Hwy 49, Camptonville; ⌚8am-4:30pm Mon-Fri).

Downieville

Downieville, the biggest town in remote Sierra County (though that's not saying much), is located at the junction of the North Yuba and Downie rivers. With a reputation that quietly rivals Moab, UT (before it got big), this is one of the premier places for mountain-bike riding in the US, and a staging area for true wilderness adventures.

As with most gold rush towns, it wasn't always fun and games: the first justice of the peace was the local barkeep, and a placard tells the story of the racist mob that hanged a Chicana named Josefa on the town bridge in 1851, the only recorded lynching of a woman in California.

Activities

The mountains and rivers in these parts beg to be explored in summer. Favorite hikes include the **Sierra Buttes Fire Lookout**, a moderate 6 miler out-and-back that joins the **Pacific Crest Trail** before a 1500ft elevation gain to epic views from the lookout tower, and **North Yuba Trail**, 12 miles along the canyon ridge, starting behind the courthouse in town. There are many more options. Pick up maps and a shuttle ride from the local outfitters.

Downieville Downhill MOUNTAIN BIKING
(www.downievilleclassic.com) This world-class mountain biking trail shoots riders over the Sierra Buttes and 5000ft down into Downieville. There are plenty of other scenic biking trails to explore, including **Chimney Rock**, **Empire Creek** and **Rattlesnake Creek**, but this route is the reason why pro-riders arrive in late July or early August for the **Downieville Classic**, a mix of cross-country and downhill racing and revelry.

Yuba Expeditions MOUNTAIN BIKING
(☎530-289-3010; www.yubaexpeditions.com; 208 Main St; bike/e-bike rentals per day $150/200, shuttle per person $25; ⌚8:30am-5:30pm Mon-Fri, 8am-6pm Sat & Sun May–mid-Nov) Yuba Expeditions is run by Sierra Buttes Trail Stewardship, a nonprofit in the center of the trail-bike scene. Rents top-of-the-line Santa Cruz bikes and e-bikes, offers all-day packages and runs a shuttle. Non-bikers will find it helpful with maps and general trail advice.

Downieville Outfitters MOUNTAIN BIKING
(☎530-289-0155; www.downievilleoutfitters.com; 312 Main St; bike rental per day $100-120, shuttle per person $30-40; ⌚8am-5pm, shuttles Jun-Oct) A good option for trail information, bike rental and shuttles in Downieville. Reservations recommended for shuttle rides.

Festivals & Events

Downieville Mountain Brewfest BEER
(www.downievillebrewfest.com; $30; ⌚Jul) This July event is focused around the consumption of craft beer, but it also involves fabulous food vendors, live music and fresh Downieville air.

Sleeping & Eating

In downtown Downieville, the soft roar of the rapids lull saddle sore bikers to sleep in several small B&Bs. More secluded options are along Hwy 49 east of town.

Tahoe National Forest Campgrounds CAMPGROUND $
(☎information 530-994-3401, reservations 877-444-6777; www.recreation.gov; tent & RV sites $24; ⌚generally May-Sep; P 🐾) West of town on Hwy 49 are a string of beautiful campsites. Most have vault toilets, running water and reservable sites along the North Yuba River. Of these, the prettiest is Fiddlecreek, which has tent-only sites right on the river.

★ **Lure Resort** CABIN, CAMPGROUND $$
(☎530-289-3465; www.lureresort.com; 100 Lure Bridge Lane; camping cabins $95, housekeeping cabins $270-330; P 📶 🐾) A great option if you want to come with biking buddies or a family, this circle of modernized log cabins is along a sublime stretch of river open to fly-fishing with big lawns for the kids to enjoy. The basic camping cabins, which are BYO sleeping bag and have shared bathrooms, sleep four tightly.

Riverside Inn HOTEL $$
(☎530-289-1000; www.downieville.us; 206 Commercial St; r $105-135, ste $200, cottage $275; P 🛜 🐾) There is a secluded, rustic charm to these 11 stove-warmed rooms and a suite overlooking the river near the heart of Downieville. About half have kitchens and all have balconies. The delightful innkeepers share excellent information about hiking and biking in the area, and in winter lend snowshoes. A nearby cottage sleeps eight.

★ **La Cocina de Oro Taqueria** MEXICAN $
(☎530-289-3584; 322 Main St; tacos from $4, burritos $11; ⊙11am-8pm Thu-Sat, 11am-5pm Sun Apr-Dec; 🖉) Chef-owner Feather Ortiz uses herbs and peppers from her garden and sources everything else from local growers to make the freshest food around. The burritos are the size of Chihuahuas. No credit cards.

Sierra City & the Lakes Basin

Sierra City is the primary supply station for people headed to the **Sierra Buttes**, a rugged, rocky shock of mountains that are probably the closest thing to the Alps you'll find in California without hoisting a backpack. It's also the last supply point for people headed into the fishing paradise of the Lakes Basin. There's information about lodging and activities at www.sierracountychamber.com.

There's just one main drag in town, and that's the Golden Chain Hwy (Hwy 49). All commerce happens here. The hotels often have the best restaurants – when they're open.

Sights & Activities

There's a vast network of trails here, including access to the **Pacific Crest Trail (PCT)**. The Sierra Country Store is the only consistently open place in town, and it welcomes trail refugees with its laundromat and deli.

To reach the Sierra Buttes, and many lakes and streams nearby, take Gold Lake Hwy north from Hwy 49 at Bassetts, 9 miles northeast of Sierra City. An excellent hiking trail leads 1.1 miles to **Haskell Peak** (8107ft), where you can see from the Sierra Buttes right to Mt Shasta and beyond. To reach the trailhead, turn right from Gold Lake Hwy at Haskell Peak Rd (Forest Rd 9) and follow it for 8.5 miles to the marked parking lot.

Sierra City's local museum, the **Kentucky Mine** (☎530-862-1310; www.sierracountyhistory.org; 100 Kentucky Mine Rd; museum adult/child $2/50¢, tour adult/child 7-17yr $7/3.50; ⊙10am-4pm late May-early Sep; P 👪), is a worthy stop that introduces the famed 'Golden Chain Hwy' (California's Hwy 49). Its gold mine and stamp mill are just northeast of town.

Sleeping & Eating

This is very much outdoorsy terrain, and the campsites are excellent. The cheapest sleeps are in the United States Forest Service (USFS) campgrounds east from Sierra City along Hwy 49. Wild Plum, Sierra, Chapman Creek and Yuba Pass all have vault toilets and running water (Sierra has river water only). If you're not bringing your tent, Buttes Resort is the best option.

Salmon Creek Campground CAMPGROUND $
(☎information 530-288-3231, reservations 877-444-6777; www.recreation.gov; Gold Lake Hwy, Calpine; tent & RV sites $24; ⊙mid-May–late Sep; P 🐾) With views of the Sierra Buttes, this USFS campground in the Tahoe National Forest is 2 miles north of Bassetts on Gold Lake Hwy, off Hwy 49. It has vault toilets, running water, and sites for tents and RVs, but no hookups.

Wild Plum Campground CAMPGROUND $
(☎877-444-6777; www.recreation.gov; tent & RV sites $24; ⊙mid-May–Sep; P) Of the handful of camping areas east of Sierra City, this is the most scenic, along a rushing stretch of Haypress Creek. The facilities – vault toilets and 47 sites – are basic but clean.

★ **Buttes Resort** CABIN, LODGE $$
(☎530-862-1170; www.buttesresort.com; 230 Main St; d $95-160; P 🚭) In the heart of Sierra City, the small Buttes Resort occupies a lovely spot overlooking the river and is a favorite with hikers looking to recharge. Most cabins have a private deck and barbecue, and some have full kitchens. You can borrow games from the wilderness-loving owners and there's a wood-lined communal area with a pool table.

Red Moose CAFE $
(☎530-862-1024; www.facebook.com/redmoosecafe; 224 Main St; $8-13; ⊙8am-2pm Thu-Sun) This rugged old-school wooden building on the main street houses a great little cafe, with an unlikely specialty in the British favorite fish and chips. It also serves big breakfast scrambles, burritos and burgers. If you arrive just behind a pack of locals at lunchtime, you might hear the cook yell, 'Tell her it's gonna be awhile!' after placing your order.

Shopping

Sierra Country Store MARKET
(☎530-862-1560; www.sierracountrystore.com; 213 Main St; ⏰8am-7pm May-Sep, 10am-6pm Oct-Apr; 📶) A welcome sight for PCT hikers and anyone else needing a laundromat, deli, groceries, ATM and wi-fi.

EL DORADO & AMADOR COUNTIES

In the heart of the pine- and oak-covered Sierra foothills, this is where gold was first discovered – Spanish-speaking settlers named El Dorado County after a mythical city of riches.

Today, SUVs en route to South Lake Tahoe pull off Hwy 50 to find a rolling hillside dotted with the historic towns, sun-soaked terraces and fertile soil of one of California's burgeoning wine-growing regions. If you make the stop, don't leave without tasting a glass of regional zinfandel, which, like the locals, is packed with earthy attitude and regional character.

Coloma-Lotus Valley

Coloma-Lotus Valley surrounds Sutter's Mill (the site of California's first gold discovery) and Marshall Gold Discovery State Historic Park. It is also a great launching pad for rafting operations. The South Fork of the American River gets the most traffic since it features exciting rapids but is still manageable. Adrenaline junkies who have never rafted before should try the Middle Fork.

Activities

Half-day rafting trips usually begin at **Chili Bar** and end close to the Marshall Gold Discovery State Historic Park. Full-day trips put in at the **Coloma Bridge** and take out at **Salmon Falls**, near Folsom Lake. The half-day options start in Class III rapids and are action-packed (full-day trips start out slowly, then build up to Class IV as a climax). Full-day trips include a lavish lunch. The season usually runs from May to mid-October, depending on water levels. Prices are lower on weekdays.

Don't want to get wet? Watch people navigate the **Troublemaker Rapids**, from the bridge near Sutter's Mill in the state park.

Monroe Ridge Trail WALKING
This 3-mile hike follows a steep route from Coloma. Take High St from the town center, then Marshall Park Way, winding through oak woodland to the Marshall Monument, via James Marshall's rugged cabin and an 1865 Catholic church and pioneer cemetery. You then join the Monroe Ridge Trail, which leads along the ridge back down into Coloma.

Whitewater Connection RAFTING
(☎530-622-6446; www.whitewaterconnection.com; half-day trips $139-169, full day $199-249; ⏰Apr-early Oct) Typical of the area's operators, with knowledgeable guides and excellent food. Prices listed are for American River trips.

Bekeart's Gun Shop OUTDOORS
(329 Hwy 49, Coloma; per person $7; ⏰10am-3pm Sat & Sun; 👪) Panning for gold is always popular at Bekeart's Gun Shop, across the street from the Gold Discovery Museum & Visitor Center. It's sometimes open on weekdays.

Sleeping & Eating

Unless you want to camp, for which you're very well served here, it's best to head south to Placerville, or get a cheap motel bed around Auburn.

American River Resort CAMPGROUND, CABIN $
(☎530-622-6700; www.americanriverresort.com; 6019 New River Rd, Coloma; tent & RV sites $20-50, cabin tents $99, cabins $185-280; P 🏊 🐾) A quarter mile off Hwy 49, just south of the Marshall Gold Discovery State Historic Park (p628), this site is more built-up than other area campgrounds. There's a small convenience store, a playground, fishing pond and pool. The sites are basic, but some are right on the river. The most spacious and pretty oak-shad ed sites are 14 to 29.

Coloma Club Cafe & Saloon AMERICAN $
(☎530-626-6390; http://colomaclub.com; 7171 Hwy 49, Coloma; mains lunch $7-15, dinner $13-17; ⏰restaurant 6:30am-9pm, bar 10am-2am; 📶) The cafe didn't exude friendliness on our visit, but the patio at this rowdy old saloon comes alive with guides and river rats when the water is high. It hosts bands and DJ nights on summer weekends.

Getting There & Away

Hwy 49 runs right through the heart of Coloma.

Coloma Shuttle (☎530-303-2404; https://colomashuttle.com; River Park Village, 7308 Suite F, Coloma; half-/full-river trips $10/15) Operated by a local nonprofit to reduce emissions and parking congestion, this shuttle connects local campsites to rafting spots on the river, with a trailer rigged up for boats and gear.

Marshall Gold Discovery State Historic Park

This **state park** (530-622-3470; www.parks.ca.gov; Hwy 49, Coloma; per car $8; 8am-8pm late May-early Sep, 8am-6pm early Sep-Oct, Mar-late May, 8am-5pm Nov-Feb;) comprises a fascinating collection of buildings in a bucolic riverside setting at the site of James Marshall's riot-inducing discovery. Buy your ticket at the **museum** (530-622-6198; http://marshallgold.com; 310 Back St, Coloma; free with park entry, guided tour adult/child $3/2; 10am-5pm Mar-Oct, 9am-4pm Nov-Feb, guided tours 11am & 1pm year-round;) to display on the dashboard, return to the museum for some background, then explore a replica of **Sutter's Mill**, mosey round the blacksmith's and Chinese store, and even try panning for gold.

Compared to the stampede of gun-toting, hill-blasting, hell-raising settlers that populate tall tales along Hwy 49, the Marshall Gold Discovery State Historic Park is a place of tranquility, with two tragic protagonists in John Sutter and James Marshall.

Sutter, who had a fort in Sacramento, partnered with Marshall to build a sawmill on this swift stretch of the American River in 1847. It was Marshall who discovered gold here on January 24, 1848, and though the men tried to keep their findings secret, prospectors from around the world stampeded into town. In one of the ironies of the gold rush, the men who made this discovery died nearly penniless. In another, many of the new immigrants who arrived seeking fortune were indentured, taxed and bamboozled out of anything they found. Meanwhile, as the site museum stresses, the world of the local Native American Nisenan tribespeople was collapsing due to disease and displacement.

In the rare moments when there aren't a million schoolkids running around, the pastoral park by the river makes for a solemn stroll. A trail leads past displays about panning and hydraulic mining, as well as the 1860 **Wah Hop Chinese Store**, to the spot on the bank of the wide American River where Marshall found gold and started the revolutionary birth of the 'Golden State.'

On a hill overlooking the park is the **James Marshall Monument**, where he was buried in 1885, a ward of the state. You can drive the circuit but it's much better to meander up to the monument on foot, and then continue on the Monroe Ridge Trail for views of the town and the river. The climb to the monument is short but steep. You can return to the park visitor center more quickly by hiking down the .5 mile Monument Trail, which begins near the Marshall Monument.

Panning for gold ($7, free if you have your own equipment) is popular. From 10am to 3pm on weekends in the summer, or by request, you get a quick training session and 45 minutes to pan.

Coloma Resort (530-621-2267; www.colomaresort.com; 6921 Mt Murphy Rd, Coloma; tent & RV sites $58-80, cabins $95-380, cottage $375-395;) is a long-established riverside campground with the feel of a summer camp and a good choice for RVs. It comes with wi-fi and a full range of activities: scavenger hunts, a rock wall, karaoke and face-painting. There's a range of accommodations, from camping to cabins and a country cottage.

Delicious soups, sandwiches, baked goods and coffee from well-known Sacramento and local purveyors find their way to **Argonaut Farm to Fork Cafe** (530-626-7345; www.argonautcafe.com; 331 Hwy 49, Coloma; items $9-14; 8am-4pm;). Crowds of school kids waiting for gelato can slow things down.

Placerville

Pronounced PLASS-er-ville, this fun city is a great little place to explore while traveling between Sacramento and Tahoe on Hwy 50. It has a thriving and well-preserved downtown with antique shops and bars, and local wags who cherish the wild reputation of 'Hangtown' – a name earned when a handful of men swung from the gallows in the mid-1800s.

Placerville has always been a travelers' town: it was originally a destination for fortune hunters who reached California by following the South Fork of the American River. In 1857 the first stagecoach to cross the Sierra Nevada linked Placerville to Nevada's Carson Valley, which eventually became part of the nation's first transcontinental stagecoach route. A placer is a mining term for deposits of heavy minerals like gold and platinum. Placer mining generally occurs in stream beds through gold panning and similar methods, all popular here during the gold rush.

Sights

Main St is the heart of downtown Placerville and runs parallel to Hwy 50 between Canal St and Cedar Ravine Rd. Hwy 49 meets Main St at the west edge of downtown. Looking like a movie set, most buildings along Main St are false fronts and sturdy brick structures from the 1850s, dominated by the spindly **Bell Tower**, a relic from 1856 that once rallied volunteer firefighters.

Hangtown's Gold Bug Park & Mine HISTORIC SITE
(☎530-642-5207; www.goldbugpark.org; 2635 Gold Bug Lane; tour adult/child $9/5; ⏰10am-4pm Apr-Oct, noon-4pm Sat & Sun Nov-Mar; P) About 1 mile north of town via Bedford Ave, this historical park stands on the site of four mining claims that yielded gold from 1849 to 1888. You can descend into the Gold Bug Mine on a self-guided audio tour with 13 stops, explore the old stamp mill, do some gem panning ($2 per hour, generally open April through October) or just picnic in the grounds for free.

Sleeping

There are some wonderful historic accommodations here, and a small number of chain motels can be found at either end of the center of Placerville along Hwy 50.

★**Camino Hotel** B&B $
(☎530-644-1800; www.caminohotel.com; 4103 Carson Rd, Camino; r $100-125, r with shared bath $75-125; P) A former lumberjack bunkhouse that's every bit as creaky as you'd hope but with rooms that have been redone. The rates are a steal, especially on weekdays, and room 4 is perfect for families with two rooms adjoined by a central sitting room. Hot breakfast included. A great spot to hunker down while touring Apple Hill's (p630) farms.

National 9 Inn MOTEL $
(☎530-622-3884; www.national9inns.com; 1500 Broadway; r $89; P) This welcoming two-story motel is the best bargain in Placerville, even if it lies at the lonely north end of town. The exterior is ho-hum, but the rooms are sparkling with refrigerators, microwaves and remodeled baths. It's a great option for travelers who want a clean, no-frills stay.

Cary House Hotel HISTORIC HOTEL $$
(☎530-622-4271; www.caryhouse.com; 300 Main St; r from $121; P@) This historic hotel in the middle of downtown Placerville has a large, comfortable lobby with backlit stained glass depicting scenes from the region's history. Once a major staging stop, it has well-worn but clean rooms (some with kitchenettes) with period decor. Ask for a room overlooking the courtyard to avoid street noise, or try room 212, a rumored supernatural haunt.

WORTH A TRIP

PLACERVILLE WINERIES

The Placerville region's high heat and rocky soil produces excellent wines, which frequently appear on California menus. Oenophiles could spend a long afternoon rambling through the welcoming vineyards of El Dorado County alone (though a full weekend of tasting could be had if it was coupled with adjoining Amador County). Details can be found at the **El Dorado Winery Association** (☎530-409-8688; www.eldoradowines.org) or Wine Smith (p630), a local shop with just about everything grown in the area.

Two noteworthy wineries, both north of Hwy 50, include **Lava Cap Winery** (☎530-621-0175; www.lavacap.com; 2221 Fruit Ridge Rd; tasting fee $5; ⏰10am-5pm; P), which has an on-hand deli for picnic supplies, and **Boeger Winery** (☎530-622-8094; www.boegerwinery.com; 1709 Carson Rd; tasting $5-15; ⏰10am-5pm; P) with its 1872 fieldstone building and blacksmith.

Eating

Sweetie Pie's BREAKFAST $
(☎530-642-0128; 577 Main St; mains $10-16, pastries $2-4, pies $21; ⏰7am-2:30pm Mon-Thu, 7am-3pm Fri & Sat, 7am-2pm Sun) Ski bunnies and bums fill this diner and bakery counter on the weekends en route to Tahoe, filling up with egg dishes and top-notch homemade baked goods including heavenly cinnamon rolls. Breakfast is the specialty, with an array of omelets, waffles, scrambles and pancakes, but it also does a capable lunch.

Farm Table Restaurant MEDITERRANEAN $$
(☎530-295-8140; https://ourfarmtable.com; 311 Main St; mains lunch $10-14, dinner $22-36; ⏰11am-3pm Mon, 11am-8pm Wed & Sun, 11am-9pm Thu-Sat; 🌿) A lovely deli-style place dishing up well-cooked farm-fresh food with a Mediterranean feel, alongside homespun fare such as duck confit raviolo. It specializes in charcuterie

WORTH A TRIP

APPLE HILL

In 1860, a miner planted a Rhode Island Greening apple tree on a hill and with it established the foundation for bountiful Apple Hill, a 20-sq-mile area east of Placerville and north of Hwy 50, where there are more than 50 orchards, farms and wineries. Apple growers sell directly to the public, usually from August to December, and some let you pick your own. Other fruits and Christmas trees are available during different seasons.

Maps of Apple Hill are available online through the **Apple Hill Association** (☎530-644-7692; www.applehill.com), or use the El Dorado **Farm Trails Guide** (http://visit-eldorado.com).

A great place to hunker down while touring the farms is the Camino Hotel (p629).

and preserving, and has plenty of gluten-free and veggie options on the menu too.

Heyday Café CAFE $$
(☎530-626-9700; www.heydaycafe.com; 325 Main St; mains lunch $13-26, dinner $13-30; ⏲11am-3pm Mon, 11am-9pm Tue-Thu, 11am-10pm Fri & Sat, 11am-8pm Sun) Fresh and well executed, the menu here leans toward simple Italian comfort food, made all the more comfortable by the wood-and-brick interior. The wine list is long on area vineyards. Locals rave about lunch.

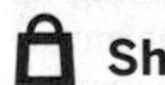

Drinking & Entertainment

Liar's Bench BAR
(☎530-622-0494; 255 Main St; ⏲8am-2am) The Liar's Bench survives as the town's classic watering hole under a neon martini sign that beckons after dark. Karaoke nights, a pool table and darts provide entertainment.

Shopping

Wine Smith WINE
(☎530-622-0516; www.thewinesmith.com; 346 Main St; tastings $8; ⏲1-7pm Mon-Thu, noon-10pm Fri & Sat, noon-7pm Sun) The Placerville wine shop that specializes in local vintages – and beers too. It pairs wines with beer and chocolate for tasting sessions.

Placerville Hardware HOMEWARES
(☎530-622-1151; 441 Main St; ⏲8am-6pm Mon-Sat, 9am-5pm Sun) The 1852 building, an anchor of Placerville's main drag, is the oldest continuously operating hardware store west of the Mississippi and a place to pick up a brochure for a self-guided tour of the town. The store has Gold Country bric-a-brac but most of what clutters the place are bona-fide goods such as hammers and buckets, plus Yeti coolers and gold-mining pans.

Bookery BOOKS
(www.facebook.com/bookeryplacerville; 326 Main St; ⏲10am-5:30pm Mon-Thu, 10am-7pm Fri & Sat, 10am-4pm Sun) A veritable warren of books, this is a great used-book store for stocking up on vacation reading, including Americana and travel and music books.

Information

El Dorado County Visitors Authority (Chamber of Commerce; ☎530-621-5885; http://visit-eldorado.com; 542 Main St; ⏲8am-5pm Mon-Fri) Maps and local information on everything from farm trails to films, breweries and Tahoe.

Getting There & Away

Amtrak (☎877-974-3322; www.capitolcorridor.org; Mosquito Rd) Runs one bus daily from the Placerville Transit Station to Sacramento ($24; 1 hour). Hop aboard in Sacramento to connect to points further along the Capital Corridor route.

El Dorado Transit (☎530-642-5383; www.eldoradotransit.com; 6565 Commerce Way, Diamond Springs; adult/child $1.50/75¢) Operates hourly weekday commuter buses roughly between 6am and 6pm to every corner of town out of the **Placerville Station Transfer Center** (2984 Mosquito Rd), a charming covered bus stop with benches and restrooms. It's about half a mile from downtown, on the north side of Hwy 50. Also runs commuter buses to Sacramento ($5) Monday through Friday.

Plymouth & Amador City

Two small, sunny villages make equally good bases for exploring Amador County's wine region. The first, Plymouth, is where the region's gold rush history is evident in its original name, Pokerville. Few card sharks haunt the slumbering town today; it wakes late when the tiny main street fills with the smell of barbecue, a few strolling tourists and the odd rumble of a motorcycle posse – although a new hotel and a new gourmet sandwich shop have energized the scene. For the real center of the action, head to the wineries and tasting rooms in the pretty Shenandoah Valley.

Six miles south, Amador City was once home to the Keystone Mine – one of the most prolific gold producers in California – but the town lay deserted from 1942 (when the mine closed) until the 1950s, when a family from Sacramento bought the dilapidated buildings and converted them into antique shops.

Sights

Chew Kee Store Museum MUSEUM
(www.fiddletown.info; Fiddletown Rd, Fiddletown; entry by donation; noon-4pm Sat Apr-Oct) Remnants of the bygone era are just outside of Plymouth. This museum, 6 miles east in Fiddletown, is an old herbal shop that once served railroad workers. The dusty collection of artifacts frozen in time are objets d'art.

Amador Whitney Museum MUSEUM
(209-267-5250; www.amador-city.com; Main St, Amador City; noon-4pm Fri-Sun) FREE This rugged little 1860s building looks like something straight out of a John Ford movie, and houses a replica schoolhouse scene and mine shaft.

Sleeping & Eating

★Rest BOUTIQUE HOTEL $$
(209-245-6315; www.hotelnest.net; 9372 Main St; r $197-279 ste $329; P) Guests sip local wines and nibble gourmet snacks from sister-property Taste during the afternoon wine hour at this new boutique property in downtown Plymouth. Staff are helpful, and the 19 rooms blend comfort and modern style. We especially like the complimentary in-room snacks. A satisfying continental breakfast is also served.

Imperial Hotel B&B $$
(209-267-9172; www.imperialamador.com; 14202 Old Hwy 49, Amador City; r $145-165, ste $155-195; P) It's a three-ghost situation at the Imperial, built in 1879. Ask the bartender for more details – but only if you're not staying here alone. This is one of the area's most inventive updates to the typical antique-cluttered hotel, with art deco touches, warm red brick, a genteel bar and a very good seasonal restaurant (dinner mains $16 to $38).

★Amador Vintage Market SANDWICHES $
(209-245-3663; www.bethsogaard.com; 9393 Main St, Plymouth; sandwiches $9-10; 9am-6pm) This big-windowed gourmet market is the place to pick up a sandwich and freshly baked cookie for your picnic at one of the wineries up the road. Also has on-site seating inside or on the small patio overlooking Main St. The curried chicken salad sells out early.

★Taste CALIFORNIAN $$$
(209-245-3463; www.restauranttaste.com; 9402 Main St, Plymouth; small plates $9-15, dinner mains $30-53; 11:30am-2pm Fri-Sun, 5-9pm Mon, Tue, Thu & Fri, 4:30-9pm Sat & Sun) Book a table at Taste, where excellent Amador County wines are paired with a fine menu of California style cooking (big on meat and game). There's open seating in the wine bar, where gregarious locals will gladly fill you in on local haunts – and maybe buy you a glass of wine. Don't miss the mushroom cigars.

Drinking & Nightlife

Drytown Club BAR
(www.facebook.com/drytown05; 15950 Hwy 49, Drytown; noon-midnight Fri-Sun) Tired of wine? Hit the Drytown Club, the local rowdy roadhouse with a Wild West vibe. The bands on weekends are bluesy, boozy and sometimes brilliant: the Doghouse Blues Band plays every Sunday at 5pm.

Sutter Creek

Perch on the balcony of one of the gracefully restored buildings on this particularly scenic Main St and view Sutter Creek, a gem of a Gold Country town with raised, arcade sidewalks and high-balconied buildings with false fronts that are perfect examples of California's 19th-century architecture. This is a good option for an overnight basecamp when visiting Amador and El Dorado County wineries.

Begin the visit at volunteer-operated Sutter Creek Visitors Center (p633) to collect a walking-tour map of historic traces left by Cornish, Yugoslavian and Italian arrivals, and pick up the handy pocket guide to the dozen wine-tasting rooms downtown. Staff will share their insights on wineries along Shenandoah Valley Rd.

Sights

The compact downtown is home to a dozen wine-tasting rooms. Most sell wines produced at vineyards in the nearby Shenandoah Valley. The vibe is friendly and intimate, and the tasting rooms are good places to try local wines if you don't have time to drive out to one of the vineyards.

Miners Bend Park PARK
(www.suttercreekfoundation.org; Old Hwy 49; P) Gold-mining equipment fills this new park at the south end of downtown. Learn about the development of Sutter Creek from its

DON'T MISS

AMADOR COUNTY WINE REGION

Amador County might be an underdog among California's winemaking regions, but a thriving circuit of family wineries, gold rush history and local characters make for excellent imbibing without a whiff of pretension. The region lays claim to the oldest zinfandel vines in the United States, and the surrounding country has a lot in common with this celebrated variety – bold, richly colored, earthy and constantly surprising.

The region has two tiny towns, Plymouth and Amador City. Start in Amador City and follow Hwy 49 north through the blip known as Drytown, continue on Hwy 49 to Plymouth, and then follow Shenandoah Rd northeast, which takes you past rolling hills of neatly pruned vines. Most hosts are exceedingly welcoming and helpful, offering information on their operations and, for the most part, free tastings.

Check the website of the Amador Vintners Association (www.amadorwine.com) for a map of the county's 40-plus wineries and a list of monthly events. All the wineries celebrate the fall harvest with food pairings and live music at the annual **Big Crush Harvest Wine Festival**, held the first weekend in October.

Deaver Vineyards (☎209-245-4099; www.deavervineyards.com; 12455 Steiner Rd, Plymouth; tasting fee $5; ⏲10:30am-5pm; P) A true family affair going back 150 years, where nearly everyone pouring has their last name on the bottles.

Jeff Runquist Wines (☎209-245-6282; www.jeffruhnquistwines.com; 10776 Shenandoah Rd, Plymouth; ⏲11am-5pm) One of the names dominating the double-gold winners list at the annual San Francisco Chronicle Wine Competition is Jeff Runquist, a long-time California winemaker who works his magic with grapes grown across California. Locally sourced favorites include the zinfandel and barbera.

Iron Hub Winery (www.ironhubwines.com; 12500 Steiner Rd, Plymouth; tastings $10-15; ⏲11am-5pm Fri-Mon; P 🐾) With its hilltop perch and sweeping views of the Sierra foothills, this chic new winery is our top pick for an afternoon of wine sipping and socializing. You can sip your barbera or old-vine zin with Fido on the sprawling patio.

Sobon Estate (☎209-245-6554; www.sobonwine.com; 14430 Shenandoah Rd, Plymouth; ⏲10am-5pm Apr-Oct, 10am-4:30pm Nov-Mar) This environmentally conscious family-run estate was founded in 1977, but its wine-making history dates to the 1850s. You'll find picnic grounds on-site as well as the small, free **Shenandoah Valley Museum**, which traces the region's wine-making history, with an emphasis on farming and wine-making tools.

Amador 360 Wine Collective (www.amador360.com; 18950 Hwy 49, Plymouth; tastings $5; ⏲11am-6pm Mon-Fri, 10am-6pm Sat & Sun) Run by the couple who organize Amador's annual barbera extravaganza (http://barberafestival.com; September), this expansive shop reserves special billing to boutique vintners who otherwise would not offer tastings.

scrappy gold rush days to its life as a full-fledged mining town in the mid-1900s, when it was home to the productive Eureka mines.

Knight Foundry MINE
(☎209-560-6160; www.knightfoundry.org; 81 Eureka St; $15; ⏲10am-3pm 2nd Sat of month) In its prime, Sutter Creek was Gold Country's main supply center for all things forged. Three foundries operating in 1873 made pans and rock crushers, but only this one operated until 1996 – it was the last water-powered foundry and machine shop in the US. You can check out the equipment up close on the second Saturday of the month on a self-guided tour.

Yorba Wines WINERY
(☎209-267-8190; www.yorbawines.com; 51 Hanford St; ⏲11am-5pm) Wines are sourced from nearby Shake Ridge Vineyards where long-time viticulturist Ann Kraemer understands the vines like they're beloved old friends. Wine tastings are informative and friendly.

Sleeping

Hotel Sutter HOTEL $$
(☎209-267-0242; www.hotelsutter.com; 53 Main St; r $180-250; P ❄ 📶) There was some controversy when they started gutting the beloved American Exchange, which had stood in repose for more than 150 years. The bricks and facade may be the only things

left, but the modern rooms, very fine restaurant (mains $13 to $27) and cool cellar bar seem to have quelled the protest.

Sutter Creek Inn B&B $$
(☎209-267-5606; www.suttercreekinn.com; 75 Main St; r $138-230; ❄📶) The 17 rooms and cottages vary in decor and amenities (antiques, fireplaces, sunny patios). All have private bathrooms. Guests can snooze in the hammock by the gardens or curl up with a book on a comfy chair on the sprawling lawn. Hot breakfast served at 9am.

Hanford House Inn B&B $$
(☎209-267-0747; www.hanfordhouse.com; 61 Hanford St; r $225-325, cottages $255-325; P❄@📶🐾) Nod off on platform beds in contemporary rooms or fireplace cottage suites. Breakfasts are harvested from the inn's garden, freshly baked goods appear every afternoon and evening brings wine tasting.

Eating & Drinking

Gold Dust Pizza PIZZA $
(☎209-267-1900; 20 Eureka St; mains $9-29; ⏰11am-8pm Mon-Wed, 11am-9pm Thu-Sun; 👪) Crisp, crusty pizza and pitchers of beer make this a favorite; it's the perfect place to hang out and chat to the locals. Combinations like the BBQ pizza put it over the top; you can order (huge) whole pizzas, or opt for slices.

Sutter Creek Cheese Shoppe MARKET $
(☎209-267-5457; www.facebook.com/SutterCreekCheese; 33b Main St; ⏰noon-5pm Mon-Thu, 10am-5pm Fri-Sun) A stop for cheeses from California and beyond. Call ahead for a picnic box of cheese, a baguette and even a little cutting board and knife to enjoy on your winery hop.

Choc-o-latte COFFEE
(www.facebook.com/chocolattesuttercreek; 48 Main St; ⏰7am-4pm Mon-Fri, 8am-4pm Sat & Sun) The namesake latte at this downtown coffee shop is an intoxicating blend of mocha and white mocha. Big windows and low-key Victorian decor make this an inviting spot for relaxing.

Entertainment

Sutter Creek Theatre PERFORMING ARTS
(☎916-425-0077; www.suttercreektheater.com; 44 Main St; tickets from $22) One of several excellent Gold Country arts venues, the theater has nearly a 100-year-long history of presenting live drama, but nowadays schedules mostly musical concerts, as well as films and other cultural events.

Information

Sutter Creek Visitors Center (☎209-267-1344; www.suttercreek.org; 71a Main St; ⏰10am-6pm) Volunteers stand by with maps, information and souvenirs. The printed walking tour through historic downtown is also available online. Grab the helpful pocket guide about the tasting rooms downtown.

Volcano

One of the fading plaques in Volcano, 12 miles upstream from Sutter Creek, tellingly calls it a place of 'quiet history.' Even though the little L-shaped village on the bank of Sutter Creek yielded tons of gold and a Civil War battle, today it slumbers away in remote solitude – where cell phone service can be iffy. Only a smattering of patinated bronze monuments and some moodily battered buildings attest to Volcano's lively past.

Large sandstone rocks line Sutter Creek, which skirts the center of town. The rocks were blasted from surrounding hills by hydraulic mining before being scraped clean of their gold. The process had dire environmental consequences, but generated miners nearly $100 of booty a day.

Sights & Activities

★Indian Grinding Rock State Historic Park HISTORIC SITE
(Chaw'se; Map p49; ☎209-296-7488; www.parks.ca.gov; 14881 Pine Grove-Volcano Rd; per car $8; ⏰park sunrise to sunset, museum 10am-4pm; P) Two miles southwest of Volcano, this sacred area for the local Miwok comprises a museum in a traditional wooden roundhouse, a village site, a limestone outcrop covered with petroglyphs – 363 originals and a few modern additions – and more than 1000 mortar holes called *chaw'se*, used for grinding acorns and seeds into meal.

Black Chasm Cavern CAVE
(☎888-488-1960; www.caverntouring.com; 15701 Pioneer Volcano Rd, Pine Grove; adult/child $6-12yr $18.50/10; ⏰9am-5pm Jun–mid-Sep, 10am-4pm mid-Sep–May; P👪) Less than 1 mile east of Volcano, this National Natural Landmark has the whiff of a tourist trap, but one look at the array of helictite crystals – rare clusters that grow horizontally – makes the crowd more sufferable. Guides for the 50-minute tours are experienced cavers. For more eye-catching rock formations, head to the Zen Garden,

where a short trail twists through a cluster of Tolkien-esque marble slabs.

Sleeping & Eating

St George Hotel HISTORIC HOTEL $

(209-296-4458; www.stgeorgevolcano.com; 16104 Main St; r $55-209) Up the crooked stairs of this charming galleried hotel are 20 rooms that vary in size and amenity (most have shared bathrooms) and are free of clutter. The restaurant (dinner Wednesday to Sunday and breakfast and lunch on weekends) has a menu anchored by steak. Hang out in the saloon and try to spot the rumored ghosts.

Volcano Union Inn HISTORIC HOTEL $$

(209-296-7711; www.volcanounion.com; 21375 Consolation St; r $139-165; P ❄ ☎) The more comfortable of the two historic hotels in Volcano: there are four lovingly updated rooms with crooked floors and private bathrooms and a large, shared balcony facing the street. Flat-screen TVs and modern touches are a bit incongruous in the old building, but it's a cozy place to stay.

The on-site **Volcano Union Pub** (mains $10-28; 5-8pm Mon, Wed & Thu, 5-9pm Fri, noon-9pm Sat, noon-8pm Sun;) has the best food in town and a lovely patio garden. The lamb burger earns raves.

Entertainment

Volcano Theatre Company PERFORMING ARTS

(209-419-0744; www.volcanotheatre.org; 16121 Main St; tickets adult/child $20/16; Sat & Sun mid-Apr–mid-Dec) On weekends between mid-April and mid-December, this highly regarded company produces live dramas in an outdoor amphitheater and in the tiny 1856 Cobblestone Theater.

Shopping

Country Store FOOD & DRINKS

(209-296-4459; 16146 Main St; 10am-6pm Mon-Sat, 11am-5pm Sun) In continuous use since 1852, this fantastically atmospheric and authentic old store has creaky floorboards, a long wooden counter and inbuilt stools, and shelves groaning with tins and bottles. The shopkeeper whips up canned beef sandwiches and hamburgers in the small cafe.

Jackson

Jackson has some historic buildings and a small downtown, but it ain't much to look at. It stands at the junction of Hwy 49 and Hwy 88, which turns east from Hwy 49 here and heads over the Sierra Nevada near the Kirkwood ski resort.

Sights

Kennedy Gold Mine HISTORIC SITE

(209-223-9542; http://kennedygoldmine.com; 12594 Kennedy Mine Rd; tours adult/child $12/6; 10am-3pm Sat & Sun Mar-Oct) You can't miss the ominous steel headframe of the mine from the road, rising to 125ft. Its pulleys lifted ore and miners from the bowels of the earth. Guided tours last about 90 minutes and take you past the stamp, gold recovery mill and massive tailing wheels. The parking lot is off North Main St.

Mokelumne Hill HISTORIC SITE

(www.mokehill.org) The somewhat undiscovered settlement of Mokelumne Hill is 7 miles south of Jackson just off Hwy 49. Settled by French trappers in the early 1840s, it's a good place to see historic buildings without the common glut of antique stores and gift shops. Stay at the old-style Hotel Leger if you want to soak up the peace and quiet.

Sleeping & Eating

Hotel Leger HERITAGE HOTEL $

(209-286-1401; www.hotelleger.com; 8304 Main St, Mokelumne Hill; r $115-145, ste $145-175;) A grand and old-fashioned place with an impressive galleried frontage and pretty decent food in the restaurant, plus characterful creaky floorboards, a stuck-in-time saloon bar and rumors of a proactive ghost situation (!). Get a room on the street side for a view of the picturesque little hillside town of Mokelumne Hill. Some rooms share a bathroom.

Mel's & Faye's Diner AMERICAN $

(209-223-0853; http://melandfayes.homestead.com; 31 Hwy 88; mains lunch $4-11, dinner $10-20; 5am-10pm) A local institution on Hwy 88 that dates back to 1956: there's a takeout window but it's not meant for quick stops. Take a seat on the bottle-green leather benches for solid diner fare that includes huge breakfasts, classic burgers, luscious milkshakes and – to balance the grease binge – a decent salad bar.

Information

Amador County Chamber of Commerce

(209-223-0350; www.amadorchamber.com; 1 Prosperity Ct; 10am-4pm Mon-Fri) Stop here to pick up information about sights and stays. To locate the office via Google maps, use Amador Economic Prosperity Center as the destination.

Getting There & Away

The only way to easily travel through this area is with your own wheels. By car, Jackson is 2½ hours from San Francisco and just over one hour from the ski resorts of South Lake Tahoe.

To connect to Sacramento, you can try **Amador Transit** (209-267-9395; http://amadortransit.com; 115 Valley View Way; fares $1-3.50; Mon-Fri), which makes weekday connections between Sacramento and the Sutter Creek Transit Station ($7, 1½ hours). If you have enough patience, you can connect to Calaveras County and southern Gold Country.

CALAVERAS COUNTY & SOUTH GOLD COUNTRY

The southern region of Gold Country is hot as blazes in the summer, so cruising through its historic gold rush hubs will demand more than one stop for ice cream. The tall tales of yesteryear come alive here through the region's famous former residents: author Mark Twain, who got his start writing about a jumping frog contest in Calaveras County, and Joaquin Murrieta, a controversial symbol of the lawlessness of the frontier era who somehow seems to have frequented every old bar and hotel in the area. Murphys is an increasingly popular wine-tasting destination, and tasting rooms line Main St.

Angels Camp

On the southern stretch of Hwy 49 one figure looms over all others: literary giant Mark Twain, who got his first big break with the story of The Celebrated Jumping Frog of Calaveras County, written and set in Angels Camp. There are differing claims as to when or where Twain heard this tale, but Angels Camp makes the most of it. There are gentlemanly Twain impersonators and statues, and bronze frogs on Main St honoring the champions of the past 80 years, as well as the **Jumping Frog Jubilee** (www.frogtown.org; 2465 Gun Club Rd; from $10; May;) on the third weekend in May (in conjunction with the county fair and something of a Harley rally). Look for the plaque of Rosie the Ribeter, who set an impressive 21ft record in 1986. Today the town is an attractive mix of buildings from the gold rush to art-deco periods.

Plan to spend at least an hour at the engaging **Angels Camp Museum** (209-736-2963; http://angelscamp.gov/museum; 753 S Main St; adult/child 5-11yr $7/3; 10am-4pm Thu-Mon; P). From Hwy 49 it looks tiny, but the museum sits on a 3-acre plot with back buildings packed tight with Gold Country artifacts. Check out the informative Mark Twain display in the main building then head out back to see stagecoaches, a model working stamp mill, a mineral collection and a mock 1800s newspaper office.

It's perhaps not the greatest natural beauty, but **Moaning Caverns** (209-736-2708; www.moaningcaverns.com; 5350 Moaning Cave Rd, Vallecito; adult/child $20/15; 11am-5pm Mon-Fri, 10am-5pm Sat & Sun), 7 miles east of Angels Camp, does have additional thrills beyond the cave, including ziplines and axe-throwing cages. Bones discovered here are some of the oldest human remains in the US. Winter events such as caroling utilize cave acoustics.

Strung out along Hwy 49 are a number of motels and hotels, including the stylish and modern **Best Western Cedar Inn & Suites** (209-736-4000; ww.bestwestern.com; 455 S Main St; r/ste from $199/209; P).

For food, the class act in downtown Angels Camp is **Crusco's** (209-736-1440; www.facebook.com/Cruscos; 1240 S Main St; mains $18-29; 11:30am-3pm & 5-9pm), which puts out a serious, authentic northern Italian menu.

There are a couple of bars in town, but your best bet is the wonderful restored art deco **cinema** (209-736-2472; www.cinemawest.com; Angels Theatres, 1228 S Main St; tickets $9.50).

Getting There & Away

Calaveras Connect (209-754-4450; www.calaverasconnect.org; one-way fare $2) operates the most reliable public transportation system in the region. Use it to connect between San Andreas, Angels Camp, Murphys, Arnold, Jackson and Sutter Creek and other surrounding towns on weekdays. You can catch it mid-route – just flag it down. The new **Saturday Hopper** (one way $3) runs between Angels Camp, Murphys and Arnold on Saturdays from mid-February through early November. It's a good option if you want to visit the wine-tasting rooms in Murphy without driving there. To connect via public transportation to the rest of California, you have to catch the Red Line to San Andreas and switch to the Purple Line to Mokelumne Hill and finally transfer to Amador Transit in Sutter Creek.

Murphys

With its white picket fences, historic downtown and old-world charm, Murphys is one of the more scenic communities along the

WORTH A TRIP

CALAVERAS BIG TREES STATE PARK

Calaveras Big Trees State Park (209-795-2334; www.parks.ca.gov; 1170 Hwy 4, Arnold; per car $10; sunrise-sunset, visitor center 10am-4pm; P) is home to giant sequoia trees that reach as high as 250ft with trunk diameters of over 25ft. These leftovers from the Mesozoic era are thought to weigh upwards of 2000 tons, or close to 10 blue whales. The giants are distributed in two large groves, one easily seen on the **North Grove Trail**, a 1.5-mile self-guided loop, near the park entrance. On the more remote **South Grove Trail**, it's a 5-mile round-trip hike to **Agassiz Tree**, the park's largest specimen.

Be sure to pick up a copy of the North Grove Trail Guide from the box at the trailhead. It shares fascinating information about the trees, local history and conservation attitudes over the years. Relax a moment at the **reclining bench**, which lets you stare up at the mighty trees and soak up their grandeur. Horses, cars and hikers used to make their way through the (human-made) tunnel bisecting the **Pioneer Cabin Tree**. Unfortunately, this tourist attraction collapsed during a rain storm in 2017.

Camping (reservations 800-444-7275; www.reserveamerica.com; off Hwy 4; tent & RV sites $25-35, cabins $185-205; generally Mar-Nov; P) is popular and reservations essential. North Grove Campground is near the park entrance; less crowded is Oak Hollow Campground, 4 miles further on the park's main road. Most atmospheric are the hike-in environmental sites. Store food and toiletries in the provided bear lockers at all times.

southern stretch of Gold Country, befitting its nickname as 'Queen of the Sierra.' It lies 8 miles east of Hwy 49 on Murphys Grade Rd, and is named for Daniel and John Murphy, who founded a trading post and mining operation on Murphy Creek in 1848. They employed the struggling local Miwok and Yokut people as laborers. While some settlers continued to persecute the tribes, John eventually married Pokela, a chieftain's daughter.

The town's Main St is refined, with tons of wine-tasting rooms, boutiques, galleries and good strolling. For information and a town overview, look to www.visitmurphys.com.

Sights & Activities

Ironstone Vineyards WINERY

(209-728-1251; www.ironstonevineyards.com; 1894 Six Mile Rd; tasting fee $5; 11am-5pm; P) The unusually family-friendly atmosphere makes the wine feel secondary at Ironstone. There's a natural spring waterfall, a mechanical pipe organ, frequent exhibits by local artists, and blooming grounds. By the deli, the museum displays the world's largest crystalline gold leaf specimen (it weighs 44lb and was found in Jamestown in 1992). The enormous tasting room accommodates crowds.

Newsome-Harlow WINERY

(209-728-9817; www.nhvino.com; 403 Main St; tasting $10; noon-5pm Mon-Thu, 11am-5:30pm Fri-Sun;) This family-run winery pours the juicy red varietals that made them famous in their lively tasting lounge. At times, the place feels like the community social club. There's an on-site chef and couch-flanked fire pits, and kids and dogs are welcome.

Murphys Old Timers Museum MUSEUM

(209-728-1160; www.murphysoldtimersmuseum.com; 470 Main St; donation requested; noon-4pm Fri-Sun) The name is a good hint that this place approaches history with a humorous touch. Housed in an 1856 building, it has an inscrutable tintype of the outlaw Joaquin Murrieta and the entertaining 'Wall of Comparative Ovations.' Guided tours of town leave from the museum every Saturday at 10am.

California Cavern CAVE

(888-488-1960; www.cavetouring.com; 9565 Cave City Rd; adult/child $16/8.50; 10am-5pm Jun–mid-Sep, 10am-4pm mid-Sep–Nov, closed Dec-May; P) In Cave City, 12 winding miles north of Murphys (take Main St to Sheep Ranch Rd to Cave City Rd), is a natural cavern, which John Muir described as 'graceful flowing folds deeply placketed like stiff silken drapery.' Regular tours take 60 to 80 minutes. Call before driving to the cavern because it may close due to weather conditions.

Mercer Caverns CAVE

(209-728-2101; www.mercercaverns.net; 1665 Sheep Ranch Rd; adult/child $19/11; 9am-5pm Jun-Aug, 10am-4:30pm Sep-May; P) For kids and adults who like a sense of adventure with their cave tour, Mercer Caverns obliges. You'll walk a quarter of a mile on 440 steps that drop, twist, turn and climb through a narrow cavern opening, which was discovered by Waller J Mercer in 1885 and soon monetized by him as tourist attraction.

Sleeping

Most accommodations in Murphys are top-end B&Bs. For the same price, there are some attractive rental cottages just off Main St, or check nearby Angels Camp or Arnold for cheaper alternatives.

★Victoria Inn B&B $$
(209-728-8933; www.victoriainn-murphys.com; 402 Main St; r $143-197, ste $237-327, cottages from $302; P) This downtown B&B has glamorous rooms with claw-foot slipper tubs, sleigh beds and balconies. Some rooms have wood-burning stoves and balconies overlooking the courtyard fountain. The common spaces have chic, modern country appeal. The free chocolate-chip cookies are delicious.

Murphys Vacation Rentals COTTAGE $$
(209-736-9372; www.murphysvacationrentals.com; 549 S Algiers St; cottages $165-395; P) For the same price as a frilly B&B, picturesque cottages clustered just off Main St are available for rent. Cleaning fee extra.

Murphys Historic Hotel INN $$
(209-728-3444; www.murphyshotel.com; 457 Main St; historic rooms $139-215, annex rooms $149-255; P) Since 1856, this hotel has been an anchor on Main St. A must-stop on the Mark-Twain-slept-here tour, the original structure is well worn, but an ongoing revamp of rooms in the adjoining buildings – after a makeover on Gordon Ramsay's *Hotel Hell* – brought new verve to the property. The Old West **saloon** is the heart of the place.

Eating & Drinking

Firewood AMERICAN, PIZZA $
(209-728-3248; www.firewoodeats.com; 420 Main St; mains $8-17; 11am-9pm Sun-Thu, 11am-9:30pm Fri & Sat;) Firewood's exposed-concrete walls and corrugated metal offer a minimalist respite from the Old West vibe downtown. There are wines by the glass, half a dozen beers on tap and basic pub fare, but the wood-fired pizzas are the hallmark. Tacos are $3 apiece.

Alchemy Market & Cafe CALIFORNIAN $$
(209-728-0700; www.alchemymurphys.com; 191 Main St; most mains $16-32; 11am-3pm Fri-Sun, 4-8pm Sun-Thu, 4-9pm Fri & Sat, bar 9pm-midnight Fri & Sat) The stellar cafe menu has a long wine list and many dishes, from calamari frites to green curry mussels, plus gourmet comfort dishes. Live music every Friday night from 6pm to 8:30pm.

Grounds AMERICAN $$
(209-728-8663; www.groundsrestaurant.com; 402 Main St; dinner mains $17-33; generally 7am-3pm daily, 5-8:30pm Wed-Sun;) This casually elegant cafe does everything competently – expert breakfast foods, a roster of light lunch mains and weekend dinners of steak and fresh fish. Iced herbal tea and fresh vegetarian options are key when temperatures outside rise. Opening hours vary.

Watering Hole CRAFT BEER
(www.murphyswateringhole.com; 223 Big Trees Rd; 11am-8pm Sun-Tue & Thu, 11am-9pm Fri & Sat) This new craft beer hall with an outdoorsy vibe serves 40 different drafts from across the US and Europe. There's an ever-changing seasonal menu of snacks and sandwiches too ($7–$15). A short walk from Main St.

Information

Wine Information Center (209-728-9467; www.calaveraswines.org; 202 Main St; 11am-5pm Thu-Sun) The Calaveras Winegrape Alliance runs this helpful information outpost. Stop by for a map to the nearby tasting rooms and suggestions to get you started.

Columbia

More than any other place in Gold Country, Columbia blurs the lines between present and past with a carefully preserved gold rush town – complete with volunteers in period dress – at the center of a modern community. In 1850 Columbia was founded over the 'Gem of the Southern Mines,' and as much as $150 million in gold was found here. The center of the town (run by the state parks system) looks almost exactly as it did in its heyday.

The blacksmith's shop, theater, old hotels and authentic bar are carefully framed windows into history, completed by stagecoach rides and breezy picnic spots.

Docents lead free hour-long tours daily at 11am from mid-June through August at the Columbia Museum. Saturdays and Sundays only the rest of the year.

Sights

Columbia State Historic Park HISTORIC SITE
(209-588-9128; www.parks.ca.gov; 11255 Jackson St; most businesses 10am-5pm; P) FREE The so-called 'Gem of the Southern

Mines' is like a miniature gold rush Disneyland, but with more authenticity and heart. Four blocks of town have been preserved, where volunteers perambulate in 19th-century dress and demonstrate gold panning. The blacksmith's shop, theater, hotels and saloon are all carefully framed windows into California's past. The yesteryear illusion of Main St is shaken only a bit by fudge shops and the occasional banjo-picker or play-acting forty-niner whose cell phone rings.

Columbia Museum HISTORIC SITE
(209-532-3184; www.parks.ca.gov; cnr Main & State Sts; 10am-5pm Apr-Sep, 10am-4pm Oct-Mar) FREE Looking rather like dinosaur bones, limestone and granite boulders are noticeable around town. These were washed out of the surrounding hills by hydraulic mining and scraped clean by prospectors. Kids can dress up in Old West–era clothes.

Sleeping & Eating

Fallon Hotel HISTORIC HOTEL $
(information 209-532-1470, reservations 800-444-7275; www.reserveamerica.com; 11175 Washington St; r $66-127;) The historic Fallon Hotel hosts the most professional theater troupe in the region, the Sierra Repertory Theatre. The building is done out in period style, with floral wallpaper, glass lanterns and gleaming wooden furnishings. Rooms have a toilet and sink, but showers are down the hall.

Cottages COTTAGE $$
(information 209-532-1479, reservations 800-444-7275; www.reserveamerica.com; 1-/2-/3-bedroom cottage $127/148/149;) A cozy alternative to staying in a hotel are these cottages, two at the end of Main St, and the largest with three bedrooms on Columbia St.

City Hotel HISTORIC HOTEL $$
(209-532-1479; www.reservecalifornia.com; 22768 Main St; r $105-127;) Among a handful of Victorian hotels in the area, City Hotel is the most elegant, with rooms that overlook a shady stretch of Main St. Adjoining the on-site restaurant Christopher's at the City Hotel (mains $12 to $38), What Cheer Saloon is an atmospheric Gold Country joint with paintings of lusty ladies and striped wallpaper.

Entertainment

Sierra Repertory Theatre THEATER
(209-532-3120; www.sierrarep.org; 11175 Washington St) This theater mixes up Shakespeare, musicals, farce and popular revues.

Sonora & Jamestown

Settled in 1848 by miners from Sonora, Mexico, this area was once a cosmopolitan center of commerce and culture with parks, elaborate saloons and the Southern Mines' largest concentration of gamblers and gold. Racial unrest drove the Mexican settlers out and their European usurpers got rich on the Big Bonanza Mine, where Sonora High School now stands. That single mine yielded 12 tons of gold in two years (including a 28lb nugget).

Today, people en route to Yosemite National Park use Sonora as a staging post. The historic center is so well preserved that it's a frequent backdrop in films.

Smaller Jamestown is 3 miles south of Sonora, just south of the Hwy 49/108 junction. Founded around the time of Tuolumne County's first gold strike in 1848, today the place limps along on tourism and antiques.

Sights & Activities

Sonora is a base for **white-water rafting**: the Upper Tuolumne River is known for Class IV and V rapids and its population of golden eagles and red-tailed hawks, while the Stanislaus River is more accessible with Class III rapids. **Sierra Mac River Trips** (209-591-8027; www.sierramac.com; 27890 Hwy 120, Groveland; one-day trips $178-309; generally Apr-Oct) and All-Outdoors (p620) both run trips of one day or more on multiple rivers.

Railtown 1897 State Historic Park STATE PARK
(209-984-3953; www.parks.ca.gov; 10501 Reservoir Rd, Jamestown; adult/child $5/3, incl train ride $15/10; 9:30am-4:30pm Apr-Oct, 10am-3pm Nov-Mar, train rides 10:30am-3pm Sat & Sun Apr-Oct;) Five blocks east of Jamestown's Main St, this 26-acre collection of trains and railroad equipment is the photogenic sister to Sacramento's rail museum. It's served as a backdrop for countless films and TV shows, including *Back to the Future III*, *Unforgiven* and *High Noon*. You can sometimes ride the narrow-gauge railroad that once transported ore, lumber and miners.

California Gold Panning Lessons OUTDOORS
(209-213-9719; www.gold-panning-california.com; 17712 Harvard Mine Rd, Jamestown; 2hr sluicing & panning from $180; by appointment 9am-3pm) Miner John and his crew provide boots and all needed equipment for a genuine experience panning at Woods Creek and beyond. Be warned: real prospecting involves

lots of digging. A couple of hours in, you'll have gold fever, a blister or both.

Sleeping & Eating

★Bradford Place Inn B&B $$
(☎209-536-6075; www.bradfordplaceinn.com; 56 W Bradford St, Sonora; r $145-265;) Gorgeous gardens and inviting porch seats surround this four-room B&B. With a two-person claw-foot tub, the Bradford Suite is the definitive, romantic B&B experience. Gourmet breakfasts can be served on the verandah.

Gunn House Hotel HISTORIC HOTEL $$
(☎209-532-3421; www.gunnhousehotel.com; 286 S Washington St, Sonora; r $169-179, ste $199;) For a lovable alternative to Gold Country's cookie-cut chains, this historic hotel hits the sweet spot. Rooms feature period decor and guests take to rocking chairs on the wide porches in the evening. A pool and a breakfast buffet make it a hit with families.

★Legends Books, Antiques & Old-Fashioned Soda Fountain CAFE $
(☎209-532-8120; www.facebook.com/legendssonora; 131 S Washington St, Sonora; sandwiches $8, ice cream $2.75; ⊙11am-5pm Thu-Tue) The place to sip sarsaparilla, snack on a Polish dog or share a scoop of huckleberry ice cream at a 26ft-long mahogany bar that's been here since 1850. Then browse antiques and books downstairs – many of them lining the old tunnel that miners used to secrete their stash directly into the former bank; there's even an in-house stream downstairs. Very cool!

Diamondback Grill AMERICAN $
(☎209-532-6661; www.thediamondbackgrill.com; 93 S Washington St, Sonora; mains $13-17; ⊙11am-9pm Mon-Thu, 11am-9:30pm Fri & Sat, 11am-8pm Sun;) With exposed brick, modern fixtures, fresh menu and contemporary details, this cafe and wine bar is a reprieve from occasionally overbearing Victorian frill along Hwy 49. Sandwiches and burgers dominate the menu (the salmon and eggplant-mozzarella are both great) and everything is homemade.

Drinking & Entertainment

The free and widely available weekend supplement of the *Union Democrat* comes out on Thursday and lists movies, music, performance art and events for Tuolumne County.

Iron Horse Lounge BAR
(☎209-532-4482; 97 S Washington St, Sonora; ⊙9am-2am) Sonora's classic and fairly rugged hangout in the center of town. Bottles glitter like gold on the backlit bar.

Sierra Repertory Theatre PERFORMING ARTS
(☎209-532-3120; www.sierrarep.com; 13891 Hwy 108, Sonora; tickets adult $25-37, child $20) Located in a restored tin warehouse in East Sonora, close to the Junction Shopping Center. This critically acclaimed company also performs in the Fallon Hotel in Columbia.

Shopping

Sierra Nevada Adventure Company SPORTS & OUTDOORS
(www.snacattack.com; 173 S Washington St, Sonora; ⊙10am-6pm) This flagship store is stocked with maps and has equipment for rent and sale. There's also friendly advice from passionate guides with knowledge of ways to get outdoors in the area.

Information

Tuolumne County Visitors Bureau (☎209-533-4420; www.yosemitegoldcountry.com; 193 S Washington St, Sonora; ⊙9am-5pm Mon-Fri 10am-4pm Sat & Sun) More so than other brochure-jammed chamber of commerce joints, the staff here offer helpful trip-planning advice throughout Gold Country as well as to Yosemite National Park and Stanislaus National Forest.

Getting There & Away

Hwy 108 is the main access road here, and it links with I-5, 55 miles west near Stockton. A summer-only entrance to Yosemite National Park lies 60 scenic miles south on Hwy 120.

A limited service is provided weekdays by **Tuolumne County Transit** (☎209-532-0404; www.tuolumnecountytransit.com; 12879 Justice Center Dr, Sonora; fare $2; ⊙Mon-Fri) buses, which make a circuit through Sonora hourly from about 7:30am to 8:30pm; they also stop in Columbia and Jamestown less frequently.

Green **trolleys** (☎209-532-0404; www.tuolumnecountytransit.com; Washington St, Sonora; ⊙8:30am-8:30pm Sat May-Sep) link the sights in Columbia, Sonora and Jamestown at no charge on Saturdays from May through September.

YARTS (☎877-989-2787; www.yarts.com; adult/child return $38/18, one-way $19/9) For Yosemite visitors staying in the Sonora area, YARTS operates three round-trip buses connecting downtown Sonora, Jamestown's Main St and Yosemite from late May through August There is just one round-trip bus in mid-May and September. Ask nicely to be dropped off at unscheduled stops in Yosemite.

AT A GLANCE

POPULATION
305,958

WATER IN LAKE TAHOE
37 trillion gallons

BEST VIEWPOINT
Inspiration Point (p656)

BEST CREEPY HISTORY
Donner Memorial State Park (p664)

BEST BREAKFAST
Fire Sign Cafe (p659)

WHEN TO GO

Jul–Aug Beach season; wildflowers bloom, and hiking and mountain-biking trails open.

Sep–Oct Cooler temperatures, colorful foliage and fewer tourists after Labor Day.

Dec–Mar Snow sports galore at resorts; storms bring hazardous roads.

Heavenly (p643) ski resort
ALISA_CH / SHUTTERSTOCK ©

Lake Tahoe

Shimmering in myriad shades of blue and green, Lake Tahoe is the USA's second-deepest lake. Sitting at 6245ft, it is also one of the highest lakes in the country. Driving around the 72-mile shoreline is a spellbinding adventure, with curves, viewpoints and beckoning trails. Generally, the north shore is quiet and upscale, the west shore, rugged and old-timey; the east shore, undeveloped; the south shore, bustling with motels and casinos. Nearby Reno is the biggest little city in the region.

The horned peaks surrounding the lake are year-round destinations. Swimming, boating, kayaking, windsurfing, stand-up paddleboarding (SUP) and boat cruises prevail in summer, as do hiking, camping and wilderness backpacking. Winter brings bundles of snow, perfect for hitting Tahoe's top-tier ski and snowboard resorts.

INCLUDES

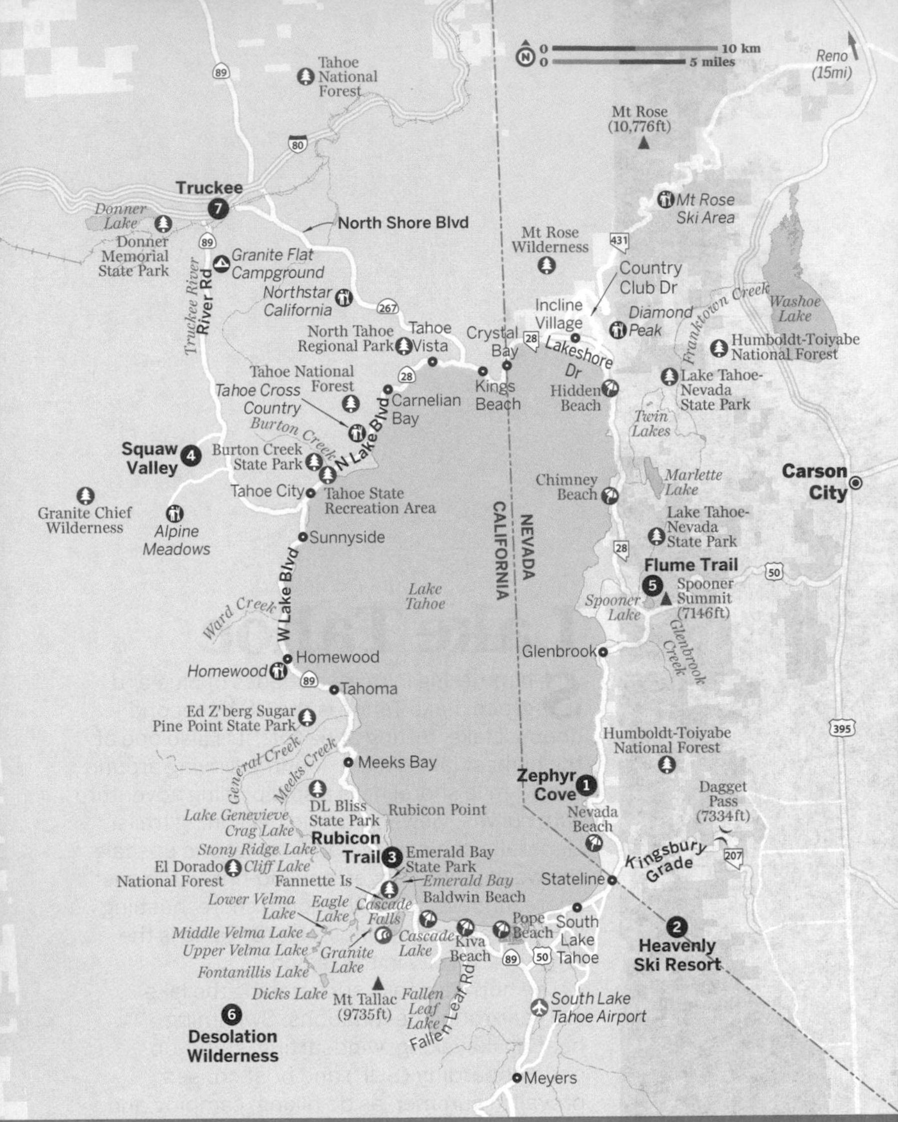

Lake Tahoe Highlights

❶ **Zephyr Cove** (p648) Surveying the shimmering expanse of Lake Tahoe from a kayak or from the sandy beach at Zephyr Cove.

❷ **Heavenly** (p643) Swooshing down the vertiginous double-black-diamond runs of this ski resort.

❸ **Rubicon Trail** (p656) Trekking this trail from Vikingsholm Castle on Emerald Bay to DL Bliss State Park.

❹ **Squaw Valley** (p662) Swimming in an outdoor lagoon or ice-skating above 8000ft atop the cable-car line.

❺ **Flume Trail** (p672) Thundering down this trail on a mountain bike to tranquil Spooner Lake.

❻ **Desolation Wilderness** (p650) Escaping summer crowds to alpine lakes and high-country meadows.

❼ **Truckee** (p664) Joining the throngs downtown for shopping, dining and conviviality.

SOUTH LAKE TAHOE & STATELINE

Highly congested and arguably overdeveloped, South Lake Tahoe is a chockablock commercial strip bordering the lake and framed by picture-perfect alpine mountains. It sits at the foot of the world-class Heavenly mountain resort, and buzzes from the gambling tables in the casinos just across the border in Stateline, NV. Lake Tahoe's south shore draws visitors with a cornucopia of activities, lodging and restaurant options, especially for summer beach access and tons of powdery winter snow.

Sights

Heavenly Gondola CABLE CAR
(Map p646; www.skiheavenly.com; Heavenly Village; adult/child 5-12yr/youth13-18yr from $64/39/50; 10am-5pm Jun-Aug, reduced off-season hours;) Soar to the top of the world as you ride this gondola, which sweeps you from Heavenly Village some 2.4 miles up the mountain in just 12 minutes. From the observation deck at 9123ft, get gobsmacking panoramic views of the entire Tahoe Basin, the Desolation Wilderness and Carson Valley, then jump back on for the final, short hop to the top.

From here there's a range of activities to enjoy (climbing, zip-lining, tubing) and decent eating at **Tamarack Lodge** restaurant and bar (mains $14 to $20), or jump on the **Tamarack Express** chairlift to get all the way to the mountain summit.

Tallac Historic Site HISTORIC SITE
(Map p646; 530-544-7383; www.tahoeheritage.org; 1 Heritage Way, South Lake Tahoe; optional tour adult/child $15/10; 10am-4pm late May-Sep;) FREE Sheltered by a pine grove and bordering a wide, sandy beach, this national historic site sits on the archaeologically excavated grounds of the former Tallac Resort, a swish vacation retreat for San Francisco's high society around the turn of the 20th century. Feel free to just amble or cycle around the breezy forested grounds, today transformed into a community arts hub, where leashed dogs are allowed.

Lake Tahoe Historical Society Museum MUSEUM
(Map p646; 530-541-5458; www.laketahoemuseum.org/the-museum.html; 3058 Lake Tahoe Blvd, South Lake Tahoe; 11am-3pm Sat May, 11am-3pm Thu-Sat Jun-Aug) FREE This small but interesting museum displays artifacts from Tahoe's pioneer past, including Washoe tribal baskets, vintage films, hoary mining memorabilia and a model of a classic Lake Tahoe steamship. On summer Saturday afternoons, check out the restored 1930s cabin out back.

Activities

Tahoe Treetop Adventure Park ADVENTURE SPORTS
(Map p644; 530-581-7563; www.tahoetreetop.com; 725 Granlibakken Rd, off Hwy 89, Tahoe City; adult/child 5-12yr $63/53; tours generally 9:15am-3:45pm Apr-Dec, hours vary seasonally;) At the Granlibakken (p661) resort, take a 2½-hour monkey-like romp between tree platforms connected by ziplines and swinging bridges. Various courses are geared to everyone from little kids (no more than 10ft off the ground) to daredevils (two 100ft ziplines and one that's 300ft). Reserve ahead. Also has locations in Tahoe Vista and Squaw Valley.

Winter Sports

★ **Heavenly** SNOW SPORTS
(Map p646; 775-586-7000; www.skiheavenly.com; 3860 Saddle Rd, South Lake Tahoe; adult/child 5-12yr/youth 13-18yr $154/85/126; 9am-4pm Mon-Fri, 8:30am 4pm Sat, Sun & holidays;) The 'mother' of all Tahoe mountains boasts the most acreage, the longest run (5.5 miles), great tree-skiing and the biggest vertical drop around. Follow the sun by skiing on the Nevada side in the morning, moving to the California side in the afternoon. Views of the lake and the high desert are heavenly indeed.

Sierra-at-Tahoe SNOW SPORTS
(530-659-7453; www.sierraattahoe.com; 1111 Sierra-at-Tahoe Rd, off Hwy 50, Twin Bridges; adult/child 5-12yr/youth 13-22yr $125/50/115; 9am-4pm Mon-Fri, 8:30am-4pm Sat, Sun & holidays;) About 18 miles southwest of South Lake Tahoe, this is snowboarding central, with six raging terrain parks and a 17ft-high superpipe. A great beginners' run meanders gently for 2.5 miles from the summit, but there are also gnarly steeps and chutes for speed demons.

Kirkwood SNOW SPORTS
(209-258-6000; www.kirkwood.com; 1501 Kirkwood Meadows Dr, off Hwy 88, Kirkwood; adult/child 5-12yr/youth 13-18yr $119/87/107; 9am-4pm) Off-the-beaten-path Kirkwood, set in a high-elevation valley, gets great snow and holds it longer than almost any other Tahoe resort. It has stellar tree-skiing, gullies, chutes and terrain parks, and is the only Tahoe resort with backcountry runs accessible by snowcats.

Lake Tahoe

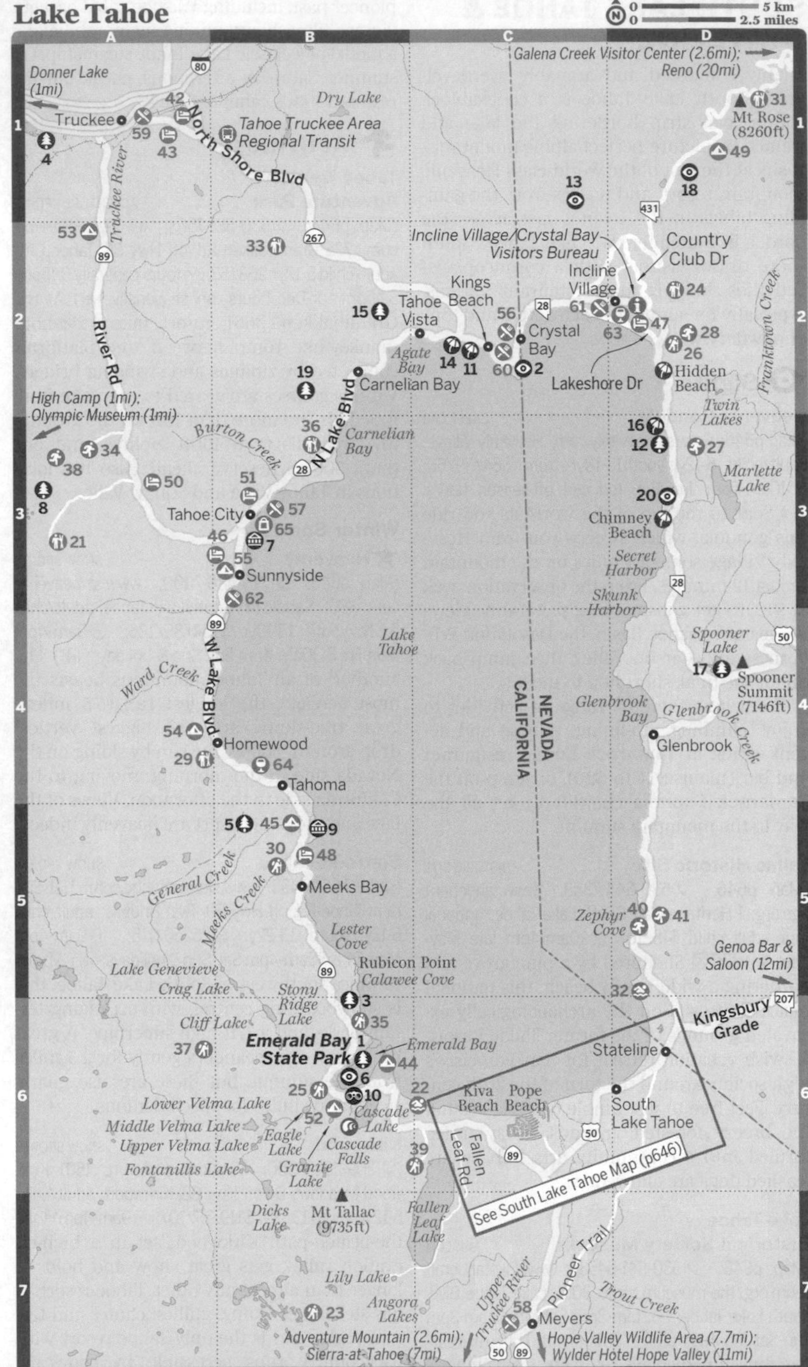

Galena Creek Visitor Center (2.6mi); Reno (20mi)
Donner Lake (1mi)
Truckee
North Shore Blvd
Tahoe Truckee Area Regional Transit
Dry Lake
Mt Rose (8260ft)
Truckee River
River Rd
Incline Village/Crystal Bay Visitors Bureau
Country Club Dr
Incline Village
Kings Beach
Tahoe Vista
Crystal Bay
Agate Bay
Carnelian Bay
Lakeshore Dr
Hidden Beach
Franktown Creek
Twin Lakes
High Camp (1mi); Olympic Museum (1mi)
Burton Creek
N Lake Blvd
Marlette Lake
Tahoe City
Chimney Beach
Secret Harbor
Skunk Harbor
Sunnyside
Lake Tahoe
Spooner Lake
Spooner Summit (7146ft)
Ward Creek
W Lake Blvd
NEVADA
CALIFORNIA
Glenbrook Bay
Glenbrook Creek
Glenbrook
Homewood
Tahoma
General Creek
Meeks Creek
Meeks Bay
Zephyr Cove
Lester Cove
Genoa Bar & Saloon (12mi)
Lake Genevieve
Rubicon Point
Calawee Cove
Crag Lake
Stony Ridge Lake
Kingsbury Grade
Cliff Lake
Emerald Bay State Park
Emerald Bay
Stateline
Lower Velma Lake
Kiva Beach
Pope Beach
South Lake Tahoe
Middle Velma Lake
Eagle Lake
Cascade Lake
Cascade Falls
Upper Velma Lake
Fallen Leaf Rd
Fontanillis Lake
Granite Lake
See South Lake Tahoe Map (p646)
Dicks Lake
Mt Tallac (9735ft)
Fallen Leaf Lake
Pioneer Trail
Lily Lake
Upper Truckee River
Trout Creek
Angora Lakes
Meyers
Adventure Mountain (2.6mi); Sierra-at-Tahoe (7mi)
Hope Valley Wildlife Area (7.7mi); Wylder Hotel Hope Valley (11mi)

Lake Tahoe

Top Sights
1 Emerald Bay State Park....B6

Sights
2 Crystal Bay Casino....C2
3 DL Bliss State Park....B6
4 Donner Memorial State Park....A1
5 Ed Z'berg Sugar Pine Point State Park....B5
6 Fannette Island....B6
7 Gatekeeper's Museum & Marion Steinbach Indian Basket Museum....B3
8 Granite Chief Wilderness....A3
9 Hellman-Ehrman Mansion....B5
10 Inspiration Point....B6
11 Kings Beach State Recreation Area....C2
12 Lake Tahoe-Nevada State Park....D3
13 Mt Rose Wilderness....C1
14 North Tahoe Beach....C2
15 North Tahoe Regional Park....B2
16 Sand Harbor....D3
17 Spooner Lake....D4
18 Tahoe Meadows....D1
19 Tahoe National Forest....B2
20 Thunderbird Lodge....D3
Vikingsholm Castle....(see 1)

Activities, Courses & Tours
21 Alpine Meadows....A3
22 Baldwin Beach....C6
Bayview Trail....(see 52)
23 Desolation Wilderness....B7
24 Diamond Peak....D2
25 Eagle Falls Trail....B6
26 East Shore Trail....D2
27 Flume Trail....D3
28 Flume Trail Bikes....D2
29 Homewood....A4
Lake Tahoe Cruises....(see 40)
30 Meeks Bay Trail....B5
31 Mt Rose....D1
32 Nevada Beach....D5
33 Northstar California....B2
Northstar Mountain Bike Park....(see 33)
34 Resort at Squaw Creek Golf Course....A3
35 Rubicon Trail....B6
Squaw Valley Alpine Meadows....(see 38)
Squaw Valley Treetop....(see 38)
36 Tahoe Cross Country....B3
37 Tahoe Rim Trail....A6
Tahoe Treetop Adventure Park....(see 46)
38 Tahoe Via Ferrata....A3
39 Tallac Trail....C6
40 Zephyr Cove....D5
Zephyr Cove Resort & Marina....(see 40)
41 Zephyr Cove Stables....D5

Sleeping
42 Best Western Plus Truckee-Tahoe....A1
43 Cedar House Sport Hotel....A1
DL Bliss State Park Campground....(see 3)
Donner Memorial State Park Campground....(see 4)
44 Eagle Point Campground....B6
45 General Creek Campground....B5
46 Granlibakken....B3
47 Hyatt Regency Lake Tahoe....D2
48 Meeks Bay Resort....B5
49 Mt Rose Campground....D1
Nevada Beach Campground....(see 32)
PlumpJack Squaw Valley Inn....(see 38)
50 River Ranch Lodge....A3
51 Tahoe City Basecamp....B3
52 USFS Bayview Campground....B6
53 USFS Campgrounds....A2
54 USFS Kaspian Campground....A4
USFS Meeks Bay Campground....(see 48)
55 USFS William Kent Campground....B3

Eating
56 Cafe Biltmore....C2
57 Christy Hill....B3
58 Getaway Cafe....C7
Le Chamois & Loft Bar....(see 38)
59 Pianeta....A1
River Ranch Lodge....(see 50)
60 Soule Domain....C2
Soupa....(see 38)
Stella....(see 43)
61 T's Rotisserie....C2
62 West Shore Market....B3
Wildflour Baking Co....(see 38)

Drinking & Nightlife
63 Alibi Ale Werks Incline Public House....D2
64 Chamber's Landing....B4
Fifty Fifty Brewing Co....(see 42)
Lone Eagle Grille....(see 47)
Tram Car Bar....(see 38)

Shopping
65 North Tahoe Arts Gift Shop & Gallery....B3

Novice out-of-bounds skiers should sign up in advance for backcountry safety-skills clinics.

Hiking

Miles of summer hiking trails start from the top of the Heavenly Gondola (p643), many with mesmerizing lake views. On the Nevada side of the state line, **Lam Watah Nature Trail** meanders for just over a mile each way across United States Forest Service (USFS) land, winding underneath pine trees and beside meadows and ponds, on its way between Hwy 50 and Nevada Beach, starting from the community park off Kahle Dr.

South Lake Tahoe

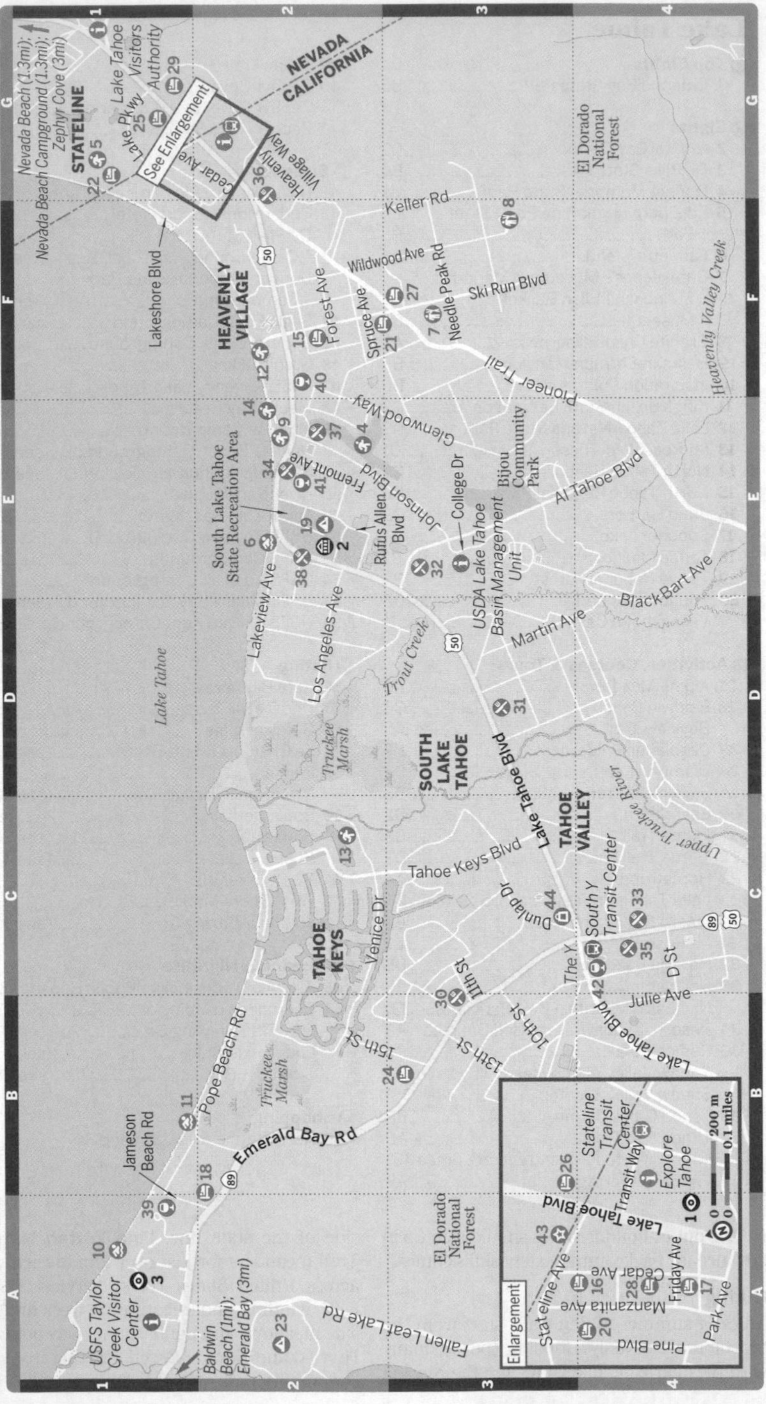

0 2 km
0 1 miles

Nevada Beach (1.3mi);
Nevada Beach Campground (1.3mi);
Zephyr Cove (3mi)
STATELINE
22
5
Lake Pkwy
25
Lake Tahoe Visitors Authority
29
Lakeshore Blvd
See Enlargement
Cedar Ave
HEAVENLY VILLAGE
36
Heavenly Village Way
NEVADA
CALIFORNIA
Lake Tahoe
USFS Taylor Creek Visitor Center
10
3
39
Jameson Beach Rd
11
18
Baldwin Beach (1mi);
Emerald Bay (3mi)
Pope Beach Rd
89
Emerald Bay Rd
Truckee Marsh
23
South Lake Tahoe State Recreation Area
6
14
34
12
Lakeview Ave
9
50
38
19
41
Fremont Ave
40
15
2
37
Forest Ave
Los Angeles Ave
4
TAHOE KEYS
Truckee Marsh
13
Fallen Leaf Lake Rd
Venice Dr
Rufus Allen Blvd
Johnson Blvd
Glenwood Way
Spruce Ave
21
27
Wildwood Ave
Keller Rd
15th St
24
Trout Creek
32
7
Needle Peak Rd
30
11th St
SOUTH LAKE TAHOE
50
College Dr
El Dorado National Forest
13th St
Tahoe Keys Blvd
USDA Lake Tahoe Basin Management Unit
Ski Run Blvd
10th St
Dunlap Dr
Lake Tahoe Blvd
31
Bijou Community Park
Pioneer Trail
8
44
TAHOE VALLEY
Martin Ave
The Y
42
South Y Transit Center
Al Tahoe Blvd
El Dorado National Forest
Lake Tahoe Blvd
Julie Ave
35
33
Upper Truckee River
Black Bart Ave
D St
Heavenly Valley Creek
89
50

Enlargement
Stateline Ave
43
Lake Tahoe Blvd
26
20
Manzanita Ave
16
Cedar Ave
Stateline Transit Center
Transit Way
28
Pine Blvd
Friday Ave
Explore Tahoe
1
17
Park Ave
0 200 m
0 0.1 miles

South Lake Tahoe

Several easy kid- and dog-friendly hikes begin near the USFS Taylor Creek Visitor Center (p655) off Hwy 89. The mile-long, mostly flat **Rainbow Trail** loops around a creek-side meadow, with educational panels about ecology and wildlife along the way. On the opposite side of Hwy 89, the gentle, rolling 1-mile **Moraine Trail** follows the shoreline of Fallen Leaf Lake; free trailhead parking is available near campsite No 75. Up at cooler elevations, the mile-long round trip to **Angora Lakes** is another popular trek with kids, especially because it ends by a sandy swimming beach and a summer snack bar selling ice-cream treats. You'll find the trailhead on Angora Ridge Rd, off Tahoe Mountain Rd, accessed from Hwy 89.

For longer and more strenuous day hikes to alpine lakes and meadows, several major trailheads provide easy access to the evocatively named Desolation Wilderness (p650): Echo Lakes (south of town); Glen Alpine (near Lily Lake, south of Fallen Leaf Lake), to visit a historic tourist resort and waterfall; and Tallac (p650), opposite the entrance to Baldwin Beach. The latter two trailheads also lead to the peak of Mt Tallac (9735ft), a strenuous 10- to 12-mile day hike. Free self-serve wilderness permits for day hikers only are available at trailheads but note that you may have to pay $5 to park at some trailheads; overnight backpacking permits are subject to quotas.

For a helpful overview of top trails in the area, visit www.tahoesouth.com.

Beaches & Swimming

On the California side, in South Lake Tahoe, the nicest strands are **Pope Beach** (Map p646; 1209 Pope Beach Dr; per car $8), **Kiva Beach** (Map p646; Tallac Point Rd) and **Baldwin Beach** (Map p644; per car $8), each with picnic tables and barbecue grills. Kiva offers free parking and allows leashed dogs too. They're all found along Emerald Bay Rd (Hwy 89), running west and east of Tallac Historic Site (p643). Nearby, **Fallen Leaf Lake**, where scenes from

Tahoe Ski Areas

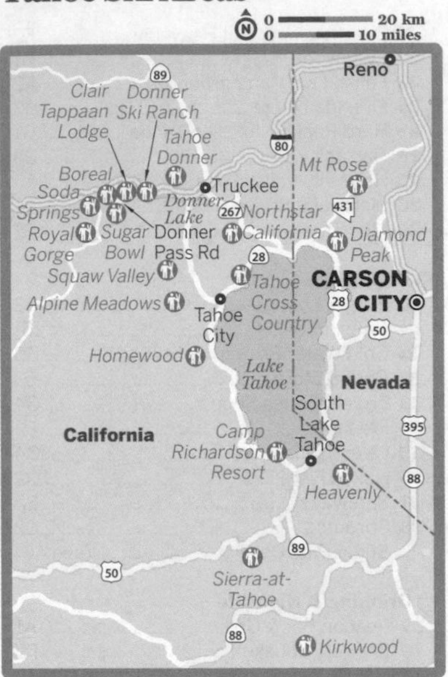

the Hollywood flicks *The Bodyguard* and *City of Angels* were filmed, is also good for summer swims. **El Dorado Beach** (Map p646; 800 El Dorado Ave) is a free public beach, just off Lake Tahoe Blvd.

Many folks prefer to head over to Stateline and keep driving north 2 miles to pretty **Nevada Beach** (Map p644; per car $8), where the wind really picks up in the afternoons, or always-busy **Zephyr Cove** (Map p644; ☎775-589-4901; www.zephyrcove.com; 760 Hwy 50, NV; per car May-Sep $10; ⏲sunrise-sunset), which has rustic resort and marina facilities along its sandy mile-long shoreline.

Boating & Water Sports

In South Lake Tahoe **Ski Run Boat Company** (Map p646; ☎530-544-0200; www.tahoesports.com; 900 Ski Run Blvd; parasailing $80-105; ⏲9am-6pm), at the **Ski Run Marina** (Map p646; ☎530-544-9500; www.skirunmarina.com; 900 Ski Run Blvd), and **Tahoe Keys Boat & Charter Rentals** (Map p646; ☎530-544-8888; www.tahoesports.com; 2435 Venice Dr; Jet Ski per hour from $149; ⏲8am-6pm), at the **Tahoe Keys Marina** (Map p646; ☎530-541-2155; www.tahoekeysmarina.net; 2435 Venice Dr E), both rent motorized powerboats, pontoons, sailboats and Jet Skis (from $149), as well as human-powered kayaks, canoes, hydro bikes, paddleboats and paddleboard sets (per hour from $25). To parasail up to 1200ft above Lake Tahoe's waves, try the Ski Run Marina branch (rides $80 to $105).

Kayak Tahoe WATER SPORTS
(Map p646; ☎530-544-2011; www.kayaktahoe.com; 3411 Lake Tahoe Blvd; kayak single/double 1hr $25/35, 1 day $65/85, lessons & tours from $50; ⏲9am-5pm Jun-Sep) Rent a kayak or a SUP, take a lesson or sign up for a guided tour, including sunset cove paddles, trips to Emerald Bay and explorations of the Upper Truckee River estuary and the eastern shore. Five seasonal locations at **Timber Cove Marina** (Map p646; ☎530-544-2942; 3411 Lake Tahoe Blvd, South Lake Tahoe), Vikingsholm (Emerald Bay) and Baldwin, Pope and Nevada Beaches.

Zephyr Cove Resort & Marina WATER SPORTS
(Map p644; ☎775-589-4901; www.zephyrcove.com; 760 Hwy 50, NV) Rents powerboats, pedal boats, wave runners, Jet Skis, canoes, kayaks and SUPs; also offers single and tandem parasailing flights.

Camp Richardson Resort Marina WATER SPORTS
(Map p646; ☎530-542-6570; www.camprichardson.com; 1900 Jameson Beach Rd, South Lake Tahoe; ⏲kayaks, paddleboats & paddleboards per hour from $30) Rents powerboats, paddleboats, water skis, kayaks and SUP gear.

Mountain Biking

For expert mountain bikers, the classic **Mr Toad's Wild Ride**, with its steep downhill sections and banked turns reminiscent of a Disneyland theme-park ride, should prove sufficiently challenging. Usually open from June until October, the one-way trail along Saxon Creek starts off Hwy 89 south of town near Grass Lake and Luther Pass.

Intermediate mountain bikers should steer toward the mostly single-track **Powerline Trail**, which traverses ravines and creeks. You can pick up the trail off Ski Run Blvd near the Heavenly (p643) resort, from the western end of Saddle Rd. For a more leisurely outing over mostly level terrain, you can pedal around scenic **Fallen Leaf Lake**. Anyone with good lungs might try the **Angora Lakes Trail**, which is steep but technically easy and rewards you with sweeping views of Mt Tallac and Fallen Leaf Lake. It starts further east, off Angora Ridge and Tahoe Mountain Ridge Rds.

For shuttle service and mountain-bike rentals for Mr Toad's Wild Ride, the Tahoe Rim Trail (p658) and other downhill adventures, as well as family-friendly tours, talk to **Wanna Ride** (☎775-790-6375; www.wannaridetahoe.com; ⌚7am-7pm). For mountain-biking trail conditions, race schedules, volunteer days and other special events, contact the Tahoe Area Mountain Biking Association (www.tamba.org).

Cycling

The **South Lake Tahoe Bike Path** is a level, leisurely ride suitable for anyone. It heads west from El Dorado Beach, eventually connecting with the **Pope-Baldwin Bike Path** past Camp Richardson (p650), Tallac Historic Site (p643) and the USFS Taylor Creek Visitor Center (p655). Visitor centers carry the excellent Lake Tahoe bike route map, available online from the Lake Tahoe Bicycle Coalition (www.tahoebike.org), which has an info-packed website for cycling enthusiasts. **Anderson's Bike Rental** (☎530-541-0500; https://andersonsbicyclerental.com; 645 Emerald Bay Rd/Hwy 89, South Lake Tahoe; per hour $10; 👪) rents hybrid bikes with helmets.

Golf

Edgewood Tahoe Golf Course GOLF
(Map p646; ☎775-588-3566; www.edgewood-tahoe.com/golf; 100 Lake Pkwy, Stateline, NV; green fee $175-300; ⌚May-Oct) Stunning lakeside scenery is a major distraction at this challenging championship 18-hole course designed by George Fazio, a favorite for celebrity golf tournaments. Tee-time reservations are required; cart and club rentals available.

Bijou Golf Course GOLF
(Map p646; ☎530-542-6097; www.cityofslt.us; 3464 Fairway Ave, South Lake Tahoe; green fee $18, club/cart rental $15/5; ⌚7am-6pm May-Oct) So you don't know your putter from your nine iron? That's OK at this laid-back, no-reservations municipal course with views of Heavenly Mountain. Built in the 1920s, it's got nine holes, which you can play twice around for an extra $11.

Horseback Riding

Both **Camp Richardson Corral & Pack Station** (Map p646; ☎530-541-3113; www.camprichardsoncorral.com; Emerald Bay Rd/Hwy 89, South Lake Tahoe; trail rides $54-95; 👪) and **Zephyr Cove Stables** (Map p644; ☎775-588-5664; www.zephyrcovestable.com; Hwy 50, Zephyr Cove, NV; trail rides $55-80; 👪), about 4 miles north of Stateline casinos, offer daily horseback rides in summer, varying from one-hour kid-friendly trips through the forest, to extended treks with meadow and lake views (reservations required).

☞ Tours

Lake Tahoe Balloons BALLOONING
(Map p646; ☎530-544-1221; www.laketahoeballoons.com; per person $299) From May through October (weather permitting), you can cruise on a catamaran launched from Tahoe Keys Marina, then clamber aboard a hot-air balloon launched right from the boat's upper deck. The lake and Sierra Nevada mountain views may take away what little breath you have left up at 10,000ft. Reservations required.

TOP WAYS TO SKI TAHOE FOR LESS MONEY

Midweek and half-day afternoon discounts on lift tickets are usually available, but expect higher prices on weekends and holidays. Lift-ticket rates go up incrementally almost every year too. Parents should ask about the interchangeable 'Parent Predicament' lift tickets offered by some resorts, which let one parent ski while the other hangs with the kids, then switch later. **Tahoe Ski Trips** (☎925-680-4386; www.tahoeskitrips.net) runs the Bay Area Ski Bus, which allows you to leave the headache of driving I-80 to others. Round trips start at $109 including lift tickets, with various add-on packages available. Pick-up locations include San Francisco and Sacramento.

In San Francisco, **Sports Basement** (https://shop.sportsbasement.com) sells deeply discounted lift tickets and has the best deals on multiday rental equipment because it doesn't charge for pickup or drop-off days.

Handy money-saving websites:

Ski Lake Tahoe (www.skilaketahoe.com) Portal for the seven biggest Tahoe resorts, with deals covering all.

Sliding on the Cheap (www.slidingonthecheap.com) Homegrown website listing discounts and deals on lift tickets.

SNOW TIRES & CHAINS

If you're driving to Lake Tahoe in winter, be aware that snow tires or chains will likely be required for your vehicle if it's been snowing. You can check the CalTrans website for more information (www.dot.ca.gov) and the California Highway Patrol – Truckee Facebook page (www.facebook.com/chp.truckee) for current snow tire and chain requirements.

Lake Tahoe Cruises CRUISE
(Map p644; ☎775-586-4906; www.zephyrcove.com; 760 Hwy 50; adult/child from $68/38) The MS *Dixie II* paddle wheeler plies Lake Tahoe's 'big blue' year-round with a variety of sightseeing, drinking, dining and dancing cruises, including a narrated two-hour daytime trip to Emerald Bay. It's based at Zephyr Cove Resort & Marina (p648) on the eastern shore in Nevada.

Action Watersports BOATING
(Map p646; ☎530-544-5387; www.action-watersports.com; 3411 Lake Tahoe Blvd, Timber Cove Marina; adult/child under 13yr $69/35) In a hurry to get to Emerald Cove? Wanna avoid those near-constant traffic jams on Hwy 89? Jump on board the *Tahoe Thunder* speedboat, which zips across the lake – watch out, though, you'll get wet! Also offers parasailing rides (from $75).

Festivals & Events

Valhalla Festival of Arts, Music & Film CULTURAL
(☎530-541-4975; www.valhallatahoe.com; ⏰Jun-Aug) A summerlong cultural bonanza of music and theater held at a 1930s Nordic hall.

Sleeping

South Lake Tahoe

South Lake Tahoe has a bazillion choices. Lodging options line Lake Tahoe Blvd (Hwy 50) between Stateline and Ski Run Blvd. Further west, closer to the intersection of Hwys 50 and 89, a string of budget motels ranges from adequate to inexcusable. For scondos and rooms near the slopes, contact Heavenly (p643).

★**Mellow Mountain Hostel** HOSTEL $
(Map p646; ☎530-600-3272; www.mellowmountainhostel.com; 3272 Cedar Ave; dm $32, r per person $96; P @) In a former life this hostel was a motel, which means all the units – from the private rooms to the four-bed dorms – have their own bathroom. Score! Amenities include breakfast, a laundry room, a full kitchen and free movies for renting. It's a friendly and well-run spot, and the gondola is a five-minute walk away.

Fallen Leaf Campground CAMPGROUND $
(Map p646; ☎info 530-544-0426, reservations 877-444-6777; www.recreation.gov; 2165 Fallen Leaf Lake Rd; tent & RV sites $36, yurts $87; ⏰mid-May–mid-Oct;) Near the north shore of stunning Fallen Leaf Lake, this is one of the biggest and most popular campgrounds on the south shore, with pay showers, 206 wooded sites and six canvas-sided yurts that can sleep a family of five (bring your own sleeping bags).

Camp Richardson Resort CABIN, CAMPGROUND $
(Map p646; ☎530-541-1801; www.camprichardson.com; 1900 Jameson Beach Rd; tent sites from $45, RV sites with partial/full hookups from $65/70, r $145-240, cabins $140-281; P) Removed from downtown's strip-mall aesthetic, this sprawling family camp is a hectic place offering seasonal camping (expect marauding bears all night long!), forested cabins rented by the week in summer, and so-so beachside hotel rooms. Sports-gear and bicycle rentals are available, and there's a popular ice-cream parlor across the road. Wi-fi in lobby, coffee shop and general store only.

Campground by the Lake CAMPGROUND $
(Map p646; ☎530-542-6096; www.cityofslt.us; 1150 Rufus Allen Blvd; tent & RV sites with/without hookups $51/41, cabins $56-81; ⏰Apr-Oct; P) Highway noise can be an around-the-clock irritant, though proximity to the city pool and ice rink make this wooded in-town campground with an RV dump station a decent choice. Basic sleeping-platform cabins are available between Memorial Day (late May) and Labor Day (early September). Pet fee is $2 per dog per night.

★**Coachman Hotel** BOUTIQUE HOTEL $$
(Map p646; ☎530-545-6460; www.coachmantahoe.com; 4100 Pine Blvd; r $224-278, ste $314; P) This modernly reimagined motel sports an appealing hunting-lodge chic. Wooden pegs for your clothes and rubber mats for your boots give rooms a functional feel, but amenities such as nightly s'mores

by the fire pit, an inviting breakfast room and a welcoming bar for coffee and alcohol encourage conversation and community.

Deerfield Lodge at Heavenly BOUTIQUE HOTEL **$$**
(Map p646; 530-544-3337; www.tahoedeerfieldlodge.com; 1200 Ski Run Blvd; r/ste from $200/285;) A small boutique hotel close to Heavenly ski resort, Deerfield has a dozen intimate rooms and spacious suites that each have a patio or balcony facing the green courtyard, along with a whirlpool tub, flickering gas fireplace and amusing coat racks crafted from skis and snowboards.

Alder Inn MOTEL **$$**
(Map p646; 530-544-4485; www.alderinn.com; 1072 Ski Run Blvd; r $190-225;) Under enthusiastic new ownership, this hospitable inn on the Heavenly ski-shuttle route charms with color schemes that pop, pillow-top mattresses, organic bath goodies, mini-refrigerators, microwaves and flat-screen TVs. Dip your toes in the kidney-shaped pool in summer.

Heavenly Valley Lodge B&B **$$**
(Map p646; 530-564-1500; www.heavenlyvalleylodge.com; 1261 Ski Run Blvd; r $209-294;) Under new and on-the-ball ownership, this family-run place along the Heavenly shuttle route perfects the balance of old Tahoe. Think fireplace rooms of knotty pine and river rock – and great amenities including DVD players and a huge movie library, a fire-pit patio and afternoon happy hour. Hot breakfast too. Some kitchenette units.

Blue Lake Inn MOTEL **$$**
(Map p646; 800-628-1829; www.thebluelakeinn.com; 944 Friday Ave; r $138-198, ste $238;) A good-value choice near the Heavenly Gondola (p643), these ample motel rooms have the core amenities: microwave, refrigerator, coffeemaker and flat-screen TV, plus a hot tub and outdoor pool.

★ **Edgewood** BOUTIQUE HOTEL **$$$**
(Map p646; 775-588-2787; www.edgewoodtahoe.com; 180 Lake Pkwy; r $549-899, ste $1549;) The view of Lake Tahoe from the big-windowed lobby is, simply put, stunning. The view gets even better from the back patios where comfy lounges and fire pits are flanked by soaring pine trees, all invigorated by crisp mountain air. Rooms are smart and inviting, if average size, and all come with gas fireplace. Staff are on-the-ball. Spa and a golf course on-site.

Wylder Hotel Hope Valley CHALET **$$$**
(530-694-2203; https://wylderhotels.com/hope-valley; 14255 Hwy 88; cabins & cottages/yurts from $275/350, campsites/RV sites $105/130;) Now under new ownership, the former Sorensen's Resort is a truly delightful option in

SKIING IN TAHOE

Lake Tahoe has phenomenal skiing, with thousands of acres of the white stuff beckoning at more than a dozen resorts. Winter sports complexes range from the giant, jet-set slopes of Squaw Valley (p663), Heavenly (p643) and Northstar (p665), to the no-less-enticing insider playgrounds of Sugar Bowl (p665) and Homewood (p658). Tahoe's simply got a hill for everybody, from kids to kamikazes. Ski season generally runs November to April, although it can start as early as October and last until the last storm whips through in May or even June. All resorts have ski schools, equipment rental and other facilities; check their websites for snow conditions, weather reports and free ski-season shuttle buses from area lodgings.

Downhill Skiing & Snowboarding

Tahoe's downhill resorts are usually open every day from December through April, weather permitting. See winter sports listings for Truckee & Donner Lake (p664), Tahoe City (p660) and South Lake Tahoe & Stateline (p643). All of them rent equipment and have places to warm up slope side and grab a quick bite or après-ski beer. Most offer group ski and snowboard lessons for adults and children (a surcharge applies, but usually no reservations are required).

Cross-Country Skiing & Snowshoeing

Tahoe's cross-country ski resorts are usually open daily from December through March, and sometimes into April. See winter sports listings for Truckee & Donner Lake, Tahoe City and South Lake Tahoe & Stateline. Most rent equipment and offer lessons; reservations typically aren't taken for either, so show up early for the best availability.

the Hope Valley, with snug pine cottages and cabins decked out with fairy lights and hammocks. Plus yurts, an Airstream and camping. There's a wealth of activities, including hiking, mountain biking and snowshoeing. Magical in the snow, but just as lovely in summer.

Basecamp South Hotel BOUTIQUE HOTEL $$$
(Map p646; 530-208-0180; www.basecamptahoesouth.com; 4143 Cedar Ave; r $299-349, ste $329, 8-person bunk r $339; P W) Recycled wood, original nature-themed canvases and artsy artifacts gussy up this stylish former motel. Lucky couples can rough it in the 'Great Indoors' room with a tented bed and a faux campfire, and families can overnight in spacious bunk-bed rooms. A rooftop deck, a beer and wine bar, and a satisfying continental breakfast sweeten the deal.

Fireside Lodge INN $$$
(Map p646; 530-544-5515; www.tahoefiresidelodge.com; 515 Emerald Bay Rd/Hwy 89; r $249-315; P) This woodsy cabin B&B wholeheartedly welcomes families, with free bikes, kayaks and snowshoes to borrow, a game room and wine and cheese. Kitchenette rooms and suites have river-rock gas fireplaces, cozy patchwork quilts and pioneer-themed touches like wagon wheels or vintage skis.

Stateline, NV

At Nevada's high-rise casinos, prices rise and fall like a gambler's luck. In winter ask about ski-and-stay packages.

Nevada Beach Campground CAMPGROUND $
(Map p644; 775-588-5562, reservations 877-444-6777; www.recreation.gov; off Hwy 50; tent & RV sites $36-38; mid-May–mid-Oct; P) Bed down on a carpet of pine needles at this tidy lakeside campground, about 3 miles north of Stateline, where 48 sites are nestled amid pines. Leashed dogs are allowed at campsites but not the beach.

Hard Rock Hotel Lake Tahoe CASINO HOTEL $$
(Map p646; 844-588-7625; www.hardrockcasinolaketahoe.com; 50 Hwy 50; r $189-259, ste $269-319; P) At Stateline's newest hotel-casino, you'll have an overnight experience that is rock-and-roll to the core. Doors to individual rooms are emblazoned with the images of rock legends, rock memorabilia and markers are scattered across the casino – Elvis was in Tahoe! – and you can play a Fender in a pop-up studio in your own room. In summer, stop by for the Saturday pool party.

Harrah's CASINO HOTEL $$
(Map p646; 775-588-6611; https://caesars.com/harrahs-tahoe; 15 Hwy 50; r from $199; P @) Clad in an oddly tasteful forest-green facade, this buzzing casino hotel is Stateline's top contender. Let yourself be swallowed up even by the standard 'luxury' rooms, which each have two bathrooms with telephones, or spring for a luxury suite with panoramic lake-vista windows. For more eye-popping views, snag a window table at one of Harrah's upper-floor restaurants.

MontBleu CASINO HOTEL $$
(Map p646; 775-588-3515; www.montbleuresort.com; 55 Hwy 50, Stateline, NV; r/ste from $230/330; P @) The public areas may sport ubercool modern boutique decor, but hallways are dim. Remodeled rooms have fluffy duvets and art deco–esque accents, and some of the marble-accented bathrooms sport hedonistic circular tubs. Rooms above the 5th floor are best, and those in the premiere category have lake views. Unwind in the lavish indoor-pool lagoon, accented by a rockscape and mini waterfalls. Spa on-site.

SNOWSHOEING UNDER STARS

A crisp quiet night with a blazing glow across the lake. What could be more magical than a full-moon snowshoe tour? Reserve ahead, as ramblings at these places are very popular.

Ed Z'Berg Sugar Pine Point State Park (p657)

Squaw Valley (p663)

Tahoe Donner (p665)

Northstar California (p665)

Kirkwood (p643)

Eating

For late-night cravings, the big casinos in Stateline have 24-hour coffee shops for hangover-helper and night-owl breakfasts. If you're just looking for filling pub grub or après-ski appetizers and cocktails, most bars and cafes serve just-OK food, some with waterfront views and live music too.

For self-catering try sandwiches and organic produce from **Grass Roots Natural Foods** (Map p646; http://grassrootstahoe.com; 2030 Dunlap Dr; 9am-8pm) or a full range

WORTH A TRIP

WORTH A TRIP: GENOA BAR & SALOON

The oldest drinking parlor (as they were once known) in Nevada, the **Genoa Bar & Saloon** (☎775-782-3870; www.genoabarandsaloon.com; 2282 Main St, Genoa, NV; ⌚10am-10pm Sun-Thu, 10am-midnight Fri & Sat) dates to 1853 and oozes charm: beer is the bonus, as are weekend bands and weekly drink specials. Be sure to examine all the dusty knickknackery. The mirror behind the bar was shipped around Cape Horn from Scotland in the 1840s. Raquel Welch's bra adorns a side wall. And there's an original wanted poster for the murderer of Abraham Lincoln (it's hanging under a boudoir painting, so be careful before posting a photo on Instagram!). The bar is in Genoa, a pretty little village at the edge of Carson Valley, at the foothills of the Sierra Nevada mountains. It was the first European settlement at the western edge of the former Utah Territory. From Stateline, follow Kingsbury Grade Rd/Hwy 207 for 11 miles over the mountains out of Tahoe. It's then a gorgeous drop to the valley, where you'll take a left onto Hwy 206. Follow it for 5.5 miles.

of groceries at **Safeway** (Map p646; www.safeway.com; 1020 Johnson Blvd; ⌚24hr).

★ Sprouts VEGETARIAN $
(Map p646; ☎530-541-6969; www.sproutscafetahoe.com; 3123 Harrison Ave, South Lake Tahoe; mains $8-12; ⌚8am-8pm; 🌿👶) Cheerful chatter greets you at this energetic, mostly organic cafe that gets extra kudos for its juices and smoothies. A healthy menu will have you noshing happily on satisfying soups, rice bowls, sandwiches, burrito wraps, tempeh burgers and fresh salads.

Sugar Pine Cakery BAKERY $
(Map p646; http://sugarpinecakery.com; 3564 Lake Tahoe Blvd, South Lake Tahoe; pastries $1-5; ⌚8am-5pm Tue-Sat, 8am-4pm Sun) Organic crunchy baguettes, ooey-gooey cinnamon rolls, fruit tarts and choco-chunk cookies.

Cork & More DELI $
(Map p646; ☎530-544-5253; www.thecorkandmore.com; 1032 Al Tahoe Blvd, South Lake Tahoe; sandwiches $8-13; ⌚10am-7pm Mon-Sat, 10am-5pm Sun) Specialty foods, gourmet deli (sandwiches, soups, salads) and picnic baskets to go.

Ernie's Coffee Shop DINER $
(Map p646; ☎530-541-2161; http://erniescoffeeshop.com; 1207 Hwy 50, South Lake Tahoe; mains $7-18; ⌚6am-2pm; 👶) A sun-filled local institution, Ernie's dishes out filling three-egg omelets, hearty biscuits with gravy, fruity and nutty waffles and bottomless cups of locally roasted coffee. Breakfast is served all day.

Burger Lounge FAST FOOD $
(Map p646; ☎530-542-2010; www.burgerloungeintahoe.com; 717 Emerald Bay Rd, South Lake Tahoe; mains $6-10; ⌚11am-7pm Thu-Mon; 👶) You can't miss that giant beer mug standing outside a shingled cabin. Step inside for the south shore's tastiest burgers, including the crazy 'Jiffy burger' (with peanut butter, cheddar cheese and bacon), the zingy pesto fries or the knockout ice-cream shakes.

Naked Fish SUSHI $$
(Map p646; ☎530-541-3474; www.thenakedfish.com; 3940 Lake Tahoe Blvd, South Lake Tahoe; sushi $6-12, mains $16-23; ⌚5-10pm Mon-Thu, 5-10:30pm Fri & Sat) With sushi chefs in ski caps, 'Rock the Casbah' rolling from the speakers and eclectic sushi-themed art adorning the walls, it's easy to feel not quite cool enough as you enter this oft-recommended raw fish joint. But then you taste the Hidden Dragon roll – with its delicious Cajun ahi – and you know you're right where you should be.

Cold Water Brewery & Grill AMERICAN $$
(Map p646; ☎530-544-4677; www.tahoecwb.com; 2544 Hwy 50, South Lake Tahoe; mains $17-22; ⌚11am-9pm Mon-Thu, 11am-10pm Fri & Sat) The vibe is welcoming and the gourmet pub grub is delicious at this airy brewery, which is earning raves as far away as Reno. Chase down the hearty roasted pork banh mi sandwich with the malty and easy-drinking Mr Toad's Wild Rye.

Freshie's FUSION $$
(Map p646; ☎530-542-3630; www.freshiestahoe.com; 3330 Lake Tahoe Blvd; mains lunch $13-18, dinner $14-28; ⌚11:30am-9pm; 🌿) From vegans to seafood-lovers, everybody should be able to find a favorite on the extensive menu at this Hawaiian fusion joint with sunset upper-deck views. Most of the produce is local and organic, and the blackened fish tacos are South Lake Tahoe's best. Check the webcam to see if there's a wait.

Getaway Cafe AMERICAN $$

(Map p644; ☎570-577-5132; www.facebook.com/TheGetawayCafe; 3140 Hwy 50, Meyers; mains $12-17; ⏰7am-3pm; 👪) On the outskirts of town, just south of the agriculture inspection checkpoint, this place really lives up to its name. Friendly waitstaff sling heaped-up buffalo chicken salads, barbecue burgers, chile relleno, coconut-encrusted French toast and more. Avoid the weekend crowds.

Lake Tahoe Pizza Co PIZZA $$

(Map p646; ☎530-544-1919; www.laketahoepizzaco.com; 1168 Emerald Bay Rd/Hwy 89, South Lake Tahoe; pizzas $12-23; ⏰4-9:30pm; 👪) Since the '70s, this classic pizza parlor has been hand rolling its housemade dough (cornmeal or whole wheat, anyone?), then piling it with crafty combos such as the meaty 'Barnyard Massacre' or vegan 'Green Giant.'

★ **Cafe Fiore** ITALIAN $$$

(Map p646; ☎530-541-2908; www.cafefiore.com; 1169 Ski Run Blvd, South Lake Tahoe; mains $24-43; ⏰5:30-10pm) Serving upscale Italian without pretension, this tiny romantic eatery pairs succulent pasta, seafood and meats with an award-winning 300-vintage wine list. Swoon over the veal scaloppine, homemade white-chocolate ice cream and near-perfect garlic bread. With only seven tables (a baker's dozen in summer when the candlelit outdoor patio opens), reservations are essential.

Drinking & Entertainment

The siren song of blackjack and slot machines calls the masses over to Stateline, NV. Published on Thursdays, the free alt-weekly newspaper *Reno News & Review* (www.newsreview.com/reno) has comprehensive Stateline entertainment and events listings. For what's going on around South Lake Tahoe, pick up a copy of the free weekly *Lake Tahoe Action,* published by the *Tahoe Daily Tribune* (www.tahoedailytribune.com).

★ **South Lake Brewing Co** MICROBREWERY

(Map p646; ☎530-578-0087; www.southlakebeer.com; 1920 Lake Tahoe Blvd, South Lake Tahoe; ⏰2-9pm Mon-Thu, noon-10pm Fri & Sat, noon-9pm Sun) Your tasting flight arrives on a ski at big-windowed South Lake Brewing, where crusty mountain men, parents with babies, dogs and their owners and connoisseurs of good beer commune in late afternoon. The citrusy Pebble Wrestler Pale Ale – with a 'marshmallow mouth feel' they say – is always a good choice. Up to 16 beers on tap daily.

Beacon Bar & Grill BAR

(Map p646; www.camprichardson.com; 1900 Jameson Beach Rd, Camp Richardson Resort, South Lake Tahoe; ⏰11:30am-8pm) Imagine all of Lake Tahoe is your very own front yard when you and your buddies sprawl across this big wraparound wooden deck. If you want to get schnockered, order the signature Rum Runner cocktail. Bands rock here in summer.

MacDuffs Pub PUB

(Map p646; ☎530-542-8777; www.macduffspub.com; 1041 Fremont Ave, South Lake Tahoe; ⏰11:30am-9:30pm) With excellent beers rotating on tap, a dartboard on the wall, and fish-and-chips and shepherd's pie (as well as gourmet burgers and wood-fired pizzas) on the menu, this dark and bustling gastropub wouldn't look out of place in Edinburgh. Sports fans and beer drinkers, step right up.

Brewery at Lake Tahoe BREWERY

(Map p646; www.brewerylaketahoe.com; 3542 Lake Tahoe Blvd, South Lake Tahoe; ⏰11am-9pm Sun-Thu, 11am-10pm Fri & Sat) This popular brewpub pumps its signature Bad Ass Ale into grateful local patrons, who may sniff at bright-eyed out-of-towners. Burgers, sandwiches, pizza and BBQ ribs on the menu, and a roadside patio in summer. Don't leave without a bumper sticker!

Opal Ultra Lounge CLUB

(Map p646; ☎775-586-2000; www.montbleuresort.com; 55 Hwy 50, MontBleu, Stateline, NV; free-$20; ⏰10pm-4am Fri & Sat) With DJ booths and go-go dancers, this Top 40 and electro dance club draws a young party crowd that enjoys getting their bodies painted in-house. Women may get in free before midnight.

Improv COMEDY

(Map p646; www.caesars.com/harveys-tahoe; 18 Hwy 50, Stateline, NV; tickets from $25; ⏰9pm Wed-Sun) Catch up-and-coming stand-up comedians doing their funny shtick at the intimate cabaret theater inside the old-school casino at Harvey's.

Information

Barton Memorial Hospital (☎530-541-3420; www.bartonhealth.org; 2170 South Ave; ⏰24hr) Around-the-clock emergency room. Barton's urgent-care clinic is inside the Stateline Medical Center at 155 Hwy 50, Stateline, NV.

Explore Tahoe (Map p646; ☎530-542-4637; www.cityofslt.us; 4114 Lake Tahoe Blvd, Heavenly Village Transit Center, South Lake Tahoe;

SOUTH LAKE TAHOE FOR CHILDREN

With oodles of outdoor activities, families will never run out of mountains to explore and beaches to dig. If the kids start to get fractious though, try one of these local favorites to mix things up a little.

Major ski resorts such as Heavenly (p643), in South Lake Tahoe, and Squaw Valley (p663) and Northstar California (p665) near Truckee, offer sledding hills for the kiddos, some with tubing rentals and thrilling rope tows. Smaller ski mountains including Sierra-at-Tahoe (p643) outside South Lake Tahoe, and Boreal (p665), Soda Springs (p665) and Tahoe Donner (p665), all near Truckee, also offer child-friendly slopes.

To avoid the crowds, bring your own sleds to designated local snow-play areas at North Tahoe Regional Park (p669) in Tahoe Vista on the north shore, or to Nevada's **Incline Village**, Tahoe Meadows (p671) off the Mt Rose Hwy (Hwy 431) or **Spooner Summit** on Hwy 50, all along the east shore. Back in California, DIY **Sno-Parks** (☎916-324-1222; http://ohv.parks.ca.gov; pass per day/year $5/25) are found along Hwy 89 at **Blackwood Canyon**, 3 miles south of Tahoe City on the west shore, and **Taylor Creek**, just north of Camp Richardson at South Lake Tahoe. Coming from Sacramento or the San Francisco Bay Area, two Sno-Parks are along I-80 at **Yuba Pass** (exit 161) and **Donner Summit** (exit 176 Castle Peak/Boreal Ridge Rd); their parking lots often fill by 11am on winter weekends. Buy required Sno-Park parking passes online or at local shops.

For private groomed sledding and tubing hills, swing by **Hansen's Resort** (Map p646; ☎530-544-3361; www.hansensresort.com; 1360 Ski Run Blvd; per person incl rental per hour $30; ⏲9am-5pm) in South Lake Tahoe or **Adventure Mountain** (☎530-659-7217; www.adventuremountaintahoe.com; 21200 Hwy 50; per car $40, tube/2-person sled per day $24/18; ⏲10am-4pm Mon-Fri, 9am-4:30pm Sat, Sun & holidays Dec-Apr), south of town at Echo Summit.

⏲9am-5pm Mon-Fri, 9am-4pm Sat & Sun) Find information on transport and recreation at the base of the gondola at Heavenly (p643). Also has a diorama of the lake and informative scientific displays. Free and very helpful maps of the entire lake area available too.

Lake Tahoe Visitors Authority (Map p646; ☎775-588-4591; www.tahoesouth.com; 169 Hwy 50, Stateline, NV; ⏲9am-5pm Mon-Fri) A full range of tourist information.

South Lake Tahoe Library (☎530-573-3185; www.eldoradolibrary.org/tahoe.htm; 1000 Rufus Allen Blvd, South Lake Tahoe; ⏲noon-5pm Mon, Thu-Sat, noon-7pm Tue & Wed; 📶) First-come, first-served free internet terminals.

Tahoe Urgent Care (☎530-553-4319; www.tahoeurgentcare.com; 2130 Lake Tahoe Blvd, South Lake Tahoe; ⏲8am-noon, 1:30-5:30pm) Walk-in medical clinic for nonemergencies.

USDA Lake Tahoe Basin Management Unit (Map p646; ☎530-543-2600; www.fs.usda.gov/ltbmu; 35 College Dr; ⏲8am-4:30pm Mon-Fri) Find out about camping and outdoor options, plus acquire permits for wilderness trips.

USFS Taylor Creek Visitor Center (Map p646; ☎530-543-2674; www.fs.usda.gov/ltbmu; Visitor Center Rd, off Hwy 89, South Lake Tahoe; ⏲8am-4:30pm late May-Oct) Outdoor information, wilderness permits and daily ranger-led walks and talks during July and August.

Getting There & Away

From Reno-Tahoe International Airport, **South Tahoe Airporter** (☎866-898-2463; www.southtahoeexpress.com; adult/child 4-12yr $33/20) operates several daily shuttle buses to Stateline casinos; the journey takes from 75 minutes to two hours.

Amtrak (☎800-872-7245; www.amtrak.com) has a daily Thruway bus service between Sacramento and South Lake Tahoe ($34, 2½ hours), stopping at the South Y Transit Center.

Getting Around

For a helpful overview of all transit options year-round around the lake, visit www.linkingtahoe.com.

South Lake Tahoe's main transportation hubs are the **South Y Transit Center** (Map p646; 1000 Emerald Bay Rd/Hwy 89), just south of the 'Y' intersection of Hwys 50 and 89; and the more central **Stateline Transit Center** (Map p646; 4114 Lake Tahoe Blvd).

Tahoe Transportation District (☎530-541-7149; www.tahoetransportation.org/transit; single/day pass $2/5) local buses operate year-round from around 6am to 8pm daily, stopping all along Hwy 50 between the two transit centers and slightly beyond.

During winter ski season, Heavenly (p643) and Sierra-at-Tahoe (p643) run free shuttles to the mountains.

NAVIGATING SOUTH TAHOE TRAFFIC

South Lake Tahoe's main east–west thoroughfare is a 5-mile stretch of Hwy 50 called Lake Tahoe Blvd. Most hotels and businesses hover around the state line and Heavenly Village. Casinos are located in Stateline, which is officially a separate city.

West of town, Hwy 50 runs into Hwy 89 at the 'Y' junction. Heavy snowfall sometimes closes Hwy 89 north of the Tallac Historic Site (p643). The section of Hwy 89 between South Lake Tahoe and Emerald Bay is also known as Emerald Bay Rd.

Traffic all along Hwy 50 between the 'Y' junction and Heavenly Village gets jammed around lunchtime and again by 5pm Monday to Friday in both summer and winter, but Sunday afternoons, when skiers head back down the mountain, are the worst.

An alternate, less crowded route through town is Pioneer Trail, which branches east off the Hwy 89/50 junction (south of the 'Y') and reconnects with Hwy 50 at Stateline.

LAKE TAHOE WESTERN SHORE

Lake Tahoe's densely forested western shore, between Emerald Bay and Tahoe City, is idyllic. Hwy 89 sinuously wends past gorgeous state parks with swimming beaches, hiking trails, pine-shaded campgrounds and historic mansions. Several trailheads also access the rugged splendor of the Desolation Wilderness (p650).

All campgrounds and many businesses shut down between November and May. Hwy 89 often closes after snowfall for plowing or due to imminent avalanche danger. Once you drive its tortuous slope-side curves, you'll understand why. The further south you are, the more of a roller coaster it is, no matter the season – so grip that steering wheel!

Emerald Bay State Park

Sheer granite cliffs and a jagged shoreline hem in glacier-carved **Emerald Bay** (Map p644; 530-541-6498; www.parks.ca.gov; parking $10; sunrise-sunset), a teardrop cove that will have you digging for your camera. Its most captivating aspect is the water, which changes from clover-leaf green to light jade depending on the angle of the sun.

Sights

You'll spy panoramic pullouts all along Hwy 89, including at **Inspiration Point** (Map p644), opposite USFS Bayview Campground. Just south, the road shoulder evaporates on both sides of a steep drop-off, revealing a postcard-perfect view of Emerald Bay to the north and Cascade Lake to the south.

Fannette Island (Map p644), an uninhabited granite speck, is Lake Tahoe's only island. It holds the vandalized remains of a tiny 1920s teahouse belonging to heir Lora Knight, who would occasionally motorboat guests to the island from **Vikingsholm Castle** (Map p644; 530-525-7232; http://vikingsholm.com; tour adult/child 7-17yr $15/12; 10:30am-4pm late May-Sep; P), her Scandinavian-style mansion on the bay. The focal point of the state park, Vikingsholm Castle, is a rare example of ancient Scandinavian-style architecture. Completed in 1929, it has trippy design elements aplenty, including sod-covered roofs that sprout wildflowers in late spring. The mansion is reached by a steep 1-mile trail, which also leads to a visitor center. Parking is $10 at the Vikingsholm lot beside Hwy 89.

Activities

Hiking

Vikingsholm Castle is the southern terminus of the famous **Rubicon Trail** (Map p644).

Two popular trailheads lead into the Desolation Wilderness. From the Eagle Falls parking lot trailhead, the **Eagle Falls Trail** (Map p644; per vehicle $5) travels one steep mile to Eagle Lake, crossing by Eagle Falls along the way. This scenic short hike often gets choked with visitors, but crowds disappear quickly as the trail continues up to the Tahoe Rim Trail and Velma, Dicks and Fontanillis Lakes (up to 10 miles round trip). From the back of USFS Bayview Campground, it's a steep 1-mile climb to glacial Granite Lake or a moderate 1.5-mile round trip to Cascade Falls, which rushes with snowmelt in early summer.

Boating

Fannette Island is accessible by boat, except during Canada goose nesting season (typically February to mid-June). Rent boats at Meeks Bay or South Lake Tahoe; from the latter, you can also catch narrated bay cruises or speedboat tours.

Scuba Diving

Established in 2018, the **Emerald Bay Maritime Heritage Underwater Trail** (www.parks.ca.gov) takes divers to sunken barges and recreational boats, complete with underwater interpretive markers. Elsewhere in the bay divers can find a submerged rockslide and other artifacts at a historic dumping ground, all part of the unique Underwater State Parks of Emerald Bay and DL Bliss State Park. Divers should be prepared for a chilly high-altitude plunge. Reno-based Sierra Diving Center (www.sierradive.com) and Adventure Scuba Center (www.renoscuba.com) offer classes and trips.

Sleeping

Eagle Point Campground CAMPGROUND $
(Map p644; ☎530-525-7277, reservations 800-444-7275; www.reserveamerica.com; Hwy 89; tent & RV sites $25-45; ⏰mid-Jun–early Sep; P 🐾) With more than 90 sites perched on the tip of Eagle Point, this state-park campground provides flush toilets, hot pay showers, beach access and bay views. Another 20 or so scattered sites are reserved for boat-in campers.

USFS Bayview Campground CAMPGROUND $
(Map p644; Hwy 89; tent & RV sites $18; ⏰Jun-Sep; P 🐾) This rustic, nay, primitive forest-service campground has 13 no-reservation sites and vault toilets, but its potable water supplies are often exhausted sometime in July. It's opposite Inspiration Point.

DL Bliss State Park

DL Bliss State Park (Map p644; ☎530-525-7277; www.parks.ca.gov; Hwy 89; per car $10; ⏰late May–mid-Oct; P) 🌿 has the western shore's nicest beaches at **Lester Beach** and **Calawee Cove**. A short nature trail leads to the **Balancing Rock**, a giant chunk of granite perched on a rocky pedestal. Pick up information from the visitor center by the park entrance.

Near Calawee Cove is the northern terminus of the scenic one-way **Rubicon Trail**. The park's **campground** (Map p644; ☎800-444-7275; www.reservecalifornia.com; tent & RV sites $35-45; ⏰mid-May–Sep; P 🐾) has 150 sites, including some coveted spots near the beach, along with flush toilets, hot pay showers, picnic tables, fire rings and an RV dump station.

The small visitor parking lot at Calawee Cove usually fills by 10am, in which case it's a 2-mile walk from the park entrance to the beach. Alternatively, ask park staff at the entrance station about closer access points to Rubicon Trail.

Meeks Bay

With a wide sweep of shoreline, sleek and shallow Meeks Bay has warm water by Tahoe standards and is fringed by a beautiful, but busy, sandy beach.

West of the highway, north of the fire station, is a trailhead for the **Meeks Bay Trail** into the Desolation Wilderness. A shaded path parallels Meeks Creek before heading steeply uphill through the forest to **Lake Genevieve** (9 miles round trip), **Crag Lake** (10 miles round trip) and other backcountry ponds, all surrounded by scenic Sierra peaks.

USFS Meeks Bay Campground CAMPGROUND $
(Map p644; ☎530-525-4733, reservations 877-444-6777; www.recreation.gov; tent & RV sites $31-33; ⏰mid-May–mid-Oct) This developed campground offers 39 reservable sites along the beach, along with flush toilets, picnic tables and fire rings. For pay showers, head to Meeks Bay Resort next door.

Meeks Bay Resort CABIN, CAMPGROUND $$
(Map p644; ☎530-525-6946; www.meeksbayresort.com; 7941 Emerald Bay Rd/Hwy 89; tent/RV sites with full hookups $45/65, cabins $225-400; ⏰mid-May–mid-Oct) The Washoe tribe offers various lodging options (cabins require minimum stays) plus kayak, canoe and paddleboat rentals. If you're hungry, swing by the waterfront grill or small market, which stocks limited groceries and camping, fishing and beach gear, as well as Native American crafts and cultural books.

Ed Z'berg Sugar Pine Point State Park

Ed Z'berg Sugar Pine Point State Park (Map p644; ☎530-525-7982; www.parks.ca.gov; Hwy 89; per car $10; P) occupies a promontory blanketed by a fragrant mix of pine, juniper, aspen and fir. It has a swimming beach, hiking trails and abundant fishing in General Creek. A paved bike path travels north to Tahoe City and Squaw Valley. In winter, 12 miles of groomed cross-country trails await inside the park; book ahead for ranger-guided full-moon snowshoe tours. In summer the park offers kayak and hiking tours through the Sierra State Parks Foundation (www.sierrastateparks.org).

DON'T MISS

HIKING & BACKPACKING THE DESOLATION WILDERNESS

Sculpted by powerful glaciers aeons ago, this relatively compact **wilderness area** (Map p644; www.fs.usda.gov/detail/eldorado/specialplaces) spreads south and west of Lake Tahoe and is the most popular in the Sierra Nevada. It's a 100-sq-mile wonderland of polished granite peaks, deep-blue alpine lakes, glacier-carved valleys and pine forests that thin quickly at the higher elevations. In summer wildflowers nudge out from between the rocks.

All this splendor makes for exquisite backcountry exploration. Six major trailheads provide access from the Lake Tahoe side: Glen Alpine, **Tallac** (Map p644; Mt Tallac Rd B trailhead), Echo Lakes (near Echo Summit on Hwy 50), **Bayview** (Map p644), Eagle Falls (p656) and **Meeks Bay** (Map p644). Tallac and Eagle Falls get the most traffic, but solitude comes quickly once you've scampered past the day hikers.

Note that **permits** (877-444-6777; www.recreation.gov; per adult $5-10) are required year-round for both day and overnight explorations in the Desolation Wilderness. Day hikers can self-register at the trailheads, but overnight permits must be either reserved online (fee $6) at www.recreation.gov and printed at home, or picked up in person at one of the three USFS offices in South Lake Tahoe and Pollack Pines. Permits cost $5 per person for one night, $10 per person for two or more nights.

Quotas are in effect from late May through the end of September. Over half of the permits for the season may be reserved online, usually starting in late March or April; the other permits are available on a first-arrival basis on the day of entry only.

Bear-proof canisters are strongly advised in all wilderness areas (hanging your food in trees will not work – these bears are too smart!). Borrow canisters for free from the USFS offices. Bring bug repellent as the mosquitoes can be merciless. Wood fires are a no-no, but portable stoves are OK. Dogs must be leashed at *all* times.

Historic sights include the modest 1872 cabin of William 'General' Phipps, an early Tahoe settler, and the considerably grander 1903 Queen Anne–style **Hellman-Ehrman Mansion** (Map p644; www.sierrastateparks.org; per vehicle $10; tours adult/child 7-17yr $12/10; 10:30am-3:30pm late May-Sep).

The park's secluded **General Creek Campground** (Map p644; 800-444-7275; www.reserveamerica.com; tent & RV sites $35; late May–mid-Sep) has 175 fairly spacious, pine-shaded sites, plus flush toilets and hot pay showers; 24 sites stay open year-round (but without showers).

Tahoma

A blink-and-you'll-miss-it lakeside outpost, Tahoma has a post office and a handful of places to stay and eat. Within striking distance of Tahoe City, Tahoma offers a more secluded base for outdoor enthusiasts.

If you don't want to camp, the best option is **Tahoma Meadows B&B Cottages** (530-525-1553; www.tahomameadows.com; 6821 W Lake Blvd; cottages $189-399; P), set in a pine grove.

You can booze all day long at **Chamber's Landing** (Map p644; 530-525-9190; 6400 W Lake Blvd; noon-8pm Jun-Sep) if you so desire.

Homewood

This quiet and very alpine-looking **resort hamlet** (Map p644; 530-525-2992; www.skihomewood.com; 5145 Westlake Blvd, off Hwy 89; adult/child 5-12yr/youth 13-19yr $134/69/94; 9am-4pm;) is popular with summertime boaters and, in winter, skiers and snowboarders. **West Shore Sports** (530-525-9920; www.westshoresports.com; 5395 W Lake Blvd; 8am-5pm) rents out all the winter and summer gear you'll need.

USFS Kaspian Campground CAMPGROUND $
(Map p644; 877-444-6777; www.recreation.gov; tent sites $22; mid-May–mid-Oct) The closest campground is this nine-site, tent-only spot set among ponderosa and fir trees; amenities include flush toilets, picnic tables and fire rings.

West Shore Inn INN $$$
(530-525-5200; www.westshorecafe.com; 5160 W Lake Blvd; r/ste from $299/429; P) Oriental rugs and arts-and-crafts decor give this luxurious six-room inn a classic, aged ambience, and the lake's so close you feel like you could dive in. It's an upscale mountain lodge where crisp, modern suites feel decadent, and each has a fire-

place and lake-view balcony. Continental breakfast included.

West Shore Café CALIFORNIAN $$$
(530-525-5200; www.westshorecafe.com; 5160 W Lake Blvd; mains lunch $17-22, dinner $29-52; 11am-9pm mid-Jun–Sep, noon-3pm, 5-8pm Oct–mid-Jun) At the West Shore Inn's cozy destination restaurant, executive chef Rob Wyss whips up worthy meals using fresh produce and ranched meats, from juicy burgers to seared scallops with crab and parmesan couscous. Dinner reservations recommended.

Sunnyside

Sunnyside is a lakeshore hamlet that may be just a dot on the map, but has several detour-worthy restaurants. To work off all that dang-good eating, rent a bicycle from an outpost of **West Shore Sports** (530-583-9920; www.westshoresports.com; 1785 W Lake Blvd), where you can get the scoop on local outdoor information. You can pedal all the way north to Tahoe City along the paved bike path, or rent a stand-up paddling set and hit the popular local beaches.

Free **Tahoe Truckee Area Regional Transit** (TART; Map p644; 530-550-1212; https://tahoetruckeetransit.com; 10183 Truckee Airport Rd; most routes free) FREE (TART) buses can take you to and from Sunnyside.

Sunnyside Lodge INN $$$
(530-583-7200; www.sunnysidetahoe.com; 1850 W Lake Blvd; r $385-539; P) This lakeside lodge features modern rooms with new bathrooms, pillow-top mattresses and flat-screen TVs, afternoon tea and cookies, and a guests-only sitting room overlooking the lake. The less expensive 'garden view' rooms lack good lake views. Note that there's lots of activity from the restaurant, and boat dock and marina next door.

Pet fee $45 per stay.

★ **Fire Sign Cafe** AMERICAN $
(www.firesigncafe.com; 1785 W Lake Blvd; mains $10-15; 7am-3pm;) For breakfast, everyone heads to the friendly Fire Sign for down-home omelets, blueberry pancakes, eggs Benedict with house-smoked salmon, fresh made-from-scratch pastries and other carbo-loading bombs, plus organic coffee. In summer, hit the outdoor patio. Lines are usually very long, so get here early.

West Shore Market SANDWICHES $
(Map p644; 530-584-2475; www.westshoremarket.com; 1780 West Lake Blvd; sandwiches $10-12; 7am-3pm daily & 5-8pm Thu-Mon) If you're headed to one of the state parks for a hike, stop here for a gourmet sandwich to go from this rustically chic neighborhood grocery. Enjoy flatbread pizzas and happy hour Thursday through Monday (5pm to 8pm); $6 kids menu available.

Sunnyside Restaurant CALIFORNIAN $$
(530-583-7200; www.sunnysidetahoe.com; 1850 W Lake Blvd; mains dining room $16-31, grill $14-19; dining room 5-8:30pm, grill varies) Classic and innovative contemporary takes on steak and seafood – think filet mignon porterhouse pork with herb salsa verde and a mixed seafood hot pot – pervade this lakeside dining room. In summer you'll probably have more fun enjoying drinks with the signature zucchini sticks and a piece of hula pie on the lakefront deck.

TAHOE CITY

The western shore's commercial hub, Tahoe City straddles the junction of Hwys 89 and 28, making it almost inevitable that you'll find yourself breezing through at least once during your round-the-lake sojourn. The town is handy for grabbing food and supplies and renting sports gear. It's also the closest lake town to Squaw Valley. The main drag, N Lake Blvd, is chockablock with outdoor outfitters, touristy shops and cafes.

Sights

You can take in downtown's top sights on a 1-mile walking loop from the North Lake Tahoe Visitor Center (p662). Follow Mackinaw Rd to Commons Beach then stroll the coastal path to the pier. Check out the clarity of the lake then walk to N Lake Blvd. Loop back toward the visitor center, passing breakfast spots, the Watson Cabin and North Tahoe Arts. Cross Fanny Bridge and explore the Gatekeeper's Museum and adjacent park.

Gatekeeper's Museum & Marion Steinbach Indian Basket Museum MUSEUM
(Map p644; 530-583-1762; www.northtahoemuseums.org; 130 N Lake Blvd/Hwy 89; adult/child under 13yr $5/free; 10am-5pm late May–mid-Oct, 11am-4pm Wed-Sat mid-Oct–Apr; P) In a reconstructed log cabin close to town,

DON'T MISS

TAHOE RIM TRAIL

The 165-mile **Tahoe Rim Trail** (Map p644; www.tahoerimtrail.org) FREE treks the lofty ridges of the Lake Tahoe Basin. Day hikers, equestrians and – in some sections – mountain bikers are rewarded by high-altitude views of the lake and Sierra Nevada peaks while tracing the footsteps of early pioneers, Basque shepherds and Washoe tribespeople.

this museum has a small but fascinating collection of Tahoe memorabilia, including Olympics history and relics from the early steamboat era and tourism explosion around the lake. In the museum's newer wing, uncover an exquisite array of Native American baskets collected from more than 85 indigenous California tribes.

Fanny Bridge BRIDGE
Just south of the always-jammed Hwy 89/28 traffic stoplight junction, the Truckee River flows through dam floodgates and passes beneath this bridge, cutely named for the most prominent feature of people leaning over the railings to look at fish (in American slang, 'fanny' means your rear end). The adjacent park and nearby dam display interpretive markers, photos and hydrological facts.

Watson Cabin MUSEUM
(☎530-583-8717; www.northtahoemuseums.org; 560 N Lake Tahoe Blvd; ⏰noon-4pm Wed-Sun Jun-Aug) FREE A few blocks east of the bridge over the Truckee River, this well-preserved 1908 settlers' cabin made from hand-hewn logs is one of the town's oldest buildings, built overlooking the beach.

Commons Beach PARK
(400 N Lake Blvd) Commons Beach is a small, attractive park with sandy and grassy areas, picnic tables, barbecue grills, a climbing rock and playground, as well as free summer concerts (www.concertsatcommonsbeach.com) and outdoor movie on Wednesday nights in July and August.

Activities

Tahoe City is within easy reach of a half dozen downhill and cross-country skiing and snowboarding resorts.

Winter Sports

Alpine Meadows SNOW SPORTS
(Map p644; ☎530-452-4356; www.skialpine.com; 2600 Alpine Meadows Rd, off Hwy 89; adult/child under 13yr/youth 13-22yr $169/110/144; ⏰9am-4pm) Though now owned by neighboring Squaw (tickets are good at both resorts and a free shuttle connects them), Alpine remains a no-nonsense resort with challenging terrain and without the fancy village, attitude or crowds. It gets more snow than Squaw and it's the most backcountry-friendly resort around. Boarders jib down the mountain in a terrain park designed by Eric Rosenwald.

Tahoe Cross Country SKIING
(Map p644; ☎530-583-5475; www.tahoexc.org; 925 Country Club Dr, off N Lake Blvd/Hwy 28; adult/child under 19yr $34/free; ⏰8:30am-5pm; 👪🐾) Run by the nonprofit Tahoe Cross Country Ski Education Association, this center has 40 miles of groomed tracks (21 trails) that wind through lovely forest, suitable for all skill levels. Group lessons come with good-value equipment-rental packages; half-day trail-pass discounts are also available. About 3 miles north of Tahoe City.

Tahoe Dave's OUTDOORS
(☎530-583-0400, 530-583-6415; www.tahoedaves.com; 590 N Lake Tahoe Blvd; ski/snowboard rentals per day from $25/22; ⏰10am-5pm Sun-Fri, 10am-6pm Sat) The main regional outfitter, with additional branches at Squaw Valley, Kings Beach, Truckee and Olympic Valley (rentals can be returned to any shop); reservations accepted. Not particularly welcoming on our visit.

River Rafting

Truckee River Raft Rentals RAFTING
(☎530-583-0123; www.truckeeriverraft.com; 185 W River Rd; adult/child 6-12yr $45/35; ⏰trips 8:30am-2:30pm Jul-early Sep; 👪) The Truckee River here is gentle and wide as it flows northwest from the lake – perfect for novice paddlers. This outfit rents rafts for the 5-mile float from Tahoe City to the **River Ranch Lodge** (Map p644; ☎530-583-4264; http://riverranchlodge.com; 2285 River Rd, Hwy 89 at Alpine Meadows Rd; mains patio & cafe $8-10, restaurant $38-44; ⏰lunch Jun-Sep, dinner year-round, call for seasonal hours), including transportation back to town. Reservations strongly advised.

Hiking

Explore the fabulous trails of the **Granite Chief Wilderness** (Map p644; www.sierrawild.gov) north and west of Tahoe City. For maps and trailhead directions, stop by the visitor center. Recommended day hikes include the moderately strenuous **Five Lakes Trail** (5 miles round trip), which starts from Alpine Meadows Rd off Hwy 89 heading toward Squaw Valley, and the easy trek to **Paige Meadows**, leading onto the Tahoe Rim Trail (p658). Paige Meadows is also good terrain for novice mountain bikers and snowshoeing. Wilderness permits are not required, even for overnight trips, but free campfire permits are needed, even for gas stoves. Leashed dogs are allowed on these trails.

Cycling

The paved 4.5-mile **Truckee River Bike Trail** runs from Tahoe City toward Squaw Valley, while the multi-use **West Shore Bike Path** heads 9 miles south to Ed Z'berg Sugar Pine Point State Park (p657), including highway-shoulder and residential-street sections. Both are fairly easy rides, but expect crowds on summer weekends. The whole family can rent bicycles from any of several shops along N Lake Blvd. Park and head out from the **64 Acres Park** trailhead behind the Tahoe City Transit Center (p662). The excellent bike-trail map of Lake Tahoe Bicycle Coalition (www.tahoebike.org) is available on its website.

Sleeping

If you show up without reservations, dingy, last-resort budget motels are along N Lake Blvd. For camping, head north to USFS campgrounds off Hwy 89 or south along Hwy 89 to state parks and small towns along the lake's western shore.

USFS William Kent Campground CAMPGROUND $

(Map p644; ☎877-444-6777; www.recreation.gov; Hwy 89; tent & RV sites $31, yurts $79; ⊙mid-May–mid-Oct; P 🐾) About 2 miles south of Tahoe City, this roadside campground offers 84 nicely shaded but cramped sites that often fill up. Amenities include flush toilets, picnic tables and fire rings, along with swimming-beach access. Also has yurts.

Mother Nature's Inn INN $$

(☎530-581-4278; www.mothernaturesinn.com; 551 N Lake Blvd; r $155-165; P 📶 🐾) Right in town behind the Cabin Fever knickknack boutique, this good-value option offers eight quiet motel-style rooms with a tidy country look, fridges and coffeemaker, eclectic furniture and comfy pillow-top mattresses. It's within walking distance of Commons Beach. Under new and very hospitable ownership.

Tahoe City Basecamp BOUTIQUE HOTEL $$$

(Map p644; ☎530-580-8430; www.basecamptahoecity.com; 955 N Lake Blvd; r from $283; P ❄ 📶 🐾) A sister property of Basecamp South Hotel (p652), this motel-style lodge celebrates the great outdoors. Look for gear racks in every room, Lake Tahoe maps adorning the walls, a fire pit ready-made for roasting s'mores (fixin's are for sale) and a rustically hip lobby. Yep, there's an invigorating appreciation for adventure here.

Granlibakken LODGE $$$

(Map p644; ☎530 583 4242; www.granlibakken.com; 725 Granlibakken Rd, off Hwy 89; r/ste from $198/460, 1-/2-/3-bedroom town house from $435/574/699; P 📶 🏊) Sleep old-school at this cross-country ski area and kitschy wedding and conference venue. Basic lodge rooms are spacious, but time-share town houses with kitchens, fireplaces and lofts can be a decent deal for families and groups. Amenities include tennis courts, a full spa, year-round outdoor pool and hot tub, and winter shuttle service to Homewood (p658).

Eating

Fat Cat CALIFORNIAN $

(☎530-583-3355; www.fatcatrestaurants.com; 599 N Lake Blvd; mains $12-38; ⊙noon-8pm Sun-Thu, 11:30am-9:30pm Fri, 11am-9:30 Sat & Sun, bar open later; 👪) This casual, family-run restaurant with local art splashed on the walls does it all: from-scratch soups, heaped salads, sandwiches, incredible burgers, pasta, steak, salmon, a paleo bowl and plenty of fried munchies for sharing. Look for live indie music on Friday and Saturday nights.

Tahoe House Bakery BAKERY $

(www.tahoe-house.com; 625 W Lake Blvd; pastries $1-3, sandwiches $9; ⊙6am-4pm; 📶) Before you take off down the western shore for a bike ride or hike, drop by this mom-and-pop shop that opened in the 1970s. Their motto: 'While you sleep, we loaf.' Sweet cookies, European pastries, fresh-baked deli sandwiches and homemade salads and soups will keep you going all afternoon on the trail.

New Moon Natural Foods DELI, HEALTH FOOD $

(www.newmoonnaturalfoods.com; 505 W Lake Blvd; mains $7-12; ⊙9am-8pm Mon-Sat, 9am-7pm Sun; 🖉) 🌿 A tiny but well-stocked natural-foods store with a gem of a deli that concocts scrumptious food to go, all packaged in biodegradable and compostable containers. Try the fish tacos or Thai salad with organic greens and spicy peanut sauce.

Dam Cafe CAFE $
(55 W Lake Blvd; mains $9-13; ⏰6am-1pm) This cute cottage is right by the Truckee River dam and Fanny Bridge (p660); stash your bikes in the racks outside and walk inside for a breakfast burrito, ice-cream fruit smoothie or pick-me-up espresso. Order at the counter.

Rosie's Cafe AMERICAN $$
(www.rosiescafe.com; 571 N Lake Blvd; breakfast $10-16, lunch & dinner $13-28; ⏰7:30am-9:30pm; 👪) With antique skis, shiny bikes and lots of pointy antlers belonging to stuffed wildlife mounted on the walls, this quirky place serves breakfast until 2:30pm. The all-American hodgepodge menu with items such as Yankee pot roast is all right, but the convivial atmosphere is a winner. Popular locals bar.

Christy Hill AMERICAN $$$
(Map p644; ☎530-583-8551; www.christyhill.com; 115 Grove St; most small plates $14-16, mains $25-42; ⏰5:45-7:30pm, bar from 5pm) Slip into your fanciest mountain-town duds for the finest dining experience in Tahoe City. Seasonal American dishes come with a creative spin, and all are accompanied by a big-windowed lake view. Solo diners can enjoy the whole experience at the bar, where sampling small plates from the happy-hour menu (5pm to 6pm; $4 to $13) is quite pleasant. The house-smoked trout is a treat.

Drinking & Nightlife

There's an unpretentious and enjoyable nightlife scene here, with several restaurants joining the fun by staging live music.

Bridgetender Tavern & Grill PUB
(☎530-583-3342; www.tahoebridgetender.com; 65 W Lake Blvd; ⏰11am-11pm Sun-Thu, 11am-midnight Fri & Sat) Après-ski crowds gather for beer, burgers and chili-cheese or garlic waffle fries at this woodsy bar (mains $10 to $13). In summer, grab a seat on the open-air patio.

Shopping

North Tahoe Arts Gift Shop & Gallery ARTS & CRAFTS
(Map p644; www.northtahoearts.com; 380 N Lake Blvd; ⏰11am-4pm) Peruse paintings, ceramics and jewelry from local artists. Open until 5pm in warmer months.

Information

North Lake Tahoe Visitor Center (Tahoe City; ☎530-581-6900; www.gotahoenorth.com; 100 N Lake Blvd; ⏰9am-5pm) At the Hwy 89/28 split, this helpful visitor center covers the North Lake Tahoe region. Stop by for maps, brochures and gifts. There are six free Tesla charging stations and one EV charging station in the adjacent parking lot.

Tahoe City Downtown Association (☎530-583-3348; www.visittahoecity.org; 425 N Lake Blvd; ⏰9am-5pm Mon-Fri) Tourist information and online events calendar.

Tahoe City Library (☎530-583-3382; www.placer.ca.gov; 740 N Lake Blvd, Boatworks Mall; ⏰10am-4pm Tue & Thu, noon-6pm Wed, noon-5pm Fri, 1-5pm Sat; 📶) Free wi-fi and walk-in internet terminals.

Tahoe Forest Health System (☎530-581-8864, ext 3; www.tfhd.com; 925 N Lake Blvd, Trading Post Center; ⏰9am-5pm Mon-Sat year-round & 9am-5pm Sun Jul & Aug) Walk-in clinic for nonemergencies.

Getting There & Away

Just south of the Hwy 28/89 split, the new **Tahoe City Transit Center** (www.tahoetruckeetransit.com; off W Lake Blvd) is the main bus terminal, with a comfy waiting room. Behind it you'll find trailhead parking for the Tahoe Rim Trail (p658) and various bike-path routes. The recommended Tahoe Truckee Area Regional Transit (TART; www.tahoetruckeetransit.com) runs free buses between Tahoe City, Incline Village and Truckee. For an overview of local transit options, visit www.linkingtahoe.com.

SQUAW VALLEY

The nirvana of the north shore, Squaw Valley played host to the 1960 Olympic Winter Games and still ranks among the world's top ski resorts. The stunning setting amid granite peaks, though, makes it a superb destination in any season, and this deluxe family-friendly resort stays almost as busy in summer as in winter.

Sights & Activities

Much summertime action centers on 8200ft **High Camp** (☎800-403-0206; http://squawalpine.com; cable car adult/child 5-17yr $49/29, all-access adventure pass adult/child 5-17yr $59/34; ⏰11am-4pm daily Nov–mid-May & Jul-Aug, Sat & Sun Sep; 🐾), reached by a cable car, which offers swimming, a hot tub, disc golf, geocaching and roller-skating. Activities down below include a ropes course with ziplines operated by **Squaw Valley Treetop** (Map p644; ☎530-807-1004; www.tahoetreetop.com; 1901 Chamonix Pl; ⊙late May-Aug). Golfers tee off at the **Resort at Squaw Creek Golf Course** (Map p644; ☎530-583-6300; www.destinationhotels.com/squawcreek; green fee incl cart $119).

Several hiking trails radiate from High Camp, or try the lovely, moderate **Shirley Lake Trail** (round trip 5 miles), which follows a sprightly creek to waterfalls, granite boulders and abundant wildflowers. It starts at the mountain base, near the end of Squaw Peak Rd, behind the cable-car building. Leashed dogs are allowed.

Olympic Museum MUSEUM
(☎800-403-0206; http://squawalpine.com; High Camp; entry incl cable car adult/child 5-17yr $49/29; ⊙11am-4pm) A fun retro exploration of the 1960 Olympics, featuring a film and much memorabilia. Located at High Camp.

★ **Squaw Valley Alpine Meadows** SNOW SPORTS
(Map p644; ☎800-403-0206; www.squawalpine.com; 1960 Squaw Valley Rd, off Hwy 89, Olympic Valley; adult/child 5-12yr/youth 13-22yr $169/110/144; ⊙9am-4pm; 👪) Few ski hounds can resist the siren call of this mega-size, world-class, see-and-be-seen resort that hosted the 1960 Winter Olympic Games. Hardcore skiers thrill to white-knuckle cornices, chutes and bowls, while beginners practice their turns in a separate area on the upper mountain. There's also a great après-ski scene, and relatively short chairlift waits.

Tahoe Via Ferrata CLIMBING
(Map p644; ☎877-873-5376; www.tahoevia.com; 1985 Squaw Valley Rd; half-/full day $99/149) Beginning in 2020, adventurers can scale the enormous cliff overlooking the Village, known as the Tram Face, on one of two via ferrata routes. Climbers are clipped to cables, which ascend the rocks across a network of steel anchors – there's more than 1000ft of elevation gain. Trips are run by Alpenglow Expeditions. Climbers must be at least 10 years old.

Festivals & Events

WinterWonderGrass Tahoe MUSIC
(www.winterwondergrasstahoe.com; ⊙Mar) Book early for this great little outdoor festival of bluegrass and acoustic roots music, the stage encircled by the snow and pines of Squaw Valley. It's a family-oriented event, with an ethos of sustainability.

Sleeping & Eating

There are some premier accommodations here, with boutique options as well as more rugged places.

River Ranch Lodge INN $$
(Map p644; ☎530-583-4264; www.riverranchlodge.com; 2285 River Rd, Hwy 89 at Alpine Meadows Rd; r $160-210; P 📶 🐾) Though there's some noise from traffic outside and the bar downstairs, request a river-facing room so you can drift off to dreamland as the Truckee River tumbles below your window. Rooms bulge with lodgepole-pine furniture; those upstairs have wistful balconies. The stone-built riverside **dining room** is a popular stop, drawing rafters and bikers to its patio for summer barbecue lunches.

★ **PlumpJack Squaw Valley Inn** BOUTIQUE HOTEL $$$
(Map p644; ☎530-583-1576; www.plumpjacksquawvalleyinn.com; 1920 Squaw Valley Rd, Olympic Valley; r/ste from $315/400; P ❄ @ 📶 🏊 🐾) Bed down at this artsy boutique hotel in the village, where every room has mountain views and extra-comfort factors such as plush terry-cloth robes and slippers. Ski-in, ski-out access doesn't hurt either, but a $150 per stay pet fee will. The chic **PlumpJack Cafe**, with its crisp linens and plush banquettes, serves seasonally inspired California cuisine with ace wines.

Wildflour Baking Co BAKERY $
(Map p644; www.squawalpine.com; 1000 Squaw Valley Rd, The Village; pastries $3-5, sandwiches $14-16; ⊙7am-7pm Mon-Sat, 7am-6pm Sun) Going strong for more than 35 years, this staple in the Olympic House is famed for its delicious desserts. We liked the chocolate chip cookies. Also sells breakfast bagels, soups and sandwiches, and Peet's Coffee. Everything is made from scratch.

Soupa HEALTH FOOD $
(Map p644; ☎530-584-6190; www.facebook.com/SoupaSquaw; 1850 Village South Rd; mains $6-12; ⊙11am-5pm) For a quick and healthy meal after a morning on the slopes, step up to the counter at tiny Soupa for quinoa bowls, soups, wraps and pressed sandwiches.

Le Chamois & Loft Bar PIZZA, PUB FOOD $
(Map p644; www.squawchamois.com; 1960 Squaw Valley Rd; mains $8-27; ⊙11am-7pm, bar to 9pm or 10pm mid-Dec–May; 👪 🐾) For a social bite after shedding your bindings, this slopeside favorite is handily positioned between the

cable-car building and the rental shop. Slide on over to devour a hot sandwich or pizza and a beer with pleasing mountain views. Open in winter only.

Drinking

Tram Car Bar BAR
(Map p644; www.squawalpine.com; Squaw Valley Rd; ⏲Sat & Sun) Sip your favorite cocktail – or a Pabst Blue Ribbon – in a restored 1970s tram car while the aerial lift glides past overhead. The bar also has a small patio. Hours are a bit irregular, but this new spot should be open by late afternoon on winter weekends.

Getting There & Away

The village at Squaw Valley, at the base of the mountain cable car, is about a 20-minute drive from Tahoe City or Truckee via Hwy 89 (turn off at Squaw Valley Rd).

Tahoe Tuckee Area Regional Transit (p659) (TART) buses between Truckee and Tahoe City, Kings Beach and Crystal Bay stop at Squaw Valley every hour or so generally between 6am and 7pm daily, with a weekend ski shuttle from late December though March.

TRUCKEE & DONNER LAKE

Cradled by mountains and the Tahoe National Forest, Truckee is a thriving town steeped in Old West history. It was put on the map by the railroad, grew rich on logging and ice harvesting, and even had its brush with Hollywood during the 1924 filming of Charlie Chaplin's *The Gold Rush*. Today tourism fills much of the city's coffers, thanks to a well-preserved historical downtown, and its proximity to Lake Tahoe and no fewer than six downhill and four cross-country ski resorts.

Sights

The aura of the Old West still lingers over Truckee's teensy one-horse downtown, where railroad workers and lumberjacks once milled about in raucous saloons, bawdy brothels and shady gambling halls. With a recent influx of families and entrepreneurs from the Bay Area, most of the late-19th-century buildings now contain restaurants and upscale boutiques. Donner Memorial State Park and **Donner Lake** (www.donnerlakemarina.com; P 👪), a busy recreational hub, are 3 miles further west.

Donner Memorial State Park STATE PARK
(Map p644; ☎530-582-7892; www.parks.ca.gov; Donner Pass Rd; per car May-Sep $10, Oct-Apr $5; ⏲visitor center 10am-5pm; P 👪) At the eastern end of Donner Lake, this state-run park occupies one of the sites where the doomed Donner Party (p666) got trapped during the fateful winter of 1846. Though its history is gruesome, the park is gorgeous and has a sandy beach, picnic tables, hiking trails and wintertime cross-country skiing and snowshoeing. The entry fee includes admission to the **visitor center**, which has fascinating, if macabre, historical exhibits and a 26-minute film reenacting their horrific plight.

Old Jail HISTORIC BUILDING
(www.truckeehistory.org; 10142 Jiboom St, cnr Spring St; suggested donation $2; ⏲10am-4pm Sat & Sun late May-early Sep) Continuously in use until the 1960s, this 1875 redbrick building is filled with relics from the wild days of yore. George 'Machine Gun' Kelly was reportedly once held here for shoplifting at a local variety store, and 'Baby Face' Nelson and 'Ma' Spinelli and her gang did time too.

Activities

Northstar Mountain Bike Park MOUNTAIN BIKING
(Map p644; ☎800-466-6784; www.northstarcalifornia.com; 5001 Northstar Dr, off Hwy 267; adult/child 9-12yr $60/40; ⏲10am-5pm Jun-Sep) Sure, there's great cross-country here, but the downhill at this lift-serviced ski resort brings on the adrenaline with lots of intermediate and expert single-track and fire roads. Over 100 miles of riding across 33 trails; bikes and body-armor rental available.

Back Country OUTDOORS
(☎530-582-0909; www.thebackcountry.net; 11400 Donner Pass Rd; ⏲8am-6pm, call ahead in winter & spring) Rents bicycles, snowshoes and paddleboards, and rents and sells new and used climbing gear, as well as backcountry ski gear.

Winter Sports

★ **Royal Gorge** SKIING
(☎530-426-3871; www.royalgorge.com; 9411 Pahatsi Rd, off I-80 exit Soda Springs/Norden, Soda Springs; adult/youth 13-22yr $37/20; ⏲8:30am-4pm; 👪 🐾) Nordic-skiing aficionados won't want to pass up a spin around North America's largest cross-country resort (now operated by Sugar Bowl), with its 85 miles of groomed track crisscrossing 6000 acres of terrain. It has great skating lanes and diagonal stride tracks, and also welcomes telemark

skiers and snowshoers. Nine warming huts are scattered about too.

Northstar California SNOW SPORTS
(Map p644; ☎530-562-1010; www.northstarcalifornia.com; 5001 Northstar Dr, off Hwy 267; adult/child 5-12yr/youth 13-18yr $169/100/139; ⏰8am-5pm) An easy 7 miles south of I-80, this hugely popular resort has great intermediate terrain as well as long black runs. Northstar's relatively sheltered location makes it a top choice when it's snowing, and the eight terrain parks and pipes are top-ranked. Advanced and expert skiers can look for tree-skiing challenges on the back of the mountain.

Sugar Bowl SNOW SPORTS
(☎530-426-9000; www.sugarbowl.com; 629 Sugar Bowl Rd, off Donner Pass Rd, Norden; adult/child 6-12yr/youth 13-22yr $121/72/100; ⏰9am-4pm) Cofounded by Walt Disney in 1939, this is one of the Sierra's oldest ski resorts and a miniature Squaw Valley in terms of variety of terrain, including plenty of exhilarating gullies and chutes. Views are stellar on sunny days, but conditions go downhill pretty quickly, so to speak, during stormy weather.

Boreal SNOW SPORTS
(☎530-426-3666; www.rideboreal.com; 19749 Boreal Ridge Rd, off I-80 exit Castle Peak/Boreal Ridge Rd; adult/child 5-12yr/youth 13-17yr $65/35/55, tubing from $29; ⏰9am-9pm; 👪) Fun for newbies and intermediate skiers, Boreal is traditionally the first resort to open each year in the Tahoe area. For boarders, there are five terrain parks including a competition-level 450ft superpipe. Boreal is the only North Tahoe downhill resort besides Squaw that offers night skiing. Stats: eight lifts, 500 vertical feet, 41 runs.

Soda Springs SNOW SPORTS
(☎530-426-3901; www.skisodasprings.com; 10244 Soda Springs Rd, off I-80 exit Soda Springs/Norden, Soda Springs; adult/child under 18yr $56/51, tubing from $25; ⏰10am-4pm Thu-Mon, daily during holidays; 👪) This cute little resort is a winner with kids, who can snow-tube, ride around in pint-size snowmobiles, or learn to ski and snowboard. Stats: two lifts, 650 vertical feet, 15 runs.

Donner Ski Ranch SNOW SPORTS
(☎530-426-3635; www.donnerskiranch.com; 19320 Donner Pass Rd, Norden; adult/child 7-12yr/youth 13-17yr $79/35/49; ⏰9am-4pm; 👪) Generations of skiers have enjoyed this itty-bitty family-owned resort. It's a great place to teach your kids how to ski, or for beginners to build skills. The ranch drops lift ticket prices after 12:30pm and on Old School Days midweek, when prices mirror those from the good old days (adult/child aged seven to 12 years $40/25). It's 3.5 miles southeast of I-80 exit Soda Springs/Norden. Stats: eight lifts, 750 vertical feet, 52 runs.

Tahoe Donner SNOW SPORTS
(☎530-587-9444; www.tahoedonner.com; 11603 Snowpeak Way, off I-80 exit Donner Pass Rd; adult/child 7-12yr/youth 13-17yr $74/44/64; ⏰9am-4pm; 👪) Small, low-key and low-tech, Tahoe Donner is a darling resort with family-friendly beginner and intermediate runs only. Stats: five lifts, 600 vertical feet, 17 runs.

Clair Tappaan Lodge SKIING
(☎530-426-3632; http://clairtappaanlodge.com; 19940 Donner Pass; day pass for nonguests $10; ⏰9am-5pm; 👪) You can ski right out the door if you're staying at this rustic mountain lodge near Donner Summit. It offers 8 miles of groomed and tracked cross-country and snowshoe trails, and connects to miles of backcountry skiing. Stop by the lodge for ski and snowshoe rentals. The lodge was built by Sierra Club members in the 1930s.

Beaches & Water Sports

Warmer than Lake Tahoe, tree-lined Donner Lake is great for swimming, boating, fishing (license required), water-skiing and windsurfing.

West End Beach SWIMMING, WATER SPORTS
(☎530-582-7777; www.tdrpd.com; 15888 S Shore Dr, off Donner Pass Rd; adult/child 2-17yr $6/5; ⏰sunrise-sunset; 👪) This Donner Lake beach is popular with families for its roped-off swimming area, snack stand, volleyball nets, and kayak, paddleboat, SUP and inner tube rentals. Lifeguards on duty May through September (9am to 5pm).

Tributary Whitewater Tours RAFTING
(☎530-346-6812; www.whitewatertours.com; half-day trip per adult/child 7-17yr $79/74; 👪) From roughly mid-May through September, this long-running outfitter operates a 7-mile, half-day rafting run on the Truckee River over class III-plus rapids that will thrill kids and their nervous parents alike.

Hiking & Climbing

Truckee is a great base for treks in the **Tahoe National Forest** (Map p644), especially around **Donner Summit**. One popular 5-mile loop hike reaches the summit of 8243ft **Mt Judah** for awesome views of

Donner Lake (p664) and the surrounding peaks. A longer, more strenuous ridge-crest hike (part of the **Pacific Crest Trail**) links **Donner Pass** to Squaw Valley (15 miles each way), skirting the base of prominent peaks, but you'll need two cars for this shuttle hike.

Donner Summit is also a major rock-climbing mecca, with more than 300 traditional and sport-climbing routes. To learn the ropes, so to speak, take a class with **Alpine Skills International** (☎530-582-9170; www.alpineskills.com; 11400 Donner Pass Rd; classes from $159; ⏲mid-Jun–early Oct).

Tours

Tahoe Adventure Company ADVENTURE
(☎530-913-9212; www.tahoeadventurecompany.com; tours per person from $60) A great option for guided Sierra adventures. Staff know the backcountry inside out and can customize any outing to your interest and skill level, from kayaking, hiking, mountain biking and rock climbing to any combination thereof. They also offer full-moon snowshoe tours, SUP lessons and guided lake paddles. There's even a lodge-to-lodge kayaking trip.

Sleeping

A few dependable midrange chain motels and hotels are found off I-80 exits. There's also a hostel behind the train station.

Redlight Historic Bunk Hotel & Speakeasy HOSTEL $
(☎530-536-0005; www.redlighttruckee.com; 10101 West River St; dm $45-49, r $109-149, ste $175-229; 📶) The name recalls this hostel's 19th-century incarnation as a brothel. With dorm beds, private rooms and even a suite with kitchenette, this is a good option for travelers on a

THE DOOMED DONNER PARTY

In the 19th century, tens of thousands of people migrated west along the Overland Trail with dreams of a better life in California. Among them was the ill-fated Donner Party.

When the families of George and Jacob Donner and their friend James Reed departed Springfield, IL, in April 1846 with six wagons and a herd of livestock, they intended to make the arduous journey as comfortable as possible. But the going was slow and, when other pioneers told them about a shortcut that would save 200 miles, they jumped at the chance.

However, there was no road for the wagons in the Wasatch Mountains, and most of the livestock succumbed under the merciless heat of the Great Salt Lake Desert. Arguments and fights broke out. James Reed killed a man, was kicked out of the group and left to trundle off to California alone. By the time the party reached the eastern foot of the Sierra Nevada, near present-day Reno, morale and food supplies were running dangerously low.

To restore their livestock's energy and stock up on provisions, the emigrants decided to rest for a few days. But an exceptionally fierce winter came early, quickly rendering what later came to be called Donner Pass impassable and forcing the pioneers to build basic shelter near today's Donner Lake. They had food to last a month and the fervent hope that the weather would clear by then. It didn't.

Snow fell for weeks, reaching a depth of 22ft. Hunting and fishing became impossible. In mid-December a small group of 15 made a desperate attempt to cross the pass. They quickly became disoriented and had to ride out a three-day storm that killed a number of them. One month later, less than half of the original group staggered into Sutter's Fort near Sacramento, having survived on one deer and their dead friends.

By the time the first rescue party arrived at Donner Lake in late February, the trapped pioneers were still surviving – barely – on boiled ox hides. The rescuers themselves fell into difficulty, and when the second rescue party, led by the banished James Reed, made it through in March, evidence of cannibalism was everywhere. Journals and reports tell of 'half-crazed people living in absolute filth, with naked, half-eaten bodies strewn about the cabins.' Many were too weak to travel.

When the last rescue party arrived in mid-April, only a sole survivor, Lewis Keseberg, was there to greet them. The rescuers found George Donner's body cleansed and wrapped in a sheet, but no sign of Tasmen Donner, George's wife. Keseberg admitted to surviving on the flesh of the dead, but denied charges that he had killed Tasmen for fresh meat. He spent the rest of his life trying to clear his name.

In the end, only 47 of the 89 members of the Donner Party survived. They settled in California, their lives forever changed by the harrowing winter at Donner Lake.

budget. Communal areas sport brocade and red drapes, and there's a kitchen, dry sauna and a small lobby bar, also known for its ice cream (5pm to 9pm Sunday to Wednesday, 4pm to 11pm Thursday to Saturday).

USFS Campgrounds CAMPGROUND $
(Map p644; ☎877-444-6777; www.recreation.gov; campsites $20-22; P 🐾) Conveniently located along Hwy 89 (though with street noise) are three minimally developed riverside camping areas within a few minutes' drive of each other: Granite Flat, Goose Meadow and Silver Creek. All have potable water and vault toilets.

Donner Memorial State Park Campground CAMPGROUND $
(Map p644; ☎530-582-7894, reservations 800-444-7275; www.reservecalifornia.com; tent & RV sites $35; ⏲late May–mid-Oct; P) Brace yourself to camp near Donner Lake (p664): this family-oriented campground has 150 campsites with flush toilets and hot pay showers.

★**Cedar House Sport Hotel** BOUTIQUE HOTEL $$
(Map p644; ☎530-582-5655; www.cedarhousesporthotel.com; 10918 Brockway Rd; r/ste from $195/315; P @ 📶 🐾) This chic, environmentally conscious contemporary lodge aims at getting folks out into nature. It boasts countertops made from recycled paper, 'rain chains' that redistribute water from the green roof garden, low-flow plumbing and in-room recycling. However, it doesn't skimp on plush robes, sexy platform beds with pillow-top mattresses, flat-screen TVs or the outdoor hot tub. It also houses Stella dining room.

Truckee Hotel HISTORIC HOTEL $$
(☎530-587-4444; www.truckeehotel.com; 10007 Bridge St; r $149-229; 📶) Tucked behind an atmospheric four-story redbrick street-front arcade, Truckee's most historic abode has welcomed weary travelers since 1873. A recent remodel has updated the carpets and furniture to genteel Victorian-infused modern luxury, and there's regular live music in its restaurant, Moody's Bistro & Lounge. Expect some train noise and no elevator. Some rooms share hall bathrooms.

Best Western Plus Truckee-Tahoe HOTEL $$
(Map p644; ☎530-587-4525; www.bestwestern.com; 11331 Brockway Rd; r $216-243; P ❄ @ 📶 🏊 🐾) Forget about retro ski-lodge kitsch as you cozy up inside these crisp, earth-toned and down-to-earth hotel rooms that abound in sunny, natural woods. Rooms come with microwaves and fridges. The hotel is 1.5 miles from downtown Truckee, but there are a couple of restaurants and a microbrewery within walking distance. Free shuttle to Northstar, 8 miles south. Hot breakfast included.

Eating & Drinking

Coffeebar CAFE $
(☎530-587-2000; www.coffeebartruckee.com; 10120 Jiboom St; mains $8-13; ⏲6am-7pm; 📶) This beatnik, bare-bones industrial coffee shop serves gelato, delectable pastries and home-brewed kombucha. Go for tantalizing breakfast crepes and overstuffed panini on herbed focaccia bread, or for a jolt of organic espresso or flavored tea lattes.

Squeeze In DINER $
(☎530-587-9814; www.squeezein.com; 10060 Donner Pass Rd; mains $11-27; ⏲7am-2pm; 👪) Across from the Amtrak station, this snug locals' favorite dishes up breakfasts big enough to feed a lumberjack. More than 60 varieties of humongous omelets – along with burgers, burritos and big salads – are served in the funky space crammed with silly tchotchkes and colorful handwritten notes on the walls.

★**Pianeta** ITALIAN $$
(Map p644; ☎530-587-4694; www.pianetarestauranttahoe.com; 10096 Donner Pass Rd; mains $20-49; ⏲5-9pm) A festive mix of locals and tourists drop in nightly at the bar for happy-hour cocktails ($7), good conversation and top-notch service. Thick stone walls, intimate booths and mountain-cool decor provide an inviting backdrop. The northern Italian dishes shine, and appreciative diners dig into pastas, steaks and seafood with gusto. Reservations recommended.

★**Moody's Bistro & Lounge** CALIFORNIAN $$
(☎530-587-8688; www.moodysbistro.com; 10007 Bridge St; mains lunch $15-19, dinner $17-49; ⏲11:30am-10pm) With its sophisticated supper-club looks and live jazz (Thursday through Saturday evenings), this gourmet restaurant in the Truckee Hotel oozes urban flair. Convivial weekend crowds bring the fun. Only fresh, organic and locally grown ingredients appear in the chef's perfectly pitched concoctions, such as pork loin with sweet potato puree, Neapolitan pizza with wild mushrooms and baby kale, and a gruyère cheeseburger.

Stella CALIFORNIAN $$$
(Map p644; ☎530-582-5665; www.cedarhousesporthotel.com; 10918 Brockway Rd; mains $12-28; ⏲5-9pm Wed-Sun) Housed at the

trendy Cedar House Sport Hotel (p667), this modern mountain-lodge dining room elevates Truckee's eating scene with Californian flair, harmonizing Asian and Mediterranean influences on its seasonal menu of housemade pastas, grilled meats and pan-roasted seafood. Bonuses: veggies grown on-site, housemade artisan bread and a killer wine list.

Fifty Fifty Brewing Co BREWERY
(Map p644; www.fiftyfiftybrewing.com; 11197 Brockway Rd; ⏲11:30am-9:30pm) Inhale the aroma of toasting grains at this brewpub south of downtown, near the Hwy 267 intersection. Sip the popular Donner Party Porter or Eclipse barrel-aged imperial stout while noshing a huge plate of nachos or other pub grub.

Shopping

Boutiques and galleries line Donner Pass Rd downtown. For unique gifts pop into **Bespoke** (10130 Donner Pass Rd). Down the block you'll find a good mix of creations from local artists at **Riverside Studios** (10076 Donner Pass Rd).

Information

Truckee Donner Chamber of Commerce (☎530-587-2757; www.truckee.com; 10065 Donner Pass Rd; computer access per 15min $3; ⏲9am-5:30pm; wi-fi) Inside the Amtrak train depot; free walking-tour maps and wi-fi.

USFS Truckee District Ranger Station (☎530-536-0417; www.fs.usda.gov/tahoe; 10811 Stockrest Springs Rd, off I-80 exit 188; ⏲8am-5pm Mon-Sat, Mon-Fri winter) Tahoe National Forest information.

Getting There & Around

Truckee straddles I-80 and is connected to the lakeshore via Hwy 89 to Tahoe City or Hwy 267 to Kings Beach. The main drag through downtown Truckee is Donner Pass Rd, where you'll find the **Amtrak Depot** (☎800-872-7245; www.amtrak.com; 10065 Donner Pass Rd) and metered on-street parking ($1.50 per hour). Visit www.townoftruckee.com for more parking information. Brockway Rd begins south of the river, connecting over to Hwy 267.

Though the Truckee Tahoe Airport has no commercial air service, **North Lake Tahoe Express** (☎866-216-5222; www.northlaketahoeexpress.com; per person to Truckee $49) shuttles to the closest airport at Reno. Buses make numerous runs daily from 6am to midnight, serving multiple northern and western shore towns and Northstar (p665) and Squaw Valley (p663) ski resorts. Make reservations in advance.

Greyhound (☎800-231-2222; www.greyhound.com; 10065 Donner Pass Rd) has once-daily Greyhound buses to Reno ($18, one hour), Sacramento ($17, 2½ hours) and San Francisco ($50, five hours). Greyhound buses stop at the train depot, as do Amtrak Thruway buses and the daily *California Zephyr* train to Sacramento ($55, 4½ hours) and Reno ($27, 1½ hours) and Emeryville/San Francisco ($49, 6½ hours).

Tahoe Truckee Area Regional Transit (☎530-550-1212; www.tahoetruckeetransit.com) (TART) links the Amtrak depot with Donner Lake hourly from about 7am to 7pm daily. Also runs free routes to the north and west shores of Lake Tahoe, including stops at Squaw Valley and Tahoe City, and to Northstar California. During ski season, additional resort shuttles run to many area ski resorts.

For a helpful overview of transportation options in Truckee and the Lake Tahoe region, visit www.linkingtahoe.com

LAKE TAHOE NORTHERN SHORE

Northeast of Tahoe City, Hwy 28 cruises through a string of cute, low-key towns, many fronting superb sandy beaches, with reasonably priced roadside motels and hotels all crowded together along the lakeshore. Oozing old-fashioned charm, the north shore is a blissful escape from the teeming crowds of South Lake Tahoe, Tahoe City and Truckee, but still puts you within easy reach of winter ski resorts and snow parks, and summertime swimming, kayaking, hiking trails and more.

The **North Lake Tahoe Visitors' Bureaus** (☎775-832-1606; www.gotahoenorth.com; 969 Tahoe Blvd, Incline Village, NV; ⏲8am-5pm Mon-Fri, 10am-4pm Sat & Sun) can help get you oriented, although the closest walk-in office is at Incline Village, NV.

Tahoe Vista

Pretty little Tahoe Vista has more public beaches than any other lakeshore town. Sandy strands along Hwy 28 include small but popular **Moon Dunes Beach**, with picnic tables and fire pits opposite the **Rustic Cottages** (☎530-546-3523; www.rusticcottages.com; 7449 N Lake Blvd; cottages $134-399; P wi-fi pets); **North Tahoe Beach** (Map p644; 7860 N Lake Blvd), near the Hwy 267 intersection, with picnic facilities, barbecue grills and beach-volleyball courts; and **Tahoe Vista Recreation Area** (www.northtahoeparks.com; 7010 N Lake Blvd;

parking $10; P), a locals' favorite with a small grassy area and marina and a branch of the Tahoe Adventure Company (p666) renting kayaks and SUP gear beside the lake.

Away from all the maddening crowds, **North Tahoe Regional Park** (Map p644; 530-546-4212; www.northtahoeparks.com; 6600 Donner Rd, off National Ave; per car $5; 7am-9pm Jun-Aug, 7am-7pm Sep & Oct, 7am-5pm Nov-May; P) offers forested hiking and mountain-biking trails, an 18-hole disc-golf course, a children's playground and tennis courts lit up for night play. In winter a sledding hill (rentals available) and ungroomed cross-country ski and snowshoe tracks beckon.

Sleeping

★Cedar Glen Lodge CABIN $$
(530-546-4281; www.tahoecedarglen.com; 6589 N Lake Blvd; r, ste & cottages $229-579; P@) Renovated and upgraded, these gorgeous cabins and rustic-themed lodge rooms across from the beach have pine paneling and granite counters, and some have kitchenettes or full kitchens. Kids go nuts over all the freebies, from ping-pong tables and volleyball to an outdoor swimming pool, a hot tub and a sauna, a putting green and toasty fire pit.

Firelite Lodge MOTEL $$
(530-546-7222; www.tahoelodge.com; 7035 N Lake Blvd; r $178; P) Upgraded with thick walls, soundproofed windows, microwaves, mini-fridges and gas fireplaces in every room, the family-run Firelite is a good-value stay in a prime walkable location, with the Tahoe Vista Recreation Area right across the street. The upstairs king-bed rooms have perfect lake-view balconies. Outside amenities include bikes to rent and a hot tub.

Franciscan Lakeside Lodge CABIN $$
(530-546-6300; www.franciscanlodge.com; 6944 N Lake Blvd; cabins $186-493; P) Spend the day on a private sandy beach or in the outdoor pool, then light the barbecue grill after sunset – ah, now that's relaxation. All of the simple cabins, cottages and suites have kitchenettes. Lakeside lodgings have better beach access and views, but roomier cabins near the back of the complex tend to be quieter and will appeal to families.

Eating & Drinking

★Old Post Office Cafe AMERICAN $
(530-546-3205; 5245 N Lake Blvd; mains $10-16; 6:30am-2pm;) Head west of town toward Carnelian Bay, where this always-packed, cheery wooden shack serves scrumptious breakfasts: buttery potatoes, eggs Benedict, biscuits with gravy, fluffy omelets with lotsa fillings and fresh-fruit smoothies. Waits for a table get long on summer and winter weekends, so roll up early.

Gar Woods Grill & Pier BAR
(530-546-3366; www.garwoods.com; 5000 N Lake Blvd; 10:30am-10:30pm) This shoreline hot spot with its own pier pays tribute to the era of classic wooden boats. Be sure to slurp a Wet Woody cocktail while watching the sun set over the lake.

Kings Beach

The utilitarian character of picturesque Kings Beach lies in its smattering of tired retro motels lined up along the highway (and belies the fact that the town has some of the area's best restaurants). This is one of the more ethnically diverse lakeshore communities, with a large Latino population, many of whom work in the tourism industry around Lake Tahoe.

In summer all eyes are on **Kings Beach State Recreation Area** (Map p644; 530-523-3203; www.parks.ca.gov; off Hwy 28; per car May-Sep $10, Oct-Apr $5; 6am-10pm; P), a seductive 700ft-long beach that often gets deluged with sunseekers and leashed dogs.

Activities

Adrift Tahoe OUTDOORS
(530-546-4112; www.standuppaddletahoe.com; 8338 N Lake Blvd; rentals per hour $25-50, per day from $80; 8am-6pm Jun-Aug, 10am-6pm Sep-May;) At Kings Beach State Recreation Area, Adrift Tahoe handles kayak, outrigger canoe and SUP rentals, and offers private lessons and tours.

Old Brockway Golf Course GOLF
(530-546-9909; www.oldbrockwaygolf.com; 400 Brassie Ave, cnr Hwys 267 & 28; green fees $40-70, club/cart rental from $25/20) Just inland from the lake, this par-36 9-hole 1920s course runs along pine-bordered fairways where Hollywood celebs once swung their clubs.

Eating & Drinking

Char-Pit FAST FOOD $
(530-546-3171; www.charpit.com; 8732 N Lake Blvd; items $3-12; 11am-9pm;) No gimmicks at this 1960s fast-food stand, which

grills juicy burgers and St Louis–style baby back ribs, and also fries up crispy onion rings and breaded mozzarella sticks. Somebody call an ambulance!

Lanza's ITALIAN **$$**

(☎530-546-2434; www.lanzastahoe.com; 7739 N Lake Blvd; mains $16-27; ⏰5-10pm, bar from 4:30pm) Next to the Safeway supermarket stands this beloved Italian trattoria, with its tantalizing aromas of garlic, rosemary and 'secret' spices perfuming the air. Dinners, though undoubtedly not the tastiest you've ever had, are hugely filling and include salad and bread. Look for the owner's sepia family photos in the entranceway.

★ **Soule Domain** AMERICAN **$$$**

(Map p644; ☎530-546-7529; www.souledomain.com; 9983 Cove St; $25-41; ⏰6-9pm) A kitschy log cabin, complete with a carved-bear totem pole, holds the most elegant restaurant on the north shore. Chef Charlie Soule puts a delicious, light-handed global spin on an appealing array of seafood and meat dishes, from sea scallops poached in champagne to curried almond chicken sautéed with snow peas and shiitake mushrooms. There's a nightly four-course classic meal for $27.

Jason's Beachside Grille BAR

(www.jasonsbeachsidegrille.com; 8338 N Lake Blvd; ⏰11am-10pm) Looking for the party around sundown? Hit this waterfront deck with a schooner of microbrew. Never mind the unexciting American fare (dinner mains $13 to $30) such as smoked chicken pasta alongside an overflowing salad bar.

ℹ Getting There & Around

Free Tahoe Truckee Area Regional Transit (p659) buses run between Tahoe City and Incline Village, making stops in Tahoe Vista, Kings Beach and Crystal Bay hourly from approximately 6am until 7:15pm daily. Another TART route connects Crystal Bay and Kings Beach with the Northstar (p665) resort every hour or so from 7am until 6pm daily. Check the website for possible seasonal changes to the routes and for details about reduced night services.

Crystal Bay (Nevada)

Crossing into Nevada, the neon starts to flash and old-school gambling palaces pant after your hard-earned cash. Though currently closed, historic Cal-Neva Resort literally straddles the California–Nevada border and has a colorful history involving ghosts, mobsters and Frank Sinatra, who once owned the joint. Oracle co-founder and billionaire Larry Ellison purchased the property in 2018, and slow-moving plans are now afoot to develop and open a new resort. Ask about the guided secret tunnel tours if it ever reopens.

Crystal Bay Casino (Map p644; ☎775-833-6333; www.crystalbaycasino.com; 14 Hwy 28; Ⓟ) *is* open, and there you can try your luck at the gambling tables, catch a live-music show or grab a burger under a mirrored ceiling at **Cafe Biltmore** (Map p644; 5 Hwy 28; most mains $9-16; ⏰7am-9pm).

For a breath of pine-scented air, flee the smoky casinos for the steep 1-mile round-trip hike up paved Forest Service Rd 1601 to Stateline Lookout. Sunset views over Lake Tahoe and the mountains are all around. A nature trail loops around the site of the former fire lookout tower – nowadays there's a stone observation platform. To find the trailhead, drive up Reservoir Rd, just east of the Tahoe Biltmore parking lot, then take a right onto Lakeview Ave and follow it uphill just over a half-mile to the iron gate on your left.

LAKE TAHOE EASTERN SHORE (NEVADA)

Lake Tahoe's eastern shore lies entirely within Nevada. Much of it is relatively undeveloped thanks to George Whittell Jr, an eccentric San Franciscan playboy who once owned a lot of this land, including 27 miles of shoreline. Upon his death in 1969, it was sold off to a private investor, who later wheeled and dealed most of it to the US Forest Service and Nevada State Parks. And lucky that is, because today the eastern shore offers some of Tahoe's best scenery and outdoor diversion.

Incline Village

One of Lake Tahoe's ritziest communities, Incline Village is the gateway to family-friendly **Diamond Peak** (Map p644; ☎775-832-1177; www.diamondpeak.com; 1210 Ski Way, off Tahoe Blvd/Hwy 28; adult/child 7-12yr/youth 13-23yr $114/49/94; ⏰9am-4pm; 👪) and high-altitude **Mt Rose** (Map p644; ☎775-849-0704; http://skirose.com; 22222 Mt Rose Hwy/Hwy 431, Reno; adult/child 6-15yr $139/69; ⏰9am-4pm) ski resorts. The latter, which has a base elevation of 8269ft, is a 12-mile drive northeast via Hwy 431 (Mt Rose Hwy). During summer, the nearby **Mt Rose**

Wilderness (Map p644; www.fs.usda.gov/ltbmu) offers miles of unspoiled terrain, including a strenuous 11-mile round trip to the summit of majestic **Mt Rose** (10,776ft). The trail starts from the deceptively named Mt Rose Summit parking lot, 9 miles uphill from Incline Village. For a more mellow meadow stroll that even young kids can handle, pull over a mile or so earlier at wildflower-strewn **Tahoe Meadows** (Map p644; Mt Rose Hwy; 🐾). Stay on the nature loop trails to avoid trampling the fragile meadows; leashed dogs are allowed. Hwy 31 between Incline Village and US 395 is also part of the 22-mile long **Mount Rose Scenic Byway** (www.travelnevada.com).

In summer, you can also visit George Whittell's mansion, **Thunderbird Lodge** (Map p644; ☎800-468-2463; http://thunderbirdtahoe.org; adult/child 6-12yr from $45/19; ⏲tours 10am-2pm Tue-Sat late Jun-late Sep, Tue, Fri & Sat mid-May–mid-Jun & late Sep–mid-Oct; 👪), where he spent summers with his pet lion, Bill.

Activities

East Shore Trail WALKING

(Map p644; www.tahoefund.org; Hwy 28) Views of the lake are up-close and gorgeous along this 3-mile paved path, which was completed in 2019. Open for walking, running, blading and biking, the trail links the southern edge of Incline Village with Sand Harbor State Park. Overlooks, interpretive markers and restrooms border the trail.

You'll find three parking lots, a **bike rental shop** (Map p644; ☎775-298-2501; http://flumetrailtahoe.com; 1115 Tunnel Creek Rd; bike rental from $25 per day, shuttle $16, state park entrance $2; ⏲8am-6pm, closed winter) and the recommended **Tunnel Creek Cafe** (mains $8 to $14) at the northern trailhead in Incline Village.

Sleeping

Hyatt Regency Lake Tahoe RESORT $$$

(Map p644; ☎775-832-1234; https://laketahoe.regency.hyatt.com; 111 Country Club Dr; r/ste/cottages from $456/606/1156; P ❄ @ 📶 ≋ 🐾) Decorated like an arts-and-crafts-style mountain lodge, every room and lakeside cottage here looks lavish, and the spa is even bigger than the casino. In summer you can sprawl on a private lakefront beach or in winter let the heated outdoor swimming lagoon warm you up after a day on the slopes. The daily resort fee is $40 and the pet fee is also $40 per day.

Eating & Drinking

T's Rotisserie MEXICAN $

(Map p644; ☎775-831-2832; www.tsrotisserie.com; 901 Tahoe Blvd; mains $3-13; ⏲11am-8pm) Fire-roasted chicken, beef and pork bring a steady stream of appreciative diners to this tacos-and-burritos joint on the main drag. Grab a seat in the small dining room or take your prize to a picnic spot. Cash only.

Bite CALIFORNIAN $$

(☎775-831-1000; www.bitetahoe.com; 907 Tahoe Blvd; shared plates $7-16, mains $15-28; ⏲5-9pm Tue-Thu, 5-10pm Fri & Sat; 🖉) Don't let the strip-mall location stop you from rocking this creative, eclectic tapas and wine bar. Mix light, seasonal, veggie-friendly dishes with modern takes on rib-sticking comfort food such as sweet chili glaze baby back ribs or garlic panko mac 'n' cheese. An après-ski crowd turns up for happy hour.

Lone Eagle Grille COCKTAIL BAR

(Map p644; ☎775-886-6899; https://laketahoe.regency.hyatt.com; 111 Country Club Dr; ⏲11:30am-10pm Sun-Thu, 11:30am-11pm Fri & Sat) At the Hyatt Regency's many-hearthed cocktail lounge, sip a divine orange-flavored margarita, then head outside for sunset and to hang out by the beach fire pit.

Alibi Ale Werks Incline Public House MICROBREWERY

(Map p644; ☎775-831-8300; www.alibialewerks.com; 931 Tahoe Blvd; ⏲noon-10pm Sun-Thu, noon-11pm Fri & Sat) Take your pick of 22 rotating drafts at this lively microbrewery and pub, where all the beer is made from Lake Tahoe water. Check the calendar for live music, trivia and comedy nights. Good pub fare too (small plates $6 to $14, mains $11 to $15). This is one of three Alibi watering holes in the region.

Lake Tahoe–Nevada State Park

Back on the lake, heading south, is **Lake Tahoe-Nevada State Park** (Map p644; ☎775-831-0494; www.parks.nv.gov; per car/bicycle $10/2; ⏲8am-1hr after sunset; P), which has beaches, lakes and miles of trails. Just 3 miles south of Incline Village is beautiful **Sand Harbor** (Map p644; ☎775-831-0494; www.parks.nv.gov/parks/sand-harbor; 2005 Hwy 28; per car $10, walk or bike in $2; P), where two sand spits have formed a shallow bay with brilliant, warm turquoise water and

WORTH A TRIP

PYRAMID LAKE

A piercingly blue expanse in an otherwise barren landscape, **Pyramid Lake** (https://pyramidlake.us; day-use permit $11) is a stunning stand-alone sight, with shores lined with beaches and eye-catching tufa formations. It's 25 miles north of Reno on the Paiute Indian Reservation. Iconic pyramid-like Anaho Island, nearer its east side, is a bird sanctuary for American white pelicans.

Permits for camping on the beach on the west side of the lake ($16) and for fishing are available online, at outdoor suppliers and CVS drugstore locations in Reno, and at the **ranger station** (775-476-1155; http://plpt.nsn.us/rangers; 2500 Lakeview Dr, Sutcliffe; 9am-1pm & 2-6pm Thu-Mon) east of SR445 in Sutcliffe. Follow all local customs and rules.

white, boulder-strewn beaches. It gets very busy here, especially during July and August, when the **Lake Tahoe Shakespeare Festival** (800-747-4697; www.laketahoeshakespeare.com; 2005 Hwy 28, Sand Harbor State Park; Jul & Aug) is underway. To avoid searching for a parking spot at the park, ride the **East Shore Express** (https://tahoetransportation.org; round trip $3; 10am-7pm Jul & Aug) from Incline Village to the park. Round-trip fare is $3 and there is free parking in Incline Village. The park can also be accessed by walking or biking 3 miles from Incline Village on the new East Shore Trail (p671).

At the park's southern end, just north of the Hwy 50/Hwy 28 junction, **Spooner Lake** (Map p644; 775-749-5980; www.parks.nv.gov; per car $10, hike & bike in $2; sunrise-sunset; P) is popular for catch-and-release fishing, picnicking, nature walks, backcountry camping and cross-country skiing. Spooner Lake is also the start of the famous 14-mile **Flume Trail** (Map p644), a holy grail for experienced mountain bikers. From the trail's end near Incline Village you can either backtrack 10 miles along the narrow, twisting shoulder of Hwy 28 or board a shuttle bus. Arrange shuttles and rent bikes by the trailhead inside the park at Flume Trail Bikes (p671).

RENO (NEVADA)

With a compact clutch of big casinos in the shadow of the Sierra Nevada, Reno has a reputation for being a poor version of Vegas. That is somewhat accurate, but these days Reno is so much more. Beyond the garish downtown, with its photo-worthy mid-century modern architecture, neon signs and alpine-fed Truckee River, sprawls a city of parks and pretty houses inhabited by a friendly bunch eager to welcome you. Only an hour from Lake Tahoe, the city is also a fun urban basecamp for exploring the lake and the Sierra foothills.

Stealing a piece of California's tech-pie, the gargantuan Tesla Gigafactory opened its doors here in 2016, bringing plenty of cashed-up youngsters to town, and Reno is ready: the transformation of the formerly gritty Midtown District continues, injecting a dose of funky new bars, top-notch restaurants and vibrant arts spaces into Reno's already unique and eclectic mix. Downtown remains a bit sketchy at night.

If you like pleasant surprises or just go for the underdog, chances are you'll love Reno.

Sights

★**National Automobile Museum** MUSEUM

(775-333-9300; www.automuseum.org; 10 S Lake St; adult/child $12/6; 9:30am-5:30pm Mon-Sat, 10am-4pm Sun; P) Stylized street scenes illustrate a century's worth of automobile history at this engaging car museum. The collection is enormous and impressive, with one-of-a-kind vehicles – including James Dean's 1949 Mercury from *Rebel Without a Cause* and a 1938 Phantom Corsair – and rotating exhibits with all kinds of souped-up and fabulously retro rides. Don't miss the 1907 Thomas Flyer in Gallery 4.

Nevada Museum of Art MUSEUM

(775-329-3333; www.nevadaart.org; 160 W Liberty St; adult/child $10/1; 10am-6pm Tue, Wed & Fri-Sun, 10am-8pm Thu; P) In a sparkling building inspired by the geological formations of the Black Rock Desert north of town, a floating staircase leads to galleries showcasing temporary exhibits and eclectic collections on the American West, labor and contemporary landscape photography. Visitors are free to explore and enjoy the Sky Room function area on the 4th floor – it's essentially a fabulous rooftop penthouse and patio with killer views. There's a bright **cafe** serving French fare off the 1st-floor entrance.

Nevada Historical Society Museum MUSEUM (☎775-688-1190; http://nvculture.org/historicalsociety; 1650 N Virginia St; adult/child $5/free; ⊙10am-4:30pm Tue-Sat) Within the main campus of the University of Nevada, the state's oldest museum includes permanent exhibits on neon signs, local American Indian culture and the presence of the federal government.

Discovery Museum MUSEUM (Terry Lee Wells Nevada Discovery Museum; ☎775-786-1000; www.nvdm.org; 490 S Center St; adult/child 1-17yr $12/10; ⊙10am-5pm Tue, Thu-Sat, 10am-8pm Wed, noon-5pm Sun; P ♿) Test your mental agility in Mindbender Mansion, create something cool in the Sparks Lab and climb a three-story model of the regional water cycle on the towering Cloud Climber. This children's museum is not as high-tech as some, but the slew of engaged kids we saw on our visit didn't seem to mind.

Activities

While gamblers feed their addictions indoors, others relish Reno's outdoor activities, from river floats and kayaking to mountain biking, climbing and skiing.

Reno is under an hour's drive from Lake Tahoe ski resorts – most hotels and casinos offer stay-and-ski packages.

For information on regional hiking and mountain-biking trails, including the Mt Rose summit trail and Tahoe-Pyramid Bikeway, download the Truckee Meadows Trails'guide (www.washoecounty.us/parks/parks and_trails/trails/index.php). Another good resource is the Galena Creek Visitor Center (p675) on the Mt Rose Scenic Byway/Hwy 431 to Incline Village.

Truckee River Whitewater Park OUTDOORS (☎775-334-2270; www.reno.gov; Wingfield Park) Mere steps from the casinos, the park's class II and III rapids are gentle enough for kids riding inner tubes, yet sufficiently challenging for professional freestyle kayakers. Two courses wrap around Wingfield Park, a small river island that hosts free concerts in summertime.

Sierra Adventures OUTDOORS (☎775-323-8928; www.wildsierra.com; 11 N Sierra St; kayak/inner tube per day from $39/19) This affable outfitter offers tons of adventure tours plus gear rentals. Tour options include kayaking, tubing, mountain biking, skiing, horseback riding and snowmobiling.

Tours

Historic Reno Preservation Society WALKING (☎775-747-4478; www.historicreno.org; $10) Dig deeper with a walking or biking tour of Reno that highlights subjects including architecture, history, literary and the movies. Check the website for the list of tours available.

Festivals & Events

Reno River Festival SPORTS (www.renoriverfestival.com; ⊙May) The world's top freestyle kayakers compete in a mad paddling dash through Whitewater Park in mid-May. Free music concerts, a craft beer village and a summer wine village as well.

Hot August Nights CULTURAL (www.hotaugustnights.net; ⊙Aug) Catch the *American Graffiti* vibe during this celebration of hot rods and rock and roll in early August, held over separate dates and various locations around Reno and Virginia City. Hotel rates skyrocket.

Sleeping

Reno has a wide range of accommodations, from budget motels to boutique hotels and decadent casino suites. Room rates in smoky casino towers can sometimes seem ridiculously inexpensive – this is to get as many people through the doors as possible. Many casinos also whack on a resort fee to your bill. Reno's prices are generally higher than in other parts of the state, especially on weekends.

Mt Rose Campground CAMPGROUND $ (Map p644; ☎877-444-6777; www.recreation.gov; Mt Rose Hwy/Hwy 431; RV & tent sites $22-50;

GREAT BALLS OF FIRE!

For a week in August during the **Burning Man** (https://burningman.org; $475; ⊙Aug-early Sep) festival, 'Burners' from around the world descend on the Black Rock Desert to build the temporary Black Rock City, only to tear it all down again and set fire to an effigy of 'the man.' In between, there's peace, love, music, art, nakedness, drugs, sex and frivolity in a safe space where attendees uphold the principles of the festival. Annual attendance tops 60,000. Reno is the closest large city to the festival site; it's about 110 miles south of Black Rock City.

THE ROW

Eldorado Properties recently completed its purchase of three hotel-casinos in downtown Reno: **Eldorado** (775-786-5700; www.eldoradoreno.com; 345 N Virginia St; 24hr), **Silver Legacy** (800-687-8733; www.silverlegacyreno.com; 407 N Virginia St; 24hr) and **Circus Circus** (775-329-0711; www.circusreno.com; 500 N Sierra St; 24hr;). The three adjacent properties are now marketed as **The Row**, a hip destination for gambling and entertainment. Although all three are connected by enclosed sky bridges, they manage to retain their unique personalities. Look for kitschy fountains at the flashy Eldorado, a giant mock-mining rig at the Victorian-themed Silver Legacy and a candy-striped big top at family-friendly Circus Circus.

mid-Jun–mid-Sep;) Reserve your spot a minimum of four days in advance for this gorgeous and popular high-altitude (9300ft) campsite overlooking Lake Tahoe. It's located within the Humboldt-Toiyabe National Forest, 28 miles from downtown Reno. Reservations can be made via the website.

Sands Regency HOTEL $
(775-348-2200; www.sandsregency.com; 345 N Arlington Ave; r from $76;) This hotel has some of the largest standard digs in town, decked out in a cheerful tropical palette of upbeat color. Empress Tower rooms are best. Rates triple on Friday and Saturday nights, but are great value during the week (especially given the 17th-floor gym and outdoor pool). There is a $15 daily resort fee.

★ **Whitney Peak** DESIGN HOTEL $$
(775-398-5400; www.whitneypeakhotel.com; 255 N Virginia St; r $237-280, ste $323;) What's not to love about this independent, inventive, funky, friendly, nonsmoking, non-gambling downtown hotel? Spacious guest rooms have a youthful, fun vibe celebrating the great outdoors and don't skimp on designer creature comforts. With an executive-level concierge lounge, an external climbing wall (if you're game), a decent on-site restaurant and friendly, professional staff, Whitney Peak is unbeatable in Reno.

Renaissance Reno Downtown HOTEL $$
(775-682-3900; www.marriott.com/hotels/travel/rnobr-renaissance-reno-downtown-hotel; 1 S Lake St; r/ste from $189/284;) It's part of a hotel group, but you could be forgiven for thinking it's a boutique hotel (in fact, it used to be). Renovated, oversized guest rooms follow a contemporary theme that's reminiscent of a stylish friend's cozy living room. With the best rooftop pool in town, this is a smart alternative to casino hotels.

★ **Jesse Hotel & Bar** BOUTIQUE HOTEL $$$
(775-507-7270; www.thejessereno.com; 306 E 4th St; r from $230;) The six rooms in this spiffy number share a spare but appealing aesthetic: exposed brick, hardwood floors, minimalist decor and big windows overlooking downtown, all softened by fluffy white linens and big windows. There's a fantastic **cocktail bar** on-site, and **Estella's Tacos Y Mezcal** (tacos $6 to $7) sells delicious street tacos across the courtyard.

Eating

Reno's dining scene is coming of age, finally going beyond the cheap casino buffets and ubiquitous old-school diners. Many downtown restaurants are open around the clock, or at least until the wee hours. The Midtown District has an impressive selection of new restaurants across a wide range of cuisines.

Peg's Glorified Ham & Eggs DINER $
(www.eatatpegs.com; 420 S Sierra St; mains $7-15; 6:30am-2pm;) Locally regarded as having the best breakfast in town, Peg's offers tasty grill food that's not too greasy.

Kwok's Bistro CHINESE $
(775-507-7270; www.kwoksbistro.com; 275 West St; mains $10-16; 11am-9:30pm) This bright box of deliciousness is the latest venture from popular local chef Kwok Chen, and the menu spotlights 'Chinese-Chinese' dishes. Dig into pork belly sliders, the chicken with onions, scallions and ginger claypot, or Singapore noodles with shrimp and BBQ pork.

★ **Old Granite Street Eatery** AMERICAN $$
(775-622-3222; www.oldgranitestreeteatery.com; 243 S Sierra St; mains lunch $11-16, dinner $14-32; 11am-9pm Mon-Fri, 10am-10pm Sat, 10am-1pm Sun;) A lovely well-lit place for organic and local comfort food, old-school artisanal cocktails and craft beers, this antique-strewn hot spot enchants diners with its stately wooden bar, water served in old liquor bottles and lengthy seasonal menu. Forgot to make a reservation? Wait at a communal table fashioned from a barn door.

Wild River Grille GRILL $$$

(☎775-284-7455; www.wildrivergrille.com; 17 S Virginia St; mains lunch $12-16, dinner $25-37; ⏲11am-9pm; ✎) You'll love the smart-casual dining and the varied menu of creative cuisine, from the sautéed elk medallions to the wild mushroom ravioli. But most wonderful of all is the patio overlooking the lovely Truckee River: it's the best spot in town for a drink on a balmy summer's evening.

Drinking & Nightlife

Reno is a fun place with plenty going on, including regular monthly pub crawls, the state's only gay bars outside Las Vegas and an emerging arts scene. The online *Reno News & Review* (www.newsreview.com/reno/home) is your best source for listings.

Chapel Tavern COCKTAIL BAR

(☎775-324-2244; www.chapeltavern.com; 1099 S Virginia St; ⏲2pm-4am) Midtown's cocktail mecca makes its own infusions – try the bourbon with fig – and a seasonal drinks menu attracts year-round interest to its antler-adorned bar and outdoor patio. DJs keep it jamming on Saturday, with occasional live music, and patrons are a diverse bunch.

Depot MICROBREWERY

(☎775-737-4330; www.thedepotreno.com; 325 E 4th St; ⏲3-10pm Mon, 11am-10pm Tue-Sat, 11am-9pm Sun) Once the headquarters for a railway company, this century-old building now houses a festive two-story brewery and distillery. Take your pick of 26 beers on tap, artisan cocktails and tasty gastro-pub selections from the restaurant (mains $10 to $34).

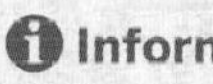

Galena Creek Visitor Center (☎775-849-4948; www.galenacreekvisitorcenter.org; 18250 Mt Rose Hwy; ⏲9am-5pm May-Oct, 9am-4pm Fri-Sun Nov-Apr) Check in with this center when you arrive at the Galena Creek Recreation Area for the latest conditions and friendly advice. Several trails can be accessed from here.

Reno-Sparks Convention & Visitors Authority Visitor Center (☎800-367-7366; www.visitrenotahoe.com; 135 N Sierra St; ⏲10am-6pm) Stop by this conveniently located center when you get to town for the latest on what's on, where and when.

Getting There & Away

About 5 miles southeast of downtown, the **Reno-Tahoe International Airport** (RNO; ☎775-328-6400; www.renoairport.com; 2001 E Plumb Ln; 📶) is served by most major airlines, with connections throughout the US to international routes.

The **North Lake Tahoe Express** (☎866-216-5222; www.northlaketahoeexpress.com; one way $49) operates a shuttle (six to eight daily, 3:30am to midnight) to and from the airport to multiple north shore Lake Tahoe locations including Truckee, Squaw Valley and Incline Village. Reserve in advance.

The **South Tahoe Airporter** (☎866-898-2463; www.southtahoeairporter.com; adult/child one way $33/20) operates several daily shuttle buses from the airport to Stateline casinos; the journey takes from 75 minutes to two hours.

RTC Washoe (☎775-348-0400; www.rtcwashoe.com; $2-5) operates six wi-fi-equipped RTC Intercity regional connector buses per day from Monday to Friday to Carson City ($5, one hour), which loosely connect to **Tahoe Transportation District** (☎775-589-5500; www.tahoetransportation.org) buses to the Stateline Transit Center in South Lake Tahoe (adult/child $4/2 with RTC Intercity transfer, one hour).

Greyhound (☎800-872-7248; www.greyhound.com; 280 N Center St) offers several direct buses a day to Reno from San Francisco (from $23, seven hours): book in advance for lowest fares.

The **Amtrak** (☎800-872-7245; www.amtrak.com; 280 N Center St) *California Zephyr* train makes one daily departure from Emeryville/San Francisco ($54, seven hours) to Reno, onwards to Chicago ($176, 52 hours): a room will set you back $425. Up to five other daily services depart Emeryville/San Francisco for Sacramento, connecting with a bus service to Reno ($60, from 5½ hours).

Getting Around

It's easy to get around Reno on foot, but parts of downtown beyond the 24-hour casino area can be sketchy after dark. Exercise caution when walking along Ralston St, between W 4th and 5th Sts, especially at night.

Casino hotels usually offer frequent free airport shuttles for guests.

The local RTC Ride buses blanket the city, and most routes converge at the RTC 4th St station downtown (between Lake St and Evans Ave). Useful routes include the RTC Rapid line for S Virginia St, 11 for Sparks and 19 for the airport. The new UNR Midtown Direct runs between the the University of Nevada, Reno, the casinos, downtown and midtown along Virginia and Sierra Sts.

AT A GLANCE

POPULATION
156,100

SKI RUNS IN MAMMOTH MOUNTAIN
150

BEST WATERFALL
Bridalveil Fall (p681)

BEST PEAK TO BAG
Mt Whitney (p732)

BEST DRIVE
Kings Canyon Scenic Byway (p699)

WHEN TO GO

May & Jun The Yosemite waterfalls are gushing and spectacular in spring.

Jul & Aug Head for the mountains for wilderness adventures and glorious sunshine.

Dec–Mar Take a wintertime romp through snowy forests.

Vernal Falls (p683)
ANNA GORIN / GETTY IMAGES ©

Yosemite & the Sierra Nevada

An outdoor-adventurer's wonderland, the Sierra Nevada is a year-round pageant of snow sports, white-water rafting, hiking, cycling and rock climbing. Skiers and snowboarders blaze through hushed pine-tree slopes, and wilderness seekers escape modern civilization.

With fierce granite mountains standing watch over high-altitude lakes, the eastern spine of California throws up a formidable but exquisite topographical barrier enclosing magnificent natural landscapes. Bubbling natural hot springs are interspersed between its river canyons and almost one dozen 14,000ft peaks.

In the majestic national parks of Yosemite and Sequoia and Kings Canyon, visitors will be humbled by the groves of solemn giant sequoias, ancient rock formations and valleys, and the ever-present opportunity to see bears and other wildlife.

INCLUDES

Yosemite & the Sierra Nevada Highlights

❶ **Yosemite National Park** (p680) Marveling at the waterfall gush in spring.

❷ **Mammoth Mountain** (p717) Whooshing down the wintertime heights of this snow-draped mountain.

❸ **Sequoia & Kings Canyon National Parks** (p698) Gazing heavenward through the celestial sequoia canopies.

❹ **Bodie State Historic Park** (p711) Ambling around this evocative ghost town.

❺ **Mono Lake** (p714) Canoeing or kayaking amid the lake's haunting tufa.

6 Devils Postpile National Monument (p722) Viewing this bizarre volcanic formation.

7 Ancient Bristlecone Pine Forest (p730) Walking amid parched groves of the earth's oldest living things.

8 Benton Hot Springs (p722) Soaking your troubles away at these hot springs.

9 Manzanar National Historic Site (p727) Visiting the museum and site of one of the darkest events in US history.

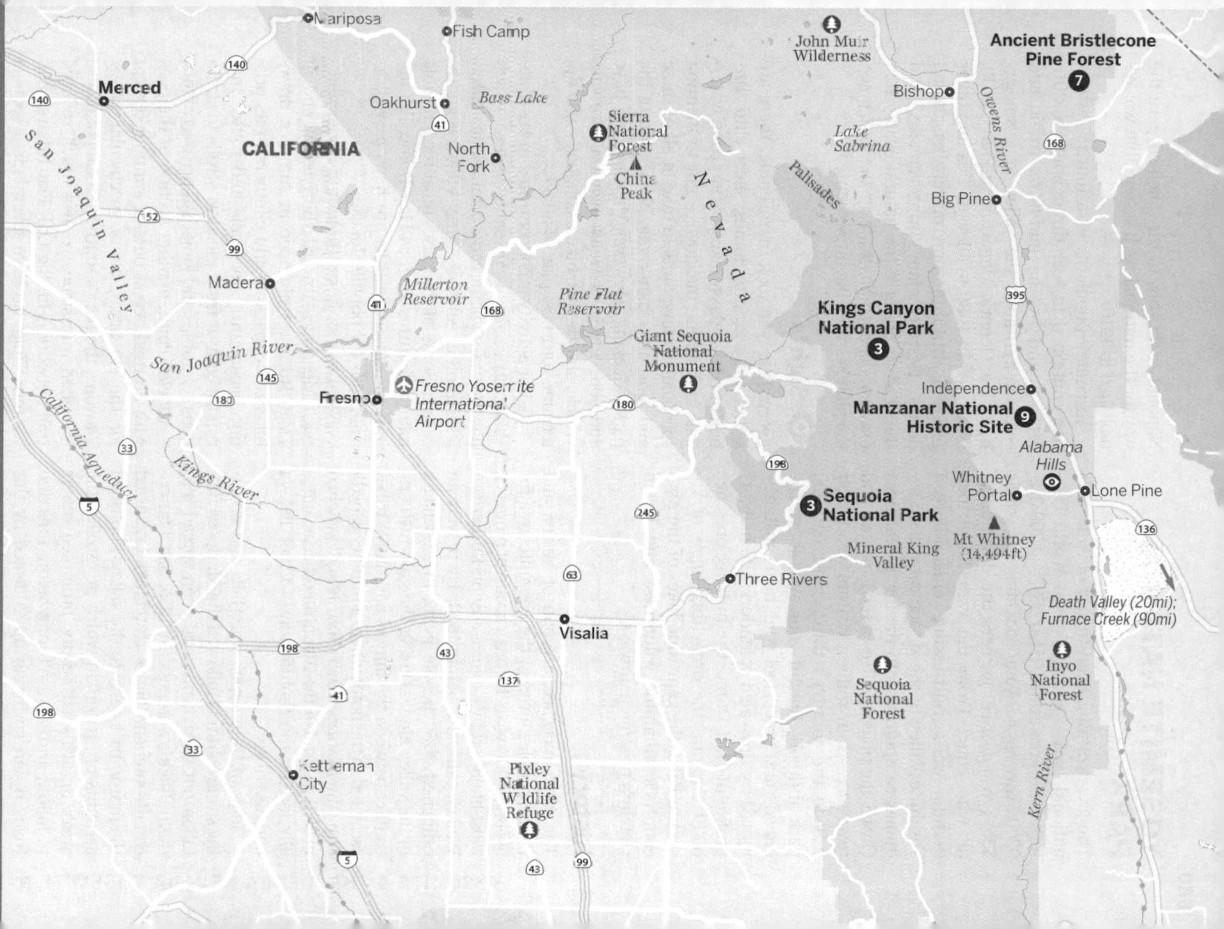

YOSEMITE NATIONAL PARK

The jaw-dropping head-turner of America's national parks, and a Unesco World Heritage site, **Yosemite** (Map p682; ☎209-372-0200; www.nps.gov/yose/index.htm; per vehicle $35) (yo-*sem*-it-ee) garners the devotion of all who enter. From the waterfall-striped granite walls buttressing emerald-green Yosemite Valley to the skyscraping giant sequoias catapulting into the air at Mariposa Grove, the place inspires a sense of awe and reverence – four million visitors wend their way to the country's third-oldest national park annually. But lift your eyes above the crowds and you'll feel your heart instantly moved by unrivaled splendors: the haughty profile of Half Dome, the hulking presence of El Capitan, the drenching mists of Yosemite Falls, the gemstone lakes of the high country's subalpine wilderness and Hetch Hetchy's pristine pathways.

History

The Ahwahneechee, a group of Miwok and Paiute peoples, lived in the Yosemite area for around 4000 years before a group of pioneers, most likely led by explorer Joseph Rutherford Walker, came through in 1833. There were an estimated 3000 people living in 22 villages in the valley alone. During the gold-rush era, conflict between the miners and native tribes escalated to the point where a military expedition (the Mariposa Battalion) was dispatched in 1851 to punish the Ahwahneechee, eventually forcing the capitulation of Chief Tenaya and his tribe.

Tales of thunderous waterfalls and towering stone columns followed the Mariposa Battalion out of Yosemite and soon spread into the public's awareness. In 1855, San Francisco entrepreneur James Hutchings organized the first tourist party to the valley. Published accounts of his trip, in which he extolled the area's untarnished beauty, prompted others to follow, and it wasn't long before inns and roads began springing up. Alarmed by this development, conservationists petitioned Congress to protect the area – with success. In 1864 President Abraham Lincoln signed the Yosemite Grant, which eventually ceded Yosemite Valley and the Mariposa Grove of Giant Sequoias to California as a state park. This landmark decision, along with the pioneering efforts of conservationist John Muir, led to a congressional act in 1890 creating Yosemite National Park; this, in turn, helped pave the way for the national-park system that was established in 1916.

Yosemite's popularity as a tourist destination continued to soar throughout the 20th century, and by the mid-1970s traffic and congestion draped the valley in a smoggy haze. The General Management Plan (GMP), developed in 1980 to alleviate this and other problems, ran into numerous challenges and delays. Despite many improvements, and the need to preserve the natural beauty that draws visitors to Yosemite in the first place, the plan is still being implemented.

Sights

Everywhere you look in Yosemite, there are sights: lofty granite domes, sheer cliffs, turbulent rivers, glassy lakes, hypnotizing waterfalls and serene meadows – not to mention spectacular viewpoints to take in all of these and more in a panorama. No section of the park is lacking. However, the time you have and your mode of transportation – private vehicle, shuttle bus, bike or on foot – will determine your best plan of attack.

Visitor activity is concentrated in Yosemite Valley, especially in Yosemite Village, which has the main visitor center, a museum, eateries and other services. Curry Village is another hub. Some of the park's most recognizable natural features such as Half Dome, El Capitan and Yosemite Falls are here, as well as trailheads for popular hikes.

Notably less busy, Tuolumne (too-*ahl*-uh-*mee*) Meadows, toward the eastern end of Tioga Rd and only open in summer, draws hikers, backpackers and climbers to its pristine backcountry for trails and routes that run the gamut from meadow strolls to strenuous scrambles and long-distance overnights.

Glacier Point, another section of the park with no road access outside summer (except for the ski area), offers spectacular views. Wawona, the park's southern focal point, also has good infrastructure, if a much reduced trail network. The Big Oak Flat Rd area and western Tioga Rd have several giant sequoia groves. In the northwestern corner, Hetch Hetchy, which has no services at all, but notably impressive waterfalls and several recommended hikes, receives the smallest number of visitors but shouldn't be overlooked.

Yosemite Valley

The park's crown jewel, spectacular, meadow-carpeted Yosemite Valley stretches 7 miles long, bisected by the rippling Merced River and hemmed in by some of the most majestic chunks of granite anywhere on earth. Ribbons of water, including some of the highest waterfalls in the US, fall dramatically before crashing in thunderous displays. At the southwestern end of the valley, **Bridalveil Fall** tumbles 620ft. The Ahwahneechee people call it Pohono (Spirit of the Puffing Wind), as gusts often blow the fall from side to side, even lifting water back up into the air. Peregrine falcons glide overhead. The waterfall usually runs year-round, though it's often reduced to a whisper by midsummer. Bring rain gear or expect to get soaked when the fall is heavy.

The counterpoint to the sublime natural scene is bustling Yosemite Village.

Yosemite Museum MUSEUM
(Map p688; www.nps.gov/yose; 9037 Village Dr, Yosemite Village; 9am-5pm summer, 10am-4pm rest of year, often closed noon-1pm) FREE The Yosemite Museum has Miwok and Paiute artifacts, including woven baskets, beaded buckskin dresses and dance capes made from feathers. Native American cultural demonstrators engage visitors with traditional basket weaving, toolmaking and crafts. There's also an **art gallery** with paintings and photographs from the museum's permanent collection. Behind the museum, a self-guided **interpretive trail** winds past the reconstructed 1870s **Indian Village of Ahwahnee**, with pounding stones, an acorn granary, a ceremonial roundhouse and a conical bark house.

Ahwahnee HISTORIC BUILDING
(Map p688; 1 Ahwahnee Dr, Yosemite Valley; shuttle stop 3) About a quarter-mile east of Yosemite Village, the Ahwahnee is a picture of rustic elegance, dating back to 1927. You don't need to be a guest to have a gawk and a wander. Built from granite, cement and steel (with hints of pine and cedar), the building is splendidly decorated with leaded glass, sculpted tiles, Native American trappings, German Gothic chandeliers and Turkish kilims. Enjoy a meal in the baronial dining room (p692) or a casual drink in the piano bar.

Around Christmas, the hotel hosts the **Bracebridge Dinner** (reservations 888-413-8869; www.bracebridgedinners.com; per person $380), a combination of banquet and Renaissance fair. Book early.

Happy Isles Art & Nature Center ART
(Map p688; 209-372-4207; artcenter@yosemiteconservancy.org; Happy Isle Loop Rd; classes $10-20) In late spring, summer and fall, the Yosemite Conservancy's art center holds daily classes featuring different artists and mediums. Register to ensure a spot, or drop in. Classes usually take place outside, and students must bring their own supplies or purchase them at the center. No experience is necessary. Contact the Yosemite Conservancy for the schedule of summer kids' classes.

Glacier Point

If you drove here, the views from 7214ft **Glacier Point** (Map p688) might make you feel like you cheated: superstar sights present themselves to you when you've made virtually no physical effort. A quick mosey up from the parking lot and you'll find the entire eastern Yosemite Valley spread out before you, from **Yosemite Falls** to **Half Dome**, as well as the distant peaks that ring Tuolumne Meadows. Half Dome looms practically at eye level, and if you might even spot hikers on its summit.

To the left of Half Dome lies the glacially carved **Tenaya Canyon**, and to its right are the wavy white ribbons of **Nevada and Vernal Falls**. On the valley floor, the Merced River snakes through green meadows and groves of trees. Sidle up to the railing, hold on tight and peer 3200ft straight down at Curry Village. **Basket Dome** and **North Dome** rise to the north of the valley, and **Liberty Cap** and the **Clark Range** can be seen to the right of Half Dome.

Almost from the park's inception, Glacier Point has been a popular destination. It used to be that getting up here was a major undertaking. That changed once the Four Mile Trail opened in 1872. A wagon road to the point was completed in 1882, and the current Glacier Point Rd was built in 1936.

At the tip of the point is **Overhanging Rock**, a huge granite slab protruding from the cliff edge like an outstretched tongue, defying gravity and once providing a scenic stage for daredevil extroverts. Through the years, many famous photos have been taken of folks performing handstands, high kicks and other wacky stunts on the rock. The precipice is now off-limits.

Tioga Road & Tuolumne Meadows

Tioga Rd (or Hwy 120 E), the only road through the park, travels through 56 miles of superb high country at elevations ranging from 6200ft at Crane Flat to 9945ft at Tioga

Yosemite National Park

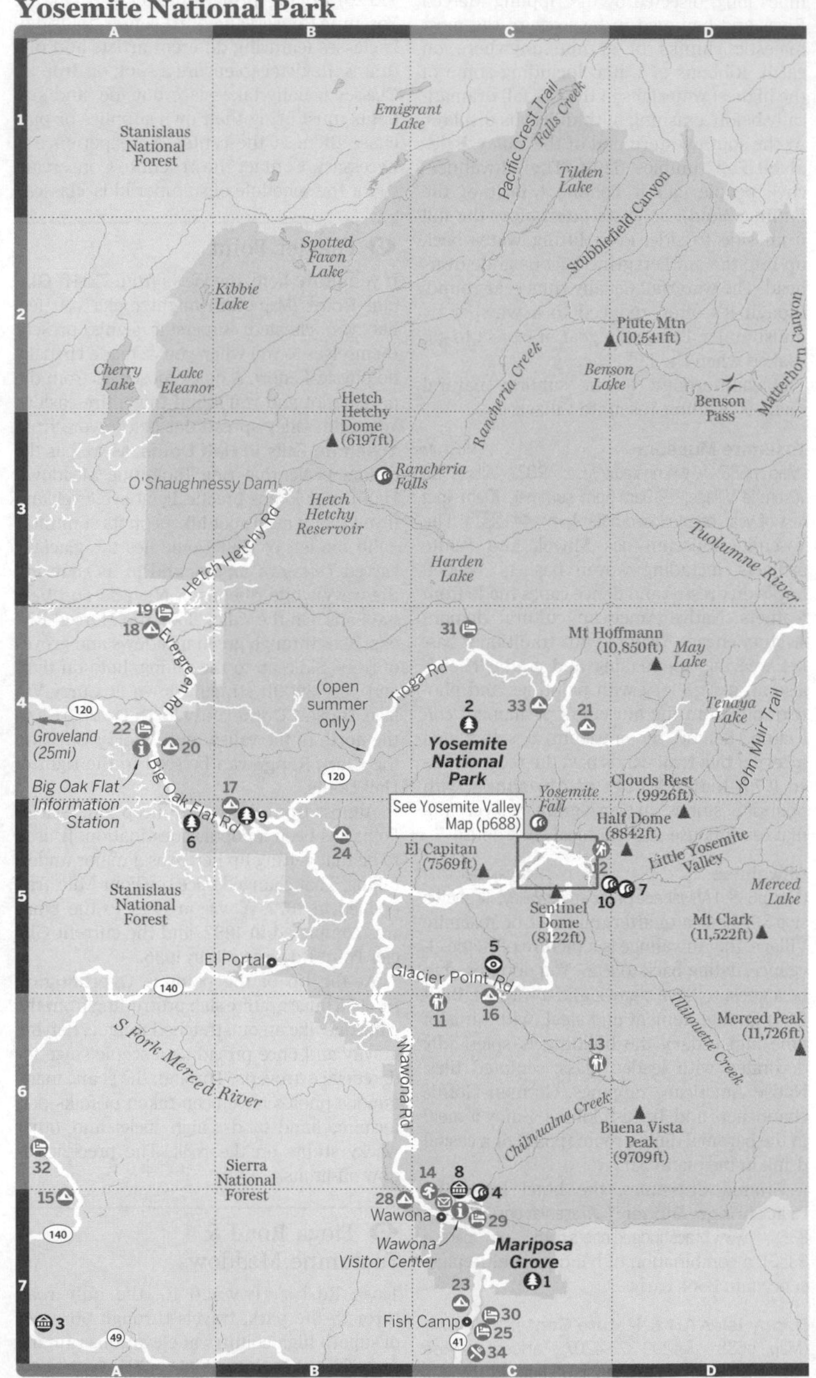

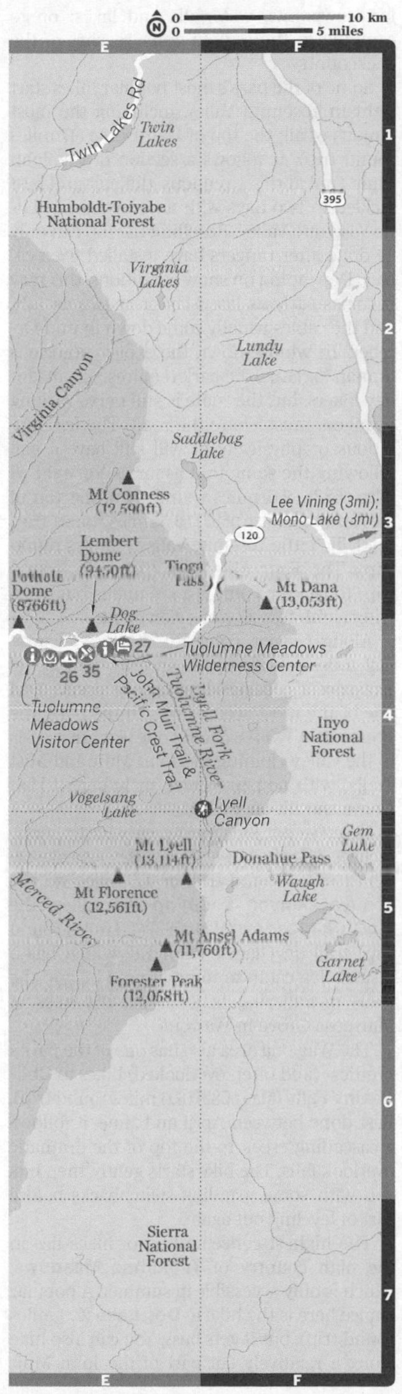

Yosemite National Park

Top Sights

1 Mariposa Grove C7
2 Yosemite National Park C4

Sights

3 California State Mining & Mineral Museum A7
4 Chilnualna Falls C7
5 McGurk Meadow C5
6 Merced Grove A5
7 Nevada Fall D5
8 Pioneer Yosemite History Center C7
9 Tuolumne Grove B5
10 Vernal Fall C5

Activities, Courses & Tours

11 Badger Pass Ski Area C6
Badger Pass Ski Area School .... (see 11)
12 Mirror Lake C5
13 Ostrander Ski Hut C6
14 Wawona Hotel Stable C7

Sleeping

15 Autocamp A7
16 Bridalveil Creek Campground C6
17 Crane Flat Campground B5
18 Dimond O Campground A4
19 Evergreen Lodge A4
20 Hodgdon Meadow Campground A4
21 Porcupine Flat Campground C4
22 Rush Creek Lodge A4
23 Summerdale Campground C7
24 Tamarack Flat Campground B5
25 Tenaya Lodge C7
26 Tuolumne Meadows Campground E4
27 Tuolumne Meadows Lodge E4
28 Wawona Campground B7
29 Wawona Hotel C7
30 White Chief Mountain Lodge C7
White Wolf Campground .... (see 31)
31 White Wolf Lodge C4
32 Yosemite Bug Rustic Mountain Resort A6
33 Yosemite Creek Campground C4

Eating

Evergreen Lodge .... (see 19)
June Bug Cafe .... (see 32)
34 Narrow Gauge Inn C7
35 Tuolumne Meadows Grill E4

Pass. Beautiful views, and giant sequoias in **Tuolumne** and **Merced** (Map p682) groves await after many a bend in the road. Heavy snowfall keeps it closed from about November until May.

Hetch Hetchy

In the park's northwestern corner, Hetch Hetchy, which is Miwok for 'place of tall grass,' gets the least amount of traffic yet sports waterfalls (Tueeulala and Wapama are easily accessible; the latter flows year-round) and granite cliffs that rival its famous counterparts in Yosemite Valley. The main difference is that Hetch Hetchy Valley is now filled with water, following a long political and environmental battle in the early 20th century.

Wawona

Wawona, about 27 miles south of Yosemite Valley, is the park's historical center, home to its first headquarters (supervised by Captain AE Wood on the site of the Wawona Campground) and its first tourist facilities. The recently restored Mariposa Grove of giant sequoias lies just inside the park's South Entrance.

★Mariposa Grove FOREST
(Map p682; 8am-8pm summer, hours vary rest of year) With their massive stature and multi-millennial maturity, the chunky high-rise sequoias of Mariposa Grove will make you feel rather insignificant. The largest grove of giant sequoias in the park, Mariposa is home to more than 500 mature trees spread over 250 acres. Walking trails wind through this very popular grove; you can usually have a more solitary experience if you come during the early evening in summer or anytime outside of summer.

Pioneer Yosemite History Center HISTORIC BUILDING
(Map p682; www.nps.gov/yose/planyourvisit; Wawona; rides adult/child $5/4; 24hr, rides 10am-2pm Wed-Sun May-Sep; P) FREE Off Wawona Rd, about 6 miles north of Mariposa Grove, you can take in the manicured grounds of the elegant Wawona Hotel and cross a covered bridge to this rustic center, where some of the park's oldest buildings were relocated. It also features stagecoaches that brought early tourists to Yosemite, and offers short horse-drawn **stagecoach rides** in summer.

Activities

Hiking

Over 800 miles of trails cater to hikers of all abilities. Take an easy half-mile stroll on the valley floor; venture out all day on a quest for viewpoints, waterfalls and lakes; or go camping in the remote outer reaches of the backcountry.

Some of the park's most popular hikes start right in Yosemite Valley, including the most famous of all: the top of Half Dome (17 miles round trip). It follows a section of the John Muir Trail and is strenuous, difficult and best tackled in two days with an overnight in Little Yosemite Valley. Reaching the top can only be done after rangers have installed fixed cables. Depending on snow conditions, this may occur as early as late May or as late as July, and the cables usually come down in mid-October. To whittle down the cables' notorious human logjams, the park requires permits for day hikers, but the route is still nerve-racking as hikers must 'share the road.' The less ambitious or physically fit will still have a ball following the same trail as far as **Vernal Fall** (Map p682) (2.6 miles round trip), the top of **Nevada Fall** (Map p682) (6.5 miles round trip) or idyllic Little Yosemite Valley (8 miles round trip). The Four Mile Trail (9.2 miles round trip) to Glacier Point is a strenuous but satisfying climb to a glorious viewpoint.

Along Glacier Point Rd, **Sentinel Dome** (2.2 miles round trip) is an easy hike to the crown of a commanding granite dome. And one of the most scenic hikes in the park, the **Panorama Trail** (8.5 miles one way), descends to the valley (joining the John Muir and Mist Trails) with nonstop views, including of Half Dome and Illilouette Fall.

If you've got kids in tow, easy destinations include **Mirror Lake** (Map p682; Yosemite Valley) (2 miles round trip, or 4.5 miles via the **Tenaya Canyon Loop**) in the valley, the **McGurk Meadow** (Map p682) (1.6 miles round trip) trail on Glacier Point Rd, which has a historic log cabin to romp around in, and the trails meandering beneath the big trees of Mariposa Grove in Wawona.

The Wawona area also has one of the park's prettiest (and often overlooked) hikes to **Chilnualna Falls** (Map p682) (8.6 miles round trip). Best done between April and June, it follows a cascading creek to the top of the dramatic overlook falls. The hike starts gently, then hits you with some grinding switchbacks before sort of leveling out again.

The highest concentration of hikes lies in the high country of **Tuolumne Meadows**, which is only accessible in summer. A popular choice here is the hike to **Dog Lake** (2.8 miles round trip), but it gets busy. You can also hike along a relatively flat part of the John Muir

DRIVING THE TIOGA PASS

Tioga Rd (Hwy 120) climbs steadily toward **Tioga Pass**, which at 9945ft is the highest autoroute over the Sierra. The short ride by car or free shuttle bus from Tuolumne Meadows takes you across dramatic, wide open spaces – a stretch of stark, windswept countryside near the timberline. You'll notice a temperature drop and, possibly, widespread patches of snow.

Tioga Rd parallels the Dana Fork of the Tuolumne River, then turns north, where it borders the beautiful Dana Meadows all the way to Tioga Pass. To the east you'll see great views of Mt Gibbs (12,764ft) and Mt Dana (13,057ft), the park's second-highest peak after Mt Lyell (13,114ft).

On most maps of California you'll find a parenthetical remark – 'closed in winter' – printed next to the pass. While true, this statement is also misleading. Tioga Rd is usually closed from the first heavy snowfall in October until May, June or even July! If you're planning a trip through Tioga Pass in spring, you're likely to be out of luck. According to official park policy, the earliest date the road will be plowed is 15 April, yet the pass has been open in April only once since 1980 (the average opening date is May 26). It's a complex and hazardous endeavor because of avalanche zones, rockfalls, fallen trees, snowpack depth and even heavy snow during the clearing process. Other mountain roads further north, such as Hwy 108, Hwy 4 and Hwy 88/89, may also be closed due to heavy snow, albeit only temporarily. Call 800-427-7623 for road and weather conditions.

Trail into lovely **Lyell Canyon** (17.6 miles round trip), following the Lyell Fork of the Tuolumne River.

Backpacks, tents and other equipment can be rented from the **Yosemite Mountaineering School** (Map p688; ☎209-372-8344; www.travelyosemite.com; Half Dome Village; ⏲8:30am-5pm Apr-Oct). The school also offers two-day, Learn to Backpack, trips for novices, and all-inclusive three- and four-day guided backpacking trips ($375 to $500 per person), which are great for inexperienced and solo travelers. In summer it operates a branch from Tuolumne Meadows.

Rock Climbing

With its sheer spires, polished domes and soaring monoliths, Yosemite is rock-climbing nirvana. The main climbing season runs from April to October. Most climbers, including some legendary stars, stay at Camp 4 (p687) near El Capitan, especially in spring and fall. In summer, another base camp springs up at Tuolumne Meadows Campground (p688). Climbers looking for partners post notices on bulletin boards at either campground.

The meadows across from El Capitan and the northeastern end of Tenaya Lake (off Tioga Rd) are good for watching climbers dangle from granite (you need binoculars for a really good view). Look for the haul bags first – they're bigger and more colorful than the climbers, and they move around more, making them easier to spot. As part of the excellent **Ask a Climber** program, climbing rangers set up telescopes at El Capitan Bridge from 12:30pm to 4:30pm (mid-May through mid-October) and answer visitors' questions.

Climbers should pay attention to routes that are temporarily closed off to protect the nesting seasons of certain protected species such as peregrine falcons and golden eagles. Closure notices are usually posted near trailheads to the sites.

Cycling

Mountain biking isn't permitted within the park, but cycling along the 12 miles of paved trails is a popular and environmentally friendly way of exploring the valley. It's also the fastest way to get around when traffic is at a standstill. Many families bring bicycles, and you'll often find kids doing laps through the campgrounds. Hard-core cyclists brave the skinny shoulders and serious altitude changes of the trans-Sierra Tioga Rd.

Swimming

On a hot summer day, nothing beats a dip in the gentle Merced River, though if chilly water doesn't float your boat, you can always pay to play in the scenic outdoor swimming pools at **Curry Village** (Map p688; adult/child $5/3; ⏲end May-Sep) and **Yosemite Valley Lodge** (Map p688; adult/child $5/3; 👪); the price of admission includes towels and showers. With a sandy beach, Tenaya Lake is a frigid but interesting option. White Wolf's Harden Lake warms up to a balmy temperature by midsummer.

MANDATORY HALF DOME PERMITS

To stem lengthy lines (and increasingly dangerous conditions) on the vertiginous cables of Half Dome, the park requires that all day hikers obtain an advance permit to climb the cables. There are currently three ways to do this, but check www.nps.gov/yose/planyourvisit/hdpermits.htm for the latest information. The season usually runs from the end of May to the first week in October. Rangers check permits at the base of the cables.

Preseason permit lottery (www.recreation.gov) Lottery applications ($10) for 225 of the 300 daily spots must be completed in March, with confirmation notification sent in mid-April; an additional fee of $10 per person confirms the permit. Applications can include up to six people and seven alternate dates.

Daily lottery Approximately 50 additional permits are distributed by lottery two days before each hiking date. Apply online at www.recreation.gov or by phone (877-444-6777) between 7am and 9pm Pacific Time; notification is available late that same evening. It's easier to score weekday permits.

Backpackers Those with Yosemite-issued wilderness permits that reasonably include Half Dome can request Half Dome permits (also $10 per person) without going through the lottery process. Backpackers with wilderness permits from a National Forest or another park can use that permit to climb the cables.

Horseback Riding

The park's concessionaire runs guided trips to such scenic locales as Mirror Lake and Chilnualna Falls from the **Wawona Hotel Stable** (Map p682; ☎209-375-6502; www.travelyosemite.com; ⏲7am-5pm mid-May–Sep), as well as four- and six-day guided trips to the park's **high-sierra camps** (☎freight 209-372-8348, lottery 888-413-8869; www.travelyosemite.com/lodging/high-sierra-camps; per person adult/child from $1320/1068, freight per pound $5). The season runs from May to October, although this varies slightly by location. No experience is needed, but reservations are advised. The high-sierra camp trips operate by lottery. Some mounts are horses, but most likely you'll be riding a sure-footed mule.

Rafting

From around late May to July, floating along the Merced River from Stoneman Meadow, near Curry Village, to Sentinel Bridge is a leisurely way to soak up Yosemite Valley views. Four-person **raft rentals** (Map p688; ☎209-372-8319; per person $28.50; ⏲10am-4pm late May-late Jul) for the 3-mile trip are available from the concessionaire in Curry Village and include equipment and a shuttle ride back to the rental kiosk. Children must be over 50lb. Or bring your own raft and pay $5 to shuttle back. This activity is suitable for the mobility impaired.

Winter Sports

The white coat of winter opens up a different set of things to do, as the valley becomes a quiet, frosty world of snow-draped evergreens, ice-coated lakes and vivid vistas of gleaming white mountains sparkling against blue skies. Winter tends to arrive in full force by mid-November and peter out in early April (an extremely dry winter in 2020 meant the valley and all but the highest elevations of the park were snow free).

A free shuttle bus connects the valley and the Badger Pass Ski Area. Roads in the valley are plowed, and Hwys 41, 120 and 140 are usually kept open, conditions permitting. Tioga Rd (Hwy 120 E), however, closes with the first snowfall. Be sure to bring snow chains with you, as prices for them double once you hit the foothills.

Ostrander Ski Hut SKIING

(Map p682; ☎209-379-5161; www.yosemiteconservancy.org) More experienced skiers can trek 10 miles out to this popular hut on Ostrander Lake. Operated by Yosemite Conservancy, the hut is staffed all winter and open to backcountry skiers and snowshoers for $50 per person, per night, on a lottery basis. See the website for details.

Badger Pass Ski Area SNOW SPORTS

(Map p682; ☎209-372-8430; www.travelyosemite.com; lift ticket adult/child $62/35; ⏲9am-4pm mid-Dec–Mar) The gentle slopes of one of California's oldest ski resorts, about 22 miles from the valley on Glacier Point Rd, are perfect for families and beginner skiers and snowboarders. There are five chairlifts, 800 vertical feet and 10 runs, a full-service lodge, and equipment rental ($30 to $42 for a full set of gear).

The excellent **Badger Pass Ski Area School** (group/private lessons from $80/89.50), where generations of novices have learned how to get down a hill safely, offers group lessons.

Sleeping

Competition for sites at one of the park's 13 campgrounds is fierce from May to September, arriving without a reservation and hoping for the best is tantamount to getting someone to lug your BarcaLounger up Half Dome. Even first-come, first-served campgrounds tend to fill by noon, especially on weekends and around holidays.

All campgrounds have flush toilets, except for Tamarack Flat, Yosemite Creek and Porcupine Flat, which have vault toilets and no potable water. Those at higher elevations get chilly at night, even in summer, so pack accordingly. The Yosemite Mountaineering School (p685) rents camping gear.

If you hold a wilderness permit, you may spend the nights before and after your trip in the backpacker campgrounds at Tuolumne Meadows, Hetch Hetchy, White Wolf and behind North Pines in Yosemite Valley. The cost is $5 per person, per night, and reservations aren't necessary.

Opening dates for seasonal campgrounds vary according to the weather.

Yosemite Valley

Camp 4 CAMPGROUND $
(Map p688; www.nps.gov/yose; Northside Dr; shared tent sites per person $6; year-round) This walk-in campground at 4000ft, entwined in climbing history and popular with climbers who tend to be long-term occupants; campsites are shared. The only park campground where pets aren't allowed.

North Pines Campground CAMPGROUND $
(Map p688; www.nps.gov/yose; tent & RV sites $26; Apr-Oct;) Within walking distance of some of the valley's most popular trailheads, North Pines (4000ft) has 81 campsites near Mirror Lake, with some spots along the Merced River; reservations required. Can feel crowded and cramped with RVs.

Upper Pines Campground CAMPGROUND $
(Map p688; www.nps.gov/yose; tent & RV sites $26; year-round;) Busy, busy, busy – and big (238 sites, 4000ft); reservations required all year. Campsites are fairly small and close to one another. However, you can find relative privacy the further back you go, toward the Happy Isles Art & Nature Center (p681).

Lower Pines Campground CAMPGROUND $
(Map p688; www.nps.gov/yose; tent & RV sites $26; Apr-Oct;) Jam-packed and noisy, with 60 sites at 4000ft, some along the Merced River; reservations required.

Housekeeping Camp CABIN $
(Map p688; www.travelyosemite.com; Southside Dr; cabins $122; Apr-Oct) This cluster of 266 cabins, each walled by concrete on three sides and lidded by a canvas roof, is crammed and noisy, but the setting along the Merced River has its merits. Each unit sleeps six and has electricity, light, a table and chairs, and a covered patio with picnic tables. Laundry (7am to 10pm) and shower facilities are open to guests and nonguests.

Bring your own sleeping bag, or linens can be rented; for the latter, be sure to have extra layers of clothes for chilly nights.

Curry Village CABIN $$
(Map p688; front desk 209-372-8333, reservations 888-413-8869; www.travelyosemite.com; tent cabins from $135, r from $260, cabins with bath from $209; mid-Mar–late Nov, Sat & Sun early Jan–mid-Mar; P) Founded in 1899 as summertime Camp Curry, this 'village' has hundreds of units squished together beneath towering evergreens. The canvas cabins (heated or unheated) – basically glorified tents – are an atmospheric compromise for those who crave a few creature comforts (bed, sheets, shelving units and safe). There are 18 motel-style rooms in Stoneman House, including a loft suite that sleeps six.

For more comfort, quiet and privacy, get one of the cozy wood cabins, which have vintage posters. Cabin 819, with its fireplace, sofa bed and king-size bed, is probably the most luxurious of the bunch. The village, which has an amphitheater for naturalist talks, several eating options, a small grocery, and bike and raft rental kiosks, is off Southside Dr.

★ **Ahwahnee** HISTORIC HOTEL $$$
(Map p688; reservations 888-413-8869; www.travelyosemite.com; 1 Ahwahnee Dr; r/ste from $580/1400; P@) The crème de la crème of Yosemite's lodging, this sumptuous historic property (briefly renamed the Majestic Hotel) dazzles with soaring ceilings and atmospheric lounges featuring mammoth stone fireplaces. Classic rooms have inspiring views of Glacier Point, Half Dome and Yosemite Falls. Cottages are scattered on the

Yosemite Valley

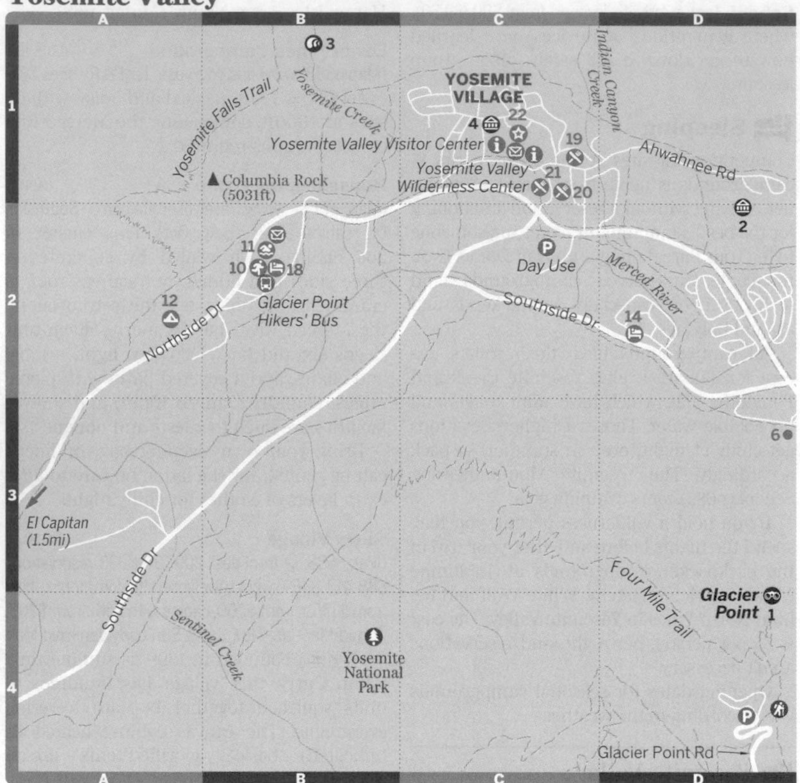

immaculate lawn next to the hotel. For high season and holidays, book a year ahead.

Ask for one of the more than 90 rooms renovated a few years ago with new carpets, curtains and bathroom fixtures; keep in mind that some rooms have more natural light than others. Suites 232 and 332 have fireplaces, chandeliers and incredible panoramic views. The Ahwahnee is the gold standard for upscale lodges, but even if you're not staying here, you can soak up the ambience during afternoon tea, a drink in the bar or ameal.

Yosemite Valley Lodge MOTEL **$$$**
(Map p688; 209-372-1001, reservations 888-413-8869; www.travelyosemite.com; 9006 Yosemite Lodge Dr; r from $260;) A short walk from Yosemite Falls, this low-slung complex contains a wide range of eateries, a lively bar, a big pool and other amenities. The rooms, spread out over 15 buildings, feel like they're a cross between a motel and a lodge, with rustic wooden furniture and nature photography. Rooms have cable TV, fridge and coffeemaker, and small patios or balcony panoramas.

Check-in can take a long time, and wi-fi is available but spotty and slow. Parking is free but fills up quickly for the day. Around 8pm it becomes easy to find a spot.

Tioga Road & Tuolumne Meadows

Tuolumne Meadows Campground CAMPGROUND **$**
(Map p682; www.nps.gov/yose; Tioga Rd; tent & RV sites $26; Jul-Sep;) At 8600ft, this is the biggest campground in the park, with 304 fairly well-spaced campsites (half of which can be reserved).

Porcupine Flat Campground CAMPGROUND **$**
(Map p682; www.nps.gov/yose; tent & RV sites $12; Jul–mid-Oct;) Primitive 52-site area at 8100ft; some campsites near the road.

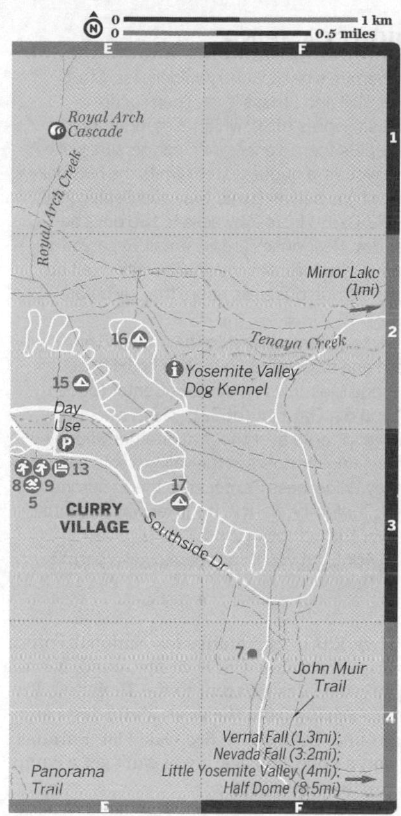

Yosemite Valley

Tamarack Flat Campground CAMPGROUND $
(Map p682; www.nps.gov/yose; Old Big Oak Flat Rd; tent sites $12; late Jun-Sep;) Quiet and primitive (pit toilets only) at 6315ft; the 52 tent sites are a rough 3-mile drive off Tioga Rd. Despite its relatively secluded location, you'll need to show up early to snag a spot, especially on weekends. Bring plenty of water.

White Wolf Campground CAMPGROUND $
(Map p682; www.nps.gov/yose; tent & RV sites $18; Jul-early Sep;) Attractive setting at 7700ft, but the 74 campsites are fairly boxed in. Trailheads for Harden and Lukens Lake hikes are nearby.

Yosemite Creek Campground CAMPGROUND $
(Map p682; www.nps.gov/yose; tent sites $12; Jul-early Sep;) The most secluded and quiet campground (7700ft) in the park is reached via a rough 4.5-mile road. There are 75 first-come, first-served primitive campsites (no potable water).

Tuolumne Meadows Lodge CABIN $$
(Map p682; reservations 888-413-8869; www.travelyosemite.com; tent cabins $160; mid-Jun–mid-Sep) Set amid the magnificent high country, about 60 miles from Yosemite Valley off Tioga Rd, this option attracts hikers to its 69 canvas tent cabins with two or four beds each, a wood-burning stove and candles (no electricity); showers available. Breakfast and dinner are offered (surcharge applies; dinner reservations required). A fork of the Tuolumne River runs through the property.

White Wolf Lodge CABIN $$
(Map p682; www.travelyosemite.com/lodging/white-wolf-lodge; White Wolf Rd; tent cabins without bath $153, cabins $185; Jun-early Sep) This complex enjoys its own little world a mile

WILDERNESS PERMITS FOR OVERNIGHT CAMPING

Shedding the high-season crowds is easiest in Yosemite's backcountry wilderness. Start by identifying a route that matches your schedule, skill and fitness level. Then secure a wilderness permit (www.nps.gov/yose/planyourvisit/wpres.htm), which is mandatory for overnight trips. The advance reservation fee is $5, plus there's a fee of $5 per person; walk-ins are free. To prevent tent cities sprouting in the woods, a quota system limits the number of people leaving from each trailhead each day. For trips between mid-May and September, 60% of the quota may be reserved by fax (209-372-0739) from 24 weeks to two days before your trip. Only one application per group per day. Responses are via email. Reservation requests made by phone (209-372-0740) are processed after the lottery. Permits must be picked up at a permit station by 10am the day of or during business hours the day before the hike.

The remainder of the permits are distributed by the office closest to the trailhead on a first-come, first-served basis (beginning at 11am one day before your planned hike) at Yosemite Valley Wilderness Center (p693), Tuolumne Meadows Wilderness Center (p692) and the information stations at Wawona (p693) and Big Oak Flat (p692). Hikers who turn up at the wilderness center nearest the trailhead get priority over those at another wilderness center. For example, if a person who's been waiting for hours in the valley wants the last permit left for Lyell Canyon, the Yosemite Valley Wilderness Center calls the Tuolumne Meadows Wilderness Center to see if any hikers in Tuolumne want it. If a hiker waltzing into the Tuolumne office says 'yes!', they get priority over the person in the valley.

Reservations are not available from October to April, but you'll still need to get a permit by self-registering at the park.

up a spur road, away from the hubbub and traffic of Hwy 120 and Yosemite Valley. There are 24 spartan four-bedded tent cabins without electricity and four very in-demand hard-walled cabins that feel like rustic motel rooms. The generator cuts out at 11pm, so you'll need a flashlight until early morning.

There's also a dining room with somewhat overpriced fare and a counter-service store.

Hetch Hetchy & Big Oak Flat Road

Crane Flat Campground CAMPGROUND $

(Map p682; www.nps.gov/yose; Big Oak Flat Rd; tent & RV sites $26; Jul–mid-Oct;) Large family campground at 6192ft, with 166 sites; reservations required. The Clark Range overlook hike, 4 miles out and back, begins here.

Hodgdon Meadow Campground CAMPGROUND $

(Map p682; www.nps.gov/yose; Tuolumne Grove Rd; tent & RV sites $18-26; year-round;) Utilitarian and crowded 105-site campground at 4900ft; reservations required mid-April to mid-October.

Dimond O Campground CAMPGROUND $

(Map p682; 877-444-6777; www.recreation.gov; Evergreen Rd; tent & RV sites $26; May-Sep) Away from the valley bustle and 4 miles off Hwy 120 in the Stanislaus National Forest, this reservable USFS campground has 35 forested sites adjacent to the Tuolumne River. Arriving from the west, it's the last campground before the Big Oak Flat Entrance, and a good fallback if you can't get a campsite inside the park.

★Rush Creek Lodge LODGE $$$

(Map p682; 209-379-2373; www.rushcreeklodge.com; 34001 Hwy 120; r & 2-bedroom villas $360-545;) Luxurious country chic sums up this fabulous family-friendly resort surrounded by the Stanislaus National Forest and situated a half-mile from Yosemite's Big Oak Flat Entrance. Most rooms have a deck with mountain views. Villas and lodge rooms feature colorful sliding barn doors, industrial-style luggage racks and internet-connected radios. The large pool and giant hot tubs are the property's social hub.

Evergreen Lodge CABIN $$$

(Map p682; 209-379-2606; www.evergreenlodge.com; 33160 Evergreen Rd, Groveland; tents $120-155, cabins $230-495; usually closed Jan–mid-Feb;) Outside Yosemite National Park, near the entrance to Hetch Hetchy, this classic, nearly century-old resort consists of lovingly decorated and comfy cabins (each with its own cache of board games) spread among the trees. Accommodations run from rustic to deluxe, and all cabins have private porches without a distracting phone or TV. Roughing-it guests can cheat with comfy, prefurnished tents.

Wawona & Glacier Point Road

Bridalveil Creek Campground CAMPGROUND $
(Map p682; www.nps.gov/yose; tent & RV sites $18; Jul-Sep;) Quieter than the Yosemite Valley campgrounds, with 110 sites at 7200ft.

Wawona Campground CAMPGROUND $
(Map p682; www.nps.gov/yose; Wawona; tent & RV sites $18-26; year-round;) Delightful riverside setting at 4000ft with 93 well-spaced campsites; reservations required May to September.

Wawona Hotel HISTORIC HOTEL $$
(Map p682; reservations 888-413-8869; www.travelyosemite.com; 8308 Wawona Rd; r with/without bath from $220/150; mid-Mar–late Nov & mid-Dec–early Jan;) This National Historic Landmark, dating from 1879, is a collection of six graceful, whitewashed New England–style buildings flanked by wide porches. The 104 rooms – with no phone or TV – have Victorian-style furniture and other period items, and about half the rooms share bathrooms, with nice robes provided for the walk there. Wi-fi is available in the annex building only.

The grounds are lovely and fairly idyllic on sunny spring days, with a spacious lawn dotted with Adirondack chairs.

Eating

You can find food options for all budgets and palates within the park, from breakfast burritos to swanky cuts of top-notch steak. All places carry good vegetarian options. The **Village Store** (Map p688; Yosemite Village; 8am-8pm, to 10pm summer) has the best selection (including health-food items and some organic produce), while stores at Curry Village, Wawona, Tuolumne Meadows and the Yosemite Valley Lodge are more limited.

Base Camp Eatery CAFETERIA $
(Map p688; Yosemite Valley Lodge, 9006 Yosemite Lodge Dr, Yosemite Valley; mains $8-17; 6:30am-10pm, to 8pm winter;) Formerly a dated and stodgy food court, this large space has been completely redesigned and modernized. Several self-service stations serve a variety of cuisines, including Asian-style noodle dishes, artisan pizzas, healthy salads and the usual burgers and chicken tenders. And whatever your view on things (park staff are generally enthused), it's a bit startling to find a Starbucks attached.

Degnan's Loft BARBECUE $
(Map p688; www.travelyosemite.com; Yosemite Village; mains $14-18; noon-9pm;) Above Degnan's Kitchen, off Village Dr, the redesigned Loft does solid portions of barbecue (ribs, pulled pork, brisket and pulled chicken) along with a small menu of appetizers. The airy space has high-beamed ceilings, a fireplace and TVs showing live sports.

Meadow Grill FAST FOOD $
(Map p688; Curry Village; mains $7.25; 7-10am & 2-7pm mid-Apr–Sep;) Order at the window on a deck near the parking window from a varied menu that includes a tasty pad Thai shrimp 'burger,' a chicken pot pie and a pork-and-lemongrass rice bowl. Even when lines are long, the food's served up fairly quickly.

Tuolumne Meadows Grill FAST FOOD $
(Map p682; Tioga Rd; mains $5-12; 8am-6pm Jun–mid-Sep;) You can hardly say you've visited Tuolumne without scoffing down a chili dog or burger in the parking lot in front of the Tuolumne Meadows Grill. The soft-serve ice-cream cones and hearty breakfasts – not to mention the people-watching at the picnic tables – are equally mandatory.

Village Grill FAST FOOD $
(Map p688; Yosemite Village; mains $6-13; 11am-6pm mid-Mar–Oct;) Fight the chipmunks for burgers, hot sandwiches, wraps, chili, salads and fries alfresco. Expect crowds and lines.

★ **Evergreen Lodge** AMERICAN $$
(Map p682; 209-379-2606; www.evergreenlodge.com; 33160 Evergreen Rd; breakfast & lunch mains $12-19, dinner mains $15-34; 7-10:30am, noon-3pm & 5-10pm;) Creative and satisfying, the Evergreen's restaurant serves some of the best meals around, with big and delicious breakfasts, three types of burger (Black Angus beef, buffalo and veggie) and dinner choices including rib-eye steak, lobster risotto and vegetarian chickpea curry.

The homey wooden tavern is a perennial favorite for evening cocktails, beers on tap over a game of pool and live music on select weekends. A general store fills the gaps with to-go sandwiches, snacks and dreamy gelato.

Ahwahnee Dining Room CALIFORNIAN $$$
(Map p688; ☎209-372-1489; Ahwahnee, 1 Ahwahnee Dr, Yosemite Valley; mains breakfast $11-19, lunch $15-22, dinner $27-48; ⏰7-10am & 11:30am-3pm Mon-Sat, 5:30-9pm daily;) The formal ambience (mind your manners!) may not be for everybody, but few would not be awed by the sumptuous decor, soaring beamed ceiling and palatial chandeliers here. The menu is constantly in flux, but most dishes have perfect pitch and are beautifully presented. There's a dress code at dinner, but otherwise shorts and sneakers are OK.

Sunday brunch (adult/child $55/22; 7am to 2pm) is amazing. Reservations highly recommended for brunch and dinner.

Drinking & Nightlife

No one will mistake Yosemite for nightlife central, but there are some nice spots to relax with a cabernet, cocktail or cold beer. Closest options outside the park include the Yosemite Bug Rustic Mountain Resort (p696), Rush Creek Lodge (p690) and Evergreen Lodge (p690), all with lively lounges in high season.

Mountain Room BAR
(Map p688; ☎209-372-1403; www.travelyosemite.com; Yosemite Valley Lodge, 9006 Yosemite Lodge Dr; ⏰4:30-10pm Mon-Fri, from noon Sat & Sun) Catch up on the latest sports news while knocking back draft brews at this large bar that buzzes in wintertime. The food menu (mains $8 to $21) features nachos, sandwiches and chili. Order a s'mores kit (graham crackers, chocolate squares and marshmallows) to roast in the open-pit Swedish-style fireplace.

Ahwahnee Bar BAR
(Map p688; ☎209-372-1489; www.travelyosemite.com; Ahwahnee, 1 Ahwahnee Dr, Yosemite Valley; ⏰11:30am-11pm) The perfect way to experience the Ahwahnee without dipping too deep into your pockets is to settle in for a drink at this cozy bar completely remodeled in 2016. Appetizers and light meals ($11 to $23) provide sustenance.

Entertainment

In addition to events at the Yosemite Theater, other activities scheduled year-round include campfire programs, twilight strolls, night-sky watching, and ranger talks and slide shows. The tavern at the Evergreen Lodge (p690) has live bands some weekends. Scan the *Yosemite Guide* for full details.

Yosemite Theater THEATER
(Map p688; www.yosemiteconservancy.org/yosemite-theater; ⏰9:30am-4:30pm; ; shuttle stops 5 & 9) FREE Behind the Yosemite Valley Visitor Center, this theater screens two films: Ken Burns' *Yosemite: A Gathering of Spirit*, a celebration of the Yosemite Grant's 150th anniversary; and the painfully dramatic but beautifully photographed *Spirit of Yosemite*. The movies alternate, starting every half-hour between 9:30am and 4:30pm (from noon on Sunday), and offer a free, air-conditioned respite from the summer heat.

At 7pm, take your pick from a rotating selection of films (adult/child $10/free). Actor Lee Stetson portrays the fascinating life and philosophy of John Muir, and park ranger Shelton Johnson recreates the experiences of a buffalo soldier. Other films explore search-and-rescue missions and rock climbing in the park. There are also special children's shows.

Information

Yosemite's entrance fee is $35 per vehicle, $30 per motorcycle or $20 for those on a bicycle or on foot and is valid for seven consecutive days. Passes are sold (you can use cash, checks, traveler's checks or credit/debit cards) at the various entrance stations, as well as at visitor centers in Oakhurst, Groveland, Mariposa and Lee Vining. Upon entering the park, you'll receive a National Park Service (NPS) map and a copy of the seasonal *Yosemite Guide* newspaper, which includes an activity schedule and current opening hours of all facilities. The official NPS website (www.nps.gov/yose) has the most comprehensive and current information.

For recorded park information, campground availability, and road and weather conditions, call 209-372-0200.

The park has a bare-bones **dog kennel** (Map p688; ☎209-372-8326; www.travelyosemite.com/discover/travel-tips/pets; Yosemite Valley Stable; per dog per day $8.75; ⏰late May-early Sep), at which dogs are kept in outdoor cages (no food is allowed, due to wildlife concerns) and stay unattended. No overnight stays are allowed. You must provide a written copy of vet immunization records. Reservations are strongly recommended.

Big Oak Flat Information Station (Map p682; ☎209-372-0200; ⏰8am-5pm late May-late Oct) Has a wilderness-permit desk.

Tuolumne Meadows Visitor Center (Map p682; ☎209-372-0263; ⏰8am-5pm Jun-Sep) Information desk, bookstore and small exhibits on the area's wildlife and history.

Tuolumne Meadows Wilderness Center (Map p682; ☎209-372-0309; ⏰8am-5pm late May–mid-Oct) Issues wilderness permits.

Wawona Visitor Center (Map p682; ☎209-375-9531; Wawona; ⊙8:30am-5pm May-Oct) Located off Wawona Rd in the historic studio of artist Thomas Hill; has information and issues wilderness permits.

Yosemite Valley Visitor Center (Map p688; ☎209-372-0200; www.nps.gov/yose; 9035 Village Dr, Yosemite Village; ⊙9am-5pm) Park's busiest information desk. Shares space with bookstore run by Yosemite Conservancy and part of the museum complex in the center of Yosemite Village.

Yosemite Valley Wilderness Center (Map p688; ☎209-372-0308; Yosemite Village; ⊙8am-5pm May-Oct) Wilderness permits, maps and back-country advice.

DANGERS & ANNOYANCES

Hiking in the wilderness is no joke. And most of Yosemite is wilderness. However, even the front country can be dangerous. There's a reason the exploits of Yosemite's search-and-rescue teams have been documented in a film and a book, *Off the Wall: Death in Yosemite*, about all of the fatalities that have occurred in the park (there were 16 in 2019, about the average for the last several years). Two experienced climbers tragically fell to their deaths from El Capitan and another was killed by rockfall in 2018. Strong winds knock down branches and trees on well-trodden valley paths and selfie-seekers take undue risks near cliff edges.

Landslides frequently close trails and steep paths get slippery after rains and flooding. Sometimes the valley itself can flood, whereupon the park closes and visitors are told to leave with little warning.

Wild animals can transmit diseases, namely lyme, rabies, plague and hantavirus cardio pulmonary syndrome (HCPS), a serious and sometimes fatal respiratory illness. Avoid direct contact with and exposure to animal droppings, especially those of rodents – even those charming-looking squirrels, chipmunks and marmots. And never touch a dead one! This means avoiding sleeping on the ground; always use a cot, hammock, sleeping bag or other surface.

Yosemite is prime black-bear habitat. However, according to the National Park Service, there has never been a bear attack resulting in a fatality or serious injury in Yosemite. Incidents do happen. However, these are down dramatically, from 165 in 2014 to only 22 in 2019. Follow park rules on proper food storage and utilize bear-proof food lockers when parked overnight.

Mountain-lion sightings are uncommon but possible. If you see one, do not run; rather, attempt to scare it away by shouting and waving your arms. The same warning applies for coyotes, which are more frequently seen. Report sightings to park dispatch (209-372-0476).

Mosquitoes can be pesky in summer, especially at high elevations in August, so bug spray's not a bad idea. And please don't feed those squirrels. They may look cute but they've got a nasty bite.

INTERNET ACCESS

Yosemite Valley Lodge (p688), Ahwahnee (p687), Curry Village (p687) and Wawona Hotel (p691) offer free wi-fi to guests.

MEDICAL SERVICES

Yosemite Medical Clinic (☎209-372-4637, emergency 911; 9000 Ahwahnee Dr, Yosemite Village; ⊙9am-7pm Mon-Fri early Jun-early Jul, 9am-7pm Mon-Sat late Jul–mid-Sep, to 5pm Mon-Fri late Sep-late May) A 24-hour emergency service is available.

MONEY

Stores in Yosemite Village, Curry Village and Wawona all have ATMs, as do Yosemite Valley Lodge (p688) and Ahwahnee (p687).

POST

The main **post office** (Map p688; 9017 Village Dr; ⊙8:30am-5pm Mon-Fri, 10am-noon Sat) is in Yosemite Village, but **Wawona** (Map p682; ☎209-375-6574; 1 Forest Dr, Wawona; ⊙9am-5pm Mon-Fri, to noon Sat) and the **Yosemite Valley Lodge** (Map p688; 9006 Yosemite Lodge Dr; ⊙12:30-2:45pm Mon-Fri) also have year-round services. A seasonal branch operates in **Tuolumne Meadows** (Map p682; ☎209-372-8236; ⊙9am-5pm Mon-Fri, to noon Sat, closed mid-Sep–mid-Jun).

TELEPHONE

There are pay phones at every developed location throughout the park. Cell-phone reception is sketchy, depending on your location; AT&T and Verizon have the only coverage and both are generally good in the Yosemite Village area.

Getting There & Away

CAR & MOTORCYCLE

Yosemite is accessible year-round from the west (via Hwys 120 W and 140) and south (Hwy 41), and in summer also from the east (via Hwy 120 E). Roads are plowed in winter, but snow chains may be required at any time. Rock slides have periodically shut down sections of road for weeks or months at a time.

Gas up year-round at Wawona or Crane Flat inside the park (you'll pay dearly), at El Portal on Hwy 140 just outside its western boundary, or at Lee Vining at the junction of Hwys 120 and 395 outside the park in the east.

PUBLIC TRANSPORTATION

Yosemite is one of the few national parks that can easily be reached by public transportation. Greyhound (p779) buses and Amtrak (p779) trains serve Merced, west of the park, where they are met by buses operated by the **Yosemite Area Regional Transportation System** (YARTS; ☎877-989-2787; www.yarts.com), and you can buy Amtrak tickets that include the YARTS segment all the way into the park. Buses travel to Yosemite Valley along Hwy 140 several times daily year-round, with a variety of stops at hotels and post offices in Midpines and El Portal along the way.

From May to September, YARTS buses also run from the Fresno airport along Hwy 41 to Yosemite Valley with stops at Tenaya Lodge in Fish Camp (one way/return $12/23), just a few miles south of the park; another at Mariposa Grove just inside the entrance; the Wawona store; and finally at Yosemite Valley Visitor Center (one way/return $18/34). The only downside is it's a slow ride: it's a full four hours from Fresno to the valley.

In summer (roughly June through September), another YARTS bus route, called the Trans-Sierra connection, runs from Mammoth Lakes along Hwy 395 to Yosemite Valley via Hwy 120. One-way tickets to Yosemite Valley are $19 ($9 child and senior, three hours) from Merced (bus route 15) and $26 ($15 child and senior, 3½ hours) from Mammoth Lakes, less if boarding in between.

YARTS fares include the park entrance fee, making them a super bargain, and drivers accept credit cards.

Getting Around

BICYCLE

Cycling is an ideal way to take in the Yosemite Valley. You can rent a wide-handled cruiser ($12/34 per hour/day) or a bike with an attached child trailer ($20/61 per hour/day) at **Yosemite Valley Lodge** (Map p688; ⏰8am-6pm summer only, weather dependent) or in **Curry Village** (Map p688; ⏰10am-4pm Mar-Oct). Strollers and wheelchairs are also rented here. Or download the Yosemite Bike Share mobile app, which has several pickup locations throughout the valley, including at Camp 4 (p687).

CAR

Roadside signs with red bears mark the many spots where bears have been hit by motorists (more than 400 collisions since 1995), so think before you hit the accelerator, and follow the poky posted speed limits – they are strictly enforced. Valley visitors are advised to park and take advantage of the Yosemite Valley Shuttle Bus. Even so, traffic in the valley can feel like rush hour in LA.

Glacier Point and Tioga Rds are closed in winter. Even if driving a rental vehicle, sometimes tire chains are required and it's recommended to always have them on hand from November to March.

Nonguests can generally park in the lots for Curry Village, Valley Lodge and the Ahwahnee during the day – dashboard parking permits for guests only are checked after 5pm.

The closest gas station to the Valley is in El Portal, which you have to leave the park to access, 15 miles away. Next best, and in the park, is at Crane Flat, a little over 17 miles away. **Wawona Chevron** (Hwy 41; ⏰24hr) has high-priced gas, but it's the only option between Oakhurst and Yosemite Valley. Electric-vehicle charging stations are located in the parking lot of the Village Store and the Ahwahnee.

Village Garage (☎209-372-8320; Village Dr; ⏰9am-5pm, towing 24hr) provides emergency repairs and even gasoline when you're in an absolute fix.

For the latest on road conditions, call the 24-hour National Park Service line at 209-372-0200.

PUBLIC TRANSPORTATION

The free, air-conditioned **Yosemite Valley Shuttle Bus** (www.nps.gov/yose/planyourvisit/publictransportation.htm; ⏰7am-10pm) is a comfortable and efficient way of traveling around the park. Buses operate year-round from 7am to 10pm at 10- to 20-minute intervals and stop at 21 numbered locations, including parking lots, campgrounds, trailheads and lodges. These get very crowded in late spring and summer. For a route map, see the *Yosemite Guide* or check www.nps.gov/yose/planyourvisit/upload/valleyshuttle.pdf.

Free buses also operate between Yosemite Valley and the Badger Pass Ski Area (winter only). The **Tuolumne Meadows Shuttle** (1 way adult/child 5-12yr $9/4.50; ⏰7am-7pm Jun–mid-Sep) runs between Tuolumne Lodge and Olmsted Point in Tuolumne Meadows (usually mid-June to early September), and the **El Capitan Shuttle** runs a summertime valley loop from Yosemite Village to El Capitan.

Two fee-based hikers' buses also travel from Yosemite Valley. For trailheads along Tioga Rd, catch the **Tuolumne Meadows Hikers' Bus** (☎888-413-8869; www.travelyosemite.com), which runs once daily in each direction. Fares depend on distance traveled; the trip to Tuolumne Meadows costs $14.50/23 one way/return. The **Glacier Point Hikers' Bus** (Map p688; ☎888-413-8869; 1 way/return $28.50/57; ⏰mid-May–Oct) is good for hikers as well as for people reluctant to drive up the long, windy road themselves. Reservations are required.

YOSEMITE GATEWAYS

Fish Camp

Fish Camp, just south of Yosemite's South entrance (and the Mariposa Grove) on Hwy 41, is more of a bend in the road than a destination, but it does have some good lodging options as well as the ever-popular **Sugar Pine Railroad** (☎559-683-7273; www.ymsprr.com; 56001 Hwy 41; rides adult/child $28/16; ⏰mid-Mar–Oct;) .

Sleeping & Eating

Summerdale Campground CAMPGROUND $
(Map p682; www.fs.usda.gov; Hwy 41; tent & RV sites $30-34; ⏰May-Sep;) The closest campground to Yosemite (only 1.5 miles away off Hwy 41), Summerdale is a pleasant spot along Big Creek, with 28 well-dispersed sites in a grassy meadow with trees for shade. Each campsite has a picnic table, a grill and a campfire ring. Vault toilets and potable water are available. It can be booked online.

White Chief Mountain Lodge MOTEL $$
(Map p682; ☎559-683-5444; www.whitechiefmountainlodge.com; 7776 White Chief Mountain Rd; r $159-179; ⏰Apr-Oct; P) The cheapest and most basic option in Fish Camp, this 1950s-era motel has 26 simple kitchenette rooms with outdated furnishings. Rooms include coffee machines, refrigerators and cable TV. It's located a few hundred yards east of Hwy 41; look for the sign and go up the wooded country road.

Tenaya Lodge HOTEL $$$
(Map p682; ☎800-514-2167, 559-683-6555; www.tenayalodge.com; 1122 Hwy 41; r $235-650; P @) A sprawling complex just 2 miles from Yosemite's south entrance, this large resort, conference center and upscale spa is ideal for families looking for a rustic luxury feel. Activities range from mountain biking and flashlight hikes to archery and movie nights. It has three pools, a games room kids won't want to leave, four restaurants and a general store.

Narrow Gauge Inn AMERICAN $$
(Map p682; ☎559-683-7720; 48571 Hwy 41; mains $15-25; ⏰7:30am-9:30 & 5:30-9pm late Apr-Oct; P) Excellent food and knockout views make the dining experience at Narrow Gauge Inn one of the finest in the Yosemite region. The dinners are creatively prepared, including dishes like seafood pasta, New York steak, and Parmesan and truffle risotto. The menu changes each season. The old-fashioned lodge-like atmosphere is casual and slightly elegant, and the windows look out on lush mountain vistas.

Oakhurst

Although only about 16 miles south of Yosemite's southern entrance (and the Mariposa Grove), at the junction of Hwys 41 and 49, Oakhurst feels worlds away from the park's natural majesty. It's the most quotidian of Yosemite's gateway towns: think strip malls and fast-food joints. For park-goers it functions primarily as a convenient service town, and it's your last chance to stock up on reasonably priced groceries, gasoline and camping supplies.

Sleeping & Eating

A mini chain-hotel building boom, all with the same owners, on Hwy 41 a few miles north of the center of town will add several hundred new rooms in the next year or so.

SIERRA VISTA SCENIC BYWAY

Set entirely within Sierra National Forest, this scenic route follows USFS roads in a 100-mile loop that takes you from 3300ft to over 7300ft. Along the way are dramatic vistas, peaks, domes, thick forest, excellent fishing, and camping almost anywhere you like (dispersed camping is allowed in most areas). It's a great way for car campers – and curious day trippers – to lose themselves within the mountains.

From its start in **North Fork**, the route takes a half-day to complete, emerging on Hwy 41 a few miles north of **Oakhurst**. Highlights include **Mile High Vista** with views of popular fishing spot Mammoth Pool, plus plenty of tranquil mountain streams and quiet hikes. The road is only open from June to November and is paved most of the way, but it's narrow and laced with curves. See www.fs.usda.gov for a map, information on sights and the best overlooks and places to explore.

★**Sierra Sky Ranch** LODGE $$
(☎559-683-8040; www.sierraskyranch.com; 50552 Road 632; r $99-304;) This 1875 former ranch is now part of the Ascend collection, and is great value. It encompasses 14 attractive acres with cozy homespun rooms and double doors that open onto shady verandas. The rambling and beautiful old lodge has vintage Western furniture, high-quality bedding and comfortable lounging areas with fruit, tea and coffee always available. The recently renovated restaurant is atmospheric at night.

Hounds Tooth Inn B&B $$
(☎559-642-6600; www.houndstoothinn.com; 42071 Hwy 41; r $140-260;) Perched on a slope just north of Oakhurst, this whitewashed garden B&B is swimming in rosebushes and Victorianesque charm. Its 12 individually designed airy rooms and two cottages, some with spas and fireplaces, have a slight English-manor-house feel. Complimentary wine, hot drinks and snacks are available in the afternoon, a chance to socialize with other travelers and experience the inn's superior service.

South Gate Brewing Company PUB FOOD $$
(☎559-692-2739; wwwsouthgatebrewco.com; 40233 Enterprise Dr; mains $12-29; 11am-8pm Sun-Thu, to 9pm Fri & Sat;) About a quarter-mile west of the junction of Hwys 41 and 49, this popular microbrewery-pub serves primo burgers (made with grass-fed beef), brick-oven pizzas, sandwiches and salads. Try a Glacier Point pale ale with a bacon Deadwood Porter barbecue burger or the blonde-ale-battered fish and chips. Steaks, meatloaf and pasta served too. Sit at the bar and chat to locals.

★**Erna's Elderberry House** CALIFORNIAN, FRENCH $$$
(☎559-683-6860; www.chateausureau.com/ernas-elderberry-house-restaurant; Château du Sureau, 48688 Victoria Lane; prix-fixe dinner $75-112, Sun brunch mains $18-24, tasting menu $68; brunch 11am-1pm Sun, dinner 5.30-8pm daily;) With wall tapestries, oil paintings and ornate chandeliers, the Californian-French restaurant at **Château du Sureau** (☎559-683-6860; www.chateausureau.com; 48688 Victoria Lane; r $385-645, 2-bedroom villas $2950;) could be a castle. But you don't have to be royalty to eat at this haute-cuisine restaurant, which boasts excellent service. Dishes change frequently and range from caramelized-onion velouté and foie-gras parfait to truffle gnocchi and dark-chocolate-raspberry torte.

Merced River Canyon

The approach to Yosemite via Hwy 140 is one of the most scenic routes to the park, especially the section that meanders through Merced River Canyon. The springtime runoff makes this a spectacular spot for **river rafting**. Right outside the Arch Rock entrance, and primarily inhabited by park employees, **El Portal** is a convenient Yosemite base.

The canyon is a top spot for **river rafting**, with many miles of class III and IV rapids (age minimums vary with water levels). Worldwide rafting operators with solid reputations run trips in the area.

Sleeping & Eating

★**Yosemite Bug Rustic Mountain Resort** HOSTEL $
(Map p682; ☎209-966-6666; www.yosemitebug.com; 6979 Hwy 140, Midpines; tent sites/dm/tent cabins from $25/39/65, r from $85, with shared bath from $65;) This friendly, folksy place, tucked away on a forested hillside about 25 miles from Yosemite, feels like an oasis. A range of accommodations lines its narrow ridges: cabins, dorms, private rooms and permanent tents. The highly recommended **June Bug Cafe** (mains $8-24; 7-10am, 11am-2pm & 6-9pm;) alone is worth the trip, as are the massages and spa with hot tub and yoga studio ($12 per day).

Autocamp CARAVAN PARK $$$
(Map p682; ☎888-405-7553; www.autocamp.com; Hwy 140, Midpines; $220-280;) This isn't your grandpa's RV park. Brought to you by a Bay Area tech start-up in partnership with REI, these Airstream trailers and canvas tents offer an experience that feels like a cross between a luxurious safari camp and a mid-century modern design store.

Mariposa

About halfway between Merced and Yosemite Valley, Mariposa (Spanish for 'butterfly') is the largest and most interesting town near Yosemite National Park. Established as a mining and railroad town during the gold rush, it has the oldest courthouse in continuous use (since 1854) west of the Mississippi, loads of Old West pioneer character and a couple of good museums dedicated to the area's heritage, plus annual festivals celebrating the history of the place.

Rock hounds should drive to the Mariposa County Fairgrounds, 2 miles south of town on Hwy 49, to see the 13lb 'Fricot Nugget' – the largest crystallized gold specimen from the California gold-rush era – and other gems and machinery at the **California State Mining & Mineral Museum** (Map p682; ☎209-742-7625; www.parks.ca.gov/?page_id=588; 5005 Fairgrounds Rd; adult/under 13yr $4/free; ⊙10am-5pm Thu-Sun May-Sep, to 4pm Oct-Apr). An exhibit on glow-in-the-dark minerals is also very cool.

Sleeping & Eating

In high season, Mariposa chain hotels, often booked several months in advance, are a distinctly bad value. Generic offerings run $200 to $400. At research time several were being upgraded and run by more upmarket brands such as Marriott.

Many of the town's restaurants have unreliable opening hours or close too early for visitors returning to Mariposa after long days in the park.

Mariposa Hotel Inn HISTORIC HOTEL **$$**
(☎209-966-7500; www.mariposahotelinn.com; 5029 Hwy 140; r $140-160;) This atmospheric, creaky 1901 building is filled with things from the past. Old photos, mirrors, newspaper clippings and an antique phone with a vintage earpiece hang on the corridor's walls, while vintage chairs, beds and dressers decorate the six king or queen rooms. Room 6 has a claw-foot tub. Hummingbirds love the flowery back patio where breakfast is served.

★**Happy Burger** DINER **$**
(☎209-966-2719; www.happyburgerdiner.com; cnr 5120 Hwy 140 & 12th St; mains $8-14; ⊙6am-9pm;) Burgers, fries and shakes served with a heavy dose of Americana kitsch. Happy Burger, decorated with old album covers, boasts the largest menu in the Sierra. It's also one of the cheaper meals in town. Besides burgers, there's sandwiches, Mexican food, salads and a ton of sinful ice-cream desserts. Patio games and a 'doggy dining area' can be found outdoors.

You can call and order in advance and pick up your food at the restaurant's to-go window.

Savoury's AMERICAN **$$**
(☎209-966-7677; 5034 Hwy 140; mains $18-43; ⊙5-9:30pm;) Upscale yet casual Savoury's is the best restaurant in town. Black-lacquered tables and contemporary art create tranquil window dressing for dishes like caramelized pork chop prepared with Sierra cider, pan-seared scallops with ginger and orange zest, Cajun-spiced New York steak with pan-seared onions, and crab cakes with cilantro-lime aioli.

Information

Mariposa County Visitor Center (☎209-966-2456; www.mariposachamber.org/visitor-center; 5158 Hwy 140, cnr Hwy 49; ⊙8am-5pm;) Helpful staff and racks of brochures; plus public restrooms and an escape-room experience.

Getting There & Away

YARTS (YARTS; ☎209-388-9589, 877-989-2787; www.yarts.com; one way $5-16) buses run year-round along Hwy 140 into Yosemite Valley ($8 one way, 1¾ hours), stopping at the Mariposa visitor center. Tickets include admission to Yosemite. There are several services per day, usually running between 6am and 8pm.

Groveland

From the Big Oak Flat entrance to Yosemite it's 22 miles to Groveland, a tiny, welcoming town with restored gold rush–era buildings and several recommended places to overnight. The approach from the west involves a fairly dramatic, steep mountain climb with switchbacks.

About 15 miles east of Groveland, in the Stanislaus National Forest, **Rainbow Pool** (www.fs.usda.gov/stanislaus; P) FREE is a popular swimming hole with a small cascade; it's signed on the south side of Hwy 120.

Sleeping

★**Groveland Hotel** HOTEL **$$**
(☎209-962-4000; www.groveland.com; 18767 Main St; r $149-200, ste $225-295; @) Run exceptionally well, the historic and tastefully decorated Groveland dates from 1850. Behind the elegant facade are 18 bright, stylish rooms with wooden platform beds and white linen; some give subtle nods to the Old West, including cow hides and carved headboards. Rooms also have wraparound verandas and coffee machines. Suites come with Murphy beds and sleep up to four.

There's plenty of patio space, and the hotel's restaurant, **Provisions Taproom & Bourbon Bar** (Groveland Hotel, 18767 Main St; mains $16-23) serves a small, chef-driven, constantly changing menu with hard-to-find craft beers in an atmospheric wood-floored room.

Hotel Charlotte BOUTIQUE HOTEL **$$**
(☎209-962-6455; www.hotelcharlotte.com; 18736 Main St; r $159-275;) Casually sophisticated and designed with a mix of contemporary touches and vintage chintz, the Charlotte, now under new ownership, is as charming as ever. Ask for one of the rooms with beautifully restored claw-foot bathtubs. For families, the Grand Suites sleep three to five. A sophisticated restaurant opened in 2019 with a new menu and chef.

Blackberry Inn Bed & Breakfast B&B **$$$**
(☎209-962-4663; www.blackberry-inn.com; 7567 Hamilton Station Loop; r $255-315; ⊙mid-Mar–Oct;) On a rural road off Hwy 120, this stunning yellow-and-white house and newer wing of suites offer sumptuous rooms with wraparound porches, stained-glass scenes of Yosemite, soaking tubs, and electric fireplaces that give off real heat and a cozy ambience. The *big* breakfasts can be delivered to your room or patio so you can spy on the hummingbirds. Two-night minimum stay.

Eating & Drinking

Mountain Sage CAFE **$**
(18653 Main St; drinks $2-6, snacks $4-8; ⊙7am-5pm summer, 7am-3pm Thu-Mon winter, later for ad hoc events;) This popular cafe, serving fair-trade coffee and tasty baked treats, is also an art gallery, nursery and live-music venue that runs an excellent summer **concert series**. It's the site of a Saturday farmers market in summertime. Smoothies, homemade quiche, cookies, breakfast burritos, oatmeal and other goodies are also available.

Cocina Michoacana MEXICAN **$**
(☎209-962-6651; 18730 Main St; mains $10-18, à la carte tacos from $4.40; ⊙10am-10pm) Quick and friendly service and large servings of tasty Mexican fare make this long-running restaurant popular with locals. There's a large menu, with familiar dishes such as carne asada, steak ranchero, burritos and fajitas. The chicken mole is especially recommended and there's a good selection of Mexican beer. Decor is simple: wooden tables, and traditional Mexican artifacts on the walls.

★Iron Door Grill & Saloon BAR
(☎209-962-8904; www.irondoorsaloon.com; 18761 Main St; ⊙restaurant 7am-10pm, bar 11am-1am, shorter hours winter) Claiming to be the oldest bar in the state (established in 1852, when it served liquor to thirsty miners), the Iron Door is a friendly, atmospheric place, with swinging doors, a giant bar, high ceilings, mounted animal heads and hundreds of dollar bills tacked to the ceiling. It has live music on some weekends and also hosts open-mic and karaoke nights.

The kitchen serves steaks, ribs and pasta dishes, as well as bar standards such as chicken fingers and burgers (mains $11 to $27).

SEQUOIA & KINGS CANYON NATIONAL PARKS

The twin parks of Sequoia and Kings Canyon (p611) dazzle with superlatives, though they're often overshadowed by Yosemite, their smaller neighbor to the north (a three-hour drive away). With towering forests of giant sequoias containing some of the largest trees in the world and the mighty Kings River careening through the depths of Kings Canyon (one of the deepest chasms in the country), the parks are lesser-visited jewels where it's easier to find quiet and solitude. Throw in opportunities for caving, rock climbing and backcountry hiking through granite-carved Sierra landscapes as well as backdoor access to 14,494ft Mt Whitney – the tallest peak in the lower 48 states – and you have all the ingredients for two of the best parks in the country.

Giant sequoia groves, underground marble caves, sculpted granite domes, jagged high-altitude peaks and wildflower meadows where mule deer and black bears graze are just a small taste of what you'll see in both the national parks and nearby national forest lands. If the weather spoils your outdoor plans, the Giant Forest Museum (p705), plus the educational exhibits and short nature films at park visitor centers, are welcome indoor diversions.

History

In 1890 Sequoia became the second national park in the USA (after Yellowstone). A few days later, the 4 sq miles around Grant Grove were declared General Grant National Park and, in 1940, absorbed into the newly created Kings Canyon National Park. In 2000, to protect additional sequoia groves, vast tracts of land in the surrounding national forest became the Giant Sequoia National Monument.

OVERNIGHT BACKPACKING

More than 850 miles of maintained trails await your footsteps in both national parks. From sun-bleached granite peaks soaring above alpine lakes to wildflower-strewn meadows and gushing waterfalls, it's backpacking heaven. Mineral King, Lodgepole and Cedar Grove offer the best backcountry trail access, while the Jennie Lakes Wilderness in the Sequoia National Forest boasts pristine meadows and lakes at lower elevations.

Park-approved, bear-proof food canisters, which are always recommended, are mandatory in some places, especially for wilderness trips (eg Rae Lakes Loop). Rent canisters at park visitor centers and trailhead ranger stations or at the Lodgepole, Grant Grove and Cedar Grove Village markets (from $5 per three day trip). To prevent wildfires, campfires are only allowed in existing campfire rings in some backcountry areas.

Kings Canyon National Park

With a dramatic cleft deeper than the Grand Canyon, rugged Kings Canyon offers true adventure to those who crave seemingly endless verdant trails, rushing streams and gargantuan rock formations. The camping, backcountry exploring and climbing here are all superb. While its neighbor, Sequoia National Park, gets all the glory, Kings Canyon also has groves of enormous sequoias and its trails are far less trafficked. Grant Grove is where you'll find General Grant, the second-largest tree in the world. Peaks more than 14,000ft high occupy other parts of the park, most of which is designated wilderness, although the main road, Kings Canyon Scenic Byway (Hwy 180; only open end April to October), is quite the drive – it twists and bends through some of the most dramatic scenery in California. The Big Stump Entrance (p704), not far from Grant Grove Village, is Kings Canyon National Park's only entrance station.

Sights & Activities

Find markets, lodging, showers and visitor information at two developed areas within Kings Canyon National Park. Grant Grove Village is only 4 miles past Big Stump Entrance (in the park's west), while **Cedar Grove Village** (Map p700), with a simple lodge, market and cafe, is 31 miles east at the bottom of the canyon. The two are separated by the Giant Sequoia National Monument and are linked by Kings Canyon Scenic Byway (Hwy 180).

General Grant Grove FOREST

(Map p700; N Grove Trail; P) This sequoia grove off Generals Hwy is astounding. The paved half-mile **General Grant Tree Trail** is an interpretive walk that visits a number of mature sequoias, including the 27-story **General Grant Tree**. This giant holds triple honors as the world's second-largest living tree, a memorial to US soldiers killed in war and the nation's official Christmas tree since 1926. The nearby **Fallen Monarch**, a massive, fire-hollowed trunk you can walk through, has been cabin, hotel, saloon and stables.

To escape the bustling crowds, follow the more secluded 1.5-mile **North Grove Loop**, which passes wildflower patches and bubbling creeks as it gently winds underneath a canopy of stately sequoias, evergreen pines and aromatic incense cedars.

The magnificence of this ancient sequoia grove was nationally recognized in 1890 when Congress first designated it General Grant National Park. It took another half-century for this tiny parcel to be absorbed into the much larger Kings Canyon National Park, established in 1940 to prevent damming of the Kings River. Information booklets are available at the trail for $1.50 (use the honesty box). The main trail takes roughly 30 minutes, with plenty of time to read information boards.

Mist Falls WATERFALL

(Map p700; Road's End, Hwy 180) One of the most popular destinations for a day hike from the Cedar Grove area of Kings Canyon, Mist Falls is an Edenic spot, with massive boulders, interesting rock formations and soaring views on the way. It's ideal for a picnic and a rest before you turn back or venture higher into the backcountry.

The trail starts next to the Road's End Wilderness Permit Station. At quieter times of the year, prescribed fires are enabled in the area; there will be notifications of these at the trails when they are happening.

Panoramic Point VIEWPOINT

(Map p700; summer only) For a breathtaking view of Kings Canyon, head 2.3 miles up

Sequoia & Kings Canyon National Parks

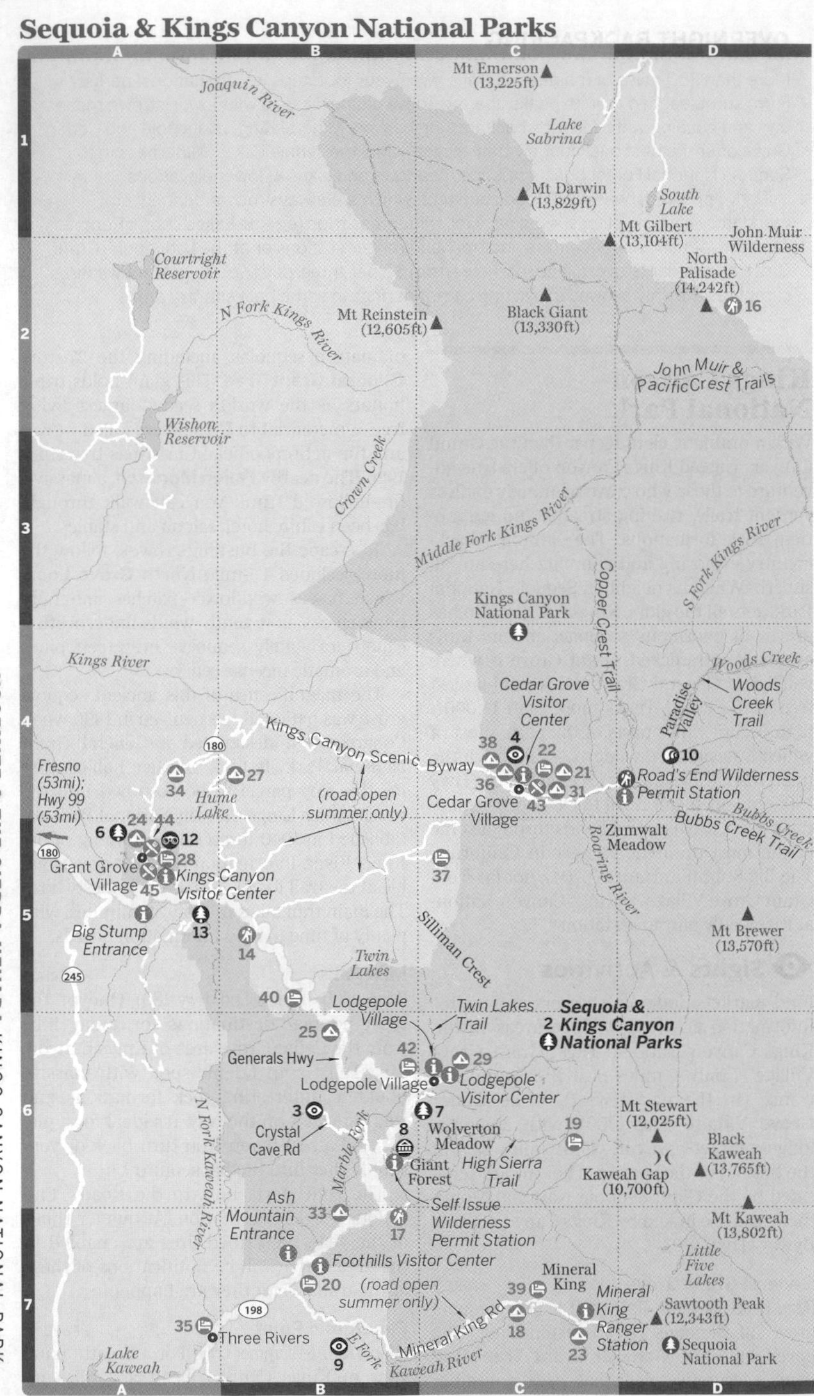

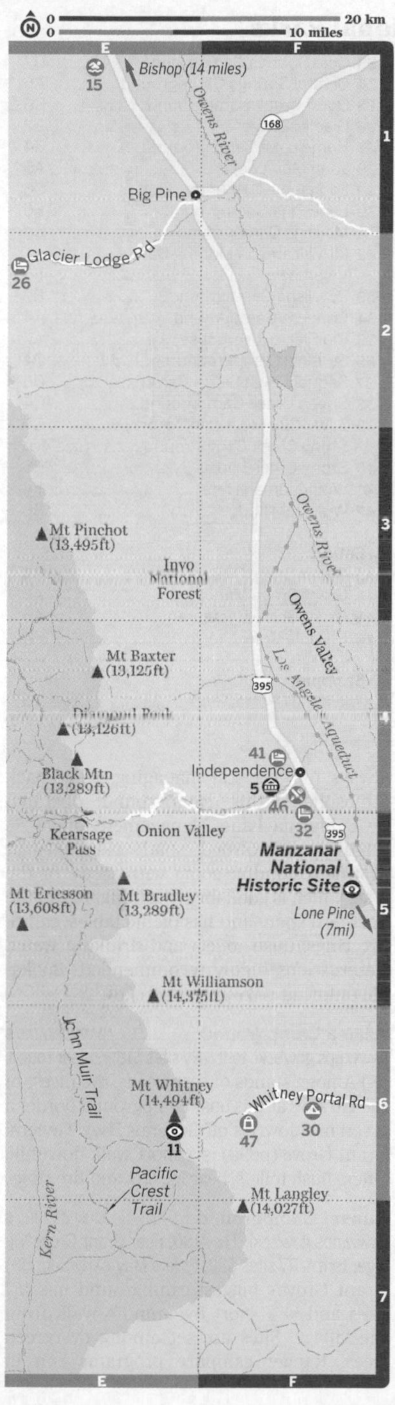

narrow, steep and winding Panoramic Point Rd (trailers and RVs aren't recommended), which branches off Hwy 180. Follow a short paved trail uphill from the parking lot to the viewpoint, where precipitous canyons and the snowcapped peaks of the Great Western Divide unfold below you. In winter, snow closes the road to vehicles and it becomes a cross-country ski, snowshoe or Yak-Trak route.

Hikers may access the road when snow levels are low. From Grant Grove's visitor center, follow the paved side road east, turning left after 0.1 miles, then right at the John Muir Lodge.

Redwood Canyon FOREST
(Map p700; road closed winter) More than 15,000 sequoias cluster in Redwood Canyon, making it one of the world's largest groves of these giant trees. In an almost-forgotten corner of the park, this secluded forest lets you revel in the grandeur of the trees away from the crowds while you hike mostly moderate trails. What you won't find here, however, are any of the California coast's redwoods – that's what early pioneers mistook these giant sequoias for, hence the erroneous name.

For the best view of this area, hike to the summit of **Big Baldy** (Map p700; Generals Hwy). Alternatively, you can walk in the forest via trailheads at the end of a bumpy 2-mile dirt road (closed in winter) that starts across from the Hume Lake/Quail Flat signed intersection on the Generals Hwy, just over 5 miles southeast of Grant Grove Village. There's also a good spot for a picnic before heading out on a hike.

Sleeping & Eating

Accommodations (and pay showers) are offered in Grant Grove and Cedar Grove Villages. Unless otherwise stated, apart from the campsites, facilities in Cedar Grove Village don't start operating until mid-May.

Potential campers should keep in mind that there are great free, uncrowded and undeveloped campgrounds off Big Meadows Rd in the Sequoia National Forest. They're some of the only empty campsites in the Sierra Nevada during the peak summer season. Free roadside car camping is also allowed near Hume Lake, but no campfires are allowed without a permit (available from the Grant Grove Visitor Center). Wilderness camping permits cost $10 (plus an additional $5 in quota season).

Sequoia & Kings Canyon National Parks

Top Sights
1 Manzanar National Historic Site F5
2 Sequoia & Kings Canyon National Parks C6

Sights
3 Cave B6
4 Cedar Grove C4
5 Eastern California Museum F4
6 General Grant Grove A5
General Sherman Tree .... (see 7)
7 Giant Forest C6
8 Giant Forest Museum B6
9 Mineral King B7
10 Mist Falls D4
11 Mt Whitney E6
12 Panoramic Point A5
13 Redwood Canyon A5

Activities, Courses & Tours
14 Big Baldy Trailhead B5
15 Keough's Hot Springs E1
16 Palisade Glacier Trail D2
17 Paradise Creek Trail B7

Sleeping
18 Atwell Mill Campground C7
19 Bearpaw High Sierra Camp C6
Buckeye Flat Campground .... (see 17)
20 Buckeye Tree Lodge B7
21 Canyon View Campground C4
22 Cedar Grove Lodge C4
23 Cold Springs Campground C7
24 Crystal Springs Campground A5
25 Dorst Creek Campground B6
26 Glacier Lodge E2
27 Hume Lake Campground B4
28 John Muir Lodge A5
29 Lodgepole Campground C6
30 Lone Pine Campground F6
31 Moraine Campground C4
32 Mt Williamson Motel & Base Camp F5
33 Potwisha Campground B7
34 Princess Campground A4
35 Rio Sierra Riverhouse A7
36 Sentinel Campground C4
37 Sequoia High Sierra Camp C5
38 Sheep Creek Campground C4
39 Silver City Mountain Resort C7
Stony Creek Campground .... (see 40)
40 Stony Creek Lodge B5
41 Winnedumah Hotel F4
42 Wuksachi Lodge B6

Eating
43 Cedar Grove Grill C4
44 Grant Grove Market A5
45 Grant Grove Restaurant A5
46 Still Life Cafe F4

Shopping
47 Whitney Portal Store F6

Grant Grove

Crystal Springs Campground CAMPGROUND $
(Map p700; www.recreation.gov; Crystal Springs Rd; tent & RV sites $18-40; mid-May–Sep;) At the smallest campground in the Grant Grove area, off Generals Hwy, 14 midsize group sites and 36 standard campsites are available. It also has picnic tables, fire rings, bear boxes, flush toilets and potable water. Online booking is possible.

Princess Campground CAMPGROUND $
(Map p700; www.fs.usda.gov; Hwy 180; tent & RV sites $27-29; late May-late Sep;) Just off the scenic byway and only a few miles from Hume Lake, almost 90 reservable sites border a pretty meadow, with sequoia stumps at the registration area. It's especially popular with RVs. Vault toilets, drinking water, picnic tables, fire rings and bear lockers are available. Reservations essential.

Hume Lake Campground CAMPGROUND $
(Map p700; www.fs.usda.gov; Hume Lake Rd; tent & RV sites $27; mid-May–mid-Sep;) Almost always full, yet still managing a laid-back atmosphere, this campground operated by California Land Management offers 65 relatively uncrowded, shady campsites at 5250ft. A handful come with views of the lake, which is good for swimming. It's on the northern shore and has picnic tables, campfire rings, flush toilets and drinking water. Reservations highly recommended. Bookable online at www.recreation.gov.

Azalea Campground CAMPGROUND $
(www.nps.gov/seki; tent & RV sites $18; year-round;) Among stands of evergreens, the nicest of the 110 sites at this busy campground border a green meadow. It's off Generals Hwy; General Grant Grove (p699) is a short walk downhill. Offers flush toilets, bear lockers and fire rings.

Sunset Campground CAMPGROUND $
(www.nps.gov/seki; Hwy 180, near Grant Grove Village; tent & RV sites $22; late May-early Sep;) Grant Grove's biggest campground has 157 sites and is a short five-minute walk from the village. Sites are set among evergreen trees. Ranger campfire programs run in

summer. Two large group sites are also available (with space for 15 to 30 people). Flush toilets, water, bear lockers, fire rings and picnic benches are available.

Grant Grove Cabins CABIN $

(877-436-9617; www.visitsequoiakingscanyon.com; 86728 Hwy 180, Grant Grove Village; cabins $100-170; May-Oct;) Set amid towering sugar pines, the accommodations here include aging tent-top shacks, rustic cabins with electricity and outdoor wood-burning stoves, and heated duplexes (a few wheelchair accessible) with private bathrooms and double beds (and new mattresses). Number 9 is the lone hard-sided, free-standing 'Honeymoon Cabin' with a queen bed, and it books up fast. Registration is at John Muir Lodge.

John Muir Lodge LODGE $$$

(Map p700; 877-436-9617; www.visitsequoiakingscanyon.com; 86728 Hwy 180, Grant Grove Village; r $250-280; P) An atmospheric building hung with historical black-and-white photographs, this is a place to lay your head and still feel like you're in the forest. Wide porches have rocking chairs, and homespun rooms contain rough-hewn wooden furniture and patchwork bedspreads. On chilly nights, cozy up to the big stone fireplace with a board game.

Grant Grove Market MARKET $

(Map p700; Hwy 180, Grant Grove Village; 8am-9pm late May-early Sep, 8am-7pm Apr-late May & early Sep-Oct) This small, newly renovated grocery store has firewood, camping supplies, sweet treats and a good range of packaged food, with a small selection of fruit and veggies, as well as sandwiches and microwavable pizza. There's also an ATM.

Grant Grove Restaurant AMERICAN $$

(Map p700; Hwy 180, Grant Grove Village; mains $8-30; 7-10am, 11:30am-3:30pm & 5-9pm late May-early Sep, to 8pm Apr-late May & early Sep-Oct;) After undergoing a top-to-bottom renovation in 2017, this is the best place for a meal (albeit competition is limited) in Grant Grove Village. The menu focuses on local produce and highlights seasonal dishes. Enjoy fresh berries, organic granola, fair-trade coffee and San Joaquin Valley–raised eggs for breakfast, and California grass-fed beef for dinner. Service can be slow.

An indoor-outdoor deck and courtyard seating are available. The lodge was constructed using materials recycled from the old structure.

Cedar Grove

Cedar Grove's **Sentinel Campground** (Map p700; www.nps.gov/seki; Hwy 180, Cedar Grove Village; tent & RV sites $22; late Apr-early Nov; P), next to the village area, is open whenever Hwy 180 is open; **Sheep Creek** (Map p700; www.nps.gov/seki; Hwy 180, Cedar Grove Village; tent & RV sites $18; late May–mid-Sep), **Canyon View** (Map p700; www.nps.gov/seki; Hwy 180; tent sites $40-60; late May-Sep) (tent only) and **Moraine** (Map p700; www.nps.gov/seki; Hwy 180; tent & RV sites $18; late May-early Sep) are opened for overflow when needed. These campgrounds are usually the last to fill up on busy summer weekends and are also good bets early and late in the season, thanks to their comparatively low elevation (4600ft). All have flush toilets.

Cedar Grove Lodge LODGE $$

(Map p700; 559-565-3096; www.visitsequoia.com; 108260 West Side Dr, Cedar Grove Village; r $150; mid-May–mid-Oct; P) The only indoor sleeping option in the canyon, this riverside lodge offers 21 simple motel-style rooms. Three ground-floor rooms with shady furnished patios have spiffy river views and kitchenettes. All rooms have phones. Guests can pick up complimentary coffee at the next-door market.

★ **Sequoia High Sierra Camp** CABIN $$$

(Map p700; 866-654-2877; www.sequoiahighsierracamp.com; tent cabins with shared bath incl all meals $500; early Jun–mid-Sep) A mile's hike into the Sequoia National Forest, this off-the-grid resort is nirvana for those who don't think luxury camping is an oxymoron. Canvas bungalows are spiffed up with pillow-top mattresses, feather pillows and cozy wool rugs. Restrooms and a shower house are shared. Reservations and usually a two-night minimum stay are required. Prices based on two people per tent.

Cedar Grove Grill AMERICAN $

(Map p700; Hwy 180, Cedar Grove Village; breakfast $6-11, lunch & dinner mains $7-19; 7am-9pm mid-May–mid-Oct;) This former greasy spoon has been reborn as a simple cafe (and gift shop with basic food supplies) with a more sophisticated menu, including breakfast burritos in the morning and trout, rice bowls and steak for lunch and dinner. Dine outside on the redesigned riverside deck. Next door are an ATM and showers (open summer only), also recently remodeled.

Information

Cedar Grove Visitor Center (Map p700; ☎559-565-3793; Hwy 180, Cedar Grove Village; ⏲9am-5pm late May-late Sep) Small, seasonal visitor center selling books and maps.

Kings Canyon Visitor Center (Map p700; ☎559-565-4307; www.nps.gov/seki; Hwy 180, Grant Grove Village; ⏲8am-5pm summer, hours vary rest of year) The park's main facility, with a bookstore and gift shop.

Road's End Wilderness Permit Station (Map p700; Hwy 180; ⏲usually 7am-3:30pm late May-late Sep) Dispenses wilderness permits, rents bear canisters and sells a few trail guides and maps. It's 6 miles east of Cedar Grove Village, at the end of Hwy 180.

Getting There & Away

BUS

There are no shuttle buses in Kings Canyon.

CAR & MOTORCYCLE

From the west, Kings Canyon Scenic Byway (Hwy 180) travels 53 miles east from Fresno through some bucolic rural scenery to the **Big Stump Entrance** (Map p700; Hwy 180; per car $30). Coming from the south, you're in for a 46-mile drive through Sequoia National Park along sinuous Generals Hwy. Budget about two hours' driving time from the Ash Mountain Entrance (p709) to Grant Grove Village. The road to Cedar Grove Village (along the eastern end of Kings Canyon Scenic Byway, otherwise known as Hwy 180), with white-knuckle twists and drop-offs, is only open from around April or May until the first snowfall.

Sequoia National Park

Picture unzipping your tent flap and crawling out into a 'front yard' of trees as high as a 20-story building and as old as the Bible. Brew some coffee as you plan your day of adventures in this extraordinary park with its soul-sustaining forests and gigantic peaks soaring above 12,000ft. Choose to gaze at dagger-sized stalactites in a 10,000-year-old cave, view the largest living tree on earth, climb 350 steps to a granite dome with soaring views of the snowcapped Great Western Divide or drive through a hole in a 2000-year-old log. All that before you've even walked a trail – where the wild scenes (and brief encounters with black bears) will give you goosebumps, charging waterfalls will leave you awestruck, and epic overnight backpacking trips will lead you to deserted lakes and idyllic backcountry camps.

Sights

Many of the park's star attractions are conveniently lined up along the Generals Hwy, which starts at the Ash Mountain Entrance (p709) and continues north into Kings Canyon and onto the Kings Canyon Scenic Byway. Most tourist activity concentrates in the Giant Forest area and in **Lodgepole Village** (Map p700). The road to remote Mineral King veers off Hwy 198 in the town of Three Rivers, just south of the park's Ash Mountain Entrance.

Giant Forest FOREST

(Map p700) This 3-sq-mile grove off Generals Hwy protects the park's most gargantuan tree specimens. Among them is the world's biggest by volume, the **General Sherman** (Map p700) tree, rocketing 275ft into the sky. Pay your respects via a short descent from the Wolverton Rd parking lot, or join the Congress Trail, a paved 2-mile pathway that takes in General Sherman, the Washington Tree (the world's second-biggest sequoia) and the see-through Telescope Tree. The 5-mile Trail of the Sequoias helps you lose the crowds.

The top destination in the park, Giant Forest was named by John Muir in 1875. At one point over 300 buildings, including campgrounds and a lodge, encroached upon the sequoias' delicate root systems. In 1997, recognizing this adverse impact, the park began to remove structures and resite parking lots. It also introduced a convenient, free seasonal visitor shuttle, significantly cutting traffic congestion and reducing the potential harm to these majestic trees.

Mineral King HISTORIC SITE

(Map p700; Mineral King Rd) A scenic subalpine valley at 7500ft, Mineral King is Sequoia's backpacking mecca and a good place to find solitude. Gorgeous and gigantic, its glacially sculpted valley is ringed by massive mountains, including the jagged 12,343ft Sawtooth Peak. The area is reached via Mineral King Rd – a slinky, steep and narrow 25-mile road not suitable for RVs or speed demons; it's usually open from late May through October. Plan on spending the night unless you don't mind driving the three-hour round trip.

Giant Forest Museum MUSEUM

(Map p700; ☎559-565-3341; www.nps.gov/seki; 47050 Generals Hwy; ⏲9am-4:30pm winter, to 6pm summer; P) FREE For a primer on the intriguing ecology and history of giant sequoias, this pint-size modern museum will entertain both kids and adults. Hands-on exhibits teach about the life stages of these big trees, which can live for more than 3000 years, and the fire cycle that releases their seeds and allows them to sprout on bare soil. The museum is housed in a historic 1920s building designed by Gilbert Stanley Underwood, famed architect of the Ahwahnee (p681).

The museum is crushed with visitors in summer. To avoid parking headaches, take the free in-park shuttle bus. You can also try the information desk here when the Lodgepole Visitor Center is closed in winter. During winter, the **self-issue wilderness permit station** is located to the right of the main entrance.

Activities

With an average elevation of about 2000ft, the foothills in the park's south are much drier and warmer than the rest of the park. Hiking here is best in spring, when the air is still cool and wildflowers put on a colorful show. Summers are buggy and muggy, but fall again brings moderate temperatures and lush foliage.

Swimming holes abound along the Marble Fork of the Kaweah River, especially near Potwisha Campground. Be careful, though – the currents can be deadly, especially when the river is swollen from the spring runoff.

Sleeping & Eating

The one lodge in the main section of the park proper also has the park's one true sit-down restaurant. Two other lodges are in the adjoining Sequoia National Forest, and Grant Grove Village in Kings Canyon has a couple of options. Three Rivers, just outside the Ash Mountain Entrance (p709), has the widest choice of accommodations. Otherwise, camping is the easiest and most inexpensive way to go.

Generals Highway

A handful of campgrounds line the highway and rarely fill up, although space may get tight on holiday weekends. Those in the foothills area in the south of the park are best in spring and fall when the higher elevations are still chilly, but they get hot and buggy in summer. Unless noted, sites are available on a first-come, first-served basis. Wilderness camping is free with permits (free between November and mid-May, $15 per permit thereafter). Stop by a visitor center or ranger station for details or for a fire permit (if you are not in a designated campsite). Lodgepole Village and Stony Creek Lodge (p708) (late May to October) have pay showers; the former also has a good **market** to stock up on food and other supplies, as well as a **cafe** serving breakfast burritos, burgers, chicken sandwiches and prepared salads.

During the summer, a mobile **food cart** stocked with sandwiches is parked near the General Sherman tree.

Stony Creek Campground CAMPGROUND $
(Map p700; www.fs.usda.gov; tent & RV sites $27; mid-May–late Sep;) A mile north of the national-park boundary near Stony Creek Lodge, this forest campground operated by California Land Management fills with families in summer. Its nearly 50 sites are spacious and shady. Flush toilets, drinking water, bear lockers, fire rings and an amphitheater are also on-site.

Lodgepole Campground CAMPGROUND $
(Map p700; www.nps.gov/seki; Lodgepole Rd; tent & RV sites $22, mid-Apr–late Nov;) Closest to the Giant Forest area, with more than 200 closely packed sites, this place fills quickly because of its proximity to Kaweah River swimming holes and Lodgepole Village amenities. The 16 walk-in sites are more private. Flush toilets, picnic tables, fire rings, drinking water and bear lockers are available.

Potwisha Campground CAMPGROUND $
(Map p700; www.recreation.gov; tent & RV sites $22; year-round;) Popular campground with decent shade near swimming spots on the Kaweah River. It's 3 miles northeast of the Ash Mountain Entrance, with 42 sites. There are flush toilets, bear lockers, picnic benches and fire pits. Reservations (highly recommended) taken May through September.

Dorst Creek Campground CAMPGROUND $
(Map p700; www.recreation.gov; Generals Hwy; tent & RV sites $22; late Jun-early Sep;) A big and busy campground with more than 200 sites. The quieter back sites are for tents only, while the front loops can fill with RVs. It's about 7 miles northwest of Wuksachi Village and is bookable online. It has picnic tables, fire rings, bear lockers and water (when water supply is low, the campsite may close).

Buckeye Flat Campground CAMPGROUND $
(Map p700; www.nps.gov/seki; Buckeye Flat Campground Access Rd; tent sites $22; Apr-late Sep;) This well-maintained, well-shaded,

HIKING IN SEQUOIA & KINGS CANYON NATIONAL PARKS

NAME	REGION	DESCRIPTION	DIFFICULTY
Big Baldy Trail	Grant Grove	hike up to a granite dome with valley views & epic soaring vistas	moderate
Big Stump Trail	Big Stump Entrance	gentle loop forest trail around grassy meadows & the history of logging	easy
Big Trees Trail	Giant Forest	paved, kid-friendly interpretive trail circling a sequoia-bordered forest meadow	easy
Crescent Meadow Loop	Giant Forest	beautiful subalpine meadow ringed by giant sequoias & summer wildflowers	easy
General Grant Tree Trail	Grant Grove	paved interpretive loop through a giant-sequoia grove	easy
General Sherman Tree to Moro Rock	Giant Forest	huge sequoias, peaceful meadows & the pinnacle of Moro Rock	moderate
High Sierra Trail to Lone Pine Creek (via Bearpaw High Sierra Camp)	Giant Forest	gorgeous sequoia-grove & canyon-view hike, crossing mountain streams	difficult
Hump Trail	Wolverton	heart-racing walk through woodland to a peaceful lake	moderate
Lakes Trail	Wolverton	forest climb to a string of gorgeous alpine lakes	moderate
Little Baldy	Lodgepole	leg-stretching climb to a granite dome with spectacular views and mountain panoramas	moderate
Marble Falls	Foothills	lower-elevation hike parallels a river canyon to a thundering cascade	moderate
Mist Falls	Cedar Grove	partly shaded forest & granite hike to a gushing waterfall	moderate
Monarch Lakes	Mineral King	high-country hike to two alpine lakes at base of Sawtooth Peak	difficult
Moro Rock	Giant Forest	steep granite dome ascent for panoramic peak & canyon views	easy
Paradise Creek Trail	Three Rivers	riverside amble through moss-covered forest, with river crossings & pleated valley views	easy
Rae Lakes Loop	Cedar Grove	passes a chain of jewel-like lakes in the heart of the Sierra Nevada high country	difficult
Tokopah Falls	Lodgepole	one of Sequoia's largest, most easily accessed scenic waterfalls	easy

DURATION	ROUND-TRIP DISTANCE (MILES)	ELEVATION CHANGE (FT)	FEATURES	FACILITIES
2-3hr	4.5	+600	woodland; views	
45min-1hr	1.9	+200	woodland; history	restrooms; picnic benches
45min	1.2	+100	wildlife-watching; great for families	restrooms; drinking water; transportation to trailhead
1hr	1.6	+200	wildlife-watching; great for families	restrooms; drinking water; transportation to trailhead
30min	0.5	+100	view; great for families	restrooms; drinking water
2½-4hr	6	+1600	wildlife-watching; view; rock climbing	restrooms; drinking water; transportation to trailhead
3 days+	32	+2200	wildlife-watching; views, water crossings	restrooms; drinking water; ranger station; backcountry campsite
3-6hr	8.2	+2000	wildlife-watching; lake	restrooms; transportation to trailhead
2 days	12.6	+2000	backpacking; lakes	restrooms; transportation to trailhead
1½-2½hr	3.8	+660	wildlife-watching; view	
3-4hr	7	+2000	view; waterfall	restrooms; drinking water
3-5hr	8	+800	view; waterfall	restrooms; drinking water; ranger station
4-6hr	8.5	+2700	wildlife-watching; view	restrooms; drinking water; backcountry campsite; swimming
40min	0.5	+300	view; great for families; rock climbing	transportation to trailhead
2-2½hr	6	+520	view; spring wildflowers; rivers	restrooms; drinking water
5 days+	40	+7000	wildlife-watching; view; waterfall	restrooms; drinking water; ranger station; backcountry campsite
2hr	3.5	+500	wildlife-watching; view; great for families; waterfall	restrooms; drinking water; transportation to trailhead

tent-only campground is off Generals Hwy about 6 miles northeast of the Ash Mountain Entrance, down a winding road that's off-limits to RVs and trailers. It has water, fire rings and grills, bear lockers and clean flush toilets. There's access to the **Paradise Creek Trail** (Map p700; Buckeye Campground, Buckeye Rd), with close passage to the rushing Paradise Creek river and falls.

Stony Creek Lodge LODGE **$$**
(Map p700; ☎877-828-1440, reservations 559-565-3388; www.sequoia-kingscanyon.com; 65569 Generals Hwy; r $210-318; ⏲mid-May–early Oct; P 📶) About halfway between Grant Grove Village and Giant Forest, this wood-and-stone lodge has a big river-rock fireplace in its lobby and 11 aging motel rooms with private bathrooms, telephones and TVs.

Wuksachi Lodge LODGE **$$**
(Map p700; ☎information 866-807-3598, reservations 888-252-5757; www.visitsequoia.com; 64740 Wuksachi Way; r $123-340; ⏲restaurant 7-10am, noon-2pm & 5:30-8pm; P 📶) Built in 1999, Wuksachi Lodge is the park's most upscale option. But don't get too excited: the wood-paneled atrium lobby has an inviting stone fireplace and forest views, but the motel-style rooms are fairly generic, with coffeemakers, mini-fridges, oak furniture and thin walls. The location near Lodgepole Village, however, is lovely, and staff members are friendly and accommodating.

Backcountry

Bearpaw High Sierra Camp CABIN **$$**
(Map p700; ☎reservations 866-807-3598; www.visitsequoia.com/bearpaw.aspx; tw tents per person incl breakfast & dinner $360; ⏲usually mid-Jun–mid-Sep) An 11.3-mile hike east of Crescent Meadow on the High Sierra Trail, this canvas-tent village at 7800ft is ideal for exploring the backcountry without lugging your own gear. Rates for each of the six tents include showers, dinner and breakfast, as well as bedding and towels. Bookings start at 7am PST every January 2 and places sell out almost immediately.

Mineral King

Mineral King's two pretty campgrounds, **Atwell Mill** (Map p700; www.nps.gov/seki; Mineral King Rd; tent sites $12; ⏲late May-late Oct; 🐾) and **Cold Springs** (Map p700; www.nps.gov/seki; Mineral King Rd; tent sites $12; ⏲late May-late Oct; 🐾), often fill up on summer weekends. Pay showers are available at the rustic **Silver City Mountain Resort** (Map p700; ☎559-561-3223; www.silvercityresort.com; Mineral King Rd; cabins with/without bath from $205/165, largest cabin from $495; ⏲late May-late Oct; 📶), the only food-and-lodging option anywhere near these parts.

Three Rivers

Named for the nearby convergence of three Kaweah River forks, Three Rivers is a friendly small town outside the park populated mostly by retirees and artsy newcomers. The town's main drag, Sierra Dr (Hwy 198), is sparsely lined with small motels, eateries and shops. Day trippers in need of supplies should fill up here before entering the park. Those in need of creature comforts will find it a convenient overnight base, with cozy lodgings, campsites, showers and plenty of wi-fi options.

South Fork Campground CAMPGROUND **$**
(www.nps.gov/seki; South Fork Rd; tent sites $6, mid-Oct–late May free; ⏲year-round) Remote, little-used, tent-only campground on the river. It's 13 miles from Three Rivers at the end of a beautiful but slightly hair-raising drive off Hwy 198. The road snakes around the mountain and becomes partly unpaved, rough and narrow. You may encounter cattle. Bear lockers, fire rings and vault toilets are available, but no water from mid-October until late May.

Rio Sierra Riverhouse INN **$$**
(Map p700; ☎833-239-7450; www.rio-sierra.com; 41997 Sierra Dr; d $195-285; ⏲Feb-Dec; ❄📶) Beside the river, a stone's throw from the national park, this cottage-style inn rents four suites, each with TV-DVD player, telephone, mini-fridge and microwave. For more privacy, you can rent the entire property (all four units). The river's beach area includes lounge chairs, a hammock, a barbecue, a river walk, campfire rings and s'mores (for those booking the whole property).

Buckeye Tree Lodge MOTEL **$$**
(Map p700; ☎559-561-5900; www.buckeyetreelodge.com; 46000 Sierra Dr; d & cabins $180-260; ❄📶🏊🐾) 🍃 Sit out on your grassy back patio or perch on the balcony and watch the river ease through a maze of boulders. Fairly generic motel rooms, one with a kitchenette, feel airy. The picnic area has barbecue grills. One cabin, a three bedroom named 'River House,' sleeps up to 10 people. Breakfast includes muffins, fruit and juice.

Information

Foothills Visitor Center (Map p700; ☎559-565-4212; 47050 Generals Hwy; ⊙8am-4:30pm, hours vary winter) Just past the Ash Mountain Entrance; a good place to stop, get your bearings, check trail info and check out campground availability further up the road.

Lodgepole Visitor Center (Map p700; ☎559-565-4436; 63100 Lodgepole Rd, Lodgepole Village; ⊙7am-5pm late May–mid-Oct) Often less helpful or informative than other park visitor centers; non-NPS staff members sell books and maps, and rangers issue wilderness permits at this seasonal tourist-info stop. Complex includes grocery store, gift shop, grab-and-go cafe, coin-operated showers and laundry facilities. Off Generals Hwy.

Mineral King Ranger Station (Map p700; ☎559-565-3768; Mineral King Rd; ⊙8am-4pm late May-late Sep) Almost 24 miles east of Three Rivers; small, seasonal ranger station issuing wilderness permits, renting bear canisters and selling a few books and maps.

Getting There & Around

BUS

Sequoia Shuttle (☎877-287-4453; www.sequoiashuttle.com; round trip incl park entry $20; ⊙6am-6:30pm late May-late Sep) buses run five times daily between the town of Visalia and the Giant Forest Museum ($20, 2½ hours) via Three Rivers; reservations required. Cost includes park admission fee. Once inside the park, the shuttle provides free transportation on four loop routes with pickups every 15 to 20 minutes.

CAR & MOTORCYCLE

Hwy 198 runs north from Visalia through Three Rivers past Mineral King Rd to the **Ash Mountain Entrance** (Map p700; Generals Hwy; car/walk-in/motorcycle $35/20/30). Beyond here, the road continues as the Generals Hwy, a narrow and windy road snaking all the way into Kings Canyon National Park, where it joins the Kings Canyon Scenic Byway (Hwy 180) near the western Big Stump Entrance (p704). Vehicles more than 22ft long may have trouble negotiating the steep road, with its many hairpin curves. Budget at least one hour to drive from the entrance to the Giant Forest/Lodgepole area and at least another hour from there to Grant Grove Village in Kings Canyon.

There are no gas stations in the park proper; fill up your tank before you arrive in the park. Those in need can find **gas** (☎559-305-7770; 64144 Hume Lake Rd; ⊙pumps 24hr, credit card only after hours, market 8am-noon & 1-5pm) year-round at Hume Lake (11 miles north of Grant Grove in Kings Canyon).

EASTERN SIERRA

Cloud-dappled hills and sun-streaked mountaintops dabbed with snow typify the landscape of the Eastern Sierra, where slashing peaks – many over 14,000ft – rush abruptly upward from the arid expanses of the Great Basin and Mojave Deserts. It's a dramatic juxtaposition that makes for a potent cocktail of scenery. Pine forests, lush meadows, ice-blue lakes, simmering hot springs and glacier-gouged canyons are only some of the beautiful sights you'll find in this region.

The Eastern Sierra Scenic Byway, officially known as Hwy 395, runs the entire length of the range. Turnoffs dead-ending at the foot of the mountains deliver you to pristine wilderness and countless trails, including the famous Pacific Crest Trail, John Muir Trail and main Mt Whitney Trail. The most important portals are the towns of Bridgeport, Mammoth Lakes, Bishop and Lone Pine. Note that in winter, when traffic thins, many facilities, attractions and smaller roads are closed.

Information

Check out www.thesierraweb.com for area events and links to local visitor information, and *Sierra Wave* (www.sierrawave.net) for regional news.

The **Eastern Sierra Interpretive Association** (www.sierraforever.org) runs talks, guided hikes and youth programs and is an overall excellent source of information on conservation and environmental issues.

Getting There & Around

The Eastern Sierra is easiest to explore under your own steam. Keep in mind that some mountain roads close in winter, as do most of the passes that take you over the Sierras from east to west, including Tioga Rd (Hwy 120) to Yosemite.

BUS

Eastern Sierra Transit Authority (☎760-872-1901; www.estransit.com) buses make a round trip between Lone Pine and Reno ($59, six hours) Monday through Friday, stopping at all Hwy 395 towns in between. Fares depend on distance, and reservations are recommended. There's also an express bus between Mammoth and Bishop ($7, one hour, around three daily) that operates Monday to Friday.

In summer, connect to Yosemite via YARTS bus (p694) in Mammoth Lakes or Lee Vining. Mammoth to Lee Vining costs $8 one way, while Mammoth to Yosemite Valley is $22 (including free park entry, plus one free under-12 ticket per adult ticket purchased), with one to two early-morning departures per day.

WILDERNESS PERMITS FOR THE EASTERN SIERRA

➡ Free wilderness permits for overnight camping are required year-round in the Ansel Adams, John Muir, Golden Trout and Hoover Wilderness areas.

➡ For the first three areas, trailhead quotas are in effect from May to October; about 60% of the quota may be reserved online at www.recreation.gov for a $6 fee (per person), or $15 (per person) if entering the Mt Whitney Zone.

➡ From November to April you can pick up permits at most ranger stations; permits are bookable around six months in advance. If you find a station closed, look for self-issue permits outside the office.

➡ Wilderness permits for the Inyo National Forest can be picked up in Lone Pine, Bishop, Mammoth Lakes or its Mono Basin ranger stations.

➡ For information, call the Inyo National Forest Wilderness Permit Office (p726) in Bishop.

➡ Yosemite's Tuolumne Meadows Wilderness Center can also issue permits for trips from Saddlebag Lake and has a self-registration permit station.

➡ Permits for Hoover Wilderness trips that depart from the Humboldt-Toiyabe National Forest (seasonal quotas on some trails) are issued at the **Bridgeport Ranger Station & Visitor Center** (Map p712; ☎760-932-7070; www.fs.usda.gov/htnf; Hwy 395; ⌚8am-4:30pm).

➡ The forums on High Sierra Topix (www.highsierratopix.com) are an excellent resource for planning trips.

Mono Lake Region

Bridgeport

Barely three blocks long, set amid an open high valley and in view of the peaks of Sawtooth Ridge, Bridgeport flaunts classic Western flair with charming old storefronts and a homey ambience. Almost everything shuts down or cuts back its hours for the usually brutal winters, but the rest of the year the town is a magnet for anglers, hikers, climbers and hot-spring devotees.

Activities

★**Travertine Hot Spring** HOT SPRINGS
(Map p712) FREE A bit southeast of town, head here to watch a panoramic Sierra sunset from three small but entirely natural hot pools set amid impressive rock formations. To get here, turn east on Jack Sawyer Rd just before the ranger station, then follow the dirt road uphill for about 1 mile. The pools are located over the mound behind the toilet block, and are free to bathe in.

Ken's Sporting Goods FISHING
(Map p712; ☎760-932-7707; www.kenssport.com; 258 Main St; ⌚7am-7pm Mon-Thu, to 8pm Fri & Sat mid-Apr–Oct, 9am-4pm Tue-Fri rest of year) Stop by Ken's for information and fishing gear. If you're trolling for trout, try the Bridgeport Reservoir and the East Walker River.

Sleeping & Eating

Silver Maple Inn & Cain House MOTEL $$
(Map p712; ☎760-932-7383; www.silvermapleinn.com; 340 Main St; r $140-200; ❄📶) Bridgeport's most upscale accommodations and always a good choice, whether you stay in one of the standard rooms in the whitewashed classic roadside motel, or one of the more contemporary and luxurious rooms in the next-door Cain House. The two share an immaculately maintained lawn with chairs laid out for enjoying sunny days.

Twin Lakes

Eager anglers line the shoreline of Twin Lakes, a gorgeous duo of basins cradled by the fittingly named Sawtooth Ridge. The area's famous for its fishing – especially since some lucky guy bagged the state's largest ever brown trout here in 1987 (it weighed in at a hefty 26lb). Lower Twin is quieter, while Upper Twin allows boating and waterskiing. Other activities include mountain biking and, of course, hiking in the Hoover Wilderness Area and on into the eastern, lake-riddled reaches of Yosemite National Park.

The main trailhead is at the end of Twin Lakes Rd (closed in winter), just past **Annett's Mono Village** (Map p682; ☎760-932-7071; www.monovillage.com; 13425 Twin Lakes Rd; tent/RV sites $28/38, r $102, cabins $115-230; ⊙late Apr-Oct; @📶); parking costs $10 per vehicle for a stay of up to one week (you have to arrive/pay during operating hours: 8am to 5pm). From here, hikers can set off along Robinson Creek for adventures in the stunning **Hoover Wilderness** (Map p682; www.fs.usda.gov) and overnight backpacking trips (wilderness permit required; can be applied for at Bridgeport Ranger Station & Visitor Center into northeastern Yosemite. The day hike to lovely **Barney Lake** (8 miles round trip) takes in magnificent views of jagged granite spires in **Little Slide Canyon** – where rock climbers detour to scale a fierce wall called the Incredible Hulk – and steep boulder rockslides on the ridge to the north.

For a hike with great views of Twin Lakes, go south from Annett's on the **Horse Creek trail**, which soon leads to the cascades of **Horsetail Falls**. It continues up to skirt the wilderness boundary and then descends back to Twin Lakes on the **Cattle Creek trail**. Loop back along the lake for 7.5 miles in total. In *Dharma Bums*, Beat author Jack Kerouac describes an ascent he made from Horse Creek Canyon to nearby Matterhorn Peak (12,300ft) with poet Gary Snyder.

A stroll down a hillside brings you to the out-of-the-way (though it can still get crowded) **Buckeye Hot Spring** (Map p712; www.monocounty.org/places-to-go/hot-springs/buckeye-hot-springs/; P) FREE. Water emerges piping hot and cools as it trickles down into several pools by lively Buckeye Creek, which is handy for taking a cooling dip. One pool is partially tucked into a small cave made from a rock overhang. Clothing is optional. The spring is off Buckeye Rd, near Hwy 395; road access may be closed during winter.

The main campgrounds in the Humboldt-Toiyabe National Forest are generally open from late April to early October. For hotels, head to Bridgeport.

Buckeye Campground (Map p712; Buckeye Rd; tent & RV sites $20; ⊙May–mid-Oct), west of Bridgeport and north of Twin Lakes in the Humboldt-Toiyabe National Forest, has tables, fire grates and toilets, but you'll need to bring or treat water. Take Twin Lakes Rd from Bridgeport for 7 miles before turning right onto Buckeye Rd. It's another 3 miles and then left at a fork to reach the campground.

Bodie State Historic Park

At **Bodie State Historic Park** (Map p712; ☎760-616-5040; www.parks.ca.gov/bodie; Hwy 270; adult/child $8/5; ⊙9am-6pm Apr-Oct, to 4pm Nov-Mar, road often closed winter; P🐕), a gold-rush ghost town is preserved in a state of 'arrested decay.' Weathered buildings sit frozen in time on a dusty, windswept plain. To get there, head east for 13 miles (the last three unpaved) on Hwy 270, about 7 miles south of Bridgeport. The access road is often closed by snow in winter.

Gold was first discovered here in 1859, and within 20 years the place grew from a rough mining camp to an even rougher boomtown with a population of 10,000 and a reputation for unbridled lawlessness. Fights and murders took place almost daily, the violence no doubt fueled by liquor dispensed in the town's 65 saloons, some of which did double duty as brothels, gambling halls or opium dens. The hills disgorged some $35 million worth of gold and silver in the 1870s and '80s, but when production plummeted, so did the population, and eventually the town was abandoned to the elements.

Peering through the windows of the 200 weather-beaten buildings, you'll see stocked stores, furnished homes, a schoolhouse with desks and books, and workshops filled with tools. The jail is still there, as are the fire station, churches, a bank vault and many other buildings.

The former Miners' Union Hall now houses a museum and visitor center. Rangers conduct free general tours. In summer, they also offer tours of the landscape and the cemetery; call for details. The second Saturday of August is **Friends of Bodie Day** (www.bodiefoundation.org), with stagecoach rides, history presentations and lots of devotees in period costume.

Lee Vining

Highway 395 skirts the western bank of Mono Lake, rolling into the gateway town of Lee Vining, where you can eat, sleep, gas up (for a pretty penny) and catch Hwy 120 to Yosemite National Park when the road's open. A superb base for exploring Mono Lake, Lee Vining is only 12 miles (about a 30-minute drive) from Yosemite's Tioga Pass entrance. **Lee Vining Canyon** is also a popular location for **ice climbing**.

Mono Lake Region

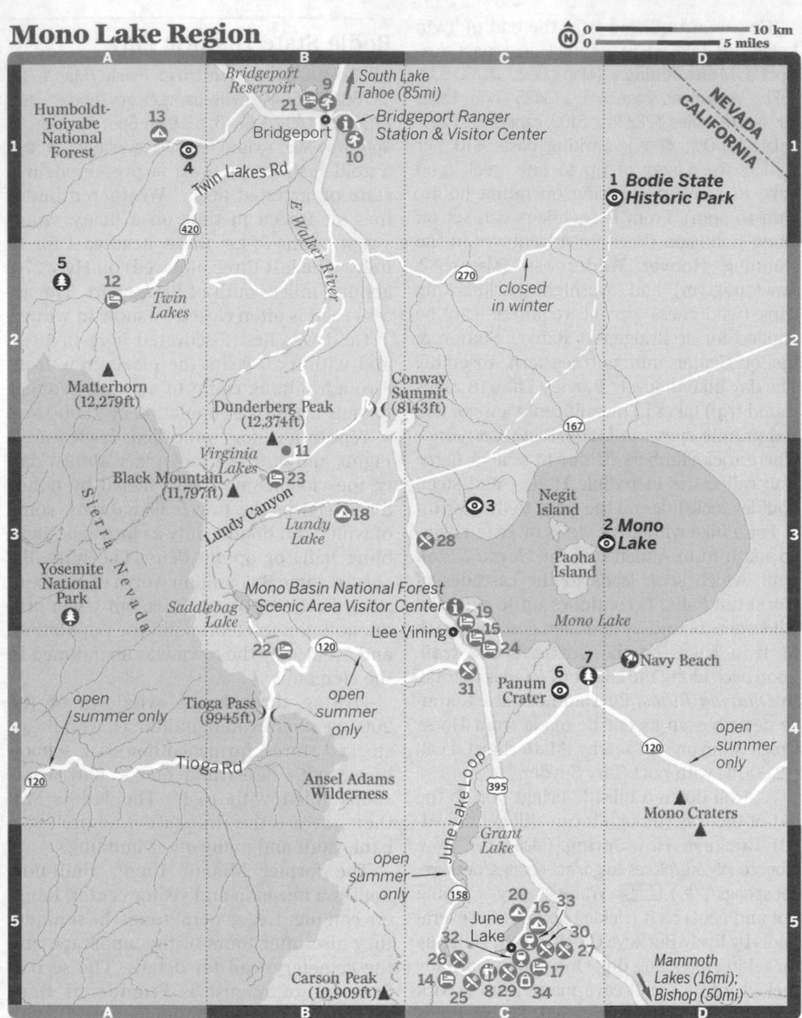

Sleeping

Lodging rates drop when Tioga Pass to Yosemite is closed. Campsites also close during the winter. Most of the lodging options in town are fairly ordinary, but winter sports fans can find a few bargains in low season. Alternatively, Mammoth Lakes, with an abundance of choice, is only 31 miles south.

★Tioga Pass Resort CABIN $$
(Map p682; www.tiogapassresort.com; Hwy 120; d $145, cabins $180-280; ⊗Jun-Sep) Situated at a whopping 9550ft and only 2 miles east of Tioga Pass, this is as close to a Yosemite experience as you can get without staying in the park. Founded in 1914, this high-country resort attracts a fiercely loyal clientele to its quiet, comfortable, woodsy cabins (most with full kitchen) beside Lee Vining Creek. Walk-ins can sometimes snag a cancellation.

Yosemite Gateway Motel MOTEL $$
(Map p712; ☎760-647-6467; www.yosemitegatewaymotel.com; 51340 Hwy 395; r $107-299;) Think vistas. This is the only motel on the eastern side of the highway, and the views of Mono Lake and surroundings from some of the rooms are phenomenal. The somewhat tired rooms have comfortable beds with

Mono Lake Region

thick duvets and big bathrooms. Family units and suites sleep up to six.

Murphey's Motel MOTEL $$
(Map p712; ☎760-647-6316; www.murpheysyosemite.com; 51493 Hwy 395; r $88-290; ❄📶🐾) At the northern end of town, this large, two-story, log-cabin-style place offers comfy but dated rooms. It's one of the few hotels in Lee Vining open year-round. Rooms have refrigerators and coffeemakers; the largest is cosy but sleeps six on three queen beds.

Eating

Latte Da Coffee Cafe CAFE $
(Map p712; ☎760-647-6310; cnr Hwy 395 & 3rd St; sandwiches from $6; ⏰7am-8pm May-Oct; 📶) Located at the **El Mono Motel** (www.elmonomotel.com; r $76-103; ⏰mid-May–Oct; 📶), this cafe is a charming spot for sandwiches, scones and good organic espresso drinks. There's a cozy wood-floored interior, a front porch and a tiny backyard garden.

★ **Whoa Nellie Deli** AMERICAN $$
(Map p712; ☎760-647-1088; www.whoanelliedeli.com; Tioga Gas Mart, 22 Vista Point Rd; mains $7.50-19; ⏰6:30am-9pm late Apr-Oct; 👪) Years after its famed chef moved on to Toomey's (p720) at Mammoth Lakes, this Mobil-gas-station restaurant off Hwy 120 is still, surprisingly, a darn good place to eat. Stop in for delicious burgers, fish tacos, wild-buffalo meatloaf and other tasty morsels, and Mono Lake views from outdoor picnic tables. There are live bands some nights.

Mono Inn AMERICAN $$$
(Map p714; ☎760-647-6581; www.themonoinn.com; 55620 Hwy 395; small plates $16-18, mains $32-38; ⏰5-9pm Fri-Sun) A restored 1922 lodge owned by the family of photographer Ansel Adams, this elegant yet casual lakefront restaurant makes everything from scratch and has correspondingly delectable lake views from inside and out. Stop in for the occasional live band on the creekside terrace. Located about 5 miles north of Lee Vining. Call reservations as opening hours are subject to change.

Mono Lake

North America's second-oldest lake is a quiet and mysterious expanse of deep blue water whose glassy surface reflects jagged Sierra peaks, young volcanic cones and the unearthly tufa (too-fah) towers that make the lake so distinctive. Jutting from the water like drip sand castles, tufas form when calcium bubbles up from subterranean springs and combines with carbonate in the alkaline lake waters.

WORTH A TRIP

VIRGINIA LAKES

South of Bridgeport, Hwy 395 gradually arrives at its highest point, Conway Summit (8143ft), where you'll be whipping out your camera to capture the awe-inspiring panorama of Mono Lake, backed by the Mono Craters, and June and Mammoth Mountains.

Also at the top is the turnout for **Virginia Lakes Road** (usually closed in winter), which parallels Virginia Creek for about 6 miles to a cluster of lakes flanked by Dunderberg Peak (12,374ft) and Black Mountain (11,797ft). A trailhead at the end of the road gives access to the Hoover Wilderness Area (p711) and the **Pacific Crest Trail**. The trail continues down Cold Canyon through to Yosemite National Park. With a car shuttle, the excellent 10.5-mile hike to **Green Creek** visits a bevy of perfect lakes; an extra mile (each way) takes you to windswept – check out the mammoth tree blowdown! – **Summit Lake** at the Yosemite border. Check with the folks at the **Virginia Lakes Resort** (Map p714; ☎760-647-6484; www.virginialakesresort.com; Virginia Lakes Rd; cabins $119-222; ⏱mid-May–mid-Oct; 🐾), opened in 1923, for maps and tips about specific trails (open seasonally between May and October). Nearby, **Virginia Lakes Pack Outfit** (Map p714; ☎760-937-0326; www.virginialakes.com; Virginia Lakes Rd; 1½hr rides from $65, half/full-day rides $105/135; ⏱Jun-Sep) offers horseback-riding trips.

In *Roughing It,* Mark Twain described **Mono Lake** (Map p712; www.monolake.org) as California's 'dead sea.' Hardly. The brackish water teems with buzzing alkali flies and brine shrimp, both considered delicacies by dozens of migratory bird species that return here year after year. So do about 85% of the state's nesting population of California gulls, which take over the lake's volcanic islands from April to August. Mono Lake has also been at the heart of a decades-long environmental controversy that involves the diversion of the lake's freshwater feeder streams to Los Angeles' drinking-water supply.

Sights & Activities

South Tufa NATURE RESERVE

(Map p712; Test Station Rd; adult/child $3/free; P 👪) Peculiar-shaped tufa spires ring shimmering Mono Lake; the biggest grove is on the southern rim, with a mile-long interpretive trail. The bizarre limestone shapes are formed when rich calcium underwater springs fuse with the carbonate-rich lake water. Visit at dusk (on wind-free days) for the most awesome scene – the surrounding mountain ranges are mirrored in the perfectly still surface. Ask about ranger-led tours and talks.

Panum Crater NATURAL FEATURE

(Map p712; Mono Crater Rd) Rising above the southern shore of Mono Lake, 640-year-old Panum Crater is the youngest, smallest and most accessible of the string of craters scattered south toward Mammoth Mountain. A panoramic trail circles the crater rim (about 30 to 45 minutes), and a short but steep 'plug trail' puts you at the crater's core.

Black Point Fissures NATURAL FEATURE

(Map p712) On the north shore of Mono Lake are the Black Point Fissures, narrow crags that opened when a lava mass cooled and contracted about 13,000 years ago. Access is from three places: east of Mono Lake County Park; from the western shore off Hwy 395; or south off Hwy 167. Check at the **Mono Basin Scenic Area Visitor Center** (Map p712; ☎760-647-3044; www.fs.usda.gov/inyo; 1 Visitor Center Dr; ⏱8am-5pm May-Sep, hours vary Oct-Dec, closed Jan-Apr; 👪) for specific directions.

Navy Beach BEACH

(Navy Beach Rd) The best place for swimming in Mono Lake is at Navy Beach, off Hwy 120. It's also the best place to put in canoes or kayaks.

June Lake Loop

Under the shadow of massive Carson Peak (10,909ft), the stunning 16-mile June Lake Loop (Hwy 158) meanders through a picture-perfect horseshoe canyon, past the relaxed resort town of **June Lake** and four sparkling, fish-rich lakes: Grant, Silver, Gull and June. It's especially scenic in fall, when the basin is ablaze with golden aspens. Catch the loop a few miles south of Lee Vining.

Activities

June Lake is backed by the Ansel Adams Wilderness area, which runs into Yosemite National Park. Hiking and horse-riding trips into the backcountry are as impressive as any in the Sierra Nevada. Mellow **June Mountain Ski Area** (Map p712; ☎888-586-3686, 24hr snow info 760-934-2224; www.junemountain.com; Hwy 158; lift tickets adult/13-22yr & senior/under 12yr $119/98/free; ⏰8:30am-4pm winter; 👪) is good for beginners; Mammoth lift passes can be used here.

Ernie's Tackle & Ski Shop SPORTS & OUTDOORS
(Map p712; ☎760-648-7756; www.ernestackleandskishop.com; 2604 Boulder Dr; ⏰7am-6pm winter, 6am-7pm rest of year) One of the most established outfitters in June Lake village, Ernie's rents fishing gear in the summer months and skiing gear in the winter months. It also sells a range of outdoor gear and clothing.

Sleeping

June Lake Campground CAMPGROUND $
(Map p712; ☎800-444-7275; www.recreation.gov; Boulder Dr; tent & RV sites $23; ⏰late Apr–mid-Oct; 🐾) On the June Lake shoreline and a short walk from town are these 28 sites with drinking water, flush toilets and bear-proof lockers. Accepts reservations.

Oh! Ridge Campground CAMPGROUND $
(Map p712; ☎800-444-7275; www.recreation.gov; off Pine Cliff Road; tent & RV sites $27.50; ⏰late Apr-Oct; 🐾) Large open-air campground popular with families because of its access to a swimming beach on June Lake. Drinking water and flush toilets, picnic tables, grills and bear-proof lockers. Accepts reservations.

June Lake Motel MOTEL $
(Map p712; ☎760-648-7547; www.junelakemotel.com; 2716 Hwy 158; r from $70, with kitchenette/kitchen $110/135; ❄@📶🐾) These 21 rooms – some enormous and most with full kitchens – catch delicious mountain breezes and have attractive light-wood furniture. There's a fish-cleaning sink and barbecues. Some times of year require a two- to three-night minimum stay.

Double Eagle Resort & Spa RESORT $$
(Map p712; ☎760-648-7004; www.doubleeagle.com; 5587 Hwy 158; r/cabins from $215/349; 📶🏊🐾) An upscale spot for these parts, Double Eagle has rustic two-bedroom log cabins and comfortable balconied hotel rooms. Worries disappear at the elegant spa, and there's a heated indoor pool and a fully equipped gym. The **restaurant** (Map p712; ☎760-648-7004; www.doubleeagle.com/eagles-landing-restaurant; mains $11-36; ⏰7:30am-9pm; P🖊) exudes rustic elegance, with cozy booths, a high ceiling and a huge fireplace.

Eating & Drinking

★**Ohanas 395** FOOD TRUCK $
(Map p712; www.ohanas395.com; 131 S Crawford Ave; mains $7-17; ⏰noon-6pm) This very good food truck, in the parking lot near June Lake Brewing (p716), serves wait-worthy 'Hawaiian soul food' with a dash of Mexican fusion. It's pretty much the only food like this on offer in the area, and you can order up dishes such as Honolulu fried noodles, slow-cooked kalua pig tacos, a classic plate lunch or an ahi poke (raw-fish salad) bowl.

Lift CAFE $
(Map p712; www.theliftjunelake.com; June Lake Loop; mains $9; ⏰6:30am-7pm Mon-Thu, to 8pm Fri-Sun; 📶) Cozy cafe with a contemporary Scandinavian-meets-Sierras aesthetic serving espresso drinks, pastries and more substantial food like egg sandwiches, vegetarian rice bowls and homemade chili. Especially popular with locals on Sunday for brunch and pasta dinners ($16). Grab a seat in the corner next to a wood-burning fireplace in winter.

Tiger Bar AMERICAN $$
(Map p712; ☎760-648-7551; www.tigerbarcafe.com; 2620 Hwy 158; mains $10-22; ⏰8am-9pm, bar to 1am) After a day on the slopes or trails, people gather at the long bar or around the pool table of this no-nonsense, no-attitude place, which has been around in some form or another since 1932. The kitchen feeds all appetites, with burgers, salads, tacos and other tasty grub, including homemade fries; there are fresh-baked pies for dessert.

Carson Peak Inn AMERICAN $$$
(Map p712; ☎760-648-7575; www.carsonpeakinn.com; 5034 Hwy 158; meals $27-48; ⏰4-8:30pm Wed-Sun) Inside a cozy house with a fireplace, this restaurant is much beloved for its tasty old-time indulgences, such as fried chicken, pan-fried trout and chopped sirloin steak. Portion sizes can be ordered for regular or 'hearty' appetites. Its opening hours are shorter during winter.

WORTH A TRIP

LUNDY LAKE

After Conway Summit, Hwy 395 twists down steeply into the Mono Basin. Before reaching Mono Lake, Lundy Lake Rd meanders west of the highway for about 5 miles to Lundy Lake. This is a gorgeous spot, especially in spring, when wildflowers carpet the canyon along Mill Creek, or in fall when the landscape is brightened by colorful foliage. Before reaching the lake, the road skirts first-come, first-served **Lundy Canyon Campground** (Map p714; www.monocounty.ca.gov/facilities/page/lundy-canyon-campground; Lundy Lake Rd; tent & RV sites $16; late Apr-Oct;). At the end of the lake there's a ramshackle resort on the site of an 1880s mining town, plus a small store and boat rentals.

Past the resort, a dirt road leads into Lundy Canyon; after 2 miles, it dead-ends at the trailhead for the Hoover Wilderness Area (p711). A fantastic 1.5-mile hike follows Mill Creek to the 200ft-high **Lundy Falls**. Industrious beavers define the landscape along the trail, with gnawed aspens scattered on the ground and a number of huge dams barricading the creek. Ambitious types can continue on via Lundy Pass to **Saddlebag Lake** and the **Twenty Lakes Basin**, though the final climb out of the canyon uses a rocky and very steep talus chute.

Note: Lundy Lake Rd can be snow covered in winter and impossible to pass.

★ **June Lake Brewing** MICROBREWERY
(Map p712; 858-668-6340; www.junelakebrewing.com; 131 S Crawford Ave; noon-8pm Mon, Wed, Thu & Sun, to 9pm Fri & Sat) A top regional draw, June Lake Brewing's open tasting room serves around 10 drafts, including Deer Beer Brown Ale and some awesome IPAs. Brewers swear the June Lake water makes all the difference. Flights are around $8 and food is available from the Ohanas 395 food truck (p715) parked close by.

T-Bar Social Club BAR
(Map p712; 760-648-7774; www.balancedrocksaloon.com/t-bar-social-club; 2588 Hwy 158, June Lake; cover $5-25) The only place to catch live music while you grab a beer is located below June Pie Pizzeria (you can enter via the pizza place or the door around the corner). Same owners means you can order a pie while enjoying the eclectic lineup. Also hosts film screenings and other town events.

Mammoth Lakes

Mammoth Lakes is a famous mountain-resort town endowed with larger-than-life scenery – active outdoorsy folks worship at the base of its imposing 11,053ft Mammoth Mountain. Long-lasting powder clings to these slopes, and when the snow finally fades, the area's an outdoor wonderland of mountain-bike trails, excellent fishing, endless alpine hiking and blissful hidden spots for hot-spring soaking. Eastern Sierra's commercial hub and a four-season resort, Mammoth is backed by a ridgeline of jutting peaks, ringed by clusters of crystalline alpine lakes and enshrouded by the dense **Inyo National Forest** (Map p724; www.fs.usda.gov/inyo).

Activities

Mammoth is an epicenter of outdoor activities, but they're seasonal so be sure to pick the right month for your visit.

McGee Creek Pack Station HORSEBACK RIDING
(760-935-4324, in winter 760 878 2207; www.mcgeecreekpackstation.com; McGee Creek Rd; 1hr/half-day/full-day rides from $50/95/165; hours vary;) Whether it's backcountry multiday packing trips or hour-long rides on nearby trails, the owners of this company offer decades of experience and knowledge. In summer, rides leave from McGee Creek Pack Station; in winter (when the road is closed) they're contactable at 8 Mile Ranch on Black Rock Springs Rd.

Rock Creek Pack Station HORSEBACK RIDING
(760-872-8331; www.rockcreekpackstation.com; 9006 Rock Creek Rd; half/full-day rides from $65/120;) Old, experienced hands run this backcountry packing company high up in the Rock Creek wilderness. Many equine activities, as well as hiking and fishing trips, are on offer.

Caldera Kayaks KAYAKING
(760-935-1691; www.calderakayak.com; 2hr hire $30, Mono Lake tours per person from $120) Cal-

dera Kayaks rents single and double kayaks for use on Lake Crowley. It also offers Mono Lake tours.

Skiing & Snowboarding

Mammoth Mountain (Map p724; ☎760-934-2571, 760-934-2571, 24hr snow report 888-766-9778; www.mammothmountain.com; adult/13-17yr/5-12yr/under 5yr from $79/65/32/free) is one of California's premier ski resorts. There's free cross-country skiing along the more than 300 miles of ungroomed trails in town and in the Inyo National Forest. Pick up a free map at the Mammoth Lakes Welcome Center (p721) or head to **Tamarack Cross-Country Ski Center** (Map p724; ☎760-934-2442; www.tamaracklodge.com/xc-ski-center; 163 Twin Lakes Rd; all-day trail pass adult/senior/child $32/25/5, rental packages adult/senior/child $32/32/27; ⏰8:30am-5pm). The season is one of the longest in the state, and typically runs from November to May, but snow has been known to stick around until June and be skiable from October.

Hiking

Mammoth Lakes rubs up against the **Ansel Adams Wilderness** (Map p724; www.fs.usda.gov) and **John Muir Wilderness** (Map p724; www.fs.usda.gov) areas, both laced with fabulous trails leading to shimmering lakes, rugged peaks and hidden canyons. Major trailheads leave from the Mammoth Lakes Basin, Reds Meadow and Agnew Meadows; the latter two are accessible only by shuttle. **Shadow Lake** is a stunning 7-mile day hike from Agnew Meadows, and **Crystal Lake** makes a worthy 2.5-mile round-trip trek from Lake George in the Lakes Basin.

From various spots along the Reds Meadow area, long-distance backpackers with wilderness permits and bear canisters can easily jump onto the **John Muir Trail** (to Yosemite to the north and Mt Whitney to the south) and the **Pacific Crest Trail** (fancy walking to Mexico or Canada?).

Cycling & Mountain Biking

When the ski slopes close, Mammoth turns into a downhill biker's paradise. Stop at

EBBETTS PASS SCENIC BYWAY

For outdoor fanatics, a scenic section of Hwys 4 and 89 called the Ebbetts Pass Scenic Byway (www.scenic4.org) is a road trip through paradise. Heading northeast from **Arnold**, gaze up at the giant sequoias of Calaveras Big Trees State Park and in winter stop at the family-friendly ski resort of **Bear Valley** (☎209-753-2301; www.bearvalley.com; 2280 Hwy 207; daily ski-lift ticket adult/6-12yr/13-19yr $105/42/85; ⏰lift 9am-3:30pm, resort end Nov-May; 👪). Nearby is the **Bear Valley Adventure Company** (☎209-753-2834; www.bvadventures.com; 1 Bear Valley Rd; snowshoes/sleds/mountain bikes/kayaks from $25/15/30/35; ⏰9am-5pm; 👪), a one-stop shop for other outdoor adventures in the area. Continuing east, the stunningly beautiful **Lake Alpine** is skirted by slabs of granite, has several great beaches, and boasts excellent water sports, fishing and hiking. A handful of campgrounds, as well as the rustic **Lake Alpine Resort** (☎209-753-6350; www.lakealpineresort.com; 4000 Hwy 4, Bear Valley; tent cabins $89-99, cabins with kitchenette or kitchen $189-339; ⏰May-Oct; P 🚭 🐾), line the lakefront.

The next stretch is the most dramatic, when the narrow highway continues past picturesque **Mosquito Lake** and the **Pacific Grade Summit** (8060ft) before slaloming through historic Hermit Valley and finally winding up and over the 8730ft summit of **Ebbetts Pass**. North on Hwy 89 and just west of **Markleeville**, you can visit the two developed pools and seasonal campground at **Grover Hot Springs State Park** (☎530-694-2248, 530-694-2249; www.parks.ca.gov; 3415 Hot Springs Rd, Markleeville; pool adult/child $10/5; ⏰10am-7pm; 👪). It's worth returning to Markleeville for dinner at the **Stone Fly** (☎530-694-9999; www.stoneflyrestaurant.com; 14821 Hwy 89; mains $15-36; ⏰5-9pm Fri-Sun) restaurant.

The relatively little-known **Hope Valley Wildlife Area** (☎916-358-2900; www.wildlife.ca.gov; P) 🌿 FREE, a gorgeous reserve of meadows, streams and forests ringed by high Sierra peaks, is not far northwest of Markleeville. Wylder Hotel Hope Valley, with a variable collection of cabins and rooms, makes an excellent base camp.

From San Francisco, it's a three-hour drive east to Arnold, via Hwys 108 and 49. Ebbetts Pass closes after the first major snowfall and doesn't reopen until June, but Hwy 4 is usually plowed from the west, often as far as Bear Valley.

Mammoth Lakes

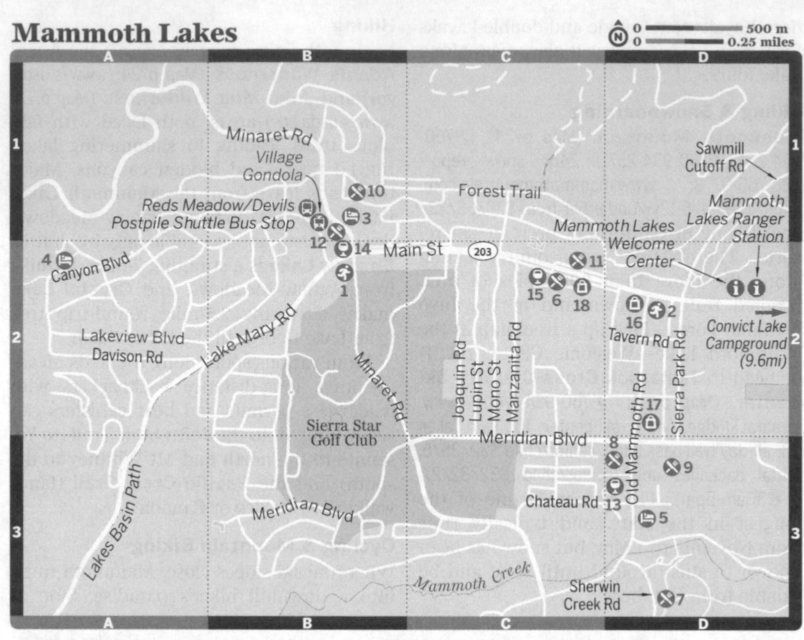

Mammoth Lakes

Activities, Courses & Tours
1 Lakes Basin Path ... B2
2 Troutfitter ... D2

Sleeping
3 Alpenhof Lodge ... B1
4 Austria Hof Lodge ... A2
5 Mammoth Creek Inn ... D3

Eating
6 Base Camp Café ... C2
7 Dos Alas CubaRican Cafe ... D3
8 El Charro Taqueria ... D3
9 Noodle-ly ... D3
Petra's Bistro & Wine Bar ... (see 3)
10 Skadi ... B1
11 Stellar Brew ... C2
12 Toomey's ... B1

Drinking & Nightlife
Clocktower Cellar ... (see 3)
13 Distant Brewing ... D3
14 Mammoth Brewing Company ... B2
15 Public House Taproom ... C2

Shopping
16 Footloose ... D2
17 Mammoth Mountaineering Supply ... D2
18 Rick's Sports Center ... C2

the Mammoth Lakes Welcome Center (p721) for a free biking map with area route descriptions.

Mammoth Mountain Bike Park MOUNTAIN BIKING
(Map p724; ☎800-626-6684; www.mammothmountain.com; day pass adult/7-12yr $45/24; ⊙9am-6pm Jun-Sep) Come summer, Mammoth Mountain morphs into the massive Mammoth Mountain Bike Park, with more than 80 miles of well-kept single-track trails. Several other trails traverse the surrounding forest. In general, Mammoth-style riding translates into plenty of hills and soft, sandy shoulders, which are best navigated with big, knobby tires.

When the park's open, it runs a free mountain-bike **shuttle** (9am to 5:30pm) from the Village area to the Main Lodge. Shuttles depart every 30 minutes, and mountain bikers with paid mountain passes get priority over pedestrians.

Lakes Basin Path CYCLING
(Map p718; cnr Lake Mary & Minaret Rds) One of Mammoth's fantastic multiuse paths, the 5.3-mile Lakes Basin Path begins at the southwestern corner of Lake Mary and Minaret Rds and heads uphill (1000ft, at a 5% to 10%

gradient) to Horseshoe Lake, skirting lovely lakes and accessing open views of the Sherwin Range. For a one-way ride, use the free Lakes Basin Trolley, which tows a bicycle trailer.

Fishing & Boating

From the last Saturday in April, the dozens of lakes that give the town its name lure in fly- and trout fishers from near and far. California fishing licenses ($15 for a single day) are available at sporting-goods stores throughout town. For equipment and advice, head to **Troutfitter** (Map p718; 760-924-3676; www.thetroutfitter.com; 2987 Main St; guided trips per half/full day from $300/390; 8am-4pm) or **Rick's Sports Center** (Map p718; 760-934-3416; 3241 Main St; per day ski rental from $28, snowshoes $12; 6am-8pm, shorter hours winter). Caldera Kayaks (p717) rents kayaks for use on Crowley Lake.

Sleeping

Mammoth B&Bs and inns rarely sell out midweek, when rates tend to be lower. During ski season, reservations are recommended at weekends and essential during holidays. Many properties offer ski-and-stay packages. Condo rentals often work out cheaper for groups. In general, good-value options are tough to find.

The Mammoth Lakes Welcome Center (p721) has a full list of campgrounds, and dispersed free camping locations (don't forget to pick up a free but mandatory fire permit for wilderness camping).

★ Mammoth Mountain Inn INN $$

(Map p724; 800-626-6684; www.themammothmountaininn.com; 10400 Minaret Rd; r $129-239, condos $259-1199;) Warm and cozy, oozing traditional ski-lodge appeal, and only steps from the base of the Panorama Gondola, this is the best address for skiers and snowboarders. Though prices come down out of ski season, at 9000ft it's a spectacular location no matter the time of year. It's a low-slung complex with a pool and hot tubs to soothe aching limbs.

Tamarack Lodge LODGE, CABIN $$

(Map p724; 760-934-2442; www.tamaracklodge.com; 163 Twin Lakes Rd; r from $140, without bathroom from $110, cabins $255-425;) In business since 1924, this charming year-round resort on Lower Twin Lake has a cozy fireplace lodge, a bar and an excellent restaurant, and 11 rustic-style rooms and 35 cabins. The cabins range from very simple to simply deluxe, and have full kitchen, private bathroom, porch and wood-burning stove. Some can sleep up to 10. Daily resort fee around $20.

Mammoth Creek Inn INN $$

(Map p718; 866-466-7000; www.themammothcreek.com; 663 Old Mammoth Rd; r $177-395;) It's amenities galore at this pretty inn at the end of a commercial strip, with down comforters and fluffy terry robes, a sauna, a hot tub and a fun pool-table room. Lofts overlook the majestic Sherwin Mountains, have full kitchens and can sleep up to six. Ski and board storage available, plus pet-friendly rooms. Resort fee $22.

Austria Hof Lodge LODGE $$

(Map p718; 866-662-6668; www.austriahof.com; 924 Canyon Blvd; r incl breakfast $100-275;) Close to Canyon Lodge, rooms here have modern knotty-pine furniture, and thick down duvets. Ski lockers, fireplaces, flat-screen TVs and a sundeck hot tub make winter stays here even sweeter. Continental breakfast is included with stays. In the evening, the lodge restaurant serves meaty gourmet German fare (such as bratwurst sampler plates and wiener schnitzel) in a cellar dining room.

Alpenhof Lodge HOTEL $$

(Map p718; 760-934-6330; www.alpenhof-lodge.com; 6080 Minaret Rd; r $150-240;) A snowball's toss from the Village, this Euro-flavored inn has updated lodge rooms with tasteful accent walls and ski racks; larger rooms and cottages have gas fireplaces or kitchens. The basement houses the Clocktower Cellar (p720).

Eating

Noodle-ly VIETNAMESE $

(Map p718; www.noodle-ly.com; 437 Old Mammoth Rd, Ste 146; mains $10-12; 11:30am-3pm & 5-8pm Thu-Mon) Welcomed by locals, this casual shop in a strip mall provides culinary variety for those looking to slurp down bowls of *pho* (Vietnamese noodle soup) with a Thai twist.

El Charro Taqueria MEXICAN $

(Map p718; 760-965-0539; 451 Old Mammoth Rd; tacos $2.75-4, mains $9; 11am-8pm) Popular with cops and locals on short lunch breaks, this family-run place serves up burritos, tacos and enchiladas with large portions of rice and beans in a no-frills dining room.

Base Camp Café AMERICAN $

(Map p718; ☎760-934-3900; 3325 Main St; mains $8-16; ⏰7:30am-4pm winter, longer hours summer; 📶✍) Fuel up with a bracing dose of organic tea or coffee and a filling breakfast (pancakes, eggs, burritos and omelets), or comfort food such as Tex-Mex jalapeño-onion straws or turkey chili in a bread bowl. The dining room is decorated with various backpacking gear, ice picks, wooden skis and beer mats. Meanwhile, the bathroom has a comical photo display of backcountry outhouses.

Stellar Brew CAFE $

(Map p718; ☎760-924-3559; www.stellarbrewnaturalcafe.com; 3280 Main St; salads & sandwiches $4.50-13; ⏰5:30am-5pm; P📶✍🐾) 🍃 Proudly locavore and mostly organic, Stellar entices you to settle into a comfy sofa for locally roasted coffee, juices, smoothies, homemade granola, breakfast burritos and scrumptious vegan (and some gluten-free) pastries. The small deck is a good place to catch some sun, even if a gas station is next door.

★Dos Alas CubaRican Cafe CUBAN $$

(Map p718; ☎760-965-0345; Sherwin Creek Rd; sandwiches $12, mains $17; ⏰11:30am-2pm & 4:30-9pm Wed, Thu & Sun, to 10pm Fri & Sat; 📶) While its setting, in a frontier-style timber building with stunning mountain views, doesn't evoke the Caribbean, this restaurant brings Cuba's flavors alive in dishes such as *escabeches* (pickled-base marinade with chicken, shrimp or vegetables) and a tasty *picadillo con arroz* (ground-beef stew). Live music from 6:30pm Wednesday.

Toomey's AMERICAN $$

(Map p718; ☎760-924-4408; www.toomeysmammoth.com; 6085 Minaret Rd; mains $16-37; ⏰7am-9pm; 👪) Since 2012 the Toomey's chef, once of legendary Whoa Nellie Deli (p713) in Lee Vining, has been preparing his eclectic menu of New Zealand elk chop, seafood jambalaya and pan-seared ahi tuna. Central location near the Panorama Gondola.

★Skadi NORWEGIAN $$$

(Map p718; ☎760-914-0962; www.skadirestaurant.com; 94 Berner St; mains $34-42; ⏰5pm-close Wed-Mon) Considering its more-than-mundane location in an industrial strip, Skadi comes as a surprise. Hip Swiss Alps decor and an innovative menu are the creation of chef Ian Algerøen, inspired by his Norwegian heritage and European fine-dining techniques. On the menu you'll find pork-belly confit and roast tenderloin, Canadian duck breast with arctic lingonberries and pan-seared day-boat scallops. Reservations required.

Lakefront Restaurant AMERICAN $$$

(Map p724; ☎760-934-2442; www.lakefrontmammoth.com; 163 Twin Lakes Rd; mains $38-60; ⏰5:30-9:30pm) The most atmospheric and romantic (and pricey) restaurant in Mammoth, this intimate dining room at Tamarack Lodge (p719) overlooks the lovely Twin Lakes. The chef crafts delights such as pecan-crusted trout, cauliflower puree, charred-tomato relish and farro. The staff is friendly and unpretentious. Menu changes each season. Reservations recommended.

Petra's Bistro & Wine Bar CALIFORNIAN $$$

(Map p718; ☎760-934-3500; www.petrasbistro.com; 6080 Minaret Rd; mains $23-36; ⏰5-9:30pm Tue-Sun) Settle in for seasonal cuisine and wines recommended by the staff sommeliers. In wintertime the best seats in the house are the cozy fireside couches. Start the evening with a cheese course, and choose from 36 wines available by the glass (250 by the bottle) or from the excellent cocktail menu. Reservations recommended.

🍷 Drinking & Nightlife

Clocktower Cellar PUB

(Map p718; ☎760-934-2725; www.clocktowercellar.com; 6080 Minaret Rd; ⏰4-11pm) In winter especially, locals throng this dive bar–pub in the basement of the Alpenhof Lodge (p719). The ceiling is tiled with a swirl of bottle caps, and the bar has 160 whiskeys, 26 beers on tap and about 50 bottled varieties.

Distant Brewing BREWERY

(Map p718; www.distantbeer.com; 568 Old Mammoth Rd; ⏰2:30-10pm Mon-Fri, from 11:30 Sat & Sun) Formerly known as Black Doubt and newly relocated to this strip-mall setting, Distant has an unsophisticated aesthetic offset by top-shelf craft beers.

Public House Taproom BAR

(Map p718; www.buccicat.com; 3399 Main St; ⏰1-11pm Sun-Thu, to midnight Fri & Sat; 📶) One of Mammoth Lakes' newest and best bars wouldn't be out of place in the big city. Pull up a stool to the very long bar with a digital screen listing nearly 50 beers and ciders on tap, with homemade pretzels and meat pies for sustenance.

DON'T MISS

BENTON HOT SPRINGS

Soak in your own hot-springs tub and snooze beneath the moonlight at the **Inn at Benton Hot Springs** (☎760-933-2287; www.bentonhotsprings.org; Hwy 120, Benton; tent & RV sites per 2 people $60-70, B&B r $92-225; P ❄ 📶 🐾), a small, historic resort in a 150-year-old former silver-mining town nestled in the White Mountains. Choose from nine well-spaced campsites with private tubs or themed, antique-filled B&B rooms with semiprivate tubs. Daytime dips ($10 per person per hour) are available. Reservations essential.

The inn is reachable from Mono Lake via Hwy 120 (in summer), Mammoth Lakes by way of Benton Crossing Rd, or Bishop via Hwy 6; the first two options are undulating drives with sweeping red-rock vistas that glow at sunset, and all take approximately one hour. An Eastern Sierra Transit Authority (p709) bus connects Bishop and Benton ($6, one hour) on Tuesday and Friday, stopping right at the resort.

If you have time, ask for directions to the Volcanic Tablelands petroglyphs off Hwy 6, where ancient drawings decorate scenic rock walls.

Mammoth Brewing Company BREWERY
(Map p718; ☎760-934-7141; www.mammothbrewingco.com; 18 Lake Mary Rd; ⊙noon-8:30pm Mon-Thu, 11:30am-9:30pm Fri, 10am-9:30pm Sat, 10am-8:30pm Sun) You be the judge whether beer is brewed best at high altitude. Boasting the highest West Coast brewery, at 8000ft, Mammoth Brewing Company offers more than a dozen brews on tap (flights around $9) – including special seasonal varieties not found elsewhere. Tasty bar food, some locals say of better quality than the beer, is available (flatbreads, burgers and mac 'n' cheese).

Shopping

Gear heads will find no shortage of shops staffed by passionate young enthusiasts indulging their own outdoor adventures on days off. Most sell ski and snowboard equipment, with great sales in low season. In-town shops are usually cheaper than those at Mammoth Mountain, especially for equipment rentals.

Footloose SPORTS & OUTDOORS
(Map p718; ☎760-934-2400; www.footloosesports.com; 3043 Main St; per day ski-rental package from $44; ⊙8am-8pm) Full range of footwear and seasonal equipment; local biking info and rentals.

Mammoth Mountaineering Supply SPORTS & OUTDOORS
(Map p718; ☎760-934-4191; www.mammothgear.com; 361 Old Mammoth Rd; snowshoe rental per day $12; ⊙8am-8pm) Offers maps and friendly advice and sells all-season equipment from winter sports to camping gear. Rentals available.

Information

The **Mammoth Lakes Welcome Center** (Map p718; ☎760-924-5500; www.visitmammoth.com; 2510 Hwy 203; ⊙8am-5pm, 8:30am-4:30pm winter) and the **Mammoth Lakes Ranger Station** (www.fs.usda.gov/inyo; 2510 Main St; ⊙9am-5pm, hours vary winter) share a site on the northern side of Hwy 203. This one-stop information center issues wilderness permits, rents bear canisters, helps visitors find accommodation and campgrounds, and provides road and trail condition updates. From May to October, when trail quotas are in effect, walk-in wilderness permits are released at 11am the day before, though numbers are given to those lined up at 8am; permits are self-issue the rest of the year.

Getting There & Away

AIR

Mammoth Yosemite Airport (MMH; www.visitmammoth.com/fly-mammoth-lakes; 1300 Airport Rd) has nonstop flights to Los Angeles, San Francisco and Denver, operating winter through spring on **United** (www.united.com). Alaska Airlines runs service to Los Angeles from April to November. However, at research time airlines were planning to redirect many commercial flights to a newly expanded airport in Bishop, 42 miles south.

From the airport, taxis meet incoming flights, while some lodgings provide free transfers. Otherwise, **Mammoth Taxi** (☎760-934-8294; www.mammoth-taxi.com) does airport runs as well as hiker shuttles throughout the Sierra.

BUS

Mammoth is easy to navigate by public transportation year-round.

YARTS (☎877-989-2787; www.yarts.com) runs buses to and from Yosemite Valley in summer.

Eastern Sierra Transit Authority (p709) has a year-round service along Hwy 395, north to Reno, NV ($46, 4½ hours), and south to Lone Pine ($14.25, just over two hours). Buses run once a day in either direction from Monday to Friday, leaving Mammoth for Reno in the morning and Lone Pine in the afternoon.

Getting Around

Eastern Sierra Transit Authority (p709) operates a year-round system of free and frequent **bus shuttles** within Mammoth Lakes that connects the whole town with the Mammoth Mountain lodges; in summer, routes with bicycle trailers service the Lakes Basin Path (p719) and Mammoth Mountain Bike Park (p718). Check the website for details on routes and schedules (usually they run every 15 to 30 minutes from around 7am to 5:30pm, with the town trolley running until 10pm).

Reds Meadow/Devils Postpile shuttle (Map p718; www.nps.gov; adult/child $8/4; approx 7am to 7pm, no service winter) provides public transportation to Reds Meadow and the Devils Postpile National Monument. From 10am to 4pm it runs nearly every 20 minutes (and every 45 minutes from 7:30am to 10am and 4pm to 7pm), departing from just under the base of the **gondola** (Map p724; ☎800-626-6684; www.mammothmountain.com; Minaret Rd; adult/13-18yr/5-12yr $34/29/12; hours vary; P) in the Village.

No app-based transportation, such as Uber or Lyft, operates in Mammoth Lakes.

Around Mammoth Lakes

Reds Meadow

One of the beautiful and varied landscapes near Mammoth Lakes is the Reds Meadow Valley, west of Mammoth Mountain. Drive on Hwy 203 as far as **Minaret Vista** (Map p724; road closed during winter) for eye-popping views (best at sunset) of the Ritter Range, the serrated Minarets and the remote reaches of Yosemite National Park.

The most fascinating attraction in Reds Meadow is the surreal volcanic formation of **Devils Postpile National Monument** (Map p724; ☎760-934-2289; www.nps.gov/depo; shuttle day pass adult/child $8/4; Jun-Oct, weather depending). The 60ft curtains of near-vertical, six-sided basalt columns formed when rivers of molten lava slowed, cooled and cracked with perplexing symmetry. This honeycomb design is best appreciated from atop the columns, reached by a short trail. The columns are an easy half-mile hike from the Devils Postpile Ranger Station.

From the monument, a 2.5-mile hike passing through fire-scarred forest leads to the spectacular **Rainbow Falls** (Map p724), where the San Joaquin River gushes over a 101ft basalt cliff. Chances of actually seeing a rainbow forming in the billowing mist are greatest at midday. The falls can also be reached via an easy 1.5-mile walk from the Reds Meadow area, which has a cafe, a store, the **Reds Meadow campground** (Map p724; 1 Reds Circle; tent & RV sites $23; closed winter;) and a pack station. Shuttle services run to the Reds Meadow area in season.

The road to Reds Meadow is only accessible from about June until September, weather permitting. To minimize impact when it's open, the road is closed to private vehicles beyond Minaret Vista unless you are camping, have lodge reservations or have a disability, in which case you must pay a $10 fee per car. Otherwise, you must use a mandatory shuttle bus.

The valley road provides access to six campgrounds along the San Joaquin River. Tranquil, willow-shaded **Minaret Falls Campground** (Map p724; www.fs.usda.gov; tent & RV sites $23; road closed winter;) is a popular fishing spot where the best riverside sites have views of the namesake cascade.

Convict Lake

One of the area's prettiest lakes, **Convict Lake** (Convict Lake Rd) has emerald water embraced by massive peaks. A hike along the gentle trail skirting the lake, through aspen and cottonwood trees, is great if you're still adjusting to the altitude. A trailhead on the southeastern shore gives access to Genevieve, Edith, Dorothy and Mildred Lakes in the John Muir Wilderness. To reach the lake, turn south from Hwy 395 on Convict Lake Rd (across from the Mammoth airport) and go 2 miles.

In 1871 Convict Lake was the site of a bloody shoot-out between a band of escaped convicts and a posse that had given chase. The posse leader, Sheriff Robert Morrison, was killed during the gunfight, and the tallest peak, Mt Morrison (12,268ft), was later named in his honor. The bad guys got away, only to be apprehended later near Bishop.

McGee Creek

Eight miles south of Mammoth Lakes, off Hwy 395, McGee Creek Rd rises into the mountains and dead-ends in a dramatic aspen-lined canyon, a particularly beautiful spot for autumn foliage. From here, the **McGee Pass Trail** enters the John Muir Wilderness, with day hikes to **Steelhead Lake** (10 miles round trip) via an easy walk to subtle **Horsetail Falls** (4 miles round trip).

On the drive up, the McGee Creek Pack Station (p716) offers trail rides. Spacious **McGee Creek Campground** (www.fs.usda.gov; McGee Creek Rd; tent & RV sites $23; late Apr-Oct;) has 28 reservable sites at 7600ft, with sun-shaded picnic tables along the creek and stunning mountain vistas.

Don't miss the coffee and home-baked goodies at the cute **East Side Bake Shop** (760-914-2696; www.eastsidebakeshop395.com; 1501 Crowley Lake Dr; mains $8-15; 6.30am-2pm Mon, Thu & Fri, to 9pm Sat, to 3pm Sun); check its calendar for fun local music at weekends.

Rock Creek

South off Hwy 395 and roughly equidistant between Mammoth Lakes and Bishop, Rock Creek Rd travels 11 miles into some of the dreamiest landscapes in the Sierra. At road's end, the Mosquito Flat trailhead into the **Little Lakes Valley** (part of the John Muir Wilderness) clocks in at a whopping 10,300ft of elevation. Mountaintops seem to be everywhere, with the 13,000ft peaks of Bear Creek Spire, Mt Dade, Mt Abbot and Mt Mills bursting out along the southwestern horizon and lush canyon meadows popping with scores of clear blue lakes. Ecstatic hikers and climbers fan out to explore – an excellent day-hike destination is the second of the **Gem Lakes** (7 miles round trip), a lovely aquamarine bowl and five-star lunch spot.

A dozen popular **USFS campgrounds** (877-444-6777; www.recreation.gov; tent & RV sites from $22; late May-Sep;) line Rock Creek Rd; most are along Rock Creek and a few are reservable. In wintertime there's a Sno-park 7 miles in, and during summer the Rock Creek Pack Station (p717) offers trail rides from its location just before the trailhead.

Fuel up on stacks of pancakes, tacos and prime rib at **Tom's Place Resort Cafe** (760-935-4239; www.tomsplaceresort.com; 8180 Crowley Lake Dr; mains $7-22; 7am-9pm, 7.30am-8pm Thu-Mon winter), an area classic, brimming with kitsch Americana. It's just off the highway at the very start of Rock Creek Rd.

The area is deservedly popular, and trailhead parking can be challenging; be prepared to trek an extra half-mile from the overflow lot.

Bishop

The second-largest town in the Eastern Sierra, Bishop is about two hours from Yosemite's Tioga Pass entrance. It's a major recreation hub, with dozens of motels and a funky and vibrant little art and outdoor community. Bishop offers access to excellent fishing in nearby lakes, climbing in the Buttermilks just west of town, and hiking in the John Muir Wilderness via Bishop Creek Canyon and the Rock Creek drainage. The area is especially lovely in fall, particularly around South Lake, when dropping temperatures cloak aspen, willow and cottonwood in myriad glowing shades.

The earliest inhabitants of the deep Owens Valley (which includes the towns of Independence, Big Pine, Bishop and Lone Pine) were Paiute and Shoshone Native Americans, who today live on four reservations in the area. White settlers came on the scene in the 1860s and began raising cattle to sell to nearby mining settlements.

Sights

★Laws Railroad Museum & Historic Site — MUSEUM

(760-873-5950; www.lawsmuseum.org; Silver Canyon Rd; suggested donation $10; 10am-4pm Sep-May;) This railroad and Old West museum recreates the village of Laws, an important stop on the route of the *Slim Princess*, a narrow-gauge train that hauled freight and passengers across the Owens Valley for nearly 80 years. On the sprawling 11 acres you'll see the original 1883 train depot, a post office, a schoolhouse and other rickety old buildings. Many contain funky and eclectic displays (dolls, fire equipment, antique stoves, even stuffed conjoined twin lambs) from the pioneer days.

Owens Valley Paiute Shoshone Cultural Center — CULTURAL CENTRE

(760-873-8844; www.bishoppaiutetribe.com/cultural-center; 2300 W Line St; 10am-6pm Tue-Fri, to 3pm Sat & Sun, call to confirm hours winter) FREE A mile west of Hwy 395, this underutilized cultural center and museum, run by the local Paiute Shoshone tribe, includes

Mammoth Lakes Area

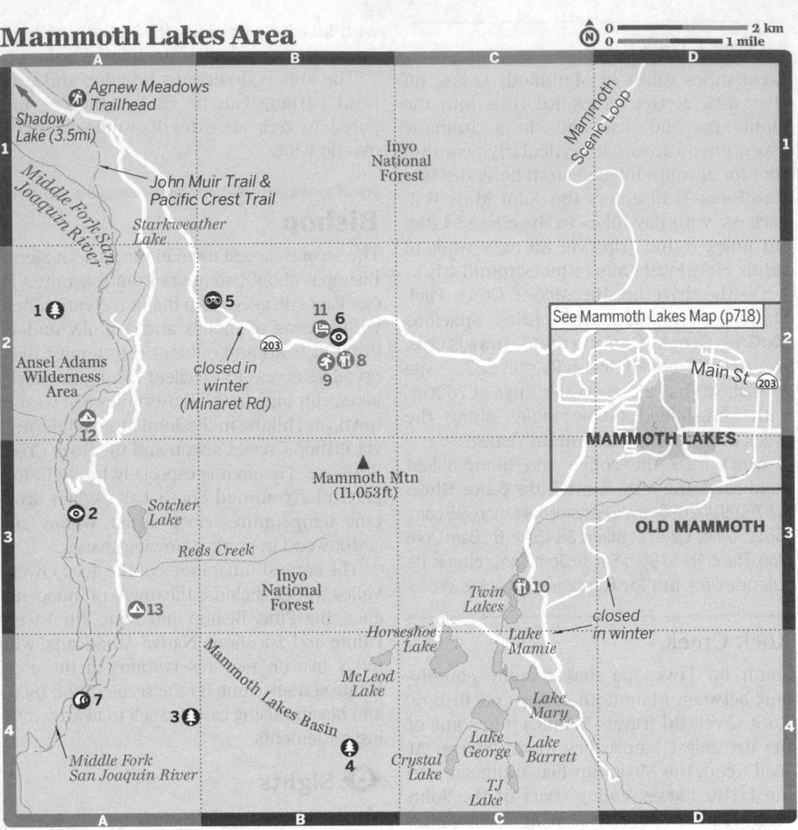

Mammoth Lakes Area

Sights
1 Ansel Adams Wilderness Area A2
2 Devils Postpile National Monument A3
3 Inyo National Forest A4
4 John Muir Wilderness Area B4
5 Minaret Vista B2
6 Panorama Gondola B2
7 Rainbow Falls A4

Activities, Courses & Tours
8 Mammoth Mountain B2
9 Mammoth Mountain Bike Park B2
10 Tamarack Cross-Country Ski Center C3

Sleeping
11 Mammoth Mountain Inn B2
12 Minaret Falls Campground A2
13 Reds Meadow Campground A3
Tamarack Lodge .... (see 10)

Eating
Lakefront Restaurant .... (see 10)

exhibits on local basketry, tools and the use of medical herbs; around the building is an interpretive native-plant walk.

Activities

The area's dry climate and varied terrain make Bishop a unique year-round destination for all manner of outdoor adventures. Road biking in winter is especially good (motorized dirt biking is very popular with locals). Several shops and organizations run avalanche training and mountaineering courses.

Climbing

Bishop is prime bouldering and rock-climbing territory, with terrain to match any level of experience and any climbing style. The main areas are the granite **Buttermilk Country**, nearly 8 miles upland and west of town on

Buttermilk Rd, and the stark **Volcanic Tablelands** and **Owens River Valley** (Happy and Sad Boulders) to the north. The tablelands are also a wellspring of Native American petroglyphs – tread lightly (two climbing rangers make daily visits to educate people on responsible practices). For climbing advice, pop into the visitors bureau (p727) or one of the many outdoor shops on Main St.

Hiking

Hikers will want to head to the high country by following Line St (Hwy 168) west along Bishop Creek Canyon, past Buttermilk Country and on to several lakes. Trailheads lead into the John Muir Wilderness and beyond to Kings Canyon National Park. Check with the White Mountain information station (p727) for suggestions, maps and wilderness permits for overnight stays.

Fishing

In the summer, fishing is good in the high-altitude lakes of **Bishop Creek Canyon** (west of town along Hwy 168). Other fine spots that are also prime locations in winter include the scenic, twisty and downright magical **Owens River** (northeast) and the **Pleasant Valley Reservoir** (Pleasant Valley Rd, north of town).

Swimming

Keough's Hot Springs SWIMMING
(Map p700; ☎760-872-4670; www.keoughshotsprings.com; 800 Keough Hot Springs Rd; adult/child 3-12yr/under 2yr $12/7/4; ⏲11am-7pm Wed-Fri & Mon, 9am-8pm Sat & Sun, longer hours Jun-Aug; 👪) About 8 miles south of Bishop, this historic green outdoor pool (dating from 1919) is filled with bath-warm water from local mineral springs. A smaller and sheltered 104°F (40°C) soaking pool sits beside it. There's a small on-site snack bar selling hot and cold sandwiches, hot dogs and ice creams.

Camping and tent cabins are also available.

Sleeping

Bishop has a handful of economically priced motels, mostly chains. The majority are located on or just off Main St. A couple of campgrounds at the foot of the Volcanic Tablelands just to the north of town are open year-round.

★Eastside Guesthouse & Bivy GUESTHOUSE $
(☎760-784-7077; www.eastsideguesthouse.com; 777 N Main St; dm $25-35, r $120-480; ❄📶) With an airy blonde-wood common area for pre- and post-hike confabs, this new guesthouse is easily Bishop's best for laid-back travelers who also want some creature comforts. The young owners have designed the property with features such as the idyllic backyard deck, barbecue spot and pond, inspired by their own world travels. Room furnishings are Ikea-like, with more upscale bathroom fixtures.

Laundry is available for $5.

USFS Campgrounds CAMPGROUND $
(www.recreation.gov; tent & RV sites $26; ⏲May-Sep; 🐾) For a scenic night, stretch out your sleeping bag beneath the stars. The closest USFS campgrounds, all but one first come, first served, are between 9 miles and 15 miles west of town on Bishop Creek along Hwy 168, at elevations between 7500ft and 9000ft.

Hostel California HOSTEL $
(☎760-399-6316; www.thehostelcalifornia.com; 213 Academy Ave; dm from $28, private r $70-140; ❄📶) A rambling Victorian house located in the center of town, this hostel packs in dusty long-distance backpackers during June and July, with a more varied mix of hikers, anglers, climbers and international travelers the rest of the year. There's a full kitchen, free coffee and bicycles for use, as well as a communal outdoors-loving atmosphere. Bikes free for guests. Adults only.

Owner Matt Meyers, an avid climber, is an excellent source of information. Hostel showers are available for use by non-guests for $5.

LEGENDARY SKIES

Created and run by Kris Hohag, a young and passionate leader and member of the local tribal council, **Legendary Skies Enterprises** (☎760-920-3389; www.legendaryskiesenterprises.com; half day per 2 people $200) is dedicated to the revitalization of indigenous languages, culture and education. As part of its mission, Kris organizes guided trips, or more accurately acts as the host to educate visitors about the land around the Owens Valley, known as the 'place of flowing water' by Paiute. As Kris points out, everywhere is sacred to the Paiute and thus needs to be protected. One way of doing this is by building a thriving tribal tourism economy and offering cultural knowledge as a career path to young tribal members. All trips involve guided tours of the Owens Valley Paiute Shoshone Cultural Center.

★**Bishop Creekside Inn** MOTEL $$
(☎760-872-3044; www.bishopcreeksideinn.com; 725 N Main St; r from $130;) At Bishop's most upscale lodging, woodsy art and Western-style leather armchairs outfit rooms that come with marble bathrooms (with walk-in glass showers), Keurig coffee-makers and thick duvet bedding. Ask for a room with a small patio alongside pretty Bishop Creek, which runs right through the grounds; it can be crossed via a bridge that leads to the pool.

Eating & Drinking

Stock up on snacks and camp-food essentials at bargain-basement prices at the **Grocery Outlet** (☎760-872-1505; 1320 N Main St; 7am-9pm). The Manor Market sells organic meat, eggs and locally grown vegetables. After the October harvest, unshelled pine nuts can be found for sale around town. And there are pick-your-own cherries, pears, peaches and apples, as well as homemade goat cheese, at Apple Hill Farms south of town.

★**Erick Schat's Bakery** BAKERY $
(☎760-873-7156; www.schatsbakery.com; 763 N Main St; sandwiches $6-10; 8:30am-3:30pm Mon-Thu, to 4pm Fri, 6am-5pm Sat & Sun;) A deservedly hyped tourist mecca filled to the rafters with racks of fresh bread, dipping oil, jams and other goodies, Schat's has been making baked goods since 1938. Some of the desserts, including the crispy cookies and bear claws, are addictive, and call for repeated trips while in town. Also has a popular sandwich bar and outdoor tables.

Holy Smoke Texas Style BBQ BARBECUE $
(☎760-872-4227; www.holysmoketexasstylebbq.com; 772 N Main St; $9-19; 11am-9pm Wed-Mon;) Tasty barbecue food, flavorful smoky pulled pork and ridiculously cheesy baked mac 'n' cheese. The redneck taco comes with homemade cornbread piled with chopped brisket, and outlaw coleslaw or potato salad on the side. Slather it in four kinds of house-made sauce: ghost pepper, spicy, hot and regular. There's country apple crisp or banana pudding for dessert.

Mercato Mexico MEXICAN $
(☎760-873-4546; 276 Warren St; mains $9; 8am-7pm Mon-Sat, 9:30am-6pm Sun) The most unassuming Mexican place in town is probably the best. The children of the owners of this mom-and-pop grocery have added a counter up front and two tiny tables in back where you can dine on quality burritos, bowls and tacos, as well as specialties like *pozole* (thick soup with pork, garlic and corn) and *mulitas* (crispy tortilla with grilled meat).

Back Alley AMERICAN $$
(☎760-873-5777; www.thebackalleybowlandgrill.com; 649 N Main St; mains $8-20; 11:30am-10pm Sun-Thu, to midnight Fri & Sat) Tucked off the main drag, behind Yamatani's Restaurant, this busy bowling-alley bar and grill (with bowling-pin carpeting!) earns the locals' affection with huge portions of fresh fish, sirloin steak and burgers. Specials come with loads of sides and the homemade desserts are surprisingly good. Bowling is $4 per person, plus $2 shoe hire.

Indy Coffee Roasting Company CAFE
(www.indyroasting.com; 307 S Main St; 8am-2pm Sun) San Francisco transplants and passionate java connoisseurs Deena and Gunner have restored the old Bishop jailhouse into a specialty coffee-bean manufacturing space that opens as a cafe on Sunday; it adjoins their hair salon. Enjoy European-style pour-overs, pastries and ping-pong out in the garden, while getting to know locals. Check out the pantry, housed in the former jail shower.

The owners, dedicated to historical and environmental conservation in the Owens Valley, have resurrected the El Camino Sierra brand and logo.

Looney Bean Coffee CAFE
(☎760-873-3311; www.looneybean.com; 399 N Main St; 5:30am-6pm;) Yes it's a small chain (there are branches in Mammoth, Oregon and Colorado too), but locals crowd the counters in the morning for fine coffee and an expanded menu of excellent salads, sandwiches and healthy bowls ($10.50), besides pancakes, bagels, tasty scones and pastries for snacking. A few street-side tables make great spots to linger on glorious sunny days.

Mountain Rambler Brewery MICROBREWERY
(☎760-258-1348; www.mountainramblerbrewery.com; 186 S Main St; 11:30am-10:30pm Sun-Thu, to 11:30pm Fri & Sat;) Rows of picnic tables and a high ceiling give this spot a beer-garden feel. Its own beers are mixed in with a rotating selection of artisan brews, and there's live music several nights a week. Visit at lunch or dinner for pub fare like burgers or more sophisticated dishes such as arugula and goat-cheese flatbread pizza ($10) and lamb empanadas ($5.50).

Information

Bishop Area Visitors Bureau (760-873-8405; www.bishopvisitor.com; 690 N Main St; 10am-5pm Mon-Sat;) Helpful and enthusiastic staff with information on accommodation and activities in Bishop and the surrounding region.

Inyo National Forest Wilderness Permit Office (760-873-2400; www.fs.usda.gov/inyo; 351 Pacu Lane, Ste 200; 8am-4:30pm daily, Mon-Fri winter) Offices for Inyo National Forest staff and wilderness-permit office.

White Mountain Public Lands Information Station (760-873-2500; www.fs.usda.gov/inyo; 798 N Main St; 8am-noon & 1-5pm daily, 8am-noon & 1-4pm Mon-Fri winter) Wilderness permits, and trail and campground information for the entire area.

Public showers are available in town at **Wash Tub** (760-873-6627; 236 N Warren St; 7am-10pm;).

Getting There & Away

Bishop sits at the junction of Hwys 395 and 6; Hwy 6 runs north into Nevada. Eastern Sierra Transit (p709) buses stop here on their way between Lone Pine ($7.25) and Reno, NV ($53); buses leave once a day in the morning Monday to Friday.

Big changes are expected in the coming years, wiht low-cost airlines aiming to fly between Bishop and major cities such as Los Angeles, Denver and San Francisco.

Big Pine

This blink-and-you've-missed-it town has a few motels and basic eateries. It mainly functions as a launchpad for the Ancient Bristlecone Pine Forest (p730) and for the granite **Palisades** in the John Muir Wilderness, a rugged cluster of peaks that includes six above 14,000ft. Stretching beneath the pinnacles is **Palisade Glacier**, (Map p700; May-Oct) the southernmost in the USA and the largest in the Sierra Nevada; pick up the trailhead at Glacier Lodge.

Glacier Lodge (Map p700; 760-938-2837; www.glacierlodge395.com; 100 Glacier Lodge Rd; tent/RV sites $28/45-55, cabins $176-334; Apr or May–mid-Nov;) is a bunch of rustic cabins with kitchens, as well as a campground. Though the original building no longer exists, it was one of the earliest Sierra getaways when it was built in 1917. Two-night minimum stay.

Independence

This sleepy highway town has been a county seat since 1866, but it's on the map because of its proximity to the Manzanar National Historic Site – the concentration camp in which Japanese people were held against their will by the US Government during WWII. West of town via Onion Valley Rd (known as Market St in town), pretty **Onion Valley** harbors the trailhead for the **Kearsarge Pass**, once a Paiute trade route. It's also the quickest east-side access to Kings Canyon National Park.

If possible, visit during Independence's blowout **4th of July parade**, when former residents return from far and wide for a day filled with classic Americana: firehouse pancake breakfast, jumping-frog races, a spelling bee open to all (including adults), historical reenactments, deep-pit barbecue in the afternoon and, of course, fireworks.

Sights

★Manzanar National Historic Site HISTORIC SITE
(Map p700; 760-878-2194; www.nps.gov/manz; 5001 Hwy 395; 9am-4:30pm;) FREE A stark wooden guard tower alerts drivers to one of US history's darkest chapters, which unfolded on a barren, windy sweep of land some 5 miles south of Independence. Little remains of the infamous war concentration camp, a dusty square mile where more than 10,000 people of Japanese ancestry were corralled during WWII. The camp's lone remaining building, the former high-school auditorium, houses a superb interpretive center. A visit is one of California's historical highlights and should not be missed.

Eastern California Museum MUSEUM
(Map p700; 760-878-0258; www.inyocounty.us/ecmsite; 155 N Grant St; donation requested; 10am-5pm;) This museum contains one of the most complete collections of Paiute and Shoshone baskets in the country, as well as artifacts from the Manzanar National Historic Site and historic photographs of primitively equipped local rock climbers scaling Sierra peaks, including Mt Whitney.

Sleeping & Eating

USFS Campgrounds CAMPGROUND $
(www.fs.usda.gov; tent & RV sites $14-21; approx May-Sep;) There are three USFS campgrounds alongside Independence Creek, including Onion Valley Campground at the

California Wildlife

Unique creatures great and small inhabit the land, sky and waters of California's diverse ecosystems. Visit them at the ocean or in the forest, or just scan the skies.

MICHAEL MIKE L. BAIRD/ GETTY IMAGES ©

1. Elephant seal
Equipped with a trunk-like nose, the enormous males noisily battle for dominance on the beach.

2. Black bear
The name is misleading, the bears' fur can be shades of brown, black, cinnamon or tawny blond.

3. California condor
A 10ft wingspan is the hallmark of these endangered carrion scavengers. Captive breeding has increased the population, and lead poisoning – once the condors' biggest threat – has become less prevalent since a 2019 law banned the use of lead ammunition for hunting in California.

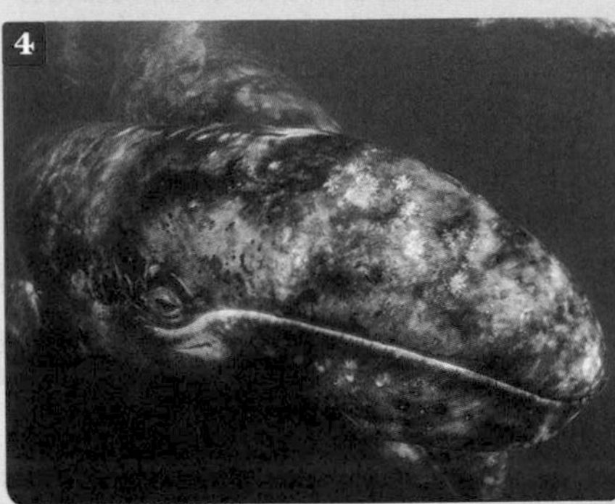

4. Gray whale
Dramatic breaches and the puffs of water spouts mark the passage of these school-bus-size mammals. Pods of whales migrate yearly between Mexico and Alaska, with peak viewing between December and April.

5. California sea lion
With dog-like faces and oversized flippers, vocal sea lions typically haul out in large social groups. The crowd-pleasing colony at San Francisco's Pier 39 mysteriously appeared soon after the 1989 Loma Prieta earthquake.

6. Mule deer
Ubiquitous throughout the state, mule deer are recognizable by their ample ears and black foreheads. Bucks wear forked antler racks.

7. Desert tortoise
Able to live for over half a century, these high-desert reptiles burrow underground to survive extreme heat and cold.

8. Hawk
Frequently seen riding the thermal currents on windy ridges, a dozen types of hawk can be found in California. These speedy birds of prey are known for their keen eyesight and strong talons.

9. Mountain lion
Also known as cougars, panthers or pumas, these territorial big cats primarily stalk and feed on deer. They hunt from dusk to dawn, and can sprint at up to 50 miles per hour.

10. Banana slug
Tread carefully along the forest floor so you don't slip on these large and squishy bright-yellow specimens.

11. Monarch butterfly
These orange-and-black beauties flutter thousands of miles to complete their annual migration.

12. Elk
Three subspecies of elk roam the state, with majestic males parading chandeliers of velvety antlers, and bugling dramatically during the fall rutting season.

JOHN LUND / GETTY IMAGES ©
STEVE JOHNSON / GETTY IMAGES ©
MICHAEL MIKE L. BAIRDCOM / GETTY IMAGES ©
OCMKA / GETTY IMAGES ©
BMSE / GETTY IMAGES ©
MOOSE HENDERSON / GETTY IMAGES ©
MAUREEN P SULLIVAN / GETTY IMAGES ©
IOANNIS STERGIOPOULOS / SHUTTERSTOCK ©

WORTH A TRIP

ANCIENT BRISTLECONE PINE FOREST

For encounters with some of the earth's oldest living things, plan at least a half-day trip to the **Ancient Bristlecone Pine Forest** (760-873-2500; www.fs.usda.gov/inyo; White Mountain Rd; trails year-round, visitor center Fri-Mon mid-May–early Nov;). These gnarled, otherworldly-looking trees thrive above 10,000ft on the slopes of the seemingly inhospitable White Mountains, a parched and stark range that once stood even higher than the Sierra Nevada. The oldest tree – called Methuselah – is estimated to be more than 4700 years old, beating even the Great Sphinx of Giza by about two centuries.

To reach the groves, take Hwy 168 east 12 miles from Big Pine to White Mountain Rd, then turn left (north) and climb the curvy road 10 miles to **Schulman Grove**, named for the scientist who first discovered the trees' age in the 1950s. The entire trip takes about one hour. There's access to self-guided trails, and a solar-powered **visitor center** (760-873-2500; www.fs.usda.gov/inyo; White Mountain Rd; per person/car $3/6; 10am-5pm Jun-Aug, to 4pm Fri-Sun May-Jun). White Mountain Rd is usually closed from November to April (if you're very fit it's possible to hike or snowshoe in). It's nicest in August, when wildflowers sneak out through the rough soil.

A second grove, the **Patriarch Grove**, is dramatically set within an open bowl and reached via a 12-mile, graded dirt road. Four miles further on you'll find a locked gate, which is the departure point for day hikes to **White Mountain Peak** – at 14,246ft, it's the third-highest mountain in California. The round trip is about 14 miles via an abandoned road, soon passing through the **Barcroft High Altitude Research Station**. Some ride the route on mountain bikes; the nontechnical and marmot-laden road winds above the tree line, though, so the high elevation makes the going tough. Allow plenty of time and bring at least two quarts of water per person. For maps and details, stop at the White Mountain ranger station (p726) in Bishop.

For altitude adjustment or some good stargazing, spend a night at the **Grandview Campground** (877-444-6777; www.recreation.gov; White Mountain Rd; donation $5;), at 8600ft. It has awesome views, tables and vault toilets, but no water. The road in may be closed during winter.

Kearsarge Pass trailhead. Reservations available at www.recreation.gov.

Mt Williamson Motel & Base Camp CABIN **$**
(Map p700; 760-878-2121; www.mtwilliamsonmotel.com; 515 S Edwards St; r $95-145;) A low-key hiker favorite, Mt Williamson has basic cabins with flat-screen TVs, calico bedspreads, tea kettles and arresting prints of the local bighorn sheep, all nestled among fruit trees. Ask about the hiker packages that include trailhead transportation. Full family-style breakfast in summer months.

Winnedumah Hotel HISTORIC HOTEL **$$**
(Map p700; 760-878-2040; www.winnedumah.com; 211 N Edwards St; d $120-165;) Young new owners have given this previously neglected grande dame from the 1920s a much-needed shot in the arm. The TV-free rooms remain sparsely and simply furnished, but the bones of the building, including handsome wood floors, staircase and lobby pillars, have been burnished and the original piano from the late 19th century restored.

Still Life Cafe FRENCH **$$**
(Map p700; 760-878-2555; 135 S Edwards St; lunch $9-16, dinner $16-29; 1-3:30pm & 5:30-9pm Wed-Sun) Fairly upscale and unexpected in such a flyspeck town, the Still Life prepares *escargot* (snails), steak *au poivre* (with peppercorn) and other French bistro faves. Dishes are served with Gallic charm in this dimly lit, eclectically decorated dining room. A number of French wines, too.

Lone Pine

Tiny Lone Pine is the gateway to big things. In the 1920s cinematographers discovered that the nearby Alabama Hills were a picture-perfect movie set for Westerns, and stars from Gary Cooper to Gregory Peck could often be spotted swaggering about town. West of Lone Pine, the jagged incisors of the Sierra surge skyward in all their raw and fierce glory. Cradled by scores of smaller pinnacles, Mt Whitney, the loftiest peak in the contiguous USA, is a bit hard to pick out from Hwy 395, so, for the best views, take a drive along Whitney Portal Rd through the Alabama Hills. The country's lowest point is only 80 miles (as the crow flies) east of here: Badwater in Death Valley. Climbing to Mt Whitney's summit is among the most popular hikes in the entire country.

Sights

★Alabama Hills NATURAL FEATURE

(Movie Flat Rd/Whitney Portal Rd; P) FREE The warm colors and rounded contours of the Alabama Hills, located on Whitney Portal Rd/Movie Flat Rd, stand in contrast to the jagged, snowy Sierras just behind. The setting for countless ride-'em-out movies, the popular *Lone Ranger* TV series and, more recently, parts of *Iron Man* (Jon Favreau, 2008) and Quentin Tarantino's *Django Unchained* (2012), the orange rock formations are a beautiful place to experience sunrise or sunset.

Museum of Western Film History MUSEUM

(760-876-9909; www.museumofwesternfilm history.org; 701 S Main St; adult/under 12yr $5/free; 10am-5pm Mon-Sat, to 4pm Sun; P) More than 400 movies, not to mention numerous commercials (mostly for rugged SUVs and Jeeps), have been shot in the area. This fascinating museum contains paraphernalia from locally set films, not just Westerns (as the name of the museum suggests). One of the most fascinating pieces in the collection is the 1928 Lincoln camera car – mounted cameras caught the action while cars drove alongside galloping horses. See items from *Django Unchained*, *Tremors*, *Star Trek* and other memorabilia in engaging exhibits.

Sleeping

★Alabama Hills Bureau of Land Management CAMPGROUND

(www.blm.gov/visit/alabama-hills; Movie Flat Rd, Alabama Hills) FREE You can't go wrong with free camping amid some of the most striking scenery in the Sierras. Go along Movie Flat Rd, then pull off onto any of the dirt roads to find a private spot behind a rock formation with snowcapped mountains towering above. Of course, services are nonexistent, but for those you can head into Lone Pine, a short drive away.

Tuttle Creek CAMPGROUND $

(Map p49; www.blm.gov/visit/tuttle-creek-campground-0; tent & RV sites $5;) Off Whitney Portal Rd, this first-come, first-served Bureau of Land Management campground has 83 primitive sites at 5120ft with panoramic 'pinch-me!' views of the Sierras, the White Mountains and the rosy Alabama Hills. There's not much shade, though. It's near a small river, so occasionally can get mosquitos and is rather windy. Drop toilets on site.

Lone Pine Campground CAMPGROUND $

(Map p700; www.fs.usda.gov; Whitney Portal Rd, tent & RV sites $22; mid-Apr–Oct;) About midway between Lone Pine and Whitney Portal, this popular creekside USFS campground (elevation 6000ft) offers vault toilets and potable water. Also has a designated family section. Can get busy in summer.

★Whitney Portal Hostel & Hotel HOSTEL, MOTEL $

(760-876-0030; www.mountwhitneyportal.com; 238 S Main St; dm/d from $34/112;) A popular launchpad for Mt Whitney trips and a locus of post-hike wash ups (public showers are available), the Whitney has the cheapest beds in town – reserve dorms months ahead for July and August. There's no common space, just well-maintained single-sex and coed bunk-bed rooms, though amenities include towels, TVs, in-room kitchenettes and stocked coffeemakers.

Dow Villa Motel HOTEL, MOTEL $$

(760-876-5521; www.dowvillamotel.com; 310 S Main St; r $85-172; P) John Wayne and Errol Flynn are among the stars who have stayed at this venerable hotel. Built in 1923, the place has been restored but retains much of its rustic charm. The rooms in the newer motel section have air-con but are also more generic. The cheaper rooms have shared bathrooms. Wi-fi in the historic wing is only guaranteed in the lobby.

Eating

Alabama Hills Cafe DINER $

(760-876-4675; www.alabamahillscafe.com; 111 W Post St; breakfast items $9.50-14; 6am-3pm Fri-Sun, to 2pm Mon-Thu;) Just off the main streets, at everyone's favorite breakfast joint, the portions are big, the bread is freshly baked and the soups are hearty. Sandwiches and fruit pies make lunch an attractive option too. You can also plan your

HIKING MT WHITNEY

The mystique of 14,494ft **Mt Whitney** (Map p700; www.fs.usda.gov/inyo; Whitney Portal Rd) captures the imagination, and conquering its hulking bulk becomes a sort of obsession for many. The main **Mt Whitney Trail** (the easiest and busiest one) leaves from Whitney Portal, about 13 miles west of Lone Pine via Whitney Portal Rd (closed in winter), and climbs about 6000ft over 11 miles. It's a super-strenuous, really, really long walk that'll wear out even experienced mountaineers, but it doesn't require technical skills if attempted in summer or early fall. Earlier or later in the season, you'll likely need an ice axe and crampons, and to overnight.

Many people in good physical condition make it to the top, although only superbly conditioned, previously acclimatized hikers should attempt this as a day hike. Breathing becomes difficult at these elevations and altitude sickness is a common problem. Rangers recommend spending a night camping at the trailhead and another at one of the two camps along the route: **Outpost Camp** at 3.5 miles or **Trail Camp** at 6 miles up the trail.

When you pick up your permit and pack-out kits (hikers must pack out their poop) at the Eastern Sierra Interagency Visitor Center in Lone Pine, get the latest info on weather and trail conditions. Near the trailhead, the **Whitney Portal Store** (Map p700; 760-876-0030; www.facebook.com/WhitneyPortalStore; hours vary May-Nov) sells groceries and snacks. It also has public showers ($5) and a cafe with enormous burgers and pancakes. The message board on its website is a good starting point for Whitney research.

The biggest obstacle in getting to the peak may be to obtain a **wilderness permit**, which is required for all overnight trips and for day hikes past Lone Pine Lake (about 2.8 miles from the trailhead). A quota system limits daily access to 60 overnight and 100 day hikers from May to October. Because of the huge demand, permits are distributed via the online **Mt Whitney lottery** (760-873-2483; www.fs.usda.gov/inyo; administration fee $6, plus per person $15; 8am-4:30pm), with applications accepted from February to mid-March.

Want to avoid the hassle of getting a permit for the main Mt Whitney Trail? Consider ascending this popular pinnacle from the west, using the **backdoor route** from Sequoia and Kings Canyon National Parks. It takes about six days from Crescent Meadow via the High Sierra Trail to the John Muir Trail – with no Whitney Zone permit required – and wilderness permits are much easier to secure.

drive through the Alabama Hills with the help of the map on the menu and rock formations painted on the walls.

Lone Pine Smokehouse BARBECUE $
(760-876-4433; www.lonepinesmokehouse.com; 325 S Main St; sandwiches & mains $8-23; noon-8pm Thu-Mon) The quality at this friendly Texas-style-barbecue place seems to be hit or miss – the beef brisket and pulled pork are most consistent. Despite the Western-themed facade, the dining room is simple, unadorned and modern. It's best to grab an outdoor table on a sunny day (dogs allowed). Regular live-music events; enquire inside.

Lone Star Bistro SANDWICHES $
(760-876-1111; 107 N Main St; sandwiches from $6; 7am-5pm Mon-Thu, to 6pm Fri-Sun) You can satisfy most of your needs at this mash-up of a gift shop, deli, ice-cream parlor and cafe. Soups, pastries and hiking fare to go are also offered.

Shopping

Elevation SPORTS & OUTDOORS
(760-876-4560; www.sierraelevation.com; 150 S Main St, cnr Whitney Portal Rd; 9am-6:30pm Sun-Thu, to 7pm Fri & Sat) Rents bear canisters and crampons, and sells hiking, backpacking and climbing gear.

Information

Eastern Sierra Interagency Visitor Center
(760-876-6222; www.fs.fed.us/r5/inyo; cnr Hwys 395 & 136; 8am-5pm, 8:30am-4:30pm winter) Well worth a stop, this USFS information center for the Sierra Nevada, Death Valley and Mt Whitney is about 1.5 miles south of town. The place to get trail info, plus self-issue wilderness permits (in the winter months) and pack-out-your-poop packs.

Understand California

History

On a Pacific island ruled by Amazon queen Califia, women warriors wear golden armor and ride dragons...recognize the story? Today the heroine of Garci Rodríguez de Montalvo's 1500 Spanish novel is better known as the namesake of California, and the basis of Hollywood superhero Wonder Woman. Califia was fictional – this land was home to 500 Native American nations. But that didn't stop generations of prospectors from searching these shores for golden treasure and wild women. Spoiler alert: they got more than they bargained for in California.

Feast & Famine

Gold was found by Native Californians on their land long before Spanish conquistadors arrived, but it had no practical use. Stone arrows, spearheads and hooks were highly effective Native Californian hunting technologies, and finely woven reed baskets could carry water and even serve as cooking vessels. Native Californian meals were seasonal and creative, featuring game sopped up with acorn-meal bread. Seashell middens on the Channel Islands are leftovers from lavish seafood feasts.

Human settlement began in Native California as early as 19,000 years ago, and communities flourished side by side. Native Californians passed knowledge of hunting grounds and turf boundaries from generation to generation in song, in at least 100 distinct languages.

Find out more about the traditions of indigenous Californians with *California Indians and Their Environment*, an engaging and accessible natural-history guide by Kent Lightfoot and Otis Parrish.

Over centuries, each nation became uniquely adapted to local ecosystems. Northern coastal fishing communities such as the Ohlone, Miwok and Pomo built snug, subterranean roundhouses and sweat lodges, where they held ceremonies, told stories and gambled for fun. Northern hunting and fishing communities like the Hupa, Karok and Wiyot constructed big houses and redwood dugout canoes, while the Modoc traveled between summer tipis and winter dugouts. Kumeyaay and Chumash villages dotted the central coast, where they fished and paddled seaworthy canoes all the way to the Channel Islands. Southern Mojave, Yuma and Cahuilla nations developed irrigation systems for farming in the desert, and made sophisticated pottery to conserve precious water.

TIMELINE

13,000–6000 BC

Native American communities settle this land, from Yurok redwood plank houses in the north to Kumeyaay thatch-domed dwellings in the south.

AD 1542–43

Portuguese navigator Juan Rodríguez Cabrillo and his Spanish crew are among the first Europeans to sail California's coast. His journey ends in the Channel Islands with a deadly gangrenous wound.

1769

Franciscan friar Junípero Serra and Captain Gaspar de Portolá lead a Spanish expedition to establish missions, rounding up Native Californians as converts and slave labor.

By the time Europeans came to their land, 300,000 Native Californians were flourishing here. Their first encounter did not bode well. When English sea captain Sir Francis Drake harbored briefly on Miwok land north of San Francisco in 1579, shamans saw their arrival as a warning of apocalypse. The omens weren't wrong, just off by a couple of centuries. By 1869, a century after Spanish colonists arrived, California's indigenous population would be decimated by 90%, due to introduced European diseases, conscripted labor, violence, marginalization and hunger in their own fertile lands.

Cowboys on a Mission

While Spanish conquistadors came to California for imperial glory, Russian and English traders came to warm up. They bartered with Native Californians for warm fur pelts, and soon business was booming – but Spain wasn't getting a cut of the action. So for the glory of God and the tax coffers of Spain, in 1769 Spain decided to establish missions across California. According to plan, these missions would be self-sustaining and run by local converts within 10 years. This venture was approved by quixotic Spanish colonial official José de Gálvez of Mexico, known for wild schemes.

Immediately after Spain's missionizing plan was approved, it began to fail. While Franciscan friar Junípero Serra and Captain Gaspar de Portolá made the overland journey to establish Mission San Diego de Alcalá in 1769, only half the sailors on their supply ships survived. Portolá headed to a fabled cove to the north, but failing to recognize Monterey Bay in the fog, he gave up and turned back.

Portolá reported to Gálvez that if the Russians or English wanted California, they were welcome to it. But Serra wouldn't give up, and secured support to set up presidios (forts) alongside missions. Soldiers weren't paid regularly, and often looted and pillaged local communities. Clergy objected to this treatment of potential converts, but relied on soldiers to round up conscripts to build missions. In exchange for their forced labor, Native Californians were promised one scant meal a day and a place in God's kingdom – which came much sooner than expected, due to diseases including smallpox, measles and syphilis that the Spanish introduced.

California's indigenous nations often rebelled against Spanish colonists, and more Native Californians died than were converted. So after building 21 missions and planting California's first vineyards, Spain stopped sending soldiers and supplies. The missions were over, but the cowboys were just getting started.

Native Californian Sites

- *Indian Canyons & Tahquitz Canyon (Palm Springs)*
- *Autry National Center (Griffith Park, LA)*
- *Indian Grinding Rock State Historic Park (Gold Country)*
- *California State Indian Museum (Sacramento)*
- *Maidu Museum & Historical Site (Roseville)*
- *Patrick's Point State Park (North Coast)*

1821

Mexican independence ends Spanish colonization of California. Mexico inherits 21 missions, along with unruly cowboys and a decimated Native Californian population.

1835

An emissary of US President Andrew Jackson makes a formal offer to buy Alta California, but Mexico unsuccessfully tries to sell it off to Britain instead.

1848

Gold is discovered near present-day Placerville by mill employees. San Francisco tabloid publisher, speculator and bigmouth Sam Brannan lets the secret out, and the gold rush is on.

1850

With hopes of solid-gold tax revenues, the US declares California the 31st state. When miners find tax loopholes, SoCal ranchers are left carrying the tax burden, creating early north–south rivalries.

Mexican Rule & Mexican Standoffs

With disease-plagued missions and flea-ridden presidios, California seemed like a minor concession when Spain lost it to Mexico in the 1810–21 Mexican War of Independence – but California's rancheros (ranchers) saw an opportunity. In 1834, Californian rancheros convinced Mexico's new government to secularize the missions and lease fertile mission lands.

By law, half the lands were supposed to go to Native Californians who worked at the missions, but few actually received their entitlements. Californian rancheros able to read and sign Spanish deeds snapped up mission property to expand their ranches, capitalizing on the growing market for cowhides and tallow (a key ingredient in soap). By 1846, most of the land and wealth in California was held by just 46 ranchero families. Rancheras (ranch women) owned many of the largest Californian ranches, rode horses as hard as men, and caused romantic scandals worthy of modern telenovelas. Ranches built by women in the 1830s to '50s became the foundations of several California cities, including San Francisco, Palo Alto, San Jose, Santa Rosa, St Helena and Healdsburg.

The distance between each of California's Spanish colonial missions equaled a day's journey by horseback. Learn more about the missions' historical significance and cultural influence at www.missionscalifornia.com.

Meanwhile, Americans were arriving at the trading post of Los Angeles via the Old Spanish Trail. Northern passes through the Sierra Nevada were trickier, as the Donner Party tragically discovered in 1846 – stranded by snow near Lake Tahoe, some survivors resorted to cannibalism. Still, the US saw potential in California. When US president Andrew Jackson offered the financially strapped Mexican government $500,000 for the territory in 1835, the offer was tersely rejected.

After the US annexed the Mexican territory of Texas in 1845, Mexico broke off diplomatic relations and ordered all foreigners without proper papers deported from California. The Mexican–American War was declared in 1846, lasting two years with very little fighting in California. Hostilities ended with the Treaty of Guadalupe Hidalgo, in which Mexico ceded much of its northern territory (including Alta California) to the US. The timing was lucky for the US, and unfortunate for Mexico: only weeks after the US took possession of California, gold was discovered.

Stranded in Sierra Nevada blizzards in 1846, some pioneers resorted to extreme survival measures – including eating their dead companions. Their harrowing tale is captured in *Desperate Passage: The Donner Party's Perilous Journey West* (2008), by Ethan Rarick.

'Gold! Gold! Gold!'

California's gold rush began with a bluff. When unscrupulous tabloid publisher Sam Brannan heard gold flakes were found near Sutter's Mill in the Sierra Nevada foothills, he published the rumor as fact, figuring it might sell some newspapers. At first Brannan's story didn't generate much excitement – gold flake had surfaced in southern California as far back as 1775. So he ran another story, this time verified by Mormon employees at Sutter's Mill who had sworn him to secrecy. Brannan

1851

The discovery of gold in Australia means cheering in the streets of Melbourne and panic in the streets of San Francisco, as the price for California gold plummets.

1869

On May 10 the 'golden spike' is nailed in place at Promontory, UT, completing the first transcontinental railroad and connecting California with the East Coast.

1882

The US Chinese Exclusion Act suspends new immigration from China, denies citizenship to those already in the country and sanctions racially discriminatory laws that remain on the books until 1943.

1906

An earthquake levels entire blocks of San Francisco in 42 seconds, setting off fires that rage for three days. Survivors start rebuilding immediately.

THE BEAR FLAG REPUBLIC

In June 1846, American settlers tanked up on liquid courage declared independence in the northern town of Sonoma. Not a shot was fired – instead, they captured the nearest Mexican official and hoisted a hastily made flag. Locals awoke to discover they were living in the independent 'Bear Republic,' under a flag painted with a grizzly that looked like a shaggy dog. The Bear Flag Republic lasted only a month before US orders telling settlers to stand down arrived.

kept his word until he reached San Francisco, where he legendarily ran through Portsmouth Sq brandishing gold entrusted to him as tithes for the Mormon church, shouting, 'Gold! Gold! Gold on the American River!'

Other newspapers around the world weren't scrupulous about the facts either, hastily publishing stories of gold discoveries near San Francisco. By 1850 – the year California was fast-tracked for admission as the 31st US state – California's non-native population had ballooned from 15,000 to 93,000. Early arrivals from around the world panned for gold side by side, slept in close quarters, guzzled locally made wine and slurped Chinese noodles.

But with each wave of new arrivals, gold became harder to find. In 1848, each prospector earned an average of about $300,000 in today's terms. By 1849 earnings were less than half that, and by 1865 they'd dropped to $35,000. When surface gold became scarce, miners picked and dynamited through mountains. The work was grueling and dangerous, and injuries often proved lethal. The cost of living in cold, filthy mining camps was sky-high – and many turned to paid company, booze and opium for consolation.

Vigilantes, Robber Barons & Railroads

The luckiest gold prospectors arrived early and got out quick, before other miners turned on them. Native Californian laborers who helped newcomers survive were denied the right to hold claims on their ancestral land. Successful Peruvians and Chileans were harassed and denied renewals to their mining claims, and most left California by 1855. Their 'Chilecito' neighborhood in San Francisco is now called Jackson Sq, but you can still order their signature drink: Pisco punch.

Criminal wrongdoing was often pinned on newcomers from Australia's penal colonies, dubbed the 'Sydney Ducks.' San Francisco's dockside 'Sydney-town' was burned down four times by arsonists, and San Francisco's self-appointed Committee of Vigilance lynched several 'Sydney Ducks' in rushed proceedings called 'kangaroo trials.' When gold was found in Australia in 1850, many Australians swiftly headed home.

Top California History Books

- *Slouching Towards Bethlehem (Joan Didion)*
- *Strangers from a Different Shore (Ronald Takaki)*
- *Alice: Memoirs of a Barbary Coast Prostitute (Ivy Anderson and Devon Angus)*
- *California: A History (Kevin Starr)*
- *City of Quartz (Mike Davis)*

1934

A longshoremen's strike ends with two strikers dead, 34 sympathizers shot and 40 gassed or beaten by police in San Francisco. After mass funeral processions and citywide strikes, shipping magnates meet union demands.

1942

Executive Order 9066 sends nearly 120,000 Japanese Americans to internment camps. Legal defenses raised by the Japanese American Citizens League lay the groundwork for the 1964 Civil Rights Act.

1955

Disneyland opens in Anaheim on July 17. As crowds swarm the park, plumbing breaks and Fantasyland springs a gas leak. Walt Disney calls a do-over, relaunching successfully the next day.

1965

20,000 National Guards are ordered to suppress the Watts Riots in LA, resulting in a six-day standoff between military and protestors. That same year, Rodney King is born.

As mining became industrialized, fewer miners were needed, and jobless prospectors turned on Chinese workers. Denied mining claims, many Chinese prospectors opened service-based businesses that survived when mining ventures went bust. By 1860, Chinese pioneers had become the second-most populous group in California after Mexicans – but this hard-won resilience met with irrational resentment. Discriminatory Californian laws restricting housing, employment and citizenship

CALIFORNIA'S CIVIL RIGHTS MOVEMENTS

Decades before the civil rights movement arrived in Washington DC, it was already underway in California. In 1942, almost 120,000 Japanese Americans living along the West Coast were ordered into internment camps by President Roosevelt – and the Japanese American Citizens League immediately filed suits that advanced all the way to the US Supreme Court. These lawsuits established groundbreaking civil rights legal precedents, and in 1992 internees received reparations and a presidential letter of apology.

Meanwhile, women and African Americans staffed California's wartime industries, and Mexican workers were recruited to fill labor shortages. By 1955, California's population had grown by almost 40%, surpassing 13 million, and an international cadre of engineers and skilled women technologists were founding California's high-tech industry. Yet at work and in civic life, California's immigrants did not always have a voice. Adopting the nonviolent resistance practices of Mahatma Gandhi and Martin Luther King Jr, labor leaders César Chávez and Dolores Huerta formed United Farm Workers in 1962 to champion the rights of immigrant laborers, bringing the issues of fair wages and pesticide health risks to the nation's attention.

California rallied for civil rights again in 2004, when then–San Francisco mayor (and future California governor) Gavin Newson began issuing marriage licenses to same-gender couples in defiance of the US Defense of Marriage Act, which limited marriage to opposite-gender couples. Court cases were appealed all the way to the Supreme Court, where the court found in favor of the California couples, and marriage equality became the law of the land nationwide.

Today civil rights remains top of mind in California, where immigrants and first-generation Americans represent over half the population – yet Immigration Customs Enforcement (ICE) raids, border camps, and other federal initiatives treat neighbors as criminals. Some California cities refuse to cooperate, citing long-standing sanctuary laws including Berkeley's trailblazing 1971 sanctuary resolution and San Francisco's 1989 citywide sanctuary law (the world's first). Under sanctuary laws, police stations, schools and hospitals don't have to assist federal authorities in deporting undocumented Californians who aren't charged with any crime. Despite threats by the Trump administration in 2017 to withhold federal funds, San Francisco and Berkeley reaffirmed their sanctuary policies – and California state legislators responded by declaring all of California a sanctuary state.

1966

Ronald Reagan is elected governor of California, setting a career precedent for C-tier entertainment figures. He serves until 1975, then becomes the 40th US president in 1981.

1967

The Summer of Love kicks off on January 14 in Golden Gate Park, where the Human Be-In blows minds and conch shells, and draft cards are used as rolling papers.

1968

Presidential candidate, former US attorney general and civil rights ally Robert Kennedy is fatally shot in Los Angeles after winning the critical California presidential primary.

1969

A UCLA computer connects to another at Stanford University, just long enough to read two characters before the system crashes. The internet is born.

for anyone born in China were passed and extended with the 1882 US Chinese Exclusion Act, which remained US law until 1943.

Immigrant rivalries were highly profitable for California's 'robber barons,' billionaire speculators notorious for union-busting and unsafe working conditions. The most notorious were 'The Big Four': Collis P Huntington, Leland Stanford, Mark Hopkins and Charles Crocker, known for their lavish estates, charitable giving to the arts and education, and cruel labor practices. To build railroads to their mines and East Coast markets, they rounded up Chinese workers for survival wages in brutal conditions. Workers were lowered down cliff faces in wicker baskets, planted lit dynamite sticks in rock crevices, then tugged the rope to be hoisted out of harm's way. Those who survived the day's work were confined to bunkhouses under armed guard in cold, remote mountain regions. With little other choice of legitimate employment, an estimated 12,000 Chinese laborers blasted through the Sierra Nevada, meeting the westbound end of the Transcontinental Railroad in 1869.

Immigrants denied entry under the Asian Exclusion Act carved heart-breaking poems into cell-block walls at Angel Island detention center. Poet Genny Lim championed the effort to preserve and translate their poignant words in *Island: Poetry and History of Chinese Immigrants on Angel Island, 1910-1940* (2014).

Oil & Water

During the US Civil War (1861–65), California couldn't count on food shipments from the East Coast, and started growing its own. California recruited homesteaders to farm the Central Valley with shameless propaganda. 'Acres of Untaken Government Land…for a Million Farmers…Health & Wealth without Cyclones or Blizzards,' trumpeted one California-boosting poster, neglecting to mention earthquakes or ongoing land disputes with rancheros and Native Californians. The hype worked: more than 120,000 homesteaders came to California in the 1870s and '80s.

Homesteaders soon discovered that California's gold rush had left the state badly tarnished. Cholera spread through open sewers of poorly drained camps, claiming many lives. Hills were stripped bare, vegetation wiped out, streams silted up, mercury washed into water supplies, and green valleys became deserts. Yet mining claims leased by the US government were tax-exempt, leaving insufficient public funds for public water works. Recognizing at last that water, not gold, was the state's most precious resource, Californians passed a pioneering environmental-protection law preventing dumping into rivers in 1884. Farmers rallied behind Southern Californian bond measures to build dams and aqueducts, transporting water all the way from the Sierras. By the 20th century, the lower one-third of the state claimed two-thirds of available water supplies.

Meanwhile, failed miner and real-estate speculator Edward Doheny made an unexpected discovery in Los Angeles: oil. In 1892, Doheny drilled his first oil well near where Dodger Stadium now stands, and within a year it was yielding 40 barrels daily. By 1900, California was producing 4 million barrels of 'black gold' annually. Downtown LA had

1977

San Francisco Supervisor Harvey Milk becomes the first openly gay man elected to public office in California. Milk sponsors a gay-rights bill before his murder by political opponent Dan White.

1989

On October 17, the Loma Prieta Earthquake hits 6.9 on the Richter scale near Santa Cruz, collapsing a two-level section of Interstate 880 and resulting in 63 deaths and almost 4000 injuries.

1992

Four white LA police officers charged with assaulting African American Rodney King are acquitted by a predominantly white jury. Six days of riots ensue.

1994

Orange County, one of the wealthiest municipalities in the US, declares bankruptcy after the county treasurer loses $1.7 billion in risky derivatives investments and pleads guilty to felony charges.

Marc Reisner's *Cadillac Desert: The American West and Its Disappearing Water* examines the contentious, sometimes violent water wars that gave rise to modern California.

boomed to 100,000 inhabitants, and California oil kickbacks greased the palms of politicians all the way to DC. Doheny's own back-door dealings were exposed in the 1920s Teapot Dome bribery scandal, inspiring Upton Sinclair's darkly satirical 1926 novel *Oil!* and the 2007 Oscar-winning drama *There Will Be Blood.*

While pastoral Southern California was urbanizing, Northern Californians who had witnessed mining and logging devastation were jump-starting the nation's first conservation movement. On a weekend visit from San Francisco to Yosemite Valley, Scottish immigrant John Muir found his calling as a naturalist. Muir founded the Sierra Club in 1892 and devoted his life to defending California wilderness against the encroachments of dams and urbanization.

After backpacking with Muir in Yosemite in 1903, President Theodore Roosevelt was convinced to preserve Yosemite as a national park. Yet despite Muir's passionate objections, Woodrow Wilson commissioned Hetch Hetchy Reservoir in 1913 to funnel water from Yosemite to the Bay Area. In drought-prone California, tensions between land developers and conservationists still run high.

Hollywood & Counterculture

By the 1920s, California's greatest export was the sunny, wholesome image it projected to the world through its homegrown film and TV industry. SoCal was a versatile stand-in for far-flung locales, and its ghost towns suited period dramas like Charlie Chaplin's *Gold Rush* (1925). But with its beach sunsets and palm-lined drives, California stole the scene in Technicolor movies and iconic TV shows. Gradually California shed its Wild West reputation to become a movie and TV star, dominating the screen behind teen surfers and beach blondes.

But Northern Californians didn't picture themselves as extras in *Beach Blanket Bingo* (1965). The Navy discharged WWII sailors for insubordination and homosexuality in San Francisco, as though that would teach them a lesson. Instead San Francisco became an outpost of free speech and free spirits, and everyone who was anyone got arrested here – including dancer Carol Doda for going topless, comedian Lenny Bruce for dropping F-bombs onstage, and City Lights Bookstore founder Lawrence Ferlinghetti for publishing Allen Ginsberg's epic poem *Howl.* Doda won and kept dancing for 45 years, Bruce was posthumously pardoned, and City Lights continues to celebrate its landmark 1957 free speech victory by publishing fresh verse and provocative prose.

To stop the spread of California counterculture, alarmed authorities turned to Hollywood. In 1947, Senator Joseph McCarthy vowed to root out suspected communists in the film industry. When 10 writers and directors refused to name names, the 'Hollywood Ten' were charged with

1994

The 6.7-magnitude Northridge earthquake strikes LA on January 17, killing 72 and causing $20 billion in property damage – one of the costliest natural disasters in US history.

2000

The Nasdaq crashes, ending the dot-com boom. Traditional industries gloat over the bubble burst, until knock-on effects lead to a devalued dollar and New York Stock Exchange slide.

2003

Republican Arnold Schwarzenegger (aka 'The Governator') is elected governor of California. Schwarzenegger breaks party ranks on environmental issues and wins re-election in 2007.

2004

Google's initial public offiersing raises a historic $1.67 billion at $85 per share. Since then share prices have increased over 900%; the company's market value now exceeds $1 trillion.

contempt of Congress and barred from working in Hollywood. But their impassioned defenses of the US Constitution were televised, generating public support nationwide. McCarthyism ended with an epic San Francisco sit-in in 1960.

California's counterculture got an unexpected boost from another government effort. To test psychoactive drugs intended to create the ultimate soldier, the CIA gave LSD to writer Ken Kesey. He saw the potential not for war but for a wild party, and spiked the punch at San Francisco's 1966 Trips Festival, organized by futurist Stewart Brand. But the all-time high was the January 14, 1967 Human Be-In in Golden Gate Park, where psychedelic trip-master Timothy Leary urged a crowd of 20,000 hippies to dream a new American dream and 'turn on, tune in, drop out.' Even after 'Flower Power' faded, other movements took root around the Bay Area, including Black Power, feminism and gay pride.

California came alive with protests, even on SoCal beaches. On January 28, 1969, an oil rig dumped 100,000 barrels of crude oil into the Santa Barbara Channel, killing dolphins, seals and thousands of birds. The laid-back SoCal beach community organized a highly effective protest, prompting the establishment of the US Environmental Protection Agency, the California Coastal Commission and pioneering pollution safeguards.

Geeking Out in California

When Silicon Valley introduced the first personal computer in 1968, advertisements gushed that Hewlett-Packard's new 'light' (40lb) machine could 'take on roots of a fifth-degree polynomial, Bessel functions, elliptic integrals and regression analysis' – all for just $33,000. Consumers didn't know quite what to do with such computers, but Trips Festival organizer Stewart Brand had a totally trippy idea: what if that technology could fit into the palm of your hand? Maybe then, the technology governments used to run countries could empower ordinary people.

When Brand shared this radical notion of 'personal computing' in his 1969 Whole Earth Catalog, it inspired a generation of technologists. At the 1977 West Coast Computer Faire, 21-year-old Steve Jobs and Steve Wozniak introduced the Apple II, a personal computer with unfathomable memory (4KB of RAM!) and microprocessor speed (1MHz!). But the question remained: what would ordinary people do with all that computing power?

By the mid-1990s an entire dot-com start-up industry boomed in Silicon Valley, and suddenly people were getting everything online. But when dot-com profits weren't forthcoming, venture-capital funding evaporated. When the Nasdaq plummeted on March 10, 2000, 23-year-old VPs and service sector employees lost their gigs overnight.

Roman Polanski's classic neo-noir thriller *Chinatown* (1974) is a fictionalized yet brutally truthful account of early-20th-century water wars waged to build Los Angeles.

2005

Antonio Villaraigosa is elected mayor of LA, becoming the first Latinx mayor since 1872. Born poor in East LA, he says in his victory speech, 'I will never forget where I came from.'

2007

Wildfires sweep drought-stricken Southern California, forcing one million people to evacuate their homes. Migrant workers, state prisoners and Tijuana firefighters help curb the blazes.

2008

California voters pass Proposition 8, defining legal marriage as between a man and a woman. California courts rule the law unconstitutional, and the Supreme Court upholds marriage equality nationwide in 2013.

2013

After years of construction delays and engineering controversies, the eastern span of the Bay Bridge opens. At more than $6 billion, it is the costliest public-works project in California history – so far.

As users searched for useful information and human connection, search engines and social media boomed. Steve Jobs was able to call Stewart Brand in 2007 with some news: he'd finally shrunk computers to fit into the palm of a hand. Smartphones took off, launching millions of apps.

Werner Herzog's documentary *Lo and Behold* (2016) explores the California origins of the internet and its impact on society.

Meanwhile, California's biotech industry has been quietly booming. Upstart company Genentech was founded in a San Francisco bar in 1976, and quickly got to work cloning human insulin and introducing the Hepatitis B vaccine. In 2004 California voters approved a $3-billion bond measure for stem-cell research, and by 2008 California had become the USA's biggest funder of stem-cell research, and the focus of Nasdaq's new Biotechnology Index. In 2020, voters re-funded the measure with $5.5 billion.

With cloud computing to store and access data, machine learning is making rapid advancements in healthcare. Covid-19 is putting these advancements to test, combining mass-testing and harm reduction strategies established in San Francisco during the HIV/AIDS epidemic with new technology-assisted testing and tracing protocols. So will machines save us all, or outlive us? That sounds like a good subject for a Hollywood movie – or at least a far-out conversation in a California marijuana dispensary (legal as of 2017). No matter what happens next, you can say you saw it coming in California.

2017

Threatened with defunding from the federal government, San Francisco and a dozen other California cities reinforce their sanctuary statutes, and California legislators declare California a sanctuary state.

2019

Firestorms sweep through LA County and NorCal Wine Country, just two years after the most destructive fires in California history. Pacific Gas and Electric is fined $2 billion for starting the fires, but has yet to pay.

2020

California is one of the first US states to declare quarantine in response to Covid-19, with key cities rapidly enacting public health measures to reduce risks.

2020

Former California attorney general and US Senator Kamala Harris is elected the nation's first female and biracial vice president.

The Way of Life

In the Southern California dreamworld, you wake up, have your shot of wheatgrass juice and roll down to the beach while the surf's up. Lifeguards wave as they jog by in their bathing suits. You skateboard down the boardwalk to your yoga class, where everyone admires your downward dog. A food truck pulls up with your favorite: sustainable fish tacos with organic mango chipotle salsa. But honestly, can you really make that SoCal dream come true?

Regional Identity

Now for the reality check. Any Northern Californian hearing your California dream is bound to get huffy. What, political protests and Silicon Valley start-ups don't factor in your dreams? But Southern Californians will also roll their eyes at these stereotypes: they didn't create NASA's Jet Propulsion Lab, SpaceX and almost half of the world's movies by slacking off.

Still, there is some truth to your California dreamscape. Nearly 70% of Californians live in coastal areas, even though California beaches aren't always sunny or swimmable. Self-help, fitness and body modification are major industries throughout the state, successfully marketed since the 1970s as 'lite' versions of religious experience – all the agony and ecstasy of the major religions, without all those heavy commandments. Exercise and healthy food help keep many Californians among the fittest in the nation. At the same time, millions of them apparently see no contradiction in consuming recreational marijuana, which was legalized in the state in 2017. Ahem.

Lifestyle

The charmed existence you dreamed about is a stretch, even in California. Few Californians can afford to spend entire days tanning and networking, what with all the aging UVA/UVB rays and sky-high rents out here. In fact, the rising cost of housing has of late reached a crisis level. Eight of the 10 most expensive US housing markets are in California, and in two of the most expensive areas, Newport Beach and Palo Alto, the average house price hovers around $2.5 million and $3 million respectively.

With a median annual household income of $71,000, buying a home these days is out of reach for many Californians. Indeed, the homeownership rate has dropped to 55%, down from a 60.7% peak in 2006. The high cost of living is also prompting more middle- and low-income Californians (especially millennials) to migrate to other states with more affordable pastures.

Thousands of Southern Californians practice Santería (also known as Lucumí), a fusion of Catholicism and Yoruba beliefs brought by West African slaves to the Caribbean, South America and sunny SoCal. Drop by a *botànica* (herbal folk-medicine shop) for charms and candles.

If you're a Californian aged 18 to 24, there's a 50/50 possibility that your roomies are your parents. Among adult Californians, one in four live alone, and about half are unmarried. If you're not impressed with your dating options in California, stick around: of those who are currently married, about a third won't be in 10 years. Increasingly Californians are shacking up: the number of unmarried cohabiting couples has increased 40% since 1990.

If you're like most Californians, you effectively live in your car. Californians commute an average of 29 minutes each way to work and spend at least $1 out of every $5 earned on car-related expenses. Small wonder that, according to the American Lung Association, six of the US cities with the highest year-round air-pollution levels are in California. But at least Californians are zooming ahead of the national energy-use curve in their smog-checked cars, buying more hybrid and fuel-efficient cars than any other state.

Around 691,000 Californians moved to another state in 2018. The most popular were Texas (86,164 people), Arizona (68,516 people) and Washington (55,467 people).

Homelessness

Surging homelessness has been a tragic consequence of the lack of affordable housing and the growing gap between income levels and the cost of living in California. In just one year, 2018 to 2019, the homeless rate jumped a whopping 17%. Living without permanent shelter is now a reality for at least 150,000 residents, or some 25% of the total US homeless population. Even in suburban and rural areas, people sleeping in cars, in tent encampments and under freeway bridges have become a common sight.

Homeless demographics are changing too. The good news: homelessness among military veterans has dropped to half of 2010 levels, helped largely by targeted public housing programs. There are also fewer homeless families with children, although 8000 families and 14,000 children are hardly numbers for rejoicing. Neither is the fact that about one third of the state's unhoused population is African American.

To counter this disturbing trend, the state government has allocated significant sums of money for emergency shelters, subsidized long-term housing, psychological counseling, job training and other measures. In 2018, voters approved Proposition 1, a $4 billion affordable housing bond, as well as Proposition 2, which funds housing for people with mental illnesses. It remains to be seen if these measures are sufficient in reversing the crisis or just the proverbial drop in the bucket.

Population

With almost 40 million residents, California is the most populous state in the USA. One in every eight Americans lives here. It is, however, no longer the fastest-growing state, adding only about 87,500 people in 2019 (0.2% vs 4.1% in Idaho, the current fastest-growing state). In fact, these days more people leave California than move here from other states, a trend that began in 2006, slowed around 2011 and picked up again in 2016.

Within California, there's a shift away from the coast to the inland areas, with the Central Valley and the Inland Empire (east of LA) posting especially robust growth rates. LA County, by contrast, lost residents in the last two years, even though it is still California's most populous. Although the High Sierras and southern deserts are sparsely populated, California's overall population density is 251 people per square mile – almost triple the national average.

Most Californians see their state as a laid-back, open-minded multicultural society that gives everyone a chance to live the American dream. Chicano pride, Black Power and LGBT+ pride all built political bases here. In 2017 then Governor Jerry Brown signed a law making California a 'sanctuary state,' thereby preventing local law enforcement from aiding federal authorities in detaining undocumented immigrants. It was upheld by the US Supreme Court in 2020.

Though written decades ago, Mike Davis' *City of Quartz* (1990) is an excoriating history of LA and a visionary glimpse into its possible future.

Immigration & Diversity

Immigration has been key to California's growth since its inception. California was a territory of Mexico and Spain before it became a US state, and has sustained one of the world's most diverse populations ever since. Today, more than 10 million Californians are immigrants. One of every four arrivals settles in California.

LATINX CALIFORNIA

The collective influence of Latinx on California life is huge. From Spanish-language billboards to radio and TV stations, you'll see, hear and experience Latinx culture all over California. Spanish is spoken everywhere from restaurant kitchens to boardrooms, and the mainstream supermarkets keep hosts of Latinx products on their shelves.

Although Latinx account for nearly 40% of the state's population, the group's political influence has so far lagged behind. Only 20% of the members of the California Legislature (State Senate and Assembly) members have Latinx roots. Leadership roles proved even more elusive, at least until 2005 when Antonio Villaraigosa became LA's first Latinx mayor since 1872. In 2014, Kevin de León became the first Latinx President pro tempore of the California State Senate in over a century. And Anthony Rendon, whose grandparents hail from Mexico, has served as Speaker of the California State Assembly since 2016. California also sends more than a dozen Latinx Congressional members to the US House of Representatives.

Most newcomers trace their origins to Mexico (four million), followed by the Philippines (848,999), China (798,000), India (532,000) and Vietnam (515,000). However, since 2010, twice as many immigrants are arriving from Asia as from Latin America. Many immigrants move to California to join family members already settled here. An estimated three million undocumented immigrants currently live in California, often with documented or naturalized family members.

Californian culture reflects the composite identity of the state. Latinx surpassed whites as the state's majority ethnic group in 2014 and now constitute 39% of the population (whites 37%). Some 15% of residents are Asian American, who make up about one third of the nation's Asian American population. There are thriving immigrant communities from China, Korea, Vietnam, Japan, Cambodia, Thailand and other parts of Asia. The greatest concentration can be found in the San Francisco Bay Area but many Asian immigrants also settled in Los Angeles, Orange, San Diego and Sacramento Counties.

As relatively late arrivals during the WWII shipping boom, California's African Americans have historically represented just 6% of the population while being a driving force in such fields as popular culture, politics, fashion, sports and more.

Religion

California is one of the most religiously diverse US states, but also one of the least religious. Less than half of Californians consider religion very important, and a quarter profess no religion at all. Of those Californians who do practice a religion, a third identify as Protestant and about 28% as Catholic. California is home to most of the nation's practicing Hindus, the biggest Jewish community outside New York, a sizable Muslim community and the largest number of Buddhists anywhere outside Asia. Californians have also established their own spiritual practices, including the Church of Satan, self-help movements and UFO cults.

Over 200 different languages are spoken in California, with English, Spanish, Chinese, Tagalog, Vietnamese and Korean in the top 10. Around 43% of state residents speak a language other than English at home.

Sports

Team Sports

California has more professional sports teams than any other state, and loyalties to National Basketball Association (NBA), National Football League (NFL) and major-league baseball teams run deep. To catch them in action, get your wallet ready. Tickets aren't cheap but sell out fast, especially for Golden State Warriors or LA Lakers basketball, Los Angeles

Chargers football, San Francisco Giants or LA Dodgers baseball, or LA Kings or San Jose Sharks hockey.

The ultimate grudge matches are between the San Francisco Giants and LA Dodgers, and the LA Lakers and LA Clippers. California college-sports rivalries are equally fierce, especially UC Berkeley's Cal Bears vs the Stanford University Cardinals, and the USC Trojans vs UCLA Bruins.

Not everything is invented in Silicon Valley: SoCal innovations include the space shuttle, Mickey Mouse, whitening toothpaste, the Hula-Hoop, Barbie, skateboard and surfboard technology and the Cobb salad.

To see small but dedicated crowds of hometown fans – and score cheaper tickets – watch women's pro basketball in LA, men's pro basketball in Sacramento, pro hockey in Anaheim or pro soccer in San Jose and LA. You may luck onto tickets for San Diego Padres and Los Angeles Angels major-league baseball games, and you can catch minor-league baseball teams up and down the state, especially the Sacramento River Cats.

A much anticipated event in 2020 was the opening of the SoFi Stadium in LA's Inglewood neighborhood. The home of the LA Rams and the LA Chargers will also host the 2022 Super Bowl and 2026 FIFA World Cup soccer games as well as the opening and closing ceremonies of the 2028 LA Summer Olympics.

LA is also poised to launch its own National Women's Soccer League team in 2022. Founded almost entirely by women, including Natalie Portman, Mia Hamm and Serena Williams, the franchise will likely be called Angel City.

Surfing, Skating & Racing

Californians have a reputation as daredevils, and if you can't join them, you can always watch them from the comfort of a beach chair. Surfing first hit California in 1914, when Irish-Hawaiian surfer George Freeth gave demonstrations at Huntington Beach in Orange County.

Between waves, bored kids along LA's Santa Monica–Venice border took to the streets with roller-skate wheels bolted onto old dresser drawers. Skateboarding took off in the 1970s, with kids breaking into SoCal's dry swimming pools to perfect their tricks, as captured in the 2001 skate-cult documentary *Dogtown and Z Boys*.

Californians like fast horses and even faster cars. San Diego County's Del Mar is the state's ritziest horse-racing track, while LA County's historic Santa Anita Park has been featured in Hollywood movies from the Marx Brothers classic *A Day at the Races* to *Seabiscuit*. The track made negative headlines in 2019 when 37 horses had to be euthanized after suffering injuries during races and training sessions.

Every April the Acura Grand Prix of Long Beach is an IndyCar race roaring through the streets of Long Beach, just south of LA. Sonoma Raceway hosts Nascar, IndyCar, motorcycle and drag racing, and Bakersfield holds Nascar and other auto-racing events year-round.

FORGING THE PATH FOR MARRIAGE EQUALITY

California was on the frontlines of civil rights during the fight for marriage equality. In open defiance of the 1996 US Defense of Marriage Act (DOMA) that defined marriage as between opposite-sex partners, then San Francisco mayor Gavin Newsom began issuing marriage certificates to same-sex couples in 2004. The issue went to the California Supreme Court, which, in 2008, found DOMA in violation of California's constitution.

However, the court ruling was overturned in November 2008 when opponents of same-sex marriage rallied to narrowly pass Proposition 8. The ballot measure proposed a state constitutional amendment barring same-sex marriage.

In 2010, a US District Court Judge struck down Proposition 8 as unconstitutional, a ruling upheld by the Ninth Circuit Court of Appeals in 2012 and the US Supreme Court in 2013. Amid celebrations, same-sex marriages resumed in California.

On Location: Film & TV

Picture Orson Welles whispering 'Rosebud,' Judy Garland clicking her ruby-red heels three times, or the Terminator threatening 'I'll be back': California is where these iconic celluloid images came to life. Shakespeare claimed 'all the world's a stage,' but in California, it's actually more of a movie set. With over 40 TV shows and scores of movies shot here annually, every palm-lined boulevard or beach seems to come with its own IMDb resume.

The Industry

You might know it as the TV and movie business, but to Southern Californians it's simply 'the Industry.' It all began in the humble orchards of Hollywoodland, a residential suburb of Los Angeles where entrepreneurial moviemakers established studios in the early 20th century. Within a few years, immigrants turned a humble orchard into Hollywood. In 1915 Polish immigrant Samuel Goldwyn joined with Cecil B DeMille to form Paramount Studios, while German-born Carl Laemmle opened nearby Universal Studios, selling lunch to curious guests to help underwrite his moving pictures. A few years later, a family of Polish immigrants arrived from Canada, and Jack Warner and his brothers soon set up a movie studio of their own.

With perpetually balmy weather and more than 315 days of sunshine a year, SoCal proved an ideal shooting location, and moviemaking flourished. In those early days, patent holders such as Thomas Edison sent agents to collect payments, or repossess movie equipment. Fledgling filmmakers saw them coming, and made runs for the Mexican border with their equipment. Palm Springs became a favorite weekend hideaway for Hollywood stars, partly because its distance from LA was as far as they could travel under restrictive studio contracts.

Seemingly overnight, Hollywood studios made movie magic. Fans lined up for premieres in LA movie palaces for red-carpet glimpses of early stars such as Charlie Chaplin and Harold Lloyd. Moviegoers nationwide celebrated the first big Hollywood wedding in 1920, when swashbuckler Douglas Fairbanks married 'America's sweetheart' Mary Pickford. Years later, their divorce would be one of Hollywood's biggest scandals, but the

MILESTONES IN CALIFORNIA FILM HISTORY

1913

Cecil B DeMille directs the first full-length Hollywood feature movie: a silent Western drama called *The Squaw Man*.

1927

The silent film era ends with the first talkie, *The Jazz Singer*. Sid Grauman opens his Chinese Theatre in Hollywood, where stars have been leaving their handprints ever since.

1939

The Wizard of Oz is the first wide-release movie shown in glorious Technicolor. It's a hit, but loses the Oscar for Best Picture to *Gone with the Wind*. Both were filmed in Culver City.

1950s

On a witch hunt for communists, the federal House Un-American Activities Committee investigates and blacklists many Hollywood actors, directors and screenwriters.

1975

The age of the modern blockbuster begins with the thriller *Jaws*, by a young filmmaker named Steven Spielberg, whose later blockbusters include *ET* and *Jurassic Park*.

2021

After major budget blowouts, the $482-million Academy Museum of Motion Pictures opens in Los Angeles. The museum's designer is award-winning Italian architect Renzo Piano.

United Artists studio they founded with Charlie Chaplin endures today. When the silent-movie era gave way to 'talkies' with the 1927 musical *The Jazz Singer*, the world hummed along.

From the 1930s to the 1950s, many famous US writers, including F Scott Fitzgerald, Dorothy Parker, Truman Capote, William Faulkner and Tennessee Williams, did stints as Hollywood screenwriters.

Hollywood & Beyond

By the 1920s Hollywood had become the industry's social and financial hub, but it's a myth that most movie production took place there. Of the major studios, only Paramount Pictures is in Hollywood proper, surrounded by block after block of production-related businesses, such as lighting and postproduction. Most movies have long been shot elsewhere around LA, in Culver City (at MGM, now Sony Pictures), Studio City (at Universal Studios) and Burbank (at Warner Bros and later Disney).

Moviemaking hasn't been limited to LA, either. Founded in 1910, the American Film Manufacturing Company (aka Flying 'A' Studios) churned out box-office hits in San Diego and then Santa Barbara. Balboa Studios in Long Beach was another major silent-era dream factory. Contemporary movie-production companies based in the San Francisco Bay Area include Francis Ford Coppola's American Zoetrope, Pixar Animation Studios and George Lucas' Industrial Light & Magic.

The high cost of filming has sent location scouts far beyond LA's San Fernando Valley (where most of California's movie and TV studios are found) to New York, Atlanta, Canada and the UK, where film production crews are welcomed with sweet deals. By the early 2010s, California began to fight back with its own series of tax credits, expanded from an annual $100 million to $330 million in 2015. In the three years that followed, 10 feature films with minimum budgets of $75 million had signed on to shoot in the state. Additionally, 15 TV series were lured from other locations, among them *American Horror Story* and *Veep*.

CALIFORNIA ON CELLULOID

From sunny capers to moody film-noir mysteries, the Golden State has proved its versatility in these movie classics:

The Maltese Falcon (1941) John Huston directs Humphrey Bogart as Sam Spade, the classic San Francisco private eye.

Sunset Boulevard (1950) Billy Wilder's classic stars Gloria Swanson and William Holden in a bonfire of Hollywood vanities.

Vertigo (1958) The Golden Gate Bridge dazzles and dizzies in Alfred Hitchcock's noir thriller.

The Graduate (1967) Dustin Hoffman flees status-obsessed California suburbia to search for meaning, heading across the Bay Bridge to Berkeley (in the wrong direction).

Chinatown (1974) Roman Polanski's gripping version of the early-20th-century water wars that made and nearly broke LA.

Blade Runner (1982) Ridley Scott's sci-fi cyberpunk thriller projects a future LA of high-rise corporate fortresses and chaotic streets.

The Player (1992) Directed by Robert Altman and starring Tim Robbins, this satire on 'the Industry' features dozens of cameos by actors spoofing themselves.

The Big Lebowski (1998) Through myriad misadventures in the Coen brothers' zany LA farce, The Dude abides.

Milk (2008) Gus Van Sant directs Sean Penn as Harvey Milk, the first openly gay man to hold a major US political office.

Once Upon a Time in Hollywood (2019) Quentin Tarantino's ode to late 1960s Hollywood, starring Leonardo DiCaprio and Brad Pitt.

Still, for Hollywood dreamers and movie buffs, LA remains *the* place for a pilgrimage. You can tour major movie studios, be part of a live TV studio audience, line up alongside the red carpet for an awards ceremony, catch movie premieres at film festivals, wander the Hollywood Walk of Fame and discover what it's like to live, dine and party with the stars.

The Art of Animation

In 1923 a young cartoonist named Walt Disney arrived in LA, and within five years he had a hit called *Steamboat Willie* and a breakout star called Mickey Mouse. That film spawned the entire Disney empire, and dozens of other California animation studios have followed with films, TV programs and special effects. Among the most beloved are Warner Bros (Bugs Bunny et al in *Looney Tunes*), Hanna-Barbera (*The Flintstones, The Jetsons, Yogi Bear* and *Scooby-Doo*), DreamWorks *(Shrek, Madagascar, Kung Fu Panda)* and Film Roman *(The Simpsons)*. Even if much of the hands-on work takes place overseas (in places such as South Korea), concept and supervision still takes place in LA and the San Francisco Bay Area.

In San Francisco, George Lucas' Industrial Light & Magic is made up of a team of high-tech wizards who produce computer-generated special effects for blockbuster series such as *Star Wars, Jurassic Park, Indiana Jones* and *Harry Potter*. Just across the San Francisco Bay, Pixar Animation Studios has produced an unbroken string of animated hits, including *Toy Story, Finding Dory, Inside Out, WALL-E, Cars* and *Soul*.

Top California Film Festivals

AFI Fest (https://fest.afi.com)

San Francisco International LGBTQ+ Film Festival (www.frameline.org)

Palm Springs International Film Festival (www.psfilmfest.org)

San Francisco International Film Festival (https://sffilm.org)

Sonoma International Film Festival (www.sonomafilmfest.org)

The Small Screen

After a year of tinkering, San Francisco inventor Philo Farnsworth transmitted the first television broadcast in 1927 of...a straight line. Giving viewers something actually interesting to watch would take a few more years. The first TV station began broadcasting in Los Angeles in 1931, beaming iconic images of California into living rooms across America and around the world with *Dragnet* (1950s), *The Beverly Hillbillies* (1960s), *The Brady Bunch* and *Charlie's Angels* (1970s), *LA Law* (1980s), *Baywatch, Buffy the Vampire Slayer* and *The Fresh Prince of Bel-Air* (1990s). *Beverly Hills 90210* (1990s) made that LA zip code into a status symbol, while *The OC* (2000s) glamorized Orange County and *Silicon Valley* (2014–19) satirized NorCal start-ups. Reality-TV fans will recognize Southern California locations from *Top Chef, Real Housewives of Orange County* and *Keeping Up with the Kardashians*.

A suburban San Francisco start-up changed the TV game in 2005, launching a streaming video on a platform called YouTube. With on-demand streaming services competing with cable channels to launch original series, we are entering a new golden age of California television. Netflix Studios (in Silicon Valley and Hollywood), Amazon Studios (Culver City) and Hulu Studios (Santa Monica) are churning out original series, feeding binge-watching cravings with futuristic dystopias such as *Stranger Things, Man in the High Castle* and *The Handmaid's Tale*. Only time will tell if streaming services will also yield breakthrough Californian comedies to compare with Showtime's sharp-witted suburban pot-growing dramedy *Weeds*, its *Californication* adventures of a successful New York novelist gone Hollywood, or HBO's *Curb Your Enthusiasm*, an insider satire of the industry featuring *Seinfeld* co-creator Larry David and Hollywood celebrities playing themselves.

Music & the Arts

When Californians thank their lucky stars – or good karma, or the goddess – that they live here, they're not just talking about the weather. The state has long been an incubator for music and the arts, mainstream, independent and occasionally outlandish, some of which has gained national and worldwide renown. In the USA's most racially and ethnically diverse state, expect eclectic playlists, involving performances and vivid shows of pride and individuality.

Music

In your California dream, you're a DJ – so what kind of music do you play? Beach Boys, West Coast rap, original punk, classic soul, hard bop, heavy metal, opera? Try all of the above. To hear the world's most eclectic playlist, just walk down a city street in California.

LA's recording industry has produced countless pop princesses, airbrushed boy bands and brooding balladeers. But the NorCal DIY tech approach is launching YouTube artists daily, not to mention wild dance parties.

Tune into the 'Morning Becomes Eclectic' show on Southern California's KCRW radio station (89.9FM, www.kcrw.com) for live in-studio performances and interviews with up-and-comers.

An Eclectic Early Soundtrack

Mexican folk music arrived in California during the rancho era, but during the gold rush rancheros had to belt to be heard over newly arrived, competing sounds of bluegrass, Chinese classical music and bawdy dancehall ragtime.

Still, it was Italian opera that became the breakout hit, with divas paid fortunes in gold dust for encores. By the early 20th century, San Francisco alone had 20 concert and opera halls, before the 1906 earthquake literally brought down the houses. Performers converged on the shattered city for marathon free public performances that turned arias into anthems for the city's rebirth.

Today, San Francisco's War Memorial Opera House is home to North America's second-largest opera company, after NYC's Metropolitan Opera, and the LA Opera is also considered one of the nation's leaders.

Swing Jazz, Blues & Soul

Swing was California's next big thing. In the 1930s and '40s, big bands sparked a Lindy Hopping craze in LA, and sailors on shore leave hit San Francisco's integrated underground jazz clubs.

California's African American community grew with the 'Great Migration' during the WWII shipping and manufacturing boom, and from this thriving scene emerged the West Coast blues sound. Texas-born bluesman T-Bone Walker worked LA's Central Ave clubs before making hit of his electric-guitar stylings for Capitol Records. Throughout the 1940s and '50s, West Coast blues was nurtured in San Francisco and Oakland by guitarists such as Pee Wee Crayton and Oklahoma-born Lowell Fulson.

With Beat poets riffing over improvised bass lines and audiences finger-snapping their approval, the cool West Coast jazz of Chet Baker and Bay Area–born Dave Brubeck emerged from San Francisco's North

Beach neighborhood in the 1950s. Meanwhile, back along LA's Central Ave, the hard bop of Charlie Parker and Charles Mingus kept SoCal's jazz scene alive and swinging.

In the 1950s and '60s, doo-wop, R&B, and soul music were all in steady rotation at nightclubs in South Central LA, considered the 'Harlem of the West.' Soulful singer Sam Cooke ran his own hit-making record label, attracting soul and gospel talent to LA.

In the 1950s, country music's hard-edged, honky-tonk Bakersfield Sound emerged inland in California's Central Valley, where Buck Owens and the Buckaroos and Merle Haggard performed their own twists on Nashville country hits for hard-drinkin' audiences of Dust Bowl migrants and cowboy ranchers.

Rockin' Out

California's first homegrown rock-and-roll talent of the 1950s was Ritchie Valens, born in LA's San Fernando Valley, whose 'La Bamba' was a rockified version of a Mexican folk song. Dick Dale experimented with reverb effects in Orange County, becoming known as 'the King of the Surf Guitar.' He topped the charts with his band the Del-Tones in the early '60s, influencing everyone from the Beach Boys to Jimi Hendrix – you might recognize 'Miserlou' from the movie *Pulp Fiction*.

Guitar got psychedelic in 1960s California. When Joan Baez and Bob Dylan had their Northern California fling in the early 1960s, Dylan plugged in his guitar and pioneered folk rock. Centered around San Francisco's Fillmore Auditorium, Janis Joplin headlined Big Brother & the Holding Company with shambling musical stylings that splintered folk rock into psychedelia, and Jefferson Airplane turned Lewis Carroll's *Alice's Adventures in Wonderland* into the psychedelic hit 'White Rabbit.' For many Fillmore headliners, the show ended too soon with drug overdoses – though the original jam band, the Grateful Dead, kept on truckin' until guitarist Jerry Garcia died in rehab in 1995.

Meanwhile, on LA's Sunset Strip, bands were blowing minds at the legendary Whisky a Go Go nightclub – especially the Byrds and the Doors, fronted by Jim Morrison. The California sound also got down with iconic funk bands War from Long Beach, Tower of Power from Oakland, and San Francisco's Sly and the Family Stone.

In '70s LA, Laurel Canyon was an enclave in the Hollywood Hills where Joni Mitchell, David Crosby and Graham Nash held legendary jam sessions. Meanwhile, down at Sunset Strip's seedy Tropicana Motel, local characters found their way into the bluesy storytelling of singer-songwriters Tom Waits and Rickie Lee Jones. Record labels produced arena bands to a high

PUNK'S NOT DEAD IN CALIFORNIA

In the 1970s, commercial arena rock on American airwaves inspired the articulate ire of California rock critics Lester Bangs and Greil Marcus, and California teens bored with prepackaged anthems started making their own with secondhand guitars, three chords and crappy amps that added a loud buzz to unleashed fury. Punk was born.

LA punk paralleled the scrappy local skate scene with the hardcore grind of Black Flag from Hermosa Beach and LA's The Germs. LA band X bridged punk and new wave from 1977 to 1987 with John Doe's rockabilly guitar, Exene Cervenka's angsty wail, and disappointed-romantic lyrics inspired by Charles Bukowski and Raymond Chandler. LA radio station KROQ put local punk front and center and launched punk-funk sensations Red Hot Chili Peppers and Jane's Addiction.

San Francisco's punk scene was arty and absurdist, not least when Dead Kennedys singer (and future San Francisco mayoral candidate) Jello Biafra mocked Golden State complacency in 'California Uber Alles.' In one legendary 1978 San Francisco punk show, the Sex Pistols broke up and the all-women Avengers took the punk scene by storm. Through the 1980s and '90s, Green Day, Blink 182 and The Offspring put pop-punk on the radio.

Even today, there's still nothing like hearing next-gen punk kids rip through all three chords they know in a grimy California club.

polish, creating the slick country-pop of the Eagles and Jackson Browne and finessing Mexican American fusion with Linda Ronstadt and Santana.

Post-Punk to Pop

The 1980s saw the rise of such influential LA crossover bands as Bad Religion (punk) and Suicidal Tendencies (hardcore/thrash), while more mainstream all-female bands the Bangles and the Go-Gos, new wavers Oingo Boingo, and California rockers Jane's Addiction and Red Hot Chili Peppers took the world by storm. Hollywood's Guns N' Roses set the '80s standard for arena rock, while San Francisco's Metallica showed the world how to head bang with a vengeance. Avant-garde rocker Frank Zappa earned a cult following and a rare hit with the 1982 single *Valley Girl*, in which his 14-year-old daughter Moon Unit taught the rest of America to say 'Omigo-o-od!' like an LA teenager.

By the 1990s California's alternative rock acts took the national stage, including songwriter Beck, political rockers Rage Against the Machine and Orange County's ska-rockers No Doubt, fronted by Gwen Stefani. Hailing from East LA, Los Lobos were the kings of the Chicano (Mexican American) bands, an honor that has since passed via Ozomatli to Chicano Batman and La Santa Cecilia.

Waiting for the Sun: A Rock 'n' Roll History of Los Angeles (1996) by Barney Hoskyns follows the twists and turns of the SoCal music scene from the Beach Boys to Black Flag. Hoskyns' *Hotel California* (2005) delves into the music (and drug-fueled times) of LA's Laurel Canyon in the 1960s and '70s.

Berkeley's 924 Gilman Street club revived punk in the '90s, launching the career of Grammy Award–winning Green Day. Riding the wave were Berkley ska-punk band Rancid, surf-punk Sublime from Long Beach, San Diego–based pop-punksters Blink 182, and Orange County's resident loudmouths, The Offspring.

Rap & Hip-Hop

Since the 1980s, West Coast rap and hip-hop have spoken truth and hit the beat. N.W.A.'s 1988 album *Straight Outta Compton* launched the careers of Eazy E, Ice Cube and Dr Dre, and established gangsta rap. Dre cofounded Death Row Records, which helped launch megawatt talents such as Long Beach bad boys Snoop Dogg, Warren G and the late Tupac Shakur. The son of a Black Panther leader who'd fallen on hard times, Tupac combined party songs and hard truths learned on Oakland streets until his untimely shooting in 1996 in a suspected East Coast/West Coast rap feud. Feuds also checkered the musical career of LA rapper Game, whose 2011 *The R.E.D. Album* brought together an all-star lineup of Diddy, Dr Dre, Snoop Dogg and more. Kendrick Lamar became one of the top hip-hop stars of the 2010s, and the 2019 murder of rapper Nipsey Hussle sent waves of grief through the South LA community as much for his activism as his music.

Throughout the 1980s and '90s, California maintained a grassroots hip-hop scene in Oakland and LA, whose breakout artist was Oakland native MC Hammer, with his landmark 1990 album *Please Hammer Don't Hurt 'Em*. Reacting against the increasing commercialization of hip-hop in the late 1990s, the Bay Area scene produced underground 'hyphy' (short for hyperactive) artists such as E-40 and Mistah F.A.B. Political commentary and funk hooks have become signatures of East Bay groups Blackalicious, The Coup and Michael Franti & Spearhead, and Oakland-based Kamaiyah is among today's chart-toppers.

Architecture

There's more to California design than beach houses and boardwalks. Californians have adapted imported styles to the climate and available materials, from cool, adobe-inspired houses in San Diego and fog-resistant redwood-shingle houses in Mendocino, to mid-century modern in Palm Springs.

MID-CENTURY MODERNISM

Starting in the 1950s, California embraced the stripped-down, glass-wall aesthetics of the International Style championed by Bauhaus architects Walter Gropius, Ludwig Mies van der Rohe and Le Corbusier. Open floor plans and floor-to-ceiling windows were ideally suited to the see-and-be-seen culture of Southern California.

Austrian-born Rudolph Schindler and Richard Neutra brought early modernism to LA and Palm Springs, which celebrates the style every February and October during Modernism Week. Neutra and Schindler were also influenced by Frank Lloyd Wright, who designed LA's Hollyhock House in a style he dubbed 'California Romanza.'

Neutra also collaborated with LA-based designers Charles and Ray Eames on the experimental open-plan Case Study Houses in Santa Monica Canyon. Many Neutra houses have appeared in the movies, as filming locations for *Boogie Nights* and *LA Confidential*.

Spanish Missions & Victorian Queens

Beginning in the late 18th century, Spanish Catholic missionaries built missions around courtyards, using materials on hand: adobe, limestone and grass. Many missions crumbled into disrepair as the church's influence waned, but the style remained practical for the climate. Early California settlers later adapted it into the *rancho* adobe style, as seen in Downtown LA's El Pueblo de Los Angeles and San Diego's Old Town.

With the mid-19th-century gold rush, California's nouveau riche imported materials to construct grand, European-style mansions. Many millionaires favored the gilded Queen Anne style, while outrageous examples of colorful, gingerbread-swagged Victorian 'Painted Ladies' can be found in San Francisco, Ferndale and Eureka.

By the turn of the 20th century, architects rejected frilly Victorian styles in favor of the simpler, classical Spanish lines. Spanish Colonial Revival architecture (also known as Mission Revival style) featured arched doors and windows, long covered porches, fountain courtyards, solid walls and red-tile roofs. Downtown Santa Barbara showcases this revival style, as do stately buildings in San Diego's Balboa Park, Scotty's Castle in Death Valley and several SoCal train depots, including in Downtown LA, San Diego, San Juan Capistrano and Santa Barbara, as well as Kelso Depot in the Mojave National Preserve.

Arts and Crafts & Art Deco

Simplicity and harmony with the natural environment were hallmarks of California's early 20th century arts-and-crafts style. Influenced by both Japanese design principles and England's arts-and-crafts movement, its woodwork and handmade touches marked a deliberate departure from the industrial revolution's mechanization. Bernard Maybeck and Julia Morgan in Northern California, and SoCal architects Charles and Henry Greene, popularized the versatile one-story bungalow. Today you'll spot them in Berkeley and Pasadena with their overhanging eaves, airy terraces and sleeping porches, and warm, livable interiors.

By the 1920s, the international art-deco style transformed elements from the ancient world – Mayan glyphs, Egyptian pillars, Babylonian ziggurats – into modern motifs to cap stark facades and outline streamlined skyscrapers in Oakland, San Francisco and LA. Streamline moderne kept decoration to a minimum, and mimicked the aerodynamic look of ocean liners and airplanes.

Postmodern Evolutions

In 1997 Richard Meier made his mark on West LA with the Getty Center, a cresting white wave of a building on a sun-baked hilltop. The billowing, sculptural Walt Disney Concert Hall (2003) by Canadian-born, LA-based

Pritzker Prize winner Frank Gehry is a signature of Downtown LA. It's across from the Broad Museum (2015), shrouded in white lattice-like shell that lifts at the corners, designed by Diller Scofidio + Renfro in collaboration with SF-based firm Gensler. A few blocks away, the Cathedral of Our Lady of the Angels (2002), designed by Spanish architect Rafael Moneo, echoes the grand churches of Mexico and Europe with a controversial deconstructivist approach. The work of another LA-based Pritzker Prize winner, Thom Mayne of the firm Morphosis, can be seen in LA's Caltrans District 7 Headquarters and Emerson College building, and the San Francisco Federal Building.

The Bay Area's iconic postmodern building is the San Francisco Museum of Modern Art (1995), which Swiss architect Mario Botta capped with a black-and-white striped, marble-clad atrium; in 2016, Norway's Snøhetta architects expanded it with wings shaped like ship sails. SF has also championed a brand of postmodernism by Pritzker Prize-winning architects who magnify and mimic the great outdoors, especially in Golden Gate Park. Swiss architects Herzog & de Meuron clad the MH de Young Memorial Museum in copper, which promises to oxidize green to match its park setting. Nearby, Renzo Piano literally raised the roof on sustainable design at the Leadership in Energy and Environmental Design (LEED) platinum-certified California Academy of Sciences, capped by a living-roof garden.

In 1919 newspaper magnate William Randolph Hearst commissioned California's first licensed female architect, Julia Morgan, to build Hearst Castle. It would take decades to finish.

Visual Arts

California has had an outsized, almost mythical presence in art since the first, fanciful drawings by cartographers accompanying early explorers. The mythologization continued through the gold-rush era, alternating between caricatures of Wild West debauchery and manifest-destiny propaganda. The completion of the Transcontinental Railroad in 1869 brought an influx of romantic painters and epic California wilderness landscapes, and in the 20th century impressionist plein-air painters gathered in art colonies in Laguna Beach and Carmel-by-the-Sea.

After the invention of photography, San Francisco–born Ansel Adams started doing justice to Yosemite and founded Group f/64 with Edward Weston and Imogen Cunningham in San Francisco. Berkeley-based Dorothea Lange turned her unflinching lens on the plight of Californian migrant workers in the Great Depression and Japanese Americans forced to enter internment camps during WWII. After WWII, Pirkle Jones saw expressive potential in California landscape photography.

As the postwar American West became crisscrossed with freeways and divided into planned communities, Californian painters captured on canvas the abstract forms of manufactured landscapes. In San Francisco, Richard Diebenkorn and David Park became leading proponents of Bay

LATINO MURAL MOVEMENTS IN CALIFORNIA

Beginning in the 1930s, when the federal Works Progress Administration sponsored schemes to uplift and beautify cities across the country, murals came to define California cityscapes. Mexican muralists Diego Rivera, David Alfaro Siqueiros and José Clemente Orozco sparked a culture of murals across LA that today number in the thousands. Rivera was also brought to San Francisco to paint murals at the San Francisco Art Institute, and his influence is reflected in the interior of San Francisco's Coit Tower and hundreds of murals across the Mission District. Murals gave voice to Chicano pride and protests over US Central American policies in the 1970s, notably in San Diego's Chicano Park, San Francisco's Balmy Alley and East LA murals by collectives such as East Los Streetscapers. The movement has inspired 21st-century muralists like Santa Monica–based Beautify Earth, which collaborates with cities and businesses to paint murals on blighted surfaces.

Area Figurative Art, while San Francisco–born sculptor Richard Serra captured urban aesthetics in massive, rusting monoliths resembling ship prows and industrial Stonehenges. Meanwhile, pop artists captured conspicuous consumerism, through Wayne Thiebaud's gumball machines, British émigré David Hockney's LA pools and, above all, Ed Ruscha's studies of SoCal pop culture. In the Bay Area, artists showed their love for rough-and-ready-made 1950s Beat collage, '60s psychedelic rock posters from Fillmore concerts, earthy '70s funk and beautiful-mess punk, and '80s graffiti art.

Today's California contemporary-art scene brings all these influences together with muralist-led social commentary, an obsessive dedication to craft and cutting-edge technology. LA's Museum of Contemporary Art and Broad Museum put on provocative and avant-garde shows, as do San Francisco's Museum of Modern Art and the Museum of Contemporary Art San Diego. To see California-made art at its most experimental, browse the galleries in Downtown LA and Culver City and the galleries and art spaces in San Francisco's Mission District and the Yerba Buena Center for the Arts.

Lastly, Burning Man, the annual late-summer self-proclaimed 'vibrant participatory metropolis' (and arts and culture festival) in the Nevada desert, is headquartered in San Francisco. The mutual influence between the two locales seems baked-in.

Theater

In your California dream you're discovered by a movie talent scout, but most Californian actors actually get their start in theater. Home to about 25% of the nation's professional actors, LA is the USA's second most influential city for theater, after NYC. Meanwhile, San Francisco has been a national hub for experimental theater since the 1960s.

Large venues to watch around LA include the Ahmanson Theatre and Mark Taper Forum in Downtown LA, Pantages in Hollywood, Geffen Playhouse close to UCLA, and the Kirk Douglas and Actors' Gang theaters in Culver City. Small theaters flourish around Hollywood, West Hollywood and North Hollywood, the West Coast's versions of off- and off-off-Broadway. Influential multicultural theaters include East West Players and Deaf West Theatre, while critically acclaimed outlying companies include the innovative Long Beach Opera and South Coast Repertory in Costa Mesa, Orange County.

San Francisco's theater heritage goes back to at least the great earthquake of 1906, when survivors were entertained in tents amid the smoldering ruins, and famous theaters were rebuilt well before City Hall. Today SF is undergoing a performing-arts renaissance, against the long odds of rising rents and federal funding cuts. Tickets are affordable and programs sensational at historic theaters, and new venues are opening mid-Market, in the Tenderloin and in North Beach. Major productions destined for Broadway and London premiere at the American Conservatory Theater and its experimental venue, The Strand. The Magic Theatre gained a national reputation in the 1970s, when Sam Shepard was the resident playwright, and it still premieres innovative California playwrights. An audience-interactive troupe, We Players, stages classic plays, including Shakespearean dramas, at unusual locations such as Alcatraz. Across the bay, the Berkeley Repertory Theatre has pushed the envelope with dozens of award-winning productions since 1968.

California's Iconic Buildings

- *Salk Institute, La Jolla*
- *Mission San Juan Capistrano*
- *Sunnylands, Rancho Mirage*
- *Getty Center, LA*
- *Walt Disney Concert Hall, LA*
- *Gamble House, Pasadena*
- *Hearst Castle, San Simeon*
- *Painted Ladies, SF*
- *de Young Museum, SF*
- *Ahwahnee Hotel, Yosemite National Park*

Mid-century modernism's photographer of record was Julius Shulman (1910–2009), with iconic black-and-white images of homes in LA and Palm Springs. His 70,000-strong photo collection is at LA's Getty Center.

By the Book

Since its earliest days, California has been a source of fascination for authors and readers alike, and its landscapes and personalities have inspired some unforgettable classics. Today's West Coast remains a magnet, now inhabited by a multicultural literary community.

Early Voices of Social Realism

Nineteenth-century California became synonymous with adventure through the talents of early chroniclers such as Mark Twain and Bret Harte. Professional hell-raiser Jack London was a wild child from the Oakland docks who traveled the world with little more than his wits and a canoe and became the world's most successful adventurer and travel writer.

Arguably early 20th century's most influential Californian author was John Steinbeck, born in Salinas in 1902. He explored the lives and struggles of the state's diverse communities: Mexican American WWI vets adjusting to civilian life in *Tortilla Flat*, flat-broke wharf characters attempting to throw a party on *Cannery Row*, and migrant farm workers just trying to survive the Great Depression in his Pulitzer Prize–winning *The Grapes of Wrath*. Acclaimed social-realist playwright Eugene O'Neill took his 1936 Nobel Prize money, sojourned near San Francisco and wrote some of his greatest successes including *Long Day's Journey into Night*.

Other novelists revealed the tarnish on the Golden State. Classics include Upton Sinclair's *Oil!*, exposing the schemes of a real-life LA oil tycoon; and Aldous Huxley's *After Many a Summer*, based on the life of William Randolph Hearst, the reclusive, vengeful media mogul who also inspired Orson Welles' film *Citizen Kane*.

LA sheltered many illustrious foreign writers in the first half of the 20th century, including Huxley and German authors Bertolt Brecht and Thomas Mann, exiled from their homeland during WWII. Meanwhile, the film industry lured literary luminaries such as William Faulkner, Dorothy Parker, Truman Capote and F Scott Fitzgerald, who found the inspiration for his final novel, *The Last Tycoon*, about a movie producer slowly working himself to death.

The writing programs at the University of California, Irvine, in Orange County, are consistently rated among the top in the nation. Among UCI's graduates are dozens of leading American novelists, including Aimee Bender, Michael Chabon, Richard Ford and Alice Sebold.

Pulp Noir & Science Fiction

Mysterious fog and neon signs created the mood for noir murder mysteries set in San Francisco and Los Angeles. Dashiell Hammett *(The Maltese Falcon)* made a cynical San Francisco private eye into a modern antihero, while hard-boiled crime writer Raymond Chandler spun tales of murder and double-crossing dames in Santa Monica. The 1990s neo-noir renaissance was led by James Ellroy *(LA Confidential)*, Elmore Leonard *(Get Shorty)* and Walter Mosley *(Devil in a Blue Dress)*, whose Easy Rawlins detective novels are set in South LA.

In science fiction, Berkeley-raised Philip K Dick imagined a Los Angeles ruled by artificial intelligence in *Do Androids Dream of Electric Sheep?*, adapted into the 1982 movie classic *Blade Runner*. Dick's novel (and now TV series) *The Man in the High Castle* imagines San Francisco circa 1962 if America had lost WWII to its fascist enemies. Berkeley-born

READING RURAL CALIFORNIA

Central Coast *Selected Poetry of Robinson Jeffers* – In the looming, windswept pines surrounding his Tor House, Jeffers found inspiration for hauntingly beautiful poems.

Central Valley *Woman Warrior: Memoirs of a Girlhood Among Ghosts* (Maxine Hong Kingston) – A tale of growing up Chinese American, and finding Californian identity.

Gold Country *Roughing It* (Mark Twain) – The master of sardonic wit tells of earthquakes, silver booms and busts, and getting by for a month on a dime in the Wild West.

Sierra Nevada *Riprap and Cold Mountain Poems* (Gary Snyder) – Influenced by Asian spirituality and classical literature, the Beat poet captures the meditative nature of open wilderness.

Ursula K Le Guin *(The Left Hand of Darkness, A Wizard of Earthsea)* brought feminism to the genre of fantasy, imagining parallel realities where heroines confront forces of darkness.

Social Movers & Shakers

After surviving WWII, the Beat Generation refused to fall in line with 1950s conformity, defying McCarthyism with poignant, poetic truths. San Francisco Beat scene luminaries included Jack Kerouac *(On the Road)*, Allen Ginsberg *(Howl)* and Lawrence Ferlinghetti, the Beats' patron publisher who cofounded the iconic City Lights Bookstore. Censors called *Howl* obscene, and Ferlinghetti was arrested for publishing it – but he won his trial in a landmark decision for free speech. Beat poets broke style rules and crossed genres, including poet-painter-playwright Kenneth Rexroth and Buddhist philosopher-poet Gary Snyder.

But no author has captured California culture with such unflinching clarity as Joan Didion, whose prose burns through the page like sun on a misty California morning. Her collection of literary nonfiction essays *Slouching Towards Bethlehem* captures 1960s flower power at the exact moment it blooms and wilts. Didion pioneered immersive first-person New Journalism alongside Hunter S Thompson and Tom Wolfe (whose *Hells Angels* and *The Electric Kool-Aid Acid Test* respectively, were defining works about '60s California).

In the 1970s Charles Bukowski's semiautobiographical novel *Post Office* captured down-and-out Downtown LA, while Richard Vasquez' *Chicano* took a dramatic look at LA's Latinx barrio. Armistead Maupin captured the rise of disco, cults, medical marijuana, feminism and gay pride in '70s San Francisco as it happened in his serialized *Tales of the City*. Bret Easton Ellis followed the short lives and fast times of coked-up Beverly Hills teenagers in *Less Than Zero*, the definitive chronicle of '80s excess. Amy Tan's *The Joy Luck Club* weaves together the stories of four Chinese immigrants and their American born daughters in a textured tale of aspiration and survival in San Francisco's Chinatown.

Since the '60s, no California bookshelf can be considered complete without graphic novels and 'zines. Throughout the state, you'll recognize characters straight out of local comics – arty, angsty teens from Daniel Clowes' *Ghostworld* and *Art School Confidential*, street-corner prophets from Wendy McNaughton's *Meanwhile in San Francisco*, and soul-searching techies from Paul Madonna's *Everything Is Its Own Reward*.

Today's California authors continue to rack up accolades. Paul Beatty bagged the Man Booker Prize and National Book Critics Circle Award for his 2015 satirical novel *The Sellout,* set in a downtrodden LA suburb. University of Southern California (USC) English professor Viet Thanh Nguyen won the 2016 Pulitzer Prize for *The Sympathizer*, about a half-Vietnamese undercover agent, and Tommy Orange was a 2019 Pulitzer Prize nominee for *There There*, about native Americans living around Oakland.

The young-adult nonfiction series *Fighting for Justice* highlights Californians who made a difference. *Fred Korematsu Speaks Up* (2004) by Laura Atkins and Stan Yogi features the chief activist for reparations for the WWII-era internment of Japanese Americans, while *Biddy Mason Speaks Up* (2019) by Atkins and Arisa White tells of an African American who escaped slavery to become a civic leader in early LA.

The Land & Wildlife

You'll never have to leave California for a change of scenery. From snowy peaks to scorching deserts, golden-sand beaches and sun-dappled redwood forests, California is the most biodiverse place in North America. Species that are rare elsewhere thrive in this balmy Mediterranean climate, with its dry summers and mild wet winters. California has more people than any other US state, which puts a tremendous strain on precious natural resources, but for more than 150 years, conservation-minded Californians have worked hard to protect the state's iconic wildlife and natural wonders.

Lay of the Land

California is the third-biggest US state after Alaska and Texas, covering more than 155,000 sq miles – if it were a country it would rank as the 59th largest in the world. It shares borders with Oregon to the north, Mexico to the south, Nevada and Arizona to the east, and has 840 miles of glorious Pacific shoreline to the west.

According to the 2015 US Geological Survey, the odds of a magnitude 6.7 or greater earthquake hitting the San Francisco Bay area in the next 30 years are 72% (in the Los Angeles area it's 60%). For what it's worth, that's good news compared to a 2008 study which concluded that it was 99% likely!

Geology & Earthquakes

California is a complex geologic landscape formed from fragments of rock and earth crust squeezed together as the North American continent drifted westward over hundreds of millions of years. Crumpled coastal ranges, fault lines rippling through the Central Valley and jagged, still-rising Sierra Nevada mountains all reveal gigantic forces at work, as the continental and ocean plates crush together.

Everything changed about 25 million years ago, when the ocean plates stopped colliding and instead started sliding against each other, creating the massive San Andreas Fault. This contact zone catches and slips, rattling California with an ongoing succession of tremors and earthquakes.

In 1906 the state's most famous earthquake measured 7.8 on the Richter scale and demolished San Francisco, leaving more than 3000 people dead. The Bay Area was again badly shaken in 1989, when the Loma Prieta earthquake (6.9) caused a section of the Bay Bridge to collapse. In Los Angeles the last 'big one' was in 1994, when the Northridge quake (6.7) caused parts of the Santa Monica Fwy to fall down, resulting in damage that made it the most costly quake in US history. Shifting fault lines far from the large urban areas periodically register high on the Richter scale, like the 2019 Ridgecrest quake, which at 6.4, along with over 100,000 aftershocks, was the strongest in Southern California in more than 20 years.

The Coast to the Central Valley

Rugged mountains take the brunt of winter storms along California's coast, leaving inland areas more protected. San Francisco marks the midpoint of the Coast Ranges, with fog swirling along the sparsely populated North Coast. To the south, beach communities enjoy balmier climates along the Central and Southern California coasts.

The northernmost reaches of the Coast Ranges get 120in of rain in a typical year, and persistent summer fog contributes another 12in of precipitation in some spots. This may not sound like the best climate for beach-going, but California's northern coastal lowlands are sublime for

Geography Map

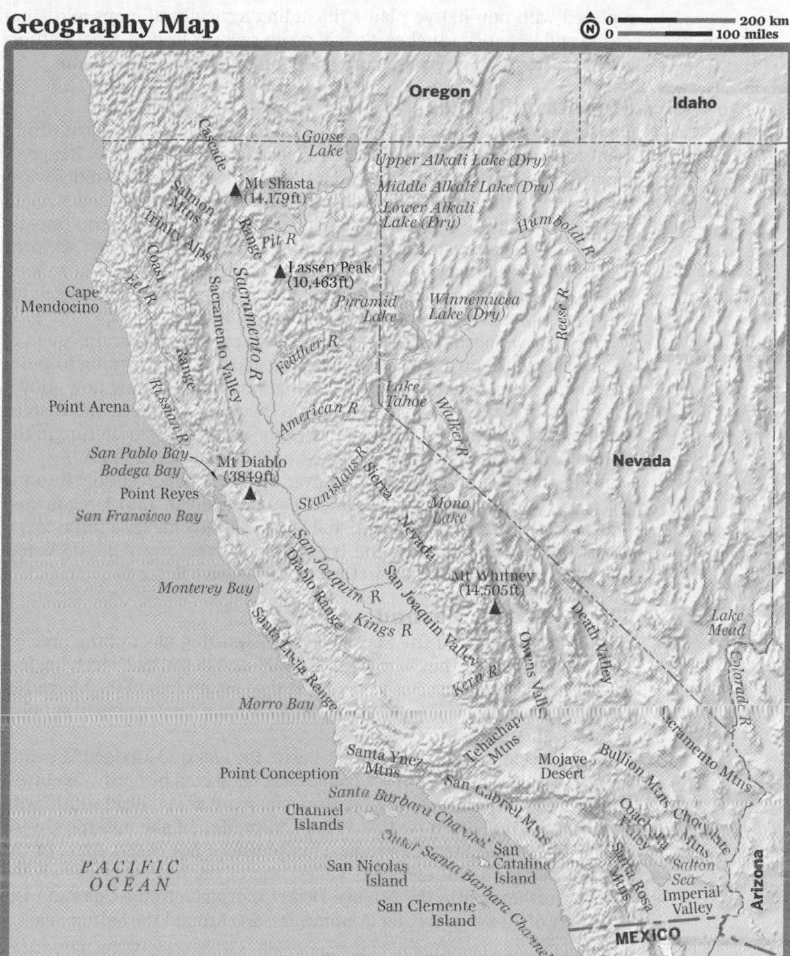

coastal wine tasting. Nutrient-rich soils and abundant moisture foster stands of towering coast redwoods, growing as far south as Big Sur and all the way north to Oregon.

On their eastern flanks, the Coast Ranges taper into gently rolling hills that slide into the sprawling Central Valley. Once an inland sea, this flat basin is now an agricultural powerhouse producing about half of America's fruits, nuts and vegetables. Stretching about 450 miles long and 50 miles wide, the valley sees about as much rainfall as a desert, but gets huge volumes of water runoff from the Sierra Nevada. The area is divided in two parts: the Sacramento Valley in the north and the San Joaquin Valley in the south.

Before the arrival of Europeans, the Central Valley was a natural wonderland – vast marshes with flocks of geese that blackened the sky, grasslands carpeted with flowers sniffed by millions of antelopes, elk and grizzly bears. Virtually this entire landscape has been plowed under and replaced with non-native plants (including agricultural crops and vineyards) and livestock ranches. So when you savor your next great California meal, raise a glass to the flora and fauna that came before you.

Browse through more than 96,000 aerial photos covering almost every mile of California's gorgeously rugged coastline, stretching from Oregon to Mexico, at www.californiacoastline.org.

Mountain Ranges

On the eastern side of the Central Valley looms California's most prominent topographic feature: the Sierra Nevada, nicknamed the 'Range of Light' by conservationist John Muir. At 400 miles long and 70 miles wide, this is one of the world's largest mountain ranges, punctuated with 13 peaks over 14,000ft high. The vast wilderness of the High Sierra (mostly above 9000ft) is an astounding landscape of shrinking glaciers, sculpted granite peaks and remote canyons. This landscape is beautiful to look at but difficult to access, and it was one of the greatest challenges for 19th-century settlers attempting to reach California.

The soaring Sierra Nevada captures storm systems and drains them of their water, with most of the precipitation above 3000ft turning to snow, creating a premier winter-sports destination. Melting snow flows down into a half-dozen major river systems on the range's western and eastern slopes, providing the vast majority of water needed for agriculture in the Central Valley and for the metro areas of San Francisco and LA.

At its northern end, the Sierra Nevada merges imperceptibly into the volcanic Cascade Mountains, which continue north into Oregon and Washington. At its southern end, the Sierra Nevada makes a funny westward hook and connects via the Transverse Ranges (one of the USA's few east–west mountain ranges) to the southern Coast Ranges.

The Deserts & Beyond

With the west slope of the Sierra Nevada capturing most of the precipitation, lands east of the Sierra crest are dry and desertlike, receiving less than 10in of rain a year. Some valleys at the eastern foot of the Sierra Nevada, however, are well watered by creeks, so that they're able to support livestock and agriculture.

At the western edge of the Great Basin, the elevated Modoc Plateau in far northeastern California is a cold desert blanketed by hardy sagebrush shrubs and juniper trees. Temperatures increase as you head south, with a prominent transition on the descent from Mono Lake into the Owens Valley east of the Sierra Nevada. This southern hot desert (part of the Mojave Desert) includes Death Valley, one of the hottest places on the planet. Further south, the Mojave Desert morphs into the Colorado Desert (part of Mexico's greater Sonoran Desert) around the Salton Sea.

California claims both the highest point in contiguous US (Mt Whitney, 14,505ft) and the lowest elevation in North America (Badwater, Death Valley, 282ft below sea level) – and they're only 90 miles apart, as the condor flies.

California's Flora & Fauna

Although the staggering numbers of animals that greeted the first foreign settlers are now distant memories, you can still easily spot wildlife thriving in California. Some are only shadow populations, and some are actually endangered – all the more reason to take the opportunity to stop by California's designated wildlife areas to appreciate their presence and support their conservation.

Marine Mammals

Spend even one day along California's coast and you may spot pods of bottlenose dolphins and porpoises swimming, canoodling and cavorting in the ocean. Playful sea otters and harbor seals typically stick closer to shore, especially around public piers and protected bays. Since the 1989 earthquake, sea lions have taken to sunbathing on San Francisco's Pier 39, where delighted tourists watch the city's resident beach bums nap, goof off and recover from their seafood dinners. To see more wild pinnipeds, visit Point Lobos State Natural Reserve near Monterey, or Channel Islands National Park in Southern California.

CALIFORNIA'S DESERT CRITTERS

California's deserts are far from deserted, but most animals are too smart to hang out in the daytime heat. Most come out only in the cool of the night, as bats do. Roadrunners (black-and-white mottled ground cuckoos) can often be spotted on roadsides – you'll recognize them from their long tails and punk-style Mohawks. Other desert inhabitants include burrowing kit foxes, tree-climbing gray foxes, hopping jackrabbits, kangaroo rats, slow-moving (and endangered) desert tortoises and a variety of snakes, lizards and spiders. Desert bighorn sheep and migrating birds flock to watering holes, often around seasonal springs and native fan-palm oases – look for them in Joshua Tree National Park and Anza-Borrego Desert State Park.

Once threatened by extinction, gray whales now migrate in growing numbers along California's coast between December and April. Adult whales live up to 60 years, grow longer than a city bus and can weigh up to 40 tons, making quite a splash when they leap out of the water. Every year they travel from summertime feeding grounds in the arctic Bering Sea, down to southern breeding grounds off Baja California then all the way back up again, making a 6000-mile round trip.

Also almost hunted to extinction by the late 19th century for their oil-rich blubber, northern elephant seals have made a remarkable comeback along California's coast. North of Santa Cruz, Año Nuevo State Reserve is a major breeding ground for northern elephant seals. California's biggest elephant seal colony is found at Piedras Blancas, south of Big Sur. There's a smaller rookery at Point Reyes National Seashore in Marin County. When marine mammals are hurt or stranded, they're cared for at Marin's Marine Mammal Center, where you can meet rescued seals and learn how you can help protect their habitats.

Land Mammals

Lumbering across California's flag is the state mascot: the grizzly bear. Grizzlies once roamed California's beaches and grasslands in large numbers, eating everything from acorns to whale carcasses. Grizzlies were particularly abundant in the Central Valley, but retreated upslope into the Sierra Nevada as they were hunted to extinction in the 1920s.

California's mountain forests are still home to an estimated 30,000 to 40,000 black bears, the grizzlies' smaller cousins. Despite their name, their fur ranges in color from black to dark brown, auburn or even blond. These burly omnivores feed on berries, nuts, roots, grasses, insects, eggs, small mammals and fish, but can become a nuisance around campgrounds and cabins where food and trash are not secured.

As settlers moved into California in the 19th century, many other large mammals fared almost as poorly as grizzlies. Immense herds of tule elk and antelope in the Central Valley were particularly hard hit, with antelope retreating in small numbers to the northeastern corner of the state, and tule elk hunted into near extinction. A small remnant herd was moved to Point Reyes, where it has since rebounded, along with another 21 other herds (totaling an estimated 5700 tule elk) scattered across the state.

Mountain lions (also called cougars) hunt throughout California's mountains and forests, especially in areas teeming with deer. Solitary lions can grow 8ft in length and weigh 175lb, and are formidable predators. Few attacks on humans have occurred, happening mostly where suburbs have encroached on the lions' wilderness hunting grounds.

Birds & Butterflies

You might think this picture-postcard state is made for tourists, but California is totally for the birds. California is an essential stop on the migratory Pacific Flyway between Alaska and Mexico. Almost half the bird species in North America use the state's wildlife refuges and nature preserves for rest and refueling. Migration peaks during the wetter winter season starting in October/November, when two million fowl gather at the Klamath Basin National Wildlife Refuges along the California-Oregon border for the world's biggest game of duck, duck, goose.

The Audubon Society's California chapter website (https://ca.audubon.org) offers helpful birding checklists, photos and descriptions of key species, conservation news and a Pacific Flyway blog (https://ca.audubon.org/audublog).

Year-round you can see birds dotting California's beaches, estuaries and bays, where herons, cormorants, shorebirds and gulls gather. Point Reyes National Seashore and the Channel Islands are prime year-round bird-watching spots.

As you drive along the Big Sur coastline, look skyward to spot endangered California condors. You may also spot condors inland, soaring over Pinnacles National Park and the Los Padres National Forest. Keep an eye out for regal bald eagles around their winter home at Big Bear Lake in the mountains near LA, and on the Channel Islands, where they've started to make a comeback.

Monarch butterflies are glorious orange creatures that take epic long-distance journeys in search of milkweed, their only source of food. They winter in California by the tens of thousands, clustering along the Central Coast at Santa Cruz, Pacific Grove, Pismo Beach and Santa Barbara County.

Wildflowers & Trees

Like human Californians, California's 6000 kinds of plants are by turns shy and flamboyant. Many species are so obscure and similar that only a dedicated botanist could tell them apart, but in the spring they merge into shimmering carpets of wildflowers that will take your breath away. The state flower is the native California poppy, which shyly closes at night and unfolds by day in a shocking display of golden orange.

The California condor is the largest flying bird in North America. In 1987 there were only two dozen or so birds left in the wild. Thanks to captive breeding and release programs, there are about 440 flying free today (an estimated 160 are in California).

California is also a region of superlative trees: the oldest (bristlecone pines of the White Mountains live to nearly 5000 years old), the tallest (coast redwoods reach 380ft) and the largest (giant sequoias of the Sierra Nevada exceed 36ft across). Sequoias are unique to California, adapted to survive in isolated groves on the Sierra Nevada's western slopes in Yosemite, Sequoia and Kings Canyon National Parks.

An astounding 20 native species of oak grow in California, including live (evergreen) oaks with holly-like leaves and scaly acorns. Other common trees include the aromatic California bay laurel, whose long slender leaves turn purple. Rare native trees include Monterey pines and Torrey pines, gnarly species that have adapted to harsh coastal conditions such as high winds, sparse rainfall and sandy, stony soils. Torrey pines only grow at Torrey Pines State Reserve near San Diego and in the Channel Islands, California's hot spot for endemic plant species.

GO WILD FOR WILDFLOWERS

The famous 'golden hills' of California are actually native plants and grasses that have adapted to local conditions over millennia, and learned to dry up in preparation for the long hot summer. Many local plants have adjusted their growing cycles to long periods of almost no rain, growing prolifically during California's mild wet winters, blooming as early as February, drying out in early summer and springing to life again with the first rains of fall.

In Southern California's desert areas, wildflower blooms usually peak in March, with carpets of wildflowers covering lowland areas of the state into April. Visit Anza-Borrego Desert State Park, Death Valley National Park, the Antelope Valley California Poppy Preserve and Carrizo Plain National Monument for some of the most spectacular annual wildflower displays.

As snows melt later at higher elevations in the Sierra Nevada, Yosemite National Park's Tuolumne Meadows is another prime spot for wildflower walks and photography, with blooms usually peaking in late June or early July.

Heading inland, the Sierra Nevada has three distinct eco-zones: the dry western foothills covered with oak and chaparral; conifer forests starting from an elevation of 2000ft; and an alpine zone above 8000ft. Almost two-dozen species of conifer grow in the Sierra Nevada, with mid-elevation forests home to massive Douglas firs, ponderosa pines and, biggest of all, the giant sequoia. Deciduous trees include the quaking aspen, a white-trunked tree with shimmering leaves that turn pale yellow in the fall, helping the Golden State live up to its name in the Eastern Sierra.

In 2006 the world's tallest-known living tree was discovered in a remote area of Redwood National Park – its location is kept secret to protect it. It's named Hyperion and stands a whopping 379ft tall.

Cacti & Other Desert Flora

In Southern California's deserts, cacti and other plants have adapted to the arid climate with thin, spiny leaves that resist moisture loss (and deter grazing animals). Their seed and flowering mechanisms kick into high gear during brief winter rains. Desert flora can bloom spectacularly in spring, carpeting valleys and drawing thousands of onlookers and shutterbugs.

One of the most common species is cholla, which looks so furry that it's nicknamed 'teddy-bear cactus,' but don't be fooled by its cuddly appearance. Cholla will bury extremely sharp, barbed spines in your skin at the slightest touch. Also watch out for the aptly named catclaw acacia, nicknamed 'wait-a-minute bush' because its small, sharp, hooked thorny spikes will try to grab your clothing or skin as you brush past.

You may also recognize prickly pear, a flat, fleshy padded cacti, the juice of which is traditionally used as medicine by Native Americans. You can hardly miss spiky ocotillo, which grows up to 20ft tall and has canelike branches that sprout blood-red flowers in spring. Creosote may look like a cactus, but it's actually a small evergreen bush with a distinctive smell.

With gangly arms and puffy green sleeves, Joshua trees look like Dr Seuss characters from afar, but up close you can see they're actually a type of yucca. In spring they burst into blossom with greenish-white flowers. Joshua trees grow throughout the Mojave Desert, although their habitat and long-term survival is severely threatened by climate change. According to local legend, they were named by Mormons who thought their crooked branches resembled the outstretched arms of a biblical prophet.

California's National & State Parks

Most Californians rate outdoor recreation as vital to their quality of life, and the amount of preserved public lands has steadily grown since the 1960s with support from key legislation. The landmark 1976 California Coastal Act saved the coastline from further development, while the controversial 1994 California Desert Protection Act passed over the objections of ranchers, miners and off highway vehicle (OHV) enthusiasts.

Today, California State Parks (www.parks.ca.gov) protects nearly a third of the state's coastline, along with redwood forests, mountain lakes, desert canyons, waterfalls, wildlife preserves and historical sites. In recent decades, state budget shortfalls and chronic underfunding of California's parks have contributed to closures, limited visitor services, increased park entry fees, as well as a near stoppage on acquiring new lands or expanding the size of the parks. But with state revenues from recreational tourism consistently outpacing resource-extraction industries such as mining, California has a considerable vested interest in protecting its wilderness tracts.

While you could be disappointed to find a park closed or full, bear in mind that some limits to public access are necessary to prevent California's parklands from being loved to death. Too many visitors can stress the natural environment. To avoid the crowds and glimpse wilderness at its most untrammeled, plan to visit popular parks such as Yosemite

California's Top Parks

Yosemite National Park

Sequoia & Kings Canyon National Parks

Death Valley National Park

Joshua Tree National Park

Lassen Volcanic National Park

Redwood National & State Parks

outside of peak season. Alternatively, less famous natural areas managed by the National Park Service (www.nps.gov/state/CA) often receive fewer visitors, which means you won't have to reserve permits, campsites or lodging many months in advance.

Co-founded by naturalist John Muir in 1892, the Sierra Club (www.sierraclub.org) was the USA's first conservation group. It remains the nation's most active, offering educational programs, group hikes, organized trips and volunteer vacations.

There are 18 national forests in California managed by the US Forest Service (www.fs.usda.gov/r5), comprising lands around Mt Whitney, Mt Shasta, Lake Tahoe, Big Bear Lake and Big Sur. Beloved by birders, national wildlife refuges (NWR), including the Salton Sea and Klamath Basin, are managed by the US Fish & Wildlife Service (www.fws.gov/refuges). More wilderness tracts in California, including the Lost Coast and Carrizo Plain, are overseen by the Bureau of Land Management (www.blm.gov/ca/st/en.html).

Conserving California

As you take in California's stunning natural landscapes, pause to appreciate the human effort it has taken to preserve and reclaim these natural wonders. In California rapid development and unchecked growth have often come at great environmental cost. Starting in 1849, gold-rush miners hacked and blasted through the California countryside in search of a lucky strike. More than 1.5 billion tons of debris and uncalculated amounts of poisonous mercury were carried downstream into the Central Valley, where rivers and streams became clogged and polluted. When you see forests in high Sierra gold country and salmon runs in the Sacramento Delta, you are admiring the resilience of nature and the work of many determined conservationists.

Water, or the lack thereof, has led to epic environmental struggles and catastrophes in California. Despite campaigning by John Muir, California's greatest environmental champion, the Tuolumne River was dammed at Hetch Hetchy in Yosemite National Park to supply Bay Area drinking water. Pipelines diverting water supplies for arid Los Angeles have contributed to the destruction of Owens Lake and its fertile wetlands, and the degradation of Mono Lake in the Eastern Sierra. Statewide, the damming of rivers and capture of water for houses and farms has ended inland salmon runs and dried up marshlands. The Central Valley's underground aquifer is subsiding, with some land sinking as much as 1ft each year. So every time you make an effort to conserve California's precious water resources, you deserve a chorus of thanks from up and down the state.

The 2015 documentary *Paya: The Water Story of the Paiute* explores the millennia-old history of the Owens Valley Paiute's usage of irrigation canals and their ongoing battle with the city of Los Angeles' diversion of this natural resource.

Altered and compromised habitats make easy targets for invasive species, including highly aggressive species that upset California's precariously balanced ecosystems. In San Francisco Bay, one of the most important estuaries in the world, there are now over 230 species choking the aquatic ecosystem, making up as much as 95% of the total biomass in some spots. Cleanup efforts are underway, and you can do your part by not dumping anything in California waterways, and recycling and composting as much of your waste as possible.

Although air quality in California has improved markedly in past decades, it's still among the worst in the country. Along with industrial emissions, the main pollutants are auto exhaust and fine particulates generated by the wearing down of vehicle tires. An even greater health hazard is ozone, the principal ingredient in smog, which makes sunny days around LA, Sacramento, the Central Valley and the western Sierra Nevada look hazy. In fact, Sequoia, Kings Canyon and Yosemite National Parks have some of the dirtiest air of any of the country's parks. California road trips are fantastic adventures, but if you rent a hybrid, take a train, carpool or hop public transit for short distances, you can breathe easier knowing you're helping to spare the air.

Survival Guide

Sustainable Travel

In California, nature's bounty is prized and locals are switched on to sustainability. This is still the USA, where car transportation reigns supreme and there's an uphill battle against single-use plastics. But it's not only easy to greenify your travels in California: it's fun, too!

Climate Challenges

According to the California Office of Environmental Health Hazard Assessment (OEHHA), annual air temperatures in California have been increasing since records began in 1895. Over the past 40 years, the mercury has been rising more quickly. Extreme weather events are more common, the winter chill has lessened, and the state has become drier overall. Aggravated by strong winds and drought, the 2018 wildfire season torched more than 2800 sq miles. It was the most destructive season on record – until the nightmare infernos two years later. By early 2020, weeks before the fire season was projected to end, more than 5800 sq miles had already burned.

Climate change is already having a significant impact on rural lifestyles, as well as on the tourist industry. With so much at stake, Californians take climate change very seriously. Visit California has spearheaded efforts to reduce car use, the National Park Service (NPS) is moving towards carbon-neutral operations in many California parks, and private businesses are getting creative (from sustainable winemaking to ecofriendly accommodations).

Ski resorts, too, are adopting a plethora of initiatives, like lower-impact snow-making machines and improved public-transport links. The Vail resorts (including Heavenly, Northstar and Kirkwood) subscribe to a 'Commitment to Zero' program with a goal of zero waste and zero net emissions by 2030. Squaw Valley has a host of measures like an increased carpooling lot and banning plastic water bottles.

Overtourism

California's beauty is also its curse. Many tourists are drawn to re-create the dreamlike snaps they've seen on Instagram, which means a dangerously high amount of footfall landing in the same spots.

In particular, Big Sur has become disturbingly overtouristed. Even in low season you might find traffic jams, in part because the iconic Bixby Bridge has become a social media darling. Travelers in a hurry for the perfect picture might park in a dangerous spot on the highway, and trample flora in their search for a vantage point. To combat this, visitors are being encouraged to sign up for the Big Sur Pledge (https://bigsurpledge.org), including careful driving and respectful approaches toward the natural environment (including fire safety).

According to the NPS, Golden Gate National Recreation Area was the USA's most visited park in 2019; crossing the bridge by bicycle or on foot can be frustratingly overcrowded. Another tourist magnet is Yosemite National Park. Yosemite drew 4.5 million visitors in 2019, making it the fifth most visited national park. Modernization of the park has brought wi-fi and increasing numbers of parking spaces for day visitors, but there are also measures to control visitor numbers: limited Wilderness Permits are issued, particularly for iconic destinations like the hike to Half Dome and the John Muir Trail.

One of the best ways to offset the damage of overtourism in California is simply to cast your net more widely when planning a trip. If you're wary about contributing to overtourism in wine country, opt for lesser-visited vineyard areas in the Central Coast, especially the Edna Valley near San Luis Obispo. Many vineyards have signed up to the Central Coast's Sustainability in Practice (SIP) initiative (www.pacificcoastfarming.com/sustainability). For a coastal road trip without the traffic, Mendocino and the North Coast offer spectacular views, redwood forests and lesser-touristed towns. In Yosemite, consider exploring less popular areas like Wawona and Hetch Hetchy.

The season can also make a huge difference: seeing Yosemite in winter has some inconveniences (one main road into the park closes, and in inclement weather you will need an all-wheel drive/4WD, snow tires, or chains). But you'll be free from summer's traffic gridlock and privy to snow-sprinkled views. Likewise, summer traffic can be intense along Generals Hwy in Sequoia National Park, and the stretch that runs from Sequoia to Kings Canyon, whereas visitor numbers ease off in winter and there are excellent snowshoeing and cross-country skiing trails.

Social media is often blamed for contributing to overtourism, but it's possible to harness hashtags for good. Use the power of Twitter, Instagram and more to highlight ecofriendly experiences and good practice – by showing images of sustainable dining, camping in designated areas, picking up litter left by others – and encourage other travelers to be part of the change.

Green Transportation

Undeniably, California is road-trip country. A car or motorcycle opens up the widest number of destinations. But it's possible to travel by train, if you intend to visit a couple of major cities and day-trip from there. The *Coast Starlight* train from Seattle, WA, passes through the Bay Area (Oakland) on its way to Los Angeles, and the *Pacific Surfliner* travels between San Luis Obispo and San Diego (via Santa Barbara and LA). Both are scenic enough to be worth their frequent delays.

Bus options exist for iconic outdoor destinations, including Yosemite Valley's public shuttle system and hiker shuttles, and Mammoth Lakes' year-round shuttle buses. In cities, it's often a relief to be vehicle-free. Traffic is notoriously bad, especially in LA and San Francisco. The rise of rideshare services like Lyft and Uber is blamed for adding even more cars to the streets. Part of the reason that rideshare services have thrived is that public transport can be sluggish and inefficient, especially if a change of bus or metro is involved. But if you aren't in a huge hurry and can avoid rush hour, public transit is still a good option. Remember, even when it appears slow going, you'll save the time, money and stress you'd have spent on parking spaces.

Jump bikes and e-scooters are available in evermore destinations, and bike lanes are increasing, even in small towns. San Francisco is fun to cycle around (if occasionally steep!), and there has been an explosion of bikes and e-bikes with an easy sign up to the service. In Santa Cruz, Monterey and San Luis Obispo, bicycles can make a good alternative to rideshare services. Some road-trip journeys translate well to two wheels, too: rather than driving 17-Mile Drive, consider negotiating the route on a rental e-bike from Monterey. It's also possible to get up and down the spine of Hwy 395 by public transport or by bike.

Lake Tahoe has an extensive paved trail network suited to cyclists: the East Shore Trail links Incline Village to Sand Harbor State Park, and at the time of writing there were plans to extend a recreational path around the whole lake. Tahoe also boasts the excellent TART buses (https://tahoetruckeetransit.com), which can get hikers to and from trailheads. Buses run along the north and west coast of the lake regularly and they're free.

Sustainable Experiences

Urban hikes Bikes & Hikes LA (https://bikesandhikesla.com) can guide you to Griffith Park for Hollywood-sign views at sunset, without worrying about grabbing an Uber back down. San Francisco is also a sweet spot for strapping on hiking boots; ramble the Presidio or step up to the lookout at Twin Peaks.

Sustainable booze Raise a glass: some 89% of Sonoma County's vineyard acreage has been certified as sustainable, while Mendocino has an emphasis on solar power and organic/biodynamic wines. The Anderson Valley has a largely solar-powered brewery, and Sacramento's Sierra Nevada Brewing Co is approaching zero-waste status.

Minibus tours Reduce the number of cars on the road by taking day trips by bus or organized tour. Look out for shared-minibus options for wineries, for example the vineyard and craft-beer scenes of San Luis Obispo and Paso Robles.

Local cafes Green travelers may be dismayed to see that one-use plastics remain the norm in many accommodations and eating establishments. Consider opting out of hotel breakfast buffets; far too many consist of one-use cups, plates and cutlery. Instead, seek out a locally owned cafe. Bring a reusable coffee cup (or buy one early into your trip) and take it along.

Resources

Green Business CA (https://greenbusinessca.org) Search for green businesses, filtering by categories like food and drink or lodging and travel.

Happy Cow (www.happycow.net) Online resource for finding vegetarian and vegan restaurants, in California and across the US and beyond.

Leave No Trace (https://lnt.org) Advice on hiking, camping and exploring protected landscapes with the lightest of footprints.

Napa Green (https://napagreen.org) Vineyards certified as sustainable at every stage of their wine production.

Directory A–Z

Climate

Los Angeles

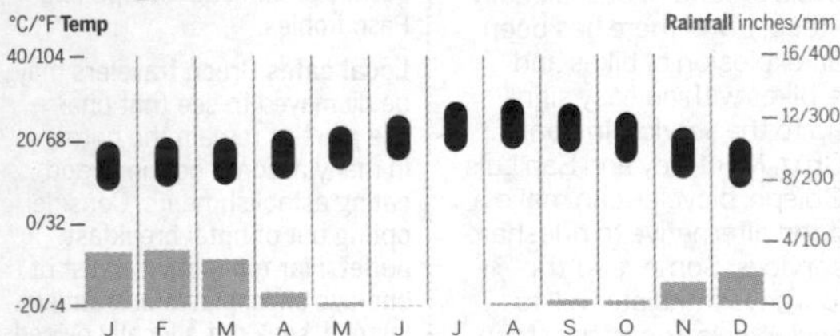

San Francisco

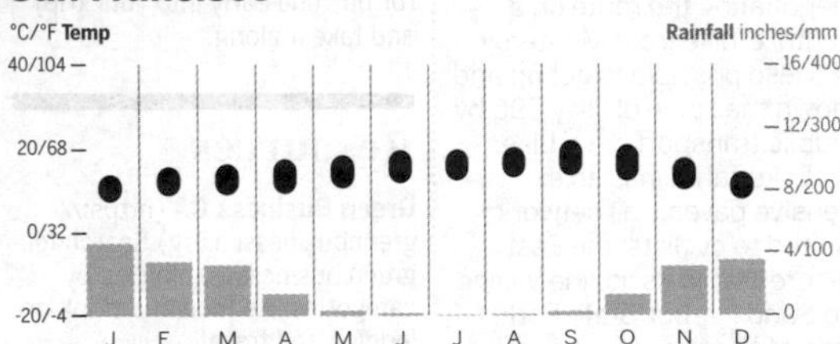

Yosemite Valley

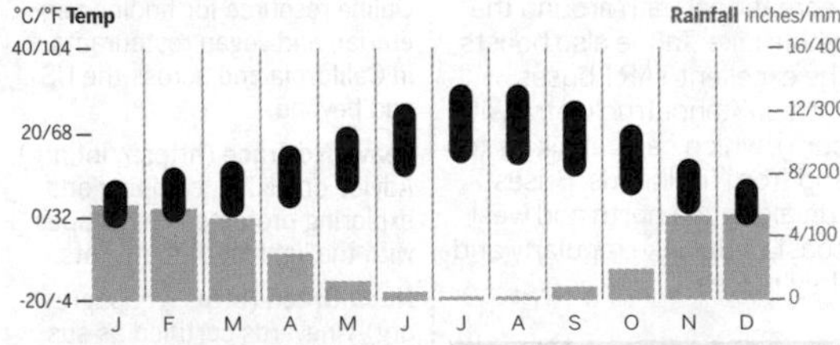

Accessible Travel

More populated areas of California are reasonably well equipped for travelers with disabilities, but facilities in smaller towns and rural areas may be limited.

Download Lonely Planet's free Accessible Travel guides from http://lptravel.to/AccessibleTravel.

Accessibility

- Most traffic intersections have dropped curbs and some have audible crossing signals.
- The Americans with Disabilities Act (ADA) requires public buildings built after 1993 to be wheelchair-accessible, including restrooms.
- Motels and hotels built after 1993 must have at least one ADA-compliant accessible room; state your specific needs when making reservations.
- For nonpublic buildings built prior to 1993, including hotels, restaurants, museums and theaters, there are no accessibility guarantees; call ahead to find out what to expect.
- Most national and many state parks and some other outdoor recreation areas offer paved or boardwalk nature trails that are graded and accessible by wheelchair.
- Many theme parks go out of their way to be accessible to wheelchairs and guests with mobility limitations and other disabilities.
- US citizens and permanent residents with a permanent disability quality for a free lifetime 'America the Beautiful' Access Pass (http://store.usgs.gov/pass/access.html), which waives entry fees to all national parks and federal recreational lands and offers discounts on some

recreation fees (eg camping). There's a $10 handling fee.

➡ California State Parks' disabled discount pass ($3.50) entitles people with permanent disabilities to 50% off day-use parking and camping fees; for an application, see www.parks.ca.gov.

Communications

➡ Telephone companies provide relay operators (dial 711) for the hearing-impaired.

➡ Many banks provide ATM instructions in Braille.

Transportation

➡ All major airlines, Greyhound buses and Amtrak trains can accommodate people with disabilities, usually with 48 hours of advance notice required.

➡ Major car-rental agencies offer hand-controlled vehicles and vans with wheelchair lifts at no extra charge, but you must reserve these well in advance.

➡ For wheelchair-accessible van rentals, also try **Wheelchair Getaways** (☎888-432-9339; www.wheelchairgetaways.com) in Sacramento, San Diego, San Francisco and LA, or **Mobility Works** (☎877-275-4915; www.mobilityworks.com) in LA, San Diego, San Francisco, Oakland, San Jose and Sacramento.

➡ Local buses, trains and subway lines usually have wheelchair lifts.

➡ Seeing-eye dogs are permitted to accompany passengers on public transportation.

➡ Taxi companies have at least one wheelchair-accessible van, but you'll usually need to call and then wait for one.

Resources

A Wheelchair Rider's Guide to the California Coast (www.wheelingcalscoast.org) Free accessibility information covering beaches, parks and trails, plus downloadable PDF guides to the San Francisco Bay Area and Los Angeles and Orange County coasts.

Access Northern California (www.accessnca.org) Extensive links to accessible-travel resources, including outdoor recreation opportunities, lodgings, tours and transportation.

Access Santa Cruz County (www.scaccessguide.com) Free online accessible-travel guide for visiting Santa Cruz and around, including restaurants, lodging, beaches, parks and outdoor recreation.

Achieve Tahoe (http://achievetahoe.org) Organizes summer and winter sports, 4WD adventures and adaptive-ski rental around Lake Tahoe in the Sierra Nevada (annual membership from $50).

California State Parks (http://access.parks.ca.gov) Searchable online map and database of accessible features at state parks.

Disabled Sports Eastern Sierra (http://disabledsportseasternsierra.org) Offers summer and winter outdoor-activity programs around Mammoth Lakes.

Los Angeles for Disabled Visitors (www.discoverlosangeles.com/search/site/disabled) Tips for accessible sightseeing, entertainment, museums and transportation.

Wheelchair Traveling (www.wheelchairtraveling.com) Travel articles, lodging and helpful California destination info.

Yosemite National Park Accessibility (www.nps.gov/yose/planyourvisit/accessibility.htm) Detailed, downloadable accessibility information for Yosemite National Park, including services for deaf visitors.

Accommodations

Amenities

➡ Budget accommodations include campgrounds, hostels and motels. Midrange properties generally offer better value for money.

➡ At midrange motels and hotels, expect clean, comfortable and decent-sized rooms with at least a private bathroom, and standard amenities such as cable TV, direct-dial telephone, a coffee maker, and perhaps a microwave and mini-fridge.

➡ Top-end lodgings offer top-notch amenities and perhaps a scenic location, high design, historical ambience, pools, fitness rooms, business centers, full-service restaurants and bars and other convenient facilities.

➡ In Southern California, nearly all lodgings have air-conditioning, but in perpetually cool Northern California most don't. In coastal areas as far south as Santa Barbara, only fans may be provided.

➡ Accommodations offering online computer terminals for guests are designated with the @ icon. A fee may apply, including at full-service hotel business centers. Rarely, there may be a fee for wireless internet or in-room access. Look for free wi-fi hot spots in hotel public areas such as the lobby or poolside.

➡ Many lodgings are now exclusively nonsmoking. Where they still exist, smoking rooms are often left unrenovated and in less desirable locations. Expect a hefty 'cleaning fee' ($100 or more) if you light up in designated nonsmoking rooms.

➡ Hotel parking fees can add up quickly, especially in big cities and at resorts.

Rates & Reservations

➡ Lodgings in national parks including Yosemite, Sequoia and Kings Canyon generally sell out months in advance for the summer, as do backcountry lodgings that operate on a lottery system.

➡ Generally midweek rates are lower, except at urban hotels geared toward business travelers. Hotels in Silicon Valley, downtown San Francisco, LA and San Diego may lure leisure travelers with weekend deals.

➡ Discount membership cards (such as AAA and AARP) may get you about 10% off standard rates at participating hotels and motels.

➡ Look for freebie-ad magazines packed with hotel and motel discount coupons at gas stations, highway rest areas, tourist offices and online.

➡ High season is from June to August everywhere, except the deserts and mountain ski areas, where December through April are the busiest months.

➡ Demand and prices spike around major holidays and for festivals, when some properties may impose multiday minimum stays.

➡ Reservations are recommended for weekend and holiday travel year-round, and every day of the week during high season.

➡ Bargaining may be possible for walk-in guests without reservations, especially at off-peak times.

Customs Regulations

Currently, non-US citizens and permanent residents may import the follwing:

➡ 1L of alcohol (if you're over 21 years of age)

➡ 200 cigarettes (one carton) or 100 cigars (if you're over 18 years)

➡ $100 worth of gifts

Amounts higher than $10,000 in cash, traveler's checks, money orders and other cash equivalents must be declared.

Don't even think about bringing in illegal drugs.

For more complete, up-to-date information, check the website of **US Customs and Border Protection** (www.cbp.gov).

Discount Cards

American Association of Retired Persons (AARP; ☎888-687-2277; www.aarp.org) This advocacy group for Americans 50 years and older offers member discounts (usually 10%) on hotels, car rentals and more. Annual membership costs $16.

American Automobile Association (AAA; ☎800-922-8228; www.aaa.com) Members of AAA and its foreign affiliates (eg CAA, AA) enjoy small discounts (usually 10%) on Amtrak trains, car rentals, motels and hotels, chain restaurants and shops, tours and theme parks. Annual membership from $52.

'America the Beautiful' Annual Pass (http://store.usgs.gov/pass; 12-month pass $80; $10 handling fee) Admits four adults and all children under 16 years for free to all national parks and federal recreational lands (eg USFS, BLM) for 12 months from the date of purchase. US citizens and permanent residents aged 62 years and older are eligible for a lifetime Senior Pass ($80; $10 handling fee), which grants free entry and 50% off some recreational-use fees such as camping.

Go Los Angeles, San Diego & San Francisco Explorer Cards (www.smartdestinations.com; 1-day pass adult/child from $78/64) The Go LA Card and pricier Go San Diego Card include admission to major SoCal theme parks (but not Disneyland). The cheaper Go San Francisco Card covers museums, bicycle rental and a bay cruise. You've got to do a lot of sightseeing over multiple days to make passes come close to paying off. Alternatively, Explorer passes give you 30 days to visit three to five attractions. For discounts, buy online.

International Student Identity, Youth Travel & Teacher Identity Cards (www.isic.org; 12-month card $25) Offers savings on airline fares, travel insurance and local attractions for full-time students (ISIC), for non-students 30 years of age or younger (IYTC) and for employed teachers (ITIC). Cards are issued online and by student unions, hosteling organizations and youth-oriented budget travel agencies.

Senior Discounts People over the age of 65 (sometimes 50, 55, 60 or 62) often qualify for the same discounts as students; any ID showing the birth date should suffice as proof.

Southern California CityPass (www.citypass.com/southern-california; adult/child from $194) If you're visiting SoCal theme parks, CityPass offers

ETIQUETTE

Californians are pretty casual by nature, but a few (unspoken) rules still apply.

Bargaining Haggling over the prices of goods usually isn't appropriate, except at outdoor markets and with sidewalk vendors.

Greetings Shaking hands with men and women when meeting for the first time may be a tad formal, but it's expected for business dealings and by some older adults.

Smoking Don't light up indoors (it's illegal) or anywhere else you don't see others doing it, unless you don't mind lots of dirty looks.

small discounts on multiday admission to Disneyland and Disney California Adventure, Legoland California and SeaWorld San Diego, with add-ons available for the San Diego Zoo or Safari Park. It's cheapest to buy them online in advance.

Student Advantage Card (☎800-333-2920; www.studentadvantage.com) For international and US students, this card offers 10% on Greyhound buses, plus discounts of 10% to 25% on some motels and hotels, rental cars, ridesharing services and shopping. A 12-month membership costs $30.

Electricity

Type A
120V/60Hz

Health

Before You Go

HEALTH INSURANCE

➡ Keep all medical receipts and documentation for billing and insurance claims and reimbursement later.

➡ Some health-insurance policies require you to get pre-authorization over the phone for medical treatment before seeking help.

➡ Overseas visitors with travel-health-insurance policies may need to contact a call center for an assessment by phone before getting medical treatment.

RECOMMENDED VACCINATIONS

Currently there are no vaccination requirements for visiting the USA. California has recently had outbreaks of measles and whooping cough, since fewer parents have been choosing to vaccinate their children. Before visiting California, make sure you've had all of the standard immunizations, including but not limited to MMR (measles, mumps and rubella), Hepatitis A and B, varicella (chickenpox) and Tdap (tetanus-diphtheria-accelluar pertussis) within the last 10 years, and the annual seasonal influenza vaccine.

Availability & Cost of Health Care

➡ Medical treatment in the USA is of the highest caliber, but the expense could kill you. Many health-care professionals demand payment at the time of service, especially from out-of-towners or international visitors.

➡ Except for medical emergencies (in which case call 911 or go to the nearest 24-hour hospital emergency room, or ER), phone around to find a doctor who will accept your insurance.

Environmental Hazards

DEHYDRATION, HEAT EXHAUSTION & HEATSTROKE

➡ Take it easy as you acclimatize, especially on hot summer days and in Southern California's deserts. Drink plenty of water. A minimum of 3 quarts per person per day is recommended when you're active outdoors. Be sure to eat a salty snack too, as sodium is necessary for rehydration.

➡ Dehydration (lack of water) or salt deficiency can cause heat exhaustion, often characterized by heavy sweating, fatigue, lethargy, headaches, nausea, vomiting, dizziness and muscle cramps.

➡ Long, continuous exposure to high temperatures can lead to possibly fatal heatstroke, when body temperatures rise to dangerous levels. Warning signs include altered mental status, hyperventilation and flushed, hot and dry skin (ie sweating stops).

➡ For heatstroke, immediate hospitalization is essential. Meanwhile, get out of the sun, remove clothing that retains heat (cotton is OK), douse the body with cool water and fan continuously. Ice packs can be applied to the neck, armpits and groin.

HYPOTHERMIA

➡ Skiers and hikers will find that temperatures in the mountains and desert can quickly drop below freezing, especially during winter. Even a sudden spring shower or high winds can lower your body temperature dangerously fast.

➡ Instead of cotton, wear synthetic or woolen clothing that retains warmth even when wet. Carry waterproof layers (eg Gore-Tex jacket, plastic poncho, rain pants) and high-energy, easily digestible snacks such as chocolate, nuts and dried fruit.

➡ Symptoms of hypothermia include exhaustion, numbness, shivering, stumbling, slurred speech, dizzy spells, muscle cramps and irrational or even violent behavior.

➡ To treat mild hypothermia, get out of bad weather and change into

PRACTICALITIES

Newspapers *Los Angeles Times* (www.latimes.com), *San Francisco Chronicle* (www.sfchronicle.com), *Mercury News* (www.mercurynews.com), *Sacramento Bee* (www.sacbee.com)

Radio National Public Radio (NPR), lower end of FM dial

TV PBS (public broadcasting); cable: CNN (news), ESPN (sports), HBO (movies), Weather Channel

Weights & Measures Imperial (except 1 US gallon equals 0.83 imperial gallons)

dry, warm clothing. Drink hot liquids (no caffeine or alcohol) and snack on high-calorie food.

➡ For more advanced hypothermia, seek immediate medical attention. Do not rub victims, who must be handled gently.

TAP WATER

It's fine to drink water from the tap anywhere in California, except at some wilderness campgrounds where the water may not be potable (look for signs or ask the campground host).

Insurance

Getting travel insurance to cover theft, loss and medical problems is highly recommended. Some policies do not cover 'risky' activities such as scuba diving, motorcycling and skiing, so read the fine print. Make sure the policy at least covers hospital stays and an emergency flight home.

Paying for your airline ticket or rental car with a credit card may provide limited travel accident insurance. If you already have private health insurance or a homeowners or renters policy, find out what those policies cover and only get supplemental insurance. If you have prepaid a large portion of your vacation, trip-cancellation insurance may be a worthwhile expense.

Worldwide travel insurance is available at www.lonelyplanet.com/travel-insurance. You can buy, extend and claim online anytime – even if you're already on the road.

Internet Access

➡ With branches in major cities and towns, **FedEx** (☎800-463-3339; www.fedex.com/us/office) offers internet access at self-service computer workstations (30¢ to 40¢ per minute) and sometimes free wi-fi, plus digital-photo printing and CD-burning stations.

➡ Free wi-fi hot spots can almost always be found at major airports, malls, hotels, motels and coffee shops (eg Starbucks) and some tourist information centers, campgrounds (eg KOA), stores (eg Apple), bars and restaurants.

➡ Free public wi-fi is proliferating and even some of California's state parks are now wi-fi–enabled (get details at www.parks.ca.gov).

➡ Public libraries have internet terminals (online time may be limited, advance sign-up required and a nominal fee charged for out-of-network visitors) and, increasingly, free wi-fi.

Legal Matters

Drugs & Alcohol

➡ Possession of up to 1oz of marijuana (if you are 21 years or older) for recreational use is no longer a crime in California, but it is still illegal to use marijuana in public (subject to fines of up to $500, as well as mandatory community-service hours and drug-education classes).

➡ Possession of any other drug or more than 1oz of marijuana is a felony punishable by lengthy jail time. For foreigners, conviction of any drug offense is grounds for deportation.

➡ Police can give roadside sobriety checks to assess if you've been drinking or using drugs. If you fail, they'll require you to take a breath, urine or blood test to determine if your blood alcohol is over the legal limit (0.08%). Refusing to be tested is treated the same as if you had taken and failed the test.

➡ Penalties for driving under the influence (DUI) of drugs or alcohol range from license suspension and fines to jail time.

➡ It's illegal to carry open containers of alcohol or marijuana inside a vehicle, even if they're empty. Unless they're full and still sealed, store them in the trunk.

➡ Consuming alcohol anywhere other than at a private residence or licensed premises is a no-no, which puts most parks and beaches off limits (although many campgrounds legally allow it).

➡ Bars, clubs and liquor stores often ask for photo ID to prove you are of legal drinking age (21 years). Being 'carded' is standard practice, so don't take it personally.

Police & Security

➡ For police, fire and ambulance emergencies, dial 911. For nonemergency police assistance, contact the nearest local police station (dial 411 for directory assistance).

➡ If you are stopped by the police, be courteous. Don't get out of the car unless asked. Keep your hands where the officer can see them (eg on the steering wheel) at all times.

➡ There is no system of paying fines on the spot. Attempting to pay the fine to the officer may lead to a charge of attempted bribery.

➡ For traffic violations the ticketing officer will explain your options. There is usually a 30-day period to pay a fine; most matters can be handled by mail or online.

➡ If you are arrested you have the right to remain silent and are presumed innocent until proven guilty. Everyone has the right to make one phone call. If you don't have a lawyer, one will be appointed to you free of charge. Foreign travelers who don't have a lawyer, friends or family to help should call their embassy or consulate; the police can provide the number upon request.

➡ Due to security concerns about terrorism, never leave your bags unattended, especially at airports or bus and train stations.

LGBT+ Travelers

California is a magnet for LGBT+ travelers. Hot spots include the Castro in San Francisco, West Hollywood (WeHo), Silver Lake, Long Beach and Downtown in LA, San Diego's Hillcrest neighborhood, the desert resort of Palm Springs, Guerneville in the Russian River Valley and Calistoga in Napa Valley.

Same-sex marriage is legal in California. Despite widespread tolerance, homophobic bigotry still exists. In small towns, especially away from the coast, tolerance often comes down to a 'don't ask, don't tell' policy.

Resources

Advocate (www.advocate.com/travel) Online news, gay travel features and destination guides.

Damron (www.damron.com) Classic, advertiser-driven gay travel guides and 'Gay Scout' mobile app.

LGBT National Hotline (888-843-4564; www.glbthotline.org) For counseling and referrals of any kind.

Misterb&b (www.misterbandb.com) Online booking site for accommodations friendly to LGBT+ travelers.

Out Traveler (www.outtraveler.com) Free online magazine articles with travel tips, destination guides and hotel reviews.

Maps

➡ GPS navigation is handy, but cannot be relied upon 100% of the time, especially in remote wilderness and rural areas.

➡ Visitor centers distribute free (but often very basic) maps. If you're doing a lot of driving around California, you'll need a more detailed road map or map atlas.

➡ Members of the **American Automobile Association** (AAA; ☎800-922-8228; www.aaa.com) or its international affiliates (bring your membership card from home) can get free driving maps from local AAA offices.

➡ National Geographic trail maps (www.natgeomaps.com/trail-maps/trails-illustrated-maps) are a good option for the Sierra Nevada.

➡ DeLorme's comprehensive *California Atlas & Gazetteer* ($25) shows campgrounds, hiking trails, recreational areas and topographical land features; it's less useful for navigating urban areas.

Money

ATMs

➡ ATMs are available 24/7 at most banks, shopping malls, airports and grocery and convenience stores.

➡ Expect a minimum surcharge of around $3 per transaction, in addition to any fees charged by your home bank.

➡ Most ATMs are connected to international networks and offer decent foreign-exchange rates.

➡ Withdrawing cash from an ATM using a credit card usually incurs a hefty fee and high interest rates; contact your credit-card company for details and a PIN number.

Cash

Most people don't carry large amounts of cash for everyday use, relying instead on credit and debit cards. Some businesses refuse to accept bills over $20.

Credit Cards

➡ Major credit cards are almost universally accepted. In fact, it's almost impossible to rent a car, book a hotel room or buy tickets over the phone without one. A credit card may also be vital in emergencies.

➡ Visa, MasterCard and American Express are the most widely accepted credit cards.

Moneychangers

➡ You can exchange money at major airports, bigger banks and currency-exchange offices such as American Express (www.americanexpress.com) or Travelex (www.travelex.com). Always inquire about rates and fees.

➡ Outside big cities, exchanging money may be

a problem, so make sure you have a credit card and sufficient cash on hand.

Taxes & Refunds

➡ California state sales tax (7.25%) is added to the retail price of most goods and services (groceries are exceptions). Local and city sales taxes may tack on up to 3%.

➡ Gasoline is heavily and increasingly taxed in California; at the time of writing drivers were paying 79¢ on the gallon.

➡ Tourist lodging taxes vary statewide, but average 10.5% to 14% in major cities.

➡ No refunds of sales or lodging taxes are available for visitors.

Post

➡ The **US Postal Service** (USPS; ☎800-275-8777; www.usps.com) is inexpensive and reliable.

➡ For sending important documents or packages internationally, try **Federal Express** (FedEx; ☎800-463-3339; www.fedex.com/us) or **United Parcel Service** (UPS; ☎800-742-5877; www.ups.com).

Public Holidays

On the following national holidays, banks, schools and government offices (including post offices) are closed, and transportation, museums and other services operate on a Sunday schedule. Holidays falling on a weekend are usually observed the following Monday.

New Year's Day January 1

Martin Luther King Jr Day Third Monday in January

Presidents' Day Third Monday in February

Cesar Chavez Day March 31

Memorial Day Last Monday in May

Independence Day July 4

Labor Day First Monday in September

Indigenous Peoples' Day Second Monday in October

Veterans Day November 11

Thanksgiving Day Fourth Thursday in November

Christmas Day December 25

School Holidays

➡ Schools take a one- or two-week 'spring break' around Easter, sometime in March or April. Some hotels and resorts, especially at beaches and near SoCal's theme parks, raise their rates during this time.

➡ School summer vacations run from mid-June until mid-August, making July and August the busiest travel months.

Safe Travel

Despite its seemingly apocalyptic list of dangers – guns, violent crime, riots, earthquakes – California is a reasonably safe place to visit. The greatest danger is posed by car accidents (buckle up – it's the law), while the biggest annoyances are metro-area traffic and crowds. When hiking or swimming in wilderness areas, be sure to understand the route, bring proper equipment and water, and read up on dangers such as rock slides, flash floods or riptides. Wildlife can also pose a threat.

Earthquakes

Earthquakes happen all the time, but most are so tiny they are detectable only by sensitive seismological instruments. Here's what to do if you're caught in a serious shaker:

➡ If indoors, get under a desk or table or stand in a doorway.

➡ Protect your head and stay clear of windows, mirrors or anything that might fall.

➡ Don't head for elevators or go running into the street.

➡ If you're in a shopping mall or large public building, expect the alarm and/or sprinkler systems to come on.

TIPPING

Tipping is *not* optional. Only withhold tips in cases of outrageously bad service.

Airport skycaps & hotel bellhops $2 or $3 per bag, minimum $5 per cart

Bartenders 15% to 20% per round, minimum $1 per drink

Concierges Nothing for simple information, up to $20 for securing last-minute restaurant reservations, sold-out show tickets, etc

Housekeeping staff $2 to $4 daily, left under the card provided; more if you're messy

Parking valets At least $2 when your car keys are handed back

Restaurant servers & room service 18% to 20%, unless a gratuity is already charged (common for groups of six or more)

Taxi drivers 10% to 15% of metered fare, rounded up to the next dollar

➡ If outdoors, get away from buildings, trees and power lines.

➡ If you're driving, pull over to the side of the road away from bridges, overpasses and power lines. Stay inside the car until the shaking stops.

➡ If you're on a sidewalk near buildings, duck into a doorway to protect yourself from falling bricks, glass and debris.

➡ Prepare for aftershocks.

➡ Turn on the radio and listen for bulletins.

➡ Use the telephone only if absolutely necessary.

Wildfires

Fire season in California has become significantly more severe in recent years, affecting travel in many areas of the state. Active fires can limit access to roads and destinations, including parks, and poor air quality can also become an issue. In 2020, the devastating fire season began in July and stretched through to November, with more than 8200 wildfires burning more than 4 million acres. Thirty-one deaths were reported, and more than 8000 structures were destroyed.

Tourist areas most affected by fires and hazardous air in 2020 included the Santa Cruz Mountains, Napa and Sonoma Wine Country, Big Sur, Yosemite National Park, Point Reyes National Seashore, San Francisco, Los Angeles, Mojave National Preserve, Sequoia & Kings Canyon National Parks, Lake Tahoe and all of the state's national forests. For updated information about how wildfires may affect your trip, check the website of Visit California (www.visitcalifornia.com/experience/california-wildfire-travel-update). For more information about road closures, air-quality readings and wildfires, visit www.fire.ca.gov/incidents.

SMOKING

➡ Smoking is generally prohibited inside all public buildings, including airports, shopping malls and train and bus stations.

➡ There is no smoking allowed inside restaurants, although lighting up may be tolerated at outdoor patio or sidewalk tables (ask first).

➡ At hotels you must specifically request a smoking room, but note some properties are entirely nonsmoking by law.

➡ In some cities and towns, smoking outdoors within a certain distance of any public business is illegal.

➡ The minimum age to legally purchase tobacco products (including e-cigarettes) in California is now 21.

Wildlife

➡ Never feed or approach any wild animal, not even harmless-looking critters – it causes them to lose their innate fear of humans which in turn makes them dangerously aggressive. Many birds and mammals, including deer and rodents such as squirrels, carry serious diseases that can be transmitted to humans through a bite.

➡ Disturbing or harassing specially protected species, including many marine mammals such as whales, dolphins and seals, is a crime, subject to enormous fines.

➡ Black bears are often attracted to campgrounds, where they may find food, trash and any other scented items left out on picnic tables or stashed in tents and cars. Always use bear-proof containers where they are provided. For more bear-country travel tips, visit the SierraWild website (http://sierrawild.gov/bears).

➡ If you encounter a black bear in the wild, don't run. Stay together, keeping small children next to you and picking up little ones. Keep back at least 100yd. If the bear starts moving toward you, back away slowly off-trail and let it pass by, being careful not to block any of the bear's escape routes or to get caught between a mother and her cubs. Sometimes a black bear will 'bluff charge' to test your dominance. Stand your ground by making yourself look as big as possible (eg waving your arms above your head) and shouting menacingly.

➡ Mountain lion attacks on humans are rare, but can be deadly. If you encounter a mountain lion stay calm, pick up small children, face the animal and retreat slowly. Make yourself appear larger by raising your arms or grabbing a stick. If the lion becomes menacing, shout or throw rocks at it. If attacked, fight back aggressively.

➡ Snakes and spiders are common throughout California, not just in wilderness areas. Always look inside your shoes before putting them back on outdoors, especially when camping. Snake bites are rare, but occur most often when a snake is stepped on or provoked (eg picked up or poked with a stick). Antivenom is available at most hospitals.

Telephone

Cell Phones

➡ You'll need a multiband LTE, GSM or UMTS phone to make calls in the USA. Popping in a US prepaid rechargeable SIM card is usually cheaper than using your network.

➡ SIM cards are sold at telecommunications and electronics stores. These stores also sell inexpensive prepaid phones, including some airtime.

➡ You can rent a cell phone at San Francisco International Airport (SFO) from TripTel (https://triptel.com); pricing plans vary, but typically are expensive.

Dialing Codes

➡ US phone numbers consist of a three-digit area code followed by a seven-digit local number.

➡ When dialing a number within the same area code, use the seven-digit number (if that doesn't work, try all 10 digits).

➡ For long-distance calls, dial 1 plus the area code plus the local number.

➡ Toll-free numbers (eg beginning with 800, 855, 866, 877 or 888) must be preceded by 1.

➡ For direct international calls, dial 011 plus the country code plus the area code (usually without the initial '0') plus the local phone number.

➡ If you're calling from abroad, the country code for the US is 1 (the same as Canada, but international rates apply between the two countries).

Payphones & Phonecards

➡ Where payphones still exist, they're usually coin-operated, though some may only accept credit cards (eg in state or national parks). Local calls cost 50¢ minimum.

➡ For long-distance and international calls, prepaid phonecards are sold at convenience stores, supermarkets, newsstands and electronics stores.

Time

Pacific Standard Time (UTC minus eight hours). Clocks are set one hour ahead during Daylight Saving Time (DST), from the second Sunday in March until the first Sunday in November.

Toilets

Free public restrooms are easy to find inside shopping malls, public buildings and some transportation hubs, as well as outdoors at parks and beaches. It's more challenging to find them in urban areas – try the nearest public library, grocery store, pharmacy, gas station, bar or coffee shop (where you might have to buy something to eat or drink before borrowing the bathroom key).

Tourist Information

➡ For pre-trip planning, peruse the information-packed website Visit California (www.visitcalifornia.com).

➡ The same government agency operates more than a dozen statewide California Welcome Centers (www.visitcwc.com), where staff dispense maps and brochures and may be able to help find accommodations.

➡ Almost every city and town has a local visitor center or a chamber of commerce where you can pick up maps, brochures and information.

Visas

➡ Visa information is highly subject to change. Depending on your country of origin, the rules for entering the USA keep changing. Double-check current visa requirements *before* coming to the USA.

➡ Currently, under the US Visa Waiver Program (VWP), visas are not required for citizens of 39 countries for stays up to 90 days (no extensions) as long as you have a machine-readable passport that meets current US standards and is valid for six months beyond your intended stay.

➡ Citizens of VWP countries must still register with the **Electronic System for Travel Authorization** (ESTA; https://esta.cbp.dhs.gov) at least 72 hours before travel. Once approved, ESTA registration ($14) is valid for up to two years or until your passport expires, whichever comes first.

➡ For most Canadian citizens traveling with Canadian passports that meet current US standards, a visa for short-term visits (usually up to six months) and ESTA registration aren't required.

➡ Citizens from all other countries, or whose passports don't meet US standards, need to apply for a visa in their home country. The process has a nonrefundable fee (minimum $160), involves a personal interview and can take several weeks, so apply as early as possible.

➡ For up-to-date information about entry requirements and eligibility, check the visa section on the website of the US Department of State (http://travel.state.gov), or contact the nearest USA embassy or consulate in your home country (for a complete list, visit www.usembassy.gov).

➡ For information about Covid-19 travel restrictions, visit the website of the Centers for Disease Control and Prevention (www.cdc.gov).

Volunteering

Casual drop-in volunteer opportunities, where you can socialize with locals while helping out nonprofit organizations, are most common in cities. Browse upcoming projects and activities and sign up online with local organizations such as One Brick (www.onebrick.org) in San Francisco and Silicon Valley, HandsOn Bay Area (www.handsonbayarea.org), LA Works (www.laworks.com) and Orange County's OneOC (www.oneoc.org). For more opportunities, check local alternative weekly tabloids and Craigslist (www.craigslist.org).

Resources

California Volunteers (www.californiavolunteers.org) State-run volunteer directory and matching service, with links to national service days and long-term programs.

Habitat for Humanity (www.habitat.org) Nonprofit organization that helps build homes for impoverished families across California; has day, weekend and weeklong projects.

Idealist (www.idealist.org) Free searchable database that includes both short- and long-term volunteer opportunities.

Sierra Club (www.sierraclub.org) Day or weekend projects and longer volunteer vacations (including for families) that focus on environmental conservation (annual membership from $15).

TreePeople (www.treepeople.org) Organizes half-day group tree planting, invasive-weed pulling and habitat-restoration projects around LA, from urban parks to mountain forests.

Wilderness Volunteers (www.wildernessvolunteers.org) Week-long trips that help maintain national parks, preserves, forests, seashores and other wilderness conservation and outdoor recreation areas.

Worldwide Opportunities on Organic Farms (www.wwoofusa.org) Long-term volunteering opportunities on local organic farms (annual membership from $40).

Work

➡ Citizens of a foreign country who want to work in California must find an employer willing to sponsor them for a temporary work visa.

➡ For full details on temporary worker visas, visit the US Department of State website (https://travel.state.gov).

➡ Don't try to work without a permit. If you're caught, it will be the end of your California dream.

Resources for potential job seekers:

USponsor Me (www.usponsorme.com)

International Student (www.internationalstudent.com)

Transportation

GETTING THERE & AWAY

Getting to California by air or overland by car, train or bus is easy, although it's not always cheap. Flights, cars and tours can be booked online at www.lonelyplanet.com/bookings.

Entering the Region

Under the US Department of Homeland Security's Orwellian-sounding Office of Biometric Identity Management, almost all foreign visitors to the USA (excluding, for now, many Canadians, some Mexican citizens, children under the age of 14 and seniors over the age of 79) will be digitally photographed and have their electronic (inkless) fingerprints scanned upon arrival.

At the time of writing, Covid-19 travel restrictions prevented the entry of foreign nationals who had in the last 14 days spent time in China, Iran, the UK, Ireland, Brazil and many countries in Europe. For updates, visit the website of the Centers for Disease Control and Prevention (www.cdc.gov).

Passport

- Under the Western Hemisphere Travel Initiative (WHTI), almost all travelers must have a valid machine-readable passport (MRP) when entering the USA by air, land or sea.
- The only exceptions are for some US, Canadian and Mexican citizens traveling by land who can present other WHTI-compliant documents (eg preapproved 'trusted traveler' cards). A regular driver's license is *not* sufficient.
- All foreign passports must meet current US standards and be valid for at least six months beyond your intended stay.
- MRPs must have a digital photo and integrated chip with biometric data (otherwise known as e-passports).

Air

- To get through airport security checkpoints (30- to 45-minute wait times are standard), you'll need a boarding pass and photo ID.
- Some travelers may be required to undergo a secondary screening, involving hand pat downs and carry-on-bag searches.
- Airport security measures restrict many common items (eg pocket knives, scissors) from being carried on planes. Check current restrictions with the Transportation Security Administration (TSA; www.tsa.gov).
- Currently the TSA requires that all carry-on liquids and gels be stored in 3.4oz or smaller bottles placed inside

CLIMATE CHANGE & TRAVEL

Every form of transport that relies on carbon-based fuel generates CO_2, the main cause of human-induced climate change. Modern travel is dependent on airplanes, which might use less fuel per kilometer per person than most cars but travel much greater distances. The altitude at which aircraft emit gases (including CO_2) and particles also contributes to their climate change impact. Many websites offer 'carbon calculators' that allow people to estimate the carbon emissions generated by their journey and, for those who wish to do so, to offset the impact of the greenhouse gases emitted with contributions to portfolios of climate-friendly initiatives throughout the world. Lonely Planet offsets the carbon footprint of all staff and author travel.

a quart-sized clear plastic zip-top bag. Exceptions, which must be declared to checkpoint security officers, include medications.

➡ All checked luggage is screened for explosives. TSA may open your suitcase for visual confirmation, breaking the lock if necessary. Leave your bags unlocked or use a TSA-approved lock.

Airports & Airlines

California's major international airports are **Los Angeles International Airport** (LAX; www.flylax.com; 1 World Way) and **San Diego International Airport** (SAN; Map p462; ☎619-400-2400; www.san.org; 3325 N Harbor Dr; Wi-Fi) in Southern California and **San Francisco International Airport** (SFO; www.flysfo.com; S McDonnell Rd), **Oakland International Airport** (OAK; ☎510-563-3300; www.oaklandairport.com; 1 Airport Dr; Wi-Fi; Ⓑ Oakland International Airport) and **Sacramento International Airport** (SMF; ☎916-929-5411; www.sacramento.aero/smf; 6900 Airport Blvd) in Northern California. Smaller regional airports throughout the state are mainly served by domestic US airlines. Many domestic and international air carriers offer direct flights to and from California.

Departure Tax

There is no separate departure tax for domestic or international flights leaving California.

Land

Border Crossings

The US Customs & Border Protection (http://bwt.cbp.gov) tracks current wait times at every US border crossing. On the US–Mexico border between San Diego and Tijuana, San Ysidro is the world's busiest land border crossing. Unless you're planning an extended stay in Mexico, taking a car across the Mexican border is usually more trouble than it's worth. Instead take the trolley from San Diego or park your car on the US side and walk across.

US citizens do not require a visa for stays of 72 hours or less within the Mexican border zone (ie as far south as Ensenada). But to reenter the USA, US citizens need to present a US passport or other WHTI-compliant travel document (see www.cbp.gov/travel); a regular US driver's license is not enough.

WARNING

In December 2019, the US State Department (http://travel.state.gov) reissued a travel warning about drug-trafficking violence and crime in Mexico. Travelers should exercise caution in Tijuana and stick to touristed areas (nontouristed areas have seen high rates of homicide, mostly related to organized crime). Cars with US license plates can be targets for carjackings, especially at night and on isolated roads.

CAR & MOTORCYCLE

➡ If you're driving into the USA from Canada or Mexico, bring your vehicle's registration papers, liability insurance and driver's license; an International Driving Permit (IDP) is a good supplement but is not required.

➡ If you're renting a car or a motorcycle, ask if the agency allows its vehicles to be taken across the Mexican or Canadian border – chances are it doesn't.

TO & FROM MEXICO

➡ You can drive into Mexico if you have your own car and insurance for Mexico. However, consider purchasing international roadside assistance, and get GPS in English set up beforehand if you don't speak Spanish (it can be tricky navigating the road signs in Mexico).

➡ Expect long border-crossing waits, especially on weekends and holidays and during weekday commuter rush hours.

➡ Also, bring your passport for reentry and be prepared to wait in line from one to three hours. Check the ever-changing passport and visa requirements with the US Department of State (http://travel.state.gov) before traveling.

TO & FROM CANADA

➡ Canadian auto insurance is typically valid in the USA and vice versa.

➡ If your papers are in order, taking your own car across the US–Canada border is usually quick and easy.

➡ On weekends and holidays, especially in summer, border-crossing traffic can be heavy and waits long.

➡ Occasionally the authorities of either country decide to search a car *thoroughly*. Remain calm and be polite.

Bus

Greyhound (☎800-231-2222; www.greyhound.com) is the major long-distance bus company, with routes throughout the USA, including to/from California. Routes trace major highways and may stop only at larger population centers, with services to many small towns having been cut. FlixBus (https://global.flixbus.com/bus/united-states) is a new competitor offering service between California and Nevada, Arizona and Utah.

Train

Amtrak (☎800-872-7245; www.amtrak.com) operates a fairly extensive rail system throughout the USA. Trains are comfortable, if a bit slow, and are equipped with dining and lounge cars and sometimes wi-fi on long-distance routes. Fares vary according to the type of train and seating (eg coach or business class, sleeping compartments).

Amtrak's major long-distance services to/from California:

California Zephyr Daily service between Chicago and Emeryville (from $176, 52 hours), near San Francisco, via Denver, Salt Lake City, Reno, Truckee and Sacramento.

Coast Starlight Travels the West Coast daily from Seattle to LA (from $141, 35 hours) via Portland, Sacramento, Oakland, San Jose, San Luis Obispo and Santa Barbara.

Southwest Chief Daily departures from Chicago and LA (from $118, 43 hours) via Kansas City, Albuquerque, Flagstaff and Barstow.

Sunset Limited Thrice-weekly service between New Orleans and LA (from $136, 48 hours) via Houston, San Antonio, El Paso, Tucson and Palm Springs.

TRAIN PASSES

Amtrak's USA Rail Pass is valid for coach-class train travel only for 15 ($459), 30 ($689) or 45 ($899) days; children aged two to 12 pay half price. For current prices, visit https://tickets.amtrak.com. Travel is limited to eight, 12 or 18 one-way 'segments' which is not the same as a one-way trip. If reaching your destination requires more than one train, you'll use multiple pass segments. Purchase passes online, then make advance reservations for each trip segment.

Sea

Several international cruise lines dock along California's coast at piers and cruise-ship terminals in San Diego, Long Beach and San Francisco.

GETTING AROUND

Air

Several major US carriers fly within California. Flights are often operated by their regional subsidiaries, such as American Eagle, Delta Connection and United Express. Alaska Airlines/Virgin America, Frontier Airlines, Horizon Air and JetBlue serve many regional airports, as do low-cost airlines Southwest and Spirit.

Bicycle

Although cycling around California is a nonpolluting 'green' way to travel, the distances involved demand a high level of fitness and make it hard to cover much ground. Forget about the deserts in summer and the mountains in winter.

Resources

Better World Club (☎866-238-1137; www.betterworldclub.com) Annual membership in the bicycle club (from $40) gets you two 24-hour emergency roadside-assistance calls and transport within a 30-mile radius.

California Bicycle Coalition (http://calbike.org) Links to cycling route maps, events, safety tips, laws, bike-sharing programs and community nonprofit bicycle shops.

Rental & Purchase

- You can rent bikes by the hour, day or week in most cities and tourist towns.
- Rentals start around $10 per day for beach cruisers, and up to $45 or more for mountain bikes; ask about multiday and weekly discounts.
- Most rental companies require a large security deposit using a credit card.
- Buy new models from specialty bike shops and sporting-goods stores, or used bicycles from noticeboards at hostels, cafes etc.

Road Rules

- Cycling is allowed on all roads and highways – even along freeways if there's no suitable alternative, such as a smaller parallel frontage road; all mandatory exits are marked.
- Some cities have designated bicycle lanes, but make sure you have your wits about you in traffic.
- Cyclists must follow the same rules of the road as vehicles. Don't expect drivers to always respect your right of way.
- Wearing a bicycle helmet is mandatory for riders under 18 years of age.
- Ensure you have proper lights and reflective gear, especially if you're pedaling at night or in fog.

Transporting Bicycles

- Greyhound transports bicycles as luggage (surcharge from $35), provided the bicycle is disassembled and placed in a rigid container ($10 box may be available for purchase at some terminals).
- Amtrak's *Cascades*, *Capitol Corridor*, *Pacific Surfliner* and *San Joaquins* trains have onboard racks where you can secure your bike unboxed; try to reserve a spot when making your ticket reservation ($5 surcharge may apply).
- On Amtrak trains without racks, bikes must be put in a box ($15 at most staffed terminals) and checked as luggage (fee $10 to $20). Not all stations or trains offer checked-baggage service, however.
- Before flying, you'll need to disassemble your bike and box it as checked baggage. Contact airlines directly for details, including surcharges ($75 to $150 or more).

Boat

Boats won't get you around California, although there are a few offshore routes, notably to Catalina Island off the coast of Los Angeles and Orange County, and to Channel Islands National Park from Ventura or Oxnard, northwest of LA heading toward Santa Barbara. On San Francisco Bay, regular ferries operate between San Francisco and Sausalito, Larkspur, Tiburon, Angel Island, Oakland, Alameda and Vallejo.

Bus

Greyhound (☎800-231-2222; www.greyhound.com) is the most popular option, and newer competitor FlixBus (https://global.flixbus.com/bus/united-states) offers service between more than a dozen destinations in California.

Buses are usually clean, comfortable and reliable. The best seats are near the front, away from the bathroom. Limited on-board amenities include freezing air-con (bring a sweater) and slightly reclining seats; select buses have electrical outlets and wi-fi. Long-distance buses stop for meal breaks and driver changes.

Bus stations are typically dreary places, often in dodgy areas. If you arrive at night, take a taxi into town or directly to your lodgings. In small towns where there's no station, know exactly where and when the bus arrives, be obvious as you flag it down, and pay the driver with exact change.

Costs

You may save money by purchasing tickets in advance and by traveling between Monday and Thursday.

Discounts (on unrestricted fares only) are offered to seniors over 62 (5% off), students with a Student Advantage card (10%) and children under 16 years (5%). Tots under two years of age ride for free only if they don't require a seat.

Special promotional discounts, such as 50% off companion fares, are often available, though they may come with restrictions or blackout periods. Check Greyhound's website for current fare specials or ask when buying tickets.

Tickets & Reservations

It's easy to buy Greyhound tickets online with a credit card then pick them up (bring photo ID) at the terminal. You can also buy tickets over the phone, or in person from a ticket agent. Greyhound terminal ticket agents also accept debit cards, personal checks and cash.

General boarding is first-come, first-served. Buying tickets in advance doesn't guarantee a seat on any particular bus unless you also purchase priority boarding, available only on some routes. Otherwise, arrive at least one hour prior to the scheduled departure to get a seat; allow extra time on weekends and holidays.

Travelers with disabilities who need special assistance should call 800-752-4841 (TDD/TTY 800-345-3109) at least 48 hours before traveling. Wheelchairs and mobility scooters are accepted as checked baggage (or carry-on, if space allows) and service animals are allowed on board.

Car & Motorcycle

Automobile Associations

For 24-hour emergency roadside assistance, free maps and discounts on lodging, attractions, entertainment, car rentals and more, consider joining an auto club.

American Automobile Association (AAA; ☎800-922-8228, emergency roadside assistance 800-222-4357; www.aaa.com) Walk-in offices throughout California, add-on coverage for recreational vehicles (RVs) and motorcycles, and reciprocal agreements with some international auto clubs (eg CAA in Canada, AA in the UK) – bring your membership card from home.

Better World Club (☎866-238-1137; www.betterworldclub.com) Ecofriendly auto club that supports environmental causes and offers add-on or stand-alone emergency roadside assistance for cyclists as well.

Driver's Licenses

➡ Visitors may legally drive a car in California for up to 12 months with their home driver's license.

➡ If you're from overseas, an International Driving Permit (IDP) will have more credibility with traffic police and simplify the car-rental process, especially if your license doesn't have a photo or isn't written in English.

➡ To ride a motorcycle, you'll need a valid US state motorcycle license, or a specially endorsed IDP.

➡ International automobile associations can issue IDPs, valid for one year, for a fee. Always carry your home license together with the IDP.

Fuel

➡ Gas stations in California, nearly all of which are self-service, are ubiquitous, except in national and state parks and some sparsely populated desert and mountain areas.

➡ Gas is sold in gallons (one US gallon equals 3.78L). At the time of writing, the average cost for mid-grade fuel was around $2.80 a gallon.

Insurance

California law requires liability insurance for all vehicles. When renting a car, check your auto-insurance policy from home or your travel insurance policy to see if you're already covered. If not, expect to pay about $10 to $20 per day.

Insurance against damage to the car itself, called Collision Damage Waiver (CDW) or Loss Damage Waiver (LDW), costs another $10 to $20 or more per day. The deductible may require you to pay the first $100 to $500 for any repairs.

Some credit cards cover CDW/LDW, provided you charge the entire cost of the car rental to the card. Check with your credit-card issuer first to determine the extent of coverage and policy exclusions. If there's an accident you may have to pay the rental-car company first, then seek reimbursement from the credit-card company.

Parking

➡ Parking is usually plentiful and free in small towns and rural areas, but often scarce and/or expensive in cities.

➡ When parking on the street, read all posted regulations and restrictions (eg street-cleaning hours, permit-only residential areas) and pay attention to colored curbs, or you may be ticketed and towed.

➡ You can pay municipal parking meters and sidewalk pay stations with coins (eg quarters) and sometimes credit or debit cards.

➡ Expect to pay $30 to $50 for overnight parking in a city lot or garage.

➡ Flat-fee valet parking at hotels, restaurants, nightclubs etc is common in major cities, especially Los Angeles and Las Vegas, NV (don't forget to tip).

Rental

CARS

Rates generally include unlimited mileage, but expect surcharges for additional drivers and one-way rentals. Child or infant safety seats are legally required; reserve them when booking for $10 to $15 per day.

If you'd like to minimize your carbon footprint, some major car-rental companies offer 'green' fleets of hybrid or biofueled rental cars, but these fuel-efficient models are in short supply. Reserve them well in advance and expect to pay significantly higher rates.

To find and compare independent car-rental companies, try Car Rental Express (www.carrentalexpress.com).

Avis (☎800-633-3469; www.avis.com)

Budget (☎800-218-7992; www.budget.com)

Dollar (☎800-800-5252; www.dollar.com)

Enterprise (☎855-266-9289; www.enterprise.com)

Fox (☎855-571-8413; www.foxrentacar.com)

Hertz (☎800-654-3131; www.hertz.com)

National (☎844-382-6875; www.nationalcar.com)

Payless (☎800-729-5377; www.paylesscar.com)

Rent-a-Wreck (☎877-877-0700; www.rentawreck.com) Minimum rental age and under-25 driver surcharges vary at six locations, including in LA and the San Francisco Bay Area.

Sixt (☎888-749-8227; www.sixt.com)

Thrifty (☎800-847-4389; www.thrifty.com)

Zipcar (☎866-494-7227; www.zipcar.com) Currently available in numerous cities across the state, this car-sharing club charges usage fees (per hour or day), including free gas, insurance (a damage fee of up to $1000 may apply) and limited mileage. Apply online (foreign drivers accepted); application fee $25, annual membership from $70.

MOTORCYCLES

Motorcycle rentals and insurance are not cheap, especially if you've got your eye on a Harley. Depending on the model, renting a motorcycle costs $100 to $250 per day plus taxes and fees, including helmets, unlimited miles and liability insurance; one-way rentals and collision insurance (CDW) cost extra. Discounts may be available for multiday and weekly rentals. Security deposits can be up to $2000 (credit card required).

Dubbelju (☎415-495-2774; www.dubbelju.com; 274 Shotwell St; per day from $99; ⊙9am-6pm Mon-Sat) San Francisco–based; rents Harley-Davidson, Japanese and European imported motorcycles, as well as scooters.

Eagle Rider (☎310-321-3180; www.eaglerider.com) Nationwide company with 11 locations in California, as well as Las Vegas, NV.

RECREATIONAL VEHICLES

Gas-guzzling RVs remain popular despite fuel prices and being cumbersome to drive. That said, they do solve transportation, accommodation and cooking needs in one fell swoop. It's easy to find RV campgrounds with electricity and water hookups, yet there are many places in national and state parks and in the mountains they can't go. In cities RVs are a nuisance, because there are few places to park or plug them in.

Book RVs as far in advance as possible. Rental costs vary by size and model, but you can expect to pay more than $100 per day. Rates often don't include mileage, bedding or kitchen kits, vehicle-prep fees or taxes. If pets are allowed, a surcharge may apply.

Cruise America (☎480-464-7300; www.cruiseamerica.com) Nationwide RV-rental company with two dozen locations statewide.

El Monte (☎888-337-2214; www.elmonterv.com) With 11 locations in California, this national RV-rental agency offers AAA discounts.

Escape Campervans (☎310-672-9909; www.escapecampervans.com) Awesomely painted campervans at economical rates in the San Francisco Bay Area, LA and Las Vegas, NV.

Jucy Rentals (☎800-650-4180; www.jucyusa.com) Campervan rentals in the San Francisco Bay Area, LA and Las Vegas, NV.

Road Bear (☎818-865-2925, 866-491-9853; www.roadbearrv.com) RV rentals in the San Francisco Bay Area and LA.

Vintage Surfari Wagons (☎714-585-7565; www.vwsurfari.com) VW campervan rentals in Orange County.

Road Rules

➡ Drive on the right-hand side of the road.

➡ Talking, texting or otherwise using a cell (mobile) phone or other mobile electronic device without hands-free technology while driving is illegal.

➡ The driver and all passengers must use seat belts in a private vehicle. In a taxi or limo, back-seat passengers are not required to buckle up.

➡ Infant and child safety seats are required for children under eight years of age, or who are less than 4ft 9in tall.

➡ All motorcyclists must wear a helmet. Scooters are not allowed on freeways.

➡ High-occupancy vehicle (HOV) lanes marked with a diamond symbol are reserved for cars with multiple occupants, sometimes only during signposted hours.

➡ Unless otherwise posted, the speed limit is 65mph on freeways, 55mph on two-lane undivided highways, 35mph on major city streets and 25mph in business and residential districts and near schools.

➡ Except where indicated, turning right at a red stoplight after coming to a full stop is permitted, although intersecting traffic still has the right of way.

➡ At four-way stop signs, cars proceed in the order in which they arrived. If two cars arrive simultaneously, the one on the right has the right of way. When in doubt, politely wave the other driver ahead.

➡ When emergency vehicles (ie police, fire or ambulance) approach from either direction, carefully pull over to the side of the road.

➡ California has strict anti-littering laws; throwing trash from a vehicle may incur a $1000 fine.

➡ Driving under the influence of alcohol or drugs is illegal. The blood alcohol limit is 0.08%. It's also illegal to carry open containers of alcohol or marijuana, even empty ones, inside a vehicle. Store them in the trunk.

Local Transportation

Except in cities, public transit is rarely the most convenient option, and coverage to outlying towns and suburbs can be sparse. However, it's usually cheap, safe and reliable.

Bicycle

Cycling is a feasible way of getting around smaller cities and towns. Even in metropolitan areas like LA, bikes can be useful for getting around neighborhoods.

Bike-sharing programs are becoming more commonplace and include Breeze Bike Share on LA's Westside (eg Santa Monica, Venice, Beverly Hills), Metro Bike Share (Downtown LA, Hollywood, Koreatown) and Long Beach BikeShare.

Bicycles may be transported on many local buses and trains, sometimes during off-peak, non-commuter hours only.

Bus, Cable Car, Streetcar & Trolley

➡ Almost all cities and larger towns have reliable local bus systems (average $1 to $3 per ride). Outside of major metro areas, service is limited in the evening and on weekends.

➡ LA's Metro Rail network consists of two subway lines, four light-rail lines and two express bus lines.

➡ In San Diego, municipal trolleys operate on three lines as far south as the Mexican border.

Taxi

Taxis cruise the streets of the busiest areas in large cities, but elsewhere you may need to call for one. Cars are metered, with flag-fall fees of $2.50 to $3.50 to start, plus around $2 to $3 per mile. Credit cards may be accepted, but bring cash just in case.

There may be an extra charge for baggage and airport pickups. Drivers expect a 10% to 15% tip, rounded up to the next dollar.

Ridesharing apps are generally cheaper than cabs and often provide better service. During peak times, waits can be long and rides are charged at a premium. This is especially true on Friday and Saturday nights and after major events.

Train

To get around the San Francisco Bay Area, hop aboard Bay Area Rapid Transit (BART) or Caltrain. Sacramento, San Jose and LA also have limited light-rail systems.

Tours

Green Tortoise (☎415-722-0471; www.greentortoise.com) Youthful budget-backpacker trips utilize converted sleeping-bunk buses for adventure tours of California's national parks, northern redwood

CALIFORNIA'S SCENIC RAILWAYS

- Railtown 1897 State Historic Park (p638)
- Roaring Camp Railroads (p299)
- Skunk Train (p253)
- California State Railroad Museum (p590)
- Napa Valley Wine Train (p178)
- Yosemite Mountain Sugar Pine Railroad (p695)

forests, southern deserts and Pacific Coast.

Train

Amtrak (☎800-872-7245; www.amtrak.com) runs comfortable, if occasionally tardy, trains and buses to major California cities and limited towns. At some stations Thruway buses provide onward connections – or replace trains (read schedules carefully). Smoking is prohibited on board.

Amtrak routes within California:

California Zephyr Daily service from Emeryville (near San Francisco) via Davis and Sacramento to Truckee (near Lake Tahoe) and Reno, NV.

Capitol Corridor Links San Francisco's East Bay (including Oakland, Emeryville and Berkeley) and San Jose with Davis and Sacramento several times daily. Thruway buses connect west to San Francisco, north to Auburn in the Gold Country and east to Truckee and Reno, NV. Transfer to BART trains in Richmond for faster rush-hour connections to San Francisco from Sacramento.

Coast Starlight Chugs north–south almost the entire length of the state. Daily stops include LA, Santa Barbara, San Luis Obispo, Paso Robles, Salinas, San Jose, Oakland, Emeryville, Davis, Sacramento, Chico, Redding and Dunsmuir.

San Joaquins Several daily trains with on-board wi-fi between Bakersfield and Oakland or Sacramento. Thruway bus connections include San Francisco, LA, Palm Springs and Yosemite National Park.

Pacific Surfliner Eight daily trains ply the San Diego–LA route via Orange County, stopping at San Diego's North County beach towns and Orange County's San Juan Capistrano and Anaheim, home of Disneyland. Three trains continue north to Santa Barbara via Burbank, Ventura and Carpinteria, with one going all the way to San Luis Obispo. Trains hug the scenic coastline for much of the route.

Costs

Purchase tickets at train stations, by phone or online (in advance for the cheapest prices). Fares depend on the day of travel, the route, the type of seating etc. Fares may be slightly higher during peak travel times (eg summer). Round-trip tickets typically cost the same as two one-way tickets.

Usually seniors over 62 and students aged 13 to 25 with a valid student ID card receive a 15% discount, while up to two children aged two to 12 who are accompanied by an adult get 50% off. AAA members save 10%. Special promotions can become available anytime, so check Amtrak's website or ask when making reservations.

Reservations

Amtrak reservations can be made up to 11 months prior to departure. In summer and around holidays, trains sell out quickly, so book tickets as early as possible. The cheapest coach fares are usually for unreserved seats; business-class fares come with guaranteed seats.

Travelers with disabilities who need special assistance, wheelchair space, transfer seats or accessible accommodations should call ☎800-872-7245 (TDD/TTY ☎800-523-6590). Also inquire about discounted fares when booking.

Train Passes

Amtrak's California Rail Pass costs $159 ($79.50 for children aged two to 12) and is valid on all trains (except certain long-distance routes) and most connecting Thruway buses for seven days of travel within a 21-day period. Pass holders must reserve each leg of travel in advance and obtain hard-copy tickets prior to boarding.

Behind the Scenes

SEND US YOUR FEEDBACK

We love to hear from travelers – your comments keep us on our toes and help make our books better. Our well-traveled team reads every word on what you loved or loathed about this book. Although we cannot reply individually to your submissions, we always guarantee that your feedback goes straight to the appropriate authors, in time for the next edition. Each person who sends us information is thanked in the next edition – the most useful submissions are rewarded with a selection of digital PDF chapters.

Visit **lonelyplanet.com/contact** to submit your updates and suggestions or to ask for help. Our award-winning website also features inspirational travel stories, news and discussions.

Note: We may edit, reproduce and incorporate your comments in Lonely Planet products such as guidebooks, websites and digital products, so let us know if you don't want your comments reproduced or your name acknowledged. For a copy of our privacy policy visit lonelyplanet.com/privacy.

OUR READERS

Many thanks to the travelers who used the last edition and wrote to us with helpful hints, useful advice and interesting anecdotes:

Kim Anning, Alain Kavenoky, Sarah Lyon and Maurits Stuyt

WRITER THANKS

Brett Atkinson

Thanks to everyone who made my exploration of California's Central Coast so enjoyable, especially Christina Glynn in Santa Cruz. The staff at the region's visitor centers were all uniformly helpful, and creative and inspired Central Coast brewers and chefs helped to make research a flavor-packed experience. At Lonely Planet, huge thanks to Grace Dobell for the opportunity to return to Big Sur.

Amy C Balfour

Big thanks to the following locals, former locals and ski fans who shared their favorite places in Tahoe, Reno and the Gold Country: Chris Crossen, Kerrie Tonking, Roy Pillay, Todd Frick, Lacy Davidson, Julee Messerich, Blakely Atherton and Tom Phillips. Special thanks to Amy & Chris Rose for your friendship, hospitality and recs for Reno and the outdoors. Thanks also to Brandon Dekema, Mike Roe and Lucy Anderson for the great local leads and contacts.

Andrew Bender

Thanks to all of the good folks of LA and Orange Counties who helped me to show off the best of my home region. In-house, thanks to Grace Dobell, Dan Bolger, Brana Vladisavljevic, Mani Ramaswamy and Kirsten Rawlings for their hard work, patience and good cheer.

Alison Bing

California bear hugs and major thanks to intrepid copilots, gourmet adventurers and ace wine-tasters Kris Boxell, Sahai Burrowes, Rosanne Lurie, Chioma Ume, Nnena Ukuku, Donald Graves, Jon Fulk, Stephanie Heald and John Lorance – plus my wonderful semi-nomadic family, Rebecca and Jennifer Bing and Marco Marinucci. Finally, a rousing toast to guidestar editors Grace Dobell, Dan Bolger and Fergus O'Shea: through firestorms & pandemics, you kept the California dream alive.

Cristian Bonetto

Muchas gracias to the Angelenos who generously shared their passion for LA, especially Daphne Barahona and Nathan Alexander, Mimi Do, Jen Berry, Sara Ventiera, Ty Holliman and Mario Ramone, Seana Corcoran, Michael Darling and Bradley Tuck. Thanks also to my sister, Barbara Bonetto, cumpà Chris Toomey and nephews Joshua and James, for helping make this trip extra special. At Lonely Planet, much gratitude to Grace Dobell for the commission.

Celeste Brash

Thanks to all of the park rangers, Aunty Kem and Susanville/Almanor friends, Anita for hippie tips, the Redding tourist office, Tevai for holding down the fort, Dana for the dog, Grace Dobell for hiring me and all the random friendly people I met along the way.

Jade Bremner

Many thanks to San Diego locals Jena Wilard, Nick Adlington and Isabella Fernandes for their insider knowledge and keeping me company on the road, plus Grace Dobell for all her LP guidebook wisdom. Massive thanks to Harriet Sinclair for the early mornings and late nights and last but not least Cheree Broughton, Darren O'Connell, Kirsten Rawlings and everyone else working hard behind the scenes.

Bailey Freeman

Thank you to everyone who made this epic California road trip an exercise in finding the beauty behind every corner. Thanks to Grace Dobell and the editorial team for trusting me with this assignment, to my sweet travel colleagues, and to MaSovaida Morgan for her guidance and expertise. And of course, thanks to my husband and mom for their unending love and support. Love you more than words can say.

Michael Grosberg

Thanks so much to the following for sharing their knowledge and experience on this beautiful region: to Jenn Edwards in Groveland; Ashlee Blocker, Kris Hohag, Tawni Thomson, Deanna and Gunner in Bishop; Neev Zaiet and Lauren Burke in Mammoth Lakes; Lisa Cesaro in Yosemite, Lindsay Kensy, Seth Mayer and Brett Archer in Kings Canyon and Sequoia. And to Rosie, Willa, Carly and Booney for cuddles and support on my return.

Ashley Harrell

Thanks to: editor Grace Dobell and my co-authors for their excellency, Reagan Parker at Visit Berkeley and ZP Zapata and Mikila Lawless at Visit Oakland for being incredibly helpful, Jeff Gilman for being the world's coolest landlord, Freda Moon for the assistance and hilarious company, Andy Wright for the Spirits Alley 'sobreakity,' Mack and Ronni Harrell for journalism school and Steve Sparapani, for being the best partner and travel sidekick a girl could ask for.

Mark Johanson

A big thanks to Vanessa Petersen for all of her help, guidance and company on my journey through Northern California. Thanks to my parents for instilling in me an insatiable thirst for travel (and joining me to taste-test the finest Mendocino wines!). And a final gracias to my partner Felipe for enduring my long absences from home.

Andrea Schulte-Peevers

Big heartfelt thank yous go to Anna Lübbe, Valerie Summers, Kirsten Schmidt and Andrew Bender for their insights and company, to Grace Dobell for putting me on the California team and to Dan Bolger for so shepherding the project through its various stages.

Wendy Yanagihara

Thanks to all the Santa Barbara area locals who mostly unwittingly helped in my research, especially the amazing professionals in the food and beverage industry who make life here so delicious. Special thanks to Grace Dobell for this project; to my research compañeros Laura Sanchez and John Adams, who made my travels delightfully less solo; and to Jason Yanagihara and Victoria Swanson for making even my short-distance sojourns possible.

ACKNOWLEDGEMENTS

Climate map data adapted from Peel MC, Finlayson BL & McMahon TA (2007) 'Updated World Map of the Köppen-Geiger Climate Classification', *Hydrology and Earth System Sciences*, 11, 1633–44.

Illustration pp82-83 by Michael Weldon

Cover photograph: Joshua Tree, Daniela Duncan/ Getty Images©

THIS BOOK

This 9th edition of Lonely Planet's *California* guidebook was researched and written by Brett Atkinson, Amy C Balfour, Andrew Bender, Alison Bing, Cristian Bonetto, Celeste Brash, Jade Bremner, Bailey Freeman, Michael Grosberg, Ashley Harrell, Anita Isalska, Mark Johanson, Andrea Schulte-Peevers and Wendy Yanagihara. The previous edition was also written by Alison, Andrea, Andrew, Brett, Celeste, Cristian, Jade and Michael. This guidebook was produced by the following:

Senior Product Editors Daniel Bolger, Grace Dobell

Senior Cartographer Alison Lyall

Product Editor Fergus O'Shea

Book Designer Fergal Condon

Assisting Editors Janet Austin, Sarah Bailey, Sasha Drew, Mani Ramaswamy, Claire Naylor, Charlotte Orr, Kirsten Rawlings, Tamara Sheward, Brana Vladisavljevic

Assisting Book Designer Gwen Cotter

Cover Researcher Fergal Condon

Thanks to Karen Henderson, Sandie Kestell, Amy Lynch, Genna Patterson, Angela Tinson

Index

C

Map Pages **000**
Photo Pages **000**

Map Pages **000**
Photo Pages **000**

N

Map Pages **000**
Photo Pages **000**

T

Map Pages **000**
Photo Pages **000**

Map Legend

Sights

- Beach
- Bird Sanctuary
- Buddhist
- Castle/Palace
- Christian
- Confucian
- Hindu
- Islamic
- Jain
- Jewish
- Monument
- Museum/Gallery/Historic Building
- Ruin
- Shinto
- Sikh
- Taoist
- Winery/Vineyard
- Zoo/Wildlife Sanctuary
- Other Sight

Activities, Courses & Tours

- Bodysurfing
- Diving
- Canoeing/Kayaking
- Course/Tour
- Sento Hot Baths/Onsen
- Skiing
- Snorkeling
- Surfing
- Swimming/Pool
- Walking
- Windsurfing
- Other Activity

Sleeping

- Sleeping
- Camping
- Hut/Shelter

Eating

- Eating

Drinking & Nightlife

- Drinking & Nightlife
- Cafe

Entertainment

- Entertainment

Shopping

- Shopping

Information

- Bank
- Embassy/Consulate
- Hospital/Medical
- Internet
- Police
- Post Office
- Telephone
- Toilet
- Tourist Information
- Other Information

Geographic

- Beach
- Gate
- Hut/Shelter
- Lighthouse
- Lookout
- Mountain/Volcano
- Oasis
- Park
- Pass
- Picnic Area
- Waterfall

Population

- Capital (National)
- Capital (State/Province)
- City/Large Town
- Town/Village

Transport

- Airport
- BART station
- Border crossing
- Boston T station
- Bus
- Cable car/Funicular
- Cycling
- Ferry
- Metro/Muni station
- Monorail
- Parking
- Petrol station
- Subway/SkyTrain station
- Taxi
- Train station/Railway
- Tram
- Underground station
- Other Transport

Routes

- Tollway
- Freeway
- Primary
- Secondary
- Tertiary
- Lane
- Unsealed road
- Road under construction
- Plaza/Mall
- Steps
- Tunnel
- Pedestrian overpass
- Walking Tour
- Walking Tour detour
- Path/Walking Trail

Boundaries

- International
- State/Province
- Disputed
- Regional/Suburb
- Marine Park
- Cliff
- Wall

Hydrography

- River, Creek
- Intermittent River
- Canal
- Water
- Dry/Salt/Intermittent Lake
- Reef

Areas

- Airport/Runway
- Beach/Desert
- Cemetery (Christian)
- Cemetery (Other)
- Glacier
- Mudflat
- Park/Forest
- Sight (Building)
- Sportsground
- Swamp/Mangrove

Note: Not all symbols displayed above appear on the maps in this book

Celeste Brash
Family Travel, Northern Mountains Like many California natives, Celeste now lives in Portland, Oregon. She arrived however, after 15 years in French Polynesia, a year and a half in Southeast Asia and a stint teaching English in Brighton, England. She's been writing guidebooks for Lonely Planet since 2005 and her travel articles have appeared in *BBC Travel* and *National Geographic*.

Jade Bremner
Beaches, Swimming & Surfing, San Diego & Around Jade has been a journalist for more than 15 years. She has lived in and reported on four different regions. Many of her favourite places have some of the best waves in the world. Jade has edited travel magazines and sections for *Time Out* and *Radio Times* and has contributed to *The Times*, CNN and *The Independent*. @jadebremner

Bailey Freeman
Sacramento & Central Valley Bailey Freeman, a wanderer who hails from Kentucky, harbors a deep love for travel in North, Central and South America, and she's happiest when she's winding her way through mountain ranges or meeting passionate folks sharing what they love. You can also find her defying gravity as an aerial acrobat (really!). Follow her at www.atravelingbee.com.

Michael Grosberg
Yosemite & the Sierra Nevada, California Wildlife, The Land & Wildlife Michael has worked on over 50 Lonely Planet guidebooks. Other international work included development on Rota in the western Pacific; South Africa where he investigated and wrote about political violence and trained newly elected government representatives. He received a Masters in Comparative Literature and taught literature and writing as an adjunct professor.

Ashley Harrell
Marin County & the Bay Area, Directory, Transport After a brief stint selling day spa coupons door-to-door in South Florida, Ashley decided she'd rather be a writer. She has traveled widely and moved often, from a tiny NYC apartment to a vast California ranch to a jungle cabin in Costa Rica, where she started writing for Lonely Planet.

Anita Isalska
Sustainable Travel Anita Isalska is a travel journalist and digital content strategist. After several merry years as a staff writer and editor – a few of them in Lonely Planet's London office – Anita now works freelance between California, the UK, and any French mountain lodge with wi-fi. Anita specialises in Eastern and Central Europe, Australia, France, and her adopted home, San Francisco. Read her stuff on www.anitaisalska.com.

Mark Johanson
North Coast & Redwoods Mark Johanson grew up in Virginia and has called five different countries home while circling the globe reporting for British newspapers (*The Guardian*), American magazines (*Men's Journal*) and global media outlets (CNN, BBC). You can also find him gazing at the Andes from his current home in Santiago, Chile. Follow Mark at www.markjohanson.com.

Andrea Schulte-Peevers
Palm Springs & the Deserts, The Way of Life Born and raised in Germany and educated in London and at UCLA, Andrea has earned her living as a professional travel writer for over two decades and authored or contributed to nearly 100 Lonely Planet titles as well as to newspapers, magazines and websites around the world. She also works as a travel consultant, translator and editor.

Wendy Yanagihara
Santa Barbara County Wendy serendipitously landed her dream job of writing for Lonely Planet in 2003 and has spent the intervening years contributing to titles including Vietnam, Japan, Mexico, Costa Rica, Cuba, Ecuador, Indonesia, and Grand Canyon National Park. In the name of research, she has explored remote valleys of West Papua, explored tiny alleys of Tokyo sprawl, and hiked the Grand Canyon from rim to rim.

OUR STORY

A beat-up old car, a few dollars in the pocket and a sense of adventure. In 1972 that's all Tony and Maureen Wheeler needed for the trip of a lifetime – across Europe and Asia overland to Australia. It took several months, and at the end – broke but inspired – they sat at their kitchen table writing and stapling together their first travel guide, *Across Asia on the Cheap*. Within a week they'd sold 1500 copies. Lonely Planet was born.

Today, Lonely Planet has offices in Tennessee, Dublin, Beijing and Delhi, with a network of over 2000 contributors in every corner of the globe. We share Tony's belief that 'a great guidebook should do three things: inform, educate and amuse'.

OUR WRITERS

Brett Atkinson

Central Coast Brett Atkinson is based in Auckland, New Zealand, but is frequently on the road for Lonely Planet. He's a full-time travel and food writer. Since becoming a Lonely Planet author in 2005, Brett has covered areas as diverse as Vietnam, Sri Lanka, the Czech Republic, New Zealand, Morocco, California and the South Pacific.

Amy C Balfour

California Camping & Outdoors, Gold Country, Lake Tahoe Amy practiced law in Virginia before moving to Los Angeles to try to break in as a screenwriter. If you listen carefully, you can still hear the horrified screams of her parents echoing through the space-time continuum. After a stint as a writer's assistant on *Law & Order*, she jumped into freelance writing, focusing on travel, food, and the outdoors.

Andrew Bender

Music & the Arts, By the Book Award-winning travel and food writer Andrew Bender has written three dozen Lonely Planet guidebooks, plus numerous articles for lonelyplanet.com. Outside of Lonely Planet, he writes the Seat 1A travel site for Forbes.com and is a frequent contributor to the *Los Angeles Times*, in-flight magazines and more.

Alison Bing

Eat & Drink Like a Local, Napa & Sonoma Wine Country, San Francisco Over 10 guidebooks and 20 years in San Francisco, author Alison Bing has spent more time on Alcatraz than some inmates, become an aficionado of drag and burritos, and willfully ignored Muni signs warning that safety requires avoiding unnecessary conversation.

Cristian Bonetto

Los Angeles, On Location: Film & TV Cristian has contributed to over 30 Lonely Planet guides to date, including New York City, Italy, Venice & the Veneto, Naples & the Amalfi Coast, Denmark, Copenhagen, Sweden and Singapore. His writing has appeared in numerous publications around the world, including *The Telegraph* (UK) and Corriere del Mezzogiorno (Italy). He lives in Melbourne. Instagram: rexcat75.

OVER PAGE MORE WRITERS

Published by Lonely Planet Global Limited
CRN 554153
9th edition – June 2021
ISBN 978 1 78701 669 9

10 9 8 7 6 5 4 3 2 1
Printed in Singapore